Henry Benjamin Wheatley

London, past and present; its history, associations, and traditions

(1891)

Henry Benjamin Wheatley

London, past and present; its history, associations, and traditions (1891)

ISBN/EAN: 9783742806680

Manufactured in Europe, USA, Canada, Australia, Japa

Cover: Foto ©Andreas Hilbeck / pixelio.de

Manufactured and distributed by brebook publishing software (www.brebook.com)

Henry Benjamin Wheatley

London, past and present; its history, associations, and traditions

(1891)

LONDON
PAST AND PRESENT

ITS HISTORY, ASSOCIATIONS, AND TRADITIONS

BY

HENRY B. WHEATLEY, F.S.A.

BASED UPON

THE HANDBOOK OF LONDON

BY THE LATE
PETER CUNNINGHAM

IN THREE VOLUMES—VOL. III

LONDON
JOHN MURRAY, ALBEMARLE STREET
1891

LONDON:

PAST AND PRESENT.

Paddington, formerly a village at the west end of London, containing, in 1801, 357 houses; now a large and increasing parish, and part of the great metropolis, having in 1881 a population of 107,098.

> Pitt is to Addington
> As London is to Paddington.—CANNING.

King Edgar gave the manor of Paddington to Westminster Abbey; the grant was confirmed by Henry I., King Stephen, and Henry II. At the Dissolution it was made part of the revenues of the Bishopric of Westminster; and when that see was abolished soon after its establishment, Edward VI. gave it to Ridley, Bishop of London, and his successors.—Newcourt's *Repertorium,* vol. i. p. 703.

Dodsley, writing in 1761, has nothing further to say of Paddington than that it is "a village in Middlesex situated on the north side of Hyde Park," and long after that artists used to come to it to sketch rural scenes and rustic figures. George Barrett, R.A. (d. 1784), one of the old school of English landscape painters, "resided in a most delightful spot, at the upper end of a field adjacent to old Paddington Canal."

Paddington was then a rural village. There were a few old houses on each side of the Edgware Road, together with some ale-houses of very picturesque appearance, being screened by high elms, with long troughs for watering the teams of the hay waggons on their way to and from market; each, too, had its large straddling sign-post stretching across the road. Paddington Green was then a complete street; and the group of magnificent elms thereon, now fast going to decay, were studies for all the landscape painters in the metropolis. The diagonal path led to the church, which was a little Gothic building, overgrown with ivy, and as completely sequestered as any village church a hundred miles from London.—*Angelo,* p. 229.

> *Hilts.* Where is thy Master?
> *Pup.* Marry he is gone
> With the picture of despair to Paddington.
> *Hilts.* Prithee run after 'un, and tell 'un he shall
> Find out my Captain lodged at the Red Lion
> In Paddington; that's the inn.
> Ben Jonson, *Tale of a Tub,* Act ii. Sc. 1.

Morland laid the scene of his popular picture of the Wearied Sportsman in an inn at Paddington; and Wilkie found in one of them materials for his Village Festival.

"At Paddington," wrote Leigh Hunt in 1843, "begins the ground of my affections, continuing through mead and green lane till it reaches beyond Hampstead."

Sequestered church and rustic ale-houses (the last of them the Horse and Sacks, removed in 1876, for the Harrow Road improvements), mead and green lane have alike disappeared, and Paddington is as town-like and uninteresting as any other London suburb. The old church (taken down in 1791) was built by Sir Joseph Sheldon and Daniel Sheldon, to whom the manor was leased by Dr. Gilbert Sheldon, successively Bishop of London and Archbishop of Canterbury in the reign of Charles II. The present church of St. Mary stands about 100 feet south of the old church. The architect was John Plaw, its builder Thomas Wapshott; the cost about £6000; the dimensions about 50 feet each way. The first stone was laid October 20, 1788, and the church consecrated April 27, 1791. *Eminent Persons interred in.*—John Bushnell, the sculptor of the figures on Temple Bar (d. 1701). Matthew Dubourg, the famous player on the violin (d. 1767). Francis Vivares, the engraver (d. 1780); in the churchyard (there was a tomb to his memory when Lysons wrote). George Barrett, the painter (d. 1784). Thomas Banks, R.A., the sculptor (d. 1805); in the churchyard on the south side. John Hall, the engraver (d. 1797). Dr. Alexander Geddes, Roman Catholic translator of the Historical Books of the Old Testament (d. 1802). Lewis Schiavonetti, the engraver (d. 1810); in the churchyard. Caleb Whitefoord (d. 1810), wine merchant, the Papyrius Cursor of the newspaper press, and the hero of Wilkie's Letter of Introduction.

> Here Whitefoord reclines, and deny it who can,
> Though he merrily liv'd, he is now a grave man!
>   .   .   .   .   .
> Ye newspaper witlings! ye pert scribbling folks!
> Who copied his squibs, and re-echoed his jokes;
> Ye tame imitators, ye servile herd, come,
> Still follow your master and visit his tomb:
> To deck it bring with you festoons of the Vine,
> And copious libations bestow on his shrine;
> Then strew all around it (you can do no less)
> Cross-Readings, Ship News, and Mistakes of the Press.
>   Goldsmith's *Retaliation.*

John Philpot Curran, the Irish orator, was buried here in 1817, but in 1840 his remains were removed to Glasnevin Cemetery near Dublin. Michael Bryan, author of the *Dictionary of Painters and Engravers* (d. 1821). Joseph Nollekens, the sculptor (d. 1823); and his father Joseph Francis, 'Old Nollekens," the painter (d. 1747). Mrs. Siddons, the celebrated actress (d. 1831). Mrs. Siddons lived for many years at Westbourne Farm, in this parish, but the *Great Western Railway* has destroyed all trace of her pretty grounds; and next her, Benjamin R. Haydon, the painter (d. June 22, 1846). William Collins, R.A. (d. 1847), distinguished for his seashore scenes; his grave is marked by a marble cross. *Observe.*—In the chancel of the church, tablet to Nollekens the sculptor (d. 1823), by Behnes; tablet to Mrs. Siddons; also in the body of the church, tablet to Richard Twiss (d. 1810), author of *Travels through Portugal and Spain*. The marriage register contains the following interesting entry: "William Hogarth, Esq., and Jane Thornhill, of St. Paul's, Covent Garden, married March 23, 1729." And on December 1796 Martin Archer Shee (the future fourth President of the Royal Academy) to Mary, daughter of Mr. James Power of Youghal. Besides the old church, Paddington parish contains about twenty churches, among which are—St. James's, now the parish church, at the end of Oxford and Cambridge Terraces; St. John's, in Southwick Crescent, possessing a good stained glass window; Holy Trinity (Thomas Cundy, architect), at the end of Westbourne Terrace; St. Mary's, 1845; Christ Church, 1855; St. Saviour's, 1856; St. Stephen, Westbourne Park, 1856; St. Matthew, Bayswater, 1858; St. Mary Magdalene, 1861; St. Peter's, Harrow Road, 1870; St. Michael and All Angels, Praed Street; St. Luke's, and one or two more. St. Mary's Hospital, a large and costly structure, was erected in 1850, but has since been altered and enlarged, and the internal arrangements greatly improved. The Great Western Railway Terminus and Hotel forms one of the chief architectural features of the place, but many other buildings of more or less architectural pretension have been erected of late years. The Paddington Canal, 13½ miles in length, was made pursuant to an Act passed in 1795, and opened July 10, 1801; it is a branch of the Grand Junction Canal.

There would be nothing to make the Canal of Venice more poetical than that of Paddington, were it not for its artificial adjuncts.—*Lord Byron.*

Paddington Street, HIGH STREET, MARYLEBONE. Here are two cemeteries appertaining to the parish of St. Marylebone. The cemetery on the south side was consecrated in 1733, that on the north in 1772.[1] Baretti, author of the Italian Dictionary which bears his name, is buried in the north cemetery. In that on the south side lies Archibald Bower, author of the *History of the Popes* (d. 1766), and Joseph Bonomi, architect (d. March 9, 1808).

Paget Place, in the STRAND, formerly *Exeter Place*, or *House*, afterwards Leicester House, and finally *Essex House*, was so called after William Paget, first Lord Paget, who bequeathed it by will, bearing date November 4, 1560, to his son and heir Sir Henry Paget, second Lord Paget. [*See* Essex House.]

Painted Chamber, or ST. EDWARD'S CHAMBER, a celebrated apartment in the old palace of the Kings of England at Westminster. It was of early or pre-Norman date, and there was a tradition that

[1] *Lysons*, vol. ii. p. 547.

Edward the Confessor died in it.[1] The chamber was 80 feet in length, 20 in breadth, and 50 in height; receiving its principal light from four windows, two at the east and two at the north. Until 1800 it was hung with tapestry, representing the Siege of Troy, when, in consequence of the Union of Great Britain and Ireland and the increased accommodation required in the House of Commons, alterations being necessary, the tapestry and wainscoting were taken down, and the interesting discovery made that the interior had been originally painted with single figures, and historical subjects from the Wars of the Maccabees and the legend of the Confessor, arranged around the chamber in a succession of subjects on six bands, somewhat similar to the Bayeux Tapestry, and on the splays and reverts of the windows. Careful drawings were made at the time by J. T. Smith, for his book on Westminster; and still more careful drawings in 1819, by Charles Stothard, since engraved in vol. vi. of the *Vetusta Monumenta*, with accompanying letterpress by John Gage Rokewoode. In very early times it was the Council Chamber of the sovereign; and in it for 800 years were held the Conferences between the two Houses of Parliament. Here, "at a conference of both Houses, July 6, 1641," Waller made his celebrated speech in Parliament upon delivering the impeachment against Mr. Justice Crawley in the matter of Ship-money. Here were held, a few years later, the private sittings of the High Court of Justice for bringing Charles I. to a public trial in Westminster Hall;[2] here the death-warrant of the King was signed by Cromwell, Dick Ingoldsby, and the rest of the regicides; and here the body of the unfortunate King rested till it was removed to Windsor. Here also the bodies of Lord Chatham and of William Pitt lay in state. After the destruction of the Houses of Parliament by fire in 1834 this place was fitted up by Sir Robert Smirke as a temporary House of Lords.

Painter-Stainers' Hall, No. 9 LITTLE TRINITY LANE. The Painter-Stainers' Company (the forerunners of the Royal Academy) existed as a licensed guild or fraternity as early as the 14th century, but they received their first Charter of Incorporation from Queen Elizabeth, July 19, 1580. The minutes of the Company commence in the early part of the reign of James I.; some of the entries are curious. Orders are made to compel the foreign painters then resident in London, Gentileschi, Steenwyck, etc., to pay certain fines for following their art without being free of the Painter-Stainers' Company. The fines, however, were never paid, the Court painters setting the Painter-Stainers in the City at defiance. Cornelius Jansen was a member, and Inigo Jones and Van Dyck occasional guests at their annual feasts.

John Browne, created Serjeant Painter to Henry VIII. by a patent dated Eltham, December 20, 1511, at a salary of 2d. a day, and four ells of cloth annually at Christmas, of the value of 6s. 8d. an ell, and elected Alderman of London, May 7, 1522, by his will dated September

---

[1] Walcott, *Memorials of Westminster*, p. 210. [2] *Whitelocke*, ed. 1732, pp. 367, 372.

17 of that year (proved December 2, 1532) conveyed to the Guild of Paynter-Stayners, of which he was a member, his house in Trinity Lane, which after his death became the hall of the Company, and so continued till it was destroyed in the Great Fire of 1666.[1] The present hall was designed by Sir C. Wren. It is large and well-proportioned, but ill lighted. The ceiling is ornamented with allegorical paintings by Isaac Fuller of Pallas or the Triumph of the Arts, and on the walls are many paintings. *Observe.*—No. 21, The Fire of London, by Waggoner; engraved in Pennant's London. No. 31, Full-length of Charles II., by John Baptist Gaspars. No. 37, Full-length of the Queen of Charles II., by Huysman. No. 33, Full-length of William III., by Sir Godfrey Kneller; presented by Sir Godfrey. No. 28, Full-length of Queen Anne, by Dahl. No. 41, Magdalen, by Sebastian Franck, (small, on copper). No. 42, Camden in his dress as Clarencieux; presented to the Company by Mr. Morgan, master in 1676. Camden left £16 by will to the Painter-Stainers, to buy them a cup, upon which he directed this inscription to be put: "Gul. Camdenus, Clarencieux, filius Sampsonis, Pictoris Londinensis, dono dedit." This loving cup of the great antiquary is produced every St. Luke's Day at the annual feast of the Company. Charles Catton, one of the original members of the Royal Academy, was master of the Company, and on October 18 (St. Luke's Day), 1784, Sir Joshua Reynolds attended and was presented with the freedom of the Company.

Palace Yard (Old), an open space between the Houses of Parliament and Henry VII.'s Chapel, and so called from the Palace of our Kings at Westminster. [*See* Westminster.] It has been the scene of many public executions. Here, January 31, 1605-1606, Guy Fawkes, T. Winter, Rookwood, and Keyes were executed for the Gunpowder Plot. Here, on Thursday, October 29, 1618—

A great and very strange scene—the last scene in the Life of Walter Raleigh. Raleigh was beheaded in Old Palace Yard: he appeared on the scaffold there about eight o'clock that morning: an immense crowd, all London, and in a sense all England looking on. A cold hoar-frosty morning. Earl of Arundel, now known to us by his Greek marbles; Earl of Doncaster ("Sardanapalus" Hay, afterwards Earl of Carlisle): these, with other Earls and dignitaries sat looking through windows near by; to whom Raleigh in his last brief, manful speech appealed, with response from them. . . . A very tragic scene. Such a man with his head grown grey, with his strong heart "breaking"—still strength enough in it to break with dignity. Somewhat proudly he laid his old grey head on the block; as if saying in better than words "There then!"—Carlyle's *Cromwell*.[2]

Here too was enacted an equally strange scene.

On the 30th of June, 1637, in Old Palace Yard, three men, gentlemen of education, of good quality, a Barrister, a Physician, and a Parish Clergyman of London, were set on three Pillories: stood openly as the scum of malefactors, for certain hours there; and then had their ears cut off,—bare knives, hot branding irons—and their cheeks stamped S.L., Seditious Libeller; in the sight of a great

---

[1] The will is printed in the *Archæologia*, vol. xxxix.

[2] See also the account by Sir John Eliot, in his *Monarchy of Man*, quoted in Forster's *Eliot*, vol. i. p. 34.

crowd, "silent" mainly, and looking "pale." The men were ... William Prynne, Barrister: Dr. John Bastwick: and the Rev. Henry Burton, Minister of Friday Street Church. Their sin was against Laud and his surplices at Allhallowtide, not against any other man or thing. . . . Bastwick's wife on the scaffold, received his ears in her lap, and kissed him. Prynne's ears the executioner "rather sawed than cut," "Cut me, tear me," cried Prynne, "I fear thee not. I fear the fire of Hell, not thee!" The June sun had shone hot on their faces. Burton, who had discoursed eloquent religion all the while, said, when they carried him, near fainting into a house in King Street, "It is too hot to last long." Too hot indeed.—*Carlyle's Cromwell*, vol. i. p. 135.

Edmund Calamy died at his house in Old Palace Yard in 1732. The landing-place by which communication was kept up with the Thames was called *Old Palace* or *Parliament Stairs*.

> Thus all the Way they row'd by Water,
> My Eyes were still directed a'ter,
> 'Till they arriv'd at *Palace Stairs*,
> The Place of Landing for our May'rs.—*Hudibras Redivivus*.

Palace Yard (New), the open space before the north entrance to Westminster Hall, so called from being the great court of the new palace begun by William II., of which Westminster Hall was the chief feature completed. The Clock-tower, long the distinguishing feature of New Palace Yard, was originally built, temp. Edward I., out of the fine imposed on Ralph de Hingham, Chief Justice of England. There is a capital view of it by Hollar. The great bell of the tower (Westminster Tom) was given by William III. to the Dean and Chapter of St. Paul's; and the metal of which it was made forms a part of the great bell of the Cathedral.

Before the Great Hall there is a large Court called the new Palace, where there is a strong tower of stone, containing a clock, which striketh on a great Bell [Great Tom of Westminster] every hour, to give notice to the Judges how the time passeth; when the wind is south-south-west, it may be heard unto any part of London, and commonly it presageth wet weather.—Howell's *Londinopolis*, fol. 1657, p. 378; and see Ned Ward, *The London Spy*, pt. 8.

The New Palace Yard being anciently inclosed with a wall, there were four gates therein; the only one at present remaining is that on the east which leads to Westminster stairs; and the three others that are demolished were that on the north which led to the Woolstaple; that on the west called Highgate (a very beautiful and stately edifice) was situate at the east end of Union Street; but it having occasioned great obstruction to the members of Parliament in their passage to and from their respective Houses, the same was taken down in the year 1706, as was also the third at the north end of St. Margaret's Lane, anno 1731, on the same account.—*Maitland*, ed. 1739, p. 729.

That ingeniose tractat [Harrington's *Oceana*], together with his and H. Nevill's smart discourses and inculcations, dayly at Coffee-houses made many Proselytes. Insomuch, that A°. 1659, the beginning of Michaelmas time, he [Harrington] had every night a meeting at the (then) Turk's Head in the New Palace Yard, where they take water, the next house to the stairs at one Miles's, where was made purposely a large ovall-table, with a passage in the middle for Miles to deliver his coffee. About it sate his disciples, and the virtuosi. The discourses in this kind were the most ingeniose and smart that ever I heard or expect to hear, and lauded with great eagernesse: the arguments in the Parlt. House were but flatt to it. Here we had (very formally) a ballotting box, and ballotted how things should be carried by way of Tentamens. The room was every evening full as it could be crammed. Mr.

Cyriack Skinner, an ingeniose young gent., scholar to John Milton, was chaire-man. —Aubrey's *Letters*, vol. iii. p. 371.

The Club, called the *Rota*, lasted little more than a year, Harrington having been arrested and sent to the Tower in 1661. Pepys records a visit he paid to it, January 10, 1660. "To the Coffee-house, where were a great confluence of gentlemen: viz., Mr. Harrington [Sir William] Poultny, chairman, Gold, Dr. Petty [Sir William Petty, ancestor of the Marquis of Lansdowne], etc., where admirable discourse till 9 at night."

The sturdy Puritan, John Stubbs of Lincoln's Inn, and his servant Robert Page, had their right hands cut off in New Palace Yard, December 3, 1580, for a seditious libel against the Queen [Elizabeth] concerning her projected marriage with the Duke of Anjou. On March 2, 1585, William Parry, convicted of high treason, was brought from the Tower to the Palace Court, and there hanged and quartered; and in February 1587, Thomas Lovelace, condemned by the Star Chamber for libellous charges, was carried about Westminster Hall and Palace Yard, set in the pillory and had one of his ears cut off. On St. Peter's Day, 1612, Robert Creighton Lord Sanquhar was hanged in front of Westminster Hall for hiring two ruffians to murder Turner, a fencing-master, by whom he had accidentally lost an eye. Dr. Alexander Leighton, the father of Archbishop Leighton, was here publicly whipped, his ears cut off, his nose slit, branded on the face with the letters S.S. (Sower of Sedition), and afterwards made to stand in the pillory, at the instigation of Laud, November 26, 1630, for a libel on the Bishops.[1] Here, March 9, 1649, the Duke of Hamilton and Lord Capel were beheaded; and here in May 1685 Titus Oates stood in the pillory and was nearly stoned to death. The last who stood in the pillory, in New Palace Yard, February 14, 1765, was Mr. John Williams, bookseller of Fleet Street, for republishing the obnoxious *North Briton*, but with him the exposure was rather a triumph than a punishment, he holding a sprig of laurel all the while in his hand, and receiving the acclamations of the assembled multitude, whilst opposite the pillory was suspended a jack-boot, a Scotch cap and an axe. At the expiration of the sentence the boot and cap were consigned to a bonfire that had been prepared for the purpose, and Williams was carried home in triumph in the hackney-coach "No. 45."

His Majesty fully authorises his most excellent Lord Eldon to give his consent to the House of Lords proceeding with these Bills, and in particular approves of the one for laying open Westminster Abbey to *Palace Yard*. Whatever makes the people more accustomed to view cathedrals must raise their veneration for the Established Church. The King will with equal pleasure consent, when it is proposed, to the *purchasing and pulling down the west* [south] *side of Bridge Street*, and the houses fronting Westminster Hall; as it will be opening to the traveller that ancient pile, which is the seat of administration of the best laws, and the most uprightly administered; and if the people really valued the religion and laws of this blessed country,

---

[1] Only half the whipping and cutting was performed in New Palace Yard; the sentence being completed eight days later at the pillory in Cheapside.

we should stand on a rock that no time could destroy.—*King George III. to Lord Chancellor Eldon*, June 8, 1804.

Sixty years were to pass away before the improvement suggested by the good old king was effected. In 1865, as a part of the scheme of Sir Charles Barry for the completion of the Houses of Parliament the area of New Palace Yard was cleared and laid out as an open place; a covered way, or cloister, for the use of members of the two Houses, was constructed along its eastern side, and the houses on the south side of Bridge Street removed, and the whole enclosed with an iron railing, the handiwork of Skidmore of Coventry, with handsome gates by Hardman of Birmingham; the whole under the directions of Sir C. Barry, R.A. A part of the design was to decorate the enclosure with bronze statues of distinguished statesmen, but the statues of Peel, Palmerston, Derby, and Beaconsfield, are at the sides of the garden plot opposite to it, called Parliament Square. Westmacott's statue of Canning, which formerly stood there, has been removed farther west. In the residence attached to the sinecure office of Yeoman-Usher of the Exchequer, in New Palace Yard, William Godwin spent the last three years of his life, and there died, April 7, 1836, at the age of eighty years.

Pall Mall, a spacious street extending from the foot of ST. JAMES'S STREET to the foot of the HAYMARKET, and so called from a game of that name, somewhat similar to croquet, introduced into England in the reign of Charles I., perhaps earlier. King James I., in his *Basilicon Doron*, recommends it as a game that Prince Henry should use. The name (Italian *palamaglio*, French *paille maille*), is given to avenues and walks in other countries, as at Utrecht in Holland. The Malls at Blois, Tours, and Lyons are mentioned by Evelyn in his Memoirs, under the year 1644.

A paille-mall is a wooden hammer set to the end of a long staffe to strike a boule with, at which game noblemen and gentlemen in France doe play much.—*The French Garden for English Ladies*, 8vo, 1621; and see *Cotgrave*, 1632.

Among all the exercises of France, I prefer none before the Paille-Maille, both because it is a gentleman-like sport, not violent, and yields good occasion and opportunity of discourse, as they walke from the one marke to the other. I marvell among many more apish and foolish toys which we have brought out of France, that we have not brought this sport also into England.—Sir Robert Dallington, *A Method for Travel*, 4to, 1598.

Pale Maille (Fr.) a game wherein a round bowle is with a mallet struck through a high arch of iron (standing at either end of an alley), which he that can do at the fewest blows, or at the number agreed on, wins. This game was heretofore used in the long alley near St. James's, and vulgarly called Pell-Mell.—Blount's *Glossographia*, ed. 1670.

It is usual to ascribe the introduction of the game, and the first formation of the *Mall*, to Charles II., but this is only a vulgar error. "The Pall of London" is mentioned by John King, Bishop of London, in 1613,[1] and Pall Mall—but whether the game or the place is not quite clear, though it was probably the latter—by Garrard in 1637.

[1] Bishop King to Carleton, February 27, 1613. *Cal. State Pap.*, 1611-1618, p. 173.

November 9, 1637.—There fell out a quarrel betwixt my Lord Philip Herbert, son of the Chamberlain, and the Lord Carr, son to the Earl of Roxborough, at *Pall Mall*, young youths both. Upon some words my Lord Philip struck him, so they fell to cuffs. It passed no further, my Lord had no notice of it who made them friends. —*Garrard to Wentworth* (*Strafford Letters*, vol. ii. p. 131).

In September 1635 a grant was made to Archibald Lumsden "for sole purchasing of all the malls, bowls, scoops, and other necessaries for the game of Pall mall, within his grounds in St. James's Fields, and that such as resort there shall pay him such sums of money as are according to the ancient order of the game."[1] A piece or parcel of pasture ground called "Pell Mell Close," part of which was planted with apple trees (Apple Tree Yard, St. James's Square, still exists), is described by the Commissioners for the Survey of the Crown Lands, in 1650, and the close must have taken its name from the particular locality where the game was played. And that this was the case is proved by the same Survey, the Commissioners valuing at £70 "All those Elm Trees standing in Pall Mall walk, in a very decent and regular manner on both sides the walk, being in number 140." In the Rate-books of St. Martin's-in-the-Fields, under the year 1656, eight names of persons are entered as living "in the Pall Mall;" and in 1657 occurs a heading, "Down the Haymarket and in the Pall Mall." Pepys (June 10, 1666), relating the dismissal of my Lady Castlemaine from the Court for some impertinent language in presence of the Queen, says that she left "presently, and went to a lodging in the Pell Mell." The Mall in the present street certainly existed as early as the reign of Charles I., and probably in that of his predecessor. The Mall in St. James's Park was made by Charles II. [*See* The Mall.]

September 16, 1660.—To the Park, where I saw how far they had proceeded in the Pell-mell, and in making a river through the Park, which I had never seen before since it was begun.—*Pepys*.

An attempt was made to compliment the Queen of Charles II. by giving the name of Catherine Street to the thoroughfare which led past the residence of Nell Gwynne to the palace of Lady Castlemaine. In the Statute of 1685 the parish of St. James is said to begin "at the Picture shop having an iron balcony at the south side of the end of *Catherine Street*, alias Pall Mall." But in the latter part of the same Act this name is dropped and Pall Mall only used. Nor does it ever appear to have come into common acceptation. In descriptions and advertisements, memoirs and letters from this time forward, the street is as far as we have been able to discover invariably called Pall Mall, with one exception. In *Letters and Miscellaneous Papers*, by Barré C. Roberts, Student of Christ Church, Oxford (4to, 1814), is a letter to Roberts, dated February 1808, from his father, who says—

I do not remember old Fribourg: he had kept a shop in the narrow part of Pall Mall, *formerly called Catherine Street*, in which he was succeeded by Pontet, a Frenchman, who told me he had married Fribourg's daughter. The shop was three

---

[1] *Cal. State Pap.*, 1631-1633, p. 286.

or four doors from the Haymarket on the right hand: I was often sent to buy snuff for my father full fifty years ago.

From which it would seem that the name of Catherine Street was occasionally used, or at least remembered, as late as the middle of the 18th century. But on the other hand Dodsley (London, 1761), whose shop was in Pall Mall, makes no reference to its having ever been so called, either under "Pall Mall" or "Catherine Street." Even in 1685, although so named in the Act of that year, it was not an accepted name.

A tauny more with short bushy hair, very well shaped, in a grey livery lined with yellow, about seventeen or eighteen years of age, with a silver collar about his neck, with these directions, "Captain George Hastings' Boy, Brigadier in the King's Horse Guards." Whoever will bring him to the Sugar Loaf in the Pall Mall shall have 40s. reward.—*London Gazette*, March 23, 1685.

One of the scenes in Wycherley's *Love in a Wood, or St. James's Park*, is laid in the *Old Pall Mall*. This is what we now call the street; for the first time that Pepys mentions Pell Mell is under July 26, 1660, where he says, "We went to Wood's at the Pell Mell (our old house for clubbing), and there we spent till ten at night." This is not only one of the earliest references to Pall Mall, as an inhabited locality, but one of the earliest uses of the word "clubbing" in its modern signification of a Club, and additionally interesting, seeing that the street still maintains what Johnson would have called its "clubbable" character.

The writing of that play [*Love in a Wood*] was the occasion of his [Wycherley's] becoming acquainted with one of King Charles's mistresses after a very particular manner. As Mr. Wycherley was going thro' Pall Mall, towards St. James's, in his chariot, he met the foresaid lady [the Duchess of Cleveland] in hers, who thrusting half her body out of her chariot, cry'd out aloud to him, "You, Wycherley, you are a son of a whore," at the same time laughing aloud and heartily. Perhaps, sir, if you never heard of this passage before, you may be surpris'd at so strange a greeting from one of the most beautiful and best bred ladies in the world. Mr. Wycherley was very much surpris'd at it, yet not so much but he soon apprehended it was spoke with allusion to the latter end of a song in the fore-mentioned play:—

When parents are slaves
Their brats cannot be any other;
Great Wits and great Braves
Have always a Punk to their Mother.

Dennis's *Letters*, 8vo, 1721, p. 215.

The Pall Mail, a fine long street. The houses on the south side have a pleasant prospect into the King's Garden; and besides they have small gardens behind them, which reach to the wall, and to many of them are raised Mounts, which give them the prospect of the said Garden and of the Park.—*Strype*, B. vi. p. 81.

Eminent Inhabitants.—Dr. Sydenham, the celebrated physician. He was living in the Pavement [on the south side of St. James's Square, and overlooking Pall Mall] in 1658, and in Pall Mall from 1664 till his death there, December 29, 1689. He is buried in St. James's Church. Mr. Fox told Mr. Rogers that Sydenham was sitting at his window looking on the Mall, with his pipe in his mouth and a silver tankard before him, when a fellow made a snatch at the tankard and ran off with it. Nor was he overtaken, said Fox, before he got among the bushes in Bond Street, and there they lost him.[1] Sydenham's executor was Thomas Malthus, afterwards apothecary to Queen Anne, and also a resident in this street. Thomas Robert Malthus, the writer on Population, was his great-grandson. Nell Gwynne, in 1670, on the "east end, north side," next to Lady Mary Howard; from 1671 to her death in 1687 in a house on the "south side," with a garden towards the Park—now No. 79; but the house has been twice rebuilt since Nell inhabited it. The "south side, west end," was inhabited in 1671 as follows :—

Mrs. Mary Knight [Madam Knight the Singer—the King's mistress],
Edward Griffin, Esq. [Treasurer of the Chamber],
Maddam Elinor Gwyn,
The Countess of Portland,
The Lady Reynelogh,
Doctor Barrow.[2]

March 5, 1671.—I thence walk'd with him [Charles II.] thro' St. James's Parke to the gardens, where I both saw and heard a very familiar discourse between [the King] and Mrs. Nellie, as they cal'd an impudent Comedian, she looking out of her garden on a terrace at the top of the wall,[3] and [the King] standing on ye greene walke under it. I was heartily sorry at this scene. Thence the King walk'd to the Duchess of Cleaveland, another lady of pleasure and curse of our nation.—*Evelyn*.

My friend Dr. Heberden has built a fine house in Pall Mall, on the Palace side; he told me it was the only freehold house on that side; that it was given by a long lease by Charles II. to Nell Gwyn, and upon her discovering it to be *only a lease* under the Crown, she returned him the lease and conveyances, saying she had always *conveyed free* under the Crown, and always would; and would not accept it till it was *conveyed free* to her by an act of Parliament made on and for that purpose. Upon Nell's death it was sold, and has been conveyed free ever since. I think Dr. Heberden purchased it of the Waldegrave family.—*W. F. Ewin to Rev. James Granger* (Granger's *Letters*, p. 308).

Henry Oldenburg, first Secretary of the Royal Society, in a house for which he paid little more than £40 a year. Sir Isaac Newton directed a letter to him (March 16, 1671-1672), "At his house about the middle of Old Pell Mail in Westminster, London." Mary Beale, portrait painter (d. December 28, 1697). Sir William Temple, in 1681, two doors eastward of Nell Gwynne. Hon. Robert Boyle, about 1668, "settled himself for life in London" in the house of his sister, Lady Ranelagh, in Pall Mall, next door to Sir William Temple, and three from Nell Gwynne. He wrote from here to Hooke in 1680, declining to be made President of the Royal Society. He died here, December 31, 1691, within a week of the sister, with whom he had lived many years, and was buried near her on the south side of the chancel of St. Martin's Church. Countess of Southesk, on the south side, in 1671. This is the celebrated Countess of De Grammont's Memoirs. Duke

---

[1] The story is told with fuller particulars in Seward's *Anecdotes*, vol. ii. p. 52.
[2] Rate-books of St. Martin's.
[3] Nell stood on a mount to speak to the King. The following advertisement from the *Postman* newspaper of April 1703 affords an interesting glimpse of this locality: "One, two, or three houses, about the middle of the Pall Mall, on the Park side, with Gardens and Mounts adjoining to the Royal Garden, to be sold or let by long lease. Enquire at the 2 Golden Balls, in the Pall Mall over against St. James's Square."

of Schomberg (d. 1690), in the large brick house known as Schomberg House, now occupied by Nos. 81 and 82 as part of the War Office. [*See* Schomberg House.] The great Duke of Marlborough, who built *Marlborough House*. George Psalmanazar had lodgings here on his first arrival, and here he was visited as an inhabitant of Formosa. Swift writes, October 1720, to the Hon. Sir Thomas Hanmer, Bart., at his house in Pall Mall. Lord Bolingbroke was living here in 1726.

October 22, 1726.—I hear that Lord Bolingbroke will be in town, at his house in Pall Mall, next week.—*Gay to Swift*.

June 4, 1727.—You will find me just returning to Crauford from the Pall Mall. —*Bolingbroke to Swift*.

Bubb Dodington, Lord Melcombe, the Bubo of Pope. "Mr. Dodington" wrote Horace Walpole, "built the house in Pall Mall which is now in front of Carlton House."

Dodington's house in Pall Mall stood close to the garden the Prince had bought there of Lord Chesterfield; and during Dodington's favour the Prince had suffered him to make a door out of his house into his garden, which, upon the first decay of his interest, the Prince shut up—building and planting before Dodington's house, and changing every lock in his own to which he had formerly given Dodington keys.—Lord Hervey's *Memoirs*, vol. i. p. 434.

He flattered Walpole at Whitehall
And damned him at Pall Mall.

Sir Robert Walpole had a freehold house in Pall Mall, which he gave to his son Edward.[1] In it lived Lady Waldegrave and Sir Edward Walpole.

Robert Dodsley, the bookseller, opened his shop in Pall Mall in 1735, under the patronage of Pope, with the sign of "Tully's Head," and dying in 1764 was buried at Durham.

To be spoke with every Thursday at Tully's head in Pall Mall, Adam Fitz-Adam.—*The World*, No. 1.

William Hunter, on his first arrival in London in 1741, took up his residence with Dr. Smellie in Pall Mall, but soon left it for the house of Dr. Douglas, the Horatian enthusiast, and owner of the "soft obstetric hand" celebrated by Pope. Smellie and Douglas were rival man-midwives, and in a paper war which arose between them the former was accused of degrading the profession by hanging out from his house in Pall Mall a paper lantern inscribed "Midwifery taught here for five shillings." The young Pretender, on his furtive visit to London in September 1750, held a secret meeting with about fifty of his friends at his lodging in Pall Mall.[2] William, Duke of Cumberland, the hero of Culloden, in Schomberg House in 1760.

October 28, 1760.—The Duke of Cumberland has taken Lord Sandwich's [house] in Pall Mall.—*Walpole to Montagu* (*Letters*), vol. iii. p. 353).

In Sir Joshua Reynolds's pocket-book for 1762 is noted an appointment, "July 17, at six with *Miss Nelly O'Brien* in Pall Mall, next door this side the Star and Garter," which is represented by the

---

[1] Horace Walpole, *Account of my Conduct*. (*Letters*, vol. i. p. lxxix.)

[2] Lord Stanhope's *Hist. of England*, vol. iv. p. 8.

present 43 A. Gibbon wrote to Holroyd, Pall Mall, December 25, 1769; and again in December 1772 immediately before he took his house in Bentinck Street. On his brief visit to England in 1787 he once more took lodgings here, and wrote to Lord Sheffield, "Virtue should never be made too difficult. I feel that a man has more friends in Pall Mall than in Bentinck Street." Sir John Pringle (President of the Royal Society, 1772-1778) frequently received the Fellows of that Society at his house until his death in 1781. Thomas Gainsborough, the painter, in the western wing of Schomberg House, from 1777 to 1783. A tablet has been placed by the Society of Arts in the house to commemorate Gainsborough's residence. David Astley, the painter, divided Schomberg House into three, and fitted up the centre in a fantastic manner for his own use, and after his death, in 1787, it was occupied by Cosway the miniature painter, whose pretty wife gave parties that were for a while extremely fashionable. In 1779, when Admiral Keppel was acquitted, and all London was illuminated, his prosecutor, Palliser, was living in Pall Mall.

February 12, 1779.—My servants, who have been out this morning, tell me that about 3 o'clock the mob found their way into Palliser's house in spite of the guards and demolished every thing in it. . . . *P.S.*—The mob entirely gutted Sir Hugh Palliser's house, but the furniture had been removed.—*Walpole to Sir H. Mann* (*Letters*, vol. vii. p. 176).

In 1782 Lord Rodney's prisoner, the Count de Grasse, took up his abode in the Royal Hotel, Pall Mall. Lord Chancellor Erskine dates a codicil of his will from "Carleton Hotel, Pall Mall, October 2, 1786." Mr. Angerstein lived at No. 102. Five doors east of it died the Right Hon. William Windham, June 3, 1810.

Windham is a Moloch among the fallen ambassadors, I was at his house on the day when the Peace procession passed in Pall Mall, and was highly gratified with his grotesque affectation of laughing at the triumph of his enemies. He laughed, but it was a laugh of agony.—*Thomas Campbell to J. Richardson*, 1802.

Lord Brougham has portrayed him under a different aspect.

His manners were the most polished and noble and courteous, without the least approach to pride, or affectation, or condescension; his spirits were, in advanced life, so gay that he was always younger than the youngest; his relish of conversation was such that, after lingering to the latest moment he joined whatever party a sultry evening (or morning as it might chance to prove) tempted to haunt the streets before retiring to rest. How often have we accompanied him to the door of his own mansion, and then been attended by him to our own, while the streets rang with the peals of his hearty merriment, or echoed the accents of his refined and universal wit. —Brougham, in *Edinburgh Review*, October 1838, p. 237.

November 18, 1805.—Wasn't you sorry for Lord Nelson? I have followed him in fancy ever since I saw him walking in Pall Mall (I was prejudiced against him before) looking just as a hero should look.—*Charles Lamb to Hazlitt*.

David Wilkie opened at No. 87, on May 1, 1812, an exhibition of his pictures and finished studies, twenty-nine in number. He lost money by it, and did not repeat the experiment, but it helped to extend his reputation. The witty, wilful Mrs. Abington died, March 4, 1815, "at her apartments in Pall Mall." Sir Charles Bunbury died at his house in Pall Mall, 1821. Sir Walter Scott, on his visit to London 1826-1827, stayed at the house of his son-in-law, Lockhart, No. 25 Pall Mall. Many entries in his Diary are dated from this house, but the whole frontage has since been altered.

Among the events which Pall Mall has witnessed, one of the most remarkable was the murder of Mr. Thynne, February 12, 1682, by Colonel Vratz and Lieutenant Stern, the hired agents of Count Konigsmark. These mean villains were hanged in Pall Mall on March 10, but the greater assassin was allowed to escape. At the Star and Garter Tavern, William, fifth Lord Byron (d. 1798), killed (1765) his neighbour and friend, Mr. Chaworth, in what was rather a broil than a duel.

June 13, 1782.—As Lady Chewton and her sisters came from the Opera, they saw two officers fighting in Pall Mall, next to Dr. Graham's and the mob trying to part them. Lord Chewton and some other young men went into the house and found a Captain Lucas of the Guards bleeding on a couch. It was a quarrel about an E. O. table : I don't know what. This officer had been struck in the face with a red-hot poker by a drawer, and this morning is dead.—*Walpole to Lady Ossory* (*Letters*, vol. viii. p. 232).

These quarrels and duels were not the only strange scenes Pall Mall beheld a century ago.

January 8, 1786.—The mail from France was robbed last night in Pall Mall,[1] at half an hour after 8. The chaise had stopped, the harness was cut, and the portmanteau was taken out of the chaise itself. A courier is gone to Paris for a copy of the despatch. What think you of banditti in the heart of such a capital?— *Walpole to Mann* (*Letters*, vol. ix. p. 35).

It was in Dalton's print warehouse, Pall Mall, in a building erected for Lamb the auctioneer, and having therefore the advantage of a "great room," that the Royal Academy had its original home. The building adjoined Old Carlton House on the east. It was here that, at the formal opening of the Academy, January 2, 1769, Sir Joshua Reynolds delivered the first of his fifteen Presidential Discourses. Here the first of the annual exhibitions was opened on April 26, 1769; and here the Academy met and the exhibitions were held till January 14, 1771, when the Academy met for the first time in their new apartments in Somerset House. The building was afterwards occupied by Christie, the picture auctioneer. At the King's Arms in Pall Mall met in 1734 the Liberty or Rump Steak Club, consisting exclusively of peers in eager opposition to Sir Robert Walpole; there is a list of the club in the *Marchmont Papers*, vol. ii. p. 20.

There was a club held at the King's Head in Pall Mall, that arrogantly called itself The World. Lord Stanhope (then (now Lord Chesterfield), Lord Herbert, etc. etc., were members. Epigrams were proposed to be written on the glasses, by each member after dinner; once when Dr. Young was invited thither, the doctor would have declined writing because he had no diamond; Lord Stanhope lent him his, and he wrote immediately:

Accept a miracle instead of wit;
See two dull lines, with Stanhope's pencil writ.

Spence's *Anecdotes*, by Singer, p. 377.

---

[1] The *foreign* Post-Office was at this time in Albemarle Street.

At the Star and Garter (1760-1770) used to meet the *Thursday Night Club*, of which the George Selwyn and Lord March set were members, as was also Sir Joshua Reynolds. Sir Joshua was regular in his attendance, although his bad whist playing, and manners the reverse of *fast*, caused him to be less highly appreciated here than he was at the Turk's Head. Another noted house was the Smyrna Coffee-house [which *see*].

> O bear me to the paths of fair Pell Mell,
> Safe are thy pavements, grateful is thy smell !
> At distance rolls along the gilded coach,
> No sturdy carmen on thy walks encroach ;
> Shops breathe perfumes : thro' sashes ribbons glow
> The mutual arms of ladies, and the beau.
> Gay's *Trivia*, B. ii. p. 257.
> Yet who the footman's arrogance can quell,
> Whose flambeau gilds the sashes of *Pell Mell*,
> When in long rank a train of torches flame,
> To light the midnight visits of the dame?
> *Ibid.*, B. iii. p. 156.

Pell Mell, it will be seen, was the genteel pronunciation of the name in the days of Queen Anne, and so it has continued to be down to the present day.

> If we must have a villa in summer to dwell,
> O give me the sweet shady side of *Pell Mell.*
> Captain Morris, *The Contrast.*

This celebrated street was, January 28, 1807, the first street in London lighted with gas, by a German named Winsor. The second was Bishopsgate Street. *Observe.*—On the south side, Marlborough House, now the residence of H.R.H. the Prince of Wales ; 69, the London Joint-Stock Bank ; 70, the Guards' Club ; 71 to 76, the Oxford and Cambridge Club ; 86, the War Office ; 94, Carlton Club ; 104, Reform Club ; 106, Travellers' Club ; 107, Athenæum Club ; 116-117, United Service Club. On the north side, 52, the Marlborough Club (formerly the British Instititution, founded 1805) ; 36-39, the Army and Navy Club ; 29, Royal Exchange Assurance, rebuilt 1884-1885, by George Aitchison, A.R.A. ; 30-35, Junior Carlton Club ; and refer to each for particular descriptions. In *Pall Mall East*, *Observe*, on north side—United University Club ; Royal Society of Painters in Water Colours ; and on the south, the Royal College of Physicians, and next to it Colnaghi's famous print-shop. Here, too, is the bronze equestrian statue of George III. by Mathew Coates Wyatt.

Palmer's Village, WESTMINSTER, the name given so late as 1831 (Elmes) to some scattered houses between the grounds of Elliot's brewery and Little James Street. *Palmer's Almshouses*, founded by James Palmer, B.D., in 1654, " at Tothill Side, Westminster," are on the north side of Victoria Street. Maitland, writing in 1739, says (p. 675), " Here is a chapel for the use of the scholars and pensioners, wherein the Founder himself, for some time, preach'd and pray'd twice a day to them." These almshouses were handsomely rebuilt in 1881.

Palsgrave Court, originally PALSGRAVE'S HEAD COURT, afterwards PALSGRAVE PLACE, in the STRAND, near Temple Bar, was so called from a tavern having for its sign the head of the Palsgrave Frederick, the husband of the Princess Elizabeth, only daughter of James I. There was also a Palatine Head in Soho. William Faithorne, the engraver, lived "at the sign of the Ship, next to the Drake, opposite to the Palsgrave Head Tavern, without Temple Bar." Here Prior and Montague make the Country Mouse and the City Mouse bilk the hackney coachman :—

> But now at Piccadilly they arrive,
> And taking coach, t'wards Temple-Bar they drive,
> But at St. Clement's Church, cat out the back ;
> And slipping through the Palsgrave, bilkt poor hack.
> Prior and Montague, *The Hind and Panther Transvers'd.*

When, 1691, Archbishop Sancroft had to quit Lambeth Palace, he took boat at Lambeth Bridge and went to "the Palgrave's Head, near Temple Bar," where he remained from June 23 to August 5, when he retired to Fressingfield in Suffolk, his native place. Tokens of the tavern are extant. This court was abolished when the large building called the Outer Temple was built partly on its site.

Pancras Lane, CITY, runs on the south and parallel to Cheapside, from Queen Street to Bucklersbury. It seems to have been so called after the Great Fire, to perpetuate the memory of the ancient church of St. Pancras, which stood on the north side of it and was not rebuilt. Previously the portion to the west of Size Lane had been called *Needelers' Lane,* and to the east *Pencritch* [Pancras] *Street,* (*Stow,* p. 98). Here are still the cemeteries of the two churches of St. Pancras and St. Benet Sherehog ; the latter is nearest to Bucklersbury.

Pancras (St.) in the Fields, a prebendal manor in Middlesex, belonging to the Dean and Chapter of St. Paul's, containing the old parish church, now made a district church, situated on the north side of the road leading from King's Cross to Kentish Town ; and a new church, the present parish church, described in a succeeding article.

St. Pancras is so called in the Domesday Survey [*Sm. Pancratium*]. The manor of Pancras belonged to the Dean and Canons or Chapter of St. Paul's ; as also did the prebendal manors of Totenhall (Tottenham Court), and Cantelows, now Kentish Town. Ruggemere, or Rugmere, was another prebend in this parish, but the site of the prebendal estate is now unknown. The parish is of great extent, reaching from St. Andrew's, Holborn, and St. George's, Bloomsbury, to Hampstead, Highgate, and Finchley, and including the Gray's Inn, Tottenham Court, Euston and Hampstead Roads, Somers Town, Camden Town, and Kentish Town, Ken (or Caen) Wood, and part of Highgate, a portion of the Regent's Park, and the whole of the extensive London and North-Western, Midland, and Great Northern Railway termini. In 1801 there were 31,779 inhabitants in the parish; in 1881 there were nearly a quarter of a million (236,209).

> Pancras Church standeth all alone, as utterly forsaken, old and weather-beaten, which, for the antiquity thereof, is thought not to yield to Paules in London. About this church have bin many buildings now decayed, leaving poor Pancras without companie or comfort, yet it is now and then visited with Kentishtowne and Highgate, which are members thereof; but they seldom come there, for they have chapels of ease within themselves; but when there is a corpse to be interred, they are forced to leave the same within this forsaken church or churchyard, where (no doubt) it resteth as secure against the day of resurrection, as if it laie in stately Paule's.—Norden, *Spec. Brit.*, 4to, 1593.

This interesting little church, partly of Norman, but in the main of Early English date, had in the course of time been greatly altered and covered with plaster. It consisted of a nave and chancel, and at the west end a tower, on which in 1750, when Chatelain's view was taken, was a short shingled spire, but which somewhat later was superseded by an odd sort of dome. In 1847-1848 the church was almost entirely rebuilt in the Norman style (Messrs. Gough and Roumieu, architects), and enlarged, with a tower on the south side at the east end of the nave. It was reopened for divine service, July 5, 1848. Whatever was of interest in the church has passed away, but the monuments deserve examination. The church was restored internally in 1888, when a chancel-screen and choir stalls were added. The old sedilia were discovered on removing the plaster from the walls. The appearance of the interior was somewhat improved, but it is still very heavy in consequence of a gallery which runs round three sides of the nave portion. *Observe.*—Against the north wall of the nave a monument, much defaced (circ. 1500), but without name or inscription; recesses for brasses alone remaining. In the south-east corner of the nave at the entrance to the chancel is a tablet, surmounted by a palette and pencils, to Samuel Cooper, the miniature painter (d. 1672): the arms are those of Sir Edward Turner, Speaker of the House of Commons in the reign of Charles II., at whose expense it is probable the monument was erected. And on the south wall of the church a monument, with two busts, to William Platt (d. 1637), the founder of an important charity, and wife, repaired at the expense of St. John's College, Cambridge, in 1743, and removed hither from the chapel at Highgate in 1833. In the churchyard have been interred an unusual number of remarkable persons. This has been in a great measure owing to its having been for a long series of years the chief burial-place for Roman Catholics resident in London, though the eminent persons buried here are by no means confined to the professors of that faith. "Of late," says Strype, writing at the beginning of the 18th century, "those of the Roman Catholic religion have affected to be buried here."[1] Till the churchyard was closed for interments, it continued to be a favourite Roman Catholic cemetery. For this preference various reasons have been assigned. A

[1] *Strype*, App., p. 136.

popular tradition was that it was the last London church in which mass was performed. Roman Catholics, said Dr. Johnson, "chose St. Pancras for their burying-place because some Catholics in Queen Elizabeth's time had been burnt there." Lysons was told that it was because "masses were said in a church in the south of France, dedicated to the same saint, for the souls of the deceased interred at St. Pancras in England." Mr. Markland dismisses all these reasons without ceremony. "I learn," he says, "*from unquestionable authority*, that it rests upon no foundation;" but is "mere prejudice."[1] This may be; but even the prejudice must have had an origin. The probable explanation is, that it having been, from accident of residence, chosen as the burial-place of some distinguished member of the church, others of a like faith wished to be laid near him, and—there being no recognised Roman Catholic burial-ground in London—the *prejudice* would every year extend and strengthen, as more and more of those who were regarded with veneration came to be laid there. These interments include many prelates and priests, members of old Catholic families, Howards and Arundels, Cliffords, Blounts, Tichbornes, Doughtys, Constables, Honars, many Jacobites and Nonjurors, and a large number of French *emigrés*, victims of the first French Revolution, who took up their residence in Somers Town.

The French Revolution tended materially to fill St. Pancras churchyard. Writing in 1811, Lysons says that "about thirty of the French clergy have on an average been buried annually at Pancras for some years past; in 1801 there were forty-one; in 1802 thirty-two."[2] Among them were several prelates and other dignitaries of the church: Angelus Franciscus de Talaru de Calmazel, Bishop of Coutance (d. 1798). Augustinus Renatus Ludovicus Le Mintier, Bishop and Count of Treguier (d. 1801). Louis André Grimaldi, Bishop of Noyon (d. 1804). Arthur Richard Dillon, Archbishop of Narbonne (d. 1806). Jean François Comte de la Marche, Bishop of St. Pol de Leon (d. 1806). The Rev. Arthur ["Father"] O'Leary (d. 1802). Father Nicholas Pisani, of the Order of St. Anthony (d. 1803). Louis Charles, Comte D'Hervilly, Field-Marshal of France, Major-General in the Russian, and Colonel in the British army, died of a wound received at Quiberon (1795). Lieut.-General Comte Montboissier (d. 1797). François Claude Amour, Marquis de Bouillé, Governor and Commander-in-Chief of the French islands in the West Indies (d. 1800). Louis Charles Bigot de St. Croix, "dernier Ministre de Louis," as the now illegible inscription on his monument recorded (d. 1803). Marie Louisa d'Esparbes de Lussan, Comtesse de Palastron, "Dame de Palais de la Reine de France" (d. 1804). Antonio Moriano Domenico Mortellari, the musical composer, "pensioner of Louis XVI., whom he served eighteen years." Henry Marquis de Lostange, "Grand Seneschal de Quercy, Mareschal des Camps et Armées de Roi de France" (d. 1807). Claude Joseph Gabriel, Viscomte de

[1] Note to Croker's *Boswell*, p. 840.   [2] *Lysons*, vol. ii. p. 619, *note* 40.

Vaulx, Field-Marshal of France and Governor of Valence in Dauphiny (d. 1809). Baroness de Montalembert (d. 1808). L. F. E. Camus, Seigneur de Pontcarré, "premier Président du Parlement de Normandie, Conseiller du Roi en tous ses conseils" (d. 1810).

Against the exterior of the church, at the south-west end of the nave, is a headstone to William Woollett the engraver (d. 1785) and his widow (d. 1819). In a part of the ground now taken by the Midland Railway Company was a pedestal-like altar-tomb to William Godwin, author of *Political Justice* and *Caleb Williams* (d. 1836), and his two wives; Mary Wolstonecraft Godwin, author of *A Vindication of the Rights of Women*, the mother of Mrs. Shelley (d. 1797); and Mary Jane (d. 1841), in whose name the "Juvenile Library" in Skinner Street was carried on. At this grave, in 1813, when it only contained the body of Mary Wolstonecraft, a remarkable scene took place:

> Shelley's anguish, his isolation, his difference from other men, his gifts of genius, and eloquent enthusiasm, made a deep impression on Godwin's daughter Mary, now a girl of sixteen, who had been accustomed to hear Shelley spoken of as something rare and strange. To her, as they met one eventful day in St. Pancras churchyard, by her Mother's grave, Bysshe, in burning words, poured forth the tale of his wild past—how he had suffered, how he had been misled, and how, if supported by her love, he hoped in future years to enrol his name with the wise and good who had done battle for their fellow men, and been true through all adverse storms, to the cause of humanity. Unhesitatingly she placed her hand in his, and linked her fortunes with his own.—Lady Shelley's *Memorials*, p. 57.

The remains of Godwin and his first wife, Mary Wolstonecraft, were removed in 1851 and laid beside those of their daughter, Mrs. Shelley, in Bournemouth churchyard. It was in Old St. Pancras Church that Godwin and Mary Wolstonecraft were married, March 29, 1797, "Marshal and the clerk of the church being the witnesses. Godwin takes no notice whatever of it in his Diary." [1]

Among the stones was one to "Daniel Tullum, gent., page of the Backstairs to the Queen of the late King James the Second," "and was abroad with them many years in all their troubles," and also with "the King's daughter Lewisa, who died in France." He died, October 14, 1730, in his seventy-seventh year. Others were those of Amy, wife of Cuthbert Constable and daughter of Hugh Lord Clifford (d. 1731); Sir James Tobin (d. 1735); Elizabeth, Countess of Castlehaven, and a few more. The plain headstone to John Walker, author of the *Pronouncing Dictionary of the English Language* and other works (d. 1807), has been replaced by a larger and more conspicuous one erected by the Baroness Burdett-Coutts. The St. Giles's portion of the ground is comparatively modern, having been consecrated in 1803. Here is the large and elaborate tomb of Sir John Soane, R.A., the architect of the Bank of England (d. June 30, 1837), his wife and son; another is that of Sir John Gurney, Baron of the Exchequer (d. March 1, 1845).

The register of burials includes those of Abraham Woodhead (d. May 4, 1678), in his day the stoutest champion of Roman Catholicism.

[1] Kegan Paul's *William Godwin*, vol. i. p. 234.

Wood gives a long account of him, and adds "that he was buried in the churchyard of St. Pancras, about 22 paces from the chancel, on the south side. Afterwards a raised altar-monument, built of brick, covered with a thick plank of blue marble, was put over his grave."[1] Obadiah Walker (d. 1699). He was buried near his friend, Abraham Woodhead, with this short inscription :— .

PER BONAM FAMAM ET INFAMIAM
OB. JAN. 31, A.D. 1699, ÆT. 86.

The interment of these prominent Catholics might be thought to have induced or favoured the preference shown for St. Pancras churchyard by others of the creed, but it is pretty certain, despite of Strype, that the practice had been for some time in existence.

> I told 'em of Pancras church where their scholars
> (When they have killed one another in duel)
> Have a churchyard to themselves for their dead.
> Davenant, *Playhouse to be Lett*, 1663 [printed 1673].

John Ernest Grabe, D.D. (d. 1711), Orientalist and editor of a valuable edition of the Septuagint. There is a monument to his memory in Westminster Abbey.

> Poor Dr. Grabe's receiving the absolution from Dr. Smalridge, the communion from Dr. Hicks, and being buried in St. Pancras church (where the Roman Catholics dying in or near this city have been commonly interred) occasions talk.—White Kennet, MSS., *Life of Robert Nelson*, p. 221.

Thomas Dungan, Earl of Limerick (d. 1715). Hon. Esme Howard, son of Henry, Earl of Arundel (d. 1728). Edward Walpole of Dunston, Lincolnshire (d. 1740). Elizabeth, Countess of Castlehaven (d. 1743). Sir Thomas Mackworth, Bart. (d. 1744). Jeremy Collier (d. 1726), the writer against the immorality of the stage in the time of Dryden. Ned Ward (d. 1731), author of the *London Spy*. He kept a punch-house in Fulwood's Rents in Holborn. His hearse was attended by a single mourning coach, containing only his wife and daughter, as he had directed it should be in his poetical will, written six years before he died. Bevil Higgons (d. 1735); he wrote against Burnet's History. Lewis Theobald (d. 1744), the hero of the early editions of the *Dunciad*, and the editor of Shakespeare.[2] Lady Henrietta Beard, daughter of an Earl of Waldegrave, widow of Lord Edward Herbert, and wife of Beard, the singer (d. 1753). Pope's Martha Blount (d. January 12, 1763, aged seventy-three) and Theresa Blount (d. October 7, 1759, aged seventy). Henry Racket (d. 1775) and Robert Racket (d. 1779), Pope's nephews, and mentioned in his will. S. F. Ravenet, the engraver (d. 1764). In this church (February 13, 1718-1719), Jonathan Wild was married to his third wife; in this churchyard he was buried in 1725.

After his execution his body was carried off in a coach and four to the sign of the Adam and Eve near Pancras Church, in order to be interred in the churchyard there, where one of his former wives was buried.—*Defoe*, vol. iii. p. 392.

---

[1] *Ath. Ox.*, ed. 1721, vol. ii. p. 618.   [2] Nichols's *Illustrations*, vol. ii. p. 745.

ST. PANCRAS IN THE FIELDS

A few nights afterwards the coffin was dug up and flung in the roadside near Kentish Town. James Leoni, the architect and editor of *Palladio* and *Alberti* (d. 1746). The Hon. Thomas Arundell, Count of the Holy Roman Empire and son of Henry, fifth Lord Arundell of Wardour (d. 1752). Peter Van Bleek, the portrait painter (d. 1764). Peter Pasqualino, a famous player on the violoncello, who first brought that instrument into fashion (d. 1766). Robert Paxton, the noted English player on that instrument (d. 1787). Thomas Mazzinghi, unrivalled in his day as a violinist (d. 1776). Maria Teresa, Duchess of Wharton (d. 1777), widow of the famous Philip, Duke of Wharton. Baron de Wenzel, the eminent oculist (d. 1790). Count Ferdinand Lucchese, Neapolitan Ambassador (d. 1790). The Duke of Sicigniano, Neapolitan Ambassador, who committed suicide at Gregnier's Hotel, May 31, 1793, shortly after his arrival in England. Count Filippo Nupumecceno Fontana, formerly Ambassador from the Court of Sardinia to that of Spain. Peter Henry Treyssac de Vergy, the opponent of the Chevalier D'Eon, died October 1, 1774, but not buried till March 3, 1775; and that anomalous personage himself, "Charles Genevieve Louis Auguste André Timothée D'Eon de Beaumont, died May 21, buried May 28, 1810, aged eighty-three years," for so the entry stands in the parish register. The French Revolution having deprived him of his pension, D'Eon's last years were spent in extreme penury.

General Pasquale de Paoli, "died February 5, 1807, aged eighty-two years, buried 13th." His remains were exhumed on August 31, 1889, and conveyed to Corsica. Edward Edwards (d. 1806), Professor of Perspective in the Royal Academy, and author of the dull but useful *Anecdotes of Painters*, which he wrote as a continuation of Horace Walpole's lively work with a nearly similar title. Henry F. J. De Cort, the landscape painter (d. 1810). Thomas Scheemakers, sculptor, the junior of that name (d. 1808). Mrs. Isabella Mills, as Miss Burchell, a famous vocalist (d. 1802). John Hayman Packer (d. 1806), an actor of celebrity in genteel comedy. Peter Woulfe, an eminent chemist (d. 1803). Tiberius Cavallo, F.R.S., a distinguished writer on physics (d. 1809). James Peller Malcolm, F.S.A., author of *Londinium Redivivum* (d. 1815).

It is greatly to be regretted that when the churchyard was converted into a garden, means were not taken to indicate the graves of the more remarkable of the persons interred here, and to renew, while renewal was possible, the inscriptions on the tombs and headstones. A memorial was erected by the Baroness Burdett-Coutts in the St. Giles's portion of the ground, on which a list of such names is inscribed—but too high and in too small characters to be read by ordinary eyes. It forms, however, a pleasing object in the garden. St. Pancras has long ceased to be "in the Fields." "Brother Kemp," says Nash in Queen Elizabeth's time to Kemp the actor, "as many alhailes to thy person as there be haicocks in Iuly at Pancredge:"[1] and Norden has left a description of the St. Pancras in 1593, which De Foe has confirmed, more than a century after, in his *History of Colonel Jack*.

> And although this place be as it were forsaken of all, and true men seldom frequent the same but upon devyne occasions, yet it is visyted and usuall haunted of roages, vagabondes, harlettes, and theeves, who assemble not ther to pray, but to wayte for praye, and manie fall into their hands clothed, that are glad when they are escaped naked. Walk not ther too late.—Norden (in 1593), "MS. Account of Middlesex," quoted by Ellis, in Norden's *Essex*, p. xiii.

Bishop Burnet, describing the locality in which Sir Edmond Berry Godfrey's body was discovered, tells us it was found "in a ditch, about a mile out of the town, near St. Pancras Church." The exact locality, as we should now describe it, was the field beyond Primrose Hill. When Burnet wrote, near St. Pancras was the best description he could give. In his lines to "Inigo Marquis Would be," Ben Jonson recommends the great architect to

> Content thee to be Pancredge Earl the while,
> An earl of show.

> It were to be hoped St. Peter would let them dwell in the suburbs of heaven; whereas, otherwise, they must keep aloofe *at Pancridge*, and not come neer the liberties by five leagues and above.—Nash, *Pierce Penilesse*, 1592.

No churchyard in London possessed so much interest as that of St. Pancras, and none has been subjected to greater outrage. After having been closed for interments it was grievously neglected. In July 1863 the Midland Railway Company, who were then planning their London extension, obtained an Act of Parliament authorising them to construct piers for carrying a viaduct across the churchyard. Further powers were granted in July 1864 enabling them to construct a tunnel underneath to join the Metropolitan Railway at King's Cross, and notwithstanding a clause in the Act restraining them from coming within 12 feet of the surface, an enormous trench about 50 feet wide was cut through a crowded portion of the ground and the tunnel built within it. In 1874 the Company sought to obtain powers to acquire the whole of the ground, including the church as well as the St. Giles's cemetery. Public indignation was thoroughly aroused, and the Bill was thrown out. Subsequently the Vestry of St. Pancras acquired the ground for the purpose of a public garden and recreation ground, and it was formally opened by the Baroness Burdett-Coutts on June 28, 1877. The St. Giles's portion was encroached upon in 1887 for the erection of a range of buildings connected with the St. Pancras Workhouse, including a mortuary and rooms for *post mortems*. To complete the story the Midland Railway Company, in 1889, acquired a large portion of the St. Pancras ground lying in the south-east corner, the boundary of the churchyard in that direction being the iron viaduct already mentioned. For this they paid £12,000, and in addition agreed to purchase a row of houses fronting St. Pancras Road, includ-

---

[1] Almond for a Parrot.

ing the site of the old Adam and Eve Tavern, to be laid out and added to the recreation ground.

Neglect and a London atmosphere have done their work in obliterating the inscriptions, and in a few years none will be legible. Fortunately many have been preserved by Mr. Cansick, in a book which he published when the graveyards were taken over by the Vestry of St. Pancras. But notwithstanding this the period is rapidly approaching when the ancient burial-ground will become a mere "open space," with a few decaying stones here and there to remind the spectator of what it once was. All the registers were transferred to the new church in the Euston Road when it became the parish church. The prebend of Pancras was held by Lancelot Andrews in the time of James I., and by Archdeacon Paley in the reign of George III.

Pancras (St.) New Church, EUSTON ROAD and EUSTON SQUARE, was designed by William Inwood, with the assistance of his son, Henry William, the Greek traveller. The foundation stone was laid by the Duke of York, July 1, 1819, and the church consecrated by the Bishop of London, April 7, 1822. The exterior is an adaptation of the Ionic temple of the Erectheion on the Acropolis at Athens, the tower being modelled from the Horologium, or Temple of the Winds, in that city. The projecting building, with the caryatides on each side of the church, and which were intended to form covered entrances to the catacombs, are adaptations of the south portico of the Pandroseion at Athens. The church is built of Portland stone, and the ornaments are chiefly of terra cotta, by C. and H. Rossi. Messrs. Inwood's model for the interior body of the church was the Erectheion. The whole structure was erected at a cost of £76,679 : 7 : 8. The pulpit and reading-desk are made of the celebrated Fairlop oak, which stood in Hainault Forest, in Essex, and gave its name to the fair long held under its branches. It was blown down in 1820. Messrs. Inwood took the greatest possible pains to make the several parts of the church accurate reproductions of the originals, as far as the difference of the materials allowed. The present elaborate chromatic decoration of the interior was carried out by Mr. J. G. Crace in 1866.

Pancras (St.), SOPER LANE, a church in the ward of Cheap, destroyed in the Great Fire, and not rebuilt. Stow describes it as "a proper small church." The name is preserved in *Pancras Lane*. The living is united with that of St. Mary-le-Bow, Cheapside. Abraham Fleming (d. 1607), the earliest translator into English verse of the Bucolics and Georgics of Virgil, was rector of this church.

Pannier, or Panyer Alley, NEWGATE STREET to PATERNOSTER ROW.

Panyer Alley, a passage out of Paternoster Row, and is called of such a sign Panyar Alley.—*Stow*, p. 128.

From a passage in Ben Jonson's *Bartholomew Fair*, Pannier Alley would seem to have been in his day inhabited by tripe-sellers; at an earlier period it was the standing-place for bakers with their bread panniers. *Observe.*—In the middle of the alley, against the east wall, a figure of a pannier or baker's basket (or perhaps a loaf) with a boy with a bunch of grapes sitting upon it, and this inscription :—

> When you have sought the City round,
> Yet still this is the highest ground.
> August 26, 1688.

Panorama, LEICESTER SQUARE. [*See* Burford's Panorama.]

Pantheon, No. 359, on the south side of OXFORD STREET, originally a theatre and public promenade, designed by James Wyatt, R.A., and opened for the first time in January 1772.[1] As at Ranelagh, the room devoted to the promenade was a rotunda, but there were fourteen other rooms. The building was Italian in style, and the decoration of the interior was intended to correspond in character. Nqorthouck described it as "a superb building . . . dedicated to the nocturnal revels of the British nobility."[2] Dr. Johnson visited it in company with Boswell, and both agreed in thinking it inferior to Ranelagh. The masquerades for which the Pantheon soon became celebrated, were on a more splendid scale than those at Chelsea.

What do you think of a winter Ranelagh, erecting in Oxford Road, at the expense of sixty thousand pounds?—*Walpole to Mann,* May 6, 1770.

The new winter Ranelagh in Oxford Road is almost finished. It amazed me myself. Imagine Balbec in all its glory! The pillars are of artificial *giallo antico.* The ceilings, even of the passages, are of the most beautiful stuccos in the best taste of grotesque. The ceilings of the ball-rooms and the panels painted like Raphael's *loggias* in the Vatican. A dome like the Pantheon glazed. It is to cost fifty thousand pounds.—*Walpole to Mann,* April 26, 1771.

February 7, 1774.—Wednesday your two sisters, Molly Cambridge, and I went to the Pantheon. It is undoubtedly the finest and most complete thing ever seen in England; such mixture of company never assembled before under the same roof. Lord Mansfield, Mrs. Baddeley, Lord Chief Baron Parker, Mrs. Abington, Sir James Porter, Mademoiselle Himell, Lords Hyde and Camden, with many other serious men, and most of the *gay* ladies in town, and ladies of the best rank and character; and he, by appearance, some very low people. Louisa is thought very like Mrs. Baddeley [a notorious *gay* lady]; Gertrude and I had our doubts whether our characters might not suffer by walking with her; but had they offered to turn her out we depended on Mrs. Hanger's protection. None of any fashion dance country dances or minuets in the great room, though there were a number of minuets and a large set of dancers. I saw Miss Wilkes dance a minuet, and that was the only name I knew; some young ladies danced cotillons in the Cotillon Gallery. I met a great many of my acquaintances, and every one complained of being tired after they had been there an hour.—*Mrs. Harris to her son, the Earl of Malmesbury* (*Letters,* vol. i. p. 247).

Mrs. Hardcastle. I'm in love with the town . . . but who can have a manner, that has never seen the *Pantheon,* the Grotto Gardens, the Borough, and such places, where the nobility chiefly resort.—Goldsmith, *She Stoops to Conquer,* 1773, Act ii.

When Gibbon was writing the first portion of his *Decline and Fall* he was a frequent visitor to the Pantheon. His plan of early rising gave him command of time, and he tells us that he never found his

---

[1] There is a large and good interior view (with figures) of the Pantheon, engraved by Earlom in 1772. There is also a view in the *European Magazine* for May 1784.

[2] *Hist. of London,* 4to, 1773, p. 737.

mind more vigorous, nor his composition more happy than in the winter hurry of society and parliament. In February 1774 he writes to Holroyd, "Don't you remember that in our *Pantheon* walks we admired the *modest* beauty of Mrs. Horneck? *Eh bien*, alas! She is," etc. This was the wife of Goldsmith's "Captain-in-lace," one of the most abandoned women of her time, who eloped with her husband's brother officer, Captain Scawen. In the following April Gibbon speaks of himself as "a very fine gentleman, a subscriber to the masquerade, . . . and now writing at Boodle's in a fine velvet coat, with ruffles of my lady's choosing." Of this entertainment he says in another letter:—

May 4, 1774.—Last night was the triumph of Boodle's. Our masquerade cost two thousand guineas; a sum that might have fertilized a province (I speak in your own style), vanished in a few hours, but not without leaving behind it the fame of the most splendid and elegant fête that was perhaps ever given in a seat of the arts and opulence. It would be as difficult to describe the magnificence of the scene, as it would be easy to record the humour of the night. The one was above, the other below all relation. I left the Pantheon about five this morning.—*Gibbon to Holroyd*.

Masquerades lost their attraction—Fashion turned her back on the Pantheon. When the Opera House was burnt down, 1789, the Pantheon was secured as a temporary home, and opened early in 1791.

February 18, 1791.—The Pantheon has opened, and is small, they say, but pretty and simple; all the rest ill-conducted and, from the singers to the scene-shifters, imperfect: the dances long and bad, and the whole performance so dilatory and tedious that it lasted from eight to half-past twelve.—*H. Walpole to Agnes Berry*.

As an opera house its existence was brief. It was entirely destroyed by fire, January 14, 1792.

It is a remarkable fact that Mr. Wyatt, who was travelling to town from the west in a post chaise with the ingenious Dixon, his clerk, saw the glare of this memorable fire illuminating the sky while crossing Salisbury Plain.—*Angelo*, p. 96.

A second but less brilliant Pantheon soon rose from the ashes of the first. The management was not successful. Theatrical performances, concerts, lectures, and miscellaneous exhibitions were successively essayed. The building was taken down in 1812, and a *third* Pantheon opened the following year. It was no more successful than its predecessor, and after being closed for some years it was reconstructed in 1834, and fitted, with then unusual splendour, as a bazaar and picture gallery. Mr. Sidney Smirke, R.A., was the architect, the cost over £30,000. The Oxford Street front is a part of Wyatt's original building, but the portico was remodelled by Mr. Smirke. After the fluctuations usual to such places it was finally closed on March 2, 1867, and is now the wine warehouse of Messrs. Gilbey.

At the Pantheon Miss Stephens, afterwards Countess of Essex, made her first appearance on the stage in the character of Barbarina.

Panton Street, HAYMARKET, and **Panton Square**, PICCADILLY, were so called after Colonel Thomas Panton, a celebrated gamester, who in one night, it is said, won as many thousands as purchased him an estate of above £1500 a year. "After this good fortune," says

Lucas, "he had such an aversion against all manner of games that he would never handle cards or dice again; but lived very handsomely on his winnings to his dying day, which was in the year 1681."[1] Colonel Panton was the last proprietor of the gaming-house called Piccadilly Hall [*see* Piccadilly], and was in possession of land on the site of the streets and buildings which bear his name as early as the year 1664. A few years later he was busy building. Sir Christopher Wren, "Surveighor Generall," had been directed to report on Colonel Panton's operations in 1671.

May it please your Majesty, in obedience to your Majesty's order of May 24, 1671, upon the petition of Thomas Panton, Esq., setting forth that he having purchased with design to build, at Piccadilly, and the two bowling greens fronting the Haymarket, and on the north of the Tennis Court, upon which several old houses were standing, which the said Thomas Panton demolished to improve the same, and make the plan more uniform: in reference to which he let out the ground, laid several foundations, and built part thereof, before his Majesty's late Proclamation; and praying his Majesty's permission, under the broad seal, to proceed in the said buildings. Upon which your Majesty ordered the Surveighor Generall to examine the truth of the allegations, and report whether the buildings will cure the noysomeness of the place; accordingly I have viewed the said place, and find the petitioner's allegations, as far as I can judge, to be true, and that the design of building shown to me may be very useful to the public, especially by opening a new street from the Haymarket into Leicester Fields, which will ease, in some measure, the great passage of the Strand, and will cure the noisomeness of that part: and I presume may not be unfit for your Majesty's licence, provided the said Thomas Panton build regularly, according to direction and according to a design to which his said licence may refer; and that he be obliged to build with brick, with party walls, with sufficient scantlings, good paving in the streets, and sufficient sewers and conveighances for the water; and that the buildings expressed in his patent be registered before the foundations are laid. All which is most humbly submitted to your Majesty's wisdom and farther order hereupon. *Christopher Wren.*

A few months after this Colonel Panton made his formal application to erect a "fair street of good buildings" between the Haymarket and Hedge Lane, marked in the manuscript to be called *Panton Street*, and other "fair buildings fronting the Haymarket upon the said ground." "Colonel Panton's Tenements" are rated for the first time in St. Martin's poor-books under the year 1672; "Panton Street North" for the first time in 1674; and "Panton Street by the Laystall" for the first time in 1675. "Madame Panton," the widow, lived in a capital mansion on the east side of the Haymarket as late as 1725. Henry, fifth Lord Arundel of Wardour (d. 1726), from whom Wardour Street derives its name, was married to Elizabeth, daughter of Thomas Panton, of St. Martin's-in-the-Fields, Esquire. In Panton Street, on the south side, was Hickford's Auction Rooms, the Christie and Manson's Rooms of the reign of George I. The great room was used also as a ballroom. On February 2, 1720-1721, the Westminster scholars performed Otway's *Orphan* at "Hickford's Dancing-Room, in Panton Street, near Leicester Fields." Prior, an old Westminster, wrote the prologue, and makes allusion to the use to which the room was ordinarily put.

[1] Lucas's *Lives of the Gamesters*, 12mo, 1714, p. 68.

> We hired this room, but none of us can dance,
> In cutting capers we shall never please;
> Our learning does not lie below our knees.
>
> Prior's *Poems*, 1733, vol. iii. p. 50.

The following curious advertisement is from the Sale Catalogue of a capital collection of pictures, sold by Hickford, March 5, 1728-1729.

N.B.—Such persons as design to be brought in chairs, are desired to come in at the back door of Mr. Hickford's Great Room (which is on a ground floor), facing the Tennis Court in St. James's Street in the Haymarket; which is so large and convenient, that, without going up or down steps, the Chair may be carried in to the very room where the Pictures, etc., are shewed.

William Hogarth engraved a "Midnight scene, in the style of the Modern Conversation," as a shop bill for "Richard Lee, at the Golden Tobacco Roll, in Panton Street, near Leicester Fields."

Panton Square, in Strype's Map (1720) is called Panton *Yard*, and is described as "a very large place for stabling and coach-houses, there being one large yard within another. This place is designed to be built into streets, taking up a large piece of ground, and according to probability will turn to better advantage than at present."[1]

1762.—The Morocco Ambassador lived in Panton Square, near Coventry Street. One of his attendants happened to displease him: he had him brought up to the garret, and there sliced his head off. It was made no secret; he and his servants thought it was very proper, but the London people, who had somewhat of Christianity were of another opinion. I saw a violent party gather before the house: they broke into it, demolished the furniture, threw everything they could lay their hands on out of the windows, and thrashed and beat the grand Moor and his retinue down the Haymarket, and afterwards attacked them wherever they found them.—O'Keefe's *Recollections*, vol. i. p. 81.

In 1868 the name Panton Square was abolished, and the name Arundel Street given to it as a portion of the street of that name leading into Coventry Street.

Paper Buildings, TEMPLE, first built "6th James I. (1609), by Mr. Edward Heyward and others." Dugdale describes them as "eastwards from the garden, 88 feet in length, 20 feet in breadth, and 4 stories high." This Edward Heyward was Selden's chamber-fellow, and Selden dedicates his *Titles of Honour* to him.

His [Selden's] chamber was in the Paper buildings which looke towards the gardens . . . staircase, uppermost story, where he had a little gallery to walke in.—Aubrey's *Anecdotes*, vol. iii. p. 531.

In one of the pleasantest papers of the *Table Talk* Selden relates the device by which he got rid of a lunatic "person of quality who came to my chambers in the Temple and told me he had two devils in his head."

The Paper Buildings, in which Selden lived, were consumed in the Great Fire, and the tenements erected (1685) in their stead destroyed, March 6, 1838, in the fire which broke out in Mr. (afterwards Justice) Maule's chambers.

[1] *Strype*, B. vi. p. 84.

Lord Campbell, when growing into practice, took chambers at—
No. 14 Paper Buildings: first floor, four excellent rooms, view up the river to Westminster Abbey, with the Surrey Hills in the distance, equally adapted for health and convenience, for pleasure and for business. The attorneys as they pass by will say: "Ah! he is getting on. He must know something about it. We will try him."—*Campbell to his father*, August 8, 1810 (*Life*, vol. i. p. 261).

Lord (then Sir John) Campbell's chambers were immediately over Maule's, and everything he had in them was consumed.

My chambers in Paper Buildings have been burned to the ground, and not an atom of anything belonging to me saved—furniture, books, briefs, MSS., Attorney-General's official documents, letters, all consumed. . . . The fire broke out in Maule's chambers. . . . He had gone to bed leaving a candle burning by his bedside.—*Life of Lord Campbell*, vol. ii. p. 107.

George Canning had chambers in Paper Buildings in 1792 when studying for the law and preparing for Parliament. Samuel Rogers lodged in Paper Buildings before removing to St. James's Place. Lord Ellenborough was the previous occupant of the chambers.

I once dined in the chambers Mr. Rogers occupied in the Temple, before he took the house in St. James's Place. The dining-room was a large and cheerful one, on the ground-floor, in Paper Buildings, and commanded a fine view of the river. He had faced the window-shutters with looking-glass, so that from every part of the room there were to be seen views of the river, up and down.—*Autob. Recollections*, by C. R. Leslie, R.A., vol. i. p. 242.

The buildings in the Elizabethan style towards the Thames were designed (1848) by Sydney Smirke, R.A., and recall "the bricky towers" of the temple of Spenser's Prothalamion, though among Templar wits they passed by the name of "Blotting-Paper Buildings."

Papey (The), a house for poor and impotent priests, by London Wall, in Aldgate Ward.

Then come you to the Papey, a proper house, wherein sometime was kept a fraternity or brotherhood of St. Charity and St. John the Evangelist called the Papey, for poor impotent priests (for in some language priests are called papes), founded in the year 1430, by William Oliver, William Barnabie, and John Stafford, chaplains or chantry priests in London, for a master, two wardens, etc., chaplains, chantry priests, conducts (unendowed chaplains), and other brethren and sisters, that should be admitted into the church of St. Augustine Papey in the Wall. The brethren of this house becoming lame, or otherwise into great poverty, were here relieved, as to have chambers, with certain allowance of bread, drink, and coal, and one old man and his wife to see them served, and keep the house clean. This brotherhood, among others, was suppressed in the reign of Edward VI.; since the which time, in this house hath been lodged Master Moris of Essex; Sir Francis Walsingham, principal secretary to her Majesty; Master Barret of Essex, etc.—*Stow*, p. 55.

Parade (The), in ST. JAMES'S PARK. The open space before the *Horse Guards*; part of the old *Tilt Yard* of *Whitehall*. [*See* Tilt Yard.]

Paradise, HATTON GARDEN, an exhibition, popular in the latter part of the 17th century, in which by mechanical contrivances figures of birds and other animals imitated the movements and sounds natural to them. John Locke in his paper of directions for a friend visiting

England sets down "Paradise by Hatton Garden" as one of the places he should visit.

September 23, 1673.—I went to see Paradise, a room in Hatton Garden furnished with the representations of all sorts of animals handsomely painted on boards or cloth, and so cut out, and made to stand, move, fly, crawl, roar, and make their several cries. The man who showed it made us laugh heartily at his formal poetry.—*Evelyn.*

Pardon Church and Churchyard, on the north side of OLD ST. PAUL'S CATHEDRAL.

There was also one great cloister, on the north side of this church, environing a plot of ground, of old time called Pardon Churchyard; whereof Thomas More, Dean of Paules, was either the first builder, or a most especial benefactor, and was buried there. About this cloister was artificially and richly painted the Dance of Machabray, or Dance of Death, commonly called the Dance of Paul's. . . . The metres, or poetry of this dance, were translated out of French into English by John Lydgate, monk of Bury (1430), and with the picture of Death leading all estates, painted about the Cloister, at the special request and at the dispence of Jenken Carpenter, in the reign of Henry VI. In this cloister were buried many persons, some of worship, and others of honour; the monuments of whom, in number and curious workmanship, passed all other that were in that church.—*Stow,* p. 122.

Over the east quadrant of the cloister was a "fair library," built by Walter Sherrington, and "well furnished with fair written books in vellum;" but of these few were left when Stow wrote. In the midst of Pardon Churchyard was the fair chapel, "first founded by Gilbert Becket, portgrave and principal magistrate in this City in the reign of King Stephen," and father of the famous English St. Thomas. The chapel was rebuilt by Dean More in the reign of Henry V. "In the year 1549, on the 10th of April," the chapel and the whole cloister, with the Dance of Death, the tombs and monuments, were begun to be pulled down by command of the Protector Somerset; so that, says Stow, "nothing thereof was left but the bare plot of ground, which is since converted into a garden for the petty canons."[1] The materials were used by Somerset in building his new house in the Strand.

There was also a *Pardon Churchyard* by the Charterhouse, formed by Ralph Stratford, Bishop of London, who on occasion of the great plague of 1348 "bought a piece of ground called No Man's Land, which he enclosed with a wall of brick and dedicated for burial of the dead," for whom there was not room in the churchyard. "In this plot of ground there was, in that year, more than 50,000 persons buried, as I have read in the charters of Edward the Third." The chapel built by the bishop was in Strype's day used as a dwelling, "and the burying plot is become a fair garden, retaining the old name of Pardon Churchyard."[2] As late as 1831 the memory of Pardon Churchyard was preserved in *Pardon Passage* and *Pardon Court,* St. John Street, Clerkenwell, "about a quarter of a mile on the right-hand side, going from Smithfield,"[3] but these have since disappeared.

Paris Garden, a manor or liberty west of the Clink on the Bank-

---

[1] *Stow,* p. 122; *Dugdale,* p. 132; *Greyfriars' Chronicle,* pp. 40, 58.
[2] *Strype,* B. iv. p. 62.　　　　　　　　　　[3] *Elmes,* p. 309.

side in Southwark. This manor was in 1113 given by Robert Marmion to the monastery of *Bermondsey*, whose property it remained till 1537, when it was conveyed to Henry VIII. It was subsequently held by Queen Jane Seymour, by Lord Hunsdon, and by Thomas Cure, founder of the almshouses in Southwark which bore his name. [*See* Cure's College.] It is almost if not quite identical with the parish of Christ Church.

The private Act 22 and 23 Charles II. (1670-1671), c. 28, is an "Act for making the Manor of Paris Garden a parish, and to enable the parishioners of St. Saviour's, Southwark, to raise a Maintenance for Ministers and for repairs of their church."

The earliest known name is Parish Garden, later on Parish or Paris Garden indifferently. Taylor the Water Poet gives a classical origin for the name :—

> How it the name of Paris Garden gained—
> The name it was from a Royall Boy,
> Brave Ilion's firebrand . . .
> From Paris, Paris Garden hath the name.

The garden was covered with trees, and was full of hiding-places with the convenience of river-side landing-places. It was therefore a suitable place for plots and conspiracies. Mr. Recorder Fleetwood, writing to the Vice-Chamberlain, July 12, 1578, describes Paris Garden as notorious for secret meetings of foreign ambassadors and their agents, and mentions instances. On the previous night, he says, the French ambassador was discovered in the company of Sir Warham St. Leger and Sir William Morgan. When questioned they resisted. "The ambassador swore great oathes that he would do many things," but the watch told him plainly that "they knewe not his dignitie," and that he and his companions were "night walkers contrary to the law."[1] To Burghley Fleetwood writes the same day that he had endeavoured to get into St. Leger's house at Chandos Place, and afterwards went on to Paris Garden, but the place there is so dark with trees that one man cannot see another, "except they have *lynceos oculos*, or els cattes eys." He repeats what he wrote to the Vice-Chamberlain as to the secret meetings of the French ambassador with Sir Warham St. Leger and Sir William Morgan, and warns Burghley that Paris Garden "is the very bower of conspiracy."[2] In consequence Burghley took examinations in person regarding these meetings.

In 1657 it was in the hands of William Angell for building purposes ; much objected to by certain influential petitioners as excessive building and injurious to them. On appeal made to the Protector Cromwell he writes with his own hand, "We refer the petition to the consideration of our Counsell desiringe the petitioners may be speedilye heard there-upon," May 22, 1657.

In 1670, when the Act was passed constituting the parish of Christ Church, three-fourths of it consisted of fields, the population a

[1] *Cal. State Pap.*, 1547-1580, p. 595.   [2] *Ibid.*, 1547-1580, p. 595.

thousand or so. The parish of the same extent now contains 13,000 people.

Paris Garden Theatre. A circus in the manor of Paris Garden, in Southwark, erected for bull and bear baitings as early as the 17th of Henry VIII., when the Earl of Northumberland is said (in the Household Book of the family) to have gone to Paris Garden to behold the bear-baiting there. Ralph and Edward Bowes were successively Masters of the Game of Paris Garden in the reign of Elizabeth.[1] The office was subsequently held and the Paris Garden leased by Henslowe and Alleyn, and under their management (when plays were all popular in the reign of James I.) occasionally converted into a theatre.

> *Tucca.* Thou hast been in Paris Garden, hast not?
> *Horace.* Yes, Captain, I ha' playd Zulziman there?
> Dekker, *The Untrussing of the Humorous Poet.*

March 20, 1611.—Warrant to pay Phil: Henslow and Edw: Allen, Masters of the Game at Paris Garden, £42 10s. and 12d. per diem in future for keeping two white bears and a young lion.—*Cal. State Pap.*, 1611-1618, p. 17.

Sunday was the day of exhibition in the reigns of Henry VIII.,[2] Mary and Elizabeth. John Bradford the martyr, preaching before Edward VI., showed

> The tokens of God's judgment at hand for the contempt of the Gospel, as that certain gentlemen upon the Sabbath day going in a wherry to Paris Garden, to the bear baiting, were drowned; and that a dog was met at Ludgate carrying a piece of a dead child in his mouth.—*Two Notable Sermons*, etc., 1574.

A terrible accident which occurred on Sunday, January 13, 1583, gave occasion for much similar comment:—

> On Sunday the stage at Paris Garden fell down all at once, being full of people, beholding the bear baiting. Many being killed thereby, more hurt, and all amazed. The godly expownd it as a due plage of God for the wickedness there usid and the Sabbath dayes profanely spent.—D'Ewes's *Diary*, p. 18.

The names and addresses of many persons killed and hurt on this occasion are given in a rare black-letter volume entitled "J. Field's Godly Exhortation, by occasion of the late Judgment of God, shewed in Paris Garden, the 13 day of January, where were assembled above 1000 persons, whereof some were slain, and one-third maimed and hurt, given to all estates for their instruction to keep the Sabbath Day" (8vo, Waldegrave, 1583). The Exhortation is dedicated to the Lord Mayor of London, the Recorder, Serjeant Fleetwood, etc. James I. prohibited performances on Sundays, and Henslowe and Alleyn represent their loss as very great in consequence. The sports not unfrequently were of a cruel character: on one occasion we hear of a pony baited with dogs with a monkey on his back; and on another of a sport called "whipping the blind bear"—tying a bear to a stake, and whipping him till the blood ran down his shoulders. Some of the bears were very famous. Harry Hunks is often referred to by our Elizabethan writers, and the name of Sackerson is known to every reader of *The Merry Wives of Windsor*.

[1] Malone's *Shakespeare*, by Boswell, vol. iii. p. 844. [2] *Strype*, B. iv. p. 6.

> Publius, student at the common law,
> Oft leaves his books, and for his recreation,
> To Paris Garden doth himself withdraw,
> Where he is ravisht with such delectation,
> As down amongst the bears and dogs he goes,
> Where, whilst he skipping cries, "To Head! To Head!"
> His satin doublet and his velvet hose,
> Are all with spittle from above be-spread:
> Then is he like his father's country hall,
> Stinking of dogges, and muted all with hawks.
> And rightly too on him this filth doth fall
> Which for such filthy sports his looks forsakes,
> Leaving old Plowden, Dyer, and Brooke alone,
> To see old Harry Hunks and Sacarson.
> <div align="right">Sir John Davies's <i>Epigrams</i> (<i>In Publium</i>).</div>

> The meat-boat of Bears'-college, Paris Garden,
> Stunk not so ill.
> Ben Jonson, <i>Epigram</i>, p. 133; and see his <i>Execration upon Vulcan</i>.

How wonderfully is the world altered! And no marvel, for it has lain sick almost five thousand years; so that it is no more like the old Theatre du Monde than old Paris Garden is like the King's Garden at Paris.—*The Gull's Hornbook* (1609), p. 8.

Here [Paris Garden] come few that either regard their credit or loss of time: the swaggering Roarer, the Cunning Cheater, the rotten Bawd, the swearing Drunkard, and the bloody Butcher have their rendezvous here, and are of chief place and respect. *London and the Country Carbonadoed*, by T. Lupton, 1632, 12mo.

Butler makes his "brave Orsin" to have been

> Bred up where discipline most rare is
> In Military Garden Paris.—*Hudibras*, vol. i. p. 2, l. 171.

"Military Garden" refers to an association instituted by James I. for training soldiers, who used to practise in Paris Garden.

The Bear Garden was closed by the Parliament at the beginning of 1642, and five years later the ground was sold. It was, however, reopened after the Restoration, and though but partially successful, the performances were continued till 1687, when the bears were sent to Hockley-in-the-Hole, and the doors of Paris Garden Theatre finally closed. The name survived for many years in "Parish Garden Stairs."

The Swan Theatre, built about 1596, was in Paris Garden [*see* Swan], and probably some of the references to the Paris Garden Theatre belong to it.

Parish Clerks' Hall, No. 24 SILVER STREET, FALCON SQUARE, the hall of the master, wardens, and fellows of the fellowship of parish clerks "of London, Westminster, Borough of Southwark, and fifteen out-parishes." The Company was licensed as a guild in 1233, by the name of the Fraternity of St. Nicholas. It was dissolved and re-incorporated by patent 24th of Henry VIII. The actual charter was granted by James I., December 31, 1611. It directs that "each parish clerk shall bring to the Clerks' Hall weekly, a note of all christenings and burials," and that only such shall be admitted to be clerks as are "able to sing the Psalms of David, and to write." The direction as to the "note of all christenings and burials" had reference to the Bills (or tables) of Mortality which the guild commenced keeping from the great plague year of 1593, and were issued as weekly bills from 1603, when London had a similar but heavier visitation. Charles I. in 1636 granted permission to the Parish Clerks to have a printing-press and employ a printer in their hall, for the purpose of printing their weekly bills.

The first hall of the Fraternity was at the sign of the Angel in Bishopsgate, and by it was an almshouse for seven poor widows of deceased members. The second hall was in Broad Lane, in Vintry Ward, and was consumed in the Great Fire of 1666, when a third hall was erected between Silver Street and Wood Street, Cheapside; this was damaged about 1844 in a fire which destroyed several great warehouses. It was restored or rebuilt in a more ornamental style, and a new entrance made in Silver Street.

Park Crescent, REGENT'S PARK. Joseph Bonaparte, the ex-king of Spain, lived at No. 23 when in London in 1833. Here is a statue of the Duke of Kent (father of the Queen) by George Gahagan.

Park Lane, HYDE PARK, runs from Piccadilly to Oxford Street, by where stood Tyburn Turnpike, and was originally called *Tyburn Lane*. Londonderry (formerly Holdernesse) House, the residence of the Marquis of Londonderry (S. and B. Wyatt, architects), is one of the finest of the London mansions, and contains many noble pictures and other works of art. In Dorchester House (bought in 1848 by R. S. Holford, Esq., and pulled down) died the Marquis of Hertford, the favourite of George IV. The present Dorchester House, designed for Mr. Holford by Lewis Vulliamy, 1852-1853, is of superior design externally and very splendid inside. Besides many admirable pictures by Claude Lorraine, Velasquez, Hobbema, Cuyp, Ostade, Vandyck, Greuze, Wilkie (the Columbus), etc., it contains a choice collection of rare and valuable books. Dudley House, the residence of Earl Dudley, is another noble mansion rich in paintings by Raphael and the earlier Italian masters. Brook House, on the other side of Upper Brook Street (T. H. Wyatt, architect), is the residence of Lord Tweedmouth; and Gloucester House of H. R. H. the Duke of Cambridge. Camelford House (at the Oxford Street end of the lane) was the town residence of Prince Leopold and the Princess Charlotte of Wales. Mrs. Fitzherbert lived in Park Lane, and it was in her drawing-room that the ceremony of her marriage with the Prince of Wales (George IV.) was performed, December 21, 1785.[1]

Park Place, ST. JAMES'S STREET. Built 1683.[2] The north side is in the parish of *St. George's, Hanover Square*; the south in *St. James's, Westminster*. The Countess of Orrery was one of the first inhabitants. No. 9 was Sir William Musgrave's, the great print-collector. William Pitt retired to No. 12 in 1801. "Old Coke of Norfolk" at No. 14. The "Mother Needham" of the *Harlot's Progress*—the "Pious Needham" of the *Dunciad*,[3] lived in Park Place.

[1] Langdale, *Mem. of Mrs. Fitzherbert*. [2] Rate-books of St. Martin's.
[3] See *Dunciad*, B. I. l. 324 and *note*.

The noted Mother Needham, convicted (April 29, 1731) for keeping a disorderly house in Park Place, St. James's, was fined 1s., to stand twice in the Pillory, viz. once in St. James's Street over against the End of Park Place, and once in the New Palace Yard, Westminster, and to find sureties for her Good Behaviour for three years.—Fog's *Weekly Journal*, Saturday, May 1, 1731.

Yesterday (May 6, 1731) the noted Mother Needham stood in the Pillory in Park Place, near St. James's Street, and was roughly handled by the populace. She was so very ill that she lay along on her face, and so evaded the law which requires that her face should be exposed.—*Grub Street Journal* (Nichols's *Hogarth*, p. 190).

She died before she could be exposed the second time.

Park Street, BOROUGH. [*See* Deadman's Lane.]

Park Street, GROSVENOR SQUARE, from South Street to Oxford Street. At No. 113 died (1827) Miss Lydia White, celebrated for her lively wit and for her blue-stocking parties, unrivalled, it is said, in the soft realm of *blue* May Fair.

At one of Miss Lydia White's small and most agreeable dinners in Park Street, the company (most of them, except the hostess, being Whigs) were discussing in rather a querulous strain, the desperate prospects of their party. "Yes," said Sydney Smith, "we are in a most deplorable condition; we must do something to help ourselves; I think we had better sacrifice a tory virgin." This was pointedly addressed to Lydia White, who, at once catching and applying the allusion to Iphigenia, answered, "I believe there is nothing the whigs would not do to raise the wind."—*Rev. W. Harness to Rev. A. Dyce* (*Remains*, p. 70, *notes*).

November 13, 1826.—Went to poor Lydia White's and found her extended on a couch, frightfully swelled, unable to stir, rouged, jesting and dying. She has a good heart, and is really a clever creature, but unhappily, or rather happily, she has set up the whole staff of her rest in keeping literary society about her. The world has not neglected her. She can always make up her circle, and generally has some people of real talent and distinction.—Sir Walter Scott, *Diary*.

Miss Nelly O'Brien, the original of three of Sir Joshua's most brilliant portraits, died here in 1768, when one of the three pictures, tradition says, was sold for three pounds, instead of the thousands it would now fetch. No. 123 was the residence of Richard Ford, author of the *Handbook for Spain*. Sir Humphry Davy lived at No. 26 from 1825 until his death. Sir William Stirling Maxwell, M.P., lived for some years at No. 7.

Park Street, WESTMINSTER, now with Queen Square renamed Queen Anne's Gate. *Eminent Inhabitants.*—The learned Stillingfleet, Bishop of Worcester, died here March 27, 1699; the equally learned Dr. Bentley. Bentley was Stillingfleet's chaplain and was residing here with him (1690) when his first publication, the *Epistle to Dr. Mill,* saw the light. These continued to be his London quarters till the beginning of 1696, when he obtained apartments in St. James's Palace.[1] William Windham, the statesman, was living at No. 5 in 1796. At No. 5 Miss Lydia White resided in 1814, and till her removal to Park Street, Grosvenor Square [which *see*]. At No. 6 William Smith, M.P. for Norwich, the champion of the Dissenters. His dinners were famous. On March 19, 1796, Samuel Rogers describes himself as meeting here Fox, Parr, Tierney, Mackintosh and Francis. "Sheridan

[1] Monk's *Bentley*, 4to, p. 55.

sent an excuse."[1] "William Wordsworth, No. 6 Park Street, Westminster," appears on an autograph visiting card of about 1835. The Rev. H. F. Cary, the translator of Dante, went to live at No. 10 in 1837, when he left the British Museum on the appointment of Panizzi as keeper of the printed books. No. 7 was the house of Charles Townley, collector of the Townley marbles, now in the British Museum; he died here January 3, 1805. Every room of Mr. Townley's house was filled with statues, bust, relievi, votive altars, sepulchral urns, inscriptions, and terra cottas; his visitors comprised a large proportion of those eminent for their rank or attainments, and his Sunday dinners, "principally for professors of the Arts, when Sir Joshua Reynolds and Zoffany generally enlivened the circle," were in their way famous. A View of Mr. Townley's Gallery was one of Zoffany's most successful pictures. The house was afterwards the residence of Spring Rice (Lord Monteagle). "The late Royal Cockpit . . . remained a next-door nuisance to Mr. Townley for many years."[2]

Parker Street, DRURY LANE to LITTLE QUEEN STREET, formerly called Parker's Lane. Mr. Philip Parker had a house here in 1623. In 1661 Mr. William Shelton purchased for £458, 10s. certain tenements on the south side of this lane, described as having been "lately in possession of the Dutch Ambassador." Here he founded a school for fifty poor boys, which continued till 1763, when the funds were declared to be inadequate to its support and the school was closed. The funds were allowed to accumulate till 1815, when a new school house was erected in Lloyd's Court, and the charity revived after a slumber of fifty-two years. The schools are abolished, and the charity was amalgamated with others in 1886.

Parker Street, PRINCES STREET, WESTMINSTER, was formerly called Benet Street, as the adjacent property belonged to Benet or Corpus Christi College, Cambridge. The old name was changed when a number of disorderly occupants were ejected about fifty years ago, and the new one was given in compliment to Archbishop Parker, who bequeathed his valuable library to Corpus Christi College.

Parliament Stairs, the landing-place for OLD PALACE YARD. In the earliest maps the name is *Old Palace Bridge*.

Parliament Street, WESTMINSTER, an open and important street, between Whitehall and the Houses of Parliament, made pursuant to 29 George II., c. 38 (1756), previously to which King Street was the only highway between Whitehall and Westminster Abbey. The spies employed to watch Wilkes reported on November 12, 1762, that "he went to Woodfall's the printers at Charing Cross; from thence to *Mr. Churchill's in Parliament Street*, but did not stay; from thence he went home to dinner."[3] The Right Hon. Henry Grattan was resident at No. 4 in 1807. [*See* King Street.]

[1] *Sharpe*, p. 17; and see Dyce's *Rogers*, p. 81. [2] Smith's *Nollekens*, vol. i. pp. 256-267.
[3] *Grenville Papers*, vol. ii. p. 160.

Parson's Court, BRIDE LANE, FLEET STREET. In 1657 the buildings of brick betwixt the Inner Temple Lane and Hare Court were set; and in 1662 those in Parson's Court, near the east end of the church.[1]

Before the Great Fire there was a parsonage house in Bride's Lane, long since leased out by the Church of Westminster, which hath the impropriation and parsonage. It is now divided into several tenements. That place is now called Parson's Court.—*Strype* (1720), B. iii. p. 267.

Patent Office, 25 SOUTHAMPTON BUILDINGS, CHANCERY LANE. The terms Patent Office, Patent Bill Office, Great Seal Patent Office, have been applied at various periods to different offices connected with the Court of Chancery to denote one of the many offices through which letters patent under the Great Seal had to pass before the grant was complete. In 1852 the procedure in connection with grants of letters patent for inventions was greatly simplified, a body of Patent Commissioners being appointed, who were put into possession of the building erected in accordance with an Act of Parliament for building an office for the Masters in Chancery (32 George III., c. 42, 1792), who were abolished in the year above mentioned. The Patent Law Amendment Act 1852, provided amongst other things that all the specifications of letters patent should be printed and published, and should be open to free inspection. This necessitated the formation of a library, and it occurred to the late Mr. Richard Prosser, of Birmingham, who took a prominent part in the question of patent law reform, that a collection of scientific works would be a valuable adjunct to the printed specifications. Accordingly he placed at the disposal of the Commissioners of Patents a very large portion of his private library, which, with a smaller collection belonging to Mr. Bennet Woodcroft, for many years the energetic head of the office, formed the nucleus of what is now the finest library of scientific and technical works in the kingdom. It was first opened to the public in April 1855 in a very humble way, and for many years there were constant complaints of the want of proper accommodation for readers. Its value was at a very early period acknowledged by the Government, and an annual grant is voted by Parliament for its maintenance. At length a new storey was added to the building, a spacious reading-room being included in the design, but the library is rapidly growing. It is open free daily from 10 A.M. to 10 P.M., and for many years it enjoyed the distinction of being the only really *free* library in London. In 1883 an Act was passed transferring the granting of patents to the Board of Trade, the registration of trademarks and designs being also added to the work of the Patent Office. Of late years the business of the office has increased enormously, the number of applications for patents amounting to nearly 20,000 annually. The *Patent Office Museum* consisted of a collection of historical relics and models connected with the history of invention, and was for many years located in one of the "Brompton Boilers," as the corrugated iron sheds which

[1] *Origines Juridiciales.*

originally formed the South Kensington Museum were irreverently nicknamed. The collection was handed over to the Science and Art Department in 1883, and is now incorporated with the Science Collection. [*See* Science and Art Department.]

Samuel Pepys mentions in his *Diary* a "Patent Office in Chancery Lane" under date March 12, 1668-1669, which was probably at the Rolls Office.

Paternoster Row, a narrow street immediately north of St. Paul's Churchyard, long inhabited by stationers, afterwards by mercers, and now chiefly by booksellers. It is familiarly known as The Row. Stow says (p. 126):—

Paternoster Row so called, because of stationers or text writers that dwelt there, who wrote and sold all sorts of books then in use, namely A.B.C., with the Pater Noster, Ave, Creed, Graces, etc.

> Should you feel any touch of poetical glow
> We've a scheme to suggest; Mr. Scott you must know,
> Who (we're sorry to say it) now works for "the Row."
>
> TOM MOORE.

But Paternoster Row was so named in the 13th century, long before any stationer settled in it. There can be no doubt that it was called Paternoster Row, as Mr. Riley observes, "from its being the residence of the trade of Paternostrers, or makers of paternosters, or prayer-beads, for the use probably, more especially, of the worshippers at St. Paul's."[1] "Paternostrer" often occurs as a designation in City archives of the 13th and 14th centuries, and there is a record in 1374 of a devise of his premises in Paternoster Row, by "Richard Russell, paternostrer."

This street, before the Fire of London, was taken up by Eminent Mercers, Silkmen and Lacemen; and their shops were so resorted unto by the nobility and gentry in their coaches, that oft times the street was so stop'd up that there was no passage for Foot Passengers. But since the said Fire, those Eminent Tradesmen have settled themselves in several other parts; especially in Covent Garden, in Bedford Street, Henrietta Street and King Street. And the inhabitants in this street are now [1720] a mixture of Trades People, and chiefly Tire-Women, for the sale of commodes, top-knots, and the like dressings for the females. There are also many shops of Mercers and Silkmen; and at the upper end some stationers, and large Warehouses for Booksellers; well situated for learned and studious men's access thither; being more retired and private.—*Stryfe*, B. iii. p. 195.

Let any man, whose years and strength of head will allow it, look back and recollect how things stood in London about fifty years ago, with respect to some particular trades, and compare it with what it is now; and he will be struck with surprise at the changes made in the time. The mercers, particularly, were few in number but great dealers; Paternoster Row was the centre of their trade; the street was built for them; the spacious shops, back-warehouses, skylights, and other conveniences, made on purpose for their trade are still to be seen; and their stocks were prodigiously great. The street was wont to be thronged with customers; the coaches were obliged to stand in two rows, one side to go in, the other to go out, for there was no turning a coach in it; and the mercers kept two beadles to keep the order of the street; about fifty principal shops took up the whole; the rest were dependents upon that trade, as about the middle of Ivy Lane, the lacemen; about

---

[1] Riley, *Memorials*, vol. xx.

the end of the street next Cheapside, the button-shops; and near at hand in Blowbladder Street, the crewel shops, silkmen, and fringe shops. They held it here in this figure, about twenty years after the Fire; and even in that line the number increasing as the gay humour came on, we saw outlying mercers set-up about Aldgate, the east-end of Lombard Street, and Covent Garden; in a few years more Covent Garden began to get a name, and at length, by degrees, intercepted the quality so much, the streets also being large and commodious for coaches, that the Court came no more into the City to buy clothes; but on the contrary the Citizens ran to the east and west; Paternoster Row began to be deserted and abandoned of its trade; and in less than two years the mercers had well nigh forsook the place, to follow the trade, seeing that the trade would not follow them. . . . The Paternoster mercers, as I remember, went all away to Covent Garden; and there for some years was the centre of trade. . . . Within about ten years more the trade shifted again; Covent Garden began to decline, and the mercers, increasing prodigiously, went back into the City; there, like bees unhived, they hovered about awhile, not knowing where to fix; but at last, as if they would come back to the old hive in Paternoster Row, but could not be admitted, the swarm settled on Ludgate Hill.—Defoe's *Complete Tradesman* (1745), chap. ii.

November 21, 1660.—My wife and I went to Paternoster Row, and there we bought some green watered moyre for a morning waistcoat.—*Pepys*.

May 17, 1662.—After dinner my Lady (Sandwich) and she [Mrs. Sanderson], and I on foot to Paternoster Row, to buy a petticoat against the Queen's coming for my lady, of plain satin.—*Pepys*.

January 8, 1665-1666.—To Bennett's in Paternoster Row, few shops there being yet open [after the plague], and there bought velvet for a coat, and camelott for a cloak for myself; and thence to a place to look over some fine counterfeit damasks to hang my wife's closet, and pitched upon one.—*Pepys*.

Pepys records other visits, but even then there were other traders than mercers there, for on one occasion he notes how, "seeing and saluting Mrs. Stokes, my little goldsmith's wife in Paternoster Row," he "there bespoke a silver chafing-dish for warming plates."

Here in 1757 lived Griffiths the bookseller, when he took in Goldsmith to bed and board, and to write criticisms for his *Monthly Review*. In a garret here Goldsmith wrote reviews of Home's *Douglas*, Wilkie's *Epigoniad*, Smollett's *History*, Burke's *Sublime and Beautiful*, and Gray's *Odes*. Griffiths's sign was the Dunciad, and Smollett speaks of "those significant emblems, the owl and long-eared animal, which Mr. Griffiths so sagely displays for the mirth and information of mankind." The Letters of Junius were addressed to "Mr. Printer Woodfall in Paternoster Row." The house was at the corner of Ivy Lane, the office door, at which the Junius letters were sometimes thrown in, was in the latter street. The Woodfalls afterwards removed into Salisbury Square. Near where *Dolly's Chop House* afterwards stood, Tarlton (d. 1588), the celebrated clown of Queen Elizabeth's reign, kept an ordinary called The Castle.[1] The house was destroyed in the Great Fire, and rebuilt on a larger scale; the great room, which was decorated in an expensive manner, being used for the concerts of the Castle Musical Society. Later the Castle was closed and the great room became the Oxford Bible warehouse. It was again burnt down, January 8, 1770. [*See* Dolly's Chop House; Chapter Coffee-house.] In Paternoster Row lived Mrs. Anne Turner, the inventor of yellow

[1] *Tarlton's Jests*, by Halliwell, p. 21.

ST. PAUL'S

starch, and a principal in the poisoning of Sir Thomas Overbury.[1] The famous booksellers Awnsham and John Churchill were located at the Black Swan in this Row in 1700. Nos. 38-41 are the premises of Messrs. Longman and Co., the eminent publishers. Thomas Longman, the founder of the house, died June 18, 1755. An edition of Rowe's *Dramatic Works*, 2 vols., 12mo, 1725, was printed for T. Longman, at the Ship and Black Swan, 1725. The present handsome building (Griffith and Dawson, architects) was erected in 1863. *Observe.*—The carvings of the Ship and Black Swan, the old sign of the house. No. 47 is Messrs. Chambers's publishing house and warehouse. This was formerly Baldwin and Cradock's. It was here, by "R. Baldwin at the Rose in Paternoster Row," that Smollett's *Critical Review* was originally published. No. 56, a spacious recent building, is the Religious Tract Society.

Paternoster Square occupies the site of Newgate Market, which *see*.

Patten-Makers Company, the seventy-sixth in order of the City Companies, was incorporated by letters patent of 22 Charles II. (1670). The Company have a small livery but no hall.

Paulet House. [*See* Winchester Street.]

Paul's (St.), the *Old* Cathedral of London, destroyed in the Great Fire, was begun to be built by Bishop Maurice, A.D. 1087, on the site of a church to the same saint, founded about A.D. 610, by Ethelbert, King of Kent, of which church Mellitus was the first, and Erkenwald (whose shrine stood at the back of the high altar) the fourth bishop. According to a tradition of the time the first church was erected on the site of a temple dedicated to Diana. Bishop Maurice's cathedral was built in part from the ruins of the Palatine Tower, or castle, which stood by the Fleet river, where afterwards was placed the monastery of the Black Friars. The ruins of the Palatine Tower were the Conqueror's contribution towards the cost of the new cathedral. The progress of the works was necessarily slow, and the church was far from being completed when, 1136, it was seriously damaged (Mathew Paris says destroyed) by fire. When resumed the works appear to have been continually carried forward, but in their progress great alterations were made in the scale and character of the several parts. The steeple is reported as finished in 1221, and a new choir in a similar style in 1240; then again it was lengthened eastward in 1255, and "nearly completed" in 1283, nearly two centuries after its commencement. It exhibited therefore examples of the Norman, of the whole period of the Early English, and of the opening years of the Decorated style. Subsequent repairs and additions carried it through the whole of the Decorated and Perpendicular periods, but the portions executed in these latter styles were unimportant: essentially the church was Norman, Early English and Early Decorated. The

[1] D'Ewes's *Memoirs*, vol. i. p. 71.

dimensions, according to the careful investigations of Mr. E. B. Ferrey,[1] were, length, from east to west, 596 feet; breadth, 104 feet; height to outer ridge of nave roof, 130 feet; of choir, 142 feet; internal height to ridge of vaulting of nave, 93 feet; of choir, 101 feet; Lady Chapel, height of tower, 285 feet; of spire, 208 feet. Dugdale, following Stow, makes the total length 690 feet, and in breadth 130. There was a Lady Chapel at the east end, with a chapel on the north of it, dedicated to St. George, and one on the south, dedicated to St. Dunstan. In the crypt below the choir was the parish church of *St. Faith*, and at the Ludgate corner (towards the Thames) the parish church of *St. Gregory*. "St. Paul's," says Fuller, "may be called the mother church indeed, having one babe in her body [*St. Faith*] and another in her arms [*St. Gregory*]." The nave of twelve bays was very long and very noble, the central tower appears to have been open as a lantern internally, the choir windows of unusual length and height, and at the east was a rich circular window. At the west end were two massive angle towers "made for bell towers,"[2] but used also as prisons. On the west side of the south transept were small cloisters, in which was painted the celebrated Dance of Death, and in the centre of the cloister garth was the Chapter House, built in 1332, "a beautiful piece of work," as Stow says, but small, its internal diameter being only 32 feet 6 inches. Next the cloisters was a charnel-house, with a chapel over it. [*See* Pardon Churchyard.] The church of St. Gregory was at the south-west angle of the cathedral. The bishop's palace was at the north-west corner of the churchyard. At the north-east end of the cathedral, "about the midst of the churchyard,"[3] stood the celebrated Cross of St. Paul's, from which sermons were regularly preached and occasionally political addresses delivered. The cathedral and precincts were encompassed by a stone wall, in which for entrance and exit were six gate-houses. [*See* St. Paul's Cross; St. Paul's Churchyard.]

Old St. Paul's was so severely injured by fire in 1561 that it was necessary to take the steeple down and roof the church anew with boards and lead. Several attempts were made to restore it, and money for the new building of the steeple was, it is said, collected.[4] James I. countenanced a sermon at *Paul's Cross* in favour of so pious an undertaking, but nothing was done till 1633, when reparations commenced with some activity, and Inigo Jones designed, at the expense of Charles I., a classic portico to a Gothic church. This portico (of itself a noble structure) was 200 feet long, 40 feet high, and 50 feet deep. It was without a pediment, Inigo intending to have it surmounted by ten statues of kings, benefactors to the church.[5] Charles designed to have built the church anew (of which Inigo's portico was only an instalment), but his thoughts were soon drawn in another direction, and Old St. Paul's, under Cromwell, was made a horse-quarter for soldiers.

[1] Longman's *Three Cathedrals of St. Paul,* p. 99, etc.
[2] *Stow*, p. 138.
[3] *Ibid.*, p. 123.
[4] *Stow*, p. 124.
[5] There is a large engraving of it by H. Hulsbergh, executed at the expense of the Earl of Burlington.

The Restoration witnessed another attempt to restore the church—a commission was appointed and a subscription opened,[1] but before a sufficient fund was raised the whole structure was destroyed in the Fire of London.

> The daring flames peep'd in, and saw from far
> The awful beauties of the sacred quire:
> But since it was profan'd by Civil War,
> Heaven thought it fit to have it purg'd by fire.—DRYDEN.

On the north side of the choir, "on whose monument hung his proper helmet and spear, as also his target, covered with horn,"[2] stood the stately tomb of John of Gaunt, Duke of Lancaster (d. 1399), with recumbent effigies of the old knight and of Constance of Castile, his second wife. In St. Dunstan's Chapel was the fine old tomb of Henry Lacy, Earl of Lincoln (d. 1310), from whom Lincoln's Inn derives its name. In the middle aisle of the nave, on the right hand, approaching the altar, stood the tomb of Sir John Beauchamp, (d. 1358), constable of Dover Castle, and son to Guy Beauchamp, Earl of Warwick. This Sir John Beauchamp lived in great state in the ward of Castle Baynard, and his house after his death was bought by Edward III., for the purposes of the royal wardrobe. [*See* Wardrobe Place.] His tomb was commonly called Duke Humphrey's Tomb, and the nave of the church, from this circumstance, Duke Humphrey's Walk. At the upper end of the nave was the mortuary chapel of Thomas Kemp, Bishop of London, who built Paul's Cross pulpit, and here and elsewhere in the nave and choir were monuments of various degrees of richness—the tombs of many other bishops of London.[3] Between the choir and south aisle was a noble monument to Sir Nicholas Bacon (d. 1578), the father of Lord Chancellor Bacon; and higher than the host and altar—for so Bishop Corbet describes it—

> Nor needs the Chancellor boast whose pyramids
> Above the host and altar reared is—*Bishop Corbet*, p. 8.

Hentzner (1598) calls it a "magnificent monument, ornamented with pyramids of marble and alabaster." Here stood (between two of the columns of the choir) the sumptuous monument of Sir Christopher Hatton, Lord Chancellor (d. 1591). Near Hatton's tomb was a tablet to Sir Philip Sydney, and another of the same unpretending description to his father-in-law, Sir Francis Walsingham. The stately appearance of Hatton's monument, and the humble nature of Walsingham's and Sidney's, occasioned the following epigram, of which, by the bye, John Stow was himself the author:—

> Philip and Francis have no tomb,
> For *great* Christopher takes all the room.

In the south aisle of the choir stood the tombs of two of the deans—Colet, founder of *St. Paul's School*, and Dr. Donne, the poet—Colet

---

[1] Harl. MS. 4941. Commission dated April 18, 1663. All subscriptions to be paid to Sir John Cutler ("His Grace's fate sage Cutler could foresee").

[2] *Dugdale*, ed. 1658, p. 47.

[3] Milman, *Annals of St. Paul's Cathedral*, p. 376.

represented as a recumbent skeleton, Donne standing in his shroud. Dean Nowell, who played so prominent a part in the controversies throughout the reign of Elizabeth, was also buried here. So also were Lily, the grammarian, the second master of St. Paul's School, and Linacre the physician, "the friend of Colet and Erasmus." Here, too, in a vault on the north side of the choir, near the tomb of John of Gaunt, was Vandyck buried (d. 1641); but the outbreak of the wars under Charles I. prevented the erection of any monument to his memory.

The "Pervyse of Paul's," or the middle aisle of the church, commonly called "Duke Humphrey's Walk" or "Paul's Walk" (a piece of naked architecture, unenriched by any other piece of sculpture than the so-called Duke Humphrey's tomb), was for a century and more (1550 to 1650) the common news-room of London, the resort of the wits and gallants about town.

It was the fashion of those times, and did so continue till these, for the principal gentry, lords and courtiers, and men of all professions not merely mechanic, to meet in St. Paul's Church by eleven, and walk in the Middle Aisle till twelve; and after dinner from three to six; during which time some discoursed of business, others of news. Now, in regard of the universal commerce there happened little that did not first or last arrive here. And I being young did associate myself at those hours with the choicest company I could pick out.—*Works of Francis Osborn*, ed. 1701, p. 403.

Here lawyers stood at their pillars (like merchants on 'Change) and received their clients.[1] Here masterless men, at the *Si quis* door, as it was called, set up their bills for service.[2] Here the rood loft, tombs and font were used as counters for payments.

If A pay B on the feast of St. Michael the Archangel next coming, in the Cathedral Church of St. Paul's in London . . . at the rood loft of the rood of the north door within the same church; or tomb of St. Erkenwald; or at the door of such a chapel, or at such a pillar within the same church, etc.—Littleton's *Tenures*, B. iii. c. v. § 342.

Here Falstaff bought Bardolph ("I bought him in Paul's"). Here the young gallant took "four turns," as Dekker prescribes, and gratified his vanity by strutting about in the most fashionable attire. Here assignations were made.

Mrs. Honeysuckle. I'll come. The hour?

Justinianus. Two: the way through Paul's; every wench take a pillar; there

---

[1] "There is a tradition that in times past there was one Inne of Court at Dowgate, called Johnson's Inn; another in Fetter Lane; and another in Paternoster Row: which last they would prove because it was next to St. Paul's Church where each Lawyer and Serjeant at his Pillar heard his client's cause, and took notes thereof upon his knee as they do in Guildhall at this day. And that after the Serjeants' Feast ended they do still go to Paul's in their habits, and there choose their Pillar whereat to hear their client's cause (if any come) in memory of that old custom."—Dugdale's *Orig. Jurid.*, ed. 1680, p. 147. "The xvij day of October [1552] was made vii. serjants of the coyffe: and after dener they went unto Powlls and so went up the stepes and so round the qwere and ther dyd they ther homage, and so [to] the north-syd of Powlles and stod a-pone the stepes ontil iiij old serjantes came to-gether and feytchyd iiij [new] and brought them unto certen pelers and left them, and then did feyched the residue unto the pelers."—*Diary of a Resident in London*, 4to, 1848, p. 76.

[2] *Pierce Penniless*, p. 43. *Every Man out of his Humour*, Act iii. Sc. 1. Hall's *Satires*, B. ii. Sat. 5.

clap on your masks: your men will be behind you; and before your prayers are half done be before you, and man you out at several doors. You'll be there.—*Westward Ho* (4to, 1607), Act ii. Sc. 1; and see Act ii. Sc. 2.

Here the penniless man dined with Duke Humphrey. Here spur money was demanded by the choristers from any person entering the cathedral during divine service with spurs on.

> Never be seen to mount the steps into the quire, but upon a high festival day, to prefer the fashion of your doublet; and especially if the singing-boys seem to take note of you; for they are able to buzz your praises above their anthems, if their voices have not lost their maidenheads: but be sure your silver spurs dog your heels, and then the boys will swarm about you like so many white butterflies; when you in the open quire shall draw forth a perfumed embroidered purse, the glorious sight of which will entice many countrymen from their devotion to wondering: and quoit silver into the boys' hands, that it may be heard above the first lesson, although it be read in a voice as big as one of the great organs.—Dekker, *Gull's Horn-book*, pp. 99, 100.

Hither Fleetwood, the Recorder of London, came "to learn some news" to convey by letter to Lord Burghley. Here Ben Jonson has laid a scene in *Every Man out of his Humour*, and here he found his Captain Bobadil, "a Paul's man," as he is called in the *dramatis personæ* before *Every Man in his Humour*. The noise was very great, and Inigo Jones's portico was built, says Dugdale,[1] "as an ambulatory for such as usually walking in the body of the church disturbed the solemn service in the choir." All this was unseemly enough in a place set apart for public worship, but the nuisance was formerly of a still greater magnitude. From the Reformation to the 1st and 2d of Philip and Mary, the nave was a common thoroughfare for people with vessels of ale and beer, baskets of bread, fish, flesh, and fruit, men leading mules, horses, and other beasts. So great, indeed, would the nuisance appear to have become, that the Mayor and Common Council, on and after August 1, 1554, prohibited the use of the church for such "unreverent" purposes, and inflicted a succession of fines on all who should offend in future.[2]

The old cathedral suffered more "unreverent" treatment under the Commonwealth. The work of reparation was at once stopped, and the funds which had been subscribed for the purpose, over £17,000, seized and appropriated to other uses. The order for the removal of crucified and superstitious images from churches was followed by a destructive clearance of the interior of St. Paul's, and in 1650 a special order was issued for casting down the statues of James I. and Charles I. from Inigo Jones's portico.

> That the statues of King James and the late King, standing now at the west end of Paule's bee throwne downe, and broken to pieces, and the inscription in the stone worke under them be deleted; And that a letter bee written to the Lord Mayor and Court of Aldermen to see this putt in execution.—*Orders of Council of State*, July 31, 1650.

To utilise the now disused cathedral the porch was let for conversion into shops for sempstresses and hucksters and other mean traders; the

---

[1] Ed. 1658, p. 160. [2] Strype's *Lond.*, B. iii. p. 169.

east end of the choir was appropriated as a meeting-house for the congregation of Dr. Burgess; and the rest of the church was made into a cavalry barrack, the horses being stabled within the sacred edifice.

The Saints in *Pauls* were the last weeke teaching their Horses to ride up the *great Steps* that lead into the *Quire*, where (as they derided) they might perhaps learne to *Chaunt* an *Antheme*; but one of them fell, and broke both his *Leg* and the *Neck* of his Rider, which hath spoiled his *Chanting*, for he was buried on *Saturday* night last. A just *Judgement* of God on such a prophane and *Sacrilegious* wretch.—*Mercurius Elencticus*, from Tuesday, January 2, till Tuesday, January 9, 1648.

With the restoration of monarchy came the resolve to restore the ruined cathedral. Much was done in the way of discussion, but no real progress was made till Wren was called in, and he after a careful survey proposed such extensive alterations in the fabric—including the formation of a spacious central rotunda, "a very proper place for a large auditory," to be covered with "a cupola, and then end in a lantern," that the debates were renewed and continued till the Great Fire put an end to the discussion by the destruction of the building. The fire broke out on September 2, 1666. On the 7th Pepys "saw all the town burned;" and had "a miserable sight of Paul's church, with all the roofs fallen, and the body of the choir fallen into St. Faith's." With the church perished all the monuments. The tower and as much of the walls as withstood the fire were removed by Wren to make way for the cathedral which "rose, phœnix-like," out of the ashes of the old. The architectural arrangement of this celebrated church has been preserved to us by the joint labours of Dugdale and Hollar. Hollar's drawings were made in September 1641, and Dugdale's book, for which they were engraved, was first published in 1658. These engravings and descriptions, and all other available sources of information, have been carefully collated, and the results presented in a clear and compact form and illustrated with many excellent engravings in Mr. William Longman's *History of the Three Cathedrals Dedicated to St. Paul* (1873), while the general history of the cathedrals is treated with a masterly hand in the *Annals of St. Paul's Cathedral*, by the late Dean of St. Paul's, the Rev. Henry Hart Milman, D.D. In these two volumes will be found ample and trustworthy information on all matters relating to the old and the present cathedrals. Dr. Sparrow Simpson's volumes on Old St. Paul's may be consulted with advantage. There is an incident connected with Old St. Paul's, remarkable in itself, but made still more so by the many celebrated writers who allude to it. In the year 1600 "a middle-sized bay English gelding," the property of Bankes, a servant to the Earl of Essex, and a vintner in Cheapside, ascended to the top of St. Paul's, to the delight, it is said by Dekker, of a "number of asses," who brayed below. Bankes had taught his horse, which went by the name of Marocco, to count and perform a variety of feats. "Certainly," says Walter Raleigh in his History, "if Bankes had lived in elder times he would have shamed all the enchanters of the world; for whosoever was most famous among them could never master or instruct any beast as he did his horse." When the novelty had somewhat lessened in London, Bankes took his wonderful beast first to Paris and afterwards to Rome. He had better have stayed at home, for both he and his horse (which was shod with silver) were burnt for witchcraft.[1] Shakespeare alludes to "the dancing horse;"[2] and in a tract called "Maroccus Extaticus," 4to, 1595, there is a rude woodcut of the unfortunate juggler and his famous gelding.

Paul's (St.) Cathedral. After the almost entire destruction of Old St. Paul's Cathedral in the Great Fire of 1666, Dr. Christopher Wren was called upon to survey and report upon its condition. There was a strong desire on the part of the authorities to restore the old building, but Wren pronounced the remaining walls unsafe, and recommended their removal with a view to the construction of a new cathedral. A committee was appointed, who decided against Wren's advice to attempt to patch up the old walls, and with the result he had predicted. Writing to Wren, April 25, 1668, Dean Sancroft says: "What you whispered in my ear at your last coming hither is come to pass. Our work at the west end of St. Paul's is fallen about our ears." On July 25 a royal warrant was issued for taking down the walls, removing the tower and choir, and clearing the ground to the foundation of the east end, with a view to the construction of a new choir for temporary use, and which might ultimately form part of a new cathedral. At Dean Sancroft's request Wren prepared a design for a cathedral, "a plan handsome and noble," which was approved by the King but objected to by the Chapter as "not sufficiently of a cathedral form." This is the design of which the model exists in the South Kensington Museum. In plan it is a Greek cross, with a spacious circular auditory at the intersection of the arms, surmounted by a dome, and at the west end a stately portico. This form Wren conceived would combine the most convenient for the Protestant ritual and service with grandeur of architectural effect; but the clergy insisted that the form should be that of a Latin cross, and that there should be both nave and aisles, and also a lofty spire. Wren therefore produced another design, in which the nave was lengthened and a curious spire placed upon the dome. This was accepted, and on May 14, 1675, a royal warrant was issued appointing Wren the architect, and authorising him to begin the work, "with the east end or quire," according to the design, "because we found it very artificial, proper, and useful." Happily, however, a clause gave the architect "liberty in the prosecution of his work to make some variations rather ornamental than essential, as from time to time he should see proper," and Wren went beyond his license in his "variations," for he produced what was in fact an entirely different and infinitely superior design. The ground was already begun to be

[1] Ben Jonson's *Epigrams*, No. cxxxiii.   [2] *Love's Labour's Lost.*

cleared, and the first stone of the new building was laid, June 21, 1675. Divine service was performed for the first time, December 2, 1697, on the day of thanksgiving for the peace of Ryswick. The King was present; the civic authorities attended in full state; and Bishop Burnet preached the sermon. The last stone was laid in 1710, thirty-five years after the first. It is frequently stated that the whole cathedral was begun and completed under one architect, Sir Christopher Wren; one master mason, Mr. Thomas Strong; and while one bishop, Dr. Henry Compton, presided over the diocese; but the latter part of the statement is not correct. Dr. Hinchman was bishop when the first stone was laid, and died the same year. Dr. Compton succeeded and was alive at the completion. Thomas Strong, mason, laid the foundation stone, June 21, 1675, and, dying 1681, was succeeded by his brother Edward, who continued and completed the work. The total cost of the building was £747,661 : 10s., which, with the exception of £68,341 in subscriptions, arrears of impropriations, and small sums coming under the head of royal gifts, fines, and forfeitures, and the sale of old materials, was defrayed by a tax on every chaldron of coal brought into the port of London, and the cathedral, it is said, deserves to wear, as it does, a smoky coat in consequence.

Exterior.—The general form or ground-plan is that of a Latin cross, with lateral projections at the west end of the nave, which give width and importance to the west front. Length from east to west, including the portico, 500 feet; breadth of the nave, 118 feet; across the transepts, 250 feet; at west end, including the Morning Chapel and that which contains the Wellington Monument, 190 feet; campanile towers at the west end, each 222 feet in height; and the height of the whole structure, from the pavement in the street to top of the cross, 404 feet. The outer diameter of the dome is 145 feet, the inner 108 feet. The outer dome is of wood, covered with lead, and does not support the lantern on the top, which rests on a cone of brick raised between the inner cupola and outer dome. The course of balustrade at the top was forced on Wren by the Commissioners for the building. "I never designed a balustrade," he says ; "ladies think nothing well without an edging." The heavy railing was also erected in opposition to his opinion. The sculpture on the entablature (the Conversion of St. Paul), the statues on the pediment (St. Paul, with St. Peter and St. James on either side), and the unfortunate statue of Queen Anne, in front of the building, with the four figures at the angles, were all by F. Bird. The statue of Queen Anne was taken away and a copy set up in 1886. The phœnix over the south door was the work of Cibber. The heavy iron railing, of more than 2500 palisades, against which Wren protested, was cast at Lamberhurst, in Kent, at a cost of £11,202 : 0 : 6, and encloses upwards of 2 acres of ground. It is a good example of cast-iron work, but its removal from the west end of the cathedral in 1873 has shown the soundness of Wren's objection to its erection. Owing to the undue proximity of houses no good near view of the cathedral as a whole is to be had. The best distant view is from the Thames, just below Blackfriars Bridge. An excellent view of it, on the whole the best obtainable, was from the bridge itself, but this was destroyed by the erection of the ugly railway viaduct, and the lofty river-side granaries and warehouses. *Observe.*—From Ludgate Hill the magnificent effect of the west front, with the dome rising above it; the double portico and grand flanking campaniles at the west end; the beautiful semicircular porticoes, north and south; the use of two orders of architecture (Composite above, Corinthian below); the exquisite outline of the dome and lantern; and the general breadth and harmony of the whole building. The circular columns at the base of the stone gallery are, it is said, too tall for the length of the pilasters in the body of the building, but they are certainly not too tall for the place they occupy. The acute observer will not fail to notice that the north and south walls are carried up exteriorly to the height of the nave roof, but on entering the cathedral it will be immediately seen that the height of the aisles bears about the same proportion to the height of the nave as is usual in Gothic edifices. On ascending the clock tower and looking towards the dome the spectator will see that the upper portion of the wall is a mere screen to hide the flying buttresses constructed to resist the thrust of the nave roof. These buttresses are also apparent in the corridor leading to the clock and bells.

Interior.—The cupola, with the paintings upon it, is of brick, two bricks thick, with stone bandings at every rise of 5 feet, and a girdle of Portland stone at the base, containing a double chain of iron strongly linked together at every 10 feet, and weighing 95 cwts. 3 qrs. 23 lbs. Wren had the inside all painted one colour to get rid of the diversity of coloured stones. The paint has now been cleaned off, and the colours are painfully apparent. A defect of the interior was forced on the architect by the Duke of York, afterwards James II.

The side oratories at St. Paul's were added to Sir Christopher Wren's original design, by order of the Duke of York [afterwards James II.], who was willing to have them ready for the popish service, when there should be occasion. It narrowed the building, and broke in very much upon the beauty of the design. Sir Christopher insisted so strongly on the prejudice they would be of, that he actually shed some tears in speaking of it; but it was all in vain. The Duke absolutely insisted upon their being inserted and he was obliged to comply.—Mr. Harding, in Spence's *Anecdotes*, ed. Singer, p. 256.

The paintings, eight in number (by Sir James Thornhill), represent the principal events in the life of St. Paul. They were never worth much, and the little interest that attached to them as Thornhill's works was destroyed when they were repainted in 1853. Wren was opposed from the first to painting the cupola with these heavy masses of monochrome. It was his wish to have decorated the cupola with the more durable ornament of mosaic work, but in this he was overruled. *Observe.*— In the choir the beautiful foliage, carved by Grinling Gibbons, and the inscription to Wren, originally over the entrance to the choir, but now on the inner porch of the north transept, ending with the line, "Si monumentum requiris, circumspice." It was first set up by Robert Mylne, architect to the Cathedral. The organ (1694) was constructed by Bernard Schmydt, the successful candidate against Harris at the Temple. It originally stood on the screen at the entrance to the choir, but is now divided and placed on each side over the stalls. The rails of the golden gallery were gilt at the expense of the Earl of Lanesborough, the "sober Lanesborough dancing with the gout" of Pope.

The chief monuments in the Cathedral are as follows :—Statue of John Howard, the philanthropist, by Bacon, R.A. (cost 1300 guineas, and was the first monument erected in St. Paul's); statue of Dr. Johnson, by Bacon, R.A.; statue of Sir Joshua Reynolds, by Flaxman, R.A.; Turner, our greatest landscape painter, by Baily, R.A.; kneeling figure of Bishop Heber, by Chantrey, R.A.; monument to Nelson, by Flaxman, R.A. (the hero's lost arm concealed by the Union Jack of England); monument to Lord Cornwallis, opposite, by Rossi, R.A. (the Indian river-gods much admired); monument to Sir Ralph Abercrombie, by Sir R. Westmacott, R.A.; General Sir Charles Napier, the conqueror of Scinde, and not far from him his brother Sir William, the author of the *History of the Peninsular War;* Sir Henry Lawrence, of Lucknow fame; Lord Melbourne the minister, and his brother the diplomatist, by Baron Marochetti; and Hallam the historian; monument to Sir John Moore, who fell at Corunna (Marshal Soult stood before this monument and wept); statue of Lord Heathfield, the gallant defender of Gibraltar; monuments to Howe and Rodney, two of our great naval heroes; monument to Nelson's favourite, the brave and pious Lord Collingwood; statue of Earl St. Vincent, the hero of the battle of Cape St. Vincent; Lord Duncan, the victor of Camperdown, and Captain Burges, who fell in that fight; Captain Mosse and "the gallant good Riou," who fell at Copenhagen, and many other of our naval heroes; monuments to Picton and Ponsonby, who fell at Waterloo; statues of Sir William Jones, the Oriental scholar; Sir Astley Cooper, the surgeon; Dr. Babington, the physician; and Lord Lyons. The monument to the Duke of Wellington, by A. Stevens, in the chapel at the west end of the south aisle, a most elaborate renaissance structure, was more than twenty years in hand, partly owing to the ill-health and mental idiosyncrasy of the artist, but also largely to the complex and difficult character of the work. It is a remarkable and beautiful production, but is seen with difficulty and at a great disadvantage in its present very unsuitable position. There are fine tombs with recumbent effigies of Bishops Blomfield and Jackson, Dean Milman and General Gordon. The monument of Dr. Donne, saved from the old cathedral—an effigy of the form of Donne, wrapped in his sepulchral shroud, has been (1873) removed from the crypt and placed in an alcove in the south-east aisle.

The crypt of St. Paul's, unlike the crypts of most other cathedrals, extends under the entire building, and is one of the most extensive and massive in structure extant. A portion of it was fitted up in 1877 as a chapel for the early morning service. In the crypt, *Observe.* —Grave of Sir Christopher Wren (d. 1723, aged ninety-one). Grave of Lord Nelson (d. 1805). The sarcophagus which contains Nelson's coffin was made at the expense of Cardinal Wolsey, for the burial of Henry VIII. in the tomb-house at Windsor; and the coffin which contains the body (made of part of the mainmast of the ship *L'Orient*), was a present to Nelson after the battle of the Nile, from his friend Ben Hallowell, captain of the *Swiftsure.* "I send it," says Hallowell, "that when you are tired of this life you may be buried in one of your own trophies." Nelson appreciated the present, and for some time had it placed upright, with the lid on, against the bulk-head of his cabin, behind the chair on which he sat at dinner. In a neighbouring alcove the sarcophagus which contains the remains of Wellington. The sarcophagus, grand in its simplicity, was wrought with infinite patience from a matchless block of Cornish porphyry. Grave of Sir John Collingwood (d. 1810), commander of the larboard division at the battle of Trafalgar. Graves of the following celebrated English painters—Sir Joshua Reynolds (d. 1792); Sir Thomas Lawrence (d. 1830); James Barry (d. 1806); John Opie (d. 1807); Benjamin West (d. 1820); Henry Fuseli (d. 1825); Joseph Mallord William Turner (d. 1851). Graves of the following eminent engineers— Robert Mylne, who built Blackfriars Bridge (d. 1811); John Rennie, who built Waterloo Bridge (d. 1821). *Monuments from Old St. Paul's,* preserved in the crypt of the present building—Dean Colet, founder of St. Paul's School; Sir Nicholas Bacon, father of the great Francis Bacon; and Sir Christopher Hatton, Queen Elizabeth's Lord Chancellor.

Ascent.—The ascent to the ball is by 616 steps, of which the first 260 are easy, and well lighted. Here the Whispering Gallery will give the visitor breath; but the rest of the ascent is a somewhat fatiguing task. *Clock Room.*—In the south-western tower is the clock, and the great bell on which it strikes. The length of the minute hand of the clock is 8 feet, and its weight 75 lbs.; the length of the hour hand is 5 feet 5 inches, and its weight 44 lbs. The diameter of the bell is about 10 feet, and its weight is generally stated at 4¼ tons. It is inscribed, "Richard Phelps made me, 1716," and is never used except for the striking of the hour, and for tolling at the deaths and funerals of any of the royal family, the Bishops of London, the Deans of St. Paul's, and should he die in his mayoralty, the Lord Mayor. The larger part of the metal of which it is made formed "Great Tom of Westminster," once in the Clock Tower at Westminster. It had long been a matter of regret and complaint that the Cathedral should be without a peal of bells, and in 1877 several of the City Companies, in conjunction with the Baroness Burdett-Coutts, determined to provide it with a complete peal of twelve bells. They were cast by Messrs. Taylor of Loughborough, weighed together about 11 tons, and cost £6000. The 1st and 2d bells were presented by the Drapers' Company; the 3d, 4th, 5th and 6th by the Baroness Burdett-Coutts and the Turners' Company; the 7th by the Salters'; the 8th by the Merchant Taylors'; the 9th by the Fishmongers'; the 10th by the Clothworkers'; the 11th by the Grocers' Company; and the 12th and largest by the Corporation. Each bell is inscribed with the motto of the donors, and with the arms of the Dean and Chapter of St. Paul's. They are hung in the northwest campanile, and ring out a full sweet peal. A new bell (Great Paul), weighing 17 tons, cast by Messrs. Taylor of Loughborough, was safely hauled into its place in the south-west campanile in May 1882.

The Library is not very valuable. *The Whispering Gallery* is so called because the slightest whisper is transmitted from one side of the gallery to the other with great rapidity and distinctness. *The Stone Gallery* is an outer gallery, and affords a fine view of London on a clear day. *The Inner Golden Gallery* is at the apex of the cupola and base of the lantern. *The Outer Golden Gallery* is at the apex of the dome. Here a noble view of London may be obtained if the ascent is made early in the morning, and on a clear day. *The Ball and Cross* stand on a cone between the cupola and dome. The construction is very interesting, and will well repay attention. The ball is 6 feet 2 inches in diameter, and will contain eight persons, "without," it is said, "particular inconvenience." This, however, may well be doubted. The weight of the ball is stated to be 5600 lbs., and that of the cross (to which there is no entrance), 3360 lbs.

The unadorned condition of the interior of St. Paul's, so different from the intention of the architect, who wished to line the cupola with mosaics by the best artists of Italy, and to place in compartments below "bas-reliefs and suchlike decorations," and complained that through insufficient funds "his wings were clipt, and the Church was deprived of its ornaments," had frequently forced itself on those interested in the worthy appearance of the fabric and its adequate employment as a great central church for public worship. Nothing practical was done, however, till the beginning of 1858, when the Bishop of London addressed a letter to the Dean and Chapter urging upon them "the advisability of instituting a series of special evening services for the benefit of those large masses of the people whom it might be impossible to attract in any other way." To this Dean Milman promptly replied, expressing for himself and the Chapter their "earnest, unanimous, and sincere desire to co-operate to the utmost of their power" in the proposed object, but showing that "the scantiness of the funds at their disposal" rendered them unable to accomplish it without extraneous help. But he further avowed the desire that "instead of the dull, cold, unedifying, unseemly appearance of the interior, the Cathedral should be made within worthy of its exterior grandeur and beauty." An appeal was made to the public, and sufficient funds obtained to fit the space under the dome for public service, to provide a magnificent organ for these special services and ceremonials, and to warm the cathedral throughout, with the result that "immense congregations of earnest and devout worshippers throng to the Cathedral, throughout even the wildest, coldest, nights of the winter months."[1] On these improvements about £10,000 were expended. A like sum was spent on ornamental alterations and decorations, but with a less satisfactory result. In 1871 an "iconographic scheme" by Burges was laid before the Executive Committee, and made public, for the complete and systematic decoration of the interior; but it proposed to overlay every part with a profusion of seraphim and cherubim with wings and bodies "fiery red" or celestial blue, princedoms, thrones and powers, archangels in armour, and angels "dressed as deacons," saints and confessors. The designs are in the Chapter House. This, in common with some other schemes of decoration, did not meet with general approval. Nothing more was formally done till June 1877, when the Executive Committee met and passed a resolution—

That it is desirable, with the funds now in hand, about £40,000, to carry into effect as far as possible the wishes of Sir Christopher Wren, by decorating the dome of St. Paul's with mosaic, in a similar style to the dome of St. Peter's at Rome.

A sub-committee was appointed to devise the best means of giving effect to this resolution: but little has since been done.

The elaborate reredos, which cost £37,000, and took eighteen months to erect, was unveiled on January 25, 1888.

The space within the railings on the north and east sides of the cathedral has been planted and laid out as a public garden, and from it some picturesque views of portions of the fabric may be obtained. When the ground was being dug over for the formation of the garden, Mr. F. C. Penrose, the architect to the Dean and Chapter, seized the opportunity to institute a careful search for any traces of the old cathedral. He came upon walls and buttresses of the cloisters and chapter-house, and was able to make out the general direction of the main structure, the central line of which, though not due east and west, inclined much less to the north-east than that of the present cathedral. He also discovered the foundations of the famous St. Paul's Cross, the site of which and the outline of its base he has marked by a stone pavement at the north-east angle of the cathedral. In the public procession to St. Paul's on occasion of the general thanksgiving for peace, Thursday, July 7, 1814, the Duke of Wellington carried the sword of state before the Prince Regent. The next public procession to St. Paul's was when the Duke of Wellington was himself carried to his grave, November 18, 1852. The latest was on February 27, 1872, when the Queen attended in state to join in the general public thanksgiving for the recovery of the Prince of Wales.

Services.—On Sundays, Good Friday, Ascension Day, and Christmas Day: Holy Communion (north-west chapel) 8; Morning Service,

[1] Dean Milman's *Annals of St. Paul's*, p. 497.

with Holy Communion, choral, 10.30; Evening Service, 3.15 and 7. On week days, except Good Friday, Ascension Day, and Christmas Day: Holy Communion (north-west chapel) 8; Morning Prayer (crypt chapel) 8; Morning Prayer, choral, 10; Short Service (north-west chapel) 1.15. Evening Prayer, choral, 4; Short Service (north-west chapel) 8. Unless otherwise stated the services are held in the choir, the entire area of the cathedral being available for worshippers. On St. Paul's Day, January 25, a selection from Mendelssohn's oratorio of *St. Paul* is performed with a full orchestra and a largely augmented choir, and on Tuesday in Holy Week Bach's Passion Music is given in like manner. During Lent the mid-day service is held in the choir, when a course of sermons, each course lasting a week, are given by eminent preachers. The services are always well-attended, about 800 persons being generally present at the daily evensong. Under Sir John Stainer, who was organist for several years, the services attained a high degree of musical excellence. On the Fridays in Lent the service is sung without the organ, and is well worth hearing. The annual meeting of the children of the Charity Schools of London has been discontinued since 1867, in consequence of the interruption to the service, rendered necessary by the erection of a huge gallery round the dome area. Haydn said that the most powerful impression he ever received from music was from their singing of the "Old Hundredth."

Paul's Bake-House Court, on the west side of GODLIMAN STREET, PAUL'S CHAIN, was so called from the bakehouse "employed in baking of bread for the Church of Paul's." [1]

On the west side of the street now called Godliman Street stood the bakehouse: it was a large building, and its place is still identified by Paul's Bakehouse Yard. The brewery probably adjoined it. There was a mill for grinding the corn, worked by horses. There were four servants in the bakehouse, three in the brewery, and two at the mill, besides a clerk of the receipts. The brewery and the bakehouse were under the charge of an officer, the Custos Bracini.—*Domesday of St. Paul's*, 1222: ed. Archdeacon Hale (*Camden Society*, 1858, p. 48).

Here was the office of the Registrar of the High Court of Admiralty, now transferred to the Royal Courts of Justice, Somerset House. The brewhouse attached to the Cathedral was converted into the Paul's Head Tavern.[2]

Paul's Chain, south side of ST. PAUL'S CHURCHYARD to CARTER LANE, a street so called from a chain or barrier drawn across the carriage-way of St. Paul's Churchyard, to preserve silence in the Cathedral during the hours of public worship. Stow (p. 137) refers to the "south chain of Paul's." The north chain is a barrier of wood. Edward Cocker ("according to Cocker") taught the arts of writing and arithmetic, "in an extraordinary manner," at "his dwelling on the south side of St. Paul's Church, over against Paul's Chain;" and here, in 1660, he wrote *The Pen's Transcendancy*, an interesting illustration of his extraordinary skill in the art of writing well.

[1] *Stow*, p. 137.   [2] *Ibid.*, p. 137.

So [they] going downe by Paules chaine, left the gentlemen going up toward Fleet Street.—R. Greene, *Cony-catching*.

The Faculties Office for granting Licenses (by Act of Parliament) to eat flesh in any part of England, is still kept at St. Paul's Chain, near St. Paul's Churchyard.— *The Kingdom's Intelligencer*, No. 8, February 23, 1663.

Paul's (St.) Churchyard, the irregular area, lined with houses, encircling St. Paul's Cathedral and burial-ground, of which the side towards the Thames is commonly called the *bow*, and the side towards Paternoster Row the *string*. The original statue of Queen Anne, before the west front of the church, was the work (1712) of Francis Bird, a poor sculptor, whose best work is his monument to Dr. Busby, in Westminster Abbey. It was the subject of an indifferent copy of verses, by a poet who could write better things, Sir Samuel Garth, author of the *Dispensary*. A couplet will suffice as a specimen of the whole:—

> With grace divine great Anna's seen to rise
> An awful form that glads a Nation's eyes.

In the area of St. Paul's Church is a noble statue erected of the late Queen in marble, though I cannot say it's extremely like Her Majesty, yet it is very masterly done, with her Crown on her head, her sceptre and globe in her hands, and adorned with her Royal Robes and ensigns of the garter. Round her Pedestal are four fine figures, also in marble, representing Great Britain, France, Ireland, and America. —Macky, *A Journey through England*, 8vo, 1722, vol. i. p. 280.

The old statue, which was worn out, has been replaced by a copy in Sicilian marble by Messrs. Mowlem, Burt, and Freeman. This was unveiled in December 1886.

At the east end of the Cathedral was *St. Paul's School*, and on the *string* or northern side is the *Chapter-house* of the Cathedral. St. Paul's Churchyard was one of the places examined for lodgings for the retinue of Charles V. previous to his coming to London in 1522, and we learn from the return the kind of houses occupied by one or two noted residents :—

Maister Lylly, scole maister : i hall, iiij chambers, iiij feather beddes, i kitchin, and other necessaries.

Poloderus [Polydore Vergil] in Paules Churche Yarde : hall, parlour, iiij chambers, iiij beddes with all necessaries.

Before the Fire, which destroyed the old Cathedral, St. Paul's Churchyard was chiefly inhabited by stationers, whose shops were then, and till the year 1760, distinguished by signs. The *Cronycle of England*, folio, 1515, was printed by Julian Notary, "dwellynge in powles chyrche yarde besyde y'' weste dore by my lordes palyes." His sign was *The Three Kinges*. At the sign of the White Greyhound, in St. Paul's Churchyard, the first editions of Shakespeare's *Venus and Adonis* and *Rape of Lucrece* were published by John Harrison ; at the Flower de Luce and the Crown appeared the first edition of the *Merry Wives of Windsor ;* at the Green Dragon the first edition of the *Merchant of Venice ;* at the Fox the first edition of *Richard II. ;* at the Angel the first edition of *Richard III. ;* at the Spread Eagle the first edition of *Troilus and Cressida ;* at the Gun the first edition of

Titus Andronicus; and at the Red Bull the first edition of *Lear.* Ben Jonson makes a reference to Purfoote the printer's sign, the Lucretia, in Paul's Churchyard :—

> He makes a face like a stabbed Lucretia.[1]

Lucretia, "with the dagger at her breast and a ridiculous expression of agony in her face, formed a vignette to most of his books," and was stamped on their covers. The earliest English book of glees and catches, *Pammelia: Musicke's Miscellanie of Pleasant Roundelays and Catches*, was published in 1609 by William Burley, at the sign of the Spread Eagle, at the north door of St. Paul's.

March 29, 1617.—Warrant to pay John Dill, Bookseller in St. Paul's Churchyard, £469 : 11 : 0 for books.—*Cal. State Pap.*, 1611-1618, p. 454.

It also appears to have been famed thus early for trunkmakers :—

> And coffin makers are well paid their rent
> For many a woefull wooden tenement
> For which the trunk makers in Paul's Church yard
> A large revenue this sad year have shared.
> Their living customers for trunks were fled
> They now made chests or coffins for the dead.
>
> Taylor (the Water Poet), *The Fearful Summer, or London's Calamitie.*

After the Fire the majority of the stationers removed to *Little Britain* and *Paternoster Row;* but the Yard was not wholly deserted. At the "Bible and Sun," or No. 65 on the north side of St. Paul's Churchyard, one door west of Canon Alley, lived John Newbery, "the philanthropic bookseller," Goldsmith's "good-natured man, with the red-pimpled face,"[2] to whose kind catering for the public we are indebted for the entertaining histories of *Mr. Thomas Trip, Giles Gingerbread,* and *Little Goody Two Shoes.* Here, for 60 guineas, Johnson (as agent for Goldsmith) sold the *Vicar of Wakefield* to Newbery's nephew. The site of Newbery's shop is now occupied by the publishing office of the Religious Tract Society. No. 81, the corner of Ludgate Hill, was the shop of Mr. Harris, another clever provider for the public entertainment in the same way, and, until 1889, occupied by Messrs. Griffiths and Farran. At No. 72 lived J. Johnson, the bookseller; and here in 1784 was published *The Task,* a poem by William Cowper. No. 62, one door east of Canon Alley, was F. and C. Rivingtons, as chronicled by Peter Pindar :—

> In Paul's Churchyard, the Bible and the Key
> This wondrous pair is always to be seen,—
> Somewhat the worse for wear—a little grey—
> One like a Saint, and one with Cæsar's mien.

In January 1757 Mrs. Carter was lodging at the house of Mr. Wallis, cabinetmaker, St. Paul's Churchyard. The house was "known as 'The Elephant,' and was situated opposite to the south door of the Cathedral." It was in St. Paul's Churchyard that Rowland Hill met William Huntington, S.S. (Sinner Saved), and ran away from him.

[1] *Cynthia's Revels,* Act v. Sc. 2; and Gifford's note to the passage.
[2] *Vicar of Wakefield,* chap. xviii.

His dislike to the S.S. was so great that, as Southey tells us, he took up one of Huntington's books with a pair of tongs, and gave it in that manner to a servant to take downstairs and use it for lighting the fire. Campbell, the poet.

June 2, 1819.—[At Longmans'] met Campbell and walked with him to a little bedroom he has taken in St. Paul's Churchyard, in order to consult medical advice about a complaint he has.—Moore's *Diary*.

The following curious picture of St. Paul's Churchyard in the time of Cromwell is from a single half-sheet in the British Museum, dated May 27, 1651 :—

Forasmuch as the Inhabitants of Paul's Churchyard are much disturbed by the souldiers and others, calling out to passingers, and examining them (though they goe peaceably and civilly along), and by playing at nine pinnes at unseasonable houres; These are therefore to command all souldiers and others whom it may concern, that hereafter there shall be no examining and calling out to persons that go peaceably on their way, unlesse they do approach their Guards, and likewise to forbeare playing at nine pinnes and other sports, from the houre of nine of the clocke in the evening till six in the morning, that so persons that are weake and indisposed to rest, may not be disturbed. Given under our hands the day and yeare above written. IOHN BARKESTEAD.
BENJAMIN BLUNDELL.

This yard, it would appear, was famous for its trees.

We have had here on Saturday night last and Sunday morning an exceeding high wind, such as seldom hath happened in any country. It hath blown down many houses in the country and many chimneys in this towne, the greatest Elme in Paul's Churchyard, and diverse Trees about the Charter-House and Westminster.—*Sir John More to Sir Ralph Winwood*, London, June 18, 1611.

In the Chapter-house of St. Paul's (on the north side of the yard) was performed, in the reign of James II., the mock ceremony of degrading Samuel Johnson, chaplain to William, Lord Russell. The divines present purposely omitted to strip him of his cassock, which rendered his degradation imperfect, and afterwards saved him his benefice. The churchyard was occasionally chosen as a place of execution for conspicuous offenders, for exposure in the pillory, and for the burning of heretical books. Major William, the loyalist, was on Friday, December 29, 1648, shot by order of the Council of the Army, "against the door that leadeth into St. Faith's Church."[1]

The Goose and Gridiron, London Yard (so called from London House, the residence of the Bishops of London), on the north side of St. Paul's, was a noted coaching inn, and the place where one of the first lodges of Freemasons was held from before 1716. Before the Great Fire the site was occupied by the *Mitre Inn*, a "musick house," famed for its concerts and musical parties. When rebuilt the new landlord gave it its present strange title, perverting according to Mr. Burn, "the Swan and Lyre, the crest and charge on the arms of the Company of Musicians, into the silly Goose and Gridiron."[2]

The erection of warehouses on the site of St. Paul's School has

[1] *Mercurius Elenticus*, December 26-January 2, 1648-1649.
[2] Burn, *London Traders' Tokens*, p. 187.

considerably altered the appearance of the east side of St. Paul's Churchyard. In 1888 considerable alterations were also made at the north-western corner. [*See* Queen's Arms Tavern; St. Paul's School.]

Paul's (St.) Coffee-house stood at the corner of the entrance from St. Paul's Churchyard to Doctors' Commons, on the site of Paul's Brewhouse and the Paul's Head Tavern. Here, in 1721, Dr. Rawlinson's books were sold. "They sold," says Thoresby, "at a prodigious rate."[1] The sale took place in the evening, after dinner.

On Tuesday I will wait on you, by one o'clock, at St. Paul's Coffee House, by Doctors' Commons gate, from whence we may go down together at the tavern next door [which was Truby's].—*Aaron Hill to David Mallet*, June 2, 1743.

Paul's (St.), COVENT GARDEN, a parish church on the west side of the market, the design of which is attributed to Inigo Jones, begun 1631[2] at the expense of the ground landlord, Francis, Earl of Bedford, and consecrated by Juxon, Bishop of London, September 27, 1638. The great delay between the period of erection and the period of consecration was owing to a dispute between the Earl of Bedford and the Rev. William Bray, Vicar of St. Martin's-in-the-Fields, on the right of presentation; the earl claiming it as his own, because he had built it at his own expense, and the vicar claiming it as his, because, not being then parochial, it was nothing more than a chapel of ease to St. Martin's. The matter was heard by the King in council, on April 6, 1638.

May 10, 1638.—The new church in the Covent Garden is now at length to be consecrated. The King, upon a petition preferred unto his Majesty by the inhabitants thereof, put an end to the long dispute which hath been betwixt the Earl of Bedford and Mr. Bray, curate or Vicar of St. Martin's-in-the-Fields. It must be a Chapel of Ease until a Parliament settle it a district parish. Mr. Bray must put in an under curate to serve the place. My Lord Bedford's £100 a year, and an house he builded for the minister in cure be presented will not be accepted.—*Garrard to Wentworth* (*Strafford Letters*, vol. ii. p. 168).

In 1645 the precinct of Covent Garden was constituted a separate parish. In consideration of the building and endowment of this church Oliver Cromwell remitted the sum of £7000 to the sons of the Earl of Bedford, out of the fines to which they were liable under the Act to prevent the multiplicity of buildings in and about London.[3]

The church was repaired in 1688, and the exterior is thus described in Hatton's *New View of London* (1708): "The walls are of brick rendered over, but the coins are stone, rustic work." The portico, which had been altered and defaced by the parishioners, was restored by the Earl of Burlington in 1727, at a cost of between three and four hundred pounds: "it had cost the inhabitants about twice as much to spoil it."[4] In 1788 the parish expended £11,000 in improving the building. An ashlering of Portland stone was added to the walls in

[1] *Thoresby's Diary*, vol. ii. p. 363.
[2] "In Covent Garden there is a particular parcel of ground laid out, in the which they intend to build a church or a chapel of ease."—
Howes, ed. 1631, p. 1049.
[3] *Northouck*, p. 733 *note*.
[4] *Parker's Penny Post*, Wednesday, April 19, 1727.

lieu of the plaster which had previously covered them, and the rustic gateways imitated by Jones from Palladio, which, like the church, were of brick and plaster, were rebuilt in stone. This work was carried out under the superintendence of Thomas Hardwick. The church was totally destroyed by fire, September 17, 1795, and rebuilt (Thomas Hardwick, architect) on the plan and in the proportions of the original building. When first erected the church was greatly admired for its classic simplicity of form and outline, and especially for its "noble Tuscan portico," exactly in accordance, as was said, with one described by Vitruvius. Gay, in his *Trivia* (1716), speaks of it as the "famous temple, with columns of plain magnificence"—

That boast the work of Jones' immortal hand.

Walpole, however, who could "see no beauty" in it, called the building a barn, and a barn it has been called ever since, and the portico "a sham."

The barn roof over the portico of the church strikes my eyes with as little idea of dignity or beauty as it could do if it covered nothing but a barn. In justice to Inigo, one must own that the defect is not in the architect, but in the order; who ever saw a beautiful Tuscan building? Would the Romans have chosen that order for a temple? Mr. Onslow, the late Speaker, told me an anecdote that corroborates my opinion of this building. When the Earl of Bedford sent for Inigo, he told him he wanted a chapel for the parishioners of Covent Garden, but added he would not go to any considerable expense; "In short," said he, "I would not have it much better than a barn." "Well! then," replied Jones, "you shall have the handsomest barn in England." The expense of building was £4500.—Horace Walpole, *Anecdotes of Painting*, ed. 1786, vol. ii. p. 274, and *note*.

For the portico being a sham, the true entrance being elsewhere, the defect is not in the architect. The architect intended it for a real entrance, but when it was decided that, for ecclesiastical reasons, the altar must occupy the usual position at the east end, the entrance at that end had of necessity to be given up. There were two small doors which were sometimes opened in the summer time.

Of the old church there is a view by Hollar, and a part of it is to be seen in Hogarth's print of "Morning." It was built of brick, with stone columns to the portico, and the roof covered with red tiles. The apex of the pediment was originally ornamented with a stone cross, preserved in Hollar's engraving, and commemorated in an old play.

Come, Sir, what do you gape and shake the head at there? I'll lay my life he has spied the little crosse upon the new church yond', and is at defiance with it.— R. Brome's *Covent Garden Weeded, or the Middlesex Justice of Peace*, 1659.

The roadway in front of the church has been widened and the footway has been carried beneath the portico. In 1888 the stone casing was cleared away and the red brick walls were exposed to view. At the same time the small bell turret at the west end was pulled down. The clock was the first long pendulum clock in Europe, and was invented and made, as an inscription in the vestry records, by Richard Harris, of London, in 1641.

The interior was rearranged, and the galleries cleared away under the superintendence of Mr. Butterfield in 1872.

Mrs. Saintly. Of what church are you?
Woodall. Why, of Covent Garden church, I think.
Gervase. How lewdly and ignorantly he answers! She means of what religion are you?—Dryden's *Limberham*, 4to, 1678.

Maggot. At your similes again! O you incorrigible wit! let me see what poetry you have about you. What's here? a Poem called a "Posie for the Ladies' Delight,"—"Distichs to write upon Ladies' Busks,"—"Epigram written in a Lady's Bible in Covent Garden Church."—*A True Widow*, by T. Shadwell, 4to, 1679; and see his *Miser*, 1672.

The parish register records the baptism of Lady Mary Wortley Montagu:—

26 May 1689.—Mary daughter of Evelyn Peirpoint, Esq., by the Lady Mary, his wife.

Also the marriage (1764) of Lady Susan Strangways to O'Brien, the handsome actor. It records also the marriage, August 29, 1773, of William Turner, of Maiden Lane, to Mary Marshall, also of the parish of St. Paul's, Covent Garden, and the baptism, May 14, 1775, of their son, Joseph Mallord William Turner, the great landscape painter. The elder Turner was buried here, 1830, and a tablet (the inscription written by the painter) records that "In the vault beneath and near this place, were deposited the remains of William Turner, many years an inhabitant of this parish." *Eminent Persons buried in.*—The notorious Robert Carr, Earl of Somerset (d. 1645). Sir Henry Herbert (d. 1673), whose "office book" as "Master of the Revels" throws so much light on the history of our stage and drama in the time of Charles I. (He was brother to Lord Herbert of Cherbury, and George Herbert.) Samuel Butler (d. 1680), author of *Hudibras*. He died in Rose Street.

He [Butler] dyed of a consumption, Septemb. 25 (Anno D^{ni} 1680), and buried 27, according to his owne appointment in the church-yard of Covent Garden; sc. in the north part next the church at the east end. His feet touch the wall. His grave, 2 yards distant from the pilaster of the dore (by his desire), 6 foot deepe. About 25 of his old acquaintance at his funerall: I myself being one.—Aubrey's *Lives*, vol. ii. 263.

Sir Peter Lely, the painter. He died (1680) in the *Piazza*. His monument, with his bust by Gibbons and his epitaph by Flatman, shared the fate of the church when destroyed by fire in 1795; and Sir Dudley North, the great merchant and political economist, afterwards occupied Lely's house, and died there, December 31, 1691. He was buried near the altar in this church, but twenty-five years afterwards his body was removed to Glemham in Suffolk. Dick Estcourt (d. 1711-1712), the actor and wit. Edward Kynaston (d. 1712), the celebrated actor of female parts at the Restoration; a complete female stage beauty, "that it has since been disputable among the judicious, whether any woman that succeeded him so sensibly touched the audience as he."[1] William Wycherley (d. 1715), the dramatist. He died in Bow Street. Pierce Tempest (d. 1717), who drew the Cries of London, known as Tempest's Cries. Grinling Gibbons (d. 1721),

[1] Downes's *Roscius Anglicanus*, 8vo, 1708.

the sculptor and carver in wood. Susannah Centlivre (d. 1723), author of *The Busy Body* and *The Wonder*. Robert Wilks (d. 1732), the original Sir Harry Wildair, celebrated by Steele for acting with the easy frankness of a gentleman. James Worsdale, the painter (d. 1767). He carried Pope's letters to Curll; and was buried in the churchyard, with an inscription (removed 1848) of his own composing:—

> Eager to get, but not to keep the pelf,
> A friend to all mankind except himself.

Dr. Thomas Arne (d. 1778), composer of "Rule Britannia." Dr. John Armstrong, author of the "Art of Preserving Health," a poem (d. 1779), in the vault under the communion table. Tom Davies, the bookseller (d. 1785), and his "very pretty wife" (d. 1801). Sir Robert Strange, the engraver (d. 1792), in the churchyard. He lived in Henrietta Street, at the sign of "The Golden Head." Thomas Girtin, the father of the school of English water-colour painting, died "at his lodgings in the Strand, November 9, 1802, at the early age of twenty-seven years; but intemperance and irregularity have no claim to longevity."[1] Charles Macklin, the actor (d. 1797), at the age of 107, buried in the vault under the communion table. There is a tablet to his memory in the church. John Wolcot (Peter Pindar), died 1819, "in a very appropriate position," says his biographer, "for it was so contrived, at his own request, that the coffin of the author of the *Lousiad* should be so near as to touch that of the bard who had produced *Hudibras*, whose genius and originality he greatly admired."[2] Fielding's "Inimitable Betty Careless," the "charming Betty Careless" of the mad scene in the *Rake's Progress*, was buried here from the parish poorhouse. William Linley (d. 1835), the celebrated musician, and father of Mrs. Sheridan. The whole of the churchyard has been levelled and all the gravestones cleared away. In front of this church the hustings were raised for the general elections of Westminster. Here, before the Reform Bill, raged those fierce contests of many days' duration in which Fox, Sir Francis Burdett, and others were popular candidates.[3] Archbishop Usher is said to have been preaching in this church when sent for by Charles I. to resolve his scruples respecting the signing of Strafford's death-warrant. The learned Simon Patrick, Bishop of Ely, was many years rector of St. Paul's, Covent Garden, and his name, in his own handwriting, is still to be seen affixed to the pages of the parish register.

Paul's Cross, a pulpit Cross of timber, mounted upon steps of stone and covered with a conical roof of lead, from which sermons were preached by learned divines every Sunday in the forenoon. "The very antiquity," says Stow, "is to me unknown." "It stood," says Dugdale, "on the north side of St. Paul's Churchyard, towards the east end." What was traditionally said to be the site was, within the last fifty years, distinguished by a lofty elm; but the exact spot was ascertained by Mr. F. C. Penrose, architect for the Cathedral, when the

---

[1] Edwards, *Anecdotes of Painting*, p. 280.
[2] *Ann. Biog.*, 1820.
[3] In the *Microcosm of London* is a good view of the election hustings in front of the portico.

burial-ground was being dug over preparatory to converting it into a garden. [*See* St. Paul's Cathedral.] At a depth of about 6 feet below the surface he came upon the octagonal stone basement, and judiciously marked the site by a pavement level with the surface, as a permanent memorial of a structure unique in its historical associations. The north-east (Cheapside) angle of the present cathedral cuts one side of the octagon. The choir of the old cathedral was a short distance from it.

In early times the three great annual Folkmotes of the Londoners were held at Paul's Cross. In the 13th century (temp. Henry III. and Edward I.) it was ordered that "if any man of London neglects to attend at one of these three folkmotes, he is to forfeit forty shillings to the King," and the sheriff is to see that such attendance is given or to enforce the fine, the ringing "of the great bell for the folkmote at St. Paul's," to be held a sufficient summons.[1] Later it was more especially employed for sermons, the promulgation of papal bulls, royal proclamations and explanations, the publication of state information, excommunications, and the public penance of important offenders, becoming, as Dean Milman observes, "the pulpit not only of the Cathedral, but almost of the Church in England," and also, in Carlyle's quaint phraseology, "a kind of Times newspaper."[2] At special sermons, or important announcements, the Lord Mayor and Aldermen attended in state, and on some occasions the Sovereign and Court were present. The congregation sat in the open air. For the King and his retinue a covered gallery was built against the wall of the Cathedral. In foul and rainy weather the sermons were preached in *The Shrowds*, or "The Crowds, according to the vulgar expression," says Dugdale. What these Shrowds were has been differently explained. Strype suggested that they were "by the side of the Cathedral church, where was covering and shelter," others have absurdly said they were the triforium; they were beyond doubt the "crypt," where was already the church of "St. Faith in the Shrowds." Shrowds is a term often used for the crypt of a church.

I read that in the year 1259 King Henry III. commanded a general assembly to be made at this Cross, where he in proper person commanded the Mayor, that on the next day following, he should cause to be sworn before the aldermen, every stripling of twelve years of age, or upward, to be true to the King and his heirs, Kings of England.—*Stow*, p. 123.

The Cross before which this assembly was brought, being defaced by a tempest of lightning in 1382, was rebuilt by Thomas Kemp, Bishop of London from 1448 to 1449, Milman says as "a more splendid stone cross with a pulpit. It became one of the buildings of which, from its grace and beauty, the City of London was most proud." This, however, is hardly borne out by contemporary statements. The platform was of stone, but the superstructure was certainly of wood. Stow says that Kemp "new built it in form as it now standeth," and he describes it as "a pulpit cross of timber, mounted upon steps of

[1] *Liber Albus*, pp. 72, 92, 105.
[2] Milman's *Annals of St. Paul's*, p. 61; Carlyle's *Cromwell*, vol. i. p. 93.

stone, and covered with lead,"[1] which agrees exactly with the contemporary painting of it in the possession of the Society of Antiquaries. At this Cross the whole battle of the Reformation in England was fought over, and the controversy between the Reformed Church and Papacy on the one hand, and Puritanism on the other, was submitted to public consideration by a succession of prelates so memorable, however different, as Ridley, Latimer, Farrar, Gardiner, Bonner, Coverdale, Sandys, Jewel, Grindal, Pilkington, and Laud, as well as by a host of divines conspicuous by their learning and oratorical and controversial powers. Before this Cross Tindall's translation of the Bible was publicly burnt, by order of Bishop Stokesley; the Pope's sentence on Martin Luther was pronounced from it, in a sermon preached by Bishop Fisher, Wolsey being present as the Pope's legate. "For the whole seven years during which the question of the King's divorce was in agitation . . . the pulpit of S. Paul's Cross rang more or less loudly with the arguments and invectives of the disputants on either side."[2] When Henry consummated his revolt from the Pope, a royal edict was issued that "Orders be taken that such as preach at Paul's Cross shall henceforth continually, Sunday after Sunday, teach and declare unto the people, that he that now calleth himself Pope, and any of his predecessors, is and were only Bishops of Rome, and have no more authority or jurisdiction, by God's laws, within this realm, than any other Bishop had, which is nothing at all."[3] The "Holy Maid of Kent" knelt in shame and silence, with her confederates the Dean of Bocking and the parson of Aldermanbury beside her, whilst her confession was read aloud; the Bishop of Bangor set forth in his sermon the heinousness of the imposture. Here four years later the famous miraculous Boxley Rood was exhibited, and all the hidden machinery exposed wherewith it had been made to bow its head and open its eyes and lips and seem to speak. Here in the reign of Mary the Protestants were anathematised, King Philip lauded by Gardiner as "the most perfect Prince," and a few years later the Perfect Prince was held up to public execration as a merciless persecutor, and the people exhorted to give thanks to God for his discomfiture in the overthrow of the "Invincible Armada," while a gaudy streamer taken from one of the ships waved over the head of the preacher. Here the Maypole, from which the church of *St. Andrew Undershaft* derives its name, was denounced as an idol by the curate of *St. Catherine Cree*, and its fate sealed. Recantations were made here; royal marriages and public victories proclaimed. It was used for other purposes: a certain Dr. Shaw, in a sermon preached here, sounded the feeling of the people in favour of the Duke of Gloucester before the ambitious Richard assumed the crown; and the memory of the Earl of Essex in Elizabeth's reign was blackened by *command* in a Sunday's sermon. When the Stuarts came to the crown the preachers at the Cross had royal listeners: King James, on one occasion, to countenance a sermon on

[1] *Stow*, pp. 121, 122. [2] *Milman*, p. 192. [3] Strype, *Memorials*, vol. i. p. 196.

the reparation of the Cathedral; and King Charles I. on the occasion of the birth of his son, afterwards Charles II. Jane Shore did penance here when accused by Richard of witchcraft; and here, in the reign of James I. (1617), Lady Markham, the wife of Sir Griffin Markham, stood in a white sheet (and was amerced in a penalty of £1000), for marrying one of her servants, her husband being still alive. A house for lodging and entertaining the preachers who came from a distance was provided in Watling Street. [*See* Shunamite's House.]

This celebrated Cross,[1] with the rest of the crosses in London and Westminster, was pulled down in 1643, by order of Parliament, Isaac Pennington being then Lord Mayor. Sermons still continued to be preached and distinguished as Paul's Cross sermons. The following document is among Archbishop Sheldon's papers in the British Museum; it was written between 1685 and 1691, and merits preservation:—

Whereas the sermon which for time immemorial hath been preach'd at St. Paul's Cross, upon pulling downe that Crosse in the time of the Rebellion was removed to St. Paul's Church, and upon the burning of that church in 1666 was by order and appointment of the Lord Bishop of London removed to St. Catherine Cree Church, and upon good reason hath since been removed by the appointment of the Lord Bishop of London aforesayd to Guild Hall Chappell; and is now thought fit by Nathaniel, Lord Bp of Duresme, Thomas Lord Bishop of Rochester, and Thomas, Lord Bishop of Peterborough, Com^{rs} for the exercise of Episcopal Jurisdiction within the city and diocess of London, during the suspension of the present Bp of the same, to be remov'd againe to some other church, and they judging that St. Mary Le Bow (one of our Peculiars) will be the most convenient for that use at present, have besought us, that our leave and license be granted thereto : Wee taking their humble request into consideracon, doe hereby give our full consent and license that the sermon commonly called the Paul's Cross Sermon be for the future preach'd at St. Mary Le Bow in Cheapside, so long as it shall be thought meet by the say'd Com^{rs}. In witness whereof wee have hereunto set our hand and seale this   day of   .—*Harleian MS.* 3788, fol. 69.

At the Restoration the Paul's Cross Sermons, with their endowments, were removed into the Cathedral itself; and they still belong to the Sunday morning preachers, now chiefly the honorary Prebendaries of the Church.—Milman's *History of St. Paul's*, p. 354.

Paul's (St.), GREAT PORTLAND STREET, or PORTLAND CHAPEL, a chapel of ease to the parish of St. Marylebone, designed by S. Leadbetter, architect, and built 1765-1766 at a cost of £5000, but not consecrated (by some unaccountable neglect) till 1831. It was restored in 1883 under the superintendence of Sir Arthur Blomfield.

At the end of Union Street, Middlesex Hospital, stood two magnificent rows of elms, one on each side of a rope walk; and beneath their shade have I frequently seen Joseph Baretti and Richard Wilson [the painter] perambulate, until Portland Chapel clock announced "five," the hour of Joseph Wilton's dinner. They both wore cocked hats and walked with canes.—J. T. Smith, *Nollekens*, vol. ii. p. 174.

Paul's (St.), KNIGHTSBRIDGE, WILTON PLACE, a Gothic edifice, surmounted by a stately tower (Thomas Cundy, architect), consecrated

---

[1] There are several very excellent views of this Cross, but the best (representing the preaching before King James) is engraved in Wilkinson (*Londina Illustrata*), and very well copied as a woodcut in Longmans' *Three Cathedrals of St. Paul's*, p. 19), from a picture in the possession of the Society of Antiquaries: a second, very good, is in Henry Farley's *St. Paul's Church, her Bill for the Parliament*, 4to, 1621.

May 30, 1843. The church cost £15,000. This was the church of the Rev. W. J. E. Bennett, during whose incumbency it was more talked about than any other church in London. It obtained its notoriety owing to the lawsuits (Westerton v. Liddell) which were brought about the ritual. The Hon. and Rev. R. Liddell was Mr. Bennett's successor.

Paul's (St.) School, a celebrated school formerly on the east side of St. Paul's Churchyard, founded in 1512 for 153 poor men's children, by Dr. John Colet, Dean of St. Paul's, the friend of Erasmus, and son of Sir Henry Colet, mercer, and Mayor of London in 1486 and 1495. The boys were to be admitted without restriction of kin, country, or station; to be taught, free of expense, by a master, sur-master, and chaplain; and the oversight of the school was committed by the founder to the Mercers' Company. The number (153) was chosen in allusion to the number of fishes taken by St. Peter. The school was dedicated by Colet to the Child Jesus, but the saint, as Strype remarks, has robbed his master of his title. The lands left by Colet to support his school were estimated by Stow in 1598 at the yearly value of £120 and better.[1] Their present value is upwards of £13,000. The education is classical, but there is now a modern side as well, and the presentations to the school are in the gift of the Master of the Mercers' Company for the time being. There are now (1890) 1000 boys in the school. Lilly, the grammarian, and friend of Erasmus, was the first master, and the grammar which he compiled, Lilly's Grammar, is still used in the school. *Eminent Scholars.*—John Leland, our earliest English antiquary; Sir Anthony Denny, the friend of Henry VIII.; William Whitaker, a famous master of St. John's College, Cambridge; William Camden, the great antiquary, after having been for a time at Christ's Hospital; John Milton, when Alexander Gill was master; the great Duke of Marlborough; Robert Nelson, author of *Fasts and Festivals;* Edmund Halley, the astronomer; Knight, the biographer of Colet; Samuel Pepys, the diarist; John Strype, the ecclesiastical historian; Sir Philip Francis (supposed to be Junius); Chief Baron Sir Frederick Pollock; Lord Chancellor Truro, who founded (1851) the Truro Prize "in grateful acknowledgment of the benefits derived by him from his education in St. Paul's School." Strype has left an interesting account of this school in his annotations upon Stow. The late school was built in 1823, from a design by George Smith, architect to the Mercers' Company, and was the third building erected on the same site. Colet's school was destroyed in the Great Fire, "but built up again," says Strype, "much after the same manner and proportion it was before."[2] The school was removed in 1880 to West Kensington, near Addison Road Station, where the Mercers' Company had purchased 16 acres and erected a new school from the designs of Mr. Barnes Williams, architect. The building in St. Paul's Churchyard has been pulled down and warehouses built on the site.

[1] *Stow*, p. 123. [2] *Strype*, B. i. p. 167.

Paul's (St.), SHADWELL, HIGH STREET, a parish so called, as belonging to the Dean and Chapter of St. Paul's, who are patrons thereof,[1] and separated from Stepney by an Act passed March 17, 1669-1670. The church was consecrated March 12, 1670-1671; taken down in 1817; and the present church designed by James Walters (d. 1821); consecrated April 5, 1821. Of the old church there are views in Wilkinson's *Londina*. Bishop Butler, as Dean of St. Paul's, nominated his nephew and namesake, Joseph Butler, to the rectory of this parish. He liked it so little that he chose for the text of his first sermon, " Woe is me that I sojourn in Mesech, that I dwell in the tents of Kedar." A canonry in St. Paul's and permission to reside in Norfolk Street, Strand, so far reconciled him to his fate that he managed to hold the rectory fifty-seven years.

Paul's Walk, a vulgar name for the middle aisle of Old St. Paul's. [*See* St. Paul's Cathedral (Old).]

Paul's Walk is the land's epitome, or you may call it the lesser aisle of Great Britain. . . . The noise in it is like that of bees, a strange humming or buzz, mixed of walking tongues and feet: it is a kind of still roar, or loud whisper. It is the great exchange of all discourse, and no business whatsoever but is here stirring and afoot. . . . It is the general mint of all famous lies, which are here, like the legends of popery, first coined and stamped in the church. All inventions are emptied here, and not a few pockets. The best sign of a temple in it is, that it is the thieves' sanctuary. . . . It is the other expence of the day, after plays, tavern, and a bawdy house; and men have still some oaths left to swear here. . . . Some make it a preface to their dinner, and travel for a stomach; but thriftier men make it their ordinary, and board here very cheap.—Earle's *Microcosmography*, 8vo, 1628.

When I past Paule's, and travell'd in that Walke
Where all oure Brittaine-sinners sweare and talk.—BP. CORBET.

Bishop Pilkington, writing in 1560 of the abuses at St. Paul's, mentions " The south alley for Popery and usury, the north for simony, and the horse-fair in the midst for all kinds of bargains, meetings, brawlings, murders, conspiracies, and the font for ordinary payments of money, as well-known to all men as the beggar knows his bush."[2] In *The Gull's Hornbook*, by Dekker, is a chapter entitled, " How a gallant should behave himself in Powle's Walkes;" and Ben Jonson lays the first scene of the third act of *Every Man out of his Humour* in "the Middle Aisle of St. Paul's." Weever (*Ancient Funeral Monuments*, 1631, p. 373) complains of the abuse, and adds, " it could be wished that walking in the middle aisle of Paules might be forborne in the time of divine service." [*See* Duke Humphrey's.]

Paul's Wharf.

Paul's Wharf is a large landing place with a common stair upon the river Thames, at the end of a street called Paul's Wharf Hill, which runneth down from Paul's Chain.—*Stow*, p. 136.

On with your riding suit, and cry *Northward Ho!* as the boy at Paul's says. —*Northward Ho*, by Thomas Dekker and John Webster, 4to, 1607.

---

[1] Strype, *Circuit Walk*, p. 105.   [2] Pilkington, *Works*, p. 210.

Sir Walter Mildmay had his house here in 1570.[1] Francis Throgmorton, the Catholic conspirator, whose revelations under the rack had such important consequences in the history of Europe, had a house at Paul's Wharf in 1583—known as the lodging of the young Lord Glenvarloch, and it was there that his papers and himself were seized.[2]

Paved Alley Chapel, LIME STREET. Paved Alley was situated at the upper end of Lime Street, by Leadenhall Street, and here the chapel with its three capacious galleries was built in 1672. The congregation first met in Anchor Lane, Lower Thames Street, and the pastor was Dr. Thomas Goodwin, chaplain to Oliver Cromwell. In 1755 the East India Company purchased a large piece of ground in the neighbourhood of Paved Alley, and the chapel was pulled down. The congregation divided into two parts—one went to Artillery Street, Finsbury, where Mr. Richardson the pastor resumed his ministry, and the other branch removed to Miles Lane, choosing the Rev. William Porter as minister. The latter congregation removed ten years later to Camomile Street, and afterwards to the Poultry. The City Temple, Holborn Viaduct, is the successor of the Poultry Chapel.

Pavilion (The), CHELSEA, a pleasant residence, surrounded by pretty gardens occupying about 20 acres of land, built by Henry Holland for his own occupation when he planned Hans Town [which *see*] at the end of the last century. After his death it was purchased by Mr. Peter Denys, after whose death it was inhabited for some years by his widow, Lady Charlotte Denys. The approach to the house was from Hans Place through an avenue of elms. Before the south front was a beautifully planted lawn and an artificial lake; on the west side of the lawn stood an imitation of the ruins of an ancient priory. The house and gardens were cleared away, and Cadogan Square was built on the site in 1882-1883.

Pavilion Road, CHELSEA. In 1870 New Road, Alfred Place, Chapel Row, and Taylor's Cottages were renamed Pavilion Road.

Paymaster-General's Office, WHITEHALL, next the Horse Guards, the office of her Majesty's Paymaster-General for the payment of army, navy, ordnance, civil service, and exchequer bills. The office is managed by the paymaster, the assistant-paymaster, and a staff of clerks. It was originally the office of the Paymaster-General of the Forces, and was not permanently enlarged till 1836.

Peabody Buildings. Mr. George Peabody, an American merchant resident in London, in a letter dated March 12, 1862, addressed to the United States Minister and four gentlemen named by him as trustees, expressed his desire "in pursuance of a long cherished determination, to attest his gratitude and attachment to the people of London, among whom he had spent the last twenty-five years of his

---
[1] Burghley's *Diary*, in *Murden*, p. 771.
[2] *Froude*, vol. xi. p. 617; and see *Fortunes of Nigel*, vol. i. p. 44.

life," by devoting a sum of £150,000 "to ameliorate the condition of the poor and needy of this great metropolis, and to promote their comfort and happiness." As regarded the expenditure, Mr. Peabody imposed "but three conditions" on the trustees who were to administer the fund, but these were "fundamental principles, from which it was his solemn injunction that those intrusted with the application of the Fund shall never under any circumstances depart." These were, "First and foremost, the limitation of its uses absolutely and exclusively to such purposes as may be calculated directly to ameliorate the condition and augment the comfort of the poor, who either by birth or established residence form a recognised portion of the population of London." Secondly, that there shall be "a rigid exclusion from the management of the Fund of any influences calculated to impart to it a character either sectarian as regards religion, or exclusive in relation to local or party politics." And thirdly, that "the sole qualification for a participation in the benefits of the Fund shall be an ascertained and continued condition of life, such as brings the individual within the description (in the ordinary sense of the word) of the poor of London; combined with moral character and good conduct as a member of society."

The trustees, of whom Lord Stanley (now Earl of Derby) was elected chairman, acting on the suggestion of Mr. Peabody, to consider whether it might not be found conducive to the realisation of the principles laid down "to apply the fund or a portion of it in the construction of such improved dwellings for the poor as may combine, in the utmost possible degree, the essentials of healthfulness, comfort, social enjoyment, and economy," decided, after careful inquiry, to erect dwellings of the kind recommended, and to "confine their attention in the first instance to that section of the labouring poor who occupy a position above the pauper." The first plot of ground obtained was in Commercial Street, Spitalfields, and on this was erected a block of dwellings affording accommodation for upwards of 200 persons. Other sites were purchased and buildings erected, which were eagerly sought for by suitable tenants, and so well satisfied was Mr. Peabody with the operations of the trustees that at different times he made additions to his first munificent gift, viz., £100,000 in 1866, £100,000 in 1868, and in 1873 £150,000, making a total of £500,000, to which has been added money received for rent and interest £465,182 : 7 : 9, making the total fund on December 31, 1888, £965,182 : 7 : 9. In 1888 the trustees expended on land and buildings £13,064 : 3 : 4, making the total expenditure to the end of the year £1,232,283 : 19 : 11. The trustees have borrowed £300,000, a portion of which amount has been paid back, so that their total indebtedness at the end of the year was £271,333 : 6 : 8. Besides those already mentioned, the trustees have erected other blocks of dwellings, several of great extent, in Shadwell, Chelsea, Islington, Bermondsey, Westminster, Blackfriars Road, Stamford Street, Southwark Street, Pimlico, Whitechapel,

Bedfordbury, Great Wild Street, Orchard Street, Whitecross Street, Clerkenwell and Little Coram Street. The trustees have provided for the artisan and labouring poor of London 11,275 rooms, besides bathrooms, laundries, and warehouses occupied by 20,413 persons. These rooms comprise 5071 separate dwellings, say 76 of four rooms, 1789 of three rooms, 2398 of two rooms, and 808 of one room. The average weekly earnings of the head of each family in residence at the close of 1888 was £1 : 3 : 9. The average rent of each dwelling was 4s. 9½d. per week, and of each room 2s. 2d. The rent in all cases includes the free use of water, laundries, sculleries, and bath-rooms.

A seated *Statue of George Peabody*, executed in bronze by Storey, the American sculptor, and regarded as an admirable likeness, was erected by public subscription at the back of the Royal Exchange in 1869.

Peckham, SURREY, a hamlet of Camberwell, now a part of the outer fringe of London. The manor of *Pecheham* is recorded in Domesday as held by the Bishop of Lisieux of Odo, Bishop of Bayeux, to whom it had been granted by King William. In the time of the Confessor it was owned by Harold and held by Alfled, and was a part of *Patricesy* [= Battersea, though from its proximity it would rather seem that Bermondsey must have been meant]. The manor is mentioned as late as the reign of Elizabeth, but no event of importance is connected with it. As late as the early years of the present century it was a district of market gardens, interspersed with citizens' villas. It is now a populous neighbourhood with many large manufactories of different kinds. In 1881 it contained 71,065 inhabitants. In place of a single chapel of ease there are half a dozen churches, mostly with ecclesiastical districts attached, numerous chapels, and several large schools. Here are the Licensed Victuallers' Asylum, an extensive pile erected in 1827, and comprising upwards of a hundred separate dwellings ; and the Girdlers' Company's Almshouses, removed here in 1852 from Pest House Row, St. Luke's. Peckham House, in Camberwell, is one of the oldest and largest lunatic asylums near London. *Peckham Rye* is a large triangular common, now secured for public use as a recreation ground. To the east of it is the Nunhead Cemetery of the London Cemetery Company. At a boarding school in Meeting House Lane, kept by the Rev. John Milner, minister of the old Presbyterian Chapel close by, Oliver Goldsmith was usher in his early London days, about 1756, and though he did not get on very well there, it was through Milner he was introduced to Griffiths and commenced his literary career. The house, which had long been known as Goldsmith's house, was with the rest of the estate purchased about 1875 by "the Sanitary Dwellings Company," who have since erected a large number of artisans' dwellings there, which they have named the Goldsmith Residences. Part of the grounds of Goldsmith House have been preserved as a recreation ground. The main Street is named Goldsmith Road.

Pedlar's Acre, the old name of the southern portion of what is now BELVEDERE ROAD, LAMBETH.

On Lambeth Wall is a spot of ground containing an Acre and nineteen poles, denominated Pedlar's Acre, which has belonged to the Parish time immemorial; 'tis said to have been given by a Pedlar, upon condition that his portrait and that of his dog be perpetually preserved in painted glass in one of the windows of the Church [St. Mary's, Lambeth], which the parishioners carefully perform in the south-east window of the middle aisle.—*Maitland*, ed. 1739, p. 791.

1607.—For mending the windows where the picture of the Pedlar stands.—*Churchwardens' Accounts of St. Mary's, Lambeth* (*Lysons*, vol. i. p. 314).

It is first entered in the Churchwardens' books of Lambeth parish in 1504, as an ozier bed named the Church Hoppys or Hope. In 1623 it is termed "the Church Oziers." In 1690 it appears for the first time as Pedlar's Acre.—Nichols's *History of Lambeth*.

[*See* St. Mary's, Lambeth.]

Peerless Pool, BALDWIN STREET, CITY ROAD, at the back of St. Luke's Hospital. A spacious public bath, formerly a spring that, overflowing its banks, caused a very dangerous pond, and which, from the number of persons who lost their lives, obtained the name of Perilous Pond, a name that seems to have been common to dangerous bathing-places; thus Stow applies the term to the Ducking Pond, Clerkenwell, the site of the Spa Road Tabernacle. The present name of "Peerless Pool" was given by Kemp, the proprietor, in 1743, when the bottom was raised and the pond enclosed. Kemp also formed a bowling green, an open fish-pond 300 feet, and bordered by a bank planted with shrubs and trees, and otherwise endeavoured to make the place attractive as a pleasure-ground. The pond and pool long remained in favour with London anglers and swimmers, but about 1805 the lease was purchased by Mr. Joseph Watts (father of Thomas Watts, the great linguist and librarian, Keeper of the Printed Books in the British Museum), who drained the fish-pond and built over a large part of the grounds. The whole is now covered with streets.

And not far from it [St. Agnes le Clair) is also one other clear water called Perillous pond, because divers youths by swimming therein have been drowned.—*Stow*, p. 7.

Gallipot. Push! let your boy lead his water-spanial along, and we'll show you the bravest sport at Parlous Pond.—T. Middleton, *The Roaring Girl*, 4to, 1611. Act 2 Sc. 1.

Hone, in his *Every-Day Book* (vol. i. pp. 970, 976), gives views of Peerless Pool and the fish-pond. The pool was 170 feet long and over 100 feet wide. The fish-pond was 320 feet long. There was also a cold bath, "the largest in England," 40 feet long and 20 feet wide.

Peerpool Lane, GRAY'S INN LANE. A corruption of Portpoole—from the manor of Portpoole, or Gray's Inn. [*See* Gray's Inn.] There is a token dated 1644 with the name Peerpool Lane inscribed upon it.

Pelham Crescent, BROMPTON. M. Guizot resided at No. 21 after the French Revolution of 1848 till July 1849. His account of the house, "almost in the country," reads rather curiously now. He writes, March 13, 1848, "I shall set to work again. I have found, close to London,—at Brompton—a little house, which is almost in the country; it is good enough for us and not expensive. I shall be able to go into London easily every day."[1] Here, on March 31, 1848, his mother, Madame Guizot, died at the age of eighty-four. In the same house afterwards lived a politician of a very different school, Mr. Ledru Rollin. At No. 10, where he had resided many years, Robert Keeley, the comedian, died February 3, 1869, in his seventy-fifth year. He made his first appearance on the stage in 1818 as Leporello in *Giovanni in London*.

Pelham Street, BRICK LANE, SPITALFIELDS. Milton's granddaughter, Mrs. Foster, kept a chandler's shop in this street.[2] [*See* Cock Lane, Shoreditch.]

Pembridge Square, BAYSWATER. Field-Marshal Sir John Fox Burgoyne, "the Moltke of England," died at No. 25, October 7, 1871, aged ninety. He was buried in the church of St. Peter ad Vincula, within the precinct of the Tower, of which he was Constable.

Penitentiary, MILLBANK. [*See* Millbank Prison.]

Penny Fields, POPLAR, between the West India Road and the High Street, of which latter it is the extension westwards. Since the construction of the West India Docks the fields have existed in name only.

Penny Post (The). A London footpost, with seven sorting houses, between four and five hundred receiving houses, and with four deliveries a day, established 1680, by Robert Murray, a clerk in the Excise, and William Dockwra, a sub-searcher in the Customs.

The Penny Post was set up on our Lady-Day (being Friday), A° D^{nl} 1680; a most ingenious and useful project, invented by Mr. Robert Murray first, and then Mr. Dockwra joined with him. The Duke of York seized on it in 1682. Mr. Murray was a citizen of London, a milliner, of the company of Clothworkers; his father a Scotchman, his mother English; born in the Strand, December 12, 1633. —Aubrey's MS. (Malone's *Inquiry*, p. 387).

Murray and Dockwra were to have entered into partnership, but both laying claim to the idea, they quarrelled and set up rival offices. Robert Murray, "the inventor and first proposer," as he called himself, received letters at Mr. Hall's Coffee-house, in Wood Street; and "Mr. Dockwra and the rest of the undertakers at the Penny Post House in Lime Street"—Dockwra's own house, formerly the mansion house of Sir Robert Abdy. Roger North assigns the merit of the invention to Dockwra, "who put it," he says, "in complete order, and used it to the satisfaction of all London, for a considerable time." The Duke of York (afterwards James II.), to whom the profits of the post-office had been assigned by the King, exhibited an information against him, for infraction of his monopoly, and the courts decided in the Duke's favour. Dockwra was afterwards appointed Comptroller, but was

---
[1] Madame de Witt's *M. Guizot in Private Life*, p. 254, Eng. trans.
[2] *Granger*, vol. v. p. 235, ed. 1824.

dismissed by the Lords of the Treasury for mismanagement in 1698. He died, September 25, 1716, aged near 100 years. See his "Case," in Harl. MS. 5954, and further particulars in Delaune's *Present State of London*, 12mo, 1681. Dockwra was the first to stamp letters with the hour at which they left his office for delivery. An additional penny was put on in 1801. [*See* Post Office.]

Penny's Gate is the name given (in an excellent map in Lockie's *Topography of London*, 1813) to the entrance from St. James's Park to the Green Park.

Pennyrich Street.

> Then Offering, he, with his dish and his tree,
> That in every great house keepeth,
> Is by my son, young Little-worth, done,
> And in Penny-rich Street he sleepeth.
> Ben Jonson, *Christmas his Masque*, 1616.

Pentecost Lane, on the north side of NEWGATE STREET, subsequently corrupted into "Pincock Lane." Stow describes it as "containing divers slaughter-houses for the butchers," and Hatton (1708) as "leading to the Bagnio,"[1] now Roman Bath Street.

Pentonville is the name given to a populous district in the parish of St. James's, Clerkenwell, which arose about the year 1773, after the formation of the New Road (now Pentonville Road) which passed through certain fields belonging to Henry Penton, Esq.[2] The first buildings were erected at Penton Villa by the New Road and in Queen's Row, Pentonville Hill, in 1773, and Dr. de Valangin, the eccentric physician, built a mansion called Hermes House, which has given its name to Hermes Street, Pentonville Road. The name of Pentonville, which, till the last twenty years, was strictly applicable to the houses built upon the property of Mr. Penton lying within the parish of Clerkenwell, has since been extended to buildings in the adjoining parish of Islington, so that it is difficult to say what is the extent of Pentonville. What was known as the Model Prison, which stands in the Caledonian Road, Islington, is styled the Pentonville Prison, although half a mile removed from the district to which the name properly belongs.

Pentonville *proper* belonged to Geoffrey de Mandeville, a Norman knight, afterwards passed to the Foliots, and by Gilbert Foliot was conveyed in the reign of Henry II. to the Knights Hospitallers of St. John of Jerusalem, at Clerkenwell. It is described by Gerard, the herbalist, as the great field called the Mantells, at the back of Islington, Mandeville being corrupted into Mantell. In St. James's Chapel, on the north side of the New Road, R. P. Bonington, one of the most promising of English landscape painters is buried ; he died in 1828, in his twenty-seventh year. Joseph Grimaldi, clown (d. 1837). Here also were

---

[1] *Stow*, p. 118; *Hatton*, p. 64.
[2] See Maps and Plans published in the year 1755 in relation to the New Road.

interred the two Storers, father and son (d. 1853 and 1837), the engravers of the Cathedrals of Great Britain and of many antiquarian and topographical views.

Pentonville Prison was built from the designs of Major R. Jebb, and cost over £84,000, but has since been enlarged and altered at a cost of £5903, making a total cost of £90,071 : 15s. The first stone was laid April 10, 1840, and the building completed in 1842. It is constructed on the radiating principle, so as to permit thorough inspection, and contains accommodation for 520 prisoners. Here prisoners condemned to penal servitude undergo the first part of their sentence. The treatment is designed to "enforce strict separation, with industrial employment and moral training." The system of imprisonment at home in place of transportation, of which this forms a part, was introduced by the Penal Servitude Act of 1853, and the amending Act of 1857. The Report of the Directors of Convict Prisons for the year 1887-1888 contains a memorandum on separate confinement by the Medical Inspector, in which extracts are made from successive reports of Pentonville Prison.

Pepper Alley Stairs, SOUTHWARK, leading from Pepper Alley to the Thames, the first landing-place west of Old London Bridge. The site is covered by the present bridge.

January 11, 1559.—The same night about 8 of the clock the Queen's Grace took her barge at Whyt Hall, and mony mo barges, and rowed along by the bank side, by my Lord of Winchester's Place, and so to Peper Alley, and so crossed over to London side with drums and trumpets playing hard beside, and so to Whyt hall again to her palace.—Machyn's *Diary*, p. 200.

July 2, 1763.—We set out this morning from Whitehall Stairs in a common wherry, landed at Pepper Alley Stairs [this was to avoid shooting the bridge] and at the other side of the bridge embarked in the Admiralty barge. . . . We got back to Greenwich to dine. We had the smallest fish I ever saw, called white-bait.—*Mrs. Harris to her Son* (the Earl of Malmesbury), *Letters of the first Earl of Malmesbury*, vol. i. p. 92.

Though Dr. Johnson owed his very life to air and exercise, yet he ever persisted in the notion that neither of them had anything to do with health. "People live as long," said he, "in Pepper Alley as on Salisbury Plain ; and they live so much happier than an inhabitant of the first would if he turned cottager, starve his understanding for want of conversation, and perish in a state of mental inferiority.—*Piozzi Anecdotes*, p. 207.

Percy Chapel, CHARLOTTE STREET, RATHBONE PLACE. This Episcopal Chapel, well known in its day, was built about 1790 for the Rev. Henry Mathew, the friend of Flaxman and Blake, and well known in the artistic and social circles of his time. It was pulled down in 1867 and its site "secularized." William Wilberforce worshipped in this chapel for some years while his daughters were at school in Bedford Square. Robert Montgomery, "the epic poet," was for several years, from 1843, the minister. It was situated opposite Windmill Street.

Percy Street, RATHBONE PLACE. At his son's house (No. 6) in this street died, in 1805, aged seventy-six, William Buchan, M.D., author of *Domestic Medicine*, of which the first edition appeared in 1769. Samuel Rose, the friend of Cowper, lived at No. 23, and here on the way back from Hayley's at Eartham the author of *The Task* visited him on September 19, 1792; Mrs. Unwin was with him. In a letter to Hayley Cowper says, "exactly at ten we reached Mr. Rose's door; we drank a dish of chocolate with him, and proceeded, Mr. Rose riding with us, as far as St. Albans." Edward Williams, the Welsh Bard, had been asked to meet him, but, says Southey, "Cowper's spirits, as might have been expected, failed him when he felt himself in London; he sate at the corner of the fire place in total silence, and manifested no other interest in the conversation than occasionally raising his eyes towards the speaker." He never saw London again. Henry Bone, R.A., the celebrated enamel painter (d. 1834), lived for some years in a house on the south side.

Pest House Field, CARNABY STREET, CARNABY MARKET, thirty-six small houses and a cemetery, founded by William, first Earl of Craven, after the Great Plague of 1665. There is a Craven Pest House Charity administered by trustees connected with the parishes of St. Clement's Danes, St. James's, Westminster, St. George's, Hanover Square, St. Martin's-in-the-Fields, and St. Paul's, Covent Garden. The income, which in 1888 was £849:17:4, is divided, after payment of expenses, between King's College and Charing Cross Hospitals. [*See* Carnaby Street.]

Pest House Row, immediately west of St. Luke's Hospital, OLD STREET, now BATH STREET; the old footway to Islington.

The Pest House beyond Bunhill Fields in the way to Islington.—Defoe's *Plague Year*, ed. Brayley, p. 63.

In Pest House Row, till the year 1737, stood the City Pest House (consisting of divers tenements), which was erected as a Lazaretto, for the reception of distressed and miserable objects, that were infected by the dreadful Plague in the year 1665.—*Maitland*, ed. 1739, p. 776.

Peter's (St.) at Paul's Wharf, a church in the ward of Queenhithe, destroyed in the Great Fire, and not rebuilt. The burying-ground at the bottom of Peter's Hill, in Thames Street, still remains.

March 25, 1649.—I heard the Common Prayer (a rare thing in these days) in St. Peter's, at Paul's Wharf, London.—*Evelyn*.

Peter's (St.) at the Cross in Cheap, a church in the ward of Farringdon Within, destroyed in the Great Fire, and not rebuilt. The open plot of ground, with a tree in it, at the corner of Wood Street, Cheapside, is part of the old churchyard. In this tree a pair of rooks built a nest in 1836, and two nests were built in 1845.[1] The church of the parish is St. Matthew's, Friday Street. Thomas Goodrich, afterwards Bishop of Ely (1534) and Lord Chancellor (1552), was rector of St. Peter's at the Cross.

[1] Harting's *Birds of Middlesex*, p. 99.

Peter's (St.), CORNHILL, at the east end, south side, a parish church in *Cornhill Ward,* destroyed in the Great Fire, and rebuilt from the designs of Sir C. Wren, and the interior of the church has been considered as among the best of his works.

> There remaineth in this church a table whereon it is written, I know not by what authority, but of a late hand, that King Lucius founded the same church to be an archbishop's see metropolitan and chief church of his kingdom, and that it so endured the space of four hundred years, unto the coming of Augustin the Monk.—*Stow,* p. 73.

The tablet was formerly suspended in the church; but is now preserved in the vestry-room. There is an engraving of it in Wilkinson's *Londina.* Bishop Beveridge was rector, 1672-1704. The rood-screen dividing the chancel from the nave was set up by his express direction, and is mentioned by him in the sermon preached at the opening of the church, November 27, 1681. Allhallows the Great is the only other City church possessing a rood-screen. There is a touching inscription to the memory of seven children, the "whole offspring of James and Mary Woodmason," burnt to death on the night of January 18, 1782. The living is in the gift of the Corporation of London. There is extant a letter, dated 1609, from James I. to the Lord Mayor and Aldermen, requesting them to present his chaplain, Mr. Theophilus Field (brother of Nat. Field), to the living of St. Peter's, Cornhill. Field got the living and afterwards rose to be Bishop of Hereford. The entry of the burial (February 16, 1722) of Sir Thomas Abney, Lord Mayor in 1700, one of the founders of the Bank of England and M.P. for the City of London, is to be found in the register. The church was extensively repaired, cleansed and redecorated in 1889, under the direction of Mr. Ernest Flint, architect.

Peter's Court, ST. MARTIN'S LANE, west side, between Nos. 110 and 111. In 1710 the goods of Mrs. Selby, sword cutler, were advertised to be sold "at the Dancing School in Peter's Court, against Tom's Coffee-house in S. Martin's Lane." This dancing school was afterwards the first studio of Roubiliac the sculptor. On his quitting it, it was converted into a drawing academy—the precursor of the Royal Academy of Arts. Hogarth may tell the story of its foundation:—

> Sir James [Thornhill] dying (1734) I became possessed of his neglected apparatus; and thinking that an academy, if conducted on moderate principles would be useful, I proposed that a number of artists should enter into a subscription for the hire of a place large enough to admit of thirty or forty persons drawing after a naked figure. This proposition having been agreed to, a room was taken in [Peter's Court] St. Martin's Lane. I lent to the society the furniture that had belonged to Sir James's Academy, and attributing the failure of the previous academies to the leading members having assumed a superiority which their fellow-students could not brook, I proposed that every member should contribute an equal sum towards the support of the establishment, and have an equal right to vote on every question relative to its affairs. By these regulations the Academy has now existed nearly thirty years, and is, for every useful purpose, equal to that in France, or any other.—Hogarth, in *Supp. Vol. to* Ireland's *Hogarth.*

In a pamphlet published by the Incorporated Society of Artists in

1771 it is stated that most of the artists of the reign of George II. and the early years of George III. were trained in this academy. It continued, in fact, to be the usual place of study for artists till the establishment of the Royal Academy in 1768. Michael Moser, keeper and treasurer of the St. Martin's Lane Academy, was appointed first keeper of the Royal Academy, and he persuaded his fellow-members to dissolve their private school and present the "anatomical figures, busts, statues, lamps," and other apparatus to the Royal Academy, to the schools of which they would have free access.

Peter's (St.), EATON SQUARE. The church was built 1824-1826, from the designs of Henry Hakewell, architect, and cost £21,515; it was nearly burnt down in 1837, and was rebuilt by Mr. Gerrard. The altar-piece, "Christ crowned with Thorns," by W. Hilton, R.A., was bought by the Royal Academy out of the Chantrey bequest, and is now deposited in the South Kensington Museum. It was purchased of the artist for 1000 guineas by the Directors of the Royal Institution, and presented by them to St. Peter's Church in 1828. On February 26, 1877, a faculty was obtained for its removal. In 1872 a new chancel and transepts in the Byzantine style were added to the nave from the designs of Mr. (now Sir) Arthur Blomfield, and they were consecrated on St. Peter's eve, 1873. Two years later the whole of the interior of the nave was remodelled under the direction of the same architect. Here was buried Admiral Sir Edward Codrington (d. 1851).

Peter's Hill, DOCTORS' COMMONS, extended from Knightrider Street to Upper Thames Street, but the southern end was cut off by the formation of Queen Victoria Street, and Peter's Hill now possesses no houses of its own, those which appear to belong to it being parts of the large and deep buildings in Queen Victoria and Knightrider Streets.

Touching lanes ascending out of Thames Street to Knightriders' Street, the first is Peter's Hill, wherein I find no matter of note, more than certain almshouses lately founded on the west side thereof by David Smith, embroiderer, for six poor widows, whereof each to have twenty shillings by the year.—*Stow,* p. 137.

Here the Master of the Revels had his office from 1611 till the time of the Civil War, and the consequent closing of the public theatres. [*See* St. Peter's at Paul's Wharf.]

Peter (St.) Le Poor, OLD BROAD STREET, a church in Broad Street Ward, of which Benjamin Hoadly, Bishop of Winchester (d. 1761), was rector from 1704 to 1720. In 1709 the House of Commons voted an address to Queen Anne, "that she would be graciously pleased to confer some dignity in the Church upon him [Hoadly] for his eminent services both to the Church and State." This unusual appeal had no effect, but Mrs. Howland, a rich widow, presented him to the rectory of Streatham, "to show that she was neither afraid nor ashamed to give him that mark of regard at that critical time." Promotion came with the next reign, but he continued to hold both these livings after he was Bishop of Bangor.

<small>Next unto Pawlet House is the parish church of St. Peter the Poor, so called for a difference from other of that name, sometime peradventure a poor parish, but at this present there be many fair houses, possessed by rich merchants and other.— *Stow*, p. 67.</small>

The church (existing in 1540), described by Stow, escaped the fire of 1666, but projected so far into the street that in 1788, when extensive repairs had become necessary, an Act of Parliament was obtained for taking it down and rebuilding it farther back, taking in the site of a court behind. The present church (a very poor one indeed) was designed by Jesse Gibson, and consecrated November 19, 1792, by Beilby Porteus, Bishop of London. It serves as well for the parish of St. Benet Fink, and the tablets were removed here when that church was pulled down in 1845. Here were buried the Rev. Edmund Gunter (d. 1626), one of the earliest and ablest of English mathematicians, and the Rev. Henry Gellibrand (d. 1636), Professor of Astronomy at Gresham College.

Peter Street, CLARE MARKET. Denzell Street was originally so called, and there is extant a token of "John Gray at Mother Shipton Peter Street in New Market, 1667."

Peter Street (Great), WESTMINSTER, between Wood Street and Rochester Row. On the front of a house facing Leg Court was recently the following inscription : "This is Saint Peter Street. 1624. R. [a heart] W."

Peter's (St.) Ad Vincula, a chapel within the precinct and liberty of the Tower, at the north end of the Tower Green, the north-west angle of the Inner Ward. Prior to 1862 the chapel was singularly mean and unsightly,[1] the result of successive alterations and additions made for the accommodation of the soldiers of the garrison. An ugly brick and plaster porch and wooden staircase leading to the soldiers' gallery disfigured the exterior ; a flat ceiling, projecting galleries and tall pews the interior. All that testified to the antiquity of the church were the Early English columns in the nave, a Decorated window in the north aisle, and a five-light Perpendicular window at the east end. In 1862 the exterior porch and staircase were removed, the galleries and the plaster ceiling cleared away, and the original timber roof opened to view and some other improvements made ; but all this only served to show that more was required, and in 1876-1877 the whole was thoroughly restored and renovated under the direction of Anthony Salvin, architect (d. 1863), and John Taylor, architect to Government Office of Works. The interest attaching to the chapel lies, however, less in the fabric than in the persons who have been interred within it.

<small>[1] I cannot refrain from expressing my disgust at the barbarous stupidity which has transformed this most interesting little church into the likeness of a meeting-house in a manufacturing town.—Macaulay, *Hist. of England*, note to chap. v.</small>

In truth, there is no sadder spot on earth than this little cemetery. Death is there associated, not, as in Westminster Abbey and St. Paul's, with genius and virtue, with public veneration and with imperishable renown; not, as in our humblest churches and churchyards, with everything that is most endearing in social and domestic charities; but with whatever is darkest in human nature and in human destiny, with the savage triumph of implacable enemies, with the inconstancy, the ingratitude, the cowardice of friends, with all the miseries of fallen greatness and of blighted fame.—Macaulay's *History of England*, chap. v.

Eminent Persons interred in.—Queen Anne Boleyn (beheaded 1536).[1]

Her body was thrown into a common chest of elm-tree, that was made to put arrows in, and was buried in the chapel within the Tower before twelve o'clock.— *Bishop Burnet*.

Queen Katherine Howard (beheaded 1542). Sir Thomas More (beheaded 1535).

His head was put upon London Bridge; his body was buried in the chapel of St. Peter in the Tower, in the belfry, or as some say, as one entereth into the vestry, near unto the body of the holy martyr Bishop Fisher.—Cresacre More's *Life of Sir Thomas More*, p. 288.

Thomas Cromwell, Earl of Essex (beheaded 1540). Gerald, ninth Earl of Kildare, Lord Deputy of Ireland (d. 1534). Margaret, Countess of Salisbury (beheaded 1541). Thomas, Lord Seymour of Sudley, the Lord Admiral (beheaded 1549), by order of his brother, the Protector Somerset. The Protector Somerset (beheaded 1552). John Dudley, Earl of Warwick and Duke of Northumberland (beheaded 1553).

There lyeth before the High Altar, in St. Peter's Church, two Dukes between two Queenes, to wit, the Duke of Somerset and the Duke of Northumberland, between Queen Anne and Queen Katherine, all four beheaded.—*Stow*, by Howes, p. 615.

Lady Jane Grey and her husband, the Lord Guilford Dudley (beheaded 1553-1554). Robert Devereux, Earl of Essex (beheaded 1600). Sir Thomas Overbury, poisoned in the Tower, and buried, according to the register, September 15, 1613. Sir Walter Raleigh (beheaded 1618). Sir John Eliot died a prisoner in the Tower, November 27, 1632; his son petitioned the King (Charles I.) that he would permit his father's body to be conveyed to Cornwall for interment, but the King's answer at the foot of the petition was, "Let Sir John Eliot's body be buried in the church of that parish where he died." Okey, the regicide (executed 1662).[2] Sir Jonas Moore, mathematician (d. 1679). Duke of Monmouth (beheaded 1685), buried beneath the communion table. John Rotier (d. 1703), the eminent medallist, the rival of Simon, and father of James and Norbert Rotier, also medallists of great merit.[3] Lords Kilmarnock and Balmerino (beheaded

[1] In Mr. Doyne Bell's *Notices of Historic Persons buried in the Chapel of St. Peter ad Vincula* is an interesting account of the discovery of the supposed remains of Anne Boleyn during the restorations of 1877.

[2] *Ludlow*, vol. iii. p. 103.

[3] When the second Lord Clarendon was a prisoner in the Tower, Rotier requested an interview with him, but the authorities refused because he was a Jesuit.—Clarendon's *Diary*.

1746), Simon, Lord Lovat (beheaded April 9, 1747); their coffin-plates are kept in the vestry, and a stone with a cross on it marks the spot where they were buried. Colonel Gurwood, editor of the *Wellington Despatches* (d. 1845). Field-Marshal Lord Combermere (d. 1865). Field-Marshal Sir John Fox Burgoyne, G.C.B., Constable of the Tower (d. 1871). *Observe.*—Altar-tomb, with effigies of Sir Richard Cholmondeley (Lieutenant of the Tower, temp. Henry VII.) and his wife. Monument, with kneeling figures, to Sir Richard Blount, Lieutenant of the Tower (d. 1564), and his son, Sir Michael Blount, his successor in the office. Monument in chancel to Sir Allen Apsley, Lieutenant of the Tower (d. 1630), the father of Mrs. Lucy Hutchinson. Inscribed stone, against south wall, over the remains of Talbot Edwards (d. 1674), Keeper of the Regalia in the Tower when Blood stole the crown. Here, in the lieutenancy of Alderman Pennington (the regicide Lord Mayor of London), one Kem, Vicar of Low Leyton, in Essex, preached in a gown over a buff coat and scarf. Archbishop Laud, who was a prisoner in the Tower at the time, records the circumstance, with becoming horror, in the *History of his Troubles.*

Peter's (St.), WALWORTH ROAD, a church semi-classic in style, designed by Sir John Soane, of which the first stone was laid June 2, 1823, by Archbishop Sutton, and the church consecrated by him February 24, 1825. It cost nearly £20,000. There is a good peal of eight bells.

Peter's (St.), WESTMINSTER. [*See* Westminster Abbey.]

Peterborough Court, FLEET STREET, on the north side, the first passage west from Shoe Lane, derives its name from the Bishops of Peterborough, who, in early times, had their town house here, and whose interest in it did not expire till 1863, when the Ecclesiastical Commissioners sold the reversion of the property to the proprietors of the *Daily Telegraph,* whose printing office occupies the whole of the Court. Here was a printing office of some note a century and a half before. "Andrew Hind, living in Peterborough Court, near Fleet Street," was declared by a committee of the House of Lords in 1711 to be the real printer of Swift's "false and scandalous" lines, beginning

An Orator dismal of Nottinghamshire.[1]

Peterborough House, MILLBANK. [*See* Millbank.]
Petre House, ALDERSGATE STREET. [*See* Aldersgate Street.]
Petticoat Lane, now MIDDLESEX STREET, WHITECHAPEL.

Petticoat Lane, formerly called Hog Lane, is near unto "Whitechapel Bars," and runs northward towards St. Mary Spittle. In ancient times, on both sides of this lane, were hedge rows and elm trees, with pleasant fields to walk in. Insomuch that some gentlemen of the Court and city built their houses here for air. Here was an House on the west side, a good way in the lane, which, when I was a boy, was commonly called the Spanish Ambassador's House, who in King James I.'s reign dwelt here: and he (I think) was the famous Gondomar. And a little way off this on the east side of the way, down a paved alley (now called Strype's Court, from my father who inhabited here), was a fair large house, with a good garden before it, built and inhabited by Hans Jacobson, the said King James's Jeweller, wherein I was born. But after French Protestants, that in the said King's reign, and before, fled their country for their religion, many planted themselves here, viz., in that part of the lane nearest Spittlefields, to follow their trades, being generally Broad Weavers of Silk, it soon became a contiguous row of buildings on both sides of the way.—*Strype*, B. ii. p. 28.

This Hog Lane stretcheth north toward St. Mary Spittle without Bishopgate, and within these forty years had on both sides fair hedge rows of elm trees, with bridges and easy stiles to pass over into the pleasant fields, very commodious for citizens therein to walk, shoot, and otherwise to recreate and refresh their dull spirits in the sweet and wholesome air, which is now within a few years made a continual building throughout of garden houses and small cottages; and the fields on either side be turned into garden plots, tenter-yards, bowling alleys, and such like.—*Stow*, p. 48.

Gherardt Van Strype (the ancestor of the ecclesiastical antiquary) was a member of the Dutch Church in London in 1567.[1] [*See* Ink Horn Court.]

Ben Jonson makes Iniquity say:—

> We will survey the suburbs, and make forth our sallies
> Down Petticoat Lane and up the Smock-Alleys,
> To Shoreditch, Whitechapel, and so to St. Kathern's,
> To drink with the Dutch there, and take forth their patterns.
> *The Devil is an Ass*, Act i. Sc. 1.

As the weavers receded from Petticoat Lane it was occupied by Jews; and for a long series of years its inhabitants have been Jews of the least respectable class, and the houses and shops receptacles for second-hand clothes and stolen goods. It is perhaps not so bad as it was a few years ago, but it is still one of the most disreputable quarters of the Metropolis. On a Saturday—the Sabbath—quiet as a City lane on a Sunday; on Sunday morning and on the afternoon of every other day it is noisy and crowded with clamorous buyers and sellers of old clothes, old jewellery, and old wares of all kinds.

Petty Burgundy, TOOLEY STREET, SOUTHWARK. This place appears in the map of 1542—reproduced in Rendle's *Old Southwark*—as The Berghené. According to G. R. Corner, the Southwark antiquary, it took the name from alien inhabitants (as in the cases of Petty France, Petty Wales, etc.), so many of whom lived in St. Olave's parish. A special burial-ground for Flemings and others in this very locality implies as much. Corner considers that the Duke of Burgundy or his representatives resided here, temp. Edward IV. When the Greenwich railway was constructed extensive brick vaults of handsome and solid construction and of ancient date were discovered, the substructure of some important mansion on this spot. In forming a new churchyard, 1582, certain godly-disposed parishioners who assisted at the work are noted as living in the "Borgyney." It is likely that this was a petty manor, a

---

[1] *Strype*, B. v. p. 300.

place of punishment, cage and pillory being shown in the map referred to (*Old Southwark*, p. 271).

Petty Calais, WESTMINSTER, was the place where the woolstaplers of Westminster dwelt. "A certain great messuage or tenement, commonly called *Pety Caleys*," is mentioned in an Act of interchange between Henry VIII. and the Abbot of Westminster. It adjoined a piece of land called *Rosamundys*.

Petty France, in BISHOPSGATE WARD, immediately without the City wall, and so called of Frenchmen dwelling there.[1] In "the new Church-yard in Petty France, given by the City, and consecrated June 4, 1617," John Lilburne (Free-born John) was interred in 1657 in the presence of 4000 persons.[2] Petty France was rebuilt in 1730, and called *New Broad Street*.

Petty France, in WESTMINSTER, now YORK STREET (from the London residence, during the early part of the last century, of the Archbishops of York).

From the entry into Totehill field the street [Tothill Street] is called Petty France, in which, and upon St. Hermit's Hill, on the south side thereof, Cornelius Van Dun (a Brabander born, yeoman of the Guard to King Henry VIII., King Edward VI., Queen Mary, and Queen Elizabeth) built twenty houses for poor women to dwell rent free; and near hereunto was a chapel of Mary Magdalen, now wholly ruinated.—*Stow*, p. 176.

He [Milton soon after took a pretty Garden-house in Petty France in Westminster, next door to the Lord Scudamore's, and opening into St. James's Park; here he remained no less than eight years, namely, from the year 1652 till within a few weeks of King Charles the 2d's Restoration. In this house, his first wife dying in childbed, he married a second, who, after a year's time, died in childbed also.—Philips's *Life of Milton*, 12mo, 1694, p. xxxiii.

Milton left his house in Petty France the first week in May 1660, and was for the next three months in "abscondance," at a friend's in Bartholomew Close. On the parapet of No. 19 William Hazlitt, who rented the house in 1811, placed a stone tablet with the inscription, "Sacred to Milton, Prince of Poets."

Lt.-Gen. The horse I rais'd in Petty France
 Shall try their chance,
 And scow'r the meadows overgrown with grass.
 The Rehearsal, Act iv.

January 6, 1709.—Walked to Westminster, and from thence to Petty France, to wait on his Grace my Lord Archbishop of York [John Sharp].—Thoresby's *Diary*, vol. ii. p. 17.

At a Tallow-Chandler's in Petty France, half-way under the blind arch: Ask for the Historian.—*Instructions to a Porter how to find Mr. Curll's Authors* (Pope and Swift's *Miscellanies*, vol. iv. p. 32).

The Bishop of Norwich was living here in 1708.[3] Aaron Hill had a house here, with a garden reaching to the park, and a grotto in it, described in his Letters at some length. John Cleland, son of the Spectator's Will Honeycomb, died in this street, aged eighty-two, in 1789.

[1] *Stow*, p. 61.   [2] Burton's *Diary*, vol. iii. p. 507.   [3] *Hatton*, p. 628.

He wrote a book of such pernicious tendency that when summoned before the Privy Council to answer for it, and pleading poverty, the President of the Council gave him an annuity of £100, on his engaging to write nothing more of the same description.

Petty Wales, the east end of THAMES STREET, by the Tower.

On the north side as well as on the south of this Thames Street, are many fair houses large for stowage, built for merchants; but towards the east end thereof, namely, over-against Galley-Key, Wool-Key and the Custom House, there have been of old time some large buildings of stone, the ruins whereof do yet remain, but the first builders and owners of them are worn out of memory, wherefore the common people affirm Julius Cæsar to be the builder thereof, as also of the Tower itself. Some are of another opinion, and that a more likely, that this great stone building was sometime the lodging appointed for the Princes of Wales, when they repaired to this City, and that therefore the street in that part is called Petty Wales, which name remaineth there most commonly until this day, even as where Kings of Scotland were used to be lodged betwixt Charing Cross and Whitehall, it is likewise called Scotland [Yard], and where the Earls of Britons were lodged without Aldersgate, the street is called Britain Street, etc. [Little Britain].—*Stow*, p. 52.

Pewterers' Hall, No. 15 LIME STREET. In the court-room is a portrait of William Smallwood, who was master of the Company in the second year of Henry VII., and gave them their hall, with a garden and six tenements adjoining. Smallwood's Hall was burnt in the Great Fire. It was replaced in 1678 by a hall which was destroyed by fire in 1840, and the present convenient but unpretending building then erected. The Pewterers' is the sixteenth in rotation of the City Companies, and was first incorporated in 1474.

Sneak. What, is Peter Primmer a candidate?
Heeltap. He is, Master Sneak.
Sneak. Lord, I know him, mun, as well as my mother: why I used to go to his Lectures to Pewterers' Hall, 'long with Deputy Firkin.—Foote's *Mayor of Garratt*, 1764.

Macklin, the actor, delivered his lectures on Elocution in this hall —whence Churchill's lines:—

> No more in Pewterers' Hall was heard
> The proper force of every word,
> Those seats were desolate become,
> And hapless Elocution dumb.
>
> Churchill, *The Ghost*, B. iii.

Philip's (St.) Chapel, REGENT STREET, near Waterloo Place. Built from the designs of J. S. Repton, at the cost of about £15,000. The first stone was laid May 15, 1819, and the chapel consecrated July 4, 1820 (St. Philip and St. James's day). The tower is an imitation of the well-known (so called) lantern of Demosthenes at Athens.

Philip Lane, LONDON WALL, to ADDLE STREET. *Felipeslane,* London Wall, occurs in the City records as early as 1291; again, as *Phelippeslane* in 1306, and often later.—(Riley, *Memorials,* xi.) Edward, twelfth and last Lord Zouch, was living in Philip Lane from 1609 to 1615. In the *Calendar of State Papers,* 1603-1610, pp. 207-209, are two letters from him to Cecil, dated *Philip Lane*, while he held the office of President of Wales; and a long correspondence afterwards, similarly dated, when he was Warden of the Cinque Ports, a busy post when, as in May 1616, pirate vessels were "captured between Broadstairs and Margate."—(*Cal. State Pap.*, 1611-1618, p. 369.) On April 18, 1619, John Hayward, the owner of the house, offers to sell it to Lord Zouch, and if he will not buy it requests him to relinquish it.—(*Cal. State Pap.*, 1619-1623, p. 37.) Sion College formerly stood at the corner of Philip Lane and London Wall.

Philpot Lane, FENCHURCH STREET, to EASTCHEAP, "So called," says Stow, "of Sir John Philpot that dwelt there, and was owner thereof."[1] He was mayor in 1378. Here lived Peter Thellusson (d. 1797), whose ambition to found a colossal fortune proved a fortune to the lawyers. In 1623, when the fleet was fitting out to bring Prince Charles and the Infanta from Spain, the Commissioners of the Navy dated their numerous letters from Philpot Lane.

> This Carol plays, and has been in his days
> A chirping boy and a kill-pot:
> Kit cobbler it is, I'm a father of his,
> And he dwells in the lane called Fill-pot.
>
> Ben Jonson, *Christmas his Masque*.

Phœnix Alley, LONG ACRE now HANOVER COURT, the passage next west of Bow Street, built circ. 1637, in which year it is mentioned for the first time in the Rate-books of St. Martin's. John Taylor, the Water Poet, kept a tavern in this alley. One of his last works (his *Journey into Wales*, 1652) he describes as "performed by John Taylor, dwelling at the sign of the Poet's Head, in Phenix Alley, near the middle of Long Aker, or Covent Garden." He supplied his own portrait and inscription:—

> There's many a head stands for a sign,
> Then, gentle Reader, why not mine?

His first sign was a "Mourning Crown," but this was too marked to be allowed. He came in 1652, and dying here in 1653, was buried, December 5, in the churchyard of *St. Martin's-in-the-Fields*. It should be noted, however, that Mr. Collier quotes a book called *Sportive Wit the Muses Merriment*, 8vo, 1656, which contains an "Epitaph on John Taylor, who was born in the City of Gloucester, died in Phœnix Alley in the 75 yere of his age: you may find him, if the worms have not devoured him, in Covent Garden Church-yard."[2] His widow, it appears from the Rate-books of St. Martin's, continued in the house, under the name of "widow Taylor," five years after his death. In 1658 "Wid[ow] Taylor" is scored out, and "Mons. Lero" written at the side. The rate they paid was 2s. 2d. a year.

Phœnix Street, SEVEN DIALS.

When William Wood obtained in 1723 his patent for coining half-pence for Ireland (which created so much dissatisfaction in that country and caused Swift to

---

[1] *Stow*, p. 77.   [2] *Memoir of Taylor*, note.

write his *Drapier's Letters*) he built a suitable factory "in Phœnix Street Seven Dials, and began the work of coining there on Monday the twenty-first of January 1723."—*Freeholders' Journal* for January 23, 1723.

Phœnix Theatre. [*See* Cockpit Theatre.]

Physic Garden, CHELSEA. [*See* Botanic Garden.]

Physicians, Royal College of, in PALL MALL EAST, corner of TRAFALGAR SQUARE, was designed by Sir R. Smirke, cost £30,000, and was opened (June 25, 1825) with a Latin oration by Sir Henry Halford. The College was founded by Linacre, physician to Henry VIII., and incorporated in 1518. By this charter and the Confirmatory Act 14 Henry VIII., it was enacted that no person, graduates of Oxford and Cambridge excepted, should practice medicine without licence from the College. This continued to be the law till 1858, when, by the Medical Act of that year, licence to practice medicine in any part of the United Kingdom was conferred on all those whose course of study and examination by either of the Universities or other special corporation entitled them to registration on the General Medical Register created by that Act.

The members, at its first institution, met in the founder's house in Knightrider Street on the site of No. 5, still (by Linacre's bequest) in the possession of the College. Here they continued till 1560, when it was taken down to make room for the new Probate Court. They then moved to Amen Corner (where Harvey read his lectures on the discovery of the circulation of the blood); from thence (1674), after the Great Fire, to Warwick Lane (this building was pulled down 1866), and from Warwick Lane to the present college. *Observe.*—In the gallery above the library seven preparations by Harvey, discoverer of the circulation of the blood, and a very large number by Dr. Matthew Baillie. The engraved portrait of Harvey, by Jansen; head of Sir Thomas Browne, author of *Religio Medici;* Sir Theodore Mayerne, physician to James I.; Sir Edmund King, the physician who bled King Charles II. in a fit, on his *own* responsibility; head of Dr. Sydenham, by Mary Beale; Dr. Radcliffe, by Kneller; Sir Hans Sloane, by Richardson; Sir Samuel Garth, by Kneller; Dr. Freind; Dr. Mead; Dr. Warren, by Gainsborough; William Hunter; Dr. Heberden. *Busts.*—George IV., by Chantrey (one of his finest); Dr. Mead, by Roubiliac; Dr. Sydenham, by Wilton (from the picture); Harvey, by Scheemakers (from the picture); Dr. Baillie, by Chantrey (from a model by Nollekens); Dr. Babington, by Behnes. Dr. Radcliffe's gold-headed cane, successively carried by Drs. Radcliffe, Mead, Askew, Pitcairn, and Matthew Baillie (presented to the College by Mrs. Baillie); and a clever picture, by Zoffany, of Hunter delivering a lecture on anatomy before the members of the Royal Academy—all portraits. The long vacant niches were in 1876 filled with statues from the chisel of Mr. Henry Weekes, R.A.; in the centre (over the doorway) that of Linacre, the founder and first president; on one side

Harvey, on the other Sydenham. *Mode of Admission.*—Order from a fellow. Almost every physician of eminence in London is a fellow.[1]

Piazza (The), in COVENT GARDEN, an open arcade on the north and east sides of Covent Garden Market place; built by Inigo Jones, circ. 1633-1634, and very fashionable when first erected, and much admired. The northern side was called the Great Piazza, the eastern side the Little Piazza. It occurs for the first time in the Rate-books of St. Martin's under the year 1634; and the leases of the two houses at the south end, next Great Russell Street (exhibited at the Society of Antiquaries in 1853), granted to Sir Edmund Verney, were dated 1634. That half of the east side of the Piazza south of Russell Street, on which the Hummums stands, was destroyed by fire in March 1769, and rebuilt without the arcade. It was again rebuilt in 1888; the northern half of the east side (including the Bedford Hotel) was pulled down in 1889 for an enlargement of the market into Bow Street. The western half of the north side (west of James Street) was pulled down about 1880, and rebuilt by Messrs. Cubitt.

Piazza—a Market place or chief street; such is that in Covent Garden, which the vulgar corruptly call the P. H., or I know not what.—Blount's *Glossographia*, 12mo, 1656.

But who should I meet at the corner of the Piazza, but Joseph Taylor;[2] he tells me, there's a new play at the Friars to-day, and I have bespoke a box for Mr. Wild and his bride.—*The Parson's Wedding*, by T. Killigrew, fol. 1663.

"In the arcade," says Walpole, "there is nothing very remarkable; the pilasters are as errant and homely stripes as any plasterer would make." This is true now, though hardly true in Walpole's time, when the arcade remained as Inigo had built it, with stone pilasters on a red brick frontage. The pilasters, as we now see them, are lost in a mass of compo and white paint; the red bricks have been stuccoed over, and the pitched roofs of red tile replaced with flat slate. The rebuilt portion to the west of James Street exhibits the red bricks.

Cockayne. Ay, Marry Sir! This is something like! These appear like buildings! Here's architecture exprest indeed! It is a most sightly situation, and fit for gentry and nobility.

Rooksbill. When it is all finished doubtless it will be handsome.

Cockayne. It will be glorious; and yond magnificent peece *the Piazza* will excel that at Venice, by hearsay (I ne'er travelled).—Brome's *Covent Garden Weeded*, 1659.

, Walking thence together to the Piazza they parted there; Eugenius and Lisideius to some pleasant appointment they had made, and Crites and Neander to their several lodgings.—Dryden, *Essay on Dramatick Poesy*, 4to, 1668.

Puh, this is nothing; why I knew the Hectors, and before them the Muns and the Tityre Tu's; they were brave fellows indeed; in those days a man could not go from the Rose Tavern to the Piazza once, but he must venture his life twice, my dear Sir Willy.—*The Scowrers*, by T. Shadwell, 4to, 1691.

London is really dangerous at this time; the pickpockets, formerly content with mere filching, make no scruple to knock people down with bludgeons in Fleet Street and the Strand, and that at no later hour than eight o'clock at night: but in the

---

[1] See the *Roll of the Royal College of Physicians of London*, by W. Munk, M.D., Fellow of the College, etc.; and *Quarterly Review*, October 1879.

[2] An actor in Shakespeare's plays as originally brought out, and one of the best.

Piazzas, Covent Garden, they come in large bodies, armed with couteaus, and attack whole parties, so that the danger of coming out of the play-houses is of some weight in the opposite scale, when I am disposed to go to them oftener than I ought.—*Shenstone to Jago*, March 1744.

Unfortunately for the fishmongers of London the Dory resides only in the Devonshire Seas; for could any of this company but convey one to the Temple of Luxury under the Piazza,[1] where Macklin the high priest daily serves up his rich offerings to the goddess, great would be the reward of that fishmonger.—Fielding, *A Voyage to Lisbon*, 1754.

Otway has laid a scene in *The Soldier's Fortune* in Covent Garden Piazza; and Wycherley a scene in *The Country Wife*. In Cocks's auction-rooms (afterwards Langford's, then George Robins's) Hogarth exhibited his "Marriage-à-la-Mode" gratis to the public; and "in the front apartments, now (1828) used as breakfast-rooms by the proprietor of the Tavistock Hotel," lived Richard Wilson, the landscape painter.[2] He had a model made of a portion of the Piazza, the whole measuring about 6 feet from the floor, which he used as a receptace for his painting implements. "The rustic work of the piers was divided into drawers, and the openings of the arches were filled with pencils and oil bottles."[3] It appears, from the baptismal register of the parish of St. Paul, Covent Garden, during the reigns of Charles II., James II., William III., and even later, that "Piazza" was a favourite name for parish children. The baptismal registers are rife with Peter and Mary Piazza, John Piazza, Paul Piazza, etc. The reason may be well imagined:—

> For, hating Covent Garden, I can hit on
> No place that's called Piazza in Great Britain.—Byron's *Beppo*.

Eminent Inhabitants.[4]—Sir William Alexander, Earl of Stirling, the poet; he was living here, in the north-west angle, in 1637. Thomas Killigrew, the wit; he was living in the north-west angle, between 1637 and 1643, and in the north-east angle, 1660-1662. Denzill Holles, in 1644, under the name of "Colonel Hollis;" and in 1666 and after in a house on the site of Evans's Hotel, afterwards inhabited by Sir Harry Vane, the younger (1647), and by Sir Kenelm Digby (1662).

> Since the restauration of Ch. II. he [Sir Kenelm Digby] lived in the last faire house westward in the north portico of Covent Garden, where my Ld Denzill Holles lived since. He had a laboratory there. I think he dyed in this house. Sed qu.—Aubrey's *Lives*, vol. ii. p. 327.

Nathaniel Crew, third and last Lord Crew, and Bishop of Durham from 1681 to 1689, in the same house. It appears, from the books of St. Paul's, Covent Garden, that almost all the foundlings of the parish were laid at the door of the house of the Bishop of Durham. Aubrey de Vere, the twentieth and last Earl of Oxford; in the north-east angle, from 1663 to 1676; he lived in what was Killigrew's house. Sir Peter Lely, from 1662 to his death in 1680; at the north-east, where Robins's auction-room afterwards was; the house

---

[1] "The Great Piazza Coffee-room in Covent Garden, late Macklin's."—Advertisement in the *Public Advertiser*, March 6, 1756.
[2] Smith's *Nollekens*, vol. ii. p. 213.
[3] *Ibid.*, vol. i. p. 142.
[4] From the Rate-books of St. Martin's and St. Paul's, Covent Garden, and other sources.

was inhabited by Roger North, the executor of Lely,[1] and by his eminent brother, Sir Dudley North, who died in it, December 31, 1691. It is now a portion of the Tavistock Hotel. Viscountess Muskerry, in 1676; in the north-west angle, corner of James Street. This was the celebrated Princess of Babylon of De Grammont's *Memoirs*. Sir Godfrey Kneller; he came into the Piazza the year after Lely died, and the house he occupied was near the steps into *Covent Garden Theatre;* he had a garden at the back, reaching as far as Dr. Radcliffe's, in *Bow Street*, "which was extremely curious and inviting, from the many exotic plants, and the variety of flowers and greens which it abounded with."[2] Here, therefore, and not in *Great Queen Street*, the scene of the well-known anecdote of Kneller's and Radcliffe's comical quarrel must be laid. Kneller lived here for twenty-one years. He had left in 1705.[3] Berkeley, Bishop of Cloyne.

I have quitted my old lodging, and desire you to direct your letters to be left for me with Mr. Smibert, painter, next door to the King's Arms Tavern, in the Little Piazza, Covent Garden.—*Berkeley, Bishop of Cloyne*, August 24, 1726 (Berkeley's *Lit. Relics*, p. 160).

Russell, Earl of Orford.

Hard by the church and at the end of the Piazza [now Evans's Hotel] is the Earl of Orford's house. He is better known by the name of Admiral Russell, who in 1692 defeated Admiral de Tourville near La Hogue, and ruined the French fleet. —*A New Guide to London*, 12mo, 1726, p. 26.

Lady Mary Wortley Montagu lived in the Piazza for some time: there is a letter from Pope addressed to her here.

Lady Mary Wortley Montagu is dangerously ill at her house in the Piazza, Covent Garden.—*Grub Street Journal*, September 17, 1730.

Lankrink and Closterman, painters; in the house lately Richardson's Hotel, now rebuilt and occupied as Lockhart's Cocoa Rooms. Sir James Thornhill, in 1733; in the second house eastward from James Street. Zoffany, the clever theatrical portrait-painter; in what was afterwards Robins's auction-room, in the north-east wing of the Piazza. Here he painted Foote, in the character of Major Sturgeon.

Piccadilly. A street consisting of shops and fashionable dwelling-houses—running east and west, which extends from the top of the Haymarket to Hyde Park Corner. The earliest allusion to it was thought to be in Gerard's *Herbal*, where we read "that the small wild buglosse grows upon the drie ditch bankes about Pickadilla," but the passage does not occur in the earliest edition, 1596, and is only to be found in that of 1633. The origin of the name is more than doubtful. Robert Baker, of the parish of St. Martin's-in-the-Fields, by his last will, dated April 14, 1623, bequeathed the sum of £2 : 10s. in money, and 10s. in bread, to the poor of the parish in which he lived. He had a wife and family and a good deal to leave. He speaks of his houses in the Strand,

---

[1] North's *Lives of the Norths*, ed. 1826, vol. iii. p. 227.
[2] *Life of Radcliffe*, by Pittis, 8vo, 1736.
[3] *Daily Courant* of March 1705.

before Britain's Burse, of a tenement in his own occupation, with its garden and cowhouse, and of a piece of land of about two acres "in the fields behind the Mews," which he had enclosed with a brick wall. The entry of the £3 in the Accounts of the Overseers of the Poor of St. Martin's tells us who Robert Baker was, and how his nameless tenement was known.

Of Robte Baeker of Pickadilley Halle gewen
by wille, iij^{lt}

Here, then, is the earliest mention of Piccadilly Hall which has yet been discovered, and the bequest and entry are additionally important, when we contrast the silence of Baker in his will when he refers to the tenement in his possession, known as Piccadilly Hall, with the particular description made by the overseers in the entry of the payment. There is reason to believe that Robert Baker did not care to have his tenement described as Piccadilly Hall; let us hear Blount :—

> A Pickadil is that round hem, or the several divisions set together about the skirt of a garment or other thing; also a kinde of stiffe collar, made in fashion of a band. Hence, perhaps, the famous ordinary near St. James's, called Pickadilly, took denomination, because it was then the utmost, or skirt house of the suburbs, that way. Others say it took name from this; that one Higgins, a Tailor, who built it, got most of his estate by Pickadilles, which in the last age were much worn in England.—Blount's *Glossographia*, ed. 1656, first ed.

Minsheu, 1627, describes it as "a peece fastened about the top of the coller of a doublet." The word occurs in several of our old dramatic writers; thus Ben Jonson :—

> Ready to cast at one whose band sits ill,
> And then leap mad on a neat pickardill.
> *Epistle to a Friend (Master Colby)*; also *The Devil is an Ass*, Act ii. Sc. 1.

His editor, Gifford, has a note upon the subject. "Piccadil," says Gifford, "is simply a diminutive of *picca* (Span. and Ital.), a spear-head, and was given to this article of foppery from a fancied resemblance of its stiffened plaits to the bristled points of those weapons." It was in fashion when Barnaby Rich wrote in 1614. "He that some fortie or fifty years sithens," says Rich, "should have asked after a Pickadilly, I wonder who could have understood him, or could have told what a Pickadilly had been, either fish or flesh."[1] Taylor the Water Poet speaks of a "Tyburn Pickadill."

Baker, it appears, had built on "the fields behind the Mews," and his widow increasing the number of tenements, the Overseers of the Poor of St. Martin's claimed Lammas money of her, for building on ground over which, after Lammas, the parishioners of St. Martin's had a right of common. In the books of the Overseers from April 18, 1640, to May 2, 1641, the sum is placed under the head of "Lamas Ground Receipts," and the entry is as follows :—

---

[1] A fresh etymology may be hazarded. In Spanish *picadillo* means hashed or minced meat, and it is as probable that Piccadilly Hall, which was a place of entertainment as well as a gaming-house, took its name from a popular dish as from a fashionable collar.

Of Mrs. Mary Baker, widdowe, in Lieu of the Lamas Common, of certaine grounds neere the Winde Mill at the Cawsey head, builded upon by her late husband deceased, and now usually called Pickadilly, xxxd.

Windmill Street preserves a recollection of "the Winde Mill at the Cawseyhead;" Panton Square and Panton Street, the name of Colonel Panton, to whom Mrs. Baker sold Piccadilly Hall; and Coventry Street, the name of Mr. Secretary Coventry of the reign of Charles II., whose garden wall ran along part of Panton Street and Oxenden Street. The situation of Piccadilly Hall, at the north-east corner of the Haymarket, is laid down in the maps of London by T. Porter and W. Faithorne, both published before 1660; and these show that over against Windmill Street stood the Gaming-house or Shaver's Hall; and at the corner of Windmill Street and Coventry Street Piccadilly Hall.

> In the afternoon of the same day [in 1641], Mr. Hyde going to a place called Piccadilly (which was a fair house for entertainment and gaming, with handsome gravel walks with shade, and where were an upper and lower bowling green, whither very many of the nobility and gentry of the best quality resorted, both for exercise and conversation), as soon as ever he came into the ground, the Earl of Bedford came to him, and told him "He was glad he was come thither, for there was a friend of his in the lower ground who needed his counsel."—Clarendon's *History of the Rebellion*, ed. 1826, vol. i. p. 422.

Sir John Suckling, the poet (d. 1641), was one of the great frequenters of Piccadilly Hall, Aubrey preserving a story of "his sisters coming to Peccadillo Bowling-green, crying for the feare he should lose all [their] portions." Another well-known person was Phil Porter.

> Farewell, my dearest Piccadilly,
> Notorious for great dinners;
> Oh, what a Tennis Court was there!
> Alas! too good for sinners.
> Phil Porter's *Farewell* (*Wit and Drollery*), 12mo, 1682, p. 39.

Lammas money was paid on account of Piccadilly House and Bowling Green as late as 1670, and the house itself pulled down circ. 1685. The Fives Court attached to the Gaming-house remained standing in Windmill Street a very few years back. The Tennis Court of Shaver's Hall remained in James Street until 1887, when it was rebuilt; a tablet now marks the place.

> *February* 7, 1638.—A sentence in the Star Chamber this term hath demolished all the houses about Piccadilly; by midsummer they must be pulled down, which have stood since the 13th of K. James (1615): they are found to be great nuisances, and much foul the springs of water which pass by those houses to Whitehall and to the City.—Garrard, *Strafford Letters*, vol. ii. p. 150.

> *April* 14, 1657.—The Clause about manners and loose persons was read.... Sir William Strickland said, "Certainly this work is very requisite, and abundance of loose persons are about town; at Piccadilly and other nurseries of vice."— *Journals of Parliament*, Burton, vol. ii. p. 35.

> *July* 31, 1662.—I sat with the Commissioners about reforming buildings and streets of London, and we ordered the paving of the way down St. James's north, which was a quagmire, and also of the Haymarket about *Piquidillo*.—*Evelyn*.

Cordelio. At last
    Volscius the great this dire resolve embraced :
    His servants he into the country sent,
    And he himself to *Piccadille* went,
    Where he's inform'd by letters that she's dead.

Baynes. So, let me see.
                Enter Prince Volscius *going out of town.*
Smith. I thought he had been gone to *Piccadille*
Baynes. Yes, he gave out so ; but that was only to cover his design.
                        The Rehearsal (1671), Act. iii.

The first Piccadilly, taking the word in its modern acceptation of a street, was a very short line of road, running no farther west than the foot of Sackville Street, and the name Piccadilly Street occurs for the first time in the Rate-books of St. Martin's under the year 1673. Sir Thomas Clarges's house, on the site of the present *Albany*, is described in the *London Gazette* of 1675 (No. 982) as "near Burlington House, above Piccadilly." From Sackville Street to Albemarle Street was originally called Portugal Street, after Catherine of Braganza, Queen of Charles II., and all beyond was the great Bath Road, or, as Agas calls it (1560), "the way to Reding." The Piccadilly of 1708 is described as "a very considerable and publick street, between Coventry Street and Portugal Street ;" and the Piccadilly of 1720 as "a large street and great thoroughfare, between Coventry Street and Albemarle Street."[1] Portugal Street gave way to Piccadilly in the reign of George I. That part of the present street, between Devonshire House and Hyde Park Corner, was taken up, as Ralph tells us, in 1734, by the shops and stone-yards of statuaries, just as the Euston Road is now—a statement confirmed by Lloyd in *The Cit's Country Box*, and by Walpole in a letter to Mann of June 6, 1746.

            And now from Hyde Park Corner come
            The Gods of Athens and of Rome ;
            Here squabby Cupids take their places,
            With Venus and the clumsy Graces.
                    Lloyd, *The Cit's Country Box*, 1757.

When do you come? If it is not soon you will find a new town. I stared to-day at Piccadilly like a country squire ; there are twenty new stone houses. At first I concluded that all the grooms that used to live there had got estates and built palaces.—*Walpole to Montagu*, November 8, 1759.

We may read the history of Piccadilly in the names of several of the surrounding streets and buildings. *Albemarle Street* was so called after Christopher Monk, second Duke of Albemarle, to whom *Clarendon House* was sold in 1675, by the sons of the great Lord Clarendon. *Bond Street* was so called after Sir Thomas Bond, of Peckham, to whom Clarendon House was sold by the Duke of Albemarle when in difficulties, a little before his death. *Jermyn Street* was so called after Henry Jermyn, Earl of St. Albans, who died 1683-1684 ; *Burlington House* after Boyle, Earl of Burlington ; *Dover Street* after Henry

[1] *Hatton*, 1708 ; *Strype*, 1720.

Jermyn, Lord Dover (d. 1708), the little Jermyn of De Grammont's *Memoirs ; Berkeley Street* and *Stratton Street* after John, Lord Berkeley of Stratton, Lord Deputy of Ireland in the reign of Charles II. ; *Clarges Street* after Sir Walter Clarges, the nephew of Ann Clarges, wife of General Monk ; and *Arlington Street* and *Bennet Street* after Henry Bennet, Earl of Arlington, one of the Cabal. *Air Street* was built in 1659; *Stratton Street* in 1693, and *Bolton Street* was, in 1708, the most westerly street in London. *Devonshire House* occupies the site of *Berkeley House*, in which the first Duke of Devonshire died (1707). *Hamilton Place* derives its name from James Hamilton, ranger of *Hyde Park* in the reign of Charles II., and brother of La Belle Hamilton. Halfmoon Street was so called from the Halfmoon Tavern. *Coventry House*, No. 106, was built on the site of an old inn, called the Greyhound, and bought by the Earl of Coventry of Sir Hugh Hunlock in 1764 for 10,000 guineas.[1] *Apsley House* was called after Apsley, Earl of Bathurst, who built it late in the last century ; and the *Albany* from the Duke of York and Albany, brother of George IV. *St. James's Church* (by Wren) was consecrated on Sunday, July 13, 1684. The sexton's book of St. Martin's informs us that the *White Bear Inn* was in existence in 1685 ; and Strype, in his new edition of *Stow*, that there was a *White Horse Cellar* in Piccadilly in 1720 ; it was so named by Williams, the landlord, in honour of the accession of the House of Hanover. This house was widely renowned in coaching days, and is still the summer starting-place of the private four-horse stage-coaches. The two Corinthian pilasters, which stood one on each side of the *Three Kings Inn gateway*, in Piccadilly (they were removed in 1864), belonged to *Clarendon House*, and were thought to be the only remains of that edifice.

Sir William Petty, our first writer of authority on political arithmetic, died in a house over against St. James's Church (1687). Next but one to Sir William Petty, Verrio, the painter, was living in 1675. In the dark red-brick rectory house, at the north side of the church, pulled down 1848, and immediately rebuilt (now No. 197), lived and died Dr. Samuel Clarke, rector of St. James's, from 1709 till his death in 1729. Here he edited *Cæsar* and *Homer ;* here he wrote his *Scripture Doctrine of the Trinity* and his *Treatise on the Being and Attributes of God*. In Coventry House, facing the Green Park, corner of Engine Street (now the St. James's Club), died in 1809, William, sixth Earl of Coventry, married, in 1752, to Maria, the elder of the two beautiful Miss Gunnings. In what was then No. 23, now No. 99, died, in 1803, Sir William Hamilton, the collector of the Hamiltonian gems, better known as the husband of Nelson's Lady Hamilton : they went there in 1800. From the house No. 80, Sir Francis Burdett was taken to the Tower, April 6, 1810 ; the arrest was made by forcing open the area windows, after a fruitless attempt

[1] Carter the Antiquary in *Gent. Mag.* for March 1816, p. 230; *Everyday Book*, vol. i. p. 578; Selwyn's *Correspondence*, vol. i. p. 339.

to get in at the first floor by a ladder. They found Sir Francis in the drawing-room with his brother, his son, and some ladies. The coach in which they carried him off was escorted by the Life Guards, with the 5th Hussars leading the way. They went round by Portland Street and the City Road through Finsbury Square and the Minories to the Tower. Windham records in his *Diary* (p. 503), "Went late to Albemarle Street. Found Life Guards in Piccadilly hunted by and hunting the mob." No. 105 was the old Pulteney Hotel; here the Emperor of Russia put up during the memorable visit of the allied sovereigns in 1814; and here the Grand Duchess of Oldenburg (the Emperor Alexander's sister) introduced Prince Leopold to the Princess Charlotte. On its site the late Marquis of Hertford built, but never occupied, Hertford House. The large brick house, No. 1 Stratton Street, was the residence of Mrs. Coutts, afterwards Duchess of St. Albans, and is now that of the Baroness Burdett-Coutts. Lord Eldon's house, at the west corner of Hamilton Place, was built by his grandfather, Lord Chancellor Eldon. Nos. 138 and 139 were all one house in the old Duke of Queensberry's time.

In the balcony of No. 138, on fine days in summer, used to sit, some forty years ago, a thin, withered old figure, with one eye, looking on all the females that passed him, and not displeased if they returned him whole winks for his single ones. . . . He had been Prince of the Jockies of his time, and was a voluptuary and millionaire. "Old Q." was his popular appellation. He died at the age of eighty-six. We have often seen him in his balcony

Sunning himself in Huncamunca's eyes;

and wondered at the longevity of his dissipation and the prosperity of his worthlessness.—*Leigh Hunt.*

Windham also mentions his habit of sitting at the window:—

September 25, 1808.—Went in to the Duke of Queensberry, whom I saw at his window; full of life but very difficult to communicate with, and greatly declined in bodily powers.—Windham's *Diary.*

He died in this house, December 23, 1810, aged eighty-six. The legacy duty on his property was £120,000.

At the corner of Park Lane, No. 137, then Lord Elgin's, the Elgin marbles were placed on their first arrival in this country. Later it was the residence of the Duchess of Gloucester. No. 94 was formerly Egremont House, then Cholmondeley House, afterwards the residence of the Duke of Cambridge (brother of George III.), and known as Cambridge House. It was then, from his first premiership, 1855, till his death, October 18, 1865, the residence of Lord Palmerston; and famed for Lady Palmerston's brilliant receptions. It is now the Naval and Military Club. Lord Palmerston, prior to 1855, lived for a short time at No. 114. The bay-fronted house which stood at the corner of Whitehorse Street was the residence of Mr. Charles Dumergue, the friend of Sir Walter Scott; until a child of his own was established in London, this was Scott's headquarters when in town. The London season of Lord Byron's married life was passed in that half of the Duke of Queensberry's house afterwards numbered 139 and pulled down in 1889. "We mean to metropolise to-morrow," says Byron, "and you will address your next to Piccadilly. We have got the Duchess of Devon's house there, she being in France." Here he brought his wife, March 18, 1815, and that bag of a housemaid, Mrs. Mule, of whom Moore has given an amusing account; and from here Lady Byron left him for ever in the middle of the following January. His affairs were so embarrassed that there had been no fewer than eight or nine executions in his house during this period. The letters of Lord Byron, written from this house, are one and all dated from No. 13 Piccadilly Terrace, and one and all of Scott's from Mr. Dumergue's, No. 15 Piccadilly West. Numbers are of little use to the local antiquary; they suffer from the caprice of the authorities. Two houses are thrown into one, the street is enlarged, or the even numbers are arranged on one side and the odd numbers on the other. Piccadilly Terrace and Piccadilly West no longer exist; and under the present system of numbering, Apsley House, Hyde Park Corner, is No. 149 Piccadilly. The Hercules Pillars public-house, where Squire Western put up his horses when in pursuit of Tom Jones, and where that bluff brave soldier, the Marquis of Granby (d. 1770), spent many a happy hour, stood long after Apsley House was built on what was Hamilton Terrace, now incorporated into Piccadilly. In Piccadilly, on the south side, facing Old Bond Street, was the shop of Wright (the publisher of the *Antijacobin*, the *Baviad*, etc.), now Ridgway's (No. 169), where Peter Pindar assaulted Gifford, and was bundled neck and crop into the muddy street for his pains. Peter Pindar, however, never ceased to assert both in print and conversation that he had "cudgelled, most soundly cudgelled" Gifford, in "one Wright's shop, a poor, ignorant and painstaking bookseller in Piccadilly." George Frederick Cooke was living at No. 9 Piccadilly West when, on February 5, 1803, he made a resolve to keep a journal, which he forgot the next day.

At the corner of Down Street was the house of Henry Thomas Hope, Esq., built 1848-1849, from the designs of M. Dusillon and Mr. T. L. Donaldson. The handsome iron railing in front was cast at Paris. The cost of the whole building is said to have been over £80,000. Here Mr. Hope kept the celebrated collection of pictures (Dutch especially) formed at the Hague by the family of the Hopes, and now chiefly at Deepdene. The Junior Athenæum Club purchased the lease for £45,000. At "No. 22 Piccadilly, late the Fantoccini Rooms," Mr. Katterfelto exhibited in 1782 the wonders of his solar microscope, whereby the "insects which have threatened this kingdom with a plague . . . and which by all accounts, caused a great plague in Italy in the year 1432 . . . will be magnified as large as an ox, and are as tough."[1]

[1] Katterfelto's *Advertisement*.

Pickaxe Street, CLERKENWELL, the name given in some old maps to GOSWELL STREET.

Pickering Place, ST. JAMES'S STREET, a small courtyard near the south-east end of the street. In Dodsley's London, 1761, it is set down as Pickering's Court. The old firm of engravers, through whose house the entrance to the Court passes, have preserved a card-plate of the Georgian era, which, without any name, states "5 Pickering Place, St. James's Street, Rouge and Roulette, French and English Hazard. Commence at one o'clock." This was one of the most notorious *Hells* in London.

Picket Street, STRAND, north side of St. Clement's Danes. Built on the site of *Butcher Row*, and so called in compliment to Alderman Picket (d. 1796, buried at Stoke Newington). Before the alteration was made the old cant name for the place among coachmen was "The Pass," or "The Straits of St. Clement's."[1] Picket Street was cleared away to make room for the new Law Courts.

A number of old, ruinous houses called Butcher Row have been taken down, and a range of new buildings erected on the north side, named Picket Street, in honour of Alderman Picket, who projected the alteration.—Priscilla Wakefield's *Perambulations in London*, 1809, p. 246.

Pickleherring Street, by the Thames Side, HORSLEYDOWN. Here, at the north end of Vine Street, is the landing-place called *Pickleherring Stairs.*

October 15, 1687.—Mr. Timothy Evans, at Pickleherring Stairs, who had been kind to my son Henry, in bringing him out of the Indies, came to me. He has been commander of merchantmen in to the Indies and Guinea, or mate, this ten years, and brought me four agates; who is desirous I would move Mr. Pepes to him into his Majesty's service.—Bishop Cartwright's *Diary*, p. 85.

Picthatch, or PICKEHATCH, a noted receptacle for prostitutes and pickpockets, generally supposed to have been in *Turnmill Street*, near Clerkenwell Green,[2] but its position is determined by a grant of the 33d of Queen Elizabeth, and a survey of 1649. What *was* Picthatch is a street at the back of a narrow turning called Middle Row (formerly Rotten Row) opposite the Charter House wall in Goswell Road. The name is still (or was till recently) preserved in "Pickax Yard" adjoining Middle Row.

In a grant by pat. 33 Eliz., p. 9, m. 25-28, appears the grant of a small enclosure occupied as a garden with a stall stable thereon built, lying in Olde Street or Pickehatch near the Charter House, in the parish of St. Giles's without Cripplegate; and in a survey of the Prebendal Manor of Finsbury (1649) is mentioned, "All that other parcel of demesne land commonly called and known by the name of Rotten Row, set, lying and being in the parish of St. Giles's without Cripplegate, in a certain street there commonly called Old Street, adjoining north upon the said street, and south upon a way or passage leading out of Old Street into the Pickthatch, and abutting east upon the Cage and Prison House in Old Street aforesaid."—T. Edlyne Tomlins (*MS. Communication to Mr. Cunningham*).

---

[1] *The Spectator*, No. 498.   [2] Gifford's *Ben Jonson*, vol. i. p. 17; Dyce's *Middleton*, vol. v. p. 512.

Falstaff [*to Pistol.*] Reason, you rogue, reason ; think'st thou I'll endanger my soul gratis ? At a word, hang no more about me ; I am no gibbet for you :—go. A short knife and a throng :—to your manor of Pickthatch, go.—*Merry Wives of Windsor*, Act ii. Sc. 2.

> Shift, here in town, not meanest among squires,
> That haunt Pict-hatch, Marsh Lambeth and Whitefriars,
> Keeps himself, with half a man, and defrays
> The charge of that state with this charm—God pays.
> Ben Jonson, *Epigram xii.* (*Lieutenant Shift*).

Shift, a thread-bare shark ; one that never was a soldier, yet lives upon lendings. His profession is skeldring and odling, his bank Paul's, and his warehouse Picthatch. —Ben Jonson, *Dram. Pers. before Every Man out of his Humour.* See also *Every Man in his Humour ;* and *Alchemist.*

Here Middleton has laid the scene of his *Black Book ;* and here there is reason to believe, from what Middleton states, Nash, the rude railing satirist, died.

I proceeded toward Pict-hatch, intending to begin there first, which (as I may fitly name it) is the very skirts of all brothel-houses.—Middleton's *Works*, vol. v. p. 513.

In the meantime, while they were ransacking his box and pockets [Sir John] Robinson fell a railing at the Colonel, giving him the base terms of Rebel and Murderer, and such language as none could have learnt, but such as had been conversant among the Civil Society of Pickt-hatch, Turnbull Street, and Billingsgate. —Mrs. Hutchinson's *Memoirs of Colonel Hutchinson*, ed. 1838, p. 132.

Pightle is a small enclosed place, and the root picht, pight seems to convey the idea of a fastening or shutting off. Pickthatch was a place parted off, where the residents were shut in and intruders shut out. It may be worth notice that Southey records in his journal of a journey in the western and south-western countries, under October 29, 1799 : "On the way [from Ringwood to Romsey in Hampshire] is the *Picket Post*, an extra-parochial alehouse, where unmarried women go to lie in, out of the reach of the constable."[1]

Pie Corner, WEST SMITHFIELD, between *Giltspur Street* and *Smithfield ;* now the Smithfield end of Giltspur Street.

Pie Corner, a place so called of such a sign, sometime a fair Inn for receipt of travellers, but now divided into tenements.—*Stow*, p. 139.

Pye corner—noted chiefly for Cook's Shops, and Pigs drest there during Bartholomew Fair.—*Strype*, B. iii. p. 283.

Hostess. I am undone by his [Falstaff's] going ; I warrant you, he's an infinitive thing upon my score.—Good master Fang, hold him sure :—good master Snare, let him not 'scape. He comes continually to Pie Corner (saving your manhood) to buy a saddle ; and he's indited to dinner to the Lubbard's Head in Lumbert Street to Master Smooth's the silkman.—Shakespeare, *Second Part of King Henry IV.*, Act ii. Sc. 1.

> *Face.* I shall put you in mind, sir ; at Pie Corner
> Taking your meal of steam in, from Cook's stalls.
> Where, like the father of hunger, you did walk
> Piteously costive.—Ben Jonson, *The Alchemist*, Act i. Sc. 1.

Littlewit. Tut, we'll have a device, a dainty one. I have it, Win, I have it, i' faith, and 'tis a fine one. Win, long to eat of a pig, sweet Win, in the Fair do you

---

[1] Southey's *Commonplace Book*, vol. iv. p. 503.

see, in the heart of the Fair, not at Pie Corner.—Ben Jonson, *Bartholomew Fair*, Act i. Sc. 1.

Whorebang. By this flesh, let's have wine, or I will cut thy head off, and have it roasted and eaten in Pie Corner next Bartholomew Tide.—Nat Field, *Amends for Ladies*, 4to, 1618.

In the Pig Market, alias Pasty Nook, or Pie Corner; where pigs are all hours of the day on the stalls piping hot, and would say (if they could speak) come eat me.—*Bartholomew Fair* (tract), 1641.

Lady Frugal. What cooks have you provided?
Holdfast. The best of the city: they've wrought at my Lord Mayor's.
Anne Frugal. Fie on them! They smell of Fleet Lane and Pie Corner.—Massinger, *The City Madam.*

Sir Humphrey Scatergood. I'll not be served so nastily as in my days of nonage, or as my father was; as if his meat had been dress'd at Pie Corner by greasy scullions there.—T. Shadwell, *The Woman Captain*, 4to, 1680; See also his *Sullen Lovers*, 4to, 1668.

Next day I through Pie Corner past:
The roast-meat on the stall
Invited me to take a taste;
My money was but small.
The Great Boobee (*Roxburghe Ballads*, p. 221).

Through a good part of the 17th century Pie Corner was noted for the manufacture of broad-sheet (or what in the next century would have been called Seven Dials) literature. Randolph, in his "Answer to Ben Jonson's Ode," speaks as contemptuously of "some Pie Corner Muse," as does Marvell, long after, in his "Rehearsal Transprosed" of "superannuated chanter of Saffron Hill and Pie Corner;" and Edward Phillips says:—

Who would grudge the slight mention of a book and its author; yet not so far as to condescend to the taking notice of every single-sheeted Pie Corner poet who comes squirting out with an elegy in mourning for every great person that dies.—Edward Phillips, *Preface to Theatrum Poetarum*, 12mo, 1675.

The Great Fire of London began at *Pudding Lane* and ended at *Pie Corner*, a singular coincidence in names, which is said to have occasioned the erection, at the corner of *Cock Lane*, of a figure of a boy upon a bracket, with his arms across his stomach, thus curiously inscribed: "This boy is in memory put up of the late Fire of London, occasioned by the sin of gluttony, 1666." There is an engraving of it by J. T. Smith, who also etched some "old houses at the south corner of Hosier Lane, drawn in April 1795," which, with the other old houses spared by the Fire, were taken down in 1809. There is still an inscription on the corner house. [*See* Cock Lane]. Long after the Fire D'Urfey calls Pie Corner "a very fine dirty place."[1]

September 4, 1666.—W. Hewer this day went to see how his mother did, and comes late home, telling us how he hath been forced to remove her to Islington, her house in Pie Corner being burned, so that the Fire is got so far that way.—*Pepys.*

A certain Company were reckoning up y⁰ families of y⁰ Pyes and named divers; at length one ask't what was Sir Edm. Py that married L⁴ Lucas sister? One answered he was Py of Py Corner.—R. Symond's *Pocket-Book*, Harl. *MS.*, 991, fol. 10.

---
[1] *Song of Bartholomew Fair.*

Pie Powder Court. [*See* Bartholomew Fair.] "A court incident to all fairs, held before the steward of the lord of the fair, for adjudicating on all contracts arising at the fair,"[1] and by 17 Edward IV., c. 2, the court is strictly prohibited from entertaining any plaint where the cause of action does not arise within the precincts and during the continuance of the fair. The Bartholomew Pie Powder Court was held in Cloth Fair, in its latter years at a public-house.

This Court has for many years been held at a public house called The Hand and Shears, in King Street at the corner of Middle Street, and near the east end of Cloth Fair.—Wilkinson's *Lond. Illust.*

The Book of the Court, now deposited in the City of London Library, Guildhall, has for its last entry:—

September 2, 1854.—The Lord Mayor not having proclaimed Bartholomew Fair, the Court of Pie Powder consequently was not held.

A like tribunal was probably held at some Southwark Inn, the part of Southwark in which the fair was held consisted mostly of inns, from the Tabard to the Swan and at the Town Hall, which was in the midst of the fair, but there is no record of any particular place. In the picture of Hogarth's Southwark Fair an actor is being arrested by an officer of the court.

Pike Garden, BANKSIDE, SOUTHWARK, a garden purchased by Philip Henslowe, the partner of Edward Alleyn the actor.[2] From Pat. 13, Car. II., we learn that William Boreman obtained a grant of "all that garden or parcel of land commonly called the *Pike* Garden, containing by estimation 3 roods and 20 perches or thereabouts in the parish of St. Saviour within the Borough of Southwark, between the common way or Bank or the River Thames, on the north, and a certayn lane called Mayden Lane on the south, including four fish-ponds or rivaries for the conservation of river fish reserved for Our Service."

Pilgrim Street, BLACKFRIARS, a narrow winding thoroughfare that follows the line of the old London Wall, from the south side of Ludgate Hill to the Broadway, Blackfriars. It has been said to owe its name to its being the road from the landing-place of pilgrims to the shrines at St. Paul's or Blackfriars. But for this there is no authority. The name is, in fact, comparatively recent. Pilgrim Street does not occur in the lists of streets in Hatton, 1708; Strype, 1720; Maitland, 1739; or Dodsley, 1761. A piece of the old City Wall, at the junction of Little Bridge Street, Pilgrim Street, and Broadway, was laid bare in 1889. Strype, without naming it, describes it as "a narrow passage out of Ludgate Street, and turning by the back-side of Ludgate prison, falleth into an open Place, with very good buildings, well inhabited by tradesmen." Its continuation by Apothecaries' Hall to the Thames (now Water Lane) he calls Water Street. In his Map what is now Pilgrim Street is marked the "Wall." Here on the south side, in an

[1] *Coke Institutes*, 4to, p. 272.   [2] Collier, *Memoirs of Alleyn*, p. 16.

old house of the reign of Charles II., with the royal arms over the door, was, a very few years back, the warehouse of "D. Price & Co., Ostrich Feather Merchants & Manufacturers," the last of the feather-makers of this once celebrated quarter. Ben Jonson has frequent references, especially in his *Bartholomew Fair*, to the Feather-Makers of Blackfriars.

> *Doll Common* (to *Face*)—Who shall take your word?
> A whoreson, upstart, apocryphal captain,
> Whom not a Puritan in Blackfriars will trust
> So much as for a feather.—Ben Jonson, *Alchemist*, Act i. Sc. 1.

Bird, a featherman in Blackfriars, is one of the characters in his *Muses' Looking-Glass*, and Marston in his *Malcontent* (4to, 1604) makes Sly say :—

> This play hath beaten all young gallants out of the feathers. Blackfriars hath almost spoil'd Blackfriars for feathers.—*Induction.*

[*See* Blackfriars.]

Pimlico, near HOXTON, a great summer resort in the early part of the 17th century, and famed for its cakes, custards and Derby ale. The name is still preserved in "Pimlico Walk," by Hoxton Church, Hoxton Street, and St. John's Road. The references to the Hoxton Pimlico are numerous in our old dramatists. Ben Jonson mentions it in *The Devil is an Ass*, *Bartholomew Fair*, *The Underwoods*, and *The Alchemist*, where he makes Lovewit say, after his neighbours have told him how his house has been abused during his absence :—

> Gallants, men and women,
> And of all sorts, tag-rag, been seen to flock here,
> In threaves, these ten weeks, as to a second Hogsden,
> In days of Pimlico and eye-bright.
> Ben Jonson, *The Alchemist*, Act v. Sc. 1.

> *Sir Lionel.* I have sent my daughter this morning as far as Pimlico, to fetch a draught of Derby ale, that it may fetch a colour in her cheeks.—Greene's *Tu Quoque*, 4to, 1614.

> *Plotwell.* We have brought you
> A gentleman of valour, who has been
> In Moorfields often : marry it has been
> To 'squire his sisters and demolish custards
> At Pimlico.—*The City Match*, fol. 1639.

Pimlico, a large district lying between St. James's Park, the river Thames, the village of Chelsea, Hyde Park Corner, and the hamlet of Knightsbridge. Buckingham Palace, Grosvenor Place and Gardens, Belgrave Square, and the Victoria Railway Station are in Pimlico.

> A place near Chelsea is still called Pimlico, and was resorted to within these few years on the same account as the former at Hogsden.—Isaac Reed (Dodsley's *Old Plays*, ed. Collier, vol. vii. p. 51).

The following extracts, from the Accounts of the Overseers of the Poor of St. Martin's-in-the-Fields, are the earliest notices yet discovered of the existing Pimlico :—

1626.—Paied for a shroud Cloathe for Goodman's wife at Pimlicoe . iij⁵ iiij ᵈ
1626.—Paied for a shrowd Cloathe for an old man dyed at Pimlico iiij ˢ
1627.—To the Constable of Pimlico to take out the Lord Cheiffe Justice's Warrant to take Mr. Burde that gott a man child one Mary Howard and borne at Pimlico . . j ˢ vj ᵈ
1630.—The iiij ᵗʰ of September 1630, paid for the hire of a horse and sledd, and a labouring man to make a grave, and to cover it at Hide pke corner, for Thomas Wood, who hanged himself at Pimplico . . . . v ˢ

Overseers' Accounts of St. Martin's-in-the-Fields.

Pimlico at this time was nearly uninhabited, nor is it introduced into the Rate-books of St. Martin's before the year 1680, when the Earl of Arlington, previously rated under the head of Mulberry Garden, is, though living in the same house, rated under the head of "Pimlico." In 1687, seven years after the first introduction of the name into the rate-books of the parish in which it was then situated, four people are described as residing in what was then called Pimlico—the Duke of Grafton, Lady Stafford, Thomas Wilkins, and Dr. Crispin. The Duke of Grafton, having married the only child of the Earl of Arlington, was residing in Arlington House, and Lady Stafford in what was then and long before called Tart Hall. In 1698 the Duke of Buckingham (then only Marquis of Normanby) bought Arlington House of the Duchess of Grafton, and rebuilding it shortly after, named it anew by its well-known title of Buckingham House. Pimlico is not mentioned in Dodsley's *London*, 1761. George IV. began the great alterations in Pimlico by rebuilding Buckingham House, and drawing the courtiers from Portland Place and Portman Square to the splendid mansions built by Thomas Cubitt and others, in what was known at that time, and long before, as the Five Fields, and is now Belgravia. But splendid as were these houses they have been eclipsed by the stately mansions erected on the Duke of Westminster's estate, between Hyde Park Corner and Victoria Railway Station. Pimlico (including Belgravia) is now the most aristocratic quarter of the Metropolis. In a small gloomy house within the gates of Elliot's Brewery, between Brewer Street, Pimlico, and York Street, Westminster, lived and died Richard Heber; here he had a portion of his extensive and noble library—a second portion occupied the whole of a house from kitchen to attic in James Street, Buckingham Gate—a third portion was at Hodnet, his country seat—and at Paris he had a fourth depôt. [*See* Davies Street.]

Pincock Lane, NEWGATE STREET, on the north side leading to The Bagnio, originally Pentecost Lane, and now Roman Bath Street. [*See* Pentecost Lane.]

Pinder of Wakefield, GRAY'S INN ROAD. This famous old country tavern stood on the *west* side of Gray's Inn Road, north of Guildford Street. The small houses between Harrison Street and Cromer Street (Nos. 235-243), Gray's Inn Road, were, till recently, named *Pindar Place*, and occupied the site. In 1705, when Tom

Brown (with the help of Ned Ward) wrote his *Comical View of London and Westminster*, the house was still in the fields. He tells how, wishing to have an hour's star-gazing one bright night, he took his "quadrant telescope and nocturnal," walked as far as Lamb's Conduit, and having seated himself on a stile had just commenced operations when "a milkmaid, crossing the fields to Pinder of Wakefield, asked me what I was looking at." The present Pinder of Wakefield public-house is on the *east* side of Gray's Inn Road.

Pine-Apple Place, MAIDA VALE, EDGWARE ROAD. In 1793-1794 George Romney the painter had a retreat here to which he used to run down to sleep and enjoy "rural breakfasts." Many of his letters to Hayley are dated from it. Another eminent painter, C. R. Leslie, R.A., lived in No. 12, from 1834 (after his return from America) till 1848, and here painted some of his best pictures.

A few days since the Duke [of Wellington] took it into his head to walk out to Leslie's, Pine Apple Place, to see the picture he is painting for the Queen, "The Christening of the Princess Royal," and I believe to give Leslie another sitting. The Duke walked all the way, which is two and a half miles, and after a great deal of trouble found Leslie's house. Leslie, who is prudent and economical keeps a cheap servant . . . and he also keeps his outer garden-gate barred and locked, and one is questioned and cross-questioned before being admitted. . . . The Duke rang the bell. After at least ten minutes out comes the servant girl, sulky at being disturbed. "Is Mr. Leslie at home?" said the Duke. "I don't know," said the girl, "but I'll see." Away she went, leaving the Duke in the dirt, without letting him into the garden, and she said to Leslie, "Here's an old man wants you, Sir." "Is there?" said Leslie; "ask him his name and what he wants." Down went the girl, "Master says you must tell your name and what you want, or I can't let you in." The Duke, by this time roused by the questioning, roared out, "I am the Duke of Wellington." The poor girl jumped up and ran back to her master, still leaving the Duke outside; out came Leslie in a fright, and at last in got his grace. He tells the story himself, and jumps up like the girl, with capital humour.—*B. R. Haydon to Wordsworth*, January 14, 1842 (*Memoir of Haydon*, by his son, vol. ii. p. 51).

Pinners', or Pinmakers' Hall, PINNERS' COURT, 54 OLD BROAD STREET, the ancient hall of the Pinners' or Pinmakers' Company, a company standing sixty-eighth on the list of City guilds, but without livery, and now defunct. The hall, a part of the Augustine priory, of which the church is known as the Dutch Church, Austin Friars, was let in the reign of Elizabeth to Verselyn for his Venetian glassworks. In the reign of Charles II. it was occupied as an Independent Meeting House, and many of the most eminent of their ministers—Baxter, Manton, Owen, Bates and Howe—preached here. Later, Isaac Watts and Pope's "Modest Foster" ministered here. It continued to be used as a dissenting chapel till 1798, when it was demolished. At Pinners' Hall was established in the 17th century the long popular "Merchants' Lecture," which was preached there at mid-day on Tuesdays. It was then delivered on the same day and hour at the Weigh-house Chapel, Fish Street Hill, and is now given at the Memorial Hall, Farringdon Street. The present Pinners' Hall is appropriated to merchants' offices.

Pit Place, Drury Lane. [*See* Cockpit Theatre.]

Plasterers' Hall, the Hall of the Ancient Fraternity of the Plasterers is No. 23 Addle Street, Wood Street, Cheapside. The company was incorporated by Henry VIII., in March 1501, by the title of the Master and Wardens of the Fraternity of the Blessed Mary of Plasterers, London. The ancient hall of the company was destroyed in the Great Fire. The present hall was designed by Sir Christopher Wren. It has been for many years occupied as a warehouse, and the ornamental features have been pretty nearly destroyed.

Playhouse Passage, Golding Lane. [*See* Fortune Theatre.]

Playhouse Yard, Blackfriars. [*See* Blackfriars Theatre.]

Playhouse Yard, Drury Lane. So called because it led to *Drury Lane Theatre.* The Rate-books of St. Martin's give the names of the actors rated to the poor for Drury Lane Theatre, at the junction of the two companies, in 1681:—

Playhouse Yard. Nicholas Burt, Robert Shattrell, Nicholas Moone, William Cartwright, Philip Griffith, Thomas Clarke, Martin Powell, Joseph Haynes, £6, Theatre Royall.

And so the names stand in 1683 and 1684. Subsequently they are omitted. Nicholas Moone was perhaps a mistake for Michael Mohun, the celebrated Major Mohun.

Playhouse Yard, Whitefriars. [*See* Whitefriars Theatre.]

Playing-Card Makers' Company. This company was incorporated by letters patent of Charles II., October 22, 1629, under the name of the Master, Wardens, and Commonalty of the Mistery of the Makers of Playing-Cards of the City of London. A livery was granted them in 1792, but they possess no hall. The card makers rank eighty-third amongst the City companies.

Plough Court, Lombard Street, runs south into Lombard Court, which itself runs west into Clement's Lane and east into Gracechurch Street. Alexander Pope is believed to have been born in this court. "The house, which by the tradition of its inmates, claims the honour of being Pope's birthplace, is at the bottom of Plough Court, and faces you as you enter the passage from Lombard Street. It belonged to the well-known William Allen, and he succeeded a Mr. Bevan."[1] Mr. Sylvanus Bevan, admitted an apothecary in 1715, first associated the house with the drug trade. He was resident in the premises in 1735. A descendant, Joseph Gurney Bevan, received first as an apprentice, afterwards as a partner, William Allen, F.R.S. (d. 1843), eminent alike as a man of science and a philanthropist, and in their hands the establishment grew into great importance. The old house was pulled down in November 1872, and its site, together with that of other houses, were re-arranged for Allen and Hanbury's drug shop, and numerous city offices.

[1] Carruthers's *Life of Pope,* p. 4.

Plowden Buildings. A row of chambers in the Temple, and so called (recently) after Edmund Plowden, an eminent lawyer in the reign of Queen Elizabeth, whose Reports and Queries are still referred to by every student of the old law. Here is Middle Temple Hall.

Plumbers' Hall, BUSH LANE, CANNON STREET, CITY; taken down to make way for the Cannon Street Railway Station, and not rebuilt. The Company, a fraternity, says Strype, "of large and very memorable antiquity," was first incorporated by James I. in 1611, and is the thirty-first in rotation of the Livery Companies of London. The hall had been rebuilt about 1830.

> The first instance of actual punishment inflicted on Protestant Dissenters was in June 1567, when a company of more than one hundred were seized during their religious exercises at Plummers' Hall, which they had hired on pretence of a wedding, and fourteen or fifteen of them were sent to prison.—Hallam, *Const. Hist. of England*, chap. iv. (10th ed.) vol. i. p. 182.

Poets' Corner, WESTMINSTER ABBEY. The eastern angle of the south transept of *Westminster Abbey* was called *Poets' Corner* from the burial there of Chaucer, Spenser, and other eminent English poets. It is not known when this name was first applied to the place. It is not used in Dart's *Westmonasterium*, 1723, and the first use of the name has been noted in Entick's *London*, 1766.

> The Poets' Corner is the place they choose,
> A false nursery for an infant muse,
> Unlike that corner where true Poets lie.
>
> Crabbe, *The Newspaper* (1785).

This is the ordinary entrance into *Westminster Abbey*. The name is also given to the houses bordering the passage from Palace Yard to the Abbey door. On May 28, 1813, Wilberforce writes to Southey from "No. 1 Poets' Corner, Westminster." The houses, four in all, are now occupied by architects, surveyors, engineers and solicitors as offices. There is an important article on Poets' Corner by Henry Poole, master mason of the abbey, in the *Antiquary*, vol. iv. p. 137.

Poland Street, OXFORD STREET, Dr. Burney (author of the *History of Music*) and Dr. Macaulay (husband of Mrs. Macaulay, the historian) both resided in this street. Dr. Burney came to live here in 1760, when his second daughter Fanny was eight years old. Seventy-two years afterwards she wrote:—

> The new establishment was in Poland Street; which was not then, as it is now, a sort of street that, like the rest of its neighbourhood, appears to be left in the lurch. House fanciers were not yet as fastidious as they are become at present, from the endless variety of new habitations. Oxford Road, as at that time Oxford Street was called, into which Poland Street terminated, had little on its further side but fields, gardeners' grounds, or uncultivated suburbs. Portman, Manchester, Russell, Belgrave Squares, Portland Place, etc.; had not yet a single stone, or brick laid, in signal of intended erection; while in plain Poland Street, Mr. Burney then had successively for his neighbours, the Duke of Chandos, Lady Augusta Bridges, the Hon. John Smith and the Miss Harrys, Sir Willoughby and the Miss Astons; and well noted by Mr. Burney's little family, on the visit of his black majesty to England, sojourned almost immediately opposite to it, the Cherokee King.—*Memoirs of Dr. Burney*, vol. i. p. 134.

In this house died his first wife, Esther Sleepe, the mother of Fanny Burney, of Dr. Charles Burney, and of that Admiral Burney who when a schoolboy had seen the handcuffs placed on the wrists of Eugene Aram, while in early manhood had witnessed the death of Captain Cook, and in his closing years was a much loved companion of Charles Lamb. Here, September 29, 1766, died the old Earl of Cromarty, who was pardoned by King George II. for the part he took in the Rebellion of 1745. Sir William Chambers, the architect, lived here before he removed to Berners Street about 1770. Gavin Hamilton, the painter, lived in this street in 1779, after his return from Italy. In 1787 William Blake took lodgings in this street—the house "No. 28 (now [1863, a tobacconist's in 1890] a cheesemonger's shop, and boasting three brass bells), not many doors from Oxford Street, on the right-hand side going towards that thoroughfare."[1] He left it for Hercules Buildings, Lambeth, in 1793. Schnebbelie, the engraver of many views of Old London, was living here in 1792. The poet Shelley on his expulsion from Oxford in 1811 took lodgings at No. 15, in this street.

Polygon (The), CLARENDON SQUARE, SOMERS TOWN, was so called from its shape. Here for several years lived William Godwin. It has been asserted that it was here he wrote *Caleb Williams* and *Political Justice;* but he did not remove to Somers Town till after the publication of the latter work, when he took a house in Chalton Street (running from the Polygon) and there wrote *Caleb Williams.* He took the house in the Polygon shortly before his marriage with Mary Wollstonecraft (March 29, 1797). She lived there, and there died (Sunday, September 10, 1797), after giving birth to the authoress of *Frankenstein,* but he continued till her death at 25 Evesham Buildings. He then moved his books to the Polygon and made his wife's room his study.[2] Godwin continued to reside in the Polygon till August 1807, when he removed to Skinner Street. J. T. Willmore, the line engraver, lived for many years at No. 23. The Polygon, now enclosed by the dirty neighbourhood of Clarendon Square, was, when Godwin lived in it, a new block of houses, pleasantly seated near fields and nursery gardens.

Polytechnic Institution, 309 REGENT STREET, built in 1837 and opened 1838 (James Thomson, architect), incorporated for the advancement of the Arts and Practical Science, especially in connection with agriculture, mining, machinery, manufactures, and other branches of industry. The collection was very miscellaneous, and there were popular lectures illustrated by dissolving views, musical entertainments, etc. The diving-bell in the Great Hall constituted a permanent attraction. The great hall was 120 feet by 40 feet, by 38 feet high in the centre. In 1848 the building was extended southward by the

---
[1] Gilchrist's *Life of Blake,* vol. i. p. 60.
[2] K. Paul's *Life of Godwin,* vol. i. p. 288; *Memoir of Mary Wollstonecraft.*

large lecture hall to seat 1200 persons, when the façade was widened by the same architect. The institution was closed on September 3, 1881. The building is now used as a Young Men's Christian Institute, partly for general education, and partly as a technical school, and the name is continued.

Pontack's, a celebrated French eating-house, in ABCHURCH LANE, CITY, where the annual dinners of the Royal Society were held till 1746, when the dinner was removed to the Devil Tavern at Temple Bar. It no longer exists.[1] Misson the French refugee, who wrote in 1697, says :—

> One word more about the cooks' shops, to give a full idea of the thing. Generally four spits, one over another, carry round each five or six pieces of butcher's meat (never anything else, if you would have a fowl or a pigeon you must bespeak it), beef, mutton, veal, pork, and lamb; you have what quantity you please cut off, fat, lean, much or little done; with this a little salt and mustard upon the side of a plate, a bottle of beer, and a roll—and there is your whole feast. Those who would dine at one or two guineas per head are handsomely accommodated at our famous Pontack's; rarely and difficultly elsewhere.—Misson, *Travels,* p. 146.

Pontack, who was somewhat of a character,—well read, according to Evelyn, in philosophy, but chiefly the rabbins, exceedingly addicted to cabalistic fancies, and "an eternal babbler,"—set up as his sign a portrait of his father, the President of Bordeaux. Pontack's portrait is introduced in Plate III. of the *Rake's Progress* as having been put up in the place of Julius Cæsar's !

> Near this Exchange [the Royal Exchange] are two very good French Eating-Houses, the one at the sign of Pontack, a President of the Parliament of Bourdeaux, from whose name the best French Clarets are called so, and where you may bespeak a dinner, from four or five shillings a head to a guinea, or what sum you please; the other is Kivat's, where there is a constant ordinary, as abroad, for all comers, without distinction, and at a very reasonable price.—Macky, *A Journey through England,* 8vo. 1722, vol. i. p. 175.

> *July* 13, 1683.—I had this day much discourse with Monsieur Pontaq, son to the famous and wise prime President of Bordeaux. This gentleman was owner of that excellent vignoble of Pontaq and Obrien, from whence come the choicest of our Bordeaux wines; and I think I may truly say of him, what was not so truly said of St. Paul, that much learning had made him mad. . . . He spake all languages, was very rich, had a handsome person, and was well bred; about 45 years of age.

> *November* 30, 1693.—Much importuned to take the office of President of the Royal Society, but I again declined it. Sir Robert Southwell was continued. We all dined at Pontac's, as usual.—*Evelyn.*

> *May* 3, 1699.—I come to wait upon you with a request that you would meet Sir Robert Southwell, Sir Christopher Wren, and other friends, at Pontac's to-day at dinner, to make an Act of Council at Gresham College.—*Bentley to Evelyn.*

The object was "to move the King" to purchase Bishop Stillingfleet's library for the Royal Society.

> What wretch would nibble on a hanging shelf,
> When at Pontack's he may regale himself?
> *The Hind and Panther Transvers'd.*

---

[1] Advertisement in *London Gazette,* 1670, and *Daily Courant,* February 3, 1722.

> Drawers must be trusted, through whose hands convey'd
> You take the liquor, or you spoil the trade;
> For sure those honest fellows have no knack
> Of putting off stum'd Claret for Pontack.—*Ibid.*

Mrs. Witwoud. I know two several companies gone into the city, one to Pontack's, and t'other to the Rummer.—Southerne, *The Wives' Excuse*, 4to, 1692.

> They all agreed that his advice
> Was honest, wholesome, grave, and wise;
> But not one man would quit his vice;
> For after all his vain attacks
> They rose and dined well at *Pontack's*.
>
> Sir C. Sedley, *The Doctor and his Patients.*

August 16, 1711.—I was this day in the City, and dined at Pontack's with Stratford and two other merchants. Pontack told us, although his wine was so good, he sold it cheaper than others; he took but seven shillings a flask. Are not these pretty rates?—Swift, *Journal to Stella*, vol. ii. p. 323.

January 26, 1713.—'Tis odd that this very day [*see* Powis House] Lord Somers, Wharton, Somerset, Halifax, and the whole club of Whig Lords, dined at Pontac's in the City, as I received private notice, they have some damned design.—*Swift to Mrs. Dingley.*

Immediately after the South Sea smash we read:—

Advices from the Royal Exchange inform us that the Minute in the great Coffee Houses, of the Routs of the Brokers, are strangely altered of late; for instead of being gone to Pontack's, gone to Brand's, gone to Caveach's; they now run, gone to the Chop House, gone to the Grill House, etc. These advices add too that the Jews and late South Sea Directors have left off boiling their Westphalia hams in Champagne and Burgundy.—Mist's *Journal* of April 1, 1721.

Read, the mountebank, who has assurance enough to come to our table up stairs at Garraway's, swears he'll stake his coach and six horses, his two blacks, and as many silver trumpets, against a dinner at Pontack's.—*Dr. Radcliffe* (Radcliffe's *Life*, 12mo, 1724, p. 41).

Pontack's successor was a lady, and a fortunate one.

Thursday, January 15, 1736.—William Pepys, banker in Lombard Street, was married at St. Clement's Church in the Strand, to Mrs. Susannah Austin, who lately kept Pontack's, where with universal esteem she acquired a considerable fortune.—*Weekly Oracle*, quoted by Burn, p. 13.

On April 19, 1740, the Duke and Duchess of Portland, with Mrs. Pendarves and five other friends, sallied out at 10 A.M., in two hackney-coaches, for a day's sight-seeing in the City. They wound up with "a very good dinner at Pontack's."[1]

Pool (The) is that part of the Thames between London Bridge and Limehouse Point where colliers and other vessels lie at anchor. From London Bridge to King's Head Stairs, Rotherhithe, is called the *Upper Pool;* from King's Head Stairs to Cuckold's Point, opposite Limehouse, the *Lower Pool.* Stations are provided in the Pool for about 250 colliers, where they can unload into lighters. Navigation in the Pool is under strict regulations. The Pool (*la Pole*) was a recognised term for this part of the river as early as the 13th century. In the Articles of Ancient Usage, collected and promulgated in the reign of Edward I., it is ordered in the article against forestallers—

[1] Delany's *Autobiography and Correspondence*, vol. ii. p. 82.

That no merchant, denizen or stranger, whatever he may be, shall go to *the Pole*, or any other place in the Thames, to meet wines or other merchandise, or go on board of vessels to buy wines or other things, until such time as they shall have come to land, under pain of losing the article.—*Liber Albus*, p. 230; and see Riley's *Memorials*, p. 298.

Goldwire. The ship is safe in the Pool then.—Massinger, *The City Madam*.

Pope's Head Alley, a footway from Cornhill—opposite the south-west corner of the Royal Exchange—to Lombard Street, and so called from the Pope's Head Tavern, of which the earliest mention occurs in the particulars of a wager made in the fourth year of Edward IV. (1464), between an Alicant goldsmith and an English goldsmith; the Alicant stranger contending, "in the tavern called the Pope's Head, in Lombard Street, that Englishmen were not so cunning in workmanship of goldsmithry as Alicant strangers," and undertaking to make good his assertion by the superior work he would produce. The wager was decided in favour of the Englishman.[1]

The Pope's Head Tavern, with other houses adjoining, strongly built of stone, hath of old time been all in one, pertaining to some great estate, or rather to the King of this realm, as may be supposed both by the largeness thereof, and by the arms, to wit, three leopards, passant, gardant, which were the whole arms of England before the reign of Edward III., that quartered them with the arms of France, three fleur-de-lis. These arms of England, supported between two angels, are fair and largely graven in stone on the fore front towards the high street, over the door or stall of one great house lately for many years possessed by Mr. Philip Gunter. The Pope's Head tavern is on the back part thereof towards the south, as also one other house called the Stone House in Lombard Street. Some say this was King John's house, which might so be; for I find in a written copy of Matthew Paris' History, that in the year 1232, Henry III. sent Hubert de Burgh, Earl of Kent, to Cornehill in London, there to answer all matters objected against him, where he wisely acquitted himself. The Pope's Head tavern hath a footway through from Cornhill into Lombard Street.—*Stow* (1603), p. 75.

In the year 1615 Sir William Craven (the father of the first Earl Craven) left the Pope's Head to the Merchant Tailors' Company, for charitable purposes, and the rents of nine houses in the alley are still received by the Company. The tavern was in existence under the same name in 1756.[2]

Early in the 17th century Pope's Head Alley was noted for its booksellers' shops. *The History of the Two Maids of More-Clacke*, 1609, was "printed by N. O. for Thomas Archer, and is to be sold at his shop in *Pope's Head Pallace*," perhaps a part of the large edifice mentioned by Stow. The first edition of Speed's *Great Britain* (fol. 1611) was "sold by John Sudbury and George Humble, in Pope's Head Alley, at the sign of the White Horse." Sudbury and Humble were the first printsellers established in London. Ben Jonson, in his *Execration upon Vulcan*, recommends "the Captain Pamphlets horse and foot

> that sally
> Upon the Exchange still out of Pope's Head Alley,"

---

[1] Herbert's *Livery Companies*, vol. ii. p. 197.   [2] *Public Advertiser* of March 16, 1756.

to the wrath of the lame Lord of Fire. Some of these were political pamphlets. On February 15, 1624, Lord Keeper Lincoln writes to Secretary Conway :—

"The King is very sensible of the wicked libel. . . . The author might perhaps be detected by employing Mr. Bill to find out by the type where it was printed. All the copies met with must be suppressed." And Conway at once sends to the Recorder of London desiring him to "make search for a book [*The Supplication of the Scottish Ministers*] *in Pope's Head Alley."—Cal. State Pap.*, 1619-1623, p. 321 ; 1623-1625, p. 163.

Peacham, in his *Compleat Gentleman*, refers the print-collector, curious in the works of Golzius, to Pope's Head Alley, where "his prints are commonly to be had."

I am old Gregory Christmas, and though I come out of Pope's Head Alley as good a Protestant as any in my parish.—Ben Jonson, *Masque of Christmas.*

Gresham. Let's step to the Pope's Head,
We shall be dropping dry if we stay here.
Heywood, *If You Know not Me.*

November 21, 1660.—I to Pope's Head and bought me an aggate-hafted knife, which cost me 5s.—*Pepys.*

February 4, 1662.—Sir W. Pen and I and my wife in his coach to Moore Fields, where we walked a great while . . . and after our walk, we went to Pope's Head, and eat cakes and other fine things.—*Pepys.*

June 20, 1662.—To Pope's Head Alley, and there bought me a pair of tweezers cost me 14s., the first thing like a bawble I have bought a good while.—*Pepys.*

July 28, 1666.—To the Pope's Head, where my Lord Brouncker and his mistress dined, and Commissioner Pett, Dr. Charleton and myself were entertained with a venison pasty by Sir W. Warren.—*Pepys.*

The Pope's Head was destroyed in the Great Fire, but rebuilt in a more costly manner.

January 18, 1668-1669.—To the Pope's Head Tavern, there to see the fine painted room which Rogerson told me of, of his doing ; but I do not like it all, though it be good for such a public room.—*Pepys.*

Before the Great Fire of 1666 Pope's Head Alley possessed a good trade for toys and turners' wares.[1] In Strype's time (thirty years later) it was chiefly inhabited by cutlers.[2]

I cannot but consider that Athens in the time of Pericles . . . held nothing that equalled the Royal or New Exchange, or Pope's Head Alley, for curiosities and toyshops.—Dr. King's *Third Letter to Lister.*

In the Pope's Head Tavern, in Cornhill, April 14, 1718, Quin, the actor, killed in self-defence his fellow comedian, Bowen. Bowen, a clever but hot-headed Irishman, was jealous of Quin's reputation, and in a moment of great anger sent for Quin to the Pope's Head Tavern, when, as soon as he had entered the room, he placed his back against the door, drew his sword, and bade Quin draw his. Quin, having mildly remonstrated to no purpose, drew in his own defence, and endeavoured to disarm his antagonist. Bowen received a wound, of which he died in three days, having acknowledged his folly and madness, when the loss of blood had reduced him to reason. Quin was tried and acquitted.

[1] *Strype*, B. ii. p. 153. [2] *Ibid.*, B. ii. p. 149.

In 1771 the New Lloyds fixed their place of meeting in Pope's Head Alley, and there they remained until March 1774, when they moved into their new rooms in the Royal Exchange. [*See* Lloyd's Subscription Rooms.]

The Pope's Head, Cornhill, was not the only house with that sign. There was a Pope's Head Tavern in Chancery Lane; and Edmund Burke, about 1756, when he met Yuseph Emin in distress in Hyde Park, gave him the only half-guinea he possessed, "took him home to his apartments *at the Pope's Head*, a bookseller's near the Temple."[1]

Poplar, a parish in Middlesex so called, originally a hamlet of Stepney, from whence it was separated in 1817, and called by the name of All Saints' Poplar. With the growth of the manufacturing industry of the district the population largely increased (in 1881 there were 55,120 inhabitants in the parish), and the district parishes of Christ Church, St. Matthias, St. Mary, St. Saviour, and St. Stephen have been formed. All Saints', the mother church, was erected from the designs of Charles Hollis and consecrated by the Bishop of London, July 3, 1823. It is a substantial stone edifice, and has a well-proportioned spire 161 feet high. The parish includes the hamlet of Blackwall, the Isle of Dogs, the East and West India and Millwall Docks, the Trinity House stores and lighthouse works, several shipbuilding yards and various large manufacturing establishments. There is a good Town Hall, Sailors' Home, Hospital, Baths, Wash-houses, stations on the North London and on the London and Blackwall Railway, and a statue of Richard Green, the shipbuilder of Blackwall Yard, and a great benefactor to the district. Here were the East India Almshouses and Chapel. In this Chapel George Steevens, the Shakespeare commentator, son of George Steevens of Poplar, mariner, was baptized on May 19, 1736, and was buried in it, January 1800. There is a fine bas-relief to his memory, by Flaxman, in the north aisle. The inscription is by Hayley. Here also were buried Robert Ainsworth (d. 1743), compiler of the Latin Dictionary which bears his name; and Dr. Gloster Ridley (d. 1774), author of the *Life of Bishop Ridley*, and for many years chaplain of Poplar Chapel. In 1866 the ecclesiastical district of St. Matthias was formed, and the East India Company's Chapel (built in 1654) was made the district church. In 1875 the church was enlarged and a chancel added to it. The chapel, cemetery and grounds of the East India Almshouses have been converted into a Public Recreation Ground.

Popler, or Poplar, is so called from the multitude of Poplar Trees (which love a moist soil) growing there in former times. And there be yet [1720] remaining, in that part of the hamlet which bordereth upon Limehouse, many old bodies of large Poplars standing, as testimonials of the truth of that etymology.—Dr. Josiah Woodward, in *Stryp* (*Circuit Walk*, p. 102).

---

[1] Prior's *Life of Burke*, ed. 1854, p. 43.

Poppin's Court, FLEET STREET, the first thoroughfare (under an archway) on the north side from Ludgate Circus. It is called *Poppin's Alley* in Hatton, 1788, but in Strype's Map, 1720, it figures as *Popinjay Court;* Dodsley, 1761, mentions a Cockpit Alley leading out of it, and the turning next to it is still called Racket Court. It appears to have been a neighbourhood devoted to manly sports; but recently a restaurant called "The Popinjay" has been built at the corner of the court, and a legend inscribed on the front which asserts that on the site stood the inn of a religious fraternity whose crest was the popinjay. The north end of Poppin's Court was cut off in 1870 in forming the new street from Holborn Circus to Ludgate Circus.

Porridge Island, a paved alley or footway, near the church of St. Martin's-in-the-Fields, destroyed in 1829, when the great rookery (of which Bedfordbury was till lately a sample) was removed from about the Strand and St. Martin's Lane. [*See* Bermudas.] It was filled with cooks' shops, and was a cant name.

<small>The fine gentleman, whose lodgings no one is acquainted with; whose dinner is served up under cover of a pewter plate, from the Cook's shop in Porridge Island; and whose annuity of a hundred pounds is made to supply a laced suit every year, and a chair every evening to a rout; returns to his bed-room on foot, and goes shivering and supperless to rest, for the pleasure of appearing among people of equal importance with the Quality of Brentford.—*The World,* Thursday, November 29, 1753.</small>

In Foote's comedy of *Taste* (1752), when Puff the auctioneer and Carmine the painter quarrel, the former exclaims, "Genius! Here's a dog! Pray how high did your genius soar? To the daubing diabolical Angels for alehouses, Dogs with chains for tanners' yards, *Rounds of Beef and Roasted Pigs for Porridge Island?*" In the Memoirs of Thomas Holcroft is an amusing account of a club called the Cameronian, which he and Shield the composer set up at a beef shop "at the corner of a little bye-court called Porridge Island."

Porridge Pot Row, OLD STREET, now ANCHOR YARD, on the north side, a few yards west of St. Luke's Church. Elmes notes it as called by the former name in 1831. Dodsley has an entry of "Porridge Pot Alley, Aldersgate Street," in 1761.

Port of London, a term frequently used very vaguely.

<small>What is legally termed the Port of London extends six-and-a-half miles below London Bridge to Bugsby's Hole beyond Blackwall; though the actual Port, consisting of the Upper, Middle, and Lower Pools, does not reach beyond Limehouse. —J. R. M'Culloch, *Dict. of Commerce,* 1851.</small>

This is the usual but scarcely the legal acceptation of the term, and is manifestly unsuitable even for mercantile purposes, as it would shut out the East India and the Albert and Victoria Docks. The strictly legal limits are much more extensive. There having been frequent disputes as to the limits of the Port an Act was passed, 13 and 14 Charles II., c. 11, for appointing Commissioners with powers to fix the limits of the Port and to make arrangements respecting quays and landing-places. The Commissioners made their Report, May 24, 1665, and in it—

> To prevent all further differences and disputes touching the extent and limits of the Port of London . . . the said Port is declared to extend and to be accounted from the promontory or point called the North Foreland in the Isle of Thanet, and from thence by a supposed right line from the opposite promontory or point called the Nase, beyond the Gun-fleet upon the coast of Essex, and continued westward, through the river Thames, and the several rivers, channels, streams, and rivers falling into it, to London Bridge.

In like manner a Commission appointed in 1819, in a Return made to the Court of Exchequer, June 30, 1819, setting out "the Limits of the Port of London," declare that eastward "The Port of London shall commence at the distance of four miles from the North Foreland Lighthouse," and on the opposite shore at a distance of three miles from the Naze Tower, and be continued "westwardly to highwater mark throughout the river Thames, and the several channels, streams, and rivers falling into it, to London Bridge."

For certain port dues "the Port of London terminates near Gravesend, at a spot called the Bound, or by corruption the Round, Tree, but this having been destroyed by time and accidents, a stone has been erected in its place."[1]

In *Reports of Committees of the House of Commons*, vol. xiv. (1803), is a full history of the Port of London.

Portland Chapel. [*See* St. Paul's, Portland Place.]

Portland Club, No. 1 STRATFORD PLACE, "the Whist Club *par éminence* since the dissolution of Graham's."[2] Members limited to 250 in number; election by ballot, one black ball in ten excludes; entrance fee, 20 guineas; annual subscription, 7 guineas. Play at whist not to exceed £1 points.

Portland Market. [*See* Oxford Market.]

Portland Place, REGENT'S PARK, a thoroughfare 125 feet wide and 600 feet long. It was designed by the brothers Adam, circ. 1778, and so named after the then Duke of Portland, the ground landlord. The Adams only built the portion of the place from Devonshire Street to Duchess Street. The great width was owing to a clause in Lord Foley's lease, which precluded the Duke of Portland from erecting any buildings to intercept the view from Foley House [which see]. The original house stood on the site of the Langham Hotel. No. 8 is now styled Foley House, but this is a modern name. When first built Portland Place was in the highest fashion.

[1] Cruden's *Hist. of Gravesend* and *Port of London*, p. 37.
[2] Hayward's *Select Essays*, vol. ii. p. 106.

> Then comes that good old character, a Wife,
> With all the dear distracting cares of life;
> A thousand cards a day at doors to leave,
> And in return a thousand cards receive;
> Rouge high, play deep, to lead the ton aspire,
> With nightly blaze set PORTLAND PLACE on fire.
>
> Sam. Rogers, *Verses spoken by Mrs. Siddons*, April 27, 1795.

Although less fashionably inhabited than when first built, Portland Place still numbers among its occupants peers, baronets, judges and privy councillors. The bronze statue of the Duke of Kent, the father of Queen Victoria, in Park Crescent, at the north end of Portland Place, was designed and cast by Gahagan. Park Crescent was called, in 1816, by Nash the architect, "the key to Marylebone Park."[1]

Eminent Inhabitants.—General Sir Henry Clinton. In 1788 his daughter eloped from this street in a hackney-coach with Mr. Dawkins, who eluded pursuit by posting half a dozen other hackney-coaches at the corners of the streets leading into Portland Place, with directions to drive off as rapidly as possible, each in a different direction, directly that started in which he and the lady were.[2] Horace Walpole wrote to Pennant from No. 5 Portland Place. At No. 25 Sir Alan Gardner was living in 1796 and 1811. James Monroe, when American Ambassador (1807), lived at No. 23. Talleyrand lived at No. 51. John Holroyd Lord Sheffield, the friend of Gibbon, and editor of his *Miscellaneous Writings*, died at his house, No. 20, May 30, 1821. Sir Humphry Davy was married, April 11, 1812, to Mrs. Apreece. The ceremony was performed at her mother's house in Portland Place by the Bishop of Carlisle. At No. 63, the house of Sir Ralph Milbanke, Lord Byron *made love* to his future wife, Miss Milbanke. At No. 2, the house of Henry Browne, F.R.S. (it is situated 51° 31' 8".4 N. Lat.), were made the original and important experiments of Captain Kater, for determining the length of the seconds pendulum, and somewhat later Sabine's elaborate observations for determining the oscillation of the pendulum in different latitudes—both sets of experiments being made with Mr. Browne's instruments and with his assistance.[3] Lord Radstock, one of the most distinguished admirals in the Great War, resided for many years in No. 10, and there died, August 20, 1825. Mark Wilks at No. 9. Lord Chief Justice Denman at No. 38. Charles Theophilus, first and last Lord Metcalfe, passed his boyhood in No. 49, the house of his father, the East India Director.

Portland Street (Great), OXFORD STREET, is now the name of the whole line of road between Oxford Street and the Euston Road, east of and parallel to Portland Place, but was originally confined to the portion between Margaret Street and Mortimer Street. South of the former it was John Street, and north of the latter Portland Road.

---

[1] *Second Report of Woods and Forests*, p. 113.
[2] There is a clever account of the elopement in the *Buckland Correspondence*, vol. i. p. 467.
[3] *Philosophical Trans.*, 1818, 1821.

This last name is preserved in the Portland Road Station of the Metropolitan Railway at the corner of the Euston Road.

Eminent Inhabitants.—William Guthrie, author of Guthrie's *Grammar*, etc., died here, March 9, 1770. Richard Wilson, the landscape painter, "at the corner of Foley Place."[1] Joseph Wilton, R.A., sculptor, "occupied the large house, Foley Place, at the south-east corner of Great Portland Street."[2] William Seward, author of Seward's *Anecdotes*, lived at No. 40.[3] James Boswell, the biographer of Johnson, died in 1795 at No. 47.[4] Carl Maria von Weber, composer of "Der Freischutz," died in Sir George Smart's house, No. 91 (now 103), June 5, 1826. No. 65 was the residence of John Jones, the engraver of the portraits of Charles James Fox, and many other fine works of Reynolds and of Romney; and father of the late Richard Jones, R.A. Sir David Wilkie was living at No. 84 in 1808-1809. William Collins, R.A., at No. 118 in 1810. Leigh Hunt at No. 35 in 1812. Joshua Brookes, the great surgeon, died at his house in Great Portland Street, January 30, 1833. On the west side (No. 131, etc.) is the Jewish *Central Synagogue*, a spacious building of Portland and red Mansfield stone, Oriental in style, with a tall campanile, erected from the designs of Mr. N. S. Joseph, and consecrated with great solemnity by Dr. Adler, the Chief Rabbi, April 7, 1870. The interior, which is very lofty, and fitted up in a rich and costly manner, is very striking.

Portman Square, between Orchard Street, Oxford Street, and Baker Street, was so called after William Henry Portman, Esq., of Orchard-Portman, in Somersetshire (d. 1796), the proprietor of an estate in Marylebone, of about 270 acres, formerly the property of the Knights of St. John of Jerusalem in England, and described in a lease granted by the last prior of the knights of St. John as "Great Gibbet Field [*see* Tyburn], Little Gibbet Field, Hawkfield, and Brock Stand, Tassel Croft, Boy's Croft, and twenty acres Fursecroft, and two closes called Shepcott Haws, parcel of the manor of Lilestone [*see* Lisson Green], in the county of Middlesex." The present proprietor of the estate is Lord Portman.

Portman Square was begun about 1764, when the north side of the square was built; but it was twenty years before the whole was finished.—*Lysons*, vol. iii. p. 257.

In Espriella's Letters (1807) Southey describes this square as "on the outskirts of the town," and approached "on one side by a road, unlit, unpaved, and inaccessible by carriages." The house in the north-west angle of the square (properly No. 1 Upper Berkeley Street) was designed, 1760, by James "Athenian" Stuart for Mrs. Montagu, authoress of the *Essay on the Genius and Writings of Shakespeare*. Here she had her public breakfasts, her Blue-stocking parties; here, on May-day, she

---

[1] Wright's *Life of Wilson*, p. 5.
[2] Smith's *Nollekens*, vol. ii. p. 172.
[3] Nichols's *Lit. Anec.*, vol. ix. p. 467.
[4] Letter from Mrs. Ogborne, of Great Portland Street, to the late John Thomas Smith, preserved in Mr. Murray's *Johnson Collections*.

used to entertain the chimney-sweeps of London; and here she died, August 25, 1800.

November 12, 1781.—Mrs. Montagu is very busy furnishing her new house; part of her family is removed into it.—Mrs. Boscawen, *Delancy*, vol. vi. p. 65; and see p. 76.

When Summer comes the bells shall ring, and flowers and hawthorns blow,
The village lasses and the lads shall all a-Maying go:
Kind-hearted lady may thy soul in heaven a blessing reap,
Whose bounty at that season flows to cheer the Little Sweep.
W. L. Bowles, *Climbing Boys' Album*, p. 347.

No. 12 (since numbered 15), was the Duke of Hamilton's, and here were some of the finest of William Beckford's pictures, removed by the duke, who was his son-in-law, from the house in which Beckford died, at Bath. No. 26 was Lady Garvagh's, where was the famous Aldobrandini Madonna of Raphael, now in the National Gallery.

Portsmouth Street, LINCOLN'S INN FIELDS. The Black Jack public-house, No. 11 in this street, was a favourite house of Joe Miller. Joe died in 1738, and the first edition of the *Jests*, which have rendered his name famous, was published the following year, "price one shilling." The Black Jack was long distinguished as "The Jump," from Jack Sheppard having once jumped from one of its first-floor windows to escape the emissaries of Jonathan Wild. No. 14 is said to be the original of Dickens's *Old Curiosity Shop*, but there is not sufficient authority for this statement.

Portsoken, one of the twenty-six wards of London, deriving its name from the "soc" or "soke" (the liberty, or separate jurisdiction), without the "port" or gate called Aldgate. This ward is without the walls, but within the liberties of the City.

In the days of King Edgar there were thirteen Knights or Soldiers, well-beloved to the King and realm, for service by them done, which requested to have a certain portion of land on the east part of the city, left desolate and forsaken by the inhabitants, by reason of too much servitude. They besought the King to have this land, with the liberty of a guild, for ever. The King granted to their request, with conditions following: that is, that each of them should victoriously accomplish three combats, one above the ground, one under ground, and the third in the water; and after this, at a certain day in East Smithfield, they should run with spears against all comers; all which was gloriously performed, and the same day the King named it Knighten Guild.—*Stow*, p. 46.

The "knightenguild" was held by the heirs of the thirteen knights till the reign of Henry I., when (A.D. 1115) the men of the guild taking upon them the brotherhood and benefits of the newly established priory of the Holy Trinity, within Aldgate, assigned their "soke" to the prior, and offered, upon the altars of the church, the several charters of their guild. Henry I. confirmed the gift, and the prior was made an alderman of London: an honour continued to his successors till the Dissolution, when the church was surrendered and the site of the priory granted by Henry VIII. to Sir Thomas Audley, Lord Chancellor. [*See* Duke's Place.] After the Dissolution the inhabitants of *Knightenguild* or Portsoken elected an alderman of their own—a privilege they enjoy to this day.[1] The name survives (corruptly) in Nightingale Lane. The principal places in the ward are Aldgate, Houndsditch, Petticoat Lane (now Middlesex Street), and the Minories.

Portugal Row, LINCOLN'S INN FIELDS, the old name of the south side of the present Lincoln's Inn Fields; built 1657, by Sir William Cowper, Robert Henley, and James Cowper, and known as Portugal Row before the marriage of Charles II. to Catherine of Portugal. In 1668 it was inhabited by the following persons:—

The Lady Arden; Wm. Perpoint, Esq.; Sir Charles Waldegrave; The Lady Fitzharding; The Lady Diana Curton; Serjeant Maynard; The Lord Cardigan; Neale, Esq.; Mrs. Ann Heron; Deane, Esq.; The Lady Mordant; Richard Adams, Esq.; The Lady Carr; The Lady Wentworth; Mr. Attorney Montague; The Lady Coventry; Judge Weld; The Lady Davenant.[2]

Sir John Maynard, the celebrated lawyer, who was living here till his death in 1690, will long be remembered for his memorable reply to William III. Lord Cardigan was the father of the infamous Countess of Shrewsbury. Sir William Davenant had "lodgings" here, says Aubrey, and here he died, April 7, 1668. "I was at his funeral: he had a coffin of walnut tree: Sir John Denham said that it was the finest coffin he ever saw." The Lady Davenant was the widow of Sir William. Wilmot, Earl of Rochester (d. 1680), lived here. "If you write to me you must direct to Lincoln's-Inn-Fields, the house next to the Duke's Playhouse in Portugal Row; there lives your humble servant, ROCHESTER."[3] On the site of what is now a part of the Museum of the Royal College of Surgeons stood the Lincoln's Inn Fields Theatre.

> This landscape of the sea—(but, by the way,
> That's an expression which might hurt our play,
> If the severer critics were in town)—
> This prospect of the sea, cannot be shown :
> Therefore be pleased to think that you are all
> Behind the Row which men call Portugal.—Sir William Davenant,
> *Epilogue to the Playhouse to be Let; see* also Davenant's *Works*, p. 74.

Portugal Street, LINCOLN'S INN FIELDS—from Serle Street to Portsmouth Street—was so called when Portugal Row, or the south side of Lincoln's Inn Fields ceased to be known by that name. In Strype's time it was without a name. He proposed to call it Playhouse Street.[4] In the burying-ground immediately opposite, belonging to St. Clement's Danes [which see], Joe Miller ("Joe Miller's *Jests*") is buried (d. 1738). The site is occupied by King's College Hospital [which see]. Here also is the High Court of Justice in Bankruptcy. Here was till a few years back the Grange public-house, with its old picturesque inn yard.

[1] "These priors have sitten and ridden amongst the aldermen of London, in livery like unto them, saving that his habit was in shape of a spiritual person, as I myself have seen in my childhood."—*Stow*, p. 53.

[2] Rate-books of St. Clement's Danes.
[3] Wharton's *Works*.
[4] *Strype*, B. iv. p. 119.

Housekeeper. The poet has a special train behind him; though they look lean and empty, yet they seem very full of invention.
Player. Let him enter, and send his train to our House Inn the Grange.—Sir William Davenant, *The Playhouse to be Let.*

Portugal Street, the old name for part of PICCADILLY; so called after Catherine of Portugal, Queen of Charles II. Portugal Street is entered in the Rate-books of St. Martin's, for the first time, under the year 1664, when the north side extended as far as Air Street. The south side was built in 1665. In 1671 it extended as far as Sackville Street, and in 1686 to Dover Street, then but newly built.

Post Office (The), ST. MARTIN'S-LE-GRAND. Although now of such immense importance to our national welfare, the English Post Office cannot be traced back through more than about 300 years of our history. Before this time the King and the nobles sent their letters by private messengers or "nuncii," whilst the commonalty, travelling little, had small need of correspondence. The merchants of the Hanse Towns have the reputation of being the first to establish a regular European letter post; and in England, although Henry VIII. paid attention to the official post, the foreign post remained for some years in the hands of the foreigners who had established it. It was on the occasion of a dispute between them as to the electing of a postmaster that James I. stepped in and appointed a Postmaster of England for foreign parts, who was to have "the sole taking up, sending, and conveying of all packets and letters concerning our service or business to be despatched to foreign parts," others being forbidden to convey letters, etc.; and since that time the business of the Post Office has remained a Government monopoly. In the reign of James I. the total annual payment for the staff of the Post Office was only £255 : 5 : 10. In 1635 a proclamation was issued "for settling the letter office of England and Scotland," in which it is enacted that there shall be "a running post or two, to run night and day, between Edinburgh and Scotland and the City of London, to go thither and come back in six days." In 1644 Edmund Prideaux, Esq., M.P., first established a weekly conveyance of letters to all parts of the nation. An Act of Parliament passed in 1656 "to settle the postage of England, Scotland and Ireland," is the real foundation of our postal system. This Act orders the "erecting of one general post office and one officer stiled the Postmaster-General of England and Comptroller of the Post Office." This Act was re-enacted 12 Car. II., c. 35, and it has been called the Post Office Charter, remaining in full force until 1710. In 1663, when the carriage of letters had become a source of income, the revenues were settled on James, Duke of York, afterwards James II.

This Conveyance by post is done in so short a time by night as well as by day that every twenty-four hours the Post goes 120 miles and in five days an Answer of a Letter may be had from a place 300 miles distant from the writer.—Delaune, *Present State of London*, 1681, p. 346.

At that time there were mails to Kent and the Downs daily; over the whole of England and Scotland three times weekly; and to the Continent from twice to thrice weekly. In 1680 a "Penny Post" was established in London by Robert Murray, a clerk in the Excise, and William Dockwra, a sub-searcher in the Customs. Murray and Dockwra quarrelled and set up rival offices, but the name of the former is soon lost sight of. When the penny post was found to be profitable the Duke of York wished to take possession of it, and after a time the Post Office succeeded in their object. Dockwra was appointed Comptroller of the Penny Post, but was dismissed by the Lords of the Treasury for mismanagement in 1698. [*See* Penny Post.] In 1708 an attempt was made by a Mr. Povey to establish a half-penny post in opposition to the official penny post, but this enterprise, like Dockwra's, was suppressed by a lawsuit. The London penny post continued until 1801, when it was made a twopenny post.

Ralph Allen of Bath, the friend of Pope and Fielding, established a system of cross roads by which he obtained a large fortune. At his death in 1764 the "bye-posts" were transferred to the care of the Post Office authorities. John Palmer in 1784 succeeded in introducing special mail coaches for the conveyance of letters, thus materially accelerating the speed of conveyance over the older plan of transmission on horseback and in carts. But the rapid growth of the postal system dates from the introduction, by Sir Rowland Hill in 1840, of the uniform penny rate of postage. Before that time the rate had been so heavy as virtually to preclude the use of the post by the mass of the population. At the same time "franking," a privilege which had been very much abused, was abolished. The opposition to the introduction of penny postage and the abolition of franks was very great, and some idea of the abuse of the latter may be gained from the statements of one or two contemporaries.

I was thereby deprived of the privilege of franking as a member of the House of Commons and I now lose the privilege of franking as a peer; but I rejoice in the sacrifice for the general good, although the loss of consequence from ceasing to be able to frank a letter for a lady in travelling, or the waiter at an inn, gave great disgust to many members of both houses, Whig as well as Tory, and made some of them openly declare that there was no longer any use in being in Parliament.— Lord Campbell, *Autobiography*, vol. ii. p. 117.

Mr. Roebuck stated in the House of Commons, June 22, 1857, that "The Ambassadors' bag in past times had been sadly weighted. Coats, lace, boots and other articles were sent by it, even a pianoforte; and not only a pianoforte but a horse."

It was also stated before a House of Commons Committee that "one man had in the course of five months counterfeited 1200 dozen of franks of Members of Parliament, and that a regular trade of buying and selling franks had been actually established with several persons in the country."

The combination of the different nations of the world to form the International Postal Union, with a uniform postage rate of 2½d. (except for very distant places, when 5d. is sometimes charged), has also done much to stimulate the growth of correspondence and the use of the

Post Office. Since the introduction of penny postage in 1840 the number of letters passing through the Post Office has increased to so great an extent that in the year ending March 31, 1889, the estimated total of letters, post-cards, book packets, newspapers and parcels was 2,362,990,000, made up as follows: 1,558,100,000 letters (or an average of 41.5 letters to each person in the United Kingdom); 201,400,000 post-cards; 412,000,000 book packets and circulars; 151,900,000 newspapers; 39,590,000 parcels. The total number of money orders during the year was 9,563,725, representing an aggregate amount of £23,869,495. The number of postal orders was 40,282,321, of the total value of £16,112,079. There are now (1889) 37,783 receptacles of all sorts for letters, of which number 17,829 are Post Offices.

The deposits in the Savings Bank Department, a branch added to the Post Office in 1860, numbered 7,540,625, and amounted to £19,052,226; the withdrawals were 2,633,808 in number, amounting to £15,802,735. The accounts remaining open on December 31, 1888, were 4,220,297; the amount standing to their credit being £58,556,394 (including interest). During the year 580 Life Insurances, amounting to £34,819, were granted, as well as 995 Immediate Annuities and 138 Deferred Annuities, of the annual values of £23,404 and £2719 respectively. The total number of Life Insurances in existence on December 31, 1888, was 6210, together with 10,358 Immediate and 1015 Deferred Annuities. The taking over the telegraphs in 1870, with the simultaneous adoption of a uniform shilling rate for the United Kingdom, largely increased the business of the Post Office; and the reduction to sixpence in 1885 still further increased it. Excluding foreign, press and free telegrams, the returns show a total of 46,816,711 inland telegrams for the year 1888-1889, the average value of which was 7.92d.

The total number of officers on the permanent establishment of the department is about 58,396; of this number 4054 are women.

With its large increase of business the Post Office has necessarily had to increase its accommodation. Originally in Cloak Lane, Dowgate Hill, the General Post Office was moved to the Black Swan, Bishopsgate, which suffered destruction in the Fire of London in 1666. The office was then transferred to Brydges Street, Covent Garden, and thence in 1690 to Lombard Street. The work to be done still increasing beyond the capacity of the building, it was decided early in this century to erect one expressly suited for a General Post Office. The site chosen was that formerly covered by the ancient monastery of St. Martin's-le-Grand. The edifice, completed after the designs of Sir Robert Smirke, is in the Ionic style, with a lofty central portico, surmounted by a pediment. This building still retains its position as the Central Office, but the large increase of business has necessitated the erection of several large auxiliary ones. The *New Post Office*, designed by Mr. J. Williams, is opposite and equal in extent to the older General Post Office. Its two fronts in St. Martin's-le-Grand and Bath Street are 286 feet long, its two ends in Newgate Street and Angel Street 146 feet, and its height from the pavement 84 feet. The building is of Portland stone on a granite basement; the two lower storeys are rusticated, with engaged shafts of the Tuscan order, the two upper Roman Corinthian. A large clearance of the whole of the west side of St. Martin's-le-Grand has been made, and new buildings for the accommodation of the Post Office are now in course of erection (1890) on this site.

Potters' Hithe. [*See* Queenhithe.]

Poulters' Company. This Company, incorporated in the reign of Henry VII., January 23, 1504, has a Master, an Upper and a Renter Warden, a Court of Assistants and a Livery. The hall of this Company is said to have been in Leadenhall Market, but was destroyed in the Fire of London, and their business is now transacted at the Guildhall. The Poulters' Company ranks thirty-fourth amongst the City Livery Companies.

Poultry. A Street connecting CHEAPSIDE and CORNHILL, and long famous for its compter. [*See* Poultry Compter.]

West from this church have ye Scalding Alley, of old time called Scalding House, or Scalding Wike, because that ground for the most part was then employed by Poulterers, that dwelt in the high street from the Stocks Market to the great Conduit. Their poultry, which they sold at their stalls, were scalded there. The street doth yet bear the name of the Poultry, and the poulterers are but lately departed from thence into other streets, as into Grasse [Gracechurch] Street, and the ends of St. Nicholas flesh shambles [Newgate Market].—*Stow*, p. 71.

In the 16th and first half of the 17th century the Poultry was famous for its taverns. The Rose Tavern was noted for its wines, and down to the days of Ned Ward and the *London Spy* maintained its reputation. The Three Cranes is often referred to as a well-known house in the pamphlets and light literature of the day. The King's Head Tavern, No. 25, was kept in Charles II.'s time by William King. His wife, happening to be in labour on the day of the King's restoration, was anxious to see the returning monarch, and Charles, in passing through the Poultry, was told of her inclination, and stopped at the tavern to salute her.[1] The letter which in 1619 "made a stir in Lancashire," respecting an apparition at Newmarket, "which the King went to see and has kept his bed ever since," was written by one Matt. Mason from "the Falchion, in Poultry." Mr. Cowden Clarke relates that in 1817, when Keats was about to publish his first little volume he lodged on "the second floor of a house in the Poultry, at the corner of the court leading to the Queen's Arms Tavern, that corner nearest to Bow Church;" but this must have been the Queen's Head in Cheapside. Few of the old taverns appear to have been rebuilt after the Great Fire. There are now none in the Poultry.

[1] Nichols's *Lit. Anec.*, vol. i. p. 3.

No. 22 Poultry was Dilly the bookseller's. Here, May 15, 1776, Dr. Johnson met Wilkes at dinner, by a manœuvre of Boswell's, of which Burke declared "that there was nothing equal to it in the whole history of the *Corps Diplomatique.*" Here Boswell's *Life of Johnson* was first published. Dilly sold his business to Mawman, a name well remembered in the book-trade. Dr. Parr took Landor to see him. In after days, however, Mawman declined to publish the *Imaginary Conversations.* No. 31 was the shop of Vernor and Hood, booksellers. Hood of this firm was father of Thomas Hood ("Comic Annual," "Song of the Shirt") who was born here in 1798. The church of *St. Mildred's-in-the-Poultry* stood on the north side, where is now the Gresham Life Assurance Office. By the removal of St. Mildred's Church, the clearing away of most of the old houses on both sides of the way, and the erection in their places of large blocks of offices and shops of considerable architectural pretensions, and the general widening of the thoroughfare, the Poultry has since 1850 been entirely changed in character and aspect.

On a portion of the site of the Poultry Compter was built in 1819 the Poultry Chapel, for Congregationalists, which under the pastoral care of Dr. Clayton long flourished. In 1872, when the "Poultry Improvements" were in full progress, it was decided to remove to another locality, and a larger chapel—the City Temple—was built for the congregation on the Holborn Viaduct. The site of the Poultry Chapel (7440 square feet) was sold by auction for £50,200.

Poultry Compter, WOOD STREET, a sheriff's prison, which stood a little to the east of Grocers' Hall Court; Chapel Place led directly to it.[1] [*See* Giltspur Street Compter and Compter in Southwark.] It was the only prison in London with a ward set apart for Jews (probably due to its proximity to the Jewry), and was the only prison left unattacked in the riots of 1780. It was a brick building of fifteen wards—the king's, the prince's, the upper, middle and women's wards, and the Jews' ward. There was a chapel, and the leads were used for exercise grounds.

John Bradford, one of the most illustrious of the Marian martyrs, was imprisoned here from January 30 to June 30, 1550. Here he was persecuted with "conferences," but as nothing could stir his fortitude, "he was suddenly conveyed out of the Compter, in the night season to Newgate; and from thence he was carried to Smithfield."[2] Dekker and Boyse, two unfortunate sons of song, were long inhabitants of the Poultry Compter. Here died Lamb, the conjuror (commonly called Dr. Lamb), of the injuries he had received from the mob, who pelted him (June 13, 1628) from Moorgate to the Windmill in the Old Jewry, where he was felled to the ground with a stone, and was thence carried to the Poultry Compter, where he died the same night. The rabble believed that the doctor dealt with the devil, and assisted the

[1] The site is carefully marked in Strype's Map of Cheap Ward.
[2] *All the Examinacions of the Constante Martir of God, M. John Bradforde,* 1561.

Duke of Buckingham in misleading the King. The City had to pay heavily for their negligence in not protecting the unfortunate man. The last slave imprisoned in England was confined (1772) in the Poultry Compter. This was Somerset, a negro, the particulars of whose case excited Sharpe and Clarkson in their useful and successful labour in the cause of negro emancipation.

> Some four houses west from this parish of St. Mildred is a prison house pertaining to one of the sheriffs of London, and is called the Compter in the Poultry. This hath been there kept and continued time out of mind, for I have not read of the original thereof.—*Stow*, p. 99.
>
> *First Officer.* Nay, we have been scholars, I can tell you,—we could not have been knaves so soon else; for as in that notable city called London, stand two most famous universities, Poultry and Wood Street, where some are of twenty years' standing, and have took all their degrees, from the Master's side, down to the Mistress's side, the Hole, so in like manner, etc.—*The Phœnix*, by T. Middleton, 4to, 1607.

Prisoners committed by the Lord Mayor were sent to the Poultry; prisoners committed by the sitting aldermen to Giltspur Street prison. The prisoners were removed from the Poultry Compter to White Cross Street prison shortly after the latter was completed.

Powis House, KNIGHTSBRIDGE, the residence of Amelia Sophia de Walmoden, the mistress of George II., who was created Countess of Yarmouth *for life.* She died 1765.

Powis House, at the north-west angle of *Lincoln's Inn Fields* and the corner of Great Queen Street; the town house of the noble family of Herbert. It was built in 1686 by William Herbert, Viscount Montgomery and Marquis of Powis, on the site of a former house burnt to the ground, October 26, 1684, "the family hardly saving themselves from being burnt." Among the Private Acts is, 1 James II., c. 3, "An Act for rebuilding the Earl of Powis' House in Lincoln's Inn Fields, lately demolished by fire." The new house (now No. 67) was designed by Captain William Winde, architect.

> Then they went to the Lord Powis' great house in Lincoln's Inn Fields, wherein was a guard, and a bill upon the door—*This house is appointed for the Lord Delamere's quarters*, and some of the company crying "*Let it alone, the Lord Powis was against the Bishops going to the Tower*," they offered no violence to it.—*English Courant*, December 1688.

Lord Powis forfeited his house to the Crown for his adherence to James II. It was inhabited for a time by the great Lord Somers; and, in February 1696-1697, was ordered to remain in the possession of the Lord Chancellor during his custody of the Great Seal. It was subsequently sold to Holles, Duke of Newcastle (d. 1711), when it received the name of *Newcastle House.* [*See* Newcastle House.]

Powis House, at the north-west end of Great Ormond Street, stood back from the street, on the site of the present *Powis Place.* It was built in the latter part of the reign of William III. by William Herbert, Marquis of Powis, son of the first Marquis of Powis, who was outlawed for his adherence to James II., and was burnt down January 26, 1713, when in the occupation of the Duc d'Aumont, ambassador from Louis XIV.

After dinner at Lord Treasurer's, the French Ambassador, Duke d'Aumont, sent Lord Treasurer word that his house was burnt to the ground. It took fire in the upper rooms, while he was at dinner with Monteleon, the Spanish Ambassador, and other persons; and soon after Lord Bolingbroke came to us with the same story. We are full of speculations upon it, but I believe it was the carelessness of his rascally French servants.—Swift to Mrs. Dingley, January 26, 1713.

The house was insured, but the French King's dignity would not permit him, it is said, to suffer a Fire-office to pay for the neglect of the domestics of his representative.[1] The front of the new house which the King erected was of stone, with eight lofty Corinthian pilasters, and surmounted on the coping by urns and statues. Over the street door was a phœnix; the ornament above the capitals of the pilasters, was the Gallic cock. The architect was Colin Campbell. The staircase was painted by Giacomo Amiconi, a Venetian painter, of some reputation in this country. He chose the story of Holofernes, and painted the personages of his story in Roman dresses. On the top was a great reservoir, used as a fish-pond and a resource against fire. Philip Yorke, Earl of Hardwicke, came to reside here in 1737, when he was appointed Lord Chancellor, and continued to occupy it during the whole time that he held the seals. In 1764-1783 it was in the occupation of the Spanish Ambassador.[2] It was taken down a few years later, and is still preserved to us in a large engraving published by Thomas Bowles (1714).

June 8, 1764.—The house of Bedford came to town last Friday, I supped with them that night at the Spanish Ambassador's, who has made Powis House magnificent.—Walpole to Lord Hertford, vol. iv. p. 247.

Nos. 50, 51, and 52 were built 1777 on part of the site.

Powis Place, GREAT ORMOND STREET. [*See* Powis House, Great Ormond Street.] John Leech was resident at No. 9 about 1848.

Pratt Place, now PRATT STREET, CAMDEN TOWN. Dr. Wolcot (Peter Pindar) lodged in the first floor of a house rented by a Mr. and Mrs. Knight in this street.

Prerogative Will Office or Court was in KNIGHTRIDER STREET, DOCTORS' COMMONS. This was the court wherein all wills were proved and all administrations granted that belonged to the Archbishop of Canterbury by his prerogative. It was removed in 1874 to Somerset House. [*See* Will Office.]

Prescot Street, GOODMAN'S FIELDS, between Leman Street and Mansell Street, is divided into "Great" and "Little." In Little Prescot Street is one of the oldest dissenting meeting-houses in London.

[1] *Noorthouck*, p. 305; *Europ. Mag.* for June 1804, p. 429. [2] *Noorthouck*, p. 746.

Prescot Street, a spacious and regular built street on the south side of the Tenter Ground in Goodman's Fields. Instead of Signs the Houses here are distinguished by numbers, as the staircases in the Inns of Court and Chancery.—*Hatton*, 1708, p. 65.

Sir Cloudesley Shovel, the old rough admiral of Queen Anne's reign, resided in this street before he removed to Soho Square; and here (August 8, 1758) the first Magdalen Hospital was opened with eight inmates, all that the Institution could then shelter. [*See* Goodman's Fields.] In Great Prescot Street are the Whitechapel County Court, a Roman Catholic Church, and the convent of St. Mary.

Primrose Hill, a hillock on the north side of the Regent's Park, from which it is divided by two roads and a canal. It belonged to the Provost and Fellows of Eton College, but has been secured by the Government and laid out as a public recreation ground. In the Register of the Stationers' Company, 1586-1587, is an entry of "A Sweete and Courtly Songe of the Flowers that grow on Prymrose Hill." In a dry ditch at the foot of this hill, on the south side, about two fields distant from the White House (Chalk Farm), the body of Sir Edmond Berry Godfrey was found on Thursday October 17, 1678. Primrose Hill was long familiarly known as Green Berry Hill, and by a curious coincidence three of the supposed murderers were named respectively Green, Berry, and Hill. Godfrey's body was removed to the White House and afterwards interred in the churchyard of St. Martin's-in-the-Fields. There is a contemporary medal of Sir Edmond, representing him, on the obverse, walking with a broken neck and a sword in his body, and on the reverse, St. Denis bearing his head in his hand, with this inscription:—

> Godfrey walks up hill after he was dead,
> Denis walks down hill carrying his head.

There is a good view on a fine day of the west end of London from this hill, though of late circumscribed by the progress of buildings. Whilst yet in the fields Primrose Hill (generally the Chalk Farm side) was often chosen for duels. Here occurred (1806) the harmless meeting between Tom Moore and Jeffrey, and here, on the night of February 16, 1821, was fought the duel between John Scott of the *London Magazine* and Mr. Christie, in which the former was killed.

There's no news that you'd care to hear of, except that the Prince is to have a villa upon Primrose Hill, connected by a fine street with Carlton House, and is so pleased with this magnificent plan that he has been heard to say, "It will quite eclipse Napoleon."—Thomas Moore, October 24, 1811 (*Memoirs*, vol. viii. p. 97).

It is needless to say that Regent Street was not carried quite so far north, and Napoleon was eclipsed in quite another fashion.

Prince's Court, GEORGE STREET, WESTMINSTER. John Wilkes had a house close to Storey's Gate, the last house on the north side, the windows looking into the park. On September 18, 1771, *Junius* wrote a long letter to Wilkes, in which he says, "My Second Letter is of public import, and must not be suppressed. I did mean that it should be buried in Prince's Court."

Prince's Hall, PICCADILLY, a large building on the south side of the street extending from the churchyard of St. James's, Piccadilly, to No. 189. It was erected in 1881 from the designs of Mr. E. R. Robson, architect, by a Limited Liability Company with a capital of £50,000, entitled the Piccadilly Art Galleries Company. There are three galleries occupied by the Royal Institute of Painters in Water-Colours and the Institute of Painters in Oil-Colours, and a hall let for concerts and entertainments. The elevation contains a series of recesses in which are placed busts of celebrated English water-colour painters. The lower part is occupied by shop fronts.

Prince's Square. [*See* Ratcliffe Highway.]

Prince's Street, BRIDGEWATER SQUARE. Edmund Halley, the astronomer, lived in this street.[1]

Prince's Street, CAVENDISH SQUARE, south-east corner to Oxford Street. Charles Lamb placed the birthplace of the immortal Elia in this street.

> Is the Parish Register nothing? Is the room in Princes Street, Cavendish Square, where we saw the light six and forty years ago, nothing?—Elia, *Postscript to the Chapter on Ears.*

Prince's Street, DRURY LANE. [*See* Drury Lane.]

> He [the first Earl of Clare, died 1637] likewise purchased one half of *Princes Street* by Drury Lane. And he caused to be routed those edificies called Lowche's Buildings, with the most part of Clement's Inn Lane, Blackmore Street by Drury Lane, and part of Clement's Inn Fields.—Gervase Holles in Collins's *Histor. Collections*, p. 85.

Pope's correspondent, Henry Cromwell, lived at "the Widow Hambleton's Coffee-house, in Prince's Street, near Drury Lane." Hence Pope speaks of "your old apartment in the Widow's Corner," and the couplet—

> To treat those nymphs like yours of Drury
> With—I protest—and I'll assure ye![2]

Prince's Street, HANOVER SQUARE, was built in the year 1719.[2] Here in 1833 died Sir John Malcolm, the historian of Persia and biographer of Lord Clive.

Prince's Street, WARDOUR STREET, was so called from the military garden of Henry, Prince of Wales, eldest son of King James I., which stood on part of Prince's Street and Gerard Street. [*See* Military Garden.] Princes Street extended from Coventry Street to Old Compton Street, where it joined Wardour Street; but in 1880 the name was abolished and the thoroughfare from Oxford Street to Coventry Street was named Wardour Street for its entire length. When all the speculations of the brilliant author of *Lacon* had failed, a fiat of bankruptcy was issued against him as the "Rev. Charles Caleb Colton, late of Prince's Street, Soho, Wine Merchant."

[1] Weld's *History of the Royal Society*, vol. I. p. 417. [2] Elwin's *Pope*, vol. vi. p. 64.

Prince of Wales Theatre, 21 TOTTENHAM STREET, Tottenham Court Road, was originally a concert room, then used for musical and miscellaneous entertainments and amateur theatrical performances. Converted into a theatre and named the Regency, it passed through many hands, and was at different times named the Fitzroy, the Royal, the West End, and the Queen's, but it was at length remodelled, and under the management of Mr. and Mrs. Bancroft became, as the Prince of Wales's, one of the most fashionable and highly patronised theatres in London. Early in 1880 Mr. and Mrs. Bancroft removed to the Haymarket Theatre, and the Tottenham Street Theatre remained empty for some years. It is now (1890) occupied by the Salvation Army. The name of Prince of Wales's Theatre has been given to what was previously the Prince's in Coventry Street.

Princess's Theatre, OXFORD Street, opposite the Pantheon, was built in 1830 as a bazaar. Forming a part of the Queen's Bazaar, as it was named, was a spacious concert room. The speculation was not successful, and in 1840 the building was remodelled by Mr. T. M. Nelson, architect for Mr. Hamlet, a well-known west-end goldsmith, and reopened in 1841 as the Princess's Theatre. Under Mr. Charles Kean's management the theatre attained celebrity for its artistic "mounting" and careful performance of the plays of Shakespeare. Later it became noted for the "realistic melodrama." In 1880 the building was almost reconstructed under the direction of Mr. C. J. Phipps, architect. The theatre itself now includes the great concert room at the back (of late the lecture hall of the Castle Street Co-operative Institute), and rendered more attractive to occupants of the dress-circle and stalls by the provision of luxurious lounge, refreshment and smoking rooms. The Oxford Street entrance has been enlarged and new entrances provided, and the working arrangements improved.

Printing House Square, BLACKFRIARS, so called from the printing office of the King's printers, formerly situated here. The first printer whose name has come down to us is John Bill, who, "at the King's Printing House in Black Friers," printed the proclamations of the reign of Charles II., and the first *London Gazette*, established in that reign. Charles Eyre and William Strahan were the last King's printers who resided here, and in February 1770[1] the King's Printing House was removed to New Street, near Gough Square, in Fleet Street, where it now is. The place still continues to deserve its name of Printing House Square, for here every day in the week (Sunday excepted) *The Times* newspaper is printed and published, and from hence distributed over the whole civilised world. This celebrated paper, finding daily employment on the premises for between 200 and 300 people, was established in 1788—the first number, price 3d., appearing on the 1st of January in that year as the successor to the *Universal Register*. In that number appeared an amusing explanation of the origin of the new title:—

[1] *London Gazette*, February 17, 1770.

The *Universal Register* from the day of its first appearance to the day of its confirmation, has like Tristram, suffered from unusual casualties, both laughable and serious, arising from its name, which on its introduction was immediately curtailed of its fair proportions by all who called for it—the word *Universal* being universally omitted, and the word *Register* being only retained. "Boy, bring me a Register." The waiter answers "Sir, we have not a Library; but you may see it at the New Exchange Coffee-house." "Then I'll see it there," answers the disappointed politician, and he goes to the New Exchange, and calls for *the Register*; upon which the waiter tells him that he cannot have it as he is not a subscriber, and presents him with the *Court and City Register*, the *Old Annual Register*, or the *New Annual Register*; or, if the coffee-house be within the purlieus of Covent Garden, or the Hundred of Drury Lane, slips into the politician's hand *Harris' Register of Ladies*. For these, and other reasons, the parents of the *Universal Register* have added to its original name that of *The Times*, which being a monosyllable, bids defiance to corruptors and mutilators of the language.—*The Times* of January 1, 1788.

The *Times* of Tuesday, November 29, 1814, was the first work ever printed by a mechanical apparatus, and the first newspaper printed by steam, the machine being the invention of a German named König. A machine erected in 1846 threw off the then almost incredible number of 6000 sheets of eight pages per hour;[1] but some years later another, by Mr. Applegarth of Dartford, was erected which threw off 10,000 an hour. Afterwards the American ten-cylinder Hoe machine was employed; but since 1869 *The Times* has been printed by the Walter Press. This remarkable machine, the most perfect printing press yet produced, was manufactured within *The Times* office, and is said to be due to the "combined ingenuity of Mr. Walter, chief proprietor, Mr. Macdonald, manager, and Mr. Calverly, chief engineer of *The Times* newspaper,"[2] nearly seven years of assiduous labour being devoted to its production. With it *The Times* is printed from a continuous roll of paper, about 4 miles long and double the width of *The Times*, which travels through the press at the rate of 1000 feet a minute—the 4 miles of paper being covered on both sides with printed matter in twenty-five minutes. The impression is taken from curved stereotype plates, cast from a paper matrix, and the machine, almost entirely automatic in its action, unrolls and damps the paper, inks the types, registers so that the columns of print range accurately on the two sides of the paper, cuts the sheets of eight pages, and delivers them printed on both sides at the rate of 17,000 an hour, and finally keeps an accurate record of the number so printed. To work this surprising apparatus only an engineer and three pressmen are required. The average number of compositors employed is 110. The process of printing is well worth witnessing, but to see it a special order must be obtained. The establishment is one of the best ordered hives of industry in the metropolis. Every part is arranged for convenient and easy working. The editor's rooms, the rooms with their excellent reference libraries appropriated to the literary staff, the printing offices with the arrange-

[1] *Times*, August 21, 1846.
[2] *English Cyclopædia, Arts and Sciences Supplement*, Art "Printing."

ments for the comfort of the workpeople, the advertisement and the publishing departments all seem designed with a view to the economy of time, labour and trouble. The buildings have been for the most part reconstructed since 1874, from the designs and under the supervision of Mr. Deacon. They are of great extent, stretching back from Queen Victoria Street, where is the advertisement office, to Playhouse Yard (the publishing office), and including the whole of Printing House Square. They are of red brick with moulded brick dressings (all made from clay dug on Mr. Walter's Bearwood estate), and Cornish granite shafts in the ornamental parts, but generally solidity rather than ornament has been sought after.

The Times—"that volume of Modern History put forth day by day," as Sir G. C. Lewis happily designated it in 1849—has taken the lead of all the London papers for very many years, and deservedly so, for the proprietors have spared no money to render it accurate, early, and comprehensive in its intelligence. It was owing to the exertions used by the proprietors of this paper, and the immense outlay which they went to, that the notorious conspiracy of Bogle and his associates was (1841) detected and laid bare. The trial of Bogle *v.* Lawson (the printer of the paper) will occupy a place in the history of the commerce of this country, whenever such a work shall be again undertaken. A Times Testimonial was subsequently raised by the merchants and bankers of London, a tablet to commemorate the trial and exposure erected in the Royal Exchange, and the bulk of the money raised (the proprietors refusing to take any pecuniary recompense) invested in the funds for certain scholarships—Times Scholarships, as they are called —at Christ's Hospital and the City of London School. Mr. John Walter, under whose superintendence *The Times* was made what it now is, died in 1847. His father, who started the paper, died in 1812.

The centenary number of the *Times*, January 1, 1888, contains a full history of the paper in its early days.

William Faithorne, the engraver, went to live in this square about 1680, chiefly employing himself in drawing from the life in crayons; here he died in 1691, and was buried in the churchyard of St. Anne's, Blackfriars.

Privy Council Office, DOWNING STREET, WHITEHALL, is part of the south end of the range of buildings known as the Treasury. Here are kept the minutes of the Privy Councils of the Crown, commencing in 1540.

Privy Garden, behind WHITEHALL, now called WHITEHALL GARDENS, a square of ground containing 3¼ acres,[1] between Parliament Street and the Thames, and appertaining to the King's Palace at Whitehall.

May 21, 1662.—In the Privy Garden saw the finest smocks and linen petticoats of my Lady Castlemaine's, laced with rich lace at the bottom, that ever I saw; and did me good to look at them.—*Pepys.*

---

[1] *Hatton*, p. 66, who describes it as "lying between the Cockpit and the Thames."

The Privy Garden, when Mr. Pepys was in it, was laid out into sixteen square compartments of grass, each compartment having a standing statue in the centre. The garden was concealed from the street by a lofty wall; from the river by the Stone Gallery and state apartments; from the court behind the Banqueting House by the lodgings of the chief attendants on the King; and from the Bowling-green, to which it led, by a row of lofty trees. It would appear to have been in every respect a private garden. In the original Privy Garden Charles I., when Prince of Wales, caused a dial to be set up, and by command of James I. there was written, "The Description and use of his Majesty's Dial in Whitehall Garden, by Edmund Gunter, London, 1624," 4to. It was defaced and went to ruin in King Charles II.'s time.

> This place for a dial was too insecure,
> Since a guard and a garden could not it defend;
> For so near to the Court they will never endure
> Any witness to show how their time they misspend.
> ANDREW MARVELL.

Other dials of glass, arranged pyramidically, were placed here by Francis Hall, *alias* Line, a Jesuit, in 1669. Vertue and Walpole speak of their remains.[1] "An explication of the diall sett up in the King's garden at London, anno 1669; in which very many sorts of dyalls are conteined, etc.," was printed at Liége, by Guillaume Henry Steel, in 1673, 4to. James II. relates in his Memoirs that on one occasion when Charles II. was rising from the Council he saw the Secretary of State lay several commissions before him, which he at once signed and passed on to the Privy Garden.

The Duke stay'd behind and took up one of the Commissions which prov'd to be that for the Duke of Monmouth's Generalship, and looking in it to see how it was drawn, he found the word *Natural* had been scrap'd out in all the places where it had been writt, and the word *Son* only left in. . . . The Duke took the Commission and carryd it immediately to the King then walking in the Garden, and withall desired his Ma^ty that the word *Natural* might again be put into the Commission as it had been, and as it ought to be. Whereupon the King taking out his sizers cutt the Commission in two, and order'd an other to be prepar'd for him to sign with the word *Natural* in it.—Clarke's *James II.*, vol. i. p. 497.

Evelyn records, May 31, 1672, that a day or two before he here took leave of "that incomparable person," the Earl of Sandwich, setting out to fight the Dutch, and full of foreboding of the death that was so close at hand. The wall that enclosed the Privy Garden was a favourite station for the display of the old ballad-sellers' wares. "I have seen Mr. Burke," said Joseph Moser, "examining the ballads, etc., upon the wall of Privy Garden, with an attention which our greatest authors might have thought it an honour to excite."[2]

The present Privy Garden, or Whitehall Gardens, consists of a row of large houses fronting the river, from which it is divided by the Victoria Embankment, and is part in the parish of St. Martin's-in-the-

---

[1] *Anecd. of Painting*, vol. ii. p. 54.   [2] *Europ. Mag.*, 1796.

Fields and part in the parish of St. Margaret's, Westminster. The centre house was the residence of Sir Robert Peel, the eminent statesman, who formed here the fine collection of Dutch and Flemish pictures, now a part of the National collection. He died in the dining-room on the ground-floor facing the river, July 2, 1850. In an action in the Court of Exchequer, February 1870, brought by the third Sir Robert Peel to recover £5355 from the Metropolitan Board of Works for damage and deterioration caused by the construction of the Thames Embankment, Sir Robert stated that the "house was built in 1824, that there were steps leading to the river, and he remembered that on one occasion, when a boy, preparations were made to remove the family and valuables by boats on occasion of a threatened attack by a riotous mob on his father's house." A house, which formed a part of the old palace, granted by William III. to the Earl of Portland, was long the town residence of the Dukes of Portland. Here lived the Duchess of Portland who purchased the Barberini Vase, and from it the house received its present name. Here the Duchess had collected an extraordinary museum, to the great disgust of her family. All the purchases were not like that of the Vase, which was kept secret from them till her death in the following year. Her museum was sold in this house, the auction beginning April 4 and ending June 7, 1786. The Duke of Portland bought the Vase for £1029, the cameo of Jupiter Serapis for £173 : 5s., and that of Augustus Cæsar for £236 : 5s. The Vase was No. 4155—the last lot. At the south end of Privy Gardens is the fine modern mansion of the Duke of Buccleuch. [*See* Montague House, Whitehall.] The minister Earl of Liverpool resided in the Privy Gardens, and here at various times have lived the Earl of Fife, the Earl of Malmesbury, the Earl of Loudon, the Earl of Harrington, Lord Gage, and many other persons of distinction.

Privy Seal Office, 1 NEW STREET, SPRING GARDENS, an office belonging to the Crown. The chief officer is called the Lord Privy Seal, and is always a cabinet minister. The Privy Seal is affixed to such grants as are required to pass the Great Seal. A grant must first pass the Privy Signet, then the Privy Seal, and lastly the Great Seal of England. The Great Seal is kept by the Lord Chancellor.

Privy Stairs, WHITEHALL, the stairs leading from the Privy Garden, by which the sovereigns and courtiers, when the King was resident at Whitehall, passed to and from the barges on the Thames. In February 1613, on the marriage of the Princess Elizabeth with the Palatine, Francis Beaumont wrote a masque for the allied houses of Gray's Inn and the Inner Temple. The subject, the nuptials of the Thames and the Rhine, appears to have been suggested by Bacon, who took the greatest interest in its progress and success. The procession was by water from Winchester Place in Southwark to Whitehall, but the King was sleepy and weary when it arrived, and it never got beyond Privy Stairs. Bacon remonstrated with the King, beseeching him "not to bury *them* quick," to which James replied that the alternative would be equivalent to "burying him quick, for he could last no longer." So, Chamberlain adds, "they came home as they went, without doing anything."

Prujean Square, OLD BAILEY, on the west side, a few doors from Ludgate Hill, so named from the residence here of Sir Francis Prujean, an eminent physician, who was President of the College of Physicians 1650-1654. In the latter year, when Harvey declined the office on account of age and infirmity, Prujean was on his advice chosen for the fifth time. In Strype's Map it is called *Prideaux Court*, Dodsley calls it *Prujean Court*. Gunner, a fashionable hairdresser and perfumer, lived here, and in 1783 advertised that "ladies' maids, valets, and servants in general," are "taught to cut and dress hair in perfection in one month, at one guinea and a half each, at Gunner's Original Academy, No. 6 Prujean Square." Further, "Mr. Gunner is always at home to dress ladies at one shilling . . . best scented powder and pomatum included."

Pudding Lane, EASTCHEAP TO LOWER THAMES STREET.

Then have ye one other lane called Rother Lane or Red Rose Lane, of such a sign there, now commonly called Pudding Lane, because the butchers of Eastcheap have their scalding houses for hogs there, and their puddings with other filth of beasts are voided down that way to their dung boats on the Thames. This lane stretcheth from Thames Street to Little East Cheap, chiefly inhabited by basket makers, turners and butchers, and is all of Billingsgate Ward.—*Stow*, p. 79.

Phil. Come, Sergeants, I'll step to my uncle's, not far off, hereby in Pudding Lane, and he shall bail me.—*Westward Ho*, Act i. Sc. 2.

Venus. Right, forsooth, I am Cupid's mother, Cupid's own mother, forsooth ; yes, forsooth. I dwell in Pudding Lane. . . .

Christmas. Good Lady Venus of Pudding Lane, you must go out for all this.— Ben Jonson, *Masque of Christmas*, 1616.

The Fire of London, commonly called the Great Fire, commenced on the east side of this lane between one and two in the morning of Sunday, September 2, 1666, in the house of Farryner, the King's baker. It was the fashion of the True Blue Protestants of the period to attribute the fire to the Roman Catholics, and when, in 1681, Oates and his plot strengthened this belief, the following inscription was affixed on the front of the house (No. 25), erected on the site of Farryner the baker's :—

Here, by y* Permission of Heaven, Hell brake loose upon this Protestant City, from the malicious hearts of barbarous Papists by y* hand of their Agent Hubert, who confessed, and on the ruines of this place declared the fact for which he was hanged, viz., That here begun that dreadful Fire which is described and perpetuated on and by the neighbouring Pillar.—Erected Anno 1681, in the Mayoralty of Sir Patience Ward, Kt.

This celebrated inscription, set up pursuant to an order of the Court of Common Council, June 17, 1681, was removed in the reign of James II., replaced in the reign of William III., and finally taken down, "on account of the stoppage of passengers to read it." Entick, who made additions to Maitland in 1756, speaks of it as "lately taken away." The house was "rebuilt in a very handsome manner."[1] The inscribed stone was buried in the cellar of the house in Pudding Lane, where it was found when the house was pulled down in 1876 and presented to the City Museum, where it is carefully preserved.

Hubert was a French Papist, of six-and-twenty years of age, the son of a watchmaker at Rouen in Normandy. He was seized in Essex, confessed he had begun the fire, and persisting in his confession, was hanged, upon no other evidence than his own. He stated in his examination that he had been "suborned at Paris to this action," and that there were "three more combined to do the same thing." They asked him if he knew the place where he had first put fire. He answered he "knew it very well, and would show it to anybody." He was then ordered to be blindfolded, and carried to several places of the City, that he might point out the house. They first led him to a place at some distance from it, opened his eyes, and asked him if that was it, to which he answered "No; it was lower, nearer to the Thames." "The house and all which were near it," says Clarendon, "were so covered and buried in ruins, that the owners themselves, without some infallible mark, could very hardly have said where their own houses had stood; but this man led them directly to the place, described how it stood, the shape of the little yard, the fashion of the door and windows, and where he first put the fire; and all this with such exactness, that they who had dwelt long near it could not so perfectly have described all particulars." Tillotson told Burnet that Howell (the then Recorder of London) accompanied Hubert on this occasion, "was with him, and had much discourse with him; and that he concluded it was impossible it could be a melancholy dream." This, however, was not the opinion of the judges who tried him. "Neither the judges," says Clarendon, "nor any present at the trial, did believe him guilty, but that he was a poor distracted wretch, weary of his life, and chose to part with it this way." We may attribute the fire with safety to another cause than a Roman Catholic conspiracy. We are to remember that the flames originated in the house of a baker; that the season had been unusually dry; that the houses were of wood, overhanging the roadway, so that the lane was even narrower than it is now, and that a strong east wind was blowing at the time. It was thought very little of at first. Pepys put out his head from his bedroom window in Seething Lane a few hours after it broke out, and returned to bed again, as if it were nothing more than an ordinary fire, a common occurrence, and likely to be soon subdued. The Lord Mayor (Sir Thomas Bludworth) seems to have thought as little of it till it was too late. People appear to have been paralysed, and no attempt of any consequence was made to check its progress. For four successive days it raged and gained ground, leaping after a prodigious manner from house to house and street to street, at great distances from one another.

[1] Dodsley's *London*, 8vo, 1761, vol. v. p. 232.

Houses were at length pulled down, and the flames still spreading westward, were at length stopped at the Temple Church, in Fleet Street, and Pie Corner in Smithfield. In these four days 13,200 houses, 400 streets, and 89 churches, including the cathedral church of St. Paul, were destroyed, and London lay literally in ruins. The loss was so enormous that we may be said still to suffer from its effects. Yet the advantages were not a few. London was freed from the plague ever after; and we owe St. Paul's, St. Bride's, St. Stephen's, Walbrook, and all the architectural glories of Sir Christopher Wren to the desolation it occasioned.

Pudding Lane is now almost entirely occupied by wholesale fruit merchants and brokers.

Puddle Dock (originally PUDDLE WHARF), at the foot of St. Andrew's Hill, Upper Thames Street, Blackfriars, in Castle Baynard Ward.

Then a water gate at Puddle Wharf, of one Puddle that kept a wharf on the west side thereof, and now of Puddle water by means of many horses watered there.—*Stow*, pp. 16, 136.

The town house of the Earl of Rutland, temp. Elizabeth, seems to have been here.[1] Rutland Place and Rutland Yard (now Rutland Wharf), to the east of Puddle Dock, commemorate the fact. Sir Dudley Carleton was living at Puddle Wharf in 1600. On December 17, 1609, the Lady Arabella Stuart wrote to Cecil from Puddle Wharf beseeching that her Patent (of the "privilege of nominating such persons as shall sell wines, aquavitæ or usquebagh" for twenty-one years) may speedily pass the Great Seal.[2] The house which Shakespeare bought in the Blackfriars, and which he bequeaths by will to his daughter, Susannah Hall, is described in the Conveyance as "abutting upon a streete leading down to Puddle Wharffe on the east part, right-against the King's Maiesty's Wardrobe"—"and now or late in the tenure or occupacon of one William Ireland, or of his assignee or assignes."[3] [*See* Ireland Yard.]

I gyve will bequeath and devise unto my daughter Susannah Hall . . . all that messuage or tenemente with the appurtenances wherein one John Robinson dwelleth scituat lying and being in the Blackfriars in London neare the Wardrobe."—*Shakespeare's Will.*

Puddle Wharf,
Which place we'll make bold with to call it our Abydos,
As the Bankside is our Sestos.

Ben Jonson, *Bartholomew Fair*, Act v; see also *Beaumont and Fletcher*, vol. ii. p. 167.

H' had been both friend and foe to crimes;

. . . .
Cartloads of bawds to prison sent
For being behind a fortnight's rent;
And many a trusty pimp and crony
To Puddle-dock for want of money.
Hudibras, pt. iii. c. 3.

---

[1] Comp. Cooper's *Athen. Cant.*, vol. ii. p. 14.   [2] *Cal. State Pap.*, 1603-1610, pp. 404, 573.
[3] Malone's *Inquiry*, p. 403.

Clodpate. Is not this better than anything in that stinking Town [London]?
Lucia. Stinking Town! I had rather be Countess of Puddle-Dock than Queen
of Sussex.—T. Shadwell, *Epsom Wells*, 4to, 1676.

Swift also introduces the Countess of Puddle Dock in his *Polite Conversation*, and Hogarth a Duke of Puddle Dock in his *Trip to Gravesend*.

> But what most pleased us was his Grace
> Of Puddle Dock, a porter grim,
> Whose portrait Hogarth in a whim
> Presented him in caricature
> And pasted on the cellar door.—Hogarth's *Trip*.

The Duke of Puddle Dock was probably at this time a notorious personage, as there was published in 1739 "The Popular Convention, a Poem by the Duchess of Puddle Dock."[1]

Puddle Hill, PUDDLE WHARF, BLACKFRIARS. Here in 1628 lived the father of Archbishop Leighton.

To his kind and loving Father, Mr. Alexander Leighton, Dr. of Medicine, at his house on the top of Pudle Hill, beyond the Black Friars Gate, near the King's Ward-robe, these.—*Archbishop Leighton to his Father from Edinburgh*, 1628.

Pullin's Row, ISLINGTON. A few houses on the east side of Upper Street, were so called.

Ben. The young gentleman in Pullin's Row, Islington, that has got the consumption, has sent to know if you can let him have a sweetbread.—Charles Lamb's farce, *The Pawnbroker's Daughter*.

Pulteney Street (Little), GOLDEN SQUARE, was originally called *Knaves Acre*.[2] Sir William Pulteney, Knt., an inhabitant of St. James's parish, held the site of this street and adjacent property by lease from the Crown, part of which he demised in 1685 to Thomas Beake, a carpenter,—hence Beak Street. A "Mr. Poultney of St. James's" is recorded as the owner of "certain messuages and tenements in a certain place called Soehoe" as early as 1645. In 1720 Strype says "The Knave's Acre is but narrow and chiefly inhabited by those that deal in old goods and glass bottles." It is still marked Knave's Acre in Roque's Map of 1745, although it is figured as Pultney Street in Strype's Map of 1720. The present *Great* Pulteney Street was of later construction. At his house here died, July 9, 1742, John Oldmixon, the historian and party writer. Great Pulteney Street is peculiarly interesting to the musician from Joseph Haydn having resided at No. 18 (lately rebuilt), when he visited England; and from Shudi (properly Tschudi), the harpsichord maker and friend of Handel, having founded his business at No. 33 as early, according to the family tradition, as 1732. The sign of the house was "The Plume of Feathers." Shudi's son-in-law, John Broadwood, who founded the pianoforte business, succeeded to it in 1769, and it still remains occupied by his descendants' firm. There is a room shown in this house to which Haydn used to retire to compose.

[1] Burn, *Tokens*, p. 495.   [2] *Hatton*, p. 66.

Pump Court, TEMPLE, was so called from the pump in the centre. The present buildings were erected in 1826.

January 27, 1678-1679.—In the night the greatest part of the Middle Temple in London, consumed by a dreadful fire which began in the south-west corner of Pump Court.—Dugdale's *Diary, in Hamper.*

In 1710, when the future Lord Chancellor Hardwicke began to study for the Bar, he took chambers in this Court; and in 1715, when commencing to practice, he moved into a fresh set of chambers, but still in Pump Court.

When, in June 1740, Fielding was called to the Bar he had chambers assigned him in this Court.

Pur Alley.

> Now Post and Pair, old Christmas heir,
> Doth make and a gingling sally;
> And wot you who, 'tis one of my two
> Sons, card-makers in Pur Alley.—
>> Ben Jonson's *Masque of Christmas.*

There was a *Pur* (or *Pur's*) Court on the east side of Old Change near Cheapside; and *Pur Field* was the old name of a portion of Lincoln's Inn Fields.

Purim Place, MILE END, on the east side of the Cambridge Road.

The names of streets will often be found connected with some singular event or the character of some person. Not long ago a Hebrew, who had a quarrel with his community about the manner of celebrating the Jewish festival in commemoration of the fate of Haman, built a neighbourhood at Bethnal Green, and retained the subject of his anger in the name which the houses bear of *Purim Place.* This may startle some theological antiquary at a remote period, who may idly lose himself in abstruse conjectures on the sanctity of a name, derived from a well known Hebrew festival; and perhaps in his imagination be induced to colonize the spot with an ancient horde of Israelites.—I. D'Israeli, *Curiosities of Literature,* vol. iii. p. 360.

On this passage Mrs. Piozzi has a note (*Piozziana,* p. 207) which may serve to show that theological antiquaries are not the only people likely to idly lose their way when embarking on abstruse etymological conjectures.

Pye Street (Old), WESTMINSTER, runs from St. Anne's Street to Duck Lane, and was so called from Sir Robert Pye (the husband of John Hampden's daughter), who resided here. Strype in 1720 described the street as "better built than inhabited." At No. 8 lived Isaac De Groot.[1] "I have known him many years," wrote Dr. Johnson. "He has all the common claims to charity, being old, poor, and infirm to a great degree. He has likewise another claim, to which no scholar can refuse attention; he is by several descents the nephew of Hugo Grotius; of him from whom, perhaps, every man of learning has learnt something."

[1] *Boswell,* by Croker, p. 335.

Quadrant (The), the eastern end of REGENT STREET, was designed when Regent Street was built by John Nash, architect. The arcade, which covered the whole footway (supported by 145 cast-iron pillars), was removed in December 1848. Thus was sacrificed the most beautiful and most original feature in the street architecture of London. The reasons assigned for this removal were, that, though picturesque in itself, and of use on a rainy day, by darkening the footpath it lessened the value of the shops and occasioned other nuisances. Traces of the arcade may still be seen at the two intersections of Leicester Street. The name was retained some years after the removal of the arcade, but is now merged in that of Regent Street.

Quebec Street, OXFORD STREET, commemorates the capture of Quebec by General Wolfe in 1759.

Queen Square, BLOOMSBURY, was so called out of compliment to Queen Anne, in whose reign it was erected.[1] The north side "was left open for the sake of the beautiful landscape formed by the hills of Highgate and Hampstead, together with the adjacent fields."[2] In 1756 Maitland calls it "Queen's Square, Red Lion Fields."

Eminent Inhabitants.—Alderman Barber, the printer, who died here in 1741 (the individual to whom Butler owes a monument in Poets' Corner). In January 1771 Barber's house was occupied by Dr. Charles Burney. Madame D'Arblay speaks of "the beautiful prospect of the hills, ever verdant and smiling, of Hampstead and Highgate, which at that period, in unobstructed view, faced the Doctor's dwelling in Queen Square."[3]

In February [1772] I had the honour of receiving the illustrious Captain Cook to dine with me in Queen Square, previously to his second voyage round the world. Observing upon table Bougainville's *Voyage autour du Monde* he turned it over and made some curious remarks on the illiberal conduct of that circumnavigator towards himself when they met and crossed each other; which made me desirous to know, in examining the Chart of M. de Bougainville, the several tracks of the two navigators; and exactly where they had crossed or approached each other. Captain Cook instantly took a pencil from his pocket-book, and said he would trace the route, which he did in so clear and scientific a manner that I would not take fifty pounds for the book. The pencil-mark having been fixed by skim-milk will always be visible.—Mem. by Dr. Burney, *Memoirs*, vol. i. p. 270.

It was on this occasion arranged that the Doctor's eldest son James (afterwards Admiral Burney, the friend of Charles Lamb) should accompany the great navigator in his approaching voyage. Charles Churchill, the poet, in 1758, after the death of his father, was engaged by Mrs. Dennis, who had a boarding-school in this square, to give "lessons in the English tongue to the young ladies," and, as Dr. Kippis says, "conducted himself in his new employment with all the decorum becoming his clerical profession." This school was at No. 31, and became so famous as to earn the name of "The Ladies' Eton." Boswell's daughter Veronica was there in 1789, and he writes of her

---

[1] *Hatton*, p. 67.
[2] *Dodsley*, 1761, vol. v. p. 240.
[3] D'Arblay's *Memoirs of Dr. Burney*, vol. i. p. 290.

with no small pride as his "Queen Square daughter." It continued to be a school of some note for nearly a century, and was finally closed about 1855. The house in the north-west corner was Heidegger's, who left it on his death in 1749 to his only daughter, the wife of Admiral Sir Peter Denis. Dr. Stukeley, who died here in 1765, was rector of the small brick church of St. George the Martyr, on the south-west side of the square [which *see*]. Dr. John Campbell, author of *The Lives of the Admirals*, and chief contributor to the *Biographia Britannica*, lived here for many years and here died, December 28, 1775.

Campbell's residence for some years before his death was the large new-built house, situate at the north-west corner of Queen Square, Bloomsbury, whither, particularly on a Sunday evening, great numbers of persons of the first eminence for science and literature were accustomed to resort for the enjoyment of conversation.— Hawkins's *Life of Johnson*, p. 210.

Johnson. I used to go pretty often to Campbell's on a Sunday evening, till I began to consider that the shoals of Scotchmen who flocked about him might probably say, when anything of mine was well done, "Ay, ay, he has learnt this of *Cawmell*." —*Boswell*, by Croker, p. 142.

Dr. Anthony Askew (d. 1774), famous as a physician, and in his own day still more widely famous as a Greek scholar. Dr. Mead gave to Askew the gold-headed cane which he had received from Radcliffe, and which, after Askew, was successively carried by Pitcairn and Baillie; it is now preserved in the Royal College of Physicians. Askew's house was a favourite resort of the leading scholars of the day, among them being enumerated Archbishop Markham, Sir William Jones, Dr. Parr, and Richard Farmer, the Shakespearian annotator.

Dr. Askew's house in Queen's Square, was said to be the most classical in London; for every passage was lined with Greek or Latin books. He had a Greek servant reckoned the finest copyist in the world.—Cradock's *Lit. Memoirs*, vol. iv. p. 135.

George III., wishing to secure the library entire, offered £5000 for it, but the family decided to submit it to auction. The sale took place in 1775 and lasted twenty days. A considerable portion of the library (including the large purchases by the King and Mr. Cracherode) came eventually to the British Museum. The Rev. George Croly, LL.D., author of *Salathiel*, was living at No. 9 Queen Square till his death in November 1860.

Queen Square has long ceased to be a fashionable place of residence, and several of the larger houses have been appropriated to commercial, educational or benevolent uses. Nos. 17-19, the Alexandra Hospital for Children with Hip Disease; Nos. 23-25, the National Hospital for the Paralysed and the Epileptic; No. 29, the College for Men and Women; Nos. 32 and 33, the School of Ecclesiastical Embroidery; No. 41, the Italian Hospital; No. 43 is the Government (District) School of Art for Ladies. General Strode erected a statue of Queen Charlotte in the centre of the square.

Queen Square, WESTMINSTER, originally QUEEN ANNE'S SQUARE,[1] and now, with Park Street, called QUEEN ANNE'S GATE. At the upper end of the square is a standing statue of Queen Anne.

> Queen Square, a beautiful new (though small) square of very fine buildings—on the north side of the Broadway, near Tuthill Street, Westminster, between which and the Broadway is a new street erecting, not yet named. There is also another square of this name designed, at the north end of Devonshire Street, near Red Lion Square.—*Hatton*, 1708, p. 67.

Queen Square was the freehold estate of Sir Theodore Jansen, one of the Directors of the South Sea Company, in the great bubble year of 1720, and was seized and sold towards the payment of the debts of the said Company, by commissioners authorised by 7 George I. c. 1, and subsequent statutes. In the early part of the 18th century Lord Grey and Lord North resided in this square, and "Lords Guernsey, Derby, and Dartmouth had town-mansions near it."[2] Admiral Edward Vernon, the captor of Portobello, was born in this square, November 12, 1684; and the Rev. C. M. Cracherode, who bequeathed his splendid library to the British Museum, was born here in 1729. When Thomson was soliciting the patronage of Speaker Compton to the second edition of the *Winter*, he wrote his letters (June 1726) from "Long's Coffee House in Queen Square, Westminster." Jonathan Richardson, the painter, and writer on painting, died at his house in Queen Square, May 28, 1745, and his son, of the same name, in 1770. Peg Woffington died here March 28, 1760. Sir William Browne, the distinguished physician, and founder of the gold medals for Greek and Latin odes and epigrams at Cambridge University, died at his house in Queen Square, May 10, 1774. At her house in this square Miss Frances Reynolds, the sister to Sir Joshua, so often mentioned by Boswell, died November 1, 1807, aged eighty. In No. 2 Queen Square Place lived the notorious Theresa Constantia Philips, and in a detached dwelling in "Queen Square Place," looking on the garden-ground of Milton's house in Petty France, Jeremy Bentham died, in 1832. He bought the property about 1772, and spent upon it "full £10,000," as he states in a Memorial to the Treasury dated 1773, against the erection of the contemplated barracks near his house. Here Sir Mark Isambard Brunel was living when working out the details of his famous block-making machinery.

> At the time when my father must have been busy working out the details of the block machinery (the idea I believe originated with him while in America) he was living in the white house which stands back from Bird-Cage Walk, near the Barracks. I believe it is now called No. 1 Queen's Square Place, and had been, I think, the house of Jeremy Bentham.—*I. K. Brunel to P. Cunningham*, April 23, 1853.

The white house was pulled down to make way for the huge *Queen Anne's Mansions*.

Queen Street, BLOOMSBURY, the old name of the north portion of MUSEUM STREET [which *see*].

---

[1] *Strype*; *Maitland*.   [2] Walcott's *Westminster*, p. 73.

Queen Street, CHEAPSIDE, "A street," says Strype, "made since the Great Fire, out of Soper Lane, for a straight passage from the water side to Guildhall." About 1667 it was named Queen Street in honour of the wife of Charles II. A trade token dated 1669 has on it "Will Clerke, 1708, at ye Cock and Bottle in Soper Lane, *alias Queen Street.*"[1]

Some call the north end of this street from Watling Street, Soper Lane.—*Hatton*, p. 67.

On the east side is the churchyard of *St. Thomas the Apostle*, a church destroyed in the Great Fire, and not rebuilt. The Rectory house of St. Thomas the Apostle and St. Mary Aldermary on the east side was designed in 1860 by Tress and Chambers, architects. At the south end of the street is *Southwark Bridge*. The end next Cheapside was widened in 1887-1889.

Queen Street (Great), extends west from the north-west corner of Lincoln's Inn Fields to Drury Lane, and is the continuation east of Long Acre. It was so named in compliment to Queen Henrietta Maria, and was commenced about 1606; fifteen houses had been erected before 1623. Howes, in his edition of *Stow* (1631), speaks of the "new fair buildings called Queene's Street leading into Drury Lane." The houses in the first instance were built on the south side only. Webb, the scholar of Inigo Jones, was the architect of some in 1640-1660, and, from the date, was most likely assisted in the designs by his great kinsman. Sir Balthazar Gerbier, in his *Counsel and Advice to all Builders* (1663), ridicules the heads of lions which are creeping through the pilasters on the houses. Vertue, however, assigned the credit to "Mr. Mills, one of the four surveyors appointed after the fire of London."

He [Inigo Jones] built Queen Street, also designed at first for a square, and, as reported, at the charge of the Jesuits; in the middle whereof was left a niche for the statue of Henrietta Maria, and this was the first uniform street, and the houses are stately and magnificent. At the other side of the way, near Little Queen Street, they began after the same manner with flower de lices on the wall, but went no further.—Bagford, *Harl. MS.*, 5900, fol. 50ᵇ.

The statue of Henrietta Maria was probably set up, and also one of the King, for on January 17, 1651-1652, the Council of State ordered "that Colonel Berkstead doe take care of the pulling downe of the gilt image of the late Queene and alsoe of the King, the one in the street commonlie called Queene's Street, and the other at the upper end of the same street towards Holborne. And the said images are to be broken in pieces."[2] One of the earliest residents must have been the Spanish Ambassador.

May 10, 1638.—The Spanish Ambassador, the Conde de Oniate, accompanied with an Irish gentleman of the order of Calatrava, in the Holy Week came to Denmark House [*i.e.* Somerset House] to do his devotions in the Queen's Chapel there. He went off thence about 10 o'clock, a dozen torches carried before him by his servants, and

---

[1] *Burn*, p. 196. [2] Sainsbury in *Fine Arts Quarterly Review*, vol. i. p. 167.

some behind him. He and the Irish gentleman were in front with their beads in their hands, which hung at a cross; some English also were among them; so that with their own company and many who followed after, they appeared a great troop. They walk from Denmark House down the Strand in great formality, turn into the Covent Garden, then to Seignior Con's house in Long Acre, so to his own house in Queen Street.—*Garrard to Wentworth* (Strafford's *Letters*, vol. ii. p. 165).

Another very early resident was John Digby, first Earl of Bristol (d. 1653), whose house here was seized by the Parliament, and granted, September 13, 1644, to the widow of Robert Lord Brooke, killed in the previous year at the siege of Lichfield. The Restoration gave it back to Lord Bristol.

May 26, 1671.—The Earl of Bristol's house in Queene Street was taken for the Commissioners of Trade and Plantations, and furnish'd with rich hangings of the King's. It consisted of seven roomes on a floore, with a long gallery, gardens, etc. This day we met; the Duke of Buckingham, Earl of Lauderdale, Lord Colpeper, Sir Geo. Carteret, Vice Chamberlaine, and myself, had the oathes given us by the Earle of Sandwich, our President. . . . We then tooke our places at the Board in the Council Chamber, a very large roome furnished with atlases, mapps, charts, globes, etc.—*Evelyn.*

The celebrated Edward, first *Lord Herbert of Cherbury*, lived on the south side, at the east corner of Great Wild Street. On July 13, 1645, Howel writes to him from the Fleet prison :—

God send you joy of your new habitation, for I understand your Lordship is removed from the King's Street to the Queen's. It may be with this enlargement of dwelling your Lordship may need a recruit of servants.

He died here in 1648.

He dyed at his house in Queen Street in the parish of St. Giles's-in-the-Fields, very serenely; asked what was o'clock, and then, sayd he, an hour hence I shall depart; he then turned his head to the other side and expired.—Aubrey's *Lives*, vol. ii. p. 387.

Sir Thomas Fairfax, the Parliament General, and his father both lived in this street, most probably in the same house. The old lord announced his second marriage in a letter dated Queen Street, October 20, 1646; and it was here that the young general on November 14, 1647, when the war was brought to a conclusion, received a congratulatory visit from both Houses of Parliament. The Lords, who arrived in a long train of coaches, had the Earl of Manchester for their spokesman, and the Commons were headed by their renowned Speaker Lenthall. Fairfax dates a printed proclamation of February 12, 1648, from his house in Queen Street. Sir Heneage Finch, Earl of Nottingham and Lord Chancellor (d. 1682), was living here when the Mace and Purse were stolen from him. [*See* Lincoln's Inn Fields.] In this house he used to receive the New Year's gift from the Bar, which, in his time, "came to near £3000 in gold." Lady Cowper in her *Diary* (p. 63) says :—

He received them standing by a table; and at the same time he took the money to lay upon the table he used to cry out "Oh, Tyrant Cuthtom!" (for he lisped). My Lord [Cowper] forbade the bringing them.

Richard, Earl Rivers, the reputed father of Richard Savage, the poet, makes mention in his will of "Rivers House, in Great Queen Street, in the parish of St. Giles's-in-the-Fields." Sir Godfrey Kneller came here from the Piazza in Covent Garden. He writes to Pope "from Great Queen Street, June 16, 1719," and sends his "humble respects to Lady Mary Whortly." Walpole and others have wrongly assigned the scene of his wit combat with Dr. Radcliffe to this residence. It really took place when Kneller was living in the Piazza, and the Doctor on the *west* side of Bow Street. Thomas Hudson (d. 1779), the portrait painter, in the house west of Freemasons' Hall, now divided and numbered 55 and 56, and which it seems certain was the one previously occupied by Kneller. Here, on October 18, 1740, the young Joshua Reynolds came to him as a house pupil, and remained under his roof till July 1743. Thomas Worlidge, the portrait painter and engraver (best known by his etchings), afterwards lived in it.[1] Hoole, the translator of Ariosto and Dante (d. 1803), was then its occupant, and after him it was rented by Chippendale the cabinet-maker, whose furniture has during the last few years been so eagerly sought after and imitated. Sir Robert Strange, the engraver, in No. 52; here he engraved his Charles I. with the horse, and the companion print of Queen Henrietta Maria; and here he died, July 5, 1792. His widow continued to reside in the house. No. 34 was in 1796 the residence of James Basire, the engraver, with whom William Blake passed his apprenticeship. According to Mr. Gilchrist,[2] the house was No. 32 (31), the more western of the two houses occupied by Messrs. Corben the coachbuilders. Blake was fond of describing a visit paid by Goldsmith to Basire at this period. Fuseli the painter was living at No. 7 in 1803. Twenty years earlier John Opie, R.A., was a resident in this street. Our great classic landscape painter, Richard Wilson, had at one time apartments in Queen Street, which were afterwards occupied by Theed, the sculptor.[3] The beautiful Perdita, when she first became Mrs. Robinson, lived here in "a large old-fashioned house, which stood on the spot where the Freemasons' Tavern has been since erected."[4] Her house was probably that in which William Hayley, the poet and friend of Cowper, resided for some years previous to his retirement to Eartham in 1774. Hayley believed his house to have been Kneller's. R. Brinsley Sheridan was living in this street in July 1780. Dr. Francklin, the translator of Lucian, in March 1784. About the same time Dr. Wolcott [Peter Pindar] was a resident.

The concealed author of *Lyrick Odes*, by Peter Pindar, Esquire, is one Woolcot, a clergyman who abjured the gown, and now lives in Great Queen Street, Lincoln's Inn Fields, under the character of a physician.—*Maloniana* (Prior's *Life of Malone*, p. 364).

---

[1] Smith (*Nollekens*, vol. ii. p. 220) says he died here; but he died at Hammersmith, and was buried in Hammersmith Churchyard, where a table records that " Here lies the body of Thomas Worlidge, painter, who died the 23d of September, 1766, aged 66 years."

Yet tho' his mortal part inactive lies,
Still Worlidge lives—for Genius never dies.

[2] *Life of Blake*, vol. i. p. 22.
[3] Wright's *Wilson*, p. 4.
[4] *Life*, vol. i. p. 74.

On the south side of this street are Freemasons' Hall and Tavern [which *see*], and a little east of it the once popular Great Queen Street Chapel, erected 1818, and the portico added in 1840. On the opposite side is the unfortunate Novelty Theatre.

The old west-end gateway entrance to this street, taken down in January 1765, was by a narrow passage under a house, familiarly known as "The Devil's Gap," or "Hell Gate."

Queen Street (Little), LINCOLN'S INN FIELDS. William, Lord Russell, was led from Holborn into this street on his way to the scaffold in Lincoln's Inn Fields.

As we came to turn into Little Queen Street, he said, "I have often turned to the other hand, with great comfort, but I now turn to this with greater," and looked towards his own house; and then, as the Dean of Canterbury [Tillotson] who sat over against him told me "he saw a tear or two fall from him."—Bishop Burnet's *Journal*.

"His own house," Southampton House (subsequently called Bedford House), he inherited through his wife, the virtuous Lady Rachel Russell, daughter of Charles II.'s Lord Treasurer, and granddaughter of Shakespeare's Earl of Southampton. No. 7 was the residence of the father and mother of Charles Lamb, September 23, 1796; and here it was that Mary Lamb, his sister, in a sudden fit of insanity—she had frequently experienced similar but less violent attacks before—stabbed her mother to the heart with a case knife snatched from the dinner table.

Queen Street (Little), now part of LANGHAM STREET, PORTLAND ROAD. No. 45 was long the residence of James Watson, the excellent engraver of the last century. Here he executed some of his best mezzotints, after Sir Joshua Reynolds.

Queen Street, MAYFAIR. At No. 12 dwelt Mrs. Elizabeth Harlow, and from here her son, George Henry Harlow, sent his first picture to the Exhibition of 1804, before he had completed his seventeenth year.

Queen Anne Square, the name given in some old maps to the square which was commenced at the south end of the present Portland Place, in front of the Langham Hotel. [*See* Portland Place.] In other maps it is called *Bentinck Square*.

Queen Anne Street East, CAVENDISH SQUARE, was the name of the street leading from Langham Place to Cleveland Street. It was afterwards named Foley Place, and now the western portion, from Langham Place to Great Portland Street, is called *Langham Street*, and the portion east of Portland Street, *Foley Street*. *Eminent Inhabitants.* —Edmond Malone, the Shakesperian commentator, went in 1779 to live at No. 55, where he remained the rest of his life; his house every year "became more and more that of a bachelor—an accumulation of books; rooms not in spruce order; furniture rather in the rear of the fashion of the age"[1]—and here he died, May 25, 1812. His very choice collection of books illustrating the Elizabethan drama is now among the cherished treasures of the Bodleian Library at Oxford. Fuseli, the painter, at No. 72, between 1788 and 1792; and in 1800 at No. 75.

Queen Anne Street, formerly QUEEN ANNE STREET WEST, CAVENDISH SQUARE—Welbeck Street to Chandos Street. Edmund Burke removed from Wimpole Street to Queen Anne Street, "next door to Mr. Fitzherbert," in 1760.[2] Richard Cumberland was living here in 1770, when his best play, the *West Indian*, was produced.

I had a house in Queen Anne Street West, at the corner of Wimpole Street, I lived there many years; my friend Mr. Fitzherbert lived in the same street, and Mr. Burke nearly opposite to me.—Cumberland's *Memoirs*, 4to, 1806, p. 238.

William Windham was living here in 1782—in March 1794 he was in Hill Street. Boswell wrote to his daughter Euphemia, December 19, 1788, "I have taken a neat, pretty, small house in Queen Anne Street West, quite a genteel neighbourhood." He was at this date busy over his *Life of Johnson*, and he found his residence in Queen Anne Street West very convenient in preparing it for the press.

February 8, 1790.—I still keep on my house in Queen Anne Street West, having taken it till Midsummer, upon my finding that chambers in the Temple, which I thought I had secured, were let to me by a person who had not a right. It is better that I am still here, for I am within a short walk of Mr. Malone [living in Queen Anne Street East] who revises my *Life of Johnson* with me.—*Boswell to Temple (Letters,* p. 319).

Among the imitations in the "Rejected Addresses" is one of a Dr. Busby,—much quizzed by the wits of that day,—of whom Horace Smith records that on his publishing a translation of the *De Naturâ Rerum* there appeared a paragraph among the *Domestic Occurrences*—"Yesterday at his house in Queen Anne Street West, Dr. Busby of a still-born Lucretius."

No. 48 was for nearly forty years (1812-1851) the residence of the greatest of our landscape painters, Joseph Mallord William Turner, and here the finest perhaps of his imaginative works were produced. His "gallery" was on the first floor. He painted in the drawing-room. The house has been rebuilt for the Duke of Portland's Estate Office. No. 31 was the town house of the late Bishop of Chichester, Dr. Gilbert (d. 1870). There was nothing to distinguish it from its plebeian neighbours. It would have been more conspicuous if he had blazoned his "bearing" over the door—"A Prester John sitting on a tombstone, with a sword in his mouth."

Queen Anne's Bounty Office, and First Fruits and Tenths' Office, 3A DEAN'S YARD, WESTMINSTER.

Queen Anne's Gate. [*See* Queen Square.]

[1] Prior's *Life of Malone,* p. 300. [2] Prior's *Life of Burke,* chap. iii.

Queen Elizabeth's Grammar School, SOUTHWARK. This school was founded in 1560* by certain inhabitants of St. Olave's parish (Henry Leeke the brewer being worthy of special note), and situated in Tooley Street. It was incorporated in 1571 and named after the reigning Queen. There are in Wilkinson's *Londina* (vol. ii.) two views and a plan of the buildings. The site being required for the approaches of New London Bridge, the building was cleared away in 1830 and a new one erected on the south side of Bermondsey Street. This was also removed in connection with some railway extension, and the present handsome and greatly enlarged building placed in Back Street Horsleydown (now named Queen Elizabeth Street). The institution is styled at present the Grammar School of St. Olave and St. John, and has an income of about £10,000. It furnishes "a liberal and useful education for the sons of parents engaged in professional, trading, or commercial pursuits." Boys are not admitted before seven or after fifteen years of age, except under very special circumstances. A new scheme is (1890) under the consideration of the Charity Commissioners.

Queen Victoria Street, CITY, from the north foot of Blackfriars Bridge to the Mansion House, forming the continuation eastward of the Thames Embankment. This noble street, one of the finest in the City, was commenced in 1867, and formally opened for traffic throughout, November 4, 1871. It proceeds in a nearly straight line from the Mansion House to Cannon Street, and thence with an easy curve to New Bridge Street, opposite the entrance to the Thames Embankment. Its width throughout is 70 feet, except by Little Earl Street, where it is somewhat narrower. Beneath it runs the Metropolitan District Railway; and along it is carried a subway for gas and water pipes. Through nearly its whole extent it is lined on both sides with large, lofty, solidly built and ornamental buildings, most of them having stone fronts, and several being structures of considerable architectural pretension. Among the larger blocks of buildings there are—starting from the Mansion House—on the north, Mansion House Buildings; Imperial Buildings; Queen's Buildings; Crown Buildings; the New Civil Service Stores; College of Arms; British and Foreign Bible Society; the church of St. Andrew-by-the-Wardrobe; the Times Advertisement Office. On the south, the remarkable structure built for the National Safe Deposit Company; Mansion House Chambers; Victoria Buildings; Albert Buildings; the Mansion House Station of the Metropolitan District Railway; Metropolitan Buildings, and Balmoral Buildings; besides on both sides many private commercial establishments.

Queen's Arms Tavern, BOW-IN-HAND COURT, between Nos. 77 and 78 CHEAPSIDE. The second floor of the houses which stretched over the passage leading to this tavern was the London lodging of John Keats, the poet. Here he wrote his magnificent sonnet on Chapman's Homer, and all the poems in his first little volume.

Queen's Arms Tavern, ST. PAUL'S CHURCHYARD.

Garrick kept up an interest in the city by appearing, about twice in a winter, at Tom's Coffee House in Cornhill, the usual rendezvous of young merchants at 'Change time; and frequented a Club, established for the sake of his company at the Queen's Arms Tavern in St. Paul's Churchyard, where were used to assemble Mr. Samuel Sharpe the surgeon, Mr. Paterson the city solicitor, Mr. Draper the bookseller, Mr. Clutterbuck a mercer, and a few others; they were none of them drinkers, and in order to make a reckoning called only for French wine. These were his standing council in theatrical affairs.—Hawkins's *Life of Johnson*, p. 433.

Here, after a thirty years' interval, Johnson renewed his intimacy with some of the members of his old Ivy Lane Club.[1] There is no Queen's Arms in St. Paul's Churchyard now.

Queen's College, 43 and 45 HARLEY STREET, so named by royal permission and under royal charter, for general female education of a high class, and for granting to governesses certificates of qualification. Incorporated 1853.

Queen's Gardens, BAYSWATER, are built on the exact site of the old Pest House. *See* Roque's Map, 1745.

Queen's Gardens, KENSINGTON. Thomas, tenth Earl of Dundonald, better known as Lord Cochrane, died at No. 12, October 31, 1860, in his eighty-fifth year. He was buried in Westminster Abbey.

Queen's Head Alley, now **Queen's Head Passage,** PATERNOSTER ROW to NEWGATE STREET, was so called from an inn or tavern with such a sign, wherein were lodged the canonists and professors of spiritual and ecclesiastical law, before Doctors' Commons was provided for them, in the reign of Queen Elizabeth. [*See* Doctors' Commons.] In this alley, in the reign of Charles II., Richard Head, author of *The English Rogue*, followed the profession of a bookseller.[2] Here, No. 8 on the west side, was Dolly's Chop House. [*See* Dolly's.]

Queen's House, another name for *Buckingham House*, so called after Queen Charlotte, Queen of George III., on whom it was settled by Act of Parliament in 1775.

Queen's Library, THE STABLE YARD, ST. JAMES'S PALACE, so called from having been built by Caroline, wife of George II. It was pulled down by Frederic, Duke of York (second son of George III.), to make way for his new house. [*See* Stafford House.] It is described as a noble room, designed by Wm. Kent, 60 feet by 30 feet, and 30 feet high. It was furnished with a choice collection of 4500 handsomely bound volumes in the various modern languages. The books were placed on the shelves in 1737.

The King [George II.], the Duke [of Cumberland], and Princess Emily saw it [the Celebration of Peace by fireworks in St. James's Park] from the Library, with their Courts; the Prince and Princess [of Wales] with their children, from Lady Middlesex's; no place being provided for them, nor any invitation given to the Library.—*Walpole to Sir Horace Mann,* May 3, 1749.

---

[1] *Boswell*, by Croker, p. 45.   [2] Winstanley's *Lives of the Poets*, p. 208.

Queen's Prison, BOROUGH ROAD, SOUTHWARK, constituted pursuant to 5 and 6 Will. IV., c. 22 (1835), and there described as "The prison of the Marshalsea of the Court of King's Bench; a prison for debtors, and for persons confined under the sentence or charged with the contempt of his Majesty's Court of King's Bench." By this Act the King's Bench, the Fleet, and Marshalsea Prisons were consolidated, and called "The King's Prison," changed on the death of the King in 1837 to "The Queen's Prison." All fees, the liberty of the rules and day rules, were abolished by the same Act. "The Brace Public-house" was abolished by the same Act. [*See* King's Bench Prison.] An Act was passed in 1862 "for discontinuing the Queen's Prison and removal of the prisoners to Whitecross Street Prison."

Queen's Road, BAYSWATER, in Roque's Map, 1745, appears as *Westbourne Green Lane.* At the south-west corner was Shaftesbury House. Mr. Whiteley's immense establishment now occupies a part of the road.

Queen's Walk is the path along the east side of the Green Park, connecting St. James's Park and Piccadilly. It appears in a map of 1783 but not of 1763. From this it might be inferred that it was named after Queen Charlotte, but it is more likely that it was after Queen Caroline, whose library overlooked it. [*See* Queen's Library.]

Queenhithe, in UPPER THAMES STREET, a short distance west of Southwark Bridge, a common quay for the landing of corn, flour, and other dry goods from the west of England,—originally called "Edred's hithe" or bank, from "Edred, owner thereof,"—but known, from a very early period as Ripa Reginæ, the Queen's bank or Queenhithe, because it pertained unto the Queen. King John is said to have given it to his mother, Eleanor, Queen of Henry II. It was long the rival of Billingsgate, and would have retained the monopoly of the wharfage of London had it been *below* instead of *above* bridge. In the 13th century it was the usual landing-place for wine, wool, hides, corn, firewood, fish, and indeed all kinds of commodities then brought by sea to London, and the City Records afford minute details as to "the Customs of Queen-Hythe," and the tolls ordered to be taken there by Edward I. But while the Queen's bailiff was authorised to take *Scavage* (or custom's toll) upon all goods landed there "in the same manner in which the Sheriffs of London take Scavage for his lordship the King in London elsewhere," it was declared that "all assizes of the City at the Hustings provided and enacted for the amendment of the City are to be enacted and observed" here.[1] As an illustration of the nature of the regulations we may cite the directions laid down for the measurement of corn :—

Every chief master-meter of all the serving people at Queen Hythe, shall find a quarter, bushel, half-bushel, strike [or strickle for smoothing the surface when the

---

[1] *Liber Albus,* B. iii. pt. i., and Riley's *Memorials.*

measure is full], and one horse. And there shall be eight chief masters, and each of such eight masters shall have three associates standing there; and each of such three so standing there shall find one horse and seven sacks, etc. . . . And of right there ought to be at Queen Hyde eight chief [or standard] measures for the measurement of corn. . . . None of the said horses [of the master-meters and their servants] shall be taken by the Sheriffs, or by any other persons in their names from the performance of their duties. . . . Also that no one of the said meters shall mete for any stranger without leave of the Bailiff of Queen Hythe. . . . Also that no meter, or any servant of theirs shall interfere between buyers and sellers, etc.[1]

For their meterage and carrying they are strictly forbidden to take "more than according to ancient custom ought to be taken," which is stated to be "for the measurement, porterage, and carriage of one quarter of wheat," as far as Westcheap, the church of Anthony in Budge Row and the like, "one halfpenny farthing," as far as Fleet Bridge, Newgate, Estchepe, and Billyngesgate, one penny, and for all streets and lanes beyond "as far as the Bar of the suburbs," one penny farthing. For measuring and carrying salt "no one of the meters shall take beyond one farthing more than for corn, and that according to the limits prescribed for corn." "And the Bailiff of Queen Hythe shall not take more than five shillings of a chief meter of corn and salt, or of his servant more than two shillings as his fee." For other merchandise the regulations are equally precise and stringent. No vessel was allowed to lie at anchor or be moored elsewhere than at Billingsgate or Queenhithe between sunset and sunrise, nor be placed near the Bankside of Southwark, on pain of the owners and masters losing the vessels and being sent to prison. The sixth charter of Henry III. confirms a grant by the Earl of Cornwall of the customs of Queenhithe to the City of London in consideration of a farm rent of £50 per annum.[2] When shipping began to stay below bridge—probably in part owing to the use of larger vessels and the difficulty of carrying them safely through the bridge—the decline of Queenhithe was rapid. Fabyan says that in the reign of Henry VII. the tolls barely amounted to £15 per annum.

Peele's chronicle-play of King Edward I. (4to, 1593) contains, among other things, "Lastly the sinking of Queen Elinor, who sunck at Charing Crosse and rose again at Pottershith, now named Queenhith." When accused by King Edward of her crimes, she replies in the words of the old ballad :—

> If that upon so vile a thing
> Her heart did ever think,
> She wish'd the ground might open wide,
> And therein she might sink!
> With that at Charing Cross she sunk
> Into the ground alive;
> And after rose with life again,
> In London at Queenhith.

It is here written "Queenhith," but our old dramatists almost always wrote it "Queenhive." Stow says nothing about "Pottershith."

[1] *Liber Albus*, p. 232.   [2] *Norton*, p. 370.

Milton refers scornfully to "That old wives tale of a certaine Queene of England that sunk at Charing Crosse and rose up at Queene-hithe."[1]

> A sleeping watchman here we stole the shoes from,
> There made a noise, at which he wakes, and follows;
> The streets are dirty, takes a Queenhithe cold,
> Hard cheese, and that, chokes him o' Monday next.
> *Beaumont and Fletcher. Monsieur Thomas (Works,* by Dyce, vol. vii. p. 375).

> From a right hand I assure you
> The eel boats here that lie before Queenhythe
> Came out of Holland.—Ben Jonson, *Staple of News.*

Mistress Birdlime. But I'll down to Queenhive and the watermen which were wont to carry you to Lambeth Marsh shall carry me thither.—*Westward Ho,* vol. iv. p. 1 (1607, 4to).

In the first quarter of the 17th century Queenhithe seems to have been the headquarters of the London watermen, whose place of assembly was an alehouse called the *Red Knight.*

In this time of Lent I being in the watermen's garrison of Queen-hive (whereof I am a souldier) and having no imployment, I went with an intent to incounter with that most valiant and hardy champion of Queen-hive commonly called by the name of *Red Knight.*—*Westward for Smelts (Percy Soc.* vol. lxxviii. p. 6).

When the Earl of Essex found that the attempt to "raise" the City was hopeless, and that he would scarce succeed in returning to Essex House by Ludgate, he made his way to Queenhithe and escaped thence in a boat. Tom Hill (Paul Pry) carried on his business as a drysalter in Queenhithe.[2]

Queenhithe (Ward of), one of the twenty-six wards of London; so called from the old wharf of the same name. This was originally a royal demesne, and is said to have been granted by Henry III. to his queen,[3] and thence to have been known as the Queen's Soke or liberty. As such it had independent jurisdiction, but like the other sokes ultimately became an electively represented ward. *General Boundaries.*—North, Knight Rider Street and Trinity Lane; south, the Thames; east, Bull Wharf Lane; west, Paul's Wharf, part of St. Peter's Hill, and the upper end of Lambert Hill. Stow enumerates seven churches in this ward: (1) church of the Holy Trinity in Trinity Lane (now united with St. Michael, Queenhithe; (2) St. Nicholas Cold Abbey, in Knight Rider Street; (3) St. Nicholas Olave, Bread Street Hill (destroyed in the Great Fire, and not rebuilt); (4) St. Mary-de-Monte-Alto, or Mounthaunt, in Old Fish Street Hill (destroyed in the Great Fire, and not rebuilt); (5) St. Michael's, Queenhithe; (6) St. Mary Summerset, in Thames Street, facing Broken Wharf (taken down and the parish united with St. Nicholas Cole Abbey); (7) St. Peter's, Paul's Wharf (destroyed in the Great Fire, and not rebuilt). And two Halls of Companies: (1) Painter Stainers' Hall; (2) Blacksmiths' Hall. The principal streets in the ward are parts of Upper Thames Street and Queen Victoria Street.

---

[1] Milton, *Premonstrant's Defence (Works,* 1641, vol. i. p. 223).

[2] Letter, dated Queenhithe, May 17, 1803.

[3] *Stow;* Norton.

Rag Fair, or, ROSEMARY LANE, now ROYAL MINT STREET (so named from its passing along the back of the Royal Mint), runs from Sparrow Corner, Tower Hill, to Cable Street, Wellclose Square, a place where old clothes and frippery are sold.[1]

> The articles of commerce by no means belie the name. There is no expressing the poverty of the goods; nor yet their cheapness. A distinguished merchant engaged with a purchaser, observing me to look on him with great attention, called out to me, as his customer was going off with his bargain, to observe that man, "For," says he, "I have actually clothed him for fourteen pence."—*Pennant*, p. 433.
>
> Where wave the tattered ensigns of Rag Fair.—Pope, *The Dunciad*.
>
> Thursday last one Mary Jenkins, who deals in old clothes in Rag Fair, sold a pair of breeches to a poor woman for sevenpence and a pint of beer. Whilst they were drinking it in a public house, the purchaser in unripping the breeches found quilted in the waistband eleven guineas in gold, Queen Anne's coin, and a thirty pound bank note, dated in 1729, which last she did not know the value of till after she sold it for a gallon of twopenny purl.—*The Public Advertiser*, February 14, 1756.

Royal Mint Street has hardly so evil a reputation as Rosemary Lane, but it is a squalid place, lined with old clothes' shops and stalls, and on Sunday mornings the aspect of Rag Fair, as it is still commonly called, is anything but edifying.

Ragged Staff Court, DRURY LANE, the last alley on the left side going towards St. Giles's, derived its name no doubt from one of the many inns which took the cognisance of the Dudleys for their sign.

> 1646.—To William Burnett in a seller in Ragged Staff Yard, being poore and very sicke . . . . 1s. 6d.
> *Vestry Books of St. Giles-in-the-Fields.*

This practice of dwelling in cellars, which thirty or forty years ago appeared to be universal in St. Giles's, is first mentioned in the Vestry Minutes of the parish in 1637.

> To prevent the great influx of poor people into the parish, ordered that the beadles do present every fortnight on the Sunday, the names of all new comers, undersetters, inmates, divided tenements, *persons that have families in cellars*, and other abuses.

The Metropolis Management Act, 1855 (cap. 120, sects. 103, 104), dealt with these cellar dwellings.

Rahere Street, GOSWELL ROAD to north end of CENTRAL STREET, belongs to the Governors of St. Bartholomew's Hospital, by whom it was built circ. 1808, and so called from Rahere, the founder of St. Bartholomew's Priory, on the site of the present hospital. The ground on which Rahere Street stands was designed, early in the present century, to have been the site of a new Smithfield Market, but the negotiation was broken off by the City authorities, and the street, as we now see it, built by the hospital authorities instead.

Railway Clearing House, SEYMOUR STREET, EUSTON SQUARE. The Clearing House was established in 1842 to do for the various Railway Companies what was done for the Bankers by their Clearing

[1] Pope, *Note to the Dunciad*.

House. It is regulated by an Act of Parliament passed in 1850. A sort of imaginary company is formed called the Clearing House, to which all the railways stand related as debtors and creditors, and which manages all the cross accounts from one company to another. The managers are elected by the Companies interested in its working. The business has grown to an enormous extent of late years, and the staff of clerks which at the foundation of the office consisted of twenty now consists of about 2000.

Rainbow Tavern, No. 15 FLEET STREET, a well-conducted and well-frequented tavern (famous for its stout), and originally established as a coffee-house by James Farr, as early as 1657.

When coffee first came in, he [Sir Henry Blount] was a great upholder of it, and hath ever since been a great frequenter of coffee-houses, especially Mr. Farr's, at the Rainbowe, by Inner Temple Gate.—Aubrey's *Lives*, vol. ii. p. 244.

I find it recorded that one James Farr, a barber, who kept the coffee-house which is now the Rainbow, by the Inner Temple Gate (one of the first in England), was, in the year 1657, presented by the Inquest of St. Dunstan's-in-the-West, for making and selling a sort of liquor called coffee, as a great nuisance and prejudice of the neighbourhood, etc. And who would then have thought that London would ever have 3000 such nuisances, and that coffee would have been (as now) so much drunk by the best of quality and physicians.—Hatton's *New View of London*, 8vo, 1708.

I have received a letter desiring me to be very satirical upon the little muff that is now in fashion; another informs me of a pair of silver garters buckled below the knee, that have been lately seen at the Rainbow Coffee House in Fleet Street.—*The Spectator*, No. 16.

The Phœnix Fire Office (the second office established in this country for insurance against fire) was located at the Rainbow Tavern in Fleet Street as early as 1682.[1]

The sign existed before the establishment of the coffee-house. There is an imprint of 1641 as follows:—" Printed by Richard Bishop for Daniel Pakeman at the sign of the Rainbow in Fleet Street near the Inner Temple Gate."

Ram Alley, now MITRE COURT, FLEET STREET, over against Fetter Lane.

Ram Alley [is] taken up by publick houses; a place of no great reputation, as being a kind of privileged place for debtors, before the late Act of Parliament [9 and 10 Will. III., c. 27, s. 15] for taking them away. It hath a passage into the Temple and into Serjeants' Inn in Fleet Street.—*Strype*, B. iii. p. 277.

It was of no great reputation a century earlier.

> Methinks he is a ruffian in his style,
> . . . .
> Cuts, thrusts, and foins at whomsoe'er he meets!
> And strows about Ram Alley meditations.
> *Character of Marston: Return from Parnassus*, 1606.

> And though Ram Alley stinks with cooks and ale,
> Yet say there's many a worthy lawyer's chamber
> 'Buts upon Ram Alley.
> *Ram Alley, or Merry Tricks*; a Comedy by Lo. Barrey, 4to, 1611.

---

[1] Delaune, *Anglia Metrop.*, 1690, p. 352; Hatton, *New View*, 1708, p. 787.

Come you to seek a virgin in Ram Alley,
So near an Inn-of-Court, and amongst cooks,
Ale-men and laundresses?—*Ibid.*

Amble. The knave thinks still he's at the Cook's shop in Ram Alley,
Where the clerks divide, and the elder is to choose;
And feeds so slovenly!—Massinger, *A New Way to Pay Old Debts.*

Ben Jonson, in his *Staple of News*, 1625, represents Lickfinger, "My cook, that unctuous rascal," as the glory of the kitchen, and master of a shop in Ram Alley. From this play we learn also that some portions at least of the City banquets were supplied from this locality, for Lickfinger had managed to convey twenty eggs from the number supplied to him for "the Custard Politic,"—the huge custard prepared for the Lord Mayor's feast. The Ram's Alley cooks also supplied dinners at the taverns; thus Lickfinger furnished "the great feast" which Penniboy junior gave at the Apollo.[1]

1627.—That Christmas the Temple Sparks had installed a Lieutenant, a thing we country folk call a Lord of Misrule. The Lieutenant had on Twelfth-eve last, late in the night, sent out to collect his rents in Ram Alley and Fleet Street, limiting five shillings to every house. At every door they winded their Temple horn, and if it procured not entrance at the second blast or summons, the word of command was—Give fire Gunner! The Gunner was a robustious Vulcan and his engine a mighty smith's hammer.—L'Estrange's *Reign of King Charles*, p. 72.

Belford, sen. Here's Mr. Cheatly shall sham and banter with you, or any one you will bring, for five hundred pound of my money.

Belford, jun. Rascally stuff, fit for no places but Ram Alley or Pye Corner.— *The Squire of Alsatia*, by T. Shadwell, 4to, 1688.

July 5, 1668.—With Sir W. Coventry, and we walked in the Park together a good while. He mighty kind to me; and hear many pretty stories of my Lord Chancellor's being heretofore made sport of by Peter Talbot, the priest, in his story of the death of Cardinal Bleau; by Lord Cottington, in his *Dolor de las Tripas*; and by Tom Killegrew in his being bred in Ram Ally, and bound prentice to Lord Cottington.—*Pepys.*

The Fire [of London] decreased, having burned all on the Thames side to the new buildings of the Inner Temple, next to Whitefriars, and having consumed them was stopped by that vacancy from proceeding further into that house; but laid hold on some old buildings which joined to Ram Alley, and swept all those into Fleet Street.—Lord Clarendon's *Autobiography*, ed. 1827, vol. iii. p. 90.

The specialty of Ram Alley did not escape Sir Walter Scott, though the reference to it comes rather curiously from the mouth of a high-born lady addressing the Queen.

The Queen said, when she stepped into the boat, that Saye's Court looked like a guard-house and smelt like an hospital.—"Like a cook's shop in Ram Alley rather," said the Countess of Rutland.—*Kenilworth*, vol. i. p. 284.

There was a Ram Alley in Leadenhall Street, and others by Smithfield, Spitalfields and Rotherhithe.

Ramilies Street. [*See* Blenheim Street.]

Ranelagh, a place of public entertainment, erected on the site of the gardens of a villa of Earl Ranelagh, at Chelsea, from the designs of William Jones, architect, in 1742. The principal room (the

[1] *Staple of News*, Act iii. Sc. 1. etc.

Rotunda) was 150 feet in diameter, with an orchestra in the centre, and tiers of boxes all round. The chief amusement was promenading (as it was called) round and round[1] the circular area below, and taking refreshments in the boxes, while the orchestra executed different pieces of music. It was a kind of "Vauxhall under cover," warmed with coal-fires. The rotunda is said to have been projected by Lacy, an actor, and the patentee of Drury Lane Theatre. The *coup d'œil*, Dr. Johnson declared, "was the finest thing he had ever seen." The last appearance (if one may use the expression) of Ranelagh was when the installation ball of the Knights of the Bath, in 1802, was given there. It was closed after July 8, 1803, and an order made, September 30, 1805, for pulling it down. The site of Ranelagh is now part of Chelsea Hospital garden, between Church Row and the river, to the east of the hospital, the roadway and the barracks. No traces of it remain.

I have been breakfasting this morning at Ranelagh Garden; they have built an immense amphitheatre, with balconies full of little ale houses; it is in rivalry to Vauxhall, and costs above twelve thousand pounds. The building is not finished, but they get great sums by people going to see it and breakfasting in the house: there were yesterday no less than three hundred and eighty persons, at eighteen pence a piece.—*Walpole to Mann*, April 22, 1742.

The invalides at Chelsea intend to present Ranelagh Gardens as a nuisance, for breaking their first sleep with the sound of fiddles. It opens I think to-night.—*Gray to Mr. Chute*, vol. ii. p. 187.

Two nights ago Ranelagh Gardens were opened at Chelsea; the prince, princess, duke, much nobility, and much mob besides were there. There is a vast amphitheatre, finely gilt, painted, and illuminated; into which everybody that loves eating, drinking, staring, or crowding is admitted for twelve pence. The building and disposition of the gardens cost sixteen thousand pounds. Twice a week there are to be ridottos at guinea tickets, for which you are to have a supper and music. I was there last night, but did not find the joy of it. Vauxhall is a little better, for the garden is pleasanter, and one goes by water.—*Walpole to Mann*, May 26, 1742.

Every night constantly I go to Ranelagh; which has totally beat Vauxhall. Nobody goes anywhere else—everybody goes there. My Lord Chesterfield is so fond of it that he says he has ordered all his letters to be directed thither.—*Walpole to Conway*, June 29, 1744.

Walpole has a great many other references to Ranelagh, and notices of it might be multiplied to any extent from other writers. Smollett, speaking from the Matt. Bramble point of view, says, "What are the amusements of Ranelagh? One half of the company are following one another's tails, in an eternal circle, like so many blind asses in an olive mill, where they can neither discourse, distinguish nor be distinguished; while the other half are drinking hot water under the denomination of tea, till nine or ten o'clock at night, to keep them awake for the rest of the evening." On the other hand, the gay young niece was in raptures with everything. The concerts and the company were the permanent attraction, but during several seasons masquerades drew the fashionable world in crowds. Bonnell Thornton's Burlesque Ode on St. Cecilia's Day, set to music by Dr. Burney, was performed

---

[1] There is a little poem of Bloomfield's describing this promenading round and round.

with great success at Ranelagh. The usual charge for admission was 2s. 6d., "tea and coffee included." When fireworks were exhibited, the charge was 5s.

There is a good view of the interior of the Rotunda, with the company at breakfast, in the 1754 edition of Stow; and the ground plan of the gardens is carefully laid down in Horwood's Map of London, 1794-1799. Several other views have been published.

Ranelagh House, CHELSEA, erected circ. 1691, to the east of the present hospital, by Richard, Earl of Ranelagh, on a piece of ground near Chelsea College, granted to him by William III., on March 12, 1689-1690, for the term of sixty-one years,[1] and built, it is said, after a design by Lord Ranelagh himself. The house was taken down in 1805. This Lord Ranelagh, who died in 1712, was the Jones of De Grammont's *Memoirs*.

Ranelagh Street, PIMLICO, now the eastern part of Ebury Street.

> I paced upon my beat
> With steady step and slow,
> All huppandownd of Ranelagh Street
> Ran'lagh Street, Pimlico.
> Thackeray, *Lines on a late Hospicious Event*.

Ratcliffe, a manor and hamlet in the parish of STEPNEY, between Shadwell and Limehouse.

Radcliffe itself hath also been encreased in building eastward (in place where I have known a large highway with fair elm trees on both the sides), that the same hath now taken hold of Limehurst or Lime host, corruptly called Lime house, some time distant a mile from Radcliffe. . . . The first building at Radcliffe in my youth (not to be forgotten) was a fair free-school and alms-houses, founded by Avice Gibson, wife to Nicholas Gibson, grocer; but of late years shipwrights and (for the most part) other marine men, have built many large and strong houses for themselves, and smaller for sailors, from thence almost to Poplar, and so to Blackwall.—*Stow* (1603), p. 157.

Ratcliffe is still for the most part occupied by marine men and those dependent upon or connected with them. But the buildings are rather places of business than dwellings, and the building space has been largely encroached upon for docks and yards. Lancelot Andrewes, the learned Bishop of Winchester of the reigns of James and Charles, received his first "education in grammar-learning in the Coopers' free-school at Ratcliffe, under Mr. Ward."[2] When Sir Walter Raleigh was organising the expedition to Cadiz in 1596, he literally lived on the river for many weeks. In his letters to Cecil this place is often referred to as *Ratleife* and *Racklieif*.

Ratcliffe Cross is mentioned by Dryden, and still exists, though it does not find a place in the Post Office Directory. It runs from the intersection of the old road from Stepney (Butchers' Row) with Broad Street, Shadwell, and Narrow Street, Limehouse, to Ratcliffe Cross Stairs, formerly a much used landing-place and ferry. At Ratcliffe

[1] *Appendix to Seventh Report of the Deputy Keeper of the Public Records*, p. 82.
[2] *Biog. Brit.*, vol. i. p. 184.

Cross, though far outside the City, was the ancient hall of the Shipwrights' Company.[1]

Tom. I have heard a ballad of him [the Protector Somerset] sung at Ratcliff Cross-*Mol.* I believe we have it at home over our kitchen mantle tree.—Dryden's *Misc. Poems*, ed. 1727, vol. iii. p. 296.

Ratcliffe Dock, on the west of Ratcliffe Cross, was one of those natural creeks so much prized by our ancestors.

Ratcliffe Highway runs from EAST SMITHFIELD to SHADWELL HIGH STREET, and was so called from the manor of Ratcliffe, in the parish of Stepney, towards which it led. Its name has been changed to ST. GEORGE STREET. From end to end the street has a maritime savour. In some way or other every shop and place of business or resort seems to be dependent on ships or sailors. The very churches and institutions—Seamen's Mission Hall, Seamen's Chapel, Seamen's Free Reading-Room, Bethel Station; and, unfortunately, flaring drinking, dancing, and music rooms, and haunts of a far worse order. Here, among other "dens," are the Chinese opium-smokers' sties. William Hogarth engraved a shop bill, in the manner of Callot, for "William Hardy, goldsmith and jeweller, in Ratcliff Highway, near Sun Tavern Fields," of which only one impression is known. 455 houses and 36 warehouses were burnt down on July 23, 1794. The murders of Marr and Williamson in Ratcliffe Highway are among the most notorious atrocities of the present century. Marr kept a lace and pelisse warehouse at 29 Ratcliffe Highway, and about twelve at night, on Saturday December 7, 1811, had sent his female servant to purchase oysters for supper, whilst he was shutting up the shop windows. On her return, in about a quarter of an hour, she rang the bell repeatedly without any person coming. The house was then broken open, and Mr. and Mrs. Marr, the shop-boy, and a child in the cradle (the only human beings in the house) were found murdered. The murders of the Marr family were followed, twelve days later, and about twelve at night, by the murders of Williamson, landlord of the King's Arms public-house, in Old Gravel Lane, Ratcliffe Highway, his wife, and female servant. A man named Williams, the only person suspected, hanged himself in prison, and was carried on a platform, placed on a high cart, past the houses of Marr and Williamson, and afterwards thrown, with a stake through his breast, into a hole dug for the purpose where the New Road crosses and Cannon Street Road begins. Sir Thomas Lawrence made a drawing of this miscreant immediately after he was cut down.[2] These murders form the subject of De Quincey's remarkable essay entitled *Murder considered as a Fine Art.*

Many of our readers can remember the state of London just after the murders of Marr and Williamson—the terror which was on every face—the careful barring of doors—the providing of blunderbusses and watchmen's rattles. We know of a shopkeeper who on that occasion sold three hundred rattles in about ten hours.—Macaulay's *Essays* (Mackintosh's *Hist. of the Revolution*).

---

[1] *Maitland*, p. 610. [2] Sale Catalogue, second day, No. 267.

At Nos. 179 and 180 Ratcliffe Highway (or St. George Street) is the remarkable establishment of Mr. "Charles Jamrach, naturalist"—the largest dealer in wild animals in Europe, where you may at any time purchase anything in that line from an elephant, giraffe, or rattlesnake to a dormouse or Java sparrow. Here and in his stores in Old Gravel Lane, close by, "you may be supplied with hyænas by the dozen, lions in neat little lots of twenty to five and twenty each; parcels of giraffes, snakes, or boa-constrictors; and samples of tigers, buffaloes, eagles, monkeys, bears and kangaroos." In one room, the late rector of St. George's tells us, 2000 paroquets "may sometimes be seen flying loosely about."[1]

In *Princes Square*, Ratcliffe Highway, is the *Swedish Protestant Church*, in which Emanuel Swedenborg (d. 1772), whose followers form the New Jerusalem Church (Swedenborgians), was buried, by the side of Dr. Solander, the companion round the world of Sir Joseph Banks. In this church, on Sunday, September 18, 1748, an order was read prohibiting all natives of Sweden and their servants from wearing gold or silver in any shape about their dress.[2]

Rathbone Place, in OXFORD STREET, was so called after a carpenter and builder of that name.[3] A stone inscribed "RATHBONES PLACE, IN OXFORD STREET, 1718," was on the front of a house at the east corner of Oxford Street, which was taken down and rebuilt in 1864. The stone was replaced in the wall of the new house.

Rathbone Place at this time (1784) entirely consisted of private houses, and its inhabitants were all of high respectability. I have heard Mrs. Mathew say (the wife of the incumbent, for whom Percy Chapel was built) that the three rebel lords, Lovat, Kilmarnock, and Balmerino, had at different times resided in it.—*A Book for a Rainy Day*, by J. T. Smith, p. 85.

Mr. Mathew's house in Rathbone Place was a favourite resort of Flaxman, Stothard, and Blake. [*See* Percy Chapel.] Flaxman as a mark of esteem decorated the parlour, Mathew's library, with "models of figures in niches, in the Gothic manner, and Oram painted the window in imitation of stained glass,"[4] the bookcases and furniture being also ornamented in a corresponding style.

Mr. Nollekens stopped at the corner of Rathbone Place, and observed that when he was a little boy [he was born August 1737] his mother often took him to the top of that street to walk by the side of a long pond, near a windmill, which then stood on the site of the chapel in Charlotte Street [*see* Percy Chapel]; and that a halfpenny was paid by every person at a hatch belonging to the miller, for the privilege of walking in his grounds.—Smith's *Life of Nollekens*, vol. i. p. 37.

In July 1742 Bolingbroke wrote from Rathbone Place to the Earl of Marchmont asking him to dine the next day with himself and Pope at Twickenham, and "carry him to Battersea in the evening." Ozias Humphrey, R.A. (d. 1810), was living at No. 29 Rathbone Place from 1777 to 1785, when he went to India. Nathaniel Hone, R.A.,

[1] Parkinson's *Places and People*; Rev. H. Jones, *East and West London*.
[2] *Gent. Mag.*, September 1748, p. 425. [3] Parton's *St. Giles's*, p. 47. [4] *Smith*, p. 84.

painter of the picture called "The Conjurer" (an attack on Sir Joshua Reynolds's method of composing his pictures), died at his house, No. 29 Rathbone Place, August 14, 1784. Baron Maseres at No. 14 in 1803. The well-known publication called the *Percy Anecdotes*, edited by Sholto and Reuben Percy, derives its name from the Percy Coffee-house, in Rathbone Place (now no more), where the idea of the work was first started by Mr. George Byerley and Mr. Joseph Clinton Robertson, the Sholto and Reuben Percy of the collection. E. H. Bailey, R.A., the sculptor, was living here in 1826, and another inhabitant was Peter De Wint, the eminent water-colour painter.

Raven Alley, WHITECHAPEL ROAD, is mentioned in *Hudibras Redivivus* (4to, 1707):—

> Yet I'm no upstart Albumazer;
> Altho' a Fool, no Planet-Gazer;
> That in this Coat has made a Sally
> From the six Steps in *Raven Alley*.

But it does not occur in Hatton's list of streets, etc., in London, Westminster, and Southwark, 1708; Maitland's, 1729; Dodsley's, 1761; or any of the maps of the early part of the 18th century.

Rawthmell's Coffee-house, HENRIETTA STREET, COVENT GARDEN, a fashionable coffee-house between 1730 and 1775, and so called after a Mr. John Rawthmell, long a respectable parishioner of St. Paul's, Covent Garden. Here the "Society of Arts" was first established (1754), and here Armstrong, the poet of the "Art of Preserving Health," was a frequent visitor.

Ray Street, CLERKENWELL, formerly *Hockley in the Hole*. The present name is derived from the proprietor. Here is, or was, the well where the parish clerks before the Reformation performed a miracle-play once a year, and from which the district of Clerkenwell derived its name. The old Ray Street was nearly swept away in the Clerkenwell improvements of 1856 and subsequent years. Some years earlier the clerks' well was discovered to be dangerously polluted by the infiltration of sewage, and closed, and shortly after the pump, which had for many years marked its site, was removed. [*See* Clerkenwell.]

Record Office (Public), FETTER LANE, was erected from the designs of Mr. (afterwards Sir James) Penniethorne, 1856-1870, to contain the national archives previously deposited in the Chapel in the White Tower [*see* Tower]; the Chapter-house, Westminster Abbey; the Rolls Chapel in Chancery Lane; Carlton Ride in St. James's Park, and the State Paper Office, St. James's Park. The building, which was erected on the Rolls estate between Chancery Lane and Fetter Lane, is a vast castellated structure, well adapted internally to the safe keeping of the inestimable documents and allowing ready access to them. The muniment rooms are "cubes of seventeen feet, fitted up in the most economical manner as to space," and filled with documents. These rooms are ranged along narrow brick-paved passages, the entrances to which on either hand are by iron doors. The shelves are of slate, and every effort has been made to render the whole fire-proof.

The documents are of great extent and of unequalled historical interest and value. They include a long series of royal charters, chancery records from the reign of John, Exchequer records, the great rolls of the Pipe, the Gascon rolls, the judicial records of the Curia Regis and other courts, the courts of the Star Chamber and Requests, the early Year-books, the documents relating to the suppression of monasteries, the vast array of documents classed under the head of Domestic Records reaching from the reign of Henry VIII., and including colonial as well as home archives, and relating to the crown and household and wardrobe expenditure, the secret service, War-office, and Admiralty. The archives may be said to commence with that unrivalled national survey, the Domesday Book of William; and among the more interesting of the later examples are the Treaty of Peace between Henry VIII. and Francis I., to which is attached the beautiful gold seal in high relief which is said to be the work of Benvenuto Cellini; the deed of recognition of Edward as Sovereign and direct Lord of Scotland, and numerous royal autograph letters.

Access to the documents may be obtained on application, and signing the name and address in a book kept for the purpose.

Red Bull Theatre stood at the upper end of *St. John Street*, on what was until recently called "Red Bull Yard," and Woodbridge Street, St. John's Street Road. Mr. Payne Collier conjectures that it was originally an inn-yard, converted into a regular theatre late in the reign of Queen Elizabeth.

Cit. Why so, Sir: go and fetch me him then, and let the Sophy of Persia come and christen him a child.

Boy. Believe me, Sir, that will not do so well: 'tis stale; it has been tried before at the Red Bull.—Beaumont and Fletcher, *The Knight of the Burning Pestle*, vol. iv. p. 1.

Last week at a puppet play, at St. John Street, the house fell, six persons were killed, and thirty or forty hurt.—*Chamberlain to Carleton*, August 23, 1599 (*Cal. State Pap.*, p. 306).

Prynne speaks of it in 1633 as a theatre that had been "lately re-edified and enlarged." It was closed during the plague of 1636-1637.

The Red Bull in St. Johns Streete, who for the present (alack the while) is not suffred to carrie the flagge in the mainetop.—*A New Book of Mistakes*, 1637.

The King's players, under Killigrew, performed within its walls till a stage in Drury Lane was ready to receive them. "The Red Bull stands empty for fencers," writes Davenant in 1663; "there are no tenants in it but old spiders."

It was afterwards employed for trials of skill. Mr. Collier possessed a printed challenge and acceptance of a trial at eight several weapons, to be performed betwixt two scholars of Benjamin Dobson and William Wright, masters of the noble science of defence. The trial was to come off "at the Red Bull, at the upper end of St. John's Street, on

Whitsun Monday, the 30th of May, 1664, beginning exactly at three of the clock in the afternoon, and the best man is to take all." The weapons were: "back-sword, single rapier, sword and dagger, rapier and dagger, sword and buckler, half pike, sword and gauntlet, single faulchion." Mr. James Greenstreet communicated to *The Athenæum*, February 21, August 29, and November 29, 1885, some important documents relating to the theatre in 1613 and 1623.

Red Cross Street, CRIPPLEGATE, from Fore Street to Barbican.

In Red Cross Street, on the west side from St. Giles's Churchyard up to the said Crosse, be many fair houses built outward, with divers alleys turning into a large plot of ground, called the Jews' Garden, as being the only place appointed them in England wherein to bury their dead, till the year 1177, the 24th of Henry II. that it was permitted to them (after long suit to the King and Parliament at Oxford) to have a special place assigned them in every quarter where they dwelt. This plot of ground remained to the said Jews till the time of their final banishment out of England, and is now turned into fair garden-plots and summer-houses for pleasure. [*See* Jewin Street.] On the east side of the Red Cross Street be also divers fair houses up to the Cross.—*Stow*, p. 113.

And first to shew you that by conjecture he [Richard III.] pretended this thing in his brother's life, you shall understand for a truth that the same night that King Edward dyed, one called Mistelbrooke, long ere the day sprung, came to the house of one Pottier, dwelling in Red Crosse Street without Cripple Gate, of London, and when he was, with hasty wrapping, quickly let in, the said Mistelbrooke shewed unto Pottier that King Edward was that night deceased. "By my truth," quoth Pottier, "then will my master the Duke of Gloucester be King, and that I warrant thee." What cause he had so to think, hard it is to say, whether he, being his servant, knew any such thing pretended, or otherwise had any inkling thereof, but of all likelihood he spake it not of nought.—Sir Thomas More (*The Pitiful Life of King Edward the Fifth*, 12mo, 1641, p. 27).

Here was Dr. Williams's Theological Library, now in Grafton Street East, Gower Street. [*See* Dr. Williams's Library.] Lady Holles's School for Girls, rebuilt 1887-1888, is in this street.

Red House, BATTERSEA, a favourite tea-garden and noted place for shooting matches, on the Surrey side of the Thames, nearly opposite Chelsea Hospital. Until the formation of Battersea Park the Red House was the headquarters of the Gun Club. It was purchased by Government in 1850 for £11,000, and pulled down in order that the site might be included in Battersea Park. It stood as nearly as possible between the south end of Chelsea Bridge and the east gate of Battersea Park.

Red Lion Court, FLEET STREET, north side, east of Fetter Lane. William Bowyer, the learned printer, moved into this court from Whitefriars in 1767. John Nichols (of the *Gentleman's Magazine*), his "apprentice, partner and successor" (and biographer), had just been admitted into partnership. When Jennens, the Shakespeare editor, visited his printers he always came in a carriage with four horses and the same number of footmen, and in his progress up the paved court the footmen preceded him to kick oyster shells or orange peel out of his way. Nichols's office was destroyed by fire, February 8, 1808.

His son and grandson continued the business in Parliament Street. Printers, publishers, bookbinders, and others connected with "the trade," still occupy the major part of the houses in Red Lion Court, and many periodicals are published here.

> One word before we part : call upon Mr. John Nichols, bookseller and printer at Cicero's Head, Red Lion Passage, Fleet Street, and ask him whether he did not, about the beginning of March, receive a very polite letter from Mr. Gibbon of Lausanne.—*Gibbon to Lord Sheffield*, May 30, 1792.

Red Lion Court, GILTSPUR STREET, a short passage of old-fashioned houses on the south side of Cock Lane, extending to the back of St. Sepulchre's churchyard, now called RED LION BUILDINGS. Here after his marriage with Miss Mead, 1749, John Wilkes lived in the house of Mrs. Mead, his wife's mother, and here, August 5, 1750, his daughter, so often referred to in his correspondence, was born. He removed to Great George Street shortly after.

Red Lion Passage leads from the south-east corner of Red Lion Square into Red Lion Street, Holborn. Erskine was living here, as a temporary arrangement, when he got his first brief.[1]

Red Lion Square, on the north side of HOLBORN. Built circ. 1698, and so called of "The Red Lion Inn," long the largest and best frequented inn in Holborn.

> He came back again unto London, where he lodged in the Red Lyon in Holborne.—*Stow*, by Howes, ed. 1631, p. 672.

> He [Andrew Marvell] lies interred under ye pewes in the south side of Saint Giles's Church in ye Fields, under the window wherein is painted in glasse a red lyon (it was given by the Inneholder of the Red Lyon Inne in Holborne).—*Aubrey's Lives*, vol. iii. p. 438.

> Thomas, a child borne under the Redd Lyon Elmes in the fields in High Holborn, baptized iij of August 1614.—*Register of St. Andrew's*, Holborn.

On the 29th of January 1661 the corpses of Oliver Cromwell, Ireton and Bradshaw were removed from Westminster to the Red Lion in Holborn, and on the following morning put upon a sledge and dragged to Tyburn, there to undergo the ignominy with which our historians have made every one familiar.[2] Rede in his *Anecdotes and Biography*, 1799, repeats a tradition that Cromwell's mutilated remains were procured by some devoted followers and reverently buried in a field on the north side of Holborn, and that the obelisk which stood in the centre of Red Lion Square marked the site of the grave. No contemporary or early writer, so far as we know, alludes to any such tradition, which has all the appearance of being a late invention. Sir Philip Yorke (Earl Hardwicke) took a house in this square in 1727, in which he resided till 1731. At this time the centre of the square was in a dirty and neglected condition, and a newspaper paragraph, quoted in the *Hardwicke Correspondence*, relates the attempt made to improve it.

> Red Lion Square in Holborn, having for some years lain in a ruinous condition, a proposal is on foot for applying to Parliament for power to beautify it, as the inhabitants of Lincoln's Inn Fields have lately done.

---

[1] Rogers's *Recollections*, p. 184.   [2] Rugge's *Diurnall, MS.*

The central area was "inclosed with iron rails, a stone watch-house" was erected "at each corner, and a plain obelisk in the centre." But the effort to beautify added little cheerfulness to the aspect of the square, if we may trust the impressions of a somewhat later writer.

Red Lion Square . . . has a very different effect on the mind. . . . I am sure I never go into it without thinking of my latter end. The rough sod that "heaves in many a mouldering heap," the dreary length of the sides, with the four watch-houses like so many family vaults at the corners, and the naked obelisk that springs from amidst the rank grass, like the sad monument of a disconsolate widow for the loss of her first husband; form altogether a *memento mori*, more powerful to me than a death's head and cross marrow-bones; and were but a parson's bull to be seen bellowing at the gate, the idea of a country church-yard in my mind would be complete.—*Critical Obs. on the Buildings and Improvements of London*, 4to, 1771, p. 13.

The watch-houses and the obelisk have long since been removed, and the enclosure was turned into a public garden, in 1885, at a cost of £327, under the superintendence of the Metropolitan Public Gardens Association.

In this square, in 1733, died Lord Chief Justice Raymond; his body was opened by Cheselden the surgeon in the presence of Dr. Mead. The benevolent Jonas Hanway, the traveller and founder of the Marine Society and Magdalen Hospital, lived and died (1786) in a house in Red Lion Square, the principal rooms of which he decorated with paintings and emblematical devices, "in a style," says his biographer, "peculiar to himself." His object was, he says, "to relieve this vacuum in social intercourse [between the time of assembling and the placing of the card tables] and prevent cards from engrossing the whole of my visitors' minds, I have presented them with objects the most attractive I could imagine—and when that fails there are the cards." Hanway was the first man who ventured to walk the streets of London with an umbrella over his head. After carrying one nearly thirty years he saw them come into general use. Dr. Parsons, the accomplished physician, died here in April 1770, in a house which he had occupied for many years. He left directions that he should not be buried till some change appeared in his corpse. He was kept unburied seventeen days. Henry Mayer, the portrait painter, lived at No. 3. Here Charles Lamb sat to him in 1826. Sharon Turner, the historian, practised for many years as an attorney at No. 32. He was living here in 1808; and here he died, February 13, 1847, aged seventy-eight. Haydon, the historical painter, was living about 1838 in a large house on the west side of Red Lion Square, immediately north of where now stands the church of St. John the Evangelist. This church, consecrated in 1878, was built from the designs of J. L. Pearson, R.A. The foundation stone was laid June 30, 1874.

Red Lion Street, CLERKENWELL GREEN, was partly built in 1719, with other buildings in the neighbourhood, by Alexander Graves, builder (d. Nov. 13, 1737). At No. 1 in this street—the Jerusalem Tavern, cleared away in forming Clerkenwell Road—John

Britton, the antiquary, was apprenticed at the beginning of 1787 to the business of a wine merchant, and served six dreary years "in the vaults . . . forcing or fining wines, bottling, corking, and binning the same."[1] He relates that while here he saw a man "pilloried and pelted on Clerkenwell Green, and in Red Lion Street another flogged at the cart's tail, both ceremonies of the most terrifying kind." The Rev. Joseph Trusler, LL.D. (d. 1820), the "moralizer" of Hogarth, at this time, says Britton,[2] "lived in Red Lion Street, a few doors from my vaulted home." He was eking out a precarious income by compiling sermons for country clergymen.

Red Lion Street, HOLBORN—north side, to Lamb's Conduit Street. [*See* Red Lion Square.] On the wall of the house, at the corner of Holborn on the west side (*The Old Red Lion*), is a block of wood let in, with the date "1611" inscribed upon it.

Red Lion Street, WHITECHAPEL, HIGH STREET to GREAT ALIE STREET, now incorporated with LEMAN STREET. Here Dick Turpin in a fray with the constables accidentally shot his friend King.

Red Lion Yard, HOUNDSDITCH. This opening was on the west side of Houndsditch, nearly opposite the present *Cock and Hoop Yard.* Here, February 15, 1748, was born Jeremy Bentham. His father and grandfather had been attorneys in this yard for a long series of years. In 1720 Strype described it as a "pretty square place with indifferent good buildings." The elder Bentham's house was the last on the left-hand side.[3]

Redriff, a corruption of Rotherhithe. [*See* Rotherhithe.] The immortal Gulliver was, as Swift tells us, long an inhabitant of Redriff.

> Have I for this thy tedious absence borne,
> And waked, and wished whole nights for thy return?
> In five long years I took no second spouse,
> What Redriff wife so long hath kept her vows?
>   Swift, *Mary Gulliver to Captain Lemuel Gulliver.*

Filch. These seven handkerchiefs, madam.
Mrs. Peachum. Coloured ones, I see. They are of sure sale from our warehouse at Redriff among the seamen.—Gay, *The Beggars Opera,* 8vo, 1728.

Reform Club, on the south side of Pall Mall, between the Travellers' Club and the Carlton Club, was founded by the Liberal members of the two Houses of Parliament about the time the Reform Bill was canvassed and carried, 1830-1832. The Club consists of 1400 members, exclusive of members of either House of Parliament. Entrance fee, 30 guineas; annual subscription, £10:10s. The house was built, 1837-1840, from the designs of Sir Charles Barry, R.A., based on the Farnese Palace. The exterior is greatly admired, though the windows, it is urged, are too small, and scarcely important enough in effect. The interior, especially the large square hall covered

---

[1] *Autob. of John Britton,* vol. i. p. 64.   [2] *Ibid.,* vol. i. p. 70.
[3] Bowring's *Life of Bentham,* p. 5.

with glass, occupying the centre of the building, is very imposing.
The water supply is from an artesian well, 360 feet deep, sunk at the
expense of the Club. The cooking establishment of the Club attained
great celebrity under the superintendence of M. Soyer, and still
sustains its reputation.

> I am here [War Office] every day; and if you should happen to come into these parts to see the National Gallery, or to look at the new building which Barry has erected for the Reform Club—a building worthy of Michel Angelo—I should be truly glad if you will look in on me.—*Macaulay to Leigh Hunt*, March 24, 1841.

Regency Theatre, TOTTENHAM STREET, TOTTENHAM COURT
ROAD, afterwards the *Prince of Wales Theatre* [which *see*], and now
occupied by the Salvation Army. Here, in 1802, Colonel Greville
instituted his Picnic Society.

Regent Square, GRAY'S INN ROAD. At the south-west angle is
the National Scottish Church, a large Gothic edifice, designed 1827-
1828 by Mr. (afterwards Sir William) Tite, architect. The cost, with
that of the freehold site, was £25,000. In the view from Hampstead
Heath it is often mistaken, from its two towers, for Westminster Abbey.
It was built for the Rev. Edward Irving. Here the "unknown tongues"
were often heard. At the east end is St. Peter's, best known as
Regent Square Church, a semi-classic building with an Ionic portico
and tower, designed 1824-1826 at a cost of £16,000, by William
and H. W. Inwood, the architects of new St. Pancras Church.

Regent Street, perhaps the most effective street in the metropolis,
was designed and carried out by John Nash, architect (d. 1835),
under an Act of Parliament obtained in 1813, 53 George III., c. 120.
It was nearly all completed in 1820. The portion up to Piccadilly
was finished in 1817. The street was intended as a communication from Carlton House to the Regent's Park, and commenced at
St. Alban's Street, facing Carlton House, thence through St. James's
Market across Piccadilly to Castle Street, where it formed a quadrant,
to intersect with Swallow Street, and then, taking the line of Swallow
Street (the site of which is about the centre of Regent Street), it
crossed Oxford Street to Foley House, where it intersected with
Portland Place. Foley House and grounds (the site of the Langham
Hotel) were bought by Mr. Nash for £70,000, as part of the plan,
but after again selling the ground, he changed the route and formed
the present turn of Langham Place, instead of the straight line into
Portland Place as was at first intended. All Souls Church was
built by Nash as a termination to the view up Regent Street from
Oxford Street. For this purpose the tower and spire are advanced
forward to the centre line of the street, and they appear almost isolated
from the church. Polytechnic Institution, erected 1838, from the
designs of Mr. J. Thomson, architect, and enlarged in 1848 [which *see*].
Argyll Rooms, at the north corner of Argyll and Regent Streets,
erected by Nash in 1816 for Joseph Welch. The large room was the

best in London for sound, and was used for the Philharmonic and all
other concerts of note until burnt down in 1834, when the present
houses, Nos. 246, 248, 250, 252, and 254 Regent Street, were erected
on the site. Argyll Place, formed at the time of making Regent
Street, by taking down a house at the south-west end of Argyll Street,
leading to Great Marlborough Street. County Fire Office [which *see*],
erected on high ground, and, when viewed from Pall Mall, apparently
terminating the lower part of Regent Street. The Quadrant was designed
by Mr. Nash (on ground leased by him from the Commissioners), and
originally consisted of two rows of shops, with bold projecting
colonnades, removed in 1848. [*See* Quadrant.] Raleigh Club (No.
16), on the east side of the lower part of the street. Junior
Constitutional Club, No. 14 (part of the same façade), late the Gallery
of Illustration, was built by Mr. Nash for his own residence. He lived
here until he retired from his profession. The gallery was decorated
with copies of Raphael's paintings, to make which (with permission of
the Pope) he had artists employed for four years at Rome. The
Junior United Service Club, north corner of Charles Street and east
side of Regent Street, was built by Sir Robert Smirke for the United
Service Club, who sold it to the Junior United Service Club when
they erected their present house in Pall Mall. The present elaborate
edifice was built from the designs of Messrs. Nelson and Innes, architects,
in 1857. Hanover Chapel, on the north-west side of Regent Street,
was built (1823-1825) from the designs of C. R. Cockerell, R.A.,
and St. Philip's Chapel (1819-1820), on the south-west side, from the
designs of G. S. Repton. St. James's Hall (No. 69) was erected in
1857 from the designs of Owen Jones.

In his designs for Regent Street Mr. Nash adopted the idea,
previously practised with success by the brothers Adam, of uniting
several dwellings into a single façade, so as to preserve a degree of
continuity essential to architectural importance. The perishable
nature of the brick and composition of which the houses in Regent
Street are built gave rise to the following epigram :—

> Augustus at Rome was for building renown'd,
> For of marble he left what of brick he had found ;
> But is not our Nash, too, a very great master ?—
> He finds us all brick and he leaves us all plaster.[1]

The last two lines are otherwise read :—

> But is not our George, too, a very great master?
> He finds London brick, and he leaves it all plaster.

Nash, it need hardly be remarked, was George IV.'s favourite
architect. Considerable alterations have been made of late years in
the appearance of the street by the rebuilding of several houses and
the heightening of others.

Regent's Canal was projected by Mr. John Nash, architect, for
the purpose of forming a continuous line of canal navigation from the

[1] *Quarterly Review* for June 1876.

Grand Junction Canal at Paddington to the River Thames at Limehouse; with basins at the Regent's Park, the City Road, St. Luke's, and at Limehouse. It was commenced October 14, 1812, opened from Paddington to the Regent's Park basin in 1814, and throughout to the Thames August 1, 1820. Mr. James Morgan was the engineer. This canal has two tunnels, and in length is rather more than 8½ miles, with a surface breadth of 45 feet, a depth of 5 feet, and a fall of 90 feet by twelve locks, exclusive of the tide lock at the Thames.

Regent's Park, a public park of 372 acres, part of old Marylebone Park, long since disparked, and familiarly known as Marylebone Farm and Fields. On the expiration of the lease from the Crown to the Duke of Portland in January 1811, the Crown obtained an Act of Parliament, and appointed a commission to form a park and to let the adjoining ground on building leases. The whole was laid out by Mr. James Morgan in 1812, from the plans of Mr. John Nash, architect, who designed all the terraces except Cornwall Terrace, which was designed by Mr. Decimus Burton. By a clause in the building leases of the Regent's Park houses the lessees covenant to renew the colouring on the stuccoed exteriors within the month of August in every fourth year; the period being the same for them all, and the tint to be that of Bath stone.

The park derives its name from the Prince Regent, afterwards George IV., who intended building a residence at the north-east side of the park. Part of Regent Street was actually designed as a communication from the Prince's residence to Carlton House, St. James's Palace, etc. The Crown property comprises, besides the park, the upper part of Portland Place from No. 8 (where there is now part of the iron railing which formerly separated Portland Place from Marylebone Fields), the Park Crescent and Square, Albany, Osnaburgh, and the adjoining cross streets, York and Cumberland Squares, Regent's Park Basin and Augustus Street, Park Villages east and west, and the outer road of the park. The Zoological Gardens are at the upper end of the park. The Holme, a villa near the centre of the park, was erected by Mr. James Burton (father of Decimus Burton), and where he resided until his decease. This Mr. Burton was a speculative builder, who covered with houses the Skinners' Company and Foundling Hospital estates; he also erected York and Cornwall Terraces, Regent's Park; Waterloo Place and the lower part of Regent Street. Through the park, on a line with Portland Place to the east side of the Zoological Gardens, runs a fine broad avenue lined with trees, and footpaths which ramify across the sward in all directions, interspersed with ornamental plantations and well stocked flower-beds. These were laid out in 1833, and opened in 1838, up to which time the public were excluded from the inside of the park. On January 15, 1867, a fearful accident occurred through the breaking of the ice on the ornamental water, when about 200 persons were immersed and nearly 40 of them lost their lives. The depth of the water has since been reduced to about four feet. Around the park runs an outer road, forming an agreeable drive nearly 2 miles long. An inner drive, in the form of a circle, encloses the *Botanic Gardens*. On the outer road is Holford House, now the Regent's Park (Baptist) College. St. Dunstan's Villa, the residence of Henry Hucks Gibbs, Esq., somewhat south of the college, erected by Decimus Burton for the late Marquis of Hertford. In the gardens of this villa are placed the identical clock and automaton strikers which once adorned St. Dunstan's Church in Fleet Street. When the marquis was a child, and a good child, his nurse, to reward him, would take him to see "the giants" at St. Dunstan's, and he used to say that when he grew to be a man "he would buy those giants." It happened when old St. Dunstan's was pulled down that the giants were put up to auction, and the marquis became their purchaser. They still do duty in striking the hours and quarters. There is a picture in the National Gallery by James Ward, R.A. (1175), which is entitled "Regent's Park, 1807." It is, in fact, a view of Marylebone Park, which afterwards became the Regent's Park.

Regent's Park Market. [*See* Cumberland Market.]

Registrar General's Office, SOMERSET HOUSE, in the rooms formerly occupied by the Royal Academy. The office of the *Registrar of Births, Marriages and Deaths* was erected pursuant to 6 and 7 William IV., c. 86. The Registrar General publishes an annual report, in which all the facts bearing on the *movement* of the population of England and Wales are minutely set forth in a tabular form, accompanied by such remarks as seem required to place the results they indicate in a clear light. He also publishes a weekly summary of the returns furnished by the local registrars throughout the country of the births, marriages, and deaths, and causes of death, particularly referring to the relative increase or otherwise of the several forms of zymotic disease; and a somewhat more general quarterly statement in which particulars are given respecting the emigration and immigration of the past three months, the fluctuations in the quality of the water-supply, and whatever seems worthy of present attention as affecting the public health. The work going on in the Registrar General's office is unintermittent, and the reports issued by him are of the utmost value not only to the sanitary student and statistician, but to those interested in all that concerns the public health and wellbeing.

Religious Tract Society, 56 PATERNOSTER ROW, and 65 St. Paul's Churchyard. Established 1799 for "the circulation of small religious books and treatises throughout the British Dominions and foreign countries." But in addition to this, its primary object, the Society has become a great trading establishment for the publication and sale of religious books and periodicals.

Rhenish Wine-house, CANNON ROW, WESTMINSTER, at the end of a passage leading from King Street. In Strype's Map of 1720

Rhenish Wine Yard opens south out of King Street, nearly opposite Charles Street. There was an entrance to it from the Privy Gardens, only open during the sittings of Parliament and the Law Courts. Pepys was "at the Rhenish Wine-house drinking," July 30, 1660, with the sword-bearer of London; and again a few days later "with Judge-Advocate Fowler, Mr. Creed, Mr. Shepley, and Captain Howard . . . and very merry." On November 24 of the same year he is again there with Creed and Shepley, and "did give them two quarts of Wormwood wine." On June 19, 1663, he is there with Mr. Moore, who showed him "the French manner, when a health is drunk . . . which is now the fashion." The last visit he records is on June 1, 1668, but he adds, "Where I have not been *in a mourning*, I think, these seven years, or more." There were other Rhenish wine-houses in London, one was in Crooked Lane and another in the Steelyard.

Richard's Coffee-house. [*See* Dick's.]

Richmond House, WHITEHALL, was so called after Charles, second Duke of Richmond of the present family (d. 1750), for whom it was built by the celebrated Earl of Burlington, but afterwards altered and enlarged by Wyatt. It stood at the southern extremity of Privy Gardens, and looked towards Charing Cross. The ground was previously occupied by the apartments of the Duchess of Portsmouth, mother (by Charles II.) of the duke's father, the first Duke of Richmond. Here the third Duke of Richmond (who died in 1806, having borne the title for fifty-six years) formed a noble collection of the very finest casts from the antique, and, with a spirit and liberality much in advance of his age, afforded every accommodation, and invited artists by advertisements to study in his gallery. This, the first[1] public school established in this country wherein the beauties of the antique could be studied, was opened on Monday, March 6, 1758, ten years before the establishment of the Royal Academy. Cipriani and Wilton (artists of eminence) attended to instruct, and silver medals were occasionally awarded. Richmond House was famous also for its entertainments and private theatricals.

May 17, 1749.—The night before last the Duke of Richmond gave a firework: a codicil to the Peace. . . . The garden lies with a slope down to the Thames, on which were lighters, from whence were thrown up, after a concert of music, a great number of rockets. Then from boats on every side were discharged water-rockets and fires of that kind; and then the wheels which were ranged along the rails of the terrace were played off; and the whole concluded with the illumination of a pavilion on the top of a slope, of two pyramids on each side, and of the whole length of the balustrade to the water. You can't conceive a prettier sight; the garden filled with everybody of fashion, the Duke [of Cumberland], the Duke of Modena and the two black Princes [of Anamaboe]. The King and Princess Emily were in their barge under the terrace; the river was covered with boats, and the shores and adjacent houses with crowds.—*Walpole to Sir Horace Mann* (*Letters*, vol. ii. pp. 155, 160).

Walpole, in one of his marginal notes on Pennant, says, "His Grace [of Richmond] having bought the adjacent house fitted up a small

[1] Sir James Thornhill opened his Art Academy in 1724, and the St. Martin's Lane School was established in 1734, but these were specially for artists to study the living model.

theatre in it, where for two winters plays were performed by people of quality." Of the performances, Peter Pindar, addressing (as usual) George III., says :—

> So much with Saving-wisdom are you taken,
> Drury and Covent Garden seem forsaken.
> Since *cost* attendeth those theatric borders,
> Content you go to Richmond House with *orders*.
>
> Peter Pindar, *Peter's Pension*.

He adds in a note: "Here is a pretty little nutshell of a Theatre, fitted up for the convenience of Ladies and Gentlemen of Quality who wish to expose themselves."

Richmond House was destroyed by fire, December 21, 1791, but rebuilt. There is an engraved view of the house by Boydell; and Edwards, in his *Anecdotes* (p. 164), mentions a drawing of the gallery by an artist of the name of Parry, which he considered curious, "being," as he says, "the only representation of the place." The lease of the house did not expire until April 1841, but the Duke, in 1819, parted with his interest in it for £4300; the house was then taken down and Richmond Terrace built on its site.

Richmond Street, LEICESTER SQUARE, runs from Wardour Street to Rupert Street. The first Earl of Macclesfield (d. 1693) was living here in 1681.[1]

Richmond Terrace, WHITEHALL, was erected on the site of Richmond House in 1824. Miss Foote, Countess of Harrington, died at No. 2, aged sixty-nine. [*See* Richmond House.]

Ring (The), a circle in Hyde Park, surrounded with trees, and forming, in the height of the season, a fashionable ride and promenade. It was made in the reign of Charles I., was situated between the Humane Society's Receiving House and Grosvenor Gate, and was partly destroyed at the time the Serpentine was formed by Caroline, Queen of George II. Oldys had seen a poem in sixteen pages, entitled "The Circus, or British Olympicks, a Satyr on the Ring in Hyde Park." "This is a poem," says Oldys, "satirising many fops under fictitious names. Near a thousand coaches," he adds, "have been seen there in an evening." Several of the trees still remain.

Wycherley was a very handsome man. His acquaintance with the famous Duchess of Cleveland commenced oddly enough. One day as he passed that Duchess's coach in the Ring, she leaned out of the window, and cried out, loud enough to be heard distinctly by him, "Sir, you're a rascal: you're a villain!" [alluding to a song in his first play]. Wycherley from that instant entertained hopes. —Pope, in *Spence* (ed. Singer, p. 16).

> Wilt thou still sparkle in the box,
> Still ogle in the Ring?
> Canst thou forget thy age and pox?
> Can all that shines on shells and rocks
> Make thee a fine young thing?
>
> *Lord Dorset's Verses on Dorinda*.

---

[1] Rate-books of St. Martin's.

Young Bellair. I know some who will give you an account of every glance that passes at a play and i' th' Circle.—Etherege, *The Man of Mode, or Sir Fopling Flutter*, 4to, 1676.

Sir Fopling. All the world will be in the Park to-night: Ladies, 'twere pity to keep so much beauty longer within doors, and rob the Ring of all those charms that should adorn it.—*Ibid.*

The next place of resort wherein the servile world are let loose, is at the entrance of Hyde Park, while the gentry are at the Ring.—*Spectator*, No. 88.

Leonora. Trifle, let's see this morning's letters.

Trifle. There are only these half dozen, madam.

Leonora. No more! Barbarity! This it is to go to Hyde Park upon a windy day, when a well-dress'd gentleman can't stir abroad. The beaus were forced to take shelter in the playhouse, I suppose. I was a fool I did not go thither; I might have made ten times the havoc in the side-boxes.

Trifle. Your ladyship's being out of humour with the Exchange woman, for shaping your ruffles so odiously, I am afraid made you a little too reserv'd, madam.

Leonora. Prithee! was there a fop in the whole Ring, that had not a side-glance from me?—Colley Cibber, *Woman's Wit, or The Lady in Fashion*, 4to, 1697.

Sir Francis Gripe (to Miranda). Pretty rogue, pretty rogue; and so thou shalt find me, if thou dost prefer thy Gardy before these caperers of the age; thou shalt outshine the Queen's box on an opera night; thou shalt be the envy of the Ring (for I will carry thee to Hyde Park), and thy equipage shall surpass the—what d'ye call 'em—Ambassadors.—Mrs. Centlivre, *The Busy Body*, 4to, 1708.

Here (1697) the people of fashion take the diversion of The Ring. In a pretty high place, which lies very open, they have surrounded a circumference of two or three hundred paces diameter with a sorry kind of balustrade, or rather with postes placed upon stakes but three feet from the ground; and the coaches drive round this. When they have turned for some time round one way they face about and turn t'other: so rowls the world!—Wilson's *Memoirs*, 8vo, 1719, p. 126.

> How lately did this celebrated Thing,
> Blaze in the box, and sparkle in the Ring.
> Garth, *The Dispensary*, 1699.

In Queen Anne's time—

The other public diversion was merely for the eyes, for it was going round and round the Ring in Hyde Park, and bowing to one another, slightly, respectfully, or tenderly, as occasion required. No woman of fashion could receive any man at her morning toilet without alarming the husband and his friends.—*Lord Chesterfield, MS.* (Stanhope's *Anne*, p. 566).

He would no more disagree with a Lord in his sentiments, than a Beau would put his hat on in Hyde-Park Ring.—Orrery's *As You Find It*, 4to, 1703.

> To all his most frequented haunts resort
> Oft dog him in the Ring, and oft to Court.
> Addison's *Prologue to Steele's Tender Husband*, 1705.

> To scandal next—what awkward thing
> Was that, last Sunday in the Ring.
> Swift, *Cadenus and Vanessa*, 1713.

> What pains to get the gaudy thing you hate,
> To swell in show, and be a wretch in state!
> At Plays you ogle, at the *Ring* you bow;
> Ev'n Churches are no sanctuaries now.
> Garth, *Epilogue to Addison's Cato*, 1713.

All the fine equipages that shine in the Ring never gave me another thought than either pity or contempt for the owners, that could place happiness in attracting the eyes of strangers.—*Lady Mary W. Montagu* (*Works*, by Lord Wharncliffe, vol. i. p. 177).

> Know, then, unnumbered spirits round thee fly,
> The light militia of the lower sky:
> These, though unseen, are ever on the wing,
> Hang o'er the Box and hover round the Ring.
> *Pope, Rape of the Lock.*
> She glares in balls, front-boxes, and the Ring,
> A vain, unquiet, glittering, wretched thing.
> *Pope, To Martha Blount, with the Works of Voiture.*

The Ring, or its immediate vicinity, was the noted Hyde Park duelling-ground of the 18th century. Here in 1712 was fought the famous duel between the Duke of Hamilton and Lord Mohun.

> My Lord [Mohun] then asked the Hackney Coachman if he knew where they could get any thing that was good, it being a cold morning; he [the Hackney Coachman] said at the House near the Ring. When they came near the house, they [Lord Mohun and his second, General Macartney] both got out of the coach, and bid the coachman get some burnt wine at the house, while they took a little walk. He went into the house and told the Drawer he brought two gentlemen, who bid him get some burnt wine against they came back; the Drawer said he would not, for very few came thither so soon in the morning but to fight.—*Duel between Duke of Hamilton and Lord Mohun (Hackney Coachman's Evidence before the Coroner).*

> "If we were not in the Park," answered Booth warmly, "I would thank you very properly for that compliment." "O, Sir!" cries the Colonel, "we can be soon in a convenient place." Upon which Booth answered, he would attend him wherever he pleased. The Colonel then bid him come along, and strutted forward directly up Constitution Hill to Hyde Park, Booth following him at first, and afterwards walking before him, till they came to that place, which may be properly called the field of blood, being that part a little to the left of *The Ring*, which heroes have chosen for the scene of their exit out of this world.—*Fielding's Amelia.*

The last circumstance of any interest connected with the Ring is the duel fought here in 1763 between John Wilkes and Samuel Martin, on account of a passage in the *North Briton*, in which Martin was stigmatised as a "low fellow and dirty tool of power." Wilkes was wounded.

Robert Street, ADELPHI. Thomas Hood and his wife, in 1824, resided in chambers at No. 2 Robert Street, Adelphi. [*See* Adelphi.]

Robin Hood Club, a discussion Club, or "Oratorical Society," which met in the last century at a house in Essex Street, Strand. [*See* Essex Street.] About the same time there was another "religious Robin Hood Society, which met every Sunday evening at Coachmakers' Hall, for free debate."[1] [*See* Coachmakers' Hall.]

Rochester House, SOUTHWARK. The inn or town house of the Bishops of Rochester. No traces remain, and the Borough Market occupies part of the site.

> Adjoining Winchester House is the Bishop of Rochester's inn or lodging, by whom first erected I do not now remember me to have read; but well I wot the same of long time hath not been frequented by any bishop, and lieth ruinous for lack of any reparations. The Abbot of Waverley had a house there.—*Stow*, p. 151.

> Rochester House was, about 40 years since, one great house and a great garden, and now consisteth of 62 tenements.—*MS. temp. James I. (Churchwardens' Accounts of St. Saviour's, Southwark).*

---

[1] *Boswell*, by Croker, p. 684.

Rochester Row, WESTMINSTER, so called after the Bishops of Rochester, several of whom (Sprat and Atterbury, for instance) held the deanery of Westminster at the same time with the see of Rochester. On the south side is the fine church of St. Stephen, erected and endowed, with the adjoining school-buildings for 400 children, by Miss (now the Baroness) Burdett-Coutts, 1847-1848; architect, Mr. B. Ferrey, F.S.A. Near it is the Westminster Police Court. On the north side are Hill's Almshouses, the Western Dispensary, and the Grenadier Guards' Hospital.

Rolls House and Chapel, CHANCERY LANE, a place where the rolls and records of the Court of Chancery were kept from the reign of Edward III. until the erection of the Record Office in Fetter Lane. [*See* Record Office.] Rolls House was the official residence of the Master of the Rolls, who also kept his court here. The Rolls Court was removed on the opening of the Royal Courts of Justice, and this building is now occupied by the officials of the Record Office. The master's house was designed by Colin Campbell in 1717-1725 at a cost of £5000, during the mastership of Sir Joseph Jekyll. The first stone was laid September 18, 1717. On the site of the present chapel Henry III. erected, in the year 1233, a House of Maintenance for converted Jews (Domus Conversorum), but the number of converts decreasing from the enactment of Edward I., in 1290, by which the Jews were banished out of the realm, Edward III., in 1377, annexed the house and chapel to the newly-created office of Custos Rotulorum, or Keeper of the Rolls. The chapel has been greatly altered and disfigured. Prior to their removal to the Record Office the Rolls of the Chancery were kept in presses ranged along the walls of this chapel, under the seats of the pews, and even behind the altar.

Observe.—Monument to Dr. John Young, Master of the Rolls in the reign of Henry VIII. Vertue and Walpole attribute it, and with great reason, to Torrigiano, the sculptor of the tomb of Henry VII. at Westminster. The Master is represented lying on an altar-tomb, with his hands crossed, and his face expressive of deep devotion. Within a recess at the back is a head of Christ, with an angel's head on each side, in high relief. Monument to Lord Bruce of Kinloss (d. 1610), Master of the Rolls in the reign of James I., and father of Edward, Lord Bruce of Kinloss, killed in a duel with Sir Edward Sackville. Monument to Sir Richard Allington of Horseheath, in Cambridgeshire (d. 1561). Conspicuous in the windows are the arms of Sir Robert Cecil and of Sir Harbottle Grimston, "under whose protection," writes Burnet (*Hist. of Own Times*, p. 104), "I lived nine years, when I was preacher at the Rolls, he being the Master of the Rolls." Among the eminent preachers at the Rolls besides Bishop Burnet were Atterbury, Bishop of Rochester, and Bishop Butler, author of the *Analogy of Religion*. Burnet's sermon at this chapel (November 5, 1684) on the text, "Save me from the lion's mouth, for thou hast heard me from the horns of the unicorns," occasioned his removal from the preachership, the King considering the Chapel of the Rolls as one of his own chapels, and the words of the text as "levelled against his coat of arms." Fifteen of Butler's sermons at the Rolls form an octavo volume. The Rolls liberty is a parish or peculiar of its own. Sir William Grant, one of the greatest judges that has adorned the Bench, lived in the Rolls House (1801-1817), but never saw more of it than the ground-floor. When his successor arrived Sir William showed him his apartments. "Here are two or three good rooms; this is my sitting-room; my library and bedroom are beyond; and I am told there are some good rooms upstairs, but I never was there."

Roman Bath. [*See* Strand Lane.]

Roman Catholic Church of St. Mary, BLOMFIELD STREET, MOORFIELDS. John Newman, architect; first stone laid August 5, 1817; consecrated April 20, 1820; cost £26,000. The body of Weber, the composer, was buried in its vaults, but removed in 1842. [*See* Finsbury Circus.] This church, up to July 2, 1869, was regarded as the pro-cathedral of the arch-diocese of Westminster; but on that day "the seat of jurisdiction was moved westward" (as Archbishop Manning worded it) to the new edifice dedicated to "Our Lady of Victories," Newland Street, Kensington. That, however, is the pro-cathedral until sufficient funds are obtained to erect a more stately permanent cathedral in Westminster.

Rood Lane, FENCHURCH STREET TO EASTCHEAP.

Rood Lane, so called of a roode there placed in the churchyard of St. Margaret Pattens, whilst the old Church was taken down and again newly built; during which time the oblations made to this rood were employed towards the building of the church; but in the year 1538, about the 23d of May, in the morning, the said rood was found to have been, on the night preceding, by people unknown, broken all to pieces, together with the tabernacle wherein it had been placed.—*Stow*, p. 79; see also *London Chronicle (Camd. Soc.)*, p. 12.

The church of St. Margaret Pattens [which *see*] is at the south-east corner. The houses in Rood Lane are now chiefly occupied as merchants' offices.

Roomland, BILLINGSGATE.

At the head of Billingsgate Dock is a square plot of ground compassed with posts, known by the name of *Roomland*, which, with the adjacent part of the street, hath been the usual place where the ship-masters, coal-merchants, wood-mongers, lightermen, and labourers, do meet every morning, in order to the buying, selling, delivering, and taking-up of sea-coals and Scotch-coals, as the principal market. This coal-market was kept on Great Tower Hill in the time of the City's late desolation [by the Great Fire].—Delaune's *Angl. Not.*, 1690, p. 355.

There was another *Roumeland* at Dowgate, for the cleansing of which an ordinance was issued in 1365. The origin of the name is uncertain. In front of several of the larger monastic establishments, as St. Albans, Waltham, Norwich, Bury St. Edmund's, and Reading, were large open spaces railed off, and sometimes, at least, as at

Waltham, used as market-places, which were called *Roomlands* or *Romelands*.¹ Mr. Walcott says they were so called "probably from *rome*, roomy, as in Romney, Romsey, etc.,"² but Romney and Romsey were certainly not so named as being roomy places, neither is it likely were the Romelands. Possibly they may have been places set apart by the Church in early times as market-places, in country towns as general, in London as special markets. The Coal Exchange, the present central coal-market, still holds its place at "the head of Billingsgate." [*See* Coal Exchange.]

Ropemakers' Alley, MOORFIELDS, now widened and called ROPEMAKER STREET, runs from the west side of Finsbury Pavement to Moor Lane. Hatton, 1708, describes it as "on the west side of Little Moorfields, a passage to Grub Street." In a Map of 1720 "Rope Walk" is given, and the alley appears to have run out from a Moorfields Holywell Street, called Rotten Row. At "his lodgings" in this alley on April 26, 1731, died Daniel Defoe, the author of *Robinson Crusoe*.

Rosamond's Pond, a sheet of water in the south-west corner of St. James's Park, "long consecrated to disastrous love and elegiac poetry."³ The earliest notice of it appears to be contained in a payment, issued from the Exchequer in 1612, of £400 "towards the charge of making and bringing a current of water from Hyde Park, in a vault of brick arched over, to fall into Rosamond's Pond at St. James's Park."⁴ It was filled up in 1770; in June of which year Mr. Whately writes to George Grenville: "Lord Suffolk is very happy that orders are given for draining the ponds near his house. Rosamond's Pond is also to be filled up and a road carried across it to [Great] George Street; the rest is to be all lawn."⁵ It lay obliquely across the west end of the present Bird Cage Walk. Lord Suffolk lived in Duke Street, Westminster, and the ponds which he was so happy to get rid of were "the places for the fowle" of the old maps.

Mrs. Friendall. His note since dinner desires you would meet him at seven at Rosamond's Pond.—Southerne, *The Wives' Excuse*, 4to, 1692.

Lady Trickitt. Was it fine walking last night, Mr. Granger? Was there good company at Rosamond's Pond?

Granger. I did not see your ladyship there.

Lady Trickitt. Me! fie, fie, a married woman there, Mr. Granger!—Southerne, *The Maid's Last Prayer, or Any rather than Fail*, 4to, 1693.

Sir Novelty (reads). Excuse, my dear Sir Novelty, the forc'd indifference I have shewn you, and let me recompense your past sufferings with an hour's

---

¹ Thorne, *Handbook to the Environs of London*, pt. ii. p. 655.
² Walcott, *Church and Conventual Arrangement*, p. 117.
³ *Warburton to Hurd*, p. 151.
⁴ Devon's *Issues from the Exchequer*, 4to, 1836, p. 150.
⁵ *Grenville Corr.*, vol. iv. p. 517. There is an engraving of Rosamond's Pond by J. T. Smith, from a drawing made in 1758, and a still better view by W. H. Toms, from a drawing by Chatelain in 1752. In the Crowle Pennant in the British Museum is a careful pen-and-ink drawing of the pond by J. Maurer, 1742. No. 86 of the Royal Academy Exhibition of 1774 was "A View of Rosamond's Pond in St. James's Park," by John Feary.

conversation, after the play, at Rosamond's Pond.—Colley Cibber, *Love's Last Shift*, 4to, 1696.

Mirabel. Meet me at one o'clock by Rosamond's Pond.—Congreve, *The Way of the World*, 4to, 1700.

Young Wou'd Be. Are the ladies come?
Serv. Half an hour ago, my lord.
Young Wou'd Be. Where did you light on 'em?
Serv. One in the passage at the old Playhouse—I found another very melancholy paring her nails by Rosamond's Pond—and a couple I got at the Chequer Alehouse in Holborn.—Farquhar, *The Twin Rivals*, 4to, 1703.

January 31, 1710-1711.—We are here in as smart a frost for the time as I have seen; delicate walking weather, and the Canal and Rosamond's Pond full of the rabble sliding, and with skates, if you know what those are. Patrick's bird's water freezes in the gally-pot, and my hands in bed.—Swift, *Journal to Stella.*

Upon the next public Thanksgiving Day it is my design to sit astride on the dragon on Bow steeple, from whence, after the discharge of the Tower guns, I intend to mount into the air, fly over Fleet Street, and pitch upon the Maypole in the Strand. From thence, by gradual descent, I shall make the best of my way for St. James's Park, and light upon the ground near Rosamond's Pond.—*The Guardian*, No. 112.

As I was last Friday taking a walk in the Park, I saw a country gentleman at the side of Rosamond's Pond, pulling a handful of oats out of his pocket, and with a great deal of pleasure gathering the ducks about him. Upon my coming up to him, who should it be but my friend the Fox-Hunter, whom I gave some account of in my 22nd paper! I immediately joined him, and partook of his diversion, until he had not an oat left in his pocket.—Addison, *The Freeholder*, No. 44, May 21, 1716.

This the Beau-monde shall from the Mall survey
. . . .
This the blest lover shall for Venus take,
And send up vows from Rosamonda's Lake.—*Rape of the Lock.*

The termination of this delectable walk [in St. James's Park] was a knot of lofty elms by a Pond side; round some of which were commodious seats for the tired ambulators to refresh their weary pedestals. Here a parcel of old worn-out Cavaliers were conning over the Civil Wars.—Ned Ward's *London Spy*, ed. 1753, p. 164.

Tom Brown speaks of the Close Walk at the head of the pond.[1] Another pond in the Green Park (nearly opposite Coventry House) bore the name of Rosamond down to 1840-1841.

Rose Street, COVENT GARDEN, a dirty and somewhat circuitous street, between King Street and Long Acre, for the most part cleared, or absorbed, in forming GARRICK STREET.

Rose Street, of which there are three, and all indifferent well-built and inhabited; but the best is that next to King Street, called White Rose Street, which is in Covent Garden Parish.—*Strype*, B. vi. p. 74.

It was in this street ("over against" which he was living at the time) that on December 18, 1679, Dryden[2] was barbarously assaulted and wounded by three persons hired for the purpose, as is now known, by Wilmot, Earl of Rochester. In the *Mercurius Domesticus*, the first

---

[1] *Amusements of London*, 8vo, 1700, p. 65.

[2] The biographers of Dryden relate that the poet was on his way home from Will's to his house in Gerard Street; but no part of Gerard Street was built in 1679, and in that year the Rate-books of St. Martin's show that Dryden was living in Long Acre, over against Rose Street. That he was on his way home from Will's is only an assumption.

number of which appeared on the following day, the affair is thus described.

Upon the 18th inst., in the evening, Mr. Dryden, the great Poet, was set upon in Rose Street, in Covent Garden, by three persons, who calling him rogue, and son of a whore, knockt him down, and dangerously wounded him, but upon his crying out murther, they made their escape; it is conceived that they had their pay beforehand, and designed not to rob him, but to execute on him som Feminine if not Popish vengeance.

Fifty pounds were offered for the discovery of the offenders, and a pardon from the King, in addition, if a principal or an accessory would come forward. Rochester took offence at a passage in Lord Mulgrave's Essay on Satire, of which he thought Dryden was the author, and, three weeks before this cowardly revenge, had written to his friend Henry Saville that he intended to "leave the repartee to *Black Will* with a cudgell." There are many allusions to this Rose Alley Ambuscade, as it is called, in our old State Poems. So famous, indeed, was the assault, that Mulgrave's poem was commonly called "The Rose Alley Satire." *Eminent Inhabitants.*—Samuel Butler, author of *Hudibras,* died here (1680) poor and neglected. Edmund Curll, the bookseller, was living here when he published *Mr. Pope's Literary Correspondence.*

Rose Street, SOHO, a street south-east of Soho Square, connecting Greek Street with Crown Street. Mrs. Delany writes that when she came to London in 1720 she found that Mr. Pendarves, her first husband, "had taken a house in a very indifferent part of the town, Rose Street, Hog Lane, Soho."[1]

Rose Tavern (The) stood in RUSSELL STREET, COVENT GARDEN, adjoining Drury Lane Theatre.[2] Part of it was taken down in 1776, when Adam, the architect, built a new front to the former theatre for Garrick, then about to part with his patent. In Charles II.'s time it was kept by a person of the name of Long (buried at St. Paul's, Covent Garden, August 5, 1661), and afterwards by his widow. Tavern tokens of the house still exist.

May 18, 1668.—It being almost twelve o'clock, or little more, to the King's Playhouse, when the doors were not then open; but presently they did open; and we in, and find many people already come in by private ways into the pit, it being the first day of Sir Charles Sedley's new play so long expected, *The Mulberry Garden;* of whom, being so reputed a wit, all the world do expect great matters. I having sat here awhile and eat nothing to-day, did slip out, getting a boy to keep my place; and to the Rose Tavern, and there got half a breast of mutton off of the spit, and dined all alone.—*Pepys.*

I left some friends of yours at the Rose.—Sedley's *Bellamira,* 4to, 1687.

Sir Fred. Frolic. Sing the catch I taught you at the Rose.—Etherege, *Love in a Tub,* 4to, 1669.

Woodcock. By the Lord Harry, Sir Positive, I do understand Mathematics better than you; and I lie over-against the Rose Tavern in Covent Garden, dear heart.—Shadwell, *The Sullen Lovers,* 4to, 1668.

Or sipping Tea while they relate
Their evening's frolic at the Rose.
The School of Politicks, p. 40, 1690.

---

[1] Mrs. Delany's *Autob.*, vol. i. p. 61.   [2] *Strype,* B. vi. pp. 67, 74.

Tope. Puh, this is nothing ; why I knew the Hectors, and before them the Muns and the Tityre Tu's ;[1] they were brave fellows indeed ; in those days a man could not go from the Rose Tavern to the Piazza once, but he must venture his life twice, my dear Sir Willy,—Shadwell, *The Scowrers,* 4to, 1691.

Whackum (a city scowrer, and imitator of Sir William Rant). Oh no, never talk on't. There will never be his fellow. O had you seen him scower, as I did, oh so delicately, so like a gentleman ! How he cleared the Rose Tavern ? I was there about law-business, compounding for a bastard, and he and two fine gentlemen came roaring in, the handsomeliest and the most genteely turned us all out of the room, and swinged us and kicked us about, I vow to God 'twould have done your heart good to have seen it.—*Ibid.*

Here Prior has laid the opening scene in *The Hind and the Panther Transversed.*

Johnson. Nay faith, we won't part so . . . let us step to the Rose for one quarter of an hour, and talk over old stories.

Bayes. I ever took you to be men of honour, and for your sakes I will transgress as far as one pint.

Johnson. Well, Mr. Bayes, many a merry bout have we had in this house, and shall have again, I hope.—Prior and Montague, *The Hind and the Panther Transversed,* 1687.

Lucy. Pray, sir, pardon me.

Brazen. I can't tell, child, till I know whether my money be safe *(searching his pocket).* Yes, yes, I do pardon you ; but if I had you in the Rose Tavern in Covent Garden, with three or four hearty rakes, and three or four smart napkins, I would tell you another story, my dear.—Farquhar, *The Recruiting Officer,* 4to, 1707.

> Suppose me dead, and then suppose
> A club assembled at the Rose,
> Where from discourse of this and that,
> I grow the subject of their chat.
>
> Swift, *Verses on his own Death.*

> Tho' he and all the world allow'd her wit,
> Her voice was shrill and rather loud than sweet ;
> When she began,—for hat and sword he'd call,
> Then after a faint kiss,—cry, 'Bye ; Dear Moll :
> Supper and friends expect me at the Rose.
>
> *Tatler,* No. 2, April 14, 1709.

He is an excellent critick, and the time of the play is his hour of business ; exactly at five he passes through New Inn, crosses through Russell Court, and takes a turn at Will's till the play begins ; he has his shoes rubbed and his periwig powdered at the Barber's as you go into the Rose.—*The Spectator,* No. 2.

The hangings [at Drury Lane Theatre] you formerly mentioned are run away ; as are likewise a set of chairs, each of which was met upon two legs going through the Rose Tavern at two this morning.—*The Spectator,* No. 36.

Mr. Hildbrand Horden was the son of Dr. Horden, minister of Twickenham in Middlesex ; and was an actor upon the stage, and had almost every gift that could make him excel in his profession, and was every day rising in the favour of the public, when, after having been about seven years upon the stage, he was unfortunately killed at the bar of the Rose Tavern, in a frivolous, rash, accidental quarrel, for which Colonel Burgess, one who was resident at Venice, and some other persons of distinction, took their trials, and were acquitted. He was remarkable for his handsome person ; and before he was buried, several ladies well dressed came in masks, which were then much worn, and some in their own coaches, to visit him in his shroud.—*List of Dramatic Authors appended to Scanderbeg, a Tragedy,* 8vo, 1747.

In this house [the Rose Tavern] George Powell spent great part of his time ;

---

[1] Bilboa and Tityre Tu are two Hectors in Wilson's popular comedy of *The Cheats* (1662), "one usurping the name of a Major, the other of a Captain."

and often toasted to intoxication his mistress, with bumpers of Nantz-brandy.—
Davies's *Dramatic Misc.*, vol. iii. p. 416.

Here (November 14, 1712) the seconds on either side arranged the duel fought the next day between the Duke of Hamilton and Lord Mohun, as "John Sisson, the drawer of the Rose Tavern," deposed in evidence before the coroner. The duke and Lord Mohun were here the same day, the duke and General Macartney (Lord Mohun's second) drinking part of a bottle of French claret together.

One Leathercoat, a porter at this tavern, has been immortalised by Hogarth in Plate III. of *The Rake's Progress*, and by Fielding in *The Covent Garden Tragedy*, 1732. On January 19, 1763, the night of the production of Mallet's tragedy of *Elvira*, Edward Gibbon and his father dined with the "only Scot whom Scotchmen did not commend."

I then undressed for the play. My father and I went to the Rose, in the passage of the play-house, where we found Mallet, with about thirty friends. We dined together, and went thence into the pit, where we took our places in a body, ready to silence all opposition. However, we had no occasion to exert ourselves.—Gibbon's *Journal*.

Rose Tavern was at the corner of THANET PLACE, without TEMPLE BAR.

At the Rose Tavern without Temple Bar there is a vine that covers an arbour where the sun very rarely comes, and has had ripe grapes upon it.—*The City Gardener*, by Thomas Fairchild, Gardener of Hoxton, 8vo, 1722, p. 55.

The Rose Tavern, a well customed house with good conveniences of rooms, and a good garden.—*Strype*, B. iv. p. 117.

The painted room at the Rose Tavern is mentioned in Walpole's letters to Cole of January 26, 1776, and March 1, 1776.

Rose Theatre, BANKSIDE, stood east of the Bear Garden and a little north-west of the site upon which the Globe was built soon afterwards. It was situated close by where the south end of Southwark Bridge now is. Here is still a Rose Alley. In 1552, as appears by a deed preserved at Dulwich College, Thomasin Symondes of London, widow, late wife of Raphe Symondes, citizen and fishmonger, sold her "messuage or tenement, called the *Little Rose*, with two gardens to the same adjoining," in the parish of St. Saviour, Southwark, to Ambrose Nicolas and others. In 1564 Nicolas let it for thirty-one years at £7 per annum, and on March 24, 1584, the remainder of his lease was purchased by Philip Hinchley [Henslowe], citizen and dyer of London.[1] The theatre, a wooden building, "done abowt with calme bordes on the outside," was opened about 1592, or a little before.

Thou hadst a breath as sweet as *the Rose* that grows by the Bear Garden.—Decker's *Satiromastix*, 1602.

A messuage or tenement, called the Rose, is mentioned in the charter of Edward VI., granting the manor of Southwark to the City of London.

Rose and Crown Court, GRAY'S INN LANE (now Gray's Inn Road, Rose and Crown Court, has long disappeared). In 1673 John

---

[1] Collier's *Memoirs of Edward Alleyn (Cam. Soc.)*, p. 189.

Aubrey, the antiquary, lodged at the house of Henry Coley in Rose and Crown Court, in Gray's Inn Lane. Coley was a tailor by trade, and astrologer, medical adviser, and fortune-teller by profession; and adopted son of William Lilly, whose *Ephemeris* he continued for several years. He published *A Key to the whole Art of Astrology*. Granger mentions his portrait inscribed " Henricus Coley, philomath," with "a celestial globe at his elbow."

Rosemary Lane, from Sparrow Corner, Minories, to Cable Street, WHITECHAPEL, since 1850 called Royal Mint Street. Here was the once notorious mart for old clothes called Rag Fair, and there are still many second-hand clothes' stores in the street. [*See* Rag Fair.] On October 31, 1631, there is a "Grant to William Bawdrick and Roger Hunt of the King's interest in certain tenements in Rosemary Lane, Middlesex, the lease of which was taken by Horatio Franchotti, an alien, but discovered and prosecuted for on His Majesty's behalf."[1] In the burial register of St. Mary's, Whitechapel, the following entry occurs:—

1646, *June* 21st. Rich. Brandon, a man out of Rosemary Lane.

To this is added, "This R. Brandon is supposed to have cut off the head of Charles the First."

He [Brandon] likewise confessed that he had thirty pounds for his pains, all paid him in half crowns within an hour after the blow was given; and that he had an orange stuck full of cloves, and a handkercher out of the King's pocket, so soon as he was carryed off from the scaffold, for which orange he was proffered twenty shillings by a gentleman in Whitehall, but refused the same, and afterwards sold it for ten shillings in Rosemary Lane.—*The Confession of Richard Brandon, the Hangman*, 4to, 1649.

This Richard Brandon was, it is said, "the only son of Gregory Brandon, and claimed the gallows by inheritance—the first he beheaded was the Earl of Strafford."[2]

"Rosemary Lane and Ratcliff" were the daily haunts, and the ashes of the neighbouring glass-house the nightly sleeping-place of Defoe's Colonel Jack, his business in "the case of some of the poorer shopkeepers" being "to look after their shops till they went up to dinner, or till they went over the way to an alehouse and the like." Goldsmith speaks of another craft than that of dealing in old clothes which was carried on here in his time.

"I beg pardon sir," cried I, "but I think I have seen you before; your face is familiar to me." "Yes, sir," replied he, " I have a good familiar face, as my friends tell me. I am as well known in every town in England as the dromedary, or live crocodile. You must understand, sir, that I have been these sixteen years Merry Andrew to a puppet-shew; last Bartholomew fair my master and I quarrelled, beat each other, and parted; he to sell his puppets to the *pincushion-makers in Rosemary Lane*, and I to starve in St. James's Park.—Goldsmith, *Essay*, p. 21.

Rosoman Street (formerly ROSOMAN ROW), CLERKENWELL, runs from Corporation Row to the New River Head. It was named after

[1] *Cal. State Pap.*, 1619-1623, p. 305.   [2] Ellis's *Letters*, 2d S., vol. iii. p. 347.

a "Mr. Rosoman, a Devonshire gentleman, the owner of the land." John Britton, in his *Autobiography* (vol. i. p. 62), under date 1787, says, "Richard Earlom [d. 1822], the eminent mezzotint engraver, who lived in Rosoman Row would have taken me [as an apprentice] with a small premium, but the opportunity was neglected." At the end of Rosoman Row was one of the series of ponds which distinguished the district of Clerkenwell and Spa Fields. By it was one of the conduits for the supply of London with water, and close at hand were the London Spa and Merlin's Cave, " places of great public resort " in the last half of the 18th century. [*See* Spa Fields.] Both these signs remain, the London Spa in Exmouth Street and Merlin's Cave in Rosoman Street, but they are now ordinary " wine vaults."

There was a reservoir at the corner of Rosoman Street, opposite the London Spaw public house, until the erection of the houses there about 1812. On the west side of this reservoir was a building with which water wheels, to aid the supply of London, were once connected ; they are represented in a small inferior print giving a north view of the Metropolis [one of a series of Views of North London from the Bowling Green at Islington], without date, but which was probably engraved about 1780.—Cromwell's *History of Clerkenwell*, 1828, p. 349.

In Rosoman Street are the Clerkenwell Vestry Hall, St. James's and Cow Cross Mission Halls, and St. Peter and St. Paul Roman Catholic Church.

Rotherhithe, corruptly REDRIFF, a manor and parish on the right bank of the Thames, in the county of Surrey, between Bermondsey and Deptford. It is not mentioned in Domesday Book, and was, at the time of the Conquest, a hamlet in the royal manor of Bermondsey. The name appears as "Ætheredes hyd" in a charter of A.D. 898, printed in Birch's *Cartularium*, vol. ii. p. 220. In the 17th century it had come to be so generally called *Redriff* that out of twenty trade tokens, recorded by Mr. Burn, nineteen spelt it Redriff; in the twentieth it was *Rothorith*, 1666.[1] Philip Henslowe used to send his horse "to grasse to Redreffe." The charge in 1600 was twentypence a week.[2]

The living is a rectory. The church, dedicated to St. Mary, was built 1714-1715 on the site of a smaller church. It was enlarged and the steeple added in 1738. It is a large brick building with stone dressings, and a lantern, and columns of the Corinthian order. The architect is unknown. In the churchyard is the monument erected by the East India Company to the memory of Prince Lee Boo, a native of the Pelew or Palas Islands, and son to Abba Thulle Rupack, or King of the Island Coo-roo-raa, who died from the smallpox in Captain Wilson's house in Paradise Row, December 29, 1784. The inscription records that the stone was erected "as a testimony of the humane and kind treatment afforded by his father to the crew of the *Antelope*, Captain Wilson, which was wrecked off the island of Coo-roo-raa on the night of the 9th of August,

[1] Burn, *Desc. Cat. of London Traders Tokens*, p. 201. [2] Henslowe's *Diary*, p. 81.

1783." Besides the mother church there are three or four district churches. Rotherhithe has always been much inhabited by seafaring people. Admiral Sir John Leake (d. 1720), distinguished on many occasions, from the Relief of Londonderry to the Battle of La Hogue and the reduction of Barcelona, was born at Rotherhithe in 1656. Manning states that the brave old Admiral Benbow was born in Wintershull Street, now Hanover Street, Rotherhithe.[1] But this is a mistake; he was born at Coton Hill, Shrewsbury. Gulliver, so Swift tells us, was long an inhabitant of the place. "It was as true as if Mr. Gulliver had spoken it," was a sort of proverb among his neighbours at Redriff. In Rotherhithe are the extensive Commercial Docks. The south entrance to the Thames Tunnel was in Swan Lane, but since the tunnel has been appropriated for the passage under the Thames of the East London Railway it has been closed to foot-passengers. Rotherhithe has many wharves, stairs, docks, yards, granaries, manufactories and shops, connected with maritime and river traffic.

On June 1, 1765, a fire broke out in a mast-yard near Rotherhithe Church, which destroyed 206 houses.

Some discussion having arisen in connection with Turner's grand picture of "The Fighting *Temeraire* tugged to her last berth to be broken up, 1838," as to where was the last berth of the good ship, the Rev. E. J. Beck, Rector of Rotherhithe, wrote a letter to the *Times* (December 20, 1877), in which is the following interesting passage:—

She was broken up not at Deptford, but at Rotherhithe, at the ship-breaking yard then in the occupation of the late Mr. John Beatson. It may interest your readers and the admirers of Turner's beautiful picture to know that the exact spot to which the good ship was towed is within a few yards of the Surrey Canal entrance of the Grand Surrey Commercial Docks. It so happened that while the *Temeraire* was still in process of destruction a chapel of ease to the old parish church of Rotherhithe was being erected within a short distance of the ship-breaker's yard, and Mr. Beatson presented to the architect (who was a relation of his own) sufficient timber to make the holy table, altar rails, and two large sanctuary chairs, which are still in use in the church of St. Paul's, Globe Street, Rotherhithe, consecrated in June 1850. The last of the wooden ships broken up in the same yard was the *Queen*, about five years since. The figure-heads of various old ships of the Fleet still adorn the entrance gates in Rotherhithe Street.—*Times*, December 20, '77.

The last line will recall another memorable picture, "Old Friends," by H. S. Marks, R.A., which attracted much notice at the Royal Academy Exhibition of 1879.

Rotten Row, HYDE PARK, a roadway for saddle-horses only, on the south side of Hyde Park, between Hyde Park Corner and Kensington; within the last few years a supplementary ride has been formed on the north side of the Serpentine, from Cumberland Gate to Victoria Gate. Many absurd etymologies have been proposed for the name, but the most probable is the apparent one, that it is called after the rotten soil of which it is composed. The privilege of *driving* along Rotten Row is confined to the Sovereign and the Hereditary Grand

[1] Manning's Surrey, vol. i. p. 229.

Falconer. In the months of May, June, and part of July, between the hours of twelve and two, and five and seven, Rotten Row is crowded with hundreds of equestrians, ladies in great numbers adding brilliancy to the scene.

> Horsed in Cheapside, scarce yet the gayer spark
> Achieves the Sunday triumph of the Park;
> Scarce yet you see him, dreading to be late,
> Scour the New Road and dash thro' Grosvenor Gate :—
> Anxious—yet timorous too !—his steed to show,
> The hack Bucephalus of Rotten Row,
> Careless he seems, yet, vigilantly sly,
> Woos the stray glance of ladies passing by,
> While his off-heel, insidiously aside,
> Provokes the caper which he seems to chide.

R. Brinsley Sheridan, *Prologue to* Lady Craven's *Comedy, The Miniature Picture*, 1781.

> When its quicksilver's down at zero,——lo !
> Coach, chariot, luggage, baggage, equipage !
> Wheels whirl from Carlton Palace to Soho,
> And happiest they who horses can engage ;
> The turnpikes glow with dust ; and Rotten Row
> Sleeps from the chivalry of this bright age ;
> And tradesmen, with long bills and longer faces,
> Sigh—as the post-boys fasten on the traces.

Don Juan, Canto xiii., stanza 44.

Round Court, ST. MARTIN'S-IN-THE-FIELDS, on the north-west side of the Strand, "almost," says Hatton, "against Buckingham Street end." It is particularly mentioned in No. 304 of the Spectator, and is carefully laid down in Strype's Map of St. Martin's-in-the-Fields. It was partly in the *Bermudas* and partly in *Porridge Island*. The site is now occupied by the Charing Cross Hospital. A once popular book, Johnson's *Lives of Highwaymen* (fol. 1736), was "Printed for and Sold by Olive Payne at Horace's Head in Round Court in the Strand, over against York Buildings."

Round House (The). [*See* St. Martin's Lane, Charing Cross.]

Rowland Hill's Chapel, the corner of Little Charlotte Street, Blackfriars Road, called also SURREY CHAPEL. The first stone of this chapel, which in plan was nearly the same as the Whitefield or Countess of Huntingdon's Tabernacles, was laid by Rowland Hill himself, June 24, 1782. The architect was William Thomas. The funds for the building were raised by a subscription, to which Lord George Gordon gave £50. It was opened for service June 8, 1783, and Hill preached his last sermon in it March 31, 1833. The building was 80 feet in diameter, and would accommodate 3000 persons. Hill died at his house adjoining the chapel on the 11th of April following, and by his own special desire a grave was dug for him beneath the pulpit which he had filled for fifty years. He was gifted with a rich flow of natural humour, which was always under perfect control, but this was merely a secondary part of the character of his preaching.

His great contemporary Robert Hall pronounced emphatically that "no man has ever drawn, since the days of our Saviour, such sublime images from nature : here Mr. Hill excells every other man."

In 1876 the congregation, presided over by the Rev. Newman Hall, removed to Christ Church, a large and costly building which they had erected at the junction of the Kennington and Westminster Bridge Roads, on a site formerly occupied by the Female Orphan Asylum, and the body of Rowland Hill was removed at the same time. Rowland Hill practised vaccination before the treatment was sanctioned by public approbation, the vestry of the chapel being then one of the chief London stations. Hannah More "asked him if it were true that he had vaccinated six thousand people with his own hand. He answered, Madam, it was nearer eight thousand."

Royal Academy of Arts, BURLINGTON HOUSE, PICCADILLY. The Academy was constituted by an instrument, which was signed by the King (George III.) as patron, December 10, 1768. In this instrument it is described as "a Society for promoting the Arts of Design," and is to "consist of forty members only, who shall be called Academicians of the Royal Academy ; they shall all of them be artists by profession at the time of their admission—that is to say, painters, sculptors, or architects." In the next clause it is said to be "His Majesty's pleasure that the following forty persons be the original members of the said society," but only thirty-six are named, of whom two are ladies, and in fact the number was not made up to forty till ten or twelve years later. In December 1769 it was decided to form a class of associates, not to exceed twenty in number, from whom in future the academicians should be chosen, and in 1770 sixteen associates were elected. It was also resolved that there should be six associate engravers, who were not however to be eligible for election to the higher grade.

The Academy established itself and opened its schools at Dillon's print warehouse, formerly Lamb's auction rooms, in Pall Mall, adjoining Carlton House, and immediately east of where the United Service Club now stands ; and here, at the first public meeting of the Academy, January 2, 1769, Sir Joshua Reynolds delivered the first of his famous Presidential Discourses. The first exhibition of the Academy was opened in these rooms on April 26, 1769, and contained 136 paintings. In 1771 the King gave the Academy apartments in Somerset House, in that part of the old mansion facing the river which had been added by Inigo Jones. But though well adapted for the ordinary purposes of the society, there were no rooms suited for the exhibitions, which continued to be held in Pall Mall till 1780, when the apartments in *New* Somerset House, built by Sir William Chambers for the use of the Academy, by special desire of the King, were ready to receive them. They remained here for fifty-eight years, and removed in May 1838 to Trafalgar Square, where they continued thirty-one years, and migrated to Burlington House in 1869.

May, 1780.—You know, I suppose, that the Royal Academy at Somerset House is opened. It is quite a Roman Palace, and finished in perfect taste as well as at boundless expense. It would have been a glorious apparition at the conclusion of the great war; now it is an insult on our poverty and degradation. . . . Gainsborough has five landscapes there, of which one especially is worthy of any collection, and of any painter that ever existed.—*Walpole to Mason.*

May 1, 1780. The Exhibition,—Now will do either to see or not to see! The Exhibition is eminently splendid. There is *contour* and *keeping*, and *grace*, and *expression*, and all the varieties of artificial excellence. The apartments are truly very noble. The pictures, for the sake of a skylight, are at the top of the house; there we dined, and I sat over against the Archbishop of York.—*Johnson to Mrs. Thrale.*

Gainsborough had sixteen pictures in this exhibition, among them the famous Horses drinking at a Trough. Reynolds contributed the portrait of Gibbon, and the almost equally well-known portrait of Miss Beauclerk as Una. The dinner to which Johnson alludes is that which was first given in Old Somerset House before the opening of the Exhibition, and has ever since formed one of the features of the London Season, and to which the highest and the most eminent deem it an honour to be invited. In the "Constitution and Laws" of the Academy it is laid down that "The guests shall consist *exclusively* of persons in elevated situations, of high rank, distinguished talents, or known patrons of the Arts," and the rule has been strictly adhered to for now more than a century. Writing to Mrs. Thrale in May 1783, Johnson says, "The Exhibition prospers so much that Sir Joshua says it will maintain the Academy." Sir Joshua's anticipations were well founded. From that time the Royal Academy has derived the whole of its funds from the produce of the annual exhibition. The members are under the superintendence and control of the Monarch, who confirms all elections, appointments, and alterations in the laws; but the Academy is regarded by the members as a "private society, though it supports a school that is open to the public,"[1] a position which the Parliamentary Commission of 1863 considered to be ambiguous. As now constituted the Royal Academy consists of forty royal academicians (including the President) and thirty associates. The honorary members—not a fixed number—comprise "honorary retired academicians," "honorary foreign academicians"—all artists of distinction, and five "honorary members" (a chaplain, two professors, an antiquary, and a foreign secretary, whose duties are as honorary as their titles). The schools "provide means of instruction for students of painting, sculpture, architecture, and engraving," and are open, without charge, to students who satisfy the authorities that they "have already attained such a proficiency as will enable them to draw or model well," and have a certain rudimentary acquaintance with anatomy, or, if a student in architecture, "a reasonable degree of proficiency" in the elementary stages of that art. The schools are under the direction of the keeper, visitors, and professors, the professorial staff comprising professors of painting, sculpture, architecture, anatomy, and chemistry, a teacher of perspective,

[1] Evidence of Mr. Howard, R.A., the Secretary, before Committee of the House of Commons, 1835.

and a master in the class of architecture. The fine library of books of prints belonging to the Academy is open to the students. Directions as to the mode of obtaining admission as a student may be obtained on application to the Secretary at Burlington House. Connected with the school is a large collection of busts from the antique. The Academy also possesses some interesting pictures and many fine drawings by the old masters, among them being a cartoon of Leda, by Michelangelo; one of a Holy Family in black chalk by Leonardo da Vinci; and a copy in oil, the size of the original, of Da Vinci's Last Supper, by Leonardo's scholar, Marco d'Oggione, which is probably of greater value than the original at Milan in its present dreadfully damaged condition. This was formerly in the Certosa at Pavia. The Academy possesses a few pieces of sculpture, the most noteworthy being a bas-relief in marble of the Holy Family by Michelangelo, presented by Sir George Beaumont. The models and casts of the works of the late John Gibson, R.A., were presented to the Academy by his widow, and are arranged in a room called the Gibson Gallery.

By a law passed in 1770 every member has on his election to present to the Academy a specimen of his art. It did not apply to those already elected, and consequently it has no "diploma work" of the thirty-six original academicians, but it has a work from the pencil or chisel of every academician elected since that year; and a very interesting collection it forms. Thus there are in the class of historical and imaginative works—Jael and Sisera, by Northcote; Age and Infancy, Opie; Thor and the Serpent of Midgard, Fuseli; Charity, Stothard; Prospero and Miranda, Thomson; Venus and Adonis, Phillips; Proclaiming Joash King, Bird; Ganymede, Hilton; Queen Katherine, Leslie; Sleeping Nymphs and Satyrs, Etty; Hagar and Ishmael, Eastlake; and St. Gregory teaching his Chant, Herbert. In works of a somewhat less ambitious order — The Fortune Teller, Ozias Humphrey; A Gipsy Girl, Sir Thomas Lawrence; Horses in a Storm, Sawrey Gilpin; Boy and Kitten, Owen; Boys digging for a Rat, Wilkie; Boy and Rabbit, Raeburn; The Village Buffoon, Mulready; The Student, Newton; The Faithful Hound, Sir Edwin Landseer; Italian Mother, Uwins; The Woodranger, Maclise; Early Lesson, Webster. Among landscapes are — Dolbadern Castle, Turner; Morning, Callcott; Young Anglers, Collins; Barge passing a Lock, Constable; On the Scheldt, Stanfield, and Baalbec, Roberts. The sculpture includes — Cupid and Psyche, by Nollekens; Sickness, Bacon; A Falling Giant, Banks; Apollo and Marpessa, Flaxman; Jupiter and Ganymede, Sir R. Westmacott; Bacchanalian Group in Bronze, Theed; Bust of Benjamin West, P.R.A., Chantrey; Eve, Baily; Narcissus, Gibson; Nymph, M'Dowell; the Elder Brother in Comus, Foley. But though there are no diploma works by the foundation members, the Academy possesses some good works by them, among others seven by Reynolds, including George III. and Queen Charlotte in their coronation robes, presented by George III.;

Portraits of himself as D.C.L., and of Sir William Chambers, presented by Reynolds and both very fine works. By Gainsborough, his own and another portrait and a landscape; and by West his Christ Blessing Little Children, and two or three more. These will now be swelled by other works of the British School dating from the present time. Sir Francis Chantrey by his will bequeathed the reversion of his property, after payment of other bequests, on the death of his widow, to the Royal Academy, to be invested and the interest laid out annually in the purchase of works of the highest merit that can be obtained, in painting and sculpture, "which may hereafter be executed by artists resident in Great Britain when they were completed." The legacy has fallen in, and already several excellent paintings, exhibited at the South Kensington Museum, and some good pieces of sculpture have been purchased.

In 1868 the eastern wing of the National Gallery, till then occupied by the Royal Academy, being required for the National pictures, the Government granted the Academy in exchange a lease for 999 years at a nominal rent of Old Burlington House with part of the garden behind. The house was altered, a new storey added and a range of spacious galleries erected in the rear, at a cost of about £120,000. The new galleries, which, with the alterations in the house, were designed by Mr. Sidney Smirke, R.A., comprise, besides the vestibule, octagonal, central hall and gallery beyond, which form the sculpture galleries, a great room, in which the annual dinner is held, a lecture hall and nine other rooms, all of which are appropriated to the Exhibition. The three galleries in the upper storey of Burlington House contain the diploma pictures, the Gibson models, and the miscellaneous pictures and works of art belonging to the Academy. The library, offices, etc., are in the body of the building, the schools are in the basement.

The Annual Exhibition of the Works of Living Artists opens to the public on the first Monday in May and closes on the first Monday in August. The annual dinner is held on the Saturday preceding the opening day. Works for exhibition are received from any artists, subject to approval or rejection by the Council. No works that have been previously exhibited, or copies of any kind are admitted. Pictures, etc., have to be sent in about five weeks before the opening of the Exhibition, but the exact days are always advertised in the newspapers and generally printed in the catalogue of the previous exhibition. On removing to Burlington House the Academy arranged for a Winter Exhibition of Works by the Old Masters and Deceased Masters of the British School, similar to those of the British Institution, which had lapsed with the close of that institution. These exhibitions are opened on the first Monday in January and close on the second Saturday in March.

Royal Academy of Music. [*See* Academy of Music.]

Royal Aquarium, TOTHILL STREET, WESTMINSTER, a large

building constructed from the designs of Mr. A. Bedborough in 1876 as an aquarium and winter garden, at a cost of nearly £200,000. The building, which is of red brick and Portland stone, is about 600 feet long and 160 wide. It was started as an institution for the moral elevation of the people by the contemplation of the wonders of nature. As a winter garden it failed completely, and it is now a sort of magnified "music hall," in which scantily dressed females go through "exciting" acrobatic performances, or are shot out of cannons, "genuine Zulus" dance, and female swimmers exhibit "aquatic feats" in the great tank, or fasting men are exhibited to a gaping crowd. Part of the western end of the building is fitted as a theatre, at present named *The Imperial*.

Royal Astronomical Society. [*See* Astronomical Society.]

Royal Exchange (The), a quadrangle and colonnade (the third building of the kind on the same site), erected for the convenience of merchants and bankers, built from the designs of Mr. (afterwards Sir William) Tite. The first stone was laid by Prince Albert, January 17, 1842, and the building was opened with great pomp by Her Majesty in person on October 28, 1844. The cost of the structure, with its sculpture, was about £150,000. Of the exterior the chief feature is the noble portico at the west end, the most imposing in its proportions and dignity of effect in the metropolis. It is octostyle (having eight Corinthian columns) with intercolumns, and the pediment is filled with emblematic sculpture in high relief by Richard Westmacott, R.A. (the younger). The portico is 96 feet wide and 74 feet high to the apex of the pediment. The columns are 4 feet 2 inches in diameter and 41 high, including the base and capital. The extreme length of the building is 308 feet. The east end is 175 feet wide, or 56 feet wider than the west end, a peculiarity which certainly adds picturesqueness to its effect when looked at from the west. The eastern entrance is marked by four Corinthian columns, from which rises a clock-tower, 170 feet high, surmounted by the Gresham grasshopper. The sides have ranges of Corinthian pilasters, between which are shops, originally deeply recessed under rusticated arches; but the shop fronts have been brought forward, much to the detriment of the architectural effect. The inner quadrangle, or *merchants' area*, is an open area 111 feet long and 53 feet wide, surrounded by an arcade about 30 feet deep. This was formerly open to the sky, but after many years of consideration it was covered about 1880 by a glass and iron roof, from the designs of Mr. Charles Barry, architect. In the centre is a marble statue—small in size and insignificant in character—of the Queen, by Lough; statues of Sir Thomas Gresham, Sir Hugh Myddelton, Sir Richard Whittington, and Queen Elizabeth, by Messrs. Behnes, Joseph, Carew, and Watson. The western part of the building is appropriated to the Royal Exchange Assurance Company; the eastern end to Lloyds. [*See* Lloyds.] The two great days on 'Change are Tuesday and Friday, and the busy period from half-past three to half-past four P.M. The

Rothschilds, the greatest people on 'Change, occupy a pillar on the south side of the Exchange. In the open space before the west front of the Royal Exchange is a colossal equestrian statue of the Duke of Wellington by Sir Francis Chantrey.

The first Royal Exchange was founded by Sir Thomas Gresham; the first stone was laid June 7, 1566, and the building opened by Queen Elizabeth in person, January 23, 1570-1571.

The Queen's Majesty, attended with her nobility, came from her house at the Strand called Somerset House, and entered the city by Temple Bar, through Fleet Street, Cheap, and so by the north side of the burse, through Threedneedle Street, to Sir Thomas Gresham's house in Bishopsgate Street, where she dined. After dinner her Majesty, returning through Cornhill, entered the burse on the south side; and after that she had viewed every part thereof above the ground, especially the pawn, which was richly furnished with all sorts of the finest wares in the city, she caused the same burse, by a herald and trumpet, to be proclaimed "The Royal Exchange," and so to be called from thenceforth, and not otherwise.—*Stow.*

After the Royal Exchange, which is now [1631] called the Eye of London, had been builded two or three years, it stood in a manner empty; and a little before her Majesty was to come thither to view the beauty thereof, and to give it a name, Sir Thomas Gresham, in his own person, went, twice in one day, round about the upper pawn, and besought those few shopkeepers then present that they would furnish and adorn with wares and wax-lights as many shops as they either could or would, and they should have all those shops so furnished rent free that year, which otherwise at that time was 40s. a shop by the year; and within two years after he raised that rent unto four marks a year; and within a while after that he raised his rent of every shop unto £4 : 10s. a year, and then all shops were well furnished according to that time; for then the milliners or haberdashers in that place sold mouse-traps, bird-cages, shoeing-horns, lanthorns, and Jews' trumps, etc. There were also at that time that kept shops in the upper pawn of the Royal Exchange, armourers that sold both old and new armour, apothecaries, booksellers, goldsmiths, and glass-sellers, although now [1631] it is as plenteously stored with all kinds of rich wares and fine commodities as any particular place in Europe, into which place many foreign princes daily send to be best served of the best sort.—*Howes*, ed. 1631, p. 869.

The materials for the construction of the Exchange were brought from Flanders, or, as Holinshed has it, Gresham "bargained for the whole mould and substance of his workmanship in Flanders," and a Flemish builder of the name of Henryke was employed.[1]

October 26, 1570.—Sir Thomas Gresham to Cecil. Requests a special license for a ship to go to Flanders with alabaster, as he had a special license for transportation of his stores from Antwerp to his Burse.—*Cal. Eliz.*, p. 394.

In general design the Exchange was not unlike the Burse at Antwerp —a quadrangle, with a cloister running round the interior of the building, a corridor or "pawn"[2] above, and attics or bedrooms at the top.

Just. Phew! excuses! You must to the Pawn to buy lawn; to St. Martin's for lace, etc.—*Westward Ho!* (1607), vol. ii. p. 1.

On the south or Cornhill front was a bell-tower, and on the north

---

[1] Burgon's *Life of Gresham*, vol. ii. p. 115.
[2] *Bahn* (German), *Baan* (Dutch), a path or walk. These were divided into stalls, and formed a kind of bazaar. In 1712 there were 160 stalls let at a yearly rent of £10 and £30 each (*Burgon*, vol. ii. p. 513). These were all vacant in 1739, when Maitland published his *History of London* (*Maitland*, p. 467).

a lofty Corinthian column, each surmounted by a grasshopper—the crest of the Greshams. The bell, in Gresham's time, was rung at twelve at noon and at six in the evening.[1] In niches within the quadrangle, and immediately above the cloister or covered walk, stood the statues of our kings and queens, from Edward the Confessor to Queen Elizabeth. James I., Charles I., and Charles II. were afterwards added. Charles I.'s statue was thrown down immediately after his execution, and on the pedestal these words were inscribed in gilt letters, *Exit tyrannus Regum ultimus*—"The tyrant is gone, the last of the Kings." Hume concludes his *History of Charles I.* with this little anecdote of City disaffection, which no doubt was in Addison's mind when he made his Tory fox-hunter satisfied that the London merchants had not turned republicans "when he spied the statue of King Charles II. standing up in the middle of the crowd, and most of the Kings in Baker's Chronicle ranged in order over their heads."[2]

According to the valuation made at Gresham's death—

The Royal Exchange with all Howses, Buildings, Pawnes, Vawtes, and Proffittes thereof, amounte to the clere yearely vallew of £751 : 5s. per ann. over all chardges and reprises.[3]

Of this, the first or Gresham's Exchange, there are two curious contemporary views in the library of the Society of Antiquaries at Burlington House. A still more interesting view, representing a full Exchange—High 'Change, as Addison calls it—was made in 1644 by Wenceslaus Hollar. It is true to Dekker's description of the Exchange in 1607. "At every turn," says Dekker, "a man is put in mind of Babel, there is such a confusion of languages." Hollar has given the picturesque dresses of the foreign merchants. There was then no necessity for printed boards to point out the particular localities set apart for different countries. The merchants of Amsterdam and Antwerp, of Hamburgh, Paris, Venice, and Vienna, were unmistakably distinguished by the dresses of their respective nations. The places of business were at this time distinguished by signs. On January 11, 1635, Cromwell addressed a letter ("Oliver's first extant letter," as Carlyle notes[4]) "To my very loving friend Mr. Storie, at the Sign of the Dog in the Royal Exchange, London."

Gresham's Exchange was destroyed in the Great Fire of 1666. Pepys describes its appearance as "a sad sight, nothing standing there of all the statues or pillars, but Sir Thomas Gresham in the corner." When the Royal Exchange was destroyed a second time by fire (January 10, 1838), the statue of Sir Thomas Gresham escaped again uninjured.

The *second* Exchange was designed by Edward Jarman or Jerman, the City surveyor. This also, like the Exchange of Gresham, was a quadrangular building, with a clock-tower of timber on the south or Cornhill front; its inner cloister, or walk; its *pawn* above, for the sale

[1] *Burgon*, vol. ii. p. 345.   [2] *Freeholder*, June 1, 1716.   [3] *Strype*, Second App., p. 6.
[4] *Carlyle's Cromwell*, vol. i. p. 129.

of fancy goods, gloves, ribbons, ruffs, bands, stomachers, etc;[1] and its series of statues (placed in niches as before) of our kings and queens, from Edward I. downwards, carved for the most part by Caius Gabriel Cibber, father of Colley. Later were added the first two Georges by Rysbrack, the third George by Wilton, and George IV. Gresham's statue was by Edward Pierce, and the statue of Charles II., in the centre of the quadrangle, by Grinling Gibbons.[2] Jarman's Exchange, which is said to have cost £58,962, was destroyed by fire, January 10, 1838.

In excavating for the new Royal Exchange the workmen came upon a remarkable hole measuring 50 feet by 34, which had apparently been a gravel pit in the time of the Romans, but closed and built over some time before they left the island. Numerous Roman remains, fragments of pottery, knives, combs, sandals, and other articles of domestic and personal use were found in it, apparently thrown there when worn out or broken. These were carefully collected by Mr. Tite (who drew up and printed an elaborate Descriptive Catalogue of them), and are now in the City Museum, Guildhall.

Royal Exchange Buildings, facing the east front of the Royal Exchange, were built in 1846 from the designs of the late Edward I'Anson. The ground is the property of Magdalen College, Oxford. At the north end of Royal Exchange Buildings was erected in 1869 a seated statue in bronze of George Peabody, an American, who so munificently provided improved dwellings for the London poor. The statue was modelled by Mr. Peabody's countryman, Mr. W. W. Story, and was cast at Munich. When first set up it was of a bright golden hue, but has already become so black as to render the features almost undistinguishable—a matter the more to be regretted as the likeness was pronounced by Mr. Peabody's friends to be both true and characteristic. Near the statue was erected in 1879 a very pretty drinking-fountain with a marble statue of Charity. It cost £1500.

Royal Free Hospital, east side of GRAY'S INN ROAD. This hospital was founded in 1828, "to receive all Destitute Sick and Diseased Persons, to whatever Nation they may belong, who may choose to present themselves as Out-Patients, and as great a number of In-Patients as the state of the Charity will permit." Previously there was no medical establishment in London into which the destitute poor, when overtaken by disease, could find instant admission without a letter of recommendation. The hospital has recently been much enlarged, and now contains 150 beds. It admits into its wards about 1900 in-patients, and administers advice and medicine to over 21,000 out-patients annually. The income in 1888 from charitable contributions and legacies was £11,250, and from invested funds £1077. The hospital relieves the sick of a very poor and thickly inhabited district.

[1] See the *Fair Maid of the Exchange*, by T. Heywood, 4to, 1607.

[2] Gibbons received £500 for it. See Wright's *Publick Transactions*, 12mo, 1685, p. 198.

Royal Geographical Society. [*See* Geographical Society, Royal.]

Royal Horticultural Society. [*See* Horticultural Society, Royal.]

Royal Humane Society. [*See* Humane Society.]

Royal Institute of British Architects. [*See* Institute of British Architects, Royal.]

Royal Institution of Great Britain, 21 ALBEMARLE STREET, PICCADILLY, established March 9, 1799, at a meeting held at the house of Sir Joseph Banks, for diffusing the knowledge and facilitating the general introduction of useful mechanical inventions and improvements, etc. Count Rumford was its earliest promoter, and in a Poetical Epistle to him some portions of the scheme were handled with considerable humour, more particularly the "Refreshment Room."

> With rapture have I visited thy house
> And marvell'd at thy vast extent of *vous*.
> Thanks to thy care that, midst its ample round,
> Soup, tea and toast, and coffee may be found ;
> And wine, and punch, and porter—freshening draught,
> Mending the monstrous *wear and tear* of thought,
> Thus a *new birth* shall Rumford's glory tell,
> And from its bowels spring a grand Hotel.

The front of the building—a row of half-engaged Corinthian columns—was designed by Mr. Lewis Vulliamy; and what, before 1837, was little better than a perforated brick wall, was thus converted into an ornamental façade. Here are a convenient lecture-theatre, one of the best for its acoustic properties of any in London, an excellent library of about 50,000 volumes, and a good reading-room, with weekly courses of lectures throughout the season, on science, philosophy, literature, and art. Members are elected by ballot. The admission fee is 5 guineas, and the annual subscription 5 guineas. Annual subscribers pay the same subscription, with an entrance fee of one guinea. A syllabus of each course may be obtained of the secretary at the Institution. The Friday evening meetings of the members, at which some eminent person is invited to deliver a popular lecture on some subject of interest connected with science, art, or literature, are well attended. Campbell delivered his lectures on poetry here in 1812, but "was nervous about his Caledonianisms." He was paid 100 guineas for the five,—then a large honorarium.[1] Moore was invited to lecture but was advised not.

July 1, 1813.—I was solicited very flatteringly to lecture at the Royal Institution next year. Campbell has just ended his lectures. I should not have disliked it, but by Rogers' advice, and that of some other friends (who thought it *infra dig.*) I declined it.—*Life of Thomas Moore*, vol. viii. p. 145.

---

[1] *Life*, vol. ii. p. 212.

In the laboratory of the Royal Institution Davy made his great discoveries on the metallic bases of the alkalies and the earths, aided by the large galvanic apparatus of the establishment. His laboratory note-books, in which these discoveries are recorded, are preserved in the library. And here his assistant and successor carried out those investigations in chemistry, electricity and magnetism which placed him in the foremost rank among the scientific men of Europe. Faraday was appointed laboratory assistant, and went to reside "in two rooms at the top of the house," on March 1, 1813; and here he resided continuously until 1858, when Her Majesty gave him a residence at Hampton Court. He delivered his last "Juvenile Course" on "The Chemistry of a Candle" in 1860, and on June 20, 1862, his last Friday evening discourse; but he retained his post as laboratory director till 1865.

Royal Military Asylum (popularly THE DUKE OF YORK'S SCHOOL), CHELSEA. Built from the designs of John Sanders in 1801. Founded for the maintenance and education of orphan children of British soldiers. The children, 500 in number, are admitted between the ages of ten and twelve and leave when fourteen.

Royal Society, BURLINGTON HOUSE. Incorporated by royal charter, April 22, 1663, as "the Royal Society of London for the advancement of Natural Science," King Charles II. and his brother the Duke of York entering their names as members of the Society. This celebrated Society (boasting of the names of Newton, Wren, Halley, Cavendish, Watt, Herschel, Davy and Faraday among its members) originated in a small attendance of men engaged in the same pursuits, and dates its beginning from certain weekly meetings held in London as early as the year 1645; "sometimes," as Wallis relates, "at Dr. Goddard's lodgings in Wood Street; sometimes at a convenient place [the Bull Head Tavern] in Cheapside; and sometimes at Gresham College, or some place near adjoining." The merit of suggesting such meetings is assigned by Wallis (himself a foundation member) to Theodore Haak, a German of the Palatinate, then resident in London. The Civil War interrupted their pursuits for a time; and Wilkins, Wallis and Goddard removing to Oxford, a second Society was established, Seth Ward, Ralph Bathurst, Dr. (afterwards Sir William) Petty and the Honourable Robert Boyle joining their number, and taking an active part in the furtherance of their views. With the Restoration of the King a fresh accession of strength was obtained, new members enlisted, meetings were again held in Gresham College, and on November 28, 1660, a resolution was adopted to establish the meetings on a regular basis, the memorandum of this meeting being, according to the Society's historian, "the first official record of the Royal Society."[1] It was agreed, December 12, 1660, to hold the meetings of the Society weekly at Gresham College, where "a subject" was

[1] Weld, *Hist. of Royal Soc.*, vol. ii. p. 63.

given out for discussion and very frequently experiments were performed. Almost from the first the King showed an active interest in the proceedings, and did the fellows "the favour and honour of offering to be entered on the Society," and on July 15, 1662, granted them a Charter of Incorporation, and when this was found to have "failed in giving the Society certain privileges essential to their welfare," granted them a new patent, which passed the Great Seal on April 22, 1663, and is the acting charter of the Society at the present day.[1] The Society continued to hold its meetings in Gresham College; and after the Great Fire, by permission of the Duke of Norfolk, in Arundel House. Subsequently the Society returned to Gresham College; but in 1710 removed to Crane Court, Fleet Street, and from thence in 1782 to Somerset House, where apartments had been assigned to them by George III. These being required for Government offices they removed in 1857 to Old Burlington House; and in 1873 to the new east wing which had been erected with especial regard to the Society's requirements.

The meetings of the Society are held weekly (on Thursdays) from November to June. From among the candidates fifteen are annually selected by the Council for election by the members. At the Anniversary Meeting in November 1889 there was a total of 518 Fellows (including 47 Honorary Foreign Members). The letters F.R.S. are the distinguishing mark of a Fellow. The patron saint of the Society is St. Andrew, and the Anniversary Meeting is held every 30th of November, being St. Andrew's Day. The Scottish saint was chosen out of compliment to Sir Robert Murray or Moray, a Scot, one of the most active of the foundation members and president of the Society before the charter. When the Society was first established it was severely ridiculed by the wits of the time, "for what reason," says Dr. Johnson, "it is hard to conceive, since the philosophers professed not to advance doctrines, but to produce facts; and the most zealous enemy of innovation must admit the gradual progress of experience, however he may oppose hypothetical temerity." Isaac D'Israeli has given an account of the hostilities it encountered, but, curiously enough, has overlooked the inimitable satire of Butler, called *The Elephant in the Moon*. The *History of the Society* was written by Sprat in 1667, by Birch in 1756, by Thomson in 1812, and by Weld in 1848. Mr. Weld has made the same omission as Mr. D'Israeli. The *Philosophical Transactions*, commenced in 1666, now occupy nearly 200 quarto volumes. The *Proceedings*, commenced in 1832, consist of forty-six volumes up to 1889. The first president after the incorporation of the Society was Viscount Brouncker, and the second Sir Joseph Williamson. Sir Christopher Wren was the third. Pepys the diarist and seven others, among whom were Halifax and Somers, came before Sir Isaac Newton, who, however, retained the chair till his death twenty-four years afterwards. Sir Hans Sloane succeeded Newton. Sir Joseph Banks was president from 1778 to 1820.

[1] Weld, *Hist. of Royal Soc.*, vol. i. p. 141.

Among the secretaries have been Bishop Wilkins, John Evelyn, Hans Sloane, Edmund Halley, Wollaston, Robert Hooke, Sir Humphry Davy, and Sir John Herschel.

The Society possesses some interesting portraits. *Observe.*—Three portraits of Sir Isaac Newton—one by C. Jervas, presented by Newton himself, and the other two by Vanderbank; Bacon, by Van Somer; two portraits of Halley, by Thomas Murray and Dahl; two of Hobbes —one taken in 1663 by, says Aubrey, "a good hand," and the other by Caspars, presented by Aubrey; Sir Christopher Wren, by Kneller; Wallis, by Soest; Flamsteed, by Gibson; Robert Boyle, by F. Kerseboom (Evelyn says it is like); Pepys, by Kneller, presented by Pepys; Lord Somers, by Kneller; Sir R. Southwell, by Kneller; Sir H. Spelman, the antiquary, by Mytens; Sir Hans Sloane, by Kneller; Sir Joseph Banks, by Phillips; Lord Brouncker, by Lely; Dr. S. Chandler, by Chamberlain; Sir John Pringle, by Reynolds. Dr. Birch, by Wells, the original of the mezzotint done by Faber in 1741, bequeathed by Birch; Martin Folkes, by Hogarth; Dr. Wollaston, by Jackson; Sir Humphry Davy, by Sir T. Lawrence; Dr. Price, by West. *Observe also.*— The mace of silver gilt (similar to the maces of the Lord Chancellor, the Speaker, and President of the College of Physicians), presented to the Society by Charles II. in 1662. The belief so long entertained that it was the mace or "bauble," as Cromwell called it, of the Long Parliament, was completely refuted by the late C. R. Weld, the assistant secretary, producing the original warrant of the year 1662, for the special making of this very mace. A solar dial, made by Sir Isaac Newton when a boy, and taken from the house at Woolsthorpe; a reflecting telescope, made in 1671 by Newton's own hands; original MS. of the *Principia;* lock of Newton's hair, silver white; MS. of the *Parentalia,* by Christopher Wren, the son; Charter Book of the Society, bound in crimson velvet, containing the signatures of the Founder and Fellows; marble busts of Charles II. and George III., by Nollekens; Newton, by Roubiliac; Sir Joseph Banks, by Chantrey, and Mrs. Somerville, by Chantrey. The Society possesses a library of about 40,000 volumes almost exclusively scientific; a Scientific Relief Fund; a Donation Fund, established to aid men of science in their researches, and distributes five gold medals in all; a biennial Rumford gold medal, two Royal medals, a Copley medal, called by Davy "the ancient olive crown of the Royal Society," and a Davy medal.

Royal Society of Literature, 21 DELAHAY STREET, ST. JAMES'S PARK. Founded in 1825 "for the advancement of Literature in its more important branches, with a special attention to the improvement of the English Language," and incorporated by royal charter, September 13, 1826. George IV. gave 1100 guineas a year to this Society, which has the merit of rescuing the last years of Coleridge's life from complete dependence on a friend, and of placing the learned Dr. Jamieson, who was fast sinking to the grave, above want. This grant was discontinued by William IV., and the Society has since become an ordinary Transaction Society. The Society, in its earlier existence, awarded gold medals to eminent writers, and published some valuable works on Egyptian hieroglyphics and on the Anglo-Saxon and Anglo-Norman periods of English literary history. The Society occupied a house in St. Martin's Place until this was required for the enlargement of the National Gallery and the opening for the new Charing Cross Road.

Royalty Theatre (New), DEAN STREET, SOHO, is a small house built in 1840 by Miss Kelly for her school of acting, and then and afterwards much used for amateur performances. It is now chiefly devoted to burlesque and farce.

Royalty Theatre, WELL STREET, WELLCLOSE SQUARE, was built by John Wilmot for John Palmer, the actor. The first stone was laid with great ceremony on Monday, December 26, 1785, the inscription declaring that "The ground selected for the purpose being situated within the Liberty of His Majesty's Fortress and Palace of the Tower of London, It has been resolved that in honour of the Magistrates, the Military Officers and Inhabitants of the said Fortress and Palace, the edifice when erected shall be called the Royalty Theatre." It was opened June 20, 1787, with a prologue by Murphy, and burnt down April 11, 1826. It was originally intended for the performance of five-act pieces, and opened with *As You Like It;* but the patentees of the other theatres memorialising the Lord Chamberlain on the subject, the new theatre was confined to pantomimes and still smaller entertainments until the restrictions on the "minor theatres" were removed. The ill-starred *Brunswick Theatre* was erected on its site.

December 5, 1806.—Having never seen the Royalty Theatre I determined that day should be devoted to that purpose. . . . The theatre is very plain but neat : the house seemed to me something larger than the Haymarket : the pit is small, but I was told the middle gallery would contain a thousand people.— George Fred. Cooke's *Journal*.

Cooke seems to have thought that Wellclose Square was at the other end of the world, for he started at eight o'clock in the morning to make his visit. At one of the public-houses into which he went for refreshment the landlady told him that she had been obliged to remove the *leaden weights* from the clock to save them from the thieves who resorted there! John Braham commenced his career as a singer at the Royalty Theatre; and here Clarkson Stanfield, the future R.A., after quitting the sea, started on his artistic course as a scene-painter. The site is now occupied by the *Sailors' Home*.

Ruffian's Hall, a cant name for *West Smithfield,* "by reason it was the usuall place of frayes and common fighting during the time that sword and bucklers were in use." [1]

[1] *Howes*, ed. 1631, p. 1023.

As if men will needes carouse, conspire and quarrel, that they may make Ruffian's Hall of Hell.—*Pierce Penilesse*, 4to, 1592 (Collier's *Reprint*, p. 35).

Beat down their weapons! My gate Ruffian's Hall?
What insolence is this?
      Massinger, *The City Madam*, Act. i. Sc. 2.

Rummer Tavern (The). A famous tavern, two doors from Locket's, between Whitehall and Charing Cross, removed to the waterside of Charing Cross in 1710, and burnt down November 7, 1750. No traces exist. It was kept in Charles II.'s reign by Samuel Prior, uncle of Matthew Prior, the poet. The Prior family ceased to be connected with it in 1702.

> My uncle, rest his soul ! when living,
> Might have contriv'd me ways of thriving :
> Taught me with cider to replenish
> My vats, or ebbing tide of Rhenish.
> So when for hock I drew prickt white-wine,
> Swear't had the flavour, and was right wine.
>   *Prior to Fleetwood Shepheard.*

There having been a false and scandalous report that Samuel Pryor, vintner at the Rummer, near Charing Cross, was accused of exchanging money for his own advantage, with such as clip and deface his Majesty's coin, and that the said Pryor had given bail to answer the same. This report being false in every part of it, if any person who shall give notice to the said Pryor, who have been the fomenters or dispersers of this malicious report, so as a legal prosecution may be made against them, the said Pryor will forthwith give 10 guineas as a reward.—*London Gazette*, May 31 to June 4, 1688.

Col. Standard. If you are my friend meet me this evening at the Rummer.—Farquhar, *The Inconstant Couple*, Act i. Sc. 1.

And again—

Col. Then meet me in half an hour hence at the Rummer.—*Ibid.*, Act. iv. Sc. 3.

Here Jack Sheppard committed his first robbery by stealing two silver spoons. The Rummer is introduced by Hogarth into his picture of "Night." There were Rummer Taverns in Henrietta Street,[1] Covent Garden, and Queen Street, Cheapside ; also a Swan and Rummer in Finch Lane, and a Rummer and Horse-shoe in Drury Lane.

Rupert Street, HAYMARKET, east side of Coventry Street to Great Crown Court, built in 1667, and so called in compliment to Prince Rupert of the Rhine, son of the King of Bohemia, and nephew to Charles I.

Russell Court, DRURY LANE, a narrow passage for foot-passengers only, leading from Drury Lane into Catherine Street, Covent Garden. [*See* Will's ; Rose.]

Towards the defraying the charge of repairing and fitting up the Chapel in Russell Court, Drury Lane, will be presented at the Theatre Royal, Drury Lane, this present Tuesday, being the 18th of June, the Tragedy of Hamlet, Prince of Denmark. With Singing by Mr. Hughes and entertainment of Dancing by Mons. Cherier, Miss Lambro, his scholar, and Mr. Evans.—*Daily Courant*, June 18, 1706, quoted in Burton's *Hist. of Queen Anne*, vol. iii. p. 309.

---

[1] Cockburn's *Letters*, vol. ii. p. 225.

This curious benefit performance called forth much comment, and Defoe, making merry with it in his Review, recommended that when the chapel was re-edified a tablet should be set up, "as is very frequent in like cases," stating when and by whose charitable aid the work was accomplished, and testified by "Lucifer, Prince of Darkness, and Hamlet, Prince of Denmark, Churchwardens."—*Review*, June 20, 1706.

Russell House, on the south side of the STRAND, was inhabited by the Russells, Earls of Bedford, prior to the erection of their house on the north side of the Strand, between it and the great square of Covent Garden. Stow, 1598, speaks of it as "Russell or Bedford House."

Russell House, near Ivye bridge, seytuate upon the Thamise now [1592] in the use of the right honorable Sir John Puckering, knight, Lord Keeper of the Prevye Seale.—Norden's *Speculum Brit. Harl. MSS.*, p. 570.

September 13, 1595.—I dyned with the Erle of Derby at Russell Howse. Mr. Thymothew, and Mr. John Hatfeldt, German, being there : [and again Sept. 22].— Dr. Dee's *Diary*, p. 53.

Russell Institution, GREAT CORAM STREET, RUSSELL SQUARE, a subscription library and reading-room. The house was erected in 1800 on speculation, for the purpose of holding assemblies and balls, and was purchased in 1808 from Mr. James Burton, the builder, by the managers of the institution, of which Sir Samuel Romilly was one of the original trustees. E. W. Brayley, author of *Londiniana* and many topographical works, was librarian from 1825 to his death in 1854.

Not Palmyra, not the Russell Institution in Great Coram Street, present more melancholy appearances of faded greatness [than the Cork Reading Room].— Thackeray, *Irish Note-Book*, p. 140.

Russell Row, SHOREDITCH, a row of houses built in the reign of Queen Elizabeth, by one Russell, a draper, on the site of certain tenements, called from their decayed appearance "Rotten Row." Originally Rotten Row "was one row of proper small houses, with gardens, for poor decayed people, there placed by the Prior of the hospital [of St. Mary, Spital]; every one tenant whereof paid one penny rent by the year at Christmas, and dined with the Prior on Christmas Day."[1]

Russell Square, BLOOMSBURY, north of Bloomsbury Square, with which it is united by Bedford Place, built circ. 1804, and so called after the Russells, Earls and Dukes of Bedford. Each side of the square is about 670 feet in length. The area was laid out by Humphrey Repton. On the south side is the statue of Francis, Duke of Bedford (the hero of Burke's *Letter to a Noble Lord*, 1796), by Sir Richard Westmacott, R.A., looking down Bedford Place on the statue of Charles James Fox which, exactly opposite to it, adorns the north side of Bloomsbury Square.

March 18, 1807.—Young Faulder and I walked over all the Duke of Bedford's new feuing grounds, Russell Square, Tavistock Place, Brunswick Square, etc. The extent of these, and the rapidity of the buildings, is beyond all comprehension. Their

---

[1] *Stow*, p. 158.

houses very inferior in appearance to our new town at Bellevue; but their squares (the areas I mean) are all most tastefully laid out with shrubs, walks, etc., which has an admirable effect.—*A. G. Hunter to A. Constable* (*A. Constable and his Literary Correspondents*, vol. i. p. 112).

Eminent Inhabitants.—Sir Samuel Romilly in No. 21, where, body and mind utterly prostrated by his wife's death on October 29, he died by his own hand, November 2, 1818. Russell Square was long in much favour with members of the bench and bar. No. 28 was the residence of Lord Chief Justice Tenterden, who died there November 4, 1832. The houses at the south corner of Guilford Street formed Baltimore House, built in 1763 (before Russell Square was formed) for George Calvert, the last Baron Baltimore, who was tried in 1768 for decoying a young milliner named Sarah Woodcock to his house in the previous year. It was afterwards occupied by the Duke of Bolton, who gave his name to the house. He was succeeded by Wedderburn, Lord Loughborough, and the name Rosslyn House, which it sometimes bore, was taken from his subsequent title, Earl of Rosslyn. No. 67, part of Baltimore House, was the residence of Sir Vicary Gibbs, C.J. of the Common Pleas, who died there February 8, 1820, "where Heath had lived and died and Talfourd afterwards held his convivialities." No. 67 was Sir T. N. Talfourd's last London residence. Charles Grant, the old East India Director and father of Lord Glenelg and Sir R. Grant, lived in No. 40. Here Francis Horner dined on May 28, 1803, and met Sir William Grant, Wilberforce and Mackintosh. Sir Thomas Lawrence, P.R.A., in No. 65, for the last twenty-five years of his life; he died here January 7, 1830.

We shall never forget the Cossacks mounted on their small white horses, with their long spears grounded, standing centinels at the door of this great painter, whilst he was taking the portrait of their General, Platoff.—Rev. John Mitford, *Gentleman's Mag.* for January, 1818.

Russell Street (Great), BLOOMSBURY, was built about 1670. In 1720 it was described as "a very handsome, large, and well-built street with the best buildings in all Bloomsbury, and the best inhabited by the nobility and gentry, especially the north side, as having gardens behind the houses, and the prospect of the pleasant fields up to Hampstead and Highgate."[1] When the first edition of this work was published it was "a street of shops," but for some years past many of the shops have been undergoing the process of reconversion into "private houses."

January 31, 1750.—People are almost afraid of stirring out after dark. My Lady Albemarle was robbed the other night in Great Russell Street by nine men.—*Walpole to Sir Horace Mann.*

Eminent Inhabitants.—Sir Christopher Wren erected a mansion for himself in this street, which was afterwards inhabited by his son and his grandson; and then by Shelden the surgeon and anatomist. Its "noble front, with its majestic cantalever cornice," writes Elmes,

[1] *Strype*, B. iv. p. 85.

"has now (1823) been taken down by a speculative builder, and common Act of Parliament fronts run up" for four houses in its stead. Ralph, first Duke of Montague (d. 1709) in Montague House [which *see*], afterwards the British Museum. William, Earl Cowper (d. 1723).

November 30, 1714.—This day was employed in packing for removing from Russell Street (where I had a delightful house, with the finest view backwards of any house in town) to the house in Lincoln's Inn Fields, where I had lived before, when my Lord had the seals, and which my Lord Harcourt lived in whilst he was Chancellor.—Lady Cowper's *Diary*.

Francis Sandford, author of the *Genealogical History*.[1] John Le Neve, author of *Monumenta Anglicana*, was born "in the house facing Montague Great Gate, December 27, 1679."[2] Lewis Theobald, in Wyan's Court, Great Russell Street. Speaker Onslow; he died here in February 1768. John Philip Kemble, in No. 89, on the north side. The house was built by Lord St. Helen's, and destroyed in 1847 to make way for the eastern wing of the British Museum. During the height of the O. P. riots, the song of "Heigh Ho, says Kemble," written by Horace Smith, was sung by ballad-singers under the windows, accompanied by "shouts and other sounds," which, Mrs. Inchbald says, nearly frightened Mrs. Kemble to death. It is of this house that Talfourd speaks when he tells us that the great actor extended his high-bred courtesy even to authors with MSS., whom he invariably attended to the door, and bade them "beware of the steps."[3]

Topham Beauclerk.

November 14, 1779.—Mr. Beauclerk has built a library in Great Russell Street that reaches half way to Highgate. Everybody goes to see it. It has put the Museum's nose quite out of joint.—*Horace Walpole to Lady Ossory*.

Beauclerk died in this house, March 11, 1780. Opposite Dyot Street was Thanet House, the residence of the Earls of Thanet. It was latterly divided into two houses. Lord Mansfield took a house in this street in 1780, after the destruction of his mansion in Bloomsbury Square. Benjamin Wilson, a portrait painter of some merit, and master painter to the Board of Ordnance, died at his house, No. 56 in this street in 1788, and there his more celebrated son, Sir Robert Wilson, was born in 1777. No. 88 was built by William Battie, M.D., the celebrated physician of St. Luke's, and author of a well-known treatise on Mental Madness (d. 1776). In the *Gentleman's Magazine* for April 1809 is printed a characteristic letter from Dr. John Jenner, the discoverer of vaccination, dated "Great Russell Street, July 8, 1808." Sir Sidney Smith, the hero of Acre, was living in No. 72 in 1828.[4] Charles Mathews (the elder) died at No. 62, June 28, 1835. At No. 105 lived, 1829, the well known publisher of works on Gothic architecture, Augustus Pugin, and there he had many pupils who became eminent in their profession. His more celebrated son, Augustus Welby Pugin, was born in Store Street, March 1, 1812.

1 *London Gazette* of 1668, No. 2339.
2 Nichols's *Lit. Anec.*, vol. i. p. 108.
3 *Letters of Charles Lamb*, p. 113.
4 Barrow's *Life*, vol. ii. p. 348.

At the chapel in this street, on June 22, 1749, David Garrick was married to Mademoiselle Violette. Dr. Francklin performed the service. The ceremony was repeated on the same day according to the Roman Catholic forms in the Chapel of the Portuguese Embassy in South Audley Street.

Russell Street, COVENT GARDEN, built 1634, and so called after the Russells, Earls and Dukes of Bedford, the ground landlords. In 1720 "it was a fine broad street, well inhabited by tradesmen;"[1] it is now rather poorly inhabited. *Remarkable Places in.*—Will's Coffee-house, on the north side of the west-end corner of Bow Street, Button's Coffee-house, "on the south side, about two doors from Covent Garden;"[2] Tom's Coffee-house, on the north side; Rose Tavern, next Drury Lane Theatre. [*See* these names.] The candidates for being touched for the King's Evil, July 1660, were required first to repair "to Mr. Knight the King's Surgeon, living at the Cross Guns in Russell Street, Covent Garden, over against the Rose Tavern." *Eminent Inhabitants.*—Carr, Earl of Somerset, implicated in the murder of Sir Thomas Overbury; he was living here, on the north side, in 1644, the year before his death. Joseph Taylor, 1634-1641, one of the original performers in Shakespeare's plays. [*See* Piazza.] John Evelyn, the Diarist.

October 18, 1659.—I came with my wife and family to London : tooke lodgings at the 3 Feathers in Russell Street, Covent Garden, for all the winter, my son being very unwell.

There is a token of "John Hatten at the Three Feathers in Russell Streete," in the Beaufoy Collection, Guildhall.[3] Evelyn was at this time acting as a secret agent in London for Charles II. Major Mohun, the actor, on the south side; in 1665 he was assessed at 10s., the highest rate levied in the street. Thomas Betterton, the actor; he died here in 1710, and here, "at his late lodgings," his "books, prints, drawings, and paintings" were sold after his death.[4] Tom Davies, the bookseller, on the south side, "over against Tom's Coffee-house," later the Caledonian Coffee-house. Tom Davies had originally a shop in Duke's Court. He began at Russell Street in 1762, and became a bankrupt in 1778.

The very place where I was fortunate enough to be introduced to the illustrious subject of this work deserves to be particularly marked. It was No. 8. I never pass by without feeling reverence and regret.—*Boswell*, by Croker, p. 133, *note*.

This [1763] is to me a memorable year ; for in it I had the happiness to obtain the acquaintance of that extraordinary man whose memoirs I am now writing. . . . Mr. Thomas Davies, the actor, who then kept a bookseller's shop in Russell Street, Covent Garden, told me that Johnson was very much his friend, and came frequently to his house, where he more than once invited me to meet him ; but by some unlucky accident or other, he was prevented from coming to us. . . . At last, on Monday, the 16th of May, when I was sitting in Mr. Davies' back parlour, after having drunk tea with him and Mrs. Davies, Johnson unexpectedly came into the

---

[1] *Strype.*
[2] Johnson's *Life of Addison.*
[3] *Burn.* p. 90.
[4] Advert. in No. 213 of 1st ed. of *The Tatler.*

shop; and Mr. Davies having perceived him through the glass door in the room in which we were sitting, advancing towards us he announced his awful approach to me somewhat in the manner of an actor on the part of Horatio when he addresses Hamlet on the appearance of his father's ghost, "Look, my Lord, it comes!"... Mr. Davies mentioned my name, and respectfully introduced me to him. I was much agitated; and recollecting his prejudice against the Scotch, of which I had heard much, I said to Davies, "Don't tell where I come from." "From Scotland," cried Davies roguishly. "Mr. Johnson," said I, "I do indeed come from Scotland, but I cannot help it."... This speech was somewhat unlucky, for with that quickness of wit, for which he was so remarkable... he retorted, "That, Sir, I find is what a great many of your countrymen cannot help."—*Boswell*, by Croker, pp. 131-133.

Another bookseller in Russell Street is remembered by association with a great English writer. When Edward Gibbon, at sixteen years of age, by solitary study of the writings of Father Parsons, had made up his mind to embrace the Roman Catholic faith, he sought counsel of "Mr. Lewis, a Roman Catholic bookseller in Russell Street, Covent Garden," who recommended him to a priest of whose name and order the great historian was ignorant when he wrote his *Memoirs*. It has since been ascertained that he was a Jesuit named Baker, one of the chaplains to the Sardinian Ambassador. The conversion of a Gentleman Commoner of Magdalen made a great stir in 1753, and the Russell Street bookseller was called before the Privy Council. The offence committed by Gibbon and Baker amounted to high treason in the statute book of those days. Baker remained unnoticed; against Gibbon "the gates of Magdalen were for ever shut." Dr. Armstrong the poet died at his house in Russell Street, September 7, 1779. Charles Lamb (Elia) took lodgings in October 1817 at "Mr. Owen's, Nos. 20 and 21 Great Russell Street, Drury Lane." The house was the west corner of Bow Street, "delightfully situated," says Talfourd, "between the two theatres:" "the house belonged," writes Procter, "to an ironmonger (or brazier) and was comfortable and clean,—and a little noisy."[1] Lamb himself describes his lookout as follows: "Drury Lane Theatre in sight from our front and Covent Garden from our back-room windows."

November 21, 1817.—We are in the individual spot I like best in all this great city. The theatres with all their noises. Covent Garden dearer to me than any gardens of Alcinous, where we are morally sure of the earliest peas and 'sparagus. Bow Street where the thieves are examined within a few yards of us. Mary had not been here four and twenty hours before she saw a thief. She sits at the window working; and casually throwing out her eyes, she sees a concourse of people coming this way, with a constable to conduct the solemnity. These little incidents agreeably diversify a female life.—*Lamb to Miss Wordsworth* (*Letters*, p. 103).

He remained here till the middle of 1823.[2] No. 19 was the shop of Barker the bookseller, at which Lamb purchased the folio *Beaumont and Fletcher*, over which as Elia he gossiped so pleasantly in his essay on "Old China." There is much wit in Wycherley's play of *The Country Wife* about Mr. Horner's lodgings in this street: that kind of wit,

[1] *H. Crabb Robinson*, vol. ii. p. 79.   [2] *Procter*, p. 249.

however, which suffers from transplanting. Russell Street was the name given to both Great and Little Russell Street in 1859. Previously Great Russell Street extended from Covent Garden Market to Brydges Street (now Catherine Street), and Little Russell Street from Brydges Street to Drury Lane.

Rutland Gate, KENSINGTON ROAD, KNIGHTSBRIDGE, built 1838-1840, and so called from a large house on the site, belonging to the Dukes of Rutland. John, third Duke of Rutland, died here in 1779. The detached house, the last on the south-west side, was built by John Sheepshanks, Esq., the distinguished patron of British Art, who here assembled that noble collection of English pictures which he afterwards presented to the nation, and which now forms one of the great attractions of the galleries at South Kensington.

Rutland House, at the upper end of ALDERSGATE STREET, near what is now called Charter House Square. Here, in 1656, "at the back part of Rutland House," the drama revived under Sir William Davenant—Cromwell, who, Carlyle says, "was very fond of music," having by the interposition of Whitelocke consented to the performance of *Declamation and Musick after the Manner of the Ancients*. The scenes were by John Webb, kinsman and executor of Inigo Jones. The first of the entertainments was published on September 3, in honour no doubt of the Protector's birthday.[1] *Rutland Place*, Charterhouse Square, commemorates the site.

Rutland Place, UPPER THAMES STREET. [*See* Puddle Dock.]

Ryder Street, ST. JAMES'S, formerly GREAT and LITTLE RYDER STREET, from St. James's Street to Bury Street, was built in 1674, and was so named after a Captain Ryder, who, as early as 1660, had set up gates on the Parish Lammas.[2] One of Swift's Letters, written from Létcombe, near Wantage, in 1714, is addressed to "Mrs. Esther Vanhomrigh, at her lodgings over against the Surgeon's in Great Ryder Street, near St. James';" and on December 13, 1712, Swift himself was living "over against the house in Little Rider Street, where D. D. lodged." Ten years later (June 1, 1722), when attempting to soothe the feelings of the unhappy Vanessa, he asks her to "remember . . . *Rider Street*."

Sablonière Hotel, LEICESTER SQUARE, occupied the south corner of the east side. The northern half of it was previously the residence of William Hogarth. [*See* Leicester Square.] The old Sablonière must not be confounded with the present *Hôtel Sablonière*, which is at the *north* corner of the east side of the square. When Kosciusko was in England he wrote to Dr. Walcott (Peter Pindar) from "Sablonière's

---

[1] "The Siege of Rhodes, made a representation by the Art of Prospective in Scenes, and the Story sung in Recitative Musick, at the back part of Rutland House, in the upper end of Aldersgate Street, London.—London, printed by J. M. for Henry Herringman, 1656," 4to.

[2] Rate-books of St. Martin's.

Hotel," requesting a visit, as he was unable, "on account of weakness from his wounds," to call on him. He could not, he told Walcott, "visit England without seeing an author who had given him so much pleasure, particularly in his prison at St. Petersburgh."[1] After that Walcott "constantly visited him." The house was pulled down in 1870, and a new building on its site was erected for Archbishop Tenison's Schoolhouse.

Sackville Street, PICCADILLY, to VIGO STREET; said to be the longest street in London of any consequence without a turning out of it on either side, and the only one without a lamp-post. It was built about 1679.[2] Sir William Petty, the earliest English writer on Political Economy, lived, in the reigns of Charles II. and James II., in the corner house on the east side, opposite St. James's Church. Dr. Joseph Warton had lodgings here in 1792.[3] Arthur Young, the father of agricultural science, lived at No. 32 for a long series of years, and died there, April 12, 1820, at the age of eighty-one. He had been blind for the last ten years of his life. The house where he lived was occupied by the Board of Agriculture, of which he was secretary. Sir Everard Home was living at No. 30 in 1809. Boswell, writing in 1785, mentions that the Literary Club, when the Turk's Head in Gerard Street was converted into a private house, "moved first to Prince's in Sackville Street," then to Baxter's (Le Telier's) in Dover Street.

Sacred Harmonic Society, established in 1832, famous for performances in Exeter Hall of the sacred oratorios of Handel, Haydn, Mendelssohn, and other great composers. With a chorus 500 strong of carefully trained voices, and an admirable orchestra, the concerts of the Society, under the direction of Sir Michael Costa, were for many years among the greatest treats which the lover of good music enjoyed. There was an important musical library in connection with the Society, now in the possession of the Royal College of Music. In 1880 Exeter Hall was purchased for the Young Men's Christian Association, and the Sacred Harmonic Society had to decide between a removal to other quarters or dissolution. After some hesitation it was resolved to continue operations, and on December 3, 1880, they commenced their forty-ninth season by a performance at St. James's Hall; but the Society is now dissolved. The Handel Festivals at the Crystal Palace, where Handel's oratorios are performed by a band and choir of unparalleled magnitude, originated with and were conducted by the Sacred Harmonic Society. They are now carried on by the Crystal Palace Company.

Saddlers' Hall, 141 CHEAPSIDE (north side, between Foster Lane and Gutter Lane), the hall of the Saddlers' Company, the twenty-fifth on the list of the City Companies, and one of the most ancient and honourable, and of the minor Companies one of the most wealthy. Herbert thinks there can be "little doubt of the Saddlers being a veri-

---

[1] *Annual Biog. and Obit.*, 1820; Peter Pindar. [2] Rate-books of St. Martin's.
[3] Nichols's *Lit. Anec.*, vol. ix. p. 473.

table Anglo-Saxon gild; and, consequently, the oldest on record of all the present Livery Companies."[1] The first Charter of Incorporation was granted to the Company, 37 Edward III., December 1363. In the persecution of 1545 Anne Askew was examined at Saddlers' Hall.[2]

Frederick, Prince of Wales (father of George III.), was a saddler, and from a balcony erected in front of the hall was once a spectator, in disguise, of the Lord Mayor's show; and when his eldest son (afterwards George III.) was christened, the Saddlers had a grand illumination and a bonfire before their hall.[3]

The Prince was desirous of seeing the Lord Mayor's Show privately, for which purpose he entered the City in disguise. At that time it was the custom for several of the City companies, particularly those who had no barges, to have stands erected in the streets through which the Lord Mayor passed in his return from Westminster; in which the freemen of companies were accustomed to assemble. It happened that his Royal Highness was discovered by some of the Saddlers' Company; in consequence of which he was invited into their stand, which invitation he accepted, and the parties were so well pleased with each other that his Royal Highness was soon after chosen Master of the Company, a compliment which he also accepted.—Edwards's Anecdotes of Painting, 4to, 1808, p. 14.

In the great hall of the Company is a full-length portrait of the Prince, by T. Frye. Sir Richard Blackmore, the poet and physician, lived either within or in a house adjoining this hall. Among the *Miscellaneous Works* of Tom Brown are epigrams and verses "To Sir R—— Bl——, on the Two Wooden Horses before Saddlers' Hall," "To the Merry Poetasters at Saddlers' Hall in Cheapside," and "To a Famous Poet and Doctor, at Saddlers' Hall." In the earliest mentioned copy occurs this couplet:—

> 'Twas kindly done of the good-natur'd cits,
> To place before thy door a brace of tits.

Two horses, *argent*, it may be stated, are the supporters of the Company's arms. With a view to identify the particular dwelling of Sir Richard Blackmore, Sir Peter Laurie (himself a member) caused the books of the Company to be examined, but without success.

The present handsome hall was erected in 1822 from the designs of Jesse Gibson. The buildings in front were erected 1863-1864, and the street façade designed by F. W. Porter, the Company's architect. The Company possesses an enriched funeral pall of crimson velvet, date about 1500.[4] When funerals were conducted with more pomp and heraldic ceremony than they now are, it was customary, on the death of a master or eminent member of a Company, for his body to lie in state in the hall; and sometimes the City halls were let on great occasions for the purposes of lyings in state. The pall of the Saddlers' and the pall of the Fishmongers' Company (a still finer one) were used on such occasions. Besides various charitable gifts the Company have a fine range of almshouses, called after the founder

[1] Herbert, *History of the Twelve Great Livery Companies*, vol. i. p. 17.
[2] *Foxe*, vol. v. p. 538.
[3] *Daily Post*, June 22, 1738.
[4] Engraved by Shaw in his *Dresses and Decorations of the Middle Ages*.

Honnor's Home, for decayed freemen of the Company, their widows and daughters, at Spring Grove, Hounslow.

Sadler's Wells, between the NEW RIVER HEAD and ST. JOHN STREET ROAD, ISLINGTON, a well-known place of public amusement; first a music house, then a theatre, and so called from a spring of mineral water, discovered by a surveyor of the highways named Sadler, who, in 1683, opened in connection with it a public music-room, and called it by his own name as "Sadler's Wells Music House," but they were more generally known as "Islington Wells." A pamphlet was published in 1684 giving an account of the discovery, with the virtues of the water, which is there said to be of a ferruginous nature, and much resembling in quality and effects the water of Tunbridge Wells.

> People may talk of Epsom Wells
> Of Tunbridge Springs which most excells:
> I'll tell you by my ten years' practice
> Plainly what the matter of fact is:
> Those are but good for *one* disease,
> To *all* distempers *this* gives ease.
>
> *A Morning Ramble, or Islington Wells Burlesqt,* 1684.

Misson, writing in 1697, describes Islington as "a large village, half a league from London, where you drink waters that do you neither good nor harm, provided you don't take too much of them." The theatre was in an outlying neighbourhood, and the playbills as late as the middle of the last century commonly announce, whenever a great performance took place, that "a horse patrol will be sent in the New Road that night for the protection of the nobility and gentry who go from the squares and that end of the town," and "that the road also towards the city will be properly guarded." For a time the place was a fashionable resort.

August 7, 1732.—Poor Lady Sunderland goes constantly to Islington Wells, where she meets abundance of good company. These waters are rising in fame, and already pretend to vie with Tunbridge. If they are as good it will be very convenient to all Londoners to have a remedy so near at hand.—*Mrs. Delany,* vol. i. p. 367.

"For some years," says Dodsley, writing a few years later, it "was honoured by the constant attendance of the Princess Amelia and many persons of quality, who drank the waters." The Princess, it is said, was always received with a salute of twenty-one guns. The charge for drinking the waters was "3d. for each person," or half a guinea for the season.[1] This place for the water drinkers was at this time called "Islington Wells," and near it was the "house of entertainment called Sadler's Wells, where, during the summer season, people are amused with balance-masters, walking on the wire, rope dancing, tumbling, and pantomime entertainments."[2] In this "Long Room opposite to Sadler's Wells," July 1765, George Alexander Stevens delivered his Lecture on Heads. The popularity of the Wells was declining when,

---

[1] *Ambulator,* 1782, p. 118. [2] *Dodsley,* 1761, vol. iii. p. 262.

in 1770, it was made the subject of George Colman's farce, *The Spleen, or Islington Spa*. The theatre continued to be only a summer house till near the end of the century.

At this time also [Easter week] opens a theatre for tumbling, rope-dancing, etc., at Sadler's Wells, Islington, and contemnes all the summer. Admittance 3s. 6d., 2s. and 1s. Each person has allowed him for his money a pint of wine or punch.—Trusler's *London Adviser and Guide*, 12mo, 1790, p. 175.

"I was afterwards," says Winifred Jenkins, "of a party at Sadler's Wells, where I saw such tumbling and dancing upon ropes and wires that I was frightened and ready to go into a fit" (*Smollett*). It was on this occasion that Humphry Clinker rescued her from the gentleman who "offered for to treat me with a pint of wind."

Sadler's Wells, writes John Britton, who at the time lived close by and was a constant attendant at the theatre, "at the end of the last century and beginning of the present, was truly a suburban theatre, being surrounded by fields. . . . There were not any public lamps, and men and boys with flambeaus were in attendance on dark nights to light persons across the fields to the nearest streets of Islington, Clerkenwell, and Gray's Inn Lane." At this time was introduced the "real water" novelty, which for many years was the special attraction of Sadler's Wells.

> Now the New River's current swells
> The reservoir of Sadler's Wells,
> And in some melodrame of slaughter
> Floats all the stage with real water.
>
> Luttrell's *Julia*, Letter iii.

The New River flowed past the theatre and means were taken to introduce "a large body of water from it to a tank beneath the floor of the stage." This floor being taken up, a broad sheet of water was displayed to the audience, and rendered very effective in naval spectacles, pantomimes, and burlettas, which were written and adapted to exhibit aquatic scenes. Among the apparently perilous and appalling incidents thus exhibited, was that of a heroine falling from the rocks into the water, and rescued by her hero-lover; a naval battle, with sailors escaping by plunging into the sea from a vessel on fire; a child thrown into the water by a nurse, who was bribed to drown it, but rescued by a Newfoundland dog.—John Britton's *Autobiography*, vol. i. p. 103.

Sensational scenes were not unknown eighty or ninety years ago. A great painter has given his impression of the aquatic drama as it was presented here a few years later.

September 14, 1812.—I have been to Sadler's Wells to see the aquatic scene that is so much talked of. Excepting by Grimaldi (the clown), I was very little entertained. I take but little delight in pantomime changes, which, to do them justice, they manage here in the greatest perfection. The afterpiece was a melodrama, the dialogue of which was in blank verse, with now and then a foolish rhyme coming out in order to call it *recitative*. [Then necessary to evade the penalties for infringement of the patent rights of the two great theatres.] The water scene pleased me better than I expected; it represented a castle with a moat and drawbridge: the castle of course attacked by troops who came on in boats. Many of the combatants contrived to get themselves into the water by the breaking of the drawbridge, where they fought up to their chins. This theatre is quite small, and ornamented in the most showy manner, with a plentiful lack of taste.—*C. R. Leslie to his Sister* (*Autob.*, vol. ii. p. 22).

Here Belzoni, the Egyptian traveller, exhibited his prodigious feats of strength as "the Patagonian Samson" (1803). Grimaldi, the most famous of clowns, achieved here his greatest triumphs (1819-1828). In 1832 T. P. Cooke made his first appearance as William in *Black-Eyed Susan*. The theatre fell into disrepute, but was restored to credit and fame under the admirable management of Mr. Phelps, who made it during many years (1844-1862) "the home of the legitimate drama."

After being for some time closed the theatre was rebuilt in 1879 on a larger scale from the designs of Mr. C. J. Phipps, the architect of many of the theatres recently built in London and the provinces. *New Sadler's Wells Theatre* was for a short time under the management of Mrs. Bateman, when the performance of the Shakesperian drama was made the leading feature. For some years past the theatre has had a very fitful existence, and has only been opened at intervals. Of the earlier houses there are views in Wilkinson's *Londina Illustrata*. The scene of Hogarth's Evening is laid at Sadler's Wells, in front of the Sir Hugh Myddelton public-house, which still exists and has a large music hall attached.

Saffron Hill, a densely inhabited neighbourhood between HOLBORN and CLERKENWELL. It was formerly a part of Ely Gardens [*see* Ely House], and derives its name from the crops of saffron which it bore. It runs from Field Lane into Vine Street, so called from the vineyard attached to old Ely House. So bad was the reputation of the locality thirty or forty years ago that the clergymen of St. Andrew's, Holborn (the parish in which the purlieu lies), were obliged, when visiting it, to be accompanied by policemen in plain clothes. Dickens described Saffron Hill and its purlieus with his darkest colours, but not darker than those who knew the neighbourhood of old felt to be deserved.

Thence into Little Saffron Hill, and so into Saffron Hill the Great. . . . A dirtier or more wretched place he had never seen. The street was very narrow and muddy, and the air was inpregnated with filthy odours. . . . The sole places that seemed to prosper amid the general blight of the place were the public houses, and in them the lowest orders of Irish were wrangling with might and main. Covered ways and yards, which here and there diverged from the main street, disclosed little knots of houses where drunken men and women were positively wallowing in filth; and from several of the doorways great ill-looking fellows were cautiously emerging, bound, to all appearance, on no very well-disposed or harmless errands.—Charles Dickens, *Oliver Twist*, 1838, chap. viii.

The street is not very clean nor very fragrant even now, nor is the appearance of its occupants reassuring, but it is a very different place to what it was when Dickens wrote. Part of it has been cleared away for the Clerkenwell improvements, and the rest has been partially cleansed and purified and brought under stricter police supervision. The church, St. Peter's, was designed 1830-1832 by Mr. (afterwards Sir Charles) Barry, and was one of his earliest works in Gothic architecture.

The Duke of Muscovy declared war against Poland, because he and his nation had been vilified by a Polish poet: but the author of the *Ecclesiastical Politie* would, it seems, disturb the peace of Christendom for the good old cause of a superannuated chanter of Saffron Hill and Pye Corner.—Andrew Marvell, *Rehearsal Transprosed*, 1674, pt. ii. p. 65.

Salisbury Court, FLEET STREET, or, as it is now written, SALISBURY SQUARE, lies to the west of St. Bride's Church, and occupies the site of the courtyard of Salisbury, or, as it was afterwards called, *Dorset House*. There is now a Salisbury Court as well as a Salisbury Square. In *The Squire of Alsatia*, by Shadwell (who was an inhabitant of the court), "Salisbury Court" and "Dorset Court" are used indiscriminately one for the other. Salisbury House was the residence of the Bishops of Salisbury, and as Seth Ward, who held the see from 1667 to 1689, told Aubrey, was got from them by the Lord Treasurer Buckhurst (d. 1608), "in exchange for a piece of land near Cricklade in Wilts, I think called Marston, but the title was not good, nor did the value answer his promise."

March 25, 1611.—Confirmation to Richard Earl of Dorset of a grant of the manor of Salisbury Court, together with Salisbury House, *alias* Sackville Place, *alias* Dorset House, and divers messuages in St. Bride's and St. Dunstan's on his compounding for defective titles.—*Cal. State Pap.*, 1611-1618.

In 1634 Bulstrode Whitelocke, when urged by his wife to have a town residence as well as one in the country, took a house in Salisbury Court. Whitelocke was absent in France when his wife died, and Edward Hyde (afterwards Lord Clarendon), writing to him about his affairs, says of his child, "My little friend at Salisbury Court is lusty, and shall give you comfort." He gave up the house on his return. In 1655 the ambassador sent from Sweden to the Protector was lodged in Salisbury Court. Here Whitelocke frequently dined with him, the ambassador complaining of feeling solitary. The large building on the south side, the Salisbury Hotel and Farmers' Club, was erected by the Agricultural Hotel Company, 1863-1864, at a cost of over £23,000, from the designs of John Giles, architect. It has about 100 rooms.

Eminent Inhabitants.—Betterton, Harris, Cave, Underhill, and Sandford the actors, next the *Duke's Theatre* in Dorset Gardens; Shadwell, the poet; Lady Davenant, the widow of Sir William Davenant; John Dryden;[1] Samuel Richardson, the novelist. "He took a range of old houses, eight in number, which he pulled down, and built an extensive and commodious range of warehouses and printing offices."[2] His dwelling-house was No. 11, in the north-west corner of the square, and his printing office and warehouse in Blue-ball Court, on the east side of the square.

My first recollection of Richardson was in the house in the centre of Salisbury Square, or Salisbury Court, as it was then called; and of being admitted as a playful child into his study, where I have often seen Dr. Young and others. . . . I

---

[1] Rate-books of St. Martin's. [2] Nichols's *Lit. Anec.*, vol. iv. p. 594.

recollect that he used to drop in at my father's, for we lived nearly opposite, late in the evening to supper; when, as he would say, he had worked as long as his eyes and nerves would let him, and was come to relax with a little friendly and domestic chat.—*Mrs. —— to Mrs. Barbauld* (Richardson's *Correspondence*, vol. i. p. 183).

It is said to have been a common practice with Richardson to hide half a crown among the types, that it might reward the diligence of the workman who should be first in the office in the morning; on the other hand, he was so sensible of his own warmth of temper that all his admonitions to his workmen were given in writing![1] Here Richardson wrote his *Pamela*. Here, for a short time—1757, in the interval between his practice as a "physician in a humble way" on the Bankside and his becoming an usher at Peckham—Goldsmith sat as press-corrector to Richardson. And here was printed Maitland's *London*, folio, 1739, the imprint on the title page being "London: Printed by Samuel Richardson, in Salisbury Court, near Fleet Street, 1739." Mrs. Delany notes, October 30, 1754, that "Richardson is very busy, removing this very day to Parson's Green. Dr. Delany called yesterday at Salisbury Court."[2] Here, in August 1732, died Mrs. Daffy, preparer of the elixir known by her name.[3]

In 1716 there were many riots in the City, mobs gathering together in processions, with the cry of "High Church and Ormond," breaking windows which were not illuminated when the cry was raised, and "demolishing houses, especially those houses then called *Mug-houses*, where those who were for King George used to hold societies."[4] One of the most noted of the Mug-houses was in Salisbury Court, and a Jacobite mob, led by one Bean, pulled down the sign-post, and then breaking into the house, tore down the bar and benches, plundered the cellar and wrecked the premises. In attempting to defend his house Robert Read, the landlord, shot one of the assailants, a weaver named Vaughan, dead. Read was tried for manslaughter and acquitted; but five of the rioters were tried at the Old Bailey, September 7, 1716, for "demolishing" Read's house, found guilty, and all five hanged in Fleet Street, at the end of Salisbury Court.[5]

Salisbury Court Theatre, SALISBURY COURT, FLEET STREET, was built in 1629, by Richard Gunnell and William Blagrove, players, and was originally the "barn" or granary at the lower end of the great back yard or court of Salisbury House.

In the yere one thousand sixe hundred [and] twenty-nine, there was builded a new faire Play-house, near the White-Fryers. And this is the seauenteenth stage or common Play-house which hath beene new made within the space of threescore yeres within London and the suburbs.—*Howes*, ed. 1631, p. 1004.

The Play-house in Salisbury Court, in Fleete Streete, was pulled down by a company of souldiers, set on by the Sectaries of these sad times, on Saturday, the 24th day of March, 1649.—*MS. Notes from Howes*, quoted in Collier's *Life of Shakespeare*, p. ccxlii.

[1] Nichols's *Lit. Anec.*, vol. iv. p. 597.
[2] *Delany Corr.*, vol. iii. p. 296.
[3] Historical Register for 1732; *The Tatler*, by Nichols, vol. vi. p. 41.
[4] Burton's *New View*, 1730.
[5] *Ibid.*

It was bought by William Beeston, a player, in 1652, and rebuilt and reopened by him in 1660. The Duke's company, under Davenant, played here till their new theatre in *Lincoln's Inn Fields* was ready to receive them. Salisbury Court Theatre was finally destroyed in the Great Fire, and not rebuilt. The *Duke's Theatre* in Dorset Gardens, opened November 9, 1671, stood facing the Thames, on a somewhat different site.

Salisbury House, in the STRAND, stood on the sites of Cecil Street and Salisbury Street, between Worcester House and Durham House, and was so called after Sir Robert Cecil, Earl of Salisbury, Lord High Treasurer to James I., by whom it was built, when only Sir Robert Cecil. Queen Elizabeth was present at the house-warming on December 6, 1602.[1]

December 7, 1602.—On Munday last the Queen dyned at Sir Robert Secil's newe house in the Strand. Shee was verry royally entertained, richely presented, and marvelous well contented; but at hir departure shee strayned her foot. His hall was well furnished with choise weapons, which her Majestie took speciall notice of. Sundry deuises; at hir entraunce, three women, a maid, a widdowe, and a wife, eache commending their owne states, but the virgin preferred;[2] an other, one attired in habit of a Turke desyrous to see hir Majestie, but as a straunger without hope of such grace, in regard of the retired manner of hir lord, complained; answere made, howe gracious hir Majestie in admitting to presence, and howe able to discourse in anie language; which the Turke admired, and, admitted, presents hir with a riche mantle, etc.—Manningham's *Diary*, p. 99.

The house was, however, far from finished at this time. Salisbury was busy building in 1608. On August 10, 1608, we find Thomas Wilson writing to Cecil on the "difference of cost between Canterbury stone [Kentish rag] and Caen stone for the works at Salisbury House,"[3] and there are several subsequent letters on the subject; one (September 9) from Leonard Lawrence to Wilson informing him that he has taken down the inner part of the gate at Canterbury, which will yield 60 or 70 loads of stone fit for London, but he refrains from meddling with the outer part till he has further instructions, because "the townspeople keeps so much ado."[4] He probably received instructions, as a few days later (September 25) he reports the demolition of the building at Canterbury and the shipment of the stones for London "for the Earl of Salisbury's use." There seems to have been as much difficulty in procuring workmen as materials, and as summary modes of procedure in order to obtain them. Sir W. Bowyer writes to the Earl from Newcastle (August 28) that he "could not obtain workmen to get stones at Berwick till Dunbar ordered three or four to be spared from the works on the bridge and castle."[5] In September 1610 are entered the specifications of a plan by a Mr. Osborne for making a portico at the south end of the Earl of Salisbury's garden in the

---

[1] Nichols's *Progresses of Queen Elizabeth*, vol. iii. p. 601; Collier's *Annals*, vol. i. p. 323.
[2] This was "a pretty Dialogue of John Davies, Twixt a Maid, a Widow, and a Wife," written for the occasion but not printed in his Works.
[3] *Cal. State Pap.*, 1603-1610, p. 451.
[4] *Ibid.*, vol. i. p. 456.
[5] *Ibid.*, p. 453.

Strand.[1] Subsequently the house was divided into "Great Salisbury House" and "Little Salisbury House," and finally pulled down in 1695.

This house afterwards became two, the one being called Great Salisbury House, as being the residence of the Earl, and the other Little Salisbury House, which was used to be let out to persons of quality; being also a large house; and this was above 28 years ago contracted for [*i.e.* 1692] of the then Earl of Salisbury for a certain term of years to build on, and accordingly it was pulled down and made into a street, called Salisbury Street, which being too narrow, and withal the descent to the Thames too uneasy, it was not so well inhabited as was expected. Another part, viz. that next to Great Salisbury House and over the long Gallery, was converted into an Exchange, and called the Middle Exchange, which consisted of a very long and large room (with shops on both sides) which from the Strand run as far as the water-side, where was a handsome pair of stairs to go down to the water-side, to take boat at, but it had the ill-luck to have the nick-name given it of the "Whore's Nest;" whereby, with the ill-fate that attended it, few or no people took shops there, and those that did were soon weary and left them. Insomuch that it lay useless except three or four shops towards the Strand; and coming into the Earl's hands, this Exchange, with Great Salisbury House, and the houses fronting the street are pulled down, and now converted into a fair street called "Cecil Street," running down to the Thames, having very good houses fit for persons of repute, and will be better ordered than Salisbury Street was.—*Strype*, B. iv. p. 120.

In "Little Salisbury House" lived William Cavendish, third Earl of Devonshire, father of the first Duke of Devonshire, who played so important a part in the Revolution of 1688, and in his house Thomas Hobbes, the philosopher, had his chamber and home.

It happened about two or three days after his Majesty's [Charles II.'s] happy returne, that as he was passing in his coach through the Strand, Mr. Hobbes was standing at Little Salisbury House Gate (where his Lord [the E. of Devonshire] then lived); the King espied him, putt off his hat very kindly to him, and asked him how he did.—Aubrey's *Life of Hobbes*.

John Pell, the mathematician, records his meeting with Hobbes in the Strand, who "led me back to Salisbury House, where he brought me into his chamber and there showed me his construction of that Probleme, which he said he had solved, namely the Doubling of a Cube."[2] There is a good river-front view of the house in Wilkinson's *Londina Illustrata*, from a drawing by Hollar, in the Pepysian Library at Cambridge.

Salisbury Square, FLEET STREET. [*See* Salisbury Court.]

Salisbury Street, STRAND, built circ. 1678, and so called from Salisbury House, the residence of Robert Cecil, first Earl of Salisbury of the Cecil family. [*See* Salisbury House.] The present street was rebuilt, James Paine, architect, 1783. Partridge the almanac maker lived in this street.

I have some thoughts of sending for him from the banks of Styx, and reinstating him in his own house, at the sign of the Globe in Salisbury Street.—*Tatler*, No. 118, January 10, 1709.

---

[1] *Cal. State Pap.*, 1603-1610, p. 637.   [2] Pell, MS. Birch, Brit. Mus.

The Salisbury estate, consisting of Salisbury and Cecil Streets, was sold by the present Marquis of Salisbury for £200,000, and preparations were made at the end of 1888 for the utilisation of the ground to the best advantage. A large hotel is being built at the end of the present street, which abuts upon the Embankment Gardens. It is proposed to build a club, theatre and chambers, with a courtyard in the centre. The entrance will be at Cecil Gate, where Cecil Street now is, and the exit at Salisbury Gate, where Salisbury Street now is.

Salmon's (Mrs.) Wax-Work, FLEET STREET, a famous wax-work exhibition on the south side of Fleet Street, between the Temple Gates. Mrs. Salmon was the Madame Tussaud of the last half of the 18th century.

> Tall Polygars
> Dwarf Zanzibars
> Mahomed's Tomb, Killarney's Lake, the Fane of Ammon,
> With all thy Kings and Queens, ingenious Mrs. Salmon!
> *Probationary Odes for the Laureateship,* 1785.

Salopian (The), CHARING CROSS, a coffee-house and tavern described in 1804 by Sir Richard Phillips as "frequented by gentlemen of the army, etc.—good dinners, wines and lodgings." When Thomas Campbell, the poet, first came to London, Thomas Telford the engineer invited him to live with him at The Salopian, but the poet said that the noise of Charing Cross was enough to drive any man crazy, and he soon left it for South Molton Street.

Saltero's (Don). [*See* Don Saltero's.]

Salters' Hall, ST. SWITHIN'S LANE, west side, the Hall of the Master, Wardens, and Commonalty of the Art or Mistery of Salters, the ninth on the list of the Twelve Great Companies of the City of London. The Salters received a grant of livery from Richard II. in 1394, and letters patent from succeeding monarchs, but the Charter of Incorporation only dates from the first of Elizabeth, 1558. The first hall of the Company was in Bread Street, but they had removed to the present site some time before the Great Fire, which destroyed the hall and its contents, including the Company's books. The present hall, 1823, was designed by Henry Carr, architect, and opened May 23, 1827. It is semi-classical in style with a portico of the Ionic order, spacious and stately. The hall itself is 72 feet by 40 feet. Oxford Court, in which it is situated, was so called from John De Vere, the sixteenth Earl of Oxford of that name, who died in 1562, and was originally the site of the inn or hostel for the Priors of Tortington, in Sussex. Empson and Dudley, notorious as the unscrupulous instruments of Henry VII.'s avarice in the later and more unpopular years of his reign, lived in Walbrook, in "two fair houses," with doors leading into the garden of the Prior of Tortington (now Salters' Garden). "Here they met," says Stow, "and consulted of matters at their pleasures."[1] Part of Salters' Hall was let in the reign of William III. to a Protestant congregation of the Presbyterian persuasion. Tom Brown alludes to the sermons here in a well-known passage:—

> A man that keeps steady to one party, though he happens to be in the wrong, is still an honest man. He that goes to a Cathedral in the morning, and Salters' Hall in the afternoon, is a rascal by his own confession.—Tom Brown's *Laconics* (*Works*, 8vo, 1709, vol. iv. p. 23).

> I Thumb'd o'er many factious Reams
> Of canting Lies, and Poets Dreams,
> All stuff'd as full of Low-Church Manners,
> As e'er was *Salters' Hall* with Sinners.
> *Hudibras Redivivus*, 4to, 1707.

Salters' Hall Chapel, adjoining the hall, continued to be one of the chief dissenting chapels in the City down to our own day. It was removed to make room for the present Salters' Hall. Lilly, the astrologer, was a freeman of this Company. *Observe.*—Full-length portrait of Adrian Charpentier, painter of the clever and only good portrait of Roubiliac, the sculptor; equestrian portrait of the Duke of Wellington; and Alderman Gibbons in his Mayoral robes, by H. T. Wells, R.A.

Salutation Tavern, No. 17 NEWGATE STREET (south side), in the reign of Anne was much resorted to for social gatherings. Somewhat later the leading booksellers and printers met here. Bowyer prints a rhyming invitation to a booksellers' supper, January 19, 1736, sent by the stewards Cave and Bowyer:—

SATURDAY, *January* 17, 1735.

SIR—

> You're desired on Monday next to meet
> At Salutation Tavern Newgate Street,
> Supper will be on table just at eight,
> One of St. John's,[2] and 'other of St. John's Gate.[3]

Along with the invitation Bowyer prints a poetical answer by Richardson the novelist, beginning:—

> For me I'm much concerned I cannot meet
> At Salutation Tavern, Newgate Street.[4]

A "late landlord preserved a tradition of the house to the effect that Sir Christopher Wren used to smoke his pipe there whilst St. Paul's was in course of rebuilding."[5]

Here, in a little smoky room, Coleridge and Lamb used to meet to enjoy Welsh-rabbits and egg-hot, and discuss poetry and philosophy, both moral and political, over pipes and orinoco.[6] And here it was that Southey discovered Coleridge in one of his gloomiest fits of melancholy, and endeavoured to rouse him to active exertion.

Some of the Sonnets which shall be carelessly turned over by the general reader,

---

[1] *Stow*, p. 84.
[2] Bowyer.
[3] Cave.
[4] Bowyer, *Anecdotes*, p. 160.
[5] A. Andrews in *Notes and Queries*, 2d S., vol. vi. p. 137.
[6] Talfourd, *Life and Letters of Charles Lamb*, pt. i. *passim*.

may happily awaken in you remembrances which I should be sorry should be ever totally extinct—the memory

> Of summer days and of delightful years, even so far back as those old suppers at our old *Salutation Inn*,—when life was fresh and topics exhaustless—and you first kindled in me, if not the power, yet the love of poetry and beauty and kindliness—
> What words have I heard
> Spoke at the Mermaid.
>
> Charles Lamb's *Dedication of his Works to Coleridge*.

Salvador House, BISHOPSGATE STREET. Here, in the office of Mr. James Edmeston, architect (d. 1867), Gilbert Scott, when a youth of sixteen, was placed, April 1827, to learn the profession of architect, and remained there till April 1831.[1]

Sambrook Court, 24 BASINGHALL STREET, so called after Sir Jeremy Sambrook, whose house was here.[2] Here practised and died, November 1, 1815, John Coakley Lettsom, M.D.[3]

Sam's Coffee-house, in EXCHANGE ALLEY; ditto in LUDGATE STREET. See, in the *State Poems* (8vo, 1697, p. 258), "A Satyr upon the French King; writ after the Peace was concluded at Reswick, anno 1697, by a Non-Swearing Parson, and said to be drop'd out of his Pocket at Sam's Coffee House." See also *State Poems*, 8vo, 1703, p. 182. Sam's was one of the City houses chosen for receiving subscriptions for the wild projects put forward during the rage for speculation resulting from the publication of the South Sea Scheme: a sample or two will show their character.

January 8, 1720.—This day at Sam's Coffee House, behind the Royal Exchange, at 3 in the afternoon, a book will be opened for entering into a joint co-partnership *on a thing* that will turn to the advantage of the concerned.

Same day.—£2,000,000 for purchasing and improving Fens in Lincolnshire—Sam's.—*Weekly Papers*, 1719-1720.

> While you at Sam's like a grave doctor sate
> Teaching the minor clergy how to prate.—*The Observatory*.

There are now two large Mulberry Trees growing in a little yard about sixteen foot square at Sam's Coffee House in Ludgate Street.—*The City Gardener*, by Thomas Fairchild, 8vo, 1722, p. 53.

Sanctuary, WESTMINSTER, a privileged precinct, under the protection of the abbot and monks of Westminster, and adjoining Westminster Abbey on the west and north side. The privileges survived the Reformation, and the bulk of the houses which composed the precinct were not taken down till 1750.[4] In this Sanctuary Edward V. was "born in sorrow, and baptized like a poor man's child;" and here Skelton, the rude-railing satirist, found shelter from the revengeful hand of Cardinal Wolsey.

Sir Thomas More's account of the taking of sanctuary by the widow of Edward IV. is very picturesque.

[1] *Personal and Professional Recollections of Sir Gilbert Scott*, pp. 55, 68.
[2] North's *Lives*, vol. iii. p. 101.
[3] Pettigrew's *Life of J. C. Lettsom*, 1817.
[4] See the oath on admission in Lansdowne MS., No. 24, Art. 84.

Therefore nowe she [Queen Elizabeth Woodville] toke her younger sonne the Duke of Yorke and her doughters and went out of the Palays of Westminster into the Sanctuary, and there lodged in the Abbote's Place, and she and all her chyldren and compaignie were registred for sanctuary persons. . . . Whereupon the Bishop [Rotheram, Archbishop of York and Lord Chancellor] called up all his servantes and toke with hym the great seale and came before day to the Quene, about whom he found much heavynesse, rumble, haste, businesse, conveighaunce, and carriage of hir stuffe into sanctuarye; every man was busye to cary, beare and conveigh stuffe, chestes, and fardelles, no man was unoccupied, and some caried more than they were commaunded to another place. The Queen sat alone belowe on the rushes all desolate and dismayde.—Sir Thomas More's *Pitifull Life of King Edward V.*, p. 49; Hall's *Union of the Two Noble and Illustre Famelies of Lancastre and Yorke*, reprint, p. 350.

What is styled the Broad Sanctuary contains St. Margaret's Church, the Guild Hall and Sessions House, and the Westminster Hospital. In the Broad Sanctuary Edmund Burke resided for many years. He begins to date from it November 7, 1772. Sir John Hawkins died, May 21, 1789, at his house by the Broad Sanctuary, formerly the residence of Admiral Vernon. Here are the Westminster Guild Hall, erected in 1805 from the designs of Mr. S. P. Cockerell; Westminster Hospital, erected in 1832 from the designs of Mr. W. Inwood. The portion styled the Sanctuary extends from the open space in front of Westminster Hospital to Great Smith Street. Here are the Central Office of the National Society; and at the south end, facing Dean's Yard, the Memorial to Old Westminsters who died in the Crimean War, designed by Sir Gilbert Scott.

Sands End, CHELSEA. Probably named from the sandy nature of the soil here, although it has been suggested that the name is derived from the Sandys family.

> All the grass that Rumney yields,
> Or the sands in Chelsey fields,
> Or the shops in silver Thames.
> Ben Jonson's Song to Celia (*The Forest*, vi.)

At a house near the creek which divided Chelsea from Fulham Addison occasionally dwelt. In a letter to the youthful Lord Warwick dated May 20, 1708, he wrote in reference to a passage in Cicero's Treatise on Friendship, "If your Lordship understand the sweetness of these words, you may assure yourself you are no ordinary Latinist; but if they have force enough to bring you to *Sandy End* I shall be very much pleased."

Sans Souci Theatre, LEICESTER PLACE, LEICESTER SQUARE, a theatre of some distinction in the early part of the present century, built by Thomas Dibdin, the song writer, and opened February 16, 1793. It was first erected behind Dibdin's music shop, in the Strand (opposite Beaufort Buildings), and afterwards removed to Leicester Place. It is now the "Hotel de Paris et de l'Europe." The first theatre was planned, painted, and decorated by Dibdin himself. Edmund Kean, when little more than a child, distinguished himself here by readings and recitations.

Saracen's Head, a celebrated tavern and coaching establishment, which stood on the north side of Snow Hill, "without Newgate." It was removed in constructing the Holborn Viaduct. On the new Snow Hill, but some distance from the old inn, another "Saracen's Head Hotel" has been erected, but it is quite unlike its predecessor in appearance and character.

Next to this church [St. Sepulchre's] is a fair and large inn for receipt of travellers, and hath to sign the Saracen's head.—*Stow*, p. 143.

In the preparations for the reception of the Emperor Charles V. in 1522, is the entry, "The signe of the Sersyns hed: xxx beddes, a stable for xl horses." This shows the importance of the inn at that time. Two other inns have the same stable room, but none make up so many beds.

Methinks, quoth he, it fits like the Saracen's Head without Newgate.—Tarlton's *Jests*, 4to, 1611.

Do not undervalue an enemy by whom you have been worsted. When our countrymen came home from fighting with the Saracens, and were beaten by them, they pictured them with huge, big, terrible faces (as you still see the sign of the Saracen's Head is), when in truth they were like other men. But this they did to save their own credits.—Selden's *Table Talk*.

At the Saracen's Head, Tom pour'd in ale and wine,
Until his face did represent the sign.
Osborn's *Works*, 8vo, 1701, p. 538.

The sign, as long as it remained, was surly and Saracenic enough to remind one of a passage in Fennor's Counter's *Commonwealth*, where a serjeant of the compter is described with "a phisnomy much resembling the Saracen's head without Newgate, and a mouth as wide vaulted as that without Bishopsgate."[1] Dickens has described the aspect of the Inn in its latter days.

Near to the jail, and by consequence near to Smithfield . . . and on that particular part of Snow Hill, where omnibus horses going eastward seriously think of falling down on purpose, and where horses in hackney cabriolets going westward not unfrequently fall by accident, is the coachyard of the Saracen's Head Inn; its portal guarded by two Saracen's heads and shoulders . . . frowning upon you from each side of the gateway. The Inn itself garnished with another Saracen's head, frowns upon you from the top of the yard. . . . When you walk up this yard you will see the booking-office on your left, and the tower of St. Sepulchre's Church darting abruptly up into the sky on your right, and a gallery of bedrooms upon both sides. Just before you you will observe a long window with the words "Coffee Room" legibly painted above it.—Dickens, *Nicholas Nickleby*, 1839, chap. iv.

Another well known inn of this name was outside Aldgate.

Nearer Aldgate is the Saracen's Head Inn, which is very large and of a considerable trade.—*Strype*, B. ii. p. 82.

Sardinia Street, LINCOLN'S INN FIELDS. Duke Street was renamed Sardinia Street in 1878, and the new name was given to it from the chapel formerly belonging to the Sardinian minister situated in the street [*see* Duke Street].

[1] Fennor's Counter's *Commonwealth*, 4to, 1617, p. 3.

Savile House, on the north side of LEICESTER SQUARE, immediately adjoining Leicester House, and so called after the Savile family, was the residence of Sir George Savile, the friend of Burke. Frederick, Prince of Wales, when living in Leicester House hired Savile House for his children. Savile's Bill for the Relief of the Roman Catholics was one of the stimulants to the Gordon Riots of June 1780, and his house was one of the first attacked by the mob, "carried by storm and given up to pillage," but the building was saved. The railings torn from it were the chief weapons and instruments of the rioters.[1] Burke, though his own house was threatened, went to the assistance of his friend.

> For four nights I kept watch at Lord Rockingham's or Sir George Savile's whose houses were garrisoned by a strong body of soldiers, together with numbers of true friends of the first rank who were willing to share the danger. Savile House, Rockingham House, Devonshire House, to be turned into garrisons!—*Burke to Shackleton (Corresp.* vol. ii. p. 355).

When Leicester Square ceased to be a fashionable place of residence, Savile House, rebuilt from the design of Mr. S. Page, was let for exhibitions and entertainments. Here for a long series of years was held Miss Linwood's exhibition of pictures in needlework. In its last years panoramas and *poses plastiques* were the leading attractions. The house was burnt down to the basement, February 28, 1865, and the site, after remaining empty for many years, was utilised about 1880 for a panorama, and subsequently reformed into the Empire Theatre.

Savile Row, BURLINGTON GARDENS to BOYLE STREET, was so called after the heiress of the Saviles, Dorothy, only daughter and heir of the celebrated George Savile, Marquis of Halifax, and wife of Richard Boyle, Earl of Burlington, the amateur architect.

> A new Pile of buildings is going to be carry'd on near Swallow Street by a Plan drawn by the Right Hon. the Earl of Burlington, and which is to be called Savile Street.—*The Daily Post,* March 12, 1733.

Eminent Inhabitants.—Henrietta Hobart, Countess of Suffolk, and mistress of George II.

> The Right Honorable the Countess of Suffolk has purchased a large house of Mr. Gray the builder, in Savile Street, Burlington Gardens for £3000.—*Daily Courant,* February 21, 1735.

Walpole, describing a fire in Vigo Street, April 28, 1761, says: "I went to my Lady Suffolk in Savile Row, and passed the whole night till 3 in the morning, between her little hot bedchamber and the spot, up to my ankles in water without taking cold."[2] Bryan Fairfax, "at the south end, in an excellent well-built brick house, held by lease under the Earl of Burlington," as appears from an advertisement of the sale of his pictures inserted in the *Public Advertiser* of April 5, 1756. Walpole speaks of it in 1761 as "that pretty house of Fairfax's, now General Waldegrave's." It must have been close to the south-east

---

[1] Walpole to Rev. W. Cole, June 15, 1780. [2] vol. iii. p. 398.

corner. In 1781 William Pitt, with his brother Lord Chatham. Writing to Wilberforce for Anderson's *Dictionary of Commerce*, he says, "If you can find it and spare it, and will trust me with it, pray send it to Savile Street."[1] Joseph Hill, the attached friend and correspondent of William Cowper, lived at No. 11. In 1797 Henry Crabb Robinson went to him as a clerk at a guinea a week. "He had no general law practice, but was steward to several noblemen."[2] Richard Brinsley Sheridan died in the front bedroom of No. 17, and was buried in Westminster Abbey. In a short note to Mr. Rogers, dated Savile Row, May 15, 1816, six weeks before his death, he says: "They are going to put the carpets out of window and break into Mrs. S.'s room and take me; for God's sake let me see you." A present of £150 from Mr. Rogers arrived in time. He had previously lived in No. 14. The Right Hon. George Tierney, a leading member of Parliament in his day, but now chiefly remembered by his duel with Mr. Pitt, fought on Putney Heath at 3 P.M. on Sunday, May 27, 1798. Mr. Tierney died at his house, No. 11 in this Row, January 25, 1830. At No. 20 lived Robert (Bobus) Smith, the brother of the Rev. Sydney Smith. No. 16 was the residence of Sir Benjamin Brodie. No. 12 was for many years the town residence of George Grote, the historian of Greece, and here he died, June 19, 1871.

Saviour's (St.) Church, for the DEAF and DUMB, 272 Oxford Street. (the corner of Queen Street), was erected in 1871 from the designs of Mr. (now Sir) A. W. Blomfield, R.A. The church, which is of red brick, Early English in style, a Maltese cross in plan and octagonal above, will accommodate a congregation of 250. The sermon is preached directly by signs, or orally, and interpreted by the sign language. Connected with the church are lecture and reading rooms, where not only lectures are delivered and evening classes taught, but a debating Society is carried on by the "deaf-mutes." The whole is a part of the organisation of the Royal Association in Aid of the Deaf and Dumb, an institution which is doing excellent work among this class of persons.

Saviour's (St.) SOUTHWARK, the church of the Augustinian Priory of St. Mary Overy, and first erected into a parish church by Act of Parliament, 32 Henry VIII. (1540-1541), when the two parishes of St. Margaret and St. Mary Magdalen in Southwark were united, and the church of the Priory of St. Mary Overy made the parish church, and called by the name of St. Saviour's. The priory church of St. Mary Overy was built by Bishop Giffard of Winchester and others about 1106, when the Augustinian Priory was established (or reorganised) by the two Norman knights, William Pont de l'Arche and William Dawncey. One hundred years after much of the borough including the church and part of London Bridge was burnt. It was rebuilt in 1208.

1208 [10th of King John]. And Seynt Marie Overeye was that yere begonne.—*Chronicle of London* (*Nicolas*, p. 7).

---

[1] *Rose*, vol. i. p. 31.   [2] *H. C. Robinson*, vol. i. p. 38.

The church had not been entirely destroyed by the fire, for a beautiful doorway and other traces of Giffard's work were discovered shortly before the demolition of the nave in 1838, and bits of earlier work which have been found at various times, indicate the existence of a church of the Saxon period. In 1238 Peter de Rupibus, then Bishop of Winchester, built the chapel afterwards set apart and used as the parish church. To stimulate the speedier completion of the building the Archbishop of York granted in 1273 an indulgence of eighty days to all who might contribute to the fabric. At the beginning of the 15th century Cardinal Beaufort, son of John of Gaunt, and Bishop of Winchester, spent large sums upon the church in repairs and alterations. His arms and Cardinal's hat are still to be seen carved on a pillar in the south transept. On February 2, 1424-1425, the marriage of James I. of Scotland and Johanna Beaufort was celebrated in this church with the customary pomp. The marriage feast was kept in the Bishop of Winchester's palace close to the church. In 1469 the stone roof of the nave fell and was replaced by the wooden roof, which lasted till the present century. Some of the bosses, curiously carved and with remains of the original colouring still upon them, are preserved in the Lady Chapel. The date of the roof is fixed by the rebus of Henry de Burton, who was Prior of St. Mary Overie in 1469.[1] The original form was Overies, and the derivation of the word is given by Somner and quoted by Bosworth. A.S. ofer (*genitive*, ofres ; *dative*, ofre) means a bank or shore, therefore the meaning of the name is St. Mary of the Bank, or on the Bankside. Overies is probably the genitive ofres, and the *s* was dropped under the erroneous supposition of its being a plural, like Chinee from Chinese.

In October 1539 the priory was suppressed, the canons were put out and their place taken by secular priests, and the property passed to Sir Anthony Brown, whose son became Viscount Montague. In 1540 the priory was made a parish church—the little church of "Marie Mawdley" (really a chapel attached to the chapel on the south side of the choir) that of St. Margaret's (in the middle of the High Street) being united with it. Some elaborate dealings protracted to the time of James I. took place between the parish and the court, in which the parish was very unfairly treated. The rectory and church buildings now became the property of the parishioners, and have remained so ever since. Alterations have been made by Acts of Parliament in 1868 and 1883, and the right of popular election of the chaplain has ceased.

The three days' "Examinacions of the Constante Martir of God, M. John Bradfourde, before the Lorde Chancellour, B. of Winchester, the B. of London, and other Commissioners," were held in this church in January 1555. Bradford was one of the most illustrious of the Marian martyrs, and no efforts were spared to convert him. After each day's examination he was taken to the "revestry" of this church

[1] *Quarterly Review*, vol. clxx. p. 397.

and assailed by fresh hands zealous to "confer" with him. Among
these was a gentleman who came "for old acquaintance sake," says
Bradford, "for I was at Muttrel tourney [the battle of Montreuil] a
paymaster, in which he was, and had often received money at my
hands." Other martyrs in the Marian persecution, such as Bishop
Hooper, John Rogers, Bishop Ferrars, Dr. Croom and Mr. Saunders
were tried in St. Saviour's Church.

After Westminster Abbey St. Saviour's contained some of the finest
specimens of Early English architecture in London. Little, however, of
the original work remains. A remarkable and conscientious restoration
of the choir and tower was made, 1822-1825, by George Gwilt, architect.

Of the many worthy names which the parish register of St. Saviour's preserves,
none deserves honour better than his. For thirty years he fought a difficult battle
against ignorance and parsimony, and it is not too much to say that although all was
not saved, we owe it to Mr. Gwilt and those who worked with him that all was not
destroyed.—*Quarterly Review*, vol. clxx. p. 407.

The nave was taken down in 1838, and in the following year it was
replaced by a very unsightly building, at a cost of £8000, erected from
the designs of Henry Rose, the floor being at a higher level than the
choir and transepts, from which it is shut off by a partition. It is
proposed to remove this portion of the church and to reconstruct the
nave as far as possible on the lines of the old one. For the complete
restoration of the building, which is projected, the services of Sir Arthur
Blomfield, R.A., have been (1890) retained as architect.

The choir is of excellent design, the lancet shaped arch being preserved throughout. On the floor cut in the stone are the names of
John Fletcher, Edmund Shakespeare, and Philip Massinger, buried in
this church, not implying the actual position of burial but simply the
fact. The altar screen (similar to the one at Winchester) was like that
one erected at the expense of Bishop Fox. In the string-course is his
famous device, the pelican. The choir was restored in 1822, but the
altar screen was not discovered until 1833, when a 17th century screen
was removed. It was restored under Robert Wallace, architect.

The Lady Chapel was restored in 1832-1834, also under George
Gwilt, architect. The woodwork divided off a corner of this chapel,
which was used by Gardiner in the time of Queen Mary as a
Consistory Court.

The church has always been famous for its bells. In 1612 the
great bell was not to weigh less than 50 cwt. At the Restoration of
1737 the weight of all the bells was about 10 tons 15 cwts. This
endangered the stability of the tower, but the danger was overcome
by the skilful use of iron ties by Mr. Gwilt.

Monuments.—Effigy of knight cross-legged, in north aisle of choir.
To John Gower, the poet (d. 1402); a perpendicular monument,
originally erected on the north side of the church, in the chapel of St.
John, where Gower founded a chantry. The monument was removed
to its present site, and repaired and coloured in 1832, at the expense of

George Granville Leveson Gower, first Duke of Sutherland. Gower's monument has always been taken care of. Peacham speaks of it in his *Compleat Gentleman*, p. 95, as " lately repaired by some good Benefactor."

He [Gower] lieth under a tomb of stone, with his image also of stone over him: the hair of his head, auburn, long to his shoulders but curling up, and a small forked beard; on his head a chaplet like a coronet of four roses; a habit of purple, damasked down to his feet; a collar of esses gold about his neck; under his head the likeness of three books which he compiled.—*Stow*, p. 152.

Thomas Cure (d. 1588), founder of Cure's Almshouses. Lancelot Andrewes, Bishop of Winchester (d. 1626); a black and white marble monument in the Lady Chapel, with his effigy at full length. The epitaph, on which Hallam remarks (*Const. Hist.*, vol. ii. p. 63, *note*, 10th ed.), claims for Bishop Andrewes "a superior reward in Heaven on account of his celibacy "—*cælebs migravit ad aureolam cælestem*, the crown of virginity in fact, was lost in the fire of 1676. When St. John's chapel was taken down his leaden coffin was found, with no other inscription than L.A. (the initials of his name). John Traherne, gentleman porter to James I. (d. 1618); half-length of himself and wife (upright), with two sons and four daughters (kneeling). John Bingham, saddler to Queen Elizabeth and James I. (d. 1625). Alderman Humble and his wife (temp. James I.), with some pretty verses, beginning—

Like to the damask rose you see.

William Austin (d. 1633); a kind of harvest-home monument, in north transept; this Austin was a gentleman of fortune and importance in Southwark in the reigns of James I. and Charles I. Lionel Lockyer, the famous empiric in Charles II.'s reign (d. 1672); a rueful full-length figure in north transept. The inscription says that his pills, well-known, will

Survive his dust, and not expire
'Till all things else, at th' universal fire.

He [a Popish Priest] sells indulgences, *like Lockyer's Pills*, with directions how they should be taken.—Butler's *Remains*, vol. ii. p. 143.

Abraham Newland, chief cashier to the Bank of England (d. 1807).

Eminent Persons buried in, and graves unmarked. — Sir Edward Dyer, the poet, in the chancel, May 11, 1607; he lived and died in Winchester House, adjoining. Edmund Shakespeare, "player" (the poet's youngest brother), buried in the church, December 31, 1607. Lawrence Fletcher, one of the leading shareholders in the Globe and Blackfriars Theatres, and William Shakespeare's "fellow," buried in the church September 12, 1608. Philip Henslowe, the manager, so well known by his curious Account Book or Diary; buried in the chancel, January 1615-1616. John Fletcher (*Beaumont and Fletcher*), buried in the church, August 29, 1625. " Philip Massinger, a stranger " (the dramatic poet), buried in the church, March 18, 1638-1639.

The houses in Dodington Grove, Kennington, were built some of them over earth removed during the renovating and rebuilding of St.

Saviour's; there probably, if anywhere, is the sacred dust of the great people buried at St. Saviour's, serving as foundations for the tenements of those who probably never heard of them.

Among notable chaplains of the parish may be mentioned Sutton, who in his sermon on the Romans, delivered in 1616 from St. Saviour's pulpit, inveighed against certain people "who dishonour God, living upon usurie, by dicing houses, and by penning and acting of playes." He was very sharply answered by Nathan Field, an actor whose name appears in the list at the beginning of the first folio of Shakespeare (1623). Moreton, fellow of Emmanuel, friend and executor to the Harvards. Crodacott, a puritan divine deprived on St. Bartholomew's Day. Sacheverell, the incendiary preacher of Queen Anne's time, who, in his famous sermon, preached at St. Paul's, November 5, 1709, described himself as Fellow of Magdalen, Oxford, and Chaplain of St. Saviour's, Southwark. Thomas Jones, of the Wesley School, and much esteemed by earnest religious people; he died young, of fever caught in visiting the sick.

Registers are well preserved and of considerable interest. Those of St. Margaret, before it became one with St. Mary Overy, begin 1538; other records of the same parish of a hundred years or so before, but in a very fragmentary state, still remain. 1553 the name of St. Saviour appears instead of St. Margaret. In these registers, among the births, marriages, and deaths, may be found names of note connected with the Shakesperian stage, and before that.

Token-books.—These at first sight appear like waste-books of some common chandler's shop—long and narrow books of common paper, in brown paper covers; they are nevertheless valuable manuscripts, containing names of all parishioners above fifteen; of streets, courts, rents, and houses in regular order; of the pence given in each case in receipt of a sacramental token of lead, having some suitable inscription, cast by the warders for the purpose of ensuring attendance at the parish church when the sacrament was administered, under penalty for neglect. The names of some sixteen of the actors of the 1623 folio appear in these books as taking the sacrament at St. Saviour's. These token-books, containing names of people in that illustrious and stirring time and in a notable district, are very valuable, but they are not cared for as they ought to be, considering that the parish contains many rich people, and that the cost of putting them in order and binding them would be trifling; to show their value as records of the past, in no other way but by these books could the actual birthplace of that pilgrim father (as he may perhaps be called), John Harvard, founder of the great University of New England, have been discovered.

From the Churchwarden's Accounts St. Saviour's, March 30, 1613:—

It.—For another quire of pap to make the token booke . . . iiijd
    For writinge the borough side token booke . . . iijs iiijd
    For writinge the bankside token booke . . . . iiijs

4800 tokens, £60. In this case the contribution was at 3d. each, and the money was generally given to the poor.

Among other burial-places belonging to St. Saviour's now entirely disused was one at the corner of Union Street and Red Cross Street, known as the Cross Bones, having an emblem of the name over the gateway. This was "the single women's churchyard," an unconsecrated place of burial appropriated, with scarcely a doubt, to the women of the stewes.

In the vestry minutes, December 1786, it is noted of the Cross Bones that some persons had dug up bodies there for dissection, that they had put them into a coach and got away with their spoil. A reward of five guineas was offered and some strong language was used in the vestry. It turned out that the sexton of the place was concerned in the traffic.

Savoy (The), in the STRAND, a house or palace on the river side (of which the chapel alone remains), built in 1245 by Peter, Earl of Savoy and Richmond, uncle unto Eleanor, wife to King Henry III. The Earl bestowed it on the fraternity of Montjoy (Fratres de Monte Jovis, or Priory de Cornuto by Havering at the Bower, in Essex), of whom it was bought by Queen Eleanor for Edmund, Earl of Lancaster, second son of King Henry III. (d. 1295). In 1293 a license to castellate was obtained.[1] Henry Plantagenet, fourth Earl and first Duke of Lancaster, "repaired, or rather new built it," at a cost of 50,000 marks, and here John, King of France, was confined after the battle of Poictiers (1356). The King, not long after his release, died on a visit to this country in his ancient prison of the Savoy. Blanche Plantagenet, daughter and co-heir of Henry, first Duke of Lancaster, married John Plantagenet, Duke of Lancaster, fourth son of King Edward III. ("Old John of Gaunt"); and while the Savoy was in his possession it was burnt and entirely destroyed by Wat Tyler and his followers (1381). Mention is made in the Accounts of 1393-1394 of the annual loss of £4 : 13 : 4, "the rent of 14 shops belonging lately to the Manor of the Savoy annexed, for each shop by the year, at four terms 6s. 8d., the accomptant had nothing, because they were burnt at the time of the Insurrection, and are not rebuilt." In the Accounts the Insurrection is spoken of as "The Rumor" (or popular murmuring, *post rumorem*). The Symeon Tower was repaired this year, as were also the "Great Gates of the Manor," and the Water Gate ; and 10s. were paid "for making one hedge for the protection of the Garden opposite the said manor of the Savoy." The "fruits and profits" of the garden were let for 13s. 4d. "Paid to divers labourers for making 2 perches of the wall on the west side of the garden, called 'mud-wall' between the Savoy and the Inn of the Bishopric of Carlisle, each perch at 9s. = 18s. ; and paid for covering 10 perches of a certain old wall on the same western side, at 18d. a perch, 15s. Mem. for the Steward to inquire whether the burden of making this wall of right belongs to the Lord or not." Also "for 82 lbs. of iron, bought and worked into the form of a lattice and placed in the wall of the

---

[1] *Thirty-first Report of the Deputy Keeper of the Records*, Appendix 1, p. 17.

aforesaid [Symeon] tower, inclosing the window towards the east, for the safe keeping of the prisoners in the said tower, at 2d. the pound, 13s. 8d."[1] The writer of the accompt received 2d. a day for wages.

The Savoy lay long neglected after this, nor would it appear to have been rebuilt, or indeed employed for any particular purpose before 1505, when it was endowed by Henry VII. as a Hospital of St John the Baptist, for the relief of 100 poor people. The King makes particular mention of it in his will. At the suppression of the hospital in 1553, the beds, bedding, and other furniture were given by Edward VI. to the Royal Hospitals of Bridewell and St. Thomas. Queen Mary re-endowed it, and it was continued and maintained as a hospital till the first of Queen Anne (1702), when it was finally dissolved. Fleetwood, the Recorder of London, describes the Savoy in 1560 in a letter to Lord Burghley as a nursery of rogues and masterless men: "The chief nurserie of all these evell people is the Savoy, and the brick-kilnes near Islington." Queen Elizabeth, when taking the air "at her woode nere Islyngton was environed with a number of roges," and sent word to the Lord Mayor and Recorder, who took summary measures for the apprehension of all rogues and masterless people. But the master of the Savoy Hospital was unwilling to allow of their apprehension in his precinct, as he was "sworne to lodge claudicantes, egrotantes, et peregrinantes;" but in spite of his "curtese letter" they were "all soundly payd" before they were sent back.[2] The Savoy, long after sanctuary was legally abrogated, continued to be a refuge for debtors and disorderly persons, and the chapel was the last place in which the so-called Fleet marriages were performed in defiance of the law. [*See* St. Mary le Savoy.]

At the Restoration the meetings of the commissioners for the revision of the Liturgy took place in the Savoy (April 15-July 25, 1661); twelve bishops appearing for the Established Church, and Calamy, Baxter, Reynolds, and others for the Presbyterians. This was called "The Savoy Conference," and under that name is matter of English history. Fuller, the author of *The Worthies*, was lecturer at the Savoy, and Cowley, the poet, a candidate at Court for the office of master. "Savoy missing Cowley" is commemorated in the State Poems of that time. The successful candidate was Dr. Killigrew, the father of Anne Killigrew, who is buried in the chapel, and who still lives in the poetry of Dryden. King Charles II. established a French church here, called "*The French Church in the Savoy.*" Now removed to Bloomsbury Street. The first sermon was preached by Dr. Durel, Sunday, July 14, 1661. The sick and wounded in the great Dutch War of 1666 were lodged in the Savoy. On the night of April 16, 1763, the recruits for the East India Service, temporarily confined in the Savoy, made a determined attempt to escape. They disarmed the guard and obtained possession of the keys, but before they could force the outer gate a detachment of soldiers arrived, and after a sharp struggle the

[1] *Archaeologia*, vol. xxiv. p. 299.   [2] Ellis's *Letters*, vol. ii. p. 285.

recruits were forced back and secured, but not till three of their number had been killed and "several mortally wounded."[1]

This Savoy House is a very great and at this present a very ruinous building. In the midst of its buildings is a very spacious Hall, the walls three foot broad at least, of stone without and brick and stone inward. The ceiling is very curiously built with wood, and having knobs in due places hanging down, and images of angels holding before their breasts coats of arms, but hardly discoverable. On one is a Cross gules between four stars or else mullets. It is covered with lead, but in divers places perished where it lies open to the weather. This large Hall is now divided into several apartments. A cooper hath a part of it for stowing of his hoops and for his work. Other parts of it serve for two Marshalseas for keeping Prisoners, as Deserters, men prest for military service, Dutch recruits, etc. Towards the east end of this Hall is a fair cupola with glass windows, but all broken, which makes it probable the Hall was as long again; since cupolas are wont to be built about the middle of great halls. In this Savoy, how ruinous soever it is, are divers good houses. First the King's Printing Press for Proclamations, Acts of Parliament, Gazettes, and such like public papers; next a Prison; thirdly a Parish Church [St. Mary-le-Savoy] and three or four of the churches and places for religious assemblies, viz. for the French, for Dutch, for High Germans and Lutherans; and lastly, for the Protestant Dissenters. Here be also harbours for many refugees and poor people.—*Strype*, ed. 1720, B. iv. p. 107.

On Tuesday a person going into the Savoy to demand a debt due from a person who had taken sanctuary there, the inhabitants seized him, and after some consultation agreed, according to the usual custom, to dip him in tar and roll him in feathers, after which they carried him in a wheelbarrow into the Strand, and bound him fast to the Maypole, but several constables and others coming in, dispersed the rabble and rescued the person from their abuses.—*The Postman* for July 1696, No. 180.

Sir Thomas Heneage appears to have removed from Bevis Marks [which *see*] to the Savoy in 1590, on being appointed Chancellor of the Duchy of Lancaster, and he died at the Duchy House in the Savoy in 1595. In 1687 the Jesuits opened a chapel and schools in the Savoy, and offered to instruct gratuitously all youths who were "fit to begin Latin" in that language, Greek, poetry and rhetoric; but schools and chapel were closed and the Jesuits dispersed on the abdication of James II. The inscription on the monument at Acton to Mrs. Barry, the celebrated actress of the reign of Charles II., describes her as "of the parish of St. Mary Savoy." Alexander Cruden, author of the *Concordance*, lived here, and here Jacob Tonson had a warehouse. The last vestiges of the Savoy buildings were swept away in forming the approaches to Waterloo Bridge.[2]

Savoy Church. [*See* St. Mary le Savoy.]

Scalding Alley, in the POULTRY, was so called from the poulterers scalding or scorching their poultry there. [*See* Poultry.]

> But who is this? O, my daughter Cis,
> Minced-pie; with her do not dally
> On pain o' your life: she's an honest cook's wife,
> And comes out of Scalding Alley.

---

[1] *Lambert*, vol. ii. p. 193.

[2] Of the Savoy there is a scarce etching by Hollar (a river front), done in 1650, and a most careful survey and view by Vertue, done in 1736, for the *Vetusta Monumenta*. Its position and the connection of the buildings are well shown in Strype's Map, B. iv. p. 108.

Schomberg House, PALL MALL, Nos. 81 and 82 on the south side, so called after Frederic Count of Schomberg, a German by birth and descent, but a Marshal of France, and Baron Teyes; Earl of Brentford, Marquis of Harwich, and Duke of Schomberg in England, as also Knight of the Garter and Master of the Ordnance. By a curious limitation in the patent he was succeeded in the dukedom by his third son, Charles, who died in 1693 of wounds received at the battle of Marsaglia, and he in his turn was succeeded by the second son of his father, although the first son was still living. This second son, and third Duke, Mindhardt Schomberg, was the actual builder of this house, which could hardly have been finished when, in 1699, a party of disbanded soldiers drew themselves up before it and threatened to pull it down.[1] After his death it passed into the possession of Lord Holderness, by whom it was let in 1760 to the Duke of Cumberland, of Culloden fame. In 1765 it was purchased for £5000 by John Astley, the handsome portrait painter. Astley was a fellow pupil with Reynolds under Hudson, and they were together in Rome. There, "poor in purse as with the pencil," he had eked out a deficient toilet by making the hinder part of his waistcoat out of one of his own canvases. On a summer's day a party of painters went for a little excursion. The day was hot, Astley incautiously threw off his coat, and his companions discovered that he was carrying on his back a terrific chasm and tremendous waterfall.[2] He had not long to resort to such shifts. Before he had been long back in England in the course of itinerant portrait-painting he attracted the notice of a wealthy widow, Lady Daniel of Duckinfield, who sat to him for her portrait and offered him her hand. Upon Schomberg House Astley spent £5000, dividing it into three, and fitting up the centre part "most whimsically," says Pennant, for his own use. Others, however, praise his architectural efforts here, as they praise the taste he displayed on his mansion at Duckinfield—at which he died, November 14, 1787. About 1780 Astley let his part of Schomberg House to Dr. Graham, the notorious quack, who converted it into what he called his "Temple of Health," with a living goddess, in the shape of a certain Mrs. Prescott, as the presiding deity. After a few years Graham found it convenient to flit to Edinburgh, where Scott, it may be remembered, was when a child subjected to his electrical treatment and earth baths.[3]

August 23, 1780.—In the morning I went to Dr. Graham's. It is the most impudent puppet-show of imposition I ever saw, and the mountebank himself the dullest of his profession, except that he makes the spectators pay a crown a-piece.— *H. Walpole to Countess of Ossory.*

In 1786 the quack doctor was succeeded in the central portion of the building by Richard Cosway, R.A., the most fascinating of miniature painters. His wonderful skill and the charms and accomplishments of his wife, Maria Hadfield, rendered the house a great resort of the fashion-

---

[1] *Vernon Corr.*, vol. ii. p. 319.   [2] Northcote's *Life of Reynolds*, vol. i. p. 44.
[3] Lockhart's *Life of Scott*, chap. iv.

able world; and the attractions of their musical parties—where the most popular singer and musician and the latest lion were sure to be found—were not diminished by the circumstance that there was a private door which communicated with the gardens of Carlton House, and that the Prince of Wales on such occasions frequently availed himself of it. These receptions were on Sunday evenings, when Pall Mall, according to Smith, "was hardly passable." Cosway gave up the house about 1799. It was then successively occupied by the Polygraphic Society, who held an exhibition here of their "wretched copies of good pictures;"[1] by Bryan, the well-known picture-dealer; by Peter Coxe, the auctioneer; and then by Payne, the bookseller, "honest Tom Payne," and Messrs. Payne and Foss, who here brought together their matchless collection of old books. Jervas, the portrait painter (d. 1730), eulogised by Pope; and Nathaniel Hone, R.A. (d. 1784), now chiefly remembered by his picture entitled the "Conjuror," were in turns tenants of Schomberg House.[2]

Another portion was more worthily occupied. In the summer of 1774, when Thomas Gainsborough removed from Bath to London, he rented the west wing of Schomberg House from Astley for £300 a year. Here Reynolds at once called upon him, and here, but after an interval of eight years, Sir Joshua had *one* sitting for his portrait, on Sunday November 3, 1782. But the portrait was never painted; and Reynolds did not again enter his door till he received that affecting letter saying that he had been "six months in a dying state," and begging as a last favour that he "would come once more under my roof and look at my things." Here then took place that interesting and solemn interview between these two illustrious painters which left the impression on the mind of the survivor that the dying man's "regret at losing life was principally the regret at leaving his art." Gainsborough died here, August 2, 1798. "We are all going to Heaven," he said, "and Vandyck is of the company." He is buried at Kew. His widow continued to reside here for some years after his death; in the spring following which an exhibition was here made of his pictures and drawings. There were 56 of the former and 148 of the latter, with their prices marked.

A Society of Arts memorial tablet in commemoration of Gainsborough's residence is placed on the house.

In 1850 part of the house was required for the enlargement of what was then called the Ordnance Office; the east wing was pulled down, and Schomberg House, which, in spite of all this "partitioning," had continued to preserve the appearance of a single fine mansion of the King William period, was reduced to a very awkward and disjointed condition. The whole of it has since been incorporated in the WAR OFFICE.

School of Design (Government), was opened May 1, 1837, at Somerset House (in rooms vacated by the Royal Academy), by and

[1] Smith's *Nollekens*, vol. ii. p. 398. [2] *Smith*, vol. ii. p. 395.

under the superintendence of the Board of Trade, for teaching the art of design or composition, with reference especially to the staple manufactures of the country. The whole arrangements were entrusted to John B. Papworth, architect, who was appointed Director, and he was succeeded by William Dyce, and then by C. H. Wilson. After some fluctuation it was in 1852 remodelled under the superintendence of Mr. (afterwards Sir Henry) Cole, and the title changed to the "Department of Practical Art." In 1841 a Branch School of Design was established at Spitalfields with the object of educating the weavers of the neighbourhood in the principles of design. In 1853 a Science Division was added; three years later the establishment ceased to be connected with the Board of Trade, and was placed under the direction of the Lord President of the Council and the Vice-President of the Committee of Council on Education. In 1857 the Department was removed to South Kensington. [*See* Science and Art Department.]

The number of students in the School of Design and branch institutions before the reorganisation in 1852 was 6997.

School Board for London (The), VICTORIA EMBANKMENT, was established in pursuance of the Elementary Education Act of 1870 (33 and 34 Vict. c. 75, ss. 37-39). The Board formerly consisted of 49 members, but the number is now fixed at 55. The members are elected by the direct (and cumulative) vote of all persons rated for the relief of the poor. The election of the Seventh Board took place on November 26, 1888. By the terms of the Act the Board have to provide sufficient accommodation in public elementary schools available for all the children resident in the metropolis for whose elementary education sufficient and suitable provision is not otherwise provided, and to furnish elementary education under such conditions as are defined in the Act. Since the Act has been in operation the Board has provided up to 1889 substantial and spacious buildings providing accommodation for upwards of 400,000 children. "Elementary" instruction is not defined in the Act, and the Board have shown themselves disposed to interpret the phrase in a liberal spirit; and some efforts have been made by the foundation of scholarships, etc., to assist promising scholars in obtaining education of a higher grade. Else as a rule the teaching is confined to the simpler branches of an ordinary English education. Drawing is taught in most of the Board Schools, and music as far as singing by the Tonic Sol-fa system. Instruction in plain needlework is a part of the regular teaching in all the girls' schools, and in some instruction is given in cookery and domestic economy. Instruction in physiology, mensuration, and other special or "extra" subjects sanctioned by the Council of Education is also in some instances given at specific times. In the Infant Schools the Kindergarten system is largely adopted. In certain centres provision is made for teaching the blind and the deaf and dumb. The Board have also for the friendless and refractory a reformatory ship and reformatory and truant schools. The number of male and female teachers employed in the Board Schools in 1889 was 6898,—2319 male and 4579 female.

There are also about 1696 pupil teachers. The annual expenditure of the Board is about £1,900,000. The office of the Board on the Victoria Embankment is a red brick "Queen Anne" building, from the designs of Mr. E. R. Robson, the Board's architect, who has superintended the erection of all and designed most of the Board Schools, which now form conspicuous features in most of the poorer districts of London.

The London School Board District, as defined by the Act, comprises ten Divisions,—City of London, Chelsea, Finsbury, Greenwich, Hackney, east and west Lambeth, Marylebone, Southwark, Tower Hamlets, and Westminster, and at the census of 1881 contained 488,995 inhabited houses and 3,832,441 inhabitants.

Science and Art Department, SOUTH KENSINGTON, founded in 1853, with offices at Marlborough House. In 1857 it was removed to South Kensington. The department grew out of the Government School of Design established in 1837 [*see* School of Design], and remodelled in 1852 as the "Department of Practical Art," in accordance with the suggestion of Mr. (afterwards Sir Henry) Cole. When the Science Division was added, the scheme, dated March 16, 1853, was intended "to extend a system of encouragement to local institutions for Practical Science similar to that already commenced in the Department of Practical Art." The Department of Science and Art remained under the control of the Board of Trade until the Education Department was constituted by an order of Council of February 25, 1856, and the 19 and 20 Vict., c. 116, to include "(*a*) the Educational Establishment of the Privy Council Office ; (*b*) the Establishment for the encouragement of Science and Art, now under the direction of the Board of Trade, and called the Department of Science and Art." These two Departments were placed under the Lord President of the Council, assisted by the Vice-President of the Committee of Council on Education.

The Parliamentary vote for the Department of Science and Art in 1856-1857 was £64,075, while that in 1888-1889 was £445,303. The Department was incorporated by Royal Charter dated April 30, 1864.

Science Division. — When the Department was constituted, the Government School of Mines, the Museum of Practical Geology, the Geological Survey, the Museum of Irish Industry and the Royal Dublin Society were constituted portions of the Department. Though the principle of granting aid to Science Schools and Classes was established in 1853, no general system of making grants applicable to the whole county was formulated until 1859, in which year the first examination for teachers was held. The staff consists of a Director for Science, an Assistant Director, an Official Examiner and two Assistant Examiners, also Professional Examiners for special subjects. The

Normal School of Science [which *see*], with its Council, Professors, Demonstrators, etc., forms a part of the Science Division.

Art Division.—In 1853 the Training Class was moved from Somerset House to Marlborough House, where temporary school-rooms were erected. In 1857 the offices of the Department and the Art Training Schools were removed from Marlborough House to South Kensington. The number of students instructed in local schools of art was then 12,500, and in the National Art Training School at South Kensington 396, besides which there were 43,312 scholars of elementary schools taught drawing by the teachers of those schools, while the number of students in the Schools of Design before the establishment of the Department of Science and Art was 6997. In 1864 a Select Committee of the House of Commons was appointed to inquire into the constitution, working, and success of Schools of Art, and its recommendations were adopted as far as they were found practicable. In 1887 there were 209 Schools of Art with 24 branch classes, and a total of 41,263 students; 584 art classes with 33,438 students; 3979 elementary schools at which 875,263 children and pupil teachers were taught drawing, of which 684,306 were examined; 51 Training Colleges with 3756 students in training examined in drawing, of whom 1012 students and teachers obtained certificates. The staff of the Art Division consists of a Director, an Assistant Director, an Official Examiner and Assistant Examiner, and an Examination Clerk. There is also the Staff of the National Art Training School.

The South Kensington Museum [which *see*] is in connection with the Science and Art Department.

Scotland Yard, WHITEHALL, was divided into Great and Little, situated between Whitehall and Northumberland Avenue. It was so called, it is said, after the Kings of Scotland and their ambassadors, who were occasionally lodged here.

On the left hand from Charing Cross be also divers fair tenements lately built, till ye come to a large plot of ground inclosed with brick, and is called Scotland, where great buildings have been for receipt of the kings of Scotland and other estates of that country; for Margaret, Queen of Scots, and sister to King Henry VIII., had her abiding there, when she came into England after the death of her husband, as the kings of Scotland had on former times, when they came to the Parliament of England.—*Stow*, p. 168.

Part of Scotland Yard was long the official residence of the Surveyor of the Works to the Crown. It was occupied by Inigo Jones. There is a letter from him dated "Office of Works, Scotland Yard, August 16, 1620, complaining that "many masons employed on the Banquetting Hall have run away." Inigo's successor, Sir John Denham, the poet of Cooper's Hill, died here, March 1668.

June 10, 1666.—He [Pierce, the surgeon] tells me further, how the Duke of York is wholly given up to his new mistress, my Lady Denham, going at noonday with all his gentlemen with him to visit her in Scotland Yard; she declaring she will not be his mistress, as Mrs. Price, to go up and down the Privy-stairs, but will be owned publicly: and so she is.—*Pepys*.

His successor, Sir C. Wren, had his office here; and in a house designed by himself and built out of the ruins of Whitehall (destroyed by fire in 1697) lived Sir John Vanburgh. It was probably built by him as comptroller of the Royal Works, for he did not succeed Sir C. Wren.

Milton, on his appointment as Latin Secretary to the Council of State in 1649, was granted an official residence in Scotland Yard, and there he continued to reside till 1652, when he removed to "a pretty garden-house" in Petty France. Whilst in Scotland Yard he lost his infant and only son, March 1650; and also the sight of his left eye. Mrs. Cibber lived in Scotland Yard, and here Charles Burney, previously a pupil of her brother Dr. Arne, was introduced to her in 1749, and laid the foundation of his fashionable career. Here in 1761 died Mrs. Dunch, known to the readers of Horace Walpole and Lady Mary Wortley Montagu. Samuel Pegge, author of the *Curialia* and of *Anecdotes of the English Language*, died here, May 22, 1800. After the death of his wife Thomas Campbell took the lease of a large house in Middle Scotland Yard from midsummer 1829; gave evening parties, and was visited by the great Cuvier, August 23, 1830. He describes the situation as "admirably convenient for all parts of London."

Scotland Yard has been much contracted of late years, and the offices of the Police Commissioners, long associated with the place, have been removed to Whitehall Place. A large building (R. N. Shaw, R.A., architect), to be used as police offices, is now (1890) in course of construction on the Thames embankment, near the old Board of Control Office. It is to be called New Scotland Yard.

Scottish Corporation, CRANE COURT, FLEET STREET, for the relief of aged and infirm natives of Scotland resident in London or its immediate neighbourhood, to give temporary aid to Scotsmen in distress, and to educate poor Scottish children. The Corporation derives its origin from a society formed a short time after the accession of James I. for relieving the less fortunate individuals of the Scottish nation. The Society continued to exercise its benevolent purpose under the designation of the "Scottish Box" until the reign of Charles II., when, in the year 1665, a Charter of Incorporation was granted, empowering the Society to hold lands, and to erect a hospital for the reception of the objects of the charity. A second Charter of Incorporation, containing more extended privileges, was granted by the same monarch in 1676. Within a few years after the date of the first charter a hospital was built in what is now Bridge Street, Blackfriars; but experience soon proved that confinement to a charity workhouse was uncongenial to the feelings and habits of the Scottish poor. The maintenance of a hospital, or receptacle for the objects of the charity, was in consequence relinquished, and the plan of assisting and relieving them at their own habitations substituted. That assistance was confined to such natives of Scotland, resident in London, as had become members by paying stated contributions to the Society, in virtue of which they were entitled to relief when in want. But the system did not work well, and the Society appearing to be fast dwindling away, a new charter was obtained in 1775, whereby the "Scottish Hospital of the Foundation of King Charles II." was reincorporated, and directed to be governed, in all time coming, by a president, six vice-presidents, a treasurer, and an unlimited number of governors. Donors of £105 and upwards are members of the committee of management for life, a donation of ten guineas and upwards constituting a governor for life, and a subscription of one guinea or more an annual governor, so long as such subscription shall continue to be paid. The necessity of contributing, as a title to admission, was dispensed with, and the corporation thus became completely a charitable institution for the relief of poor natives of Scotland, who might be reduced to poverty and want. The income is about £6000, and about 165 pensions are paid annually, besides about 340 petitioners relieved monthly.

The premises belonging to the corporation in Crane Court were bought from the Royal Society in 1782. The hall was the great meeting-room of the Royal Society when Sir Isaac Newton was president. [*See* Crane Court.] This interesting building was destroyed by fire on Wednesday, November 14, 1877. A more commodious building of red brick and stone was erected on the site from the designs of Professor T. L. Donaldson, and opened in 1880.

Scriveners' Company, the forty-fourth in rank of the City guilds, was originally known as the Writers of the Court Letter of the City of London, and was incorporated 14 James I. (1616) as the Society of Writers of the City of London. The Company has a livery and a few charities. It had a hall in Noble Street, but "being reduced to low circumstances" sold it to the Company of Coachmakers.

Scroope's (or Scrope's) Inn, HOLBORN, a serjeants' inn, over against St. Andrew's Church, in Holborn, so called after the noble family of the Scropes of Bolton. It ceased, it is said, to be a serjeants' inn about the year 1498. Scroope's Inn was succeeded by *Scroope's Court*, known in the present century as *Union Court*. In Scroope's Court died, 1632, Sir Oliver Butler. The Holborn (or Scroope's Inn) end of Union Court, was cleared away for the Holborn Viaduct.

Seacoal Lane, a lane 180 yards in length, between *Snow Hill* (north) and *Fleet Lane* (south), swept away in extending the London, Chatham, and Dover Railway from Ludgate Hill to the Holborn Viaduct.

The next is Seacoal Lane, I think called Limeburners' Lane, of burning lime there with seacoal; for I read a record of such a lane to have been in the parish of St. Sepulchre, and there yet remaineth in this lane an alley called Limeburners' Alley.—*Stow*, p. 145.

Seacoal Lane is named in the Pipe Rolls, 12 Henry III. (1228), being no doubt then used as a landing-place for sea coal from the barges on the Fleet River; and in the Patent Rolls, 41 Henry III. (1257) mention is made of ship-loads of sea coal imported into London. These facts dispose of the assertion which has been made that sea coal was not used in London earlier than the time of Edward I. or II.—*Riley Memorials*, p. xvi. *note* 7.

In the 17th of Edward III. (1343), "a piece of land in the lane called *Secollane* near the water of Flete," was granted upon lease to the Butchers of St. Nicholas Shambles, "for the purpose of there in such water cleansing the entrails of beasts . . . they paying yearly to the Lord Mayor, at the Feast of our Lord's Nativity, one boar's head"—(Riley). In the reign of Henry IV. we find it again mentioned in a "Writ for the repair of one foot of Flete Bridge, towards Secollane."[1]

The she doctor that cured Abel Drugger of the effects of "fat ram mutton" supper, lived here.

> Yes faith—she dwells in Seacoal Lane,—did cure me,
> With sodden ale, and pellitory of the wall;
> Cost me but twopence.—Ben Jonson, *Alchemist*, Act iii. Sc. 2.

"The Jest of George and the Barber," in *The Merry Conceited Jests of George Peele, Gentleman*, is said to have taken place "at a blind ale-house in Sealcoal Lane," where he found "George in a green jerkin, a Spanish platter-fashioned hat, all alone at a peck of oysters."[2]

Searle Street. [*See* Serle Street.]

Seething Lane, GREAT TOWER STREET (east end) to CRUTCHED FRIARS.
The church of Allhallows Barking is at the corner in Tower Street. *Sieuthenestrate*, or *Suiethenestrate*, is mentioned in the City records as early as A.D. 1281; Stow's conjecture that it was originally Sidon Lane would seem, therefore, to be unfounded. Sir Francis Walsingham lived and died in this lane:—

> Sidon Lane, now corruptly called Sything Lane. . . . In this Sidon Lane divers fair and large houses are built, namely, one by Sir John Allen, some time mayor of London, and of council unto King Henry VIII.; Sir Francis Walsingham, Knight, principal secretary to the Queen's Majesty that now is was lodged there, and so was the Earl of Essex.—*Stow*, p. 50.

> The 6 of April [1590] about midnight deceased Sir Francis Walsingham, Knight, at his house in Seeding Lane, and was about ten of the clocke in the next night following, buried in Paules Church without solemnity.—*Stow*, by Howes, ed. 1631, p. 761.

Walsingham's widow continued to live in Seething Lane, and at her house here Robert Devereux, Earl of Essex, was baptized by Lancelot Andrewes.[3]

> Seething or Sything Lane runneth northwards from Tower Street unto Crutched Friars. It is now [1720] a place of no great account; but amongst the inhabitants some are merchants. Here is the Navy Office; but the chief gate for entrance is out of Crutched Friars.—*Strype*, B. ii. p. 53.

Pepys lived at the Navy Office in this lane during the nine years, 1660-1669, over which his *Diary* extends.

---

[1] *Liber Albus*, p. 502.   [2] Dyce's *Peele*, vol. ii. p. 271.
[3] *Life of Bishop Andrewes*, p. 34.

July 4, 1660.—Up early and with Commissioner Pett to view the houses in Seething Lane belonging to the Navy, where I find the worst very good, and had great fears that they will shuffle me out of them, which troubles me.—*Pepys.*

July 18, 1660.—This morning we met at the [Navy] Office: I dined at my house in Seething Lane.—*Pepys.*

September 5, 1666.—About two in the morning my wife calls me up and tells me of new cryes of fire, it being come to Barking Church, which is at the bottom of our lane.—*Pepys.*

May 9, 1667.—In our street, at the Three Tuns Tavern, I find a great hub-bub; and what was it but two brothers had fallen out, and one killed the other. And who should they be but the two Fieldings; one whereof, Bazill, was page to my Lady Sandwich; and hath killed the other, himself being very drunk, and so was sent to Newgate.—*Pepys.*

It was *Basil* who was killed. They were sons of George Fielding, Earl of Desmond, and uncles of the father of Henry Fielding the novelist. Seething Lane has now many corn, wine, and general merchants among its inhabitants. Here are the Corn Exchange Chambers and Subscription Room. Pepys's Three Tuns Tavern has disappeared. [*See* Navy Office; Allhallows Barking.]

Sepulchre (St.) in the BAILEY (occasionally written ST. 'PULCHER's), a church at the western end of Newgate Street, and in the ward of Farringdon Without. About a fifth of the parish of St. Sepulchre lies "without the liberties" of the City of London, and the church is in consequence in the anomalous position of having two sets of church-wardens. A church existed here in the 12th century; but the oldest part of the present edifice, the tower and south-west porch, is of the middle of the 15th century. The body of the church was destroyed in the Great Fire of 1666, and was rebuilt and the tower repaired, it is said, by Sir C. Wren, the works being completed in 1670. The fire itself was stopped at Pie Corner, a few yards north of the church. In 1338 William of Newcastle-under-Lyme bequeathed an estate to the parish for the maintenance of the fabric. With the process of time the estate has increased in value, and now yields, it is said, nearly £2000 a year. The consequence has been frequent repairs and restorations, by the last of which the church has been thoroughly transformed. Large repairs were done in 1738. The body of the church was in a great measure rebuilt and a new roof put on in 1837. In 1863 and following years considerable alterations were made; but the most material were effected in 1875 and 1878. In 1875 the tower and porch—a separate building of three floors, projecting from the tower on the south—had new window tracery inserted, pinnacles to the tower rebuilt, a new oriel on the south front of the porch, where Popham's statue stood, and the whole refaced and completely restored, the architect being Mr. W. P. Griffith. In 1878-1880 the body of the church was restored under Mr. Robert Billing, architect. New windows filled with tracery of a very florid type were inserted, new buttresses, battlements, and pinnacles added, and the interior made conformable. The church is now Gothic throughout, but Gothic of the last quarter of the 19th century. The tower was 152 feet 9 inches to the cap of the pinnacles; as restored it is 149 feet 11 inches. The organ, a very fine instrument, originally built by Renatus Harris in 1670, was repaired and enlarged by the elder Byfield about 1730. Subsequently improvements have been made, and new stops added by Hancock, and by Gray and Davison in the present century. The case is attributed to Grinling Gibbons. It is now entirely remodelled and placed in St. Stephen's Chapel. For many years past it has been the custom for the organist to give a recital after the Sunday evening service. The church is 150 feet long by 62 wide, and with St. Stephen's Chapel 81 feet.

A tablet is preserved in the church with a list of charitable donations and gifts, containing the following item :—

> 1605.—Mr. Robert Dowe gave for ringing the greatest bell in this church on the day the condemned prisoners are executed, and for other services for ever, concerning such condemned prisoners, for which services the sexton is paid £1 : 6 : 8 . . . £50 0 0

This has now been appropriated by the Charity Commissioners.

It was the custom formerly for the clerk or bellman of St. Sepulchre's to go under Newgate on the night preceding the execution of a criminal, and ringing his bell to repeat the following verses :—

> All you that in the condemned hold do lie,
> Prepare you, for to-morrow you shall die;
> Watch all and pray, the hour is drawing near,
> That you before the Almighty must appear;
> Examine well yourselves, in time repent,
> That you may not to eternall flames be sent.
> And when St. Sepulchre's bell to-morrow tolls,
> The Lord above have mercy on your souls.
> Past twelve o'clock !

This is further explained by a passage in Munday's edition of *Stow* :—

> Robert Dowe, citizen and merchant taylor of London, gave to the parish church of St. Sepulchre's, the somme of £50, that after the several sessions of London, when the prisoners remain in the gnol as condemned men to death, expecting execution on the morning following : the clarke of the church should come in the night time, and likewise early in the morning to the window of the prison where they lye, and there ringing certain tolls with a hand-bell, appointed for the purpose, he doth afterwards (in most Christian manner) put them in mind of their present condition, and ensuing execution, desiring them to be prepared therefore as they ought to be. When they are in the cart, and brought before the wall of the church, there he standeth ready with the same bell, and after certain tolls, rehearseth an appointed prayer, desiring all the people there present to pray for them. The Beadle also of Merchant Taylors' Hall hath an honest stipend allowed him to see that this is duly done.—Munday's *Stow*, ed. 1618, p. 25.

Hatton has printed (*New View*, p. 707) the "Exhortation" and "Admonition" used on this occasion. The former he calls "The Words said in the Gateway of the Prison the night before Execution;" the latter, "The Words said in St. Sepulchre's Churchyard as the prisoners are drawn by [to Tyburn] to be executed." Dowe is buried in the church of St. Botolph, Aldgate, where there is a portrait-monument to his memory. Another curious custom observed at this church was that of presenting a nosegay to every criminal on his way to Tyburn. One of the last given was presented from the steps of St. Sepulchre's to Sixteen-stringed Jack, *alias* John Rann, executed in 1774 for robbing the Rev. Dr. Bell in Gunnersbury Lane, on the road to Brentford. He wore it in his button-hole. The clock of St. Sepulchre's still regulates the execution of criminals in Newgate.

John Rogers, the Marian protomartyr, was vicar of this church. On April 11, 1600, William Dodington, a brother-in-law of Sir Francis Walsingham, and an officer in the Exchequer, threw himself from the tower and was killed. "If I do break my neck," said Bacon to Queen Elizabeth, "I shall do it in a manner as Mr. Dodington did it, which walked on the battlements of the church many days, and took a view and survey where he should fall."[1]

Saturday, April 12, 1600.—Dorrington, rich Dorrington, yesterday morning, went up to St. Sepulchre's steeple, and threw himself over the battlement, and broke his neck. There was found a paper sealed, with this superscription, "Lord save my soule, and I will praise thy name."—*Rowland Whyte to Sir Robert Sydney*, vol. ii. p. 187.

It was that William Dodington that wilfully brake his neck by casting himself down headlong from the battlements of St. Sepulchre's steeple, upon the sight of certain depositions touching a cause in controversy between him and one Drunker in Chancery.—*Marginal Note to a letter from Dodington to Hatton*, p. 362.

Eminent Persons buried in St. Sepulchre's. — Roger Ascham (d. December 30, 1568), author of *Toxophilus* (1545) and *The Schoolmaster* (1570); William Gravet, vicar of St. Sepulchre's, watched over him as he was dying. When Elizabeth was told of his death she said she would rather have lost ten thousand pounds than her old tutor. Captain John Smith, author of the *General History of Virginia* (fol. 1626), (d. 1631); his epitaph in doggrel verse is no longer legible: it is printed in *Strype* and elsewhere. Sir Robert Peake, the engraver, Faithorne's master, and Governor of Basing House for the King during the Civil War under Charles I. (d. 1667). Fleetwood, the Recorder of London, writes to inform Lord Burghley, July 1585, that when Awfield was executed at Tyburn for "sparcinge abroad certen lewd sedicious and traytorous bookes," his body "was brought to St. 'Pulchers to be buryed, but the parishioners would not suffer a traytor's corpes to be layed in the earthe where theire parents, wyeffs, chyldren, kynred, maisters, and old neighbours did rest," and so "his carcase was retourned to the buryall grounde necre Tyborne."[2] A century and a half later the parishioners, less scrupulous, permitted the body of Sarah Malcolm, the murderess, to be buried, 1733, in their churchyard. Thomas Lord Dacre was beheaded at the Tower and his body buried in this church.

The churchyard, till the middle of the 18th century, extended on the south side far into the street, and was bounded by a high wall, leaving no footway for passengers. In 1760 the wall was removed and a portion of the churchyard levelled. When the Holborn Viaduct

[1] Cooper, *Ath. Cant.*, vol. ii. p. 164.   [2] Ellis's *Letters*, vol. ii. p. 298.

was formed, 1871, a further portion was laid into the street, the bodies exhumed being reinterred in the City Cemetery at Ilford, where a monument was erected to their memory. Since then the churchyard has been levelled and planted as a flower-garden. In Johnson's *Highwaymen* (fol. 1736) is a characteristic view of St. Sepulchre's; it is entitled "Jonathan Wild going to the place of Execution."

Payne Fisher, "Paganus Piscator," 1616-1693, was buried in the churchyard.

Serjeants' Inn, CHANCERY LANE; **Serjeants' Inn,** FLEET STREET, houses of law originally set apart for the Honourable Society of Judges and Serjeants-at-Law. The serjeants always addressed one another as "brother." One of Chaucer's Canterbury Pilgrims is a "serjeant-of-law." No person could be made a justice of the Queen's Bench or Common Pleas who was not "of the degree of the coif"; a phrase taken from the peculiar cap which was the distinctive badge or emblem of the serjeant-at-law. When, as of late years was commonly the case, a justice was appointed who was not of the degree of the coif, before taking the oaths as judge he went through the ceremony of admission as a serjeant, and at the same time received a retainer from his own inn to plead as their serjeant.

<small>First I was made a serjeant, and then my patent writ as Chief Justice was handed to me, and, having taken many strange oaths, my title to hang, draw, and quarter was complete. . . . Brougham tried to play me a dog's trick, by running away with my fee of ten guineas as a retainer to plead when become a serjeant for the Society of Lincoln's Inn. I made him disgorge. . . . I have dined twice at Serjeants' Inn, my admission to which cost me near £700.—Lord Campbell (*Letter and Journal*, November 1850), *Life*, vol. ii. pp. 274, 276.</small>

Mr. Foss, following Dugdale, is of opinion that the Chancery Lane Inn was not an Inn for Serjeants before the 2d of Henry V. (1414-1415), and that it was earlier occupied by serjeants than the inn in Fleet Street.[1] The Fleet Street Inn appears to have been a private dwelling in the reign of Henry VIII. It ceased to be occupied by the serjeants towards the end of the 18th century. The hall was purchased by the Amicable Assurance Society, and the rest of the inn rebuilt as private houses. The Fleet Street front of the building is now occupied by the Norwich Union Office. On one of the houses in the square behind (No. 9) is a stone with a coat of arms, S. I. and the date 1669 cut on it. No. 13, occupied by the Church of England Sunday School Institute, has a handsome elevation. The Chancery Lane Inn was retained till the dissolution of the Society in 1876. The premises, including the hall, a spacious and lofty dining-room,— lighted by five painted glass windows,—chapel and robing rooms, were sold by auction, February 23, 1877, for £57,100, the proceeds being divided amongst the members, a transaction which gave rise to some comment at the time. The portraits, twenty-six in number, of eminent members of the inn, including Lord Chancellors King,

---

[1] Foss, *Judges*, vol. iv. p. 247.

Camden, Eldon, Truro, Lyndhurst, and Campbell; Sir Edward Coke, Sir Matthew Hale, the Earl of Mansfield, Lord Denman and other distinguished judges, were presented by the Society to the National Portrait Gallery.

Lord Chief Justice Coke was living in Serjeants' Inn during the Overbury inquiries. Lord Chief Justice Hyde and Lord Keeper Guildford also lived here.

> His Lordship by the means of his brother in law Mr. Robert Hyde, settled himself in the great brick house near Serjeants' Inn in Chancery Lane, which was formerly the Lord Chief Justice Hyde's; and that he held it till he had the Great Seal, and some time after.... His house was to his mind, and having, with leave, a door into Serjeants' Inn Garden, he passed daily to his chambers, dedicated to business and study.... But being scandalised at the poorness of the Hall [Serjeants' Inn Hall], which was very small and withal ruinous, he never left till he brought his brethren to agree to the new building of it; which he saw done, with as much elegance and capacity as the place would admit of, and thereby gained a decent avenue, with stone steps, to his chambers, as may be seen at this day.—North's *Life of Lord Keeper Guildford*, pp. 164, 165.

Serle Street, LINCOLN'S INN FIELDS to CAREY STREET, was so called from a Mr. Henry Serle, who died intestate (circ. 1690), much in debt, and his lands heavily mortgaged.[1] He acquired his property in this neighbourhood partly by purchase from the sons and from the executors of Sir John Birkenhead, the writer of *Mercurius Aulicus*, during the Civil War under Charles I., who died in 1679, seized in fee of two-thirds of Fickett's Field. The second edition of *Barnabæ Itinerarium*, or *Barnaby's Journal* (the first edition with a printer's name and date upon it), was printed in 1716, for "S. Illidge, under Searle's Gate, Lincoln's Inn New Square." Sir James Mackintosh removed from Portland Place to 14 Serle Street, after Michaelmas Term, 1795. In an invitation to Canning he calls it his "black-letter neighbourhood." His wife died here, April 8, 1797. There is a monument to her in St. Clement's Danes with an inscription by Dr. Parr. Parr tells Landor, April 1801, that his daughter "Catherine is at Mackintosh's, 14 Serle Street."[2]

Serle's Coffee-house, LINCOLN'S INN. [*See* Serle Street.]

> I do not know that I meet in any of my walks objects which move both my spleen and laughter so effectually as those young fellows at the Grecian, Squire's, Serle's, and all other Coffee-houses adjacent to the law, who rise early for no other purpose but to publish their laziness.—*The Spectator*, No. 49.

Mr. Dyce has printed a letter from Akenside, the poet, addressed "To Mr. Dyson, at Serle's Coffee House, Lincoln's Inn;" this was Jeremiah Dyson, the poet's friend and patron.

Serle's Court, LINCOLN'S INN. This was the old name for New Square, and was so called from the Henry Serle noticed under *Serle Street*. The arms of Serle with those of the inn are over the gateway next Carey Street.

---

[1] *Autob. of Sir John Bramston*, p. 359.   [2] Parr's *Life and Corr.*, vol. i. p. 160.

July 29, 1714.— With the Society for Promoting Christian Knowledge at their new apartments at Lincoln's Inn (*No. 6 in Serle's Court*). After the business was over I looked at the curious and noble models of many churches proposed to be built ; this pleasant room being that where the Commissioners meet upon that account in the forenoons (as the Bishop of London, Mr. Nelson, etc., did this day) and the Society in the afternoon.—Thoresby's *Diary.*

Lord Eldon (when Sir John Scott and Solicitor-General) in the summer of 1791 took "a set of chambers at No. 11 Serle's Court, commonly called The New Square, Lincoln's Inn, under a lease to him, dated September 1 in that year."

Sermon Lane, ST. PAUL'S, or SERMON LANE, DOCTORS' COMMONS, from Carter Lane to Knightrider Street.

Corruptly called Sermon Lane for Sheremoniers' Lane, for I find it by that name recorded in the 14th of Edward I., and in that lane a place to be called the Blacke loft (of melting silver) with four shops adjoining. It may therefore be well supposed that lane to take name of Sheremonyars, such as cut and rounded the plates to be coined or stamped into sterling pence ; for the place of coining was the Old Exchange, near unto the said Sheremoniars Lane.—*Stow*, p. 138.

Serpentine River, 50 acres of water, partly in *Hyde Park* and partly in *Kensington Gardens*, formed 1730-1733, by Caroline, Queen of George II., who threw several ponds into one, and carried a stream into it which had its rise near Westend, in the parish of Hampstead. This small tributary stream, for many years the Bayswater sewer, was cut off (except the storm water) from the Serpentine in 1834, and the loss of water was supplied from the Thames by the Chelsea Waterworks Company. After quitting the park at Albert Gate by a waterfall made in 1820, the Serpentine is now absorbed in the main drainage system of London.

The earliest reference to the Hyde Park ponds occurs perhaps in the Works Accounts for 1628-1629, when a payment is entered "for making a new sluice and mending other sluices at the Pond Heads in Hyde Park." In the evidence before the coroner, on the subject of the fatal duel between the Duke of Hamilton and Lord Mohun, in 1712, it is stated that the duke got out of his coach "on the road that goes to Kensington, over against Price's lodge, and walked over the grass and between the two ponds." Twenty years later the lodge 'was removed.

The old Lodge in Hyde Park, together with part of the grove, is to be taken down in order to compleat the Serpentine River.—*The Daily Post*, April 20, 1733.

The stone bridge separating Kensington Gardens from Hyde Park was built by J. and G. Rennie in 1826, of Bramley Fall stone, at a cost of £45,469, besides £3100 for the approaches. On the north side is the neat semi-classic edifice erected in 1834 and enlarged in 1837 by John B. Bunning, architect, as the receiving-house of the *Royal Humane Society.* Near it the Boat-house, where boats are let for hire. The Serpentine is the most resorted to of all the London waters for bathing and skating. It is estimated that nearly 1,000,000 persons bathe in the Serpentine during the year. Many lives are endangered of both bathers and skaters, but, thanks to the vigilance and skill of the Humane Society's officers, very few lives are lost. When young Benjamin West arrived in England he was told that he could get excellent skating on "the Serpentine River in Hyde Park" or the Basin in Kensington Gardens. Skating in those days was much better understood in New than in Old England, and the performance of the handsome young American made a great sensation. He was recognised by General Howe, who had known him at Philadelphia, and requested by him to show the bystanders what was called in Pennsylvania "The Salute." "Out of this trivial incident an acquaintance arose between him and the young noblemen present," and, as he told Galt, "he perhaps received more encouragement as a portrait-painter on account of his accomplishment as a skater than he could have hoped by any ordinary means to obtain."[1] Franklin won equal admiration by his skating on the Serpentine. The carriage drive along the north bank is called *The Ladies' Mile*.

Seven Dials, an open area in the parish of St. Giles-in-the-Fields, on what was once "Cock and Pye Fields," from which seven streets— Great Earl Street, Little Earl Street, Great White Lion Street, Little White Lion Street, Great St. Andrew's Street, Little St. Andrew's Street, Queen Street—radiate, and so called because there was formerly a column in the centre, on the summit of which were (as was always said) seven sun-dials, with a dial facing each of the streets.

October 5, 1694.—I went to see the building beginning neere St. Giles's, where 7 streets make a star from a Doric pillar placed in the middle of a circular area; said to be built by Mr. Neale, introducer of the late Lotteries in imitation of those at Venice.—*Evelyn*.

> Where fam'd St. Giles's ancient limits spread,
> An inrail'd column rears its lofty head;
> Here to seven streets seven dials count the day,
> And from each other catch the circling ray:
> Here oft the peasant with inquiring face,
> Bewilder'd trudges on from place to place;
> He dwells on every sign with stupid gaze,
> Enters the narrow alley's doubtful maze;
> Tries every winding court and street in vain,
> And doubles o'er his weary steps again.—Gay's *Trivia*.

The column on which the seven dials stood was removed in July 1773, on the supposition that a considerable sum of money was lodged at the base. But the search was ineffectual, and the pillar was removed to Sayes Court, Addlestone, with a view to its erection in the park. This, however, was not done, and it lay there neglected until the death of Frederica, Duchess of York, in 1820, when the inhabitants of Weybridge, desiring to commemorate her thirty years' residence at Oatlands and her active benevolence to the poor of the neighbourhood, bethought them of the prostrate column, purchased it, placed a coronet instead of the dials on the summit, and a suitable inscription on the

---

[1] Galt's *Life of West*, vol. ii. p. 31.

base, and erected it, August 1822, on the green. The stone on which were the dials not being required was utilised as the horse-block at a neighbouring inn, but has been removed and now reposes on the edge of the green, opposite the column. The most curious thing is that, notwithstanding the concurrent testimony of all who described it during the eighty years it stood at Seven Dials, it is a hexagonal block, and has most distinctly only *six* faces—too much battered to make out what was on them, but which are said to have had the marks where the styles were fixed plainly discernible when the column was erected.[1]

The accounts are not so certain of the exact time and place of his [Martinus Scriblerus's] birth. As to the first he had the common frailty of old men to conceal his age; as to the second, I only remember to have heard him say, that he first saw the light in Saint Giles's parish. But in the investigation of this point, Fortune hath favoured our diligence. For one day as I was passing by the Seven Dials I overheard a dispute concerning the place of nativity of a great astrologer, which each man alleged to have been in his own street. The circumstances of the time and the description of the person, made me imagine it might be that universal genius whose life I am writing. I returned home, and having maturely considered their several arguments, which I found to be of equal weight, I quieted my curiosity with this natural conclusion, that he was born in some point common to all the seven streets: which must be that on which the Column is now erected. And it is with infinite pleasure that I since find my conjecture confirmed by the following passage in the codicil to Mr. Neale's will: "I appoint my executors to engrave the following inscription on the Column in the centre of the Seven Streets which I erected: 'LOC, NAT. INCLYT. PHILOS. MAR. SCR.'" But Mr. Neale's order was never performed, because the Executors durst not administer.—*Memoirs of Martinus Scriblerus*.

Seven Dials was long famous for its ballad-mongers and ballad-printers. The Churchwardens' Accounts of St. Giles's, between the years 1640 and 1657, exhibit the payment of small sums to "Tottenham Court Meg" and "Ballet-singing Cobler," and the sum of two shillings and sixpence "for a shroude for oulde Guy, the poet." The late Mr. Catnach, whose name is affixed to a large collection of ballads, lived in the Seven Dials.

Portraits that cost twenty, thirty, sixty guineas, and that proudly take possession of the drawing-room, give way in the next generation to those of the new married couples, descending into the parlour, where they are slightly mentioned as my father's and mother's pictures. When they become my grandfather and grandmother, they mount to the two pair of stairs; and then unless dispatched to the mansion-house in the country, or crowded into the housekeeper's room, they perish among the lumber of garrets, or flutter into rags before a broker's shop in the Seven Dials.—Walpole's *Anecdotes of Painting*, vol. iv. p. 22.

Here Taylor has laid the scene of his *Monsieur Tonson*.

Be gar there's Monsieur Tonson come again.

and

One night our hero, rambling with a friend,
Near famed St. Giles's chanced his course to bend,
Just by that spot the *Seven Dials* hight:
'Twas silence all around, and clear the coast,
The watch as usual dozing on his post,
And scarce a lamp displayed a twinkling light.

---

[1] Thorne, *Handbook to the Environs*, p. 692.

Dickens, in one of his earliest sketches, doubts whether any Frenchman ever lived in the Seven Dials, and then goes on to describe the neighbourhood :—

> The stranger who finds himself in the Dials for the first time, and stands, Belzoni like, at the entrance of seven obscure passages, uncertain which to take, will see enough around him to keep his curiosity and attention awake for no inconsiderable time. From the irregular square into which he has plunged, the streets and courts dart in all directions, until they are lost in the unwholesome vapour which hangs over the house-tops, and renders the dirty perspective uncertain and confined ; and lounging at every corner, as if they came there to take a few gasps of such fresh air as has found its way so far, but is too much exhausted already to be enabled to force itself into the narrow alleys around, are groups of people, whose appearance and dwellings would fill any mind but a regular Londoner's with astonishment. . . . In addition to the numerous groups who are idling about the ginshops, and squabbling in the centre of the road, every post in the open space has its occupant who leans against it for hours with listless perseverance.—*Sketches by Boz*, 1836.

Of late years the Seven Dials has been greatly improved. Much of the district, however, has been cleared away to make room for Charing Cross Road and Shaftesbury Avenue.

Seymour Street (West), PORTMAN SQUARE to CONNAUGHT SQUARE, was so called from the noble family of the Seymours, Dukes of Somerset, connected by marriage with the Portman family, the ground landlords of the Seymour Street property. *Eminent Inhabitants.*— General Paoli.[1] In the drawing-room of No. 45, the residence of Lady Floyd, Sir Robert Peel was married, in 1820, to Julia, her step-daughter, and daughter of the late General Sir John Floyd, Bart. Campbell, author of *The Pleasures of Hope*, at No. 10. He came to live here in 1823.

> *September* 5, 1823.—Every article of the drawing room is now purchased : the most amiable curtains—the sweetest of carpets—the most accomplished chairs—and a highly interesting set of tongs and fenders ! I hope to have the pleasure of showing you through the magnificent suite of chambers—the front one of which is actually 16 feet long !—*Campbell to Mr. Gray.*

Some of Campbell's saddest days were spent in this house ; for here his only son became a hopeless lunatic, and here (May 9, 1828) his wife sank into the grave.

Shades, UPPER THAMES STREET and OLD SWAN STAIRS, LONDON BRIDGE, a tavern of great civic celebrity for the purity and flavour of its wines. The coffee-room was a dark, low room built out from the Old Fishmongers' Hall, and divided into compartments, overlooking the river. The wine was drawn from the butt into silver tankards, the Shades being said to be the last of the old taverns that retained that custom.

Shadwell, on the left bank of the Thames, between Wapping and Limehouse, formerly a hamlet of Stepney, but created a distinct parish

---

[1] See a letter from Boswell to Lord Thurlow, dated from "General Paoli's, Upper Seymour Street, Portman Square, June 24, 1784."—Croker's *Boswell*, p. 773.

in 1670. [*See* St. Paul's, Shadwell.] London Docks are partly within this parish. The occupations are chiefly maritime. The population, 11,702 in 1851, had decreased to 10,395 in 1881, owing mainly to the demolition of small houses for the London Docks' extensions.

Shaftesbury Avenue, a new road leading from Piccadilly to New Oxford Street, which was completed and opened to the public in June 1886. The line of route cuts through Seven Dials and includes the old Dudley Street, King Street, and Richmond Street. At the point where Shaftesbury Avenue intersects Charing Cross Road has been built Cambridge Circus (named after the Duke of Cambridge, who opened Charing Cross Road in January 1887). The opening up of these poor neighbourhoods has constituted one of the greatest improvements in Western London during the second half of the present century, and the need of these thoroughfares is shown by the use made of them as new routes for omnibuses, etc. There are three theatres in Shaftesbury Avenue, viz. the Lyric (near the Piccadilly Circus end of the Road), built from the designs of C. J. Phipps, architect; the Shaftesbury (near Cambridge Circus), which is isolated on four sides, also built from the designs of Mr. Phipps; and a theatre built for Mr. D'Oyley Carte, which is not yet (1890) named. This building is also isolated on four sides, and fronts Cambridge Circus, Shaftesbury Avenue, Greek Street and Church Street. It is built from the designs of T. E. Collcutt, architect.

Shaftesbury House, ALDERSGATE STREET. [*See* Aldersgate Street.]

Shakespeare Gallery. [*See* British Institution.]

Shanley's, a Coffee-house in COVENT GARDEN.

The two theatres, and all the public Coffee-houses I shall constantly frequent, but principally the Coffee-house under my lodge, Button's, and the play-house in Covent Garden: but as I set up for the judge of pleasures, I think it necessary to assign particular places of resort to my young gentlemen as they come to town, who cannot expect to pop in at Button's on the first day of their arrival in town. I recommend it, therefore, to young men to frequent SHANLEY'S some days before they take upon them to appear at Button's.—Steele's *Lover*, No. 5, March 6, 1714 (and see No. 2].

Shaver's Hall, the cant and common name for the celebrated gaming-house, erected in the reign of Charles I. by a gentleman-barber, servant to Philip Herbert, Earl of Pembroke and Montgomery. It faced Piccadilly Hall, and occupied the whole south side of the present Coventry Street, between the Haymarket and Hedge Lane.

Since Spring Gardens was put down, we have, by a servant of the Lord Chamberlain's, a new Spring Gardens, erected in the fielde beyond the Mews, where is built a fair house and two bowling greens, made to entertain gamesters and bowlers at an excessive rate, for I believe it hath cost him above four thousand pounds, a dear undertaking for a gentleman barber. My Lord Chamberlain [Pembroke] much frequents this place, where they bowl great matches.—*Garrard to Lord Strafford*, June 24, 1635.

All that Tenem^t called Shaver's Hall, strongly built wth Brick, and covered with lead, consistinge of one Large Seller, commodiously devided into 6 Roomes, and over the same fower fair Roomes, 10 stepps in ascent from ye ground, at 3 seurall wayes to the goeinge into the said house, all very well paved wth Purbeck stone well fitted and joynted, and above stayres in the first story 4 spacious Roomes; also out of one of the said Roomes one faire Belcony, opening wth a pleasant prospect southwards to the Bowling Alleyes, and in the second story 6 Roomes, and over the same a fair walk leaded and inclosed wth Rayles, very curiously carved and wrought; alsoe one very fayr Mayr Case, very strong and curiously wrought, leadinge from the bottome of the said house, very conveniently and pleasantly upp into all the said Roomes, and upp to one Leaded walk at the topp of the said house; as alsoe adioyninge to a Wall on the west part thereof, one shedd devided into 6 Roomes, and adioyninge to the North part, one Rainge consisting of 3 Large Roomes, used for Kitchens, and one other room, used for a coale house, and over the Kitchens 2 Lofts, devided into faire chambers; as alsoe one faire Tennis Court, very strongly built wth Brick and covered with Tyle, well accommodated with all things fitting for the same; as alsoe one Tenement thereunto adioyninge, consisting of 3 Roomes below stayres, and 3 Roomes above stayres; alsoe at the gate, or comeing in to the upper Bowlinge Alley, one Parlour Lodge, consisting of one faire Roome at each side of the gate; as alsoe one faire pair of stayres wth 12 stepps of Descent leading down into the Lower Bowlinge Alley 2 wayes, and meeting at the bottom in a faire Roome under the Highway or footpath, leading between the 2 bowlinge Alleys, between two brick walls east and west, and the Lower ground, one fair bowling Alley and one Orchard wall, planted wth seurall choyce of fruite trees; as also one pleasant banquetting house and one other faire and pleasant Roome, called the greene Roome, and one other Conduit house and 2 other Turretts adioyninge to the walls, consisting of 2 Roomes in each of them, one above the other. The ground whereon the said buildings stand, together wth 2 fayre Bowlinge Alleyes, orchard gardens, gravily walks, and other green walks and Courts and Courtyards, containinge, by estimacon, 3 acres and ¼, lyeing betweene a Road way leading from Charinge Crosse to Knightsbridge west, and a high way leadinge from Charinge crosse towards So-Hoe, abutting on the Earl of Suffolk's brick wall south, and a way leading from St. Gyles to Knightsbridge west, now in the occupacon of Captayne Geeres, and is worth per ann. cl^{li}.—*A Survey [made in 1650] of Certain Lands and Tenements, scituate and being at Pickadilley, the Blue Muse and others thereunto adioyninge (No. 73 of the Augmentation Records).*

[*See* Piccadilly.]

Shepherd's Market, MAY FAIR (south of Curzon Street), was formed about 1735, and was so called after "Edward Shepherd, Esq., an architect, owner of Shepherd's Market and many other buildings about May Fair," who died September 24, 1747.[1]

Shepherdess Walk, CITY ROAD to PACKINGTON STREET, ISLINGTON, formerly SHEPHERD and SHEPHERDESS WALK. The walk led across the Shepherd and Shepherdess Fields and Hoxton Fields, appropriated as grounds for the archery practice of the Royal Artillery Company. On the east of the walk was the old manor-house of Wenlocksbarn, known in the early part of the present century as Wenlock Farm; Wenlock Street marks the site. At the south-east corner of the walk, by the City Road, stood the Shepherd and Shepherdess Tavern and Tea-gardens, long a popular place of resort—

> To the Shepherd and Shepherdess then they go,
> To tea with their wives for a constant rule.

---

[1] *Gent. Mag.*, October 1747, vol. xvii. p. 496.

The site was afterwards occupied by the Eagle Tavern and Grecian Theatre. At the opposite corner is St. Luke's Workhouse, rebuilt on a larger scale in 1871 for the Holborn Union. The fields on either side of the walk (now a broad street) have been built over, and a district church, Holy Trinity, erected in the walk itself. Here are Lumley's Almshouses, erected in 1672 in Pest House Field by the Viscountess Lumley for six poor women of the parishes of Aldgate and Bishopsgate.

Sherborne Lane, CITY — King William Street to Abchurch Lane. Here is the City Carlton Club.

Langborne Ward, so called of a long bourne of sweet water, which of old time breaking out into Fenchurch Street, ran down the same street and Lombard Street, to the west end of St. Mary Woolnoth's church, where turning south and breaking into small shares, rills, or streams, it left the name of Share-borne Lane or Southborne Lane (as I have read) because it ran south to the river of Thames.—*Stow*, p. 75.

Scire-burne (*scir*, a share; *scrir-an*, to divide) is the more likely etymology.

All those that will send letters to the most parts of the habitable world, or to any parts of our King of Great Britaine's Dominions, let them repaire to the Generall Post-Master Thomas Withering at his house in Sherburne Lane, neere Abchurch.—*The Carrier's Cosmographie*, by John Taylor, the Water Poet, 4to, 1637.

Sherrard Street, GOLDEN SQUARE. [*See* Sherwood Street.]

Sherwood Street, GOLDEN SQUARE, from Brewer Street to Glasshouse Street. Built circ. 1679,[1] and so called after "Esquire Sherwood," who lived in Brewer Street in 1680. In the last century it was commonly called *Sherrard* Street. Many of Walpole's early letters to George Montagu are addressed to Sherrard Street.

After Mr. Dryden's decease, the Lady Elizabeth, his widow, took a lesser house in *Sherrard Street*, Golden Square, and had wherewithal to live frugally genteel, and keep two servants to the day of her death.—*Mrs. Thomas* (Wilson's *Memoirs of Congreve*, 8vo, 1730, pt. 2, p. 9).

Ship, at CHARING CROSS, a long established tavern and coach office over against Scotland Yard. Part of it, with property in Spring Gardens, 3250 feet, was sold June 1874 for £30,000 to Messrs. Drummond for their new banking premises.

Ship Court, OLD BAILEY, west side, near Ludgate Hill; now absorbed in the Railway Companies' and carriers' yards and stables. Richard Hogarth kept a school in this Court, and here most probably his son William, the celebrated painter, was born.

Ship Yard, in the STRAND, without TEMPLE BAR. It led past the Ship Tavern into Little Shire Lane. It was particularised as "Without Temple Bar," to distinguish it from another tavern of the same sign within the Bar. In the London *Gazette* of September 8, 1666, the first issued after the Great Fire is the following:—

[1] Rate-books of St. Martin's-in-the-Fields.

Mr. Thomas Nevil, Comptroller of the Petty Customs in the Port of London, who formerly dwelt at the Crown in St. Paul's Churchyard, is now removed to the Ship, between Temple Bar and Chancery Lane End, over against the hither Temple Gate.

In 1571 an Inn near Temple Bar called the Ship, lands in Yorkshire and Dorsetshire, and the Wardship of a minor, were granted to him [Sir Christopher Hatton].—*Life and Times of Sir Christopher Hatton*, by Nicolas, p. 7.

Faithorne now set up in a new shop, at the sign of the Ship next to the Drake, opposite to the Palsgrave's Head Tavern, without Temple Bar, where he not only followed his art, but sold Italian, Dutch, and English prints, and worked for booksellers.—*Walpole*, ed. Dallaway, vol. v. p. 132.

A tavern token exists of "The Ship without Temple Bar," with the date upon it of 1649. In Wilkinson's *Londina Illustrata* is a "south-west view of an ancient structure in Ship Yard, Temple Bar, supposed to have been the residence of Elias Ashmole, the celebrated antiquary." Ashmole's house was in *Shire Lane*.

Shipwrights' Company, the fifty-ninth in order of the City guilds, was a fraternity by ancient prescription, and was granted ordinances for its government from the Court of Mayor and Aldermen in 1456, and a Patent of Incorporation from James I. in 1605. The Company has a livery but no hall. The hall it once possessed was at Ratcliff Cross.

Shire Lane (vulgarly SHEER LANE), TEMPLE BAR. In James I.'s time, as appears from a list of houses, taverns, etc., in Fleet Street and the Strand, it was known by the name of Shire Lane, *alias* Rogue Lane.[1] Despite the name it had respectable inhabitants. In it lived Sir John Sedley, and here his son Sir Charles Sedley, the dramatic poet, was born. "Neere the Globe in Sheer Lane"[2] lived Elias Ashmole, the antiquary; here Antony à Wood records his having dined with him;[3] and here Seth Ward, Bishop of Salisbury, sought him out in February 1677 to apprise him that Garter King-at-Arms was dead. At the upper end of Shire Lane Steele placed the residence of Isaac Bickerstaff, who dates many of his *Tatlers* from it. The Tatler Club met at the Trumpet[4] in Shire Lane; and from it he led his company of Twaddlers on their immortal march. In Shire Lane is said to have originated the famous Kit-Cat Club, commemorated on Kneller's most famous canvases. [*See* Kit-Cat Club.] But whatever Shire Lane may have been in its prime, in its later days it became utterly abominable. So disreputable a place had it become that at one time a man was employed to stand at the end of it, with a lanthorn lighted in broad day, warning passengers not to enter it. In July 1845, in the hope that by another name it would lose some of its evil fragrance, the name was changed to LOWER SERLE'S PLACE, as the *Tempest* for a like reason had altered its sign to the Duke of York. Under the supervision of the New Police there was some improvement, but it remained a disreputable place. Happily the last vestige of it was cleared away for the New Law Courts.

[1] Harleian MS., 6850.
[2] *Lives of Leland, Hearne, and Wood*, vol. ii. p. 234.
[3] *Hamper*, p. 393.
[4] *Tatler*, No. 132.

Then hard by the Bar is another lane called Shire Lane, because it divideth the City from the Shire.—*Stow*, p. 139.

Shear Lane cometh out of Little Lincoln's Inn Fields, and falleth into Fleet Street by Temple Bar: the upper part hath good old buildings, well inhabited; but the lower part is very narrow and more ordinary.—*Strype*, B. iv. p. 72.

Even then at the same time he sounds another *trumpet* than that in Sheer Lane, to horse and hem in his auditory.—Andrew Marvell.

In this order we marched down *Sheer Lane*, at the upper end of which I lodge. When we came to Temple Bar, Sir Harry and Sir Giles got over; but a run of the coaches kept the rest of us on this side the street: However we all at last landed and drew up in very good order before Ben Tooke's shop, who favoured our rallying with great humanity.—*Tatler*, No. 86, October 25-27, 1709.

> And oft repuls'd, as oft attack the great
> With painful art, and application warm,
> And take at last some little place by storm;
> Enough to keep two shoes on Sunday clean,
> And starve upon discreetly, in *Sheer Lane*.—Young, Sat. iii.

In the dwelling and spunging-house of a sheriff's officer of the name of Hemp in this lane, Theodore Hook, while under arrest for a defalcation in his accounts as Treasurer of the Mauritius, made the acquaintance of Dr. William Maginn.[1] The time passed "pleasantly," he said, and there was "an agreeable prospect, *barring* the windows."

Shoe Lane, FLEET STREET, runs due north from Fleet Street into Holborn, by St. Andrew's Church. The earliest mention of Shoe Lane in the City records is in 4 Edward II. (1310), when a writ is sent from the King on the 8th of July commanding that "you cause to come before us, or the person holding our place, at the church of St. Brigit without Ludgate, on the Saturday next after the Feast of the Translation of St. Thomas the Martyr, eighteen good and lawful men of the venue of *Scolane* in the ward without Ludgate; to make inquisition on oath as to a certain tenement with its appurtenances in *Scholane*, which the Abbot of Rievaulx is said to have appropriated without leave of our Lord the King," etc.[2] This writ was not in accordance with custom and was evaded by the City authorities. A similar one was sent on the 10th of October, but the result is not recorded. The next notice is in the 19th of Edward III. (1345), when Thomas de Donyngtone is condemned to be hanged for stealing one furred surcoat and two double hoods, value 4s., and two linen sheets, value 40d., in *Sholane near* Holbourne. The name again occurs in the 21st of Edward III. (1347), when John Tournour of *Sholane* is ordered not to make his wine-measures for the future "of any wood but dried," and to stamp his name, or his mark, on the bottom of them.

In this Shoe Lane, on the left hand [the east side] is one old house called Oldborne Hall; it is now letten out into tenements.—*Stow*, p. 145.[3]

1610.—Thomas Penkithman of Warrington, Co. Lancaster, has expended money in building houses in Shoe Lane, on the ground of the Earl of Derby. They have

---

[1] *Quarterly Review*, No. 143, p. 86.
[2] Riley, *Memorials*, p. 75.
[3] See a view of the exterior (circ. 1800) in Wilkinson's *Londina Illustrata*. The same work contains a chimney-piece and ceiling in the old hall, the latter with the date 1617.

been taken possession of by one Shute under pretence, etc.—*Cal. State Pap.*, 1611-1618, p. 132.

In the 17th century there was a noted cock-pit in Shoe Lane. It was sometimes visited by persons we should not have expected to meet there. Writing to his nephew from "St. Martin's Lane by the Fields," June 3, 1633, Sir Henry Wotton says: "This other day at the Cock-pit in Shoe Lane (where myself am *rara avis*) your Nephew, Mr. Robert Bacon came very kindly to me, with whom I was glad to refresh my acquaintance, though I had rather it had been in the theatre of Redgrave."[1] Thirty years later the company was less refined.

December 21, 1663.—To Shoe Lane to see a cocke-fighting at a new pit there, a spot I was never at in my life: but Lord! to see the strange variety of people, from Parliament man by name Wildes that was Deputy Governor of the tower when Robinson was Lord Mayor, to the poorest 'prentices, bakers, brewers, butchers, draymen, and what not; and all these fellows one with another cursing and betting. I soon had enough of it.—*Pepys*.[2]

About this time Shoe Lane appears to have been the centre for the designers of the rude woodcuts which figured at the heads of ballads and broad-sheets.

A ballad-monger is the ignominious nickname of a penurious poet, of whom he partakes in nothing but in poverty. . . . For want of truer relations, for a need, he can find you out a Sussex dragon, some sea or inland monster, drawn out by some *Shoe Lane man*, in a Gorgon-like feature, to enforce more horror in the beholder.—*Whimsies: or a New Cast of Characters*, 1631.

The sign-painters, a busy race when every shop in London had its painted sign, also congregated here, and Harp Alley, Shoe Lane, was the great mart for ready-made and second-hand signs.[3] Thackeray, in his Lecture on Steele, repeats a story "as exceedingly characteristic" of the men and times, narrated by Dr. John Hoadley, of his father, when Bishop of Bangor, being present by invitation "at one of the Whig meetings held at the Trumpet in Shoe Lane, when Sir Richard [Steele] in his zeal rather exposed himself, having the double duty of the day upon him, as well to celebrate the immortal memory of King William, it being the 4th of November, as to drink his friend Addison up to conversation pitch." But the meeting, if not fabulous, must be transferred to the Trumpet in *Shire Lane*, where the Tatler's Club met. [*See* Shire Lane.] George Colman makes Dr. Pangloss say—

I'm dead to the fascinations of beauty: since that unguarded day of dalliance, when being full of Bacchus,—*Bacchi plenus*—*Horace*—Hem! my pocket was picked of a metal watch at the sign of the Sceptre in Shoe Lane.—*Heir at Law*, Act iv. Sc. 3.

At the back of Walkden's ink manufactory an extensive range of vaulted cellars still remain. They belonged apparently to some large house which stood upon the spot.

Eminent Inhabitants.—John Decreetz (or De Critz), serjeant painter to James I. and Charles I. "Resolute" John Florio, author of the well-known Dictionary which bears his name. His house in Shoe Lane is

---

[1] *Reliq. Wottonianæ*, p. 463.   [2] See also *Anecdotes and Traditions*, by Thoms, p. 47.
[3] Edwards, *Anecdotes of Painting*, p. 138.

mentioned in his will. In 1676 Praise-God Barebones was paying £25 a year for a house in Shoe Lane. He states himself to be eighty years of age, and to have resided twenty-five years in the parish of St. Dunstan in the West.[1] In an obscure lodging, near Shoe Lane, died, in 1749, Samuel Boyce, the poet. When almost perishing with hunger he is said to have been unable to eat some roast beef that was brought for him because there was no ketchup. Oliver Goldsmith mentions Shoe Lane as though he had himself lived in it :—" Nor will I forget the beauties of Shoe Lane in which I myself have resided since my arrival."[2]

Observe.—No. 3, the Ben Jonson Tavern, with the poet's head for a sign. Nos. 103-105, the *Standard* newspaper printing and publishing office, a large and massive new building. On the site of Farringdon Market, on the east side of Shoe Lane, in what was once the burying-ground of Shoe Lane workhouse (added during Hacket's ministry, and by Hacket's interest), Thomas Chatterton was buried. The northern half of Shoe Lane has been greatly changed in appearance by the construction of the Holborn Viaduct and its approaches, and Farringdon Market, or what remains of it, is destined to be cleared away as soon as the new City Fruit and Vegetable Market is completed. [*See* Bangor Court ; Farringdon Market ; Gunpowder Alley ; Harp Lane.]

Shoemakers' Row, WEST SMITHFIELD.

> Then at Smithfield Bars, 'twixt the ground and the stars,
> There's a place they call Shoemaker Row,
> Whereat you may buy shoes every day
> Or go barefoot all the year thro'.
> Tom D'Urfey, *Ancient Song for Bartholomew Fair.*

Probably this was a cant name for a row of stalls where shoes were on sale during Bartholomew Fair. The only Shoemakers' Rows we find extant in D'Urfey's day were between Great Carter Lane and Blackfriars, in Aldgate, and by Deadman's Place, Bankside, Southwark. Sir Christopher Wren is said to have rented a house in *Shoemakers' Row, Carter Lane,* during the building of St. Paul's, for convenience in watching the progress of the works.

Shoreditch, a manor and populous parish, at the north-east end of London, between Norton Folgate, Hoxton, and Hackney. The old way of spelling the name is Soersditch, but the derivation is uncertain. That it was so called after Jane Shore, the mistress of Edward IV., is a vulgar error, perpetuated by Haywood's "King Edward IV." and a ballad in Percy's *Reliques :—*

> Thus weary of my life, at lengthe
> I yielded up my vital strength
> Within a ditch of loathsome scent,
> Where carrion dogs did much frequent :
> The which now since my dying daye,
> Is Shoreditch call'd, as writers saye ;
> Which is a witnesse of my sinne,
> For being concubine to a King.—Percy's *Reliques,* vol. ii. Book 2.

---

[1] *Notes and Queries,* 3d S., vol. i. p. 253. [2] *Citizen of the World,* Letter 122.

> *Richard.* But, Catesby, say, where died Shore and his wife?
> *Catesby.* Where Ayre was hanged for giving her relief,
> There both of them round circling his cold grave,
> And arm in arm, departed from this life.
> The people, from the love they bear to her
> And her kind husband, pitying his wrongs,
> For ever after mean to call the ditch
> Shore's Ditch, as in the memory of them.
> Haywood's *King Edward IV.*, 2d part, p. 192 (*Shak. Soc.*)

The popular notion had early taken material form in the Jane Shore Inn, of which there are 17th-century tokens extant. The inn still exists—No. 103 Shoreditch High Street.

Soersditch, so called more than four hundred years since, as I can prove by record.—*Stow*, p. 158.

The Manour of Soersditch with the Polehowse and Bowes (so expressed in the Record), lately belonging to John de Northampton of London, Draper, was granted 15 Richard II. to Edmund Duke of York, and Earl of Cambridge, and Edward Earl of Roteland [Rutland], son of the same Edmund and Isabel.—*Strype*, B. iv. p. 50.

I read of the King's Manour, called, Shoresditch Place, in the parish of Hackney. But how it took that name I know not. This house is now called Shore Place. The vulgar tradition goes that Jane Shore lived here; and here her royal lover used to visit her. But we have the credit of Mr. Stow that the true name was Shorditch Place, and 'tis not unlikely to have been the place of a Knight called Sir John de Sordich, a great man in Edward the Third his days, who was with that King in his wars in France, and is remembered in our Annals in 14 Edw. III. He was owner of lands in Hackney as well in demesne as in service: which he gave to Croston his chaplain. This Weever notes; who thinks Shorditch to be named from the said Knight.—*Strype*, B. iv. p. 53.

The mock title "Duke of Shoreditch" used to be bestowed on the most successful archer in the annual trials of skill. It was said to have been applied in the first instance by Henry VIII. In the "Poor Man's Petition" of 1603, one item is that the King should not make the "good Lord of Lincoln Duke of Shoreditch." The title appears to have been given from the circumstance that the fields at Shoreditch with those at Finsbury and Hoxton were the chief practising grounds of the London archers, and hence, whilst the Duke of Shoreditch was the premier archer, those of somewhat inferior fame were dubbed Marquis of Hogsden (Hoxton), Earl of Pancridge (St. Pancras), and the like. The archers who practised in the fields at Mile End called their chief bowman Prince Arthur, and others his knights.

And another time at a shooting match at Windsor, the King [Henry VIII.] was present; and the game being well nigh finished, and the upshot thought to be given, one Barlo, a citizen and inhabitant of Shoreditch, shot and won them all. Whereat the King greatly rejoiced, and told him he should be named The Duke of Shoreditch. On which account the Captain of the Company of Archers of London, for a long time after, was styled by that name.—*Strype*, B. i. p. 250.

In 1598 was published "A Martiall Conference pleasantly discussed between two Souldiers only practised in Finsbury Fields, in the modern Wars of the renowned Duke of Shoreditch and the mighty Prince Arthur. Newly translated out of Essex into English by Barnaby Rich, Gent. 1598."—*Collier*, vol. i. p. xxxvi.

In July 1553, when Dudley Duke of Northumberland set out with a goodly following to seize Queen Mary in the Eastern Counties—"As they went throughe

Shordyke, saieth the duke to one that rid by him, 'the people prece to se us, but not one sayeth God spede us.'"—*Queen Jane and Queen Mary* (Camden Soc.), p. 8.

Two of the witnesses in the inquiry into the mysterious death of Richard Hunn, who was found hanged in the Lollards' Tower, St. Paul's, where he was imprisoned on a charge of heresy, were "Robert Johnson and his wife dwelling at the Bell in Shoreditch." The back of the inn must at that time have opened upon the country, for it is deposed that one Charles Joseph leaped upon his horse in the inn yard and "prayed the host to let him out of his back gate, that he might ride out by the field side; which the host so did."[1] Lying on the main road to the Eastern Counties, the inns of Shoreditch, the nearest point to the City, were numerous and much frequented by travellers.

Monopoly. Gad's-so, dost hear? I'm to sup this night at the Lion in Shoreditch with certain gallants.—*Westward Ho*, Act ii. Sc. 3 (1607, 4to).

Newton dates a remarkable letter to Locke "At the Bull, in *Shoreditch*, London, September 16, 1693." Shoreditch was formerly notorious for the easy character of its women. To die in Shoreditch was not a mere metaphorical term for dying in a sewer.

"Call a leete at Bishopsgate, and examine how every second house in Shoreditch is mayntayned; make a privie search in Southwarke, and tell me how many shee inmates you finde." In another passage Nash couples "Shoreditch, the Spittle, Southwarke, Westminster, and Turnbull Street."—Nash's *Pierce Pennilesse*, 1592.

Well said, daughter: lift up your voices and sing like nightingales, you Tory-rory jades. Courage, I say; as long as the merry pence hold out, you shall none of you die in Shoreditch.—Dryden, *The Kind Keeper, or Mr. Limberham*, 4to, 1680.

Here, next door unto The Gun, lived Mrs. Millwood, who led George Barnwell astray.

> Good Barnwell, then quoth she,
> Do thou to Shoreditch come,
> And ask for Mrs. Millwood's house,
> Next door unto the Gun.—Percy's *Reliques*, vol. iii. Book 3.

When Chatterton first came to London, 1770, he lodged in the house of Walmsley, a plasterer, in Shoreditch, where his kinswoman, Mrs. Ballance, also lived. He remained here from May to July, when he removed to Brook Street, where in the following month came the unhappy end.

> Harwood, my townsman, who invented first
> *Porter* to rival wine, and quench the thirst,

was a brewer on the east side of High Street, Shoreditch, and his famous beverage was first *retailed* at the Blue Last at the corner of New Inn Yard in the neighbouring Curtain Road. New Inn Yard remains, but the Blue Last has departed. Shoreditch High Street has been much improved in appearance of late years by the widening of its northern end, the formation of Commercial Street, and the new street from Old Street, and especially by the extensive works in connection with the new Goods Station of the Great Eastern Railway. [*See* Hog Lane; Holywell Street; St. Leonard's, Shoreditch; Standard Theatre.]

[1] *Foss*, vol. iv. p. 193

Short's Gardens, DRURY LANE, to King Street, St. Giles's, said to have been so named from a "mansion built there by Dudley Short, Esq., an eminent parishioner in the reign of Charles II., with garden attached."[1] But another Mr. Short had built here much earlier.

July 7, 1618.—The Justices of Middlesex report to the Council that they have examined the state of the large building lately erected in Drury Lane, assigned by Wm Short of Gray's Inn to Edw. Smith, and find that it is erected on the foundations of the former tenements.—*Cal. State Pap.*, 1611-1618, p. 551, and comp. under July 18.

Here, in "a hole," as he calls it, Charles Mathews the elder made one of his first attempts as an actor.

Shrouds (The), the crypt at St. Paul's. [*See* St. Paul's Cathedral.] There is a sermon of Latimer's "preached in the Shrouds at St. Paul's Church, in London, January 18, 1548."

Shug Lane, PICCADILLY, afterwards Tichborne Street (which *see*).

Chatelain, the celebrated engraver, died [1770] of an indigestion after a hearty supper of lobsters: he then lodged at a carpenter's in a court near Shug Lane: going home after his supper of lobsters, he bought and eat a hundred of asparagus; he was buried by subscription.—Captain Grose, *Biographical Anecdotes*, p. 166.

Shunamite's House, WATLING STREET. The maintenance of the sermons at St. Paul's Cross, and the ensuring of suitable preachers, was from an early period a matter of much interest. Aylmer, Bishop of London, and other benefactors contributed liberally to a fund for the purpose, and the Lord Mayor and Court of Aldermen ordered that every minister who should preach at the Cross,—"considering the journies some of them might take from the Universities, or elsewhere, —should at his pleasure be freely entertained for five days' space, with sweet and convenient lodging, fire, candle, and all other necessaries: viz. from Thursday, before their day of preaching, to Thursday morning following."[2] The house provided for their lodging was called the Shunamite's House from the hospitable entertainment of Elisha by the Shunamite woman.[3] The character of the house is very well shown in the interesting story told by Izaak Walton in his *Life of Richard Hooker*, which the reader of that book cannot fail to remember, of Hooker's coming to town to preach at Paul's Cross, soon after he had taken his degree (1581); how he arrived "at the Shunamite's House in Watling Street" (then kept by John Churchman, sometime a draper of note); "wet and weary and weather-beaten;" how he took a cold, and how Mrs. Churchman cured him; how she persuaded him that he was a man of a tender constitution, and that it was best for him to have a wife, that might prove a nurse to him; how Mr. Hooker acceded to her opinion, and how Mrs. Churchman

---

[1] Dobie's *St. Giles*, 2d ed., p. 61.
[2] *Strype*, B. iii. p. 149.
[3] "And she [the Shunamite woman] said unto her husband, . . . Let us make a little chamber, I pray thee, on the wall; and let us set for him [Elisha] there a bed, and a table, and a stool, and a candlestick: and it shall be, when he cometh to us, that he shall turn in thither. And it fell on a day, that he came thither, and he turned into the chamber, and lay there."—2 Kings, iv. 9-11.]

recommended her daughter Joan; how Mr. Hooker married her, and had so little cause to rejoice in the wife he obtained on the occasion of his *Paul's Cross* sermon, that he might with the Psalmist liken his habitation to the tents of Kedar. The Paul's Cross Sermons were continued after the Cross was destroyed; but the Shunamite's House was abandoned. The date of its discontinuance is not stated, but Strype (1720) says, "This good custom continued, till of late times it hath been taken away, or disused."

Siam's, an India House in St. James's Street, kept by a Mrs. Siam, for the sale of teas, toys, shawls, Indian screens, cabinets, and other oriental goods. It is mentioned by several of our Queen Anne writers; but the name has long been removed, and the site of the house long since forgotten.

Lady Malapert. O law! what should I do in the country? There's no levees, no Mall, no plays, no tea at Siam's, no Hyde Park.—Southern, *The Maid's Last Prayer*, 4to, 1693.

Leonora. I will write to him to meet me within half an hour at Mrs. Siam's the India House, in St. James's Street.—Cibber, *Woman's Wit or the Lady in Fashion*, 4to, 1697.

Leonora [Scene, an India House]. Come, Mrs. Siam, what new Indian toys have you?—*Ibid.*

India, or as they were at first called China, houses monopolised the *shopping* of the fine ladies of London from early in the 17th to the middle of the 18th century. Ben Jonson more than once refers to them:—

> [She] is served
> Upon the knee!—And has her pages, ushers,
> Footmen, and coaches—her six mares—nay eight,
> To hurry her through London, to the Exchange,
> Bethlem, *the China-houses.*
>
> Ben Jonson, *The Alchemist*, 1610, Act iv. Sc. 2.

So in *The Silent Woman* (Act iv. Sc. 2) he makes Lady Haughty say: "And go with us to Bedlam, to the China-houses, and to the Exchange." Scandal imputed other motives to the monopoly than

> To cheapen tea or buy a screen.—PRIOR.

King William III. severely reprehended Queen Mary for being persuaded to go to one.[1] Cibber makes Lady Townley "take a flying jaunt to an India house," as one of the dashing gaieties of a fine lady's London life.

> There are no Indian-houses, to drop in
> And fancy stuffs, and chuse a pretty Screen,
> To while away an hour or so—"*I swear
> These cups are pretty, but they're deadly dear:*"
> And if some unexpected friend appear
> "The Devil!—Who could have thought to meet you here?"
> *Epilogue to Rowe's Ulysses*, 1706, 4to.

---

[1] Dalrymple's *Memoirs*, vol. ii. p. 79, Appendix.

> Straight then I'll dress, and take my wonted range
> Through India shops, to Motteux's, or the Change,
> Where the tall jar erects its stately pride,
> With antic shapes in China's azure dyed.
> There careless lies a rich brocade unroll'd,
> Here shines a cabinet with burnish'd gold.
> *Lady M. W. Montagu, The Toilet,* by Gay.

In reprinting this as a "Town Eclogue" Gay makes a few alterations, and adds a couplet which notices one of the chief temptations of these shops—the raffle—

> But then remembrance will my grief renew
> 'Twas there *the raffling dice* false Damon threw.

Sidney Alley, LEICESTER SQUARE, now Sidney Place, from the north-west corner of the square to Coventry Street, was so called from the Sidneys, Earls of Leicester. [*See* Leicester House.]

Sidney House, the first known London residence of the Sidney family was in the Old Bailey.

Silver Street, CHEAPSIDE, from Wood Street to Falcon Square.

Down lower in Wood Street is Silver Street (I think of silversmiths dwelling there), in which be divers fair houses.—*Stow,* p. 112.

Gossip Censure. A notable tough rascal, this old Pennyboy! right city-bred.
Gossip Mirth. In Silver Street, the region of money, a good seat for an usurer.—Ben Jonson, *The Staple of News.*

It must also have been famous for its wig-makers.

Otter. All her teeth were made in the Blackfriars; both her eyebrows in the Strand, and her hair in Silver Street.—Ben Jonson, *The Silent Woman,* Act iv. Sc. 1.

On the south side of Silver Street (No. 24) is the Parish Clerks' Hall [which *see*]. A large fire occurred here in 1884.

Silver Street, GOLDEN SQUARE, from Beak Street to Cambridge Street. Canaletto, the great landscape painter, was living here in 1752, when he issued the following advertisement:—

Signior Canaletto gives notice that he has painted Chelsea College, Ranelagh House, and the River Thames; which if any gentleman or others are pleased to favour him with seeing the same, he will attend at his lodgings at Mr. Viggan's in Silver Street, Golden Square, for fifteen days from this day, July 31, from 8 to 1, and from 3 to 6 at night each day.

Sion College, VICTORIA EMBANKMENT, E.C., near the north end of Blackfriars Bridge and next building on the west to the City of London School, was founded 1623 as a College and Almshouse pursuant to the will of Dr. Thomas White, who therein describes himself as "Minister of God's Word and Vicar of St. Dunstan in the West." This, however, was perhaps the least important of his preferments, as he held the prebend of Mora in the cathedral church of St. Paul's, and as he was also Treasurer of Salisbury, Canon of Ch. Ch. Oxford, and of Windsor. To the College and almshouse was added, by the munificence of Dr. John Simson, rector of St. Olave, Hart

Street, and one of the executors of Dr. White, a library. Letters patent incorporating the College were granted by Charles I., July 3, 1630. Other letters patent containing an exemplification of the former Charter of Incorporation of 1630, and in no way altering it, were granted by Charles II., June 20, 1664. The College consists of the incumbents of the City of London and its suburbs. By prescription the suburbs are taken to be the parishes which touched the City walls in any part of its circumference at the date of the foundation of the College, and parishes which, as time has gone on, have been carved out of the original suburban parishes. The Governing Body is elected annually on the third Tuesday after Easter Tuesday, and consists of a President, two Deans, and four Assistants. The objects for which the College was incorporated are thus set forth in Dr. White's will: "For the Glory of God the good of his Church and redress of many inconveniences not prejudicial to the Lord Bp. of London's jurisdiction whom I would have visitor he and his Successors for ever, but to maintain truth in Doctrine, love in conversing together, and to repress such sins as follow us as men; that they might be admonished and ordered there rather to make them amend or else the College to send them and their cause to the Bishop to be punished accordingly."

The almshouse was to shelter ten poor men and ten poor women; of these eight were to be of the Merchant Taylors' Company, six from the parish of St. Dunstan in the West, four from the City of Bristol, and two from the parish of St. Gregory by St. Paul's. Besides their rooms the almsfolk were to receive a small pension.

The Library, coeval with the College, though no part of the original foundation, has from the first been the chief glory of the College. The late Lord Campbell, when summing up in a case in which the President and Court had to defend their dismissal of an unsatisfactory employé thus spoke of it: "The Corporation of Sion College is one of the most venerable institutions of the country, the library being very splendid and one that has been of very great service both to literature and to science. It is most excellent, and I think the public are indebted to the Governors of Sion College in seeing that the public have the full benefit of that noble library."

From the first the Library, though belonging to the President and Fellows of the College, has always been considered to have a public character. The times during which it is open are 10 A.M. to 4 P.M. on every week day except Saturday, when it closes at 2 P.M. During these hours students are freely admitted to consult such works as they may desire to see, though, if it seems to the Librarian desirable, he may require the production of a recommendation from a beneficed clergyman. Upon payment of half a guinea per annum the Fellows and all licensed curates in the metropolis acquire the privilege of borrowing books from the Library, and of using the Common Room, which is well supplied with all the leading periodicals, with newspapers and with writing materials. To obtain the same privileges incumbents not being Fellows are required to pay an annual guinea. Up to the date of the first Copyright Act the Library depended for its supply of books upon voluntary contributions in money and in kind, and a small entrance fee paid by the Fellows. These contributions were very liberal, and resulted in the formation of the nucleus of a library of exceptional interest. To mention a few of the principal benefactors—Elizabeth, Viscountess Camden, gave £200, and there were various contributions of £100 and of £50 each. Nathaniel Torporley, Walter Travers, Simeon Ashe, George, Earl of Berkeley, John Lawson, Eleanor, relict of the celebrated printer, Thomas James, gave whole libraries to the college. Mrs. James as many as 3000 volumes, Earl Berkeley 1676 volumes, many of them very choice. The Rev. E. Waple close upon 1900 volumes, besides duplicates, which sold for £155. In 1679 King Charles II. presented a Jesuit library seized at Holbeck in the West Riding; few, however, of these volumes reached the College, and these in a very sorry condition, the greater part were made away with by pursuivants, etc. A new source of supply was opened up in the reign of Queen Anne, as Sion College Library was one of those named in the first Copyright Act, and so became entitled to a copy of every work entered at Stationers' Hall until 1836, when under 6 and 7 William IV., c. 110, this privilege was taken away and a money compensation voted to replace it. At present the sum annually spent in the purchase of additions to the library is £370. The new buildings of the College upon the Victoria Embankment were formally opened by H.R.H. the Prince and Princess of Wales on December 15, 1886. Previous to this the College had occupied premises situated in London Wall between Aldermanbury on the east and Philip Lane on the west, the former site of Elsing Spital. The old library was built along the east side of Philip Lane; it was 125 feet in length, 25 feet in width. The hall, a building of no architectural interest, stood back in the College garden. The only feature in the old buildings of any artistic merit was the gateway.

In the short period which elapsed between the opening in 1630 of the original buildings of the College (of which those just spoken of were apparently a tolerably faithful reproduction) and the Great Fire of London, there were several sets of chambers for students in the College gardens. In one of these sets lived Thomas Fuller whilst collecting materials for his Church History. This book is dated from Sion College. Up to the year 1845 the rooms occupied by the almsfolk were under the Library, to which they were a constant source of danger from fire. In 1845 a new almshouse was built in another part of the College property, some of the rooms looking into Philip Lane.

With the view, however, of removing the College and its valuable Library to a more accessible site, an Act of Parliament was obtained in 1884, which sanctioned the assignment to the almsfolk of a definite portion of the property in place of a somewhat vague claim to a small proportionate share of the whole. The Act also sanctioned the abolition of the almshouse, the almsfolk to receive premiums of much larger amount than those payable to them before. The arrangement thus sanctioned has worked so well that there are now forty instead of twenty pensioners, with pensions of from £30 to £40 a year instead of £17. At the same time a new Governing Body was provided for what had now become Sion Hospital. This set the President and Court of Governors free to purchase the present freehold side of the College, which they acquired from the City for £31,625, and to erect the new building thereon from the designs of Mr. (now Sir) Arthur Blomfield at a cost of £26,000, the money for the purpose being raised by the sale of a large part of the freehold of the old site. In the new buildings the library is well housed and the other business of the College is carried on as it was carried on heretofore in London Wall.

Sion Hill. [*See* College Hill.]

Sise Lane, CITY, from Bridge Row to Queen Victoria Street, a corruption of St. Syth's Lane or St. Osyth's Lane; from the church of *St. Bennet Sherehog* or *Syth*, destroyed in the Great Fire, and not rebuilt. A large part of the northern end of Sise Lane was swept away in constructing Queen Victoria Street.

Skinner Street, HOLBORN, was formed in 1802, and received its name from Alderman Skinner, through whose exertions it was built. The old highway between Newgate Street and Holborn Bridge, before Skinner Street was made, was Snow Hill, a circuitous, very narrow, very steep, and very dangerous roadway. William Godwin, author of *Caleb Williams*, kept a bookseller's shop for several years in this street in the name of his wife. Charles Lamb's *Tales from Shakespeare*, and Mary Lamb's *Mrs. Leicester's School* were published by "M. J. Godwin, at the Juvenile Library, 41 Skinner Street."

Popular Works for the Amusement and Instruction of Young Persons Published by M. J. Godwin & Co., French and English City Juvenile and School Library, No. 41 Skinner Street, Snow Hill (a Corner House).—*Advertisement at the end of Lamb's Adventures of Ulysses, 1819.*

The house was on the north side, at the angle of Snow Hill, and nearly opposite Turnagain Lane. It was swept away for the London, Chatham and Dover Railway; and what remained of Skinner Street was cleared away in 1867 for the Holborn Viaduct.

Skinners' Hall, DOWGATE HILL. The hall of the Skinners' Company, the sixth on the list of the Twelve Great Companies of London. The Company was incorporated in 1327, and the government vested in a master, four wardens, and a court of assistants. The hall, mentioned as early as the reign of Henry III., was destroyed in the Great Fire, and rebuilt shortly after at a cost of over £1800. The East India Company held their meetings for a time in this hall, for which they paid a yearly rent of £300. The present front, Ionic in character, with the Skinners' arms in the pediment, was added by Richard Jupp, the Company's architect, in 1790. The dining-hall was rebuilt 1847-1850 under the direction of G. B. Moore. The drawing-room is lined with cedar wood, traditionally said to have been given by the East India Company to the Skinners Company. A few years since (under the mastership of Charles Barry, architect) the old ceiling was removed, and a new decorated carved ceiling added, and the old work redecorated, making a very handsome apartment. The mode of electing a master is curious. A cap of maintenance is carried into the hall in great state, and is tried on by the old master, who announces that it "will not fit" him. He then passes it on to be tried by several next him. Two or three more misfits occur, till at last the cap is handed to the intended new master, for whom it was made. The wardens are elected in the same manner. *Observe.*—Portrait of Sir Andrew Judd, Lord Mayor of London in 1551, and founder of the large and excellent school at Tunbridge, of which the Skinners' Company have the patronage and supervision. [*See* Skinners' Well.]

Skinners' Well, CLERKENWELL, on the west side of the church, but now closed; one of six wells forming the River of Wells, which had its rise in the high ground about Clerkenwell, and, running due south, fell into the Fleet river at the bottom of Holborn Bridge and Snow hill. It was so called, says Stow, "for the skinners of London held there certain plays yearly, played of Holy Scripture." In Rocque's Map of 1745 a *Skin Market* occupies the ground on both sides of what is now Perceval Street. Its memory is preserved in *Skinner Street* and *Market Street*. The latter occupies part of the site and the former leads to it.

In the year 1390, the 14th of Richard II., I read the Parish Clerks of London, on the 18th of July, played interludes at Skinners' Well, near unto Clarkes' Well, which play continued three days together; the king, queen, and nobles being present.[1] Also in the year 1409, the 10th of Henry IV., they played a play at the Skinners' Well, which lasted eight days and was of matter from the Creation of the world. There were to see the same the most part of the nobles and gentles in England.—*Stow*, p. 7.

Skinners' Well is almost quite lost, and so it was in Stow's time. But I am certainly informed, by a knowing parishioner, that it lies on the west of the church, enclosed within certain houses there. The parish would fain recover the well again, but cannot tell where the pipes lie. Dr. Rogers, who formerly lived in an house there, shewed Mr. E. H., late churchwarden, two marks in a wall in the Close where these pipes (as he affirmed) laid, that it might be known after his death.—*Stryfe*, B. iv. p. 69.

Slaughter's Coffee-house, a famous coffee-house at the upper end of the west side of St. Martin's Lane, three doors from Newport

---

[1] It appears by Devon's *Issues of the Exchequer from Henry III. to Henry VI.* (8vo, 1837, p. 244), that the sum of £10 was paid to the Parish Clerks and others on account of the play of the *Passion of our Lord*, and the *Creation of the World*, performed by them at Skinners' Well, in 1391, after the Feast of St. Bartholomew (Shaks. *Soc. Pap.*, vol. i. p. 43).

Street, so called after Thomas Slaughter, the landlord by whom it was established in the year 1692. Slaughter died in or about the year 1740, and in 1741 was succeeded in his business by Humphrey Bailey. A second Slaughter's (New Slaughter's, as it was called) was established in the same street about 1760, when the original establishment adopted the name of "Old Slaughter's," by which designation it was known till within a few years of the final demolition of the house to make way for the new avenue between Long Acre and Leicester Square made 1843-1844. The chief frequenters of the house were artists living in St. Martin's Lane. Here Roubiliac was often to be found, and Wilson was an occasional visitor; and here, in early life, Wilkie would enjoy a small dinner at a small cost. Abraham De Moivre, the great mathematician, in his old age and penury (he died in 1754, aged eighty-seven), used to attend at Slaughter's Coffee-house to pick up a pittance by the solution of questions relative to games of chance. Goldsmith, in his Account of Various Clubs (Essay VI.): says "If a man be passionate, he may vent his rage among the old orators at Slaughter's coffee-house, and damn the nation because it keeps him from starving."

Sloane Street, a very long street lying between Knightsbridge and the King's Road, and so called after Sir Hans Sloane, the physician, and Lord of the Manor of Chelsea. It was planned in 1780 by the architect Henry Holland. [*See* Cadogan Place; Chelsea; Hans Place.]

On the 26th of October (1818) Mrs. Inchbald went once more into private lodgings at No. 48 in Sloane Street; a situation to which she had always professed uncommon dislike.—Boaden, *Life of Mrs. Inchbald*, vol. ii. p. 230.

Originally on the east side, near Sloane Square, was Holy Trinity Church, erected from the designs of James Savage, architect, and consecrated May 8, 1830. This church was pulled down in 1889, and replaced by a new one, built from the designs of J. D. Sedding, architect, at a cost of nearly £35,000, defrayed by Earl Cadogan. Consecrated by the Bishop of London, May 13, 1890.

In *Sloane Square*, at the south end of Sloane Street, lived (1790-1797) Francis Legat, the engraver of Northcote's Murder of the Princes in the Tower and other excellent plates.

When Lord Byron, at ten years of age, was brought to London for the benefit of Dr. Matthew Baillie's advice, his mother took apartments in *Sloane Terrace*, the second turning south of Cadogan Place, on the east side of Sloane Street. Here too he came for the Saturdays and Sundays, and for all holidays, during the two years he was at Dr. Glennie's School at Dulwich.

Smart's Quay, LOWER THAMES STREET, east of Billingsgate.

Smart's Key, so called of one Smart sometime owner thereof.—*Stow*, p. 78.

One Wotton, a gentilman borne and sometyme a marchauntt of good credyte, who fallinge by tyme into decay, kepte an alehowse at Smart's keye, neere Byllingesgate, and after, for some mysdemeanor beinge put downe, he reared upp a new trade of lyffe, and in the same howse he procured all the cuttpurses abowt this Cittie to repaire to his said howse. There was a schole howse sett upp to learn younge boyes to cutt purses. There were hung up two devices, the one was a pockett, the other was a purse. The pocket had in yt certen cowntens and was hunge abowte with hawkes bells, and over the toppe did hangge a little searing bell; and he that could take owt a counter without any noyse was allowed to be a publique Hoyster; and he that could take a piece of sylver owt of the purse without the noyse of any of the bells, he was adjudged a judiciall Nypper. Nota, that a Hoister is a Pick-pockett, and a Nypper is termed a Pickpurse or a Cutpurse.

Memorand. That in Wotton's howse at Smart's keye are wryten in a table divers Poysies, and among the rest one is this—
"Si spie sporte, al non spie, tunc steale."
Another is thus—
"Si spie, si non spie, Hoyste, nyppe, lyfte, shave and spare not."

Note, that Hoyste is to cutt a pockett, nyppe is to cutt a purse, lyft is to robbe a shoppe or a gentilman's chamber, shave is to take a cloake, a sword, a sylver spoone, or such like that is negligentlie looked unto.—*Fleetwood (the Recorder) to Lord Burghley,* July 7, 1585 (*Ellis,* vol. ii. p. 298).

Smithfield, or, SMOOTHFIELD, the "campus planus re et nomine" of Fitzstephen, an open area in the form of an irregular polygon containing 5¾ acres,[1] for centuries, and until 1855, used as a market for sheep, horses, cattle and hay. It is sometimes called *West Smithfield,* to distinguish it from a place of smaller consequence of the same name in the east of London.

Est ibi extra unam portarum, statim in suburbio, quidam planus campus, re et nomine.—*Fitzstephen* (temp. Henry II.)

And this Sommer, 1615,[2] the City of London reduced the rude vast place of Smithfield into a faire and comely order, which formerly was neuer held possible to be done, and paved it all ouer, and made diuers sewers, to conuey the water from the new channels which were made by reason of the new pavement: they also made strong rayles round about Smithfield, and sequestred the middle part of the said Smithfield into a very faire and ciuill walk, and rayled it round about with strong rayles to defend the place from annoyance and danger, as well from carts as all manner of cattell, because it was intended hereafter, that in time it might proue a faire and peaceable Market Place, by reason that Newgate Market, Cheapside, Leadenhall, and Gracechurche Street, were unmeasurably pestred with the unimaginable increase and multiplicity of market-folkes. And this field, commonly called West Smithfield, was for many yeares called "Ruffian's Hall," by reason it was the usual place of Frayes and common fighting during the time that sword and bucklers were in use. But the ensuing deadly fight of Rapier and Dagger suddenly suppressed the fighting with Sword and Buckler.—*Howes,* ed. 1631, p. 1023.

Falstaff. Where's Bardolph?
Page. He's gone into Smithfield to buy your worship a horse.
Falstaff. I bought him in Paul's, and he'll buy me a horse in Smithfield: an I could get me but a wife in the Stews, I were manned, horsed, and wived.—*Second Part of Henry IV.,* Act i. Sc. 2.

This town two bargains has not worth one farthing,
A Smithfield horse—and wife of Covent Garden.
Epilogue to Dryden's *Limberham.*

And if some *Smithfield Ruffian* take up some strange going: some new mowing with the mouth; some wrinching with the shoulder; some brave proverb; some

---

[1] Answer 1372 to Question of Committee of House of Commons on Smithfield Enquiry, 1849-1850.
[2] The work began, Antony Munday informs us, on February 4, 1614-1615. "The citizens charge thereof (as I have been credibly told by Master Arthur Strangewaies) amounting well near to sixteen hundred pounds."

fresh new oath that is not stale but will run round in the mouth ; some new disguised garment, or desperate hat, fond in fashion, or garish in colour, whatsoever it cost, how small soever his living be, by what shift soever it be gotten, gotten must it be, and used with the first, or else the grace of it is stale and gone.—Roger Ascham's *Scholemaster*, 1570 (*Arber*, p. 54).

December 4, 1668.—Mr. Pickering meets me at Smithfield, and I, and W. Hewer and a friend of his, a jockey, did go about to see several pairs of horses, for my coach; but it was late and we agreed on none, but left it to another time : but here I do see instances of a piece of craft and cunning that I never dreamed of, concerning the buying and choosing of horses.—*Pepys*.

Smithfield is famous in history for its jousts, tournaments, executions and burnings, and until 1855 for its market,—the great cattle market of the largest city in the world. Here Wallace and the gentle Mortimer were executed. [*See* The Elms.] Here, on Saturday, June 15, 1381, Sir William Walworth slew Wat Tyler. "The King," says Stow, "stood towards the east near St. Bartholomew's Priory, and the Commons towards the west in form of battle."[1]

1357.—In the winter following [the Battle of Poictiers] were great and royall justs, holden in Smithfield, where many knightly feats of armes were done, to the great honour of the king and realme, at the which were present the kings of England, France, and Scotland, with many noble estates of all those kingdomes, whereof the more part of the strangers were prisoners.—*Stow*, by Howes, p. 263.

"Sir William Chatris, otherwise called Santre, parish priest of the church of St. Scithe [Osyth] the Virgin in London," was the first person burned for heresy in England. The decree of Henry IV., dated February 26, 1400-1401, directs that he shall be "put into the fire in some public or open place within the liberties of your City." There can be no doubt that Smithfield was the place selected. The next victim (March 1609) was John Badley, a tailor in the diocese of Rochester. According to Foxe Prince Henry (Henry V.) was present at Smithfield and did his best to save him, going so far even as to have the fire extinguished for a time.

1410 (11th Henry IV.)—This same yere there was a clerk that beleved nought on the sacrament of the Auter, that is to seye, Godes body, which was dampned and brought into Smythfield to be brent, and was bounde to a stake where as he schulde be brent. And Henry, prynce of Walys, thanne the kynge's eldest sone, consailed hym for to forsake his heresye and holde the righte wey of holy chirche. And the prior of seynt Bertelmewes in Smythfeld broughte the holy sacrament of Godes body, with xij torches lyght before, and in this wyse cam to this cursed heretyk : and it was asked hym how he beleved ; and he ansuerde, that he beleved well that it was halowed bred and nought Godes body ; and thanne was the toune put over hym, and fyre kyndled therein : and whanne the wrecche felte the fyre he cryed mercy ; and anon the prynce comanded to take awey the toune and to quenche the fyre, the whiche was don anon at his comandement : and thanne the prynce asked hym if he wolde forsake his heresye and taken hym to the feith of holy chirche, whiche if he wolde don, he schulde have hys lyf and good ynow to liven by : and the cursed shrewe wold nought, but contynued forth in his heresye ; wherefore he was brent.— *A Chronicle of London from* 1089 *to* 1483, p. 92, edited by Sir N. H. Nicolas.

In May 1538 Forrest, the Prior of the Observant Convent at Greenwich, was burnt for denying the King's [Henry VIII.'s] supremacy ;

[1] *Stow's Annals*, by Howes, ed. 1631, p. 288.

and for some reason his punishment was made to differ from the usual form. A wooden image of a Welsh saint which had been regarded with peculiar reverence throughout North Wales had recently been brought to London, and was hewed into billets to serve as fuel for the occasion. Forrest was suspended over the fire in an iron cage and roasted to death. On July 28, 1540, three eminent Protestant divines, Barnes, Garret and Jerome, were burnt at Smithfield for heresy; and three papists, Powel, Fetherstone and Abel, were, at the same time and place hanged, drawn and quartered, for denying the King's supremacy. The Marian burnings, some 270 in all, were too numerous to particularise. The last of the burnings for heresy in Smithfield was in the reign of James I., when, on March 25, 1612, "Bartholomew Legate, the Arian" so suffered. For other crimes Smithfield witnessed burnings, at least occasionally, for many years longer.

May 10, 1652.—Passing by Smithfield, I saw a miserable creature burning who had murdered her husband.—*Evelyn*.

In March 1849, during excavations necessary for a new sewer, and at a depth of 3 feet below the surface, immediately opposite the entrance to the church of St. Bartholomew the Great, the workmen laid open a mass of unhewn stones, blackened as if by fire, and covered with ashes and human bones charred and partially consumed. This was doubtless the spot generally used for the Smithfield burnings —the face of the sufferer being turned to the east and to the great gate of St. Bartholomew, the prior of which was generally present on such occasions. Many bones were carried away as relics. The spot is indicated by a granite memorial with a suitable inscription placed (1870) in the wall of St. Bartholomew's Hospital (on the left of the entrance), nearly opposite the above site. A "Smithfield Martyrs' Memorial Church" was about the same time erected in St. John's Street Road, the nearest site available. In the first English edition of Foxe's *Acts and Monuments* there is a view, accurate enough as to the locality, representing the burning of Anne Askew and her two companions. The market-place was paved, drained and railed in 1685.

The sharp practices in the horse and cattle markets early made Smithfield bargains a byword.

He [Gay] had made a pretty good bargain (that is a Smithfield) for a little pace in the Custom House.—*Swift to Arbuthnot*, November 30, 1727.

Shall I stand still and tamely see
Such *Smithfield* bargains made of me?
Is not my heart my own?
H. Carey, *The Honest Yorkshireman*.

The inconvenience of holding the great horse and cattle market of the metropolis within the City was every year more obvious. The space was insufficient to meet the ever increasing growth of the trade, and the interference with the ordinary traffic and the public comfort had become almost intolerable. The place itself had, moreover, come to be a moral and physical nuisance. It was surrounded by bone-houses, cat-gut manufactures, slaughter-houses, and knackers' yards, and of the sixty-seven houses about it thirteen were public-houses. On market-days it was dangerous to pass and painful to witness. None too dark for the latter years of its existence was Dickens's sketch of Smithfield Market in 1838:—

> It was market morning. The ground was covered, nearly ankle-deep, with filth and mire; a thick steam perpetually rising from the reeking bodies of the cattle, and mingling with the fog, which seemed to rest upon the chimney-tops, hung heavily above. All the pens in the centre of the large area, and as many temporary pens as could be crowded into the vacant space, were filled with sheep; tied up to posts by the gutter side were long lines of beasts and oxen, three or four deep. Countrymen, butchers, drovers, hawkers, boys, thieves, idlers and vagabonds of every low grade, were mingled together in a mass; the whistling of drovers, the barking of dogs, the bellowing and plunging of oxen, the bleating of sheep, the grunting and squeaking of pigs, the cries of hawkers, the shouts, oaths, and quarrelling on all sides; the ringing of bells and roar of voices, that issued from every public-house; the crowding, pushing, driving, beating, whooping and yelling; the hideous and discordant din that resounded from every corner of the market; and the unwashed, unshaven, squalid, and dirty figures constantly running to and fro, and bursting in and out of the throng; rendered it a stunning and bewildering scene, which quite confounded the senses.—*Oliver Twist*, chap. xxi.

At length the Corporation decided to remove the market. The necessary Parliamentary powers were obtained. A site of about 30 acres was obtained in what was known as the Copenhagen Fields and a new market constructed. On June 11, 1855, the last market for horses, cattle and sheep was held, and Smithfield Market finally closed; and two days later, June 13, the New Smithfield or Metropolitan Cattle Market was opened in Copenhagen Fields. [*See* Metropolitan Cattle Market.] On January 19, 1857, a large meeting of unemployed workmen of London was held in Smithfield. It was stated that the numbers were: carpenters, 9000; plasterers, 4000; painters, 4000; stone masons, 1000; bricklayers and labourers, 15,000; smiths, moulding decorators, etc., 2000, making a total of 35,000 men.

The general aspect of Smithfield has since greatly changed. It is still preserved as an open space, the hay market being still held here; but the area has been contracted by the appropriation of that portion of it lying north of Long Lane to the construction of the Central Meat, Poultry, and Provision Markets, a very remarkable structure described elsewhere. [*See* London Central Markets.] The centre of Smithfield has been laid out as a garden, with a handsome drinking fountain, etc. The greater part of the public-houses have been cleared away; a bank and other good buildings have been erected, and the approaches improved.

Smithfield Bars, a wooden barrier on the north side of Smithfield, like Holborn Bars, Temple Bar, etc. The name survived till the erection of the new Central Meat Market (1868), but the barrier had long disappeared.

Smithfield Bars, so called from the Bars there set up for the severing of the City Liberty from that of the County.—*Strype*, B. iii. p. 284.

June 23, 1580.— The French Imbasidore, Mounswer Mouiser (Malvoisier) ridinge to take the ayer, in his returne cam thowrowe Smithfild; and ther, at the Bars, was steayed by those ofisers that sitteth to cut sourds, by reason his raper was longer than the statute. He was in a great feaurie, and dreawe his raper; in the meane season my Lord Henry Seamore cam, and so steayed the matt^r. Hir Matie is greatlie ofended wth the ofisers, in that they wanted jugement.—*Letter of Lord Talbot* (Lodge, *Ill. Br. Hist.*, vol. ii. p. 228).

Smithfield (East). Spenser, author of *The Faerie Queen*, is said to have been born here.

On the east and by north of the Tower lieth East Smithfield and Tower Hill, two plots of ground so called without the walls of the city.—*Stow*, p. 47.

Strype mentions the "lands and mills." In early times it was a haunt of river-pirates, and very appropriately their place of execution.

Concerning Pyrates: I read, that in the year 1440 in the Lent season, certain persons with six ships brought from beyond the seas fish to victual the City of London; which fish when they had delivered, and were returning homeward, a number of sea-thieves in a barge, in the night came upon them, when they were asleep in their vessels, riding at anchor on the river Thames, and slew them, cut their throats, cast them over board, took their money, and drowned their ships, for that no one should espy or accuse them. Two of these thieves were after taken and hanged in chains upon a gallows set upon a raised hill, for the purpose made, in the field beyond East Smithfield, so that they might be seen far into the river Thames.—*Strype*, B. iv. p. 43.

Smith Square, WESTMINSTER, the houses round St. John's Church [which *see*]. John Fawcett, the actor, was born at No. 5, February 6, 1824.

Smith Street, WESTMINSTER.

Smith Street, a new street of good buildings, so called from Sir James Smith, the ground landlord, who has here a fine house. It is situate in Westminster fronting the Bowling Alley on the west side Peter Street.—*Hatton*, 1708, p. 76.

From "Smith Street, Westminster, 1707," Steele writes to assure the future Mrs. Steele that he lies down to rest with her image in his thoughts, and awakes in the morning in the same contemplation.[1] Thomas Southerne, author of *Oroonoko* and the *Fatal Marriage*, died in 1746 at his house in this street. The Westminster Literary, Scientific, and Mechanics Institute was built 1840. It is now a Free Library and School of Art in connection with South Kensington.

Smyrna Coffee-house, a celebrated coffee-house of the time of Queen Anne. It was situated on the north side of Pall Mall, at the corner of Crown Court, over against Marlborough House—where is now No. 59, Messrs. Harrisons, the booksellers.

My brother Isaac designs, for the use of our sex, to give the exact characters of all the chief politicians who frequent any of the coffee-houses from St. James's to the 'Change; but designs to begin with that cluster of wise-heads, as they are found sitting every evening, from the left side of the fire at the Smyrna to the door.—*The Tatler*, No. 10, May 3, 1709.

---

[1] *Corresp.*, by Nichols, vol. i. p. 104.

The seat of learning [at the Smyrna] is now removed from the corner of the chimney on the left hand towards the window, to the round table in the middle of the floor, over-against the fire; a revolution much lamented by the porters and chairmen, who were much edified through a pane of glass that remained broken all the last summer.—*The Tatler*, No. 78, October 8, 1709.

I have known Peter publishing the whisper of the day by eight o'clock in the morning at Garaway's, by twelve at Will's, and before two at the Smyrna.—*The Spectator*, No. 457.

Prior and I came away at nine, and sat at the Smyrna till eleven receiving acquaintance.—Swift, *Journal to Stella* (Scott, vol. ii. p. 49).

February 19, 1711.—I walked a little in the Park till Prior made me go with him to the Smyrna Coffee House.—*Ibid.* (Scott, vol. ii. p. 180).

If it is fine weather, we take a turn in the Park till two, when we go to dinner; and if it be dirty, you are entertained at picket or basset at White's; or you may talk politics at the Smyrna and St. James's.—Macky, *A Journey through England*, 8vo, 1722, vol. i. p. 168.

I have known him [Beau Nash] wait a whole day at a window in the Smyrna Coffee House, in order to receive a bow from the Prince, or the Duchess of Marlborough as they passed by where he was standing, and he would then look round upon the company for admiration and respect.—Goldsmith, *Life of Nash*.

To the printed copy of Thomson's Proposals for publishing, by subscription, the *Four Seasons* with a hymn on their succession, the following note is appended: "Subscriptions are taken in by the author at the Smyrna Coffee House in Pall Mall."

Snow Hill, HOLBORN, the confined, circuitous, narrow and steep highway between Holborn Bridge and Newgate. Stow writes it *Snor Hill* and *Snore Hill* (pp. 144, 145); Howell, *Sore Hill*, adding, "now vulgarly called Snow Hill;"[1] but Hatton writes *Snow Hill* without any comment. When Skinner Street was built in 1802 Snow Hill ceased to be the highway between Newgate Street and Holborn. It remained little improved till cleared away in forming the Holborn Viaduct and approaches, 1867. The present Snow Hill is a new and wider street, carried partly on the old lines, from the eastern end of the Holborn Viaduct to Farringdon Street. The steepness of Snow Hill is suggestive of a species of ruffianly violence which Gay has described in his account of the "Scowrers" and "Mohocks" in his *Trivia*:—

> I pass their desp'rate deeds, and mischiefs done
> Where from Snow Hill black steepy torrents run;
> How matrons hooped within the hogshead's womb
> Were tumbled furious thence.—Gay's *Trivia*, B. iii. p. 329, etc.

Snow Hill in Charles II.'s days was famous for its ballads and ballad-mongers. Dorset asks Howard:—

> Whence
> Does all this mighty mass of dulness spring
> Which in such loads thou to the stage dost bring?
> Is't all thy own? or hast thou from Snow Hill
> The assistance of some ballad-making quill?
> Buckingham, *Misc.* p. 75.

---

[1] *Londinopolis*, fol. 1657, p. 341. In a contemporary document describing property destroyed in the Great Fire of 1666, it is written "Snore Hill, *alias* Snow Hill."—*Additional MSS., Brit. Mus.*, No. 5063, fol. 37.

I knew a Unitarian minister who was generally to be seen upon Snow Hill (as yet Skinner Street was *not*) between the hours of ten and eleven in the morning, studying a volume of Lardner. I own this to have been a strain of abstraction beyond my reach. I used to admire how he sidled along keeping clear of secular contacts.—Elia's *Essays*, " Detached Thoughts."

Where Snow Hill joined Holborn Bridge and Cow Lane (near the end of the present Cock Lane) the roadway widened, and in the midst was a conduit about which idlers used to gather and gossip and occasionally to quarrel. Here in 1715, on the anniversary of Queen Anne's coronation, a Jacobite mob collected, and with banners and trumpets toasted the memory of King James, drank Queen Anne and High Church, cursed King William and abused King George, and beat and stripped all passers-by who would not do the same.[1]

By the advantage of copying some pictures of Titian and Vandyck, Dobson profited so much that a picture he had drawn being exposed in the window of a shop on Snow Hill, Vandyck passing by was struck with it ; and inquiring for the author, found him at work in a poor garret, from whence he took him and recommended him to the king.—Walpole's *Anecdotes*, 1st ed., 4to, 1762, vol. ii. p. 106 ; ed. 4to, 1798, vol. iii. p. 235.

John Bunyan, author of the *Pilgrim's Progress*, died (1688) at the house of his friend, Mr. Strudwick, a grocer at the sign of the Star on Snow Hill. Thomas Cromwell, great grandson of the Protector and grandson of Henry Cromwell, the Lord Deputy, carried on the business of a grocer on Snow Hill, and there died in 1748.

Soane Museum (Sir John Soane's Museum), 13 LINCOLN'S INN FIELDS, north side ; formed by Sir John Soane, architect of the *Bank of England* (d. 1837). The house was built by Sir John Soane in 1812, and the collection is distributed over twenty-four rooms. Every corner and passage is turned to account. On the north and west sides of the picture-room are cabinets, and on the south are movable shutters, with sufficient space between for pictures. By this arrangement the small space of 13 feet 8 inches in length, 12 feet 4 inches in breadth, and 19 feet 6 inches high, is rendered capable of containing as many pictures as a gallery of the same height 45 feet long and 20 feet broad.

Observe.—The Egyptian sarcophagus, discovered by Belzoni, October 18, 1815, in a tomb in the valley of Biban el Molook, near Gournou. It is formed of one single piece of alabaster, or arragonite, measuring 9 feet 4 inches in length by 3 feet 8 inches in width, and 2 feet 8 inches in depth, and covered internally and externally with elaborate hieroglyphics. When a lamp is placed within it the light shines through, though it is 2½ to 4 inches in thickness. On the interior of the bottom is a full-length figure, representing the Egyptian Isis, the guardian of the dead. It was purchased by Soane from Mr. Salt in 1824 for £2000. The lid or cover has been broken into numerous pieces, of which there are seventeen in the Museum ; it was itself a hollowed

[1] Doran, *London in Jacobite Times*, vol. i. p. 69.

block, which when placed upon the chest added 15 inches to its height. The pieces were put together by Joseph Bonomi. Sixteen original sketches and models, by Flaxman, including one of the few casts in plaster of the Shield of Achilles. Six original sketches and models by T. Banks, R.A., including the Boothby Monument, one of his finest works. A large collection of ancient gems, intaglios, etc., under glass, and in a good light. Set of the Napoleon medals, selected by the Baron Denon for the Empress Josephine, and once in her possession. Sir Christopher Wren's watch. Carved and gilt ivory table and four ivory chairs, formerly in Tippoo Saib's palace at Seringapatam. Richly mounted pistol, said to have been taken by Peter the Great from the Bey, Commander of the Turkish army at Azof, 1696, and presented by the Emperor Alexander to Napoleon at the Treaty of Tilsit in 1807. Napoleon took it to St. Helena, from whence it was brought by a French officer, to whom he had presented it. The original copy of the *Gerusalemme Liberata*, in the handwriting of Tasso. The first four folio editions of *Shakespeare* (J. P. Kemble's copies). An exceedingly interesting folio of designs for Elizabethan and James I. houses by John Thorpe, an architect of those reigns. Fauntleroy's Illustrated copy of Pennant's *London*; purchased by Soane for 650 guineas. *Commentary on St. Paul's Epistles*, illuminated by Giulio Clovio for Cardinal Grimani. Three Canalettis—one A View on the Grand Canal of Venice, extremely fine. The Snake in the Grass, or Love unloosing the Zone of Beauty, by Sir Joshua Reynolds; purchased at the sale of the Marchioness of Thomond's pictures for £500. The Rake's Progress, by Hogarth, a series of eight pictures; purchased by Soane in 1802 for £598. The Election, by Hogarth, a series of four pictures; purchased by Soane, at Mrs. Garrick's sale in 1823 for £1732 : 10s. Van Tromp's Barge entering the Texel, by J. M. W. Turner, R.A. Portrait of Napoleon in 1797, by Francesco Goma. Miniature of Napoleon, painted at Elba in 1814, by Isabey. In the dining-room is a portrait of Soane, by Sir T. Lawrence; and in the gallery under the dome a bust of him by Sir F. Chantrey. The contents of the Museum are very crowded, but the trustees having succeeded in obtaining some additional premises near, new rooms are now (1890) in course of completion which will give more space and cause some rearrangement of the Museum.

Admission by tickets, which may be obtained on application at the hall. The Museum is open to general visitors on Tuesdays, Wednesdays, Thursdays and Saturdays from ten to five during the months of April, May, June, July, and August; and on Tuesdays and Thursdays in February and March. Access to the Books, Drawings, MSS., or permission to copy Pictures or other Works of Art, is to be obtained by special application to the Curator.

Society for Promoting Christian Knowledge. [*See* Christian Knowledge Society.]

Society for the Propagation of the Gospel in Foreign Parts; Office, 19 Delahay Street, Westminster. An offshoot of the Society for Promoting Christian Knowledge; this Society was founded in 1701 to establish and support Church of England Missions in the colonies and heathen countries. Its income in 1888 was £138,366.

Society of Painters in Water Colours, PALL MALL EAST, was established in 1805, and held its first exhibition at No. 20 Lower Brook Street, Bond Street.

Here (at the house of Samuel Shelley, a miniature painter of considerable eminence in his day), Shelley, W. F. Wills, W. H. Pyne, and R. Hills first laid their heads together and projected the institution of a Society of Painters in Water Colours. This was about the years 1800-1802, and it was not till 1804 that they had succeeded in getting nine others to join them in the speculation.—*MS. Letter of the late Robert Hills, President of the Society of Painters in Water Colours.*

The original members were George Barrett, Joshua Cristall, W. S. Gilpin, John Glover, William Havell, Robert Hills, J. Holworthy, J. C. Nattes, F. Nicholson, N. Pocock, W. H. Pyne, S. Rigaud, S. Shelley, J. Varley, and W. F. Wells. The annual spring exhibition of this Society, commonly called the *Old* Water Colour Society, is one of the most agreeable and attractive in London. They also have a winter exhibition of the members' studies and sketches. [*See* Institute of Painters in Water Colours.]

Soho Bazaar. [*See* Soho Square.]

Soho Square, on the south side of OXFORD STREET, contains some good houses, well inhabited till within the last fifty or sixty years. *So-ho,* or *So-how,* was an old cry in hunting when the hare was found. Pennant gives a very erroneous account of the square:—

Soho Square was begun in the time of Charles II. The Duke of Monmouth lived in the centre house [on the South side] facing the statue. Originally the square was called in honour of him Monmouth Square; and afterwards changed to that of King Square. I have a tradition [1] that on his death, the admirers of that unfortunate man changed it to Soho, being the word of the day at the field of Sedgemoor. The house was purchased by the late Lord Bateman [hence Bateman's Buildings] and let by the present Lord [1791] to the Comte de Guerchy, the French ambassador. After which it was let on building leases. The form of the house is preserved by Mr. Nathaniel Smith, in the first number of the *Illustrations of London.* The name of the unfortunate Duke is still preserved in Monmouth Street.—*Pennant.*

The square was not named from "the word of the day at Sedgemoor," but "the word" at Sedgemoor was given from the name of the neighbourhood in which Monmouth dwelt. The battle of Sedgemoor was fought in 1685, and the ground on which Soho Square stands was called "Soho" or *So-hoe* as early as the year 1632,[2] and perhaps before. So-hoe frequently occurs in the Records and in the parish books from that time onwards. In 1634 there is a grant of the lease of a "watercourse of spring water coming and rising from a place called So-howe," etc. In 1636 people were living at the "Brick-kilns near Sohoe,"[3] and in

---

[1] S. Pegge, Esq., to whom I am indebted for several interesting remarks.—*Pennant.* The reverse of Pegge's tradition is the fact.
[2] Rate-books of St. Martin's.
[3] *Ibid.*

1650 Shavers' Hall, or Piccadilly Hall, is described in the Commonwealth Survey as "lying between a roadway leading from Charing Cross to Knightsbridge West, and a high-way leading from Charing Cross towards So-Hoe." In the burial register of St. Paul's, Covent Garden, is the following entry—

1660. Dec. 16. A pr'sh child from Soeho in chy'd.

"The fields about So-Hoe" are mentioned in a proclamation of April 7, 1671, prohibiting the further erecting of small habitations and cottages in the fields, called the Windmill Fields, Dog Felds, and the fields adjoining to "So-Hoe," which building, it is said, "choak up the air of his Majesty's palaces and parks, and endanger the total loss of the waters, which, by expensive conduits, etc., are conveyed from those fields to his Majesty's Palace at Whitehall." In 1675 the fields about Soho were so much built upon that there was a separate receiver of the rates of this part of the then parish of St. Martin's-in-the-Fields; and the book in which the rates are entered is called the "Soho Book." To this information it may be added that Alexander Radcliffe's Epistle from Hypsipyle to Jason, in his *Ovid Travestie* (4to, 1680), is dated from "So-hoe Fields, February 27th, 1679-1680;"— that Soho, and certain fields adjoining, south of the present Oxford Street, were granted (July 17, 1672) by the trustees of Henrietta Maria to Henry Jermyn, Earl of St. Albans; by Charles II. to the Duke of Monmouth; by James II., after the duke's attainder, to his duchess; and by William III. (May 13, 1700) to William Bentinck, Earl of Portland, and his heirs for ever. The grant to the Earl of Portland includes "all those pieces or parcels of land situate, lying, and being in or near the parish of St. Anne, within the liberty of Westminster, anciently called or known by the names of Kemp's Field and Bunches Close, Coleman Hedge, or Coleman Hedge Field, containing together by estimation 220 acres, and Doghouse Field, *alias* Brown's Close, containing by estimation 5½ acres, and were since more lately called or known by the name or names of Soho or Soho Fields, which premises are now laid out into streets and other places, with many tenements and buildings erected thereon, the chief of which are at present known and distinguished by the names following—King's Square, *alias* Soho Square, Greek Street, Church Street, Moor Street, Compton Street, Frith Street, Charles Street, Sutton Street, Queen Street, Dean Street, King's Court, Falconberg Court, Rose Street, north side of King Street, west side of Crown Street, *alias* Hog Lane, south side of the road called Acton Road [Oxford Street], leading from St. Giles's towards Tyburn, the whole ground aforesaid being limited and bounded as followeth, viz.—by the said high road leading to Tyburn on the north; by the said lane or street, called Crown Street, *alias* Hog Lane, towards the east; by the said street or high road leading towards Piccadilly, called King Street, over against the land called the Military Ground (now also built upon), towards the south; and by the back part of houses and lands late in the tenure of Sir William Pulteney, deceased, or his assigns, in a street called Old Soho, *alias* Wardour Street, in part, and by a lane called Hedge Lane (now Princes Street), towards the west." This, it will be seen by a reference to the map, includes the whole of Soho, and nearly the whole of the present parish of St. Anne's. So much for the Pennant tradition.

The square was built in 1681, and contained at that time the following inhabitants :—

Duke of Monmouth ; Colonel Rumsey ; Mr. Pilcher ; ——Broughton, Esq ; Sir Henry Inglesby ; Earl of Stamford.—*Rate-books of St. Martin's.*

It is called King's Square (1694) in the quotation below. Hatton describes it in 1708 as "King's or Soho Square" (p. 43); Strype in 1720, and Maitland in 1739, as "a stately quadrate designated King's Square, but vulgarly Soho Square ;" in the index to Strype it is entered as "Soho Square," though the name never occurs in the description. In Strype's Map the present Carlisle Street is called King Square Street and King Square Court ; and the latter name by Smith in his *Life of Nollekens,* 1829.

The design also of that Fountain in the middle of King's Square in *Sor-Hoe-Fields-Buildings,* deserves observation ; where on a high pedestal is His Majesty's statue, and at his feet lie the representatives of the four principal rivers of England, Thames, Trent, Humber, and Severn, with subscriptions under each.—*Anglia Notitia,* 1694.

November 27, 1690.—I went to London with my family to winter at Soho in the great Square.—*Evelyn.*

Sir Will. That's the coxcombly Alderman [Sir Humphrey Maggot], that marry'd my termagant Aunt : she has this dolt under correction and has forced him out of Mark Lane to live in Soho Square.—*The Scowrers,* by T. Shadwell, 4to, 1691, and so in two other places in the same play.

The first of our Society is a gentleman of Worcestershire, of ancient descent, a Baronet : his name Sir Roger de Coverley. When he is in town he lives in Soho Square.—*The Spectator,* No. 2 (March 2, 1710-1711).

> And when I flatter, let my dirty leaves
> Clothe spice, line trunks, or, fluttering in a row,
> Befringe the rails of Bedlam and Soho.—POPE.

Eminent Inhabitants.—The Duke of Monmouth, natural son of Charles II., by Lucy Walters (beheaded 1685). In 1717 Monmouth House was an auction-room. J. T. Smith visited the house with Nollekens about 1773, when the workmen were beginning to pull it down.

It was on the south side [between Frith Street and Greek Street] and occupied the site of the houses which now stand in Bateman's Buildings. . . . The gate entrance was of massive ironwork supported by stone piers, surmounted by the crest of the owner of the house ; and within the gates there was a spacious court-yard for carriages. The hall was ascended by steps. There were eight rooms on the ground floor ; the principal one was a dining-room towards the south, the carved and gilt panels of which had contained whole-length portraits. At the corners of the ornamented ceiling, which was of plaster, and over the chimney-piece, the Duke of Monmouth's arms were displayed. . . . The staircase was of oak, the steps very low, and the landing-places were tesselated with woods of light and dark colours. . . . As I ascended, I remember Mr. Nollekens noticing the busts of Seneca, Caracalla, Trajan, Adrian, and several others, upon ornamented brackets. The principal room on the first floor, which had not been disturbed by the workmen, was lined with blue satin, superbly decorated with pheasants and other birds in gold. The chimney-piece was richly ornamented with fruit and foliage. . . . In the centre over this chimney-piece, within a wreath of oak leaves, there was a circular recess which evidently had been designed for the reception of a bust. The heads of the panels of the brown window-shutters, which were very lofty, were gilt; and the piers between the windows, from stains upon the silk, had probably been filled with looking-glasses. The workmen were demolishing the upper part, so that it was dangerous for us to go higher, or see more of this most interesting house.—Smith's *Nollekens*, vol. i. pp. 30-32.

There is an engraving of the front in Smith's *Antiquities of London*. Gilbert Burnet, Bishop of Salisbury.

January 22, 1708-1709.—Walked to Soho Square to the Bishop of Salisbury's, who entertained me most agreeably with the sight of several valuable curiosities, as the original Magna Charta of King John, supposed to be the very same that he granted to the nobles in the field, it wanting that article about the Church, which in the exemplars afterwards was always inserted first; it has part of the great seal also remaining.—Thoresby's *Diary*, vol. ii. p. 27.

Sir Cloudesley Shovel (d. 1707.) Here his body, after his melancholy shipwreck, was laid in state previous to interment in Westminster Abbey. On the south side Daniel Finch, Earl of Winchelsea and Nottingham, 1708. Ripperda, the Dutch adventurer, once Prime Minister of Spain, lived here in great magnificence, 1726. Lord Chancellor Macclesfield; he died here in 1732. His son, the President of the Royal Society, afterwards resided in the same house. Alderman Beckford (father of William Beckford, author of *Vathek*), in the house the corner of Greek Street, sold in 1861 to the Sisters of Charity. [*See* Greek Street.]

The Lord Mayor had enjoined tranquillity—as Mayor. As Beckford, his own house in Soho Square was embroidered with "*Liberty*" in white letters three feet high. Luckily the evening was very wet, and not a mouse stirred.—*Walpole to Mann*, April 19, 1770.

Walpole's correspondent, Field-Marshal Conway (d. 1795), on the south side, in the right-hand corner, leading from Greek Street. Mrs. Teresa Cornelys, "the Heidegger of the age,"[1] in "Carlisle House" (so called from Charles Howard, Earl of Carlisle, who built the house between 1786 and 1790), on the east side, corner of Sutton Street; Mrs. Cornelys purchased the house in 1760, and built some additional rooms in 1769. Here were given a series of balls, concerts, and masquerades, unparalleled in the annals of public fashion. At one of these (February 26, 1770) the Duke of Gloucester (brother of George III.) appeared in the character of Edward IV., with Lady Waldegrave as Elizabeth Woodville; and though their disguise was not made known till two or three years later, "methinks," says Horace Walpole, "it was not very difficult to make out the meaning of the masks."[2] Mrs. Cornelys was a German by birth, and by profession a public singer. She was a bankrupt in 1772, and the house was sold by auction, but in 1776 she re-obtained temporary possession of it. The house was pulled down in 1788, but the ballroom was kept

[1] *Walpole to Mann*, February, 22, 1771.   [2] *Letters*, vol. v. p. 227.

standing, and in 1792 St. Patrick's R. C. Chapel was consecrated. Sir John Hawkins says in his *Life of Johnson*, published in 1787, that she was a prisoner for debt to a large amount, "but in the riots of 1780 found means to escape from confinement, and has not since been heard of." She turned up again, however, as a "vender of asses' milk" at Knightsbridge, but she sank still lower, and died (1797) in the Fleet Prison. The staircase of the house was painted by Henry Cook (d. 1700). Wedgwood thought of taking this house for a warehouse and showrooms. On November 14, 1772, he wrote to his partner, Bentley, "What has become of Mrs. Cornelys's rooms? She is, I hear, to remain in prison, and I cannot think anybody else will venture to take up her place. Soho Square is not a bad situation I think, but then you know better than I do." They ultimately settled in Greek Street. George Colman the elder, at No. 28, left-hand corner of Bateman's Buildings. Sir Joseph Banks, in the house No. 32 in the south-west corner, by Frith Street. Here he gave his public breakfasts and Sunday evening receptions.

> On Sundays at Sir Joseph's never failed.
> Matthias, *Pursuits of Literature*, pt. iv. L. 275.

Sir Joseph Banks's house, as Gifford remarked to Moore,[1] was in science what Holland House was in politics and literature. Peter Pindar made merry with the President of the Royal Society and his Sunday gatherings.

> One morning at his house in Soho Square,
> As with a solemn awe-inspiring air,
> Amidst some Royal sycophants he sat ;
> Most manfully their masticators using,
> Most pleasantly their greasy mouths amusing,
> With coffee, butter'd toast, and birds' nest chat.—
> Peter Pindar, *Sir Joseph Banks and the Boiled Fleas.*

> To give a breakfast in Soho,
> Sir Joseph's very bitterest foe
> Must certainly allow him peerless merit :
> Where on a wagtail and tom-tit
> He shines, and sometimes on a nit ;
> Displaying powers few gentlemen inherit.
> Peter Pindar, *Sir Joseph Banks a Privy Counsellor!* (an Ode).

By a codicil to his will, dated January 21, 1820, Sir Joseph left the use of his large library and collections to Robert Brown, the eminent botanist, during life, and to the British Museum on his death.[2] Brown occupied the apartments in which Banks held his meetings, and there died, June 10, 1858. The front part of the house, overlooking the square, was occupied by the Linnæan Society till its removal to Burlington House. It is now the Hospital for Diseases of the Heart.

Richard Payne Knight, the famous collector and writer of many works on art and taste, died, April 24, 1824, at his house No. 3 in this

[1] *Diary*, vol. ii. p. 230.   [2] Weld, *Hist. of Royal Society*, vol. ii. p. 115.

square, now Messrs. Kirkman's pianoforte warehouse. Here he formed, at a cost of over £50,000, the remarkable collection of bronzes and Greek coins, drawings, etc., which he bequeathed to the British Museum. No. 12 was the residence of Sir Anthony Carlisle the great surgeon.

> In this solitary sullen life Barry [the painter] continued till he fell ill, very probably from want of food sufficiently nourishing; and after lying two or three days under his blanket, he had just strength enough to crawl to his own door, with a paper in his hand on which he had written his wish to be carried to the house of Mr. Carlisle in Soho Square. There he was taken care of, and the danger which he had thus escaped seems to have cured his mental hallucinations.—*Southey to A. Cunningham.*

Hatton (1708) gives the following as the aristocratic inhabitants of the square at that date: *on the east side*, Lord Berkeley, Lord Carlisle; *on the west side*, Lord George Howard, Sir Thomas Mansel, comptroller of the Household; *on the south side*, Lord Nottingham; and *on the north side*, Lord Leicester, whose house in Leicester Square was then let to the Imperial ambassador.

The White House opposite Mrs. Cornelys had long a very unsavoury reputation. It is now included in Messrs. Crosse and Blackwell's premises. No. 18 on the east side was occupied in 1824, and for many years, by W. H. Pickersgill, R.A., portrait painter. In 1811, when Sir Charles Bell, the great anatomist, married, he took the house No. 34 Soho Square.

Here, on the west side, is the Soho Bazaar, established 1815 by Mr. Trotter. This the chief bazaar in London was offered for sale by auction in July 1879, but the reserved price was not reached, and the bazaar, to the great delight of young folks (and their elderly relations), still keeps its doors open, although its proportions are somewhat contracted, the upper rooms being closed.

The statue of Charles II. which stood in the centre of the square was removed in the summer of 1876 to the grounds of Mr. Frederick Goodall, R.A., at Harrow Weald, and an octagonal tool-house erected on the site.[1]

Sol's Row. [*See* Hampstead Road.]

Somers Town, a poorly inhabited suburb of London, on the north-west side, built in 1786 and following years, and so called from the noble family of Somers, whose freehold property it is, or was, when it was named. "The Brill," or, as Dr. Stukeley has called it, Cæsar's Camp, was a part of the present Somers Town, but the district called the Brill and a considerable portion of the rest of Somers Town has been cleared away during the last twenty years in order to construct the Midland Railway Terminus and goods depôt. Towards the end of the last century Somers Town became a great resort of Roman Catholic priests and other refugees from the French Revolution, attracted probably by the low rents of houses in the unfinished "town,"

[1] *Builder,* July 29, 1876

and the proximity of the St. Pancras burial-ground. A chapel and various benevolent institutions were established here by the Abbé Caron, a man of great influence among his compatriots. In the chapel were interred the Princess of Condé, M. Caron and his brother, and other persons of note, but the majority were buried at St. Pancras. The chapel remains, but all other vestiges of the French colony have disappeared. William Godwin lived in Somers Town from the beginning of 1793, first in Chalton Street, where he wrote *Caleb Williams* and published *Political Justice;* afterwards (1797), when he married Mary Wollstonecraft, in Evesham Buildings, and then in the Polygon. Dr. Wolcott (Peter Pindar) died at his house in Somers Town, January 14, 1819. He had gone there to live when the house was in the midst of nursery grounds, and remained when it was surrounded by dull lines of streets. Leslie the painter visited him shortly before his death.

A short time before Dr. Wolcott's death I became acquainted with a young Irishman, a literary man, named Desmoulins, who was intimate with him, and who, knowing my admiration of his poems, offered to take me to see him. The doctor appointed a day to receive us, and we called at his lodgings in a small house in an obscure street in Somers Town. But he was too ill to see a stranger. Mr. Desmoulins went up to his bedroom, and I stayed in his little sitting-room which was furnished as might be expected. There were shelves with books, a piano on which lay a violin, and there were pictures and drawings on the walls, of which some were small copies from Reynolds, and some landscapes in water-colours by Wolcott himself.—*Autob. Recollections of C. R. Leslie, R.A.*, vol. i. p. 248.

Somerset Coffee-house, in the STRAND, east corner of the entrance to King's College. The letters of Junius were occasionally left at the bar of this coffee-house, sometimes at the bar of the New Exchange, and now and then at Munday's in Maiden Lane. The waiters received occasional fees for taking them in.

Somerset House, in the STRAND (the old building), "a large and goodly house,"[1] built by the Protector Somerset, brother of Queen Jane Seymour, and maternal uncle of Edward VI. Two inns, appertaining to the sees of Worcester and Lichfield, and several tenements adjoining, were pulled down in 1549 to make way for it; and the great cloister on the north side of St. Paul's, containing "The Dance of Death," and the priory church of the Knights Hospitallers (of St. John of Jerusalem), Clerkenwell, were demolished to find stones to erect it. The present *Somerset House* occupies the same site. The Protector began his palace in the Strand very soon after the death of Henry VIII. Letters exist dated from "Somerset Place" as early as 1547; Foxe tells of speeches in "the Gallery at his Grace's house in the Strand," and of his examining prisoners there;[2] and one of the "Articles objected against the Lord Protector" was that "you had and held, against the law, in your own house, a Court of Requests." But this house may have been an inn seized and new named—not an uncommon circumstance at this time, or indeed for many years after.

[1] *Stow.*   [2] *Foxe*, vol. vi. pp. 198, 246.

1551.—Master Bradford spared not the proudest, and among many many others will't them to tak example be the last Duck of Somerset, who became so cold in hearing God's word, that the yeir before his last apprehension hee wold goe visit his masonis, and wold not dinye himself to goe from his Gallerie to his hall for hearing of a sermon.—*John Knox to the Faithful in London.*

What portion of the work was completed when the Protector was beheaded, January 22, 1552, no research has yet been able to discover. In an account of the duke's expenditure between April 1, 1548, and October 7, 1551, the amount expended on Somerset House is stated as £10,091 : 9 : 2, equal at least to £50,000 of our present money.[1] The name of the architect is unknown. The Clerk of the Works was Robert Lawes, described in a roll of the duke's debts as "late Clerke of the Duke's Woorkes at Strand Place and at Syon."[2] There is a plot or plan of the house among the drawings of Thorpe, preserved in Sir John Soane's Museum. Of this very interesting old building there are several views; that by Moss is considered the best. One by Knyff is early and curious. The picture at Dulwich (engraved in Wilkinson) represents the river front before Inigo Jones's chapel and alterations destroyed the uniform character of the building. In the Fitzwilliam Museum at Cambridge is a cork model of the façade and back, presented in 1826 by the Rev. E. B. Elliot of Trinity College. After the attainder of the duke, when Somerset House became the property of the Crown, little, if anything, was done to complete the building. The screen prepared for the hall was bought for the church of St. Bride's, where it no doubt remained till destroyed in the Great Fire.[3] During a portion at least of Mary's reign it was appropriated to her sister Elizabeth.

[On February 25, 1557] the Lady Elizabeth came riding from her house at Hatfield to London, attended with a great company of lords, and nobles, and gentlemen, unto her place called *Somerset Place*, beyond Strand Bridge.—*MS. Journal*, quoted by Strype, *Eccl. Mem.*, vol. iii. p. 444.

In 1566-1567 Queen Elizabeth listened to the promises of an alchemist who undertook to manufacture precious gems and to transmute any metal into gold. His letters were addressed direct to the Queen. Cecil writes in his Diary, February 10, 1567 : "Cornelius de la Noye, an alchemist, wrought in Somerset House, and abused many." In 1596 Elizabeth granted the keeping of Somerset House to her kinsman, Lord Hunsdon, during life.[4] James I. granted Somerset House to his Queen, Anne of Denmark, and in 1616 commanded it to be called Denmark House.[5]

August 14, 1604.—Grant by Queen Anne to John Gerard, Surgeon and Herbalist, of lease of a garden plot adjoining Somerset House, on condition of his supplying her with herbs, flowers, and fruit. With an endorsement of surrender to the Queen of the said plot, 27 June 1611, by Robert Earl of Salisbury to whom it was granted by Gerard.—*Cal. State Pap.*, 1603-10, p. 141.

[1] *Letters to Granger*, p. 108.
[2] Account of Thomas Blagrave, Esq., preserved in the Audit Office, Somerset House.
[3] *Stow*, p. 147.
[4] Burghley's *Diary in Murden*, p. 811. Norden's *Essex*, p. 13.
[5] *Stow*, by Howes, ed. 1631, p. 1026.

June 22, 1608.—Grant to Earl of Salisbury of the office of Keeper of Somerset House and Garden during the Queen's life.—*Cal. State Pap.*, 1603-1610, p. 441.

February 8, 1609.—Warrant to pay to William Goodrowse, Sergeant Surgeon £400 for laying out the gardens of Somerset House.—*Ibid.*, p. 490.

Charles I. assigned it to his Queen (Henrietta Maria) in the ninth year of his reign, and caused a chapel to be added to the building, for the free use of the Roman Catholic religion. The chapel was designed by Inigo Jones, and the first stone laid September 14, 1632.[1] It was consecrated with much ceremony at the end of 1635.

January 8, 1636.—This last month the Queen's Chapel in Somerset House Yard was consecrated by her Bishop; the ceremonies lasted three days, massing, preaching, and singing of Litanies, and such a glorious scene built over their altar, the Glory of Heaven, Inigo Jones neer presented a more curious piece in any of the Masques at Whitehall; with this our English ignorant papists are mightily taken.—*Garrard to Wentworth (Strafford Letters*, vol. i. p. 505).

May 10, 1638.—The Lieutenant of the Tower, Sir William Balfour, beat a priest lately for seeking to convert his wife: he had a suspicion that she resorted a little too much to Denmark House, and staid long abroad, which made him one day send after her. Word being brought him where she was, he goes thither, finds her at her devotions in the Chapel; he beckons her out: finds her accompanied with a priest, who somewhat too saucily reprehended the Lieutenant for disturbing his Lady in her devotions; for which he struck him two or three sound blows with his Battoon, and the next day came and told the King the whole passage: so it passed over.—*Garrard to Wentworth (Strafford Letters*, vol. ii. p. 165).

A few tombs of her French Roman Catholic attendants are built into the cellars of the present building, immediately beneath the great square. Here, in the Christmas festivities of 1632-1633, Henrietta Maria took a part in a masque (the last in which she played); Here, in 1652, died Inigo Jones, the great architect. Here, in 1658, Oliver Cromwell's body lay in state.

This folly and profusion so far provoked the people that they threw dirt in the night on his escutcheon that was placed over the great gate of Somerset House.—*Ludlow*, vol. ii. p. 615.

After Cromwell's death it was in contemplation to sell Somerset House. Ludlow, not always a safe authority, says it was sold.

Col. Henry Martin moved at the same time that the Chapel belonging to Somerset House might not be sold, because it was the place of meeting for the French Church, and this request was granted; but the House itself was sold for the sum of ten thousand pounds.—*Ludlow*, vol. ii. p. 679.

A project was formed to purchase it for the Quakers, but George Fox put his foot upon it:—

1658.—When some forward spirits that came among us would have bought Somerset House, that we might have meetings in it, I forbade them to do so: for I then foresaw the King's coming in again.—*George Fox*, vol. i. p. 490.

On November 2, 1660, Henrietta Maria resumed her residence in Somerset House, and Cowley and Waller wrote copies of verses on the repairs she had made in her old palace. The former makes the renovated edifice sing its own praises. After speaking of the desolate condition in which she had found it, he continues:—

[1] Ellis's *Letters*, vol. iii. p. 271, 2d S.

And now I dare
Ev'n with the proudest palaces compare.

Before my gate a street's broad channel goes,
Which still with waves of crowding people flows.
And every day there passes by my side,
Up to its western rench, the London tide,
The Spring-tides of the term ; my front looks down
On all the pride and business of the town.

My other fair and more majestic face
(Who can the Fair to more advantage place ?)
For ever gazes on itself below ;
In the best mirror that the world can show.

Cowley, *On the Queen's Repairing Somerset House.*

Here, in May 1665, on Henrietta Maria's farewell to England, Catharine of Braganza took up her residence, although the formal grant by letters patent was not made by Charles II. till after his mother's death in 1669. Here, in January 1669-1670, the body of Monk, Duke of Albemarle, lay in state. Sir Samuel Tuke, author of *Adventures of Five Hours*, died in Somerset House, January 26, 1673, and was buried in the chapel. Here, on October 17, 1678, the famous Sir Edmund Berry Godfrey, is said to have been murdered, and his body carried hence to the field where it was found near *Primrose Hill*. Two of the supposed murderers were attendants belonging to the chapel in Somerset House. Charles II. died, February 2, 1685, and on April 8 Evelyn "met the Queen - Dowager going now first from Whitehall to dwell at Somerset House. When she left England for Portugal, in May 1692 (never to return), Somerset House became a nest of lodgings (as Hampton Court at the present day) for some of the nobility and poorer persons about the Court ; though it would appear to have been always recognised as part of the jointure of the consort of the sovereign.

They passed that building which of old
Queen Mothers were designed to hold,
At present a mere lodging pen,
A palace turn'd into a den,
To barracks turn'd, and soldiers tread
Where Dowagers have laid their head.

Churchill, *The Ghost*, B. iv.

Lewis de Duras, Earl of Feversham, who commanded King James's troops at the battle of Sedgemoor, and Lady Arlington, widow of Secretary Bennet, were living here in 1708.[1] Mrs. Gunning, the mother of the three celebrated beauties—the Duchess of Argyll and Hamilton, the Countess of Coventry, and Mrs. Travers—held the appointment of housekeeper, and here she died in 1770, and her husband John Gunning in 1767. Here, in the reign of George III., Charlotte Lennox, author of the *Female Quixote*, had apartments.

Addison (*Spectator*, No. 77) represents himself as walking " in

[1] *Hatton*, p. 633.

Somerset Garden a little before our Club time," when he saw Will Honeycomb "squirt away his watch a considerable way into the Thames," thinking it was the pebble he had just picked up from the grand walk.

Buckingham House, in St. James's Park, was settled on Queen Charlotte, in lieu of Somerset House, by an Act passed in 1775, and the old palace of the Protector and of the Queens of England immediately destroyed, to erect the present pile of public offices still distinguished as Somerset House. [*See* Denmark House; Somerset Stairs.]

Somerset House, in the STRAND (present building). A pile of public offices, erected between the years 1776 and 1786, on the site of the palace of the Protector Somerset. [*See* preceding article.] The architect was Sir William Chambers. The general proportions of the building are good, and some of the details of great elegance. The entrance archway or vestibule from the Strand has deservedly found many admirers.[1] The terrace elevation towards the Thames was made, like the Adelphi Terrace of the brothers Adam, in anticipation of the long projected embankment of the river, and is one of the noblest façades in London. The building is in the form of a quadrangle, with wings. The Strand front is 155 feet long, the river front 600 feet. The inner quadrangle is 319 by 224 feet. Wings have been added to Chambers's building; the east wing, which contains King's College, by Sir R. Smirke in 1828-1831; the west wing, devoted to the Inland Revenue Department, by Sir James Pennethorne in 1853. *Observe*—under the vestibule, on your left as you enter (distinguished by a bust of Sir Isaac Newton), the entrance doorway to the apartments formerly occupied by the Royal Society and Society of Antiquaries; Herschel and Watt, and Davy and Wollaston, and Walpole and Hallam have often entered by this door. *Observe*—under the same vestibule, on your right as you enter, the entrance doorway of the apartments, from 1780 to 1838, of the Royal Academy of Arts. Some of the best pictures of the English school have passed under this doorway to the great room of the yearly exhibition; and under the same doorway, and up the same steps, Reynolds, Wilkie, Flaxman and Chantrey have often passed. The last and best of Reynolds's Discourses were delivered, by Sir Joshua himself, in the great room of the Academy, at the top of the building. Somerset House is now wholly appropriated as Government offices. The principal are the Exchequer and Audit Department; the Probate Office; the Legacy Duty Office, where the several payments are made on bequests by wills of personal property; the Inland Revenue Office, where stamps are issued, and public taxes and excise duties received from the several district collectors; Accountant and Comptroller-General's Office; and the Registrar-General's Office is for the registration of the births, marriages, and deaths of the United Kingdom. In the basement are

[1] The keystone masques of river deities on the Strand front were carved by Carlini and Wilton, two of the early Royal Academicians.

produced by steam and hand presses all the various stamps issued from the several Government departments, with the exception of the adhesive postage stamps, which are prepared by private firms. Here also is the Chemical Laboratory of the Inland Revenue Office. The bronze statue of George III. and figure of Father Thames, by John Bacon, R.A., cost £2000.

A little above the entrance door to the Stamps and Taxes is a white watch-face, regarding which the popular belief has been, and is, that it was left there by a labouring man who fell from a scaffold at the top of the building, and was only saved from destruction by the ribbon of his watch, which caught in a piece of projecting work. In thankful remembrance (so the story runs) of his wonderful escape, he afterwards desired that his watch might be placed as near as possible to the spot where his life had been saved. The story is utterly unfounded. The watch-face was placed where it is by the Royal Society as a meridian mark for a portable transit instrument in one of the windows of their ante-room.

To this account of Somerset House may be added a little circumstance of interest which Mr. Cunningham was told by an old clerk on the establishment of the Audit Office. "When I first came to this building," he said, "I was in the habit of seeing, for many mornings, a thin, spare, naval officer, with only one arm, enter the vestibule at a smart step, and make direct for the Admiralty, over the rough round stones of the quadrangle, instead of taking what others generally took, and continue to take, the smooth pavement at the sides. His thin, frail figure shook at every step, and I often wondered why he chose so rough a footway; but I ceased to wonder when I heard that the thin, frail officer was no other than Lord Nelson—who always took," continued my informant, "the nearest way to the place he wanted to go to."

July 15, 1817.—Wrote some lines in the solitude of Somerset House, not fifty yards from the Thames on one side, and the Strand on the other; but as quiet as the sands of Arabia.—Crabbe's *Journal.*

But the record is wrongly dated by Crabbe: it should be *Sunday* the 13th,—which explains the quiet.

Somerset Stairs, SOMERSET HOUSE.

Neander was pursuing this discourse so eagerly, that Eugenius had called to him twice or thrice, ere he took notice that the barge stood still, and that they were at the foot of Somerset Stairs, where they had appointed it to land. The company were all sorry to separate so soon, though a great part of the evening was already spent; and stood awhile looking back on the water, upon which the moonbeams played and made it look like floating quicksilver; at last they went up through a crowd of French people who were merrily dancing in the open air, and walking thence to the Piazza, they parted there.—Dryden's *Essay on Dramatick Poesy*, 4to, 1668.

Somerset Street, PORTMAN SQUARE, from Orchard Street to Duke Street. ' George Stubbs, A.R.A. [elected R.A. in 1781, but declined the honour, d. 1806], the eminent animal painter, lived here for some years.

Soper Lane, now QUEEN STREET, CHEAPSIDE, Stow says, "took that name not of soap-making as some have supposed, but of Alen le Sopar, in the 9th of Edward II." But he is in error. It was called Soper Lane as early as 1288, and undoubtedly from the sopers, or soapmakers, dwelling there. The pepperers succeeded them.

In this Soper's Lane the Pepperers anciently dwelt, wealthy Tradesmen who dwelt in spices and Drugs. Two of this trade were divers times Mayors in the reign of King Henry III.; viz. Andrew Bocherel and John de Gisorcio or Gisors. In the reign of King Edward II. anno 1315, they came to be governed by rules and orders, which are extant in one of the books of the Chamber under this title, *Ordinatio Piperrarum de Soper's Lane.—Strype*, B. iii. p. 15.

When Mary and Philip rode through the City, they were accompanied by Cardinal Pole and Gardiner. Before the Cardinal was carried a cross, and as the party rode on, the Cardinal ostentatiously blessed the multitude; but these only "greatly laughed him to scorn" for his pains, and would neither take off their caps nor bow to the cross. This manifestation, from the houses as well as the streets, fired Gardiner with unseemly rage; and his cry to his servants was, "Mark that house!" "Take this knave, and have him to the Compter!" "Such a sort of heretics, who ever saw?" "I will teach them, an I live." "This did I hear him say," writes Mowntayne, "I standing at Soper Lane end."—J. G. Nichols, *Narratives of the Reformation (Camd. Soc.)*

Sir Baptist Hicks, Viscount Campden, of the time of James I., whose name is preserved in *Hicks's Hall* and Campden Hill, Kensington, was a mercer, at the sign of the White Bear, at Soper Lane End, in Cheapside.[1] Bulstrode Whitelocke was residing in Soper Lane in 1631, when his son James was born. [*See* Queen Street.]

South Bank, REGENT'S PARK, a row of cottages on the south bank of the Regent's Canal, west of the Regent's Park. One of these was built by Ugo Foscolo, and named *Digamma Cottage*, to commemorate his share in that celebrated controversy. The neighbouring *Alpha Road* and *Beta Place* probably owe their names to this Digamma Cottage.

South Eastern Railway. The original terminus of this Company was on the Surrey or Southwark side of London Bridge. The first 1½ mile ran on arches side by side with the East Greenwich Railway, the next 8 miles on the Croydon Railway, and the continuation to Reigate Station, 20½ miles from London, on the Brighton Railway. The South Eastern works began at Reigate Station (Redhill is the junction now) and ran to Tunbridge, Ashford, Canterbury, Ramsgate, Deal, Folkestone, and Dover. The whole line to Dover was opened in February 1844. It is now carried to the Cannon Street Station in the City and the Charing Cross Station at the west end—both large and costly structures with magnificent hotels attached. To reach each of these the Thames is crossed by an iron girder bridge. Besides the original line the Company have constructed branch lines to

[1] *Strype*, B. i. p. 287.

Tunbridge Wells and Hastings; a Mid-Kent line to Bickley; North Kent to Dartford, Gravesend, and Maidstone; a line to Guildford, Aldershot, and Reading, and suburban lines to Greenwich, Woolwich, Peckham Rye, etc. Pleasant excursions, returning the same day, may be made by this line to Box Hill and Dorking, Penshurst, Hever Castle, Tunbridge Wells, Knole and Canterbury.

South Kensington, a new district so named, formed chiefly out of Brompton and Brompton West, and having for its nucleus the estate purchased by the Commissioners of the Great Exhibition of 1851. The district has no very definite limits, but is generally considered to extend from the west end of the Brompton Road to Kensington proper, and to have for its north and south boundaries Kensington Gore and the Harrington estate. It is traversed by broad roads, lined by spacious and high-rented dwellings, intermingled with still more costly mansions and "gardens"; and within its limits are the South Kensington Museum and Schools of Science and Art, the Natural History Museum, and the Imperial Institute; also the South Kensington and Gloucester Road Stations of the Metropolitan Railway.

South Kensington Museum has grown out of the collection of models, casts, prints, and other examples purchased for the purpose of Instruction in Design and Ornamental Art in the Schools of Design. In 1851 the Board of Trade appointed a committee to select objects for purchase, notable "entirely for the excellence of their art or workmanship," to the amount of £5000, from the Great Exhibition of that year. These objects were exhibited at Marlborough House and opened in September 1852 as a Museum of Ornamental Art. It was then decided to take an annual vote for the formation of a systematic collection representing the application of fine art to industry of all periods. In 1856 Parliament voted £10,000 for the transference of the Science and Art Department [which *see*] to the estate at South Kensington purchased by the Commissioners of the Exhibition of 1851, and an iron building was erected, under the superintendence of Sir William Cubitt, upon the south-eastern portion of the estate, at a cost of £15,000. The Museum was opened on June 22, 1857, by the Queen, accompanied by the Prince Consort. Immediately after the opening the erection of permanent buildings was commenced, and the Picture Galleries, the Schools of Art, the North and Central Courts, the Keramic Gallery, Lecture Theatre, and Refreshment Rooms were completed and opened in successive years. The greater portion of the iron building was taken down in 1868 and re-erected as a Branch Museum at Bethnal Green [which *see*]. The South Kensington Museum stands on 12 acres of land, and the site was acquired by Government at a cost of £60,000.

At either end of the South Court are the two fine frescoes by Sir Frederick Leighton, Bart., P.R.A., executed in a process, called by its inventor, Mr. Gambier Parry, "Spirit fresco." The subject at the north end is *The Industrial Arts as applied to War*, and that at the south end *The Industrial Arts as applied to Peace*. The contents of the Museum have now grown to vast dimensions, and it will only be possible to indicate very briefly the character of the chief collections. An admirable series of Guides to the contents of the Museum, each forming a handbook to a particular subject, has been published by the Department.

Pictures.—Mr. John Sheepshanks presented his fine collection of pictures of English painters in 1857, "with a view to the establishment of a collection of pictures and other works of art fully representing British art and worthy of national support." The Sheepshanks' gallery includes 26 of the finest works of Mulready, 16 by Landseer, 20 by Leslie, and 4 by Turner.

The collection of water-colour paintings is of great value, and is composed of the gift of Mrs. Ellison, Mr. William Smith, Mr. C. T. Maud, and the bequests of the Rev. C. H. Townshend and Mr. J. M. Parsons. The gallery contains works by Paul Sandby, T. Girtin, J. S. Cotman, Turner, Varley, David Cox, De Wint, Copley Fielding, Prout, W. Hunt, etc.

The Raphael Cartoons, which were exhibited at Hampton Court from the reign of William III. till 1865, were in that year allowed by Her Majesty to be removed to the Museum, when a special gallery was prepared for them.

Architectural Court.—The majority of the objects are full-sized reproductions in plaster of architectural works of large dimensions. In 1884 a series of casts illustrative of the history of antique sculpture, copies of the best examples in the principal continental galleries, was added to the Museum.

Pottery.—The Keramic Gallery contains a fine collection of earthenware, stoneware, and porcelain. There are no less than five pieces of the famous Oiron (or Henri Deux) ware. A fine collection of English pottery was presented by Lady Charlotte Schreiber and the late Mr. C. Schreiber.

Jones Collection.—In 1882 the Museum was enriched by the important bequest of Mr. John Jones of Piccadilly, which consisted of a collection of furniture, Sèvres and other porcelain, enamelled miniatures by Janet, Petitot, and others; paintings, sculpture, bronzes, etc.

The Japanese and Chinese collections in the South and Oriental Court are of great value and interest. The historical collection of Japanese pottery was formed by the Japanese Government for the Museum.

Mention must also be made of the Della Robbia ware, majolica, bronzes, woodwork of various countries, textiles, and the fine collection of historical musical instruments in the west Arcade.

National Art Library.—This library contains upwards of 70,000 volumes bearing directly upon art, and in addition 240,000 drawings, prints, engravings of ornaments, and photographs of art objects. A range of galleries on the first floor has lately been specially erected for this library.

Science and Educational Library.—The nucleus of this library is the collection which formed part of the Educational Exhibition held in St. Martin's Hall in 1854; a portion of the library of the Royal School of Mines in Jermyn Street has recently been added. The library contains over 64,000 volumes.

Dyce and Forster Collections.—The valuable libraries of the Rev. Alexander Dyce, the Shakespearian scholar, and John Forster, the critic and biographer of Dickens, are kept distinct from the other collections, and a reading-room is attached to them. The Dyce collection consists of oil paintings, miniatures, engravings, a few manuscripts, and upwards of 11,000 volumes of printed books. The Forster collection consists of oil and water-colour paintings, drawings, engravings, manuscripts, autographs, and upwards of 18,000 volumes of printed books.

Science Collections.—A Museum of Science was contemplated as an integral part of the Science and Art Department from its creation, but owing to a variety of circumstances the collections were not developed as much as the art collections. Some (among them the food collection) were removed to the Bethnal Green Museum, and the development of the science collections remained in abeyance till 1881. The Patents, Designs, and Trade Marks Act of 1883 having transferred the control and management of the Patent Museum to the Science and Art Department, the iron building which had hitherto contained the Patent Museum was vacated in 1886, and the collections were rearranged in the Exhibition galleries between the Imperial Institute and the Natural History Museum.

India Museum [which *see*] is temporarily placed in the Exhibition galleries.

The remarkable growth of the South Kensington Museum was largely due to the untiring energy of the late Sir Henry Cole, K.C.B., who occupied the position of Director for many years. He was succeeded by Sir Philip Cunliffe Owen, K.C.B., K.C.M.G., the present director.

The Museum is open on Mondays, Tuesdays and Saturdays from 10 A.M. till 10 P.M., *free;* and on Wednesdays, Thursdays and Fridays from 10 A.M. till 4, 5, or 6 P.M., according to the daylight, on payment of sixpence for each person. The Exhibition galleries and Indian section are open free daily from 10 A.M. till 4, 5, or 6 P.M., according to the season.

South Molton Street, NEW BOND STREET, from Brook Street to Oxford Street. William Blake, the poet and eccentric painter, lived for seventeen years at No. 17 in this street. Here he had interviews with angels and persons of scarcely inferior distinction. "South Molton Street, Sunday, August 1807.—My wife was told by a spirit to look for her fortune by opening by chance a book which she had in her hand. It was Bysshe's *Art of Poetry.* She opened the following. . . . I was so well pleased with her luck that I thought I would try my own."

In excavating, a few years back, in front of a public-house at the east corner of this street, at a depth of about 6 feet from the pavement, an old conduit head was discovered, having on it the City arms with the date 1627.

> I can cut watch-papers and work cat-gut ; make quadrille baskets with pins, and take profiles in shade ; ay, as well as the Lady at No. 62 South Molton Street, Grosvenor Square.—Mrs. Cowley's *Belle's Stratagem,* 1780.

On the front of No. 36 (the third house from Oxford Street) is an inscription: "This is South Molton Street 1721."

South Place, FINSBURY, north of Finsbury Circus. Mr. W. J. Fox, M.P. (Publicola), was for many years minister of South Place Chapel.

South Place, KNIGHTSBRIDGE, on the south side of what is now known as the Kensington Road. Here was the residence of the elder Sterling, that "gallant shewy stirring gentleman the Magus of the Times," to whom and to whose house reference is so often made in Carlyle's *Life of John Sterling.*

South Sea House, north-east end of THREADNEEDLE STREET, the hall or place of business of "The Governor and Company of Merchants of Great Britain trading to the South Seas and other parts of America." The Company, incorporated in 1711, consisted of holders of navy and army bills and other unfunded debts, to the amount of £9,177,967 : 15 : 4, who were induced to fund their debts on reasonable terms, by being incorporated into a Company, with the monopoly of the trade to the South Sea and Spanish America. Government, says Mr. M'Culloch, was far from blameless in the affair. The word "bubble," as applied to any ruinous speculation, was first applied to the transactions of the South Sea Company, and, often as the word has been used since, never was it more applicable to any scheme than to the South Sea project of the disastrous year of 1720.

> When Sir Isaac Newton was asked about the continuance of the rising of the South Sea Stock, he answered, that he could not calculate the madness of the people.—Spence's *Anecdotes,* p. 368.
>
> What made Directors cheat in South-Sea year?
> To live on venison when it sold so dear.
> Pope, *Works,* vol. iv. p. 242.
>
> In the extravagance and luxury of the South Sea Year, the price of a haunch of venison was from three to five Pounds.—*Ibid.*

Adam Anderson, author of the *History of Commerce* (d. 1765), was forty years a clerk in the South Sea House. The Company has long ceased to be a trading body, and its remaining stock has been converted into annuity stock.

At the north east extremity of Threadneedle Street, where it enters Bishopsgate Street, is situated the South Sea House. This house stands upon a large extent of ground ; running back as far as Old Broad Street facing St. Peter le Poor. The back-front was formerly the Excise Office; then the South Sea Company's Office; and hence is distinguished by the name of the Old South Sea House. As to the new building in which the Company's affairs are now transacted, it is a magnificent structure.—Noorthouck's *History of London*, 4to, 1773, p. 569.

Reader, in thy passage from the Bank—where thou hast been receiving thy half-yearly dividend (supposing thou art a lean annuitant like myself)—to the Flower Pot to secure a place for Dalston, or Shacklewell, or some other thy suburban retreat northerly, didst thou never observe a melancholy looking, handsome, brick and stone edifice, to the left—where Threadneedle Street abuts upon Bishopsgate? I dare say thou hast often admired its magnificent portals ever gaping wide, and disclosing to view a grave court, with cloisters, and pillars, with few or no traces of goers-in or comers-out—a desolation something like Balclutha's.

This was once a house of trade,—a centre of busy interests. The throng of merchants was here—the quick pulse of gain—and here some forms of business are still kept up, though the soul be long since fled. Here are still to be seen stately porticos, imposing staircases, offices as roomy as the state apartments in palaces—deserted, or thinly peopled with a few straggling clerks; the still more sacred interiors of court and committee-rooms, with venerable faces of beadles, door-keepers —directors seated on forms on solemn days (to proclaim a dead dividend) at long worm-eaten tables, that have been mahogany, with tarnished gilt-leather coverings, supporting massy silver inkstands long since dry; the oaken wainscot hung with pictures of deceased governors and sub-governors, of Queen Anne, and the two first monarchs of the Brunswick dynasty; huge charts, which subsequent discoveries have antiquated; dusty maps of Mexico, dim as dreams,—and soundings of the Bay of Panama!—Charles Lamb, *Elia*, 1st S.

John Lamb, the elder brother of Charles, was a clerk in the South Sea House, and through his influence Elia himself was admitted to learn bookkeeping in the office—hence his familiarity with its interior economy. Portions of the interior and exterior have been remodelled, 1855-1856, and the South Sea House is now a nest of mercantile offices, it having been sold for £55,700.

South Street, GROSVENOR SQUARE, Farm Street to Park Lane. *Eminent Inhabitants.*—Charles James Fox at No. 26, in 1792. The Duke of Orleans (Philippe Egalité), at No. 31. Lady Holland died, November 16, 1845, at No. 33; and here died, April 10, 1843, John Allen, M.D., of Holland House celebrity. George Bryan (Beau) Brummell was living at No. 24 in 1809. Lord Melbourne, at No. 39, during the whole of the Melbourne administration (1835-1841); it is said that Lord Melbourne for many years never gave a dinner, or even had a joint cooked for himself, in this house.

His cooks with long disuse their trade forgot;
Cool was his kitchen.

Southampton Buildings, HOLBORN to CHANCERY LANE, a row of tenements so called after the Wriothesleys, Earls of Southampton, and entitled "Old" to distinguish them from the "New" buildings in High Holborn, erected by Thomas Wriothesley, Earl of Southampton (d. 1667), son of Shakespeare's patron, and father of Lady Rachel Russell. [*See* Southampton House, Holborn.] On August 16, 1673, the Holborn property of the Southampton family was assigned, in trust, to Arthur, Earl of Essex, and others, for and on behoof of Elizabeth,

Countess-Dowager of Northumberland, on her marriage with the Honourable Ralph Montague, eldest son and heir of Edward, Lord Montague. On July 17, 1690, it was assigned in mortgage by Ralph, Earl of Montague, and Elizabeth, Countess of Montague, to Edward Rudge and Edward Littleton. In 1723 it was granted by John, Duke of Montague, as a portion to his eldest daughter, Lady Isabella, on her marriage to William, Duke of Manchester. On March 22, 1727, it was sold and assigned in fee by William and Isabella, Duke and Duchess of Manchester; John, Duke of Montague; Scroop, Duke of Bridgewater; Robert, Earl of Sunderland; and Francis, Earl of Godolphin, to Jacob de Bouverie, Esq., and Sir Edward de Bouverie, Bart., ancestors of the present proprietor, the Earl of Radnor. On March 3, 1740, Sir Jacob de Bouverie, Bart., granted a lease to Edward Bootle, for a term of 230 years, of those premises. After that the present buildings were erected by Edward Bootle, who left them by will to Robert Bootle; who left them by will to trustees; and by divers assignments they became vested in Edward Smith Bigg, Esq., who granted them on lease to the trustees of the London Mechanics' Institute, for the whole of his term of 146 years, from September 1, 1824, at a rent of £229 per annum, with liberty to purchase down to £29 per annum, at any time, for the sum of £350.[1] They are now held by the Birkbeck Bank. The Birkbeck Institution, a reconstitution of the London Mechanics' Institution, and so named in honour of Dr. Birkbeck, the original founder, has been removed to a new house in Bream's Buildings.

This yeare [1650] Jacob, a Jew, opened a Coffey house at the Angel, in the Parish of S. Peter in the East Oxon, and there it was by some, who delighted in Noveltie, drank. When he left Oxon, he sold it in Old Southampton buildings in Holborne near London, and was living there in 1671.—Autobiography of Antony à Wood, vol. ii. p. 65.

Here, in the house of a relative, Edmund Ludlow, the Parliamentary general, lay concealed at the time of the Restoration till he succeeded in escaping to the Continent. In 1696, when Sir George Barclay was arranging the plot for the murder of William III., he took lodgings under the name of Brown in Southampton Buildings, "over against the arch" which led to Staple Inn, the meeting-place of the conspirators being the Griffin Tavern close by.[2] Thomas Holcroft, the dramatist, about 1780 kept a lodging-house in this street. Charles Lamb was living at No. 34 in 1809, after he left Mitre Court Buildings and before he went to Inner Temple Lane. Twenty-one years afterwards, in 1830, when he made a last attempt to reside in London, he once more took up his abode in the same No. 34. In March 1811, when Coleridge was lecturing, he resided in Southampton Buildings, and, as he was in daily intercourse with the Lambs, very probably in No. 34, to which they themselves twice resorted. Here, in the Southampton Coffee-house, at the Chancery Lane end, Hazlitt has laid the scene of his

[1] *Mechanics' Register*, vol. ii. pp. 179, 180.　　[2] *Blackmore*, pp. 135, 136.

Essay on Coffee-house Politicians; and here he occasionally held a kind of evening levee.[1]

> For several years Mr. Hazlitt was a very regular visitor to the Southampton Coffee House. . . . He always came in the evening, occupied a particular place reserved for him as scrupulously as his seat at Covent Garden, called for what he wanted, and settled the score whenever it happened to be convenient.—W. C. Hazlitt, *Memoirs of William Hazlitt*, vol. i. p. 292.

In the year 1820 Hazlitt took apartments at No. 9, at the house of a tailor named Walker. Here, on August 16, he "first saw the sweet apparition" of Miss Sarah, the landlord's daughter, bringing up the tea-tray, and at once fell in love with her. She would not listen to his advances; and after a while he made a journey to Edinburgh to procure a divorce, but the young lady remained unmoved. The great writer then "threw out his clamorous anguish to the clouds and to the winds and to the air" in his *Liber Amoris, or the New Pygmalion* (12mo, 1823), and returned no more to Southampton Buildings.

At Nos. 25 and 26 are the Patent Office, the Registries of Design and Trade Marks Offices, and the Patent Library and Reading Room. At No. 10 is the Office of the Commissioners for Affidavits in the Irish Law Courts, and Registry of Deeds in Ireland. [*See* Patent Office.]

Southampton House, BLOOMSBURY, occupied the whole of the north side of the present Bloomsbury Square.

> Southampton House, a large building with a spacious court before it for the reception of coaches, and a curious garden behind, which lieth open to the fields, enjoying a wholesome and pleasant air.—*Strype*, B. iv. p. 84.
>
> *October* 2, 1664.—To my Lady Sandwich's through my Lord Southampton's new buildings in the fields behind Gray's Inn, and indeed they are very great and a noble work.—*Pepys*.
>
> *February* 9, 1665.—Din'd at my Lo. Treasurer's the Earle of Southampton in Blomesbury, where he was building a noble Square or Piazza, a little Towne; his owne house stands too low, some noble roomes, a pretty cedar chapell, a naked garden to the north, but good aire.—*Evelyn*.

> If you're displeas'd with what you've seen to-night
> Behind Southampton House we'll do you right;
> Who is't dares draw 'gainst me and Mrs. Knight?
> *Epilogue to Mountfort's Greenwich Park*, 4to, 1691.

Rachel, Lady Russell, whose letters invest this house with many delightful associations, died in it September 29, 1723, aged eighty-six. [*See* Bedford House, Bloomsbury.]

Southampton House, HOLBORN, the town house of the Wriothesleys, Earls of Southampton, on the south side of Holborn, a little above Holborn Bars. It was taken down circ. 1652. Parts remained as late as 1850 in Mr. Griffith's, a whipmaker's warehouse, 322 Holborn, and some fragments existed in the Blue Posts Tavern, No. 47 Southampton Buildings, Holborn. On May 17, 1847, Mr. Griffith showed Mr. Cunningham what is still called "the chapel" of

[1] Patmore, in *Jerrold's Mag*. No. 2.

the house, with rubble walls and a flat-timbered roof. Mr. Griffith informed Mr. Cunningham at the same time that his father remembered a pulpit in the chapel, and that he himself, when forming the foundation of a workshop adjoining, had seen portions of a circular building which he supposed to be part of the ruins of the old Temple mentioned by Stow. He was probably right, for in pulling down some old houses early in the last century in the immediate neighbourhood unmistakable remains of the first Temple church were discovered. These remains were of Caen stone.

Beyond the bars [Holborn Bars] had ye in old time a Temple built by the Templars, whose order first began in 1118, in the 19th of Henry I. This Temple was left and fell to ruin since the year 1184, when the Templars had built them a new Temple in Fleet Street, near to the river of Thames. A great part of this old Temple was pulled down but of late in the year 1595. Adjoining to this old Temple was sometime the Bishop of Lincoln's Inn, wherein he lodged when he repaired to this city. Robert de Curars, Bishop of Lincoln, built it about the year 1147. John Russell, Bishop of Lincoln, Chancellor of England in the reign of Richard III., was lodged there. It hath of late years belonged to the Earls of Southampton, and therefore called Southampton House. Master Ropar hath of late built much there; by means whereof part of the ruins of the old Temple were seen to remain, built of Caen stone, round in form as the new Temple by Temple Bar, and other Temples in England.—*Stow*, p. 163.

Southampton House was conveyed in Fee to the Lord Wriothesley, Earl of Southampton, and Lord Chancellor in the time of King Edward VI. For which the Bishop hath no other house in or near London, as is thought.—*Strype*, B. iv. p. 69.

This Wriothesley, Earl of Southampton, died at Southampton House in 1550.

1617.—James I. to Sir Henry Yelverton, Attorney-General. Orders him to prepare a Bill confirming certain privileges to Henry Earl of Southampton, etc., . . . and to extend the liberties of Southampton House from Holborn Bars to the Rolls in Chancery Lane.—*Cal. State Pap.*, 1611-1618, p. 507.

My Lord of Southampton moved the king by petition, that he might have leave to pull down his house in Holborn, and build it into tenements, which would have been much advantage to him, and his fortune hath need of some helps. His Majesty brought his petition with him to the Council Table, and recommended it to the Lords, telling their lordships that my Lord of Southampton was a person whom he much respected, etc.; but upon debate it was dashed.—*Garrard to Lord Strafford*, March 23, 1636, vol. ii. p. 57.

And lately it [Southampton House] hath bin quite taken down and turned to several private tenements.—Howell's *Londinopolis*, fol. 1657, p. 344.

Tuesday, August 28, 1649.—There is a well found by a souldier (and so called the Souldier's Well) near Southampton House in Holburne, doth wonderfull cures to the blind and lame.—*Perfect Occurrences from August* 24 *to August* 31, 1649.

Southampton Market, BLOOMSBURY, better known in later years as *Bloomsbury Market* [which *see*].

December 9, 1668.—Abroad with my wife to the Temple . . . and so to see Mr. Spong, and found him out by *Southampton Market*, and there carried my wife, and up to his chamber, a bye place, but with a good prospect of the fields.—*Pepys*.

Southampton Row, from HIGH HOLBORN to RUSSELL SQUARE. Under this name are now included *King Street* and *Upper King Street*.

---

[1] Herbert's *Inns of Court*, p. 259, *note*.

The former included the portion between High Holborn and Hart Street, and the latter the portion northwards to Bloomsbury Place. The remainder is the original Southampton Row, of which the east side of Russell Square is a prolongation. Here, about 1750 (nine doors north of Cosmo Place), was the residence of Ashley Cowper, the uncle of the poet, and the father of Lady Hesketh and Theodora Jane Cowper, whom the poet loved so tenderly, and who retained for him a life-long affection. "The most popular poet of his generation" was then articled to a solicitor in the neighbourhood, and he and his fellow-clerk, Edward Thurlow, afterwards Lord Chancellor, passed most of their time with this family.

I did actually live three years with Mr. Chapman, a solicitor, that is to say I slept three years in his house; but I lived, that is to say I spent my days, *in Southampton Row*, as you very well remember. There was I and the future Lord Chancellor, constantly employed from morning to night, in giggling and making giggle, instead of studying the law.—*Cowper to Lady Hesketh.*

Here, "at Mr. Jauncey's," on the east side of the Row, when the British Museum was first opened to the public, Gray the poet took apartments which had previously been occupied by his friend Dr. Wharton.

I am now settled in my new territories, commanding Bedford Gardens and all the fields as far as Highgate and Hampstead, with such a concourse of moving pictures as would astonish you; so rus-in-urbe-ish, that I believe I shall stay here, except little excursions and vagaries, for a year to come. What though I am separated from the fashionable world by Broad St. Giles' and many a dirty court and alley, yet here is air and sunshine, and quiet however to comfort you: I shall confess that I am basking all the summer, and I suppose shall be blown down all the winter, besides being robbed every night; I think, however, that the Museum, with all its manuscripts, and rarities by the cart load, will make ample amends for all the aforesaid inconveniences.—*Gray to Mr. Palgrave,* July 24, 1759.

The unhappy Dr. Dodd at one time kept a "Select Academy" in this Row. Dodd, the actor, celebrated as Sir Andrew Aguecheek, died at his lodgings in this Row in 1796.

Southampton Square. [*See* Bloomsbury Square.]

Southampton Street, BLOOMSBURY, runs from Holborn into Bloomsbury Square.

I was born in London on November 6, 1671, in Southampton Street, facing Southampton House.—Colley Cibber's *Apology.*

Southampton Street, PENTONVILLE, from Pentonville Road to Caledonian Road. Dickens relates that Joe Grimaldi, the King of Clowns, passed his last days in a "neat little dwelling" in this street. A few doors off was the "Marquis Cornwallis Tavern," the landlord of which used to call for him every evening and return with him at night. Grimaldi was crippled in his lower limbs, and the friendly landlord carried him on his back. Grimaldi died here in 1837. In this street Thomas Carlyle had lodgings ("my own rooms in Southampton Street")[1] on his first visit to London, 1824.

[1] Carlyle's *Reminiscences,* p. 241.

Southampton Street, STRAND to COVENT GARDEN MARKET, was so called in compliment to Lady Rachel Russell, daughter of Thomas Wriothesley, Earl of Southampton, and wife of William, Lord Russell, the patriot. *Eminent Inhabitants.*—Mrs. Oldfield, the actress; Arthur Maynwaring, in his will (dated 1712), describes her as residing in "New Southampton Street, in the parish of St. Paul's, Covent Garden." David Garrick in No. 27, from his marriage in 1749 until 1772, during the most brilliant part of his career, intermediately between King Street and the Adelphi. The house still bears the same number and will be easily recognised. It is on the west side near the top; is of red brick, and has four front windows in each of the upper storeys. Thomas Linley, the composer, and father of Mrs. Sheridan and Mrs. Tickell, died, 1795, at No. 11 (pulled down in 1890). Dick Estcourt, the actor, died (1713) at his lodgings on the west side. Dr. Lemprière, of Classical Dictionary celebrity, died at a house in this street in 1824. No. 31, Godfrey and Cooke's (established 1680), the oldest chemist and druggist's shop in London,—is now occupied by a publisher,—lasted till about 1860, when the firm discontinued this house and retained the business in Conduit Street. There was a bar at the south end of the street which was taken away about thirty years ago.

Southwark, Borough of, on the south of the Thames, long known as *the* Borough, takes its name from being originally the fortification of London on the south. Being on the high road to London from the Continent it appears to have been inhabited from the earliest times. During the Roman occupation many villas were built here for the wealthier Roman colonists. George Gwilt's Map, compiled in 1819, shows some twenty distinct finds of Roman remains about 10 feet below the present surface, and connected with villas and burial-places, and more have been discovered since. In the construction of Southwark Street evidences of dwellings built on piles (like lake dwellings) came to light.

Southwark was at the first confined to within a short distance of the river, known as the gildable manor, and was from time immemorial a borough. "The burgesses in 1356 say they had formerly a charter franchise which was destroyed by fire, they pray an exemplification of the same, and it was allowed." Bit by bit Southwark came under the City jurisdiction, but never completely so; and although made a ward—Bridge Ward Without—it was never like other wards, it conferred no citizenship on the inhabitants and gave them no privileges.[1] On a vacancy in Bridge Ward Without it is offered to the senior alderman, as being in the category of an honorary dignity. [*See* Bridge Ward Without.] The ward has no representatives in the Common Council.

The Borough is in shape somewhat like the map of Italy, St. George's Road and Bethlem being at the toe of the boot. It lies entirely south of the Thames, having Lambeth to the west and Deptford to the east.

[1] The first alderman of the ward was Sir John Ayliffe, barber surgeon, who was appointed in 1550.

The older borough comprised the parishes of St. George, St. John, Horselydown, St. Olave, St. Thomas and St. Saviour, exclusive of the Clink and Christ Church (Paris Garden); later on it included, as it does now, Christ Church, the Church Liberty, Bermondsey, and Rotherhithe. In 1631, during a time of scarcity, the Lord Mayor counted 16,880 mouths in Southwark, but the area then was so much smaller than it is now that it can scarcely be compared with the Southwark of the census of 1881, which showed a population of 221,946.

The town or village which had grown up in Saxon times where the Roman villas had previously stood was burnt by William the Conqueror, and little seems to have remained of it when the Domesday Survey was made. Odo, Bishop of Bayeux, then had "a monastery and tide-way in Southwark." These he seems to have acquired by somewhat sharp practice. In Edward the Confessor's time "of the produce of the port where ships resort, the King received two parts, Earl Godwin the third," but now the Bishop seems to have appropriated the whole to himself. Edward III., by a charter of the first year of his reign (1327), granted the vill of Southwark to the citizens of London who, as recited, in a petition to the King in Parliament had complained that malefactors escaped there out of the jurisdiction of the City, and prayed that such vill might be given to them. With consent of his Parliament the King grants the said vill in fee farm. The grant—against which the inhabitants of Southwark petitioned in vain—was confirmed in a second charter of the 11th year (1337), and in fuller terms in a third of the 50th of the same King's reign (1376). Several charters in later reigns confirmed, extended, or varied the terms of the grant, the last, which vests the entire control of the borough in the Lord Mayor and Corporation of London, being that of 5th Edward VI., 1551.[1] Southwark sent representatives to Parliament from the 23d of Edward I., 1296.[2]

Southwark, from the earliest times, was the chief thoroughfare to and from London and the southern counties and towns, including Canterbury and the cities of the Continent. This is sufficient to account for the large number of inns, such as the Bear at the Bridge foot, the King's Head, the Talbot or Tabard of Chaucer's "Canterbury Pilgrims" [*see* Tabard], and the White Hart, which was the headquarters of Jack Cade during his brief occupancy of the City and Borough (1450). Cade's inn was destroyed in the great Southwark fire of 1676, but was rebuilt, and it was at this White Hart that Sam Weller was first introduced to a world of admirers. The inn was cleared away in 1889.

The Duke of Hamilton of the time of Charles I., while knocking for admittance at an inn gate in Southwark, about four in the morning, was arrested by a party of soldiers searching for Sir Lewis Dyves.

He told them a very formal story of himself and his business, which at first satisfied them; but they observed that as he took a pipe of tobacco by them, he burned several great papers to fire it, whereupon they searched him, and found such

---

[1] Manning and Bray, and Brayley's *Surrey*; *Liber Albus*; Riley's *Memorials*; *Norton*.
[2] Manning and Bray, vol. iii. p. 649.

papers about him as discovered him.—Burnet's *Memoirs of the Dukes of Hamilton*, p. 384.

Some of the inns bore odd signs. Andrews, in *Anecdote History of Great Britain* (1794), mentions that "in the borough of Southwark is a sign on which is inscribed *The Old Pick-my-toe.*" Mrs. Piozzi, who long dwelt in the Borough, wrote in the margin, "So it is: I knew the sign and was probably then the only person who could have guessed the derivation." The figure represented the ancient statue of the Roman slave seeking for the thorn in his foot.[1] In the 16th century there were here many town houses of persons of importance, such as abbots, priors and others. There were Suffolk House, by St. George's Church, for Brandon, Duke of Suffolk, and his wife, the Princess Mary; and Winchester House for the Bishops of Winchester. West of the latter place were playhouses, bear and bull baiting circuses, and stews or licensed brothels.

In the old poem of "Cock Lorell's Bote," printed by Wynkyn de Worde in the reign of Henry VIII., the Bankside, Southwark, is called "The Stewes Banke." They were of very old standing. As early as the reign of Edward I. there was an ordinance of the City providing—

That no boatman shall have his boat moored and standing over the water after sunset; but they shall have all their boats moored on this [the City] side of the water that so thieves or other misdoers may not be carried by them under pain of imprisonment: nor may they carry any man or woman, either denizens or strangers, unto the Stews [of Southwark] except in the day-time under pain of imprisonment. *Liber Albus*, B. iii. pt. ii. p. 242.

Southwark had also an unenviable celebrity for its prisons. These prisons were the King's Bench (Queen's Prison), the Marshalsea, the White Lion, the Borough Compter, and the Clink, or prison of the Clink Liberty, as the Manor of Southwark was of old called. [*See* those names.] "I live," said Mr. Highland, member for Southwark, speaking in the House of Commons, June 6, 1667,—"I live amongst prisoners. In three prisons near me there are above one thousand prisoners."[2] Taylor, the Water Poet, thus refers to these prisons :—

> Five jayles or prisons are in Southwark placed,
> The Counter, once St. Margarets church defaced,
> The Marshalsea, the Kings Bench and White Lyon—
> Then thers the Clinke, where handsome lodgings be,
> And much good may it do them all for me.

It is pleasanter to remember that the first English Bible printed in England was "Imprynted in Southwarke for James Nycolson," 1536. Southwark being the last stage towards London was necessarily the chosen resort of reformers, disturbers, and lovers of change. Godwin and his sons made incursions in 1052. Simon de Montfort was here in 1264 during the Barons' Wars; attempts were made to take him by surprise at his lodgings, but they failed. In 1554 Sir Thomas Wyatt found his way to Tower Hill through Southwark. In 1666 Colonel Thompson and 2000 of people gathered here "for King Jesus."

[1] *Piozziana*, p. 183. [2] *Burton's Diary*, vol. ii. p. 191.

A great change was made in the appearance of Southwark when George Dance the younger, R.A., "Clerk of yᵉ City's Works" at the end of the last century, laid out the Bridge House estate of the Corporation in St. George's Fields. Since then changes have been continuous, and very little of the old-fashioned character of the Borough is now left. [*See* also Bankside, Barclay and Perkins's Brewery, Bear Garden, Bridge Ward Without, George (St.) the Martyr, Globe Theatre, Guy's Hospital, Hope Theatre, Horselydown, Mint, Olave (St.), Paris Garden, Rose, Saviour (St.), Thomas (St.) à Waterings, Thomas's (St.) Hospital, Winchester House.]

Southwark Bridge, a bridge over the Thames, was of three cast-iron arches, resting on stone piers, at the narrowest part of the river, between London and Blackfriars Bridges. It was designed by Sir John Rennie, and erected by a public company, at an expense of about £800,000. The first stone was laid April 23, 1815, by Admiral Viscount Keith. The bridge was opened without any public ceremony at midnight of March 24, 1819. The span of the centre arch is 240 feet, of the side arches each 210 feet. The entire weight of iron employed in upholding the bridge is about 5780 tons. The roadway is 700 feet long and 42 wide. The approach from the City is by Queen Street, Cheapside. Southwark Bridge was purchased by the Corporation of London in 1866 for £218,868, and made free of toll. A good general account of the bridge and its erection will be found in the *Autobiography of Sir John Rennie*, pp. 7 and 22-26.

Southwark Fair, called also the Lady Fair and St. Margaret's Fair. It was one of the three great fairs of special importance described in a Proclamation of Charles I., "unto which there is usually extraordinary resort out of all parts of the kingdom."[1] The three fairs were Bartholomew Fair, Sturbridge Fair, near Cambridge, and Our Lady Fair, in the borough of Southwark. Liberty to hold an annual fair in Southwark, on September 7, 8, and 9, was granted to the City of London by the charter of 2 Edward IV. (November 2, 1462), but it was probably held long before in a loose informal manner. The charter was confirmed by that of 5 Edward VI. (April 23, 1551), together with a Court of piepoudre for the determination of all suits and offences occurring during the fair. [*See* Bartholomew Fair ; Pie-powder Court.] The fair was held in the public ways, courts and inn-yards from above the Tabard to St. George's Church. Though the allowed time for its continuance by charter was only three days, it generally continued, like other fairs, for fourteen days. It was famous for its drolls, puppet shows, rope dancing, music booths, and tippling houses.

September 21, 1668.—To Southwark Fair, very dirty, and there saw the puppet-shew of Whittington, which was pretty to see ; and how that idle thing do work upon people that see it, and even myself too ! And thence to Jacob Hall's dancing

---

[1] *Rymer*, vol. xix. p. 185.

on the ropes, where I saw such action as I never saw before, and mightily worth seeing; and here took acquaintance with a fellow that carried me to a tavern, whither came the music of this booth, and by and by Jacob Hall himself, with whom I had a mind to speak, to hear whether he had ever any mischief by falls in his time. He told me, "Yes, many, but never to the breaking of a limb." He seems a mighty strong man. So giving them a bottle or two of wine, I away.—*Pepys.*

Before going into the fair Pepys had taken the precaution to leave his purse with Bland his waterman, "at the Beare," for "fear of his pocket being cut."

September 13, 1660.—I saw in Southwark at St. Margaret's Faire, monkies and apes dance and do other feates of activity on ye high rope; they were gallantly clad *à la mode*, went upright, saluted the company, bowing and pulling off their hatts; they saluted one another with as good a grace as if instructed by a daunceing-master. They turn'd heels over head with a basket having eggs in it without breaking any; also with lighted candles in their hands and on their heads without extinguishing them, and with vessells of water without spilling a drop. I also saw an Italian wench daunce and performe all the tricks on ye high rope to admiration; all the Court went to see her. Likewise here was a man who tooke up a piece of iron cannon of about 400 lb. (*sic*) weight with the haire of his head onely.—*Evelyn.*

It was studied for its low life by Hogarth and Gay, who have left us the celebrated picture of Southwark Fair and the popular *Beggar's Opera.* Powell, Booth, and Macklin were all three introduced at the fair.

His [Boheme's] first appearance was at a Booth in *Southwark Fair*, which in those days, lasted two weeks, and was much frequented by persons of all distinctions, of both sexes; he acted the part of Menelaus in the best droll I ever saw, called the Siege of Troy.—Victor's *History of the Theatres* (1761), vol. ii. p. 74.

Timothy Fielding, the actor (who has been confused with Henry Fielding, the author), had a booth at Southwark Fair. [*See* BLUE MAID ALLEY.] The bellman by order of the Justices cried down the fair in 1743, and it was prohibited for the future by the Common Council in 1762, having long been scandalous for its scenes of riot and immorality; it was finally suppressed by the Corporation in September 1763.

Southwark Park, of 63 acres, was formed by the Metropolitan Board of Works and opened to the public in 1869. The name has the same misappropriateness as that of Finsbury Park. Southwark Park is situated immediately west of the Commercial Docks and the Deptford Lower Road, with the whole of Bermondsey between it and Southwark. The park is in the midst of a dense and very poor population, to whom it is a great boon, and by whom it appears to be thoroughly appreciated. It cost about £96,000. There was an old Southwark Park, an appendage to Suffolk House and a part of the King's Manor, which was excepted from the grant of the borough of Southwark to the City of London in the charter of Edward VI.[1]

Southwark Place, SOUTHWARK. [*See* Suffolk House, Southwark.]

Southwark Street, a broad and handsome street (but disfigured at its western end by the London, Chatham and Dover Railway

---

[1] *Norton*, p. 388.

bridge which crosses it there), constructed by the Metropolitan Board of Works and opened in 1864. It cost £555,922. It is 70 feet wide and 3450 feet long, and runs from the Borough High Street, a little south of the Borough Market, in an easy curve to the Blackfriars Road, opposite Stamford Street, and is lined for the most part with large and substantial warehouses and offices, some of them of considerable architectural pretension. Such are the Hop Exchange (opened 1867), the Southwark and the Alliance Chambers, etc. The east end is much occupied by hop merchants and factors; farther west are wholesale stationers, druggists, oil-merchants, engineers, and other large business establishments.

Spa Fields, CLERKENWELL, so called from the *London Spa*, a mineral spring of some celebrity in the 17th and first half of the 18th century. The Spa House stood at the angle where Exmouth and Rosoman Streets meet. [*See* London Spa.] The fields were also known as *Ducking Pond Fields, Clerkenwell Fields*, and *Pipe Fields*. They were an open waste, notorious for bull-baiting, duck-hunting, pugilism, wrestling and other rough sports, and a favourite Sunday promenade for Londoners. They began to be built over in 1817, and were in a few years covered thickly with houses.

March 27 (Lord's Day), 1664.—It being church-time walked to St. James's, to try if I could see the belle Butler, but could not; only saw her sister, who indeed is pretty, with a fine Roman nose. Thence walked through the Ducking Pond Fields; but they are so altered since my father used to carry us to Islington, to the old man at the King's Head, to eat cakes and ale (his name was Pitts), that I did not know which was the Ducking Pond, nor where I was.—*Pepys*.

On Wednesday last two women fought for a new shift, valued at half a guinea, in the Spaw Fields, near Islington. The battle was won by the woman called Bruising Peg, who beat her antagonist in a terrible manner.—*Daily Advertiser*, June 22, 1768.

On Sabbath-day who has not seen
In colours of the rainbow dizen'd
The prentice beaux and belles I ween,
Fatigued with heat with dust half poisen'd
To *Dobney's* strolling, or *Pantheon*
Their tea to sip or else regale,
As on the way they shall agree on,
With syllabubs or bottled ale.
London Evening Post, August 1776.

Malcolm, in his *Anecdotes of Manners in London in the Eighteenth Century* (1803), speaks of Spa Fields as still a great Sunday resort.

The *Ducking Pond* was a little west of the London Spa, and by it was *Ducking Pond House*. This was taken down in 1770, and the *Pantheon*, a large circular assembly room, erected on its site. The grounds were laid out as a sort of minor Vauxhall or Ranelagh, the Ducking Pond being now called the lake, and furnished with boats. After a time the Pantheon acquired an evil reputation, and in 1776 was closed as a place of entertainment, to become shortly the birth-place and cradle of a new and influential sect. It was taken by two "evangelical" clergymen and reopened as *Northampton Chapel*; the lake being drained and, with the grounds, turned into a cemetery. This provoked the incumbent of the parish, and the clergymen were inhibited by the Ecclesiastical Courts (February 1779) from preaching in an unconsecrated place. The chapel was transferred to the Countess of Huntingdon and immediately reopened, she making the adjoining house her residence with a view to cover, by privilege of peerage, clergymen preaching there. The Ecclesiastical Courts, however, decided against the claim, and two of her clergy having seceded from the Establishment, the chapel became the first chapel of "The Countess of Huntingdon's Connexion." It was a plain brick building, with a high domical roof and lantern, and had on the front a stone inscribed *Spa Fields Chapel*. It was pulled down 1879. It was capable of holding 2000 persons.

Selina, Countess of Huntingdon, died in the house adjoining, June 17, 1791. Spa Fields burial-ground became notorious in 1845 in consequence of the proprietors burning the bodies of the dead to make room for fresh interments. About 1350 bodies, it appeared, were annually buried there. The ground was shortly after closed by an Order in Council.

In 1886 a new Spa Fields chapel was built in Lloyd Square, the site and building costing £15,000.

The Spa Fields Reform Meetings of 1816, which led to the suspension of the Habeas Corpus Act in the following spring, were held on the site of the present *Wilmington Square* (erected 1818). The first meeting was held November 15, when the crowd dispersed quietly after being addressed by Orator Hunt from the first floor window of the Merlin's Cave public-house. At the second meeting on December 2 the Watsons, father and son, spoke from a waggon drawn up in front of Merlin's Cave. After much noise and riot young Watson called on the mob to follow him and seize the Tower. Having sacked the shop of Beckwith, a gunsmith at Snow Hill, on their way, they reached Tower Hill, but were there quickly dispersed. In the following June young Watson was tried for high treason before Lord Ellenborough and acquitted. A *Merlin's Cave* still occupies the site of the old house, the present building being a "gin palace" marked by a bust, meant no doubt for Merlin, but which would serve as well for Homer, with the equally authentic date, "A.D. 516." It stands at the junction of Merlin's Place with Upper Rosoman Street. *Wilmington Square* is immediately south.

Spanish Place, MANCHESTER SQUARE, is at the north-east corner of the square and extends into Charles Street. At its own north-east corner is the chapel built for the Spanish Embassy in 1792 from the design of Joseph Bonomi, A.R.A., architect, and renovated and decorated in 1866 under the superintendence of C. J. Wray, when a new and powerful organ by Gray and Davison was added. The campanile was raised, 1846, by Charles Parker, architect. In the time of the first

French Empire No. 3 was the residence of the Maréchal duc de Coigny, and a great resort of the leading emigrés. Michael Faraday, who spent his early days in this neighbourhood, often pointed out the spot in this street where he used to play marbles.

'Sparagus Garden, a place of amusement in LAMBETH MARSH, adjoining Cuper's Gardens, and now only known, even by name, to local antiquaries and the readers of our seventeenth century literature. It was a narrow strip running up from the river, a little east of Queen's Arms Stairs, the landing-place opposite and answering to Whitehall Stairs. Richard Brome wrote a play, called the *'Sparagus Garden*, acted in 1635 at Salisbury Court, and printed in 4to, 1640.

April 22, 1668.—To the fishmonger's and bought a couple of lobsters, and over to the 'Sparagus Garden, thinking to have met Mr. Pierce and his wife, and Knipp.—*Pepys.*

Spectacle Makers' Company, the sixtieth on the list of the City Companies, an ancient fraternity by prescription, but first incorporated by letters patent of Charles I., dated May 16, 1630. The Company has a livery, granted by the Court of Aldermen in 1809, but no hall.

Spencer House, ST. JAMES'S PLACE and the GREEN PARK, was built for John Spencer, first Lord Spencer of Althorp (d. 1783). The statues on the pediment are by M. H. Spang. The Green Park front designed by John Vardy, and the St. James's Place front by James Stuart. [*See* St. James's Place.]

Spitalfields, a district and parish in the east of London, between Bishopsgate and Bethnal Green, inhabited by weavers of silk and other poor people. It was a place of sepulture for Roman London, and received its name from the fields having once belonged to the Priory and Hospital of St. Mary Spital, founded in 1197 by Walter Brune and Rosia his wife, and dedicated to the honour of Jesus Christ and the Virgin Mary by the name of Domus Dei et Beatæ Mariæ, extra Bishopsgate, in the parish of St. Botolph. Hence the present parish of Christ Church, Spitalfields. The old name was *Lolesworth*, according to Stow, who gives a long and particular account of the discovery of a large number of Roman cinerary urns, bones, vestiges of coffins and various other remains made in excavating on the east side of the church for brick-earth in 1576. Stow was himself present during some of the diggings, and carried with him a small "pot of white earth . . . made in the shape of a hare squatted upon her legs, and between her ears the mouth of the pot; also the lower jaw of a man, some iron nails," etc.[1] The fields were covered with buildings between 1650 and 1660.

The silk manufacture was planted in Spitalfields by French emigrants, expelled from their own country upon the revocation of the Edict of Nantes in 1685, a measure which transferred to this country

[1] *Stow*, p. 64.

the families of Auriol, Barré, Boileau, Bouverie, Ligonier, Labouchere, Romilly, Houblon, Lefroy, Levesque, De la Haye, Garnault, Ouvry, etc. In Spitalfields are found many French names, as Bataille, Lafontaine, Strachan, Fontaneau, etc., by weavers, enamellers, jewellers, etc., both masters and workpeople, down to our own day; while still more, perhaps, translations of the original French names of their ancestors, as Masters (Le Maitre), Young (Le Jeune), Black (Lenoir), King (Le Roi), and the like; but the traces of French descent have been fast fading away in recent years. The Dollonds were French refugees, and John Dollond, the inventor of the achromatic telescope, was born in Spitalfields and worked with his father at the loom. In the churchyard of the priory (now Spital Square), was a pulpit cross, "somewhat like," says Stow, "to that in St. Paul's churchyard," where the celebrated Spital sermons were originally preached. The cross was rebuilt in 1594, and destroyed during the troubles of Charles I. The sermons, however, have been continued to the present time, and are still preached every Easter Monday and Easter Tuesday, before the Lord Mayor and Aldermen, at Christ Church, Newgate Street. The Christ's Hospital or Blue Coat Boys were regular attendants, in the reign of Queen Elizabeth,[1] at the Spital sermons at the old cross in Spital Square.

A hospital or spital signified a charitable institution for the advantage of poor, infirm, and aged persons—an almshouse, in short; while spittles were mere lazarhouses, receptacles for wretches in the leprosy, and other loathsome diseases the consequence of debauchery and vice.—Gifford (*Note in Massinger's Works*).

On Easter Sunday the ancient custom is that all the children of the Hospital go before my Lord Mayor to the Spittle, that the world may witness the works of God and man, in maintenence of so many poor people, the better to stir up living men's minds to the same good.—*A Nest of Ninnies*, by Robert Armin, 4to, 1680.

> That other
> That, in pure madrigal, unto his mother
> Commended the French hood and scarlet gown
> The Lady May'ress passed in through the town,
> Unto the Spittle Sermon.—Ben Jonson, *Underwoods*, No. lxi.

But the sermon of the greatest length was that concerning Charity before the Lord Mayor and Aldermen at the Spittle: in speaking which he [Dr. Barrow] spent three hours and a half. Being asked after he came down from the pulpit whether he was not tired: "Yes, indeed," said he, "I began to be weary with standing so long."— Pope's *Life of Seth Ward*, 12mo, 1697, p. 148.

The population of Spitalfields in 1881 was 22,585. No district in or about London contains a similar mass of low-rented houses to that of Spitalfields and Bethnal Green. The weavers' houses generally consist of two rooms on the ground floor and a workroom above. This workroom always has a window the whole length of the room for the admission of light to the loom; in these small, crowded, and often dirty rooms some of the most delicate and exquisitely wrought velvets, satins, and brocaded silks have been produced. But the weaving population of Spitalfields has been for some years declining. Many of the houses above described have been swept away in constructing Commercial

---

[1] *Stow*, p. 119.

Street, the formation and extension of the Great Eastern Railway, and in various local alterations and improvements, and few if any such houses have been built in their place. The character of the district has undergone a marked change in the last few years, but it remains distinctively a region of small, low-rented and overcrowded houses, inhabited by a very poor population. [*See* Christ Church, Spitalfields; Pelham Street, Spital Square, Wheeler Street.]

"In 1870, when the promulgation of the celebrated decree of papal infallibility had been resolved upon, it was deemed necessary that the Pope should wear at the attendant ceremony a new vestment woven entirely in one piece. Italy, France, and other European countries were vainly searched for a weaver capable of executing this work, and at last the order came to England, where in Spitalfields was found the only man able to make the garment, and he, by a strange irony of fate, one of the erstwhile persecuted Huguenot race."—Booth's *Labour and Life of the People*, 1889, vol. i. p. 394, *note*.

Bishop Wilson of Calcutta was born in Church Street, Spitalfields, July 22, 1778. A view of the house is given in his *Life*, vol. i. p. 3.

Spital Square, SPITALFIELDS, is an open place on the east side of Norton Folgate, formerly a centre of the silk and velvet trade. Thomas Stothard, R.A., passed a seven years' apprenticeship with a "draftsman of patterns for brocaded silk" in this square; and here his genius was first discovered by Harrison, the publisher of the *Novelist's Magazine*, which was to owe its popularity to his graceful pencil.[1]

Spittle Croft, a burying ground of 13 acres, consecrated in 1349 by Dr. Ralph Stratford, Bishop of London, situated near Charterhouse Square.

And the Plague coming on with great fury in the year 1349, Sir Walter de Manny . . . purchased of the Master and Brethren of St. Bartholomew's Spittle, a piece of ground called Spittle Croft, containing thirteen acres and a rod . . . and there were buried in that year more than fifty thousand corpses in these thirteen acres and a rod of ground.—Bearcroft's *Sutton and Charter House*, 1737, p. 164.

Spring Gardens, between ST. JAMES'S PARK and CHARING CROSS and WHITEHALL, a garden dating at latest from the reign of James I., with butts, bathing-pond, pheasant-yard, and bowling-green, attached to the King's Palace at Whitehall, and so called from a jet or spring of water, which sprung with the pressure of the foot, and wetted whoever was foolish or ignorant enough to tread upon it.

In March 1610, there is a "Grant to Geo. Johnson, Keeper of the *King's Spring Garden*;" and in the same month funds are assigned for "making defence for orange and other fruit trees in the Park and Spring Garden." In March, 1611, the minion Robert Carr was created Viscount Rochester, and appointed *Keeper of the Palace of Westminster*, part of the duty being to "keep and preserve wild beasts and fowl in St. James's Park and Garden and Spring Garden" (*Cal. State Pap.*, 1611-1618, p. 57, etc.) Among the Egerton MSS., No. 806, in the British Museum, is an account of "Charges don in doeinge of sundry needful reparacons about the I'ke and Springe Garden, beginninge primo Julij, 1614, and ending ultimo Septem. next." The water was supplied by pipes of lead from St. James's Fields. Among other charges at the

---

[1] *Life*, by Mrs. Bray, p. 9.

end is one, "For two clucking henns to sett upon the pheasant eggs, iiij⁵." On the 29th of November, 1601, a payment was made to George Johnson, keeper of the Spring Garden, for a scaffold which he had erected against the Park wall in the Tilt Yard, for "the Countie Egmond" to see the tilters (Chalmer's *Apology*, vol. i. p. 340). And in 1630 Simon Osbaldeston was appointed keeper of the King's Garden called the Spring Garden and of His Majesty's Bowling-green there. It appears by the patent (Pat. 7 Car., pt. 8, No. 4) that the garden was made a Bowling-green by command of Charles I—Lysons's *Environs*, vol. i. p. 324; Lord Chamberlain's *Warrant Book*, vol. i. p. 252.

In a garden joining to this Palace [Whitehall] there is a jet d'eau, with a sun-dial, at which, while strangers are looking, a quantity of water forced by a wheel, which the gardener turns at a distance through a number of little pipes, plentifully sprinkles those that are standing round.—Hentzner's *Travels*, anno, 1598.

Water-springs of this description were not uncommon in gardens of the time of Queen Elizabeth, and even later. One of this character existed at Chatsworth; and Nares, in his Glossary, says that the spring-garden described by Plot was to be seen at Enstone, in Oxfordshire, in 1822.

> But look thee, Martius; not a vein runs here,
> From head to foot, but Sophocles would unseam,
> And like a Spring Garden, shoot his scornful blood
> Into their eyes, durst come to tread on him.
> *Beaumont and Fletcher*, ed. Dyce, vol. ii. p. 484.

To John Sweate, carpenter, for framing and putting up two Sluces of tymber in the Spring Garden, and a new Bridge with tymber and plankes and nailes on each side, ix foote in length, to lead to the Duck Pond Island, and for framing and setting up a Sluce at the Pond in Scotland Yard . . . £6:13:4.—*Crown Works at Whitehall*, 1634-1635.

April 18, 1633.—The Earl of Holland was on Saturday last very solemnly restord at Council Table (the King present) from a kind of eclipse wherein he had stood since the Tuesday fortnight before. . . . All the cause yet known was a verbal challenge sent from him by Mr. Henry Germain to the now Lord Weston, newly returned from his foreign imployments, that . . . he did him at such a time, even in the Spring Garden (close under his father's window) with his sword by his side.—*Sir H. Wotton to Sir Edmund Bacon* (*Rel. Wott.*, p. 455).

The great bowling green in this garden, and a "new garden house for his Majesty to repose in," were made in 1629 by William Walker for Charles I., the bowling green with turf from Blackheath.[1]

June 3, 1634.—The Bowling-green in the Spring Garden was, by the King's command, put down for one day, but by the intercession of the Queen it was reprieved for this year; but hereafter it shall be no common bowling-place. There was kept in it an ordinary of six shillings a meal (when the King's proclamation allows but two elsewhere), continual bibbing and drinking wine all day under the trees; two or three quarrels every week. It was grown scandalous and insufferable; besides my Lord Digby being reprehended for striking [Will. Crofts] in the King's garden, he answered that he took it for a common bowling-place, where all paid money for their coming in.—*Garrard to Lord Strafford* (*Strafford Papers*, vol. i. p. 262).

Since the Spring Garden was put down, we have, by a servant of the Lord Chamberlain's, a new Spring Garden erected in the fields behind the Muse [*See* Piccadilly], where is built a fair house, and two bowling greens made, to entertain gamesters and bowlers at an excessive rate; for I believe it has cost him £4000,—a

---

[1] Accounts, favoured by Lord Chamberlain's office.

dear undertaking for a gentleman barber. My Lord Chamberlain much frequents that place, where they bowl great matches.—*Garrard to Lord Strafford* (*Strafford Papers*, vol. i. p. 435).

When James, Duke of York, made his escape from St. James's Palace, April 20, 1648, he and Colonel Bamfield passed into and out of the Spring Garden "as gallants come to hear the nightingale."

> As for the pastimes of my sisters, when they were in the country, it was to read, work, walk, and discourse with each other. Commonly they lived half the year in London. Their customs were in winter time to go sometimes to plays or to ride in their coaches about the streets, to see the concourse and recourse of people, and in the spring time to visit the Spring Garden, Hyde Park, and the like places; and sometimes they would have music and sup in barges upon the water.—*Margaret Lucas, Duchess of Newcastle* (temp. Charles I.)

> *June* 13, 1649.—I dined with my worthy friend Sir John Owen. . . . Afterwards I treated ladies of my relations in Spring Garden.—*Evelyn*.

> Shall we make a fling to London, and see how the spring appears there in the Spring Garden; and in Hyde Park, to see the races, horse and foot?—R. Brome, *A Joviall Crew*, 4to, 1652.

> *May* 10, 1654.—My Lady Gerrard treated us at Mulberry Garden, now ye onely place of refreshment about the toune for persons of the best quality to be exceedingly cheated at; Cromwell and his partizans having shut up and seized on Spring Garden, wch till now had been ye usual rendezvous for the ladys and gallants at this season. —*Evelyn*.

> *May* 20, 1658.—I went to see a coach race in Hyde Park, and collationed in Spring Garden.—*Evelyn*.

> The manner is as the company returns [from Hyde Park] to alight at the Spring Garden so called, in order to the Parke, as our Thuilleries is to the Course; the inclosure not disagreeable, for the solemnness of the grove, the warbling of the birds, and as it opens into the spacious walks at St. James's; but the company walk in it at such a rate, you would think that all the ladies were so many Atalantas contending with their wooers . . . But as fast as they run they stay there so long as if they wanted not time to finish the race; for it is usual here to find some of the young company till midnight; and the thickets of the garden seem to be contrived to all advantages of gallantry, after they have been refreshed with the collation, which is here seldom omitted, at a certain cabaret, in the middle of this paradise, where the forbidden fruits are certain trifling tarts, neats' tongues, salacious meats, and bad Rhenish; for which the gallants pay sauce, as indeed they do at all such houses throughout England.—*A Character of England*, etc. (attributed to Evelyn), 12mo, 1659, p. 56.

After the Restoration the Spring Garden at Charing Cross was called the Old Spring Garden, the ground built upon, and the entertainments removed to the New Spring Garden at Lambeth, since called *Vauxhall*.[1] Pepys preferred the new Spring Garden to the old one.

> *May* 29, 1662.—To the old Spring Garden, and there walked long, and the wenches [his wife's two maids] gathered pinks. Here we staid and seeing that we could not have anything to eate, but very dear and with long stay, we went forth again without any notice taken of us, and so we might have done if we had had anything. Thence to the new one, where I never was before, which much exceeds the other.—*Pepys*.

In the early part of the 18th century there was another Spring Garden at Knightsbridge,—like the Old and the New Spring Gardens,

---

[1] *London Gazette* of 1675, No. 981.

a place of public resort.[1] The ground built upon was called "Inner Spring Garden" and "Outer Spring Garden."[2]

The *Blue Posts* in Spring Garden was the rendezvous of the conspirators in the plot to assassinate William III., in the spring of 1696.

Eminent Inhabitants.—Sir Philip Warwick, in 1661, etc., author of the Memoirs which bear his name; he lived in Outer Spring Garden. *Warwick Street,* adjoining, was named after him. Sir William Morris, in 1662, etc., in Outer Spring Garden. Philip, Earl of Chesterfield, 1667-1670, in Outer Spring Garden. Prince Rupert, from 1674 to his death in November 1682. The Lord Crofts, "mad Lord Crofts," 1674, etc. In the books of the Lord Steward's office he is described as living, in 1677, "in the place commonly called the Old Spring Garden." Sir Edward Hungerford, in 1681, after his removal from the site of *Hungerford Market.* Colley Cibber, from 1711 to 1714.

In or near the old Play-house in Drury Lane, on Monday last, the 19th of January, a watch was dropp'd having a Tortoise-shell Case inlaid with silver, a silver chain, and a gold seal ring, the arms a cross wavy and chequer. Whoever brings it to Mr. Cibber, at his House near the Bull Head Tavern in Old Spring Garden at Charing Cross, shall have three guineas reward.—*The Daily Courant,* January 20, 1703.

The Earls of Berkeley from 1772. [*See* Berkeley House.] Admiral Sir Charles Saunders, one of the most distinguished on our long roll of seamen, died at his house in Spring Gardens, December 7, 1775. Sir Gilbert Elliott (first Earl of Minto) was living here before his expedition to Toulon, 1793. George Canning at No. 13 (right-hand corner of Cockspur Street). On March 12, 1799, he writes to Malone asking him to take his place in the chair at "The Club."[3]

A lady having put to Canning the silly question—"Why have they the spaces in the iron gate at Spring Gardens so narrow?" he replied, "Oh Ma'am, because such very fat people tried to go through,"—a reply concerning which Tom Moore said that the person who does not relish it can have no perception of real wit.—Dyce's *Rogers,* p. 160.

The first Earl of Malmesbury at No. 14.

Sunday, November 3, 1805.—Mr. Pitt and Lord Mulgrave came to me in Spring Gardens, about 10 o'clock, with a Dutch newspaper in which the capitulation of Ulm was inserted at full length. As they neither of them understood Dutch, and all the offices were empty, they came to me to translate it, which I did as well as I could; and I observed but too clearly the effect which it had on Pitt, though he did his utmost to conceal it. This was the last time I saw him.—Lord Malmesbury's *Diary.*

Sir Robert Taylor, the architect of the Bank of England and founder of the Taylor Institute, Oxford, died at his house in Spring Gardens, September 27, 1788, leaving a fortune of £180,000, though, as he used to say, he began life with hardly eighteenpence. His son, Michael Angelo Taylor, whose name is attached to the well-

---

[1] He carried me to the *Spring Garden* at Knightsbridge, where we walked in the gardens, and he treated me very handsomely.—Defoe's *Moll Flanders,* Talboy s ed., p. 243.
[2] Rate-books of St. Martin's-in-the-Fields.
[3] Prior, *Life of Malone,* p. 256.

known Act of Parliament 1816-1817, relating to paving, also died here in 1834. In June 1838 another eminent and equally prosperous architect, Sir George Gilbert Scott, "settled down," as he wrote, shortly after his marriage, at No. 20 (now 31) Spring Gardens, and continued to live there till 1844, when he removed to St. John's Wood; but the house in Spring Gardens continued to be his professional office till his death. The houses are now principally used as offices. No. 24 is the Land Revenue Records and Enrolments Office, and the Admiralty has No. 26. At the Park end, Nos. 10 to 14, was the office of the Metropolitan Board of Works, erected in 1860, from the designs of Fred. Marrable, architect to the Board. It is a large Palladian edifice, now occupied by the London County Council. The meeting-room has been (1890) enlarged to afford accommodation for the increased number of representatives at a cost of over £16,500. "The Great Room in Spring Garden," where the Society of Artists held their exhibitions for several years, now forms a part of the offices of the London County Council. Hogarth designed a frontispiece for the second exhibition in 1761. St. Matthew's Episcopal Chapel, at the corner of New Street, was built by an ancestor of Lord Clifford, and occasioned a dispute in 1792 between Lord Clifford and the vicar of St. Martin's-in-the-Fields, who claimed the right of presentation. It is now closed as a place of worship, and is filled with Admiralty Records. [*See* Bull Head Tavern.]

Spur Alley, in the STRAND, an opening under the Salutation Tavern,[1] now *Craven Street*, in the Strand, and so called since 1742.[2]

Vertue had received two different accounts of his [Grinling Gibbons's] birth; from Murray the painter, that he was born in Holland of English parents, and came over at the age of nineteen; from Stoakes (relation of the Stones), that his father was a Dutchman, but that Gibbons himself was born in Spur Alley in the Strand.—*Horace Walpole.*

The truth is, Gibbons was born at Rotterdam on April 4, 1648.[3]

Spur Inn, No. 129 BOROUGH HIGH STREET, SOUTHWARK. Spur Inn Yard still remains; and there is a 17th-century token of the Spur Inn in the Guildhall Collection.

From thence [the Marshalsea] towards London Bridge, on the same side, be many fair inns for receipt of travellers by these signs, the Spurre, Christopher, Bull, Queene's Head, Tabarde, George, Hart, Kinge's Head, etc. Amongst the which the most ancient is the Tabard.—*Stow*, p. 154.

This inn is shown in the plan of the borough in 1542, reproduced in Rendle's *Old Southwark*.

Spurriers' Lane, TOWER STREET. [*See* Water Lane.]
Spurriers' Row, LUDGATE HILL. [*See* Creed Lane.]
Squire's Coffee-house, FULWOOD'S RENTS, was so called from a Mr. Squire, "a noted coffee man in Fuller's Rents," who died

---

[1] Harleian MS., 6850, temp. James I.
[2] Rate-books of St. Martin's-in-the-Fields.
[3] Black's *Catalogue of the Ashmolean MSS.* col. 209.

September 18, 1717. It was patronised by the benchers and students of Gray's Inn.

I do not know that I meet, in any of my walks, objects which move both my spleen and laughter so effectually, as those young fellows at the Grecian, Squire's, Serle's, and all other coffee houses adjacent to the Law.—*The Spectator*, No. 49.

Having passed away the greatest part of the morning in hearing the Knight's [Sir Roger de Coverley's] reflections, he asked me if I would smoke a pipe with him over a dish of coffee at 'Squire's.—*The Spectator*, No. 269.

Stafford House, in ST. JAMES'S PARK, between St. James's Palace and the Green Park, occupies the site of the library built by Caroline, wife of George II. [*See* Queen's Library], and partly that of Godolphin House. It was built, all but the upper storey, for the Duke of York (second son of George III.), with money advanced for that purpose by the Marquis of Stafford, afterwards first Duke of Sutherland (d. 1833), Benj. Wyatt, architect. The Duke of York did not live to inhabit it, and the Crown lease, pursuant to 4 and 5 Vict. c. 27, was sold to the Duke of Sutherland on July 6, 1841, for the sum of £72,000, the original cost of the building. The purchase money was spent in the formation of Victoria Park. The upper storey was added for the Duke of Sutherland, by Sir Charles Barry, R.A., architect. This is said to be the finest private mansion in the metropolis. The great dining-room is worthy of Versailles. The internal arrangements were also planned by Barry. The pictures, too, are very fine; but the collection is private, to which admission is obtained only by the express invitation or permission of the duke. The collection is distributed throughout the house. The Sutherland Gallery, as it is called, is a noble and splendidly decorated room, 136 feet long by 32 feet wide.

PRINCIPAL PICTURES.

RAPHAEL.—Christ bearing His Cross, a small full-length figure, seen against a sky background adorned with pilasters adorned with arabesques.
GUIDO.—Head of the Magdalen. Study for the large picture of Atalanta in the Royal Palace at Naples. The Circumcision.
GUERCINO.—St. Gregory. St. Grisogono. A Landscape.
PARMEGIANO.—Head of a Young Man (very fine).
TINTORETTO.—A Lady at her Toilet.
TITIAN.—Mercury teaching Cupid to read in the presence of Venus (an Orleans picture, figures life size). St. Jerome in the Desert. Three Portraits.
MORONI.—Head of a Jesuit (very fine).
MURILLO (5).—Two from Marshal Soult's Collection—the Return of the Prodigal Son (a composition of nine figures). Abraham and the Angels. Cost £3000.
F. ZURBARAN (4).—Three from Soult's Collection (very fine).
VELASQUEZ (2).—Duke of Gandia at the Door of a Convent, eight figures, life size, from the Soult Collection. Landscape.
ALBERT DÜRER.—The Death of the Virgin.
HONTHORST.—Christ before Pilate (Honthorst's *chef d'œuvre*), from the Lucca Collection.
N. POUSSIN (3).
G. POUSSIN (1).
RUBENS (4).—Holy Family. Marriage of St. Catherine. Sketch, *en grisaille*,

for the great picture in the Louvre, of the Marriage of Henry IV. and Marie de Medicis.

VAN DYCK (4).—Three-quarter portrait of Thomas Howard, Earl of Arundel, seated in an arm-chair (very fine and admirably engraved by Sharp). Two Portraits. St. Martin dividing his Cloak (in a circle).

WATTEAU (5).—All fine.

D. TENIERS (2).—A Witch performing her Cantations. Ducks in a Reedy Pool.

TERBURG.—Gentleman bowing to a Lady (very fine).

SIR JOSHUA REYNOLDS.—Dr. Johnson without his Wig, and with his hands up.

SIR D. WILKIE. — The Breakfast Table, painted for the first Duke of Sutherland.

SIR T. LAWRENCE.—Lady Gower and Child (afterwards Duchess of Sutherland, and her daughter, the Duchess of Argyll).

E. BIRD, R.A.—Day after the Battle of Chevy Chase.

E. LANDSEER, R.A.—Lord Stafford and Lady Evelyn Gower (Lady Blantyre).

W. ETTY, R.A.—Festival before the Flood.

JOHN MARTIN.—The Assuaging of the Waters.

PAUL DELAROCHE.—Lord Strafford on his way to the Scaffold receives the blessing of Archbishop Laud.

WINTERHALTER.—Scene from the Decameron.

A collection of 150 portraits, illustrative of French history and French memoirs.

The land on which Stafford House stands belongs to the Crown, and the duke pays an annual ground rent for the same of £758. At least £250,000 were spent on Stafford House up to 1850.

Stafford Row, PIMLICO, extended from Buckingham Palace Gate to Brewer Street, and was so called after Sir William Howard, Lord Viscount Stafford, beheaded (1680) on the perjured evidence of Titus Oates and others. [*See* Tart Hall.] Stafford Row has been pretty well cleared away for the office of the Duchy of Cornwall, the Buckingham Palace Hotel, etc., and is now included in Buckingham Palace Gate and Buckingham Palace Road. Here (1767) lived William Wynne Ryland, the engraver, executed for forgery, August 29, 1783. Here lived for many years; and died, December 1781, Judith Cowper (Mrs. Madan), Pope's correspondent. No. 9 was the residence of Grosvenor Bedford, the correspondent of Horace Walpole. O'Keefe, the actor, was for some time a resident in Stafford Row. Here too resided Anna Maria Yates, the celebrated tragic actress. Her house was a favourite resort of Arthur Murphy, John Home, Richard Cumberland, and other literary men connected with the stage. She died here in 1787; and in 1796 was followed by her husband, Richard Yates, also actor, and famous for his old men's parts. Yates had ordered eels for dinner, and died the same day of rage and disappointment because his housekeeper was unable to obtain them. The actor's great-nephew was, a few months after, August 22, 1796, killed while endeavouring to force an entry into the house of his uncle, to whose property he thought, as heir at law, he had a just claim. He was a lieutenant in the navy, and an artist of some merit. Mrs. Radcliffe, author of the *Mysteries of Udolpho*, died here, February 7, 1823, in her sixty-second year.

Stafford Street, OLD BOND STREET to ALBEMARLE STREET, occupies the exact site of the Chancellor Clarendon's mansion. A public-house, "The Duke of Albemarle," perpetuates the name of the next possessor. A stone was formerly let into the wall with the inscription, "This is Stafford Street, 1686."

Staining Lane, WOOD STREET, Gresham Street West to Oat Lane.

Staining Lane of old time so called, as may be supposed, of painter stainers dwelling there.—*Stow,* p. 114.

When Charles V. was about to visit England in 1522 an inventory was taken of the accommodation afforded by the London, when "The signe of the Egle in Stanyng Lane," was returned as having "vi beddes, and a stable for xvi horses."[1] The old church of St. Mary Staining was at the north end of the lane. [*See* St. Mary Staining.] The hall and chapel of the Haberdashers' Company are on the east side. The houses in the lane are chiefly occupied by wholesale warehousemen.

Stamford Bridge, FULHAM ROAD, nearly opposite the Chelsea Station of the West London Extension Railway. Here, on the west of the West London Cemetery, and close to the Lillie Bridge Grounds, are the grounds of the London Athletic Club, opened February 3, 1878, one of the principal metropolitan places for the practice of general athletic sports, lawn tennis, and the like.

Stamford Street runs from WATERLOO ROAD to the BLACKFRIARS BRIDGE ROAD, and was built in the present century on part of Lambeth Marsh. John Rennie, the engineer, the builder of Waterloo and Southwark Bridges, lived at No. 52 (now 18), and died there, October 16, 1821, in his sixty-first year. He was buried in St. Paul's Cathedral. On the east side are the Stamford Street Unitarian Chapel (1827) noticeable by its massive Doric portico, and a Gothic Wesleyan Chapel. On the north side is the Hospital for Diseases of the Skin. In Duke Street, Stamford Street, is Messrs. Clowes's vast printing-office.

Standard in Cheap, a water standard or conduit, situated "about the midst of this street" [Cheapside], opposite Honey Lane, but "of what antiquity the first foundation," added Stow, " I have not read." The Standard in Cheap was a place for the execution of capital and minor punishments, the making of proclamations, etc. Stow mentions that in 1293 "three men had their right hands smitten off there, for rescuing of a prisoner arrested by an officer of the City." Wat Tyler in 1381 beheaded Richard Lions and others ; and in 1450 Jack Cade beheaded Lord Saye at the Standard in Cheap.[2]

Also the same yere [17 Hen. VI., 1439], in hervest tyme were brent at the Standard in Chepe diverse nettes, cappes, sadelys and other chaffare, for they were falsely mad and deseyvebly to the peple.—*London Chronicle,* edited by Sir N. H. Nicolas.

[*See* Cheapside.]

[1] *Rutland Papers,* p. 29. [2] *Stow,* p. 100.

Standard in Cornhill, a water-standard, with four spouts, made (1582) by Peter Morris, a German, and supplied with water conveyed from the Thames, by pipes of lead. It stood at the east end of Cornhill, at its junction with Gracechurch Street, Bishopsgate Street, and Leadenhall Street, and with the waste water from its four spouts cleansed the channels of the four streets. The water ceased to run between 1598 and 1603; but the Standard itself remained for a long time after. It was long in use as a point of measurement for distances from the City, and several of our suburban milestones were, but a very few years ago, and some perhaps are still, inscribed with so many miles "from the Standard in Cornhill." There was a Standard in Cornhill as early as the 2d of Henry V.[1] [*See* Cornhill.]

Standard Theatre, SHOREDITCH, opposite the former terminus, now the Goods Station of the Great Eastern Railway, with an entrance from Holywell Street, occupies in part the site of the old Curtain Theatre. It was burnt down in October 1866, but immediately rebuilt on an improved plan, and is now one of the largest theatres in London. It will, it is said, accommodate an audience of 4500 persons.

Stangate, LAMBETH, from the west foot of Westminster Bridge to Lambeth Marsh. Stukeley, who calls it Stanega Ferry, traces the old Roman road from Chester to Dover through St. James's Park and Old Palace Yard to Stanegate and Canterbury, and so to the three famous seaports, Rutupiæ, Dubris, and Lemanis.[2] His itinerary is not quite accurate, but Stangate was a part of or on the Roman road to the South Coast, and it has been stated that "from Lambeth to Fisher's Gate on the Sussex Coast, the word *Gate* is added to the names of nearly all the places through which the Roman road passes."[3]

Had they a standynge at Shooter's Hill, or at *Stangat* Hole to take a pourse? Why: dyd they stande by hyghe waye? Did they robbe? or break open any man's house or dore?—Latimer's *Third Sermon to Edward VI.*, 1549.

A large tract of ground was here rescued from the river, upon which the new St. Thomas's Hospital was built, 1868-1871.

Stanhope House, WHITEHALL, the residence of George Monk, Duke of Albemarle.

There was a Trunk on Saturday last, being the 18th inst. [July, 1672-1673] cut off from behind the Duke of Albemarle's coach, wherein there was a Gold George, 18 Shirts, a Tennis Sute laced, with several fronts and laced Cravats and other Linen; if any can give tidings of them to Mr. Lymbyery the Duke's Steward at Stanhope House near Whitehall, they shall have five pounds for their pains and all charges otherwise defrayed.—*London Gazette*, No. 748.

Stanhope Street, CLARE MARKET, so called after Ann Stanhope, wife of John Holles, first Earl of Clare, and mother of the celebrated Denzil Holles: she died in 1651 in "the corner house of the Middle

[1] *Stow*, p. 71; *London Chronicle* (Nicholas), p. 99.
[2] *Iter. Curiosum*, p. 113. [3] *Edinb. Rev.*, May 1828, p. 515.

Piazza in Covent Garden." Joe Grimaldi, the greatest of clowns, was born in this street, December 18, 1778.[1] He was baptized at St. Clement Danes. John [Lord] Campbell rented, Michaelmas 1800, "the second floor [Scoticè, the third storey] of No. 6 Stanhope Street, Clare Market . . . I get it, unfurnished, at the rate of £18 a year, including £2 a year for service. . . . I have three rooms—a parlour, a bedroom, and a large dressing closet."[2]

Stanhope Street, MAY FAIR, now **Great Stanhope Street,** consists of fifteen spacious houses, built on ground belonging to the Dean and Chapter of Westminster, and runs from South Audley Street to Park Lane. No. 1 is the town residence of the Duke of Manchester; No. 3 of the Earl of Jersey; No. 8 of the Earl of Lanesborough.

Eminent Inhabitants.—Right Hon. Charles Townshend in 1777. George Canning writes to Crabbe the poet from "Stanhope Street, November 13, 1817." Colonel Barré, Adjutant-General of Wolfe's army at Quebec, and, as a politician, the faithful adherent of Chatham, lived and died (1802) at No. 12 in this street. In this house Sir Robert Peel the statesman lived (1820-1825), and here his heroic son, William, was born, November 2, 1824, as is recorded on his tomb at Cawnpore. Lord Palmerston at No. 9. Henry Fitzroy, first Lord Raglan (died before Sebastopol, June 28, 1855), at No. 5. Field-Marshal Henry, first Viscount Hardinge (died, September 24, 1856), at No. 15.

Staple Inn, HOLBORN, an Inn of Chancery (before 1415) appertaining to *Gray's Inn,* extends from No. 2 Holborn Bars to Southampton Buildings, Chancery Lane. The houses are built about an open quadrangle, and behind is a pleasant garden.

Staple Inn was the Inne or Hostell of the Merchants of the Staple (as the tradition is), wherewith until I can learne better matter, concerning the antiquity and foundation thereof, I must rest satisfied. But for latter matters I cannot chuse but make report, and much to the prayse and commendation of the Gentlemen of this House, that they have bestowed great costs in new-building a fayre Hall of brick, and two parts of the outward Courtyards, besides other lodging in the garden and elsewhere, and have thereby made it the fayrest Inne of Chauncery in this Universitie.—*Sir George Buc (Howes,* ed. 1631, p. 1065).

Staple Inn was purchased by the Benchers of Gray's Inn in 1529. In Elizabeth's reign there were 145 students in term and 69 out of term. Sir Simond D'Ewes mentions that on February 17, 1624, in the morning, he went to Staple Inn and there argued a moot point or law case with others, and was engaged until near 3 P.M. The inn was sold in 1884 to the Prudential Assurance Company for £68,000, and the Holborn front was restored and cleared from the plaster covering the timber beams. The houses are let as offices and chambers, and are largely tenanted by solicitors. The new buildings on the terrace leading into Southampton Buildings were erected in 1843 (Messrs.

---

[1] *Life, by Dickens.*   [2] *Life,* vol. I. pp. 56, 57.

Wigg and Parnell architects) for the Taxing Masters, but are now occupied by the Patent Office and the Land Registry Office.

Dr. Johnson was living here in 1758; in 1759 he removed to Gray's Inn. Isaac Reed, the Shakespeare commentator, had chambers at No. 11, where he died, January 5, 1807. In Reed's chambers Steevens corrected the proof sheets of his edition of Shakespeare. He used to leave his house at Hampstead at one in the morning, and walk to Staple Inn. Reed, who went to bed at the usual hour, allowed his fellow-commentator a key to the chambers, so that Steevens stole quietly to his proof sheets, without, it is said, disturbing the repose of his friend.

Star Chamber, a judicial court in the palace of our Kings at Westminster, commonly said to have been erected by Henry VIII., but which was in fact, as Hallam pointed out, the old *Concilium Regis* or *Ordinarium*, and the object of statute 3, Henry VII. c. 1, was to revive the Council and place its jurisdiction on a permanent and unquestionable basis. "The Judges of the Court" were "the Privy Council and the Messengers of the Court, the Warden of the Fleet's servants, the Chancellor, Treasurer, and Keeper of the Privy Seal, with a Bishop and temporal Lord of the Council; and the Chief Justices of the King's Bench and Common Pleas, or two other justices in their absence," are empowered to summon before them certain specified offenders, and after examination to punish them "as if convicted by course of law." But the jurisdiction of the court soon stretched far beyond the boundaries assigned by law. It took cognisance among other offences of " forgery, perjury, riot, maintenance, fraud, libel, and conspiracy." The King was often present at the sittings of the court, and both the Stuarts too often acted the part of prosecutor. Under the Tudors the Star Chamber formed a terrible instrument for the punishment, short of death, of any who had fallen under the displeasure of the Government, but its full capacity in this respect only became manifest under the Stuarts, when by its means, as Macaulay remarks, "the Government was able to fine, imprison, pillory, and mutilate at pleasure." The most famous prosecution of this court was that of the learned Puritan lawyer Prynne, in the reign of Charles I., by the Attorney-General Noy, at the instigation of Archbishop Laud. Prynne had published a bulky volume called *Histriomastix*, in condemnation of plays and actors, full of erudition, and if possible fuller of invective, some of which were specially directed against female actors. Unfortunately for the author the Queen took part in a court masque about the time of the publication of his book, when attention was directed to an entry in the index, " Women Actors notorious whores." The reference was to the Roman courtesans, but Prynne was summoned before the Star Chamber; other offensive passages were cited, and he was condemned and sentenced to stand twice in the pillory, to have both his ears cut off by the common hangman, to be branded in the forehead, pay a fine of £5000, and to be imprisoned for life. This was perhaps the most atrocious of the sentences inflicted by the court, but others nearly as severe and quite as iniquitous were about this time not infrequent. The Chamber had become in fact an intolerable tyranny. It was abolished by the Act of 16 Charles I. c. 10, the first year of the Long Parliament, and the memory of its misdeeds contributed powerfully to bring about the tragic fate of Laud, if not that of his royal Master.[1]

> In the Chamber of Stars
> All matters there be ² mars ;
> Clapping his rod on the board,
> No man dare speak a word ;
> For he hath all the saying,
> Without any renaying.
> He rolleth in his Records ;
> He sayeth how say ye my Lords,
> Is not my reason good?
> . . . . .
> Some say yes, and some
> Sit still as they were dumb.
>   Skelton, *Why Come ye not to Court?* 85-96 (Dyce's
>   *Skelton*), vol. ii. p. 32.

Then is there the Star Chamber, where in the Term time, every week once at the least, which is commonly on Fridays and Wednesdays, and on the next day after the term endeth, the Lord Chancellor, and the Lords and other of the Privy Council, and the Chief Justices of England from nine of the clock till it be eleven do sit. This place is called the Star Chamber, because the roof thereof is decked with the likeness of stars gilt.—*Stow*, p. 175.

The Starre Chamber is a chamber at the one End of Westminster Hall. It is written the Starred Chamber. Now it hath the signe of a Starre ouer the doore as you one way enter therein.—*Minsheu*, ed. 1617.

Lord Carew writes to Sir Thomas Roe, then absent on his embassy to the Great Mogul, that on June 20, 1616, the King, James I., sat in person in the Star Chamber and "made a large speeche to the admiration of the hearers, speaking more like an angel than a man."[3] About this time James purposed building a new Star Chamber. There is a Council Warrant of June 27, 1619, for payment to Inigo Jones of £37, "for making two several models, the one for the Star Chamber, the other for the Banqueting House;" but the design had been prepared by him at least two years earlier.

June 21, 1617.—The Queen is building at Greenwich after a plan of Inigo Jones: he has a design for a new Star Chamber which the King would fain have built if there were money.—*Cal. Stat. Pap.*, 1611-18, p. 473.

The building itself was evidently of the Elizabethan age, and the date 1602, with the initials E. R. separated by an open rose on a star, was carved over one of the doorways. The ceiling was of oak, and had been very curiously devised in moulded compartments, ornamented with roses, pomegranates, portcullises and fleurs-des-lys : it had also been gilt and diversely coloured.—Britton and Brayley's *Westminster Palace*, p. 443.

---

[1] Hallam, *Const. Hist. of England*, chaps. i., viii., ix.; Sir F. Palgrave, *Original Authority of the King's Council*; "Account of Star Chamber," by John Bruce, *Archaeo.*, vol. v. p. xxv.

[2] Cardinal Wolsey, who made much use of the Star Chamber.

[3] *Cal. State Pap.*, 1611-18, p. 425.

There is an engraving of the ceiling by J. T. Smith, and an interesting view of the Chamber in Britton and Brayley's *Westminster*, Plate XX. In the curious Illumination[1] in the Lambeth Library of Earl Rivers presenting his book, and Caxton his printer, to King Edward IV., the King is represented seated in a chamber, the roof of which is powdered with stars.

Star and Garter, PALL MALL, a tavern of considerable note in the 18th century. Smollett makes Matthew Bramble say that the servants at private houses were so greedy and rapacious that he could "dine better, and for less expense, at the Star and Garter in Pall Mall than at our Cousin's castle in Yorkshire." Swift has also a good opinion of the house and the moderation of the charges.

March 20, 1712.—I made our Society change their house, and we met to-day at the Star and Garter in the Pelmall. Lord Arran was president. The other day was so extravagant in his bills that for four dishes, and four, first and second course, without wine or desert, he charged £21 : 6 : 8 to the Duke of Ormond.—*Swift to Stella.*

Here, 1760-1770 met George Selwyn's Thursday Club, famous for wit and whist. "There is nobody at White's," writes Gilly Williams to George Selwyn, July 18, 1763; "our jovial club meets at the Star-in-Garter." The Dilettanti Society met here, at least occasionally. The instructions for the famous Classical Mission sent out by the Society are dated, "Star and Garter, May 17, 1764." The meeting of another club at the Star and Garter had a melancholy termination. Ten members of the Nottinghamshire Club sat down to their weekly dinner one afternoon in January, in "a mighty odd-shaped room on the second floor." Dinner was served precisely at a quarter after four. About seven o'clock a dispute arose between William, fifth Lord Byron, and Mr. Chaworth,—neighbours and hitherto friends,—about the game on their respective estates. Hot words were exchanged, but it was thought the quarrel had died away. About eight o'clock Mr. Chaworth left the room, and five minutes after was followed by Lord Byron. They met on the first floor landing, and asked the waiter for an empty room. He showed them into the back room on that floor, placed a very small tallow candle on the table, and closed the door upon them. The room was about 16 feet square, with one corner cut off for the fireplace and chimney. They drew, fought, and Mr. Chaworth fell mortally wounded. Lord Byron was tried for murder and acquitted. "So far was he from feeling any remorse for having killed Mr. Chaworth," wrote his grand-nephew, Lord Byron, the poet, that "he always kept the sword which he used upon that occasion in his bedchamber, and there it still was when he died."

State Paper Office, in ST. JAMES'S PARK, at the bottom of Duke Street West, where a flight of stone steps now leads into the Parade,

[1] Engraved as a frontispiece to Walpole's *Royal and Noble Authors*.

was a repository for the reception and arrangement of the documents accumulating in the offices of the Privy Council and the Secretaries of state, at whose disposal the documents are held. The office was established in 1578, and enlarged and made into a "set form or library" in the reign of James I. The papers were originally kept in the uppermost rooms of the Gate House at Whitehall, and were first put in order during the Grenville administration in the reign of George III. They are now deposited in the Record Office, Fetter Lane. [*See* Record Office.] The building in St. James's Park, the last design by Sir John Soane, R.A., was erected in 1829-1833, and demolished in 1862 to make way for the New India Office.

Stationers' Hall, STATIONERS' HALL COURT, LUDGATE HILL. The Stationers' Company was incorporated May 4, 1557, by letters patent of Philip and Mary, under the title of "The Master and Keepers, or Wardens, and Commonalty of the Mistery or Art of Stationers of the City of London," and a livery was granted by the Court of Mayor and Aldermen, February 1, 1560. Its foundation, however, took place at a much earlier date, as we find it mentioned in 1403, when a set of by-laws were allowed by the Court of Aldermen. The first hall of the Brotherhood was situate in Milk Street, Cheapside; and in 1553 they moved to St. Peter's College, near the Deanery of St. Paul's. In 1611 the Stationers' Company purchased the site of their present hall, which was then occupied by Abergavenny House, the residence successively of the Dukes of Brittany and the Earls of Pembroke and Abergavenny. The house was renovated and enlarged for the purposes of the Company, but was destroyed in the Great Fire of 1666, when the Stationers' Company suffered heavy losses.

<blockquote>Only the poor booksellers have been indeed ill-treated by Vulcan: so many noble impressions consumed by their trusting them to the churches, as the loss is estimated near two hundred thousand pounds, which will be an extraordinary detriment to the whole republic of learning.—*Evelyn to Sir S. Tuke*, September 27, 1666.</blockquote>

The first meeting of the court after the Fire was held at Cook's Hall, and the subsequent courts until the hall was rebuilt were held at the Lame Hospital Hall, *i.e.* St. Bartholomew's Hospital. The present edifice was erected on the site of the former hall in 1670. It was built of brick, but in 1800 received a casing of Portland stone, from the designs of Robert Mylne, architect. St. Cecilia's Feast and several County Feasts were annually held in Stationers' Hall. Various lotteries have been drawn here, and in 1745 the Surgeons' Company were allowed the use of the hall. Alterations were made in 1888, when a new wing was added.

Observe.—Painted window by Eginton, given by Alderman Cadell; portraits of Prior and Steele (good), presented by John Nichols; of Richardson, the novelist, Master of the Company in 1754, and of Mrs. Richardson, the novelist's wife (both by Highmore); of Alderman

Boydell, by Graham; portrait of Tycho Wing, son of Vincent Wing, the astrologer; he died in 1668, but his name is still continued on one of the sheet almanacks of the Stationers' Company.

The Stationers' Company, for two important centuries in English history, occupied by the terms of their charters a commanding position in literature. Printers were obliged to serve their time to a member of the Company, and publications were required to be "Entered at Stationers' Hall." This was, however, far from always being the case, as during the reigns of Elizabeth and succeeding sovereigns special letters patent of permission to print specified works were issued, and these letters patent really exempted them from the jurisdiction of the Stationers' Company, the fees being in such cases paid to the Crown. Thus, to give one example, Elizabeth granted Richard Tottel, the publisher of the first Poetical Miscellany, the privilege of printing every law-book published in England. Registration is not compulsory, but under the Copyright Act of 1842 the proprietor of every published work is required to register his claim, for his own protection, in the books of the Stationers' Company before any legal proceedings can take place. The Stationers' is not a wealthy Company, but it possesses an important treasure in the series of registers of works entered for publication at Stationers' Hall from 1557, which constitutes a most valuable source of information relating to the history of literature of the last 300 years. These registers, however, do not by any means include every work since their introduction, for, as already mentioned, many works issued by special license were not entered therein. Mr. J. Payne Collier's two volumes of carefully selected extracts from their earlier pages, and the accurate "Transcripts" edited by Mr. Edward Arber, have opened up a mass of interesting matter previously lying hidden. There are several charities connected with the Company, and a Grammar School in Bolt Court, founded in 1858.

Stationery Office (Her Majesty's), PRINCES STREET, STOREY'S GATE, WESTMINSTER, was established in 1785 for the supply of stationery, books and printing to the several public departments of Government, prior to which time the chief offices of Government were supplied by private individuals, under patents from the Crown. The printing of the Excise was long executed under patent by Jacob Tonson, the eminent bookseller, and in 1757 a patent was granted to George Walpole, Earl of Orford, for the supply of stationery to the Treasury for the period of forty years. The old office was in James Street, Buckingham Gate, in the house long the residence of Lord Milford, where Mr. J. R. M'Culloch (1780-1864), comptroller, lived for many years. The present Stationery Office was erected about 1847, from the designs of Sir J. Pennethorne, at a cost of £25,792.

Statistical Society (Royal), ADELPHI TERRACE, founded 1834; incorporated 1887. The members are styled "Fellows," and pay

2 guineas annually. The Society issues a quarterly *Journal*, which contains many papers of great research and permanent value.

Steaks (The). [*See* Beaf Steak Society.]

Steelyard, STEELYARD, or STILLIARD in UPPER THAMES STREET, in the ward of Dowgate (facing the river), where the Cannon Street Railway Station now stands. "Their hall," says Stow, "is large, built of stone, with three arched gates towards the street, the middlemost whereof is far bigger than the others, and is seldom opened; the other two bemured up; the same is now called the old hall."[1]

The Steelyard, a place for merchants of Almaine, that used to bring hither as well wheat, rye, and other grain, as cables, ropes, masts, pitch, tar, flax, hemp, linen cloth, wainscots, wax, steel, and other profitable merchandises.—*Stow*, p. 87.

Steelyard, a place in London where the fraternity of the Easterling Merchants, otherwise the Merchants of the Hannse and Almaine are wont to have their abode. It is so called Stilliard of a broad place or court, wherein steele was much sold.—*Minsheu*, ed. 1617, and H. Blount both in his *Law Dictionary* and his *Glossographia*.

The Steelyard was lately famous for Rhenish Wines, Neats' Tongues, etc.—Blount's *Glossographia*, ed. 1670.

Other writers derive the name from its being the place where the King's steelyard, or beam, for weighing the tonnage of goods imported into London, was erected before its transference to Cornhill.

Lambecius explains the name Steel-yard (or as he calls it Stealhof) to be only a contraction of Stapelhof, softened into Stafelhof, and synonymous with the English word Staple, which is in the civil law Latin style of Edward III. termed *Stabile emporium*, a fixed port depôt.- Herbert's *Twelve Livery Companies*, p. 12, *note*.

This latter derivation is by far the most likely; Minsheu is without doubt wrong, as steel until long after the adoption of the name Steelyard for their guild by the Merchants of the Hanse was only quite a secondary item in their trade.

In their hall were the two great pictures by Holbein, the triumphs of Riches and Poverty, thus described by Walpole: "The former was represented by Plutus riding in a golden car; before him sat Fortune scattering money, the chariot being loaded with coin, and drawn by four white horses, but blind and led by women, whose names were written beneath; round the car were crowds with extended hands catching at the favours of the god. Fame and Fortune attended him, and the procession was closed by Crœsus and Midas, and other avaricious persons of note. . . . Poverty was an old woman, sitting in a vehicle as shattered as the other was superb; her garments squalid, and every emblem of wretchedness around her. She was drawn by asses and oxen, which were guided by Hope and Diligence, and other emblematic figures, and attended by mechanics and labourers. It was on the sight of these pictures that Zucchero expressed such esteem of this master. . . . The large pictures themselves Felibien and Depiles say were carried into France and Flanders, whither they were trans-

[1] *Stow*, p. 88.

ported I suppose after the destruction of the Company. The Triumph of Poverty was engraved by Vosterman, and copies of both are now at Strawberry Hill."—Walpole's *Anecdotes*, ed. Dallaway, vol. i. p. 152.

The merchants of the Steelyard formed a branch of the great Hanseatic League, and probably originally gave rise to this League. As early as 967 a regulation of King Ethelred ordains that "the emperor's men, or Easterlings, coming with their ships to Belingsgate, shall be accounted worthy of good laws." In the first charter of which we have record as being granted to the members of the Steelyard was that given by Henry III. in the following words:—

Henry by the Grace of God, King of England, Lord of Ireland, Duke of Aquitain, etc. To the citizens of London to whom these Presents shall come, greeting: Know ye that, at the Instance of the most Serene Prince of the Roman Empire, our Brother, we have granted to these Merchants of Almain who have a House in our City of London, which is called commonly Guilda Aula Theutonicorum, that we will maintain them all and every one, and preserve them through our whole Kingdom, in all their Liberties and free Customs, which they have used in our Times, and in the Times of our Progenitors, and will not withdraw such Liberties and free Customs from them, nor suffer them to be at all withdrawn from them, etc. Witness my Self at Westminster the 15th of June in the 44th year of our Reign.

It is thus clear that at that date the Merchants of the Hanse were a fully recognised body possessed of distinct privileges. The term Steelyard as applied to the Guildhall of these merchants came into use towards the end of the 14th century.

Other privileges were granted to them by the citizens of London, on condition of their maintaining one of the gates of the City, called *Bishopsgate*, in repair, and their sustaining a third of the charges, in money and men to defend it, "when need were." These privileges remained unimpaired till the reign of Edward VI., when, on the complaint of a society of English merchants called "The Merchant Adventurers," "sentence was given that they had forfeited their liberties and were in like case with other strangers."[1] Great interest was made to rescind this sentence, and ambassadors from Hamburg and Lubeck came to the King, "to speak on the behalf of the Stilliard Merchants."[2] Their intercession was ineffectual. "The Stilliard men," says the King, "received their answer, which was to confirm the former judgment of my council."[3] This sentence, though it broke up their monopoly, did not injure their Low Country trade in any great degree, and the merchants of the Steelyard still continued to export English woollen clothes, and to find as ample a market for their goods as either the Merchant Adventurers or the English merchants not Merchant Adventurers. The trade, however, was effectually broken by a proclamation of Queen Elizabeth, by which the merchants of the Steelyard were expelled the kingdom, and commanded to depart by February 28, 1597-1598.[4] The after history of the building I find recorded in the Privy Council Register of the year 1598-1599, wherein, under

[1] King Edward's *Diary*, in Burnet, February 23, 1551.
[2] *Ibid.*, February 28.
[3] *Ibid.*, May 7.
[4] *Egerton Papers*, p. 273.

January 30 in that year, the register records that a letter was sent to the Lord Mayor, requiring him to deliver up the house of the Steelyard to the officers of Her Majesty's navy, "after the avoydinge and departinge of the strangers that did possess the house. That the said house of the Stiliards should be used and employed for the better bestowing and safe custodie of divers provisions of the navy. The rent to be paid by the officers of the navy."[1] In the church of *Allhallows the Great*, adjoining, is a handsome screen of oak, manufactured at Hamburg, and presented to the parish by the Hanse Merchants, in memory of the former connection which existed between them and this country. Sir Thomas More held the office of agent for the associated merchants.

Stephen's Alley, KING STREET, WESTMINSTER, ran between King Street and Canon Row. It was swept away when Parliament Street was formed: Derby Street, then called Derby Court, was a prolongation of it. Here lived and died (1650) Thomas May, the poet, and historian of the Long Parliament.

> As one put drunk into the Packet boat,
> Tom May was hurried hence and did not know't,
> But was amaz'd on the Elysian side,
> And with an eye uncertain gazing wide,
> Could not determine in what place he was,
> For whence in Steven's Alley, trees or grass,
> Nor where the Pope's Head or the Mitre lay
> Signs by which still he found and lost his way.

Andrew Marvell's lines "On Tom May's Death," *Miscellaneous Poems*, folio 1681, p. 35.

Stephen's (St.) Chapel. [*See* Houses of Parliament.]

Stephen's (St.), COLEMAN STREET, a church in Coleman Street Ward (on the left-hand side of Coleman Street, going up to London Wall), destroyed in the Great Fire and rebuilt in 1676, from the designs of Sir C. Wren.

John Hayward, at that time under-sexton of the parish of St. Stephen Coleman Street, carried or assisted to carry all the dead to their graves, which were buried in that large parish and who were carried in form; and after that form of burying was stopped, he went with the Dead-Cart and the Bell to fetch the dead-bodies from the houses where they lay, and fetched many of them out of the chambers and houses. For the parish was and is still remarkable, particularly above all the parishes in London, for a great number of alleys and thoroughfares, very long, into which no carts could come, and where they were obliged to go and fetch the bodies a very long way; such as White's Alley, Cross Key Court, Swan Alley, Bell Alley, White Horse Alley, and many more. Here he went with a kind of hand-barrow, and laid the dead bodies on it, and carried them out to the carts; which work he performed and never had the distemper at all, but lived about twenty years after it, and was sexton of the parish to the time of his death.—*Memoirs of the Plague*, by Defoe, ed. Brayley, p. 128.

The old church contained a monument "To the Memory of that antient servant to the City with his Pen, in divers employments, especially the *Survey of London*, Master Anthony Munday, Citizen and

[1] Harl. MS., 4181, fol. 185 B.

Draper of London" (d. 1633). Over the gateway into the churchyard is a representation in high-relief of the Last Judgment, a relic probably of the old church. The living is a vicarage. The right of presentation belongs to the parishioners, who in 1823 elected the Rev. Josiah Pratt, a popular evangelical preacher of that time. On his death in 1879 the parishioners elected his son, the Rev. J. W. Pratt, to succeed him. The church was cleaned and decorated in 1879.

Stephen's (St.), WALBROOK, in the ward of Walbrook, immediately behind the Mansion House, one of Sir C. Wren's most celebrated churches, of which the first stone was laid October 16, 1672. It was completed in 1679, and cost only £7652. The church was erected at the public expense; but the pews and wainscoting were supplied by the Grocers' Company, the patrons of the living, against the wish of the architect. The exterior is unpromising, but the interior is all elegance and even grandeur. The interior is an oblong, 75 feet by 56, with a circular dome on an octagonal base, which rests on eight Corinthian columns—an arrangement at once original and singularly rich, varied and graceful. The cupola—a little St. Paul's—is very effective; the lights are admirably disposed, and every one can see and hear to perfection. The walls and columns are of stone; the dome only of timber and lead. The dimensions of the church are 60 feet wide, 83 feet long, and 60 feet high. The diameter of the dome at the springing is 43 feet.

August 24, 1679.—Ordered that a present of Twenty Guineas be made to the lady of Sir Christopher Wren, as a testimony of the regard the parish has for the great care and skill that Sir Christopher Wren showed in the rebuilding of our church.—Ward's *Lives of the Gresham Professors*, p. 104.

On the north wall hangs West's masterpiece—the Martyrdom of St. Stephen, painted originally as the altarpiece. The east window is now filled with painted glass, by Willement, the gift of the Grocers' Company. Sir John Vanbrugh, the architect and wit, was buried (1726) in the family vault of the Vanbrughs in the north aisle. The church serves as well for the parish of St. Benet Sherehog.

Sir Robert Chicheley, alderman and twice Lord Mayor (1411, 1421), purchased the ground whereon St. Stephen's Church stands, and built the previous church. He gave the advowson to the Grocers' Company.[1] Thomas Becon was instituted rector of this church, March 24, 1547, on the presentation of the Grocers' Company, but was ejected after the accession of Mary as a "married priest" and imprisoned in the tower. There is a tablet to the memory of Nathaniel Hodges, a physician and writer on the Plague (1629-1688). Dr. Wilson, rector of St. Stephen's in the last half of the 18th century, erected in the chancel of his church a statue of Mrs. Macaulay, the republican historian, while she was yet living. It was removed by his successor.[2] Dr. Croly (d. 1860), author of *Salathiel* and other works

[1] William Ravenhill's *Short Account of the Company of Grocers*, 1689.
[2] Wright's *Note to Walpole*, vol. v. p. 146.

of fancy and imagination, was rector for many years. There is a monument and bust by Behnes to his memory.

The church underwent a restoration in 1847-1848 (John Turner, architect). The high pews were removed and Mosaic pavement laid down in 1888, when extensive alterations were carried out under the direction of A. M. Peebles, architect.

Stephen's (St.), WESTMINSTER, on the south side of Rochester Row, between Greycoat Street and Vincent Square, a spacious Gothic church, erected and endowed, with the adjacent schools and buildings, by Miss (now the Baroness) Burdett Coutts. The first stone of the church was laid July 1, 1847, and it was completed in 1849. It was designed by Benjamin Ferrey, F.S.A.; is Decorated in style; a substantial stone structure, carefully finished in all the details and richly ornamented throughout. The body of the church is 82 feet long with a chancel 47 feet deep. The tower and spire are 200 feet high. The windows are filled with painted glass by Willement—some of his best work. The altar cloth was the gift of the Duke of Wellington. The adjoining schools, for 400 children, and connected buildings, correspond in style with the church, and the whole form an architectural and picturesque group.

Stephen Street, TOTTENHAM COURT ROAD, west side, the next street south of Percy Street. George Morland, the painter, was living with his father, Henry Robert Morland, at No. 14 in this street (now a rag and bottle merchant's) in the years 1780-1786.[1] Stephen Street and the adjacent Gresse Street were so named from Stephen Gaspar Gresse (father of John Alexander Gresse, drawing-master to the daughters of George III.), who purchased a long lease of the site— which was then "divided into small portions and let for smoke-a-pipe gardens to various tradesfolks"[2]—and let it on building leases.

Stepney, a parish lying east of Whitechapel, was originally of very much larger extent than at present, and included Stratford-le-Bow, Whitechapel, Shadwell, Mile End, Poplar, Blackwall, Spitalfields, Ratcliff, Limehouse, and Bethnal Green. It is the mother parish of the whole of what is now called "East London." The etymology of the name Stepney is doubtful. In the Domesday Book this parish is entered as a manor under the name of Stibenhede. It has been variously written as Stevenhethe,[3] Stebenhuthe,[4] Stebenhethe,[5] Stebenhythe and Stebunhethe.[6] That the termination is the old Saxon word *hyth,* a wharf or haven, there can be little doubt, but the rest of the word is by no means so clear. Lysons suggests that it may be derived from *steb,* a trunk, and thus be the *timber-wharf;* others believe it to be a corruption of Steven, and the word thus means St. Stephen's Haven.

[1] Catalogues of the Royal Academy.
[2] MS. Recollections of the late Robert Hills, the water-colour painter.
[3] *Liber Albus,* p. 204.
[4] *Ibid.,* p. 80.
[5] Riley's *Memorials,* p. 28.
[6] Lysons's *Environs,* vol. iv. p. 678.

The whole parish in 1794 contained about 1530 acres of land (exclusively of the site of buildings), of which about 80 acres were then arable, about 50 occupied by market-gardeners, and the remainder meadow-pasture and marsh land.—Lysons's *Environs*, vol. iv. p. 678.

All its pastures and market-gardens have long since disappeared, and Stepney is now one of the most populous parishes in London. In 1881 its population was 58,500.

The great plague of 1665 was particularly severe in this part of London. Clarendon, in speaking of the difficulty of obtaining seamen in the following year, says that "Stepney and the places adjacent, which were their common habitations, were almost depopulated."

The church is dedicated to St. Dunstan (which *see*). Stepney meeting-house was erected for Mathew Mead (buried in the churchyard of St. Dunstan's), and during his time was one of the most noted of the nonconformist places of worship. It has lately been rebuilt. Near the church stood a spacious mansion, the seat of Henry, first Marquis of Worcester. It was in the two-storied dwelling above the gateway of this mansion that Mathew Mead lived, and here that his still more famous son, Dr. Richard Mead,—the "prince of English physicians," and the friend and successor in practice of Dr. Radcliffe, the founder of the Radcliffe Library at Oxford—was born in 1673. William King, LL.D., who delivered the Latin oration at the dedication of the above library in 1749, was also a native of Stepney.

Sterling Club, a social club, founded in 1838 by John Sterling as the Anonymous Club, where he and his friends might meet monthly and talk together over a frugal dinner. The original members included, besides the founder and James Spedding the secretary, Thomas Carlyle, Alfred Tennyson, Frederick Maurice, John Stuart Mill, Archdeacon Hare, Bishop Thirlwall, Lord Lyttleton, Monckton Milnes (Lord Houghton), and Sir C. L. Eastlake; to whom were shortly afterwards added Bishop Wilberforce, Chenevix Trench (Archbishop of Dublin), and Archdeacon (now Cardinal) Manning.[1] The history of the club is sufficiently told by Carlyle :—

In order to meet the most or a good many of his friends at once on such occasions [his visits to London], he now, furthermore, contrived the scheme of a little Club where monthly over a frugal dinner some reunion might take place; that is, where friends of his, and withal such friends of theirs as suited—and in fine, where a small select company definable as persons to whom it was pleasant to talk together,—might have a little opportunity of talking. The scheme was approved by the persons concerned: I have a copy of the Original Regulations, probably drawn up by Sterling, a very solid lucid piece of economics; and the List of the proposed Members, signed "James Spedding, Secretary," and dated "August 8, 1838." The Club grew; was at first called the *Anonymous Club*; then, after some months of success, in compliment to the founder, who had now left us again, the *Sterling Club*, under which latter name, it once lately, for a time, owing to the Religious Newspapers, became rather famous in the world! In which strange circumstances the name was again altered, to suit weak brethren; and the Club still subsists, in a sufficiently flourishing, though happily once more a private condition. That is the origin and genesis of poor

[1] Carlyle's *Life of Sterling*, p. 208; Ashwill's *Life of Bishop Wilberforce*, vol. i. p. 142.

Sterling's Club; which, having honestly paid the shot for itself at Wills' Coffee-house or elsewhere, fancied its bits of affairs were quite settled; and once little thought of getting into Books of History with them!—Carlyle's *Life of Sterling*, 2d ed., 1852, p. 208.

Stew Lane, a narrow passage between No. 51 and No. 52 LOWER THAMES STREET, leading to *Stew Quay* by the Thames. This name was given to the passage as leading to a landing-place to which the Doll Tearsheets were probably restricted in passing to or from the Stews on the opposite bank.

January 20, 1608.—Grant to George Chester and Wingfield Moulsworth to use *Stew Quay* and Seannocke Quay, near the Custom House, as free quays for lading and unlading goods.—*Cal. State Pap.*, 1603-1610, p. 396.

Stews, or STEWES BANK. [*See* Winchester House, Southwark; Cardinal's Cap Alley.] A small district on the Bankside in Southwark, the houses of which were "whited and painted, with signes on the front, for a token of the said houses."[1] "The Bordello or Stews," says Stow, "a place so called of certain stew-houses privileged there, for the repair of incontinent men and the like women." These "allowed stew-houses" were originally eighteen in number, and were situated between the Bear Gardens and the Clink prison. They "had signs on their fronts towards the Thames, not hanged out but painted on the walls, as the Boar's Head, the Cross Keys, the Gun, the Castle, the Crane, the Cardinal's Hat, the Bell, the Swan, etc."[2] The houses were under strict parliamentary and municipal regulations, dating from the 8th Henry II., and confirmed or modified in several later reigns. On the City side were such ordinances as that (temp. Edward I.) which directs that "no boatman shall have his boat moored and standing over the water after sunset; but they shall have all their boats moored on this [the City] side of the water . . . nor may they carry any man or woman, either denizens or strangers, unto the Stews, except in the day-time, under pain of imprisonment."[3] These houses, which then belonged to William Walworth, Lord Mayor of London, who leased them from the Bishop of Winchester, were "spoiled" by Wat Tyler and the Kentish rebels—a circumstance that may have helped to nerve the arm of the loyal mayor when he encountered Tyler in Smithfield a few days later. In 1506 a royal ordinance closed the doors of the Stews, but shortly after they were allowed to be reopened, the number being reduced from eighteen to twelve. Forty years later (1546) they were finally suppressed and all similar privileges abolished.

Latimer, in his third sermon before Edward VI. (March 22, 1549), alludes to the suppression of the Stews. "You have put downe the Stues, but I praye you what is the matter amended. . . . I dare say there is now more whoredom in London than ever there was on the Bancke. These be the newes I have to tell you, I feare they be true." So also says Alexander Barclay in his *Eclogue of the Cytezen and Uplondysman*, printed by Wynkyn de Worde.[4]

[1] Proclamation of April 13 (37th Henry VIII.) in the Library of the Society of Antiquarians.
[2] *Stow*, p. 151. [3] *Liber Albus*, p. 242. [4] *See* the Percy Society reprint, p. 29.

> Blessed Saynt Saviour
> For his naughty behaviour
>   That dwelt not far from the Stewes
> For causyng infidelitie
> Hath lost his dignitie
>   Of him we shall have more newes.

A Booke entitled the Fantassie of Idolatrie (circ. 1540); Foxe, vol. v. p. 406.

In the time of Henry II. (1154) the Stews, regulated hitherto by Custom ("Customarie" of long before is quoted), were legally recognised, and they so continued to be until 1535, when they were proclaimed by sound of trumpet and *as far as possible* publicly and entirely suppressed. In the reign of Richard II. the rebels under Wat Tyler "brake down the Stews near London Bridge," then held by frowes of Flanders of the Lord Mayor, Sir William Walworth.

The Castle and the Cardinal's Hat, two of these houses, are noted in the book of expenses of Sir John Howard, the first Duke of Norfolk of that time.

Stinking Lane, NEWGATE STREET to LITTLE BRITAIN, now *King Edward Street*, was so called as leading to the slaughter-houses of St. Nicholas Shambles, and probably not often visited by the scavenger.

> Then is Stinking Lane so called, or Chick Lane, at the East End of the Grey Friars Church, and there is the Butchers' Hall.—*Stow*, p. 118.

It was afterwards called *Blowbladder Street*, next *Butcher Hall Lane*, and last of all, about 1844, *King Edward Street*.

Stock Exchange, CAPEL COURT, and 7, 8, 9 Throgmorton Street. The ready-money market of the world, which had its origin in the National Debt. The Stockbrokers originally met at New Jonathan's Coffee-house in Change Alley, and on July 14, 1773, they "came to a resolution that instead of being called New Jonathan's it should be called 'The Stock Exchange,' which is to be wrote over the door, the brokers then collected sixpence each, and christened the house with punch." In 1801 a new building was erected, and opened March 1802. In 1854 this gave place to the present edifice, erected after the designs of Thomas Allason, jun., which, after being enlarged on two several occasions, was supplemented in and after 1884 by a magnificent annexe, equal in size to, but of an entirely different shape from, that of the original building. This was designed by J. J. Cole, architect, and comprises the additions in Throgmorton Street and in Old Broad Street. The interior of the New Exchange with its second dome is lined with marbles. Capel Court, in which it stands, was so called from the London residence and place of business of Sir William Capel, ancestor of the Capels, Earls of Essex, and Lord Mayor of London in 1504. The members of the Stock Exchange, about 3200 in number, consist of brokers and dealers (or jobbers) in British and foreign funds, railway and other shares exclusively; each member paying an annual subscription of £10. A notice is posted at every entrance that none but members are admitted. A stranger is soon detected, and by the custom of the place is made to understand that he is an intruder, and turned out. The admission of a member takes place in committee, and is by ballot. The election is only for one year, so that each member has to be re-elected every Lady-day. The committee, consisting of thirty, and called the "Committee for General Purposes," is elected by the members at the same time. Every new member of the "house," as it is called, must be introduced by three members, of not less than four years standing, each of whom enters into security in £500 for four years. An applicant for admission who has been a clerk to a member for the space of four years has to provide only two securities, each to enter into a similar engagement for £300. A bankrupt member immediately ceases to be a member, and cannot be re-elected unless all his liabilities have been discharged in full. The usual commission charged by a broker is one-eighth per cent upon the stock sold or purchased; but on foreign stocks, railway bonds and shares, it varies according to the value of the securities. The broker generally deals with the "jobbers," as they are called, a class of members who are dealers or middle men, who remain in the Stock Exchange in readiness to act upon the appearance of the brokers, but the market is entirely open to all the members, so that a broker is not compelled to deal with a jobber, but can treat with another broker if he can do so more advantageously to his client. The fluctuations of price are produced by sales and purchases, by continental news, and domestic politics and finance. Those who buy stock which they cannot receive are called "Bulls," or who sell stock which they have not, are in *Exchange Alley* called "Bears." These nicknames were in use as early as the reign of Queen Anne, but their meaning is now somewhat altered; a Bull is one who speculates for a *rise*, and a Bear one who speculates for a *fall*.

Stocking Weavers' Hall. [*See* Weavers' Hall.]

Stocks Market. A market for fish and flesh in Walbrook Ward, on the site of the present *Mansion House*. It was established in 1282 by Henry Walis, Lord Mayor, "where some time had stood (the way being very large and broad) a pair of stocks for punishment of offenders; this building took name of these stocks."[1]

On November 1, 1319, the "sworn wardens for overseeing the flesh-meat brought to the shambles called 'les Stokkes' . . . caused to be brought before the said Mayor and Aldermen two beef carcasses, putrid and poisonous, the same having been taken from William Sperlyng of West Hamme, he intending to sell the same at the said shambles."—Riley's *Memorials of London*, p. 133.

The Stocks Market remained a market for the sale of meat and fish until destroyed in the Great Fire of 1666. When rebuilt it was converted into a market for fruit and vegetables.

Instead of Flesh and Fish sold there before the Fire, are now sold Fruits, Roots and Herbs; for which it is very considerable and much resorted unto, being of note

[1] Stow, p. 85.

for having the choicest in their kind of all sorts, surpassing all other markets in London.—*Strype*, B. ii. p. 199.

In the market stood a statue of Charles I. and one intended to be taken for Charles II., of which latter, however, Pennant [1] gives the following account:—

> In it stood the famous equestrian statue, erected in honour of Charles II. by his most loyal subject Sir Robert Viner, lord mayor. Fortunately his lordship discovered one (made at Leghorn) of John Sobieski trampling on a Turk. The good knight caused some alterations to be made, and christened the Polish monarch by the name of Charles, and bestowed on the turbaned Turk that of Oliver Cromwell.

Walpole [2] says that the statue "came over unfinished, and a new head was added by Latham." Stocks Market was removed at Michaelmas, 1737, to the site of the present *Farringdon Street*. Here it lost its name, and was known as *Fleet Market* (which *see*). The mutilated statue, after remaining for some time among rubbish, was presented by the Common Council to Mr. Robert Vyner, a descendant of the Lord Mayor, who removed it to his county seat in Gautby Park, Lincolnshire.

Stockwell (Surrey), an ecclesiastical parish, but one of the eight wards of the parish of Lambeth, lies between Wandsworth and Brixton. Lysons, writing in 1810, says "the hamlet of Stockwell contains about one hundred houses." At that time Stockwell was a surburban hamlet, but it has now lost all its rural character. Rather more than a century ago (in 1772) this place became noted as the scene of the famous "Stockwell Ghost," who created a great sensation by causing the furniture, etc., to dance. The maid-servant is said to have afterwards acknowledged to having practised the imposition, but after the death of the lady of the house in 1790 the "dancing furniture" sold at extravagant prices.[3]

The parish church of St. Michael was erected in 1840, and enlarged in 1864, and accommodates about 1400 persons. Here in the Clapham Road is Mr. Spurgeon's Stockwell Orphanage, founded in 1867. Stockwell Green, formerly an open space at the junction of Stockwell Road and Landor Road, fell a prey to the builder in 1874, after a struggle with the inhabitants.

Stoke Newington (MIDDLESEX), in the Finsbury division of Ossulstone Hundred, is bounded by Hornsey, Islington, Hackney, and Tottenham. Lysons describes Stoke Newington as containing in 1810 "about 550 acres of land, 18 of which are occupied by market gardeners; the remainder almost wholly meadow and pasture." Now it is a populous suburb of London, and contained, in 1881, 3544 inhabited houses and a population of 22,780. In old records the name is written Newtone, or Neweton. The word Stoke occurs in the names of several places as a distinguishing addition, and is probably derived from the

---

[1] *London*, p. 577.
[2] *Annals*, ed. Dallaway, vol. iii. p. 152. 237; and Hone's *Every Day Book*, vol. i. (January
[3] See Lysons's *Environs of London*, vol. I. p. 7, 1825), p. 62.

Saxon *Stoc*, a wood. It was first prefixed to the name of this place in the 15th century, at which time the manor contained about 100 acres of woodland.[1] Morris explains the word Stoke as denominating "a place by the water."

The old parish church, dedicated to St. Mary, was a low Gothic structure, and according to Stow repaired or "rather rebuilded" in 1562. Further enlargements and alterations were made in subsequent years, and in 1858 a new church was erected exactly facing the old one. The new church, also dedicated to St. Mary, now serves as the parish church, but divine service is likewise performed in the old church, which still retains many of the characteristics of a rural place of worship. The new church, a handsome edifice of the Early Decorated style, was built after the designs of Sir Gilbert Scott. In the old church are monuments to John Dudley (d. 1580), with effigies of himself and his wife (who afterwards married Thomas Sutton, the founder of the Charter House); Sir John Hartopp, Bart. (d. 1762), the monument by Banks; Dr. Samuel Wright (d. 1787), the famous nonconformist preacher, etc. Amongst the ministers at the presbyterian chapel on Newington Green may be mentioned Dr. Price (d. 1791), famed for his moral and metaphysical writings, but especially for his "Treatise on Reversionary Payments" and his "Observations on Civil Liberty, and the Justice and Policy of the War with America;" Dr. Towers (d. 1799), the author of *British Biography* and other works; Rochemont Barbauld (d. 1808), husband of the more noted Mrs. Barbauld, who was buried in the churchyard. Clissold Park, or Newington Park as it was formerly called, which was for many years the residence of the Crawshays, was acquired as a public park in 1889. The New River passes through the grounds.

Eminent Inhabitants.—Here in 1817, at the school of the Rev. John Bransby, Edgar Allan Poe, the American poet, "was for the first time placed under the restraint of regular school discipline."[2] Poe has himself described the house in his "partly autobiographical" story of "William Wilson." There, however, he speaks of "the *five* years of my residence in the quaint old building," and adds, "Encompassed by the massy walls of this venerable academy, I passed, yet not in tedium or disgust, the years of the third lustrum of my life." But this must be taken as a poetic fiction, as his biographer expressly states that he was only two years in England,—1817-1819, *i.e.* from his ninth to eleventh year. Daniel Defoe resided in Church Street about 1710.[3] The house was pulled down some years ago to make room for a new street, which was named after him Defoe Street. Thomas Day (d. 1789), the author of *Sandford* and *Merton*. John Howard, the philanthropist and pioneer of prison reform in England, took lodgings here after his first tour abroad, and after being nursed by his landlady through a severe illness, married her, although twenty-seven years her junior. Lord Chief Justice

[1] Lysons's *Environs*, vol. iv. p. 15, etc.   [2] Gill's *Life of Poe*, pp. 26, 28.
[3] Harl. MSS., No. 7001.

Popham and Sir Francis Popham resided here. Bridget Fleetwood, the eldest daughter of Oliver Cromwell, was buried here September 5, 1681. She married General Ireton, and after his death General Fleetwood, and resided many years at Stoke Newington. Dr. Isaac Watts was from 1696 to 1702 tutor in the family of Sir John Hartopp here, and afterwards spent the last thirty years of his life in the house of Sir Thomas and Lady Abney. A spot containing an arbour said to have been a favourite haunt of the great divine, and where many of his hymns were written, is still railed off; and a statue, erected to his memory by public subscription in 1845, stands in one of the principal walks. The old manor house belonged to the prebendaries of Newington, but was leased at the beginning of the 16th century to William Paten, and in 1571 assigned by him to John Dudley. After Dudley's death his widow appears to have let the house to the Earl of Leicester about 1582, and to the Earl of Oxford a few years later. It was probably a visit made by Elizabeth to one of these courtiers that gave rise to her association with an avenue in this estate, which still bears her name. Mrs. Dudley, after her second marriage to Thomas Sutton, again lived on her Newington estate. Through the marriage of John Dudley's daughter Anne to Sir Francis Popham the manor passed into the Popham family, in which it remained till 1669, when it passed by sale to Thomas Gunstor. He built a new mansion, and in 1695 the old one was pulled down and part of the estate let on building leases. His sister Mary, who inherited the manor, married Sir Thomas Abney, some time Lord Mayor of London. The Abney estate was converted into a cemetery under the title of Abney Park Cemetery, and opened in 1840. [*See* Abney Park Cemetery.]

Stone Buildings, LINCOLN'S INN, a handsome range of stone houses (hence the name) built 1756 from the designs of Sir Robert Taylor. The working drawings were made by a young man of the name of Leach, then a clerk in Taylor's office, who afterwards became a student of Lincoln's Inn, and died filling the high and lucrative office in the law of Master of the Rolls. Leach's drawings are preserved in the library of Lincoln's Inn. Pitt's chambers appear to have been in Stone Buildings. Canning's father was "for some time with a Serjeant Walker who then resided in Stone Buildings." The south end was added 1844-1845 under the direction of Philip Hardwick, R.A.

Store Street, TOTTENHAM COURT ROAD to GOWER STREET. Mary Wollstonecraft went to live here in 1791, and, according to Godwin—

In a commodious apartment, added to the neatness and cleanliness which she had always scrupulously observed, a certain degree of elegance, and those temperate indulgences in furniture and accommodation, from which a sound and uncorrupted taste never fails to derive pleasure.—Godwin's *Memoir*, p. 95.

Storey's Gate, BIRDCAGE WALK, ST. JAMES'S PARK, was so called after Edward Storey, who lived in a house on the site of the present gate, and was keeper of the Volary (Aviary) to King Charles II. He died in 1684 and was buried in St. Margaret's, Westminster.

April 25, 1682.—About nine, this night, it began to lighten, thunder, and rain. The next morning, there was the greatest flood in S. James's Park ever remembered. It came round about the fences, and up to the gravel walks—people could not walk to *Webb's* and *Storie's*.

April 3, 1685.—This afternoon nine or ten houses were burned or blown up, that looked into S. James's Park, between *Webb's* and *Storie's*.—*Diary of Philip Madox*, *MS.*, formerly in the possession of Thorpe, the bookseller (*Notes and Queries*, No. 8).

Their late Maties King William and Queen Mary by L^{res} Patents under the Great Seale bearing date the 7th of June, 1690, did demise to Richard Kent and Thomas Musgrave, Esqrs., at the nominacon of Sr Henry Fane, A certain Peece of Land in the Parish of St. Margarett's Westm^r. without the wall of S^t. James's Parke extending in length from the north end of a Ten^ement late in the Tenure in the poss^{ion} of John Webb to the south end of some shedds late in the Tenure of William Storey, Five Hundred and Seaventy Feet or thereabouts To hold for Fifty years from the date at the Yearly Rent of Six Shillings and Eight Pence.—*Harl. MS.*, No. 6811, Art. 3.

Dropt in St. James's Park, September the 3d, 1705, betwixt Mr. Story's and the Duke of Buckingham's House, a Gold Minuit Pendulum Watch, etc.; if offered to be Sold or pawn'd you are desired to stop the same and give notice to Mr. Padington at his house in Princes Court near Mr. Story's.—*The Daily Courant*, September 5, 1705.

From nine to eleven I allow them to walk from Story's to Rosamond's Pond in the Park.—*Tatler*, No. 113.[1]

August 5, 1746.—I don't know whether I told you that the man at the Tennis Court protests that he has known Lord Balmerino dine with the man that sells pamphlets at Storey's Gate, and says "he would often have been glad if I would have taken him home to dinner."—*Walpole to Montagu*, vol. ii. p. 46.

Strand (The), one of the main arteries of London, reaching from Charing Cross to the site of Temple Bar (now marked by a huge decorated pedestal). The portion between King William Street and Charing Cross is now called West Strand. In the last century it only reached "from Charing Cross to Essex Street,"[2] the portion of the road from Essex Street to Temple Bar being called "Temple Bar Without." The Strand was originally a low-lying road running near the banks of the Thames, and hence it obtained its name.

> I send, I send here my supremest kiss
> To thee my silver footed Thamasis.
> No more shall I reiterate thy *Strand*
> Whereon so many stately structures stand.
>
> Herrick, *Teares to Thamasis*.

At the digging a Foundation for the present Church (St. Mary-le-Strand), the Virgin Earth was discovered at the Depth of Nineteen Feet; whereby 'tis manifest that the Ground in this Neighbourhood originally was not much higher than the River *Thames*; therefore this Village was truly denominated the *Strand*, from its Situation on the Bank of the River.—Maitland's *History of London*, p. 739.

In 1315 a petition of the inhabitants of Westminster represented the footway from Temple Bar to the King's Palace at Westminster as so bad that the feet of horses and rich and poor men received constant damage, and that the footway was interrupted by thickets and bushes.

---

[1] Pennant has an erroneous statement about the origin of the name. "Where the iron gates at the bottom of that noble street, George Street, are placed, stood a storehouse for the Ordnance in the time of Queen Mary. I remember a dirty dark passage leading into the Park, which preserves its memory, but was corruptly called Storey's Gate."

[2] Parish Clerks' Survey, 12mo, 1732.

An ordinance of Edward III. in council, dated 1353, directs the laying of a tax on all goods carried by land or water from the City to West minster, "in order for the repairing the highway leading from the gate of London called Temple Bar to the gate of the Abbey at Westminster, that highway being . . . become so deep and miry, and the pavement so broken and worn as to be very dangerous both to men and carriages."[1] The Strand was long very little more than "a way or street"[2] between the cities of Westminster and London, and was not paved before Henry VIII.'s reign, when (1532), it being then "full of pits and sloughs, very perilous and noisome," an Act was passed for "paving the streetway between Charing Cross and Strand Cross, at the charge of the owners of the land."

One of the first ascertained inhabitants of the Strand was Peter of Savoy, uncle of Henry III., to whom that king, in the thirtieth year of his reign (1245), granted "all those houses upon the Thames, which sometime pertained to Briane de Insula, or Lisle, without the walls of the City of London, in the way or street called the Strand." The Bishops were the next great dignitaries who had inns or houses in the Strand, connecting, as it were, the City with the King's Palace at Westminster. "Anciently," says Selden in his *Table Talk*, "the noblemen lay within the City for safety and security; but the bishops' houses were by the waterside, because they were held sacred persons whom nobody would hurt." As many as nine bishops possessed inns or hostels on the south or water side of the present Strand, at the period of the Reformation. The Bishop of Exeter's inn was afterwards Essex House. The Bishop of Bath's inn was afterwards Arundel House. The inns of the three Bishops of Llandaff, Chester, and Worcester were swallowed up by the palace of the Protector Somerset, on the site of the present Somerset House. Near the site of the present church of St. Mary's stood "Strand Cross."

Opposite to Chester Inn stood an antient cross . . . in the year 1294 and at other times the Judges sat without the city, on this cross, to administer justice. Pennant's *London*, p. 144.

The Bishop of Carlisle's inn (west of the Savoy) was afterwards Worcester House, the mansion of the Dukes of Beaufort, hence the present Beaufort Buildings. The Bishop of Durham's inn occupied the site of the Adelphi; and the inn of the Archbishop of York was conveyed, in the reign of James I., to Villiers, first Duke of Buckingham, whose name and titles are preserved in several streets between the Adelphi and Charing Cross. The upper or north side of the road lay open to the fields, to St. Martin's-in-the-Fields, St. Giles-in-the-Fields, and Covent Garden, as late as the reign of Charles I. A few noblemen's mansions, however, had been previously erected. Burghley House, the London lodging of the great Lord Burghley, on the site of the present Exeter Street and Exeter 'Change, and Bedford House, on the site of the present Southampton Street and Bedford Street, were built

[1] Rymer's *Fœdera*, vol. v. p. 762.   [2] Stow, p. 164.

in the reign of Elizabeth. Salisbury House, on the site of the present Cecil Street and Salisbury Street, and Northampton, now Northumberland House, were built in the reign of James I. Middleton, the dramatist, describes it not untruly at this time as "the luxurious Strand."[1] The stables of Durham House were taken down in 1610 to erect the New Exchange; York House was taken down in 1675; and Burghley, or Exeter House, in 1676, and Exeter 'Change erected the next year on the principal site. Arundel House was taken down in 1678; Worcester House in 1683; Salisbury House in 1696; Bedford House in 1704; Essex House in 1710; the New Exchange in 1737, and the Adelphi afterwards erected on the same site: old Somerset House was taken down in 1775; Butcher Row in 1813; and Exeter 'Change in 1829, when the great Strand improvements at the West End were made pursuant to 7 Geo. IV., c. 77.

The Lawyer embraced our young gentleman and gave him many riotous instructions how to carry himself: told him he must acquaint himself with many gallants of the Inns of Court, and keep rank with those that spend most, always wearing a bountiful disposition about him, lofty and liberal; his lodging must be about the Strand, in any case, being remote from the handicraft scent of the City.—*Father Hubburd's Tales*, 4to, 1604 (Middleton's *Works*, vol. v. p. 573).

For divers yeares of late certain fishmongers have erected and set up fishstalles in the middle of the street in the Strand, almost over against Denmark House, all which were broken down by speciall Commission, this moneth of May, 1630, least in short space they might grow from stalles to shedds, and then to dwelling houses, as the like was in former time in Olde Fish Street, and in Saint Nicholas Shambles, and in other places.—*Howes*, ed. 1631, p. 1045.

> [1] Come let us leave the Temple's silent walls,
> The business to my distant lodging calls:
> Through the long Strand together let us stray,
> With thee conversing I forget the way.
> Behold that narrow street, which steep descends,
> Whose building to the shining shore extends;
> Here Arundel's fam'd structure rear'd its frame,
> The street alone retains an empty name:
> Where Titian's glowing paint the canvas warm'd,
> And Raphael's fair design with judgment charm'd,
> Now hangs the Bell-man's song, and pasted here,
> The coloured prints of Overton appear.
> Where statues breath'd the work of Phidias' hands,
> A wooden pump or lonely watch-house stands;
> There Essex' stately pile adorn'd the shore,
> There Cecil's, Bedford's, Villiers',—now no more.—Gay, *Trivia*.
>
> Where the fair columns of St. Clement stand,
> Whose straitened bounds incroach upon the Strand;
> Where the low pent-house bows the walker's head,
> And the rough pavement wounds the yielding tread;
> Where not a post protects the narrow space,
> And strung in twines combs dangle in thy face;
> Summon at once thy courage, rouse thy care,
> Stand firm, look back, be resolute, beware.
> Forth issuing from steep lanes,[2] the Collier's steeds

---

[1] Middleton's *Works*, by Dyce, vol. v. p. 578.   [2] Milford Lane.

> Drag the black load ; another cart succeeds,
> Team follows team, crowds heap'd on crowds appear.—*Ibid.*

The Strand is now given up entirely to business purposes, and the "luxurious" mansions of the nobility and gentry must be sought for farther westward. The Strand is remarkable as containing more theatres than any other street in London. In it are to be noticed—north side: Adelphi, Nos. 410, 411; Vaudeville, No. 404; Lyceum, No. 354; Gaiety, No. 345; Opera Comique, No. 299. South side: Strand, No. 168; and Terry's, Nos. 105, 106. Besides these the Royal Italian Opera House, Drury Lane, Theatre, the Globe, the Savoy, Toole's, and the Avenue only lie a short distance off the Strand. [*See* these respective headings.] The business of the Strand now forms a kind of connecting link between the hurry and bustle of the City and the comfort and leisure of the West End.

Eminent Inhabitants (not already mentioned).—Sir Harry Vane the elder (temp. Charles I.), next door to Northumberland House (then Suffolk House), where now stands the Grand Hotel;[1] this was long the official residence of the Secretary of State. Mr. Secretary Nicholas was living here in Charles II.'s reign. William Lilly, the astrologer (d. 1681), at "the corner house, over against Strand Bridge." He was servant for some time to a man of the name of Gilbert Wright, and performed many of the menial offices of his house—swept the street before his door, cleaned his shoes, scraped the trenchers, and played the part of tub-boy to the Thames in carrying water for his master's use. "I have helped," he says, "to carry eighteen tubs of water in one morning." Lilly got on in life, married his master's widow, and came at last to possess the house in which he had performed so many menial occupations. William Faithorne, the engraver (d. 1691), "at the sign of the Ship, next to the Drake, opposite to the Palsgrave Head Tavern, without Temple Bar." Pierce Tempest, the engraver of the Cries of London, which bear his name :—

There is now Published the Cryes and Habits of London, lately drawn after the Life in great Variety of Actions, Curiously Engraved upon 50 Copper Plates, fit for the Ingenious and Lovers of Art. Printed and Sold by P. Tempest over against Somerset House in the Strand.—*The London Gazette*, May 28 to 31, 1688.

At "No. 18 in the Strand" lived J. Mathews the bookseller, and father of Charles Mathews the actor, and in this house the latter was born. Jacob Tonson, the bookseller and friend of Dryden, at "Shakespeare's Head, over against Catherine Street, in the Strand," now No. 141; the house (since rebuilt) was afterwards occupied by Andrew Millar, the publisher, and friend of Thomson, Fielding, Hume, and Robertson; and after Millar's death by Thomas Cadell, his apprentice, and friend, and the publisher of Gibbon. Thomson's *Seasons*, Fielding's *Tom Jones*, and the Histories of Hume, Robertson, and Gibbon were first published at this house. Millar was a Scotchman, and distinguished his house by the sign of "Buchanan's Head." James Northcote, R.A.,

[1] This house was No. 1 in the Strand, and was the first house in London that was numbered.—Smith's *Nollekens*, vol. i. p. 236.

on his first coming to London in 1771 lodged at "Mrs. Lefty's, Grocer in the Strand." Six shillings a week gained by colouring prints of flowers covered all his expenses. "At the corner of Beaufort Buildings, in the Strand," lived Charles Lillie, the perfumer, known to every reader of *The Tatler* and *The Spectator*. [*See* Beaufort Buildings.] Mrs. Inchbald, the actress and dramatic writer, was living in 1809 at No. 163, "by the side of the new Church," and from the top of this house was a witness of the burning of Drury Lane Theatre. No. 332, now the printing-offices of *The Weekly Times* and *Echo*, was during its flourishing epoch the office of *The Morning Chronicle*,—the upper floors being the Editor's rooms and the residence of Mr. John Black during his long editorship of that journal.[1] No. 346 (corner of Wellington Street), now the offices of *The Field* and *The Queen*, was formerly Doyley's warehouse for woollen goods. Dryden in his *Limberham* speaks of "Doily Petticoats," and Steele in *The Guardian* (No. 102) of his "Doily Suit," while Gay in his *Trivia* describes a Doily as a poor defence against the cold. No. 277 was in the time of Queen Anne the shop of Bat Pidgeon, known to every reader of *The Spectator*.[2] At No. 132 Bathoe the bookseller established in 1740 the first circulating library in London. On the first floor of a house at the eastern corner of Castle Court (where Agar Street now stands) the Society of Arts held their meetings in 1756, and there they erected assaying furnaces. Nathaniel Smith and Joseph Nollekens were playfellows here. Adjoining Temple Bar and on a part of the site of the New Law Courts, stood the small pent-house of lath and plaster occupied for many years by Crockford[3] (d. 1844) as a shell-fish shop; here he made the money with which he established the Club in St. James's Street which bore his name. [*See* Crockford's.] The Banking House of Messrs. Coutts and Company is numbered 59.

The business hitherto carried on in St. Martin's Lane was removed by Middleton to its present site in 1757—in a house erected for it, the central house of eleven which formed the New Exchange, or Britain's Bourse. The house itself was at this time known as the Three Crowns. In 1755 Mr. James Coutts of Edinburgh was admitted as a partner, the firm being then entitled Campbell and Coutts. By the death of George Campbell in 1760 Coutts was left sole partner. Soon after his brother Thomas was admitted, and he, surviving his brother, became the head of the firm,—the Old Coutts of boundless wealth. By his death in 1822 the male line of Coutts became extinct.—"Account of Coutts Family," by Robert Chambers, *Chambers's Journal*, November 7, 1874.

[*See* the various buildings mentioned under their several names, and also the several streets along the line.]

Strand Bridge, the original name for the fine bridge by John Rennie, but changed by Act of Parliament, and now universally known as *Waterloo Bridge*. It was previously applied to a bridge over the

---

[1] See *Forty Years' Recollections*, by Charles Mackay, LL.D., vol. i. p. 71.
[2] Smith's *Nollekens*, vol. i. p. 3; vol. ii. p. 217.
[3] There is a good view of the house in No. 1 of J. W. Archer's *Vestiges of Old London*.

streamlet from St. Clement's Well, where it crossed the Strand; and afterwards to a landing-pier at the foot of Strand Lane. [*See* Strand Lane.]

Then had ye in the high street a fair bridge called Strand Bridge, and under it a lane or way down to the landing-place on the bank of the Thames.—*Stow*, p. 165.

February 25, 1527.—The Lady Elizabeth came riding from her house at Hatfield to London . . . unto her place called Somerset Place, beyond Strand Bridge.—Strype, *Hist. Mem.*, vol. iii. p. 444; *Machyn*, p. 167.

I landed with ten sail of Apricock boats at Strand Bridge, after having put in at Nine Elms, and taken in Melons, consigned by Mr. Cuffe of that place to Sarah Sewell and Company at their stall in Covent Garden.—*The Spectator*, No. 454.

There was a third bridge in the Strand in addition to Ivy Bridge and Strand Bridge, the remains of which were discovered in 1832 during the construction of a sewer a little east of St. Clement's Church. "It was of stone and consisted of one arch about 11 feet long, very antique in its appearance and of the most durable construction."[1] It is difficult for us to conceive what a London roadway must have been in the time of the Tudors and Stuarts. When James Naylor, the weak-minded Quaker enthusiast, was flogged by the direct order of Parliament, the historian of the sect records that

The 18th December [1656] J. Naylor suffered part: and after having stood full two hours with his head in the Pillory, was stripped, and whipped at a cart's tail, from Palace Yard to the Old Exchange, and received three hundred and ten stripes; and the executioner would have given him one more (as he confessed to the Sheriff), *there being three hundred and eleven kennels*, but his foot slipping, the stroke fell upon his own hand, which hurt him much.—Sewel's *Hist. of the Quakers*, 4to, 1709, vol. i. p. 239.

There were thus no fewer than 311 open channels crossing the roadway between Westminster Hall and the Royal Exchange; and after heavy rains every lane leading to the Thames must have been an open watercourse. Perhaps the largest of the unbridged channels was at Milford (Mill Ford) Lane.

Strand Inn, an Inn of Court belonging to the Middle Temple. It was pulled down by the Protector Somerset, and part of the present Somerset House occupies the site.

Strand Lane, in the STRAND, east of Somerset House, and opposite the east end of St. Mary's Church, was originally the channel of the rivulet which crossed the great thoroughfare under Strand Bridge. It must be remembered that the Strand at this part has been raised fully 20 feet above the ancient level. The lane led to the landing-place, at one time known as Strand Bridge; but this was destroyed in forming the Thames Embankment and the lane is no longer a thoroughfare. On the east side of this lane is a genuine ancient *Roman Bath*, which is well worth inspection. The bath is 13 feet long and 6 feet wide, and is supplied by a spring of beautifully clear, cold water. The bricks of which it is constructed are similar to those of the City Wall, but smaller in size.[2]

[1] *Knight*, vol. ii. p. 151.
[2] There is an engraving of the bath in Knight's *London*, vol. ii. p. 164, 1842. It has been little altered since.

Strand Theatre, on the south side of the Strand, four doors west of Surrey Street, formerly called Punch's Playhouse, is principally devoted to burlesque and farce. The exterior is unpretentious, the interior well appointed.

Stratford Le Bow, (the Stratford atte Bowe of our old writers of the 14th and 15th centuries), now commonly called Bow, formerly a hamlet of Stepney, but made into a separate parish in 1720, lies a mile east of Mile End. The name Stratford or Straet-ford is derived from a ford through the Lea at the place where it was crossed by the old Roman Road to Colchester. About the beginning of the 12th century Queen Matilda built a bridge over the Lea near the "Old Ford," and from the shape of this bridge the name of the village took the addition of "atte Bow."

> Matilda, wife of Henry I., having herself been well washed in the water, caused two bridges to be builded in a place one mile distant from the Old Ford, of the which one was situated over Lee at the head of the town of Stratford nowe called Bowe, because the bridge was arched like unto a bowe, a rare piece of work, for before that time the like had never been seen in England. The other over the little brooke, commonly called Chanelse Bridge.—Leland's *Collections*.

The old bridge, consisting of three narrow arches, had been so often repaired as to leave little of the original structure when taken down in 1835. The present one, a substantial structure in Aberdeen granite, of a single elliptical arch, 70 feet in span, was erected from the designs of Messrs. Walker and Burges, and formally opened February 14, 1839. The French of Chaucer's "Prioress" was spoken in the Stratford manner:—

> And Frensch sche spak ful faire and fetysly,
> After the scole of Stratford atte Bowe,
> For Frensch of Parys was to hire unknowe.
> *Prologue to Canterbury Tales*, l. 124.

Bakers living at Stratford-le-Bow supplied London with bread as late as the reign of Henry VIII.

> A custome which many holde that Mile-End is no walke without a recreation at Stratford Bow with creame and cakes.—Kemp's *Nine Days' Wonder*, 4to, 1600.
>
> William de Croton, of the county of Suffolk, was attached for pretending to be a sergeant of the Sheriffs of London. Meeting Richolda of Stratford and Mabel of Stratford, bakeresses, who were bringing bread to the City with their carts, for sale, he arrested the carts of the said Richolda and Mabel until they had paid him a fine.—Riley's *Memorials*, p. 79.

This parish was also for some time the resort of the butchers of London, "who do rent their houses at Stratforde and around Stratforde." In 1371 the air of the City having been "greatly corrupted and infected" by the slaughtering of cattle therein, Edward III. ordained that

> All oxen, sheep, swine and other large animals, for the sustenance of our city aforesaid to be slaughtered, should be taken to the village of Stretteford, on the one side and the village of Knyghtebrugge on the other side of the said city and there be slaughtered.—Riley's *Memorials*, p. 356.

The parish church, dedicated to St. Mary, was originally built about the beginning of the 14th century as a chapel of ease to Stepney, and was consecrated as a parish church March 16, 1719.

What is now known as Stratford, a mile or so farther east, is more properly Stratford Langthorn.

Stratford Place, OXFORD STREET, north side, opposite South Molton Street, was built about 1775 by Edward Stratford second Earl of Aldborough, and others, to whom a ground-lease, renewable for ever under certain conditions, had been granted by the Corporation of London. In the mansion that terminates the place, and fronts the entrance from *Oxford Street*, the Earl of Aldborough resided for many years.[1] Here stood the Lord Mayor's Banqueting House, erected for the Mayor and Corporation to dine in after their periodical visits to the Bayswater and Paddington Conduits, and the Conduit Head adjacent to the Banqueting House, which supplied the City with water.

> A conduit head
> Hard by the place toward Tyburn, which they call
> My Lord Mayor's Banqueting House.
> Ben Jonson, *The Devil is an Ass*, Act v. Sc. 1.

Strype preserves a curious picture of a visit made by the Mayor to the Conduit Heads in the year 1562. Before dinner they hunted the hare and killed her, and after dinner they went to hunting the fox; "there was a cry for a mile, and at length the hounds killed him at the end of St. Giles'; great hallooing at his death and blowing of horns." The Banqueting House was taken down in 1737, and the cisterns arched over at the same time.[2] Here General Strode (the same who set up the statue in Cavendish Square) erected a pillar to commemorate the naval victories of Britain, which it did for a very brief period, as the foundations gave way in 1805.

About 1792 Richard Cosway, R.A., removed from Schomberg House, Pall Mall, to the south-western corner of Stratford Place. The house has a lion on the outside, and hardly had he taken possession of his new abode when a pasquinade, attributed to Peter Pindar, was affixed to his door :—

> When a man to a fair for a show brings a lion,
> 'Tis usual a monkey the sign post to tie on :
> But here the old custom reversed is seen
> For the lion's without, and the monkey's within !

Cosway, one of the vainest of men, was so mortified that he removed shortly after to No. 20. This he fitted up and furnished in a style then scarcely known in the houses of professional men. His marble chimneypieces were all carved by Thomas Banks, R.A. The rooms —each fitted in a different manner—"were more like scenes of enchantment pencilled by a poet's fancy, than anything, perhaps, before displayed in a domestic habitation."

[1] *Londiniana*, vol. iii. p. 40.   [2] *Maitland*, ed. 1739, p. 779.

> His furniture consisted of ancient chairs, couches, and conversation stools, elaborately carved and gilt and covered with the most costly Genoa velvets; escritoires of ebony, inlaid with mother-of-pearl; and rich caskets for antique gems, exquisitely enamelled, and adorned with onyxes, opals, rubies and emeralds. There were cabinets of ivory, curiously wrought; mosaic tables set with jasper, blood-stone, and lapis-lazuli; having their feet carved into the claws of lions and eagles; screens of old raised oriental Japan; massive musical clocks richly chased with or-molu and tortoise-shell; ottomans superbly damasked; Persian and other carpets . . . and rich hangings of English tapestry. The chimney-pieces, carved by Banks, were further adorned with the choicest bronzes and models in wax and terra-cotta; the tables covered with old Sèvres, blue, Mandarin, Nankin, and Dresden china; and the cabinets were surmounted with crystal cups adorned with the York and Lancaster roses, which might probably have graced the splendid banquets of the proud Wolsey. —Smith's *Nollekens*, vol. ii. p. 401.

In his drawing-room was a marble sarcophagus in which was the embalmed body of his deceased daughter; but this Mrs. Cosway, on her return from her long sojourn in Italy, got rid of, sending the body to the Bunhill Fields cemetery, and the sarcophagus to Nollekens, the sculptor. Cosway resided here to the last. His death occurred in Miss Udney's carriage, on July 4, 1821, while taking an airing on the Edgeware Road. Madame D'Arblay records[1] meeting Sir Joshua Reynolds at a dinner at Mrs. Walsingham's (a daughter of Sir Hanbury Williams) in Stratford Place. Henry Addington (Lord Sidmouth) was living here in 1792. Sydney Smith at No. 18 in 1835. No. 1 is the Portland Club House. R. W. Elliston, the celebrated actor, dated from Stratford Place in June 1822.

Stratton Street, PICCADILLY, west side of Devonshire House. Built circ. 1693,[2] and so called after John, Baron Berkeley of Stratton, the hero of Stratton Fight, fought at Stratton in Cornwall during the Civil Wars under Charles I. This Lord Berkeley built Berkeley House in Piccadilly (on the site of Devonshire House); hence Berkeley Street and Berkeley Square. Thomas Graham, Lord Lynedoch, the hero of Barossa, and Wellington's second in command in the Peninsula, lived at No. 12 in this street, and died here, December 18, 1843, in his ninety-sixth year. No. 1, on the left-hand side, is the residence of the Baroness Burdett Coutts. Here the Duchess of St. Alban's (Mrs. Coutts) gave her magnificent entertainments; and here she died in 1837. For two months before her death she lay in the great dining-room towards Piccadilly, without pain, but weak and tranquil. James Douglas, the author of *Nenia Britannica*, lived in this street. Thomas Campbell writes to Dr. Currie from No. 2, April 13, 1802.

Streights i' the Strand, a cant name, as Gifford says, given to a "nest of obscure courts, alleys and avenues running between the bottom of St. Martin's Lane, Half-Moon, and Chandos Street," frequented by bullies, knights of the post, and fencing masters, now cleared away. [*See* Bermudas; Butcher Row; Porridge Island.]

[1] *Diary*, vol. ii. p. 164. [2] Rate-books of St. Martin's-in-the-Fields.

Justice Overdo. Look into any angle of the town, the Streights, or the Bermudas, where the quarrelling lesson is read, and how do they entertain the time but with bottle-ale and tobacco?—Ben Jonson, *Bartholomew Fair.*

> Their very trade
> Is borrowing; that but stopt they do invade
> All as their prize, turn pirates here at land,
> Have their Bermudas, and their Streights i' the Strand.
> *Ben Jonson to Sir Edward Sackville.*

Strombello or Strumbello (STRUMBELS, Dodsley) is the name given in Sayer's Map of 1769 to some buildings in the Chelsea Road, on the left of the present church of St. Barnabas. Intermediately the ground was occupied by a small playhouse of the lowest description, called the Orange Theatre.

1762.—At Cromwell House, Brompton, once the seat of Oliver, was also a tea-garden concert; and at *Strombolo Tea-gardens* near Chelsea was a fine fountain. —*O'Keefe*, vol. i. p. 88.

The place was called Queen Street in 1794.

Strutton Ground, WESTMINSTER, Victoria Street (south side) to Great Peter Street, a corruption of Stourton Ground, from Stourton House, the mansion of the Lords Dacre of the South. [*See* Emanuel Hospital.]

Strype's Court, PETTICOAT LANE, the second turning on the right hand from Aldgate, is said to have been so called after the father of Strype, the historian, a merchant and silk throwster, and long an inhabitant of the court. The historian was born in this court in 1643.[1] But it should be noted that in Strype's own Map (1720) it is called *Tripe Yard;* and that Dodsley (1761) enters it as *Trype Yard*, but also as *Strype's Yard*. It is now known as *Tripe Court*. [*See* Petticoat Lane.]

Suffolk House, CHARING CROSS. The second name of what was afterwards known as *Northumberland House.*

On Thursday, May 8th, 1539, "when all the citizens of London mustered in harnes afore the Kinge," Henry VIII. was stationed at the Whitehall Gateway, and "the Lord Chancellor, the Duke of Norfolke, Duke of Suffolke, and other Lords of the Kinge's householde, stood at the Duke of Suffolke's place by Charing Cross to see them as they passed by."—Wriothesley's *Chronicle*, p. 96.

On the left hand of Charing Crosse, there are divers fair houses built of late years, specially the most stately palace of Suffolk or Northampton House, built by Henry of Northampton, son to the Duke of Norfolk and Lord Privie Seal to King James. —Howell's *Londinopolis*, fol. 1657, p. 350.

Suckling refers to this house in his famous ballad on the Wedding of Roger Boyle, Lord Broghill, afterwards first Earl of Orrery, with Lady Margaret Howard, daughter of Theophilus, Earl of Suffolk.

> At Charing Cross, hard by the way
> Where we (thou know'st), do sell our hay,
> There is a house with stairs.

---

[1] *Lysons*, vol. iv. p. 175.

And there did I see coming down
Such folks as are not in our town,
Forty at least in pairs.

March 15, 1617.—Grant to the Earl of Suffolk to have a small pipe for conveying water to Suffolk House, inserted in the main pipe from Hyde Park to Westminster Palace.—*Cal. State Pap.*, 1611-1618, p. 447.

Evelyn, under June 9, 1658, records that he "went to see the Earl of Northumberland's pictures . . . in Suffolk House," and he observes that "the new front towards the gardens is tolerable, were it not drown'd by a too massive and clumsie pair of stayres of stone, without any neate invention." A second, perhaps an earlier house belonging to the same noble family, stood on the site of the present *Suffolk Street*, Haymarket. [*See* Suffolk Street.]

Suffolk House, SOUTHWARK.

Almost directly over-against St. George's Church, was sometime a large and most sumptuous house, built by Charles Brandon, late Duke of Suffolk, in the reign of Henry VIII., which was called Suffolk House; but coming afterwards into the King's hands, the same was called Southwarke Place, and a Mint of coinage [*see* The Mint] was there kept for the King. To this Place came King Edward VI., in the second of his reign, from Hampton Court, and dined in it. . . . Queen Mary gave this house to Nicholas Heath, Archbishop of Yorke, and to his successors, for ever, to be their Inn or Lodging for their repair to London, in recompense of York House, near to Westminster, which King Henry her father had taken from Cardinal Wolsey, and from the see of York. Archbishop Heath sold the same house to a merchant or to merchants that pulled it down, sold the lead, stone, iron, etc., and in place thereof built many small cottages of great rents, to the increasing of beggars in that borough. The archbishop bought Norwich House or Suffolk Place, near unto Charing Cross, because it was near unto the Court, and left it to his successors.—*Stow*, p. 153.

The said Archbishop, August the 6th, 1557, obtained a license for the alienation of this capital messuage of Suffolk Place; and to apply the price thereof for the buying of other houses called also Suffolk Place, lying near Charing Cross; as appears from a Register belonging to the Dean and Chapter of York.—*Strype*, B. iv. p. 17.

It appears, however, from the Charter of Edward VI. (*Norton*, p. 386), that Henry VIII. purchased these "lands, tenements, and premises" from Charles, Duke of Suffolk. Edward granted them to the City, and they were attached to the Bridge House estate. The house with its park is shown in Wyngaerde's View of London (ab. 1550). The name still survives in Great Suffolk Street. "Brandonne's Place in Southwerke" is mentioned in Sir John Howard's Expenses, under the year 1465, but this does not refer to Suffolk House, which was not built until about 1516. This is Sir Thomas Brandon's Place in another part of Southwark, afterwards given by Sir Thomas in 1510 to Lady Guildford, hence the name of Great Guildford Street.

Suffolk Lane, UPPER THAMES STREET, to Laurence Pountney Lane.

Suffolk Lane, well known by the Grammar School, founded and supported there by the Merchant Taylors' Company, took its denomination from the noble family of Suffolk [De la Pole], who anciently had property on this spot; and it is not unlikely that what is called Duck's Foot Lane was originally the Duke's foot-lane, or narrow way to and from his mansion.—Dr. Wilson's *St. Lawrence Poultney*, 4to, 1831, p. 5.

The Merchant Taylors' School was removed in 1875 to the site of the old Charterhouse School. [*See* Merchant Taylors' School.] The pious Robert Nelson, author of the *Fasts and Festivals*, was born in this lane, June 22, 1656. His father, John Nelson, was a wealthy trader to the Levant.

Suffolk Street, HAYMARKET to PALL MALL EAST; built circ. 1664,[1] and "so called," says Strype, "as being built on the ground where stood a large house belonging to the Earls of Suffolk. It is a very good street," he continues, "with handsome houses, well inhabited, and resorted unto by lodgers."[2] It was originally called "Suffolk Yard Buildings."[3] Horace Walpole, in a MS. note to Pennant, says that this street "used to be known for the residence of foreigners, who were but ill lodged here: of late years hotels have been introduced where they are better accommodated and in better streets. In the reign of George the First an Italian warehouse was kept at the upper end of Suffolk Street by one Corticelli, much frequented by people of fashion for raffles and purchases and gallant meetings. It is mentioned in Lady M. W. Montagu's Letters." Fifty years later Theodore Hook, in *Gilbert Gurney*, writes—

I [Gilbert Gurney] took a first floor in Suffolk Street, Charing Cross, then extremely unlike what it afterwards became in the course of the improvements in that neighbourhood. At that period it consisted for the most part of tailors' houses, the upper floors of which were tenanted in their different degrees by gentlemen loose upon town, visitors to the metropolis, and officers on half-pay, of which it appeared the greater portion were considered to be "frae the North," inasmuch as Suffolk Street was nicknamed in that day *the Scottish Barracks*.

Evelyn notes, December 23, 1671, that "the Councillors of the Board of Trade dined together at the Cock in Suffolk Street." Besides Evelyn, Shaftesbury and Waller were of the number, and Locke was their secretary. The Golden Eagle, Suffolk Street, was the scene of the so-called "Calf's Head Club" riot, January 30, 1735, when a mob broke the windows and wrecked the house under the belief that a number of young noblemen and gentlemen who were dining there were having a "calf's-head dinner" in commemoration of the execution of Charles I. The Cock and the Golden Eagle have both disappeared, and there is no tavern in Suffolk Street now; but there are three or four private hotels and several lodging-houses. At the Pall Mall corner is the *University Club House*, built, 1822-1826, from the designs of W. Wilkins and J. P. Gandy-Deering, and No. 6 the gallery of the *Society of British Artists*, built by J. Nash, 1823-1824. The street was rebuilt in 1822. *Eminent Inhabitants.*—Moll Davis, from 1667 to 1674, when she removed to St. James's Square.

January 14, 1667-1668.—The King [Charles II.], it seems, hath given her [Moll Davis] a ring of £700, which she shows to every body, and owns that the

---
[1] Rate-books of St. Martin's.   [2] *Strype*, B. vi. p. 68.   [3] Rate-books of St. Martin's.

King did give it her; and he hath furnished a house in Suffolke Street most richly for her; which is a most infinite shame.—*Pepys*.

February 15, 1668-1669.—In Suffolk Street lives Moll Davis; and we did see her coach come for her to her door, a mighty pretty fine coach.—*Pepys*.

Thomas Stanley, the editor of *Æschylus;* he died at his lodgings in this street in 1678, and was buried in the adjoining churchyard of St. Martin's-in-the-Fields. Sir John Coventry, who was on his way to his own house in Suffolk Street, from the Cock Tavern in Bow Street, where he had supped,[1] when his nose was cut to the bone at the corner of the street " for reflecting on the King." A motion had been made in the House of Commons to lay a tax on playhouses. The Court opposed the motion. The players, it was said (by Sir John Birkenhead), were the King's servants, and a part of his pleasure. Coventry asked, " Whether did the King's pleasure lie among the men or the women that acted ?"—perhaps recollecting more particularly the King's visits to Moll Davis in the street he himself lived in. The King determined to *leave a mark* upon Sir John Coventry, who was watched on his way home. " He stood up to the wall," says Burnet, "and snatched the flambeau out of the servant's hands; and with that in one hand, and his sword in the other, he defended himself so well, that he got more credit by it than by all the actions of his life. He wounded some of them, but was soon disarmed, and then they cut his nose to the bone, to teach him to remember what respect he owed to the King."[2] Burnet adds that his nose was so well sewed up that the scar was scarce to be discerned. The famous " Coventry Act," against cutting and maiming, had its origin in this piece of barbarous revenge. Sir Philip Howard and the Earl of Suffolk; the former from 1665 to 1672; the latter from 1666. Henry Coventry (Mr. Secretary Coventry), from 1669 to 1686. Coventry Street derives its name from this Mr. Secretary Coventry. Sir Edward Spragg, one of the Admirals of the Dutch war under Charles II. Dean Swift, on July 6, 1711, took lodgings here, five doors from Mrs. Vanhomrigh, the mother of Vanessa. During the previous two months he had been living at Chelsea for his health, but kept his gown and periwig at Mrs. Vanhomrigh's for paying visits. Swift left Suffolk Street in October for a lodging by Leicester Fields. In his " Cadenus and Vanessa " he gives a lively picture of a morning reception in Vanessa's apartment, where

<blockquote>
Vanessa held Montaigne and read,
While Mrs. Susan combed her head.
</blockquote>

Horace Walpole writes to Conway, September 9, 1762, " By this time I suppose the Duke de Nivernois is unpacking his portion of olive dans la rue de Suffolk Street." At this time the Venetian ambassador resided in Suffolk Street, and, as Dodsley notes, had a Popish Chapel in his house. Samuel Foote was living in Suffolk Street when young Holcroft found him at breakfast in 1770; and here his body was brought after his death at Dover in 1777. James Barry, R.A., at No. 29, between the years 1773 and 1776.

[1] Marvell's *Letters*.   [2] *Burnet*, ed. 1823, vol. I. p. 468.

James Barry, member of the Royal Academy and of the Clementini Academy of Bologna, informs such of the young nobility and gentry as may be desirous of forming a taste for the Arts, and a knowledge and practice of drawing, that he will wait upon such as will honour him with their commands, and give lessons twice a week at three guineas per month. He continues his business as usual in Suffolk Street, No. 29, Haymarket, where he is to be met with Mondays and Tuesdays excepted.—*Public Advertiser*, June 4, 1774; *Gentleman's Magazine*, August 1834.

George Frederick Cooke was living at No. 38 in September 1803. Lord Winchilsea was living at No. 7 when challenged in 1829 by the Duke of Wellington. Richard Cobden, the Apostle of Free Trade, died "at his lodgings in Suffolk Street," April 2, 1865, aged sixty. The house of Edward Cresy, architect, was designed by him in imitation of Andrea Palladio's at Vicenza.

Suffolk Street, MIDDLESEX HOSPITAL—the first turning west of the hospital, now called Nassau Street. Major Rennell, the celebrated geographer, was living at No. 23 in this street in 1792.

Suffolk Street, SOUTHWARK, was so called after *Suffolk House*, afterwards called *Southwark Place*. [*See* Suffolk House, Southwark.] The last barber who extracted teeth in London (the last of the barber-surgeons) lived in this street, and died here about the year 1824. This thoroughfare is now called *Little Suffolk Street*. The present *Great Suffolk Street* is set down as *Dirty Lane* in the Map of 1720, and is one of ten enjoying that distinction in Dodsley's *London*, 1761. The Post Office Directory recognises no Dirty Lane in 1890.

Suffolk Street Gallery. [*See* Artists (Society of British).]

Sugar Loaf Alley, now SUGAR LOAF COURT, on the south side of Leadenhall Street, near Aldgate, to Fenchurch Buildings.

Then have ye an alley called Sprinckle Alley, now named Sugarloafe Alley of the like sign.—*Stow*, p. 52.

Sun Fire and Life Office, No. 63 THREADNEEDLE STREET, the corner of Bartholomew Lane and opposite the Bank and Royal Exchange. The building was erected 1842 from the designs of C. R. Cockerell, R.A., at a cost of about £18,500, and stands partly on the site of the old church of St. Bartholomew by the Exchange. This, the third office for the insurance of houses from fire established in this country, was projected by John Povey in 1706. The poet Pope held thirty-one shares in this office, for which he paid £1011 : 7s. It deserves to be recorded that a well-known and useful work, *The Historical Register*, was published by the Sun Fire Office between the years 1714 and 1738, "to save their subscribers the expense of taking in a newspaper."

Sun Tavern, FISH STREET HILL (west side), was in existence in Pepys's days and noted then as a dining-house.

December 22, 1660.—Went to the Sunne Taverne on Fish Street Hill to a Dinner of Captain Teddiman's, where was my Lord Inchiquin, Sir W. Penn, etc., and other good company, where we had a very fine dinner, good musique, and a great deal of wine. I very merry. Went to bed my head aching all night.—*Pepys*.

Sun Tavern. [*See* Fulwood's Rents.]

Sun Tavern behind the Royal Exchange, was built immediately after the Great Fire of 1666, at the expense of John Wadloe, son of old Simon Wadloe and his successor as landlord of the Devil Tavern.

June 28, 1667.—Mr. Lowther tells me that the Duke of Buckingham do dine publicly at Wadlow's at the Sun Tavern.—*Pepys.*

In *Wit and Drollery* (12mo, 1682, p. 28) is a poem "Upon Mr. Wadloe's New Tavern and Sign behind the Royal Exchange." The sign, it appears from this, was painted by Isaac Fuller. Among the *Luttrell Ballads* and *Broadsides* was a poem, called "The Glory of the Sun Tavern behind the Exchange" (1672). It seems to have been built in a very magnificent manner. The writer calls Wadloe the Wolsey of tavern magnificence.

Sun Tavern Fields, UPPER SHADWELL, east of King David Lane, notorious a century ago as a meeting-place for East End roughs, but long since built over. In 1768, when the London coal-whippers "struck" for higher wages, seven of them were hanged in these fields for shooting at the landlord of the Roundabout Tavern in Shadwell. The sailors who manned the colliers in the Pool being detained by the strike of the coal-whippers, began to unload the cargoes themselves, and were set upon in consequence.

Surgeons, Royal College of, LINCOLN'S INN FIELDS, south side. In the year 1745 the barbers and surgeons, who from 1540 until that date had formed one company, separated, and the latter were incorporated under the title of "The Masters, Governors and Commonalty of the Art and Science of Surgery." At the dissolution the barbers retained the hall in Monkwell Street [*see* Barber-Surgeons' Hall], the surgeons finding a temporary home at Stationers' Hall until 1751, when their premises, known as Surgeons' Hall in the Old Bailey, were ready for occupation. In 1796 the Company came to a premature end through their holding an illegal court. It was attempted to put matters right by a Bill in Parliament, but there was so much opposition from those persons who were practising without the diploma of the Corporation, that the Bill, after passing safely through the Commons, was thrown out by the Lords. In the following year attempts were made to come to terms with the opponents of the Bill, and finally it was agreed to petition for a Charter from the Crown to establish a Royal College of Surgeons in London. These negotiations were successfully carried out in 1800, and the old corporation having disposed of their Old Bailey property to the City authorities, the College took possession of a house in Lincoln's Inn Fields, the site of the present building.

The Hunterian collection, which forms the basis and still a large proportion of the contents of the present Museum, was originally arranged in a building which its founder, John Hunter, erected for it in 1785, behind his house in Leicester Square. In 1787 he had completed its arrangement, the principle of which is still adhered to; and the Museum was opened for inspection during the month of October to the medical profession, and in May to non-professional patrons, cultivators, or lovers of physiology and natural history.

John Hunter died October 16, 1793, aged sixty-four. By his will he directed his Museum to be offered in the first instance to the British Government, on such terms as might be considered reasonable, and in case of refusal, to be sold in one lot, either to some foreign state, or as his executors might think proper.

In the year 1799 Parliament voted the sum of £15,000 for the Museum, and an offer of it being made to the Corporation of Surgeons, it was accepted on the terms proposed by Government.

In 1806 the sum of £15,000 was voted by Parliament in aid of the erection of an edifice for the display and arrangement of the Hunterian Collection; a second grant of £12,500 was subsequently voted, and upwards of £21,000 having been supplied from the funds of the College, George Dance, jun., and James Lewis designed the building in Lincoln's Inn Fields, 1806-1813, and in this the Museum was opened for the inspection of visitors in the year 1813.

From the number of the additions the Museum became too small for their adequate display and arrangement, and more space being at the same time required for the rapidly increasing Library, the greater portion of the present building was erected by Sir Charles Barry, wholly at the expense of the College, in 1835, at a cost of about £40,000, and the Hunterian and Collegiate Collections were rearranged in what are now termed the Western and Middle Museums, which were opened for the inspection of visitors in 1836.

Further enlargement of the building having become necessary by the continued increase of the collection, the College, in 1847, purchased the premises of Mr. Alderman Copeland, in Portugal Street, in the rear, for the sum of £16,000, and in 1852 proceeded to the erection of the Eastern Museum at the expense of £25,000, Parliament granting £15,000 in aid thereof.

Through the munificence of the late Sir Erasmus Wilson the College has been able to again materially extend its premises. In 1888 the house at the east end of the front building was pulled down, and on its site a handsome addition to the Library was erected, the already existing premises being at the same time greatly improved. Two new museums are now (1890) in course of erection; in the upper gallery of these will be displayed a collection of drawings and photographs illustrating rare or curious diseases.

The collection is arranged in three apartments: the *Western* contains on the ground-floor the Anthropological series—specimens illustrating human anatomy and the external forms of Invertebrata; the gallery is devoted to Pathology. In the *Middle Museum* will be found on the ground-floor the commencement of the Comparative Osteological series;

in the first gallery part of the Physiological series, and in the upper gallery Entozoa and specimens illustrating Teratology. The remaining portions of Comparative Osteology and Physiology are in the *Eastern Museum.*

The College possesses a fine Library of 45,000 volumes of books relating to medicine, surgery and the allied sciences; there is also a good collection of portraits of medical men. On the staircase are several busts of eminent surgeons, the majority of them past presidents of the College; and also the cartoon of the so-called Holbein's picture representing Henry VIII. granting the Charter to the Barber-Surgeons; the painting itself is in Barber-Surgeons' Hall. In the council room and office are portraits of celebrated surgeons, including Reynolds's well-known painting of John Hunter.

The Museum is open to the members of the College, to the trustees of the Hunterian Collection, and to visitors introduced by them personally or by written orders on the public days, which are Monday, Tuesday, Wednesday and Thursday in each week, from eleven to five o'clock from March 1 to August 31; and from eleven to four o'clock from October 1 to the last day of February.

The Library is open to members of the College and to persons personally introduced by them. On the recommendation of a member tickets may be granted to non-members. In the case of students, the application must be accompanied by a recommendation signed by two of their teachers, members of the College. During the month of September both the Museum and Library are closed.

Surrey Chapel. [*See* Blackfriars Road.]

Surrey Institution, BLACKFRIARS ROAD, a few doors over the bridge, on the right passing into Surrey, was founded in 1808 on a similar plan to that of the Royal Institution. The premises were those of the old Leverian Museum. Dr. Adam Clarke was appointed Principal Librarian and Secretary, but he resigned in 1809. Here Coleridge delivered his lectures on Shakespeare, and Hazlitt his lectures on the Comic Writers of England. The Surrey Institution died of slow decay, and the building was let for occasional concerts and lectures; and eventually the "Rotunda," as it came to be called, obtained an evil fame as the theatre of the exhibitions of the Rev. Robert Taylor, known as "the Devil's Chaplain," and other infidel lecturers. It is now converted into business premises.

Surrey Street, STRAND, to the Victoria Embankment.

Surrey Street, also, replenished with good buildings, especially that of Nevison Fox, Esq., towards the Strand, which is a fine, large, and curious house of his own building; and the two houses that front the Thames; that on the East Side being the House of the Honourable Charles Howard, Esq., brother to Henry Duke of Norfolk, both fine houses with pleasant though small gardens towards the Thames.—*Strype*, B. iv. p. 118.

John Evelyn was residing in this street in 1696. His house is particularised as "William Draper's, Esq., Surrey Street, near Norfolk

Buildings." William Congreve the dramatist. He writes, June 26, 1706, "I am removed to Mr. Porter's in Surrey Steeet."[1] It was here that Voltaire paid him the oft-cited visit.

He was infirm and come to the verge of life when I knew him. . . . He spoke of his Works as of Trifles that were beneath him; and hinted to me in our first conversation that I should visit him upon no other foot than that of a Gentleman, who led a life of plainness and simplicity. I answered that had he been so unfortunate as to be a mere Gentleman I should never have come to see him; and I was very much disgusted at so unseasonable a piece of Vanity.—Voltaire, *Letters Concerning the English Nation*, London, 8vo, 1733, p. 188.

"It is worthy of remark," says Thackeray, "that the anecdote does not appear in the text of the same letters in the edition of Voltaire's *Œuvres Complètes*, Paris, 1837." It will be found, however, in the first French edition, published at Basle in 1734. Congreve died here, January 29, 1728-1729, and was buried in Westminster Abbey. George Sale, translator of the *Koran*, died here in 1736. The commissioners appointed for the regulation of hackney-coaches held their office in Surrey Street. This will explain the allusion in Book iv. of the *Ghost*. Churchill no doubt had many disputes with the cabmen of his day.

> Why should we mention Surrey Street,
> Where every week grave judges meet
> All fitted out with hum and ha,
> In proper form to drawl out law,
> To see all causes duly tried
> 'Twixt knaves who drive and fools who ride.

Surrey Theatre (The), south end of the BLACKFRIARS ROAD, was opened November 7, 1782, by Messrs. Hughes and Charles Dibdin, in opposition to the elder Astley. It was originally called the Royal Circus and Equestrian Philharmonic Academy, and was long an unsuccessful speculation.

> And burnt the Royal Circus in a hurry,
> ('Twas called the Circus then, but now the Surrey).
> *Rejected Addresses.*

The interior was rebuilt in 1799, and the whole theatre burnt, August 12, 1805; the insurance had run out, and there was a consequent loss of £25,000. The new theatre, built at a cost of £14,500 from the designs of Rudolph Cabanel, jun., was opened Easter Monday, 1806. Elliston, who held it from February 1809 to March 1814, changed its name to *The Surrey*. Tom Dibdin was lessee from 1816 to 1822, and quitted it, a loser of £18,000 by the speculation. He was well acquainted with all the London theatres, and he said of the Surrey that "the house itself is without exception the best constructed, both for audience and actors, in or near the metropolis."[2] Subsequently Mr. Davidge acquired a handsome fortune by his management; and later, under the management of Mr. Creswick, it obtained some distinction for the performance of the legitimate drama. This theatre, like its predecessor, was destroyed by fire, January 30, 1865; and the present,

[1] Berkeley's *Relics*, p. 347.   [2] T. Dibdin's *Autob.* vol. ii. p. 113.

erected at a cost of £25,000 from the designs of Mr. J. Ellis, was opened on December 26 of the same year.

John Palmer, the actor (d. 1798), was stage manager, and played in the second theatre (1789) while a prisoner within the Rules of the King's Bench. His salary, £20 a week, and the way in which he squandered his money, are said to have suggested the clause in the then Debtors' Act, which made all public-houses and places of amusement *out* of the Rules.

Surrey Zoological Gardens, PANTON PLACE, KENNINGTON, contained the menagerie of Mr. Cross, by whom the grounds were laid out in 1831-1832, after the demolition of Exeter 'Change and the Mews at Charing Cross. The collection of animals was a very good one, the lions and tigers having been especially noted. The fêtes and exhibitions in the summer months in these gardens were among the attractions of the Surrey side of London. The grounds were about 15 acres in extent, with a sheet of water of nearly 3 acres. The building for the animals was 300 feet in circumference. In 1837 fireworks were introduced and a series of fire spectacles were exhibited for many years. The Surrey Music Hall was erected on a portion of the ground in 1856 at a cost of about £18,000, Sir Horace Jones, architect; it was very successful in its acoustic properties. Jullien was manager for a time, and Thackeray gave here some readings of his *Four Georges*. The hall was not long successful, and it was temporarily used for St. Thomas's Hospital while the building at Stangate was being erected; subsequently it was occupied by the Rev. C. H. Spurgeon during the building of his Tabernacle at Newington Butts. During a religious service a panic was caused by a false alarm of fire, which caused the death and serious injury of about forty persons. It was destroyed by fire, June 11, 1861, and the Gardens were purchased for building purposes in 1877, and have been since built upon.

Sussex Place, REGENT'S PARK. At No. 24 lived from 1826 to 1853 J. G. Lockhart, editor of the *Quarterly Review*.

Sutton's Hospital. [*See* Charter House.]

Swallow Street, PICCADILLY, was so called from "Swallow Close," referred to in the grant from the Crown in 1664 of lands in Westminster to Lord Chancellor Clarendon.[1] But an earlier mention is to be found in the Vestry Minutes of St. Martin's, where, under April 29, 1658, the "Lamas of Swallow field" is referred to; and in the Patent Roll, dated July 1, 1536, reciting the exchange of lands between Henry VIII. and the Abbey of Westminster, mention is made of "two acres of land in Charyng crosse Felde now in the tenure of Thomas Swallow."

Swallow Street, very long, coming out of Pickadilly, and runneth northwards, to Tyburn Road, against Neb's Pound, but of no great account for buildings or inhabitants.—*Strype*, B. vi. p. 84.

---

[1] Lister's *Life of Clarendon*, vol. iii. p. 125.

The larger portion of the original street is included in the present *Regent Street*. What is now called Swallow Street was formerly *Little Swallow Street*. Swallow Street proper commenced where Glasshouse Street (the west portion of which is now called Vigo Street) crossed it, and ended in Oxford Street, exactly opposite Princes Street. The houses on the west side of Regent Street are built on its roadway. A sufficient notion of its former importance will be supplied by mentioning that in the great trial in 1792 between Charles Fox and Horne Tooke, no fewer than five of the twelve jurymen were residents of Swallow Street. Of the remaining seven, three were furnished by Piccadilly.

When Richard Baxter was excluded, 1675, from the meeting-house he had built in Oxenden Street he hired another in Swallow Street, but was prevented from using it, a guard being placed there for many Sundays to hinder him from entering it. In 1690 the French congregation which had previously worshipped in the French Ambassador's chapel in Monmouth House, Soho Square, removed to a building in Swallow Street. The registers of this church are preserved at Somerset House and are full of interesting entries. In 1770 the chapel was sold to Dr. James Anderson, and was for many years subsequently used as a chapel of the Established Kirk of Scotland. Dr. Chalmers frequently preached from its pulpit. It is now the Theistic Church, founded by the Rev. C. Voysey. John K. Sherwin, the eminent engraver, died in extreme poverty, 1790, at the alehouse called the Hog in the Pound at the corner of Swallow Street and the Oxford Road, where he was hiding from his creditors. Remains of the northern end of Swallow Street exist in *Swallow Place* and *Swallow Passage*, Oxford Circus.

Swan Alley (now GREAT SWAN ALLEY) COLEMAN STREET, City, runs from between Nos. 66 and 67 Coleman Street to Little Bell Alley. Swan Alley was severed into two parts and the central portion swept away in the formation of Moorgate Street, which was carried across it. Most of the houses left are on the east side of Moorgate Street. About the middle of the 17th century Swan Alley acquired notoriety from occurrences connected with a Puritan meeting-house in it.

Upon the first day of the second month, commonly called April, 1658, many of the Lord's people being assembled together in *Swan Alley*, in Coleman Street (a public place where Saints have met many years): as they were waiting upon the Lord in prayer and other holy duties, on a sudden the Marshal of the City, with several other officers, rushed in with great violence upon them. . . . Old brother Canne was then in the pulpit and had read a place of Scripture, but spoken nothing to it. Now he perceiving that they came in at both doors, with their halberts, pikes, staves, etc., and fearing that there might be some hurt done to the Lord's poor and naked people, desired the brethren and sisters to be all quiet, and to make no stir; for his part he feared them not, but was assured the Lord would eminently stand by them. While he was thus speaking to the people, exhorting them to patience, one of the officers (breaking through the crowd) came furiously upon him, and with great violence plucked him out of the pulpit, and when he had so done, hurled him over the benches and forms in a very barbarous manner.—*A Narrative published by a Friend to the Prisoners*, 1658.

This strange scene took place five months before the death of

Oliver Cromwell. John Canne was pastor at Amsterdam, and a leading man among the Baptists; but had apparently ceased to officiate in Swan Alley before January 6, 1661, when Venner and his brother fanatics sallied from this building and put all London in terror. Such was their desperate courage, skill and activity, that it took three days to master them, and yet Pepys records :—

January 10, 1661.—Mr. Davis told us the particular examinations of these Fanatiques that are taken : and in short it is this, these Fanatiques, that have routed all the train-bands that they met with, put the King's life-guards to the run, killed about twenty men, broke through the City gates twice ; and all this in the day-time, when all the City was in arms ;—are not in all above thirty-one. Whereas we did believe them (because they were seen up and down in every place almost in the City, and had been in Highgate two or three days, and in several other places) to be at least 500. . . . Their word was " The King Jesus, and their heads upon the gates." Few of them would receive any quarter.—*Pepys.*

Venner, with Hodgkins, another prominent Fifth-Monarchy man, was hanged, drawn and quartered at the end of Swan Alley in Coleman Street, on January 19, 1661 ; two others, Pritchard and Oxman, at the end of Wood Street, on the same day, and "many more" two days later. Entick (1766) says that Oliver Cromwell had resided in a large house which stood at the east end of the alley, and was pulled down about 1750 ; but this was probably only one of the idle traditions which associate so many of the large old houses about London with the great Protector.

Swan Alley, near the WARDROBE, BLACKFRIARS. The Swan was the cognisance of the Beauchamp family, long distinguished residents in this part of London. The so-called Duke Humphrey's tomb, in old St. Paul's, was really the tomb of Sir John Beauchamp.

In the Council Register of the 18th August, 1618, there may be seen "a list of buildings and foundations since 1615." It is therein said, "That Edward Allen, Esq., dwelling at Dulwich [the well-known player and founder of Dulwich College], had built six tenements of timber upon new foundations, within two years past, in Swan Alley near the Wardrobe.—Chalmers's *Apology*, vol. i. p. 280.

Swan Stairs, or, The Old Swan, UPPER THAMES STREET, a celebrated landing-place on the Middlesex side of the river Thames, a little "above bridge," where people used to land and walk to the other side of old London Bridge, rather than run the risk of what was called "shooting the bridge." [*See* London Bridge.] In 1441, when the Duchess of Gloucester did penance at Christchurch by Aldgate, she landed at these stairs and walked the rest of the way.

And on the Wednesday next sueing she [Aleanor Cobham] com fro Westm', be barge unto the Swan in Tempse strete, and there she londyd.—*A Chronicle of London from* 1089 *to* 1483, 4to, p. 129.

March 25, 1661.—Come Mr. Salisbury to see me. . . . I took him to Whitehall with me by water, but he could not by any means be moved to go through the bridge, and we were fain to go round by the old Swan.—*Pepys.*

We [Johnson and Boswell] landed at the Old Swan, and walked to Billingsgate, where we took oars [for Greenwich].—*Boswell*, by Croker, vol. i. p. 469.

I scarcely ever pass over London Bridge without glancing my eye towards those highly-favoured rooms appertaining to Joseph Hardcastle's counting-house at *Old Swan Stairs*, and feeling a glow of pleasure at the recollection that there the London Missionary Society, the Religious Tract Society and the Hibernian Society formed their plans of Christian benevolence, on which Divine Providence has so signally smiled. This pleasure is greatly heightened when I also recollect that in these favoured rooms was brought forth that gigantic agent of moral and spiritual good, the British and Foreign Bible Society. These rooms in my judgment are second to none but those in which the Disciples met after their Master's ascension, and from whence they went forth to enlighten and to bless a dark and guilty world !—*Jubilee Memorial of the Religious Tract Society*, p. 113.

Swan Tavern, at CHARING CROSS. No. 383 of Mr. Akerman's curious collection of "Tradesmen's Tokens, current in London and its vicinity between the years 1648 and 1672 "—No. 303 of the Beaufoy Catalogue—is a swan crowned, and holding a bunch of grapes in its bill, with the inscription, "Marke Rider at the Swan against the Mewes, 1665. His Halfe Penny." The Swan was a tavern of repute in the 15th century. In the Stewards' Account-Book of John Howard, Duke of Norfolk, is the entry :—

xxj day of Feverer 1466-7. Item my Mastyr payd for his costes at the Swan at Westemenstre . . . iis. 1jd.

It is the subject of a good anecdote preserved by Aubrey and confirmed by Powell, the actor, in the dedication to his *Treacherous Brothers*, 4to, 1696.

A GRACE BY BEN JONSON, EXTEMPORE, BEFORE KING JAMES.

Our King and Queen, the Lord God blesse,
The Palsgrave and the Lady Besse ;
And God blesse every living thing
That lives and breathes and loves the King.
God blesse the Councill of estate,
And Buckingham the fortunate.
God blesse them all, and keepe them safe,
And God blesse me, and God blesse Raph.

The King was mighty inquisitive to know who this Ralph was. Ben told him 'twas the drawer at the Swanne Taverne by Charing Crosse, who drew him good Canarie. For this drollery his Matie gave him an hundred poundes.—*Aubrey*, vol. iii. p. 415.

Swan Theatre, SOUTHWARK, in the liberty of Paris Garden, built about 1596, and used as an amphitheatre for bull and bear baiting, as well as for the acting of plays by the insertion of a movable stage when required. It was one of the largest London theatres, and a view of the exterior is found in Visscher's View of London (1616). A contemporary view of the interior has been discovered in the University Library at Utrecht, which is of the greatest interest as the only view known to exist of the interior of a Shakespearian theatre. This was first issued in a pamphlet by Dr. Gaedertz in 1888, and a more accurate reproduction of the original is given in the *Transactions of the New Shakspere Society* (1887-1891, p. 215).

The drawing shows a portion of the round with the movable stage in the centre. There are three tiers of seats called *sedilia*, separated by two galleries without seats called *porticus*. The galleries are covered by a roof, but the centre of the building is open to the sky. John De Witt, who wrote a short description to accompany the drawing, says that the building was capable of seating 3000 persons, but this is scarcely probable.

The theatre fell into decay and appears to have been swept away about 1633. In Holland's *Leaguer*, 1632, we read that the Lady of the Leaguer can almost "shake hands with the playhouse, which like a dying Swanne hangs her head and sings her own dirge." It stood where Holland Street now is, and not far from the present Blackfriars Road.

Swan with two Necks, LAD LANE, an old inn, tavern, and booking and parcel office, from which coaches and waggons started to the north of England; a corruption of Swan with two Nicks, the mark (*cygninota*) of the Vintners' Company for their "game of swans" on the Thames. [*See* Vintners' Company; Dyers' Company.] By an old law (or custom, rather) every swan that swam under London Bridge belonged, by right of office, to the Lieutenant of the Tower. Lad Lane is now incorporated with Gresham Street.

The Carriers of Manchester doe lodge at the Two Neck'd Swan in Lad Lane, between Great Wood Street, and Milk Street End.—Taylor's *Carrier's Cosmographie*, 4to, 1637.

There was a house with this sign, in 1632, in Swan Alley, Southwark.[1]

Swedish Church, PRINCE'S SQUARE, St. George's-in-the-East. The date 1728 is on the front of the church. Emanuel Swedenborg (d. March 20, 1772), founder of the "New Church" or Society of Swedenborgians, lies buried in this church, and alongside Dr. Solander, the companion of Sir Joseph Banks (d. 1782).

Sweeting's Alley, originally SWEETING'S RENTS, CORNHILL, at the east end of the Royal Exchange, was so called after Henry Swieten or Sweeting, a Dutch merchant who owned considerable property on this spot at the time of the Great Fire of 1666.[2]

August 6, 1731.—Died Mr. Charles Sweeting, an eminent grocer Without Bishopgate, and Deputy of that part of the ward, possessed of a plentiful Estate at the East End of the Royal Exchange.—*Universal Spectator*, August 14, 1731.

That excellent and by all physicians approved China drink, called by the Chineans Tcha, by other nations Tay alias Tee is sold at the Sultaness Head Cophee House in Sweeting's Rents, by the Royal Exchange, London.—*Mercurius Politicus*, September 30, 1651.

Knight's in Sweeting's Alley; Fairburn's in a court off Ludgate Hill; Howe's in Fleet Street—bright enchanted palaces, which George Cruikshank used to people with grinning fantastical imps and merry harmless sprites,—where are they? Fairburn's shop knows him no more; not only has Knight disappeared from Sweeting's Alley, but, as we are given [to understand, Sweeting's Alley has dis-

---

[1] Churchwardens' Accounts of St. Saviour's.
[2] *Addit. MS. in the British Museum*, No. 5065, fol. 138.

appeared from the face of the Globe.—Thackeray, *Westminster Review*, June 1840, art. "George Cruikshank."

Sweeting's Alley was swept away for the new Royal Exchange. The site is covered by the paved area of Exchange Buildings.

Swithin's (St.) by London Stone, a church in CANNON STREET, in Walbrook Ward, destroyed in the Great Fire and rebuilt from Sir C. Wren's designs in 1678. The church is chiefly remarkable for the constructive skill and ingenuity of the architect. In 1869 the interior was "restored"—*i.e.* remodelled in 19th-century Gothic fashion, and in 1879 a new chancel and vestry were added. After the Great Fire the parish of St. Mary Bothaw was united to St. Swithin's, and this church serves for both parishes. The Rev. William Elstob, the Saxon scholar (d. 1715), was rector of St. Swithin's. The last leaf of a mouldering register records (December 1, 1663) the marriage of Dryden, the poet, to the Lady Elizabeth Howard. This interesting entry escaped the anxious researches of Malone. They were married in the old church, by license obtained only the day before. In the Register the poet's name is spelt Draydon, and the lady's Haward. No reason has been disclosed for the selection of this church for the ceremony. In the entry of the license, which is preserved in the Vicar-General's office, it is recorded that "appeared personally John Driden of St. Clement Danes, in the County of Middlesex, Esq., aged about 30 years and a Batchelor, and alleged that he intendeth to marry with Dame Elizabeth Howard of St. Martin's in the Fields, aged about 25 years." So neither party belonged to 'the parish. There is a monument in the church to Michael Godfrey (1658-1695), Deputy Governor of the Bank of England, who was killed by a cannon ball at the Siege of Namur. [*See* London Stone.]

Swithin's (St.) Lane, LOMBARD STREET and KING WILLIAM STREET to CANNON STREET. On the west side of this lane are Founders' Hall and Salters' Hall; and (standing back) New Court, the counting-house of Messrs. Rothschild, the great money merchants and the Austro-Hungarian Consulate. At the south-west corner of the lane is the church of St. Swithin. One of the bubble companies of 1720, with a proposed capital of two millions, was for a general insurance on houses and merchandise, at the Three Tuns, *Swithin's Alley*, but this was then a colloquialism for *Sweeting's Alley*.

Symond's Inn, CHANCERY LANE (east side), a series of private tenements let to students of the law and others, and so called, it is thought, from Thomas Simonds, gentleman, buried in St. Dunstan's-in-the-West in June 1621. He was apparently the great-uncle of Sir Symonds D'Ewes. The Masters in Chancery had formerly their offices here. The ground rents of this inn are received by the Bishop of Chichester. [*See* Chichester Rents.] Symonds Inn was demolished in 1873-1874, and a stately pile of 110 chambers, with a front of

Portland stone, 60 feet high, towards Chancery Lane, erected on the site.

Sythe (St.), or St. Osyth. [*See* St. Bennet Sherehog; Sise Lane.]

Tabard (The). This celebrated inn of Southwark, always associated in our minds with Chaucer and the "Canterbury Pilgrims," was built most probably in the 14th century, as a neighbouring inn, the Bear, certainly was. It was on the eastern side of the High Street (Long Southwark), exactly opposite St. Margaret's Church.

A tabard is a jaquet or sleeveless coat, worne of times past by Noblemen in the warres, but now only by Heraults, and is called theyre coate of Armes in servise. It is the signe of an Inn in Southwarke by London, within the which was the lodging of the Abbott of Hyde by Winchester. This was the Hostelry where Chaucer and the other Pilgrims met together, and with Henry Baily their hoste, accorded about the manner of their journey to Canterbury. And whereas through time it hath been much decaied, it is now by Master J. Preston, with the Abbot's house thereto adjoyned, newly repaired, and with convenient rooms much encreased, for the receipt of many guests.—Speght's *Chaucer*, fol. 1598, and *see Stow*, p. 154.

> Befel that in that sesoun on a day,
> In Southwerk at the Tabard, as I lay,
> Redy to wenden on my Pilgrimage
> To Canterburie with full devout corage,
> At night was come into that hostelrie,
> Well nyne-and-twentie in a companye,
> Of sondry folk, by adventure i-falle,
> In felawschipe, and pilgryms were they alle,
> That toward Canterburie wolden ryde ;
> The chambres and the stables weren wyde,
> And wel we weren esed atte beste, etc.
>
> Chaucer, *Prologue to Canterbury Tales*.

In the great fire which broke out, May 26, 1676, and destroyed the Town Hall and above six houses, Chaucer's Tabard, which was situated in the midst of the part where the fire raged fiercest, was, there can be no doubt, destroyed. It was rebuilt, and probably nearly on the old lines, for, as it came down to our own day, it consisted of open wooden galleries with chambers behind, surrounding an open court, and a large room which continued to be called the Pilgrims' Room. But the landlord of the new house, deeming the Tabard too antiquated a sign, or perhaps unacquainted with its signification, changed the sign to The Talbot, and Betterton describes it under its new name in his modernised version of Chaucer's Prologue. The Tabard and The Talbot are two such distinct names, that a succeeding landlord found it necessary to distinguish Chaucer's inn by the following inscription on the frieze of the beams which hung across the road, and from the centre of which the sign was suspended : "This is the inne where Sir Jeffry Chaucer and the nine and twenty pilgrims lay in their journey to Canterbury, anno 1383." In 1763, when the signs of London were taken down, this inscription was set up over the gateway, but was painted out in 1831. As late as the middle of the 18th century plays were acted in "The Talbot Inn Yard" during Southwark Fair. Timothy Fielding had his "Great Theatrical Booth in the Talbot Inn Yard," and played *The Beggar's Opera*, the parts "by the Company of Comedians from the new Theatre in Lincoln's Inn Fields," with "all the songs and dances . . . as performed at" that theatre, "during the time of the Fair" of 1728. Like most of the old inns, whose main dependence was on the coach and country waggon traffic, the Tabard suffered greatly from the introduction of railways. It gradually fell into a dilapidated, dirty condition; the greater part of it was let for stables, carmen's warerooms, and railway stores. At length in 1873 it was sold by auction, and in 1875-1876 the whole was swept away. A new inn, *The Old Tabard* (No. 85 Boro' High Street), has been built, and the site of the old one is marked by *Talbot Inn Yard*, let out chiefly as hop-merchants' offices; and the name is further preserved in *Tabard Street*, of old notorious as *Kent* Street. The best and oldest view of The Tabard is in Urry's "Chaucer" (fol. 1721).[1]

Tabernacle Row, Tabernacle Square, Tabernacle Walk, CITY ROAD (east side) and FINSBURY, all derived their name from the original temporary preaching-place run up for George Whitefield on the west side of what was then called Windmill Hill, and is now Tabernacle Walk.

<small>Shortly after Whitefield's separation from Wesley, some Calvinistic Dissenters built a large shed for him near the Foundry, upon a piece of ground which was lent for the purpose till he should return from America. From the temporary nature of the structure they called it a *Tabernacle*, in allusion to the movable place of worship of the Israelites during their journey in the wilderness; and the name being in puritanical taste became the designation of all the chapels of the Calvinistic Methodists.—Southey's *Life of Wesley*.</small>

The permanent *Whitefield's Tabernacle* stands on the north side of Tabernacle Row. Other of Whitefield's, or the Countess of Huntingdon's Tabernacles were in Spa Fields, Tottenham Court Road, etc. But there was a Tabernacle in London before that of Whitefield, and in it Bentley delivered his second series of Boyle Lectures.

<small>*December* 3, 1693.—Mr. Bentley preach'd at the *Tabernacle neere Golden Square*. I gave my voice for him to proceed on his former subject the following yeare in Mr. Boyle's Lecture."—*Evelyn*.</small>

[*See* Tenison's Chapel; Whitefield's Tabernacle.]

Talbot (The). [*See* The Tabard.]

Tallow Chandlers' Hall, No. 5, on the west side of Dowgate Hill. The Company, the twenty-first on the City list, was incorporated by Edward IV., but it had existed as a brotherhood for a considerable time previously. Henry VI. granted them arms and a crest in 1456, and Elizabeth added supporters. Both the grants are preserved in the Hall, the latter bearing the signature of William Camden, *Clarencieux*.

---

[1] *The Inns of Old Southwark*, by William Rendle and Philip Norman, London, 1888, has a chapter devoted to the Tabard.

The old hall was destroyed in the Great Fire, and was rebuilt from the designs of Sir C. Wren in 1672. It is a large and handsome building, with a Tuscan colonnade, and was in great part rebuilt in 1871.

Tanfield Court, TEMPLE. These buildings were first erected by Henry Bradshaw, Treasurer, in 26 Henry VIII. (1534-1535), and were long known as Bradshaw's Rents. The present name is derived from Sir Laurence Tanfield, Chief Baron of the Exchequer in 1607,[1] whose residence was here. His daughter was the mother of Lucius Carey, Lord Falkland, who inherited Tanfield's large fortune. At No. 3 lived Robert Keck, who bought the Chandos portrait of Shakespeare from Mrs. Barry. Keck died at Paris in 1719, leaving his chambers ("No 3 Tanfield Court, Temple") and the contents of them to his cousin, Francis Keck, of Great Tew, in Oxfordshire, Esq. On Sunday morning, February 4, 1732, Mrs. Lydia Duncombe, aged eighty, and Elizabeth Harrison, aged sixty, were found strangled, and their maid, Ann Price, aged seventeen, with her throat cut, in their beds, at a house in Tanfield Court. The laundress was Sarah Malcolm, who was executed for the murders, and whose portrait Hogarth painted in Newgate. He said afterwards, "This woman by her features is capable of any wickedness." Sir James Thornhill accompanied him. [*See* Mitre Court.]

Tart Hall, "without the gate of ST. JAMES'S PARK, near Buckingham House," was built (the new part at least) in 1638, by Nicholas Stone, the sculptor,[2] for Alathea, Countess of Arundel, wife to Thomas, the magnificent Earl of Arundel, and descended to her second son, the unfortunate William, Lord Viscount Stafford, beheaded in 1680, on the perjured evidence of Titus Oates and others. The gateway was never again opened after the last time Lord Stafford passed through it. The house, after being for some time used as a place of entertainment, was taken down in 1720. A memory of it is still preserved in *Stafford Row* adjoining. The name is difficult to account for. The adjoining Mulberry Garden was above all things famous for its tarts [*see* Mulberry Garden], and this, it has been suggested, gave rise to the popular name of this ancient mansion, but it would hardly account for the early and general use of the name.

The Committee of Lords being informed that some important papers were hid in a wall at Tart Hall, they sent to break it, and in a copper box found those which the Attorney-General says give more light into the plot than all they had formerly seen, but most particularly against the Lord Stafford.—*Algernon Sidney's Letters to Henry Savile,* p. 74.

The parish of St. Martin's-in-the-Fields crosseth James Street against Tart Hall, which it passeth through, and on the garden wall at the processioning there is a boy whipt (a custom used to remember the parish bounds), for which he hath some small matter, as about 2d., given him: the like custom is observed at or by Tyburn gallows.—*Strype,* B. vi. p. 67.

The remainder of the Arundelian Collection was preserved at Tart Hall, without the gate of St. James's Park, near Buckingham House. These curiosities, too, were

---

[1] Dugdale's *Origines Juridiciales,* p. 146.   [2] Walpole's *Anecdotes,* vol. ii. p. 63.

sold by auction in 1720, and the house itself had been lately demolished. Dr. Mead bought the head of Homer, now in the British Museum. The sale produced £6535. —Walpole's *Anecdotes*, ed. *Dallaway*, vol. ii. p. 153.

Some carved seats, by Inigo Jones, were purchased from Tart Hall, and placed in a temple at Chiswick by Lord Burlington.—*Ibid.*, vol. ii. p. 148.

Mr. Walpole, who saw Tart Hall at the time of the second sale, informed me that it was very large, and had a very venerable appearance.—*Pennant*.

Among the Harleian MSS. (No. 6272) is "A Memorial of all the Roomes at Tart Hall: And an Inventory of all the Household Stuffs and goods there, except of six Roomes at the north end of the ould Building (wch the Right Honorable the Countess of Arundell hath reserved unto her peculiar use) and Mr. Thomas Howard's closett, etc.: 8° September, 1641." In the "Footmen's Hall," were "Foure pictures hanging on the walls thereof—1st. A Gundelowe; 2d. A Mountebanke; 3d. A Brave. 4th. King Henry 7, his wife and children." "The Great Roome, or Hall," was situated "next to the Banketing House." "My Lord's Room" was hanged with yellow and green taffeta. A closet on the west side had the floor covered with a carpet of yellow leather. The *roof* of one of the rooms was decorated with a "picture of the Fall of Phaëton." Mr. Arden's room was "hanged with Scotch plad." Several pictures are mentioned with their artists' names—Diana and Actæon, by Titian (now in the Bridgewater Gallery?); Jacob's Travelling, by Bassano (now at Hampton Court?); A Martyrdom, by Tintoret; the Nativity of our Saviour, by Honthorst. No statues are mentioned. The site is marked in Faithorne's Map of London, 1658.

Tasel Close. [*See* Artillery Ground.]

Tatnam Court. [*See* Tottenham Court.]

An Elegy on the most execrable murder of Mr. Clun, one of the comedians of the Theatre Royal, who was robbed and most inhumanly killed, on Tuesday night, being the 2d August, 1664, *neare Tatnam Court*, as he was riding to his country-house at Kentish-town.—Hazlitt's *Handbook of E. E. Lit.*, p. 112 B.

Tattersall's, in GROSVENOR PLACE, entered by a narrow lane, at the side of St. George's Hospital, was for many years a celebrated mart for the sale of horses, and so called after Richard Tattersall (d. 1795), originally a training groom to the second and last Duke of Kingston. Tattersall acquired the foundation of his fortune by the purchase, for £2500, of the celebrated horse "Highflyer." Here was a subscription room, under the supervision of the Jockey Club, and attended by all the patrons of the turf, from noblemen down to innkeepers; and the betting here regulated the betting throughout the country. The lease having run out the building was pulled down in 1866, and the site covered by the new wing of St. George's Hospital. Tattersall's was removed to Knightsbridge Green. [*See* Grosvenor Place; Knightsbridge.]

Flutter. Oh yes, I stopt at Tattersall's as I came by, and there I found Lord James Jessamy, Sir William Wilding and Mr. ——.—Mrs. Cowley's *Belle's Stratagem*, p. 178.

Tavistock Place, between WOBURN PLACE and MARCHMONT STREET, was so called after the second title of the Dukes of Bedford, the ground landlords. It first appears in the Court Guide in 1807. *Eminent Inhabitants.*—John Pinkerton, the historian, at No. 9; here his depraved mode of life was the cause of continual quarrels with abandoned women. Mary Anne Clarke, while mistress of the Duke of York, lived for some time at No. 31. Galt, the novelist, and Douce, the antiquary, lived at No. 32. Francis Baily, President of the Royal Astronomical Society, at No. 37, from 1825 till his death here, August 30, 1844.

The house stands isolated in a garden, so as to be free from any material tremor from passing carriages. A small observatory was constructed in the upper part. The building in which the earth was weighed and its bulk and figure calculated, the standard measure of the British nation perpetuated, and the pendulum experiments rescued from their chief source of inaccuracy, can never cease to be an object of interest to astronomers of future generations.—Sir John Herschel.

Here were held the weekly meetings of the society of distinguished and scientific men, chiefly mathematicians and astronomers, known as the Baily Club. The house was subsequently the residence of Sir Matthew Digby Wyatt, architect; until his death in 1877. John Britton, the antiquary, was long resident at No. 10; and Sir Harris Nicolas lived for some years at No. 19.

Tavistock Row, COVENT GARDEN, a row of houses, fourteen in number, on the south side of Covent Garden Market, now (1890) entirely cleared away. In No. 4 lived Miss Martha Reay, the mistress of Lord Sandwich, killed in the Piazza (1779), by the Rev. James Hackman, in a fit of frantic jealousy.

> A Sandwich favourite was this fair,
> And her he dearly loved;
> By whom six children had, we hear;
> This story fatal proved.
>
> A clergyman, O wicked one,
> In Covent Garden shot her;
> No time to cry upon her God,
> Its hop'd he's not forgot her.
>
> *Grub Street Ballad on Miss Ray,* quoted by Sir Walter Scott in his *Essay on Imitations of the Ancient Ballad.*

Hackman was recruiting at Huntingdon; appeared at the ball; was asked by Lord Sandwich to Hinchinbrooke; was introduced to Miss Reay, became violently enamoured of her, made proposals, and was sent into Ireland, where his regiment was. He sold out; took orders, but could not bend the inflexible fair in a black coat more than in a red. He could not live, he said, without her. He meant only to kill himself, and that in her presence; but seeing her coquet at the play with Macnamara, a young Irish Templar, he determined suddenly to dispatch her too. [*See* Tyburn.] In the upper part of the same house died, July 11, 1797, Charles Macklin, at the great age of ninety-seven. Here the elder Mathews called to give the aged actor a taste of his boyish quality for the stage. In No. 5 William Vandervelde the younger died, in 1707:[1] and in 1799, in the front room of the second floor of the same house, died Thomas Major, the engraver.[2] It was afterwards occupied by "Irish Johnstone," the actor. No. 13 was Zincke's, the celebrated miniature painter; and Dr. Wolcot (Peter Pindar), wrote many of his invectives against George III. and the Royal Academy in the garret of the same house. William Godwin was living in Tavistock Row in 1755. One of John [Lord] Campbell's early London lodgings was at No. 3, "a couple of rooms," he wrote to his father, February 17, 1800, "for which I pay only nine shillings a week."

Tavistock Square, north of Russell Square, was built about the same time as Tavistock Place, and like it named from the second title of the Duke of Bedford. Prince Hoare resided at No. 3 in 1807. In the same house from 1816 to 1821 lived John Braham, the famous singer, and father of the Countess Waldegrave. Charles Knight at No. 51 in 1828.

"Tavistock House," in the open space at the north-east corner of Tavistock Square, was long the residence of James Perry, editor of the *Morning Chronicle*, and Tavistock House was noted for its reunions of men of political and literary distinction during the great days of that celebrated Whig paper. The house was afterwards divided and the moiety, which still retained the name of Tavistock, became the residence of Frank Stone, A.R.A., the painter, of whom the lease was purchased by Charles Dickens towards the end of 1850. During the next ten years it was his London abode. He built a little theatre in the garden and gave in it a series of brilliant amateur performances, in which he himself played the leading parts. The play-bills were headed "The Smallest Theatre in the World, Tavistock House." In the summer of 1860 Dickens sold the lease, and on September 4 wrote to Mr. Wills, "Tavistock House is closed to-day and possession delivered up."[3] He now made Gad's Hill his home, hiring a furnished house in London for a few weeks each year. Later it was for a time the residence of M. Gounod the composer.

Tavistock Street, COVENT GARDEN, runs from Southampton Street to Wellington Street. Richard Leveridge, the celebrated singer, kept a tavern in this street after his retirement from the stage. Here he brought out "A Collection of Songs, with the Music by Mr. Leveridge. In two volumes. London: Engraved and Printed for the Author, in Tavistock Street, Covent Garden, 1727."

Tavistock Street, Covent Garden, was once the street of fashionable shops—what Bond Street was till lately, and what Bond Street and Regent Street together are now. I remember hearing an old lady say that in her young days the crowd of handsome equipages in Tavistock Street was considered one of the sights of London.

---

[1] Smith's *Nollekens*, vol. i. p. 229. [2] *Ibid.*, vol. ii. p. 335.
[3] *Letters of Charles Dickens*, vol. ii. p. 120.

I have had the curiosity to stride it. It is about 160 yards long, and before the footways were widened would have admitted three carriages abreast.—Walker, *The Original*, No. 3, June 3, 1835.

> Returning thence the disappointed fleet
> Anchors in Tavistock's fantastic street:
> There under Folly's colours gaily rides
> Where Humour points or veering Fashion guides.
> *Cumberland (Cradock*, vol. iv. p. 262).

When he [Lord Thurlow] was young he would do the kindest things and at an expense to himself which at that time he could ill afford, and he w^d do them, too, in the most secret manner. I know not what is become of her now, but in those days there was a certain Miss Christian, the daughter, if I mistake not, of a Norfolk clergyman, who had been a friend of Thurlow's father. The girl was left pennyless, and he established her in Tavistock Street as a milliner, disbursing three hundred pounds to furnish a shop for her. I went with him to the house, and having seen her, am ready to swear that his motives were not, nor could be, of the amorous kind, for she was ugly to a wonder.—*Cowper to Carwardine*, June 11, 1792; Southey's *Cowper*, vol. vii. p. 127.

It is on such occasions snuff takers delight to solace themselves with a pinch of Thirty seven; and we accordingly do so in imagination at our friend Fliddon's in Tavistock Street, who is a higher kind of Lilly to the *Indicator*—our papers lying among the piquant snuffs, as those of our illustrious predecessor, the *Tatler*, did among Mr. Lilly's perfumes at the corner of Beaufort Buildings.—*Leigh Hunt*.

A large building used as a flower market has been erected on the north side of the street, but all that side west of the flower market now (1890) lies an open space.

Technical Institute, and Technical College. [*See* City and Guilds of London.]

Temple (The). A liberty or district between FLEET STREET and the Thames, and so called from the Knights Templars, who made their first London habitation in Holborn, in 1118, and removed to Fleet Street, or the New Temple, 1184. Spenser alludes to this London locality in his beautiful "Prothalamion":—

> those bricky towres [1]
> The which on Themmes brode aged back doe ryde,
> Where now the studious lawyers have their bowers,
> There whylome wont the Templer Knights to byde,
> Till they decayd through pride.

At the downfall of the Templars, in 1313, the New Temple in Fleet Street was given by Edward II. to Aymer de Valence, Earl of Pembroke, whose tomb, in Westminster Abbey, has called forth the eulogistic criticism of the classic Flaxman. At the Earl of Pembroke's death in 1323 the property passed to the Knights of St. John of Jerusalem [*see* St. John's Gate], by whom the Inner and Middle Temples were leased to the students of the Common Law, and the Outer Temple to Walter Stapleton, Bishop of Exeter, and Lord Treasurer, beheaded by the citizens of London in 1326. No change took place when the Temple property passed to the Crown at the dissolution of religious houses in

---

[1] The Fire of London was stopped in its march westward by the brick buildings of the Temple. The houses in Fleet Street were of wood. [*See* Ram Alley.]

the reign of Henry VIII., and the students of the two Inns of Court remained the tenants of the Crown till 1608, when James I. by letters patent conferred the two Temples on the Benchers of the two societies and their successors for ever. There are two edifices in the Temple specially worthy of a visit: the Temple Church (serving for both Temples), and the Middle Temple Hall.

The Temple Church was the church of the Knights Templars, and consists of two parts, the Round Church and the Choir. The Round Church (transition Norman work) was built in the year 1185, as an inscription in Saxon characters, formerly on the stonework over the little door next the cloister, recorded, and dedicated by Heraclius, Patriarch of Jerusalem; the Choir (pure Early English) was finished in 1240. The restorations and alterations, made 1839-1842, at a cost of £70,000, are in correct 12th and 13th century taste; but it is much to be lamented that the changes were of so sweeping a character that the interest of association was not regarded, and that the monuments to several great men (though architecturally out of place) were not suffered to remain in the arcades and compartments in which they were first erected. Many of these monuments were removed to the triforium. *Observe.*—Entrance doorway (very fine); two groups of monumental effigies, in Round Church, of Knights Templars, cross-legged (names unknown, at least very uncertain); the figure between the two columns on the south-east having a foliage-ornament about the cushion supporting the head, and the feet resting upon a lion, represents, it is said, William Marshall, Earl of Pembroke (d. 1119), Earl Marshal and Protector of England during the minority of Henry III.; monument of white marble, left of the altar, to the learned Selden [1] (d. 1654; he was buried beneath); and in the triforium (ascended by a narrow staircase), the tombs of Plowden, the jurist; Richard Martin (d. 1618), to whom Ben Jonson dedicates his *Poetaster;* James Howell, the letter-writer (d. 1666); Edmund Gibbon.

My family arms are the same which were borne by the Gibbons of Kent in an age when the College of Heralds religiously guarded the distinctions of blood and name; a lion rampant, gardant, between three schallop shells argent, on a field azure. I should not, however, have been tempted to blazon my coat of arms were it not connected with a whimsical anecdote. About the reign of James I. the three harmless schallop shells were changed by Edmund Gibbon, Esq., into there ogresses, or female cannibals, with a design of stigmatising three ladies, his kinswomen, who had provoked him by an unjust lawsuit. But this singular mode of revenge, for which he obtained the sanction of Sir William Seager, king at arms, soon expired with its author; and on his own monument in the Temple Church the monsters vanish, and the three schallop shells resume their proper and hereditary place.—*Gibbon.*

[1] "His grave was about ten foot deepe or better, walled up a good way with bricks, of which also the bottome was paved, but the sides at the bottome for about two foot high were of black polished marble, wherein his coffin (covered with black bayes) lyeth, and upon that wall of marble was presently lett downe a huge black marble stone of great thicknesse, with this inscription: 'Hic jacet corpus Johannis Seldeni, qui obijt 30 die Novembris, 1654.' Over this was turned an arch of brick (for the House would not lose their ground) and upon that was throwne the earth etc."—*Aubrey,* vol. iii. p. 533.

The so-called Penitential Cell, off the corkscrew stairs leading to the gallery. In the burial-ground east of the Choir, and without the building, Oliver Goldsmith was buried, on April 9, 1774, at 5 o'clock in the evening. There is a coped gravestone with an inscription to his memory in the graveyard on the north side, but the exact place of his interment is unknown, although the inscription says "Here lies." Lord Chancellor Thurlow was buried with unusual pomp under the south aisle, September 1806.[1] The Round was used as a place where lawyers received their clients, each occupying his particular post, like a merchant upon 'Change.

> *Face.* Here's one from Captain Face, sir [*to Surly*],
> Desires you meet him in the Temple Church
> Some half hour hence, and upon earnest business.
>   Ben Jonson, *The Alchemist*, Act ii. Sc. 1.
>
> *Face.* I have walk'd the Round
> Till now, and no such thing.—*Ibid.*, Act iii. Sc. 2.

And for advice 'twixt him and us he had made choice of a lawyer, a mercer, and a merchant, who that morning were appointed to meet him in the Temple Church. Middleton, *Father Hubburd's Tales*, 4to, 1604.

> Retain all sorts of witnesses
> That ply i' the Temples under trees,
> Or walk the Round with Knights o' th' Posts
> About the cross-legg'd knights their hosts ;
> Or wait for customers between
> The pillar rows in Lincoln's Inn.—*Hudibras*, pt. iii. c. iii.

Courtin. I shall be ere long as greasy as an Alsatian bully ; this flapping hat, pinned up on one side, with a sandy weather-beaten peruke, dirty linen, and to complete the figure, a long scandalous iron sword jarring at my heels. My companions the worthy Knights of the most noble order of the Post, your peripatetic philosophers of the Temple Walks.—Otway, *The Soldier's Fortune*, 4to, 1681.

Nor was this custom forgotten when the present cloisters were rebuilt, after the Great Fire of 1666.

I remember that after the fire of the Temple, it was considered whether the old cloister walks should be rebuilt, or rather improved into chambers ; which latter had been for the benefit of the Middle Temple. But in regard it could not be done without the consent of the Inner houses, the Masters of the Middle houses waited upon the then Mr. Attorney Finch, to desire the concurrence of his society, upon a proposition of some benefit to be thrown in on his side. But Mr. Attorney would by no means give way to it, and reproved the Middle Templars very bitterly and eloquently upon the subject of students walking in evenings there, and putting cases "which," he said, "was done in his time, as mean and low as the buildings were then, however it comes," said he, "that such a benefit to students is now made so little account of."[2] And thereupon the cloisters, by the order and disposition of Sir Christopher Wren, were built as they now stand.—North's *Life of Lord Keeper Guildford*, ed. 1826, vol. i. p. 27.

The preacher at the Temple is called Master of the Temple, and this was once an appointment of greater dignity and expectations than

---

[1] Campbell, *Lives of the Chancellors*, vol. v. p. 631.

[2] Evelyn received the first rudiments of his education in the church porch at Wotton.

it is now.[1] The "judicious" Hooker, author of the *Ecclesiastical Polity*, was for six years Master of the Temple—"a place," says Izaak Walton, "which he accepted rather than desired." Travers, a disciple of Cartwright, the Nonconformist, was then lecturer; and Hooker, it was said, preached Canterbury in the forenoon, and Travers Geneva in the afternoon. The Benchers were divided; and Travers, being first silenced by the Archbishop, Hooker resigned and retired to the quiet parsonage of Boscombe to complete his great work, the *Ecclesiastical Polity*. In this church Archbishop Ussher preached the funeral sermon of the learned Selden. The organ was made by Father Schmydt, or Smith, in honourable competition with his great rival Renatus Harris. Blow and Purcell, then in their prime, performed on Father Smith's organ on appointed days; and till Harris's was heard every one believed that Smith's must be chosen. Harris employed Baptiste Draghi, organist to Queen Catherine, "to touch his organ," which brought it into favour; and thus the two continued vying with each other for near a twelvemonth. The decision at length was left to the notorious Judge Jeffreys, who decided in favour of Father Smith. Smith excelled in the diapason, or foundation stops; Harris principally in the reed stops. The choral services on a Sunday are well performed and well attended. The Round of the church is open to all, but the Choir is reserved for the Benchers, barristers, and students. Strangers are admitted by the introduction of a Bencher of either Temple. Shakespeare (or the writer of the *First Part of King Henry VI.*) has made the "Temple Gardens"—a fine open space, fronting the Thames—the place in which the distinctive badges (the white rose and red rose) of the houses of York and Lancaster were first assumed by their respective partisans.

Suffolk. Within the Temple Hall we were too loud:
The garden here is more convenient.

Plantagenet. Let him that is a true-born gentleman,
And stands upon the honour of his birth,
If he suppose that I have pleaded truth,
From off this brier pluck a white rose with me.
Somerset. Let him that is no coward, nor no flatterer,
But dare maintain the party of the truth,
Pluck a red rose from off this thorn with me.

Plantagenet. Hath not thy rose a canker, Somerset?
Somerset. Hath not thy rose a thorn, Plantagenet?

Warwick. This brawl to-day,
Grown to this faction in the Temple Gardens,

---

[1] When Sherlock, Bishop of Salisbury, was Master of the Temple, the sees of Canterbury and London were vacant about the same time (1748); this occasioned an epigram upon Sherlock:—

At the Temple one day Sherlock taking a boat,
The waterman asked him, "Which way will you float?"

"Which way?" says the doctor; "why, fool, with the stream!"
To St. Paul's or to Lambeth was all one to him.
The tide in favour of Sherlock was running to St. Paul's. He was made Bishop of London.

> Shall send, between the red rose and the white,
> A thousand souls to death and deadly night.
>
> *First Part of Henry VI.*, Act ii. Sc. 4.

It would be impossible to revive the scene in the supposed place of its origin, for such is the smoke and foul air of London that the commonest and hardiest kind of rose has long ceased to put forth a bud in the Temple Gardens, but these gardens have become the home of the chrysanthemum, and every year a fine exhibition of these flowers is to be seen here. The Temple is walled in on every side, and protected with gates. There is no poor-law within its precinct. [*See* Inner Temple Lane; Middle Temple Lane; King's Bench Walk; Paper Buildings; Hare Court; Elm Court; Ram Alley; Crown Office Row; Fig Tree Court; Brick Court.]

THE INNER TEMPLE is an Inn of Court, with three Inns of Chancery attached—Clifford's Inn, Clement's Inn, and Lyon's Inn, the latter now cleared away. The Gate House in Fleet Street, erected 5th of King James I., carries the feathers of Henry, Prince of Wales, eldest son of James I., in relief upon the front. It is now a hairdresser's, and is thus erroneously inscribed: "Formerly the Palace of Henry VIII. and Cardinal Wolsey." The greater part of the Inner Temple was destroyed in the Great Fire of 1666, the flames stopping within a very few yards of the Temple Church.

Eminent Members.—Littleton (the famous judge). Sir Edward Coke. Sir Christopher Hatton. Lord Buckhurst (Lord High Treasurer). John Bradford ("But for the grace of God, there goes John Bradford"), admitted 1547. John Selden ("a long scabby-poled boy, but a good student," as Sir Giles Mompesson told Aubrey), removed from Clifford's Inn to the Inner Temple in May 1604. His chambers were in *Paper Buildings* [which *see*]. He was elected a Bencher in 1632. When he died in 1654 his executors wished to present his library to the Society, and with that view lodged it in some chambers in the King's Bench Walk, where it remained for five years without any arrangement being made for receiving it. It was then bestowed upon the Bodleian Library and welcomed with all due honour. Heneage Finch, Judge Jeffreys, Francis Beaumont (*Beaumont and Fletcher*), Lord Mansfield, William Browne (author of *Britannia's Pastorals*), William Cowper (the poet). The hall, a poor mock Gothic building as "restored" in 1816, was demolished in 1869, and the present more spacious hall erected in its place from the designs of Sydney Smirke, R.A. This is a substantial structure of Portland stone, Perpendicular in style, 94 feet long, 41 feet wide, and 40 feet high to the wall plate, and has an open oak roof resembling that of Westminster Hall. The fine oriel at the upper end is filled with heraldic painted glass. Under the north end is an ancient crypt, which has been carefully restored. In olden times the Inner Temple Hall was famous for its revels and banquets. The revels are over but the banquets are still given, and on Grand Days with much state and ceremony. When Sir Heneage Finch, afterwards Lord Chancellor Nottingham, was Reader of the Society of the Inner Temple, King Charles II. dined with him in Inner Temple Hall; an honour, it is said, never before granted by a King in this country. The last Reader who read was Sir William Whitelocke in 1684.[1]

"The last revel in any of the *Inns of Court* was in the Inner Temple, held in honour of Mr. Talbot, when he took leave of that house, of which he was a bencher, on having the Great Seal delivered to him. A friend, who was present during the whole entertainment, obliged me with the following account, which, with some circumstances supplied by another gentleman then likewise present, seemed worth adding here, by way of comparison with those in former times, and as it may probably be the last of the kind:—

"On the 2nd of February, 1733, the Lord Chancellor came into the Inner Temple Hall about two of the clock, preceded by the Master of the Revels (Mr. Wollaston), and followed by the Master of the Temple (Dr. Sherlock), then Bishop of Bangor, and by the Judges and Serjeants who had been members of that house. There was a very elegant dinner provided for them and the Lord Chancellor's officers; but the Barristers and Students of the house had no other dinner got for them than what is usual on all Grand Days; but each mess had a flask of claret, besides the common allowance of port and sack. Fourteen students waited on the Bench Table, among whom was Mr. Talbot, the Lord Chancellor's eldest son; and by their means any sort of provision was easily obtained from the upper table by those at the rest. A large gallery was built over the screen, and was filled with ladies, who came, for the most part, a considerable time before the dinner began; and the music was placed in the little gallery, at the upper end of the Hall, and played all dinner time.

"As soon as dinner was ended the play began, which was *Love for Love*, with the farce of *The Devil To Pay*. The actors who performed in them all came from the Haymarket, in chairs, ready dressed; and, as it was said, refused any gratuity for the trouble, looking upon the honour of distinguishing themselves on this occasion as sufficient.

"After the play the Lord Chancellor, the Master of the Temple, the Judges and Benchers, retired into their Parliament Chamber, and in about half an hour afterwards came into the Hall again, and a large ring was formed round the fire-place (but no fire nor embers were on it); then the Master of the Revels, who went first, took the Lord Chancellor by the right hand, and he with his left took Mr. J[ustice] Page, who, joined to the other Judges, Serjeants, and Benchers present, danced, or rather walked, round about the coal fire, according to the old ceremony, three times, during which they were aided in the figure of the dance by Mr. George Cooke, the Prothonotary, then upwards of 60; and all the time of the dance the *ancient song*, accompanied with music, was sung by one Tony Aston [an actor], dressed in a bar gown, whose father had been formerly Master of the Plea Office in the King's Bench.

"When this was over, the ladies came down from the gallery, went into the Parliament Chamber, and stayed about a quarter of an hour, while the Hall was putting in order; then they went into the Hall and danced a few minutes; country dances began about ten, and at twelve a very fine collation was provided for the whole company: from which they returned to dancing, which they continued as long as they pleased; and the whole day's entertainment was generally thought to be very genteelly and liberally conducted. The Prince of Wales honoured the performance with his company part of the time : he came into the music gallery wing about the middle of the play, and went away as soon as the farce of walking round the coal fire was over."—Wynne's *Eunomus*, ed. 1774, vol. iv. p. 104.

It was at a banquet at the Inner Temple Hall (July 6, 1846) that

[1] Pegge's *Curialia Misc.*, p. 236.

Brougham stole a famous joke of Dr. Arbuthnot's, and while eulogising Lyndhurst said, in allusion to Lord Campbell's presence, that "to an expiring Chancellor, Death was now armed with a new terror." Samuel Rogers had chambers in Paper Buildings [which *see*]. The reader will not forget Charles Lamb's delightful essay on "The Old Benchers of the Inner Temple," the Inner Temple itself, "the most elegant spot in the metropolis," with its hall and library, garden, terrace, and fountain.

THE MIDDLE TEMPLE is an Inn of Court, with two Inns of Chancery attached—New Inn and Strand Inn. The former alone remains. The entrance from Fleet Street is by a heavy red brick front with stone dressings, built in 1684, from the design of Sir Christopher Wren, in place of the old portal which Sir Amias Paulet, while Wolsey's prisoner in the gate-house of the Temple, "had re-edified very sumptuously; garnishing the same," says Cavendish, "on the outside thereof, with cardinal's hats and arms, and divers other devices, in so glorious a sort, that he thought thereby to have appeased his old unkind displeasure."

> He [Wolsey] layed a fine upon Sir Amias to build the gate of the Middle Temple; the arms of Pawlet with the quarterings are in glass there to this day [1680]. The Cardinall's armes were, as the storie sayes, on the outside in stone, but time has long since defaced that, only you may still discerne the place; it was carv'd in a very mouldering stone.—Aubrey's *Lives*, vol. iii. p. 588.

The great hall of the Society, known as "Middle Temple Hall," was built in 1572, while Plowden, the well known jurist, was treasurer of the Inn. It is 100 feet long, 42 feet wide, and 47 feet high, and is one of the best specimens of an Elizabethan hall we possess. The roof, put up in 1575, open hammer-beam design with pendants, is the best Elizabethan roof in London. The screen, a very rich piece of Renaissance work, is said to have been formed in exact imitation of the Strand front of old Somerset House, but this is a vulgar error, like the tradition which relates that it was made of the spoils of the Spanish Armada, the records of the Society proving that it was set up thirteen years before the Armada put to sea. *Observe.*—Busts of Lords Eldon and Stowell, by Behnes. The portraits are chiefly copies, and not good. The exterior was dressed with stone, in wretched taste, in 1757. We first hear of Shakespeare's *Twelfth Night* in connection with this fine old hall, a student of the Middle Temple, of the name of Manningham, making the following entry in his diary:—

> *February* 2, 1601 [1601-1602].—At our feast we had a play called *Twelve Night or what you will*. Much like the *Comedy of Errors*; or Menechmi in *Plautus*; but most like and neere to that in Italian, called *Inganni.*—*Harl. MS.*, 5353.

Sir John Davies, the poet, whose *Nosce Teipsum* forms one of the glories of Queen Elizabeth's reign, was expelled the Society of the Middle Temple for thrashing his friend, Mr. Richard Martin (d. 1618), also a member of the Inn, during dinner-time, in the Middle Temple Hall. Davies was afterwards, on proper submission, re-admitted, and Martin is still remembered, not by his thrashing, but by Ben Jonson's noble dedication to him of his *Poetaster*. It deserves to be mentioned, in illustration of the revels at Christmas, which used to be held in the halls of the Inns of Court, that in taking up the floor of the Middle Temple Hall, about the year 1764, near one hundred pair of dice were found, which had dropt, on different occasions, through the chinks or joints of the boards. The dice were very small, at least one third less than those now in use. Members of this Inn are summoned to dinner during Term by sounding a horn.

Prince Henry. Jack, meet me to-morrow in the Temple Hall.
  Shakespeare, *First Part of Henry IV.*, Act iii. Sc. 1.

On Thursday, the 10th day of July, 1623, after our supper in the Middle Temple Hall ended, with another utter-barrister I argued a moot at the bench to the great satisfaction of such as heard me. Two gentlemen under the bar arguing at first in law French, bareheaded, as I did myself before I was called to the bar at the cupboard.—*D'Ewes*, vol. i. p. 232.

On Wensday the 23 of Febru. 1635, the Prince d'Amours gave a masque to the Prince Elector and his brother in the Middle Temple, wher the Queene [Henrietta Maria] was pleasd to grace the entertaynment, by putting of [off] majesty to putt on a citizen's habitt, and to sett upon the scaffold on the right hand amongst her subjects.—Sir H. Herbert (*Shak. by Boswell*, vol. iii. p. 237).

Manly. I hate this place [Westminster Hall] worse than a man that has inherited a Chancery Suit.

Freeman. Methinks 'tis like one of their halls in Christmas time, whither from all parts fools bring their money to try by the dice (not the worst judges) whether it shall be their own or no.—Wycherley, *The Plain Dealer*, 4to, 1676.

The Middle Temple Library, erected from the designs of Mr. H. R. Abraham, was opened by the Prince of Wales, October 31, 1861, on which occasion his Royal Highness was called to the Bar and admitted a Bencher of the Middle Temple. The Library is Collegiate Gothic in style, and a good building, but looks short and stilted from there being two floors of offices beneath the great hall. This, the Library proper, is a handsome room 86 feet long (with on oriel of 10 feet), 42 feet wide, and 63 feet high. It has seven tall windows on each side, a bay of five lights, overlooking the Thames, and a large window of seven lights on the north filled with heraldic glass. The open timber roof is after the model of that of Westminster Hall.

The regulations for admission, call to the Bar, etc., are similar to those of the other Inns of Court. [*See* Inns of Court.]

Eminent Members.—Plowden; Sir Walter Raleigh (who calls himself "Walter Rawely of the Middle Temple" in his "Commendation" of Gascoigne's *Steele Glas*, circ. 1570); Sir Thomas Overbury; Sir John Davies, the poet; John Ford, the dramatist (admitted November 16, 1602); John Pym (admitted April 23, 1602); Lord Chancellor Clarendon (admitted in 1625, when his uncle, Sir Nicholas Hyde, was treasurer); Bulstrode Whitelocke; Ireton (Cromwell's son-in-law); Evelyn (admitted February 13, 1636); John Aubrey, the antiquary (admitted 1646); Lord Keeper Guildford (admitted November 27, 1655); Lord Chancellor Somers; Wycherley; Shadwell; Congreve; Elias Ashmole, the antiquary (called to the bar, November 2, 1660); Southerne; Edmund Burke; R. B. Sheridan; Sir William Blackstone;

Dunning Lord Ashburton (d. 1783); Lord Chancellor Eldon; Lord Stowell; Thomas Moore, the poet; Sir Henry Havelock, the Indian hero, was a fellow-pupil with Judge Talfourd in Chitty's chambers in the Middle Temple.

Temple Bar, a gateway of Portland stone which, until 1878, separated the Strand from Fleet Street. The first mention of Temple Bar occurs in 1301 in a grant of land in the parish of St. Clement Danes, *extra Barram Novi Templi*. At that time the *gate* of the City was Ludgate, and the *bar* or chain put up at the end of Fleet Street by the Knights Templars marked the boundary of the territory under the control of the City, but without its walls. As the City increased in population the space within the walls became too limited, and these extra-mural lands were put under the control of the ward which they adjoined; hence the *without* and *within* added to the names of certain of the wards.

Temple Bar is the place where the freedom of the City of London and the Liberty of the City of Westminster doth part: which separation was anciently only Posts, Rails and a Chain; such as now are at Holbourn, Smithfield and Whitechapel Bars. Afterwards there was a House of Timber, erected cross the street, with a narrow gateway, and an entry on the south side of it under the house.—*Strype*, B. iii. p. 278.

The gate, described by Strype, of which a drawing is given in Hollar's seven-sheet Map of London, was taken down after the Great Fire, and a new Bar erected 1670-1672 from the designs of Sir Christopher Wren. On the east side, in niches, were the statues of King James I. and his Queen, Anne of Denmark, and on the west side those of Charles I. and Charles II., all by John Bushnell, who died in 1701. This gate was removed in the winter of 1878-1879, and the stones (about 1000) remained exposed to the weather for ten years. The work of re-erecting Temple Bar at the entrance to Sir Henry B. Meux's private grounds, Theobalds, Waltham Cross, was completed December 3, 1888. There was an old custom connected with Temple Bar which deserves mention. The gates were invariably closed by the City authorities whenever the Sovereign had occasion to enter the City. A herald sounded a trumpet before the gate— another herald knocked—a parley ensued—the gates were then thrown open, and the Lord Mayor for the time being made over the sword of the City to the Sovereign, who graciously returned it to the Mayor. Stow describes in his *Annales* a scene like this, when Queen Elizabeth was on her way to St. Paul's to return thanks for the defeat of the Armada.

When Cromwell and the Parliament dined in the City in state, on June 7, 1649, the same ceremony was observed; the Mayor, says Whitelocke, delivering up the sword to the Speaker, "as he used to do to the King." The last observance of this ceremony was on February 27, 1872, when Queen Victoria went to St. Paul's to the Thanksgiving Service for the recovery of the Prince of Wales from typhoid fever.

At many periods the decorations of the Gate were of a very ghastly character. The mangled remains of Sir Thomas Armstrong, hanged at Tyburn June 20, 1684, the head and quarters of Sir William Parkins, and the quarters of John Freind were among the early ornaments of the present Bar. Armstrong was concerned in the Rye House Plot; Parkins and Freind in the assassination Plot against William III. The heads of the victims of the fatal "45" were the last placed upon the Bar. "I have been this morning at the Tower," Walpole writes to Montague, August 16, 1746, "and passed under the new heads at Temple Bar, where people make a trade of letting spying-glasses at a halfpenny a look." "I remember," said Johnson,[1] "once being with Goldsmith in Westminster Abbey. While we surveyed the Poets' Corner, I said to him :—

Forsitan et nostrum nomen miscebitur istis.

When we got to the Temple Bar he stopped me, pointed to the heads upon it, and slily whispered me :—

Forsitan et nostrum nomen miscebitur istis."

The last heads which remained on the Bar were those of Townley and Fletcher.[2] "Yesterday," says a news-writer of April 1, 1772, "one of the rebels' heads on Temple Bar fell down. There is only one head now remaining." This last head fell shortly after. The interior of the Bar was leased from the City (at a yearly rental of £50) by Messrs. Child, the bankers, as a repository for the ledgers and cash-books of their house. Pynson the printer lived here, and (*see* Fleet Street) his first work states in the colophon that it was printed "the v day July the year of our lord god 1493 by me Richarde Pynson at the Temple barre of London."

The "Temple Bar Memorial," which marks the site of the old building, was unveiled, September 8, 1880, by H.R.H. the late Prince Leopold (afterwards Duke of Albany). It is 31 feet 6 inches high, 5 feet wide, and 7 feet 8 inches long, and is surmounted by a bronze dragon (commonly styled "the griffin") by C. B. Birch, A.R.A. The architect was Sir Horace Jones, and the marble statues of the Queen and the Prince of Wales are the work of Mr. (now Sir E.) Boehm. The portrait medallions on the east and west sides are of the Prince of Wales and Sir Francis Wyatt Truscott, Lord Mayor. The last of the four reliefs, that on the south side, representing the procession of the Queen to the Guildhall Banquet on November 9, 1837, was inserted in place in December 1882, thus completing the memorial, the total cost of which was £10,690 : 6 : 5.

Temple Church. [*See* The Temple.]

Temple Exchange Coffee-house, near TEMPLE BAR. Here the Fire of London stopped. Four of Goldsmith's letters (in 1757-1758) are dated from this house, which ceased to be a coffee-house about the year 1810.

[1] *Boswell*, by Croker, p. 258. [2] *Ann. Reg.*, fol. 1766, p. 50.

Temple Stairs, or Temple Bridge, was a landing-place extending across two stone arches well into the Thames, within the Temple Grounds.[1]

In 18 Jac. [1621] the bridge and stairs to the Thames were made.—Dugdale's *Origines Juridiciales.*

We were no sooner come to the Temple Stairs but we were surrounded with a crowd of Watermen, offering us their respective services. Sir Roger, after having looked about him very attentively, spied one with a wooden leg, and immediately gave him orders to get his boat ready.—*Spectator,* No. 283.

For some time there appears to have existed a right-of-way through the "Templegate to Tempelbrygge," and in 1360 a complaint was made against the possessors of the Temple for preventing the use of this way. The petitioners were John de Hydyngham and eleven others:—

> Who say upon their oath that time out of mind the commonalty of the city aforesaid have been wont to have free ingress and egress with horses and carts, from sunrise to sunset, for carrying and carting all manner of victuals and wares therefrom to the water of Thames, and from the said water of Thames to the city aforesaid, through the Great Gate of the Templars, situate within Temple Bar in the Ward aforesaid, in the suburb of London; and that the possessors of the Temple were wont, and by right ought, to maintain a bridge at the water aforesaid.—Riley's *Memorials,* p. 308.

Tenison's (Archbishop) Chapel is situated on the west side of King Street, Golden Square. The approach from Regent Street is by Chapel Court, formerly called Hide Court. In Strype's *Stow,* 1720, this building is spoken of as "the Chapel of Ease, by some called The Tabernacle." It had a front in Regent Street, which was designed in 1823 by C. R. Cockerell, architect, and was turned into a shop about 1861.

February 19, 1693.—The Bishop of Lincoln [Tenison] preached in the afternoon at the Tabernacle near Golden Square, set up by him.—*Evelyn.*

December 3, 1693.—Mr. Bentley [the great critic] preached at the Tabernacle near Golden Square.—*Evelyn.*

Tenison's (Archbishop) Grammar School, LEICESTER SQUARE. The school was founded in 1685, and occupied the same building as Archbishop Tenison's Library. It was removed to Leicester Square when Castle Street was pulled down, and it now occupies the site of Hogarth's house and the Sablonière Hotel. The school was reconstituted in 1871. In 1887 the income from payments for pupils was £1320, and endowment and interest only £220.

Tenison's (Archbishop) Library, CASTLE STREET, ST. MARTIN'S LANE, immediately behind the National Gallery, founded in 1684, and partly endowed by Dr. Tenison, then vicar of St. Martin's-in-the-Fields, and afterwards Archbishop of Canterbury. The origin of the library is related by Evelyn:—

February 15, 1683-1684.—Dr. Tenison communicated to me his intention of erecting a Library in St. Martin's parish, for the public use, and desired my assistance, with

---

[1] A good view of the Temple Stairs is given in the *Gentleman's Magazine,* October 1768.

Sir Christopher Wren, about the placing and structure thereof. A worthy and laudable design. He told me there were 30 or 40 young men in Orders in his parish, either governors to young gentlemen, or chaplains to noblemen, who being reproved by him on occasion for frequenting taverns or coffee-houses, told him they would study or employ their time better if they had books. This put the pious Doctor on this design.—*Evelyn*.

February 23, 1683-1684.—Afterwards I went with Sir Christopher Wren to Dr. Tenison, where we made the drawing and estimate of the expence of the Library, to be begun this next Spring neere the Mewes.—*Evelyn*.

The library, of 4000 volumes, was open to the parishioners of St. Martin's-in-the-Fields; St. James's, Westminster; St. Anne's, Soho; and St. George's, Hanover Square. An early Chaucer MS. was the chief treasure of the collection; but there were also early editions of Wiclif, Bacon, and other old writers, and copies of many rare and valuable theological works. The house was pulled down in 1861 to make room for the extension of the National Gallery; and the MSS. and printed books were, by order of the Charity Commissioners, sold by Messrs. Sotheby and Wilkinson.

Tennis Court, HOLBORN, on the south side of the street, nearly opposite Gray's Inn Lane. It led into Southampton Buildings, but is now closed. It marks the site of the Tennis Court of Southampton House.

Mr. Julian Marshall, in his *Annals of Tennis* (1878), gives a curious list of fourteen Tennis Courts in London in 1615 from a MS. of Lord Leconfield's at Petworth. They are as follows: Whitehall (two, covered and uncovered), Somerset House, Essex House, Fetter Lane, Fleet Street, Blackfriars, Southampton, Charterhouse, Powles Chaine, Abchurch Lane, Lawrence Pountney, Fenchurch Street and Crutched Friars.

Tennis Court Theatre, SOUTHWARK.

Afterwards [1778] I acted for a few nights at the Tennis Court in the Borough, which was soon shut up by the Surrey Magistrates.—George F. Cooke, *Life*, vol. i. p. 26.

There is still a place named Tennis Court between 56 and 57 Newcomen Street, Borough.

Terry's Theatre, 105 and 106 STRAND, was built in 1887 (Walter Emden, architect). The accommodation is for 800 persons, and special arrangements are made for escape in case of fire, and the total exit accommodation is equal to 3500 persons. The whole building, including the roof, is constructed of concrete and iron, no wood being used in the auditorium except for doors and windows.

Thames (The), the longest of our rivers, to which London is so largely indebted for its commercial importance, rises on the southeastern slopes of the Cotswold Hills, and after an easterly course of 225 miles in length, in which it passes Oxford, Windsor, Hampton Court, Twickenham, Richmond, London and Greenwich, etc., flows into the North Sea at the Nore, a distance of 60 miles below London. The derivation of the word Thames was for a long time almost universally misunderstood. When Spenser in his *Faerie Queene* made the word a combination of Thame and Isis, he only put into a poetic form the idea then generally current that this river only bore the name Thames after the confluence of the Thame and Isis at Dorchester.

> Soon after whom the lovely bridegroom came,
> The noble Thames, with all his goodly traine,
> But him before there went, as best became,
> His auncient parents, namely th' auncient Thame;
> But much more aged was his wife than he,
> The Ouze,' whom men do Isis rightly name.
>   *Faerie Queene*, B. iv. canto xi. stanza 24.

Bishop Gibson in his *Additions to Camden* first pointed out the error and showed that *Isis* is quite a misnomer, and that the river is the *Thames* from its source to its mouth.

Upon this first mention of the river Thames, it will not be improper to observe, that, though the current opinion is that it had that name from the conjunction of the Thame and the Isis, it plainly appears that the river was always called Thames or Tems, before it came near the Thame. For instance, in an ancient charter granted to Abbot Aldhelm, there is particular mention made of certain lands upon the east part of the river, "cujus vocabulum Temis, juxta vadum qui appellatur Summerford" (the name of which is Thames, near the ford called Somerford), and this ford is in Wiltshire. The same thing appears from several other charters granted to the Abbot of Malmesbury, as well as that of Evesham; and from old deeds relating to Cricklade. And, perhaps, it may with safety be affirmed, that in any charter or authentic history it does not ever occur under the name of Isis, which, indeed, is not so much as heard of but among scholars; the common people all along from the head of it to Oxford calling it by no other name but that of Thames. So also the Saxon Tamese (from whence our Tems immediately comes) is a plain evidence that people never dreamt of any such conjunction. But further, all our historians who mention the incursions of Aethelwold into Wiltshire, A.D. 905, or of Canute, A.D. 1016, tell us that they passed over the Thames at Cricklade.—Gibson's *Camden's Britannia*, vol. i. p. 194, ed. 1772.

The scholarly name Isis for the upper river was probably taken from the ending of the Latin form *Tamesis* or *Tamisis*.

From London Bridge to King's Head Stairs, at *Rotherhithe*, is called the Upper Pool; from thence to *Cuckold's Point*, the Lower Pool; thence to Deptford, Limehouse Reach; thence to Enderby's Ropehouse, Greenwich Reach; thence to Blackwall Point, Blackwall Reach. At very high tides, and after long easterly winds, the water at London Bridge is very often brackish. Spenser calls it "The silver-streaming Thames;" Middleton and Herrick, "The silver-footed Thamasis." Denham has sung its praises in some noble couplets:—

> O could I flow like thee, and make thy stream
> My great example, as it is my theme!
> Though deep yet clear, though gentle yet not dull,
> Strong without rage, without o'erflowing full.
>   SIR JOHN DENHAM.

and Pope described its banks with the accuracy of a Dutch painter in his ludicrous imitation of Spenser's manner.

I take it ill you should say anything against the Mole; it is a reflection, I see, cast at the Thames. Do you think that rivers which have lived in London and its neighbourhood all their days, will run roaring and tumbling about like your Tramontane torrents in the North. No, they only glide and whisper.—*Gray (the poet) to Mr. Wharton*, August 13, 1754.

The morning was fair and bright, and we had a passage thither [from London to Gravesend] I think as pleasant as can be conceived; for take it with all its advantages, particularly the number of fine ships you are always sure of seeing by the way, there is nothing to equal it in all the rivers of the world. The yards of Deptford and Woolwich are noble sights. . . . We saw likewise several Indiamen just returned from their voyage. . . . The colliers likewise, which are very numerous and even assemble in fleets, are ships of great bulk; and if we descend to those used in the American, African, and European trades, and pass through those which visit our own coasts, to the small craft that plie between Chatham and the Tower, the whole forms a most pleasing object to the eye, as well as highly warming to the heart of an Englishman, who has any degree of love for his country, or can recognise any effect of the patriot in his constitution.—Fielding, *A Voyage to Lisbon*.

An alderman of London reasonably (as methought) affirmed that although London received great nourishment by the residence of the prince, the repair of the parliament and the courts of justice, yet it stood principally by the advantage of the situation upon the river; for when, as on a time, it was told him by a courtier that Queen Mary, in her displeasure against London, had appointed to remove with the parliament and term to Oxford, this plain man demanded whether she meant also to divert the river Thames from London or no? and when the gentleman had answered "No;" "Then," quoth the alderman, "by God's grace we shall do well enough at London whatsoever become of the term and parliament.—*An Apology for the City of London*: in Stow's *Survey*, 1598.

Queen Elizabeth died at Richmond, and her body was brought with great pomp by water to Whitehall:—

> The Queen was brought by water to Whitehall;
> At every stroke the oars did tears let fall:
> More clung about the barge; fish under water
> Wept out their eyes of pearl, and swum blind after.
> I think the bargemen might with easier thighs
> Have rowed her thither in her people's eyes.
> For howsoe'er, thus much my thoughts have scan'd
> Sh'ad come by water, had she come by land.
> *Contemporary Epitaph*, in Camden's *Remains*, p. 388.

Cowley died at Chertsey, on the Thames, and his body was carried by water to Whitehall:—

> Oh, early lost! what tears the river shed
> When the sad pomp along his banks was led,
> Pope, *Windsor Forest*.

Nelson's body was brought in great state by water from Greenwich to Whitehall. State prisoners, committed from the Council Chamber to the Tower or the Fleet, were invariably taken by water. The Thames, that carried, in the reign of James II., the seven bishops to the Tower, was made the repository of the Great Seal of England, which James, in his flight, threw into the river while crossing in a small boat from Millbank to Lambeth. It was accidentally fished up a few months after. The Thames was frozen over in the winters of 1564, 1608, 1634-1635, 1683-1684, 1715-1716, 1739-1740, 1789, and 1814. The frost of 1683-1684 is known as Frost or Blanket Fair, and was kept with peculiar honours, such as the establishment of a printing-press and the roasting of an ox whole.

The weather is so very sharp and the frost so great, that the river here is quite frozen over, so that for these three days last past, people have gone over it, in several places, and many booths are built on it between Lambeth and Westminster, where they roast meat and sell drink.—*The Duke of York (James II.) to the Prince of Orange (William III.),* January 4, 1683-1684.

There is little chance of the Thames being frozen *over* again, since the removal of Old London Bridge, whose piers, by obstructing the passage of the floating ice, caused it to coagulate into one mass; the current likewise is so much stronger since the bridge was removed and the river embanked for a considerable distance. The bridges were opened to the public in the following order: *Old* London in 1209; *Old* Westminster in 1750; *Old* Blackfriars in 1769; *Old* Battersea in 1771; Vauxhall in 1816; Waterloo in 1817; Southwark in 1819; *New* London in 1831; Hungerford Suspension in 1846; Chelsea Suspension in 1856; Lambeth in 1862; Charing Cross (which replaced Hungerford Bridge) in 1863; *New* Westminster in 1862; *New* Blackfriars in 1869; Albert Suspension in 1873; and *New* Battersea in 1890. The Thames Tunnel was opened in 1843. [*See* all these names.] Taylor, the Water Poet, was a licensed sculler or waterman on the Thames in the reign of James I. The scene of Dryden's Essay on Dramatic Poesy is laid on a boat on the Thames at London. It was on August 1, 1716, that Doggett, the actor, first gave "an orange-coloured livery with a badge representing Liberty," to be rowed for by six watermen that are out of their time within the year past, "they are to row from London Bridge to Chelsea," the gift being in honour of the accession of the house of Hanover, and "it will be continued," as he announced, "annually on the same day for ever," a continuance for which he made due provision in his will. The first regatta seen in this country took place on the Thames before *Ranelagh Gardens,* June 23, 1775. The first steamboat seen on the Thames was in 1816. The Thames was formerly famous for its water dialect, or mob language, one of the privileges of the river assumed by watermen, of which Ned Ward and Tom Brown have both left specimens, and of which Fielding complains so touchingly in his voyage to Lisbon.

Leatherhead. There's no talking to these watermen, they will have the last word. —*Ben Jonson.*

May 14, 1669.—My wife and I by water, with my brother, as high as Fulham, talking and singing and playing the rogue with the western bargemen, about the women of Woolwich which made them. [*See* also May 28, 1669.]—*Pepys.*

Many ladies will take a broad jest cheerfully as from the watermen.—Wycherley, Dedication of *Plain Dealer.*

To the knight's great surprise, as he gave the good night to two or three young fellows a little before our landing, one of them instead of returning the civility asked us what green old Put we had in the boat, and whether he was not ashamed to go a wenching at his years? with a great deal of the like Thames ribaldry. Sir Roger seemed a little shocked at first, but at length assuming a face of magistracy told us, That if he were a Middlesex Justice he would make such vagrants know that her Majesty's subjects were to be no more abused by water than by land.—*The Spectator,* No. 383.

It is well-known that there was formerly a rude custom for those who were sailing upon the Thames to accost each other as they passed in the most abusive language they could invent; generally however with as much satirical humour as they were capable of producing. Johnson was once eminently successful in this species of contest. A fellow having attacked him with some coarse raillery, Johnson answered him thus, "Sir, your wife, under pretence of keeping a bawdy house, is a receiver of stolen goods."—*Boswell.*

The sewerage of London, and the restless state of the stream from the number of steamboats passing up and down, have materially contributed to poison the purity of the water. Yet the Thames was once famous for its fish. "What should I speake," says Harrison, in 1586, "of the fat and sweet salmons, daily taken in this streame, and that in such plentie (after the time of the smelt be past) as no river in Europe is able to exceed it."[1] The first salmon of the season was invariably carried to the King's table, by the fishermen of the Thames; and a sturgeon caught below London Bridge was carried to the table of the Lord Mayor; if above bridge, to the table of the King or Lord High Admiral.[2] Evelyn records the curious circumstance that a whale 58 feet in length was killed in the Thames between Deptford and Greenwich on June 3, 1658. The wind had been blowing northerly for nearly six months. Now, however, it is very different; a salmon has not been taken in the Thames for many years; and the produce of the river in and near London is confined to flounders, eels, and whitebait. The eels are small, but sweet; and the whitebait is almost peculiar to the Thames. [*See* Blackwall; York House.] The fishing-tackle shops in *Crooked Lane*, leading to *Old Swan Stairs*, where the Thames fishermen lived who attended on the London disciples of Izaak Walton were famous, but the shoals of roach that frequented the starlings of Old London Bridge were of rare occurrence before the removal of the bridge, and are now no longer to be seen. The impurity of the stream has driven bathers away—yet it was once very different. Lord Northampton, in the reign of Charles I., was taken ill of the colic, of which he died, while washing himself in the Thames, after he had waited on the King at supper, and had supped himself. Blood concealed himself among the reeds at Battersea, in order to shoot King Charles II. while bathing in the Thames over against Chelsea. One of the darling recreations of Sir Dudley North was swimming in the Thames.

He used that so much, that he became quite a master of it. He could live in the water an afternoon with as much ease as others walk upon land. He shot the bridge [old London Bridge] divers times at low water, which showed him not only active, but intrepid; for courage is required to bear the very sight of that tremendous cascade, which few can endure to pass in a boat.—Roger North's *Lives of the Norths*, 8vo, 1826, vol. ii. p. 294.

The polite Earl of Chesterfield directed a letter to Lord Pembroke (the collector), who was always swimming, "To the Earl of Pembroke, in the Thames, over against Whitehall."[3] "Last week," says Lord

[1] Harrison's *Description of England* before Holinshed, ed. 1586, p. 46
[2] MS. in Lord Steward's office, dated February 1786.
21, 1607; Dugdale's *Troubles*, fol. 1681, p. 580.
[3] Walpole to Lady Craven, November 27,

Byron, the poet, in a letter dated August 11, 1807, "I swam in the Thames from Lambeth through the two bridges, Westminster and Blackfriars, a distance, including the different turns and tacks made on the way, of three miles." The London visitor should make a point of descending the Thames by a steamboat from Chelsea to Blackwall (the work of an hour and a half), and of observing the following places, principally on the left or Middlesex bank: Chelsea Old Church, Chelsea Hospital, Vauxhall Bridge; Penitentiary; (right) St. Thomas's Hospital; Lambeth Palace; (left) church of St. John's, Westminster, and Houses of Parliament, Westminster Bridge; York Water-gate, the Adelphi Terrace (Garrick's house is the centre one), Waterloo Bridge; Somerset House, Temple Gardens, and roof of Middle Temple Hall, St. Bride's Church—the steeple one of Wren's great works; Whitefriars, the site of *Alsatia*, Blackfriars Bridge; here is a very fine view of St. Paul's and the City churches; *observe* how grandly Bow steeple, with its dragon on the top, towers above them all, and commands attention by the harmony of its proportions; Southwark Bridge; here the right or Surrey side, commonly called the Bankside, becomes interesting from its fine associations—here stood the Globe Theatre, the Bear Garden and Winchester House, and (right) here is the church of St. Saviour's, Southwark. You now pass under London Bridge, and should *observe* (left) the steeple of St. Magnus and the Monument. Here begins the Pool. *Observe.*—(left) The Tower, St. Katherine's Docks; (right) Rotherhithe Church; here you pass over the Thames Tunnel; (right) Greenwich Hospital, one of Wren's great masterpieces; the Observatory at Greenwich, Blackwall Reach, etc. [*See* all these places, Greenwich excepted. *See* also Folly; Pool; Cuckold's Point, etc.]

Thames Embankment (The.) The embanking of the Thames formed a part of Sir Christopher Wren's scheme for the rebuilding of London after the Great Fire, and since then has figured in most large plans of London improvements, but it was only in 1862 that a Bill was obtained and the necessary works commenced by the Metropolitan Board of Works for the construction of an embankment on the north bank of the river from Blackfriars Bridge to Westminster Bridge. Since then two further embankments, on the south bank from Westminster Bridge to Vauxhall, and on the north bank from Battersea Bridge to Chelsea Bridge, have been constructed.

The *Victoria Embankment*, the official name given to the northern embankment between Blackfriars and Westminster Bridges, was commenced in 1862 and opened in 1870 by the Prince of Wales as the representative of the Queen. This magnificent piece of engineering, designed by and carried out under the supervision of Sir Joseph Bazalgette, engineer to the Metropolitan Board of Works, consists of a solid granite river wall 8 feet thick, with foundations carried down from 16 to 30 feet below low-water mark. About 1¼ mile in length, backed by a roadway 100 feet wide and following the easy curve of the river, with Blackfriars Bridge at the one end and the Houses of Parliament at the other, Waterloo Bridge and Somerset House midway, and all along the wide and animated Thames, the Victoria Embankment forms perhaps the finest and most characteristic roadway in the metropolis. Underneath the roadway runs the Metropolitan District Railway, and between this and the wall itself are carried two tunnels, the lower the great intercepting or low-level sewer of the main drainage system, the upper for water and gas pipes and telegraph wires, which can thus be repaired without necessitating the breaking up of the roadway. From the river the Embankment is marked by the simplicity and dignity befitting such a work. Beyond the massive bronze lions' heads, holding large mooring-rings, which are placed on the pedestals at intervals of 60 feet, the ornament is reserved for the landing-places. And even here, with the exception of the *proposed* sculptural groups, it is wholly constructional. The cost was about £2,000,000. The space gained from the river, and which was formerly at low tide a pestiferous slime, varies in width from 200 to 450 feet, and amounts to about 30 acres. A part of this reclaimed land has been laid out as public gardens, and in them have been erected various statues of public men, none of which, however, call for special notice. The Embankment is gradually becoming lined with more or less pretentious buildings, both public and private. At the Blackfriars end is the large building occupied by De Keyser's Royal Hotel; a little farther along we come to the new City of London School and Sion College; then follow the offices of the London School Board; the Examination Hall of the Royal Colleges of Physicians and Surgeons, the Savoy Hotel, and other new buildings occupied as offices. At the corner of the new approach, Northumberland Avenue (which *see*), is the Avenue Theatre (opened in March 1882); and at the Westminster Bridge end were for many years the unfinished walls of the ill-fated Grand Opera House. The new Police Offices, to be called New Scotland Yard, are now (1890) in course of completion. At the foot of Cecil Street stands the Egyptian obelisk, or so called Cleopatra's Needle, presented to the English Government by Mehemet Ali, but, owing to the difficulty of removal, it was allowed to remain lying in the sand of Alexandria until 1877, when the public-spirited munificence of Sir Erasmus Wilson (who spent £10,000 for the purpose) and the engineering skill of Mr. Dixon succeeded in removing all difficulties and transferring the unwieldy gift to its present site on the Embankment.

Together with its broad and handsome approach on the City side— Queen Victoria Street—the Victoria Embankment opens up a wide and convenient roadway from the heart of the City to the seat of Legislature at Westminster.

The *Albert Embankment*, on the south side of the river from Westminster Bridge to Vauxhall, is almost identical in character and equal in dignity and grandeur with that just described. It was opened in 1870, is about 4300 feet long, with a roadway 60 feet wide, and was constructed at a cost of a little over £1,000,000. Flanking the

Westminster end of this embankment is the imposing range of buildings forming St. Thomas's Hospital, but after passing Lambeth Palace and Doulton's Pottery Works there is nothing worthy of note.

The *Chelsea Embankment*, from Battersea Bridge to Chelsea Bridge, was finished in 1874. It is faced with mill-stone grit towards the river, is about a mile long, and cost about £250,000. Underneath the roadway is the main sewer.

Thames Street, on the north bank of the THAMES, stretches from Blackfriars Bridge to the Tower, and is rather more than a mile in length. That part of the street below London Bridge is called Lower Thames Street, that above, Upper Thames Street. The eastern end of Thames Street was sometimes called Petty Wales (which *see*), and also occasionally Galley Row.[1] That part of Thames Street which lies in Bridge Ward formerly bore the name of Stockfishmonger Row.

Some excavations made for sewers in Thames Street led to discoveries which confirm the truth of Fitz Stephen's assertion that London was formerly walled on the water side, and although in his time the wall was no longer standing, at least in an entire state, there was probably enough left to trace its course by. This wall was first noticed at the foot of Lambeth Hill, forming an angle with Thames Street, and extending, with occasional breaks, to Queenhithe; and some walling of similar character, probably a part of the above, has been noticed in Thames Street, opposite Queen Street. It was from eight to ten feet thick, and about eight deep, reckoning the top at nine feet from the present street level, and composed of ragstone and flint, with alternate layers of red and yellow, plain and curve-edged tiles, cemented by mortar, as firm and hard as the tiles, from which it could not be separated. For the foundation strong oaken piles were used, upon which was laid a stratum of chalk and stones, and then a course of hewn sand-stones, from three to four feet long, by two and a half in width.—C. Roach Smith, *Arch. Journal*, vol. i. p. 114.

I had rather live all my days among the cheesemongers' shops in Thames Street, than pass such another spring in this filthy country.—*The Connoisseur*, June 13, 1754.

John Chaucer, the poet's father, was a vintner in Thames Street, and the poet himself lived there for many years. In the 14th century the river front of Thames Street exhibited numerous handsome buildings, but these were destroyed by the fire and not rebuilt.

March 19, 1668.—Walked all along Thames Street, which I have not done since it was burned, as far as Billingsgate; and there do see a brave street likely to be, many brave houses being built, and of them a great many by Mr. Jaggard; but the raising of the street will make it mighty fine.—*Pepys*.

In Thames Street stood formerly Baynard's Castle, and the Steelyard (which *see*).

Observe—In Upper Thames Street, walking eastward to *The Tower:* church of *St. Benet, Paul's Wharf*, rebuilt after the fire, by Wren: here Inigo Jones is buried; churchyard of *St. Peter's, Paul's Wharf* (this church was destroyed in the Great Fire, and not rebuilt); *Trig Lane; Castle Baynard* (name alone); *Broken Wharf; Queenhithe;* warehouse, No. 46, as a successful adaptation of Gothic to ordinary business purposes, architect W. Burges. Church of *St. James, Garlickhithe; Vintners'*

---

[1] *Stow*, p. 50.

Hall; College Hill; Dowgate; Allhallows the Great; Coldharbour; Steelyard; Suffolk Lane; Lawrence Poultney Hill; Old Swan Stairs (here was the Shades, at London Bridge, noted for the excellent flavour of its wines and its moderate charges). Here the street passes under *London Bridge. Observe*—In Lower Thames Street, *Fish Street Hill,* church of *St. Magnus* (built by Wren); *Pudding Lane* (where the Great Fire of 1666 broke out); *Botolph Lane*, so called from the church of St. Botolph, destroyed in the Great Fire; *Billingsate; St. Mary-at-Hill* (so called from the church on the hill, on the left as you ascend); church of *St. Dunstan's-in-the-East* (built by Wren); *Custom House; the Tower.*

Thames Subway. [*See* Tower Subway.]

Thames Tunnel (two miles below London Bridge). A tunnel 1300 feet in length and 35 feet in width, beneath the bed of the river Thames, connecting Wapping on the left side of the river with Rotherhithe, or Redriff, on the right. This work was projected and carried out under enormous difficulties by Sir Mark Isambard Brunel. It was commenced in January 1825, closed for seven years by an inundation; recommenced in 1835 and opened for public traffic March 25, 1843. It cost over £600,000, of which £270,000 was lent by Government. Only about £100,000 of this advance was repaid, and a Treasury Warrant remitted the balance of over £150,000. As a footway for passengers this tunnel never more than paid the bare expenses of working, and was sold in 1865 to the East London Railway Company for £200,000. Sloping approaches were added by this Company, and trains now run through the Tunnel, connecting the Great Eastern and other lines north of the Thames with the Brighton and those on the south. The Tunnel consists of two arched passages 1200 feet long, 14 feet wide, 16½ feet high, separated by a wall of brick 4 feet thick, with 64 arched openings in it. The crown of the arch is 16 feet below the bottom of the river.

Thanet House, ALDERSGATE STREET.

And the 7 day of May 1664, being Saturdaie, about 3 o'clock in the morning dyed my sonne-in-law John Tufton Earle of Thanet in his house called Thanet House, in Aldersgate Street at London in those lodgings that look towards the street, which he had about 20 years since built with freestone very magnificently.—*True Memorials of Anne Pembroke, Dorset, and Montgomery.*

[*See* Aldersgate Street.]

Thanet Place, 231 STRAND, a few doors west of Temple Bar, was so called after the Tuftons, Earls of Thanet. John Martin the painter was living here in 1811. [*See* Rose Tavern.]

Thatched House Club (formerly Civil Service Club), No. 86 ST. JAMES'S STREET—west side, next the Conservative Club House. The Club (established 1865) comprises 1200 members, who are elected by ballot. Entrance fee, 25 guineas; annual subscription, 10 guineas.

Thatched House Tavern, ST. JAMES'S STREET, a celebrated tavern, with a large room for public meetings, stood from 1711 up to about 1843 on the site of the present *Conservative Clubhouse.* It then occupied the adjoining premises from 1845 to 1865, when it was pulled down and the Civil Service Club (now the Thatched House Club) and Thatched House Chambers were built on the site.

> The Deanery House may well be match'd,
> Under correction, with the Thatch'd.
>
> Swift, *Birthday Verses on Mr. Ford.*

December 27, 1711.—I entertained our Society at the Thatched House Tavern to-day at dinner; but brother Bathurst sent for wine, the house affording none.— Swift, *Journal to Stella.*

In the debates on the Regency, a prim peer, remarkable for his finical delicacy and formal adherence to etiquette, having cited pompously certain resolutions which he said had been passed by a party of noblemen and gentlemen of great distinction at the Thatched House Tavern, the Lord Chancellor Thurlow, in adverting to these, said, "As to what the noble lord in the red riband told us he had heard at the alehouse."—Lord Campbell's *Lives of the Chancellors,* vol. v. p. 643.

In this tavern Gildon has laid the scene of his *Comparison between the Two Stages* (12mo, 1702). The Society of Dilettanti met at the Thatched House, and here were kept their famous portraits until the removal to Willis's Rooms. [*See* Dilettanti Society.]

Thavie's Inn, HOLBORN CIRCUS, an Inn of Chancery appertaining to *Lincoln's Inn,* but sold by that society in 1771 to a Mr. Middleton. It derives its name from John Thavie, of the Armourers' Company, who in 1348 bequeathed certain houses in Holborn towards the fabric of the adjoining church of St. Andrew, still possessed by the parish. The north end of the Inn was cut off in forming the Holborn Viaduct.

I must and will begin with Thavis Inne, for besides that at my first coming to London I was admitted for probation into that good house, I take it to be the oldest Inn of Chancery, at the least in Holborn. It was before the dwelling of an honest citizen called John Thavie an armorer, and was rented of him in the time of King Edward the 3 by the chief Professors then of the Law, viz., Apprentices, as it is yet extant in a record in the Hustings, and whereof my Lord Coke shewed to me the transcript, but since that time it was purchased for the students and other professors of the Law of Chancery by the Benchers of Lincoln's Inn, about the reign of King Henry the Seventh, and retaineth the name of the old Landlord or owner Master Thavie.—*Sir George Buc,* in Howes, ed. 1631, p. 1074.

Thavie's Inn was purchased by the Society of Lincoln's Inn in 1550 of Gregory Nichols, citizen and mercer, for the sum of "three score and fifteen pounds," for the use of students of the law.[1] It was sold to Mr. Middleton in 1769 for £4100. The scene of Hogarth's *Second Stage of Cruelty* is laid at the gate of Thavie's Inn. The longest "shilling fare" in London was from this Inn to Westminster, and the foreground of the picture is occupied by four lawyers in wigs and gowns, who have clubbed their threepence each for the Hackney Coach, *No.* 24, *F. Nero driver,* to carry them to Westminster. But—

> The generous steed in hoary age
> Subdued by labour lies,

---

[1] Cooper's *Melmoth,* p. 335.

And mourns a cruel master's rage
While Nature strength denies.—*Inscription under Print.*

Thayer Street, MANCHESTER SQUARE (Hinde Street to George Street). Here, at No. 4, was the Venetian Embassy in 1796—the last of the long line. And here at his lodgings, in No. 16, died (1857) Long Tylney Wellesley Pole, known as the last and prodigal owner of Wanstead, and condemned to lasting fame by the "Rejected Addresses."

Theatre (The), HOLYWELL LANE, SHOREDITCH, the earliest building erected in or near London purposely for theatrical entertainments, stood on "certain howsing and void grounds lying and being in Holywell, in the county of Middlesex," let (April 13, 1576) by Giles Allein, of Haseleigh, in Essex, gentleman, to "James Burbadge, late of London, joiner," for twenty-one years, at the yearly rent of £14. The house was erected at the cost of John Braynes, the father-in-law of Burbadge, who advanced £600 on condition that Burbadge should assign to him a moiety of the theatre and its profits. That assignment does not seem to have been executed in the lifetime of Braynes, and his widow was obliged to commence proceedings in equity, to compel a fulfilment of the contract. The point in dispute was afterwards moved to the Star Chamber, Allein, the ground landlord, complaining to the Privy Council that the rent was partly unpaid, and that Cuthbert Burbadge, the son, had, December 28, 1598, "carried the wood to the Bankside, and there erected a new playhouse with the said wood." Allein's bill was referred to Francis Bacon, Esq. (afterwards Earl of St. Alban), whose decision was that "the said bill is very uncertain and insufficient, and that no further answer need to be made thereto."[1] The "new playhouse" was the Globe. The present Standard Theatre is said to occupy, at least in part, the site of the Theatre in Holywell Lane.

In the *Middlesex County Records* (edited by J. C. Jeaffreson, vol. ii. p. xlvii.) there is a notice of an indictment against John Braynes and John Burbadge in Elizabeth's reign on account of commotions and riots, etc., which had taken place at the theatre. We have no description of either the exterior or interior of the building, but in De Witt's later description of the London Theatres, 1596, it is described as one of four amphitheatres (See *Transactions of the New Shakspere Society*, 1887-1891, p. 218).

Theobalds Road, RED LION SQUARE to GRAY'S INN LANE, was so called because it led towards Theobalds, in Hertfordshire, the favourite hunting-seat of King James I. The King, on leaving Whitehall, went through the Strand, up Drury Lane, and so on into Holborn, Kingsgate Street, and the King's Way or Theobalds Road. Hatton (1708), speaking of Kingsgate Street and the King's Way, says, "This street and way are so called because the King used to go this way to Newmarket: some call the easterly end of this street Theobalds Road."[2] John le Neve

[1] Proceedings in the Star Chamber preserved in the Chapter House; *Shakspere Society's Papers*, vol. iv. p. 63.
[2] *Hatton*, p. 44.

lived in this road, and here he advertised that his *Monumenta Anglicana* (5 vols. 8vo, 1717-1719) might be bought. Theobalds Road has within the last few years been in parts much widened and altered to fit it to form part of the great thoroughfare from Oxford Street to Old Street and Shoreditch. In 1878 King's Road was renamed and included in Theobalds Road.

Thieving (or Thieven, *i.e. Thieves*) **Lane,** WESTMINSTER. Great George Street nearly represents it.

And now to pass to the famous monastery of Westminster: at the very entrance of the Close thereof, is a lane that leadeth toward the west, called *Thieving Lane*, for that thieves were led that way to the Gate House, while the Sanctuary continued in force.—*Stow*, p. 169.

This place by some is called Bow Lane, from its turning passage into Broken Cross, or Long Ditch, like a bent bow. The houses are not over well built, and divers of its inhabitants drive a trade in second hand goods.—*Strype*, B. vi. p. 63.

Thomas (St.) of Acon or Acres, was a *Militia Hospitalis* "on the north side of Chepe," on the ground now occupied by Mercers' Chapel, founded by Agnes, sister of Thomas à Becket, and named after that popular saint. St. Thomas was named of Acon or Acre in consequence of the belief that Acon or Acre in Syria was captured through his miraculous interposition. The house in which à Becket was born stood on the site of the chapel dedicated to him. In the early ordinances of the City the Mayor and Alderman are directed on divers feasts and other solemn occasions to go in procession "from the church of St. Thomas de Acon to St. Paul's," and on the Wednesday "in the week of Pentecost, from St. Thomas de Acres to Saint Paul's," the terms being used indifferently.[1] The site of the chapel is now merged in Mercers' Hall and chapel [which *see*].

In the 13th Henry VIII. (1521) when the Mercers borrowed a large sum from the Prior of the Charterhouse, "the annuity or yearly rent" due upon it was to be paid "at the aulter of Seynt Thomas the Martyr, in the northe parte of the body of the chyrche of Seynt Thomas the Martyr in London, called Seynt Thomas of Acon."

In the sermon preached by Bishop Latimer before Edward VI. on April 12, 1547, he related the following anecdote:—

I had rather ye shoulde come of a naughtye minde to heare the worde of God, for noveltye, or for curiositie to here some pastime than to be awaye. I had rather ye shoulde come, as the tale is, by the gentlewoman of London. One of her neighbours mette her in the streate, and sayed Mestres whither go ye? Marry, sayed she, I am goynge to S. *Tomas of Acres*, to the sermon. I coulde not slepe al thys laste nyghte, and I am goynge now thether, I never fayled of a good nap there. And so I had rather ye shoulde go a napping to the sermons than not go at al.

Thomas (St.) The Apostle, "a proper church" in Knightrider Street, by Wringwren Lane,[2] in the ward of Vintry, destroyed in the Great Fire and not rebuilt. The church of the parish is St. Mary Aldermary.

[1] *Liber Albus*, p. 6, etc; Erasmus speaks of Becket as "Thomas Acrensis."—*Life*, by Jortin, vol. i. p. 33.   [2] *Stow*, p. 92.

Thomas (St.) Apostle, SOUTHWARK, on the north side of St. Thomas Street. The church of the dissolved Monastery or Hospital of St. Thomas in Southwark; made parochial after the dissolution of religious houses. In 1360 (34 Edward I.) the brethren of St. Thomas were allowed to celebrate divine service. Before 1489 a church was here, with chapels and altars and statues, and in 1521 the parish was known as "the parish of St. Thomas's Hospital." The living is in the gift of the governors of *St. Thomas's Hospital.* The register records the marriage, January 27, 1613, of the father and mother of John Evelyn. In 1700 the church had long been unfit for its purpose, and in 1703 a new one was erected at a cost of £3043 : 2 : 8, allowed out of the duty upon "coales and culm."

The parish is the smallest in Southwark, but it included within it the two magnificent hospitals of St. Thomas and Guy's, until the former was removed to make room for the extension of the South Eastern Railway. The sculptor of the monument of Mary Queen of Scots in Westminster Abbey, and of the remarkable tomb of Sir Roger Aston and his wives in Crayford, describes himself in the agreement, dated January 4, 1612-1613, for making and setting up the latter work, as "of St. Thomas the Apostle in Southwarke." The sculptor of the monumental bust and tomb of Shakespeare at Stratford-upon-Avon was "Gerard Johnson, a Hollander, in St. Thomas Apostells."[1] In the first edition of this work Mr. Cunningham assumed that this was St. Thomas the Apostle in the Ward of Vintry, but further inquiries convinced him that he was mistaken, and that "Gerard Johnson lived, liked Cure, in St. Thomas the Apostle, Southwark, near to the Globe Theatre, and that he must have often *seen* Shakespeare. If I am right in this conjecture, the Stratford bust becomes additionally valuable as a likeness."[2] The register of neither parish throw any light on the subject.

Thomas (St.) Hospital, ALBERT EMBANKMENT; rebuilt on 8½ acres of ground recovered from the river by the construction of the Albert Embankment, lies between Westminster Bridge and Lambeth Palace.

The old Hospital in High Street, Southwark, was founded in 1213 by Richard, Prior of Bermondsey, as an Almonry; bought at the dissolution of religious houses by the citizens of London, and opened by them as a Hospital for poor and impotent people in 1552. The building having fallen into disrepair was entirely rebuilt in 1701-1706 by public subscription. In 1862 the South Eastern Railway, requiring a portion of the site for their branch line to Charing Cross, gave by award £296,000 for the building and ground. The new building was commenced in 1868 and opened by the Queen in June 1871. It consists of 7 blocks (or pavilions as they are technically designated) of about equal size, with a smaller one between the fourth and fifth, and

[1] *Dugdale's Diary,* by Hamper, 1653, p. 79; and App. 2, 1592.   [2] Letter in *Builder,* April 4, 1866.

the medical school, a long low building with a ventilation shaft, at the Lambeth end. These pavilions have each four wards above the ground floor, with their ends towards the river, and are 125 feet long, 28 feet wide, and 15 feet high. A lower range of buildings between the pavilions and Palace Road contains meeting hall, chapel, out-patients' department, residences, etc. The building, of red brick, was constructed by Mr. H. Currey, at a cost of £500,000, of which £90,000 was paid to the Metropolitan Board for the site. The number of beds is 572, and the gross income, derived from rents aided by voluntary contributions, is about £42,200. The number of patients in 1887 was, in, 5058; out, 24,826; casualties, 62,775.

Mr. W. Rendle communicated some interesting articles in the Records of St. Thomas's Hospital to the *Antiquary* in 1889. (See vol. xx.)

Thomas (St.) à Waterings, a place of execution for the county of Surrey, situated close to the second milestone on the *Old Kent Road*, and so called from a brook, or spring, dedicated to St. Thomas à Becket. Chaucer's pilgrims passed it on their way to the shrine of St. Thomas à Becket at Canterbury:—

> And forth we riden a litel more than paas,
> Unto the waterynge of Seint Thomas,
> And there our host began his hors arreste.
> *Prologue to Canterbury Tales,* l. 820, etc.

Gerard found white saxifrage, burr-reedes, etc., "in the ditch, right against the place of execution, at the end of Southwarke, nere London called St. Thomas Waterings."

> And yf they do in dede, I pray God they may spede,
> Even as honestly
> As he that from steyling, goth to Sent Thomas Watryng
> In his yong age
> So they from pytter pattour, may come to tytter totur,
> Even the same pilgrimage.

A New Enterlude, drawen out of the Holy Scripture of Godly Queene Hester, 1561.

> For at Saynt Thomas of Watrynge, an' they strike a sayle
> Then must they ryde in the haven of hempe without fayle.
> *Morality of Hycke Scorner.*

> Host. These are the arts
> Or seven liberal deadly sciences
> Of pagery, or rather paganism,
> As the tides run! to which if he apply him,
> He may perhaps take a degree at Tyburn,
> A year the earlier; come to read a lecture
> Upon Aquinas at St. Thomas à Waterings,
> And so go forth a laureat in hemp circle![1]
> Ben Jonson, *The New Inn,* Act i. Sc. 1.

Whitehall, June 20, 1663.—The fellow that stole the heiress, was hanged on Tuesday at St. Thomas Waterings, and could get no pardon or reprieve, though the

---

[1] It is perhaps necessary to point out the punning connection which Ben Jonson strikes out between Thomas Aquinas and Thomas à Waterings'.

King by chance went by, and was told 'twas the custom then to reprieve at least, but the City petition weighed down that consideration.—Sir J. Williamson, *Corr.* vol. i. p. 55; *Cam. Soc.*, 1874.

John Henry, *alias ap* Henry, a Welchman, and author of many of the Martin Mar-Prelate tracts, was hanged at St. Thomas à Waterings, May 29, 1593; and Franklin, one of the inferior agents implicated in the murder of Sir Thomas Overbury, was executed at the same place on December 9, 1615. In 1834 occurred a remarkable recurrence to the old form. Two men had been condemned to death for a murder at Chester, but a dispute arose as to whether the execution should be carried into effect by the sheriff of the county or the sheriff of the city of Chester. Neither functionary would give way, and as, in the then state of the law, "years might elapse before this dispute could be legally determined," the Attorney-General, Sir John (afterwards Lord) Campbell, resorted to an expedient which he may relate in his own words :—

There was a great outcry by reason of the law being thus defeated. I boldly brought the convicts to the bar of the King's Bench, and prayed that execution should be awarded against them by the judges of that court. After a demurrer and long argument they were ordered to be executed by the Marshal of the King's Bench, *at St. Thomas à Waterings* in the borough of Southwark, aided by the Sheriff of Surrey, a form of proceeding which had not been resorted to for many ages. The execution took place accordingly amidst an immense assemblage, not only from the metropolis, but from remote parts of the kingdom.—*Life of Lord Campbell*, 1881, vol. ii. p. 58.

Threadneedle Street, from Princes Street, between the Bank of England and the Royal Exchange, to Bishopsgate Street. Stow calls it *Threeneedle Street*,[1] "I suppose," says Hatton, "from such a sign."[2]

The origin of the name presents considerable difficulty. Some see it in the connection with Merchant Taylors' Hall, while others suppose it refers to the arms of the needlemakers' Company—"three needles in fesse argent."

Threadneedle Street was originally *Thridneedle Street*, as Samuel Clarke dates it from his study there.—D'Israeli, *Cur. of Lit.*, 1 vol. ed., p. 259.

Dr. Plot writes it *Thredneedle Street in 1693.[3] Threadneedle Street runs from Bishopsgate Street, between the Royal Exchange and the Bank, to Princes Street; formerly it ran to the Stocks Market, the site of the present Mansion House; but the enlargement of the Bank of England and the rebuilding of the Royal Exchange curtailed it considerably. "The Old Lady in Threadneedle Street" has long been a familiar name for the Bank of England. *Observe*.—Consolidated Bank (No. 52), formerly the Hall of Commerce, on the north side, as marking where the French Church stood, and the Hospital of St. Anthony before that; Sun Fire Office, corner of Bartholomew Lane, on the site of St. Bartholomew's Church, taken down in 1840; Merchant Taylors' Hall, on the south side, entirely hid from view by a

[1] *Stow*, p. 69. [2] *Hatton*, p. 82. [3] *Letter to Evelyn*, October 2, 1693.

narrow frontage of modern buildings; the Baltic; the South Sea House. [*See* all these names.] Messrs. Prescott's Bank, No. 62.

The records of the Brewers' Company, under date 1421, relate the misconduct of one William Payne, at "the sign of the Swan by St. Anthony's Hospital, Threadneedle Street," who refused to contribute a barrel of ale to be sent to King Henry V. in France. He was fined 3s. 4d. for a swan for the Master's breakfast. Threadneedle Street was of old noted for its taverns. Sir John Hawkins, writing near the middle of the last century, says that "in that space near the Royal Exchange and Threadneedle Street, the number of taverns was not so few as twenty; on the side of the Bank there stood four; and at one of them, the Crown, it was not unusual to draw a butt of mountain, containing one hundred and twenty gallons, in gills, in a morning." The Crown was the house where Pepys was wont to "sup at the [Royal Society] Club, with my Lord Brouncker, Sir George Ent and others." It stood "behind the 'Change," on part of what is now the Threadneedle Street entrance to the Bank of England.[1] The Cock Tavern, another wine and dining house, "behind the Exchange," was built against the south wall of St. Bartholomew's Church, immediately west of Prescott and Grote's bank. It was cleared away in 1840. The Antwerp Tavern, a famous house in the early part of the 17th century, did not survive the Great Fire. Of the King's Arms and one or two more there are tokens or other memorials still extant.

The grandfather and father of Sir Philip Sidney lived in this street, in "a tenement called Lady Tate's house," on the site of a part of the House and Hospital of St. Anthony, annexed by Edward IV. to the collegiate church of St. George, in Windsor. The Dean and Canons of Windsor demised this house to Sir Henry Sidney, by an indenture, dated May 26, 1563, for the further term of sixty years, at the yearly rent of £6 : 13 : 4.[2] Sir Dudley North, before he went to the Levant, lived with "one Mr. Andrews, a packer in Threadneedle Street."

<blockquote>
This I you tell is our jolly Wassel,
And for Twelfth-night more meet too:
She works by the ell, and her name is Nell,
And she dwells in Threadneedle Street too.
Ben Jonson, *Masque of Christmas*.
</blockquote>

Three Cranes in the Vintry, "the most topping tavern in London," as Sir Walter Scott makes mine host of the Black Bear at Cumnor describe it, was situated in Upper Thames Street at the top of what is still known as *Three Cranes Lane*, immediately below Southwark Bridge. It derived its name from "three strong cranes of timber placed on the Vintry wharf by the Thames side to crane up wines there."[3] These three cranes, very clumsy machines too, are represented in Visscher's *View of London* (1616). It is probable that two out of the three were not erected till the beginning of the reign of Elizabeth,

---

[1] Burn's *Tokens*, p. 240.   [2] This indenture is now Ashmole MS., No. 1519.
[3] Stow, p. 90.

as in the times of Henry VIII.,[1] Edward VI., and Mary, one only is spoken of, and the tavern appears to have been called the Crane. Then an entry in the books of the Drapers' Company, August 14, 1518, records the burial this day of "Mrs. Elizabeth Peke, widow, from the Crayne in the Vintre," in St. Michael's Church; the Company's "best beryall clothe" being lent for the occasion, and "every of the vj berers had a sylver spoone for his labor."[2]

1552.—Thus the good Duke [Somerset], passing through a great part of the City, landing at the Crane in the Vintry, was conveyed to the tower.—Foxe's *Martyrs*, vol. vi. p. 293.

1554.—Then the first day of February the queene's grace came in hare owne persone unto the Gilde halle of Londone, and showyd hare mynde unto the Mayor, aldermen and the hole craftes of London in hare owne persone, with hare captes in hare honde in tokyn of love and pes, and went home agayne by water at the Crane in the Ventre.—*Chronicle of the Grey Friars*, p. 86.

The colophon to a black letter edition of Sir Bevis of Hampton, in David Garrick's collection, bears witness that it was "Imprynted at London in the Vinetre upon the thre Crane Wharfe by William Coplande;" but it is unluckily without date. The locality became a favourite one with the booksellers, as combining the attractions of a busy landing-place and a "topping tavern." *The Workes of a young wyt trust up with a Fardell of pretty fancies* was printed in 1577 "nigh unto the Three Cranes in the Vintree;" in 1599 E. Venge was a bookseller at the Black Bull in the same locality, and others might be enumerated.

> In whom are as much virtue, truth and honestie
> As there are true fathers in the Three Cranes of the Vintree.—
> *Damon and Pithias*, 1571.

A pox o' these pretenders to wit! Your Three Cranes, Mitre, and Mermaid men! Not a corn of true salt, not a grain of right mustard amongst them all.—Ben Jonson, *Bartholomew Fair* (1614), Act. i. Sc. 1.

> *Iniquity.* Nay, boy, I will bring thee to the bawds and the roysters
> At Billingsgate, feasting with claret-wine and oysters;
> From thence shoot the Bridge, child, to the Cranes in the Vintry,
> And see there the gimblets how they make their entry.
> Ben Jonson, *The Devil is an Ass*, 1616.

May 14, 1660.—Information was given to the Council of State that several of His Majesty's goods were kept at a fruiterer's warehouse near the Three Cranes, in Thames Street, for the use of Mistress Elizabeth Cromwell, wife to Oliver Cromwell, some time called Protector; and the Council ordered that persons be appointed to view them, and seventeen carts load of rich house stuff was taken from thence, and brought to Whitehall, from whence they were stolen.—*Mercurius Politicus Redivivus*, *Addit. MS.* in British Museum, 10, 116.

Here, after the battle of Worcester, Charles II. and Lord Wilmot had agreed to meet if they found their way to London. They were to inquire for Will Ashburnham.[3]

January 23, 1662.—After choosing our gloves we all went over to the Three Cranes Taverne, and, though the best room in the house, in such a narrow dogg-hole

---

[1] Cavendish's *Wolsey*, p. 108.   [2] Quoted by Burn, p. 241.
[3] Dalrymple, *Charles II.*, p. 108.

we were crammed, and I believe we were near forty, that it made me loath my company and victuals, and a sorry poor dinner it was too.—*Pepys.*

New Queen Street, commonly called the Three Cranes in the Vintry, a good open street, especially that part next Cheapside, which is best built and inhabited. At the lowest end of the street, next the Thames, is a pair of stairs, the usual place for the Lord Mayor and Aldermen to take water at, to go to Westminster Hall, for the new Lord Mayor to be sworn before the Barons of the Exchequer. This place with the Three Cranes is now of some account for the Costermongers, where they have their warehouses for their fruit.—*Strype,* B. iii. p. 13.

There were several other Three Crane Taverns in London. In Strype's Map of Chepe Ward (1720) a large Three Crane Tavern is represented as occupying a courtyard on the south side of the Poultry, opposite St. Mildred's Church; others were in the Old Bailey, The Savoy, St. Olave's Street, Southwark, etc. Their signs were all birds. Decker in his *Belman of London,* 1608, informs us that "the beggars of London called one of their places of rendesvous by this name."

Three Cups (The), a favourite London sign. Hatton enumerates three: on the east side of St. John Street, near Hicks's Hall; on the west side of Bread Street, near the middle; on the east side of Goswell Street, near Aldersgate Street. A fourth is mentioned by Beaumont and Fletcher:—

> You know our meetings,
> At the Three Cups in St. Giles'.
> *Beaumont and Fletcher's Works,* by Dyce, vol. iv. p. 42.

And a fifth (in Holborn), by Winstanley, in his *Lives of the Poets* (12mo, 1687, p. 208). The six houses, Nos. 16 to 21 Featherstone Buildings, occupy the site of the Three Cups Inn in High Holborn. Three shillings weekly for ever are payable out of the rents of these houses to the poor of Holborn, under the will of Lewis Owen, who died in 1624.

Three Leg Alley, FETTER LANE—Great New Street to Gough Square. In Three Leg Alley (now Pemberton Row), in the parish of St. Bride's, lived and died Thomas Flatman, the miniature painter and poet.[1]

> Flatman who Cowley imitates with pains,
> And rides a jaded Muse whipt with loose reins.—*Lord Rochester.*

In the time of Charles II., when Flatman lived in the parish of St. Bride's, Three Leg Alley was one of the best inhabited parts of the parish.

Three Nuns Inn, Nos. 10 to 13 ALDGATE HIGH STREET, is mentioned by Defoe in his Plague Year, it was a great coaching inn, and long famous for its punch. The Aldgate Station of the Metropolitan Railway occupies a part of the site of the old inn. It was rebuilt in 1880.

I doubt not but there may be some ancient persons alive in the parish who can justify the fact of this, and are able to show even in what part of the churchyard the pit lay better than I can; the mark of it also was many years to be seen in the

---

[1] Rate-books of St. Bride's, Fleet Street.

churchyard, on the surface lying in length, which goes by the west wall of the churchyard, out of Houndsditch, and turns east again into Whitechapel, coming out near the Three Nuns Inn.—Defoe, *Memoirs of the Plague*, ed. Brayley, p. 90.

Three Tuns, a famous Tavern in GUILDHALL YARD.

> Ah Ben !
> Say how or when
> Shall we thy Guests,
> Meet at those lyrick feasts
>   Made at the Sun
> The Dog, the Triple Tunne ;
> Where we such clusters had
> As made us nobly wild, not mad ?—*Herrick*, p. 413.

Compass. Three Tuns do you call this Tavern? It has a good neighbour of Guildhall, Master Pettifog.—Show a room, Boy.—Webster, *A Cure for a Cuckold*, Act. iv. Sc. 1.

General Monk lodged at this tavern on a memorable occasion in 1660.

But the next morning early, February 9 (1660), the General commanded the march of his army up into the City, without advising with any of his own officers. And having placed his main guards at the old Exchange, and other convenient places, he retired himself to the *Three Tuns Tavern*, near Guildhall, where he dispatched his orders.—Skinner's *Life of Monk*, p. 233.

Three Tuns are the arms of the Vintners' Company, and were consequently a favourite sign with Vintners. Besides the Guildhall Tavern there were in the City in the 17th century the Three Tuns in Ludgate Hill, in St. Paul's Churchyard, by the Conduit in Cheapside, in Cloth Fair, in Gracechurch Street, and one or two other places ; and there are half a dozen Three Tuns in the City now.

I went to a little eating or chop house called *The Three Tuns*, where I used to dine for 13d., including a penny to the waiter.—Jeremy Bentham, *Life*, p. 133.

Three Tuns Tavern, ST. MARGARET's HILL, SOUTHWARK. On April 27, 1768, when Wilkes was taken into custody and ordered to be committed to the King's Bench prison, the mob took out the horses on Westminster Bridge, and drew his coach along the Strand, Fleet Street, etc., to Spitalfields, where they turned the two tip-staves out of it. They then dragged the carriage to this tavern, where Wilkes alighted and made a speech to them from one of the upper windows. When he had persuaded the mob to disperse he walked quietly over to the King's Bench Prison and delivered himself to the Marshal. The house, afterwards known as " The Three Tuns Hotel and Tavern," has recently been removed in the course of local improvements, but the site is marked by *Three Tun Passage*, No. 110 Borough High Street.

Thrift Street. [*See* Frith Street, Soho.]

Throgmorton Street, LOTHBURY, the north-east corner of the Bank of England, to BROAD STREET, was so called after Sir Nicholas Throgmorton, who is said to have been poisoned by Dudley, Earl of Leicester, Queen Elizabeth's favourite. There is a monument to his memory in the Church of St. Catherine Cree. The pious Robert Nelson was living here with his mother towards the end of the 17th century.

August 6, 1694.—I directed my letter to be left for you with Madam Nelson, at her house in Throgmorton Street behind the Old Exchange.—*Bishop Bull to Robert Nelson.*

Alexander Chalmers, author of the *Biographical Dictionary*, was living here June 13, 1815. Throgmorton Street is now chiefly inhabited by stockbrokers and jobbers. *Observe.*—Drapers' Hall, on north side, and near to it the Imperial Ottoman Bank (No. 26), a handsome semi-oriental edifice erected in 1871 from the designs of Mr. Burnet, and the adjoining offices, Italian Gothic in style, built in 1870 from the designs of Mr. Chatfeild Clarke. On the south side in New Court is an entrance to the Stock Exchange, and also the back of the new buildings of the Stock Exchange. West of Drapers' Hall is the handsome new thoroughfare called *Throgmorton Avenue*, carried across the Drapers' Hall Gardens (*see* Drapers' Hall) to London Wall by Carpenters' Hall.

Tichborne Street, HAYMARKET. This once crowded thoroughfare connecting Coventry Street and Regent Street is set down as *Shug Lane* by Hatton, 1708, in Strype's Map of 1720, and in Dodsley's *London*, 1761. Strype describes it as "but meanly built, neither are its inhabitants much to be boasted of." A century and half later the description was equally applicable. In 1726 "Winter, a Poem, price 1s.," was published by J. Millar, at Locke's Head in Shug Lane, near the Haymarket, and the next bookseller to the Horse Guards. This cannot mean that there was no other book shop between Shug Lane and the Horse Guards, so must refer to a second place of business of Millar's. The north side was pulled down in connection with the opening up of Regent Circus, Piccadilly, and the formation of the Shaftesbury Avenue, and the south side was incorporated with Piccadilly.

Tilers' and Bricklayers' Company. This ancient fraternity received its first Charter of Incorporation from Queen Elizabeth, August 3, 1568. The old hall of the Company, No. 52 Leadenhall Street, has been rebuilt and is now known as *Sussex Hall*.

Tilney Street, MAY FAIR—South Audley Street to Park Lane. Soame Jenyns died here, December 18, 1787.

Tiltyard (The), at WHITEHALL, an open space over against the Banqueting House, and including part of the present Parade in St. James's Park; "a large tiltyard for noblemen and others to exercise themselves in justing, turning, and fighting at barriers."[1] Henry VIII. on May-day 1540 held a tournay here to which knights were invited from all parts of Europe, "all comers that would fight against the challengers of England." The festival lasted several days, the knights

[1] *Stow*, p. 168.

on one day jousting on horseback with swords, on another fighting on foot at the barriers; and the whole was wound up by a magnificent banquet given by the King and Queen to all the knights who had taken part in the tourney, and another on the next day to the Lord Mayor and Aldermen and their wives. Here for many years were held the annual exercises in arms in celebration of Queen Elizabeth's birthday. They were commenced by Sir Henry Lee of Ditchley and continued by Clifford, Earl of Cumberland :—

> On the 17th day of November, anno 1590, this honourable gentleman [Sir Henry Lee] together with the Earl of Cumberland [Clifford], having first performed their service in Armes, presented themselves unto her Highness [Queen Elizabeth] at the foot of the staires under the gallery window in the Tilt Yard at Westminster, where at that time her Majestie did sit, accompanied with the Viscount Turyn [Turenne], Ambassador of France, many Ladies and the chiefest Nobilitie. — *Honour, Military and Civill*, by Sir William Segar, Norroy, 1602.

In the reign of James I. there was tilting at Court on March 24, 1620, at which Prince Charles distinguished himself by his handsome display and gallant running. "He hurt Lord Montgomery in the arm." "The French Ambassador was absent because he was not allowed the preference of place over the Spanish Ambassador."[1] But to make amends to the French Ambassador, on

> *January* 8, 1621—Four couples ran to tilt to show the French Ambassador that martial pastime. Prince Charles himself ran first with Richard Buckhurst, Earl of Dorset, and broke their staves very successfully. The next couple that ran were the beloved Marquis of Buckingham and Philip Lord Herbert . . . but had very bad success in all the courses they made.—Sir S. D'Ewes's *Autobiography*, vol. i. p. 166.
>
> In April 1622—The tilting is postponed on account of the King's illness: the Prince [Charles] is disappointed, wishing to make show of a feather he received from his Spanish mistress.—*Cal. State Pap.*, 1619-1623, p. 380.
>
> *Falstaff.* And now is this Vice's dagger (Justice Shallow) become a squire; and talks as familiarly of John of Gaunt, as if he had been sworn brother to him; and I'll be sworn he never saw him but once in the Tiltyard, and then he burst his head for crowding among the Marshal's men. I saw it; and told John of Gaunt, he beat his own name, for you might have truss'd him and all his apparel into an eel-skin.—Shakespeare, *Second Part of Henry IV.*, Act iii. Sc. 2.
>
> She had a tale how Cupid struck her in love with a great Lord in the Tilt-Yard, but he never saw her; yet she in kindness would needs wear a willow-garland at his wedding.—Beaumont and Fletcher, *The Scornful Lady*, Act i. Sc. 1.
>
> The best I have seen have been the devices of Tilting whereof many were till of late reserved in the Private Gallery at Whitehall, of Sir Philip Sydney, the Earl of Cumberland, Sir Henry Leigh, the Earl of Essex, with many others; most of which I once collected with intent to publish them, but the charge dissuaded me.— Peacham, *The Compleat Gent.*, ch. xviii. p. 277, ed. 1661.
>
> And then his [Essex's] glorious feather-triumph when he caused two thousand orange-tawny feathers, in despite of Sir Walter Raleigh, to be worn in the Tilt-Yard before her Majestie's own face.—Sir Henry Wotton, *Rel. Wott.*, ed. 1685, p. 190.
>
> *Mr. Sage.* If it were in my power, every man that drew his sword, unless in the Service, or purely to defend his life, person or goods, from violence (I mean abstracted from all puncto's or whims of honour), should ride the wooden horse in the Tiltyard for such first offence.—*The Tatler*, No. 39.

---

[1] *Cal. State Pap.*, 1619-1623, pp. 133, 135.

This predecessor of ours [said Sir Roger de Coverley] you see is dressed after this manner, and his cheeks would be no larger than mine, were he in a hat as I am. He was the last man that won a prize in the Tiltyard (which is now a common street before Whitehall). You see the broken lance that lies there by his right foot; he shivered that lance of his adversary all to pieces. . . . I don't know but it might be exactly where the Coffee House [Man's] is now.—*The Spectator*, No. 109.

In the 17th century there was a Monk's Head in the Tiltyard, and as late as 1762 there was a tavern there.

Your brother . . . is excessively enamoured of London. . He says there is no wit except at the Bedford ; no military genius but at George's ; no wine but at the Star and Garter ; no turbot except at the Tilt-Yard.—*Boswell to the Hon. Andrew Erskine*, February 16, 1762.

Times Newspaper Office (The). [*See* Printing House Square.]

Tin-Plate Workers' Company. This fraternity was first incorporated by letters patent of 22 Charles II., December 29, 1670, by the title of the Master, Warden, Assistants and Commonalty of the Art and Mystery of Tin-plate Workers and Wireworkers of the City of London. A livery was first granted them in 1796. They have no hall. The tin-plate workers rank seventy-second of the City Companies.

Titchfield Street (Great), MARYLEBONE—Oxford Street to Carburton Street. *Eminent Inhabitants.*—Richard Wilson, R.A., the landscape painter, at No. 85, in 1779. P. J. Loutherbourg, R.A., the landscape painter, at No. 45, from 1776 to 1780.[1] At No. 76, the house of Joseph Bonomi, A.R.A., died James Barry, the painter and friend of Edmund Burke, February 22, 1806. William Collins, R.A., so favourably known by his English scenes of coast and country life, was born in this street in 1787. William Huntington's (S.S.) first chapel, erected by subscription in this street, was burnt down in 1810, when his followers built him a much more spacious edifice in Gray's Inn Road.

Titchfield Street (Little), GREAT PORTLAND STREET. At No. 4 lived (1779) William Doughty, who engraved so many capital mezzotint portraits after Sir Joshua Reynolds. At No. 9, under the care of a Mrs. Gibson, Lord Nelson's daughter by Lady Hamilton, Horatia Nelson Ward Thompson was brought up. She died Sunday, March 6, 1881, at Beaufort Villa, Woodriding, Pinner, Middlesex, in her 81st year.

Token House Yard, LOTHBURY (north side of the Bank of England) to TELEGRAPH STREET, was so called from a mint-house, or office established here for the issue and change of the royal farthing tokens coined under a patent granted in 1635-1636 by Charles I. to Henry Howard, Lord Maltravers and Sir Francis Crane, Knights.[2] It may have been placed here on account of its proximity to Lothbury, where the brassfounders resided, but here was the house and garden of Thomas Howard, Earl of Arundel, the father of Lord Maltravers, who was

---

[1] Royal Academy Catalogues for these years. [2] Burn's *Tokens*, p. xlvii.

believed at the time to have an interest in the patent. Token House Yard was built on the site of the Earl of Arundel's ground by Sir William Petty, our earliest writer on Political Economy, and ancestor of the Marquis of Lansdowne. It is mentioned by Hatton, 1708; and Strype, 1720, describes it as "a large place, with well built houses, fit for good inhabitants, especially the row on the east side, which have courtyards with brick walls before them. At the upper end of this yard is a small passage down steps into Bell Alley in Coleman Street Ward."

Passing through Token House Yard in Lothbury, of a sudden a casement violently opened just over my head, and a woman gave three frightful screeches, and then cried, "Oh Death, Death, Death!" in a most inimitable tone, and which struck me with a horror and a chillness in my very blood. There was nobody to be seen in the whole street, neither did any other window open; for people had no curiosity now in any case; nor could any body help one another; so I went on to pass into Bell Alley.—Defoe, *Memoirs of the Plague*, ed. Brayley, p. 117.

Token House Yard now consists of "well built houses" and offices, mostly occupied by stock and share brokers and solicitors. Observe on the west side the *Auction Mart*, erected in 1864, from the designs of Mr. S. Clarke, on the removal of the old Auction Mart in Bartholomew Lane. [*See* Auction Mart.]

Tom's Coffee-house, in BIRCHIN LANE, CORNHILL.

After all that has been said of Mr. Garrick, envy must own that he owed his celebrity to his merit; and yet, of that himself seemed so diffident that he practised sundry little but innocent arts to insure the favour of the public. He kept up an interest in the city by appearing, about twice in a winter, at Tom's Coffee House in Cornhill, the usual rendezvous of young merchants at 'Change time; and frequented a club established for the sake of his company in the Queen's Arms Tavern in St. Paul's Church Yard.—Hawkins's *Life of Johnson*, p. 433.

Tom's Coffee House, May 30th, 1770.—There is such a noise of business and politics in the room that my inaccuracy in writing here is highly excusable. My present profession obliges me to frequent places of the best resort.—*Chatterton to his Sister* (Dix's *Life*, p. 275).

It is not, however, certain which was the Tom's Coffee-house that Chatterton felt himself called upon to frequent as a place of the best resort.

Tom's Coffee-house, in DEVEREUX COURT. [*See* Devereux Court.]

There is a letter of Pope's in print, addressed to Fortescue, his "counsel learned in the law," at this coffee-house.[1]

Tom's Coffee-house, No. 17 RUSSELL STREET, formerly GREAT-RUSSELL STREET, COVENT GARDEN,

stood on the north side over-against *Button's*, and was so called after Captain Thomas West, the landlord, who, November 26, 1722, threw himself in a delirium, occasioned by gout, out of a back-window two stories high, and died immediately.[2]

---

[1] Bowles's *Pope*, vol. x. p. 206.   [2] *Historical Register* for 1722, p. 52.

With careful brows at Tom's and Will's they meet,
And ask, who did elections lose or get.
                                    Rowe, *Epilogue to Tamerlane*, 4to, 1703

After the Play the best company generally go to Tom's and Will's Coffee Houses near adjoining, where there is playing at Picket, and the best of conversation till midnight. Here you will see blue and green ribbons and Stars sitting familiarly, and talking with the same freedom as if they had left their quality and degrees of distance at home.—Macky, *A Journey through England*, 8vo, 1722, vol. i. p. 172.

Mr. Murphy said he remembered when there were several people alive in London who enjoyed a considerable reputation merely from having written a paper in *The Spectator*. He mentioned particularly Mr. Ince, who used to frequent Tom's Coffee House.—Boswell. *Life of Johnson*, 8vo ed., p. 505.

The house in which I reside (17 Great Russell Street, Covent Garden) was the famous Tom's Coffee House, memorable in the reign of Queen Anne; and for more than half a century afterwards: the room in which I conduct my business as a coin dealer, is that which, in 1764, by a guinea subscription among nearly seven hundred of the nobility, foreign ministers, gentry, and geniuses of the age—was made the card-room, and place of meeting for many of the now illustrious dead, and remained so till 1768, when a voluntary subscription among its members induced Mr. Haines, the then proprietor (and the father of the present occupier of the house), to take in the next room westward, as a coffee-room; and the whole floor *en suite* was constructed into card and conversation rooms.—William Till, *Descriptive Particulars of English Coronation Medals*.

The Craftsman in 1727 was printed for R. Francklin "under Tom's Coffee-house in Covent Garden;" and here lived Lewis, the bookseller, the original publisher of Pope's "Essay on Criticism."[1] The house was pulled down and rebuilt in 1865.

Tomlin's Town, or TOMLIN'S NEW TOWN, has now vanished from the Directories, but in Maps of 1810-1819 it is the name given to the site of the present Oxford Square and Cambridge Square, at the back of the St. George's burial-ground and west of the Edgeware Road.

Took's Court, CHANCERY LANE—Cursitor Street to Furnival Street. Richard Brinsley Sheridan, in the last year of his life, was an inhabitant of a spunging-house in this court. Here he wrote his angry letter to Whitbread, printed in Moore's *Life* (vol. ii. p. 242). The court is now largely occupied by law stationers and law writers. No. 21 is the Chiswick Press or Whittingham's well-known printing office, and the offices of the *Athenæum* and *Notes and Queries* are next door.

Tooley Street, SOUTHWARK, near the south foot of London Bridge, is a corruption of St. Olave's Street,[2] and derives its name from the adjoining church of *St. Olave, Southwark*. To the advertisement put forth in Cromwell's time by Thomas Garway, the founder of Garraway's Coffee-house, is appended the following notice:—

Advertisement.—That Nicholas Brook, living at the sign of the Frying-Pan in St. Tulies Street against the Church, is the only known man for making of Mills for grinding of Coffee powder, which Mills are by him sold from 40 to 45 shillings the Mill.—Ellis's *Letters*, second series, vol. iv. p. 61.

---

[1] Prospectus of Carte's *Life of Ormond*, dated February 2, 1733.
[2] Henry Machyn's *Diary*, p. 303, speaks of "Sent Towllys in Southwarke." In the 17th century such transitional forms as St. Tules, St. Soules, St. Tooleys, are to be met with.

Tooley Street was known as Short Southwark, to distinguish it from the High Street or Long Southwark; about the church was a small liberty called the Berghené or Little Burgundy. [*See* Berghené.] It will long continue to be famous from the well-known story related by Canning of "the three tailors of Tooley Street," who formed a meeting for redress of popular grievances, and began their petition to the House of Commons, "*We* the people of England." On the south side, approached by a narrow court, was St. Saviour's Grammar School, removed for the railways. In White Horse Court, immediately adjoining, was the inn of the Prior of Lewes, in Suffolk. A transition Norman crypt, part of the inn, was remaining within the last forty years. East of St. Olave's Church was the inn of the Abbot of St. Augustine, afterwards in the possession of the St. Leger, Grenville and Fletcher families, a memorial of it being preserved to our own day in *Sillinger* Wharf. Tooley Street has been much altered of late years, and a portion of the south side swept away for the approaches and extensions of the South Eastern and London and Brighton Railways. On the north side are several new piles of large and substantial warehouses. Here is a memorial tablet to "James Braidwood, Superintendent of the London Fire Brigade, who was killed near this spot in the execution of his duty, at the great fire on the 22nd June, 1861, erected by the "M" Division of Police."

Torrington Square. No. 55 was the last London residence of Sir Nicholas Harris Nicolas, editor of Nelson's Despatches and Letters, and author of the very useful *Chronology of History*. He died at Boulogne in 1848. The Rev. Joseph Hunter, also a well-known antiquary (d. 1861), resided at No. 30.

Tothill, a manor in Westminster, possessed, in the reign of Henry III., by John Maunsel, who rose to the dignity of Chancellor of England. Here he entertained the King and his court, the company being so numerous that they were accommodated in a large tent, or tents; his own manor-house being too small.

"'Toot hills" occurs in many parts of England, in the several forms of "Toot," Tut, Tot, Tote, etc. The origin of Tothill, in this instance, appears to be that given in an ancient lease, which particularises a close called the Toothill, otherwise the Beacon Field. There is a place of the same name near Caernarvon Castle also called the Beacon Hill. The Toot Hill was the highest ground in a locality, which would be used as a post of observation, for the erection of a beacon, or a stronghold. Thus in the second book of Samuel, v. 7, where the authorised version has "Nevertheless David took the stronghold of Zion," Wicliffe renders it "Forsooth David toke the *tote hill* Syon"; and in verse 9, "So David dwelt in the fort, and called it the city of David," Wicliffe has "David dwelt in *the tote hill*." Canon Isaac Taylor [1] thinks that "places called Tot Hill, Toot Hill or Tooter Hill . .

[1] *Words and Places*, p. 326.

may possibly have been seats of Celtic worship." It has been supposed by Mr. G. Lawrence Gomme that this was the site of the Folk-moot at Westminster. (*See Antiquary*, voL xi., p. 6.)

Tothill Fields (particularly so called) comprised that portion of land between Tothill Street, Pimlico, and the river Thames; this is a somewhat uncertain boundary—but it is the best that can be given, or, as Jeremy Bentham says, writing in 1798, "If a place could exist of which it could be said that it was in no neighbourhood, it would be Tothill Fields." [1]

In early times Tothill Fields was the theatre of great tournaments and ceremonies. On occasion of the coronation of Eleanor, Queen of Henry III., 1236, "royal solemnities and goodly jousts" were held in Tothill Fields; and in 1256—

> John Mansell, the King's councillor and priest, did invite to a stately dinner the Kings and Queens of England and Scotland, Edward the King's son, Earls, Barons, and Knights, the Bishop of London, and divers citizens, whereby his guests did grow to such a number, that his house at Totehill could not receive them, but that he was forced to set up tents and pavilions to receive his guests, whereof there was such a multitude that seven hundred messes of meat did not serve for the first dinner.—*Stow*, p. 176.

It was also the place in which were held wagers of battle.

> In the same yere [1441] was a fightyng at the Tothill between too thefes, a pelour and a defendant, and the pelour hadde the field and victory of the defendant withinne thre strokes.—*A Chronicle of London*, 4to, 1827, p. 128.

Such scenes were not uncommon in Tothill Fields. Stow describes a challenge of this kind, which should have been fought in Trinity term, 1571, respecting "a certain Manour, and demaine lands belonging thereunto, in the Isle of Harty, adjoining to the Isle of Sheppey in Kent," with all his usual interesting minuteness of dress and circumstance, but the passage is too long to cite.[2] Later it was a frequent scene of more private combats.

> *Staines.* I accept it: the meeting place?
> *Spendall.* Beyond the Maze in Tuttle.
> *Staines.* What weapon?
> *Spendall.* Single rapier.
> *Staines.* The time?
> *Spendall.* To morrow.
> *Staines.* The hour?
> *Spendall.* 'Twixt nine and ten.
> *Staines.* 'Tis good. I shall expect you.—*Greene's Tu Quoque.*

> *Lod.* I have expected you these two hours, which is more than I have done to all the men I have fought withal since I slew the High German in Tuttle.—Shirley, *The Wedding*, Act iv. Sc. 3 (1629).

The last duel in Tothill Fields of which we have any account took place, May 9, 1711, between Sir Cholmley Dering, Knight of the Shire for Kent, and a gentleman of the name of Thornhill. Swift tells Stella on the same day, on the authority of Dr. Freind (who had just left the dying man), "They fought at sword and pistol this morning in Tuttle

---

[1] *Twenty-eighth Report of Finance Committee*, p. 79.   [2] *Stow*, by Howes, ed. 1631, p. 669.

Fields, the pistols so near that the muzzles touched. Thornhill discharged first, and Dering having received the shot discharged his pistol as he was falling, so it went into the air. . . . This makes a noise here, but you don't value it." On the 21st of the following August Swift completes the story. "Thornhill, who killed Sir Cholmley Dering, was murdered by two men at Turnham Green last Monday night: as they stabbed him they bid him remember Sir Cholmley Dering." Dering was to have been married the week after the duel.

Punishments for various offences, and particularly, as would seem, for necromancy and witchcraft, were often inflicted here;[1] and archery and other sports practised.

> According to my Lord's saying, my cousin Thomas and I, the Sunday after I had your letters, when the King [Henry VIII.] *schote yn Tothylle* [no date, but before 1514], I spoke two times unto the King's Grace for your servants, and he asked of me where they were, "let me see them," and I called them unto the King and Nott shot afore him. My Lord Treasurer said good words of you and them both, and so did Mr. Cumton [William Compton], M. Brandon [Duke of Suffolk] and Mr. Garnys.
> —*Trevelyan Papers*, vol. ii. p. 10.

The privilege of holding a weekly market and an annual fair was granted to the Abbot of Westminster by Henry III. in 1248, the market to be held in Tuthill, the fair in St. Margaret's churchyard, but in 1542 the fair also was removed to Tothill Fields. As long as they remained unbuilt on Tothill Fields were used for military musters and as public playing-ground.

> The men of Hartfordshire lie at Mile-End,
> Suffolk and Essex traine in Tuttle Fields,
> The Londoners and those of Middlesex
> All gallantly prepar'd in Finsbury.
> Decker, *The Gentle Craft*, vol. i. p. 11.

> *August* 25, 1651.—The Trained Bands of London, Westminster, etc., drew out into Tuttle Fields, in all about 14,000, the Speaker and divers members of the Parliament were there to see them.—*Whitelocke*.

> We have done him no injury, but once I stroke his shins at foot-ball in Tuttle.—Randolph, *Hey for Honesty* (1651), *Works*, p. 474.

Locke in the directions for a foreigner visiting London, which he wrote in 1679, says he may see "shooting in the long-bow and stobball in Tothill Fields." Howell refers to the gardens.

> *July* 25, 1629.—I have sent you herewith a hamper of melons, the best I could find in any of Tothill Field Gardens.—*Howell to Sir Arthur Ingram* (*Letters*, p. 214).

The Maze, represented in Hollar's View of Tothill Fields, was made anew in 1672.[2]

> There is a Maze at this day in Tuthill Fields, Westminster, and much frequented in the summer time in fair afternoons.—Aubrey, *Anec. and Trad.*, p. 105.

In emergencies Tothill Fields were used as a place of sepulture after a fashion very strange to modern notions. Thus, in the plague year of 1665, Pepys writes:—

[1] Walcott's *Westminster*, p. 325. [2] Churchwardens' Accounts of St. Margaret's, Westminster.

July 18.—I was much troubled this day to hear at Westminster how the officers do bury the dead in the open Tuttle-fields, pretending want of room elsewhere; whereas the new chapel churchyard was walled-in at the publick charge in the last plague time, merely for want of room; and now none, but such as are able to pay dear for it, can be buried there.—*Pepys.*

The churchwardens' Accounts of St. Margaret's, Westminster, exhibit a payment of thirty shillings to Thomas Wright, for sixty-seven loads of soil "laid on the graves in Tothill Fields, wherein 1200 Scotch prisoners, taken at the Battle of Worcester, were buried."

A Bridewell House of Correction or Prison was built here in 1655, enlarged in 1788, and continued to be used till the opening of the New Prison in 1834. On the side of the Sessions House, Broad Sanctuary, is fixed the doorway of the old Tothill Fields Prison, which was removed in 1836. A bear-garden was in existence here as late as 1793.[1] Vincent Square occupies part of the site.

Tothill, Tuthill, or Tuttle Street, from the Broad Sanctuary to the Broadway, WESTMINSTER.

Tothill Street, a large street in Westminster, between Petty France (west) and the Old Gate House (east).—*Hatton,* 8vo, 1708, p. 84.

Such is Hatton's description; but the *Gatehouse* has long been level with the ground, and *Petty France* has since been transformed into *York Street.* Our notions have also changed about its size—no one would call it "a large street" now. In the 16th and 17th centuries there were mansions on both sides of Tothill Street, those on the south having gardens reaching to the Park. Stourton House, at the southwest end of the street, was the residence of the Lords Dacre of the South; opposite to it lived Lord Grey de Wilton; and at Caron House died, 1612, Sir George Carew. At Lincoln House Sir Henry Herbert had his office as Master of the Revels in 1664-1665.[2] On May 28, 1623, Endymion Porter wrote to his wife Olive that "Lady Carey in Tuttle Street" is to pay her "£112 for money lent by him to her son in Spain."[3] Before the middle of the 17th century smaller houses were beginning to be built here.

1634.—The tobacco licences go on apace, they yield a good fine and a constant yearly rent, but the buildings yield not that profit that was expected as yet. My Lord Maynard compounded for £500 for some twenty houses built in Tuttle Street.—Garrard, *Strafford Letters,* vol. i. p. 263.

Betterton, the actor, was born in this street some time in 1635. Thomas Amory, the author of *John Buncle,* died here in 1789, aged ninety-seven. In a house near the Gate House Edmund Burke lived for some time.

Ben Jonson, in the *Staple of News,* speaks of—

All the news of Tuttle Street, and both the Alm'ries, the two Sanctuaries, long and round Woolstaple, with King's Street and Cannon Row to boot.

---

[1] Walcott's *Westminster,* p. 329.   [2] *Walcott,* p. 282.   [3] *Cal. State Pap.,* 1619-1623, p. 590.

On the north side, No. 72, was a curious old inn, *The Cock* [*see the Cock Tavern*], but it was cleared away in 1873, with all the other houses on that side, to make way for the Royal Aquarium. No. 4 was a later Cock Tavern, and is now the Aquarium Tavern. This is a modern house with an old stone, dated 1671, let into the front. In the old house Thomas Southerne, the poet (1660-1746)

> Tom sent down to raise
> The price of prologues and of plays—

lived for many years at Mr. Whyte's, an oilman in Tothill Street, against Dartmouth Street.[1] He died there, May 26, 1746. The house, was still an oilman's shop in 1850. It has been pulled down some years. The destruction on the south side has not been so sweeping; but several houses at the east end were taken down for the formation of Victoria Street and the Westminster Palace Hotel. In all there are only eighteen houses left in Tothill Street.

Tottenham Court Road, a market road, or street, leading from Oxford Street to the prebendal manor of Tothill, Totenhall, or Totenham Court, described in Domesday, and originally appertaining to the Dean and Chapter of St. Paul's. In 1560 the manor was demised to Queen Elizabeth for ninety-nine years, in the name of Sir Robert Dudley. In 1639, twenty years before the expiration of Queen Elizabeth's term, a lease was granted to Charles I., in the name of Sir Henry Vane. In 1649, being seized as Crown land, the manor was sold to Ralph Harrison, Esq., of London, for the sum of £3318 : 3 : 11. At the Restoration it reverted to the Crown; and in 1661 was granted by Charles II., for the term of forty-one years, in payment of a debt, to Sir Henry Wood. The lease was next possessed by Isabella, Countess of Arlington, in the reign of Charles II., from whom it descended to her daughter, the Duchess of Grafton; and in this way was inherited by the family of the Fitzroys, Dukes of Grafton, descended from Barbara Villiers, Duchess of Cleveland, the notorious mistress of Charles II. The fee-simple of the manor, subject to the payment of £300 per annum to the prebendary of Tottenham, was subsequently vested in the Hon. Charles Fitzroy, first Lord Southampton, and his heirs, by an Act passed in 1768, and *Grafton Street, Fitzroy Square*, etc., not long after erected on the grounds belonging to the manor. The Manor House stood at the north-west extremity of the present road, and was subsequently transformed into a public house, known as the Adam and Eve, now in the Hampstead Road. There is a view of it in Wilkinson, with a plan exhibiting the exact locality of the house. Here, in Tottenham Court Road, and in front of the Adam and Eve tea gardens, Hogarth has laid the scene of his *March to Finchley*. Here "the famous pugilistic skill of Broughton and Slack was publickly exhibited, upon an uncovered stage, in a yard open to the North Road;"[2] and here, in the tea-gardens,

[1] Letter to Dr. Richard Rawlinson (Malone's *Life of Dryden*, p. 176.)
[2] Smith, *Book for a Rainy Day*, p. 26.

(May 16, 1785), Lunardi effected his second descent from his balloon. The grounds attached to the Adam and Eve were spacious and convenient, and the company at one time respectable. As the new buildings increased it became a place of a more promiscuous resort—so much so, indeed, that the music-room was abolished, the skittle-grounds destroyed, and the gardens dug up for the foundation of the present "Eden Street, *Hampstead Road*," the first turning on the left hand from Tottenham Court Road. The first notice of Tottenham Court, as a place of public entertainment, contained in the books of the parish of St. Giles's-in-the-Fields, occurs under the year 1645, when Mrs. Stacye's maid, and two others, were fined a shilling a-piece "for drinking at *Tottenhall Court* on the Sabbath daie,"[1] but Ben Jonson seems to refer to this road when he makes Quarlous say to Win-wife in *Bartholomew Fair*, 1614, "Because she is in possibility to be your daughter-in-law, and may ask your blessing hereafter when she courts it to Totnam to eat cream."[2] Tottenham Fields were until a comparatively recent date a favourite place of resort.

> When the sweet-breathing spring unfolds the buds,
> Love flies the dusty town for shady woods.
> Then Tottenham fields with roving beauty swarm.
> Gay, *Epistle to Pulteney.*

1773.—Notwithstanding Tottenham Court Road was so infested by the lowest order, who kept what they called a *Gooseberry Fair*, it was famous at certain times of the year, particularly in summer, for its booths of regular theatrical performers, who deserted the empty benches of Drury Lane Theatre, under the mismanagement of Mr. Fleetwood, and condescended to admit the audience at sixpence each. Mr. Yates, and several other eminent performers had their names painted on their booths.—J. T. Smith, *Book for a Rainy Day*, p. 27.

Tottenham Court Road does not boast an illustrious roll of inhabitants. Pinkerton writes to Lord Buchan, January 29, 1793, "My address is 120 Tottenham Court Road;" and Chateaubriand said that about the same time he lodged in a garret in Tottenham Court Road for six shillings a week.

December 5, 1818.—On passing through Tottenham Court Road we saw an unusual congregation of blackguards at the entrance of a passage called Cock Court. Asked what was the matter? "Randall lives here, Sir." It was the Conqueror's levée.—Thomas Moore's *Diary*.

Moore had been at a fight between this Randall and another the day before, and was now on his way to visit his daughter's grave at Hornsey. Moore's "congregation of blackguards" were not the worst of that colour who have been met with here. Brothers the Prophet declared that he "had seen the Devil walking leisurely up Tottenham Court Road."[3]

Observe.—Meux's brewhouse at the south-east corner, famous for its porter vats and artesian well. Opposite to it :—

A large circular boundary stone, let into the pavement in the middle of the highway, exactly where Oxford Street and Tottenham Court Road meet in a right angle.

---

[1] Parton's *History of St. Giles's*, p. 139.   [2] Ben Jonson, *Bartholomew Fair*, Act i. Sc. 1.
[3] Southey's *Espriella's Letters*, vol. ii. p. 231.

When the charity boys of St. Giles's parish walk the boundaries, those who have deserved flogging are whipped at this 'stone,[1] in order that as they grow up they may remember the place, and be competent to give evidence should any dispute arise with the adjoining parishes. Near this stone stood St. Giles's Pound.—*J. T. Smith*, p. 22.

On the west side of Tottenham Court Road was Whitefield's Tabernacle, built by subscription under the auspices of the Rev. George Whitefield, the founder of the Calvinistic Methodists. The first stone was laid May 10, 1756, and the chapel opened November 7 following—Whitefield preaching on the occasion to a very crowded audience. Mrs. Whitefield (d. 1768) is buried here; and here, on a monument to her memory, is an inscription to her husband, who, dying in New England in 1770, was buried at Newbury Port, near Boston. John Bacon, R.A., the celebrated sculptor, died August 7, 1799, is buried under the north gallery; here too lies the once popular preacher and writer, the Rev. A. M. Toplady, who died August 11, 1788. The chapel was pulled down in April 1890.

Tottenham Street, TOTTENHAM COURT ROAD, west side, near Whitefield's Tabernacle. Richard Wilson, the landscape painter's "last abode in London was at a mean house in Tottenham Street, Tottenham Court Road, in which he occupied the first and second floors, almost without furniture."[2] The *Prince of Wales Theatre* (which *see*) was formerly Francis Pasquale's concert-room. It was afterwards purchased and enlarged by the directors of the Concerts of Antient Music, and subsequently converted into a theatre, under the names of the Tottenham Street, Regency, Royal West London, Queen's, and finally the Prince of Wales Theatre.

> Muse are the Tottenham Street subscribers poor?
> Will Drury keep some pence from Tottenham's pocket?
> Does threatening bankruptcy extend a gloom
> O'er the proud walls of Tottenham's royal room?
> Peter Pindar, *Ode upon Ode*.

Tower (The) of London, the most celebrated fortress in Great Britain, stands immediately without the City walls, on the left or Middlesex bank of the Thames, about ½ mile below London Bridge.

This Tower is a citadel to defend or command the city; a royal palace for assemblies or treaties; a prison of state for the most dangerous offenders; the only place of coinage for all England at this time; the armoury for warlike provisions; the treasury of the ornaments and jewels of the crown; and general conserver of the most records of the King's courts of justice at Westminster.—*Stow*, p. 23.

Tradition has carried its erection many centuries earlier than our records:—

> This way the king will come, this is the way
> To Julius Cæsar's ill-erected Tower.
> Shakespeare, *King Richard II.*, Act v. Sc. 1.
> *Prince.* Where shall we sojourn till our coronation?
> *Gloster.* Where it seems best unto your royal self.

---

[1] This refers to the last quarter of the 18th century. The boys do not now receive their whippings here. [2] Wright's *Life of Wilson*, p. 5.

> If I may counsel you, some day or two
> Your highness shall repose you at the Tower.
> *Prince.* I do not like the Tower, of any place.
> Did Julius Cæsar build that place, my lord?
> *Buck.* He did, my gracious lord, begin that place,
> Which, since, succeeding ages have re-edified.
> *Prince.* Is it upon record, or else reported
> Successively from age to age, he built it?
> *Buck.* Upon record, my gracious lord.
>   Shakespeare, *King Richard III.*, Act iii. Sc. 1.
>
> Ye towers of Julius, London's lasting shame,
> With many a foul and midnight murder fed.
>   Gray, *The Bard.*

There is no authority, however, to confirm tradition in the remote antiquity assigned to the Tower. No part of the existing structure is of a date anterior to the keep, or the great square tower in the centre called the White Tower, and this, it is well known, was built by William the Conqueror, circ. 1078. During excavations made for building purposes in 1772 and 1777 some ruins of an old stone wall 9 feet in thickness, and of which the cement was exceedingly hard, were found near the White Tower, and these were either the remains of an earlier edifice, or a portion of the bulwarks of the old wall. Some old Roman coins were also found at the same time.

> I find in a fair register book, containing the acts of the Bishops of Rochester, set down by Edmond de Hadenham, that William I., surnamed Conqueror, built the Tower of London, to wit, the great white and square tower there, about the year of Christ 1078, appointing Gundulph, then Bishop of Rochester, to be principal surveyor and overseer of that work.—*Stow*, p. 17.

Rochester Castle has been commonly ascribed to Gundulph, Bishop of Rochester (the William of Wykeham of his age), but it is now known to be of later date. The keep (now a shell) of the castle at Malling is the only known example left of his military architecture.

The Tower is surrounded by a dry ditch, capable of being flooded at high water, running all round the outer wall. The western, northern and eastern sides are protected by casemated ramparts rising from the ditch, with bastions at the angles, and surmounted with short heavy guns. The defence along the southern or river front consists of a low rampart, guarded by a chain of small forts.

The "Ballium wall," of great thickness and solidity, and varying from 30 to 40 feet in height, is probably of about the same date as the White Tower. It formerly formed a continuous inner bulwark, but when Cromwell obtained possession of the Tower he caused the Royal Palace, which occupied the south-eastern portion of the space enclosed by this wall, to be pulled down, and with this went a great part of the Ballium wall on the eastern and southern sides. The wall has lately been rebuilt on the eastern side. The only vestige of the Palace left is the buttress of an old archway adjoining the Salt Tower. This inner wall was flanked with thirteen protecting towers, of which twelve still remain in a more or less "restored" form. The *Lanthorn Tower*, which stood between the Salt and Wakefield Towers, was removed on the erection of the Ordnance Office. In 1882 these warehouses were removed, and the Lanthorn Tower rebuilt, the general effect of the buildings from the river being thus greatly improved.

The principal entrance to the Tower is from Great Tower Hill, at the south-east angle of the outer wall, through the Middle and Byward Towers. The Lion Tower formerly stood just without the Middle Tower, and it was here the Menagerie was kept. On the south or river front are two entrances, the *Queen's Stairs* by the Byward Tower, and *Traitors' Gate*, under St. Thomas Tower (used only for the reception of prisoners of rank).

> On through that gate misnamed, through which before
> Went Sidney, Russell, Raleigh, Cranmer, More.
>
> Roger's *Human Life*.

At the south-east angle is the Irongate, "a great and strong gate, but not usually opened," facing Little Tower Hill.

The *White Tower* was restored by Sir Christopher Wren, who faced the windows with stone in the Italian style and otherwise modernised the exterior, but the interior has been but little altered. This Tower is 116 feet from north to south by 96 from east to west, and is three storeys high. The exterior walls are 15 feet in thickness, and the interior is divided by a wall 7 feet thick, running north and south; another running east and west subdivides the eastern of these divisions into unequal parts. These partition walls, extending through all three storeys, form one large and two smaller rooms on each floor. The smallest division of the ground floor, known as Queen Elizabeth's armoury, is a vaulted room, and in reality forms the crypt of St. John's Chapel. On the north side of this room is a cell 10 feet long and 8 wide in the thickness of the wall, and receiving light only through the doorway. These rooms are said to have been Sir Walter Raleigh's prison, where he wrote the *History of the World*. Over this room, on the first floor, and extending through both first and second floors, is St. John's Chapel, one of the finest specimens of Norman ecclesiastical architecture which we possess. The massive columns and general simplicity of character of this chapel give it a very solemn and impressive appearance. A triforium, extending over the aisles and semicircular east end, probably served to allow the queen and her ladies to attend the celebration of mass unseen by the congregation below. The chapel is 55 feet in length, 31 feet wide, and 32 feet high to the crown of the vault. The nave between the pillars is 14 feet 6 inches wide; the aisles are about half the width, and 13 feet 6 inches high. The triforium is 11 feet 9 inches high. It was dismantled in 1558. At the foot of the winding stairs leading up to St. John's Chapel and situate in the centre of the south side of the White Tower, two skeletons were found in July 1674, supposed to be the remains of the two murdered princes, sons of Edward IV. They were removed in 1678 by Charles II.'s orders to Westminster Abbey, and placed in a small sarcophagus against the east wall of the north side of Henry VII.'s chapel.

St. John's Chapel was long used as a repository for records, but on the erection of the Record Office the records were transferred thither in 1857, and the chapel once more dedicated to its proper uses, divine service being now occasionally celebrated therein. It was in this chapel that, at the creation of the Order of the Bath by Henry IV. at his coronation, the forty-six noblemen and gentlemen first installed knights thereof performed the chivalrous ceremony of watching their armour from sunset to sunrise. Here, kneeling at his prayers before the altar, Brackenbury is said to have received and rejected Richard's proposal to murder the young princes. And here the remains of Elizabeth of York, Queen to Henry VII., lay in state in 1503 previous to her magnificent funeral. The Council Chamber, in the second storey, and communicating directly with the triforium of the chapel, was the old council room of the English Sovereigns. Here Richard II. was compelled formally to resign his crown to Henry of Bolingbroke.

I have been King of England, Duke of Aquitaine and Lord of Ireland about twenty-one years, which seigniory, royalty, sceptre, crown, and heritage I clearly resign here to my cousin Henry of Lancaster; and I desire him here in this open presence, in entering of the same possession, to take this sceptre.—Froissart.

Here also was Hastings denounced, arrested and hurried to the block by Crookback Richard: the gallery which, cut in the solid wall, runs round the whole of the Council Chamber probably serving as the hiding-place for the soldiers whom Richard had in readiness to carry out his foul plans. The vaults of this Tower formed dungeons of the most dismal kind. Here was one called by the suggestive name of "Cold Harbour"; another "Little Ease," where Guy Fawkes was for some time confined, was a mere hole in the wall closed by a heavy door, and was so small that the prisoner could neither stand upright nor lie down, but was obliged to remain in a bent and cramped position. In another of these dungeons was placed the rack, and here the victims could be tortured without fear of their cries being heard. The principal tower in the outer line of defence is the *St. Thomas Tower*, a fine old edifice, under which extends the wide stone archway, guarded by two strong water-gates, already mentioned as Traitors' Gate. From the landing-place here a flight of stone steps leads to the gate of the *Bloody Tower*. The heavy portcullis of this latter gateway is one of the very few still to be found in England in working order. The Bloody Tower, the only rectangular tower of the inner ward, is the traditional scene of the murder of the young princes Edward and Richard. The *Bell Tower* is asserted to have been Elizabeth's lodging when confined in the Tower by her sister: here also Bishop Fisher is said to have been confined; but during the restoration of the White Tower a few years ago a small cell was discovered in the vaults with an inscription, pointing to the White Tower as the Bishop's more probable prison. The *Beauchamp* or *Cobham Tower* was probably built about the beginning of the 13th century, and received its name from Thomas de Beauchamp, Earl of Warwick, confined here in 1397 previous to his banishment to the Isle of Man. This tower was for many years the principal state prison, and the walls of the prison room (with its two recesses probably formerly used as cells) on the first floor are covered with inscriptions chiselled in it by various occupants. Amongst the innumerable prisoners from time to time confined here may be mentioned : Anne Boleyn (in the upper chamber) 1554; John Dudley, Earl of Warwick, eldest son of the Duke of Northumberland, condemned to death for his part in the conspiracy to place Lady Jane Grey on the throne, was reprieved but died shortly afterwards in his prison room: he left a most elaborate carving, in which his brothers Ambrose, Robert, Guilford, and Henry are symbolised by twigs of oak with acorns, roses, geraniums and honeysuckle. Guilford Dudley, 1554; and Lady Jane Grey (who probably inscribed her name " Jane " on the north wall), 1554; Edmund and Arthur Poole (the great grandsons of George, Duke of Clarence and brother of King Edward IV.), who were confined here from 1562 till their death; Philip Howard, Earl of Arundel, confined here from 1584 to his death in 1595; his body was buried in St. Peter's ad Vincula, but removed to Arundel in 1624; Dr. John Store, Chancellor of Oxford under Queen Mary, and noted for his cruel persecution of the Protestants, executed at Tyburn for high treason 1571, etc. etc. The *Devereux Tower*, standing at the north-west angle of the inner Ballium wall, derives its name from Robert Devereux, Earl of Essex. The *Flint Tower*, of which all but the foundation walls are of modern date, contained dungeons of such a rigorous character as to receive the designation of Little Hell. The *Bowyer Tower*, formerly the residence of the King's Bowyer or " Master Provider of the King's Bows," is the reported scene of the murder of George Duke of Clarence in 1474. The fire of 1841, which destroyed the barracks and great storehouse, originated in the Bowyer Tower. The *Brick Tower* is assigned as the place of confinement of Lady Jane Grey during a portion of the period of her incarceration. In the *Jewel* or *Martin Tower* the Crown jewels were formerly kept; it also served as a prison-house. The *Constable* and *Broad Arrow Towers* served the same purpose. The *Salt Tower* is probably of Norman origin, and contains the curious sphere with the signs of the zodiack engraved on its walls, May 30, 1561, by Hugh Draper of Bristol, committed on a charge of sorcery. The *Wakefield Tower*, which received its name from the imprisonment of the Yorkists after the battle of Wakefield, is now the receptacle for the jewels.

The *Jewel House* within the Tower was kept by a particular officer called "The Master of the Jewel House." He was charged with the custody of all the Regalia, had the appointment in his gift of goldsmith to the King, and "was even esteemed the first Knight Bachelor of

England, and took place accordingly."[1] The office was held by Thomas Cromwell, afterwards Earl of Essex. The perquisites and profits were formerly very large, but after the Restoration they diminished so much that Sir Gilbert Talbot, the then Master, was tacitly permitted by the King to show the Regalia to strangers.

> The Master of the Jewel House hath a particular Servant in the Tower intrusted with that great Treasure, to whom (because Sr Gilbert Talbot was retrenched in all the perquisites and profitts of his place, and not able to allow him a Competent Salary) his Majesty doth tacitly allow him that he shall shew the Regalia to Strangers ; which furnished him with so plentifull a livelyhood that Sr Gilbert Talbot, upon the death of his Servant there, had an offer made to him off 500 old broad peeces of gold for the place.—*Harl. MS.*, 6859, p. 29.

The treasures of the jewel house were diminished during the Civil Wars under Charles I. The plate amongst the Regalia "which had crucifixes or superstitious pictures" was disposed of for the public service;[2] and what remained of the plate itself was subsequently delivered up to the trustees for sale of the King's goods to raise money for the service of Ireland.[3] The Regalia is arranged in the centre of a well-lighted room, with an ample passage for visitors to walk round. *Observe*—St. Edward's Crown, made for the coronation of Charles II. to replace the old crown (lost in the confusion of the Civil Wars), which Edward the Confessor was supposed to have worn, and used in the coronations of all our Sovereigns since his time. This is the crown placed by the Archbishop of Canterbury on the head of the Sovereign at the altar, and the identical crown which Blood stole from the Tower on May 9, 1671. The New State Crown, made for the coronation of Queen Victoria; composed of a cap of purple velvet, enclosed by hoops of silver, and studded with a profusion of diamonds; it weighs one pound and three-quarters. The large unpolished ruby is said to have been worn by Edward the Black Prince; the sapphire is of great value, and the whole crown is estimated at £111,900. The Prince of Wales's coronet, of pure gold, unadorned by jewels. The Queen Consort's Crown, of gold, set with diamonds, pearls, etc. The Queen's Diadem, or circlet of gold, made for the coronation of Mary of Modena, Queen of James II. St. Edward's staff, of beaten gold, 4 feet 7 inches in length, surmounted by an orb and cross, and shod with a steel spike. The orb is said to contain a fragment of the true Cross. The Royal Sceptre, or Sceptre with the Cross, of gold, 2 feet 9 inches in length; the staff is plain, large table diamond; The Rod of Equity, or Sceptre with the Dove, of gold, 3 feet 7 inches in length, set with diamonds, etc. At the top is an orb, banded with rose diamonds, and surmounted with a cross, on which is the figure of a dove with expanded wings. The Queen's Sceptre with the Cross, smaller in size, but of rich workmanship, and set with precious stones. The Queen's Ivory Sceptre (but called the Sceptre of Queen Anne Boleyn), made for Mary of Modena, consort of James II. It is

---

[1] *Harl. MS.*, 6859, p. 17; MS. dated 1680. [2] *Whitelocke*, ed. 1732, p. 106. [3] *Ibid.*, p. 418.

mounted in gold, and terminated by a golden cross, bearing a dove of white onyx. Sceptre found behind the wainscoting of the old Jewel Office in 1814; supposed to have been made for Queen Mary, consort of William III. The Orb, of gold, 6 inches in diameter, banded with a fillet of the same metal, set with pearls, and surmounted by a large amethyst supporting a cross of gold. The Queen's Orb, of smaller dimensions, but of similar fashion and materials. The Sword of Mercy, or Curtana, of steel, ornamented with gold, and pointless. The Swords of Justice, Ecclesiastical and Temporal. The Armillæ, or Coronation Bracelets, of gold, chased with the rose, fleur-de-lys, and harp, and edged with pearls. The Royal Spurs, of gold, used in the coronation ceremony whether the Sovereign be King or Queen. The Ampulla for the Holy Oil, in shape of an eagle. The Gold Coronation Spoon, used for receiving the sacred oil from the ampulla at the anointing of the Sovereign, and supposed to be the sole relic of the ancient regalia.[1] The Golden Salt Cellar of State, in the shape of a castle. Baptismal Font, of silver gilt, used at the christening of the Royal children. Silver Wine Fountain, presented to Charles II. by the corporation of Plymouth.

The Tower Menagerie was one of the sights of London up to the reign of William IV. and the removal of the few animals that remained to the Zoological Gardens in the Regent's Park. Henry I. kept lions and leopards, and Henry III. added to the collection.

I read that in the year 1235, Frederick the emperor sent to Henry III. three leopards, in token of his regal shield of arms wherein those leopards were pictured; since the which time those lions and others have been kept in a part of this bulwark [the Tower], now called the Lion Tower, and their keepers there lodged. King Edward II., in the 12th of his reign, commanded the Sheriffs of London to pay to the keepers of the King's leopard in the Tower of London sixpence the day for the sustenance of the leopard, and three halfpence a day for diet of the said keeper. More in the 16th of Edward III., one lion, one lioness, and one leopard, and two cat lions in the said Tower, were committed to the custody of Robert, the son of John Bowre.—*Stow*, p. 19.

September, 1586.—The keeping of the Lyones in the Tower graunted to Thomas Gyll and Rafe Gyll with the Fee of 12*d*. per diem, and 6*d*. for the Meat of those Lyons.—Lord Burghley's *Diary* in Murdin, p. 785.

A century ago the lions in the Tower were named after the reigning Kings; and it was long a vulgar belief "that when the King dies, the lion of that name dies after him." Addison alludes to this popular error in his own inimitable way :—

Our first visit was to the lions. My friend [the Tory Fox Hunter], who had a great deal of talk with their keeper, enquired very much after their health, and whether none of them had fallen sick upon the taking of Perth, and the flight of the Pretender? and hearing they were never better in their lives, I found he was extremely startled: for he had learned from his cradle that the lions in the Tower were the best judges of the title of our British Kings, and always sympathised with our Sovereigns.—Addison, *The Freeholder*, No. 47.

The Menagerie was removed in November 1834. The present refreshment-room, by the ticket-house, occupies the site.

[1] *Archæological Journal*, vol. i. p. 269.

The Armouries contain a very fine and valuable collection of armour and weapons. This collection was historically arranged by Sir Samuel Meyrick, and rearranged and classified by J. R. Planché in 1869. Amongst this collection are also many of the old instruments of torture, etc., but we must refer to the Official Catalogue for particulars.

Eminent Persons confined in the Tower.—Wallace; Roger Mortimer, 1324; John, King of France; Charles, Duke of Orleans, father of Louis XII.; The duke, who was taken prisoner at the battle of Agincourt, acquired a very great proficiency in our language. A volume of his English poems, preserved among the Royal MSS. in the British Museum, contains the earliest known representation of the Tower, and has often been engraved. Queen Anne Boleyn, executed May 19, 1536, by the hangman of Calais, on a scaffold erected within the walls of the Tower; Queen Katherine Howard, fourth wife of Henry VIII., beheaded on a scaffold erected within the walls of the Tower, February 14, 1541-1542; Lady Rochford was executed at the same time. Sir Thomas More, 1534; Archbishop Cranmer; Protector Somerset, 1551-1552; Lady Jane Grey, beheaded on a scaffold erected within the walls of the Tower, February 12, 1554; Sir Thomas Wyatt, beheaded on Tower Hill, April 11, 1554; Robert Devereux, Earl of Essex, beheaded on a scaffold erected within the walls of the Tower, February 25, 1601.

It is said I was a prosecutor of the death of the Earl of Essex, and stood in a window over-against him when he suffered, and puffed out tobacco in disdain of him. But I take God to witness I had no hand in his blood, and was none of those that procured his death. My Lord of Essex did not see my face at the time of his death, for I had retired far off into the Armoury, where I indeed saw him, and shed tears for him, but he saw not me.—Sir Walter Raleigh's Last Speech.

Sir Walter Raleigh. He was on three different occasions a prisoner in the Tower; once in the reign of Queen Elizabeth, on account of his marriage, and twice in the reign of King James I. Here he began his *History of the World;* here he amused himself with his chemical experiments; and here his son, Carew Raleigh, was born. Lady Arabella Stuart, and her husband William Seymour, afterwards Duke of Somerset. Seymour escaped from the Tower.

In the meane while Mr. Seymour, with a Perruque and a Beard of blacke Hair, and in a tauny cloth suit, walked alone without suspition from his lodging out at the great Weste Doore of the Tower, following a Cart that had brought him billets. From thence he walked along by the Tower Wharf by the Warders of the South Gate, and so to the Iron Gate, where Rodney was ready with oares for to receive him. —*Mr. John More to Sir Ralph Winwood,* June 8, 1611 (*Winwood,* vol. iii. p. 280).

Sir Thomas Overbury: he was committed to the Tower on April 21, 1613, and found dead on September 14 following, having been poisoned at the instigation of the profligate Countess of Somerset. Sir John Eliot, who wrote here his *Monarchy of Man;* he died in the Tower, November 27, 1632. Earl of Strafford, 1641. Archbishop Laud, 1640-1543. John Selden. Lucy Barlow, the mother of the Duke of Monmouth. Cromwell discharged her from the Tower in July 1656.[1] Sir William Davenant. Villiers, second Duke of Buckingham. Sir Harry Vane, the younger. Sir William Coventry.

March 11, 1668-1669.—Up and to Sir W. Coventry to the Tower. . . . We walked down to the Stone Walk, which is called, it seems, my Lord of Northumberland's walk, being paved by some one [2] of that title who was prisoner there: and at the end of it there is a piece of iron upon the wall with his armes upon it, and holes to put in a peg for every turn they make upon that walk.—*Pepys.*

Earl of Shaftesbury; Earl of Salisbury, temp. Charles II. When Lord Salisbury was offered his attendants in the Tower he only asked for his cook. The King was very angry. William, Lord Russell, 1683; Algernon Sidney, 1683; Seven bishops, June 8, 1688; Lord Chancellor Jeffreys, 1688; the great Duke of Marlborough, 1692. Sir Robert Walpole, 1712 (Granville, Lord Lansdowne, the poet, was afterwards confined in the same apartment, and has left a copy of verses on the occasion.) Harley, Earl of Oxford, 1715; William Shippen, M.P. for Saltash, for saying, in the House of Commons, of a speech from the throne by George I., "that the second paragraph of the King's speech seemed rather to be calculated for the meridian of Germany than Great Britain; and that 'twas a great misfortune that the King was a stranger to our language and constitution." He is the "downright Shippen" of Pope's poems. Bishop Atterbury, 1722.

How pleasing Atterbury's softer hour,
How shone his soul unconquered in the Tower!—POPE.

At his last interview with Pope Atterbury presented Pope with a Bible. When Atterbury was in the Tower Lord Cadogan was asked, "What shall we do with the man?" His reply was, "Fling him to the lions." Dr. Freind; here he wrote his *History of Medicine.* Earl of Derwentwater; Earl of Nithsdale; Lord Kenmuir. Lord Nithsdale escaped from the Tower, February 28, 1715, dressed in a woman's cloak and hood, provided by his heroic wife, which were for some time after called "Nithsdales." The Earl of Derwentwater and Lord Kenmuir were executed on Tower Hill. The history of the Earl of Nithsdale's escape, contrived and effected by his countess with admirable coolness and intrepidity, is given by the countess herself, in a letter to her sister, printed in the appendix to Cromek's *Remains of Nithsdale and Galloway Song,* p. 311. Lords Kilmarnock, Balmerino, and Lovat, 1746. The block on which Lord Lovat was beheaded is preserved in the Armoury. John Wilkes, 1762; Lord George Gordon, 1780; Sir Francis Burdett, April 6, 1810. [*See* Piccadilly.] Arthur Thistlewood, March 3, 1820. [*See* Cato Street.

Persons born in.—Carew Raleigh (Sir Walter Raleigh's son); Mrs. Hutchinson, the biographer of her husband; Countess of Bedford, (daughter of the infamous Countess of Somerset, and mother of William Lord Russell).

The chief officer of the Tower is the Constable, a dignity dating from the Conquest, and first held by Geoffrey de Mandeville. Langton,

[1] *Whitelocke,* p. 649.   [2] Henry, ninth Earl.

Archbishop of Canterbury, Hubert de Burgh, Sir Thomas Fairfax, the Duke of Wellington, Sir John Fox Burgoyne, and Lord Napier of Magdala, are amongst the familiar historical characters who have held the post of Constable of the Tower. The present (1890) Constable is Field-Marshal Sir Daniel Lysons. [*See* St. Peter's ad Vincula.]

The entrance to the Tower is from Tower Hill by the western gate. Admission from ten to four by tickets, for the Armoury and White Tower, 6d.; and for the Crown Jewels 6d. each person; but on Mondays and Saturdays free.

Tower Hamlets (The), certain parishes, or hamlets, and liberties without the jurisdiction of the City of London, and formerly within the liberties of the Lieutenant of the Tower. These liberties include Hackney, Norton Folgate, Shoreditch, Spitalfields, Whitechapel, East Smithfield, St. Katherine's, Wapping, Ratcliffe, Shadwell, Limehouse, Poplar, Blackwall, Bromley, Old Ford, Mile End, Bethnal Green, etc. By the Reform Act of 1831 they were constituted a Parliamentary Borough, returning two members to represent their interests in the House of Commons. By the Reform Act of 1867 the borough was divided into the parliamentary boroughs of Hackney and the Tower Hamlets, each to return two members to Parliament. At the census of 1881 the parliamentary borough contained 438,910 inhabitants. By the Reform Act of 1885 Hackney was divided into north, central, and south, each returning one member; and the Tower Hamlets into Whitechapel, St. George's, Limehouse, Mile End, Stepney, Bow, and Bromley and Poplar, each returning one member.

Tower Hill, the high ground to the north-west of the *Tower*.

From and without the Tower ditch west and north is the Tower Hill, sometime a large plot of ground, now greatly straitened by encroachments (unlawfully made and suffered) for gardens and houses. . . . Upon this Hill is always readily prepared, at the charges of the City, a large scaffold and gallows of timber, for the execution of such traitors or transgressors as are delivered out of the Tower, or otherwise, to the sheriffs of London, by writ, there to be executed.—*Stow*, p. 49.

When we came upon the Hill, the first object that more particularly affected us, was that emblem of destruction, the scaffold.—Ned Ward's *London Spy*, pt. 13.

The scaffold was removed about the middle of the last century.

In 1543 Marillac the French Ambassador lived on Tower Hill, and the Duke of Norfolk (son of the victor of Flodden) and his brother, Lord William Howard, frequently paid him "mysterious midnight visits."[1] Lady Raleigh lodged on Tower Hill while her husband was a prisoner in the *Tower*.

The Lady Raleighe must understand his Ma⁹ Expresse Will and comandment that she resort to her house on Tower Hill or ellswhere wth her women and sonnes to remayne there, and not to lodge hereafter w^thin the Tower.—*Orders concerning the Tower of London, to be observed by the Lieutenant* (Sir W. Wade's *Reg.*, 1605, 1611; *Addit. MSS. Brit. Mus.*, No. 14,044).

William Penn, the founder of Pennsylvania, was born on Tower Hill, October 14, 1644.

[1] *Froude*, vol. iv. p. 250.

Your late honoured father dwelt upon Great Tower Hill on the east side, within a court adjoining to London Wall.—*P. Gibson to William Penn, the Quaker* (Sir W. Penn's *Life*, vol. ii. p. 615).

At a public-house on Tower Hill, known by the sign of the Bull, whither he had withdrawn to avoid his creditors, Otway, the poet, died (it is said of want), April 14, 1685. In a cutler's shop on Tower Hill Felton bought the knife with which he stabbed the first Duke of Buckingham of the Villiers family; it was a broad, sharp, hunting knife, and cost one shilling. The second duke often repaired in disguise to the lodging of a poor person, "about Tower Hill," who professed skill in horoscopes.[1] Smith has engraved a view of a curious old house on Tower Hill, enriched with medallions evidently of the age of Henry VIII., and similar to those at old Whitehall and at Hampton Court.

Executions on Tower Hill.—Bishop Fisher, June 22, 1535; Sir Thomas More, July 6, 1535.

Going up the scaffold, which was so weak that it was ready to fall, he said hurriedly to the Lieutenant, "I pray you, Master Lieutenant, see me safe up, and for my coming down let me shift for myself."—Roper's *Life*.

Cromwell, Earl of Essex, July 28, 1540; Margaret, Countess of Shrewsbury, mother of Cardinal Pole, May 27, 1541; Earl of Surrey, the poet, January 21, 1547; Thomas, Lord Seymour of Sudeley, the Lord Admiral, beheaded March 20, 1549, by order of his brother the Protector Somerset; The Protector Somerset, January 22, 1552; Sir Thomas Wyatt, 1554; John Dudley, Earl of Warwick and Northumberland, 1553; Lord Guilford Dudley (husband of Lady Jane Grey), February 12, 1553-1554; Sir Gervase Elways or Helwys, Lieutenant of the Tower, hanged for his share in the murder of Sir Thomas Overbury; Earl of Strafford, May 12, 1641; Archbishop Laud, January 10, 1644-1645; Sir Harry Vane, the younger, June 14, 1662; "The trumpets were brought under the scaffold that he might not be heard"[2]; William Howard, Lord Viscount Stafford, December 29, 1680, beheaded on the perjured evidence of Titus Oates and others; Algernon Sidney, December 7, 1683.

Algernon Sidney was beheaded this day; died very resolutely, and like a true rebel, and republican.—*Duke of York to Prince of Orange*, December 7, 1683.

Duke of Monmouth, July 15, 1685; Sir John Fenwick, January 28, 1697; Earl of Derwentwater and Lord Kenmuir, implicated in the Rebellion of 1715; Lords Kilmarnock and Balmerino, August 18, 1746.

Kilmarnock was executed first, and then the scaffold was immediately new strewn with sawdust, the block new covered, the executioner new dressed, and a new axe brought. Then old Balmerino appeared, treading the scaffold with the air of a general, and reading undisturbed the inscription on his coffin.—*Walpole to Mann*, August 21, 1746.

Simon, Lord Lovat, April 9, 1747. He was not only the last person beheaded on Tower Hill, but the last person beheaded in this country.

[1] Clarendon's *Autobiography*, vol. iii. p. 27.   [2] *Pepys*, June 14, 1662.

The Tribulation on Tower Hill, mentioned by Shakespeare, has puzzled his commentators; the reference seems to be to a Puritan congregation, but it is hard to see why they should be ready to endure "the youths that thunder at a playhouse."

Porter. These are the youths that thunder at a playhouse, and fight for bitten apples; that no audience but the Tribulation of Tower Hill, or the limbs of Limehouse, their dear brothers, are able to endure.— Shakespeare, *Henry VIII.*, Act v. Sc. 3.

Among the miscellaneous titles of City ordinances in Book iv. of the *Liber Albus* is one of a "Grant of the Hermitage near the garden of his lordship the King upon Towrhille."[1]

Tower Royal, WATLING STREET, in Vintry Ward, so called, according to Stow, from an ancient tower or messuage of the Kings of England, but really from the adjacent street of the *Reole* or *Riole*, "which was built (in the 13th century probably) by the Merchants of the Vintry, who imported wine from the town of La Reole, near Bordeaux."[2]

Tower Royal was of old time the King's House. King Stephen was there lodged; but sithence called the Queen's Wardrobe. The princess, mother to King Richard II., in the fourth year of his reign was lodged there; being forced to fly from the Tower of London, when the rebels possessed it.—*Stow*, p. 27.

This Tower and great place was so called of pertaining to the kings of this realm, but by whom the same was first built, or of what antiquity continued, I have not read more than that in the reign of Edward I., the 2nd, 4th, and 7th years, it was the tenement of Simon Beawmes [Beauvais]; also that in the 36th of Edward III., the same was called the Royal [the Riole] in the parish of S^t. Michael de Paternoster, and that in the 43rd of his reign, he gave it by the name of his inn called the Royal, in the city of London, in value twenty pounds by year, unto his college of S^t. Stephen at Westminster.—*Stow*, p. 92.

In early records it is invariably called "la Real," "la Reole," "la Riole," or "la Ryal or Ryole;" and it is described simply as a "tenement;" I have never found an instance of its being called a "tower." At the close of the reign of Henry III. it was held by one Thomas Bat, citizen of London, who demised it to Master Simon of Beauvais, surgeon to Edward I.; this grant was confirmed by that sovereign by charter in 1277 (Rot. Cart. 5 Edw. I. m. 17.—*Placita de Quo Warranto*, p. 461). This Simon of *Beauvais* figures in Stow and Pennant as Simon de Beawmes. In 1331 Edward III. granted "la Real" to his consort Philippa, for the term of her life, that it might be used as a depository for her wardrobe (Rot. Pat. 4 Edw. III., 2d part, m. 15). By Queen Philippa it was extensively repaired, if not rebuilt, and the particulars of the works executed there by her direction, may be seen in the Wardrobe Account of the sixth year of her reign, preserved in the Cottonian MS. Galba E. iii., fo. 177, et seq.; this account is erroneously attributed in the catalogue to Eleanor, consort of Edward I. One Maria de Beauvais, probably a descendant of Master Simon, received compensation for quitting a tenement which she held at the time Philippa's operations commenced. In 1365 Edward III. granted to Robert de Corby, in fee, "one tenement in the street of la Ryole, London," to hold by the accustomed services. Finally, in 1370, Edward gave the "inn (hospitium) with its appurtenances called le Reole, in the city of London," to the canons of St. Stephen's, Westminster, as of the yearly value of £20 (Rot. Pat. 43 Edw. III., m. 24).

It is thus sufficiently clear that in the thirteenth and fourteenth centuries this place was not called *Tower Royal:* nor does there appear to be any ground for sup-

---

[1] *Liber Albus*, p. 477.   [2] Riley, *Memorials*, vol. xx.

posing that it was so named in earlier times, or, indeed, that it was ever occupied by royalty before it became Philippa's wardrobe.—T. Hudson Turner, in *Notes and Queries*, No. 8.

The earliest notices of the building Mr. Riley discovered in the City archives are of A.D. 1318 and 1320, in both of which it is called *La Riole*. When Stow wrote it had been "neglected and turned into stabling for the King's horses; and is now (1598) letten out to divers men, and divided into tenements." What remained of it was entirely destroyed in the Great Fire.

Tower Street (Great), TOWER HILL to LITTLE TOWER STREET by Idol Lane.

> This is the way
> To Julius Cæsar's ill-erected Tower.
> Shakespeare, *Richard II.*, Act v. Sc. 1.

When the profligate Earl of Rochester, under the name of "Alexander Bendo," played the part of a mountebank physician in the City, he took up his lodgings in Tower Street, next door to the Black Swan, at a goldsmith's house, where he gave out that he was sure of being seen "from 3 of the clock in the afternoon till 8 at night."

Being under an unlucky accident, which obliged him to keep out of the way, he disguised himself so that his nearest friends could not have known him, and set up in Tower Street for an Italian mountebank, where he (had a stage and) practised physic some weeks not without success.—Burnet's *Life*, p. 37, ed. 1680.

Observe.—On the south side, No. 48, the Czar's Head.

Having finished their day's work [Peter the Great and his boon companions] they used to resort to a public-house in Great Tower Street, close to Tower Hill, to smoke their pipes and drink beer and brandy. The landlord had the Czar of Muscovy's head painted and put up for his sign, which continued till the year 1808, when a person of the name of Waxel took a fancy to the old sign, and offered the then occupier of the house to paint him a new one for it. A copy was accordingly made from the original, which maintains its station to the present day as the sign of the "Tzar of Muscovy."—Barrow's *Life of Peter the Great*, p. 83.

The house has since been rebuilt, and the sign removed, but the name remains; and out of Trinity Square is Muscovy Court. On the north side, by Tower Hill, is the church of Allhallows, Barking.

Tower Street (Little), from GREAT TOWER STREET to EASTCHEAP. Here Thomson composed his poem of *Summer*.

I go on Saturday next to reside at Mr. Watts's academy in Little Tower Street, in quality of Tutor to a young gentleman there.—*Thomson to Aaron Hill*, May 24, 1726.

When you honour me with an answer, please to direct for me at Mr. Watts's academy in Little Tower Street.—*Ibid.*, June 7, 1726.

Tower Street Ward, one of the twenty-six wards of London, and so called from its contiguity to the *Tower of London*. It is bounded on the north by *Fenchurch Street*, on the south by the *Thames*, on the east by *Tower Hill*, and on the west by *Billingsgate*. Stow enumerates three churches in this ward — *Allhallows, Barking ; St. Olave's, Hart*

Street; St. Dunstan's-in-the-East. The *Custom House,* and two Halls of Companies, the *Clothworkers'* and *Bakers',* are also in this ward—the extreme ward of the City to the east upon the Thames.

Tower Subway (The), a tunnel under the Thames from Tower Hill to Tooley Street, constructed in 1869-1870 by Mr. P. Barlow, C.E. The subway is remarkable for simplicity, celerity, and economy of construction rather than for commercial success. It was formed by excavating a tunnel through the clay bed of the Thames by means of a wrought-iron tubular shield, 8 feet in diameter, which was pushed forward, as the cutting advanced, by powerful screw-jacks. The tunnel was lined with a tube formed of cast-iron rings, 7 feet in diameter, firmly bolted together, the space between this tube and the clay being filled with an impermeable blue-lias cement. The work was carried through at the average rate of 9 feet a day, and completed for £16,000. The tunnel is reached at each end by a shaft about 60 feet deep. When first opened passengers were conveyed through the tunnel in an omnibus drawn by small steam-engines fixed at the Tower and Tooley Street ends. Some difficulties occurring in the working this plan was abandoned and it was found necessary to make passengers walk.

Town Ditch.

Town Ditch, a broad passage just without the City wall, between Christ's Hospital and Little Britain . . . and so called from the ditch that was formerly without the walls of the City.—*Hatton,* p. 83.

The Town Ditch, without the wall of the City, which partly now remaineth, and compassed the wall of the City, was begun to be made by the Londoners in the year 1211, and was finished in the year 1213, the 15th of King John. This ditch was then made of 200[1] feet broad . . . was long carefully cleansed and maintained, as need required; but now of late neglected and forced either to a very narrow and the same a filthy channel, or altogether stopped up for gardens planted and houses built thereon.—*Stow,* p. 8.

A portion of the playground fronting the grammar school at Christ's Hospital is still called "The Ditch." [*See* Houndsditch.]

Town's End (The), an old name for that part of Pall Mall west of the Haymarket. Sir Robert Naunton, author of *Fragmenta Regalia,* was living in "The Town's End" in 1632.[2] There was also a Town's End Lane at Hockley in the Hole; and another in Thames Street, in which two pirates are reported to be concealed in December 1616.

Toynbee Hall, 28 COMMERCIAL STREET E., was founded in 1884, and is supported by voluntary contributions. The institution is managed by a council elected by members of the Universities Settlement Association and by committees of the residents. The objects are "to educate citizens in the knowledge of one another, to provide teaching for those willing to learn, and recreation to those who are weary."

[1] At p. 186 he says 204 feet.   [2] Rate-books of St. Martin's.

Trafalgar Square, CHARING CROSS, a spacious square at the junction of Whitehall, Cockspur Street, the Strand, St. Martin's Lane, and Pall Mall East, where the *Royal Mews* and the *Bermudas* stood, commenced in 1829, and completed, as it now appears, from designs furnished in 1841 by Sir Charles Barry; Barry's original designs (rejected as too costly) were on a much grander scale.[1] The square derives its name from Lord Nelson's last victory. It is said to have cost, in granite work alone, upwards of £10,000. The north side of the square is occupied by the National Gallery; on the west side are the Union Club and the College of Physicians, both designed by Sir Robert Smirke; at the north-east angle is the fine portico of St. Martin's-in-the-Fields, by James Gibbs, and on the east side are Morley's Hotel and the west central branch Post Office. The south side is open to Whitehall. The fountains, of Peterhead granite, were designed by Barry and made by Messrs. M'Donald and Leslie of Aberdeen. They are supplied with water by two artesian wells, one 395 feet deep, in front of the National Gallery, the other 300 feet deep, in Orange Street, which are carried by a tunnel to a tank capable of containing 70,000 gallons. The Nelson column, on the south side of the square, was designed by William Railton, and carried out 1840-1843, but not completed until 1846-1849. The statue on the top (18 feet high, and formed of two stones from the Granton Quarry) was the work of E. H. Baily, R.A. It has been styled "the beau ideal of a Greenwich pensioner." The capital is of bronze, cast from cannon recovered from the wreck of the *Royal George.* The statue was set up November 4, 1843.

The bronze bas-reliefs on the four sides of the base of the column are—the Death of Nelson, by Mr. Carew; the Battle of the Nile, by Mr. Woodington; the Bombardment of Copenhagen, by Mr. Ternouth; and the Battle of St. Vincent, by Mr. Watson. The colossal bronze lions erected in 1867 on the salient pedestals at the four angles—studies from nature by Sir Edwin Landseer, are grand in their majestic repose. It is to be regretted, however, that they are repetitions of the same model. The total cost of the column has been about £46,000. The equestrian statue of George IV., by Sir Francis Chantrey, at the north-east corner of the square, was originally ordered for "the top of the marble arch" in front of Buckingham Palace—now at the Oxford Street entrance to Hyde Park. The statue was commenced in 1829, under an express order from the King himself, and the sum agreed upon was 9000 guineas. Of this sum one-third was paid, in January 1830, by the King himself; a second instalment, upon the completion of a certain portion of the work, by the Department of Woods and Forests; and the third and last instalment, in 1843, after the artist's death, by the Lords of the Treasury. The statue of General Sir Henry Havelock, at the south-east, is by W. Behnes; and that of Sir Charles Napier, at the south-west, by G. G. Adams. The statue

[1] *Life of Sir C. Barry*, by his son, p. 122.

of General Gordon in the centre of the square is the work of Hamo Thornycroft, R.A. (1888). In 1875 were set up, under the direction of the Astronomer Royal, official "Secondary Standards of Length," along a solid granite platform erected for the purpose at the foot of the north wall of the square, for its entire length of 259½ feet. The measures comprise standards of the surveying land-chain of 66 feet, with divisions of 10 links each; and the building land-chain of 100 feet, with divisions of 10 feet, the first division of 10 feet being subdivided into feet; mural standards of the imperial yard, 2 feet, 1 foot, and subdivided inches. The defining lines of the several measures are bronze blocks let into the granite, and the exact measurement is in the middle of each line.

Traitors' Gate. [*See* Tower.]

Travellers' Club (The), PALL MALL, next door to *The Athenæum*, originated soon after the peace of 1814, in a suggestion of Lord Londonderry, then Lord Castlereagh, for the resort of gentlemen who had resided or travelled abroad, as well as with a view to the accommodation of foreigners, who, when properly recommended, receive an invitation for the period of their stay.[1] Here Prince Talleyrand often played a game at whist. With all the advantage of his great imperturbability of face, he is said to have been an indifferent player. The present Club House, designed by Sir Charles Barry—the design based on that of the Villa Pandolfini at Florence—in 1830-1832, is deservedly admired. The Carlton Terrace front has been injured by the erection of a smoking-room on the attic. The Club is limited to 800 members. Each member pays 30 guineas on admission, and an annual subscription of 10 guineas. Rule 6 directs, "That no person be considered eligible to the Travellers' Club who shall not have travelled out of the British Islands to a distance of at least 500 miles from London in a direct line."

Treasury Buildings, WHITEHALL, a range of buildings between the Horse Guards on one side and Downing Street on the other, and now consisting of the Treasury, Education, and Privy Council offices. The Treasury is so called from its being the office of the Lord Treasurer or Lord High Treasurer: an office of great importance, first put into commission in 1612, on Lord Salisbury's death, and so continued with very few exceptions till abolished in 1816. The last Lord Treasurer was the Duke of Shrewsbury, in the reign of Queen Anne, but the last acting Lord Treasurer was the duke's predecessor, Harley, Earl of Oxford, the friend of Pope and Swift. The Prime Minister of the country is usually First Lord of the Treasury. He has a salary of £5000 a year, and an official residence in Downing Street. In the Treasury all the national money transactions are conducted. The Lord High Treasurer used formerly to carry a white staff, as the mark of his office. The royal throne still

[1] *Quarterly Review*, No. cx. p. 481.

remains at the head of the Treasury table. The present *façade* towards the street was designed (1846-1847) by Sir Charles Barry, R.A., replacing a *façade*, the work of Sir John Soane in 1824-1828, for the Council Chamber, a handsome room incorporated in the new buildings. The old Treasury, a stone building fronting the Horse Guards' Parade, was erected in 1733, from the designs of W. Kent, and is only a portion of a much more extensive front.

Trig Stairs, TRIG LANE, UPPER THAMES STREET; so called after John Trigge, owner of the stairs in the reign of Edward III. Trigg Lane is on the south side of Upper Thames Street, opposite Lambeth Hill. There is a Trig Wharf still, but the stairs have disappeared.

> A pair of stairs they found, not big stairs,
> Just such another pair as Trig Stairs.—
> Cotton's *Virgil Travestie*, B. 1.

The motion or puppet show of Hero and Leander, in Ben Jonson's *Bartholomew Fair*, is thus described by Littlewit, the author:—

> I have only made it a little easy and modern for the times, that's all. As for the Hellespont, I imagine our Thames, here; and the Leander I make a dyer's son about Puddle Wharf, and Hero a wench o' the Bankside, who going over one morning to Old Fish Street, Leander spies her land at Trig Stairs, and falls in love with her.

And again—

> Leander does ask, Sir, what fairest of fairs,
> Was the fare he landed but now at Trig Stairs.

For Calamy's Adventure at Trig Stairs, *see* his *Autobiography*, vol. ii. p. 138.

Trinity Chapel, CONDUIT STREET. [*See* Conduit Street.]

Trinity Church, CHURCH STREET, MINORIES (formerly Little Minories)—the first turning on the left hand from Aldgate—the church of the Priory of the Holy Trinity, founded by Matilda, Queen of Henry I., A.D. 1108. It escaped the Fire of 1666, and being very old, was taken down in the year 1706, and rebuilt.[1]

> Here [in the Little Minories] is the Trinity Minories Church, which pretends to privileges, as marrying without license.—*R. B., in Strype*, B. ii. p. 28.

On the north side of the chancel is a monument to William Legge, groom of the bedchamber and lieutenant-general of the ordnance to King Charles I. (d. 1672). Here his son, the first Earl of Dartmouth, and his grandson, the second earl, and annotator of Burnet, are both buried. In the church is preserved in a tin box a man's head, which the tradition of the place affirms to be that of Henry Grey, Duke of Suffolk, father of Lady Jane Grey, who was beheaded February 23, 1554.

Trinity Court, ALDERSGATE STREET. [*See* Aldersgate Street.]

Trinity House, on the north or upper side of TOWER HILL, was built, 1793-1795, from the designs of Samuel Wyatt. The principal

[1] *Hatton*, p. 573.

front consists of a main body and wings of the Ionic order on a rusticated basement. Over the windows are medallions with portraits in low relief of George III. and Queen Charlotte, representations of lighthouses and emblematic devices. The house belongs to a Company or Corporation founded by Sir Thomas Spert, Comptroller of the Navy to Henry VIII., and commander of the *Harry Grace de Dieu*,[1] who was appointed its first master. It was incorporated (March 20, 1514) by the name of "The Guild or Fraternity of the most Glorious and Undividable Trinity of St. Clement," which name was extended by a later charter (James II. 1685) into "The Master, Wardens, and Assistants of the Guild, Fraternity, or Brotherhood, of the Most Glorious and Undivided Trinity, and of St. Clement, in the parish of Deptford Strond, in the county of Kent." The Corporation consists of a Master, Deputy-Master, Wardens, Assistants, and Elder Brethren, twenty-four in all, and an unlimited number of inferior members, and has for its object the increase and encouragement of navigation, etc., the regulation of lighthouses and sea-marks, the securing of a body of skilled and efficient pilots for the navy and mercantile service, and the general management of nautical matters not immediately connected with the Admiralty. The revenue of the Corporation, arising from tonnage, beaconage, etc., is applied (after defraying the expenses of lighthouses, buoys, etc.) to the purposes of the Mercantile Marine Fund, as provided by the Merchant Shipping Acts since 1853. Other funds, derived from estates and bequests, are administered for the relief of decayed pilots and seamen, their widows and children. The Duke of Edinburgh is the present master, and the Prince of Wales an elder brother. The old hall at Deptford in which the Company met was pulled down in 1787, and was replaced by another building which is still standing. Their first London house appears to have been at Ratcliffe. In 1618 a petition to James I. from the "Merchant Adventurers of Newcastle for leave to freight in strangers' bottoms" was sent to the Master, Wardens, etc., for report; and their reply to the Council is dated "Trinity House, Ratcliffe, June 3d."[2] Again, there is a certificate of May 13, 1620, also dated from Trinity House, Ratcliffe, describing the "boundaries of the Mediterranean or Levant Sea, and declaring that Malaga distinctly lies within that sea, and that the Malaga wines are rolled into the Levant Sea to be shipped."[3] Fifty years later their house was in Water Lane, Lower Thames Street, the site and name of which are still preserved. Hatton describes it as "a stately building of brick and stone (adorned with ten bustos), built anno 1671."[4] In the court-room of the present house are busts of Nelson, St. Vincent, Howe, and Duncan; portraits of James I., James II., Sir Francis Drake, William Pitt, the Earl of Sandwich, etc., and a large painting by Gainsborough Dupont, representing the Members

---

[1] The *Harry Grace de Dieu* had four masts, and is represented with great minuteness in the picture at Hampton Court of Henry VIII.'s embarkation at Dover.
[2] *Cal. State Pap.*, 1611-1618, p. 343.
[3] *Ibid.*, 1619-1623, p. 145.
[4] *Hatton*, p. 373.

of the Board in 1794. There is also a museum of maritime relics and curiosities. To ensure the greatest possible efficiency in the lighting of the lighthouses round the coast, as also of the fog-signals and other appliances, the Trinity House has generally an adviser of the highest scientific eminence. Prof. Faraday held this post, and used to say that there was no part of his life that gave him more delight.

Trinity Lane, UPPER THAMES STREET, so called from the church of the Holy Trinity, destroyed in the Great Fire, and not rebuilt, but united to *St. Michael's, Queenhithe*. At the corner of Trinity Lane and Upper Thames Street was the church of St. Michael Queenhithe; and in Little Trinity Lane, No. 9, is *Painter Stainers' Hall*.

Trinity Square, TOWER HILL. Behind the houses in this square, on the west side of a vacant plot of ground in George Street, Tower Hill, stands one of the most perfect of the very few remaining portions of the old wall of London. [*See* London Wall.]

Tufnell Park, UPPER HOLLOWAY, a collection of modern villas, so called after the Tufnell family, lords of the Manor of Barnsbury [which *see*]. It is built on a portion of the demesne lands, under powers of a private Act (3 George IV. cap. 18, 1832), "enabling the trustee under the will of the late William Tufnell, Esq., to reduce the fines of the copyholds held of the Manor of Barnsbury, and to grant building and repairing leases of the devised estates," etc. St. George's, Tufnell Park, a rather elegant circular church, with a short transept, an apsidal chancel, and detached tower and spire, was erected in 1867 from the designs of Mr. G. Truefitt, architect.

Tufton Street, WESTMINSTER, built by Sir Richard Tufton of Tothill Street (d. 1631), runs from Great College Street to Horseferry Road, Westminster. Here was the "Royal Cock Pit;" (which *see*) probably the last in London.

Tun (The), CORNHILL, "a prison for night-walkers and other suspicious persons," built of stone and castellated by Henry le Waleis, Lord Mayor of London in the year 1283, and "called the Tun, because the same was built somewhat in the shape of a tun standing on one end."[1] The Tun formed a part of the structure known as the Conduit. An Ordinance of Edward respecting "persons wandering at night" was to the effect that any person found in the streets of the City after curfew, armed or of suspicious appearance—"unless it be a great lord, or other substantial person of good reputation," or some one of their household and having a warranty from them, and who "is going from one to another with a light to guide them,"—and any stranger who shall have no occasion to come so late into the City, shall "be taken by the keepers of the peace and put into the Tun, which for such misdoers is assigned," and on the morrow be taken before the mayor

[1] *Stow*, p. 71.

and aldermen to be by them dealt with according to law. But the Tun was not for night-wanderers only. Another Ordinance directs that "such bakers and millers as shall steal dough or flour shall be drawn on a hurdle, and be committed to the Tun on Cornhulle and there confined."[1] "*Item*—If any priest be found with a woman he shall be taken unto the Tun on Cornhulle, with minstrels" playing before him.[2] The Tun was in fact the ordinary prison for persons charged with incontinence, against which the City laws were in the Middle Ages very severe.

Turf Club, PICCADILLY—the corner of Clarges Street. This club, formerly the Arlington, had its house in Grafton Street till 1876, when it purchased the lease of No. 47 Clarges Street, till then the residence of the Dukes of Grafton, and fitted it up sumptuously as a first-class club-house. The Turf Club ranks next to the Portland as the great whist club of London. Members are elected by ballot, two black balls excluding. The entrance fee is 30 guineas, the annual subscription 15 guineas.

Turk's Head Coffee-house, "the next house to the Stairs," NEW PALACE YARD, WESTMINSTER. Here, about 1659, James Harrington's celebrated Rota Club met. Among the members were Cyriac Skinner, Major Wildman, and Sir William Petty. For them "was made purposely," says Aubrey, "a large oval table with a passage in the middle for Miles [the landlord] to deliver his coffee. About it sate his [Harrington's] disciples and the virtuosi. We many times adjourned to the Rhenish Wine-house."[3]

Turk's Head Coffee-house, STRAND, opposite Catherine Street. A modern building (No. 142) occupies the site.

July 21, 1763.—At night Mr. Johnson and I supped in a private room at the Turk's Head Coffee-house in the Strand. "I encourage this house," said he, "for the mistress of it is a good civil woman, and has not much business."—Croker's *Boswell*, p. 152.

They again supped together at the Turk's Head on July 28, and on the 30th concluded the day there "very socially."

On Wednesday August 3 [1763] we had our last social meeting at the Turk's Head Coffee-house, before my setting out for foreign parts.—*Ibid.*, p. 158.

Turk's Head, GERARD STREET. [*See* Gerard Street.] Gibbon wrote to Malone from the "Turk's Head, Gerard Street, February 5, 1782."

Turk's Row, CHELSEA. On the front of a house at the south-west corner a stone is let in with the inscription, "Garden Row, anno 1733."

Turnagain Lane.

Near unto this Seacoal Lane, in the turning towards Holborn Conduit, is Turnagain Lane, or rather, as in a record of the 5th of Edward III., Windagain Lane,

---

[1] *Liber Albus*, pp. 145, 240.   [2] *Ibid.*, p. 396.   [3] *Aubrey*, vol. iii. p. 375.

for that it goeth down west to Fleet Dike, from whence men must turn again the same way they came, for there it stopped.—*Stow*, p. 145.

There is an old proverb, " He must take him a house in Turnagain Lane." Turnagain Lane may still be found, though sadly shorn of it's ancient proportions, on the east side of Farringdon Street, near the Holborn Viaduct bridge.

February 28, 1560 (Ash Wednesday).—In Turnagayne Lane, in Sent Pulker's [St. Sepulchre's] paryche, a lame woman with a knef kylled a proper man.
March 8, 1560.—Rode to hanging the woman that killed the man in Turnagayne Lane.—Machyn's *Diary*, p. 227.

Turnbull Street (properly TURNMILL STREET), between *Clerkenwell Green* and *Cow Cross*, and long a noted haunt for harlots and disorderly people. Middleton in his *Black Book* (1604) calls it *Tunbold Street*. The west side of Turnmill Street has been cleared away for the Metropolitan Railway.

Under Fleet Bridge runneth a water, sometimes called the river of the Wells, since Turnmill or Tremill brook, for that divers mills were erected upon it, as appeareth by a fair register book of the priory at Clerkenwell, and donation of the lands thereunto belonging, as also by divers other records.—*Stow*, pp. 6, 11.

Falstaff. This same starved justice [Shallow] hath done nothing but prate to me of the wildness of his youth, and the fents he hath done about Turnbull Street; and every third word a lie, duer paid to the hearer than the Turk's tribute.—Shakespeare, *Second Part of Henry IV.*, Act iii. Sc. 2.

One of the characters in Ben Jonson's *Bartholomew Fair* is " Dan Jordan Knockem, a horse-courser and a ranger of Turnbull;" and there are many uncleanly references to it in *Beaumont and Fletcher*, Taylor the Water Poet, *London Carbonadoed*, etc.

Ursula. You are one of those horse-leeches that gave out I was dead in Turnbull Street, of a surfeit of bottle-ale and tripes.
Knockem. No, 'twas better meat, Urse: cows' udders, cows' udders!—Ben Jonson, *Bartholomew Fair*.

Turners' Company, the fifty-first in order of precedence of the City Companies. Though by repute an ancient fraternity, the Company received its first Charter of Incorporation in the 2d of James I. (June 12, 1604) by the appellation of the Masters, Wardens, and Commonalty of the Art or Mystery de lez Turners of London. The Company has a livery but no hall. The old hall (long since sold) was on College Hill. Of late years the Company has taken great interest in the furtherance of technical instruction, and instituted prizes, including the freedom of the Company, for the best specimens of the turners' art, and the freedom of the Company has been presented to many distinguished men.

Turnmill Street. [*See* Turnbull Street.]

Turnstile (Great), on the south side of HOLBORN, a passage to, and in a straight line with, the east side of Lincoln's Inn Fields. The place derives its name from the turnstile, or revolving barrier, erected for the purpose of excluding horses, but admitting pedestrians to pass between Holborn and Lincoln's Inn Fields. Occasionally the name occurs as *Turningstile*. In a Presentment of the Jury of Middlesex, 1 Edward VI., mention is made of "twoe tenements at the Turne style in Holborne."[1]

> *The Lives of the Roman Emperors.*—Sold by George Hutton at the sign of the Sun, within Turning-Stile in Holborne, 1636.

And here he published Sir Edwin Sandys's *Europæ Speculum* in 1637.

> Great Turnstile Alley, a great thoroughfare which leadeth into Holborn, a place inhabited by shoemakers, sempsters, and milliners, for which it is of considerable trade, and well noted.—*R. B., in Strype*, B. iv. p. 75.
>
> Mr. Bagford [the celebrated antiquary] was first a shoe-maker at Turnstile, but that would not do; then a bookseller at the same place, and that as little.—*J. Sotheby to Thomas Hearne*, May 19, 1716 (*Letters from the Bodleian*, vol. ii. p. 21).
>
> *Lump.* I will not break my method for the world; I have these twenty years walked through Turn-stile Alley to Holborn Fields at four: all the good women observe me, and set their bread into the oven by me.—*A True Widow*; a Comedy, by T. Shadwell, 4to, 1679.
>
> At Dulwich College is a Library having a collection of plays, given by one Cartwright, bred a bookseller, and afterwards turned player. He kept a shop at the end of Turn Stile Alley, which was first designed as a 'Change for vending Welsh flannels, friezes, etc., as may be seen by the left side going from Lincoln's Inn Fields. The house being now divided remains still turned with arches. Cartwright was an excellent actor, and in his latter days gave y^m not only plays, but many good pictures, and intended to have been a further benefactor with money, and been buried there, but was prevented by a turbulent woman there.—Bagford, *Harl. MS.* 5900, fol. 54 b.

Here, in Great Turnstile, about 1750-1760, John Smeaton, the builder of the Eddystone Lighthouse, kept a shop for making and selling philosophical instruments. John Britton was in the habit of meeting the Chevalier d'Eon (who dressed as a female and was respectable and respected) "at an eating-house in Great Turnstile, Holborn."

Turnstile (Little), on the south side of HOLBORN, a passage to the west side of Lincoln's Inn Fields.

> These much frequented thoroughfares (Great and Little Turnstile) derived their names from the Turning Stiles which, two centuries ago, stood at their respective ends next Lincoln's Inn Fields, and which were so placed both for the conveniency of foot passengers, and to prevent the straying of cattle, the fields being at that period used for pasturage.—Brayley's *Londiniana*, vol. ii. p. 125.

Turnstile (New), on the south side of HOLBORN, the next opening west of *Little Turnstile.* A stone let in to the wall is inscribed "New Turnstile, 1688." There was yet another *Turnstile* out of Lincoln's Inn Fields, on the south side. In 1661 Leonard Sowerby was a publisher at "the Turn-stile near New-Market [*i.e.* Clare Market] in Lincoln's Inn Fields."

Tussaud's Waxworks, MARYLEBONE ROAD. This exhibition, which is said to be the oldest in Europe, was opened on the Boulevard

---

[1] *Notes and Queries*, 7th S., vol. v. p. 415.

du Temple at Paris in 1780, and was first shown in London at the Lyceum in 1802. It was located for many years at the Bazaar in Baker Street, Portman Square, but in 1884 the present building was erected by Mr. H. W. Williams, from the designs of Mr. F. W. Hunt, for the reception of the continually increasing collection of waxworks. It has an average depth of 60 feet and a frontage of 400 feet. The white marble staircase was brought from the huge residence at Kensington built by Baron Albert Grant, when the materials of that house were publicly sold. Madame Tussaud (niece of M. Curtius, who modelled figures in wax and taught her the art), was born at Berne in 1760. She was in Paris during the period of the great French Revolution and modelled the heads of the celebrated and notorious men and women whose figures form so characteristic a portion of the gallery. Madame Tussaud died in London, April 15, 1850. The relics of Napoleon I. are of great interest.

Tuthill Street. [*See* Tothill Street.]

Tyburn (*Aye-bourne*, *'t Aye-bourne*), a brook, or bourne, that rose near Hampstead, and, after receiving several tributary streamlets, ran south into the Thames at a place called King's Scholars' Pond, a little below Chelsea. Crossing Oxford Street, near Stratford Place, it made its way by Lower Brook Street and the foot of Hay Hill (Aye Hill) through Lansdowne Gardens, down Half Moon Street, and through the hollow of Piccadilly, where it was crossed by a stone bridge, into the Green Park. Here it expanded into a large pond, from whence it ran past the present Buckingham Palace in three distinct branches into the Thames, first, in early times, spreading into a marsh and surrounding the wooded Thorney, or Isle of Thorns, on which the Abbey of Westminster was built. It formed one of the main sewers. *Rosamond's Pond*, in St. James's Park, was in part supplied by the Tyburn waters. When Tyburn church was rebuilt it was dedicated to the Virgin by the name of *St. Mary-le-bourne*—hence the present *Marylebone*. [*See* Hay Hill.]

Tyburn Lane, PICCADILLY, the original name for what is now *Park Lane*, between *Piccadilly* and *Oxford Street;* and so called because it led to Tyburn. It is introduced into the rate-books of the parish of St. Martin's-in-the-Fields for the first time in 1679, and was then called "Tyburn Road:" in 1686 it is called Tyburn Lane.

Tyburn, TYBURN GALLOWS, or TYBURN TREE (or DEADLY NEVER GREEN), a celebrated gallows or public place of execution for criminals convicted in the county of Middlesex. It existed as early as the reign of Henry IV., and derives its name from Tyburn Brook, described above. It stood, there is reason to believe, on the site of Connaught Place, and near its south-west corner, though No. 49 Connaught Square is said to be the spot.[1] [*See* Connaught Square.]

[1] The question was discussed in *Notes and Queries*, 1860, without any definite result.

Teyborne, so called of bornes and springs, and tying men up there.—Minsheu's *Dictionary*, fol. 1617.

Tieburne, some will have it so called from Tie and Burne, because the poor Lollards for whom this instrument (of cruelty to them, though of justice to malefactors) was first set up, had their necks tied to the beame, and their lower parts burnt in the fire. Others will have it called from Twa and Burne, that is two rivulets, which it seems meet near to the place.—Fuller's *Worthies* (*Middlesex*).

The first year of his [Henry IV.'s] reign (1399-1400) Sir Barnardo Brokkas was beheaded at London in Cheppesyde, and Sir Thomas Shellé, Knight, Mandlyne and Ferlyby, clarkes, were hangyd at Tyborne.—*Grayfriars Chronicle*, p. 9.

1403-1404.—The prior of Lanndes, Sir Robert Claryndon, Knight, and eight freer minores were hongyd at Tyborne. . . . And William Serle that was cheffe yomane with King Richard was drawne and hongyd at Tyborne, and the quarters salted.—*Ibid.*, p. 10.

Tyburn Gallows was a triangle in plan, having three legs to stand on, and appears to have been a permanent erection.

> *Biron.* Thou mak'st the triumviry, the corner cap of society,
> The shape of Love's Tyburn, that hangs up simplicity.
>
> Shakespeare, *Love's Labour's Lost.*

There's one with a lame wit, which will not wear a four-corner'd cap. Then let him put on Tyburn, that hath but three corners.—*Pappe with a Hatchet*, 4to, 1589.

It was made like the shape of Tiborne, three square.—Tarlton's *Jests*, 4to, 1611.

Rawbone. I do imagine myself apprehended already: now the constable is carrying me to Newgate—now, now, I'm at the Sessions House, in the dock:—now I'm called—"Not guilty, my Lord." The jury has found the indictment, *billa vera*. Now, now, comes my sentence. Now I'm in the cart riding up Holborn in a two-wheeled chariot, with a guard of halberdiers. "There goes a proper fellow," says one; "Good people, pray for me;" now I'm at the three wooden stilts [Tyburn]. Hey! now I feel my toes hang i' the cart; now 'tis drawn away; now, now, now! —I am gone.—Shirley, *The Wedding*, 4to, 1629, Act iv. Sc. 3.

Others take a more crooked path yet, the King's highway, where at length their vizzard is plucked off, and they strike fair for Tyburne.—Bishop Earle's *Microcosmographie*, 1628.

Bishop Latimer preaching before Edward VI., April 5, 1576, concerning corrupt judges, said, "There lacks a fourth thing to make up the mess, which so God help me if I were judge, should be *hangum tuum a Tyburne Typpet* to take with him; an it were the judge of the King's Bench, My Lord Chief Justice of England, yea an it were my Lord Chancellor himself, to Tyburne with him."

Gascoigne, in his *Steel Glas* (1576), has another euphemism for hanging—

> That souldiours starve or preck at *Tyborne Crosse*.

Celebrated Persons executed at Tyburn.—In 1499 Perkin Warbeck, that "little cockatrice of a king," as Bacon calls him. Elizabeth Barton, the Holy Maid of Kent, and five others, were beheaded for high treason, April 21, 1534. The Nun's head was fixed on London Bridge. May 4, 1535, Haughton, the last prior of the Charterhouse, with others of his brethren, was executed for high treason. This was "the first time in English history that ecclesiastics were brought out to suffer in their habits, without undergoing the previous ceremony of degradation."[1] In 1536 the Fitzgeralds, for their share in the Irish insurrection. In 1541, the youthful Thomas Fienes, ninth Lord Dacre,

---

[1] *Froude*, vol. ii. p. 359.

for killing a man in a brawl. In 1581, the Jesuits Campion and Harte; fragments of their habits, and drops of blood spilt in the quartering, were eagerly collected and carried away as relics. Campion had a friend in the Harrow Road whom he used to visit, and in passing the Tyburn gallows a presentiment of what would be his fate led him always to raise his hat. In 1587 Doctor Lopes for compassing the death of the Queen (Elizabeth) by poison; and in 1589 one Squire for a like crime. February 21, 1595, Robert Southwell the poet and Jesuit. November 14, 1615, Mrs. Turner, implicated in the murder of Sir Thomas Overbury; she was the inventress of yellow starch, and was executed in a cobweb lawn ruff of that colour.[1]

> The hangman had his bands and cuffs of yellow, which made many after that day, of either sex, to forbear the use of that coloured starch, till it at last grew generally to be detested and disused.—*Autobiography of Sir S. D'Ewes*, vol. i. p. 69.

Weston, Overbury's keeper. John Felton, the assassin of Villiers, Duke of Buckingham (1628); his body was afterwards hanged in chains at Portsmouth. Hacker and Axtell (October 19, 1660) and Okey, Barkstead and Corbet (April 19, 1662), five of fifty-nine who signed the death warrant of Charles I. Thomas Sadler (1677), for stealing the mace and purse of the Lord Chancellor. [*See* Lincoln's Inn Fields.] Oliver Plunket, Archbishop of Armagh (1681), for an assumed design of bringing a French army over to Ireland to murder all the Protestants in that kingdom. Sir Thomas Armstrong (June 20, 1684), who was concerned in the Rye House Plot, and his head was set on Temple Bar. Sir William Parkyns and Sir John Freind (1686), for conspiring to assassinate William III.; Jeremy Collier and two other nonjuring clergymen were with them in the cart under the gallows, and 'produced a greater sensation than the execution itself" by laying hands on them and pronouncing a form of absolution just before the hangman did his office.[2] Robert Young (1700), the deviser of the Association Plot ("the flower-pot contrivance") against Bishop Sprat, Marlborough and others; he was hanged for coining. John Smith:

> On the 12th of Decr 1705, one John Smith, being condemned for felony, and burglary, being conveyed to Tyburn; after he hanged aboute a quarter of an hour, a reprieve coming, he was cut down, and being cut down came to himself, to the great admiration of the spectators, the executioner having pulled him by the legs, and used other means to put a speedy period to his life.—*Hatton*, 1708.

Ferdinando, Marquis Paleotti (1718), for the murder of his servant. Jack Sheppard, in the presence of 200,000 persons (November 16, 1724). Jonathan Wild (May 24, 1725); Fielding's "Jonathan Wild the Great" picked the parson's pocket of his corkscrew, at his execution, which he carried out of the world in his hand. Defoe says there was a greater concourse of spectators at his execution than on any previous occasion. "Jack Sheppard had a tolerable number to attend his exit; but no more to be compared to the present than a regiment to an army."[3] Lord Ferrers, for the murder of his land-steward (May 5,

[1] Howell's *Letters*, ed. 1705, p. 3. [2] *Macaulay*, chap. xxi. [3] Applebee's *Journal*, May 29, 1725.

1760); he wore his wedding clothes to Tyburn; as good an occasion, he observed, for putting them on as that for which they were first made.[1] The earl had behaved in so brutal a manner to his wife that they had been separated by Act of Parliament, and the estate placed in the hands of trustees, who had appointed Johnson the land-steward, to receive the rents. On the day of the murder the earl sent for Johnson (who was an old man) to his room, turned the key in the door, ordered him to kneel down, and shot him through the body with a pistol. He then lifted him into a chair and sent for a surgeon. Johnson survived nine hours and told the story. Dr. Cameron, July 1753. John Wesket (January 9, 1795), for robbing the house of his master, the Earl of Harrington.

> Harrington's porter was condemned yesterday. Cadogan and I have already bespoke places at the Brazier's. I presume we shall have your honour's company, if your stomach is not too squeamish for a single swing.—*Gilly Williams to George Selwyn (Selwyn's Correspondence*, vol. i. p. 323).
>
> Harrington's man was hanged last Wednesday. The dog died game—went in the cart in a blue and gold frock, and, as the emblem of innocence, had a white cockade in his hat. He ate several oranges on his passage, inquired if his hearse was ready, and then, as old Rowe used to say, was launched into eternity.—*Gilly Williams to George Selwyn (Selwyn's Correspondence*, vol. i. p. 355).

Mrs. Brownrigg (September 14, 1767), for whipping two of her female apprentices to death. [*See* Flower de Luce Court.] John Rann, *alias* "Sixteen Stringed Jack," a noted highwayman (November 30, 1774), for robbing the Rev. Dr. Bell, the Princess Amelia's chaplain, in Gunnersbury Lane, near Brentford; he was remarkable for foppery in his dress, and particularly for wearing a bunch of sixteen strings at the knees of his breeches.

> The malefactor's coat was a bright pea-green; he had an immense nosegay, which he had received from the hand of one of the frail sisterhood, whose practice it was in those days to present flowers to their favourites from the steps of St. Sepulchre's church.—Smith's *Book for a Rainy Day*, p. 29.

Daniel and Robert Perreau (January 17, 1776), for forgery. Daniel lived with the notorious Mrs. Rudd, who was said to have incited him to the crime and then betrayed him. Boswell described her as "a lady universally celebrated for extraordinary address and insinuation."[2] Dr. Dodd (June 27, 1777), for forging a bond in the name of the Earl of Chesterfield for £4200. He came in a coach, and a very heavy shower of rain fell just upon his entering the cart, and another just at his putting on his nightcap. During the shower an umbrella was held over his head, which Gilly Williams, who was present, observed was quite unnecessary, as the doctor was going to a place where he might be dried.

> He was a considerable time in praying, which some people standing about seemed rather tired with; they rather wished for a more interesting part of the tragedy. . . . There were two clergymen attending on him, one of whom seemed very much affected

---

[1] Walpole's *Letters*, vol. iv. p. 50. His wife was burned to death in 1807.
[2] Croker's *Boswell*, p. 544.

The other I suppose was the ordinary of Newgate, as he was perfectly indifferent and unfeeling in everything he said and did. The executioner took both the hat and wig off at the same time. Why he put on his wig again I do not know, but he did; and the doctor took off his wig a second time, and then tied on a nightcap which did not fit him; but whether he stretched that or took another, I could not perceive. He then put on his nightcap himself, and upon his taking it he certainly had a smile on his countenance, and very soon afterwards there was an end of all his hopes and fears on this side the grave. He never moved from the place he first took in the cart; seemed absorbed in despair and utterly dejected; without any other signs of animation but in praying. I stayed till he was cut down and put into the hearse.—*A. Storer to George Selwyn (Selwyn's Correspondence*, vol. iii. p. 197).

Very different is the account given by the excellent John Wesley:—

After some time spent in prayer, he pulled his cap over his eyes, and falling down seemed to die in a moment. I make no doubt but at that moment the angels were ready to carry him into Abraham's bosom.

The Rev. James Hackman (April 19, 1779), for the murder of Miss Reay, in the Piazza of Covent Garden; he was taken to Tyburn in a mourning-coach, containing, besides the prisoner, the ordinary of Newgate, a sheriff's officer, and James Boswell, the biographer of Johnson: Boswell, like Selwyn, was fond of seeing executions. [*See* Tavistock Row.] William Wynne Ryland, the line engraver (August 29, 1783), for a forgery on the East India Company.

The last woman who suffered death in England for a political offence was Elizabeth Gaunt, an ancient matron of the Anabaptist persuasion, burned to death at Tyburn for harbouring a person concerned in the Rye House Plot. The last person executed at Tyburn was John Austin, on November 7, 1783. The first execution before Newgate was on December 9 following.

The earliest hangman whose name is known was called Derrick. He lived in the reign of James I., and is mentioned by Dekker in his *Gull's Hornbook*, and by Middleton in his *Black Book*. He was succeeded by Gregory Brandon, who, as has been said, "had arms confirmed to him by the College of Heralds, and became an esquire by virtue of his office." This otherwise incredible legend is explained in the following extract from one of Lord Carew's "overland letters" to Sir Thomas Roe, when on his embassy to the Great Mogul.

December 1616.—York Herald played a trick on Garter King-at-Arms by sending him a coat of arms drawn up for Gregory Brandon, said to be a merchant of London and well descended, which Garter subscribed, and then found that Brandon was the hangman: Garter and York are both suspended, one for foolery, the other for knavery.—*Cal. State Pap.*, 1611-1618, p. 428.

Chamberlain adds a little detail:—

January 4, 1616.—I had almost forgotten that the two principal heralds, Garter and York, are both in the Marshalsea, for a trick of fooling and knavery, in giving one Gregory Brandon, the hangman of London, a fair coat of arms. The one is for plotting such a device; the other for being so grossly overtaken.—*John Chamberlain to Sir Dudley Carleton.*

Brandon was succeeded by Dun, "Esquire Dun," as he is called;

and Dun, in 1684, by John Ketch, commemorated by Dryden,[1] and whose name is now synonymous with hangman.

The hangman's rope was commonly called "a riding knot an inch below the ear," or, "a Tyburn tippet," as we have seen it was termed by Latimer, or "an anodyne necklace"; and the sum of 13½d. is still distinguished as "hangman's wages."

> A Tyborne checke
> Shall breke his necke.—*Skelton*, vol. i. p. 255.

Trials, condemnations, confessions, and last dying speeches were first printed in 1624; and "Tyburn's elegiac lines" have found an enduring celebrity in *The Dunciad*.

> With my estate, I'll tell you how it stands,
> Jack Ketch must have my clothes, the king my lands.
> The last Will and Testament of Anthony, King of Poland
> [Shaftesbury], (*State Poems*, 8vo, 1703, p. 119).

In the early part of the last century the hangman did his office in a very perfunctory manner.

> The hangman does not give himself the trouble to put them out of their pain; but some of their friends or relatives do it for them. They pull the dying person by the legs and beat his breast to despatch him as soon as possible.—Misson's *Memoirs*, 1719, p. 123.

> Here was one Peter Lambert, a swaggering companion, hanged the week before Easter, for killing one Hamden, a Low Country Lieutenant, and dyed forsooth a Roman Catholick. His friends carryed him in a coach from the gallows, and would have buryed him the next day in Christ's Church, but were forbidden by the Bishop. Now upon a rumour that he was seen in France, the King suspected that there might be cunning, and cautelous dealing in his execution, and would not be satisfied till the Sheriffs of London, in the presence of much people, took him up where he was buryed; and upon view found he was sufficiently hanged.—*Mr. Chamberlain to Sir Ralph Winwood*, May 2, 1610.

> *On Tyburn.*
> O Tyburn! could'st thou reason and dispute,
> Could'st thou but judge as well as execute;
> How often would'st thou change the Felon's doom,
> And truss some stern Chief Justice in his room.
> Then should thy sturdy Posts support the Laws;
> No promise, frown, or popular applause,
> Should sway the Bench to favour a bad cause;
> Nor scarlet gown, swell'd with poetic fury,
> Scare a false verdict from a trembling jury.
> Justice, with steady hand and even scales,
> Should stand upright as if sustained by Hales;
> Yet still in matters doubtful to decide,
> A little bearing towards the milder side.
> Dryden's *Miscellaneous Poems*, ed. 1727, vol. v. p. 126.

> The Devil who brought him to the shame takes part:
> Sits cheek by jowl, in black, to cheer his heart,
> Like thief and parson in a Tyburn cart.
> Dryden, *Epilogue to the Loyal Brother*, 1682.

Henrietta Maria, Queen of Charles I., is said, on very insufficient

---

[1] *Epilogue to the Duke of Guise*; and *Essay on Satire*.

authority, to have walked barefooted through Hyde Park to Tyburn
and to have done penance there, though the fact of her having
done so has been denied by the Marshal de Bassompierre, the French
ambassador in England at the time. On the three wooden stilts of
Tyburn the bodies of Oliver Cromwell, Ireton, and Bradshaw were
hung on the first anniversary (January 30, 1660-1661) of the execution
of Charles I. after the Restoration. Their bodies were dragged from
their graves in Henry VII.'s Chapel, in Westminster Abbey, and
removed at night to the Red Lion Inn, in Holborn, from whence
they were carried next morning in sledges to Tyburn, and there, in
their shrouds and cere-cloths, suspended till sunset at the several angles
of the gallows. They were then taken down and beheaded, their
bodies buried beneath the gallows, and their heads set upon poles on
the top of Westminster Hall.[1]

The last plate of Hogarth's "Idle and Industrious Apprentice"
represents an execution at Tyburn's triple tree. [*See* Bowl Yard,
Holborn.]

Tyburn Road, the old name for *Oxford Street*.

Tyburn Road betⁿ St. Giles's Pound E. and the Lane leading to the Gallows W.,
length 350 yards.—*Hatton*, 8vo, 1708, p. 84.

Having purchased the body of a malefactor, he hired a room for its dissection near
the Pest Fields in St. Giles's, at a little distance from Tyburn Road.—*Memoirs of
Martinus Scriblerus*.

My Lord Dorset was set upon on Saturday night by four or five footpads, as he
came by Tyburn. He says little of it himself; but I hear they took from him to the
value of fifty or sixty pounds, with his gold George. They, seeing him fumbling in
his pockets, told him it was not honourable to *sink* upon them, and they must search
him; whereon he threw his money out of the coach, and bid them pick it up. One
of them told him, that if they did not know him they should use him worse.—
Secretary Vernon to Duke of Shrewsbury, July 25, 1699, vol. ii. p. 327.

Tyburnia, the conventional name of a part of Bayswater lying
between the Edgware Road and Pembridge Road, and reaching north
from the Bayswater Road to the Westbourne district, and for the most
part covered during the last thirty years with large and costly mansions,
and laid out in roads, squares, gardens, and terraces. Like its
more aristocratic rival *Belgravia*, its name, extent and boundaries are
merely conventional, but are very well understood by the residents.

Uncumber (Saint), an altar or rood in old ST. PAUL'S, popularly
so called, and much resorted to by women of the poorer classes, whose
offering, curiously enough, was *oats*. The saint, whose proper name,
says Sir Thomas More, was St. Wylgeforte, had the credit of being able
to "*uncumber* them of their husbands." An old popular rhyme says—

    If ye cannot slepe but slumber
    Give otes unto Saynt Uncumber.
    If a wife were weary of her husband she offered oats
    At St. Paul's, at London, to St. Uncumber.
    Michael Wood, quoted in Wordsworth's *Eccl. Biog.*, vol. i. p. 166.

---

[1] Wharton's *Gesta Britannorum*, p. 490, add. MSS. British Museum 10,116. Wood's *Athenæ Oxonienses*, art. "Ireton."

Union Club House, TRAFALGAR PLACE, at the south-west end of Trafalgar Square (Sir Robert Smirke, R.A., architect). The club is chiefly composed of merchants, lawyers, Members of Parliament, and, as James Smith, who was a member, writes, "of gentlemen at large." The cellars are said to contain a larger stock of wine than those of any other club in London. Entrance fee, 38 guineas ; annual subscription, 7 guineas. The house is built on ground let by the Crown, for ninety-nine years, from October 10, 1822.

Union Court, HOLBORN, opposite St. Andrew's Church, was formerly called Scroope's Court, after the noble family of Scroope of Bolton, who had a town house here, afterwards let to the serjeants-at-law. [*See* Scroope's Inn.] Only the northern part now exists, the Holborn end having been swept away in forming the Holborn Viaduct and its approaches. In Union Court lived William Henry Toms, the engraver (1700-1750), a name dear to London topographers.

Union Street, MIDDLESEX HOSPITAL, from Great Titchfield Street to Norfolk Street, now called Cleveland Street.

At the end of Union Street, Middlesex Hospital, stood two magnificent rows of elms, one on each side of a rope-walk ; and beneath their shade I have frequently seen Joseph Baretti and Richard Wilson perambulate until Portland Chapel clock announced *five*, the hour of Joseph Wilton's dinner.—Smith's *Nollekins*, vol. ii. p. 177.

The "magnificent rows of elms" were felled to clear the ground for the Strand Union Workhouse.

Union Street, SOUTHWARK (formerly Duke Street), connects the Borough High Street with Charlotte Street and the Blackfriars Road. No. 88 is a public-house, distinguished by the sign of "King Henry VIII.'s Head." The house, as an inn, is coeval with Henry VIII.'s reign. The structure is modern. The Police Court, which had long been fixed in this street, was removed in January 1845.

United Service Club, at the south-east corner of PALL MALL and WATERLOO PLACE, was erected 1826 from the designs of John Nash, architect, for officers not under the rank of Major in the Army and of Commander in the Navy. The exterior was redecorated and the interior remodelled, and an addition made on the east side from the designs of Decimus Burton in 1858-1859. The club was established in 1815. This is still considered to be one of the most commodious, economical and best managed of all the London Club Houses. In it are hung Stanfield's Battle of Trafalgar and several portraits. The members are limited to 1600. Entrance fee, £40 ; annual subscription £8.

United Service Club (JUNIOR), north-west corner of CHARLES STREET and east side of REGENT STREET, was designed by Sir Robert Smirke for the *Senior* United Service Club, but was found too small for the purposes of that Club. It was rebuilt on an enlarged scale and in a more sumptuous style in 1855-1857; architects Messrs. Nelson and Innes. It comprises 2000 members, who pay an entrance fee of £40 and an annual subscription of 7 guineas.

United Service Institution, WHITEHALL YARD, founded 1830, as a central repository for objects of the military and naval arts, science, natural history, books and documents relating to those objects, and for the delivery of lectures on appropriate subjects. Member's entrance fee, £1; annual subscription, 10s.; life subscription, £6. *Hours of Admission for Visitors.*—Daily (Fridays excepted) during the summer months, April to September, from eleven to five; winter months, from eleven to four. *Mode of Admission.*—Member's order, easily procurable. The members are above 4000 in number. The museum of the institution contains much that will repay a visit. The Asiatic Room contains a large and rich collection of Indian and Afghan arms, armour, etc., Chinese and Japanese weapons, and the ruder weapons of the natives of Borneo and the South Sea Islands. The African Room displays an equally varied collection of Moorish, Abyssinian, Ashantee and Central African arms and armour. Other rooms exhibit the early and recent military weapons and accoutrements of different European countries, while others again are devoted to the arms used of old and at the present time in the navy, models of ships of various countries, including some of our recent gunboats and iron-clads. *Observe.* — Basket-hilted cut-and-thrust sword, used by Oliver Cromwell at the siege of Drogheda (1649),— the blade bears the marks of two musket-balls ; sword worn by General Wolfe when he fell at Quebec (1759); Sir Francis Drake's walking stick; sash used in carrying Sir John Moore from the field, and lowering him into his grave on the ramparts at Corunna; Captain Cook's chronometer; part of the deck of the *Victory* on which Nelson fell, his sword and other relics; rudder of the *Royal George* sunk at Spithead; skeleton of Marengo, the barb-horse which Napoleon rode at Waterloo; Captain Siborne's elaborate and faithful model of the field and battle of Waterloo, containing 100,000 metal figures; large model of the Battle of Trafalgar; Colonel Hamilton's model of Sebastopol; relics of Sir John Franklin's Arctic expedition. There is an excellent library.

United University Club House, SUFFOLK STREET and PALL MALL EAST, was built from the designs of William Wilkins, R.A., and J. P. Gandy Deering, and opened February 13, 1826. A storey was added in 1850. The members, limited to 1000, belong to the two universities of Oxford and Cambridge. Entrance fee, 30 guineas; annual subscription, 8 guineas.

University Club (New), 57 ST. JAMES STREET, a handsome Gothic building erected from the designs of Alfred Waterhouse, R.A. It was established in 1863, and consists of 1100 members. Entrance fee, 30 guineas; annual subscription, 8 guineas.

University College, LONDON, on the east side of GOWER STREET, a proprietary institution, "for the general advancement of literature and science, by affording to young men adequate opportunities for obtaining literary and scientific education at a moderate expense." It was founded in 1826 as the *London University* by the exertions of Lord Brougham, Thomas Campbell the poet, and others, but the title was changed under the Charter of Incorporation to University College. It was reincorporated with the same title in 1865. The central building was erected 1827-1828 from the designs of W. Wilkins, R.A. The hall at the rear having been burnt down, a library with staircase approach was erected 1848-1851 from the designs of Professor T. L. Donaldson at a cost of £6173. The central vestibule or Flaxman Hall, 1848, by Professor C. R. Cockerell and Professor T. L. Donaldson. About 1867 a south wing was added from the designs of Professor T. Hayter Lewis; and the north wing was opened in February 1881, and cost £35,000. The course of instruction in University College is of the most comprehensive kind. The college is open to all, and everything is taught that falls within a university curriculum, except theology, which by its constitution is strictly excluded. Science is made a special feature. The School of Medicine is deservedly distinguished. There is a department of Engineering and the Constructive Arts, and of late years a Slade School of the Fine Arts has been added with marked success. The staff of professors are men of high reputation in their respective departments. There are scholarships, exhibitions and prizes in the several schools, and the students have the use of an extensive library and medical museum.

The *Junior School* for boys between seven and fifteen years of age, under the government of the Council of the College, is entered by a separate entrance in Upper Gower Street. The school session is divided into three terms; and the payment is 8 guineas a term, with some "extras." Boys are admitted to the school at any age under fifteen, if they are competent to enter the lowest class. When a boy has attained his sixteenth year he will not be allowed to remain in the school beyond the end of the current session. The subjects taught include the usual branches of a liberal education, and the work of the higher classes is arranged with special regard to matriculation at the University of London. Full information as to all matters connected with the school may be obtained of the Secretary.

University College (or North London) Hospital, opposite University College, GOWER STREET, was founded in 1833 for the gratuitous relief of poor, sick, and maimed persons, and the delivery of poor married women at their own homes, and for furthering the objects of the College, by affording improved means of instruction in medicine and surgery to the medical students of University College, under the superintendence of its professors. The front looking east was designed, 1833-1834, by Alfred Ainger, as also the north wing, of which the first stone was laid by Lord Brougham, May 20, 1846.

The building was altered and the number of beds increased from 160 to 200 in the summer and autumn of 1879. The hospital has separate departments for diseases of women; of children—fourteen beds being devoted to children under twelve years of age in separate wards; diseases of the skin; of the eye; of the ear; the throat and the teeth. The number of persons treated during the year 1888 was 38,487, of whom 2701 were in-patients. The annual cost of maintaining the Hospital in its present state is over £15,000, whilst its settled income amounts to only about £8000.

University of London, BURLINGTON GARDENS, established by Royal Charter in 1837 "for the advancement of religion and morality and the promotion of useful knowledge, without distinction of rank, sect, or party." The government of the University is vested in a Chancellor (Earl Granville), Vice-Chancellor, and Senate of thirty-six Fellows. The University is not a teaching but an examining body; conferring degrees after examination — considered to be more severe and searching than in the older universities—upon members of the various colleges throughout the kingdom, and private students who have previously matriculated at this university. The examiners are paid by Government. Degrees are conferred in Arts (bachelor and master), Literature (doctor), Science (bachelor and doctor), Laws (bachelor and doctor), Medicine (bachelor and doctor), Surgery (bachelor and master), and Music (bachelor). There are also examinations in Scriptural subjects, and subjects relating to public health.

The building, the principal façade of which is one of the most elegant and most characteristic for its purpose in London, was completed in 1870 from the designs of Mr. (afterwards Sir James) Pennethorne. It is of Portland stone, with columns of red Mansfield stone, and mouldings and carvings of Hopton stone; Palladian in style, the principal storey of the Corinthian order on a rusticated basement. Along the front are statues of men who may be regarded as impersonations of the University studies. On the roof line of the east wing are Galileo, La Place and Goethe (all by Mr. E. W. Wyon); on the centre Aristotle, Galen and Cicero, by Mr. J. S. Westmacott; Justinian, Archimedes and Plato, by Mr. F. Woodington; on the west wing David Hume, John Hunter and Sir Humphry Davy, by Mr. Noble. In the niches of the east wing are Cuvier, Liebnitz and Linnæus, by Mr. P. M'Dowell, R.A.; in the western niches Locke, Bacon and Adam Smith, by Mr. W. Theed. In the portico are seated statues of Harvey, Newton, Milton and Jeremy Bentham. The principal rooms of the interior are the Theatre, in the east wing, used on public occasions for conferring degrees, etc., and the examination rooms in the west wing, each about 72 feet by 56 feet; the waiting and secondary examination rooms, each 62 feet by 33 feet; laboratory and anatomical rooms, of about the same dimensions, and a spacious and handsome library—in which is an excellant collection of books, very largely due to the liberality of the late Lord Overstone and of

George Grote the historian. It also includes the valuable library of the late Professor Augustus De Morgan.

University Street, TOTTENHAM COURT ROAD and GOWER STREET. At No. 22 in this street died, March 8, 1833, John Thomas Smith, Keeper of Prints in the British Museum, whose services to London topography must be honourably mentioned in every account of the great City.

Upholders' Company. This Company was founded between 1460 and 1465, and a coat of arms was granted on December 11 of that year. A charter was given by Charles I. in 1626 to the Company under the title of the Master, Wardens and Commonalty of the Mystery or Art of the Upholders of the City of London. This Company ranks forty-ninth among the City Guilds. They have a livery but no hall.

Uxbridge House, BURLINGTON GARDENS, the corner of Old Burlington Street, was designed 1790-1792 by John Vardy, who was assisted in the front by Joseph Bonomi, A.R.A., on the site of Queensberry House (designed by G. Leoni,[1] 1726), the London residence of the Duke and Duchess of Queensberry, who befriended Gay. It was the town residence of the Earl of Uxbridge (Marquis of Anglesea), who was living here in 1815 immediately before the battle of Waterloo, where he commanded the British cavalry and lost his leg. He died here, April 29, 1854, in his eighty-sixth year. The house is now the *Western Branch of the Bank of England*, and has of course been greatly altered to adapt it to banking purposes, and offices have been added at the back and fronting Savile Row, but the principal rooms on the first floor retain their stately carved marble fireplaces and other decorative features.

Vandon Street, WESTMINSTER. This was formerly Little George Street, and on a stone on the front of one of the houses is the inscription, "This is George Street, 1717."

Vandun's Almshouses, PETTY FRANCE, afterwards YORK STREET, WESTMINSTER, so called after their founder, Cornelius Van Dun, a native of Breda, in Brabant, and a soldier under Henry VIII. at the siege of Tournay (d. 1577). His monument in the church of St. Margaret, Westminster (engraved by J. T. Smith), represents him in his dress as one of the yeomen of the guard to Queen Elizabeth. The almshouses which were for eight poor women have been abolished, and the "Vandon Charity" is otherwise appropriated.

Vaudeville Theatre, 404 STRAND, a small theatre, insignificant outside, but with a pretty and convenient interior, was erected in 1870, and is chiefly devoted to comedy and burlesque. It has been lately distinguished by the production of plays grounded on Fielding's novels.

[1] There is an engraving of it by Picart, 1726.

Vauxhall, FAUKESHALL, or FOXHALL, a manor in Surrey, properly Fulke's Hall, and so called from **Fulke de Breauté,** the celebrated mercenary follower of King John.

Fulke de Breauté married Margaret, Earl Baldwin's mother, and thus obtained the wardship of her son; he appears to have built a hall, or mansion-house, in the manor of South Lambeth during his tenure of it; and from his time it was called indifferently Faukeshall, or South Lambeth, and is so termed in the tenth year of Edward I.—T. Hudson Turner, *Archæol. Journal,* No. xv. p. 275.

Edward II. granted the manor of Faukeshall to Roger Damorie. Upon his attainder, for taking part with the Barons against the King about two years afterwards, it was granted to Hugh le Despencer; who being executed in 1326, the manor appears to have been restored to the widow of Roger Damorie, who gave it to King Edward III. in exchange for some lands in Suffolk. It was afterwards granted to Edward the Black Prince, and by him given to the church of Canterbury, to which it still belongs; King Henry VIII. having given it to the Dean and Chapter on the suppression of the Monastery.—*Lysons,* vol. i. p. 231.

There is a view of the old manor-house in Wilkinson's *Londina Illustrata.* It was afterwards known as Copped or Copt Hall; and here Lady Arabella Stuart was confined, under the custody of Sir Thomas Parry.

The Earl of Worcester is buying Fauxhall from Mr. Trenchard, to bestow the use of that house upon Gaspar Calehof and his son as long as they shall live; for he intends to make it a college of artizans.—*Hartlib to Boyle,* May, 1654 (Weld's *Royal Society,* vol. i. p. 53).

At Vaux Hall, Sir Samuel Moreland built a fine Room, anno 1667; the inside all of Looking Glass, and Fountains very pleasant to behold, which is much visited by strangers; it stands in the middle of the Garden, . . . Foot square, . . . high, covered with Cornish Slate; on the front whereof he placed a Punchanello, very well carved, which held a Dial; but the winds have demolished it.—Aubrey's *Surrey,* vol. i. p. 12.

Lysons says that Morland's house was converted into a distillery in 1725, and it was still used as a distillery when he wrote in 1790; but there is some uncertainty as to the exact site of the house. Tradition has associated the name of Guido Fawkes with Vauxhall, but it is certain that he never had any connection with the place. It appears, however, that a house or store by the waterside at Vauxhall was hired by Robert Kayes, who was hanged and quartered along with Fawkes, Rookwood and Winter in Old Palace Yard, January 31, 1606. This house, which stood on a part of the present Nine Elms Station of the South-Western Railway, " was casually burnt down to the ground by powder" in 1634.[1]

Ambrose Phillips, the poet, died at his lodgings, Vauxhall, June 18, 1749. When every movement of Wilkes was watched and reported upon to the Secretaries of State, he frequently went to "one Mr. Kerr's at Vauxhall, where Mr. Churchill lodges."[2]

Vauxhall Bridge, an iron bridge over the Thames at Vauxhall, communicating with Millbank on the left bank of the river. It was built from the designs of James Walker, C.E.; and was originally called

[1] Sermon by Dr. Featley quoted by *Lysons,* vol. i. p. 233; and by Brayley, *History of Surrey* vol. iii. p. 348.   [2] *Grenville Papers,* vol. ii. p. 156.

Regent's Bridge, the first stone having been laid, May 9, 1811, by Lord Dundas as proxy for the Prince Regent. The works were suspended for a time, and on August 21, 1813, Prince Charles of Brunswick laid the first stone of the abutments on the Surrey side. The bridge was opened June 4, 1816. It consists of nine arches, each of 78 feet span, and cost about £300,000. In 1879 it was purchased by the Metropolitan Board of Works for £255,230, and opened to the public toll free.

Vauxhall Bridge Road extends from Vauxhall Bridge and Besborough Gardens, the western end of Victoria Street. A portion of the site formerly occupied by the Neathouse Gardens was raised to a level with Pimlico by the use of soil transported from St. Katherine's when the docks were formed. On this made ground the upper part of the road was built. In 1865 several terraces and places were renamed, and 325 houses renumbered as Vauxhall Bridge Road.

Vauxhall Gardens, on the Surrey side of the Thames, and a short distance east of Vauxhall Bridge, over against Millbank, a place of public resort from the reign of Charles II. almost to the present time, and celebrated for its walks, lit with thousands of lamps; its musical and other performances; its suppers, including ham cut in wafery slices, and its fireworks. The Gardens were formed circ. 1661, and originally called "The New Spring Gardens," to distinguish them from the *Old Spring Gardens* at Charing Cross.

Not much unlike what His Majesty has already begun by the wall from Old Spring Gardens to St. James's in that Park, and is somewhat resembled in the New Spring Garden at Lambeth.—Evelyn's *Fumifugium*, 1661.

July 2, 1661.—I went to see the New Spring Garden at Lambeth, a pretty contrived plantation.—*Evelyn*.

Balthazar Monconys, in his *Voyage d'Angleterre*, 1633, describes the *Jardins Printemps* at Lambeth as having "lawns and gravel walks, dividing squares of 20 or 30 yards enclosed with hedges of gooseberry trees, within which were planted roses" and other flowers and shrubs.

June 20, 1665.—Thanksgiving Day for victory over the Dutch. . . . By water to Fox Hall [Vauxhall], and there walked an hour alone, observing the several humours of the citizens that were there this holyday, pulling off cherries, and God knows what.—*Pepys*.

May 28, 1667.—I by water to Foxhall and there walked in Spring Garden. A great deal of company, and the weather and garden pleasant, and it is very pleasant and cheap going thither, for a man may go to spend what he will, or nothing, all is one. But to hear the nightingale and other birds, and other fiddles and there a harp, and here a Jew's trump, and here laughing and there fine people walking is mighty divertising.—*Pepys*.

May 30, 1668.—Over to Fox Hall, and there fell into the company of Harry Killigrew, a rogue newly come back out of France, but still in disgrace at our Court, and young Newport and others, as very rogues as any in the town, who were ready to take hold of every woman that come by them. And so to supper in an arbour: but Lord! their mad talk did make my heart ake.—*Pepys*.

Pepys moralises as he makes the entry in his Journal, "But Lord! what loose company was this, that I was in to-night, though full of wit;

and worth a man's being in for once, to know the nature of it, and their manner of talk and lives." And then he went again, the next day but one (the next day was "the Lord's Day," so he could not go then), to learn a little more of the nature of it.

June 1, 1668.—Alone to Fox Hall, and walked and saw young Newport and two more rogues of the town seize on two ladies, who walked with them an hour with their masks on (perhaps civil ladies); and there I left them.—*Pepys.*

July 27, 1668.—Over the water with my wife and Deb and Mercer to Spring Garden, and there eat and walked; and observe how rude some of the young gallants of the town are become, to go into people's arbors where there are not men, and almost force the women; which troubled me, to see the confidence of the vice of the age: and so we away by water with much pleasure home.—*Pepys.*

Hippolita. Not suffered to see a play in a twelvemonth !—
Prue. Nor go to Punchinello, nor Paradise !—
Hippolita. Nor to take a ramble to the Park nor Mulberry Garden !—
Prue. Nor to Totnam Court, nor Islington !—
Hippolita. Nor to eat a syllabub in New Spring Garden with cousin !—Wycherley, *The Gentleman Dancing Master,* 4to, 1673.

Cunningham. No, Madam, you conquer like the King of France. Your subjects for ever after are at rest.
Thisbe. You said as much to the flame-coloured Petticoat in New Spring Garden.—Sedley, *Bellamira,* 4to, 1687.

Mrs. Frail. A great piece of business to go to Covent Garden Square in a hackney-coach, and take a turn with one's friend ! If I had gone to Knightsbridge, or to Chelsea, or to Spring Garden or to Barn Elms, with a man alone, something might have been said.—Congreve, *Love for Love,* 4to, 1695.

Lady Fancyful. 'Tis infallibly some intrigue that brings them to Spring Garden.—Vanbrugh, *The Provoked Wife,* 4to, 1697.

Wycherley has other references besides that we have quoted. Vanbrugh lays one of his liveliest scenes in the Spring Garden ; Etherege, in his *She Would if She Could ;* and other dramatists speak of Foxhall or Spring Gardens in passages indicating with sufficient plainness the character of the place.

The Great Spring Garden, commonly called the New Spring Garden at Fox Hall, with several acres of Land, and Houses, is to be sold. Inquire of Mrs. Eliz. Plant at Fox Hall near the Garden.—*London Gazette,* No. 3006, p. 1694.

The ladies that have an inclination to be private take delight in the close walks of Spring Gardens,—where both sexes meet, and mutually serve one another as guides to lose their way, and the windings and turnings in the little Wildernesses are so intricate, that the most experienced mothers have often lost themselves in looking for their daughters.—Tom Brown's *Amusements,* 8vo, 1700, p. 54.

May 17, 1711.—I was this evening with Lady Kerry and Miss Pratt at Vauxhall to hear the nightingales, but they are almost past singing.—*Swift to Stella.*

May 24, 1714.—We went by water to Fox Hall and the Spring Garden. I was surprised with so many pleasant walks, etc., so near London.—Thoresby's *Diary,* vol. ii. p. 215.

I immediately recollected that it was my good friend Sir Roger's voice, and that I had promised to go with him on the water to Spring Garden, in case it proved a good evening. . . . We were now arrived at Spring Garden, which is exquisitely pleasant at this time of the year. When I considered the fragrancy of the walks and bowers, with the choirs of birds that sung upon the trees, and the loose tribe of people that walked under their shades, I could not but look on the place as a kind of Mahometan Paradise. Sir Roger told me it put him in mind of a little coppice

by his house in the country, which his chaplain used to call an Aviary of Nightingales.
. . . He here fetched a deep sigh, and was falling into a fit of musing, when a
Mask who came behind him, gave him a gentle tap on the shoulder, and asked him
if he would drink a bottle of Mead with her? But the Knight being startled at so
unexpected a familiarity, and displeased to be interrupted in his thoughts of the
widow, told her "she was a wanton baggage," and bid her go about her business.
We concluded our walk with a glass of Burton ale and a slice of hung beef.—*The
Spectator*, No. 383.

We hear very little of New Spring Gardens between 1712 and the
great period of their reopening, under the management of Jonathan
Tyers, on June 7, 1732, with an entertainment called *Ridotto al fresco*,
at which the Prince of Wales was present, two-thirds of the company
appearing in masks, dominoes, or lawyers' gowns. Admission tickets
were charged a guinea each. Tyers was unceasing in his endeavours
to enlarge the beauty and attractions of the grounds. Hogarth executed
several pictures for the rooms, and Tyers presented him with a gold
admission medal for himself and friends, bearing the inscription, *In
perpetuam Beneficii Memoriam*. Roubiliac's first work in England was
a statue of Handel made for Vauxhall Gardens. Roubiliac is said to
have owed his introduction to his first patron, Sir Edward Walpole, to
an advertisement he put forth of his having found, on his way home
from Vauxhall, a pocket-book containing a considerable number of bank-
notes, and some papers, apparently of consequence to the owner;
their owner was Sir Edward Walpole. The price of admission was 1s.
up to the summer of 1792, when it was raised to 2s. Subsequently
it was raised to 4s., but in 1850 it was 1s. again. Vocal music was
introduced for the first time by Mr. Tyers in 1745. Fireworks were
not exhibited till 1798, and even then not constantly displayed.

The coaches being come to the water-side, they all alighted, and getting into one
boat, proceeded to Vauxhall. The extreme beauty and elegance of this place is well
known to almost every one of my readers; and happy is it for me that it is so; since
to give an adequate idea of it would exceed my power of description.—Fielding,
Amelia, B. ix. chap. ix.

Tom Tyers was the son of Mr. Jonathan Tyers, the founder of that excellent
place of public amusement, Vauxhall Gardens, which must ever be an estate to its
proprietor, as it is peculiarly adapted to the taste of the English nation; there being
a mixture of curious show, gay exhibition, musick, vocal and instrumental, not too
refined for the general ear,—for all which only a shilling is paid,—and though last
not least, good eating and drinking for those who choose to purchase that regale.—
Boswell, by Croker, p. 599.

Friday, April 21, 1749, was performed at Vauxhall Gardens the rehearsal of the
music for the fireworks, by a band of 100 musicians, to an audience of above 12,000
persons (tickets 2s. 6d.) So great a resort occasioned such a stoppage on London
Bridge [then the only bridge over the Thames below Kingston], that no carriage
could pass for three hours. The footmen were so numerous as to obstruct the
passage, so that a scuffle happened, in which some gentlemen were wounded.—
Gent. Mag., 1749, vol. xix. p. 185.

June 23, 1750.—I had a card from Lady Caroline Petersham to go with her to
Vauxhall. I went accordingly to her house and found her and the little Ashe, or
the Pollard Ashe as they call her; they had just finished their last layer of red, and
looked as handsome as crimson could make them. . . . We marched to our
barge, with a boat of French horns attending and little Ashe singing. We paraded

some time up the river, and at last debarked at Vauxhall. . . . Here we picked up Lord Granby, arrived very drunk from Jenny's Whim. . . . At last we assembled in our booth, Lady Caroline in the front, with the visor of her hat erect, and looking gloriously jolly and handsome. She had fetched my brother Orford from the next box, where he was enjoying himself with his *petite partie*, to help us to mince chickens. We minced seven chickens into a China dish, which Lady Caroline stewed over a lamp with three pats of butter and a flagon of water, stirring and rattling and laughing, and we every minute expecting the dish to fly about our ears. She had brought Betty the fruit-girl, with hampers of strawberries and cherries from Rogers's, and made her wait upon us, and then made her sup by us at a little table. . . . In short, the whole air of our party was sufficient, as you will easily imagine, to take up the whole attention of the Garden ; so much so, that from 11 o'clock till half an hour after 1 we had the whole concourse round our booth ; at last, they came into the little gardens of each booth on the sides of ours, till Harry Vane took up a bumper and drank their healths, and was proceeding to treat them with still greater freedoms. It was 3 o'clock before we got home.— *Walpole to Montague*, vol. ii. p. 211-214.

This [Foxhall] is the place where are those called Spring Gardens, laid out in so grand a taste, that they are frequented in the three summer months by most of the nobility and gentry, then in and near London ; and are often honoured with some of the royal family, who are here entertained with the sweet song of numbers of nightingales, in concert with the best band of musick in England. Here are fine pavilions, shady groves, and most delightful walks, illuminated by above 1000 lamps, so disposed that they all take fire together, almost as quick as lightning, and dart such a sudden blaze as is perfectly surprising. Here are among others, 2 curious statues of Apollo the god, and Mr. Handel the master of musick ; and in the centre of the area, where the walks terminate, is erected the temple for the musicians, which is encompassed all round with handsome seats, decorated with pleasant paintings, on subjects most happily adapted to the season, place, and company.—*England's Gazetteer*, 12mo, 1751 (art. "Foxhall").

> There oft returning from the green retreats
> Where fair Vauxhallia decks her sylvan seats ;
> Where each spruce nymph from city Counters free,
> Sips the frothed syllabub, or fragrant tea ;
> While with sliced ham, scraped beef, and burnt champagne,
> Her prentice lover soothes his amorous pain.
>
> Canning's *Loves of the Triangles*, 1798.

The title Spring Garden was retained till 1785, when it was changed to Vauxhall Gardens ; but the annual licence was to the last taken out in the name of the *Spring Gardens*. The gardens continued to be a place of fashionable amusement nearly to the end of the reign of George III. ; and after they ceased to be fashionable they were long a popular resort. In their later years they were a favourite place for balloon ascents. M. Garnerin ascended several times from these gardens, and on one occasion, September 21, 1802, he descended from a great height in a parachute. It was at Vauxhall that Green became famous as an aeronaut. His voyage to the continent, with Messrs. Monck Mason and Holland, was made in his great balloon, 80 feet high, from Vauxhall, at half-past one in the afternoon of November 7, 1836, and the descent near Weilburg in Nassau about half-past seven next morning. After many changes of managers and fluctuations in prosperity Vauxhall Gardens were opened for the last time on the night of Monday, July 25, 1859. Then, as the advertisements ran,

"Farewell to Vauxhall. The last night for ever! ... The last Dancing! the last Suppers! the last Punch! And no extra charge!"

Soon after the closing of the gardens the site was laid out in streets, and the whole is now covered with houses, schools, and a church (St. Peter's) designed by J. L. Pearson, architect. The memory of the gardens is preserved in Vauxhall Walk, Tyer Street, etc. There is a capital old view of the gardens by J. Müller, after Wall, and another by S. Maurer, dated 1744; but the best of all is "A general Prospect of Vauxhall Gardens, showing at one view the disposition of the whole Gardens," engraved for the 1754 edition of *Stow*. Later views abound.

Vauxhall Park, SOUTH LAMBETH, a small park of about 8 acres in the South Lambeth Road, opened by H.R.H. the Prince of Wales on Monday, July 7, 1890. The cost was about £45,000, raised partly from the rates but largely by private subscriptions. The park includes the garden of the Right Hon. Henry Fawcett and the house in which he died. The park has been handed over to the vestry of Lambeth and laid out at the expense of the Kyrle Society.

Vedast's (St.), FOSTER LANE, a church in the ward of *Farringdon Within*; destroyed in the Great Fire, and rebuilt from the design of Sir Christopher Wren. The lane as well as the church originally bore the name of St. Vedast; this was corrupted into Fauster and then into Foster. In the 17th century the correct name of the church was revived with the *alias* of St. Foster's, but the lane retained the corrupted form. It serves as well for the parish of *St. Michael-le-Querne*. The right of presentation belongs alternately to the Archbishop of Canterbury and the Dean and Chapter of St. Paul's.

The church is noteworthy as having one of the most original and picturesque of Wren's spires. The steeple of the old church, being only partially injured by the fire of 1666, was retained when the new church was built, but in 1694 it was found necessary to take it down, when the present one was erected. Like most of Wren's towers it is quite plain till it rises above the houses. The spire is square in plan, but the lower stage is slightly concave, the second convex, and considerable character is given by clusters of engaged shafts projecting boldly from the angles, thus producing great play of light and shade. The entire height is 150 feet. The interior of the church has also some peculiarities. It consists of a nave (70 feet by 34) and south aisle (50 feet by 20, the tower being taken out of it); and in order to make the most of the site the walls are not exactly at right angles, the north side being a few feet longer than the south, which, again, is a little out of a straight line. *Observe*—the altar with its Corinthian columns, vase-like finials, carved scrolls and festoons, a characteristic work of Grinling Gibbons.

John Scott *alias* Rotherham, Archbishop of York and Lord Chancellor, was buried here in 1465. Robert Herrick, the poet (d.

1674), was baptized here on August 24, 1591. His father, Nicholas, was a goldsmith in Cheapside.

Vere Street, CLARE MARKET, was so called after Elizabeth Vere, (d. 1683), daughter of Horatio; Lord Vere, of Tilbury, and wife of John Holles, second Earl of Clare. Sir Thomas Lyttelton was living in this street in 1688.[1] Here stood *Gibbons's Tennis Court*, converted into a theatre by Thomas Killigrew; and in this temporary building his company performed from 1660 till April 1663, when the new theatre in Drury Lane was ready to receive them. They furnished a list of twenty pieces, which they termed their *stock* plays. Of these three only were Shakespeare's, but one of them, *Henry IV.*, was acted on the opening night, November 8, 1660. Dryden's first play, the *Wild Gallant*, was brought out here in February 1663.

> Rest you merry
> There is another play-house to let in Vere Street.
> Davenant, *The Play-house to be Let*, 1663 (*Works*, p. 72).

Ogilby, the poet, drew a lottery of books on Tuesday, June 2, 1668, "at the Old Theatre, between Lincoln's Inn Fields and Vere Street." He describes the books in his advertisement as "all of his own designment and composure." One of the many "lock-ups" with which Sir Richard Steele became acquainted was situated in this street. On October 24, 1740, he writes to his wife from "the Bull Head, Clare Market," and again on the 30th from "Vere Street." He was out the next day.

Vere Street, OXFORD STREET to CAVENDISH SQUARE, derives its name from the Veres, Earls of Oxford. In St. Peter's Chapel, in this street (designed by James Gibbs, 1721-1724), cost £7000, William, second Duke of Portland, was married (July 11, 1734) to the Lady Margaret Cavendish Harley, only daughter and heir of Edward Harley, Earl of Oxford and Mortimer, by his wife, the Lady Henrietta Cavendish, only daughter and heir of John Holles, Duke of Newcastle. The surrounding streets preserve many of these names. This Duchess of Portland formed the celebrated museum which bore her name. The celebrated Rev. Frederick Denison Maurice was incumbent of this chapel from 1860 until his death, 1872. John Michael Rysbrack, the sculptor, lived for forty years in this street, and died at Bristol 1770.

Mr. Rysbrach's house is in the further end of Bond Street, and up cross Tyburne Rode [Oxford Street], in Ld. Oxford's grownd upon the right hand going to his Chaple.—*Gibbs, the Architect, to Pope* (supp. vol. to *Works of Pope*, 8vo. 1825, p. 154).

Edward Askew Sothern, the celebrated comedian (Lord Dundreary), died at his residence, No. 1 Vere Street, January 19, 1881, of consumption.

Verge, Court of The, was instituted by James I. on June 8, 1611, apparently by the advice of Sir Francis Bacon, to take cognisance

[1] Rate-books of St. Clement's Danes.

"of personal actions which concern persons not being, or which hereafter shall not be, of our household," but which are within the verge of the King's house; there being some doubt as to the powers of the Marshalsea in such cases. Sir Thomas Vavasour and Sir Francis Bacon were the first judges.

For nuisances and grievances I will for the present only single out one, that ye present the decays of highways and bridges, for where the majesty of the King's House brings recourse and access it is both disgraceful to the King and disuseful to the people if the ways near abouts be not fair and good: whereas it is strange to see the chargeable pavements, causeways in the avenues and entrances of the towns abroad beyond the seas; whereas London, the second City (at the least) of Europe, in glory, in greatness, and in wealth, cannot be discerned by the fairness of the ways, though a little, perhaps, by the badness of them, from a village.—Bacon's *Charge to the Jury on opening the Court of the Verge*, 1611 (*Works*, vol. ii. p. 288).

Moria. There should not a nymph or a widow be got with child in *the Verge* but I would guess, within one or two, who was the right father.—Ben Jonson, *Cynthia's Revels*, Act iv. Sc. 1.

The Verge of the Court was a place privileged from arrests by ordinary officers of the law, and retained its rights till all privileges of sanctuary were abolished.

The Verge of the Court was that ground about Whitehall and St. James's which belongs to the Crown, and which is privileged from arrests. The privileged place includes Charing Cross on the north side of the way, from the corner of St. Martin's Lane to Hedge Lane, and both the King's Mews. On the south side from the street leading into Spring Gardens to the public house beyond the Treasury, and all Spring Gardens; on the opposite side of the way from Northumberland House to the end of Privy Garden, taking in all Scotland Yard, Whitehall, and Privy Garden. It further includes all the Parks, the Stable-Yard, St. James's, Cleveland Court and all Hyde Park, except the mere crossing from the Green Park to Hyde Park. Most houses in the Verge let lodgings; and I knew an artful fellow once that eluded all his creditors by residing there; if he wanted to go out of it he took water at Whitehall Stairs, which place is privileged; and as no writ can be served on the water without a water-bailiff's warrant, which cannot be immediately procured, he would land safely in the City or on the Surrey side; for a Middlesex writ loses its force in the City and in Surrey, unless backed by a City or a Surrey magistrate, which requires time and preparation to get done.—Trusler's *London Adviser and Guide*, 12mo, 1790.

Victoria Docks, PLAISTOW LEVEL, east of Bow Creek, were authorised by Parliament in 1850-1851, and opened in 1856. Excavated from the comparatively valueless marshes, the surface of which was below high-water mark, the docks were constructed on a larger scale, with greater facility and at less cost than the older docks in London. The area secured by the Company was about 600 acres, of which 200 acres were appropriated to dock purposes and the rest retained for building on and for future extension if necessary. The water area of the new docks was 100 acres, a little over that of the West India Docks, and exceeding the united area of all the other docks on the left bank of the Thames. The docks were especially fitted for vessels of the largest size, the intention being to save such vessels the risks attending the navigation of the narrow and crowded upper reaches of the river. The entrance lock, below Blackwall, is 325 feet long, 80 feet wide, and 28 feet deep. Quays and warehouses were carefully arranged and encircled with a complete system of railways and telegraphs, and hydraulic machinery was for the first time introduced—it is now employed in all the London Docks. The Company was empowered to raise a capital of £1,000,000 and borrow £200,000. The works were completed for about £1,000,000. The docks were found to answer the anticipations of the projectors, and have been steadily growing in favour with merchants and shipowners.

This increasing competition of the Victoria Docks led to the union of the East and West India Docks, the London Docks, and the St. Katharine's Dock Companies in 1863, and after some negotiations to the amalgamation with them of the Victoria Docks, the latter undertaking being purchased in 1869 for £1,062,000. Since then the united Company has expended on the Victoria Dock a very large sum in the construction of warehouses and on various appliances; and in 1876-1880 it added a magnificent new dock to the east of the former, and with it uniting the Bugsby and Galleon Reaches of the Thames by a straight water-way 2¾ miles long, and saving steamers of the larger class the intricate navigation of the narrow upper reaches of the Thames.

The Albert Dock as this extension of the Victoria Dock is named, was formally opened, May 7, 1880. The great basin is 6500 feet long, 490 wide, and has a depth of 27 feet below Trinity high-water mark. The entrance lock, by the Beckton Gas Works opposite Triphook Point, a short distance below Woolwich, is 800 feet long and 80 feet wide. A cut 200 feet long and 80 feet wide connects the two. The Albert Dock has proved of immense value as an auxiliary to Woolwich Arsenal in affording the means of rapidly victualling and preparing the large Government troop and store ships for sea with previously unequalled ease and quickness. Connected with the Albert Dock are two graving docks, respectively 500 and 410 feet long. The total water area of the Victoria and Albert Docks is about 185 acres; the land area is 430 acres.

About these docks has grown up the large and populous districts of Canning Town and Silvertown, with half a dozen churches, and many chapels, schools, halls, institutes, and hotels, inns and public-houses of all grades. The "uptown" warehouses of the Victoria Docks are on the line of the Blackwall Railway by the Minories.

Victoria Embankment. [*See* Thames Embankment.]

Victoria Gardens, WESTMINSTER. The long vacant piece of ground on the south of the Victoria Tower of the Houses of Parliament, between Abingdon Street and the Thames, about an acre in extent, was laid out, 1880-1881, by Her Majesty's Board of Works, as a summer garden for public use and enjoyment, and named the Victoria Gardens. A vote of £2400 was made for laying and planting the ground, March 1881, in addition to which the Rt. Hon. W. H. Smith, M.P., contributed £1000 towards the cost.

Victoria Park, BETHNAL GREEN and HACKNEY, was formed under the authority of an Act passed in 1842. The first cost of formation was covered by the purchase-money of York House, St. James's, received from the Marquis of Stafford (afterwards Duke of Sutherland), to whom the remainder of the Crown lease was sold in 1841 for £72,000. The entire cost was about £100,000. A plot of land was purchased 265 acres in extent, bounded on the south by Sir George Duckett's canal (sometimes called the Lea Union Canal); on the west by the Regent's Canal; on the east by Old Ford Lane, leading from Old Ford to Hackney Wick; and on the north by an irregular line of fields, but of this a sixth (45 acres) was by the Act reserved for building sites. Twenty-one acres were so employed, but in 1872 the Metropolitan Board of Works purchased the remaining 24 acres for £24,000, and these by an Act of that year were incorporated with the park, which now, therefore, comprises 244 acres.

The ground, a long and comparatively narrow, curved area, was laid out with much judgment and taste, every irregularity of form and inequality of surface being turned to account, planted with trees, shrubs, and flowers in prettily arranged beds, and two moderate sized sheets of water formed, with islands for the shelter of aquatic birds, and boats for the recreation of juvenile oarsmen. A portion of the park is set aside as cricket and play grounds. Formed out of open fields, it had necessarily at first a somewhat bare aspect, but it is now a very fine park, and an immense and thoroughly appreciated boon to a poor and thickly-populated district. It serves as a lung to the north-east part of London, and is said to have perceptibly improved the health as well as added to the enjoyment of the inhabitants of Bethnal Green and Spitalfields. It is said by the "Parks Preservation Society"—which was a main instrument in procuring the addition in 1872—that the population of the districts surrounding the park, which was 309,367 at the census of 1841, had increased to 839,647 in 1871.

Near the Hackney entrance is a large and handsome Gothic Drinking Fountain, designed by Mr. H. A. Darbyshire, and erected by the Baroness Burdett-Coutts in 1862 at a cost of over £5000. It is an octagon in plan, 28 feet in diameter, crowned by a cupola 60 feet high. The base is of granite, the columns of coloured red granite; marble figures pour water from vases into a capacious basin, and at the angles are vases for holding living flowers. On the skirts of the park have been erected the French Hospital (Hospital for poor French Protestants and their descendants) [*see* French Hospital], and the City of London Hospital for Diseases of the Chest (founded 1848), opened by the Prince Consort in 1855.

Victoria Railway Station. [*See* Victoria Street, Westminster.]

Victoria Square, BUCKINGHAM PALACE ROAD, PIMLICO, was built circ. 1836, or rather scooped out of the back gardens of Arabella Row and Ranelagh Street. The last London residence of Thomas Campbell, author of the *Pleasures of Hope*, was at No. 8 in this square. He went there in January 1841, and left in September 1843.

Victoria Street, HOLBORN, the name first given to the continuation of Farringdon Street northward. It is now called FARRINGDON ROAD, and extends from the Holborn Viaduct, or Charterhouse Street, to King's Cross Road. The church seen at the distance is *St. James's, Clerkenwell;* the dome adjoining is part of *Clerkenwell Sessions House.*

Victoria Street, WESTMINSTER, a street 3080 feet long and 80 feet wide between the kerbs, with footways 20 feet wide, extending from the Broad Sanctuary, Westminster, to Pimlico. It was projected 1844 by H. R. Abraham, architect, and opened in August 1851, at a cost of £215,000. It was at a standstill for some years and took slowly for building purposes, in fact it was only completely filled up in 1887. The street is lined with lofty "mansions" let out in "flats" as residences—at the time of their erection a novelty in London—and large blocks of chambers. At the Westminster end is the spacious Westminster Palace Hotel. At the Pimlico end is the Victoria Station of the London, Chatham and Dover; and London, Brighton and South Coast Railways, connected with which, by a subterranean passage, is the Victoria Station of the Metropolitan District Railway. Near the centre of Victoria Street, north side, is *Christ Church.*

Victoria Theatre, WATERLOO ROAD, LAMBETH, originally *The Cobourg,* and called *The Victoria* for the first time in the reign of William IV., when her present Majesty was only heir-presumptive to the crown. The first stone of the *Cobourg Theatre* was laid September 14, 1816 (Rudolph Cabanel, architect), and the house opened in 1818. It was opened as the *Victoria Theatre,* July 1, 1833, with the play of *Black-eyed Susan,* T. P. Cooke sustaining the part of William. It was for many years a favourite resort of the inhabitants of the district, and was noted for the blood and thunder character of the entertainments, widely known as the "Vic." After being some time closed, the lease was purchased by a limited association with the view of trying whether the working classes of that part of London could be attracted by musical entertainments of a popular character, but divested of what was objectionable in the lower class of music halls. It was accordingly altered and handsomely decorated at the cost of a few friends interested in the experiment, and opened early in 1881 as the *Royal Victoria Coffee Music Hall.* Smoking is allowed; and tea, coffee, and light beverages are provided, but all "alcoholic drinks" are prohibited. [*See* Cobourg Theatre].

Vigo Street, REGENT STREET. The original name was *Vigo Lane,* bestowed in honour of the action at Vigo Bay in 1702, and it applied to the whole lane from Bond Street to Glasshouse Street. The portion behind Burlington House was afterwards called *Burlington Gardens.*

Lane was not changed to *Street* for many years after the formation of Regent Street; it stands, indeed, as *Vigo Lane* in Elmes's London Streets, 1831.

April 28, 1761.—There has been a terrible fire in the little traverse street at the upper end of Sackville Street. Last Friday night, between 11 and 12, I was sitting with Lord Digby in the coffee-room at Arthur's: they told us there was a great fire somewhere about Burlington Gardens. I, who am as constant at a fire as George Selwyn at an execution, proposed to Lord Digby to go and see where it was. We found it within two doors of that pretty house of Fairfax, now General Waldegrave's. I sent for the latter, who was at Arthur's, and for the Guard from St. James's. Four houses were in flames before they could find a drop of water: eight were burnt.—*Walpole to Montagu*, vol. iii. p. 397.

Villiers Street, STRAND, built circ. 1674,[1] and so called after George Villiers, second and last Duke of Buckingham of the Villiers family. [*See* York House.] *Eminent Inhabitants.*—John Evelyn.

November 17, 1683.—I tooke a house in Villiers Streete, York Buildings, for the winter, having many important concerns to dispatch, and for the education of my daughters.—*Evelyn*.

Sir Richard Steele, after his wife's death, from 1721 to 1724. In 1725 the rate-books of St. Martin's have the word "gone" against his name. He died in Wales in 1729.

In this street was a Music Room almost as celebrated in its day as the Hanover Square Room at a later period. There was also for a time a Music Room in Charles Street, Covent Garden, which was frequently coupled with it. Among Aaron Hill's *Miscellanies* (vol. iv. p. 106) is "A Prologue for the third night of Zara, when first played at the *Great Musick Room*, in Villars Street, York Buildings," 1735. On this occasion a gentleman named Bond, who was acting the part of Lusignan, fell dead upon the stage.

About three years previous to Mr. Garrick's appearing at the Theatre in Goodman's Fields, he performed Chamont in the Tragedy of the Orphan, at a small house called the Duke's Theatre, in Villiers Street, York Buildings, which was situated within a few doors of the bottom of the street, on the right-hand side. The play was got up by the Scholars of Eton College. The ladies who were present at Mr. Garrick's professional debut were so fascinated by his splendid powers that they offered him their purses and trinkets from the Boxes.—Anthony Pasquin, *Children of Thespis*, p. 208, *note*.

All the houses on the right-hand side of Villiers Street were removed to make way for the Charing Cross Station and Hotel.

Vincent Square, WESTMINSTER, built early in this century on the site of the Bear Garden in Tothill Fields, was so called after William Vincent, Dean of Westminster (d. 1816). The church of St. Mary the Virgin was designed by Edward Blore, F.S.A., and consecrated October 12, 1837. Here is the Westminster Police Court, removed, 1845, from Queen Square, where it had been fixed so long as to be quite identified with the locality. Here, too, are the Coldstream Guards' Hospital, and a hospital for women and children.

---

[1] Rate-books of St. Martin's.

Vine Court, MIDDLE TEMPLE. *Finetti Philoxenis,* a curious little book of Court Ceremonies of the time of James I. and Charles I., was printed in 1656 "by T. R. for H. Twyford and G. Bedell, and are to be sold at their shops in Vine Court, Middle Temple, and the Middle Temple Gate." The author was Sir John Finett, master of the ceremonies to James I. and Charles I. The first edition of Cocker's *Arithmetic,* 1671, was also published by "Henry Twyford in Vine Court, Middle Temple."

Vine Street, PICCADILLY. Here, after his removal from Old Palace Yard, was the studio of Scheemakers the sculptor, in which Joseph Nollekens learned his art. Mrs. Scheemakers had such an opinion of her husband's pupil that she declared "Joey was so honest she could trust him to stone the raisins."

Little Vine Street now contains little more than the back of St. James's Hall and the Police Office. The old Watch-house was pulled down in 1868 and rebuilt on a larger scale.

Vine Street, SAFFRON HILL, so called from the vineyard of old Ely Gardens. [*See* Ely Place.]

Vine Street, WESTMINSTER, on the south side of St. John's Church, was so called from the vineyard belonging to the Palace of our Kings at Westminster. It was renamed *Romney Street* in 1869-1870. The Vine-garden, within the Mill-ditch of Westminster, is mentioned in a Privy Seal granted by Charles II. to Edward Billing.[1] Charles Churchill, the satirist, was born, in 1731, in this street.

> Famed Vine Street,
> Where Heaven, the utmost wish of man to grant,
> Gave me an old house and an older aunt.

So he sang to lose a legacy by the allusion. The poet's father was curate and evening lecturer of the neighbouring church of *St. John the Evangelist.*

Vinegar Yard, DRURY LANE, properly Vine Garden Yard, or Vineyard, was built circ. 1621.[2]

February 4, 1624.—Buried Blind John out of Vinagre Yard.—*Burial Register of St. Martin's-in-the-Fields.*

In the *Beggar's Opera* this yard is mentioned as a rival to Lewknor's Lane and Hockley in the Hole; and in Pope's "Instructions to a Porter how to find Mr. Curll's authors," "the schoolmaster with carbuncles on his nose" is made a resident of "the Hercules and Hell in Vinegar Yard." Clayrender's letter, in Roderick Random, to her "Dear Kreeter," is written from "Wingar Yeard, Droory Lane." Its contiguity to the theatre is not overlooked in the *Rejected Addresses:*—

> And one, the leader of the band,
> From Charing Cross along the Strand,
> Like stag by beagles hunted hard,
> Ran till he stopp'd at Vin'gar Yard.

---

[1] *Harleian MS.,* 7341.   [2] Rate-books of St. Martin's.

"The Crown Tavern," in the yard, was a favourite place of "The Eccentrics," a celebrated Club of Londoners, who allowed drink and eccentricities to prevail. The club does not now exist.

Vintners' Hall, No. 68, on the south side of UPPER THAMES STREET. The Vintners' Company is the eleventh on the list of the twelve Great Companies of London. The Vintners, comprising the *Vinetarii*, or wine importers and merchants, and the *Tabernarii*, tavern-keepers or retailers of wine, were an ancient fraternity, and were incorporated in the 15th of Henry VI. (1436-1437). They are a wealthy company, maintain considerable hospitality, and dispense large charities. John de Stody, who held the lordship of the village of Stody, in Norfolk, 1344, was Sheriff of London 1352, free of the Vintners' Company, and Lord Mayor 1357. "He gave the company the site of the quadrant, where the Vintners' Hall is built, yet called Stody's Lane."[1] The hall was burnt down in the Great Fire and rebuilt from the designs of Sir Christopher Wren in 1671. It is of moderate size and comparatively plain, but has some good carved oak in the great room. Only the Council Chamber remains, as the hall was rebuilt 1820-1823. In the court-room are full-length portraits of Charles II., James II., Marie d'Este, and Prince George of Denmark, and a painting ascribed to Vandyck of St. Martin, the patron saint of the Company, dividing his cloak with a beggar. There is also a good and well-preserved piece of tapestry representing St. Martin. Among the Company's plate is a remarkably fine parcel gilt salt-cellar ascribed to Cellini. One of the churches in the ward of Vintry is dedicated to the Company's patron saint. It is called *St. Martin-in-the-Vintry*.

Vintry (The), says Stow, was—

A part of the bank of the river Thames, where the merchants of Burdeaux craned their wines out of lighters and other vessels, and there landed and made sale of them. —*Stow*, p. 89.

Prior to the 28th of Edward I. the merchants had to make sale of their wines within forty days of unlading from the ships, but in that year, on their setting forth the loss and inconvenience they suffered, their complaint was "redressed by virtue of the King's writ . . . since the which time many fair and large houses, with vaults and cellars for stowage of wines, and lodging of the Bordeaux merchants have been built" along the wharfs on the river's side, and the place acquired the name it retained for centuries of the Vintry. This was the first patent of the kind granted to foreign merchants, but it was followed three years later by another extending cognate privileges to all foreign merchants who "sell by wholesale only."

In the reign of Henry IV., the young Prince Henry [Shakespeare's Prince Hal], Thomas, Duke of Clarence, John, Duke of Bedford, and Humfrey, Duke of Glocester, the King's sons, being at supper among the merchants of London in *the Vintry*, in the house of Lewes John, Henry Scogan sent them a ballad beginning thus:—

"My noble Sonnes and eke my lordes deare."—*Stow*, p. 90.

---

[1] *Norfolk Tour*, p. 792.

This was "ballad-royal," which, Ben Jonson says, Scogan "For the King's sons writ daintily well."[1]

Vintry (Ward of), one of the twenty-six wards into which the City of London is divided, was so named as containing the *Vintry* [which *see*]. It is bounded on the north by Cannon Street, south by the Thames, east by Dowgate, and west by *Queenhithe*. Stow enumerates four churches and four Halls of Companies as situated in this ward: St. Michael's, called Paternoster Church-in-the-Royal, College Hill; St. Thomas the Apostle (destroyed in the Fire, and not rebuilt); St. Martin's-in-the-Vintry (destroyed in the Fire, and not rebuilt); St. James's, Garlickhithe; Vintners' Hall; Cutlers' Hall; Glaziers' Hall, but this Company now has no hall; Parish Clerks' Hall (now in Silver Street, Cripplegate Ward). [*See* all these names.] *Southwark Bridge* abuts from near the centre of this ward, and the larger part of the Cannon Street terminus of the South Eastern Railway is within it.

Wager Hall.
<blockquote>Wits, cheats, and fops are free of Wager Hall,</blockquote>
says Dryden in his Prologue to King Arthur (1691), but we find no other trace of such a place, which is probably an imaginary one invented by the poet for the purpose of his attack on the prevalent vice of betting.

Walbrook was in early days, as Stow tells us, a "fair brook of sweet water, which came from out the north fields, through the wall and midst of the City, into the river of Thames, and which Division is till this day constantly and without change maintained." Thus in the City ordinances we find that "when a person is bound to clear himself under the Great Law," or under pleas of the Crown, it is declared that there must be a jury provided of "six-and-thirty reputable men of the City"; and in choosing these six-and-thirty men "the procedure, according to the ancient usage of the City of London, is wont to be, and should be," that "eighteen men must be chosen from the east side of the Walebroke, and eighteen men from the west side of Walebroke."[2] But important as it must have been as a boundary mark, it must very early have ceased to be "a fair brook of sweet water," and was, in fact, the first of the many similar streamlets which have fallen victims to the exigences of the growing city, being first polluted and then blotted out. As early as 16 Edward I. A.D. 1288, it was ordained "that the watercourse of Walbrook should be made free from dung and other nuisances, and that the rakes [jakes?] should be put back again upon every tenement extending from the Moor [of Finsbury] to the Thames." At this time it had been partially covered in, and in 28 Edward I. 1300, it was ordered that the portion of "the covering over the water-course of *Walebroc*, over against the chancel of the church of St. Stephen," should be repaired at the cost of that parish; and it had been previously determined by whom the bridges over the brook should be kept in

---
[1] Ben Jonson, *Fortunate Isles*. [2] *Liber Albus*, pp. 51, 98.

order.[1] Seventy-four years later, in 48 Edward III. (1374), the Moor of Finsbury was leased to Thomas atte Ram, a brewer, "for seven years then next ensuing, without paying any rent therefor: upon the understanding that the same Thomas shall keep the said moor well and properly, and shall have the Watercourse of Walbrok cleansed for the whole of the term aforesaid; and shall have the same cleared of dung and other filth thrown or deposited therein, or that may be there placed during the term aforesaid: he taking for every latrine built upon the said watercourse 12 pence yearly, during such term, for his trouble, as from of old has been wont to be paid. And if in so cleansing it, as aforesaid, he shall find aught therein, he shall have for his own all that he shall so find in the dung and filth thereof."[2] But even this last liberal concession was insufficient to procure the desired end; and in 6 Richard II. (1383) the nuisance had become greater than ever, although the charge for latrines had been doubled.

Up to this time its name as a stream, Wall Brook, is still preserved, but in 3 Henry V. (1415) the "fair brook of sweet water" has sunk into the "Foss of Walbrooke" (as Fleet River became the Fleet Ditch); its "horrible, infected and corrupt" atmosphere is spoken of; and provision is made for the construction of a *scluys* or *speye*,[3] by which it might from time to time be flooded by water little less filthy than its own. Later it was in part vaulted over, and by the end of the reign of Elizabeth the whole was covered over and hidden from view.

This water was called not Galus, brook of a Roman Captain, slain by Asclepiodatus, and thrown therein as some have fabled, but of running through and from the wall of the city, the course whereof, to prosecute it particularly, was and is from the said [city] wall to St. Margaret's Church in Lothbury; from thence beneath the lower part of the Grocers' Hall about the East part of their Kitchen under St. Mildred's Church, somewhat west from the Stocks' Market; from thence through Buckelsbury, by one great house built of stone and timber, called the Old Barge, because barges out of the river of Thames were rowed up so far into this brook . . . and so behind the other houses to Elbow Lane, and by a part thereof down Greenwich Lane into the river of Thames.—*Stow*, p. 45.

This water-course having divers bridges, was afterwards vaulted over with brick, and paved level with the streets and lanes wherethrough it passed; and since that, also houses have been built thereon, so that the course of Walbrook is now hidden under ground, and thereby hardly known.—*Stow*, p. 6.

The writer of Sir Richard Phillips's *History of London*[4] says, that he saw the Walbrook in November 1803, "still trickling among the foundations of the new buildings at the Bank." In digging for the foundations of new buildings in recent years, stout timber piles have been at different times excavated in the course of the old Walbrook, and it has been suggested that a cluster of these had formed the basis of a primeval pile dwelling or dwellings; but the piles bore no marks of such extreme antiquity, and there can be little doubt that they were the supports of some of the structures that we know abounded along the banks of "the fair brook."

[1] Riley, *Memorials*, pp. 23, 43-47.
[2] *Ibid.*, p. 379; and see *Liber Albus*, p. 501.
[3] Riley, p. 615.
[4] *History of London*, 4to, 1805, p. 20.

Walbrook, a street in the City, running from the POULTRY into BUDGE ROW and CANNON STREET. In 35 Edward I. (1307) "John Le Marischale of Walebroke" is associated with the Aldermen and other good men of the City in a business of importance. In 39 Edward III. (1365), when ordinances were made for *Pelterers* and *Pelliperes*, or furriers and skinners, as they would now be called, it was specially directed that "all the freemen of the said trade shall dwell in Walebroke, Cornehulle, and Bogerowe" [Walbrook, Cornhill, and Budge Row]; and later it was ordered "that no one shall cause his furs to be scoured in the high streets in the day-time."[1]

Sir Christopher Wren is said to have lived in a house subsequently No. 5. *Observe.*—Church of *St. Stephen's Walbrook* [which *see*]. No. 5, the handsome new building of the *City Liberal Club*. On a house (No. 11) on the west side is a tablet with bracket and cornice dated 1668.

Walbrook Ward, one of the twenty-six wards of London, and so called from the brook by the City wall, described in the preceding article. Stow enumerates five churches in this ward: *St. Swithin-by-London-Stone; St. Mary Woolchurch; St. Stephen's, Walbrook; St. John-upon-Walbrook; St. Mary Bothaw.* The *Mansion House* is in this ward.

In 1382 (5 Richard II.) an occurrence took place which is amusingly illustrative of old City ways.

> Whereas the Mayor and Aldermen with common assent had agreed that all the Aldermen of London, for the dignity of the said City, should be arrayed upon the Feast of Pentecost, in the 5th year, etc., in cloaks of green, lined with green taffeta or tartaryn [a thin silk] under a penalty, at the discretion of the Mayor and the other Aldermen, so arrayed, to be assessed :—On Monday, the same Feast, when the said Mayor and Aldermen went to the Church of St. Peter on Cornhill, to go in procession from thence through the City, according to the ancient custom, to the Church of St. Paul, *John Sely, the Alderman of Walbrook*, appeared there in a cloak that was single and without a lining, contrary to the Ordinance and assent aforesaid. Whereupon, by the advice of the Mayor and other Aldermen, it was then adjudged and assented to, that the said Mayor and other Aldermen should dine with the same John at his house, and that at the proper costs of the said John, on the Thursday following, and further the said John was to line his cloak in manner aforesaid : and so it was done. And this judgment shall extend to all other Aldermen, hereafter to come, without sparing any one, if any person among them shall act contrary to the Ordinance aforesaid.—Riley, *Memorials*, p. 466.

Wallingford House stood on the site of the present *Admiralty*, and was so called after Sir William Knollys, Treasurer of the Household to Queen Elizabeth and King James, Baron Knollys, Viscount Wallingford, and Earl of Banbury. His father was Treasurer of the Household before him, and inhabited the same official house at the end of the *Tilt Yard*. The first Duke of Buckingham of the Villiers family purchased the house from Lord Wallingford in 1621-1622. Carleton's correspondent, John Chamberlain, says that he paid partly by "some money" and partly by "making Sir Thomas Howard

[1] Riley's *Memorials; Liber Albus.*

Baron of Charlton and Viscount Andover; and some think the relieving of the Lord of Somerset and his Lady out of the Tower."[1] Buckingham's first child, called *Jacobina* after the King, was born here in March 1622. "During the illness of the Marchioness," we are told, "the King prayed heartily for her, and was at Wallingford House early and late." Here Buckingham's eldest son, the author of the *Rehearsal*, was born January 30, 1627. Bassompierre calls the house *Valinforth*. The house assumed the character of an official residence very early. When Buckingham was created Lord High Admiral he established at Wallingford House a Council of the Sea, or Board of Admiralty. The Duke was assassinated August 23, 1628, and the young Duke being a minor the Council was continued at Wallingford House.[2] The Lord Treasurer's Office[3] was also here. Warrants are extant addressed to the Auditors of the Imprests, and signed "R. Weston," and "Fra. Cottington"; and "Portland" and "Fra. Cottington," dated from Wallingford House, April 21, 1632, and April 29, 1634. Weston (afterwards Earl of Portland) was treasurer and Cottington under-treasurer at this time, so that Wallingford House must, during those years, have continued to serve as a Government office. Whether it continued to be thus employed in the following years is not so certain.

April 14, 1635.—The Duchess of Buckingham was married about a week since to the Lord Dunluce, and are to live at Wallingford House, whence the Treasurer's family removes. My Lord Chamberlain takes home his daughter, and the King places the young Duke and his brother with the Archbishop of Canterbury to be bred up there.—*Garrard to Wentworth* (*Strafford Letters*, vol. i. p. 413).

The infamous Countess of Essex is said to have died in this house, but this is a mistake; she died in 1632 at Chiswick. From the roof of Wallingford House, then in the occupation of the Earl and Countess of Peterborough, Archbishop Ussher saw Charles I. led to execution. Ussher swooned at the sight and was carried to his apartments.[4]

The "General Council of the Officers of the Army," otherwise known as *the Wallingford House Party*, assembled here after Cromwell's death. Their chief object seems to have been to frustrate the designs of Monk, but they had no settled plan, and the party, though supported by Fleetwood and Vane, was a powerless faction. Ludlow describes their movements with great minuteness in his *Memoirs*. Fleetwood was at this time living in the house. Wallingford House reverted to the second Duke of Buckingham at the Restoration; here the corpse of Cowley, his brother-collegian and intimate friend, lay in state, and here the Duke was living in 1671, when the following advertisement appeared in the *London Gazette* of that year:—

On Wednesday, March 26, 1671, was lost from Brentwood in Essex, a couple of young Hounds of his Grace the Duke of Buckingham; the one a black Tanned, with a little white under his neck; the other a white one, with black spots, both marked

---

[1] *Cal. State Papers*, 1603-1610, p. 317. [3] *Ibid.*, vol. i. p. 291.
[2] *Strafford Letters*, vol. i. p. 209. [4] Parr's *Life of Ussher*, fol. 1686.

with B. on the left shoulder; whoever can give notice of them to the Porter at Wallingford House in the Strand, shall be well rewarded for their pains.—*London Gazette*, No. 563.

Lord Clifford, the Lord Treasurer, afterwards inhabited it, and here Evelyn called to take leave of his lordship.

> *August* 18, 1673.—I went to take leave of him [My Lord Clifford] at Wallingford House. He was packing up pictures, most of which were of hunting wild beasts, and vast pieces of bull-baiting, beare-baiting, etc. I found him in his study, and restored to him several papers of state and others of importance, which he had furnished me with, on engaging me to write the *Historie of the Holland War*. .
> Taking leave of my Lord Clifford he wrung me by the hand, and looking earnestly on me, bid me God b'ye, adding, "Mr. E., I shall never see thee more." "No!" said I. "My Lord, what is the meaning of this? I hope I shall see you often, and as greate a person againe." "No, Mr. E., do not expect it, I will never see this place, this City, or Courte againe." . . . In this manner, not without almost mutual tears, I parted from him; nor was it long after but the news was that he was dead, and I heard from some one, who I believe knew, he made himself away, after an extraordinary melancholy.—*Evelyn*.

The Lord Treasurer dated public documents from this house, 1674-1676. Wallingford House was sold to the Crown in 1680, and about 1726 the present *Admiralty* was erected where it stood.

To Sir Christopher Wren.

> S^r—My Lord Treasurer has ordered me to let you know that he would have the Duke of Buckingham's building at *Wallingford House* and so on, in what relates to the building itself, but as to the way out of the street into Old Spring Gardens, that must be stopt up till my Lord is satisfied that it may be legally made into that ground.— I am S^r yours etc., H. G. Tunbridge Wells,
> *Treasury Letter Book.* July 26, 1686.

Walnut Tree Tavern, Tooley Street, Southwark.

> Over against this parish church (St. Olave's), on the south side of the street, was sometime one great house built of stone, with arched gates, pertaining to the Prior of Lewes in Sussex, and was his lodging when he came to London: it is now a common hostelrie for travellers, and hath to sign the Walnut Tree.—*Stow*, p. 154.

Walnut Tree Alley preserved the memory of the old hostelry, and when this alley was swept away for the approaches to New London Bridge, a vaulted chamber, or crypt, was discovered underneath the houses, curiously confirming the statement of Stow that the Walnut Tree Inn was the mansion of the Priors of Lewes. Cuthbert Beeston, citizen and girdler of London, died in 1582, seized of the Walnut Tree Inn, together with the garden belonging thereto, and fifteen messuages in Walnut Tree Lane, otherwise Carter Lane, in St. Olave's, Southwark, "held of the Queen in chief, worth yearly £5 : 6 : 8." It appears that the Walnut Tree Inn occupied the east side of the building. The west wing was purchased by the parish for the use of the Grammar School of St. Olave's, founded in 1571.[1]

Walworth, a manor so named in Domesday, now and for about 500 years included in Newington and Newington Butts, the birthplace, Lysons thought, of the celebrated citizen who bore its name. Two

---
[1] *Archæologia*, vol. v. p. xxiii.

commons were comprised in the manor: Walworth Common, about 48 acres, and Lowenmoor Common, of about 19 acres. It is now the property of the Dean and Chapter of Canterbury. The church, dedicated to St. Peter, a classical structure erected from the designs of Sir John Soane at a cost of £19,126, was consecrated by Archbishop Sutton, February 28, 1825. There are besides the district churches of St. John, St. Paul, St. Mark, and St. Stephen, the last a Gothic edifice of florid design erected in 1871 by Messrs. Jarvis. The fields and open spaces about Walworth have all been covered with houses, and at the census of 1881 the registration sub-district contained 59,562 inhabitants. The population is mostly of the artisan and labouring class, and many parts of the district are ill-built, crowded, and unwholesome. A worthy attempt to provide better accommodation for the inhabitants of one of these districts was made by the Fishmongers' Company, who, in 1876, erected, at a cost of £13,000, ten admirably fitted blocks of dwellings on their estate in Lock's Fields, providing comfortable tenements for 800 families.

In Manor Place, Walworth, died, November 1, 1835, aged seventy-seven, the friend and correspondent of Southey, Thomas Taylor, the Platonist.

Wapping, a hamlet of St. Mary, Whitechapel, on the Middlesex side of the River Thames, a little below *The Tower*, "and chiefly inhabited by seafaring men and tradesmen dealing in commodities for the supply of shipping and shipmen."[1] It was originally a great wash, watered by the Thames, and was first recovered in the reign of Queen Elizabeth. Stow calls it "Wapping in the Wose"[2] (really Wapping in the Ooze), signifying as much, says Strype, "as in the wash or in the drain."[3] The usual place of execution for pirates was at "Wapping in the Wose."[4] [*See* Execution Dock.] But other offenders sometimes suffered here.

March 10, 1618.—Sir George Sandys hanged at Wapping for taking purses on the highway, having been formerly pardoned for like offences: his lady and son in prison as accomplices.—*Sir G. Herbert to Sir Dudley Carleton (Cal. State Pap., 1611-1618, p. 527.*

Lord Chancellor Jeffreys attempting, after the abdication of King James, to make his escape in the disguise of a common seaman— having on a "furre cap, a seaman's neckcloth, and a dirty coat "— was captured in an obscure alehouse, called the Red Cow, in Anchor-and-Hope Alley, near King Edward's Stairs in Wapping. He was found by a scrivener he had formerly insulted, lolling out of window in all the confidence of misplaced security. Among the papers preserved in the Record Office connected with the great Overbury poisoning case, is one in which the "Old Man of Wapping" is denounced as an "eminent Witch." Strype relates at length the curious history of "a large house of timber" which was built by the river side "in this

---

[1] *Strype*, B. iv. p. 39.   [2] *Stow*, p. 157. In the second edition it is misprinted "in the West."
[3] *Strype*, B. iv. p. 37.   [4] *Stow*, by Howes, ed. 1631, p. 697.

hamlet of Wappin, anno 1626 . . . for the making of allom, and which grew to such an inconvenience and annoyance . . . that upon complaint of the inhabitants to the King and Council, it was proceeded withal as appeareth." He gives this "complaint," which set forth as a special case, that "a lighter of allom grease lying in the Hermitage Dock, which was taken out of a ship lying there overthwart the mouth of the Dock; and upon the emptying of the water out of the lighter, which issued from the grease, there did arise a most noysome stinking . . . and it did so stink that we were not able to endure the scent of it, insomuch that it endangered all the ponds and wells thereabouts." Another petition from the inhabitants of the hamlet of Wapping and the neighbouring parishes declares, with a fine redundancy of expletives, that "being continually choaked and poysoned up with the daily and continual stink and most noisome and infectious smell that is lately begun among us by a workhouse for making of allome," we "are not able to live in our houses, nor keep our families at work about us, the detestable stink thereof is so infectious and intolerable." If allowed to be continued they affirm "it is generally thought it will be a decay and dangerous infection to all inhabitants both on this side and the other side the water within two miles' compass of the place it standeth." And they conclude by asking that "reformation be given," otherwise "we shall be compelled to leave our houses and dwellings to our utter undoings, for the noysome smell is so dangerous, that no man will dwell thereabouts, if he might have his house rent free!" Then there is another petition of his "Majesty's liege subjects, being in number many thousands," which points out the injury done to the "many great brewhouses, which breweth beer for the use and service of your Majesty's navy," to "all passengers that way, or by the River of Thames," many of whom have already been "cast into extremity of great sicknesses and diseases"; that "of late many fishes in the Thames have been found ready to die and dead, supposed to be poysoned by some ill substance issuing into the River of Thames;" that "all the pasture ground lying near thereabouts is tainted and spoiled in such manner that the cattel do refuse to feed on the same;" and they ask for "speedy redress in that behalf, the same annoyance being so great and unsavoury that otherwise your poor subjects, being many thousands in number, shall be compelled to forsake their houses, and abandon their dwellings, to the loss of their trades and lives, and the utter undoing of them and their families."

These petitions were considered in Council at Whitehall, July 25, 1627, and an order made that the works should be continued until Lady Day next ensuing, and no longer, and in the meantime no new works should be erected. The inhabitants demurred to the delay, and on their further petition an Order in Council was issued, September 12, that "the said Allome works should be presently suppressed from working," and the farmers thereof are commanded to "see the same duly executed; and of the performance thereof to give account to their

Lordships within ten or twelve days after the date hereof." Still the works went on, and the Council at their meeting, December 12, 1627, for reasons stated, authorise the continuance of the works to Lady Day, 1628, when they are to be removed "to some other place more remote from the City of London and the suburbs thereof;" and this, we may suppose, was done, as nothing more is said on the subject.[1]

Friday, July 24, 1629.—King Charles having hunted a Stag or Hart from Wansted in Essex, killed him in Nightingale Lane in the hamlet of Wappin, in a garden belonging to one ——, who had some damage among his herbs, by reason the multitude of people there assembled suddenly.—*Strype*, B. iv. p. 39.

The first (Pope's) Duke of Chandos married the widow of Sir Thomas Duval, regarding whom Mrs. Pendarves [Mrs. Delaney] writes to Swift, April 22, 1736, "The marriage has made a great noise, and the poor Duchess is often reproached with being bred up in *Burr Street, Wapping.*" Oddly enough, Swift, in writing to Mrs. Pendarves in January 1736, says, "A woman of quality, who had excellent good sense, was formerly my correspondent, but she scrawled and spelt like a Wapping wench."

He [Johnson] talked to-day [April 12, 1783] a good deal of the wonderful extent and variety of London, and observed that men of curious inquiry might see in it such modes of life as very few could ever imagine. He in particular recommended us to *explore Wapping*, which we resolved to do. [We accordingly carried our scheme into execution in October 1792, but whether from that uniformity which has in a great degree spread through every part of the metropolis, or from our want of sufficient exertion, we were disappointed.]—Croker's *Boswell*, p. 724, and Boswell's note.

Any one seeking to "explore Wapping" now, would find less to repay his trouble than Boswell might have discovered in 1792. There must then have been much that was curious and characteristic in the low-lying semi-maritime suburb, with its narrow ways, quaint shops, and river-side manners. But all this has been swept away by the recent rapid march of improvement. A few years ago the notoriety of the "Claimant" and his asserted riparian origin led many to visit Wapping, if not to explore its byways. But even the Orton house has now disappeared. It was pulled down in 1876, and it may save the future annotator of our criminal annals some trouble to record its exact site.

It stood near the Wapping entrance of the London Docks, and adjoined that in which it is said Lord Nelson got his outfit when he first went to sea. Both are now demolished to make way for warehouses, which promise to displace most of the old residences by the river-side in these parts. Indeed, the High Street of Wapping is gradually being skirted by enormous piles of these buildings, and before long few beyond the model lodging-houses of Sir Sidney Waterlow and the residences of the dock officers will be left for domestic use.—Rev. H. Jones, *East and West London*, p. 50.

In Wapping High Street was the entrance to the Thames Tunnel [which *see*].

Much of Wapping is considerably below high-water level, and as very inadequate provision has been made to prevent overflows, the

[1] *Strype*, vol. ii. pp. 39-43.

streets are flooded and the basements of the houses filled with water whenever the spring tides rise above the ordinary level. It can hardly be regretted, therefore, that dwellings are giving place to warehouses. When these are general their owners and occupants will take care that a sufficient embankment is provided. Joseph Ames, the antiquary, and author of *Typographical Antiquities, or the History of Printing in England*, "lived in a strange alley or lane in Wapping."[1] His very useful work, first printed in 1749, has been edited and enlarged by William Herbert, and again in the present century by T. F. Dibdin. The church is dedicated to St. John the Baptist. The Rev. Francis Willis, the "mad doctor," whose treatment of George III. was considered to be so beneficial that he was rewarded with a pension of £1500 a year for twenty-nine years, was rector of Wapping. So later was Dr. Le Bas.

War Office, PALL MALL. The War Office, of which the headquarters were formerly at the Horse Guards, now occupies the old Ordnance Office, built for the Duke of Cumberland, brother of George III., and the adjoining Buckingham House to the east and Schomberg House to the west, on the south side of Pall Mall. Here are concentrated the offices of the Adjutant-General, the Quarter-Master-General, the Inspector-General of Artillery, the Chaplain-General, and other heads of departments. [*See* Horse Guards.] In the front of the old Ordnance Office is a bronze statue of Sidney Herbert, Lord Herbert of Lea, by Foley, erected in 1867. [*See* Ordnance Office, Pall Mall, Schomberg House.]

Wardour Street, SOHO, or, WARDOUR STREET, OXFORD STREET, ran from Oxford Street to Compton Street, but now, by the incorporation of Princes Street, extends to Coventry Street. [*See* Princes Street.] It was built circ. 1686,[2] and so called after Henry, third Lord Arundel of Wardour (d. 1694), a steady adherent to the cause of King James II. Henry, the fifth Lord Arundel, married Elizabeth, daughter of Thomas Panton, of St. Martin's-in-the-Fields. [*See* Panton Square.] Flaxman, the sculptor, lived at No. 27, a small house in this street, from 1781 to 1787. No. 99, the corner of Peter Street, is *The Intrepid Fox*, so called in honour of Charles James Fox, by the landlord, Sam House, one of his most enthusiastic worshippers. House died in 1785, and on the day of his death Mr. Fox sat for a considerable time by his bedside. He is celebrated in the *Rolliad*.

> Why should I tell the Election's honest tale,
> That scene of libels, riots, blood and ale?
> There, of *Sam House* the horrid form appeared;
> Round his white apron howling monsters reared
> Their angry clubs; and broken heads they polled,
> And Hood's best sailors in the kennel rolled.
>   Charles Jenkinson, *Political Eclogues*.

---

[1] Brydges' *Restituta*, vol. iv. p. 235.   [2] Stone, corner of Edward Street.

Wardour Street is famous for book-stalls and curiosity-shops. Charles Lamb was fond of this street; and Hazlitt lies on the other side of the wall which encloses the burial ground of St. Anne's. I have heard Lamb expatiate on the pleasure of strolling up "Wardour Street on a summer's day."—*Leigh Hunt.*

Rummaging over the contents of an old stall at a half *book,* half *old-iron shop,* in an alley leading from Wardour Street to Soho Square, yesterday, I lit upon a ragged duodecimo, which had been the strange delight of my infancy. . . . The price demanded was sixpence, which the owner (a little squab duodecimo of a character himself) enforced with the assurance that his "own mother should not have it for a farthing less."—*Elia: The Months.*

The *York* Chop House in this street was the favourite (and inexpensive) resort of successive generations of young painters and art students attending the schools in St. Martin's Lane and the Royal Academy.

Nothing could be more agreeable than my daily intercourse at this period (the Spring of 1820) with Irving and Newton. We visited in the same families, chiefly Americans resident in London, and generally dined together at the *York Chop House* in Wardour Street.—Leslie, R.A., *Autob. Recollections,* vol. i. p. 63.

Here are many shops exclusively devoted to the sale of old furniture, pictures, china, and other articles of vertu. Rumour says that the back premises of Wardour Street are largely devoted to the manufacture of sham antiques of all kinds. [*See* St. Anne's, Soho.]

Wardrobe (The), a house near Puddle Wharf, Blackfriars, built by Sir John Beauchamp (d. 1359), whose tomb in old St. Paul's was mistaken for the tomb of the good Duke Humphrey. Beauchamp's executors sold it to Edward III., and it was subsequently converted into the office of the Master of the Wardrobe and the repository for the royal clothes. When Stow drew up his *Survey,* Sir John Fortescue was lodged in the house as Master of the Wardrobe.

Lord's Day, June 9, 1661.—By and by we got a sculler, and landing at Worcester House, went to the Wardrobe. I went up to Jane Shore's Tower, and there W. Howe and I sang.—*Pepys.*

There were also kept in this place the ancient cloathes of our English Kings, which they wore on great festivals; so that this Wardrobe was in effect a Library for Antiquaries, therein to read the mode and fashion of garments in all ages. These King James in the beginning of his reign gave to the Earl of Dunbar, by whom they were sold, re-sold, and re-re-sold at as many hands almost as Briareus had, some gaining vast estates thereby.—Fuller's *Worthies,* ed. 1662, p. 193.

I gyve, will, bequeath, and devise unto my daughter, Susannah Hall, all that messuage or tenement, with the appurtenances, wherein one John Robinson dwelleth, situat, lying, and being in the Blackfriers in London, nere the Wardrobe.—Shakespeare's *Will.*

After the Great Fire the Wardrobe was removed, first to the Savoy, and afterwards to Buckingham Street in the Strand.[1] It was the duty of the officers of the Wardrobe to provide "proper furniture for coronations, marriages, and funerals" of the sovereign and royal family, "cloaths of state, beds, hangings, and other necessaries for the houses of foreign ambassadors, cloaths of state for Lord Lieutenant of Ireland, Prince of Wales, and ambassadors abroad," as also to provide robes for

[1] *Chamberlayne,* ed. 1669, p. 263; *Hatton,* p. 729.

ministers of state, Knights of the Garter, etc. The last Master of the Wardrobe was Ralph, Duke of Montague, died 1709. [*See* Swan Alley.]

Warner Street, COLD BATH FIELDS. Henry Carey (natural son of Savile, Marquis of Halifax, the famous "Trimmer," and great-grandfather of Edmund Kean), author of *Chrononhotonthologos*, and the ever popular ballad of "Sally in our Alley," died by his own hand in this street on October 4, 1743.

Warren Street, FITZROY SQUARE, Tottenham Court Road to Cleveland Street. Dr. William Kitchener, author of the *Cook's Oracle*, lived and died at No. 43 in this street, and here were held what he called his "Committee of Taste" dinners. The hour was five minutes past five, and no guest arriving late was admitted. The last of these pleasant meetings was held on February 20, 1827, and six days later Kitchener was dead. He was buried in the family vault at St. Clement Danes. It was for his weekly conversazione that the directions "come at seven, go at eleven" were prepared. For some time this was a favourite locality with artists. Leslie settled here when he first came to London at the end of 1811.

I was solitary, and began to feel that even in London it was possible to be unhappy. I did not, however, feel this in its full force until I was settled in lodgings, consisting of two desolate-looking rooms up two pair of stairs in Warren Street, Fitzroy Square.—C. R. Leslie, R.A., *Autobiographical Recollections*, vol. i. p. 29.

Charles Turner, one of the best of the great school of mezzotint engravers, lived for many years at No. 50. Abraham Raimbach, the line engraver, was living at No. 10 whilst engaged in Wilkie's Village Politicians; James Boaden, author of the *Life of Mrs. Siddons* and other theatrical biographies, at No. 60; Frederick Reynolds, the dramatist, at No. 48; the Rev. F. W. Robertson of Brighton was born at No. 70, February 3, 1816.

Warwick Crescent, PADDINGTON. Robert Browning lived at No. 19 from the time of his return out of Italy after the death of his wife in 1861, until the summer of 1887, when he removed to 29 De Vere Gardens. Much of his poetry was therefore written in Warwick Crescent, notably "The Ring and the Book." A memorial tablet was placed upon the front of the house by the Society of Arts in August 1890.

Warwick House, CHARING CROSS, stood at the end of Warwick Street, an *impasse* running out of Cockspur Street, parallel to Pall Mall, and terminating in a stable yard. This was the site of Warwick House, the birthplace (1608) and residence of Sir Philip Warwick, the well-known royalist memoir writer (d. 1683). The mansion, however, is best known as the residence of the Princess Charlotte of Wales. At that time (1815) "the entrance of Warwick House was secured by bars of iron in the inside; and the Princess goes through the Court of Carlton House."[1]

[1] *Miss Knight*, vol. ii. p. 55.

> Warwick House, in which Princess Charlotte and I, with an excellent family of old servants, were now the only residents, was an old moderate-sized dwelling, at that time [January 1813] miserably out of repair, and almost falling to ruins. It was situated at the extremity of a narrow lane with a small court-yard and gates, at which two sentinels were placed. On the ground floor was a hall, dining-room, library, comptroller's room, and two very small rooms, with a good staircase, and two back staircases much the reverse. Above was what was called the waiting-room, of very moderate dimensions, where Princess Charlotte took her lessons in the morning; a good drawing-room, her Royal Highness's bedroom and dressing-room, or closet off it for a maid; my sitting-room adjoining, and my bedroom, both small, the latter particularly so. Yet for a private family it was far from being uncomfortable, though anything rather than royal. The drawing-room and Princess Charlotte's bedroom, with bay windows, looked on a small garden with a wall, and a road which divided it from the gardens of Carlton House, to which there was a door of communication. Nothing could more perfectly resemble a convent than this residence, but it was a seat of happiness to Princess Charlotte compared with the Lower Lodge at Windsor.—*Autobiography of Miss Cornelia Knight*, vol. i. p. 200.

It was from Warwick House that the Princess, "wearied out by a series of acts, all proceeding from the spirit of petty tyranny, and each more vexatious than another," made her escape in a hackney coach, July 16, 1814, to the house of her mother in Connaught Place; but was induced, chiefly by the arguments and persuasion of Mr. (afterwards Lord) Brougham, and the entreaties of the Duke of Sussex and of her mother, to submit to her father and return to Warwick House, which she did in a royal carriage that had been sent for, accompanied by the Duke of York and her governess, between four and five o'clock in the morning.[1]

Warwick House, in HOLBORN (north side), where is now *Warwick Court*, a short distance west of Gray's Inn Gateway, and leading into Gray's Inn. The Earl of Warwick was living in Warwick House in 1646, but it must have passed into other hands not long after.

> Dame Shusan, lady to the Rt. Honble Robert Lord Rich, Earl of Warwick, died in Warwick House in Holborn, the 16th January 1645-1646, and was buried at St. Lawrence Church, near Guildhall, on the 24th of the same.—*Parish Register of St. Andrew's, Holborn.*
>
> *March* 3, 1659-1660.—After dinner I to Warwick House in Holborn, to my Lord [the Earl of Sandwich], where he dined with my Lord of Manchester, Sir Dudley North, my Lord Fiennes, and my Lord Barkly.—*Pepys.*
>
> As we came by Warwick House, observing all shut up there, he [William Lord Russell] asked if my Lord Clare was out of town. I told him he could not think any windows would be open there on this occasion.—Bp. Burnet's *Journal* (William Lord Russell on his way to execution in Lincoln's-Inn-fields).[2]

The Earl of Clare was living in Warwick House in 1688. Warwick House had given place to Warwick Court in 1708.

Warwick Lane, NEWGATE STREET to PATERNOSTER ROW; originally (1311) *Eldedeneslane*, *i.e.* Old Dean's Lane.

> Then is Eldenese Lane, which stretcheth north to the high street of Newgate Market; the same is now called Warwick Lane, of an ancient house there built by an Earl of Warwick, and was since called Warwick Inn. It is in record called

---

[1] Lord Brougham.   [2] *London Gazette*, No. 2350.

a messuage in Eldenese Lane, in the parish of St. Sepulchre, the 28th of Henry VI. Cicille, Duchess of Warwick, possessed it.—*Stow*, p. 128.

I read that in the 36th of Henry VI. that the greater estates of the realm being called up to London . . . Richard Nevill, Earl of Warwick [the King-maker], came with six hundred men all in red jackets, embroidered with ragged staves before and behind, and was lodged in Warwick Lane; in whose house there was oftentimes six oxen eaten at a breakfast, and every tavern was full of his meat; for he that had any acquaintance in that house, might have there so much of sodden and roast meat as he could prick and carry up on a long dagger.—*Stow*, p. 33.

On the house at the corner of Newgate Street is a stone with the effigy in low relief of Guy, Earl of Warwick, and the date, 1668. Just beyond, on the west side, was the College of Physicians—the old College, with its "gilded pill" on the top, designed by Wren. [*See* Physicians, Royal College of.] On the east side was *the Bell Inn*.

He [Archbishop Leighton] used often to say that if he were to choose a place to die in, it should be an Inn; it looking like a pilgrim's going home, to whom this world was all as an Inn, and who was weary of the noise and confusion in it. He added that the officious tenderness and care of friends was an entanglement to a dying man; and that the unconcerned attendance of those that could be procured in such a place would give less disturbance. And he obtained what he desired; for he died [1684] at the Bell Inn in Warwick Lane.—Burnet's *Own Times*, ed. 1823, vol. ii. p. 426.

The Inn has gone, but *Old Bell Inn Yard*, now a railway booking-office waggon yard, is there to mark the site. On the west side was an equally famous inn, the *Oxford Arms*.

These are to give notice that Edward Bartlet, Oxford Carrier, hath removed his Inn in London, from the Swan at Holborn Bridge to the Oxford Armes in Warwick Lane, where he did Inn before the Fire. His coaches and waggons going forth on their usual days, Mondays, Wednesdays, and Frydays. He hath also a Hearse, with all things convenient to carry a Corps to any part of England.—*London Gazette* for March 1672-1673, No. 762.

"At the Oxford Arms in Warwick Lane" lived John Roberts, the bookseller, from whose shop issued the majority of the squibs and libels on Pope, and the publisher, 1744, of Johnson's *Life of Savage*. The Oxford Arms Inn, with its quaint galleries, chambers, and carved fireplaces, was sold in 1875 and pulled down in 1876, but its memory survives in *Oxford Arms Passage*.

Warwick Street, COCKSPUR STREET, Charing Cross, was built circ. 1675.[1] The street, which had no thoroughfare, was so called from the house of Sir Philip Warwick, author of the *Memoirs* which bear his name.

Over against St. Alban's Street is Stone Cutter's Alley, paved with free-stone, which leads into Warwick Street, and likewise to the back gate of the King's garden, for the conveniency of Mr. George London, her late Majesty's principal gardener, there inhabiting in a neat and pleasant house.—*Strype*, B. vi. p. 81.

This George London was a landscape-gardener of great celebrity before the time of Kent or "Capability" Brown. In conjunction with Wise he introduced what Walpole calls "verdant sculpture" among us, stocking our gardens with giants, animals, monsters, coats of arms, and mottoes,

[1] It is mentioned by Ogilby of that date.

in yew, box, and holly. At the end of this street stood *Warwick House*, inhabited for a time by the Princess Charlotte. [*See* Warwick House, Charing Cross.] At No. 4 Little Warwick Street lived General Conway, the cousin and correspondent of Horace Walpole.[1]

Warwick Street, GOLDEN SQUARE. Roman Catholic Chapel, formerly the chapel of the Bavarian. Embassy, now called the Church of the Assumption. This chapel was gutted in the riots of 1780. Hogarth collectors greatly value a shop bill executed by him for a tobacconist in this street. On the top is a label with the words, "La Croix's, the Corner of Warwick Street, near Swallow Street, St. James's." Here, when John (afterwards Lord) Campbell came to London to push his fortune (1798) he had his first London lodgings —first at No. 35, then at No. 18.[2]

Water Gate (The), at the TOWER.

One other water-gate there is by the bulwark of the Tower, and this is the last and farthest water-gate eastward on the river of Thames, so far as the city of London extendeth within the walls.—*Stow*, p. 17; see also *Stryp*, Appendix, p. 68.

Water Gruel Row, HACKNEY. Here lived William Caslon, the celebrated typefounder (b. 1692, d. 1766).

Water Lane, BLACKFRIARS, from Broadway to Queen Victoria Street. On the east side is Apothecaries Hall; and from it run Playhouse Lane and Printing-house Yard.

Water Lane, FLEET STREET, changed November 5, 1844, into *Whitefriars Street*, by consent of the Commissioners of the Sewers and at the request of the freeholders of the lane. Thomas Tompion, the famous watchmaker, kept shop at the corner of Water Lane, died here in 1713, and was buried in the centre of the nave of Westminster Abbey.

Well, let me tell you (said Goldsmith), when my tailor brought home my bloom-coloured coat, be said, "Sir, I have a favour to beg of you. When anybody asks you who made your clothes, be pleased to mention John Filby, at the Harrow in Water Lane." *Johnson:* Why, Sir, that was because he knew the strange colour would attract crowds to gaze at it, and then they might hear of him, and see how well he could make a coat even of so absurd a colour.—*Boswell*, ed. Croker, p. 203.

Filby also supplied him with "a pair of bloom-coloured breeches," for which he charged him £1 : 4 : 6.

Water Lane, GREAT TOWER STREET, formerly called *Spurrier Lane*.

The next is Sporiar Lane, of old time so called, but since and later time named Water Lane, because it runneth down to the water-gate by the Custom House in Thames Street.—*Stow*, p. 51.

Here was the house of Sir Marmaduke Rawdon, a great merchant of the time of James I. and Charles I.; and uncle of the M. Rawdon whose life has been published by the Camden Society (1863). In

[1] *See* Walpole's *Letters*, vol. iii. p. 343; vol. vii. p. 391.
[2] *Life*, by Hon. Mrs. Hardcastle, vol. i. pp. 39, 41.

this lane was the *Old* Trinity House, burned down in the Great Fire, and again in 1718, and each time rebuilt. The site is marked by the site of merchants' offices (No. 5), called "The Old Trinity House."

Waterloo Bridge, a bridge over the Thames, between Wellington Street, Strand, and the Waterloo Road (at first called *the Strand* Bridge), the noblest stone bridge in the world, was built by a public company pursuant to an Act passed in 1809. The first stone was laid October 11, 1811, and the bridge publicly opened by the Prince Regent on the second anniversary of the battle of Waterloo, June 18, 1817. The engineer was John Rennie, son of a farmer at Phantassie, in East Lothian—the engineer of many of our celebrated docks and of the breakwater at Plymouth. He died in 1821, and is buried in St. Paul's Cathedral by the side of Sir C. Wren. Ralph Dodd, C.E., stated (*Gentleman's Magazine,* 1817, vol. i. p. 482), that the design was approved by the proprietors before Rennie had anything to do with the work.

Canova, when he was asked during his visit to England what struck him most forcibly, is said to have replied—that the trumpery Chinese Bridge, then in St. James's Park, should be the production of the Government, whilst that of Waterloo was the work of a Private Company.—*Quarterly Review,* No. 112, p. 309.

> Speak ye, too, Works of Peace
> For ye too have a voice,
> Which shall be heard by ages ! The proud Bridge
> Through whose broad arches, worthy of their name
> And place, his rising and his refluent tide
> Majestic Thames, the royal river, rolls.
> Southey, *Ode on Visit of George IV. to Scotland.*

This celebrated bridge, "a colossal monument worthy of Sesostris and the Cæsars" (*M. Dupin*), consists of nine equal elliptical arches, each of 120 feet span and a rise of 24 feet 6 inches, supported on piers 20 feet wide at the springing of the arches. The entire length is 2456 feet, the bridge and abutments being 1380 feet, the approach from the Strand, 310 feet, and the causeway on the Surrey side, as far as supported by the land-arches, 766 feet. The bridge is therefore on a level with the *Strand,* and one uniform level throughout.

The total cost of the bridge was £565,000. . . . The approaches, besides the land and buildings, cost a further sum of £112,000; so that the total cost of the bridge and approaches was £677,000, and the land and buildings and contingences, £373,000, making a total of £1,050,000.—*Autob. of Sir John Rennie, F.R.S.,* p. 35.

As a commercial speculation the bridge was so far from successful that in January 1872 two shares, of £100 each, were sold by auction for £10.[1] Under powers conveyed by the Metropolitan Bridges Act, 1877, the Metropolitan Board of Works purchased the bridge and all the bridge company's rights for £475,000, and on October 5, 1878, opened the bridge to the public free of toll.

Waterloo Place, PALL MALL. The second-floor window of No. 11, looking into Charles Street, marks the bedroom and sitting-room

[1] *City Press,* January 6, 1872.

of James Hogg, the Ettrick Shepherd, during his first and only visit to London, in the winter of 1831-1832. No. 13 was the west-end establishment of Messrs. Taylor and Hessey, the publishers of the *London Magazine*, in which the *Essays of Elia* and the *Confessions of an English Opium Eater* first appeared.

> It was then that [circ. 1823] the contributors met once a month over an excellent dinner given by the firm; and consulted and talked on literary matters together. . . . Charles Lamb came to most of these dinners, always dressed in black (his snuff-coloured suit having been dismissed for years), always kind and genial.

Until the middle of the year 1890 Messrs. Rivington's business was carried on at No. 3. Waterloo Place now boasts among other publishers' firms W. H. Allen and Co., No. 13; and Smith, Elder and Co., No. 15. Other noteworthy houses of somewhat earlier date are commemorated in Hood's verses:—

> Thy first great trial in this mighty town
> Was, if I rightly recollect, upon
> That gentle hill which goeth
> Down from the "County" to the Palace[1] gate.
> And, like a river, thanks to thee, now floweth
> Past the old Horticultural Society,
> The Chemist Cobb's, the house of Howell and James,
> Where ladies play high shawl and satin games,
> A little *Hell* of lace!
> And past the Athenæum, made of late,
> Severs a sweet variety
> Of milliners and booksellers who grace
> Waterloo Place,
> Making division, the Muse fears and guesses,
> 'Twixt Mr. Rivington's and Mr. Hessey's.
> Thomas Hood, *Ode to Mr. MacAdam*.

The lower end of Waterloo Place is a favoured place for statues and memorials. At the junction with Pall Mall is the Guards' Memorial, by John Bell, erected in honour of the officers and men of the three regiments of Foot Guards who fell in the Crimea; three bronze statues of guardsmen on a pedestal of granite surmounted by a Victory of marble; the Russian cannon taken at Sebastopol. South of Pall Mall, statues of Lord Clyde, by Marochetti; Sir John Franklin, by Noble; Field-Marshal Sir John Burgoyne, by Sir Edgar Boehm, and opposite to it at the south-east corner Lord Lawrence, by the same sculptor. At the end of the place, on the steps leading into St. James's Park, is the Duke of York's column and statue [which *see*].

Watermen's Hall, No. 18 ST. MARY AT HILL, LOWER THAMES STREET, is a neat unpretentious building of brick and stone, erected in 1786. The old hall of the Company was in *Cold Harbour*, Upper Thames Street, and faced the river. Taylor, the Water Poet, tells us that in his time "the number of watermen, and those that lived and were maintained by them, and by the only labour of the oar and scull, betwixt the bridge of Windsor and Gravesend, could not be fewer than 40,000." This was in

[1] Carlton House—long removed.

the reign of Queen Elizabeth ; and in the reign of Anne the number was said to be the same. "There be," says Strype, " 40,000 watermen upon the rolls of the Company, as I have been told by one of the Company ; and that upon occasion they can furnish 20,000 men for the fleet ; and that there were 8000 then in the service." In 6 Henry VIII. (1514) an Act was passed for regulating the fares, charges, etc., of watermen, wherrymen, bargemen, etc., in the City of London and on the river Thames, but the watermen of London were first made a Company by virtue of an Act of Parliament passed in the 2d and 3d of Philip and Mary (1515). The watermen rank ninety-first of the City Companies. The Company has no livery. The licensing and registration of boats and barges, the licensing and control of the watermen, and the direction of the pilotage, navigation of barges and lighters, are vested in the Watermen's Company. When Blackfriars Bridge was built the Company accepted the sum of £13,650 in the Three Per Cents in compensation for the loss of the Sunday ferry, maintained by the Company for charitable purposes. The introduction of steam-boats has changed the whole character of the passenger traffic on the Thames, and watermen proper are greatly reduced. But the watermen and river pilots licensed by the Watermen's Company number nearly 12,000.

Watling Street, from BUDGE ROW, CANNON STREET, to ST. PAUL'S CHURCHYARD.

Then for Watheling Street, which Leland called Atheling, or Noble Street ; but since he showeth no reason why, I rather take it to be so named of that great highway of the same calling. True it is that at the present the inhabitants thereof are wealthy drapers, retaillers of woollen cloths, both broad and narrow, of all sorts, more than in any one street of this city.—*Stow*, p. 129.

In Maxwell Lyte's Report on the MSS. of St. Paul's, *Hist. MSS. Comm.* (Appendix to Ninth Report), of the end of the 13th century and middle of the 14th century, are registers in which we find the form Athelyng Street.

He fills his belly, and never asks what's to pay : wears broad cloth and yet dares walk *Watling Street* without any fear of his draper.—*Green's Tu Quoque (Old Plays,* vol. xi. p. 207).

Watling Street was two centuries ago notorious, as it still is, for its inconvenient and almost dangerous narrowness. Thus Moxon, speaking of the Milky Way in his *Treatise of Astronomy,* 1670, says, "Some in a sportive manner call it *Watling Street,* but why they call it so I cannot tell, except it be in regard of the narrowness it seemeth to have."

<blockquote>
Who would of Watling Street the dangers share,
When the broad pavement of Cheapside is near ?—Gay, *Trivia.*
</blockquote>

In this street were the following churches, walking eastward into *Budge Row : St. Augustine's, Watling Street* (near St. Paul's) ; *Allhallows, Bread Street ; St. Mary's, Aldermary ; St. Anthony's,* or *St. Antholin's.* But within the last few years Allhallows, Bread Street, and St. Antholin's have been pulled down. [*See* those places.] Nos.

63, 64, are the headquarters of the London Salvage Corps, and at Nos. 64-69 was the chief station of the Metropolitan Fire Brigade, now removed to Southwark Bridge Road. Dr. Nathaniel Hodges, so honourably distinguished for his conduct during the plague of 1665, dates his account of it from his house in Watling Street, May 8, 1666.

Wax Chandlers' Hall, GRESHAM STREET WEST, was built in 1852 from the designs of Charles Fowler. The Wax Chandlers were recognised as a fraternity and their bylaws allowed by the Court of Aldermen in 1372, but the Company, the twenty-ninth in precedence among the City Companies, was first incorporated in 1 Richard III., 1684. The mercurial Duke of Wharton, when anxious, like Shaftesbury and Buckingham before him, to foment a spirit of opposition in the City, became a member of this Company. A previous hall in Gutter Lane was new built in 1657.

Weavers' Company, the forty-second in order, and the most ancient of the Livery Companies of London—a Company possessing the exclusive privilege of admitting to the freedom and livery of the Company persons not free of the City of London. The first Charter of Incorporation was granted by Henry II. in 1184 to the cloth and tapestry weavers of London, and has affixed to it the seal of Thomas à Becket. The guild consists of two Bailiffs (an upper and under), two Wardens, a court of eighteen assistants, livery and freemen. The old hall of the Company was destroyed in the Great Fire, rebuilt on the same site, and taken down in 1856, when a block of merchants' offices were built on the site, No. 22 Basinghall Street (east side) and named Weavers' Hall. In the 17th century the hall, like the halls of some of the other Companies, seems to have been used as a Presbyterian meeting-house.

'That Paul's shall to the Consistory call
A Dean and Chapter out of Weavers' Hall?
Cleaveland's *Hue and Cry after Sir John Presbyter*, p. 75.

Weighhouse Yard, LITTLE EASTCHEAP, so called from the King's Weighhouse.

In this Lane [Love Lane] on the north-west corner entering into Little Eastcheap, is the Weighhouse, built on the ground where the church of St. Andrew Hubbard stood before the Fire of 1666. Which said Weighhouse was before in Cornhill. In this House are weighed merchandises brought from beyond seas to the King's Beam, to which doth belong a Master, and under him four Master Porters, with labouring Porters under them. They have Carts and Horses to fetch the goods from the Merchants' Warehouses to the Beam, and to carry them back. The house belongeth to the Company of Grocers, in whose gifts the several Porters', etc., places are. But of late years little is done in this office, as wanting a compulsive power to constrain the merchants to have their goods weighed; they alleging it to be an unnecessary trouble and charge.—*Strype*, B. ii. p. 173. See also *Stow*, p. 73; and *Strype*, B. v. p. 421, etc.

It is accorded, that the King shall have his weights in a certain place, or in two places, or in three or four if necessary, within the City; and that all merchandise sold by weight that exceeds five-and-twenty pounds, shall be weighed with the King's weights in weighing for the custom that pertains thereunto, according as shall thereon be ordained. And unto such weights of the King as well buyers as sellers are to resort, after the form above stated. And if any person shall be found weighing merchandize, that is weighable, above the weight of five-and-twenty pounds, otherwise than by the King's weights, and be convicted of the same, let the merchandize of such person be forfeited to the King, in whatever hands the same shall be found; and let the other party be heavily amerced unto the King. And let the weighers be sworn unto the King lawfully to weigh for vendor and for seller.—*Ordinance*, 13 Edward I., 1285 (*Liber Albus*, p. 248).

In the early part of the 18th century a congregation of Independents had their "commodious meeting-house" in a "large room over the Weigh-house;" hence the title of a later meeting-house, the *King's Weigh-house* Chapel, Fish Street Hill, not far from the old Weighhouse, which became famous during the ministry of the Rev. Thomas Binney. This was taken by the Metropolitan and District Railway Companies for the completion of the Inner Circle Railway. The compensation was £37,000. In April 1888 the Duke of Westminster offered a site in Duke Street, Grosvenor Square, at a peppercorn rent for 99 years' lease, the freehold of which was valued at £25,000. The new chapel is now in course of erection.

Welbeck Street, CAVENDISH SQUARE, from Great Marylebone Street to Henrietta Street, was so called after Welbeck in Nottinghamshire, the ancient seat of the noble family of Cavendish, now the residence of the Duke of Portland. *Eminent Inhabitants.*—The mother of Martha and Theresa Blount.

Item, I give and devise to Mrs. Martha Blount, younger daughter of Mrs. Martha Blount, late of Welbeck Street, Cavendish Square, the sum of one thousand pounds.—Pope's *Will*.

Edmund Hoyle, who wrote on Whist; he died here in August 1769, aged ninety-seven, and was buried in the cemetery in Paddington Street. Lord George Gordon, the hero of the riots of 1780. Tyrwhitt, editor of the *Canterbury Tales* of Chaucer, died here, August 15, 1786. Mrs. Thrale came to reside at No. 33 on her marriage with Piozzi, and from here she wrote her last note to Fanny Burney, August 13, 1784. Miss Thrale (Queeney) was living at No. 12 in 1792. Maclean, the highwayman who robbed Horace Walpole, and carried off the Earl of Eglinton's blunderbuss, had been a grocer in Welbeck Street. His father was an Irish dean. Dr. Thomas Young lived here in 1815.

At No. 32 is the Chapel of the Russian Embassy; No. 71 is a Chapel of the Plymouth Brethren. No. 73, the West End Hospital for the Paralysed and Epileptic.

Weld House. [*See* Wild House.]

Well Street, JEWIN STREET, CRIPPLEGATE. [*See* Crowders' Well Alley.]

Well Street, WELLCLOSE SQUARE, runs from Cable Street to East Smithfield. Here, on the west side, stood the unfortunate *Royalty Theatre* [*see* that heading]. On the site stands that very useful institution, the Sailors' Home, where provision is made for lodging and boarding 500 seamen, and providing them with home, club and social comfort, and recreation adapted to the maritime taste. Upwards of 9000 seamen avail themselves annually of the Home, which is now self-supporting. Close to it, and conducted under the same auspices, the Destitute Sailors Asylum, which, during 1880, gave shelter to 599 shipwrecked seamen, and in which, since its opening in 1827, above 60,000 seamen of all nations, "utterly destitute, have been sheltered, fed and clothed, and sent forth again in a condition to battle with the peculiar hardships of their calling."

Wellclose Square, ST. GEORGE STREET, WHITECHAPEL. "It has also been called *Marine Square*, from the number of sea officers residing there."[1] The old Danish Church which from 1696 stood in the centre of this square—and during part of his latter days was the Seamen's Church with "Bo'son" Smith as its minister—was pulled down in 1869, and the *Seamen's Children Day Schools* (in connection with the church of St. Paul, Dock Street, Whitechapel) erected on the site. These schools, which have room for 700 children, and cost £5000, were opened by the Prince and Princess of Wales on June 30, 1870. [*See* Danish Church.] The first Magdalen Chapel was in this square, with Dr. Dodd for its chaplain.

The Sessions House for the Liberty of the Tower is at No. 33 in this square. Thomas Day, the author of what was once the delight of all schoolboys, *Sandford and Merton*, was born at No. 36 in 1748. Mr. W. B. Ward, the inventor of the Wardian Case, was a medical practitioner in Wellclose Square.

Wellings Farm, the name given in old maps to the site of the present Inner Circle of the Regent's Park, and the gardens of the Royal Botanic Society.

Wells Street, OXFORD STREET. Dr. Beattie, author of *The Minstrel*, lodged at No. 64 in the year 1771. Here are St. Andrew's Church, famous for its musical services, built 1845-1847 (Messrs. Dankes and Hamilton, architects); St. Andrew's Choir and Middle Class School, and St. Andrew's National Schools.

Weltzie's Club. [*See* St. James's Street.]

Wenlock's Barn appears in the old maps three-quarters of a mile direct north of the present Finsbury Square, near the footbridge in Shepherd and Shepherdess Walk. It was the manor-house of the ancient prebendal manor of Wenlock's Barn belonging to the Dean and Chapter of St. Paul's, and has bequeathed its name to *Wenlock Basin*, *Road*, and *Street*, City Road.

Wesley's (John) Chapel. [*See* City Road.]

[1] *Harrison*, circ. 1777

Wesleyan Centenary Hall and Mission House, BISHOPSGATE STREET WITHIN, facing Threadneedle Street, erected from the designs of W. F. Pocock, 1839-1840, provides offices for transacting the ordinary business of the Society, and a large hall for holding public meetings and occasional religious services.

West India Docks, at the time of construction the most magnificent in the world (William Jessop, engineer), cover 295 acres, and lie between Limehouse and Blackwall, on the left bank of the Thames. The first stone was laid by William Pitt, July 12, 1800, and the Import Dock was opened for business August 21, 1802. The docks as a whole were formally opened by Lord Minto, July 12, 1806, exactly six years from the laying of the first stone. The northern, or Import Dock, is 170 yards long by 166 wide, and will hold 204 vessels of 300 tons each; and the southern, or Export Dock, is 170 yards long by 135 yards wide, and will hold 195 vessels. South of the Export Dock is a canal nearly three-quarters of a mile long, cutting off the great bend of the river, connecting Limehouse Reach with Blackwall Reach, and forming the northern boundary of the Isle of Dogs. It was originally constructed by the Corporation of London, and called the *City Canal*. Being unremunerative as a ship canal it was sold to the West India Dock Company in 1829. The two docks, with their warehouses, are enclosed by a lofty wall 5 feet in thickness, and have held at one time 148,563 casks of sugar, 70,875 barrels and 433,648 bags of coffee, 35,158 pipes of rum and Madeira, 14,021 logs of mahogany, and 21,350 tons of logwood. The water area of the West India Docks is about 98 acres; the storage capacity of the warehouses 31,531,725 cubic feet. Though they retain their old name the docks belong to the East and West India Dock Company—formed by the amalgamation of the two companies in 1838—and are used by every kind of shipping. [*See* East India Docks.]

West Street, UPPER ST. MARTIN'S LANE to CAMBRIDGE CIRCUS. West Street Chapel, between Nos. 10 and 11, was *La Tremblade*, one of the original Huguenot churches in London.[1] John Wesley frequently preached in this chapel between the years 1743 and 1793. The pulpit was also filled at various times by Whitefield, Romaine, and Fletcher of Madeley. The chapel is now opened as a free church in connection with St. Giles's parish. On the corner house of West Street and St. Martin's Lane is a parish mark with the date 1691.

Westbourne, a bourne, brook, or streamlet of water rising a little north of Paddington, and passing Bayswater and the east end of the present Serpentine, through the Five Fields (or what is now called Belgravia) on to Westbourne Place, Sloane Square, direct to the Thames at Chelsea. It is now the Ranelagh sewer. Here, from

[1] Smiles, *Huguenots*, p. 266.

1805 to 1817, Mrs. Siddons had a cottage, called Westbourne Farm, on which her husband wrote verses. General Lord Hill occupied a house by Paddington, pleasantly situated in the fields, with country all around it. The construction of the *Great Western Railway* altered the appearance of the place, and every part has since been built over.

Westminster, a city, constituted by royal charter and by many public privileges, but since swallowed up in the general vortex of modern London. It extends as far as Kensington and Chelsea westward, to the City of London boundary (Temple Bar) eastward, to the Thames southward, and to Marylebone northward. It therefore embraces the whole of St. Paul's, Covent Garden; St. Clement's Danes; St. Mary-le-Strand; the precinct of the Savoy; St. Martin's-in-the-Fields; St. James's, Westminster; St. George's, Hanover Square; St. Margaret's, and St. John the Evangelist. Here was a Benedictine monastery (Westminster Abbey), from which it derives its name, and here the Kings and Queens of England, from Edward the Confessor to Queen Elizabeth, had their principal palace (*Westminster Palace*).

Thorney may be defined as an island lying off the coast of Middlesex in the estuary of the Thames. It was very scientifically described for us about half a century ago by William Bardwell of Park Street, Westminster, one of the architects of the "Westminster Improvement Company." He says it is about 470 yards long and 370 yards wide, and is washed on the east side by the Thames, on the south by a rivulet running down College Street, on the north by another stream which flows or flowed through Gardener's Lane, the two being joined by the "Long Ditch" which formed a western boundary, as nearly as possible where Prince's Street is now. Within the narrow limits thus described stand both the Abbey and the Houses of Parliament and other familiar buildings.—Loftie's *Westminster Abbey* (Portfolio, 1889, p. 21).

Three hundred years before Domesday Book (1086) the extent of the rural manor of Westminster was mentioned in a Charter of Offa King of Mercia dated 785. . . . In the 6 Henry III. (1222) a decree of Cardinal Archbishop Langton and certain Bishops and Priors, who appear to have sat in arbitration on some difference which had arisen on the question, curtails from the east side of the parish all the precinct of the Savoy, the entire area of St. Mary le Strand and St. Clement Danes, and . . . parts of St. Giles and St. Andrew Holborn . . . St. Margaret Westminster as thus left comprised the present parishes of St. Paul Covent Garden, St. Martin-in-the Fields, St. James Piccadilly, St. Anne Soho, St. George Hanover Square and St. John the Evangelist, Westminster; and as if in compensation for the detachment of the east side, three manors were added to the parish on the west and north-west. Paddington had also been confirmed as an appendage of Westminster by Stephen (1135) and Henry II. (1154). By a charter of 17 Richard II. (1393) the parishes of St. Mary le Strand and St. Clement Danes, together with that of St. Martin's-in-the-Fields, then newly formed, were declared to be possessed by the Abbot as part of the manor of Westminster. Further changes were also made by Letters Patent in the reigns of Henry VIII. (1534) and James I. (1604).—*Report of the Vestry of the United Parish of St. Margaret and St. John the Evangelist*, 1889, pp. 3, 4.

Though a city Westminster has no municipality, but is governed by a High Steward, elected by the Dean of the collegiate church of St. Peter's, Westminster (*Westminster Abbey*), and by a High Bailiff, also elected by the Dean, and by sixteen burgesses and the like number of assistants. Henry VIII. made it the seat of a bishop, who was called the Bishop of Westminster, but only one person received that distinction, Thomas Thurleby, or Thirlby, afterwards Bishop of Ely. Westminster returned two members to Parliament since the time of Henry VIII. until the Reform Act of 1885, and was long almost a nomination borough of the Court, but for nearly a century was notorious for generally returning radical members to Parliament after contests so severe that the Westminster elections of Mr. Fox and Sir Francis Burdett are points of importance in the history of the British Constitution.[1]

By the last Reform Act it was divided into St. George's, Hanover Square, Strand, and Westminster, each division returning one member. From being the seat of the Courts of Law the name of Westminster became at an early date synonymous with the law itself.

> Not much unlyke the bargayne that I herd of late shoulde be betwixt two fryndes for a horse.... Thus thys bargayne became a *Westminster matter*: the lawyers gote twyse the valewe of the horse.—Bp. Latimer's *First Sermon*, p. 28.

The very valuable report of the Vestry already quoted from in this article contains notes on local government in Westminster from pre-Reformation times to the present day. The compiler (Mr. John Edward Smith, Vestry Clerk) writes, "Several Charters, each under the Great Seal of the Monarch of the time, the earliest dates from 1256 (40 Henry III.), have been brought to light during the past five years. The parish muniment room at the Town Hall also contains thousands of manuscript books and records of parochial affairs from the year 1464 (3 Edward IV.) to the present day, in addition to the Vestry Minutes dating from 1585."

Westminster Abbey, the Collegiate Church or Abbey of St. Peter's, Westminster—the "minster west" of St. Paul's, London, is said, on somewhat legendary authority, to have been founded by Sebert, King of the East Saxons, circ. 616. It is, however, mentioned in a charter of Offa, King of Mercia, A.D. 785, and must have existed before that date. The present abbey was founded by King Edward the Confessor, and dedicated to St. Peter. It was fifteen years in building, and only completed in time to permit of its consecration on Innocents' Day, December 28, 1065, a week before the King died. The church was built in the Norman style, and was regarded as a structure of matchless grandeur and beauty. "Its very size—occupying as it did almost the whole area of the present building—was in itself portentous.... The east end was rounded into an apse. A tower rose in the centre crowned with a cupola of wood. At the western end were erected two smaller towers, with five large bells.

---

[1] Some curious particulars concerning early Westminster Elections will be found in the correspondence of Secretary Vernon, vol. ii. pp. 135-137, and vol. iii. p. 159. Vernon (who sat for Westminster), speaking of the opposition of Sir Harry Colt, observes—" We had a mighty appearance against him in the field, both of horse and foot, who ran down his men at a strange rate, and cudgelled him into ditches full of water, and yet we say they were the aggressors." The poll was taken in Covent Garden Church porch for the first time in November 1701. The election generally lasted forty days.

The hard strong stones were richly sculptured. The windows were filled with stained glass. The roof was covered with lead. The cloisters, chapter-house, refectory, dormitory, the infirmary with its spacious chapel, if not completed by Edward, were all begun and finished in the next generation on the same plan."[1] But of this goodly edifice hardly anything remains except a few fragments of the substructure. In this abbey our kings and queens have been crowned, from Edward the Confessor to Queen Victoria; and here very many of them are buried, some with and others without monuments.

> A man may read a sermon, the best and most passionate that ever man preached, if he shall but enter into the sepulchre of kings. . . . Where our kings have been crowned, their ancestors lie interred, and they must walk over their grandsire's head to take his crown. There is an acre sown with royal seed, the copy of the greatest change—from rich to naked, from cieled roof to arched coffins, from living like gods to die like men. . . . There the warlike and the peaceful, the fortunate and the miserable, the beloved and the despised princes mingle their dust, and pay down their symbol of mortality; and tell all the world, that when we die our ashes shall be equal to kings, and our accounts easier, and our pains or our crowns shall be less.
> —Jeremy Taylor's *Holy Dying*, chap. i. sect. 2.

The abbey is 511 feet long (or 403 exclusive of Henry VII.'s Chapel); the transepts, 203 feet across; height of roof, 101 feet 8 inches from the pavement; height of towers, 225 feet. The choir, which extends far west of the transepts, is 155 feet long; the nave, 154 feet. What remains exist of the Confessor's church are the substructure of the Dormitory, or Chapel of the Pyx, and the dark cloister south of the south transept. Of the existing church the oldest parts are Edward the Confessor's Chapel, or Chapel of the Kings, choir, and transepts, which were built by Henry III., and are Early English, or First Pointed, in style. The four bays west of the transept (including the west end of the choir and the first bay of the nave) are of the time of Edward I., and are Early Decorated, or Second Pointed, in style. The remainder of the nave, to the west door, was built in the 15th century, under Sir Richard Whittington as Commissioner. Henry VII.'s Chapel is late Perpendicular, very richly ornamented with panelling, etc. The lower part of the western towers and the façade were fairly well repaired by Sir C. Wren, who had been appointed surveyor in 1698. This work was begun about 1713, and completed about 1723. Nicholas Hawksmoor succeeded Wren, and in 1735 he proposed the raising of the towers, which was completed 1739, in a mixture of Gothic and Italian details.[2] Sir Gilbert Scott was appointed architect to Westminster Abbey in 1849, and retained that office till his death in 1878. During those years not only did he pay unremitting attention to the maintenance of the fabric, but carried out a continuous though gradual restoration of its ornamental details as well as

---

[1] Dean Stanley's *Historical Memorials of Westminster Abbey*, p. 25.

[2] The best (and a very sufficient) guide to the architecture of the Abbey is Sir Gilbert Scott's *Gleanings from Westminster Abbey*, as in all other matters is Dean Stanley's most interesting *Historical Memorials of Westminster Abbey*, 4th edition, 1876. The Misses Bradley, daughters of the present Dean, have compiled a very useful guide.

constructive features. His chief works here, as enumerated by himself, were "two pulpits, three grilles, altar rails, the gable and pinnacles of the south transept, sundry tops of pinnacles, a new altar-table in the sanctuary of the church, and another in Henry VII.'s Chapel." Also "the hardening of the decayed internal surfaces with shellac dissolved in spirits of wine;" the cleansing and renovating the "bronze effigies of Kings and others;" the portals of the north transept, being the so-called Solomon's Porch," and, perhaps the greatest triumph of all, the entire restoration of the beautiful Chapter House.[1] The upper part of the north transept has just (August 1890) been completed by Mr. J. L. Pearson, R.A., the present architect.

The following eminent persons are buried in Westminster Abbey. (The names of those persons buried without monuments or inscribed gravestones are printed in italics.) KINGS AND QUEENS.—King Sebert, —his tomb was certainly here if his body was not; Edward the Confessor; Henry III.; Edward I. and Queen Eleanor; Edward III. and Queen Philippa; Richard II. and his Queen; Henry V.; Henry VII. and his Queen; Anne of Cleves, Queen of Henry VIII.; *Edward VI.; Mary I.;* Mary, Queen of Scots; Queen Elizabeth; *James I.* and *his Queen; Queen of Bohemia,* daughter of James I. and mother of Prince Rupert; *Charles II.; Anne Hyde,* first wife of James II.; *William III.* and *Queen Mary;* Queen Anne; *George II.* and *Queen Caroline.* EMINENT MODERN STATESMEN.—Lord Chancellor Clarendon; Savile Lord Halifax; Sir William Temple; Craggs; Pulteney, Earl of Bath; the great Lord Chatham; William Pitt; Fox; Canning; Castlereagh; Wilberforce; Palmerston. EMINENT SOLDIERS.—Aymer de Valence, Earl of Pembroke; Sir Francis Vere; *Prince Rupert;* Monk, Duke of Albemarle; *William, Duke of Cumberland,* the hero of Culloden; Marshal Wade. The INDIAN STATESMEN.—Sir George Staunton and Lord Lawrence; and the INDIAN GENERALS.—Lord Clyde; Sir James Outram; and Sir George Pollock. EMINENT SEAMEN.—*Admiral Blake; Admiral Dean; Sir E. Spragg; Montague, Earl of Sandwich;* Sir Cloudesley Shovel; Earl of Dundonald (Lord Cochrane). EMINENT POETS.—Chaucer; Spenser; *Beaumont;* Ben Jonson; Michael Drayton; Sir Robert Ayton; Sir W. Davenant; Cowley; *Denham; Roscommon;* Dryden; Prior; Congreve; Addison; Rowe; Gay; Macpherson, who gave "Ossian" to the public; R. B. Sheridan; and Thomas Campbell. EMINENT ANTIQUARIES, HISTORIANS, and PROSE WRITERS generally.—Camden; Spelman; Isaac Casaubon; Archbishop Ussher; Dr. Samuel Johnson; Lord Lytton; Bishop Thirlwall; Grote; Macaulay; Charles Dickens; Rennell, the geographer; Thomas Telford and Robert Stephenson, the engineers; Sir William Chambers, James Wyatt, Sir Charles Barry, and Sir Gilbert Scott, the architects; Banks, the sculptor; David Livingstone, the African missionary and traveller; and Sir Rowland Hill, the originator of the penny post. EMINENT MEN OF SCIENCE.—

---

[1] Scott, *Autob. Recollections,* p. 287, etc.; *Gleanings from Westminster Abbey.*

Sir Isaac Newton; John Woodward, the founder of the professorship of geology at Cambridge; Richard Mead; John Hunter, the great anatomist, brought here in 1859 from the vaults of St. Martin's-in-the-Fields; Herschel; Sir Charles Lyell. EMINENT ACTORS AND ACTRESSES. —*Betterton;* the second *Mrs. Barry; Mrs. Oldfield; Mrs. Bracegirdle; Mrs. Cibber; Henderson; Samuel Foote;* and David Garrick. EMINENT MUSICIANS.— Henry Purcell; Dr. Blow; William Croft; William Shield; Samuel Arnold; Sir Sterndale Bennett; and, greatest name of all in music, Handel. EMINENT DIVINES.—Dr. Barrow; Dr. South. OTHER EMINENT PERSONS.—*Mountjoy, Earl of Devonshire,* of the time of Queen Elizabeth; the unfortunate *Arabella Stuart;* the mother of Henry VII.; the mother of Lady Jane Grey; the mother of Lord Darnley; the wife of the Protector Somerset; the wife of the great Lord Burghley; the wife of Sir Robert Cecil; Sir Dudley Carleton, ambassador and letter writer, temp. James I.; the Duke and Duchess of Newcastle (the poet and poetess); the father and mother of Villiers, Duke of Buckingham; Villiers, first Duke of Buckingham, and his two sons, the profligate second duke, and Francis, killed when a boy in the Civil Wars; the *Duchess of Richmond* (La Belle Stuart); the second Duke of Ormond, and *Atterbury, Bishop of Rochester,* all of whom died in banishment; Sheffield, Duke of Buckingham; *Hakluyt,* who collected the early voyages which bear his name; Dr. Busby, the schoolmaster; *Tom Killigrew* and M. St. Evremont, the English and French epicurean wits; *Aubrey de Vere,* the twentieth and last Earl of Oxford of the house of Vere; and old Parr, who died (1635), as was very positively affirmed, at the great age of 152.

"Victory or Westminster Abbey" was Nelson's exclamation at Trafalgar; and when we reflect on the many eminent persons buried within its walls, it is indeed an honour. There is, however, some truth in the dying observation of Sir Godfrey Kneller—"By God, I will not be buried in Westminster! They do bury fools there."

CHAPELS.— *Observe* that in each chapel are placed plans of its monuments mounted on cards, which will be found very convenient for reference, as they show at once the name and position of every monument.

I. *Chapel of St. Benedict* (the first south - east end of Poets' Corner). *Observe.*—Under glass, and on the left in entering, is part of an altar-decoration of the 13th or 14th century, 11 feet long by 3 feet high.

The work is divided into two similar portions; in the centre is a figure, which appears to be intended for Christ, holding the globe, and in the act of blessing; an angel with a palm branch is on each side. The single figure at the left hand of the whole decoration is St. Peter; the figure that should correspond on the right, and all the Scripture subjects on that side, are gone. In the compartments to the left, between the figure of St. Peter and the centre figures, portions of those subjects remain: the fourth is destroyed. These single figures and subjects are worthy of a good Italian artist of the fourteenth century. The remaining decorations were splendid and costly; the small compartments in the architectural enrichments are filled with variously-coloured pieces of glass, inlaid on tinfoil, and have still a brilliant effect. The compartments not occupied by figures were adorned with a deep-blue glass resembling lapis lazuli, with gold lines of foliage executed on it. The smaller spaces and mouldings were enriched with cameos and gems, some of which still remain. That the work was executed in England there can be little doubt.—*Eastlake on Oil Painting*, p. 176.

This is commonly called the "Chapel of the Deans of the College," several of whom are buried here. The principal tombs are those of Langham, Archbishop of Canterbury (d. 1376); the Countess of Hertford, sister to the Lord High Admiral Nottingham, so famous for his share in the defeat of the Spanish Armada (d. 1598); and Lionel Cranfield, Earl of Middlesex, and Lord High Treasurer in the reign of James I. (d. 1645). Here are also the tombs of Archbishop Spottiswoode, Abbot Carlington, and Deans Bill and Goodman.

II. *Chapel of St. Edmund.*—Contains twenty monuments, of which that on the right on entering, to William de Valence, Earl of Pembroke, half-brother to Henry III., and father of Aymer de Valence, Earl of Pembroke (d. 1296), is the first in point of time and also the most important; the effigy exhibits the earliest existing instance in this country of the use of enamelled metal for monumental purposes. The other tombs and monuments of importance in this chapel are: tomb of John of Eltham, son of Edward II.; tomb, with two alabaster figures, 20 inches in length, representing William of Windsor and Blanche de la Tour, children of Edward III.; monumental brass (the best in the Abbey), representing Eleanora de Bohun, Duchess of Gloucester, in her conventual dress as a nun of Barking Abbey (d. 1399); monumental brass of Robert de Waldeby, Archbishop of York (d. 1397); effigy of Frances Grey, Duchess of Suffolk, grand-daughter of Henry VII., and mother of Lady Jane Grey; alabaster statue of Elizabeth Russell, of the Bedford family—foolishly shown for many years as the lady who died by the prick of a needle. Edward Bulwer Lytton—Lord Lytton, the novelist and statesman—was interred here in 1873.

III. *Chapel of St. Nicholas.*—Contains the monument of Anne, wife of the Protector Somerset; the great Lord Burghley's monument to his wife Mildred, and their daughter Anne; Sir Robert Cecil's monument to his wife; tomb of Lady Jane Clifford; a large altar-tomb, in the area of the chapel, to the father and mother of the celebrated Villiers, Duke of Buckingham, the "Steenie" of James I.; Philippa, Duchess of York (d. 1433); under it lies the body of Queen Catherine of Valois, removed here in 1776.

IV. *Chapel of the Blessed Virgin*, generally known as *Henry VII.'s Chapel*, is entered by a flight of steps beneath the chantry of Henry V. The entrance gates are of oak, overlaid with brass, gilt, and wrought into various devices—the portcullis exhibiting the descent of the founder from the Beaufort family, and the crown and twisted roses the union that took place, on Henry's marriage, of the White Rose of York with the Red Rose of Lancaster. The chapel consists of a central aisle, with five small chapels at the east end, and two side aisles, north and south. The banners and stalls appertain to the Knights of the Most Honourable Military Order of the Bath, an order of merit next in rank in this country to the Most Noble Order of the Garter: the knights were formerly installed in this chapel; and the Dean of Westminster is Dean of the Order. The statues in the architecture of this chapel are commended by Flaxman for "their natural simplicity and grandeur of character and drapery;" and speaking of the fan-vaulting of the roof, Sir Gilbert Scott says it is here seen in "its most perfect beauty."

The principal monuments in Henry VII.'s Chapel are: altar-tomb with effigies of Henry VII. and Queen (in the centre of the chapel), the work of Peter Torrigiano, an Italian sculptor. Lord Bacon calls it "one of the stateliest and daintiest tombs in Europe;" the heads of the King and Queen were originally surmounted with crowns; the enclosure or screen, of earlier date, is of brass, and the supposed work of English artists. In the vault below was placed the body of James I., the coffins of Henry and his Queen being "stripped of their cases and coverings" and removed from their places "to give convenient entry to the enormous bulk of the coffin of James."[1] In the *South Aisle*.— Altar-tomb, with effigy (by Peter Torrigiano) of Margaret, Countess of Richmond, mother of Henry VII.; altar-tomb, with effigy of the mother of Lord Darnley, husband of Mary, Queen of Scots; tomb, with effigy (by Cornelius Cure) of Mary, Queen of Scots, erected by James I., who brought his mother's body from Peterborough Cathedral and buried it here. The painting and gilding of Mary's monument cost £265; the tomb [sarcophagus and effigy] £825 : 10s.; the iron grate £195. Monument to George Villiers, Duke of Buckingham, and his duchess; the duke was assassinated by Felton in 1628; his youngest son, Francis, who was killed in the Civil Wars, and his eldest son, the second and profligate duke, are buried with their father in the vault beneath. Statue of the first wife of Sir Robert Walpole, erected by her son Horace Walpole, the great letter-writer. In the *North Aisle*.— Tomb, with effigy (by Maximilian Coult) of Queen Elizabeth (the lion-hearted Queen); her coffin is placed on that of her sister, Queen Mary, in a low narrow vault, affording room only for the two coffins; alabaster cradle, with effigy of Sophia, daughter of James I., who died when only three days old. Beneath, in the vault of the Stuarts, was found, on opening it in 1869, "a vast pile of coffins" of all sizes, rudely huddled together; "a chaos of royal mortality," is Dean Stanley's striking expression. On a careful examination there could be identified the coffins of Henry, Prince of Wales; Mary, Queen of Scots, with that of Arabella Stuart upon it; Henry of Oatlands; Mary, Princess of Orange; Prince Rupert; Anne Hyde, first wife of James II.; Elizabeth, Queen of Bohemia; ten children of James II. (including his "natural son James Darnley"); and the eighteen children of Queen Anne.

[1] *Dean Stanley*, p. 339.

James I. and his Queen lie elsewhere—Anne of Denmark, in a lonely vault, and James, as we have seen, in that of Henry VII.[1] Monument to Lodowick Stuart, Duke of Richmond and Lennox, and his duchess, of the time of James I.: La Belle Stuart is buried beneath this monument; monument to George Monk, Duke of Albemarle, who restored King Charles II.; sarcophagus of white marble, containing certain bones accidentally discovered (July 1674) in a wooden chest below the stairs of the White Tower, and believed to be the remains of Edward V. and his brother Richard, Duke of York, murdered by order of their uncle, King Richard III.; monuments to Savile, Marquis of Halifax, the statesman and wit (d. 1695);[2] to Montague, Earl of Halifax, the universal patron of the men of genius of his time (d. 1715); here Addison and Craggs are buried; to Sheffield, Duke of Buckingham, the patron of Dryden, with its inscription, "Dubius, sed non Improbus, Vixi," which suggested to Prior his well-known lines—

> *On Bishop Atterbury's burying the Duke of Buckingham.*
>
> "I have no hopes," the Duke he says and dies;
> "In sure and certain hope," the Prelate cries:
> Of these two learned Peers, I pr'ythee, say man,
> Who is the lying knave, the Priest or Layman!
> The Duke he stands an infidel confest,
> "He's our dear brother," quoth the lordly priest;
> The Duke, though knave, still "Brother dear" he cries,
> And who can say the reverend Prelate lies?

In the vault at the base of the monument lie the Duke and his family—usually spoken of as deposited in the Ormond Vault. Northeast of Henry VII.'s tomb is the Argyll vault, in which, and not under the Sheffield Chapel as commonly supposed, are deposited the coffins of the great Duke of Argyll and his Duchess, side by side, and on them those of their two daughters (*Stanley*.) Recumbent figure, by Sir R. Westmacott, of the Duke of Montpensier, brother to Louis Philippe, King of the French. King Charles II., William and Mary, and Queen Anne, are buried in a vault at the east end of the south aisle of the chapel. King George II. and Queen Caroline; Frederick, Prince of Wales, the father of George III., his wife Augusta, and three of their children; and William, Duke of Cumberland, the hero of Culloden, in a vault in the centre of the nave of the chapel. The remains of King George II. and his Queen lie mingled together, a side having been taken by the King's own direction from each of the coffins for this purpose: the two sides which were withdrawn were seen standing against the wall when the vault was opened for the last time in 1871. In a vault south-west of Henry VII.'s tomb was found, during the search for the coffin of James I., a leaden coffin rudely shaped to the form, with an inscribed plate showing that it contained

---

[1] *See* the very interesting "Account of the Search for the Grave of King James I.," printed as an Appendix to Dean Stanley's *Historical Memorials*, p. 535, etc.

[2] "I am not sure that the head of Halifax in Westminster Abbey does not give a more lively notion of him than any painting or engraving that I have seen."—*Macaulay*.

the undisturbed remains of Elizabeth Claypole, the favourite daughter of Oliver Cromwell. The great Protector himself was interred at the extreme eastern end of Henry VII.'s chapel, but, as is too well known, his corpse was exhumed after the Restoration and treated with every possible contumely.

V. *Chapel of St. Paul.*—Contains altar-tomb on the right on entering to Lodowick Robsart, Lord Bourchier, standard-bearer to Henry V. at the battle of Agincourt; altar-tomb of Sir Giles Daubeny (Lord-Chamberlain to Henry VII.) and his lady. Stately monument against the wall to Sir Thomas Bromley, Lord-Chancellor of England in the reign of Queen Elizabeth; he sat as Chancellor at the trial of Mary, Queen of Scots, at Fotheringay. Monuments to Sir Dudley Carleton, ambassador to Spain, from James I.; to Viscount Dorchester, and Francis, Lord Cottington, of the time of Charles I. Colossal portrait-statue of James Watt, the great engineer, by Sir Francis Chantrey, cost £6000; quite out of harmony with the rest of the monuments and out of proportion to the size of the chapel. As the huge mass was being moved across the threshold the arch of the vault beneath gave way, disclosing to the eyes of the astonished workmen rows upon rows of gilded coffins in the vaults beneath; into which, but for the precaution of planking the area, workmen and work must have descended, joining the dead in the chamber of death. The long inscription on the pedestal was written by Lord Brougham. A marble bust (by W. D. Kayworth) bears the inscription, "Underneath is interred Sir Rowland Hill. Born December 8, 1795, died August 27, 1879. Originater of the Penny Postal System." Archbishop Ussher is buried in this chapel; his funeral was conducted with great pomp by command of Cromwell, who bore half the expense of it; the other half fell heavily on his relations.

VI. *Chapel of St. Edward the Confessor,* also called the *Chapel of the Kings*, in many respects the most interesting of all the chapels, occupies the space at the back of the high altar of the Abbey, and is entered from the north Ambulatory by a temporary staircase. The centre of this chapel is taken up by the shrine of King Edward the Confessor, erected in the reign of Henry III., and richly inlaid with mosaic work: of the original Latin inscription only a few letters remain. The wainscot addition at the top was erected in the reign of Mary I. by Abbot Fekenham. Henry IV. was seized with his last illness while performing his devotions at this shrine. No part of this chapel should be overlooked. *Observe.*—Altar-tomb, with bronze effigy of Henry III. (the effigy of the King very fine); altar-tomb of Edward I., composed of five large slabs of Purbeck marble, and carrying this appropriate inscription:—

"EDWARDVS PRIMVS SCOTORVM MALLEUS—HIC EST."

When the tomb was opened in 1774, the body of the King was discovered almost entire, with a crown of tin gilt upon his head, a sceptre of copper gilt in his right hand, and a sceptre and dove of the same materials in his left; and in this state he is still lying. Altar-tomb, with effigy of Eleanor, Queen of Edward I.; the figure of the Queen was the work of Master William Torell, goldsmith, *i.e.* Torelli, an Italian, and is much and deservedly admired for its simplicity and beauty; the original iron-work was the work of a smith, Thomas le Leghtone, living at Leighton Buzzard, in Bedfordshire. On the south side, altar-tomb, with effigy of Edward III.; the sword and shield of state, carried before the King in France, are placed by the side of the tomb.

> Sir Roger in the next place laid his hand upon Edward III.'s sword, and leaning upon the pommel of it, gave us the whole history of the Black Prince; concluding that, in Sir Richard Baker's opinion, Edward III. was one of the greatest princes that ever sate on the English throne.—*Addison.*

Altar-tomb, with effigy of Philippa, Queen of Edward III. The tomb was the work of Hawkin de Liège, and of John Orchard, a stone-mason of London.[1] Altar-tomb, with effigies of Richard II. and his Queen. Altar-tomb and chantry of Henry V., the hero of Agincourt; the head of the King was of solid silver, and the figure was plated with the same metal; the head was stolen at the Reformation; the helmet, shield, and saddle of the King are still to be seen on a bar above the turrets of the chantry. Gray slab, formerly adorned with a rich brass figure (a few nails are still to be seen), covering the remains of Thomas of Woodstock, Duke of Gloucester, youngest son of Edward III., murdered by order of his nephew, Richard II. Small altar-tomb of Margaret of York, infant daughter of Edward IV. Small altar-tomb of Elizabeth Tudor, infant daughter of Henry VII. Brass, much worn, representing John de Waltham, Bishop of Salisbury, and Lord High Treasurer of England in the reign of Richard II.; by whose command he was buried in the Chapel of the Kings. At the west end of the Chapel are the two coronation chairs, still used at the coronations of the sovereigns of Great Britain—one containing the famous stone of Scone on which the Scottish Kings were wont to be crowned, and which Edward I. carried away with him as an evidence of his absolute conquest of Scotland: this stone is 26 inches long, 16 inches wide, and 11 inches thick, and is fixed in the bottom of the chair by cramps of iron; it is simply a block of the reddish-gray sandstone of the western coasts of Scotland,[2] squared and smoothed. "In this chair and on this stone every English sovereign from Edward I. to Queen Victoria has been inaugurated" (*Stanley*). The other chair was made for the coronation of Mary, Queen of William III. Between the chairs are placed the great two-handed sword borne before Edward III. in France.

> We were then conveyed to the two coronation chairs, where my old friend [Sir Roger de Coverley], after having heard that the stone underneath the most ancient

---

[1] Devon's *Issues of the Exchequer from Henry III. to Henry VI.*
[2] Professor Ramsay, see *Stanley*, p. 58.

of them, which was brought from Scotland, was called Jacob's pillow, sat himself down in the chair; and looking like the figure of an old Gothic king, asked our interpreter what authority they had to say that Jacob had ever been in Scotland? The fellow, instead of returning him an answer, told him that he hoped his honour would pay the forfeit. I could observe Sir Roger a little ruffled at being thus trepanned; but our guide not insisting upon his demand, the knight soon recovered his good humour, and whispered in my ear, that if Will Wimble were with us, and saw those two chairs, it would go hard but he would get a tobacco-stopper out of one or t' other of them.—*Addison.*

The Screen dividing the chapel from the Choir was erected in the reign of Henry VI.; beneath the cornice runs a series of fourteen sculptures in bas-relief, representing the principal events, real and imaginary, in the life of Edward the Confessor; the pavement of the chapel, much worn, is contemporary with the shrine of the Confessor.

VII. *Chapel of St. John the Baptist* contains the tombs of several early Abbots of Westminster: Abbot William de Colchester (d. 1420); Abbot Mylling (d. 1492); and Abbot Fascet (d. 1500). The large and stately monument to Henry Carey, Lord Hunsdon, first cousin and Chamberlain to Queen Elizabeth. Large altar-tomb of Cecil, Earl of Exeter (eldest son of the great Lord Burghley), and his two wives; the vacant space is said to have been intended for the statue of his second countess, but outliving him, she disdainfully refused to be represented on the left side, though she is buried below. Monument to Colonel Popham, one of Cromwell's officers at sea, and the only monument to any of the Parliamentary party suffered to remain in the Abbey at the Restoration of Charles II.; the inscription, however, was turned to the wall; his remains were removed at the same time with those of Cromwell, Ireton, Bradshaw, Blake, and the great Parliamentary leader John Pym, who was buried in this chapel, December 15, 1643, with extraordinary magnificence, the two Houses of Parliament and the Assembly of Divines being in attendance. By Pym's body were laid those of Devereux, Earl of Essex, and Sir William Strode.

VIII. *The Chapel of Abbot Islip* contains the altar-tomb of Islip himself (d. 1532), and the monument to the great-nephew and eventually heir of Sir Christopher Hatton, Queen Elizabeth's Lord Chancellor. The Hatton vault was purchased by William Pulteney, the celebrated Earl of Bath, who is here interred, and whose monument, by the side of General Wolfe's, is without the chapel, in the aisle of the Abbey. The Wolfe monument was the work of Joseph Wilton, and cost £3000; the bas-relief (in lead, bronzed over) represents the march of the British troops from the river bank to the Heights of Abraham; this portion of the monument is by Capizzoldi.

The East Aisle of the North Transept was formerly divided by screens into the *Chapels of St. John, St. Michael,* and *St. Andrew.* Here are two of the most remarkable monuments in the Abbey. One is that of Sir Francis Vere, the great Low Country soldier of Queen Elizabeth's reign. Four knights kneeling, support on their shoulders a table, on which lie the several parts of a complete suit of armour;

beneath is the recumbent figure of Vere; the whole full of vigour and admirably executed. The sculptor is unknown. The other is the monument by Roubiliac (one of the last and best of his works) to Mr. and Mrs. Nightingale. The bottom of the monument is represented as throwing open its marble doors, and a sheeted skeleton is seen launching his dart at the lady, who has sunk affrighted into her husband's arms.

The dying woman would do honour to any artist. Her right arm and hand are considered by sculptors as the perfection of fine workmanship. Life seems slowly receding from her tapering fingers and quivering wrist.—*Allan Cunningham.*

When Roubiliac was erecting this monument, he was found one day by Gayfere, the Abbey mason, standing with his arms folded, and his looks fixed on one of the knightly figures which support the table over the statue of Sir Francis Vere. As Gayfere approached, the enthusiastic Frenchman laid his hand on his arm, pointed to the figure, and said, in a whisper, "Hush! hush! he vil speak presently."[1] The monument to Lord Norris, another of Elizabeth's generals, near the north end, is also a noteworthy work, not less magnificent though less beautiful than that of Sir Francis Vere. The kneeling figures which support the slab are those of Lord Norris's six sons, who had all, but the youngest, died in their father's lifetime; they are praying, he is praising God. Behind the Norris tomb are statues of Mrs. Siddons by Chantrey, and of her brother John Philip Kemble, modelled by Flaxman, and sculptured after his death by Hinchcliffe (removed from the South Transept); both, however, are buried elsewhere. Against the walls are a bust of Sir Humphry Davy, the great chemist, and a medallion of Dr. Thomas Young, the pioneer in deciphering Egyptian hieroglyphics and author of the undulatory theory of light. On the west side are monuments to Admiral Kempenfelt, lost in the *Royal George;* Sir John Franklin, the Arctic voyager; and a bust of Dr. Matthew Baillie.

The *Choir* affords the best point of view for examining the architecture of the Abbey. The view from here is very grand. In the centre, under the tower, is the spot where the sovereigns of England, from the Conqueror downwards, have been crowned. The altar, erected in 1867, from the designs of Sir G. G. Scott, has in the reredos a mosaic of the Last Supper, executed by Messrs. Clayton and Bell, and is altogether a most elaborate and costly work. *Observe.*—Tomb of Sebert, King of the East Saxons, erected by the abbots and monks of Westminster in 1308. Portrait of Richard II., a contemporary painting lately and skilfully restored by G. Richmond, R.A. Tomb of Edmund Crouchback, Earl of Lancaster, second son of Edward III., and of his countess. Tomb of Aymer de Valence, Earl of Pembroke (very fine— one of the best views of it is from the north aisle).

The monuments of Aymer de Valence and Edmund Crouchback are specimens of the magnificence of our sculpture in the reign of the two first Edwards. The

---

[1] Smith, *Nollekens and his Times,* vol. ii. p. 90, says that Gayfere related this anecdote to him, with the difference that Roubiliac's eyes were "rivetted to the kneeling figure at the north-west corner of Lord Norris's monument."

loftiness of the work, the number of arches and pinnacles, the lightness of the spires, the richness and profusion of foliage and crockets, the solemn repose of the principal statue, the delicacy of thought in the group of angels bearing the soul, and the tender sentiment of concern variously expressed in the relations ranged in order round the basement, forcibly arrest the attention, and carry the thoughts not only to other ages, but to other states of existence.—*Flaxman.*

Tomb of Ann of Cleves, one of King Henry VIII.'s six wives.

The rich mosaic pavement is an excellent specimen of the Opus Alexandrinum, and was placed here at the expense of Henry III., in the year 1268. The black and white pavement was laid at the expense of Dr. Busby, master of Westminster School.

The organ is divided and placed above the stalls. It is blown by the action of a gas engine fixed in the centre of the cloisters. The visitor now enters the *North Transept*, where inscribed stones mark the graves of the rival statesmen, Pitt and Fox.

> The mighty chiefs sleep side by side;
> Drop upon Fox's grave the tear,
> 'Twill trickle to his rival's bier.—*Sir Walter Scott.*

Grattan, Canning, Castlereagh, and Palmerston.—The monuments to the Duke and Duchess of Newcastle, of the time of Charles I. and II. Roubiliac's monument to Sir Peter Warren, containing his fine figure of Navigation. Rysbrack's monument to Admiral Vernon, who distinguished himself at Carthagena. Bacon's noble monument to the great Lord Chatham, erected by the King and Parliament at a cost of £6000.

> Bacon there
> Gives more than female beauty to a stone,
> And Chatham's eloquence to marble lips.
> *Cowper, The Task.*

Nollekens's large monument to the three naval captains who fell in Rodney's great victory of April 12, 1782, erected by the King and Parliament, cost £4000. Flaxman's grand portrait-statue of the great Lord Mansfield, with Wisdom on one side, Justice on the other, and behind the figure of a youth, a criminal, by Wisdom delivered up to Justice—erected by a private person, who bequeathed £2500 for the purpose. Statue of Sir W. Follett, by Behnes. Small monument, with bust, to Warren Hastings—erected by his widow. Sir R. Westmacott's Mrs. Warren and Child—one of the best of Sir Richard's works. Chantrey's three portrait-statues of Francis Horner, George Canning, and Sir John Malcolm. Statue, by Gibson, of Sir Robert Peel, disguised, by a pedantic anachronism, in a Roman toga; and statue of Lord Palmerston robed as a Knight of the Garter, by Jackson.

On the way to the Nave, and in the *North Aisle of the Choir*, are tablets to Henry Purcell (d. 1695), and Dr. Blow (d. 1708), two of our greatest English musicians. The Purcell monument was erected at the expense of the wife of Sir Robert Howard, the poet; the inscription is attributed to Dryden. Portrait-statues of Sir Stamford Raffles, by Chantrey; and of Wilberforce, by S. Joseph.

The *Nave*.—Entering the nave on the right is the monument to Sir John Herschel. A small stone, in the middle of the north aisle (fronting Killigrew's monument), inscribed, "O Rare Ben Jonson," marks the grave of the poet. He is buried here standing on his feet, and the inscription was done, as Aubrey relates, "in a pavement-square of blue marble, about fourteen inches square . . . at the charge of Jack Young (afterwards knighted), who, walking here when the grave was covering, gave the fellow eighteenpence to cut it." When the nave was repaved in 1821, the stone was taken up and the present uninteresting square placed in its stead. The original stone was, however, recovered from the stoneyard in the time of Dean Buckland, who caused it to be affixed to the north wall of the nave. In 1849, when Sir Robert Wilson was buried, and again when John Hunter's grave was dug a little to the west, the loose sand in which Ben Jonson was interred gave way, and the poet's skull, with "the red hair still upon it," rolled down; but upon each occasion was reverently replaced.[1] Tom Killigrew, the wit, is buried by the side of Jonson; and his son, who fell at the battle of Almanza in 1707, has a monument immediately opposite. East of Ben Jonson's grave is that of David Livingstone, the African traveller; and near his those of Telford and Stephenson, the engineers, the latter commemorated by an incised brass on the floor, and both by a memorial window just above. In the south aisle are—Monument to Sir Palmes Fairborne, with a fine epitaph in verse by Dryden. Monument to Sir William Temple, the statesman and author, his wife, sister-in-law, and child;—this was erected pursuant to Temple's will. Monument to Sprat, the poet, and friend of Cowley. (Bishop Atterbury is buried opposite this monument, in a vault which he made for himself when Dean of Westminster, "as far," he says to Pope, "from kings and kæsars as the space will admit of.") Monument, with bust, of Sidney, Earl of Godolphin, chief minister to Queen Anne "during the first nine glorious years of her reign." Monument to Heneage Twysden, who wrote the genealogy of the Bickerstaff family in the *Tatler*, and fell at the battle of Blaregnies in 1709. Monument to Congreve, the poet, erected at the expense of Henrietta, Duchess of Marlborough, to whom, for reasons not known or mentioned, he bequeathed a legacy of about £10,000.

When the younger Duchess exposed herself by placing a monument and silly epitaph of her own composing and bad spelling to Congreve in Westminster Abbey, her mother, quoting the words, said "I know not what pleasure she might have had in his company, but I am sure it was no honour."—*Horace Walpole*.

In the Baptistery, at the west end of the south aisle, are the monuments to Atterbury; to Secretary Craggs (with an epitaph in verse by Pope), and Dean Wilcocks; a seated statue of the poet Wordsworth by Lough, and a bust of Keble, author of the *Christian Year*, by Woolner. In front of Congreve's monument Mrs. Oldfield, the actress, is buried, "in a very fine Brussells lace head," says her maid; "a Holland shift

[1] Frank Buckland's *Curiosities of Natural History*, 3d S., vol. ii. pp. 181-189.

with a tucker and double ruffles of the same lace; a pair of new kid gloves, and her body wrapped up in a winding-sheet." Hence the allusion of the satirist—

> Odious! in woollen! 'twould a saint provoke!
> (Were the last words that poor Narcissa spoke)—
> No, let a charming chintz and Brussells lace
> Wrap my cold limbs, and shade my lifeless face;
> One would not, sure, be frightful when one's dead—
> And—Betty—give this cheek a little red.—POPE.

Under the organ-screen—Monuments to Sir Isaac Newton, designed by Kent, and executed by Rysbrack—cost £500; and to Earl Stanhope. Monument to Dr. Mead, the famous physician (d. 1754). Three monuments, by Roubiliac, in three successive windows; to Field-Marshal Wade, whose part in putting down the Rebellion of 1745 is matter of history; to Major-General Fleming; and Lieutenant General Hargrave. The absurd monument, by Nicholas Read, to Rear-Admiral Tyrrell (d. 1766); its common name is "The Pancake Monument." Heaven is represented with clouds and cherubs, the depths of the sea with rocks of coral and madrepore; the admiral is seen ascending into heaven, while Hibernia sits in the sea with her attendants, and points to the spot where the admiral's body was committed to the deep. The upper part of this monument has now been taken away.

Monument of Major-General Stringer Lawrence, erected by the East India Company, "in testimony of their gratitude for his eminent services in the command of their forces on the coast of Coromandel, from 1746 to 1756." Monument, by Flaxman, to Captain Montagu, who fell in Lord Howe's victory of June 1. Monumental group of Lord Clyde, Sir James Outram, and Sir Henry Havelock. Bust of Sir James Outram. Monument to Major André, executed by the Americans as a spy in the year 1780. The monument was erected at the expense of George III., and the figure of Washington on the bas-relief has been renewed with a head, on three different occasions, "the wanton mischief of some schoolboy," says Charles Lamb, "fired, perhaps, with raw notions of transatlantic freedom. The mischief was done," he adds,— he is addressing Southey,—"about the time that you were a scholar there. Do you know anything about the unfortunate relic?" This sly allusion to the early political principles of the poet caused a temporary cessation of his friendship with the essayist. Sir R. Westmacott's monument to Spencer Perceval, First Lord of the Treasury and Chancellor of the Exchequer, shot by Bellingham in the lobby of the House of Commons in 1812, cost £5250. Monuments to William Pitt, cost £6300; and C. J. Fox (there is no inscription); both by Sir Richard Westmacott. Monument, by E. H. Baily, R.A, to the third Lord Holland.

In *South Aisle of Choir*, recumbent figure of William Thynn, Receiver of the Marches in the reign of Henry VIII. Good bust, by

Le Sœur, of Sir Thomas Richardson, Lord Chief Justice in the reign of Charles I. Monument to Thomas Thynn, of Longleat, who was shot in his coach on Sunday, February 12, 1682. [*See* Haymarket.] The bas-relief contains a representation of the event.

A Welshman bragging of his family, said his father's effigy was set up in Westminster Abbey; being asked whereabouts, he said, "In the same monument with Squire Thynn, for he was his coachman."—Joe Miller's Jests.

Monument to Dr. South, the great preacher (d. 1716); he was a prebendary of this church. Monument, by F. Bird, to Sir Cloudesley Shovel (d. 1707).

Sir Cloudesley Shovel's monument has very often given me great offence. Instead of the brave rough English Admiral, which was the distinguishing character of that plain gallant man, he is represented on his tomb by the figure of a beau, dressed in a long periwig, and reposing himself upon velvet cushions under a canopy of state. The inscription is answerable to the monument ; for, instead of celebrating the many remarkable actions he had performed in the service of his country, it acquaints us only with the manner of his death, in which it was impossible for him to reap any honour.—Addison.

Bird bestowed busts and bas-reliefs on those he decorated, but Sir Cloudesley Shovel's, and other monuments by him, made men of taste dread such honours.— Horace Walpole.

Monuments to Dr. Busby, master of Westminster School (d. 1695); to Sir Godfrey Kneller, with epitaph in verse by Pope; and by T. Banks, R.A., to Dr. Isaac Watts, who is buried in *Bunhill Fields*. Bust, by Flaxman, of Pasquale de Paoli, the Corsican chief (d. 1807). Monument to Charles Burney, D.D., the Greek scholar (d. 1817); the inscription by Dr. Parr.

Poets' Corner is the name given to the eastern angle of the South Transept, from the tombs and honorary monuments of Chaucer, Spenser, Shakespeare, and several of our greatest poets. [*See* Poet's Corner.] Tomb of Geoffrey Chaucer, the father of English poetry (d. 1400); erected in 1555, by Nicholas Brigham, a scholar of Oxford, and himself a poet; Chaucer was originally buried in this spot, Brigham removing his bones to a more honourable tomb. A portrait of Chaucer originally ornamented the back of the tomb. Its loss was in part supplied in the painted glass window above the tomb, erected in 1868, in which are medallions of Chaucer and Gower and scenes from Chaucer's poems. Monument (at south end) to Edmund Spenser, author of *The Faerie Queene;* executed by Nich. Stone at the expense of "Anne Pembroke, Dorset, and Montgomery" (the cost was £40), and renewed in 1778 at the instigation of Mason, the poet; Spenser died in King Street, Westminster, "from lack of bread," and was buried here at the expense of Queen Elizabeth's Earl of Essex. Monument to Shakespeare in the west aisle—his bones, as all know, repose at Stratford-on-Avon; erected in the reign of George II. from the designs of Kent. When Pope was asked for an inscription, he wrote—

Thus Britons love me, and preserve my fame,
Free from a Barber's or a Benson's name.

We shall see the sting of this presently: Shakespeare stands like a sentimental dandy. Beaumont rests here in an unrecorded grave. Monument at the south-east end to Michael Drayton, a poet of Queen Elizabeth's reign, erected by the same Anne, Countess of Pembroke, Dorset, and Montgomery; the epitaph in verse by Ben Jonson, and very fine. Close to it a tablet to Ben Jonson, erected in the reign of George II., a century after the poet's death: Jonson, as we have seen, was buried in the north aisle of the nave. At the south end, bust of Milton (buried at St. Giles's, Cripplegate), erected in 1737, at the expense of Auditor Benson: "In the inscription," says Dr. Johnson, "Mr. Benson has bestowed more words upon himself than upon Milton;" a circumstance that Pope has called attention to in the *Dunciad*—

On poets' tombs see Benson's titles writ.

Next to Milton's is a monument to Butler, author of *Hudibras* (buried at St. Paul's, Covent Garden), erected in 1732 by John Barber, a printer, and Lord Mayor of London. Grave of Sir William Davenant, with the inscription, imitated from Ben Jonson's, "O rare Sir William Davenant." Monument to Cowley (north of Chaucer's), erected at the expense of the second and last Villiers, Duke of Buckingham; the epitaph by Sprat. North of Cowley's monument is a bust of Dryden, erected at the expense of Sheffield, Duke of Buckingham.

This Sheffield raised: the sacred dust below
Was Dryden once: the rest who does not know.—POPE.

The bust by Scheemakers is very fine. Honorary monument to Shadwell, the antagonist of Dryden, erected by his son, Sir John Shadwell, in front of Milton's. South of Chaucer's tomb is a monument to John Philips, author of *The Splendid Shilling* (d. 1708).

When the inscription for the monument of Philips, in which he was said to be *uni Miltono secundus*, was exhibited to Dr. Sprat, then Dean of Westminster, he refused to admit it; the name of Milton was in his opinion too detestable to be read on the wall of a building dedicated to devotion. Atterbury, who succeeded him, being author of the inscription,[1] permitted its reception. "And such has been the change of public opinion," said Dr. Gregory, from whom I heard this account, "that I have seen erected in the church a bust of that man whose name I once knew was considered as a pollution of its walls."—*Dr. Johnson.*

Monument (near Shadwell's) of Matthew Prior, erected, according to his own desire, "as a last piece of human vanity," by his son. The bust, by A. Coysevox, was a present to Prior from Louis XIV., and the epitaph, written by Dr. Freind, famous for long epitaphs, for which he has been immortalised by Pope—

Freind, for your epitaphs I griev'd,
Where still so much is said;
One half will never be believ'd,
The other never read.

Monument (south-east corner of the west aisle) to Nicholas Rowe, author of the tragedy of *Jane Shore*, erected by his widow; epitaph by Pope. Monument (next to Rowe's) to John Gay, author of *The*

[1] Dean Stanley, on the authority of Crull the antiquary (who copied the inscription before the offending words were erased), says it was written by Dr. Smalridge.

Beggar's Opera; the short and irreverent epitaph, *Life is a jest,* etc., is his own composition; the verses beneath it are by Pope. Statue of Addison, by Sir R. Westmacott, erected 1809. Close to the statue of Shakespeare is a monument to Thomson, author of *The Seasons* (buried at Richmond), erected 1762; from the proceeds of a subscription edition of his works. Tablet, by Nollekens, to Oliver Goldsmith (buried in the Temple). The Latin inscription is by Dr. Johnson, who, in reply to a request that he would celebrate the fame of an author in the language in which he wrote, observed, that he never would consent to disgrace the walls of Westminster Abbey with an English inscription. Monument, near the bust of Milton, to Gray, author of *An Elegy in a Country Churchyard,* who lies in his own churchyard of Stoke-Poges. The verse by Mason, the monument by Bacon, R.A. Monument to Mason, the poet, and biographer of Gray (buried at Aston); the inscription by Bishop Hurd. Monument to Christopher Anstey, author of the *New Bath Guide* (buried at Bath). Inscribed gravestone over Richard Brinsley Sheridan. Bust of Robert Southey (buried at Keswick), by H. Weekes. Inscribed gravestone over Thomas Campbell, author of *The Pleasures of Hope,* and statue by W. C. Marshall, A.R.A. Beside him, in an unmarked grave, was laid Henry Cary, the translator of Dante. At the foot of the statue of Addison lies Lord Macaulay. Close by is the bust of William Makepeace Thackeray, the novelist, himself resting at Kensal Green; and below his bust is the grave of Charles Dickens.

The wall of the South Transept has been named by Dean Stanley —following a hint of Fuller's—the *Historical Aisle.* Here, on the west side, is the monument of Isaac Casaubon (d. 1614), the learned editor of Persius and Polybius.

On Isaac Casaubon's tablet is left the trace of another "candid and simple nature." Izaak Walton . . . forty years afterwards, wandering through the South Transept, scratched his well-known monogram on the marble, with the date 1658, earliest of those unhappy inscriptions of names of visitors, which have defaced so many a sacred space in the Abbey. *O si sic omnia!"—Dean Stanley,* p. 290.

Next to Casaubon's is a monument to William Camden, the great English antiquary (d. 1623). The monument was defaced and the nose broken off the bust when the hearse and effigy of Essex, the Parliamentary general, were destroyed in 1646, by some of the Cavalier party, who lurked at night in the Abbey to be revenged on the dead. The monument was piously restored by the University of Oxford in 1780. "Opposite his friend Camden's monument," but outside the transept, is the grave of Sir Henry Spelman, an antiquary scarcely less famous. At the foot of Camden's monument the Parliamentary historian May was buried, but afterwards exhumed. "Close by the bust of Camden and Casaubon lie, in the same grave, Grote and Thirlwall, both scholars together at the Charter House, both historians of Greece, the philosophic statesman and the judicial theologian."[1]

[1] *Stanley,* p. 303.

Under a white gravestone in the centre of the South Transept lies Thomas Parr. "Old Parr," who, if we may trust the record on his gravestone, died in 1652, at the great age of one hundred and fifty-two, having lived in the reigns of ten princes, viz. Edward IV., Edward V., Richard III., Henry VII., Henry VIII., Edward VI., Mary, Elizabeth, James I., and Charles I. Gravestone over the body of Thomas Chiffinch, closet-keeper to Charles II. (d. 1666). Monument to M. St. Evremont, a French epicurean wit, who fled to England to escape a government arrest in his own country (d. 1703). Bust of Dr. Barrow, the great divine (d. 1677). Gravestone over the body of the second wife of Sir Richard Steele, the "Prue" of his correspondence. Monument, by Roubiliac, to John, Duke of Argyll and Greenwich (d. 1743); the figure of Eloquence, with her supplicating hand and earnest brow is very masterly. Canova was struck with its beauty; he stood before it full ten minutes, muttered his surprise in his native language, passed on, and returning in a few minutes, said, "That is one of the noblest statues I have seen in England." Monument by Roubiliac (his last work) to George Frederick Handel, the great musician (d. 1759). Monument to Barton Booth (buried at Cowley), the original Cato in Addison's play. Monument to Mrs. Pritchard, the actress, famous in the characters of Lady Macbeth, Zara, and Mrs. Oakley (d. 1768). Inscribed gravestones over the bodies of David Garrick and Samuel Johnson. Monument to David Garrick, by H. Webber, erected at the expense of Albany Wallis, the executor of Garrick.

> Taking a turn the other day in the Abbey, I was struck with the affected attitude of a figure which I do not remember to have seen before, and which, upon examination, proved to be a whole-length of the celebrated Mr. Garrick. Though I would not go so far with some good Catholics abroad as to shut players altogether out of consecrated ground, yet I own I was not a little scandalised at the introduction of theatrical airs and gestures into a place set apart to remind us of the saddest realities. Going nearer, I found inscribed under this harlequin figure a farrago of false thoughts and nonsense.—*Charles Lamb.*

Inscribed gravestones over the remains of James Macpherson, the translator of *Ossian;* and of William Gifford, the editor of the *Quarterly Review.*

The painted glass in the Abbey is mostly modern. The older (but not ancient) glass in the north rose window is richer in colour.

The exhibition of the wax figures was discontinued in 1830. They originated in the old custom of making a lively effigy in wax of the deceased in robes of state—a part of the torchlight funeral procession of every great person—and of leaving the effigy over the grave as a kind of temporary monument. Some of these effigies were executed at great cost and with considerable skill. That of La Belle Stuart, one of the last that was set up, was the work of a Mrs. Goldsmith. The effigy of General Monk used to stand by his monument close to Charles II.'s grave, and the showman used to hand Monk's cap round to receive the visitors' contributions.

> This here's the cap of General Monk ! Sir, please put summut in.—Barham, *Ingoldsby Legends*.

This kind of exhibition was found so profitable to the Minor Canons and Lay Vicars, that they manufactured effigies (such as those of the great Earl of Chatham and Lord Nelson) to add to the popularity of their series.

> Another time he [Dr. Barrow] preached at the Abbey on a holiday. Here I must inform the reader that it is a custom for the servants of the church upon all Hollidays, Sundays excepted, betwixt the Sermon and Evening Prayers, to show the Tombs and Effigies of the Kings and Queens in Wax, to the meaner sort of people, who then flock thither from all the corners of the town, and pay their twopence to see The Play of the Dead Volks, as I have heard a Devonshire Clown most improperly call it. These perceiving Dr. Barrow in the pulpit after the hour was past, and fearing to lose that time in hearing which they thought they could more profitably employ in receiving—these, I say, became impatient, and caused the organ to be struck up against him, and would not give over playing till they had blow'd him down.—Dr. Pope's *Life of Seth Ward*, 12mo, 1697, p. 147.

Many of the effigies, for the most part very dilapidated, are preserved in the wainscot presses over the Islip Chapel, and only shown by special permission. Now leave the interior of the Abbey, for the purpose of visiting the Cloisters, walking through St. Margaret's churchyard, and entering Dean's Yard, where, on the left, next the west front of the Abbey, is the *Jerusalem Chamber*, in which King Henry IV. died.

> *King Henry.* Doth any name particular belong
> Unto the lodging where I first did swoon?
> *Warwick.* 'Tis called Jerusalem, my noble lord.
> *King Henry.* Laud be to God !—even there my life must end.
> It hath been prophesied to me many years,
> I should not die but in Jerusalem;
> Which vainly I supposed the Holy Land :—
> But bear me to that chamber; there I'll lie;
> In that Jerusalem shall Harry die.
> Shakespeare, *Second Part of King Henry IV.*

It was of old the Abbot's private withdrawing room, with doors leading to the refectory and the garden. After the dissolution of the Abbey and the appropriation of the Chapter House to national purposes, the Jerusalem Chamber became the place where the Dean and Chapter met to discuss their business matters. Occasionally it was used for the reception of distinguished guests and for holiday festivals. Conferences were held in it, and in it met the famous Assembly of Divines.

> Out of these walls came the Directory, the Longer and Shorter Catechism, and that famous *Confession of Faith* which, alone within these Islands, was imposed by law on the whole kingdom; and which alone of all Protestant Confessions, still, in spite of its sternness and narrowness, retains a hold in the minds of its adherents, to which its fervour and its logical coherence in some measure entitle it.—*Stanley*, p. 467.

Here were held conferences and convocations of bishops and clergy, here met the commissioners for the revision of the Liturgy, and here the Prayer Book received its final form, and here in our own day have sat that band of learned theologians and philologists who were occupied in the grave task of revising the received translation of the Old and New Testaments. Convocation has met here since its renewal in 1854. Another purpose to which the Jerusalem Chamber was formerly applied, and which has invested it with associations very different to those just mentioned, was that of being the occasional depository of the bodies of eminent persons about to be buried in the Abbey. Here lay in solemn state the famous anti-puritan pulpit wit Robert South; Sir Isaac Newton; and for the days before the torchlight procession at dead of night to the grave in Henry VII.'s chapel, Joseph Addison.

The *South Cloister* may be entered from a door in the south aisle of the nave, or from Dean's Yard. The cloisters were the cemetery of the abbots, the centre or open space that of the monks. In the south cloister are effigies of several of the early abbots. A large blue stone, uninscribed, marks the grave, it is said, of Long Meg of Westminster, a noted virago of the reign of Henry VIII. Note the quaint epitaph in verse, in north cloister, to William Lawrence, by Thomas Randolph. Monument, in east cloister, to Sir Edmund Berry Godfrey, murdered in the reign of Charles II. In the east cloister is a tablet to the mother of Addison. Monument, in east cloister, to Lieutenant-General Withers, with epitaph by Pope. Monument, in west cloister, to George Vertue, the antiquary and engraver. Medallion monument to Bonnell Thornton, editor of the *Connoisseur*—inscription by Joseph Warton. In the west cloister is a monument by T. Banks, R.A., to William Woollett, the engraver (buried at St. Pancras). Tablet to Dr. Buchan (west cloister), author of a work on *Domestic Medicine* (d. 1805). "Under a blue marble stone, against the first pillar in the east ambulatory," Aphra Behn was buried, April 20, 1689, and alongside of her, in fitting companionship, the scurrilous wit Tom Brown. Under stones no longer carrying inscriptions, are buried Henry Lawes, "one who called Milton friend;" Betterton, the great actor; Mrs. Bracegirdle, the beautiful actress; and Samuel Foote, the famous comedian. At the south-east corner of the cloister are remains of the Confessor's buildings, including the Chapel of the Pyx, an interesting specimen of the earliest Anglo-Norman architecture; it was of old a treasury office, and still permission to enter the building can only be obtained through the Lords of the Treasury. A small wooden door, in the south cloister, leads to *Ashburnham House*, and the richly ornamented doorway in the east cloister to the *Chapter House*. This is open to the public, and should by all means be visited. [*See* Ashburnham House; Chapter House; Sanctuary.]

The hours of *Divine Service* are: *Sundays*, 8 A.M., 10 A.M., and 3 P.M., also at certain seasons 7 P.M. (in choir or nave); *Week-days*, 8.30 A.M., 9 A.M. (Westminster School Service), 10 A.M., and 3 P.M. The chapels are open free on Mondays and Tuesdays.

Westminster Bridge, the second stone bridge in point of time over the Thames at London. When we read in our old writers—and the allusions are common enough — of Ivy Bridge, Strand Bridge, Whitehall Bridge, Westminster Bridge, and Lambeth Bridge, landing piers alone are meant.

Ralph Morice, Archbishop Cranmer's secretary, "went over" from Lambeth "unto *Westminster Bridge* with a sculler, where he entered into a wherry that went to London, wherein were four of the Gard, who meant to land at Paules Wharfe, and to passe by the King's highnesse, who then was in his barge, with a great number of barges and boates about him, then baiting of beares in the water over against the bank."—Fox, *Mart.* ed. 1597, p. 1081.

Latimer in preaching to Edward VI., April 12, 1549, on Christ's words to Peter, says, " I dar saye there is never a wherriman at Westminster Bridge but he can answere to thys ; " and the Order of Crowning of James I. and Anne of Denmark opens with, "The King and Queen came from Westminster Bridge to the West door of the Minster Church." Great opposition was made by the citizens of London to a second bridge over the Thames, at or even near London; and in 1671, when a bill for building a bridge over the Thames at Putney was read, a curious debate took place, recorded by Grey (vol. i. p. 415). The Bill was rejected, fifty-four voting for it and sixty-seven against it.

The Act for constructing a bridge from Old Palace Yard, Westminster, to the opposite shore in Surrey was passed in 1736. The architect employed to construct it was Charles Labelye, a native of Switzerland, naturalised in England. The first stone was laid January 29, 1738-1739, and the bridge first opened for foot-passengers, horses, etc., November 18, 1750. It was 1223 feet long and 44 feet wide, and consisted of thirteen semicircular arches, the centre being 76 feet span, as well as a small one at each end. The piers were built on caissons or rafts of timber, which were floated to the spot destined for them. It was originally surmounted by a lofty parapet, which M. Grosley, a French traveller, has gravely asserted was placed there in order to prevent the English propensity to suicide. It was on this bridge that Wordsworth wrote his famous sonnet—

COMPOSED UPON WESTMINSTER BRIDGE,
September 3, 1803.

Earth has not anything to show more fair :
Dull would he be of soul who could pass by
A sight so touching in its majesty :
This City now doth like a garment wear
The beauty of the morning ; silent, bare,
Ships, towers, domes, theatres and temples lie
Open unto the fields, and to the sky ;
All bright and glittering in the smokeless air.
Never did sun more beautifully steep
In his first splendour valley, rock, or hill ;
Ne'er saw I, never felt, a calm so deep !
The river glideth at his own sweet will :
Dear God ! the very houses seem asleep ;
And all that mighty heart is lying still.

When Gibbon lost his place at the Board of Trade, and again set out for Lausanne to finish the *Decline and Fall*, he says, "As my post-chaise moved over Westminster Bridge, I bade a long farewell to the *fumum et opes strepitumque Romæ.*" Crabbe, the night after he left his letter at Burke's door, "walked Westminster Bridge backwards and forwards until daylight." Burke's reply saved him from suicide.

The soil was deepened or washed away after London Bridge was removed, and in consequence ten piers settled down. In 1846, it was found necessary to close the bridge entirely, until it could be lightened of much superincumbent material and fitted to serve as a temporary structure. During six and thirty years upwards of £200,000 are said to have been spent on its maintenance and repairs. After many delays a new bridge was commenced, May 1854, from the designs of Mr. Thomas Page, C.E. As it was to be of unusual width, the engineer conceived the bold plan of constructing in the first instance one half the bridge (about 40 feet in width) from end to end, and opening it for traffic while the other was being built. Owing to obstructions and a temporary suspension of the works, the first half was not opened for traffic till March 1860. The second half was completed and formally opened at four o'clock in the morning of May 24, 1862, "that being the day and hour on which her Majesty was born" in 1819.

The present bridge is 1160 feet long and 85 feet wide, and so nearly level that the rise in the centre is little over 5 feet. It consists of seven low segmental wrought and cast iron arches — the central arch 120 feet in span, and the shore arches 95 feet — borne on granite piers. The foundations of each pier are formed by 145 bearing piles driven through the gravel to an average depth of nearly 30 feet into the London clay, and around them 44 cast-iron cylinder piles and as many sheeting plates, forming a sort of permanent coffer-dam, the intermediate spaces and area up to low water level being filled with a concrete of hydraulic lime. A base course of blocks of granite was laid on this, and then the pier carried up, the core of brick, the casing granite. The total cost of the bridge did not exceed £250,000. From Westminster Bridge is obtained the best view of the Houses of Parliament; their towers, mingling with those of Westminster Abbey, stand out grandly as the bridge is crossed from the Surrey side. The river front of the Houses on the one hand and St. Thomas's Hospital and Lambeth Palace on the other, are well seen from the south side of the bridge.

Westminster Bridge Road extends from Westminster Bridge to the Obelisk, Blackfriars Road. In this road, on the south side, is the entrance to St. Thomas's Hospital, Sanger's Amphitheatre (late Astley's), Canterbury Theatre of Varieties (late Canterbury Hall), and Christ Church, the handsome successor of Rowland Hill's Surrey Chapel. On the north side are some houses, on one of which (No. 266) is a stone inscribed "Coade's Row, 1798." The name was given from its neighbourhood to Coade's manufactory of artificial stone, situated in Narrow Wall (now Belvedere Road), and at one time an establishment of much merit.

Westminster Hall, the old hall of the palace of our kings at Westminster, incorporated by Sir Charles Barry into the new Houses of Parliament, to serve as their vestibule. It was originally built in the reign of William Rufus, and is supposed to have been a nave and aisles divided by timber ports; and during the refacing of the outer walls, a Norman arcade of the time of Rufus was uncovered, but destroyed. Rufus's Hall was intended as the commencement of a new Westminster Palace to supersede that of Edward the Confessor. The present hall was formed 1397-1399 (in the last three years of Richard II.), when the walls were carried up 2 feet higher, the windows altered, and a stately porch and new roof constructed according to the design of Master Henry de Yeveley, master mason. The stone moulding or string-course that runs round the hall preserves the white hart couchant, the favourite device of Richard II. The roof, with its hammer beams (carved with angels), is of oak, and the finest of its kind in this country. Fuller speaks of its "cobwebless beams," alluding to the vulgar belief that it was built of a particular kind of wood (Irish oak) in which spiders cannot live.[1] The early Parliaments, and the still earlier Grand Councils, were often held in this hall. The Law Courts of England were of old held in the open hall; the Exchequer Court at the entrance end, and the Courts of Chancery and Kings at the opposite end; and here, in certain courts built by Sir John Soane, on the west of the hall, they continued to be held until the opening of the New Law Courts in 1882. These courts were—the Court of Chancery, in which the Lord Chancellor sat; the Court of Queen's Bench, in which the Lord Chief Justice of the King's Bench[2] sat; the Court of Common Pleas, presided over by a Lord Chief Justice, and called by Coke "the pillow whereon the attorney doth rest his head"; and the Court of Exchequer, presided over by a Lord Chief Baron. The name Westminster Hall was not unfrequently used for the law itself.

> Whatever Bishops do otherwise than the Law permits, Westminster Hall can control or send them to absolve.—Selden's *Table Talk.*

When Peter the Great was taken into Westminster Hall, he inquired who those busy people were in wigs and black gowns. He was answered they are lawyers. "Lawyers!" said he, with a face of astonishment: "why, I have but *two* in my whole dominions, and I believe I shall hang one of them the moment I get home."[3]

> It is reported that John Whiddon, a Justice of the Court of King's Bench in 1 Mariæ, was the first of the Judges who rode to Westminster Hall on a Horse or Gelding; for before that time they rode on mules.—Dugdale's *Orig. Jur.* ed. 1680, p. 38.
>
> *Manly.* I hate this place [Westminster Hall] worse than a man that has inherited a Chancery suit: I wish I were well out on't again.
>
> *Freeman.* Why, you need not be afraid of this place; for a man without money

---

[1] Ned Ward's *London Spy*, part viii.
[2] Sir Edward Coke was the last Lord Chief Justice of England. His successor was Lord Chief Justice of the King's Bench.
[3] *Fog's Journal*, quoted in *Gentleman's Magazine*, 1737, p. 193.

needs no more fear a crowd of lawyers than a crowd of pickpockets.—Wycherley, *The Plain Dealer*, 4to, 1676.

Colonel Standard. What! a soldier stay here. To look like an old pair of Colours in Westminster Hall, ragged and rusty.—Farquhar, *The Constant Couple*, 4to, 1707.

I remember, when I was a boy, I saw the Hall hung full on one side with colours and standards taken from the Scots at Worcester fight, but upon King Charles the Second his coming to his just right, all taken down.—*Strype*, B. vi. p. 49.

The late Mr. Jekyll told me that soon after he was called to the bar a strange solicitor coming up to him in Westminster Hall, begged him to step into the Court of Chancery to make a motion of course, and gave him a fee. The young barrister, looking pleased but a little surprised, the solicitor said to him, "I thought you had a sort of right, Sir, to this motion, for the bill was drawn by Sir Joseph Jekyll, your great grand-uncle, in the reign of Queen Anne."—Lord Campbell's *Lives of the Chancellors*.

October 27, 1621.—A high tide swept through Westminster Hall, and did much harm.—*Cal. State Papers*, 1619-1623, p. 303.

March 1625.—The highest tide ever known has done great harm along the Thames side. Westminster Hall was three feet in water.—*Cal. State Papers*, 1623-1625, p. 497.

The Thames Embankment has effectually got rid of that danger; but as late as October 21, 1812, Speaker Abbot records in his *Diary* that—

> About half-past 2, returning to Palace Yard, I saw the tide rushing in. It soon rose to the door of Westminster Hall; flowed into it; and three or four boats full of men went into the Hall. The tide still continued to rise for three-quarters of an hour. It filled my Court Yard, and the horses were up to their bellies in water in the stable.—vol. ii. p. 406.

Besides the Law Courts, a part of Westminster Hall was taken up with the stalls of booksellers, law stationers, sempstresses, and dealers in toys and smallwares, the rents' and profits of which belonged by right of office to the Warden of the Fleet.[1] The Hall was found on fire, Sunday, February 20, 1630-1631, "by the burning," as Laud records in his *Diary*, "of the little shops or stalls kept therein." In the curious account of Master [afterwards Sir] Henry Blount's *Voyage into the Levant*, made in 1634 (published 1638), he says that he gave one of the boys (pages) attached to the Turkish commander in the Danube, "a pocket looking-glass in a little ivory case, with a comb; such as are sold at *Westminster Hall* for four or five shillings a piece."

January 20, 1659-1660.—At Westminster Hall, where Mrs. Lane and the rest of the maids had their white scarfs, all having been at the burial of a young bookseller in the Hall.—*Pepys*.

In Hall of Westminster
Sleek sempstress vends amidst the Courts her ware.
Wycherley, *Epilogue to the Plain Dealer*.

We entered into a great Hall where my Indian was surprised to see in the same place, men on the one side with baubles and toys, and on the other taken up with the fear of judgment, on which depends their inevitable destiny. In this shop are to be sold ribbons and gloves, towers and commodes by word of mouth: in another shop lands and tenements are disposed of by decree. On your left hand you hear a nimble-tongued painted sempstress with her charming treble invite you to buy some

---

[1] Laud's *Diary*, p. 45; *Strype*, B. iii. p. 280.

of her knick-knacks, and on your right a deep-mouthed cryer, commanding impossibilities, viz., silence to be kept among women and lawyers.—Tom Brown's *Amusements*, etc., 8vo, 1700.

The duodecimo volume of Sir Walter Raleigh's *Remains* was printed in 1675, for Henry Mortlock, at the Phœnix in St. Paul's Churchyard, and at the White Hart in Westminster Hall.[1]

Let the spectator picture to himself the appearance which this venerable hall has presented on many occasions. Here were hung the banners taken from Charles I. at the battle of Naseby;[2] from Charles II. at the battle of Worcester;[3] at Preston and Dunbar;[4] and, somewhat later, those taken at the battle of Blenheim.[5] Here, at the upper end of the hall, Oliver Cromwell was inaugurated as Lord Protector, sitting in a robe of purple velvet lined with ermine, on a rich cloth of state, with the gold sceptre in one hand, the Bible richly gilt and bossed in the other, and his sword at his side; and here, four years later, at the top of the hall fronting Palace Yard, his head was set on a pole, with the skull of Ireton on one side of it and the skull of Bradshaw on the other. Here shameless ruffians sought employment as hired witnesses, or to act as bail, and walked openly in the hall with a straw in the shoe to denote their quality;[6] and here the good, the great, the brave, the wise and the abandoned have been brought to trial. Here (in the Hall of Rufus) Sir William Wallace was tried and condemned. Here, in this very hall, Sir Thomas More and the Protector Somerset were doomed to the scaffold. Here, in Henry VIII.'s reign (1517), entered the City apprentices implicated in the murders on "Evil May Day" of the aliens settled in London, each with a halter round his neck, and crying "Mercy, gracious Lord, mercy," while Wolsey stood by, and the King, beneath his cloth of state, heard their defence and pronounced their pardon—the prisoners shouting with delight and casting up their halters to the hall roof, "so that the King," as the chroniclers observe, "might perceive they were none of the discreetest sort."[7] Here too, on "a scaffold" erected for the purpose, took place, in the same presence, the trial of Queen Anne Boleyn. Here the notorious Earl and Countess of Somerset were tried in the reign of James I. for the murder of Sir Thomas Overbury. Here the great Earl of Strafford was condemned:—

> Each seemed to act the part he came to see,
> And none was more a looker-on than he.—*Sir John Denham.*

the King being present, and the Commons, sitting bareheaded all the time.[8] Here the High Court of Justice sat which condemned King Charles I., the upper part of the hall hung with scarlet cloth, and the

---

[1] There is an old engraving of the hall by Gravelot, representing the bookstalls.
[2] *Ludlow*, Vevay ed., vol. I. p. 156.
[3] *Strype*, B. vi. p. 49.   [4] *Ibid.*
[5] *Whitelocke*, p. 471.
[6] Charity took to husband an eminent gentleman, whose name I cannot learn, but who was famous for so friendly a disposition that he was bail for above a hundred persons in one year. He had likewise the remarkable humour of walking in Westminster Hall with a straw in his shoe.—*Jonathan Wild*, chap. ii.
[7] Hall's *Chronicle*, ed. 1548, fol. lxi.
[8] *Sir E. Walker*, p. 219.

King sitting covered, with the Naseby banners above his head. Here Lily, the astrologer, who was present, saw the silver top fall from the King's staff, and others heard Lady Fairfax exclaim, when her husband's name was called over, "He has more wit than to be here." Here, in the reign of James II., the seven bishops were acquitted. Here Dr. Sacheverel was tried and pronounced guilty by a majority of seventeen. Here the rebel Lords of 1745—Kilmarnock, Balmerino and Lovat—were heard and condemned. Here Lord Byron was tried for killing Mr. Chaworth; Lord Ferrers for murdering his steward; and the Duchess of Kingston, 1776, for bigamy. Here Warren Hastings was tried, and Burke and Sheridan grew eloquent and impassioned, while senators by birth and election, and the beauty and rank of Great Britain, sat earnest spectators and listeners of the extraordinary scene. The last public trial in the hall itself was Lord Melville's in 1806; and the last coronation dinner in the hall was that of George IV., when for the last time, probably, according to the custom maintained for ages, the King's champion (young Dymocke) rode on horseback into the hall in full armour, and threw down the gauntlet on the floor, challenging the world in a King's behalf.

At the upper end of Westminster Hall is a long marble stone of twelve foot in length and three foot in breadth. And there is also a marble chair, where the Kings of England formerly sate at their Coronation Dinners; and at other solemn times the Lord Chancellor. But now not to be seen, being built over by the two Courts of Chancery and King's Bench.—*Strype*, B. vi. p. 49.

Access to St. Stephen's Crypt at the south-east corner is by a flight of steps.

This noble hall is 290 feet long by 68 feet broad. It is said to be the largest apartment in the world not supported by pillars —save the Hall of Justice at Padua, and railway stations. The floor was renewed by Sir Charles Barry, R.A., to something like its original elevation in relation to the height of the building; and somewhat altered to make the hall serve as the vestibule to the new Palace of Westminster. Barry pulled down the south wall of the hall and formed the archway and steps into his St. Stephen's chamber. [*See* Heaven and Hell.] Sir John Soane's Law Courts were sold in January 1883 for about £2400. The clearing away of these left one side of Westminster Hall in a very bald, unfinished condition, and new so-called cloisters have been built after the designs of J. L. Pearson, R.A., architect.

Westminster Hospital, BROAD SANCTUARY, opposite WESTMINSTER ABBEY, an Elizabethan Gothic edifice, erected 1832, from the designs of Messrs. Inwood. The hospital was instituted 1719, and was the first in this kingdom established and supported by voluntary contributions. It was established in Petty France, April 1720; removed to Chapel Street, Westminster, in 1724; to James Street in 1734; and to Broad Sanctuary in 1834. The hospital has been lately enlarged and improved; and has now 205 beds. In 1888 the number of in-patients was 2684, of out-patients 22,103, of lying-in cases 256. The total income, £12,537. The Medical School connected with the hospital was opened in Caxton Street in 1885, and enlarged in 1886 and 1887. The number of students is over 100.

Westminster Ophthalmic Hospital, KING WILLIAM STREET, STRAND, founded 1816, by the eminent ophthalmic surgeon, G. J. Guthrie, F.R.S., for the relief of indigent persons afflicted with diseases of the eye, who are received on their own application without letters of recommendation. The income in 1887 was £1688; the number of in-patients, 363, and out-patients, 7852.

Westminster Palace, the principal seat and palace of the Kings of England, from Edward the Confessor to Henry VIII. The bulk of the building was destroyed by fire in 1512, and Henry VIII., after Wolsey's disgrace, removed his palace to Whitehall; but still much of the rambling old palace remained until the burning of the Houses of Parliament. The only remaining portions are Westminster Hall and the crypt of St. Stephen's Chapel; the fire which destroyed the Houses of Parliament, October 16, 1834, having destroyed the Painted Chamber, the Star Chamber, St. Stephen's Chapel and cloisters, the cellar of Guy Fawkes, the Armada hangings, and the other less important vestiges of the original building. Other apartments in the old palace bore the names of Antioch Chamber, Cage Chamber, Chamber of the Holy Ghost, Great Exchequer Chamber, Jewry, etc. The name survives in the Palace Yards—Old Palace Yard, the court of the old palace; and new Palace Yard, the court of the new palace, projected by William Rufus. The ground plan, measured and drawn by William Capon, between 1793 and 1823, is engraved in volume v. of the *Vetusta Monumenta*. St. Stephen's Chapel was founded by Stephen, King of England, for a dean and canons. The chapel was rebuilt in the reign of Edward II., between 1320 and 1352, and till its destruction in 1834 was always looked upon as an excellent example of Decorated architecture of very fine and rich work.[1] This was the House of Commons from the reign of Edward VI. to its destruction by fire in 1834; and was the scene of Cromwell's dismissal of the Parliament. The House of Lords, destroyed in 1834, was the old Court of Requests. [*See* Houses of Parliament.] The crypt of St. Stephen's Chapel was restored by the late E. M. Barry, R.A., in a rich and costly style, and fitted up as a chapel for the use of Members of Parliament.

Westminster School, or ST. PETER'S COLLEGE, DEAN'S YARD, WESTMINSTER, "A publique schoole for Grammar, Rethoricke, Poetrie, and for the Latin and Greek languages," founded by Queen

---

[1] The oldest view of the river-front of St. Stephen's Chapel is before the second volume of Nalson's *Impartial Collection* (fol. 1683), since re-engraved by J. T. Smith. But the most splendid work on St. Stephen's Chapel is Mr. F. Mackenzie's account, large atlas folio, with its numerous engravings from actual measurements made in 1844, by direction of the Woods and Forests. The engravings from Billings's drawings in Brayley and Britton's *Westminster Palace* are also good.

Elizabeth, 1560, on an older foundation,[1] and attached to the collegiate church of St. Peter at Westminster. A school connected with the collegiate church was kept in the west cloister of the Abbey as early as the 14th century, and in some form or other was no doubt continued down to the dissolution of the Abbey. The College consists of a dean, twelve prebendaries, twelve almsmen, and forty scholars; with a master and an usher. This is the foundation, but the school consists of a larger number of masters and of a much larger number of boys. The forty are called Queen's scholars, and after an examination, which takes place on the first Tuesday after Rogation Sunday, four are elected to Trinity College, Cambridge, and four to Christ Church, Oxford; and "in the former years of my mastership" (of Trinity), Bentley writes to the Dean of Westminster, "the Westminster scholars got the major part of our fellowships. Of later years they have not so succeeded." A parent wishing to place a boy at this school will get every necessary information from the headmaster; boys are not placed on the foundation under twelve, or above thirteen years of age. *Eminent Masters.* — Alexander Nowell, headmaster, 1543; Nicholas Udall, author of *Roister Doister*, was appointed Master by Queen Mary about 1555, having been expelled from the same position at Eton in 1543; Camden, the antiquary—second master, 1575, headmaster, 1593; Dr. Busby, for over half a century (1640-1695); Vincent Bourne; Jordan (Cowley has a copy of verses on his death). *Eminent Men educated at.*— *Poets:* Ben Jonson; Bishop Corbet; George Herbert; Giles Fletcher; Jasper Mayne; William Cartwright; Cowley; Dryden; Nat Lee; Rowe; Prior; Churchill; Dyer, author of *Grongar Hill;* Cowper; Southey. Cowley published a volume of poems whilst a scholar at Westminster. *Other great Men.* —Sir Harry Vane, the younger; Hakluyt, the collector of the voyages which bear his name; Sir Christopher Wren; Charles Montague, Earl of Halifax; George Stepney; Locke; South; Atterbury; Warren Hastings; Gibbon, the historian; Cumberland; Horne Tooke, before going to Eton; Lord Mansfield; Marquis of Rockingham; Marquis of Anglesey; Lord Raglan; Lord Combermere; Lord Keppel; Earl Russell; the elder Colman.

Cumberland and I boarded together in the same house at Westminster.—COWPER.

> At Westminster, where little poets strive
> To set a distitch upon six and five,
> Where Discipline helps opening buds of sense,
> And makes his pupils proud with silver pence,
> I was a poet too.—Cowper, *Table Talk.*

He who cannot look forward with comfort, must find what comfort he can in looking backward. Upon this principle I the other day sent my imagination upon a trip thirty years behind me. She was very obedient, and very swift of foot, presently performed her journey, and at last set me down on the sixth form at Westminster. . . . Accordingly I was a schoolboy in high favour with the master, received a

[1] Appendix to *Report of the Cathedral and Collegiate Church Comm.*, 1854.

silver groat for my exercise, and had the pleasure of seeing it sent from form to form for the admiration of all who were able to understand it.—*Cowper*.

This custom [of sending from form to form] was not practised at Westminster in the days of Dr. Vincent. But "sweet remuneration" was still dispensed in silver pence; and those pence produced still "goodlier guerdon" by an established rate of exchange at which the mistress of the boarding-house received them, and returned current coin in the proportion of six to one. My first literary profits were thus obtained, and, like Cowper, I remember the pleasure with which I received them. But there was this difference, that his rewards were probably for Latin verse, in which he excelled, and mine were always for English composition.—Southey, *Life of Cowper*, vol. i. p. 17, *note*.

The boys on the foundation were formerly separated from the town boys when in school by a bar or curtain. The schoolroom was a dormitory belonging to the Abbey, and retained certain traces of its former ornaments. New buildings have been erected, in which the boys are now taught in distinct and separate classes, and the old schoolroom is no longer used. The College hall, originally the Abbot's refectory, was built by Abbot Litlington, in the reign of Edward III. The dormitory was built by the Earl of Burlington in 1722. The Dean and Chapter hold a house and estate at Chiswick, to which the boys are to be removed in case of the plague; the house (or hospital as it was called) cost £500 when first built, in the reign of Queen Elizabeth.[1] It has long been let; and was for many years well known as the Chiswick Press of Charles Whittingham. It was pulled down a few years ago and applied to other uses.

In conformity with an old custom, the Queen's scholars perform a play of Terence or Plautus every year at Christmas, with a Latin prologue and epilogue new on each occasion. A school oration on Dr. South was pirated in 1716 by the notorious Edmund Curll, and printed with false Latin. The boys accordingly invited him to Westminster to get a corrected copy, and first whipped him and then tossed him in a blanket. There is a curious poem on the subject, with three representations, of the blanket, the scourge, and Curll upon his knees.

The Westminster Boys were long notorious for their rough behaviour in the Abbey, where visitors of all ranks stood very much in awe of them.

July 9, 1754.—Will you believe that I have not yet seen the Tomb [of his mother in Westminster Abbey]? None of my acquaintance were in town, and I literally had not courage to venture alone among the Westminster boys at the Abbey; they are as formidable to me as the ship carpenters at Portsmouth.—*Walpole to Bentley*, vol. ii. p. 394.

The privilege of Westminster Boys to be present at Coronations in Westminster Abbey is recognised by the authorities, who provide seats for them; and Dean Stanley observes in their presence a remarkable case of survival: "Even the assent of the people of England to the election of the Sovereign has found its voice in modern days, through the shouts of the Westminster scholars, from their recognised seats in the Abbey.[2]

[1] *Lansdowne MS.*, 4, art. 11. [2] Stanley, *Hist. Memorials of Westminster Abbey*, p. 46.

Weymouth Street, PORTLAND PLACE to HIGH STREET, MARYLE-
BONE. Prof. Faraday's father died at No. 18 in this street in 1810.
The Rev. Sidney Smith was living here in 1810. From 1861 till his
death, October 4, 1874, Bryan Waller Proctor (Barry Cornwall) lived
at No. 32.

Wheeler Street, SPITALFIELDS, WHITE LION STREET and COM-
MERCIAL STREET. The principal meeting-house of the early Quakers—
William Penn, George Whitehead, Thomas Ellwood, etc., was in this
street.[1] On June 23, 1657, an Act was passed of which one clause
enabled "William Wheeler, Esq., who is by lease and contract engaged
to build certain houses in and upon his lands in Spitalfields, in the
parish of Stepney, at any time before October 1, 1660, to erect, new
build and finish, upon eight acres of the said fields, on part whereof
divers houses and edifices are already built, and streets and highways
set out, several houses, buildings, and other appurtenances."[2]

Wheelwrights' Company (The), was incorporated February 3,
1670, under letters patent of Charles II., by the name of "The Master,
Wardens, Assistants and Commonalty of the Art and Mistery of Wheel-
wrights of the City of London," but a livery was not granted till 1773.
This Company possesses no hall, and its business is transacted at
Guildhall.

Whetstone Park, a narrow roadway in the parish of St. Giles-
in-the-Fields, formed between the north side of *Lincoln's Inn Fields*
and the south side of *Holborn*, and so called after William Whetstone,
a tobacconist, and overseer of the parish of St. Giles-in-the-Fields, in
the time of Charles I. and the Commonwealth. There is a token of
William Whetstone at the Black Boy in Holborn, dated 1653. It was
long notorious, and was attacked, on account of its great immorality,
by the London apprentices in 1682. Since 1708, however, it has
chiefly consisted of stables and workshops.[3] There is still, however,
an alehouse, the Horse and Groom, in Whetstone Park. The west
part of Whetstone Park was called *Phillips' Rents* from one Phillips,
who built it, as what is now Feathers' Court, running north into
Holborn, was called Pargiter's Court for a similar reason.[4] Milton's
garden, when in 1645 "he removed to a smaller house in Holborn,
which opened backward into Lincoln's Inn Fields," must have been
built over by these unhallowed houses.

> And makes a brothel of a palace,
> Where harlots ply, as many tell us,
> Like brimstones in a Whetstone alehouse.—BUTLER.

> Near Holborn lies a Park of great renown,
> The place I do suppose is not unknown.
> For brevity's sake the name I shall not tell,
> Because most genteel readers know it well.

---

[1] *Ellwood*, p. 187. [2] *See* note to Barton's *Diary*, vol. ii. p. 283.
[3] Hatton's *New View of London*, 8vo, 1708, p. 88. [4] Dobie's *St. Giles and St. George*, p. 56.

(Since Middle Park near Charing Cross was made
They say there is a great decay of trade);
'Twas there a flock of Dukes, by fury brought,
With bloody mind a sickly damsel sought, etc.

On the three Dukes killing the Beadle on Sunday Morning, February 26, 1670-1671,
(*State Poems*, 8vo, 1697, p. 147).

Lady Flippant. But why do you look as if you were jealous then?

Dapperwit. If I had met you in Whetstone's Park, with a drunken foot soldier,
I should not have been jealous of you.—Wycherley, *Love in a Wood*, 4to, 1672.[1]

After I had gone a little way in a great broad street, I turned into a tavern hard
by a place they call a Park; and just as one park is all trees, that park is all houses—
I asked if they had any deer in it, and they told me not half so many as they used
to have; but that if I had a mind to a doe, they would put a doe to me.—*The
Country Wit*, by J. Crowne, 4to, 1675.

Aldo. 'Tis very well, Sir; I find you have been searching for your relations then
in Whetstone's Park.

Woodall. No, Sir; I made some scruple of going to the foresaid place, for fear of
meeting my own father there.—Dryden's *Kind Keeper, or Mr. Limberham*, 4to,
1680.[2]

Bedlam—'tis a new Whetstone's Park, now the old one's plough'd up.—Ned
Ward, *The London Spy*, pt. iii.

Whitcomb Street, PALL MALL EAST to COVENTRY STREET,
originally *Hedge Lane*, is mentioned under its present designation in a
Vestry Minute of St. Martin's-in-the-Fields of March 14, 1677, fixing
the proposed boundaries of St. James's, Piccadilly, and St. Anne's, Soho.
It is so named also in Strype's Map, 1710. A stone high up on the
house No. 14 has the initials I. A. and the date 1692.

White Bear Inn, PICCADILLY, stood on the south side of
Piccadilly, between the Haymarket and Regent Street. Luke
Sullivan, Hogarth's assistant in many of his plates, and J. B. Chatelain,
engravers, died here.[3]

White's, a celebrated Club-house, Nos. 37 and 38 ST. JAMES'S
STREET, originally White's Chocolate-house, under which name it was
established circ. 1698, on the west side of the present street, five doors
from the bottom, in the house that was previously the residence of the
stately Countess of Northumberland—"the last who kept up the
ceremonious state of the old peerage." Pope fixes the locality as being
between the Chapel Royal and Mother Needham's in Park Place.

> She ceased. Then swells the Chapel Royal throat
> "God save King Cibber!" mounts in every note.
> Familiar White's "God save King Colley!" cries;
> "God save King Colley!" Drury Lane replies:
> To Needham's quick the voice triumphal rode
> But pious Needham dropt the name of God.
>
> Pope, *Dunciad*, vol. i. p. 308.

Very early in the 18th century it had become notorious as an
aristocratic gaming-house. Swift says that "The late Earl of Oxford

---

[1] See also Shadwell's *Miser*, 4to, 1672.
[2] See also his *Prologue to the Wild Gallant*, when revised); also Nat Lee's *Dedication of Princess of Cleve*, 4to, 1689, etc., but the references might be endless and the result worthless or worse.
[3] Smith's *Antiquarian Ramble*, vol. i. p. 26.

[Robert Harley, who died 1724], in the time of his ministry, never passed by White's Chocolate-house (the common Rendezvous of infamous Sharpers and noble Cullies) without bestowing a curse upon that famous academy, as the bane of half the English nobility."[1] And William Whitehead (who quotes this passage in a note) calls it in his *Manners, a Satire* (1739), "a Den of Thieves." The first White's was destroyed by fire, April 28, 1733, at which time the house was kept by a person of the name of Arthur.

On Saturday morning [April 28, 1733], about four o'clock, a fire broke out at Mr. Arthur's, at White's Chocolate House, in St. James's Street, which burnt with great violence, and in a short time entirely consumed that house, with two others, and much damaged several others adjoining.—*The Daily Courant*, April 30, 1733.

Young Mr. Arthur's wife leaped out of a window two pair of stairs upon a feather bed without much hurt. A fine collection of paintings belonging to Sir Andrew Fountaine, valued at £3000 at the least, was entirely destroyed. His Majesty and the Prince of Wales were present above an hour, and encouraged the Firemen and People to work at the Engines—a guard being ordered from St. James's to keep off the populace. His Majesty ordered 20 guineas among the Firemen and others that worked at the Engines and 5 guineas to the Guard; and the Prince ordered the Firemen 10 guineas.—*Gent. Mag.* for 1733.[2]

This is to acquaint all noblemen and gentlemen that Mr. Arthur, having had the misfortune to be burnt out of White's Chocolate House, is removed to Gaunt's Coffee House, next the St. James's Coffee House, in St. James's Street, where he humbly begs they will favour him with their company as usual.—*The Daily Post*, May 3, 1733.

All accounts of gallantry, pleasure and entertainment, shall be under the article of White's Chocolate House; poetry under that of Will's Coffee House; learning under the title of the Grecian; foreign and domestic news you will have from St. James's Coffee House.—*The Tatler*, No. 1.

> To all his most frequented haunts resort,
> Oft dog him to the Ring, and oft to Court;
> As love of pleasure, or of place invites:
> And sometimes catch him taking snuff at White's.
> Addison, *Prologue to* Steele's *Tender Husband*.

As a Club White's dates from 1736, when the house ceased to be an open Chocolate-house that any one might enter who was prepared to pay for what he had. It was made a private house for the convenience of the chief frequenters of the place, whose annual subscriptions towards its support were paid to Arthur, the proprietor of the house, by whom the Club was formed. Arthur died in June 1761, and was succeeded by Robert Mackreth, who married Mary Arthur, the only child of the former proprietor.

> When Bob Mackreth served Arthur's crew,
> "Rumbold," he cried, "come black my shoe!"
> And Rumbold answer'd, "Yes, Bob!"

---

[1] Swift's *Essay on Modern Education*.

[2] The incident of the fire was made use of by Hogarth in Plate VI. of the *Rake's Progress*, representing a room at White's. The total abstraction of the gamblers is well expressed by their utter inattention to the alarm of fire given by watchmen who are bursting open the doors. Plate IV. of the same pictured moral represents a group of chimney-sweepers and shoe-blacks gambling on the ground over against White's. To indicate the Club more fully, Hogarth has inserted the name *Black's*, and it is irradiated by a flash of lightning pointed directly at it.

> But now returned from India's land,
> He scorns t' obey the proud command,
> And boldly answers, " Na-bob."

Sir E. Brydges's *Autobiography*, vol. i. p. 194 (*Lord Camden ?*). For variations in the Epigram, see *Walpole to Mason*, November 1, 1780.

Mackreth retired in 1763 with an unenviable fame,[1] transferring the property to his kinsman the Cherubim.

> That puts me in mind to inform your Grace of a great event, which is that Bob retires from business at Lady Day, and the Cherubim is to keep the house.—*Rigby to the Duke of Bedford*.

> *April* 5, 1763.—Sir—Having quitted business entirely and let my house to the Cherubim, who is my near relation, I humbly beg leave, after returning you my most grateful thanks for all favours, to recommend him to your patronage, not doubting by the long experience I have had of his fidelity but that he will strenuously endeavour to oblige.—*Robert Mackreth to George Selwyn*.

The property passed, in 1784, to John Martindale, who was bankrupt in 1797; and in 1812 to Mr. Ragget. From him it descended to his son. The Club was removed to the present house in 1755. The front alterations were made in 1850, and the four bas-reliefs of the seasons, from the designs of Mr. George Scharf, were added. The freehold of White's Club-house was sold at the auction mart, March 7, 1871, for £46,000, to H. W. Eaton, Esq., M.P.

The earliest record in the Club is a book of rules and list of members "of the old Club at White's," dated October 30, 1736. The principal members were the Duke of Devonshire, the Earls of Cholmondeley, Chesterfield, and Rockingham, Sir John Cope, Major-General Churchill, Bubb Dodington, and Colley Cibber. The Rules direct—

> That every member is to pay one guinea a year towards having a good Cook.
> The supper to be upon Table at 10 o'Clock and the Bill at 12.
> That every member who is in the room after 7 o'Clock and plays is to pay Half a Crown.

From 1736 the records of the Club are nearly complete. Many of the rules are curiously characteristic of the state of society at the time.

> *December* 26, 1755.—That the Picket Cards be charged in the Dinner or Supper Bill.
> *March* 22, 1755.—That the names of all Candidates are to be deposited with Mr. Arthur or Bob [Mackreth].
> *May* 20, 1758.—To prevent those invidious conjectures which disappointed candidates are apt to make concerning the respective votes of their Electors, or to render at least such surmises more difficult and doubtful, it is ordered that Every Member present at the time of Balloting shall put in his Ball, and such person or persons who refuse to comply with it shall pay the supper reckoning of that night.
> *February* 11, 1762.—It was this night ordered that the Quinze players shall pay for their own cards.

---

[1] See two leading cases in Equity, Fox *v.* Mackreth; and Mackreth *v.* Symmons, 1 W. and Tudor, 92 and 235.

February 15, 1769.—It was this night agreed by a majority of nineteen balls, that Every Member of this Club who is in the Billiard Room at the time Supper is declared upon table shall pay his reckoning if he does not Sup at the Young Club.[1]

In 1775 the Club was restricted to 151 members, and the annual subscription raised to 10 guineas. In 1780 it was ordered that a dinner should be ready every day at five o'clock during the sitting of Parliament, at a reckoning of twelve shillings per head. In 1781 the Club was enlarged to 300 members, and in 1797, when it was enlarged to 400, the following rules were added to the book:—

No person to be balloted for but between the hours of 11 and 12 at Night.

Dinner at Ten Shillings and Sixpence per head (Malt Liquor, Biscuits, oranges, apples, and olives included) to be on Table at Six o'Clock. The Bill to be brought at nine. The price and qualities of the Wines to be approved by the Manager.

That no Member of the Club shall hold a Faro Bank.

That the Dice used at Hazard shall be paid for by Boxes, that is, every Player who holds in three hands to pay a Guinea for Dice.

That no hot suppers be provided unless particularly ordered, and then be paid for at the rate of Eight Shillings per head. That in one of the rooms there be laid every night (from the Queen's to the King's Birthday) a Table with Cold Meat, Oysters, etc. Each person partaking thereof to pay four shillings—Malt Liquor only included.

That Every Member who plays at Chess, Draughts, or Backgammon do pay One Shilling Each time of playing by day-light and half a crown Each by Candle-light.

The distinction between the Young and the Old Clubs seems to have ceased about this time. In 1800 it was enlarged to 450 members, and in 1813 to 500 members. The present limitation is 750. Walpole, writing to Mason (June 18, 1751), describes "an extravagant dinner at White's," which is the talk of the town. The Club, on June 20, 1814, gave a ball at Burlington House to the Emperor of Russia, the King of Prussia, and the allied Sovereigns then in England, which cost £9849 : 2 : 6. Covers were laid for 2400 people. Three weeks after this (July 6, 1814) the Club gave a dinner to the Duke of Wellington, which cost £2480 : 10 : 9.

At its foundation and long after White's was essentially a gaming club. Walpole tells us that the celebrated Earl of Chesterfield, after he gave up the Seals in 1748, lived "at White's, gaming and pronouncing witticisms among the boys of quality;"[2] and yet he says to his son that "a member of a gaming club should be a cheat or he will soon be a beggar."[3]

The most fashionable as well as the common people at that time dined at an early hour, and a supper was then an indispensable meal. White's became a great supper-house, where gaming, both before and after, was carried on to a late hour and to heavy amounts. The least difference of opinion invariably ended in a bet, and a book for entering the particulars of all bets was always laid upon the table. One of

[1] See on the subject of the "Old Club," *Walpole to Mann*, February 2, 1752. It appears that the two clubs were kept quite distinct, although they seem to have been held in the same house. Probably, as the old club was very select and small in its numbers, the young club was considered as an adjunct from which it could be replenished as members died or resigned.

[2] Walpole's *George II.*, vol. i. p. 51.

[3] *Works*, by Lord Stanhope, vol. ii. p. 429.

these, with entries of a date as early as 1744, has been preserved. The marriage of a young lady of rank would occasion a bet of a hundred guineas, that she would give birth to a live child before the Countess of ——, who had been married three or even more months before her. Heavy bets were pending that Arthur, who was then a widower, would be married before a member of the Club of about the same age and also a widower; that Sarah, Duchess of Marlborough, would outlive the old Duchess of Cleveland; that Colley Cibber would outlive both Beau Nash and old Mr. Swinney; and that a certain minister would cease to be in the Cabinet by a certain time.[1]

> What can I now? my Fletcher cast aside,
> Take up the Bible, once my better guide?
> Or tread the path by vent'rous heroes trod,
> This box my thunder, this right hand my god?
> Or chair'd at White's, amidst the Doctors sit,
> Teach oaths to Gamesters, and to Nobles wit?
> Pope, *The Dunciad*.

> As oft I overheard the Demon say,
> Who daily met the loiterer in his way,
> " I'll meet thee youth at *White's*"; the youth replies,
> " I'll meet thee there,"—and falls his sacrifice.—*Young to Pope.*

There is a man about town, a Sir William Burdett, a man of very good family but most infamous character. In short, to give you his character at once, there is a wager entered in the bet book at White's (a MS. of which I may one day or other give you an account) that the first baronet that will be hanged is this Sir William Burdett.—*Walpole to Mann*, December 16, 1748.

They have put in the papers a good story made on White's. A man dropped down dead at the door was carried in; the club immediately made bets whether he was dead or not, and when they were going to bleed him the wagerers for his death interposed, and said it would affect the fairness of the bet.—*Walpole to Mann*, September 1, 1750.

March 21, 1755.—I t'other night at White found a very remarkable entry in our very remarkable wager book, "Lord Mountford bets Sir John Bland twenty guineas that Nash outlives Cibber." How odd that these two old creatures, selected for their antiquities, should live to see both their wagerers put an end to their own lives.—*Walpole to Mason*, vol. ii. p. 481.

White's was formerly distinguished for gallantry and intrigue. During the publication of *The Tatler*, Sir Richard Steele thought proper to date all his love-news from that quarter: but it would now be as absurd to pretend to gather any intelligence from White's, as to send to Batson's for a lawyer, or to the Rolls Coffee House for a man-midwife.—*The Connoisseur* of May 9, 1754.

Mr. Pelham [the Prime Minister] was originally an officer in the army and a professed gamester; of a narrow mind, low parts, etc. . . . By long experience and attendance he became experienced as a Parliament man; and even when Minister, divided his time to the last between his office and the Club of gamesters at White's. —*Glover the Poet's Autobiography*, p. 48.

The Dryads of Hagley are at present pretty secure, but I sometimes tremble to think that the rattling of a dice-box at White's may one day or other (if my son should be a member of that noble academy) shake down all our fine oaks. It is dreadful to see not only there, but almost in every house in town, what devastations are made by that destructive Fury, the spirit of Play.—*Lord Lyttelton to Dr. Doddridge*, April 1750 (*Lyttelton Correspondence*, p. 421).

---

[1] See *Walpole to Bentley*, October 31, 1756.

> From hence to White's our virtuous Cato flies,
> There sits with countenance erect and wise,
> And talks of games of whist and pig-tail pies.
>
> Soame Jenyns, *The Modern Fine Gentleman*, 1746.

March 3, 1763.—White's goes on as usual; play there is rather more moderate, ready money being established this winter at quinze. Lord Masham was fool enough to lose three thousand at hazard to Lord Bolingbroke the night before last : I guess that was not all ready money.—*Rigby to Duke of Bedford.*

March 2, 1818.—Let me here relate what I heard of one of the Clubs—White's —the great Tory Club in St. James's. Somebody spoke of the lights kept burning there all night : "Yes," said a member, "they have not been out, I should think, since the reign of Charles the Second.—Rush, *Residence at the Court of London.*

With reference to the great spirit of gaming which prevailed at White's, the arms of the Club were designed by Horace Walpole, Dick Edgcumbe, George Selwyn, etc., at Strawberry Hill, in 1756.[1] The blazon is vert (for a card table); three parolis proper on a chevron sable (for a hazard table); two rouleaus in saltier, between two dice proper, on a canton sable; a white ball (for election) argent. The supporters are an old and young knave of clubs; the crest, an arm out of an earl's coronet shaking a dice-box; and the motto, "Cogit Amor Nummi." Round the arms is a claret bottle ticket by way of order. Edgcumbe made "a very pretty painting" of these arms, which they entitled "The Old and Young Club at Arthurs." At the Strawberry Hill sale it was bought by the Club for twenty-two shillings.

White's Coffee-house, near the ROYAL EXCHANGE, was the daily resort of Colonel Blood and his associates during that mysterious period of his being in favour at Court.

White Conduit House, PENTONVILLE, a popular place of entertainment and tea-gardens, was so named from a conduit of flint and brick, faced with stone, built over a reservoir, the water from which was conveyed by pipes to the Charterhouse.[2] When the Charterhouse was supplied from other sources the conduit was suffered to go to ruin. A view of it, when in the last stage of neglect (1827), by Mr. J. Fussell, is given in Hone's *Every-Day Book* (vol. ii. p. 1202). It was finally demolished in 1831, and the site built over. White Conduit House was a kind of minor Vauxhall for the Londoners who went for cakes and cream to Islington and Hornsey. The gardens were a favourite Sunday afternoon resort for small tradesmen and their families.

> Time was when satin waistcoats and scratch wigs,
> Enough distinguished all the City prigs
> Whilst every sunshine Sunday saw them run
> To club their sixpences at Islington;
> When graver citizens, in suits of brown,
> Lined every dusty avenue to town,

---

[1] *Walpole to Montagu*, April 20, 1756.
[2] In 1430 John Feriby and Margery his wife enfeoffed the Prior, etc., of the Charterhouse of the well-spring in Overmead to make an aqueduct at the rent service of 12d.—Tomlins, *Yseldon*, p. 161.

Or led the children and the loving spouse,
To spend two shillings at White Conduit House.
Rev. Charles Jenner, Eclogue 2, *Time Was*.

William Woty, 1760, celebrated in delectable verse the "tea and cream and buttered rolls" served "in china with gilt spoons" at White Conduit House "on Sunday afternoons." The gardens lost their character early in the present century, and the house, before it was pulled down (January 1849) to make way for a new street, was nothing more than a large tavern, with a large room, for suburban entertainments and political meetings. A public-house called White Conduit was built on the north end of the gardens, now No. 14 Barnsbury Road, and the name is further preserved in White Conduit Street, running from Barnsbury Road to Cloudesley Road, Islington.

White Hart Court, LOMBARD STREET, was the last turning on the right hand from the Mansion House, but has been swept away in recent improvements. In it lived from 1740 till 1767 Dr. John Fothergill, the celebrated Quaker physician.

White Hart Inn, BISHOPSGATE STREET WITHOUT, "next unto the parish church of St. Botolph." "Bishopsgate," says Stow, "is a fair inn for receipt of travellers." Next to it was "the Hospital of St. Mary of Bethleham."[1] The hospital—Bedlam—was removed in 1814. By that time the White Hart seems to have lost much of its reputation as an inn for travellers. The courtyard was in part taken for the building of White Hart Court; but the inn remained down to 1829—a large, rambling, half-timber structure, having three broad bays in the front, with a lofty central archway as the principal and carriage entrance. On the central bay was the date 1480. The old inn was pulled down in 1829, when Bedlam Gate was removed and the broad thoroughfare called Liverpool Street formed. A new White Hart—a smart "wine and spirit" tavern, was built on what remained of the site of the old inn. An engraving of the Old White Hart is given in the *European Magazine* for March 1787; and another, showing the house as it appeared before its demolition in 1829, but somewhat changed in appearance from 1778, in the *Mirror* for 1830 (vol. xv. p. 177).

White Hart Inn, SOUTHWARK, is mentioned in the *Greyfriars Chronicle,* p. 19;[2] in the *Paston Letters,* vol. i. p. 61; in Shakespeare's *Second Part of Henry VI.,* Act iv. Sc. 8; and by Sam Weller in the *Pickwick Papers.* Hatton describes it as standing "on the east side of the Borough of Southwark, towards the south end;" and adds (p. 90), "This is the largest sign about London, except the Castle Tavern, in Fleet Street." There are many interesting pictures of the old inn, taken at different times, and descriptions, notably in the *Pickwick Papers.* The White Hart no doubt existed as an inn before 1406, and was Cade's headquarters in 1450. In 1669 it was partly burnt down and

---

[1] *Stow,* p. 62.
[2] And there was beheddyd . . . one Haway-dyne of Sent Martyns, at the Whyt Harte in Southwarke.—*Greyfriars Chron.,* p. 19.

in 1676 wholly so. It remained until July 1889, when it was pulled down. It was a fair specimen of the inn with large courtyard and galleries.

White Hart Inn, STRAND, has given its name to Hart Street, Covent Garden, and is mentioned in a lease to Sir William Cecil (Lord Burghley) of September 7, 1570, and is there described as being "scituate in the high streete of Westm'. commonly called the Stronde."[1]

Weever has preserved an epitaph in the Savoy Church on an old vintner of the White Hart.

> Here lieth Humphrey Gosling, of London, vintnor,
> Of the Whyt Hart of this parish a neghbor,
> Of vertuous behauiour, a very good archer,
> And of honest mirth, a good company keeper.
> So well inclyned to poore and rich,
> God send more Goslings to be sich.

Gosling died in 1586.

White Horse Cellar, PICCADILLY (south side), near Arlington Street, famous as the starting-place, in coaching days, of the mail-coaches and finely-appointed stages to Oxford, Bristol, and the western towns generally. An excellent representation of it in its palmy days, by George Cruikshank, will be found at the end of Pierce Egan's *Tom and Jerry*, and a verbal description by Charles Dickens in the *Pickwick Papers*. The old White Horse Cellar faded before the progress of railways; but "Hatchett's Hotel and New White Horse Cellar" at the corner of Dover Street still flourishes, and is the stabling-place of the summer four-horse coaches that are now so much in vogue for plaseure traffic. The hotel and cellar have been lately rebuilt.

White Lion, near ST. GEORGE'S CHURCH, SOUTHWARK.

The White Lion, a gaol, so called for that the same was a common hosterie for the receipt of travellers by that sign. This house was first used as a gaol within these forty years [1598] last past.—*Stow*, p. 153.

There was formerly in Southwark but one prison, particularly serving for the whole county of Surrey, and that called the White Lion, which was for the custody of murtherers, felons, and other notorious malefactors. It was situate at the south end of St. Margaret's Hill, near unto St. George's church; but that being an old decayed house, within less than twenty years past the county gaol is removed to the Marshalsea Prison, more towards the Bridge.—*Strype*, B. iv. p. 29.

Lent unto Frances Henslow, to discharge hime seallfe owt of the Whitte Lion, from a hat-macker in barmsey [Bermondsey] streete, abowt his horsse which was stolen from hime—v⁸.—Henslowe's *Diary*, p. 192.

Some confusion has arisen on account of an inn near the bridge and a gaol near the church, a quarter of a mile apart, being of the same name.

Robert Cooke Keeper of the Whit lyon, a suter for the amendment of a partye gutter betwyxt the blacke bull and the sayd Whytt lyon, was answeryd that y¹ shold be vewyd by yᵉ surveyors on day, of this week, yf God send fayre wether.—*MS. Notes of Weekly Meetings of Governors of St. Thomas's Hospital*, July 16, 1571.

---

[1] *Archæologia*, vol. xxx. p. 497.

This was afterwards represented by 149 High Street, near St. George's Church, and is identical with the site of the prison of 1560, which served for the county of Surrey for felons, recusants, Quakers, and religious nonconformists generally. The rabble apprentices, who in the year 1640 attacked Lambeth Palace, were sent to this prison.

The daye before the triall some of that companye came in the daye time, brake open the prison, the White Lion in Southwark, lett out all the prisoners, the rest as well as their own companye. One of them hath been taken since, and on Saturdaye last was hanged and quartered.—*Laud to Lord Conway*, May 25, 1640; *Gent. Mag.*, 1850, vol. i. p. 349.

In 1718 the White Lion is described as "a strong place for fettered felons," but towards the end of the century it was unfit for use. Ultimately the White Lion gave place to the New Bridewell at Hangman's Acre, by Higler's Lane and Dirty Lane (Suffolk Street), shown on Horwood's Map 1799. In 1811 £8000 was spent on the site of the old prison in building the New Marshalsea, the prison immortalised by Dickens.

White Lion Street (Great), SEVEN DIALS, north-west side, to Dudley Street. Here, in 1746, at the sign of the Dove, in "a pretty decent room," for which she paid "three pounds a year," lived Mrs. Pilkington, known by her Memoirs. Here she advertised that she drew petitions and wrote letters "on any subject except the law."

White Tower. [*See* The Tower.]

Whitechapel, a parish lying east of ALDGATE, originally a chapelry in the parish of Stepney, but constituted a separate parish in the 17th century. It is large, stretching away to Mile End; populous, it had 71,350 inhabitants in 1881; commercial, but, as regards the bulk of the inhabitants, poor.

Whitechapel is a spacious fair street for entrance into the city Eastward, and somewhat long, reckoning from the laystall East unto the bars West. It is a great thorough-fare, being the Essex road, and well resorted unto, which occasions it to be the better inhabited, and accommodated with good Inns for the reception of travellers and for horses, coaches, carts, and waggons.—*Strype*, B. ii. p. 27.

The great street in Whitechapel is one of the broadest and most public streets in London; and the side where the butchers lived more like a green field than a paved street; toward Whitechapel church the street was not all paved, but the part that was paved was full of grass.—*The City Remembrancer*, vol. i. p. 357.

Ralph. March fair, my hearts!—Lieutenant, beat the rear up.—Ancient, let your colours fly; but have a great care of the butchers' hooks at Whitechapel; they have been the death of many a fair ancient [ensign].—Beaumont and Fletcher, *The Knight of the Burning Pestle* (ed. Dyce, vol. ii. p. 218).

I lived without Aldgate, about midway between Aldgate Church and Whitechapel Bars, on the left hand or north side of the street; and as the Distemper had not reached to that side of the City, our neighbourhood continued very easy; but at the other end of the town the consternation was very great; and the richer sort of people, especially the nobility and gentry, from the west part of the city, thronged out of town with their families and servants in an unusual manner; and this was more particularly seen in Whitechapel; that is to say, the broad street where I lived.—Defoe, *Memoirs of the Plague*.

In the High Street of Whitechapel is held the largest hay and straw market in the kingdom. So large is the influx of carts and waggons on market days that the broad street is insufficient to contain them, and they crowd the neighbouring thoroughfares to overflowing. Till within memory the district north of the High Street—extending from Petticoat Lane to Osborn Street, and stretching back to (and including) Wentworth Street—was one of the very worst localities in London ; a region of narrow and filthy streets, yards and alleys, many of them wholly occupied by thieves' dens, the receptacles of stolen property, gin-spinning dog-holes, low brothels, and putrescent lodging-houses, —a district unwholesome to approach and unsafe for a decent person to traverse even in the daytime. In George Yard, one of the worst of these dark ways, was "Cadgers' Hall," notorious as a haunt where mendicants who live on assumed sores met and regaled. The construction of the broad Commercial Street across the centre of the district swept away some of the worst of the rookeries and let light into others, and the supervision of the new police did even more to mitigate its dangers and improve its general character, but it is still one of the foul spots of London.

Here [leaving Spitalfields, which lies to the north] you lose sight of the dwarfish and dwindled weavers, and are moving among men of might—fellows of thews and sinews, genuine specimens of the stuff of which common men are made—no porcelain and brittle ware, but unqualified English clay and flint-stone, roughly annealed, but strong, solid, and serviceable. A Whitechapel Bird was once a well-understood definition of a thorough-paced rascal—one versed in all the accomplishments of bull-baiting, dog-fancying and dog-stealing, Sunday-morning boxing-matches, larcenies great and small, duffing, chaffering, and all other kinds and degrees of high and low villany. Thirty years ago no Smithfield Market day passed over without what is called a *bull hank*, which consisted in selecting a likely beast to afford sport from any drove entering Whitechapel, and hunting him through the streets till he became infuriated ;—when the ruffians had had their fun out, and enough fright and alarm were spread around to satisfy them, the poor beast was knocked on the head and delivered over to its owner, if they could find him.—*Cornelius Webbe*, 1836.

Mr. Webbe was misinformed as to the frequency of these *bull hanks*. They were mostly confined to the Monday droves and the summer months. The Whitechapel Birds were usually assisted on such occasions by a contingent of Spitalfields' Weavers, lithe of body, light of foot, and fond of sport, and all armed with long, light ash sticks. The beast was generally picked out from a drove taking the Sun Street and Brick Lane route, the favourite spot being the junction of Brick Lane and Osborn Street, when the birds would swoop down on their quarry from Montague and Wentworth Streets in irresistible numbers. The unfortunate animal was invariably turned down the Whitechapel Road towards Stepney or Bow-Fair Fields (fields no longer), and we have heard of some of exceptional wind and vigour running as far as Wanstead Flats. If a run was anticipated (and Rumour's voice was seldom silent), the Whitechapel headborough with his crown-tipt staff and one or two officers would most likely make their appearance, but conveniently be elsewhere when a fray was imminent. With the appointment of the "New Police" bull hanks disappeared for ever.

Perhaps the term Whitechapel Bird was only a variation of the term jail-bird—a jail-bird of a lower stamp. At any rate, there was a jail of no very high repute in Whitechapel in the 17th century, and Taylor the Water Poet, in his " Praise and Virtue of a Jayle," puts up a pious petition that he may be saved from it :—

> Lord Wentworth's Jayle within White-Chappell stands,
> And Finsbury, God bless me from their hands!

Hatton speaks of it in 1708 as "a prison for debtors in the manor of Stepney, under £5 per annum"[1]—whatever that may mean. The terrible outrages on poor women in 1888 and 1889, known as the Whitechapel murders, created a widespread terror in the district as well as a feeling of horror over the whole country. The murderer or murderers still remain undiscovered.

The Parliament in 1642 erected fortifications in Whitechapel, then called Mile End. The mound was large and surrounded by a trench. While watching its formation in disguise, Sir Kenelm Digby was arrested here. "A mistaken idea," says Lysons, " has prevailed that this mount was made of the rubbish occasioned by the Great Fire of London in 1666."[2] A more persistent tradition was that the mount was a great burial-ground for the victims of the plague of 1665. The site is marked by Mount Place on the south side of Whitechapel Road, a little west of the London Hospital.

The church, dedicated to St. Mary Matfellon, was rebuilt on a larger scale and more costly fashion in 1875-1877, and burnt down in August 1880. It has again been rebuilt. [*See* St. Mary Matfellon.] There are also two district churches, St. Mark's and St. Jude's, and many chapels. On the south side of Whitechapel Road is the London Hospital. On the same side, No. 235, is the New East London Theatre, and next door were Meggs' Almshouses; the Pavilion Theatre is on the opposite side of the road. There are in the parish a Court House, station of the East London Railway, and the Proof-house of the gun-makers of London, where all gun-barrels made in London have to be proved and stamped before being issued for sale. In the Jews' burial-ground in Brady Street, Whitechapel Road, N. M. Rothschild (d. 1836), the leading stockbroker of Europe and founder of the Rothschild family, was buried. [*See* Mile End.]

Whitecross Street, CRIPPLEGATE (*Whytcrouchstrete*, 1339), runs from Fore Street, City, to Old Street, St. Luke's. The City End, Fore Street to Beech Street, is known as *Lower Whitecross Street;* the northern extensions, a region of costermongers, from Beech Street to Old Street, is called *Upper Whitecross Street.* The name was derived from a stone cross which stood near Beech Lane.

---

[1] Hatton, *New View*, p. 787.   [2] *Lysons*, vol. ii. p. 714.

In this street was a white cross; and near it was built an arch of stone, under which was a course of water down to the Moor, called now Moorfields. Which being too narrow for the free course of the water, and so an annoyance to the inhabitants, the twelve men presented it at an Inquisition of the King's Justices, 3 Edward I. (1275). And they presented the Abbot of Ramsey, and the Prior of St. Trinity, whose predecessors, for six years past had built (as the Inquisition ran) a certain stone arch at White Cross . . . which arch the foresaid Abbot and Prior and their successors ought to maintain and repair. . . . Hereupon it was commanded the Sheriffs to distrain the said Abbot and Convent, to mend the arch.—*Strype*, B. iii. p. 88.

In White Crosse Street King Henry V. built one fair house, and founded there a brotherhood of St. Giles. . . . But the said brotherhood was suppressed by Henry VIII.; since which time Sir John Gresham, mayor, purchased the lands and gave part thereof to the maintenance of a free school which he had founded at Holt, a market-town in Norfolk.—*Stow*, p. 113.

On the west side of Lower Whitecross Street stood the well-known debtors' prison—"Whitecross Street Prison," appertaining to the Sheriffs of London and Middlesex, built 1813-1815, from the designs of William Mountague, Clerk of the City Works. It was calculated to hold 400 prisoners, and was a large gloomy and unwholesome-looking place. The alterations in the law as respects imprisonment for debt rendered Whitecross Prison unnecessary, and it was closed in July 1870 and shortly after demolished, the prisoners for debt being transferred to the City Prison, Holloway. The site is now occupied by the City Goods Station of the Midland Railway, a vast structure of red brick and stone, covering an area of 2000 square yards, erected in 1874-1875 at a cost of £130,000. On the opposite side of the way was the City Green Yard or Pound, which was built over about 1883. [*See* Greenyard.] The new red brick Fire Brigade Station at the Beech Street end marks the City boundary.

In Upper Whitecross Street extensive clearances have been made among the costermongers' yards and alleys, and blocks of model dwellings are intended to supply their place.

Whitefield Street, FITZROY SQUARE, runs from Windmill Street to Warren Street, parallel with the Tottenham Court Road and Charlotte Street, and midway between the two. The name was formerly *John Street*, but was changed about 1870 in honour of the famous preacher, at the back of whose Tabernacle it passes. Public feeling has changed since the time when Cowper wrote—

Leuconomus—beneath well-sounding Greek
I slur a name a poet must not speak.
Cowper, *Hope* (1782), l. 554, and see the following lines.

Whitefield's Tabernacle, TOTTENHAM COURT ROAD, for some time known as *Tottenham Court Road Chapel*, on the west side, about half-way up, was erected by the Rev. George Whitefield, the popular preacher, A.D. 1756, and enlarged in 1759. The chapel was built on the site of an immense pond, called in Pine and Tinney's Maps (1742 and 1746) "The Little Sea." There were several interesting monuments—to Whitefield's wife, to Augustus Toplady, and to John Bacon,

R.A. The latter was buried under the north gallery. There was also a good bas-relief by him of the Woman touching the hem of the Saviour's Garment.

The property is copyhold, and was sold in 1827 for £19,500; after this the chapel was closed for a time. It was afterwards purchased by trustees and much altered in appearance. In 1860 it was enlarged and refronted; in 1889 the building showed serious signs of decay, and it was found necessary to close it, and it was pulled down in April 1890. A temporary iron chapel has been built on the ground adjoining for use until a new chapel can be erected.

Whitefriars, a precinct or liberty, between Fleet Street and the Thames, the Temple walls and Water Lane. Here was the White Friars' Church, called "Fratres Beatæ Mariæ de Monte Carmeli," first founded by Sir Richard Gray in 1241. Among the benefactors were King Edward I., who gave the ground; Hugh Courtenay, Earl of Devon, who rebuilt the church; and Robert Marshall, Bishop of Hereford, who built the choir, presbytery, and steeple. The church was surrendered at the Reformation, and in place thereof were "many fair houses built, lodgings for noblemen and others."[1] The hall was used as the first *Whitefriars Theatre* (1609). The privileges of sanctuary, continued to this precinct after the Dissolution, were confirmed and enlarged in 1608 by royal charter. Fraudulent debtors, gamblers, prostitutes, and other outcasts of society made it a favourite retreat. Here they formed a community of their own, adopted the language of pickpockets, openly resisted the execution of every legal process, and extending their cant terms to the place they lived in, new-named their precinct by the well-known appellation of *Alsatia*, after the province which formed a debateable land between Germany and France. [*See* Alsatia.]

<small>Though the immunities legally belonging to the place extended only to cases of debt, cheats, false witnesses, forgers and highwaymen found refuge there. For amidst a rabble so desperate no peace officer's life was in safety. At the cry of "Rescue," bullies with swords and cudgels, and termagant hags with spits and broom-sticks, poured forth by hundreds; and the intruder was fortunate if he escaped back into Fleet Street, hustled, stripped, and pumped upon. Even the warrant of the Chief Justice of England could not be executed without the help of a company of musketeers. Such relics of the barbarism of the darkest ages were to be found within a short walk of the chambers where Somers was studying history and law, of the chapel where Tillotson was preaching, of the coffee-house where Dryden was passing judgment on poems and plays, and of the hall where the Royal Society was examining the astronomical system of Isaac Newton.—Macaulay's *Hist.*, chap. iii.</small>

This vicious privilege was at length abolished by the Act 8 and 9 William III., c. 27 (1697), but it was only by slow degrees that Whitefriars was cleared of its lawless inhabitants and became a safe resort and dwelling-place for respectable citizens. There had, however, at all times been a portion of the old precinct wholly removed from this lawless community. Many of the Greys were buried in the monastery, and at the Dissolution the Friary House seems to have been secured

---

[1] *Stow*, p. 148.

by the head of this powerful family. Henry Grey, the ninth Earl of Kent (d. 1639), the friend of Selden, and his widow, the something more than friend, lived here *in ædibus carmeliticis*. At the death of the Countess (1651) the mansion was bequeathed to Selden, who continued to live in it till his death in 1654. Here, in the reign of James I., Turner, the fencing-master, kept his school, and here, while drinking with a friend at a tavern door on a fine evening in May, he was shot through the heart by assassins hired for the purpose by Lord Crichton of Sanquhar. Turner had accidentally put out the eye of Lord Sanquhar while fencing at Rycote, in Oxfordshire, and was never forgiven. The actual assassins were hanged in Fleet Street at the Whitefriars Gate, and Lord Sanquhar himself in Old Palace Yard. In another part of the Whitefriars Sir Balthazar Gerbier established his Academy for Foreign Languages;[1] and here, in Charles II.'s reign, Banister established a music school, and Ogilby, the poet, a warehouse for his maps. Banister's music-room was "a large room near the Temple back-gate."[2] The George Tavern in Whitefriars—in which Shadwell laid some of the scenes of his *Squire of Alsatia*, and which Mrs. Behn mentioned in *The Lucky Chance* (1687)—became the printing-office of William Bowyer, the elder. The house, which he converted into a printing-office, was situated in Dogwell Court. On January 30, 1713, the premises were entirely destroyed by fire, and so high did Bowyer's character stand, that his brother stationers, the Stationers' Company and the two Universities assisting, subscribed enough to set him up again in business. The unusual course was taken of issuing a "Brief," which produced £1514; this, with the amount contributed by his friends, made a total sum of £2539 received by Mr. Bowyer. His loss was estimated at £5146.[3] In this house the second and more eminent William Bowyer, "the learned printer," was born, December 17, 1699, and lived in it for sixty-seven years, only quitting it for a roomier house in Red Lion Passage in 1767. The house was occupied later by Thomas Davison, and is now a part of the establishment of Messrs. Bradbury and Agnew, famed as printers, and the proprietors of *Punch*.

During recent years great changes have been made within the precinct of Whitefriars. On the eastern side considerable spaces have been cleared and large offices and warehouses erected. The Thames Embankment has been carried along its southern border, and here, instead of gas-works, coal wharfs, and river-side rookeries, the ground is now occupied by the City of London School and Sion College.

Gentleman. Towards Chertsey, noble lord?
D. of Gloucester. No, to Whitefriars; there attend my coming.
Shakespeare, *Richard III*.

Whitefriars Theatre. Three of our early theatres stood between the Thames and Fleet Street. The first was called the *Whitefriars*

[1] *Whitelocke*, ed. 1732, p. 441.   [2] Roger North's *Memoirs of Musick*.
[3] Nichols's *Literary Anecdotes*, vol. i. pp. 59-63.

Theatre, the second the *Salisbury Court Theatre*, and the third the *Duke's Theatre in Dorset Gardens*. The Whitefriars Theatre was the old hall or refectory belonging to the dissolved Monastery of Whitefriars, and stood without the garden wall of Salisbury or *Dorset House*, the old inn or hostel of the Bishops of Salisbury. The patent mentioning the Whitefriars as a theatre is dated in January 1610, and the alteration appears to have been made in 1609. Little that is certain is known of the old playhouse, although it has been stated that plays were acted at Whitefriars as early as 1580, which was before the theatre was opened. [*See* Dorset Gardens Theatre and Salisbury Court Theatre.]

Whitehall, WESTMINSTER, the Palace of the Kings of England from Henry VIII. to William III. Nothing remains of it but Inigo Jones's Banqueting House, James II.'s statue, and the name, in the broad thoroughfare called *Whitehall*, and *Whitehall Gardens, Place*, and *Yard*. It was originally called *York House;* was delivered and demised to the King by charter, February 7 (21st of Henry VIII.), on the disgrace of Cardinal Wolsey, Archbishop of York,[1] and was then first called Whitehall. "There is another place of this name," says Minsheu, "where the Court of Requests is kept in the palace at Westminster."

Whitehall occupied a large space of ground, having one front towards the *Thames*, and another of a humbler character towards *St. James's Park; Scotland Yard* was the boundary one way, and *Canon Row, Westminster*, the boundary on the other. There was a public thoroughfare through the Palace from Charing Cross to Westminster, crossed by two gates, one known as Whitehall Gate, the other as the King Street Gate. This arrangement was long an eyesore, and Henry VIII., offended with the number of funerals which passed before his Palace on their way from Charing Cross to the churchyard of *St. Margaret's, Westminster*, erected a new cemetery on the other side of Whitehall, in the parish of *St. Martin's-in-the-Fields*.

Henry VIII.'s Whitehall was a building in the Tudor or Hampton Court style of architecture, with a succession of galleries and courts, a large hall, a chapel, tennis-court, cockpit, orchard, and banqueting house. Hentzner, who saw Whitehall in the reign of Elizabeth (1598), says:—

> This Palace is truly royal; inclosed on one side by the Thames, on the other by a Park, which connects it with St. James's, another royal palace. . . . Near the Palace are seen an immense number of swans, who wander up and down the river for some miles in great security. . . . In the Park is great plenty of deer. . . . In a garden adjoining to this Palace is a *jet d'eau*, which while strangers are looking at it, a quantity of water forced by a wheel, which the gardener turns at a distance, through a number of little pipes, plentifully sprinkles those that are standing round.

James I. intended to have rebuilt the whole Palace, and Inigo Jones designed a new Whitehall for that king, worthy of the nation and his

[1] Archbishop Warham acknowledges the receipt of Wolsey's "loving letters dated at your Grace's *place beside* Westminster."—Ellis's *Letters*, vol. ii. p. 43.

own great name. But nothing was built beyond the Banqueting House. Charles I. contemplated a similar reconstruction, but poverty at first prevented him, and the Civil War soon after was a more effectual prohibition. Charles II. preserved what money he could spare from his pleasures to build a palace at Winchester. James II. was too busy about religion to attend to architecture, and in William III.'s reign the whole of Whitehall, Inigo Jones's Banqueting House excepted, was destroyed by fire. William talked of rebuilding it after Inigo's designs, and a model by Mr. Weedon was laid before him.[1] Nothing, however, was done. Anne, his successor, took up her abode in St. James's Palace, and Sir John Vanbrugh built a house at Whitehall—the house ridiculed by Swift with such inimitable drollery. The first fire was in 1619 (when the Banqueting House was burnt); the second in 1686; and the third in 1708 was owing to the negligence of a maid-servant, who, about eight at night, to save the labour of cutting a candle from a pound, burnt it off and carelessly threw the rest aside before the flame was out.

April 10, 1691.—This [last] night a sudden and terrible fire burnt down all the buildings over the stone gallery at Whitehall to the water side, beginning at the apartment of the late Duchess of Portsmouth (which had been pulled down and rebuilt no less than three times to please her), and consuming other lodgings of such lewd creatures whó debauched K. Charles 2 and others, and were his destruction.— *Evelyn; see also Bramston*, p. 365.

But the great (or fourth) fire which finally destroyed Whitehall broke out on Tuesday, January 4, 1697-1698, about four in the afternoon, through the neglect of a Dutchwoman who had left some linen to dry before the fire in Colonel Stanley's lodgings. The fire lasted seventeen hours.

The tide at times rose so high at Whitehall that it flooded the kitchen. Pepys illustrates this by a curious story of the Countess of Castlemaine, when the King was to sup with her soon after the birth of her son, the Duke of Grafton. The cook came and told the imperious countess that the water had flooded the kitchen, and the chine of beef for the supper could not be roasted. "Zounds!" was her reply, "she must set the house on fire, but it should be roasted." So it was carried, adds Pepys, to Mrs. Sarah's husband's, and there roasted.[2] A still more curious picture of the water rising at Whitehall is contained in a speech of Charles II.'s to the House of Commons, entitled, "His Majestie's Gracious Speech to the Honourable House of Commons in the Banqueting House at Whitehall, March 1, 1661[2]." . . . "The mention of my wife's arrival," says the King, "puts me in minde to desire you to put that compliment upon her, that her entrance into the town may be with more decency than the ways will now suffer it to be; and for that purpose, I pray you would quickly pass such laws as are before you, in order to the amending those ways, and that she may not find Whitehall surrounded with water." Lord Dorset alludes to these

[1] *Strype*, B. vi. p. 6.   [2] *Pepys*, October 13, 1663.

periodical inundations in his well-known song, "To all you ladies now at land":—

> The King, with wonder and surprize,
>   Will swear the seas grow bold ;
> Because the tides will higher rise
>   Than e'er they did of old ;
> But let him know it is our tears
> Bring floods of grief to Whitehall Stairs.
>   With a fa la, la, la, la.

Three of the best of the several engravings of Whitehall are copied with great care in Wilkinson's *Londina Illustrata*. A good view of the water front (showing the Privy Stairs) is engraved at the top of Morden and Lea's large Map, published in the reign of William III. ; and in Kip's *Nouveau Theatre* is an interesting view of the Banqueting House, inscribed "H. Terasson delin. et sculp. 1713," showing the curious entrance gate on the north side, and on the south a wall bristling with cannon. Another valuable view is preserved in the famous caricature of "The Motion," executed in 1742, and which Horace Walpole commends so highly in his letters. But the engraving which preserves Whitehall to us in all its parts is the ground-plan of the Palace, from a survey made in the reign of Charles II. by John Fisher, and engraved by Vertue (1747), who might have dated it with safety before 1670, not, as he has done, 1680, seeing that Sir John Denham and the Duke of Albemarle, whose apartments are marked, were both dead before 1670 ; and in 1680 Dr. Wren was Sir Christopher Wren, and the Countess of Castlemaine Duchess of Cleveland.[1] In filling up the plan preserved by Vertue, Pepys comes to our aid with some of his minute allusions. He refers oftener than once to the following places : Henry VIII.'s Gallery, the Boarded Gallery, the Matted Gallery, the Shield Gallery, the Stone Gallery, and the Vane Room. Lilly, the astrologer, mentions the Guard Room. The Adam and Eve Gallery was so called from a picture by Mabuse, now at Hampton Court. In the Matted Gallery was a ceiling by Holbein ;[2] and on a wall in the Privy Chamber a painting of Henry VII. and Henry VIII., with their Queens, by the same artist, of which a copy in small is preserved at Hampton Court.[3] On another wall was a Dance of Death, also by Holbein, of which Douce has given a description ; and in the bed-chamber of Charles II. a representation by Wright of the King's birth, his right to his dominions, and his miraculous preservation, with this motto, *Terras Astræa revisit*.[4] Manningham in his Diary gives thirty-six of "Certayne devises and empresses taken by the scucheons in the Gallery at Whitehall ;" and Hentzner enumerates among the objects to be observed in Whitehall a "variety of emblems on paper, cut in the shape of shields, used by the nobility at tilts and tournaments, hung up there for a memorial." Considering that the age was that of Elizabeth, and that

---

[1] The original drawing (or a reduced copy) by Vertue is preserved in the Library of the Society of Antiquaries.
[2] *Pepys*, August 18, 1668.
[3] Sanderson's *Graphice*, p. 24.
[4] *Cal. of Ashm. MSS.*, coll. 475.

such men as Sidney and Raleigh and Devereux were among the knights who hung up these shields, it is worth while to give a specimen of what Manningham made note of on March 19, 1602.

The scucheon, twoe windmilles crosse sailed, and all the verge of the scucheon poudered with crosses crosselets, the word [motto] *Vndique Cruciatus*. Under written these verses—

> When most I rest beholde howe I stand crost,
> When most I move I toyle for others' gayne,
> The one declares my labour to be lost,
> The other showes my quiet is but payne.
> Unhappy then whose destiny are crosses
> When standing still and moveing breedes but losses.

Another specimen is much less romantic—"An empty bagpipe. The word *Si impleveris*."

Whitehall, March 30, 1604.—Grant with survivorship to And : Bright and Samuel Doubleday, of the offices of distilling herbs and sweet waters at the Palace of Whitehall *and of keeping the library there.*—*Cal. State Pap.*, 1603-1610, p. 89.

Whitehall, Oct. 27, 1604.—Grant to Sir Th : Knyvet of £20 per annum, for life, on consideration of his giving up his lodgings at Whitehall for the use of Prince Charles.—*Ibid.*, vol. i. p. 161.

The old Banqueting House was burnt down on Tuesday, January 12, 1618-1619, and the present Banqueting House, designed by Inigo Jones, commenced June 1, 1619, and finished March 31, 1622. From the roll of the account of the Paymaster of the Works, of the "Charges in building a Banqueting House at Whitehall, and erecting a new Pier in the Isle of Portland, for conveyance of stone from thence to Whitehall," formerly preserved at the Audit Office among the Declared Accounts, it appears that the sum received by the paymaster "for the new building of the Banqueting House, and the erecting a Pier at Portland," was £15,648 : 3s. The expense of the pier was £712 : 19 : 2, and of the Banqueting House, £14,940 : 4 : 1 ; the expenditure exceeding the receipts by £5 : 0 : 3. The account, it deserves to be mentioned, was not declared (*i.e.* finally settled) till June 29, 1633, eleven years after the completion of the building, and eight after the death of King James I. : a delay confirmatory of the unwillingness of the father and son to bring the works at Whitehall to a final settlement. Inigo's great masterpiece is described in this account as "a new building, with a vault under the same, in length 110 feet, and in width 55 feet within ; the wall of the foundation being in thickness 14 feet, and in depth 10 feet within ground, brought up with brick ; the first storey to the height of 16 feet, wrought of Oxfordshire stone, cut into rustique on the outside, and brick on the inside ; the walls 8 feet thick, with a vault turned over on great square pillars of brick, and paved in the bottom with Purbeck stone ; the walls and vaulting laid with finishing mortar ; the upper storey being the Banqueting House, 55 feet in height, to the laying on of the roof ; the walls 5 feet thick, and wrought of Northamptonshire stone, cut in rustique, with two orders of columns and pilasters, Ionic and Composite, with their architrave, frieze, and cornice, and other ornaments ; also rails and ballasters round about the top of the building, all of Portland stone, with fourteen windows on each side, and one great window at the upper end, and five doors of stone with frontispiece and cartoozes; the inside brought up with brick, finished over with two orders of columns and pilasters, part of stone and part of brick, with their architectural frieze and cornice, with a gallery upon the two sides, and the lower end borne upon great cartoozes of timber carved, with rails and ballasters of timber, and the floor laid with spruce deals; a strong timber roof covered with lead, and under it a ceiling divided into a fret made of great cornices enriched with carving; with painting, glazing, etc.; for performance thereof a great quantity of stone hath been digged at Portland quarry, in the county of Dorset, and Huddlestone quarry, in the county of York." As surveyor-general Inigo Jones had for salary 8s. 4d. per day, with an allowance of £46 a year for house rent, besides a clerk and incidental expenses. The master mason was Nicholas Stone. His pay was 4s. 10d. the day. The masons' wages were from 12d. to 2s. 6d. the man per diem; the carpenters were paid at the same rate; while the bricklayers received from 14d. to 2s. 2d. the day.[1]

The ceiling of the Banqueting House is lined with pictures on canvas, representing the apotheosis of James I., painted abroad by Rubens in 1635. Sir Godfrey Kneller had heard that Rubens was assisted by Jordaens in the execution. The sum he received was £3000. In 1785 G. B. Cipriani, R.A., received £2000 for cleaning and "restoring" these paintings. His repaintings were removed by Seguier, and the painting again cleaned and restored by Rigaud. The figures in these works are of colossal dimensions. Smith, who examined them closely when Seguier's scaffold was erected for cleaning them in 1832, says that "the children are more than 9 feet, and the full-grown figures from 20 to 25 feet in height." Within, and over the principal entrance, is a bust, in bronze, of James I., by Le Sœur, it is said. The Banqueting House was converted into a chapel in the reign of George I. (about 1724). It has never been consecrated. Here, on every Maundy-Thursday (the day before Good Friday), is the Royal Maundy distributed to as many poor and aged men and women as the Sovereign may be years of age. James Wyatt added the staircase on the north side in 1798. Sir John Soane restored the building in 1829-1830. The services at the Chapel Royal, Whitehall, are Sunday morning at 11, afternoon at 3. The Boyle Lectures are given here in May and June in the afternoon. The old chapel of the palace was situated near the river.

During several years of the reign of Henry VIII. Whitehall was the scene of many of those splendid jousts and revels in which he delighted till age and sickness had soured his temper. Here too passed before him those mighty musters of the citizens and train-bands which contemporary annalists describe with so much enjoyment. It was in Whitehall that at midnight, on January 25, 1533, the unfortunate Anne

[1] *Walpole*, by Dallaway, vol. ii. p. 58.

Boleyn was married to the wife-slaying monarch. Edward VI. held a Parliament here, and here listened to the preaching of Latimer. At the outset of the reign of Mary, Whitehall was attacked by a party of Wyatt's followers; and a few days after the Queen had the satisfaction of seeing the misguided rabble kneel in the mire in front of Whitehall, with halters round their necks, and crave her mercy, which she, looking over the gate, graciously accorded, whereat they set up a mighty shout of "God save Queen Mary." Mary spent many solitary days here, and here her ecclesiastical adviser, Bishop Gardiner, died, November 15, 1556. Elizabeth restored to Whitehall its former splendour and festivity. She built a new Banqueting House and gave magnificent feasts; held tourneys and jousts, where knights like Sir Harry Lee, Sir Christopher Hatton (afterwards Chancellor), Sir Philip Sidney, Sir Fulke Greville, Sir Walter Raleigh, and Sir Robert Devereux kept the barriers against all comers; and saw grave tragedies and courtly masques, and sometimes baitings of bulls and bears and the performances of mimes and tumblers. Of the serious matters of state transacted here it is needless to speak.

These courtly amusements her successor continued. Several of Ben Jonson's masques were written for performance before their Majesties at Whitehall, Inigo Jones contriving the properties and machinery. Even the mighty intellect of Bacon bent itself to the preparation of a masque to be performed at Whitehall by the members of the Inns of Court. Sometimes the masques followed weddings, as after the marriage of Philip Herbert, Earl of Montgomery, to the Lady Susan Vere, December 27, 1600; of the abandoned Countess of Essex to the King's worthless favourite, Robert Carr, Earl of Somerset, December 26, 1613; and, most splendid of all, that of the King's only daughter, Elizabeth, to Frederick Prince Palatine, afterwards the luckless King of Bohemia. For a few years Charles I. kept Whitehall brilliant with masques and plays, the King and Queen taking part, and lawyers as well as courtiers assisting.

February 27, 1634.—On Monday after Candlemas Day the Gentlemen of the Inns of Court performed their Masque at Court. They were sixteen in number, who rode through the streets in four chariots, and two others to carry their pages and musicians, attended by an hundred gentlemen on great horses, as well clad as ever I saw any. They far exceeded in bravery any masque that had formerly been presented by those Societies, and performed the dancing part with much applause. In their company there was one Mr. Read of Grays Inn, whom all the women, and some men, cried up for as handsome as the Duke of Buckingham. They were well used at Court by the King and Queen, no disgust given them, only this one Accident fell, Mr. May of Grays Inn, a fine poet, he who translated Lucan, came athwart my Lord Chamberlain in the Banqueting House, and he broke his staff over his shoulders, not knowing who he was, the King present, who knew him, for he calls him his Poet, and told the Chamberlain of it, who sent for him the next morning, and fairly excused himself to him, and gave him fifty pounds in pieces.—*Garrard to Lord Deputy Wentworth* (*Strafford Letters*), vol. i. p. 207.

November 9, 1637.—Here are to be two masques this winter; one at Christmas, which the King with the young nobless do make; the other at Shrovetide, which the Queen and her ladies do present to the King. A great room is now in building only for this use, betwixt the Guard Chamber and Banquetting House, of fir, only weather boarded and slightly covered. At the marriage of the Queen of Bohemia I saw one set up there, but not of that vastness that this is, which will cost too much money to be pulled down, and yet down it must when the masques are over.—*Garrard to Wentworth* (*ibid.*), vol. ii. p. 130.

A few weeks later (November 16) Garrard tells Wentworth that the King is busy practising his part, and that "most of the young lords, who are good dancers, attend his Majesty in this business."[1]

The event which is most closely associated in the popular mind with Whitehall is the execution of King Charles I., which took place on January 30, 1649, on a scaffold erected in front of the Banqueting House, towards the Park. The warrant directs that he should be executed "in the open street before Whitehall." Lord Leicester tells us in his Journal that he was "beheaded at Whitehall Gate." Dugdale, in his Diary, that he was "beheaded at the gate of Whitehall;" and a broadside of the time, preserved in the British Museum, that "the King was beheaded at Whitehall Gate."[2] There cannot, therefore, be a doubt that the scaffold was erected in front of the building facing the present Horse Guards. Another point has excited some discussion. It appears from Herbert's account of the King's last moments, that "the King was led all along the galleries and Banqueting House, and there was a passage *broken through the wall*, by which the King passed unto the scaffold." On the other hand, Ludlow relates in his *Memoirs* that the King "was conducted to the scaffold out of the window of the Banqueting House."[3] The following memorandum of Vertue's on the copy of Terasson's large engraving of the Banqueting House is preserved in the library of the Society of Antiquaries : "It is, according to the truest reports, said that out of this window K. Charles went upon the scaffold to be beheaded, the window-frame being taken out purposely to make the passage on to the scaffold, which is equal to the landing-place of the Hall within side." The window marked by Vertue belonged to a small building abutting from the north side of the present Banqueting House, and he was certainly in error. It is almost certain that Charles went out of an opening made in the centre blank window of the front, next the park. It must be remembered that all the windows were then blank. As late as 1761 the centre window only was glazed.

On Tuesday, March 31, 1657, the Speaker, at the head of the whole House of Parliament, "repaired to the Banqueting House at Whitehall, to present unto his Highness the Lord Protecter the humble Petition and Advice" of the House. " H. H. attended by the Lord President of the Council and other Officers of State came thither" to receive them; listened to the address of the Speaker, accepted the petition, and promised an early reply.[4] The humble petition and

[1] *Strafford Letters*, vol. ii. 140.
[2] So also in his *History of the Troubles in England*, fol. 1681, p. 373. Dugdale says the scaffold was erected "before the Great Gate at Whitehall."
[3] *Memoirs*, Vevey ed., vol. i. p. 283.
[4] *Journal of Parliament*.

advice was a proffer of the crown; the reply came in writing on April 3, gratefully declining the proffered gift.

The residence of the second Charles at Whitehall is marked by gifts to harlots, advertisements of lost and stolen dogs, and a variety of unseemly scenes. Charles built a new playhouse at Whitehall, to which Pepys went, and saw there "the King and Queen, Duke and Duchess, and all the great ladies of the Court, which, indeed, was a fine sight," but, "above all, my Lady Castlemaine." It is a curious illustration of the extent of the panic caused by the Great Fire of London that Pepys notes (under September 6, 1666) that he went "to Sir W. Coventry at St. James's, who lay without curtains having removed all his goods; *as the King at Whitehall* and everybody had done, and was doing." Evelyn records a scene he witnessed at Whitehall when James II. was king, the sequel to which affords a remarkable exemplification of the punishment inflicted for striking in the King's Court.

July 9, 1685.—Just as I was coming into the lodgings at Whitehall, a little before dinner, my Lord of Devonshire, standing very near his Majesty's bedchamber door in the lobby, came Col. Culpepper and in a rude manner looking my lord in the face, asked whether this was a time and place for *excluders* to appear: my Lord at first took little notice of what he said, knowing him to be a hot-headed fellow, but he reiterating it, my Lord asked Culpepper whether he meant him; he said, yes, he meant his Lordship. My Lord told him he was no excluder (as indeed he was not); the other affirming it again, my Lord told him he lied, on which Culpepper struck him a box on the ear, which my Lord return'd and fell'd him. They were soon parted, Culpepper was seiz'd, and his Majesty, who was all the while in his bedchamber, order'd him to be carried to the Green Cloth Officer, who sent him to the Marshalsea, as he deserv'd. My Lord of Devonshire had nothing said to him.—*Evelyn*.

But the earl escaped only for the moment. Culpepper, it was intimated, should not be again admitted to the presence-chamber. But after a while he was there, as little abashed as ever. The two again met in the drawing-room at Whitehall. There had been disputes in the interval between their respective adherents, and threats had passed on both sides. They at once withdrew from the royal presence. At the door the old quarrel was renewed, and the earl struck Culpepper in the face with a cane. The earl was in disfavour at Court on account of his politics, and a criminal information was filed against him in the King's Bench. He pleaded privilege of peerage, but this was disallowed. He then pleaded guilty; and Jeffreys sentenced him to a fine of £30,000 and to imprisonment till payment should be made.[1] It was at Whitehall that Monmouth after his capture was brought, "his arms bound behind him with a silken cord," into the presence of his uncle, James II., in order that the mean-spirited monarch might enjoy the abject submission of the nephew whom he had already resolved no submission should save from the scaffold. A little later Whitehall witnessed his own craven terrors and final flight from his crown and country (December

[1] *Macaulay*, ch. vii.

18, 1668). "On the morning of Wednesday the 13th of February (1669), the court of Whitehall and all the neighbouring streets were filled with gazers." The Lords and Commons in Convention had agreed to offer the crown to William of Orange and the Princess Mary. The formal tender was that day made in the Banqueting House, which had been duly prepared for the great ceremony. With this solemnity the glory of Whitehall passed away. Thenceforth no monarch resided in it, and it was not again the scene of courtly ceremonials. A large part of the Palace, as we have seen, was destroyed by fire in January 1697, and not rebuilt. The ground was assigned to private uses, and in August 1759 the fine old gatehouse, known as Holbein's Gate, was demolished to make way for the present Parliament Street; and with it may be said to have disappeared the last vestige, except the Banqueting House, of Royal Whitehall.

Of Holbein's Gate there is an interesting view, by Vertue, in the *Vetusta Monumenta*, a second in Wilkinson's *Londina Illustrata*, a third in Smith's *Westminster*, and a fourth by Wale in Dodsley's *London*. William, Duke of Cumberland (the hero of Culloden), had every brick removed to Windsor Great Park, and talked of re-erecting it at the end of the Long Walk, with additions at the sides, from designs by Thomas Sandby. Nothing, however, was done. Sandby's design may be seen in Smith's work. There were eight medallions on this gate (four on each side) made of baked clay, and glazed like delft-ware. Three of these (then and still at Hatfield Priory, Hatfield Peverell, in Essex) are engraved in Smith's *Westminster*, and represent, it is said, Henry VII., Henry VIII., and Bishop Fisher. Two (worked into keepers' lodges at Windsor) are now, by Mr. Jesse's exertions, at Hampton Court, where they are made to do duty as two of the Roman Emperors. That they were of Italian workmanship, and like the medallions at Hampton Court, probably the work of John de Maiano, has been pretty well determined by Sir Henry Ellis.[1] When Strype drew up his additions to Stow's *London*, "the uppermost room, in Holbein's Gateway, was used as the State Paper Office."[2]

The lead statue of James II., behind Whitehall, was the work of Grinling Gibbons, and was set up December 31, 1686, at the charge of Tobias Rustat.[3] The King, it is said, is pointing to the spot where his father was executed; but this vulgar error has been exposed long ago, though it is still repeated. Nothing can illustrate better the mild character of the Revolution of 1688 than the fact that the statue of the abdicated and exiled King was allowed to stand in the innermost courtyard of what was once his own Palace.

Whitehall Gardens. [*See* Privy Gardens.]

Whitehall Stairs, the stairs leading from the Thames to Whitehall Palace. Here Vanbrugh has laid a scene in *The Relapse, or Virtue in Danger*. [*See* Whitehall.]

[1] Ellis's *Letters*, 3d S., vol. i. p. 249.   [2] *Strype*, B. vi. p. 5.   [3] *Bramston*, p. 253.

The Court used to take the water from the stairs at Whitehall Palace in Summer evenings when the heat and dust prevented their walking in the Park. An infinite number of open boats filled with the Court and City beauties attended the barges in which were the royal family; collations, music and fireworks completed the scene.—*Grammont Memoirs.*

Whitehall Yard, north of the Chapel Royal (Banqueting House). Here is the Royal United Service Institution, but a great change has been made in the yard lately by reason of the demolition of houses, and the erection of a large range of mansions on the river side.

Whitelands, CHELSEA. An old house on the north side of Marlborough Road; large buildings are now attached to it, and it is occupied by a paper-hanging factory. Whitelands Training College is in the King's Road.

Whittington's College. [*See* College Hill.]

Wigmore Street, CAVENDISH SQUARE to PORTMAN SQUARE, was so called after Robert Harley, Earl of Oxford, Earl Mortimer, and Baron Harley of Wigmore Castle, the stronghold of the ancient Mortimers. "Wigmore shall fly to set my uncle free!" exclaims young Mortimer in Marlowe's *Edward II.*

Wild Court, GREAT WILD STREET. Here, at No. 12, lived Theophilus Cibber and his wife, the daughter of Dr. Arne, and one of the best tragic actresses the English stage has produced. The fact of their residence here is derived from their own bills for their benefits, and from the famous trial of December 5, 1738.

Wild House, properly WELD HOUSE, on the site of what is now LITTLE WILD STREET, LINCOLN'S INN FIELDS, was built in the early part of the reign of Charles I. by Sir Edward Stradling, on ground then called "Oldwick close," and sold, in 1651, to Humphrey Weld, Esq., a rich parishioner of St. Giles's-in-the-Fields, son of Sir Humphrey Weld, Lord Mayor of London in 1608. The form of the house was a centre with two wings, possessing a street front of 150 feet, and a depth behind, with the garden, of 300 feet.[1] It was subsequently let by the Weld family to persons of distinction, foreign ambassadors, etc. The Duchess of Ormond was living in Wild House in 1655,[2] and Ronquillo, the Spanish ambassador, in another wing of the building in the reigns of Charles II. and James II. In the rioting which followed the news of the flight of James II., the mob wrecked Ronquillo's house and chapel, and the ambassador had to make his escape by a back door.[3]

The rich plate of the Chapel Royal had been deposited at Wild House, near Lincoln's-Inn-Fields, the residence of the Spanish Ambassador, Ronquillo. Ronquillo, conscious that he and his court had not deserved ill of the English nation, had thought it unnecessary to ask for soldiers; but the mob was not in a mood to make nice distinctions. . . . . His house was, therefore, sacked without mercy; and a noble library, which he had collected, perished in the flames. His only comfort

---

[1] Heath's *Grocers' Company,* p. 225.   [2] *Life of Duke of Ormond,* 8vo, 1747, p. 167.
[3] Bramston, *Autob.* (*Cam.l. Soc.*), p. 339.

was, that the host in his chapel was rescued from the same fate.—Macaulay's *History of England*, ch. x.

April 26, 1681.—I din'd at Don Pietro Ronquillo's, the Spanish Ambassador, at Wild House, Drury Lane, who used me with extraordinary civility. The dinner was plentiful, half after the Spanish, half after the English way. After dinner he led me into his bed-chamber, where we fell into a long discourse concerning religion.—*Evelyn*.

Weld House is to be lett, containing 33 rooms, garrets, and cellars, with other suitable conveniences in Weld Street, near Lincoln's Inn Fields. Enquire at Weld House, or at Marybone House.—*London Gazette* for 1694, No. 3010.

Wild House and gardens were let on a building lease for ninety-nine years in 1695; and the present Great and Little Wild Street erected on the site. The property was the subject of the leading Chancery case of Lister *v.* Foxcroft (*White and Tudor*, 625), which was not finally decided by the House of Lords until April 7, 1701.

Wild Street (Great), LINCOLN'S INN, Drury Lane end of Great Queen Street to Sardinia Street. [*See* Wild House.] Pope's correspondent, Henry Cromwell, was living, July 17, 1709, at "the Blue Bull in Great Wild Street, near Drury Lane, London."[1]

March 18, 1708.—In the town it is ten to one, but a young fellow may find his strayed heart again, with some Wild Street or Drury Lane damsel.—*Pope (æt.* 20) *to Cromwell.*

Wild Street (Little). [*See* Wild House.] In the Baptist Chapel in this street, between Nos. 23 and 24 (now a mission hall), a sermon was annually preached commemorative of the great storm of 1703—the storm celebrated by Addison in his poem of "The Campaign."

Wilderness Row, CLERKENWELL, from Goswell Street opposite Old Street, to St. John Street, was so named from the houses facing the northern portion of the Charterhouse grounds, which being planted with shrubs and laid out in walks overshadowed by trees was called the *Wilderness*. Wilderness Row has been widened by setting back the Charterhouse wall and was incorporated in 1878 with that portion of the new road from Oxford Street to Old Street called *Clerkenwell Road*, of which it forms the northern half. The Row covered in part the site of Pardon churchyard, the chapel attached to which stood near its western end, near where Zion Chapel now stands. In excavating at various times large quantities of human bones have been found. When Wilderness Row was built the land was partly open fields; and here as late as about 1825 was the Cherry Tree Inn, with its once noted tea-gardens.

Wildman's, a Coffee-house in BEDFORD STREET, STRAND, the favourite headquarters of John Wilkes's supporters.

> What Patron shall I choose? . . . .
> Shall I prefer the grand retreat of Stowe,
> Or, seeking patriots, to friend *Wildman's* go?

---

[1] Elwin's *Pope*, vol. vi. p. 80.

> To Wildman's! cried Discretion (who had heard
> Close standing at my elbow, ev'ry word)
> To Wildman's! art thou mad? can'st thou be sure
> One moment there to have thy head secure?
>
> Each dish at Wildman's of sedition smacks;
> Blasphemy may be Gospel at Almacks.
>   Peace, good Discretion, peace—thy fears are vain;
> Ne'er will I herd with Wildman's factious train.
>   Churchill, *The Candidate.*

It is incredible what pains Monsieur Beaumont has taken to *see.* He has seen Oxford, Bath, Blenheim, Stowe, Jews, Quakers, Mr. Pitt, the Royal Society, the Robin Hood, Lord Chief Justice Pratt, the Arts and Sciences, *has dined at Wildman's,* and I think with my Lord Mayor.—*H. Walpole to Earl of Hertford,* November 9, 1764.

Will Office, SOMERSET HOUSE, occupies the centre of the south side of the great quadrangle, and was removed from Knightrider Street, Doctors' Commons, in 1874. At this office wills are proved and administrations granted, and here are preserved all wills granted within the prerogative of the Archbishop of Canterbury. The earliest copy of a will preserved in the strong room of the Probate Registry is of the year 1383, and the earliest original of the year 1484.

Here is the original will of Shakespeare, on three folio sheets of paper, with his signature to each sheet—the first signature being, however, so damaged as to be only in part legible. The wills of Van Dyck, the painter, of Inigo Jones, Sir Isaac Newton, Dr. Johnson, Izaak Walton; and, in short, of all the great men of this country who died possessed of property in the south of England are also here. The will of Napoleon I., in which he bequeathed 10,000 francs to Cantillon, the man who tried to assassinate the Duke of Wellington in Paris, was given up to the French Government in 1853. It was proved by Count Antholin in August 1824, and the assets within the province of Canterbury were sworn to be under the value of £600. The office abounds in matter of great biographical importance—illustrative of the lives of eminent men, of the descent of property, and of the manners and customs of bygone times. Since 1861 any person entitled to do so may prove a will and take out probate, at the *Department for Personal Application,* without the assistance of Proctor or Solicitor.

The *Department for Literary Inquiry* is in a room set apart for that purpose. It is open (except on holidays) from 10 A.M. to 3.30 P.M. between October 10 and August 10, and between 11 A.M. and 2.30 P.M. between August and October. On payment of a fee of one shilling visitors may search the calendars and read registered copies of wills from 1383 to the present time.

The office hours at the Will Office are from ten to four, excepting during the vacation, when they are from eleven to three. The charges for searching the calendars of names is one shilling for every name. The charge for seeing the original will is a shilling extra. Plain copies of wills may be had at sixpence per folio.

Will's Coffee-house, No. 1 Bow Street, Covent Garden, on the west side, corner of Russell Street, and so called from William Urwin, who kept it. " It seems," says Sir Walter Scott, "that the original sign of the house had been a *Cow*. It was changed, however, to a *Rose* in Dryden's time."[1] Scott appears to have confused two houses. The Rose Tavern was on the *south* side of Russell Street, at the east corner of Bridges Street; Will's Coffee-house was, as said above, on the *north* side, at the corner of Bow Street. The change from the *Cow* to the *Rose* is also very doubtful. It certainly must have taken place, if at all, before Dryden's time. William Long is entered in the parish books as landlord of *The Rose* as early as 1651. [*See* Rose Tavern.] The lower part of Will's was let in 1693 to a woollen draper, " Mr. Philip Brent, woollen draper, under Will's Coffee-house in Russell Street, Covent Garden."[2] In 1722 it was occupied by a bookseller, " James Woodman, at Camden's Head, under Will's Coffee-house in Bow Street, Covent Garden." The wits' room was upstairs on the first floor.

In the Churchwardens' Accounts of St. Paul's, Covent Garden, under the year 1675, are the following entries:—

An accompt of money received for misdemeanors.

July 8, 1675.—Of William Urwin . . . 4s.

"Will" kept at times, it appears, a disorderly coffee-house. He was alive in 1695.

Nowhere was the smoking more constant than at Will's. That celebrated house, situated between Covent Garden and Bow Street, was sacred to polite letters. There the talk was about poetical justice and the unities of place and time. There was a faction for Perrault and the moderns, a faction for Boileau and the ancients. One group debated whether *Paradise Lost* ought not to have been in rhyme. To another an envious poetaster demonstrated that *Venice Preserved* ought to have been hooted from the stage. Under no roof was a greater variety of figures to be seen. There were earls in stars and garters, clergymen in cassocks and bands, pert Templars, sheepish lads from the Universities, translators and index-makers in ragged coats of frieze. The great press was to get near the Chair where John Dryden sate. In winter that chair was always in the warmest nook by the fire; in summer it stood in the balcony. To bow to the Laureate, and to hear his opinion of Racine's last tragedy, or of Bossu's treatise on epic poetry, was thought a privilege. A pinch from his snuff-box was an honour sufficient to turn the head of a young enthusiast.—Macaulay, *Hist. of England*, chap. iii.

February 3, 1663-1664.—In Covent Garden to-night, going to fetch home my wife, I stopped at the Great Coffee-house there, where I never was before: where Dryden, the poet (I knew at Cambridge), and all the wits of the town, and Harris the player, and Mr. Hoole of our College. And had I had time then, or could at other times, it will be good coming thither; for there, I perceive, is very witty and pleasant discourse.—*Pepys*.

This sort of men you shall hear say in the Pit, or at *the Coffee House* (speaking of an author) Damn me! How can he write? He's a raw young fellow newly come from the university. . . . Of another they say S'death, he's no scholar, can't write true grammar, etc.—Ravenscroft (To the Reader), *The Careless Lovers*, 4to, 1673.

A boy of about 14 years old, being threatened, run away from his Master in Bow

---

[1] Scott's *Life of Dryden* (in *Misc. Prose Works*, vol. I. p. 382).
[2] *London Gazette* for 1693, No. 2957.

Street yesterday being the first of November [1674] . . . ; his name Thomas Parsons. Whoever shall give notice of him where he is to William Urwin's Coffee House in Bow Street in Covent Garden, shall be well rewarded for his pains.—*London Gazette*, No. 934.

Johnson. Faith, sir, 'tis mighty pretty, I saw it at the Coffee-house.

Bays. 'Tis a trifle hardly worth owning ; I was t'other day at Will's throwing out something of that nature ; and I' gad, the hint was taken, and out came that picture ; indeed, the poor fellow was so civil to present me with a dozen of 'em for my friends : I think I have one here in my pocket ; would you please to accept it, Mr. Johnson.—Prior and Montague, *The Hind and the Panther Transvers'd.*

> But granting matters should be spoke
> By method rather than by luck ;
> This may confine their younger stiles,
> Whom Dryden pedagogues at Will's :
> But never could be meant to tie
> Authentic wits like you and I.
>
> Prior to *Fleetwood Shepheard.*

> As I remember said the sober mouse
> I've heard much talk of the Wits' Coffee House.
> Thither, says Brindle, thou shalt go and see
> Priests sipping coffee, Sparks and Poets tea ;
> Here rugged frieze, there Quality well drest,
> These baffling the Grand Seigneur, those the Test.
> And here shrewd guesses made, and reasons given
> That human laws were never made in heaven.
> But above all, what shall oblige thy sight
> And fill thy eye-balls with a vast delight,
> Is the Poetic Judge of sacred wit
> Who does i' the darkness of his glory sit.
>
> Prior, *Town and Country Mouse.*

I had been listening what objections had been made against the conduct of the play [Don Sebastian] ; but found them all so trivial, that if I should name them, a true critic would imagine that I had played booby, and only raised up phantoms for myself to conquer.—Dryden, *Preface to Don Sebastian.*

Dryden, in various prefaces, takes notice of objections that had been made by critics to his Plays ; which one naturally expects to find in some of the pamphlets published in his time. But the passage before us (ut sup.) inclines me to believe that most of the criticisms which he has noticed were made at his favourite haunt, Will's Coffee House.—Malone (*Dryden*, vol. iii. p. 191).

Bays. But if you please to give me the meeting at Will's Coffee House, about three in the afternoon, we'll remove into a private room, where, over a dish of tea, we may debate this important affair with all the solitude imaginable.

The Reasons of Mr. Bays's [Dryden's] changing his Religion, 4to, 1688.

I cannot omit to tell you, that a Wit of the Town, a friend of mine, at Will's Coffee House, the first night of the play, cry'd it down as much as in him lay, who before had read it and assured me he never saw a prettier comedy.—Mrs. Behn's *Preface to The Lucky Chance,* 4to, 1687.

A Wit and a Beau set up with little or no expense. A pair of red stockings and a sword-knot sets up one, and peeping once a day in at Will's, and two or three second-hand sayings, the other.—Tom Brown's *Laconics.*

From thence we adjourned to the Wits' Coffee-house. . . . Accordingly up stairs we went, and found much company, but little talk. . . . We shuffled through this moving crowd of philosophical mutes to the other end of the room, where three or four wits of the upper class were rendezvous'd at a table, and were disturbing the ashes of the old poets by perverting their sense. . . . At another table were seated a parcel of young, raw, second-rate beaus and wits, who were conceited if they had but the honour to dip a finger and thumb into Mr. Dryden's snuff-box.—Ned Ward, *The London Spy*, part x.

It was in returning home from Will's that Dryden was set upon and beaten by the dastardly Lord Rochester's hired ruffians.

> To Will's I went, where Beau and Wit
> In mutual contemplation sit;
> But which were Wits, and which were Beaus,
> The Devil sure's in him who knows,
> For either may be which you please,
> These look like those who talk'd like these;
> To make amends, there I saw Dryden.

A Day's Ramble in Covent Garden, 1691. *Poems in Burlesque*, 4to, 1692.

> Will's is the mother church: From thence their creed
> And as that censures poets must succeed.

Verses prefixed to "Sir Noisy Parrot," 4to, 1693.

I am by no means free of the Poet's Company, having never kissed their Governor's hands nor made the least court to the Committee that sits in Covent Garden.—Sir Richard Blackmore, *Preface to King Arthur*, fol. 1697.

> Had but the people, scar'd with danger, run
> To shut up Will's, where the sore plague begun,
> Had they the first infected men convey'd
> Straight to Moorfields!

Blackmore, *A Satire upon Wit*, 1700.

Blackmore has another gird at Will's in connection with his proposed Bank for Wit.

> The Bank when thus establish'd will supply
> Small places for the little loitering fry,
> That follow G[arth], or at Will Ur[wi]n's ply.

Blackmore, *ibid*.

Why should a poet fetter the business of his plot, and starve his action, for the nicety of an hour or the change of a scene; since the thought of man can fly over a thousand years with the same ease, and in the same instant of time, that your eye glances from the figure of six to seven on the dial-plate, and can glide from the Cape of Good Hope to the Bay of St. Nicholas, which is quite across the world, with the same quickness and activity, as between Covent Garden Church and *Will's Coffee-house?*—Farquhar, *A Discourse upon Comedy*, 1702.

> Whate'er success this play from Will's may meet,
> We still must crave the favour of the Pit.

Prologue to Orrery's *As You find It*, 4to, 1703.

I am sensible by experience, that there's a great deal of artifice and accomplishment required in a gentleman that will write for the Theatre;—and 'tis a mighty presumption in any one to attempt it, who has not ingratiated himself among the Quality, or been conversant at Will's.—Walker's *Preface to Marry or do Worse*, 4to, 1704.

I think our business done and to some purpose,—to put one King out and another in within the year! I meant only to relieve the Duke of Savoy, and then—Will's Coffee House in Winter.—Earl of Peterborough, *Valencia*. July 2, 1706 (Mahon's *War of the Succession*, p. 198).

> Now view the beaus at Will's, the men of wit,
> By nature nice, and for discerning fit,
> The finished fops, the men of wig and snuff,
> Knights of the famous Oyster-barrel snuff.

Defoe's *Reformation of Manners*.

I was about seventeen when I first came up to town, an odd-looking boy, with short rough hair, and that sort of awkwardness which one always brings up at first out of the country. However, in spite of my bashfulness and appearance, I used now and then to thrust myself into Will's to have the pleasure of seeing the most celebrated wits of that time, who then resorted thither. The second time that ever I was there, Mr. Dryden was speaking of his own things, as he frequently did, especially of such as had been lately published. "If anything of mine is good," says he, "'tis Mac Flecknoe; and I value myself the more upon it, because it is the first piece of ridicule written in Heroics." On hearing this, I plucked up my spirit so far as to say, in a voice but just loud enough to be heard, that "Mac Flecknoe was a very fine poem; but that I had not imagined it to be the first that ever was writ that way." On this, Dryden turned short upon me, as surprised at my interposing; asked me how long I had been a dealer in poetry; and added, with a smile, "Pray, sir, what is it that you *did* imagine to have been writ so before?" I named Boileau's *Lutrin*, and Tassoni's *Secchia Rapita*, which I had read, and knew Dryden had borrowed some strokes from each. "'Tis true," said Dryden, "I had forgot them." A little after Dryden went out, and in going spoke to me again, and desired me to come and see him next day. I was highly delighted with the invitation; went to see him accordingly, and was well acquainted with him after, as long as he lived.— Dean Lockier (*Spence*, by Singer, p. 59).

I had the honour of bringing Mr. Pope from our retreat in the Forest of Windsor, to dress *à la mode*, and introduce at Will's Coffee House.—*Sir Charles Wogan to Swift* (Scott's *Swift*, vol. xviii. p. 21).

It was Dryden who made Will's Coffee-house the great resort of the wits of his time. After his death, Addison transferred it to Button's, who had been a servant of his; they were opposite each other, in Russell Street, Covent Garden.—*Pope* (*Spence*, by Singer), p. 263.

Addison passed each day alike, and much in the manner that Dryden did. Dryden employed his mornings in writing, dined *en famille*, and then went to Will's : only he came home earlier a' nights.—*Pope* (*Spence*, by Singer), p. 286.

Let us see if we can find anything in his rhymes, which may direct us to his Coffee House or to his Bookseller's. By his taking three opportunities to commend Mr. Dryden in so small a compass, I fancy we may hear of him at Shakspeare's Head [Tonson's], or at Will's.—Dennis, *Reflections on Pope's Essay on Criticism*, 1712, p. 27.

The translator [Pope] seems to think a good genius and a good ear to be the same thing. Dryden himself was more sensible of the difference between them, and when it was *in debate at Will's Coffee House* what character he would have with posterity; he said, with a sullen modesty, I believe they will allow me to be a good versifier.—Oldmixon, *An Essay on Criticism*, 8vo, 1728, p. 24.

I find, that upon his [Pope's] first coming to Town, out of pure Compassion for his exotick Figuor, narrow circumstances, and humble appearance, the late Mr. Wycherley admitted him into his society, and suffered him, notwithstanding his make, to be his humble admirer at Will's.—Pope, *Alexander's Supremacy and Infallibility Examined*, 4to, 1729, p. 13.

When I was a young fellow, I wanted to write the *Life of Dryden*; and in order to get materials, I applied to the only two persons then alive who had seen him; these were old Swinney and old Cibber. Swinney's information was no more than this, "That at Will's Coffee House Dryden had a particular chair for himself, which was set by the fire in winter, and was then called his winter-chair; and that it was carried out for him to the balcony in summer, and was then called his summer-chair." Cibber could tell no more but "that he remembered him a decent old man, arbiter of critical disputes at Will's."—Dr. Johnson, in *Boswell*, ed. Croker, vol. iii. p. 435.

When Steele started the *Tatler*, 1709, he announced that—

All accounts of gallantry, pleasure, and entertainment shall be under the article of White's Chocolate House; poetry under that of Will's Coffee House; learning under the title of Grecian; foreign and domestic news you will have from St. James's

Coffee House. And goes on with a statement which may be taken to indicate the comparative expenses of the four establishments.—"I cannot keep the ingenious man to go daily to *Will's*, under two-pence each day merely for his charges; to *White's*, under sixpence; nor to the *Grecian*, without some plain Spanish, to be as able as others at the learned table; and that a good observer cannot speak with even kidney at *St. James's* without clean linen.—*The Tatler*, No. 1 (1709).

This place [Will's] is very much altered since Mr. Dryden frequented it; where you used to see songs, epigrams, and satires in the hands of every man you met, you have now only a pack of cards; and instead of the cavils about the turn of the expression, the elegance of the style, and the like, the learned now dispute only about the truth of the game.—*The Tatler*, No. 1, April 8, 1709.

> Rail on, ye triflers, who to Will's repair,
> For new lampoons, fresh cant, or modish air.
>
> E. Smith, *On John Phillips's Death*.

> Be sure at Will's the following day,
> Lie snug, and hear what critics say;
> And if you find the general vogue
> Pronounces you a stupid rogue,
> Damns all your thoughts as low and little,
> Sit still, and swallow down your spittle.
>
> Swift, *On Poetry; a Rhapsody*.

After the Play, the best company go to Tom's and Will's Coffee House near adjoining, where there is playing at Picket, and the best of conversation till midnight. Here you will see blue and green ribbons and stars sitting familiarly, and talking with the same freedom as if they had left their quality and degrees of distance at home.—Macky, *A Journey through England*, 8vo, 1722, p. 172.

There is no place of general resort wherein I do not often make my appearance; sometimes I am seen thrusting my head into a round of Politicians at Will's, and listening with great attention to the narratives that are made in those little circular audiences.—*The Spectator*, No. 1.

Would it not employ a Beau prettily enough, if, instead of playing eternally with a snuff box, he spent some part of his time in making one? Such a method as this would very much conduce to the public emolument, by making every man living good for something; for there would then be no one member of human society but would have some little pretension for some degree in it; like him who came to Will's Coffee House upon the merit of having writ a Posie of a ring.—*The Spectator*, No. 43.

Robin the porter, who waits at Will's Coffee House, is the best man in town for carrying a billet; the fellow has a thin body, swift step, demure looks, sufficient sense, and knows the town.—*The Spectator*, No. 398.

Before five in the afternoon I left the City, and came to my common scene of Covent Garden, and passed the evening at Will's in attending the discourses of several sets of people who relieved each other within my hearing on the subjects of cards, dice, love, learning, and politics. The last subject kept me till I heard the streets in the possession of the bell-man, who had now the world to himself, and cried *past two o'clock*.—*The Spectator*, No. 454, August 11, 1712.

Truewit. Just as it was I find when I us'd Will's; but pray, Sir, does that ancient rendezvous of the *Beaux Esprits* hold its ground? And do men now, as formerly, become Wits by sipping coffee and tea with Wycherley and the reigning poets?

Freeman. No, no; there have been great revolutions in this state of affairs since you left us: *Button's* is now the established Wit's Coffee-house, and all the young scribblers of the times pay their attendance nightly there to keep up their pretensions to sense and understanding.—Gildon, *A New Rehearsal*, 12mo, 1714.

Why, Faith (answered I), the Controversy [about Pope's *Homer*] as yet remains undecided: Will's Coffee House gives it to the four Books, Button's to the one.

But leaving the division of the merits of the cause to those two sovereign tribunals of Will's and Button's.—Gildon, *Art of Poetry*, 1718.

William Street, LOWNDES SQUARE. Lady Morgan, the authoress of the *Wild Irish Girl*, went to reside at No. 11 in 1838, and died there, April 16, 1859. She was buried in the Brompton Cemetery.

Williams's (Dr.) Library, No. 16 GRAFTON STREET (Tottenham Court Road and Gower Street), of about 25,000 volumes, and exceedingly rich in old and especially Puritan and patristic theology, was founded by the Rev. Daniel Williams, D.D., an eminent Protestant dissenting minister of the Presbyterian denomination. Dr. Williams was born at Wrexham, in Denbighshire, 1664, and died in London, January 24, 1716. Dr. Williams possessed considerable property, and, leaving his widow a life interest therein, bequeathed the bulk of it after her death to various religious and educational uses. The bequest which founded the Williams's Library was intended to carry out a long-cherished purpose of the founder to establish a library which might be available for general use, but be particularly for the service of the London ministers. He had himself formed a good collection of books, and he added to it, by purchases, the library of Dr. Bates. He directed the trustees to erect a suitable building, for which they purchased a site in *Redcross Street*, and there opened the library in 1724. In 1864 the library was removed to a temporary home in Queen's Square, Bloomsbury, until the building in Grafton Street was ready, and the old house was pulled down. There is a good printed catalogue, in three volumes. Admission is readily granted to suitable persons, though nominally a trustee's nomination is required. The library is open from Monday till Friday (both inclusive) throughout the year, except during the month of August and the Christmas and Whitsun weeks. Among its treasures the library possesses a fine copy of the first folio edition of Shakespeare; an original portrait of Richard Baxter; and the "glass basin which held the water wherewith Queen Elizabeth was baptized."

Willis's Rooms, No. 26 KING STREET, ST. JAMES; a suite of assembly rooms, built 1765-1771 (Robert Mylne, architect) for Almack's balls. [*See* Almack's Rooms.] Since the dissolution of the Almack's committee in 1863, the rooms have been known exclusively as "Willis's," but that name (from the proprietor who succeeded Almack) was used, at least occasionally, as early as 1790.[1] Willis's Rooms were long celebrated for high-class dinners, meetings, concerts, and balls. Here the meetings of the Society of Dilettanti were held, and the famous portraits of the original members were hung. [*See* Dilettanti Society.] The establishment, however, ceased to supply dinners in 1889, and the dining clubs which met here have now removed. It is said that the place has been leased (1890) to a German syndicate, who intend to establish a system of German health baths of every description.

[1] *See* Trusler's *London Adviser and Guide*, 12mo, 1790, p. 174.

Willow Walk, now WILLOW STREET, PIMLICO, mentioned for the first time in the rate-books of St. Martin's-in-the-Fields, under the year 1723, was, till 1829-1839, a low-lying footpath west of Tothill Fields, with long cuts or reservoirs on either side, belonging to the Chelsea Waterworks Company. The cuts were drained in 1829-1831, and the ground raised for the present terraces and squares by the soil excavated from St. Katherine's Docks. A lonely cottage in the Willow Walk, long the haunt of Jerry Abershaw, the notorious highwayman, and his associates, was standing as late as 1836.

Wilton Crescent, BELGRAVE SQUARE. No. 24 was the residence of Henry Hallam, the historian, died January 1859.

Wilton Place, north of Wilton Crescent, KNIGHTSBRIDGE. The church, dedicated to *St. Paul*, has acquired a prominent place in ritualistic annals.

Wimbledon House, STRAND, a mansion erected on a part of the Exeter House property by Sir Edward Cecil (d. 1638), first and last Baron Putney and Viscount Wimbledon, a grandson of the great Lord Burghley. It stood at the east corner of Wellington Street North, and while still quite new was burned to the ground in November 1628, a portion of the same viscount's house at Wimbledon having been destroyed by gunpowder on the previous day. In 1720 Strype describes it as "a very handsome house." It is said [1] to have been built from a design by Inigo Jones, and, with its covered up-and-down entrance projecting into the carriage way, makes a prominent feature in old pictures of the Strand. It was pulled down about 1782.

Wimpole Street, CAVENDISH SQUARE, so called from Wimpole, in Cambridgeshire, sold by the second Earl of Oxford to Lord Chancellor Hardwicke. In No. 12 lived Admiral Lord Hood; in 1809 he was living in No. 37. In No. 67 Henry Hallam wrote his *History of the Middle Ages*, and his *Constitutional History of England*. In No. 65 lived, in 1792, Sir Elijah Impey. Here (then the house of his brother-in-law, Sir Benjamin Hall) was the first London residence of Baron Bunsen. Early in 1759 Edmund Burke was resident in Wimpole Street, "the chief expenses of housekeeping being sustained by Dr. Nugent." [2]

William Wilkie Collins, the novelist, died at his house, No. 82, on September 23, 1889.

Winchester House, AUSTIN FRIARS, more generally called Pawlet or Powlet House, after William Paulet, first Marquis of Winchester, Lord High Treasurer of England in the reigns of Edward VI., Mary, and Elizabeth, on the site of the house, cloister and gardens of the Augustine Friars. [*See* Austin Friars.] When the marquis was asked

---

[1] *See Wine and Walnuts*, vol. i. p. 149; *Notes and Queries*, 2d S., vol. ii. p. 476.

[2] Prior's *Life of Burke*, p. 56, and see Forster's *Goldsmith*, vol. i. p. 294.

by what means he had managed to retain so important an office as that of Lord Treasurer for so long a time, his reply was, " By being a willow and not an oak." A portion of this noble old mansion, though deformed by modern alterations and divided into warehouses, remained as late as 1844.

Then east from the Carriers' Row is a long and high wall of stone, inclosing the north side of a large garden adjoining to as large an house built in the reign of King Henry VIII. and of Edward VI. by Sir William Powlet, Lord Treasurer of England. Through this garden, which of old time consisted of divers parts, now united, was sometimes a fair footway, leading by the west end of the Augustine Friars' church straight north, and opened somewhat west from Allhallows church against London Wall towards Moorgate; which footway had gates at either end, locked up every night: but now the same way being taken into those gardens, the gates are closed up with stone, whereby the people are forced to go about by St. Peter's church, and the east end of the said Friar's church, and all the great place and garden of Sir William Powlet to London Wall and so to Moorgate. This great house . . . stretcheth to the north corner of Brode [Broad] Street, and then turneth up Brode Street, and all that side to and beyond the east end of the said Friars' church.—*Stow*, p. 66.

Winchester House, CHELSEA, the palace of the Bishops of Winchester from 1663 to 1820, was situated across what is now the river end of Oakley Street. It was a large red brick building erected by James, Duke of Hamilton, in the reign of Charles I., and formed a continuation of the Manor House. It was bought by Government for the see of Winchester, when the old palace at Southwark was given up, under powers of an Act of Parliament in 1663. Bishop North died here in 1820, and the house was then sold to the Lord of the Manor. It was pulled down soon afterwards.

Winchester House, SOUTHWARK. In 1107 William Giffard, Bishop of Winchester and also Lord Chancellor, built this spacious palace on the Bankside, to the west of St. Mary Overies, on a plot of ground belonging to the priory of Bermondsey, and it became the town residence of the Bishops of Winchester for five hundred and thirty years. During a vacancy in the see it was assigned as a residence to Simon de Montfort and his wife, the daughter of King John. In 1424 James Stuart, King of Scotland, liberated from his prison, was married to Johanna Beaufort, and the wedding feast was held at the house of her uncle, Cardinal Beaufort, who was then Bishop of Winchester. In 1427 the Cardinal, returning from beyond sea, was met by the mayor, aldermen and citizens, and conducted with much pomp to Southwark. In May 1451 William Waynflete, "in a certain lofty roome commonly called *le Peynted Chamber* in his manor house of Southwark," made a solemn declaration regarding his tenure of the see of Winchester.[1] Gardiner, in his turn, lived here in great style. He had a number of young gentlemen of family as his pages, whose education he superintended. His establishment was the last of the sort in England, as after the Reformation the bishops' palaces were mostly occupied by their families (*Lord Campbell*).

[1] *Life of Bishop Waynflete*, p. 66.

In 1551 Gardiner was imprisoned in his own house, and in the next year he entertained at a great feast the Ambassador of Spain and the Council in the same place. In 1554 he was dead: "There are grand obsequies a sermon and a mass, after which the peple go to his place to dener."

Stow (1598) describes Winchester House as "a very fair house, well repaired," with "a large wharf and a landing place called the Bishop of Winchester's Stairs," shown by Rocque in his map of 1726 as St. Mary Overy's Stairs, and only closed of late years. The principal frontage of the palace was towards the river. It was bounded south and west by gardens decorated with statues and fountains, and by a park of about 70 acres, which extended to the manor of Paris Garden.

The last bishop of the see who lived at Winchester House was Lancelot Andrewes, who died here in 1626, and was buried at St. Saviour's Church in the so-called bishop's chapel.

Winchester House has been occupied by several persons either as a residence or as a prison. Sir Edward Dyer, the poet, and friend of Sir Philip Sidney.

I have been this morning to Winchester House to seek you.—*Robert, Earl of Essex to Mr. Dyer,* July 21, 1587.

Add hereunto that very lately by a wind-furnace greene glass for windows is made as well by pit-coale at Winchester House in Southwarke as it is done in other places with much wast and consuming of infinite store of billetts and other wood-feull. —Sturtevant's *Metallica,* 1612, p. 4 (ed. 1858).

In 1642 the Parliament converted Winchester House into a prison, and among the prisoners confined in it was Sir Kenelm Digby, who here wrote his *Critical Remarks on Sir Thomas Browne's Religio Medici.* His letter to Browne is dated "Winchester House, March 20, 1642."

Sir Kenelm Digby was several times taken and let go again ; at last imprisoned in Winchester House. I can compare him to nothing but a great fish that we catch and let go again, but still he will come to the bait ; at last therefore we put him into some great pond for store.—Selden's *Table Talk.*

For a time it was the home of Lieut.-Col. Lilburne. In 1649 he was allowed to leave his prison in the Tower to visit his sick and distressed family at Winchester House, "mine own house in Southwark." In 1647 the manor and Winchester House were sold to Thomas Walker of Camberwell for £4380 : 8 : 3, but at the Restoration it reverted to the See. The bishops, however, no longer used it as a residence, and an Act was passed in 1663 permitting them to let it in tenements. The park was dismantled in this year, and a noble old tree furnished timber for seven houses in Gracechurch Street.

In 1814 a great fire destroyed nearly all the remains of this once noble place, and there were disclosed the solid and noble proportions of the great hall, and the remains of a fine circular window. The site is now covered with wharves, warehouses and other business premises.

Winchester Street, CITY, BROAD STREET to LONDON WALL, was so called after Paulet or Winchester House. [*See* Winchester House.]

John Archer, the author of *Every Man his own Physician*, 1673, lived at the "Golden Ball, Winchester Street, near Broad Street." In this work he makes the number of the senses six. Edmund Halley, the astronomer, was the son of a soap-boiler in this street, but was born at his father's country house at Haggerstone. The earliest of his published observations were made, July 25, 1675, on an eclipse of the moon, from the house in Winchester Street. Richard Gough, the antiquary, in the obituary notice which he himself selected for insertion in the *Gentleman's Magazine*, is stated to have been born in 1735 "in a large house in Winchester Street, London, on the site of the Monastery of Austin Friars." The houses, including some large recent blocks of many-storied "Buildings," are now mostly occupied as offices and chambers by merchants, solicitors, commercial and mining companies, and the like. In Great Winchester Street is Pinners' Hall; in Little Winchester Street was the Greek Church, with an entrance in London Wall, pulled down and removed to Bayswater.

Windham Club, ST. JAMES'S SQUARE, established in 1828. The object of the Club, as stated in Rule I., "is to secure a convenient and agreeable place of meeting for a society of gentlemen, all connected with each other by a common bond of literary or personal acquaintance." The number of members is limited to 650. Election is by ballot; one black ball in ten excludes. Admission fee 30 guineas, and 1 guinea to the library fund; annual payment 10 pounds.

Windmill Street, FINSBURY SQUARE, the north-west corner to CASTLE STREET, was so called after three windmills, erected in the reign of Queen Elizabeth, on a deposit made in Finsbury field of "more than one thousand cartloads" of bones removed from the charnel of old St. Paul's when the charnel-house was destroyed in 1549 by order of the Duke of Somerset. On these bones "the soilage of the city," as Stow calls it, was subsequently laid, and the three windmills "in short space after raised."[1] It was also for some years used as a burial-place for criminals who had perished at the hands of the hangman. Middleton alludes to these windmills in his *Father Hubbard's Tales*,[2] and Shirley in his play of *The Wedding*,[3] though neither Gifford nor Dyce appears to have understood the reference. Agas represents them in his map. The royal foundry for casting cannon in the reign of George I. was situated on Windmill Hill, in Upper Moorfields.

Windmill Street (Great), PICCADILLY, leading from the west end of Coventry Street to Pulteney Street, derives its name from a windmill represented in Faithorne's map of London, 1658, which windmill gave its name to certain fields mentioned in a printed proclamation of April 7, 1671: "The fields, commonly called the Windmill Fields,

[1] *Stow*, pp. 125, 159; *Strype*, B. iv. p. 102.   [2] *Middleton's Works*, by Dyce, vol. v. p. 592.
[3] *Shirley's Works*, by Gifford, vol. i. p. 421.

Dog Fields, and the fields adjoining to So Hoe." Windmill Street was, however, then laid out. In 1671 Colonel Panton craved license to

Build and finish certain houses in the continuation of a street called *Windmill Street*, from the upper end of the Haymarket to the highway leading from Soho to Ayre Street and Paddington; on the east corner towards the Haymarket, about 100 feet in front, also on the same side about 200 feet in front, opposite *Windmill Yard*; and to build on both sides a short street, leading from out of Windmill Street, opposite Windmill Yard, towards St. Giles's, on the west side of Windmill Street, in the two bowling-greens, between the Haymarket and Leicester Fields.—*Trans. of Privy Council*, Elmes's Wren, p. 305.

Eminent Inhabitants.—Colonel Charles Godfrey, in 1683; he married Arabella Churchill, mistress of James II. and mother of the Duke of Berwick. Sir John Shadwell, in 1729, a celebrated physician of his time, and son of Shadwell, the poet laureate. Dr. William Hunter, in the large house on the east side still standing and incorporated with the Lyric Theatre; the doctor in this house closed his life, March 30, 1783, with a memorable speech: "If I had strength enough," said he, "to hold a pen, I would write how easy and pleasant a thing it is to die."

Having failed in his application to Government for a site in the Mews, William Hunter purchased this piece of ground, and on it built a spacious house, into which he removed in 1770. Attached to the house were dissecting rooms and a museum of anatomical and pathological preparations at the time unrivalled. Here he established a school of anatomy, his famous brother, John Hunter, being his assistant first and afterwards his partner. Hunter bequeathed the museum to Dr. Baillie, with the reversion after his death to Glasgow University. Mr. Wilson, who later became proprietor of the "School of Anatomy, Great Windmill Street," offered in 1812 to sell the whole establishment to Charles Bell for £10,000. Bell purchased it for a much less sum, and he speaks of it as "an institution which, founded by the Hunters, has made all the anatomists of the present day, at home and abroad." The museum (largely augmented by him) was sold by Sir Charles Bell, about 1825, to the Edinburgh College of Surgeons, who built a spacious hall for its reception. Bell removed to Edinburgh in 1826. On the east side of Great Windmill Street is St. Peter's Church, designed by Raphael Brandon, and next to it the dancing saloon, called the Argyll Rooms, existed for some years.

Windmill Street, TOTTENHAM COURT ROAD to CHARLOTTE STREET, was so named from a windmill which stood in the fields at the west end of the street. Nollekens, the sculptor, when an old man, walking one day with J. T. Smith, "stopped at the corner of Rathbone Place, and observed that when he was a little boy, his mother often took him to the top of that street to walk by the side of a long pond, near a windmill which then stood on the site of the chapel in Charlotte Street; and that a halfpenny was paid by every person at a hatch belonging to the miller for the privilege of walking in his grounds."[1]

[1] Smith, *Life of Nollekens*, vol. i. p. 37.

In Smith's day "Windmill Street was strongly recommended by physicians for the salubrity of the air."[1] Maitland, writing in 1756, describes the Middlesex Hospital as being in this street. It was established here in "two convenient houses adjoining each other" in 1745, and removed to its present site "in Marybon fields" in the year in which Maitland wrote.

Windmill Tavern, OLD JEWRY, a noted tavern at the corner of Old Jewry and Lothbury. Stow says it had originally been a synagogue; and, in 1291, when Edward I. banished the Jews from England, it was made over to a new order of friars called *De Pænitentia Jesu*, or *Fratres de Sacca*. From them it passed in 1305 to Robert Fitzwalter; and from him to Robert Lange, mercer, Lord Mayor in 1439, and to Hugh Clopton, mercer, who kept his mayoralty there in 1492.

It is now a tavern and hath to sign a Windmill and thus much for this house, sometime the Jews' synagogue, since a house of friars, then a nobleman's house, after that a merchant's house, wherein mayoralties have been kept, and now a wine tavern. —*Stow*, p. 105.

In 1522, when arrangements were being made for the reception of the Emperor Charles V., "the *Wyndemylne* in the Old Jury" was set down as being able to supply fourteen feather-beds, and stabling for twenty horses. *Wellbred*, in the first act of *Every Man in his Humour*, dates a letter "from the Windmill," and asks *Young Knowell* whether he has "forsworn all his friends in the Old Jewry," and whether he has "conceived that antipathy between us and Hogsden as was between Jews and hog's flesh." In 1628, when the wretched Dr. Lamb, the Duke of Buckingham's "devil," was pursued by the mob from the Fortune Theatre through Moorgate into Old Jewry, he took refuge in this tavern, but after a time was thrust out by the vintner, and so maltreated that he died at the Compter the next day.

Windsor Court, MONKWELL STREET. James Percy, the trunk-maker of Dublin, was living here when pressing his claim to the peerage of Northumberland. His pursuit, which he followed up for twenty years, ended by his being ordered, in 1689, by the House of Lords to wear on his breast before the Four Courts in Westminster Hall, a paper inscribed, "The false and impudent Pretender to the Earldom of Northumberland." The order was carried out. His son, Anthony, is said to have been subsequently Lord Mayor of Dublin.[2]

Wine Office Court, FLEET STREET.

About the middle of the year 1760, he [Goldsmith] left Green Arbour Court for respectable lodgings in Wine Office Court, Fleet Street, where for about two years he remained with an acquaintance or relation of the friendly bookseller, Newbery. Here he was often visited by Dr. Percy.—Prior's *Life of Goldsmith*, vol. i. p. 368.

Here Johnson and Percy supped with him on May 31, 1761. Percy called for Johnson on his way, and found him dressed in a new suit of clothes and well-powdered wig. Noticing his unusual smartness John-

---
[1] *Recollections*, p. 25.   [2] *See* Craik's *Romance of the Peerage*, vol. iv. p. 312.

son said, "Sir, Goldsmith is a great sloven and justifies his disregard of propriety by my practice. To-night I desire to show him a better example." Mr. Forster says that the *Vicar of Wakefield* was written here. On the right, in this court, is the Old Cheshire Cheese, one of the oldest, and for many years the most popular, of our London chop-houses.

Woburn Square, between RUSSELL SQUARE and GORDON SQUARE, was originally intended to be called Rothesay Square.[1] Mrs. Bentley, the actress, died at her house in this square, January 14, 1850, in her sixty-fifth year. Christ Church, on the east side of the square, was designed by Lewis Vulliamy, architect.

Wonder (The), a Tavern near LUDGATE, which Roger North mentions as frequented by his celebrated brother, Sir Dudley North, who "loved a chirping glass in an evening." On one occasion, when he had been taking more than enough of these *chirping glasses* "with the citizens then called Tories," he met with an accident which had nearly proved fatal.

Wood Street, CHEAPSIDE, runs from Cheapside into London Wall. Stow has two suppositions about the origin of the name: first, that it was so called because it was built throughout of *wood;* and secondly, and more probably, that it was so called after Thomas Wood, one of the sheriffs in the year 1491, who dwelt in this street, an especial benefactor to the church of *St. Peter-in-Cheap,* and the individual at whose expense "the beautiful front of houses in Cheap over against Wood Street end were built." "His predecessors," says Stow, "might be the first builders, owners, and namers of this street."[2] Entering Wood Street from Cheapside, the yard on the left, with a tree in it, marks the site of the church of *St. Peter-in-Cheap.* For many years a pair of rooks built their nest in this tree. The Cross Keys Inn derives its name from the church of St. Peter. A little higher up, on the right-hand side (where the street indents a little), stood *Wood Street Compter.* At the corner of *Hugin Lane* (so called of one Hugan, who dwelt there) is the church of *St. Michael, Wood Street,* the final repository of the head of James IV., who fell at Flodden. *Gresham Street,* lying to the right, was called *Lad Lane,* or *Ladle Lane ;* and that part lying to left, Maiden Lane, from a sign of the Virgin. Still higher up on the right, and at the corner of *Love Lane,* is the church of *St. Alban, Wood Street.* In 1569 the Dean and Chapter of St. Paul's leased three houses in Wood Street to the Corporation *in reversion for ninety-nine years after* 1602, at the rent of £8 per annum.[3] In Strype's time the street was famous for the manufacture of wedding-cakes.[4]

February 29, 1663-1664.—To one Royall, a stone cutter, over against the Spur, at the upper end of Wood Street. I eat for my dinner a Wood-street cake, which cakes are famous for being well made.—*Journal of Sir Thomas Browne's Son, Edward* (Browne's *Works,* i. 52).

---

[1] Dobie's *St. Giles,* p. 199. [2] *Stow,* p. 3. [3] *Cal. State Papers,* 1547-1580, p. 377.
[4] *Strype,* B. iii. p. 91.

The street is now largely occupied by warehouses (drapery, lace, silk, and hosiery), many of the warehouses being spacious and costly structures.

Sir John Cheke, who taught "Cambridge and King Edward Greek," died from shame at his own moral cowardice in renouncing Protestantism on September 13, 1557, at the house of his friend, Mr. Peter Osborne, in Wood Street. There is a letter from him of July 16, 1657, "from my house in Wood Streete." In 1645-1648 Dr. Wallis and other eminent scientific men used to meet weekly at the house of Dr. Goddard in Wood Street, "on account of his having a workman skilled in grinding glasses for microscopes and telescopes." Thomas Ripley, the architect (d. 1758), kept in early life a carpenter's shop and a coffee-house in this street.[1] *Cheapside Cross* stood at *Wood Street* end. Here proclamations continued to be read long after the cross was taken down. The Castle here, on the east side, is mentioned in 1684 as one of the most important of London inns. It is still standing, and is used as an office for Pickford vans.

> At the corner of Wood Street, when daylight appears,
> Hangs a thrush that sings loud, it has sung for three years:
> Poor Susan has passed by the spot, and has heard
> In the silence of morning, the song of the Bird.
>
> 'Tis a note of enchantment; what ails her? She sees
> A mountain ascending, a vision of trees;
> Bright volumes of vapour through Lothbury glide,
> And a river flows on through the vale of Cheapside.

Wordsworth, *The Reverie of Poor Susan*, 1797 (*Works*, vol. ii. p. 95).

Wood Street Compter was first established in 1555, when, on the feast of St. Michael the Archangel in that year, the prisoners were removed from the old Compter in Bread Street to the new Compter in Wood Street, Cheapside.[2] This Compter was burnt down in the Great Fire.[3] It stood on the east side of the street, where the houses recede a little, and was removed to *Giltspur Street* in 1791. There were two Compters in London: the Compter in Wood Street, under the control of one of the sheriffs, and the Compter in the Poultry, under the superintendence of the other. Under each sheriff was a secondary, a clerk of the papers, four clerk sitters, eighteen serjeants-at-mace (each serjeant having his yeoman), a master keeper, and two turnkeys. The serjeants wore blue-coloured cloth gowns, and the words of arrest were, "Sir, we arrest you in the King's Majesty's name, and we charge you to obey us." In the reign of Henry VI. it was ordered that the sheriffs might exact payment from prisoners electing to be in "the Compter rather than go to Newgate or to Ludgate . . . four pence, six pence, eight pence, or twelve pence per week each person, towards the rent of the said house, without more."[4] But this tariff speedily fell into oblivion. There were three sides: the knights' ward (the dearest of all), the master's side (a little cheaper), and the Hole (the cheapest of all). The register of entries was called The

---

[1] Hawkins's *Life of Johnson*, p. 375.　　[2] *Stow*, p. 3.
[3] Of the building erected after the Fire, there is a view by J. T. Smith.　　[4] *Liber Albus*, p. 447.

Black Book. *Garnish* was demanded at every step, and the hall, at least the hall of the Wood Street Compter, was hung with the story of the Prodigal Son.[1]

The scene of *The Counter Scuffle*, a piece of low humour inserted in Dryden's *Third Miscellany*, and quoted by Scott in the *Fortunes of Nigel*, is laid in Wood Street Compter. One of the most amusing passages in the novel is founded on it :—

> And now let each one listen well,
> While I the famous battel tell
> In Wood Street Counter that befell
> In High Lent.
>
> *Alex.* Sir Davy send your Son to Wood Street College,
> A Gentleman can nowhere get more knowledge.
> *Sir Davy.* There Gallants study hard.
>   Decker, *The Roaring Girle*, vol. iii. p. 189.

Wooden Bridge, PIMLICO, the old bridge over the principal "cut" in the great Pimlico marsh—now drained and dry. This is the bridge to which Flaxman refers in the following description of the residence in 1807 of Anker Smith, the celebrated engraver: "In case you should desire to know his address, it is above the Water-works, nearer to the Bridge, on the opposite side of the road, Chelsea, name on the door." [*See* Jenny's Whim.] The bridge exists still in a vastly altered form as *Ebury Bridge*.

Woodmongers' Hall, DUKE'S PLACE, ALDGATE.

After the fall of the church [Trinity Church, Duke's Place] the inhabitants had service in the Woodmongers' Hall, then called the Duke's Hall, in Duke's Place.— *Cal. Jac. Dom. Add.*, p. 648.

The ancient fraternity of Woodmongers or Fuellers, who were also the vendors of sea coal, were incorporated as a company, 3 James I. (August 29, 1605), and were entrusted with the government of the cars and carts to be employed in the City and Liberties of London; but on complaints of the carmen and others this trust was taken from them and given to the President and Governors of Christ's Hospital. In 1665 the Company surrendered their Charter, but by an Act of the Common Council in 1694, they obtained the privilege of keeping 120 carts "for the more effectual carrying on their business" (*Strype, Maitland*, etc.) The Company has long been practically extinct, or merged in that of the Carmen.

Woodstock Street, on the south side of OXFORD STREET, between New Bond Street and South Molton Street. Dr. Johnson was living in this street in the year 1737.[2]

Woodyard (The), WHITEHALL, an outlying portion of the palace, between the Thames and Scotland Yard. In Vertue's plan it is sur-

---

[1] "*The Compter's Commonwealth*, by William Fennor, his Majesty's servant," 4to, 1617 ; *Strype*, B. iii. p. 51 ; Dodsley's *Old Plays*, ed. Collier, vol. v. p. 43 ; Heywood's play of the *Fair Maid of the Exchange*; and Dyce's *Middleton*, vol. i. p. 392.
[2] Croker's *Boswell*, p. 30.

rounded by buildings—the Small Beer Buttery, the Great Bakehouse, the Queen's Bakehouse, the Charcoal House, the Spicery, the Cyder House, etc. On the west side is "Lady Churchill's Laundry," and on the east a set of apartments belonging to Mrs. Churchill (mother of the Duke of Berwick).

September 12, 1676.—To London, to take order about the building of an house, or rather an apartment, which had all the conveniences of an house, for my deare friende, Mr. Godolphin and lady, which I undertooke to contrive and survey, and employ workmen, till it should be quite finished; it being just over against his Majestie's Woodyard by the Thames side, leading to Scotland Yard.—*Evelyn.*

Woolmen, Company of, ranks forty-third in the City Companies. The fraternity of Woolmen, sometimes called Woolmongers, was established by prescription in the 2d Edward IV., 1462, and empowered to grant licences to woolwinders in the City and Liberties—the last licence so granted being in 1770. The Company has no hall, but obtained a grant of livery from the Court of Aldermen in 1825.

Woolsack (The), a tavern WITHOUT ALDGATE, famous for its pies. Ben Jonson mentions it in *The Alchemist,* and in *The Devil is an Ass;* and Machyn records that its "goodman" was carried to the Tower early in the morning of July 20, 1555. There are 17th-century tokens of a Woolsack in Houndsditch, perhaps the same.

Woolstaple (The), WESTMINSTER, occupied as nearly as possible the site of the present Bridge Street, outside the north wall of New Palace Yard. Wool was in the 13th and 14th centuries the great article of export from England, and the war-making Plantagenets kept the trade in it under their immediate control. Stow says that the staple was here in the reign of Edward I., and that the merchants of the staple with the parishioners of St. Margaret's "built of new the said church, the great chancel excepted, which was lately before new built by the Abbot of Westminster." By 17 Edward III. (1343) it was enacted that "no silver be carried out of the realm on pain of death; and that whosoever transporteth wool should bring over for every sack four nobles of silver bullion." Edward was preparing at this time for his great invasion of France. Ten years later (1353), by a new Act, the staple of wool, before kept at Bruges, was ordained to be kept at Westminster, to begin on "the next morrow after the Feast of St. Peter ad Vincula" (August 1), to the "great benefit of the King," says Stow, "and loss unto strangers and merchants; for there grew unto the King by this means (as it was said) the sum of one thousand one hundred and two pounds by the year more than any his predecessors had received." Next year the Parliament granted the King, for the prosecution of the French war, "fifty shillings of every sack of wool transported over seas, for the space of six years next ensuing." At this time all wool sent from London had to be brought for "trowage" to the Westminster Woolstaple. The imposition was in no long time remitted in favour of the City of London; but as late as Henry VI. the King had "six wool-houses within the Staple at Westminster," which he granted to the Dean and Canons of St. Stephen at Westminster.[1] Out of this endowment, apparently, Henry VIII. founded on the site St. Stephen's Hospital for eight maimed soldiers. This was removed in 1735, and eight almshouses built in St. Anne's Lane, bearing the inscription, "Woolstaple Pensioners, 1741."[2]

Ben Jonson, in enumerating Westminster localities, speaks of "Tuttle Street, and both the Alm'ries, the two Sanctuaries, long and round, *Woolstaple*, with Kinges Street and Cannon Row to boot."[3]

Worcester House, in the STRAND, stood on the site of the present *Beaufort Buildings*. An earlier Worcester House was in St. James, Garlickhithe, overhanging the river.[4] The Strand house originally belonged to the see of Carlisle, but, at the Reformation, was presented by the Crown to the noble founder of the Bedford family. Under the Earls of Bedford it was known as *Bedford* or *Russell House*, a name which it bore till the family moved over the way and built a second *Bedford House*, on the site of the present Southampton Street, when the inn of the see of Carlisle took the name of its new occupant, Edward, second Marquis of Worcester, the Earl of Glamorgan of the Civil Wars, and the author of the *Century of Inventions*. The Marquis of Worcester died in 1667, and his son Henry was created, in 1682, Duke of Beaufort; hence *Beaufort Buildings*. During the Commonwealth, Worcester House in the Strand was used for committees of all kinds, and furnished by Parliament for the Scotch commissioners.[5] Subsequently, according to Whitelocke, it was sold by Parliament to the Earl of Salisbury, "at the rate of Bishop's Lands."[6] But on May 2, 1657, there was brought into Parliament a "Bill for settling of Worcester House in the Strand upon Margaret Countess of Worcester, during the life of Edward Earl of Worcester"; and on April 14, 1659, it was resolved that " Margaret Countess of Worcester, shall have the actual possession of Worcester House delivered up to her on March 25 next; and in the mean time the rent of £300 be paid her for the said house for this year; and that the sum of £400 be paid in recompense of all demands for detaining of Worcester House from her since her title thereunto by the late Acts of Parliament."[7] Twelve days after the entrance of Charles II. into London on his Restoration, the Marquis of Worcester wrote and offered his house (free of rent) to the great Lord Clarendon.

In a word, if that your Lordship pleased to accept of me, I am the most real and affectionate servant, and as a little token of it, be pleased to accept of Worcester House to live in, far more commodious for your Lordship than where you now are [Dorset House], though not in so good reparation, but such as it is, without requiring from your Lordship one penny rent (yet that only known between your Lordship

---

[1] *Stow*, pp. 168, 169.
[2] Wallcot, *Memorials of Westminster*, p. 79.
[3] Ben Jonson, *Staple of News*, Act iii. Sc. 2.
[4] Machyn's *Diary*, p. 301; *Stow*.
[5] *Whitelocke*, ed. 1732, p. 80.
[6] *Ibid.* p. 289.
[7] Burton's *Diary*.

and me). It is during my life at your service, for I am but a tenant in tail; but were my interest longer, it should be as readily at your Lordship's command.—*Marquis of Worcester to Lord Clarendon* (Lister, vol. iii. p. 108).

The Chancellor leased the house of the marquis, as he tells us in his *Life*, at a yearly rent of £500; and here, in Worcester House, on September 3, 1660, between eleven and two at night, Anne Hyde, the Chancellor's daughter, was married to the Duke of York, according to the rites of the English Church.

> *December* 22, 1660.—The marriage of the Chancellor's daughter being now newly owned, I went to see her. . . . She was now at her father's at Worcester House in the Strand. We all kiss'd her hand, as did also my Lord Chamberlain (Manchester) and Countess of Northumberland. This was a strange change—can it succeed well?—*Evelyn.*

The Chancellor was surrounded by all sorts of seekers — "the creatures of Worcester House," as they are called by Mrs. Hutchinson in her Memoirs of her husband. After Clarendon's removal to his new house in Piccadilly, near the top of St. James's Street, Worcester House would appear to have been left unoccupied, or let for installations and state receptions. On August 26, 1669, the Duke of Ormond was installed Chancellor of the University of Oxford, and on September 3, 1674, the Duke of Monmouth Chancellor of the University of Cambridge, in this house. The great hall is mentioned by Pepys (August 20, 1660), and the "Conference at Worcester House betwixt the Episcopal and the Nonconformist Divines, by His Majesty's Commission," of the reign of Charles II., by Andrew Marvell in his *Rehearsal Transprosed*.[1]

Worcester Place, the residence of John Tiptoft, Earl of Worcester, Lord High Treasurer of England, stood near Vintner's Hall, Upper Thames Street (1485).

Worship Street, SHOREDITCH, to FINSBURY SQUARE and CITY ROAD; formerly *Hog Lane*. It appears as Worship Street in *Dodsley*, 1761, but in a map dated 1767 it is still figured as Hog Lane. The name was perhaps changed out of compliment to Wesley's place of *Worship* in the Old Foundry, which occupied the site of the present Providence Row. The name is now solely suggestive of the Police Court.

> And sure enough at *Worship Street*
> That Friday week they stood;
> She said *had* language he had used—
> And thus she made it *good.*—THOMAS HOOD.

Wyan's Court—in *Maitland*, 1739, and *Dodsley*, 1761, called WYNAM'S COURT—GREAT RUSSELL STREET, BLOOMSBURY. In this court (it no longer exists) lived Lewis Theobald, the editor of *Shakespeare*, and the hero of the early editions of *The Dunciad*. There is a long letter written by him in defence of his notes on *Shakespeare*, dated, "Wyan's Court, in Great Russell Street, April 16, 1729." In this court also lived Elizabeth Thomas, "Curll's Corinna," the go-

[1] Ed. 1674, part ii. p. 344.

between in the publication of Pope's letters to Cromwell, and in consequence condemned to everlasting infamy in the *Dunciad.*

Wych Street, DRURY LANE. The old name for Drury Lane was *Via de Aldewych;* hence Wych Street, a street in continuation of Drury Lane.[1] Among the St. Paul's MSS., calendared by H. C. Maxwell Lyte (Appendix to *Ninth Report Hist. MSS. Comm.*, p. 7), is an "acquittance of the dean and chapter of St. Paul's for rent issuing from a new garden lately belonging to John Bosham, adjoining his great inn in Aldewych *extra la Temple Barre* on which three houses formerly stood. 6 Henry IV." From the Angel Inn, at the bottom of this street, Bishop Hooper was taken to his martyrdom at Gloucester in 1554. Zachary Macaulay gives Wilberforce (November 21, 1795) an amusing narrative of the proceedings at a "Debating Society in Wych Street, Drury Lane."[2] Mark Lemon, the dramatic writer, and for many years editor of *Punch*, was previously for some years landlord of the Shakespeare's Head, No. 31 Wych Street, and under his genial rule it became a very favourite resort of actors, dramatic critics and journalists. Douglas Jerrold and Charles Dickens shining the bright particular stars of the Drury empyrean. Most of the old houses have been pulled down and rebuilt.

York Buildings, STRAND, a general name for the streets and houses erected on the site of old York House, but now restricted to one street, which was originally named George Street. Here was established by patent, 27 Charles II., p. 11, n. 11, the "York Waterworks," designed to supply the west end of London with water from the Thames. In 1690 the works were burnt down and re-erected, and in 1691 an Act of 2 and 3 William and Mary was obtained, by which the proprietors of the waterworks were incorporated under the name of "the Governor and Company of Undertakers for raising the Thames water in York Buildings." Savery's fire-engine was set up here, but proved a failure, and was reconstructed by Smeaton on the Newcomen model.[3] The works resulted in a heavy loss. There are several engraved views of the waterworks. About 1719 the Company's charter was used for a different purpose from that for which it was granted, and the forfeited estates of the Jacobites were purchased at a very small sum by the Company. In consequence of these proceedings the £10 shares rose in value to £305.

> You that are blest with wealth, by your Creator,
> And want to drown your money in Thames Water,
> Buy but York Buildings, and the cistern there,
> Will sink more pence than any fool can spare.

South Sea Playing Cards (Five of Spades), *Notes and Queries*, vol. v. (1852), p. 217.

In 1829 the Corporation was dissolved by Act of Parliament. A full account of the curious proceedings here alluded to is given in a pamphlet by David Murray (*The York Buildings Company, a Chapter*

---
[1] Parton, *Hist. of St. Giles-in-the-Fields*, p. 113. [2] Wilberforce Corr., vol. i. p. 118.
[3] Smiles, *Boulton and Watt*, pp. 56, 57, 206, 216, 217.

in *Scotch History*, Glasgow, 1883). *Eminent Inhabitants.*—Peter the Great, in 1698, "in a large house at the bottom of York Buildings," now occupied by the Charity Organisation Society, and numbered 15 Buckingham Street. There are some fine painted ceilings in the house. Robert Harley, Earl of Oxford, in 1708, "in York Buildings, near the water-side"; Samuel Pepys. [*See* Buckingham Street, Strand.] Plate 22 of Boydell's *Views* affords a peep of Mr. Pepys's house; and in his printed *Diary* an engraving of the interior of his library. These houses are now chiefly occupied as chambers.

York Column, CARLTON GARDENS, a column of Scotch granite, erected (1830-1833) by public subscription, and surmounted with a bronze statue of the Duke of York, the second son of George III. The column, 124 feet high, was designed by Mr. B. Wyatt, and the statue, 14 feet high, executed by Sir Richard Westmacott. There is a staircase to a gallery affording a fine view of the west end of London and the Surrey Hills, but during the last few years no one has been allowed to ascend.

York House, BATTERSEA. In the reign of Edward IV. Lawrence Booth, afterwards Archbishop of York, bought one moiety, nearly 400 acres, of the estate belonging to the Stanley family, in this parish. This he annexed to the see of York, and built a house by the Thames as a residence for the archbishops in their visits to the south. It continued to be occasionally used by them down to the end of the 17th century, after which it was let to tenants. Under the Parliament it was seized and sold to Sir Allen Apsley and Colonel Hutchinson for £1806, but was reclaimed by the see after the Restoration. All signs of the old house have disappeared, but its memory is preserved in York Road.

York House, CITY. Baynard's Castle was known for a period by this name, no doubt from having been, after the death of Humphrey, Duke of Gloucester, granted by Henry VI. to Richard, Duke of York, who, writes Stow, "in the year 1457, lodged there as in his own house." [*See* Baynard's Castle.]

York House, STABLE YARD, ST. JAMES'S. Built by Frederick, Duke of York, second son of George III., on a piece of ground leased from the Crown for 999 years, from October 10, 1825, at the yearly rent of £758 : 15s., and sold in 1841 to the Marquis of Stafford (afterwards Duke of Sutherland) for £72,000. [*See* Stafford House.]

York House, in the STRAND, or YORK PLACE, CHARING CROSS, an old London lodging of the Archbishops of York, obtained by Heath, Archbishop of York and Lord Chancellor in Queen Mary's reign, in exchange for Suffolk House, in Southwark, presented to the see of York by Queen Mary, "in recompense of Yorke House [Whitehall], near to Westminster, which King Henry, her father, had taken from Cardinal Wolsey, and from the see of York."[1]

The said Archbishop, August 6, 1557, obtained a license for the alienation of this capital messuage of Suffolk Place; and to apply the price thereof for the buying of other houses called also Suffolk Place, lying near Charing Cross; as appears from a register belonging to the Dean and Chapter of York.—*Strype*, B. iv. p. 17.

This York House does not appear to have been inhabited by any Archbishop of York except Heath, and by him only for a very short time. Young, Grindall, Sandys, Piers, and Hutton, successively Archbishops of York (1561 and 1606), appear to have let it to the Lord Keepers of the Great Seal. Lord Chancellor Bacon, the son of Sir Nicholas Bacon, Lord Keeper, was born at York House, in the Strand, in 1560-1561, and here his father, the Lord Keeper, died in 1579. Lord Keeper Puckering died here in 1596; Lord Chancellor Egerton in 1616-1617. The Commissioners to inquire into the cause of the death of Sir Thomas Overbury sat at York House; and from here are dated the Orders, October 17, 1615, to Somerset "to keep his chamber near the Cockpit," and to his countess "to keep her chamber at the Blackfriars, or at Lord Knollys's house near the Tiltyard."

An attempt was made, in 1588, to obtain the House from Queen Elizabeth, probably by the Earl of Essex, to whom the custody of the House was subsequently committed, as Norden mentions in his *Survey of Middlesex*. Strype has printed part of a secret letter from Archbishop Sandys to Lord Burghley, entreating his lordship "to be a means to the Queen that he might refuse his yielding therein."[2] The Earl of Essex, when committed to the charge of Lord Keeper Egerton, was for six months—October 6, 1599 to March 20, 1600—under surveillance or ward in York House. When the Duke of Lennox wished to bargain for his life interest in York House, Lord Bacon replied: "For this you will pardon me: York House is the house wherein my father died, and wherein I first breathed, and there will I yield my last breath, if so please God and the King will give me leave."[3]

Bacon's Latin letter to the University of Cambridge, on sending them his *Novum Organon*, is dated *Ex Ædibus Eborac*. 3*mo October* 1620. Aubrey says that Bacon built an aviary at York House which cost him £300; but the story of his jesting with the fishermen, which Aubrey says occurred in the garden here, Bacon himself places at Chelsea.[4] It was from York House that, May 1, 1621, the Great Seal was "fetched from" Lord Bacon. A few months later the disgraced Chancellor had "leave to repair to York House for a fortnight, but remained so long that he had warning to return to Gorhambury."[5] The next summer (July 1, 1622) we find that "Viscount St. Albans has filed a bill in Chancery against Buckingham, on account of the non-performance of his contract for taking York House."[6] Somehow York

[1] *Stow*, p. 153.
[2] *Strype*, B. vi. p. 3.
[3] Letter in *Lamb MSS.*, vol. viii. No. 936.
[4] Aubrey, *Lives*, vol. ii. pp. 223, 224; Bacon, *Apoph.*, p. 95.
[5] *Cal. State Papers*, 1619-1623, p. 301.
[6] *Ibid*, p. 418.

House passed to Buckingham, the first Duke of the Villiers family. He obtained it not apparently from Bacon, having, as was said, "borrowed" it of Archbishop Matthew, till such time as he could persuade him "to accept as good a seat as that was in lieu of the same, which could not be so soon compassed, as the Duke of Buckingham had occasion to make use of rooms for the entertainment of foreign princes."[1] An exchange, however, was subsequently effected.

May 15, 1624.—Whitson-Eve. The Bill passed in Parliament for the King to have York House in exchange for other lands. This was for the Lord Duke of Buckingham.—Archbishop Laud's *Diary*.[2]

The duke pulled down the house and erected a large and temporary structure to supply its place, the walls of which were "covered with huge panes of glasse," as mirrors were then rather commonly called.[3] The Water Gate, on the margin of the Thames, at the bottom of Buckingham Street, which, though nearly entombed by the Thames Embankment, still remains to show the stately scale on which the whole house was designed to have been erected, is attributed to Inigo Jones.

I am confident there are some that live, who will not deny that they have heard the King of blessed memory, graciously pleased to avouch he had seen in Anno 1628, close to the Gate of York House, in a roome not above 35 foot square, as much as could be represented as to Sceans, in the great Banqueting Room of Whitehall.—Sir Balthazar Gerbier, *Discourse on Building*, 1662.

Thursday, October 8, 1626.—Towards night I went to see the Duke of Boukingham at his residence called Jorschaux [York House], which is extremely fine, and was the most richly fitted up than any other I saw.—Bassompierre's *Embassy to England in* 1626.

For the more magnificent adornment of York House, Buckingham purchased of Rubens for a hundred thousand florins the splendid collection of paintings, antiques, gems, etc., "more like that of a prince than a private gentleman," with which the great painter of Antwerp had enriched his own dwelling. Among the pictures were no fewer than 19 by Titian; 21 by Bassano; 13 by Paul Veronese; 17 by Tintoretto; 3 by Raphael; 3 by Leonardo da Vinci; and 13 by Rubens himself.

The duke did not live in York House, but used it only for state occasions. He was assassinated August 23, 1628. His son, the second Duke of Buckingham, was born in *Wallingford House* in 1627.

At York House, also, the galleries and rooms are ennobled with the possession of those Roman Heads and statues which lately belonged to Sir Peter Paul Rubens, Knight, that exquisite painter of Antwerp: and the garden will be renowned so long as John de Bologna's Cain and Abel stand there, a piece of wondrous art and workmanship. The King of Spain gave it to his Majesty at his being there, who bestowed it on the late Duke of Buckingham.—Peacham, *Compleat Gentleman*, ed. 1661, p. 108.

The "superstitious pictures in York House" were ordered to be sold, August 20, 1645;[4] but not before, as Brian Fairfax tells us, his

[1] Sir B. Gerbier.
[2] See also Rushworth's *Histor. Collect.*, fol. 1650, p. 149; and Strype, B. vi. p. 4.
[3] *MS. Contemporary Poem* "Uppon severall pieces of Worke in the Duke's gallery at Yorke House," formerly in the possession of the late Mr. W. J. Thoms.
[4] *Whitelocke*, p. 167.

"old trusty servant Mr. John Trayleman" had contrived to smuggle some of the best of them over to Holland, where they were purchased by the Archduke Leopold, and are now in the Belvedere Gallery at Vienna.[1] The house itself was given by Cromwell and his colleagues to General Fairfax, whose daughter and heiress married the second and last Duke of Buckingham of the Villiers family. The young Duke of Buckingham thought the easiest way to regain the estate was to marry the heiress. He came over to England the year before Oliver died, proposed, was accepted, and, September 1657, was married at Nun Appleton, near York. When the Protector was told of the marriage he gave the duke liberty to reside at York House, but not to quit it without permission. Buckingham broke his promise and was sent to the Tower. Lord Fairfax went to remonstrate with Cromwell, lost his temper, and the Protector and his old General parted in anger, never to meet in life again.

November 27, 1655.—I went to see York House and gardens, belonging to the former greate Buckingham, but now much ruin'd thro' neglect.—*Evelyn.*
He [Lord Fairfax] lived in York House, where every chamber was adorned with the arms of Villiers and Manners, lions and peacocks. He was descended from the same ancestors, Earls of Rutland.—Brian Fairfax, *Memoirs of the Life of the D. of Buckingham.*

In 1661 it was occupied by Baron de Batteville, the Spanish ambassador; in 1663 the Russian ambassador was lodging here.

May 19, 1661 (Lord's Day).—I walked in the morning towards Westminster, and, seeing many people at York House, I went down and found them at masse, it being the Spanish Ambassador's; and so I got into one of the gallerys, and there heard two masses done, I think not in so much state as I have seen them heretofore. After that, into the garden, and walked an hour or two, but found it not so fine a place as I always took it for by the outside.—*Pepys.*
June 6, 1663.—To York House, where the Russia Embassader do lie. . . . That that pleased me best, was the remains of the noble soul of the late Duke of Buckingham appearing in his house, in every place, in the door cases and the windows.—*Pepys.*

By a deed, dated January 1, 1672, the duke sold York House and gardens for the sum of £30,000, to Roger Higgs, of St. Margaret's, Westminster, Esq.; Emery Hill, of Westminster, gentleman; Nicholas Eddyn, of Westminster, woodmonger; and John Green, of Westminster, brewer, by whom the house was pulled down, and the grounds and gardens converted into streets and tenements, bearing the names and titles of the last possessor of the house, *George Street, Villiers Street, Duke Street, Of Alley, Buckingham Street.* The rental, in 1668, of "York House and tenements, in the Strand," was £1359: 10s. There is an engraving of York House in the *Londina Illustrata*, from a drawing by Hollar, in the Pepysian Library at Cambridge. [*See* York Watergate.]

York Place, the old name for *Whitehall.*

[1] *Walpole*, vol. ii. p. 99; *Smith*, vol. xxxi. etc.; Sainsbury, *Rubens's Papers*, p. 65.

1st Gent.   Sir,
You must no more call it York Place, that is past:
For, since the cardinal fell, that title's lost;
'Tis now the king's, and call'd—Whitehall.
   3rd. Gent.   I know it;
But 'tis so lately alter'd, that the old name
Is fresh about me.—Shakespeare, *Henry VIII.*, Act iv. Sc. 1.

The bitter satirist of Wolsey wrote—

> Why come ye nat to Court?
> To whyche Court?
> To the kinges Courte
> Or to Hampton Court?
> Nay, to the Kinges Court:
> The kynges courte
> Should have the excellence;
> But Hampton Court
> Hath the preemynence,
> And *Yorkes Place*,
> With my lordes grace,
> To whose magnifycence
> Is all the conflewence, etc.

Skelton, *Why Come ye Nat to Courte?* (Skelton's *Works*, by Dyce, vol. ii. p. 39).

York Place, PORTMAN SQUARE, is the continuation of Baker Street northwards. William Pitt resided at No. 14 during the Addington administration, and here Lord Eldon found him at breakfast when he carried the King's "commands for Mr. Pitt to attend him."[1] No. 8, the house looking down York Street, was the residence of Cardinal Wiseman, and here he died, February 15, 1865. He previously lived in Golden Square.

York Stairs, BUCKINGHAM STREET. [*See* York Watergate.]

York Street, COVENT GARDEN, was so called in compliment to James, Duke of York, afterwards James II. Hatton describes it, 1708, as "a very short, but broad and pleasant street," and Strype, 1720, as "very short, but well built and inhabited." Beneath the parapet ledge of the house well known as Mr. H. G. Bohn, the bookseller's, now Messrs. George Bell and Sons (Nos. 4 and 5) is a stone inscribed with the name of the street and the year of its erection—"1636." The vaults of this house are very extensive, and are said to cover part of the burial-ground of the ancient convent from whence *Covent Garden* derives its name. *Eminent Inhabitants.*—Dr. Donne's son, in 1640.[2] Mrs. Pritchard, the actress, when she advertised her benefit at Drury Lane, in the *Public Advertiser* of March 13, 1756. At No. 4 De Quincey wrote "bit by bit" his *Confessions of an Opium Eater.* No. 5 was the residence of Elliston when lessee of Drury Lane Theatre.

York Street, KENSINGTON, so called from "Thomas York, Citizen and Joyner of London," who, in 1687, was in possession of the land in this neighbourhood.[3] Thackeray was living at No. 13 in this street

[1] *Eldon's Life*, by Twiss, vol. i. p. 446.
[2] Rate-books of St. Paul's, Covent Garden.
[3] Title-deeds in possession of John J. Merriman, Esq.

when *Vanity Fair* was in course of publication. His writings at that period are full of allusions to the neighbourhood. The house is the one with two bay windows at the south-west end of the street. The shop at the north-east end—an ironmonger's—is frequently spoken of by Cobbett in his *Rural Rides*, etc.

York Street, ST. JAMES'S SQUARE to JERMYN STREET, was so called in compliment to James, Duke of York, afterwards James II. Here is *Ormond Yard*, and here, on the east side, was the chapel of the Spanish Embassy. The chapel with the arms of Castile on the walls was turned into a house in 1877. Apple-tree Yard, in this street, derives its name from an orchard of apple-trees, for which St. James's Fields were famous in the reign of Charles I. Ridgway, the publisher of the *Rolliad*, had his shop at No. 1 York Street, St. James's Square.

York Street, BROADWAY, WESTMINSTER, was so called after John Sharp, Archbishop of York, whose town-house was in 1708 in this street. It was formerly known as *Petty France*, and was so marked in Rocque's Map. Milton, whilst Latin Secretary to Oliver and Richard Cromwell, 1651-1660, lived at No. 19 in this street, in "a pretty garden-house next door to the Lord Scudamore's, and opening into St. James's Park."

Here his blindness came on; here was the brief period of his happy second marriage; here he wrote his *Defensio Secunda*, some of his other pamphlets, and some of the most famous of his Sonnets; and here he began his "Paradise Lost."— David Masson, Letter in *The Times*, October 22, 1875.

Jeremy Bentham bought the house and added the garden to his own house, leaving nothing but a narrow area at the back, overhung by a cotton willow-tree, said to have been planted by Milton. Near the back attic-window Bentham affixed a stone inscribed with—"SACRED TO MILTON, PRINCE OF POETS." Among Bentham's tenants in Milton's house was William Hazlitt, the critic, who occupied it from June 1812 to 1819. He made "a large wainscoted room upstairs his study," because he fancied it might have been Milton's. Milton's house was demolished in 1877 to make way for the huge Queen Anne Mansions. It had fallen into a neglected and dilapidated condition.

York Terrace, QUEEN'S ELM, BROMPTON. Thomas Moore was living here in 1811, the year of his marriage. Mrs. Moore described it to Mr. S. C. Hall as a pretty house, the terrace being then isolated, with nursery gardens opposite. Long afterwards the poet went to Brompton "to indulge himself with a sight of that house." Mr. Hall says "it is now a house in a row. I regret that I cannot indicate the number, but believe it to be No. 5."

York Waterworks. [*See* York Buildings.]

York Watergate, at the Thames end of BUCKINGHAM STREET, CHARING CROSS, is commonly said from an early date to have been designed by Inigo Jones for George Villiers, Duke of Buckingham, the "Steenie" of James I. But Sir Balthazar Gerbier appears to have acted as architect to the Duke at York House, and was probably the responsible architect of the Watergate. Whether he actually designed it is doubtful. It was built by Nicholas Stone, "master mason" of Whitehall and Windsor, who also claims the design. In his *Works Book*, preserved in Sir John Soane's Museum, is the entry—

<small>The Watergate at York House bee dessined and built ; and ye right hand lion hee did, fronting y Thames. Mr. Kearne, a Jarman, his brother by marrying, did ye shee lion.</small>

The Watergate has always been admired for its proportions and suitability to the purpose. Now sunk in a hollow and thrust aside by the Thames Embankment works, it is seen to a great disadvantage. On the street front is the Villiers' motto—*Fidei coticula Crux*. [*See* York House.]

Yorkshire Stingo, MARYLEBONE ROAD, on the south side where the road takes a turn south to join the Edgware Road, nearly opposite where is now the Metropolitan Railway Station. There is still a tavern with the sign of the Yorkshire Stingo at 183 Marylebone Road.

<small>The second cast iron bridge [ever constructed] was designed by the celebrated Thomas Paine. It was executed at Rotherham in 1789, was brought to London in 1790, and set up in the bowling green of the Yorkshire Stingo, Lisson Green ; but as Mr. Paine was not able to pay the expense, the arch was taken to pieces and carried back to Rotherham, where some of the parts were applied to the famous bridge afterwards erected at Sunderland.—Cooke's *Old London Bridge*, p. 7.</small>

From here the first pair of London omnibuses were started, July 4, 1829; they ran to the Bank and back; the fare was one shilling, or sixpence for half the distance. Mr. Shillibeer was the owner.

Zoological Gardens (The), REGENT'S PARK, belong to the Zoological Society of London, a Society instituted in 1826, and incorporated by Royal Charter in 1829, for the advancement of Zoology, and the introduction and exhibition of the Animal Kingdom alive or properly preserved. The principal founders were Sir Humphry Davy and Sir Stamford Raffles. The gardens were first opened in 1828.

Visitors are admitted to the gardens of the Society every week-day from nine in the morning till sunset : on Mondays, at sixpence each ; on the following days at one shilling each; children at sixpence. On Sundays the gardens are open only to members and their friends. Every member can introduce two friends personally, or by special order. A military band performs in the gardens on Saturday afternoons at 4 P.M. during the summer.

These gardens contain the largest and most complete collection of living animals in the world, and afford one of the greatest attractions to the sightseer in London. The collection of snakes is the finest ever brought together. The great centres of attraction are the large new lion house, where the carnivora are fed at 4 P.M. ; the great monkey house; the houses of the elephants, hippopotami, giraffes, zebras, and antelopes; the snake room; the bear pits and seal ponds; and the aquarium.

The Society's House is at No. 11 Hanover Square. Fellows are elected by ballot, and pay an admission fee of £5 and an annual subscription of £3. The annual income of the Society is about £27,500, of which about five-sixths are derived from payments for admission to the gardens, the rest from the subscriptions of fellows. The annual expenditure on the gardens and museums is about £25,000. The Society has a library for the use of its members; and lectures are delivered at the theatre in the gardens during the season.

INDEX

ABBADIE, John, buried, ii. 495
Abbot, Abp., ii. 362; portrait, 363
Abdy, Sir Robert, lived, iii. 69
Abel, hanged, iii. 256
Abel, Sir John, i. 443
Abercorn, Marquis of, lived, i. 388
Abercrombie, John, died, i. 345
Abercrombie, Sir Ralph, monument, iii. 48
Aberdeen, Earl of, Prime Minister, i. 254; lived, 59
Abergavenny, Henry Nevill, sixth Earl of, lived, i. 2
Abergavenny, Marquis of, i. 518
Abernethy, John, i. 119; lived, 146
Abershaw, Jerry, iii. 523; executed, ii. 324
Abinger, Lord, lived, ii. 586
Abington, Mrs., lived, ii. 4; died, iii. 13
Abney, Sir Thomas, lived, i. 3; iii. 319; buried, 73
Abraham, H. R., architect, ii. 385; iii. 352, 435
Abraham, Robert, architect, i. 460; ii. 299, 600
Achilles, statue, ii. 253
Achley, Roger, lived, i. 458
Ackermann, Rudolph, lived, i. 140; buried, 415
Adam, Brothers, builders of Adelphi, i. 4, 521, 526, 542; ii. 50, 255, 366, 462; iii. 108
Adam, James, died, i. 15
Adam, John, ii. 310
Adam, Robert, architect, i. 8; 163, 222, 250, 517; ii. 188, 604; iii. 170; died, i. 15
Adam, William, duel with Fox, ii. 253
Adams, John, burned, i. 116
Adams, John Quincy, married, i. 31
Addams, Dr. Jesse, Merchant Taylors' School, ii. 526
Addington, Dr., lived, i. 424
Addington, H. See Sidmouth
Addison, Joseph, school, i. 365; church, ii. 326; coffee-house, 281; married, 7; lived, i. 3, 380; ii. 198, 224, 296; iii. 209; buried, 463, 467; statue, 477; memorial tablet to his mother, 480

Adelaide, Queen, i. 4
Aders, Charles, ii. 20
Adolphus, John Leycester, ii. 526
Agar, William, i. 9
Aikin, Dr. John, lived, i. 277
Aikman, William, lived, ii. 382
Ainger, Alfred, architect, iii. 422
Ainsworth, Robert, lived, i. 179; buried, iii. 106
Aiton, W., landscape-gardener, ii. 329
Akenside, Dr. Mark, i. 497; lived, 209, 473; died, 309; buried, ii. 280
Akerman, Governor of Newgate, buried, i. 392
Alba, Bishop of, ii. 503
Albano, Benedict, architect, i. 466
Albemarle, Ann, Duchess of, ii. 48; marriage to Thomas Radford, 372; lived, 582
Albemarle, Elizabeth, Duchess of (d. 1734), i. 13
Albemarle, George, first Duke of, i. 278, 300; ii. 143; lived, i. 438, 520; ii. 62, 286; iii. 301, 379; married, ii. 103; body lay in state, iii. 271; buried, 463; monument, 467; wax effigy, 478
Albemarle, Christopher, second Duke of, i. 13; iii. 88; lived, i. 411
Albemarle, Earl of, duel (1760), ii. 511
Albert, Prince Consort, stones laid and buildings opened by him, i. 428, 430, 452; ii. 529, 568; iii. 181; portrait, i. 386, 395; statues, ii. 223, 235, 410
Alcock, Bishop, rector, ii. 66
Aldborough, Edward, Earl of, lived, iii. 327
Alderson, Baron, school, i. 365
Aldrich, Henry, baptized, ii. 468
Aldrich, Rev. Mr., i. 432
Aldrich, Robert, Bishop of Carlisle, lived, i. 329
Aldridge's Horse Mart, ii. 489
Alerton, Ralph, burned, ii. 269
Alfieri, Count Vittorio, duel, ii. 151
Alfune, ii. 109
Allason, Thomas, jun., architect, iii. 315

INDEX

Allein, Giles, iii. 321
Allen, soldier, ii. 254
Allen, George, architect, ii. 610
Allen, John, club, i. 480; died, iii. 279
Allen, Ralph, i. 146; Post-office, iii. 114
Allen, Sir John, Lord Mayor (1521), ii. 520
Allen, Sir Thomas, Lord Mayor, lived, ii. 327
Allen, Thomas, buried, ii. 450
Allen, William, F.R.S., iii. 99
Alleyn, Edward, i. 125, 137; ii. 68, 116; iii. 31; baptism, i. 227; lord of manor, ii. 323; marriage, i. 318; lived, 102, 426; buried, 227
Alleyn, William, born, i. 502
Allington, Mrs., i. 37
Allington, Sir Richard, monument, iii. 166
Allix, Rev. Dr. Peter, ii. 309
Allston, W., lived, i. 295
Alsop, Bernard, lived, ii. 168
Althorp, Lord, lived, i. 12
Alwyne, Bishop, ii. 203
Amelia, Princess, lived, i. 341, 342; visitor at Sadler's Wells, iii. 199
Ames, Joseph, lived, ii. 212; iii. 447; died, i. 417; buried, ii. 98
Amherst, General, lived, ii. 519
Amhurst, Nicholas, ii. 526
Amiconi, Giacomo, painter, iii. 119
Amory, Thomas, lived, ii. 616; died, iii. 388
Amyot, Thomas, died, ii. 274
Ancaster, Duke of, lived, ii. 401
Anderson, Adam, iii. 278
Anderson, Dr. James, minister, iii. 339
Anderson, J. Macvicar, architect, i. 331
Anderson, Mrs., i. 250
André, Major, born, ii. 179; monument, iii. 424
Andrewes, Lancelot, Bishop of Winchester, born, i. 32; Merchant Taylors' School, ii. 526; iii. 149; lived, 525; preacher, ii. 609; prebend, iii. 23; rector, ii. 110; monument, iii. 215
Angell, Frederick, i. 285
Angell, Samuel, architect, i. 498
Angell, William, iii. 30
Angelo, Henry, lived, i. 330
Angerstein, John Julius, ii. 572; lived, 13
Anglesey, Arthur Annesley, Earl of, school, iii. 488; lived, i. 99, 523
Anglesey, Marquis of, lived, iii. 424; died, 424
Angoulême, Duc d', lived, ii. 93
Anketin de Auvergne, ii. 32
Anne, Queen, ii. 328; lived, i. 74, 162, 320, 438; ii. 430; married, 277; died, 330; buried, iii. 463, 467; portrait, ii. 523, 608; iii. 5; statue, 46, 53, 134
Anne of Cleves, i. 375, 378; buried, iii. 463; tomb, 472
Anne of Denmark, lived, i. 495; iii. 269; buried, 463, 467; portrait, 358

Anson, Admiral Lord, i. 8; lived, iii. 187
Anstey, Christopher, monument, iii. 477
Anstey, John, lived, ii. 213
Anstis, John, ii. 210; lived, i. 74
Anthony, Dr. Francis, died, i. 110
Apsley, Sir Allen, i. 127; iii. 536; lived, ii. 298; monument, iii. 77
Arbuthnot, Dr., physician, i. 384; ii. 622; lived, i. 379, 517, 400; died, 455; buried, ii. 280
Arbuthnot, George, died, i. 140
Archer, John, lived, iii. 526
Archer, Thomas, bookseller, lived, iii. 104
Archer, Thomas, architect, ii. 190, 311
Archer, Thomas, Lord, lived, i. 463; ii. 21
Arden, Lady, lived, iii. 112
Arderne, Thomas, ii. 102
Argand, Ami, lived, i. 289
Argyll, Elizabeth, Duchess of, died, i. 59
Argyll and Greenwich, Duke of (d. 1743), i. 289; buried, iii. 467; monument, 478
Argyll, Archibald, seventh Earl of, marriage, i. 227; lived (1615), ii. 47
Argyll, Archibald, Marquis of, lived, i. 523
Arlington, Countess of, lived, iii. 871
Arlington, Henry Bennet, Earl of, ii. 566; iii. 89; lived, i. 60; ii. 130
Armistead, Mrs., ii. 122
Armstrong, Dr. John, ii. 163, 235; iii. 152; died, 195; buried, 59
Armstrong, Sir Thomas, hanged, iii. 359, 415
Arne, Dr., ii. 513; lived, i. 472; ii. 336; buried, iii. 59
Arne, Thomas, upholsterer, lived, ii. 336
Arnold, Dr. Samuel, ii. 452, 513; buried, iii. 464
Arthur, proprietor of White's Club, iii. 492
Arundel, Alathea, Countess of, lived, iii. 346
Arundel, Fitz-Alans, Earls of, i. 228
Arundel, Henry Fitz-Alan, Earl of, lived, i. 72
Arundel, Master, ii. 373
Arundel, Hon. Thomas, buried, iii. 21
Arundel, Howards, Earls of, ii. 244
Arundel, Philip Howard, Earl of, lived, i. 72; buried, iii. 395
Arundel, Thomas Howard, Earl of, i. 125; lived, 73, 137; iii. 382
Arundel, Thomas, Archbishop of Canterbury, ii. 10; lived, i. 140; portrait, ii. 361
Arundel of Wardour, Thomas, first Lord, lived, ii. 221
Arundel of Wardour, Henry, third Lord, iii. 447
Arundel of Wardour, Henry, fifth Lord, (d. 1726), iii. 26

INDEX 547

Ascham, Roger, buried, iii. 230
Ascu, Anne, prisoner, ii. 591
Asgill, John, ii. 399; student, 390
Ashburnham, Earl of, i. 517
Ashburton, Alexander Baring Lord, lived, i. 123
Ashburton, John Dunning Lord, Middle Temple, iii. 358; died, ii. 396
Ashe, Elizabeth, married to Edward Wortley Montague, ii. 517
Ashley, James, i. 75
Ashmole, Elias, ii. 182, 210; lived, 537; iii. 240; Middle Temple, 357; marriage, i. 159; ii. 392; monument, 495
Aske, Robert, i. 75
Askew, Anne, i. 116; examined, iii. 198; trial, ii. 172; burned, iii. 256
Askew, Dr. Anthony, lived, iii. 133
Astle, Thomas, tablet, i. 128
Astley, David, lived, iii. 13
Astley, John, lived, iii. 220
Astley, Philip, i. 76; ii. 182, 615
Aston, Walter, Lord, ii. 566
Athole, Duke of, lived, ii. 301
Atkinson, Robert, lived, i. 346; school, iii. 488
Atkinson, William, architect, i. 530
Atterbury, Dr., Bishop of Rochester, lived, i. 379, 400; preacher, iii. 166; prisoner, 399; buried, 464; monument, 473
Aubert, Alexander, F.R.S., lived, ii. 214
Aubrey, John, i. 92; ii. 142; lived, 144; iii. 172; Middle Temple, 357
Audley, Hugh, i. 79; ii. 131
Audley, Lord Chancellor, i. 363, 532; iii. 111
Aufrere, George, lived, i. 379
Augusta, Princess of Wales, mother of George III., buried, iii. 467
Aumont, Duc d', French Ambassador, iii. 119
Auriol, Rev. E., rector, i. 536
Austen, Dr., lived, i. 344
Austen, Jane, lived, ii. 189, 208
Austen, Thomas, ii. 386, 509
Austin, John, executed, iii. 417
Austin, William, monument, iii. 215
Austo, James, burned, ii. 269
Austo, Margery, burned, ii. 269
Awdeley, John, lived, ii. 405
Awfield, parishioners would not allow his body to be buried at St. Sepulchre's, iii. 230
Axtell, executed, iii. 415
Aylesbury, Bruces, Earls of, lived, i. 85, 418
Aylesbury, Earl of, lived, ii. 382
Aylmer, Bishop of London, iii. 246
Aylophe, Sir John, i. 246
Ayscough, Rev. Samuel, buried, ii. 97
Ayton, Sir Robert, ii. 320; buried, iii. 463

BABBAGE, Charles, F.R.S., lived, i. 503; buried, ii. 325
Babington, Dr., bust, iii. 82; monument, 48
Babington, hiding-place, ii. 317
Bach and Abel, i. 330
Bach, Sebastian, ii. 188
Bachhoffner, Dr., i. 446
Backwell, Alderman, Edward, i. 348; ii. 63; lived, 22
Bacon, Anthony, i. 299; ii. 140; lived, i. 196, 378
Bacon, Captain Francis, i. 278
Bacon, John, R.A., modelled for Coade, i. 430; lived, 228; ii. 594; buried, iii. 391; monument, 502; ii. 2
Bacon, John, sen., sculptor, i. 47
Bacon, Justice Sir Francis, i. 109
Bacon, Lord Chancellor, i. 364, 443; ii. 140, 144; iii. 371, 432; born, 537; baptized, ii. 479; married, 495; commissioner, 393; lived, i. 325, 515; ii. 82; portrait, iii. 188
Bacon, Lord-keeper, Sir Nicholas, ii. 140; founder, i. 485; lived, 2, 86; ii. 600; died, iii. 537; monument, 41, 49
Bacon, Robert, iii. 242
Baddeley, ii. 88
Badley, John, burned, iii. 255
Bagford, John, born, ii. 37; lived, i. 365
Baggallay, Justice, portrait, ii. 523
Bailey, Captain (1634), ii. 517
Bailey, Humphrey, iii. 253
Bailey, Thomas, i. 276
Baillie, Dr. Matthew, lived, ii. 165; died, i. 342; preparation, iii. 82; bust, 82, 471
Baily, E. H., R.A., i. 294; iii. 405; lived, i. 492; iii. 152
Baily, Francis, died, iii. 348
Bainham, James, i. 228
Baker, Henry, born, i. 346
Baker, Jesuit, iii. 195
Baker, Mrs. Mary, iii. 87
Baker, Robert, ii. 211
Baker, Robert, iii. 85
Baker, R. W., ii. 348
Baker, Sir Edward, i. 90
Baker, Sir Richard, lived, ii. 543; prison, 59; burial, i. 239
Baker, William, benefactor, ii. 176
Bakewell, Thomas, i. 92
Baldwin, Richard, i. 92
Balendin, murderer, ii. 51
Bales, hanged, ii. 64
Bales, Peter, lived, ii. 612
Balfe, Michael, buried, ii. 325
Ball, John, token, i. 93
Ballard, Edward, died, ii. 407
Balmerino, Lord, i. 357; trial, iii. 486; prisoner, 399; executed, 401; buried, 76
Balthrope, Robert, monument, i. 116

INDEX

Baltimore, George Calvert, first Lord, iii. 192; buried, i. 538; lay in state, ii. 25
Baltinglass, Lady, lived, i. 207
Bambridge, Thomas, ii. 58
Bamfield, Colonel, in Spring Gardens, iii. 295
Bamfield, confessor, ii. 271, 286, 401
Bampfylde, John, lived, ii. 336
Banbury, Sir William Knollys, Earl of, lived, iii. 441
Bancroft, Archbishop, Gray's Inn, ii. 140; Lambeth Palace, 362; tomb, 495
Bancroft, Francis, i. 93; tomb, ii. 205, 613
Bancroft, Mr. and Mrs., Prince of Wales's Theatre, ii. 201; iii. 122
Bangor, Bishops of, i. 94
Banim, John, lived, i. 42
Bankes and his horse, i. 156; ii. 136; iii. 44
Banks and Barry, architects, i. 308
Banks, Lady, i. 254
Banks, Sir Joseph, i. 254; iii. 185; born, i. 60; lived, 308, 493; ii. 401; iii. 266; club, ii. 484; President of the Royal Society, iii. 187; bust, 188; portrait, 188; statue, i. 274
Banks, Thomas, R.A., lived, i. 187; ii. 594; buried, iii. 2; 463
Bannister, Charles, buried, ii. 479
Bannister, Jack, i. 406; ii. 201; died, 134
Bannister, John, the younger, i. 288
Bannister, Mr., ii. 19; his music school, iii. 504
Banquelle, John de, i. 92
Barbauld, Mrs., lived, i. 334; ii. 594; buried, iii. 318
Barbauld, Rochemount, minister, ii. 594; iii. 318
Barber, Alderman, erector of monument to Butler in Westminster Abbey, iii. 476; died, 132
Barclay, Alexander, rector, i. 35
Barclay, Sir George, i. 439; lived, iii. 280
Barebone, Nicholas, ii. 17; lived, 299, 399
Barebone, Praise-God, lived, ii. 37, 62; iii. 243
Baretti, Joseph, stabs a man in a broil, ii. 199; died, 7; buried, iii. 3; monument, ii. 496
Barham, Rev. R. H., rector, i. 81; ii. 502
Barker, bookseller, iii. 195
Barker, John, preacher, ii. 179
Barker, J. K., architect, ii. 275
Barker, Robert, i. 304; died, ii. 357; tomb, 495
Barker, Thomas, lived, i. 283
Barkstead, executed, iii. 415
Barlow, Dr., Bishop of Lincoln, consecrated, ii. 13
Barlow, Lucy, prisoner, iii. 398
Barlow, P., engineer, iii. 404
Barlow, P. W., engineer, ii. 358

Barlow, W. H., engineer, ii. 518
Barnaby, Grace, i. 415
Barnard, Lady Anne, lived, i. 165
Barnard, Sir Andrew, buried, i. 384
Barnes, burned, iii. 256
Barnes, Joshua, "Grecian," i. 396
Barnes, Thomas, "Grecian," i. 396; lived, ii. 578; buried, 325
Barnwell, George, i. 3
Baro, Peter, lived, i. 481
Barowe, Alice, ii. 214
Barré, Colonel, lived, ii. 460; iii. 302
Barrett, George, R.A., lived, iii. 1; buried, 2
Barrington, Daines, lived, ii. 343
Barrington, Shute, Bishop of Durham, lived, i. 342
Barrington, Viscount, lived, i. 342
Barrow, Dr. Isaac, school, i. 365; preached, ii. 377; professor, 155; lived, iii. 11; died, i. 357; buried, iii. 464; bust, 478
Barrow, Sir John, lived, ii. 586; buried, i. 320
Barry, Bishop, ii. 344
Barry, Sir Charles, R.A., born, i. 245; lived, ii. 14, 67, 92; buried, iii. 463; architect, i. 93, 246, 429; ii. 227, 239; iii. 8, 157, 181, 201, 298, 335, 405, 406, 407, 482, 486
Barry, Charles, architect, ii. 146, 429; iii. 252
Barry, E. M., R.A., architect, i. 323, 359, 466; ii. 15, 65, 242, 572, 618; iii. 487
Barry, James, R.A., i. 71; lived, 338; ii. 616; iii. 332; died, 382; grave, 49
Barry, Ann (1734-1801) buried, iii. 464
Barry, Elizabeth (1658-1713), died, iii. 219
Barry, Spranger, lived, i. 229; ii. 601; died, i. 343
Bartleman, James, died, i. 170
Bartlett, Thomas, i. 121
Bartolozzi, Francis, lived, i. 161, 277
Barton, Elizabeth, holy maid of Kent, executed, iii. 414
Basevi, George, architect, i. 153, 451; ii. 303
Basevi, Nathan, lived, i. 185
Basing, William, ii. 203
Basire, James, lived, iii. 137
Basyngstoke, Richard de, i. 235
Bateman, Lord, lived, i. 127
Bateman, Miss, Sadler's Wells, iii. 201
Bates, Dr., library, iii. 522; minister, 98; preacher, ii. 179
Bates, executed, ii. 431, 448
Bath, Bishops of, residences, i. 72, 124; iii. 321
Bath, William Bourchier, Earl of, lived, i. 284
Bath, William Pulteney, Earl of, lived, i. 62, 123; duel, ii. 151; buried, iii. 463, 470
Bathurst, Earl, lived, i. 56; ii. 254, 300; iii. 89; portrait, ii. 398

INDEX 549

Battersby, Mr., ii. 35
Batteville, Baron de, Spanish Ambassador, lived, iii. 539
Battie, William, M.D., iii. 193
Battishill, organist, i. 415
Bawdrick, William, iii. 173
Baxter, Richard, i. 336; ii. 37; marriage, i. 157, 226; lived, 207, 366; preacher, ii. 284; pastor, 619; minister, iii. 98, 339; prisoner, ii. 341; burial, i. 392; his wife's burial, 392
Baynard, Ralph, i. 131, 133
Baynard, William, i. 131
Baynings, Lord, lived, ii. 471
Bazalgette, Sir Joseph, engineer, i. 383; iii. 366
Beachcroft, Samuel, architect, ii. 522
Beaconsfield, Earl of, born, i. 6, 281; baptism, 44; lived, 487; ii. 273; statue, iii. 8
Beake, Thomas, i. 135; iii. 130
Beale, Mary, lived, iii. 11
Beard, John, i. 213
Beard, Lady Henrietta, buried, iii. 20
Beattie, Dr., lived, iii. 458
Beatty, Sir William, buried, ii. 325
Beauchamp, Sir John, iii. 340; lived, 448; tomb, 41
Beauclerk, Topham, died, i. 6; iii. 193; quoted, i. 287; his children, 321
Beaufort, Cardinal, iii. 213; lived, 524
Beaufort, Henry, first Duke of, lived, i. 140, 141, 328
Beaufort, Dukes of, residence, iii. 321
Beaufort, Johanna, married to James I. of Scotland, iii. 213
Beaumont, Colonel, duel, ii. 299
Beaumont, Earl of, lived, i. 313
Beaumont, Francis, lived, i. 101, 365, Inner Temple, iii. 354; buried, 463, 476
Beaumont, J. T. Barber, ii. 542
Beaumont, Sir George, ii. 572; lived, 164
Beazley, Samuel, architect, ii. 305, 451
Beck, William, architect, i. 222
Becket, Agnes à, iii. 372
Becket, Gilbert, iii. 29
Becket, Thomas à, born, ii. 521; iii. 456; lived, i. 6; image, ii. 361
Beckford, Alderman, i. 184; lived, ii. 149, 547; iii. 265; memorial, ii. 95; monument, 170; statue, 264
Beckford, William, lived, i. 502; ii. 165
Becon, Thomas, i. 392; rector, 505; iii. 311
Bedborough, A., architect, i. 58; iii. 181
Bedford, Captain, ii. 607
Bedford, Countess of, born, iii. 399
Bedford, Lucy, Countess of, marriage, i. 539
Bedford, Duchess of, ii. 199
Bedford, Dukes of, i. 144, 145
Bedford, John Plantagenet, Duke of, i. 451

Bedford, William, first Duke of, i. 463
Bedford, John, fourth Duke of, portrait, ii. 575
Bedford, Francis, fifth Duke of, statue, iii. 191
Bedford, Earls of, i. 145, 330; residence, iii. 533
Bedford, John, first Earl of, i. 460
Bedford, Edward Russell, third Earl of, marriage, i. 539
Bedford, Francis, fourth Earl of, i. 461; iii. 56
Bedford, Francis, architect, ii. 312
Bedford, Grosvenor, lived, i. 276; iii. 299
Beechey, Sir William, R.A., lived, ii. 93, 192
Beeston, Cuthbert, iii. 443
Beeston, William, iii. 204
Behn, Aphra, buried, iii. 480
Behnes, William, i. 374; lived, 492; ii. 619; buried, 325
Belasyse, John, first Lord, i. 361
Belcher, J., architect, ii. 418
Belcher, Messrs., architects, i. 485
Belenian, Nicholas, burned, i. 116
Bell, Robert, bequest, ii. 573
Bell, Sir Charles, surgeon, ii. 538; lived, 66, 386, 426; iii. 267, 527; died, i. 383
Bell, William, parson, ii. 540
Bellamont, Lord, duel, ii. 513
Bellamy, George Anne, lived, i. 170, 534
Bellamy, Thomas, architect, ii. 344
Bellew, Rev. John, i. 142
Bellieure, Mons, lived, ii. 130
Bellingham, lived, ii. 546; trial, 611; executed, 592
Beloe, Rev. William, i. 29; ii. 15; lived, i. 281; died, ii. 327; tablet, i. 35
Belzoni, iii. 260; exhibited, ii. 8; iii. 201
Benbow, Admiral, iii. 175
Benedict, Sir Julius, buried, ii. 325
Benet, Sir John, lived, ii. 299
Bennett, Rev. W. J. E., iii. 63
Bennett, Sir Sterndale, buried, iii. 464
Benson, Auditor, erector of the bust of Milton in Westminster Abbey, iii. 476
Benson, William, abbot and dean, i. 192
Bentham, Jeremy, ii. 545; born, iii. 157; married, ii. 468; lived, iii. 541; died, 134
Bentham, William, lived, ii. 134
Bentinck, Lord George, married to Mary Davies (1753), ii. 517; statue, i. 341
Bentinck, Ven. W. H. E., ii. 545
Bentley, Mrs., actor, lived, iii. 529
Bentley, Richard, i. 44, 253; lived, i. 2, 25; iii. 34
Berenger, De, swindler, ii. 296
Beresford, Viscount, i. 342
Berkeley, Dr., Bishop of Cloyne, lived, i. 14; ii. 307; iii. 85; buried, i. 414
Berkeley, Earls of, lived, iii. 296

INDEX

Berkeley, George, first Earl, **benefactor,** iii. 250; "grocer," ii. 161
Berkeley, Fred. Augustus, fifth Earl of, i. 163
Berkeley, Hon. George, ii. 320
Berkeley, Lady Elizabeth, i. 166; **monument,** ii. 277
Berkeley, John, Lord, of Stratton, iii. 89
Berkeley, Lords, i. 166; iii. 328; lived, i. 162, 288; iii. 267
Berkshire, Howards, Earls of, i. 166
Berkstead, Colonel, iii. 235
Bernal, Ralph, died, ii. 4
Bernard, Francis, M.D., **buried,** i. 159; monument, 226
Bernard, Sir Thomas, i. 169; buried, ii. 73
Bernardiston, Sir Samuel, lived, i. 190
Berners, Charles, ii. 537
Berners, Ralph de, i. 325
Berners, William, i. 169
Berti, Duc de, lived, ii. 93
Berry, Mr., (d. 1735), i. 310
Berry, Agnes, lived, i. 80, 487
Berry, Dame Rebecca, monument, i. 540
Berry, Mary, lived, i. 80, 487
Best, Captain, duel with Lord **Camelford,** i. 450; ii. 328
Bettenham, Jeremiah, ii. 144
Betterton, Thomas, i. 357; born, iii. 388; baptized, ii. 468; lived, iii. 202; died, 194; buried, 464, 480; portrait, ii. 575
Betty, Henry West, died, i. 43
Bevan, Joseph Gurney, iii. 99
Bevan, Sylvanus, iii. 99
Bevan, W. C., ii. 39
Beveridge, William, Bishop of St. **Asaph,** rector, iii. 73; died, i. 494
Bigg, Edward Smith, iii. 280
Biggin, George, lived, i. 361
Bigland, Sir Ralph, buried, i. 159
Bigods, Earls of Norfolk, i. 280
Bill, Dean, tomb, iii. 465
Bill, John, printer, lived, iii. 54, 122; died, i. 42
Billing, Edward, iii. 437
Billings, Robert, architect, iii. 228
Billington, Mrs., lived, i. 281
Bindley, James, memorial, ii. 501
Bingham, John, monument, iii. 215
Bingley, Benson, Lord, lived, ii. 190
Binney, Rev. Thomas, minister, iii. 457
Birch, Alderman, lived, i. 458
Birch, C. B., A.R.A., iii. 359
Birch, Dr. Samuel, Merchant **Taylors'** School, ii. 526
Birch, Dr. Thomas, i. 254, 497; lived, ii. 601; buried, 466; portrait, iii. 188
Birch, Samuel, Lord Mayor, ii. 431
Bird, William, ii. 485
Birkbeck, George, M.D., i. 188; buried, ii. 325
Birkenhead, Sir John, iii. 232; buried, ii. 479

Bish, lottery agent, i. 458; ii. 417
Bishop, Sir Henry R., died, i. 319
Black, John, lived, iii. 324
Black, W. H., minister, i. 485; ii. 546
Blackall, Alderman, lived, i. 489
Blackall, Offspring, Bishop of Exeter, born, i. 489
Blackborough, lived, ii. 486
Blackburn, E. L., architect, i. 478; ii. 317
Blackmore, Sir Richard, i. 125; lived, 374; iii. 198
Blackstone, Sir William, school, i. 365; Middle Temple, iii. 357; lived, i. 237, 327, 374; died, ii. 396
Blackwell, Mrs., lived, i. 380
Blackwell, William, ii. 262
Blades, Sheriff, i. 238
Blagden, carpenter, i. 474
Blagden, Sir C., club, ii. 484
Blagrove, William, iii. 203
Blake, Admiral, buried, ii. 468; iii. 463
Blake, William, painter, ii. 20; born, i. 277; apprenticed, iii. 137; **marriage,** i. 128; lived, ii. 210; iii. 101, 277; died, ii. 75; buried, i. 304
Blanche de la Tour, tomb, iii. 465
Blanchard (d. 1835), actor, ii. 450
Blanchard, Richard, banker, lived, ii. 63
Bleek, Peter van, buried, iii. 21
Blemund, William, lived, i. 206
Blemunds, family of, i. 143, 205
Blessington, Countess of, lived, ii. 130
Bligh, Admiral, tomb, ii. 495
Bliss, Dr., Merchant Taylors' School, ii. 526
Blizard, Sir William, i. 126, 278; **brass,** 227
Blomfield, Bishop, ii. 507; tomb, iii. 48
Blomfield, Sir Arthur, R.A., architect, i. 46, 49, 149, 393; ii. 368, 371, 498, 600; iii. 62, 74, 212, 214, 251
Blood, Colonel, ii. 304, 404; iii. 496; died, i. 232; buried, ii. 579
Blood, Fanny, lived, ii. 594
Bloomfield, Robert, poet, ii. 25; lived, i. 154, 424, 444
Blore, Edward, architect, i. 171, 293, 366; ii. 363, 471; iii. 436
Blount, Martha, lived, i. 218; died, 165; buried, iii. 20
Blount, Mrs. Martha, mother of Martha and Theresa Blount, lived, iii. 457
Blount, Sir Michael, monument, ii. 77
Blount, Sir Richard, monument, iii. 77
Blount, Theresa, lived, i. 218; ii. 337; buried, iii. 20
Blow, Dr., buried, iii. 464; memorial tablet, 472
Blucher, Marshal, lived, ii. 287
Bludworth, Sir Thomas, Lord Mayor at time of the Fire, iii. 128
Boaden, James, lived, iii. 449
Bodeley Master (killed 1560), i. 336

INDEX

Bodley, Lady, tablet, i. 116
Bodley, Sir Thomas, lived, ii. 405
Boehm, Sir Edgar, R.A., statues, i. 274; ii. 256; iii. 359
Boffe, Joseph de, lived, ii. 107
Bohn, Henry G., bookseller, iii. 540
Bohun, Humphry de, Earl of Hereford and Essex, i. 203
Bokerels or Bukerels, i. 297
Bole, Richard, ii. 508
Boleyn, Anne, married to Henry VIII., iii. 510; prisoner, 395, 398; trial, 485; buried, 76
Bolingbroke, Viscount, lived, i. 517; ii. 121; iii. 12, 151; monument, i. 128
Bollein, Geffrey, buried, ii. 370
Bollinbrooke, Earl of, lived, ii. 596
Bolton, Duke of, lived, iii. 192; duel, ii. 511
Bolton, Prior, i. 115, 325, 326
Bonaparte, Joseph, ex-king of Spain, lived, iii. 33
Bond, Alderman William (d. 1576), i. 477; monument, ii. 205
Bond, Alexander, i. 133
Bond, G., architect, ii. 337
Bond, Martin, monument, ii. 205
Bond, Sir Thomas, i. 14, 218; iii. 88
Bone, Henry, R.A., lived, i. 125, 169; iii. 72
Boniface, Archbishop of Canterbury, ii. 360
Bonington, R. P., buried, iii. 70
Bonner, Bishop, i. 179, 221; prisoner, ii. 476; buried, 102
Bonomi, Joseph, A.R.A., iii. 261; architect, 290, 424; lived, 382; buried, ii. 496; iii. 3
Bonvici, Antonio, lived, i. 477
Booth, Barton, died, i. 360; monument, 121; iii. 478
Booth, Charles, Bishop of Hereford, ii. 46
Booth, Lawrence, Archbishop of York, iii. 536
Bootle, Edward, iii. 280
Boreman, John, ii. 289
Boreman, William, iii. 95
Boron, Duc de, lived, i. 477
Boroski, murderer of Tom Thynne, ii. 198
Borrell, H. P., i. 266
Boscawen, Admiral, lived, ii. 300
Bosset, Colonel de, i. 266
Bossy, Peter James, pillory, ii. 611
Boswell, James, ii. 137; club, i. 480; lived, 80, 219, 450; ii. 181, 258; iii. 139; died, 110
Boswell, James, jun., died, ii. 85
Boswell, Ralph, lived, i. 223
Boswell, Sir Alexander, lived, i. 91
Boswell, Veronica, iii. 132
Bothmar, Baron, lived, i. 519
Boucher, Catherine S., baptism, i. 128
Boufflers, Madame de, lived, ii. 307
Boughton, murderer, ii. 58

Bouillé, Marquis de, buried, iii. 18
Boulter, Archbishop, Merchant Taylors' School, ii. 526
Boulton, M., i. 18
Bourchier, Lodowick Robsart, Lord, altar-tomb, iii. 468
Bourgeois, Sir Francis, born, ii. 484
Bourne, Vincent, master, Westminster School, iii. 488
Bouverie, Sir Jacob de, iii. 280
Bovy, James, i. 543
Bowack, lived, i. 400
Bowen, killed by Quin in self-defence, iii. 105
Bower, Archibald, lived, i. 219; buried, ii. 496; iii. 3
Bowes, Edward, iii. 31
Bowes, Lady Anna Maria, lived, ii. 66
Bowes, Sir Martin, ii. 417; buried, 508
Bowes, Ralph, iii. 31
Bowles, William Lisle, ii. 555
Bowman, coffee-house, ii. 532
Bowman, Sir William, ii. 344
Bowyer, Sir Edmund, lived, i. 318
Bowyer, William, the elder, lived, iii. 504
Bowyer, William, the younger, born, ii. 407; iii. 504; lived, 154
Box, Simon, burial, i. 385
Boyce, Samuel, died, iii. 243
Boydell, Alderman, John, i. 251; lived, 374; ii. 263; buried, 610; monument, 610; portrait, iii. 306
Boyer, Abel, died, i. 380; ii. 50; buried, 450
Boyer, Rev. James, buried, i. 392
Boyle, Hon. Robert, died, iii. 11; buried, ii. 478; portrait, iii. 188
Boyse, S., the poet (d. 1749), lived, ii. 158; prisoner, iii. 117
Bracegirdle, Mrs., i. 407, 524; ii. 397; lived, ii. 245; buried, iii. 464, 480
Brackenbury, iii. 394
Brackston, John, ii. 387
Bradborne, i. 370
Bradford, John, Inner Temple, iii. 354; preacher, 31; lived, ii. 61; prisoner, i. 426; ii. 341; iii. 117; examination, 213
Bradshaw, Henry (1534-1535), iii. 346
Bradshaw, John, regicide, Gray's Inn, ii. 140; corpse, iii. 155; body at Tyburn, 419
Bradshaw, Lucretia, married, ii. 205
Bradwardine, Archbishop, i. 328
Brady, Nicholas, D.D., rector, ii. 322; preacher, 450
Brady, Sir Antonio, i. 180
Braham, John, ii. 128; iii. 189; lived, i. 91, 280; iii. 349; manager, ii. 305
Braidwood, James, memorial, iii. 385
Bramah, lived, ii. 400
Bramston, Sir John, lived, ii. 149
Branch, William, burned, ii. 460

INDEX

Brand, John, rector, ii. 492
Brand, Sir Matthew, ii. 117
Brandon, David, architect, i. 331
Brandon, Gregory, hangman, iii. 417
Brandon, Raphael, architect, ii. 351; iii. 527
Brandon and Ritchie, architects, ii. 129
Brandon, Richard, buried, ii. 504; iii. 173
Brandon, Sir Thomas, K.G., lived, iii. 330; buried, i. 197
Bray, Mrs., died, i. 281
Bray, of Eaton, tomb, ii. 448
Bray, Rev. William, iii. 56
Bray, Sir Reginald, i. 375
Braybrooke, Bishop, i. 221; ii. 495
Brayley, E. W., librarian, iii. 191
Braynse, John, iii. 371
Breauté, Fulke de, iii. 425
Brent, John, brass, ii. 481
Brent, Philip, iii. 517
Brett, Miss, lived, ii. 287
Brettingham, Matthew, architect, ii. 299, 600
Brewster, Sir David, lived, i. 515
Briane de Insula, or Lisle, iii. 321
Bridgewater, Francis, Duke of, i. 248; lived, i. 422, 473
Bridgewater, John, third Earl of, lived, i. 106, 248
Bridgman, landscape-gardener, ii. 329
Bridgman, Sir Orlando, lived, ii. 17
Bridport, Viscount, lived, ii. 191
Bright, John, portrait, ii. 575
Brinsden, John, i. 544
Briset, Jordan, ii. 313
Bristol, Countess of, i. 378
Bristol, Frederick Digby, Earl of, Bishop of Down, lived, ii. 299
Bristol, John Digby, Earl of, i. 141; lived, ii. 395; iii. 136
Britain, Earls of, ii. 443
Britton, John, iii. 412; lived, i. 419; ii. 435; iii. 157, 348; died, i. 316
Britton, Thomas, lived, i. 85
Broadwood, John, pianoforte maker, iii. 130
Brockedon, William, lived, i. 334, 503
Brocklesby, Dr., ii. 106; lived, 601
Brodie, Sir Benjamin, lived, iii. 212
Brome, Alexander, ii. 613; buried, 392
Bromley, Sir Thomas, Lord Chancellor, monument, iii. 468
Brontë, Anne, i. 351
Brontë, Charlotte, i. 351
Brook, Nicholas, lived, iii. 384
Brooke, Christopher, prisoner, ii. 477
Brooke, Fulke Greville, first Lord, lived, i. 284; ii. 156
Brooke, William, seventh Lord, lived, ii. 186
Brooke, John Charles, buried, i. 159
Brooke, Lady, lived (1644), iii. 136

Brooke, Rev. Stopford, i. 142
Brookes, Joshua, lived, i. 205; ii. 474; died, iii. 110; buried, ii. 281
Brooks, wine merchant, i. 286
Brooks, John, ii. 438
Brooks, Shirley, lived, i. 281; buried, ii. 325
Brooks, William, architect, ii. 431
Brothers, Richard, lived, i. 141; buried, ii. 318
Brougham, Lord, i. 403; student, ii. 391; lived, i. 164; ii. 137, 396; founder, iii. 422; joke on Campbell's *Lives of the Chancellors*, 356; his daughter buried, ii. 392
Broughton, John, i. 288; died, ii. 357
Broughton, Lady, keeper of the gatehouse, ii. 90
Broughton, lived, iii. 264
Broughton, prize-fighter, ii. 510
Brouncker, Viscount, President of the Royal Society, ii. 187; died, ii. 303; buried, 320; portrait, iii. 188
Brown, Lancelot, ii. 329; died, 212
Brown, Robert, ii. 266; died, i. 493
Brown, Sir Anthony, iii. 213
Brown, Tom, lived, i. 92; died, 95; buried, iii. 480
Browne, Alderman John, Serjeant Painter to Henry VIII., iii. 4
Browne, Dr. Edward, lived, i. 471
Browne, Henry, F.R.S., lived, iii. 109
Browne, Isaac Hawkins, lived, i. 2
Browne, John, buried, ii. 112
Browne, Sir Anthony, ii. 577
Browne, Sir Thomas, baptized, ii. 536; portrait, iii. 82
Browne, Sir William, lived, i. 126; died, iii. 134
Browne, William (1590-1645), Inner Temple, iii. 354
Browning, Robert, lived, iii. 449
Brownlow, Sir John, i. 288
Brownrigg, Mrs., lived, ii. 37, 65; executed, iii. 416
Bruce, Lord, of Kinloss, monument, iii. 166
Bruges, William, lived, ii. 333
Brummell, Beau, lived, i. 349, 359, 389; iii. 379
Brummell, William, died, i. 359
Brune, Walter, iii. 291
Brune, William, ii. 605
Brunel, Isambard Kingdom, engineer, ii. 147, 249; lived, 400; buried, 325
Brunel, Sir Marc Isambard, engineer, iii. 369; lived, i. 147; ii. 400; died, i. 535; buried, ii. 325
Brunswick, Augusta, Duchess of, lived, ii. 187
Brunswick, Duke of, lived, ii. 191
Bryan, picture dealer, lived, iii. 221

INDEX

Bryan, Michael, buried, iii. 2
Bryan, Sir Francis, i. 194
Bryson, J. M., architect, ii. 196
Bubb, Captain, lived, ii. 357
Bubb, G., ii. 199
Buc, Sir George, i. 508
Buccleuch, Dukes of, residence, iii. 126
Buchan, William, M.D., died, iii. 71, memorial tablet, 480
Bock, Samuel, buried, i. 415
Buckerel, Andrew, i. 297
Buckhurst, Lord, i. 231
Buckingham, Duchess of, lived, i. 62, 292
Buckingham, Villiers, Dukes of, residence, iii. 321, 441
Buckingham, George Villiers, first Duke of, i. 141, 290, 378; ii. 608; rebuilt York House, iii. 538; buried, 464; monument, 466
Buckingham, George Villiers, second Duke of, i. 141, 378, 533; ii. 182; iii. 539; married, ii. 451; lived, i. 291, 296, 348, 438, 445; at Tower Hill, iii. 401; prisoner, 399; buried, 464, 466; portrait, i. 366
Buckingham, John Sheffield, Duke of, Master of Grocers' Company, ii. 161; at Marylebone, 512; duel, 352; lived, i. 61, 291; ii. 130, 400; buried, iii. 464, monument, 467; portrait, i. 366
Buckingham, George Grenville, first Marquis of, lived, i. 291
Buckland, Frank, died, i. 13; buried, 281
Buckland, George, i. 446
Buckle, Henry Thomas, lived, ii. 601, 622
Buckley, Samuel, lived, ii. 406
Buckstone, manager, ii. 201
Budd, Dr., lived, i. 367
Budgell, Eustace, lived, i. 74
Buggin, Sir George (d. 1825), monument, i. 536
Bull, John, i. 429
Bull, Mr., lived, ii. 545
Buller, Right Hon. Charles, died, i. 387
Buller, William and Richard, buried, ii. 109
Bullock, William, ii. 7
Bulmer, Bevis, water-works, i. 280
Bulmer, W., printer, buried, i. 415
Bulwer, Lady, school, ii. 189
Bunbury, Sir Charles, died, iii. 13
Bunning, J. B., architect, i. 182, 403, 494, 430; ii. 32, 247, 530; iii. 233
Bunsen, Baron, i. 478; lived, 80, 333, 487; iii. 523
Bunyan, John, ii. 138; died, iii. 260; buried, i. 303
Burbadge, Cuthbert, i. 199; iii. 371
Burbadge, James, i. 199; iii. 371; buried, ii. 387
Burbadge, Richard, ii. 116; died, 228; buried, 387

Burbadge, Winifrid, i. 199
Burdett, Sir Francis, lived, iii. 89; prisoner, 399; died, ii. 297
Burdett-Coutts, Baroness, i. 178, 446; ii. 606; iii. 21, 49, 50, 90, 166, 312; residence, 328; benefactor, 434
Burford, John, i. 304
Burges, Captain, monument, iii. 48
Burges, Robert, buried, i. 158
Burges, William, A.R.A., i. 255, 265, 266; St. Paul's, iii. 51
Burgess, Daniel, preacher, i. 524
Burgess, Dr., pastor, iii. 44
Burgh, Hubert de, i. 193, 197; Constable of the Tower, iii. 400
Burghley, Mildred, Lady, monument, iii. 465
Burghley, Sir William Cecil, Lord, i. 141, 377, 460; ii. 140; iii. 30, 498; lived, i. 304; iii. 321; died, i. 343
Burgoyne, Field-Marshal, Sir John Fox, Constable of the Tower, iii. 400; died, 69; buried, 77; statue, 454
Burgoyne, General, ii. 284; died, 213
Burke, Edmund, i. 184, 287, 464, 476; ii. 18; member of Brooks's, i. 287 note, Middle Temple, iii. 357; lived, i. 283, 361, 494, 534; ii. 66, 106; iii. 139, 209, 106, 188, 523; statue, ii. 242
Burke, Richard, born, i. 127; died, 476
Burley, Sir Simon, ii. 531
Burley, William, lived, iii. 54
Burlington, Countess Dowager of, i. 320, 331
Burlington, Richard, first Earl of, i. 305
Burlington, Richard, third Earl of, i. 80, 102, 306, 331, 455, 450; ii. 454, 463; iii. 162, 489; restored St. Paul's Church, Covent Garden, 56
Burlington, Lord George Cavendish, Earl of, i. 306
Burn, William, architect, ii. 557
Burnet, Bishop, ii. 276, 371; preacher, iii. 46, 166; lived, 265; died, i. 419; ii. 316; buried, 277
Burnet, Dr. Thomas, lived, i. 365; portrait, 366; ii. 35
Burnet, Mr., architect, iii. 380
Burney, Admiral James, died, ii. 274
Burney, Charles, D.D. (d. 1817), monument, iii. 475
Burney, Dr. Charles, organist, i. 505; lived, ii. 384, 489; iii. 100, 132; died, i. 385
Burney, Fanny. See D'Arblay
Burrowes, Dr., rector, i. 473
Burt, Nicholas, lived, iii. 99
Burton, Decimus, architect, i. 78, 225, 258, 408, 446; ii. 254; iii. 160, 161
Burton, Henry, rector, ii. 514; iii. 213
Burton, James, builder, i. 309; iii. 160, 191

Busby, Dr. Richard, iii. 472; benefactor, ii. 150; headmaster, Westminster School, iii. 488; buried, 464; monument, 475
Busby, Dr. Thomas, translator of Lucretius, lived, iii. 139
Bushill, Fred. K., architect, ii. 615
Bushnell, John, statues, iii. 358; buried, iii. 2
Busk, Captain Hans, lived, i. 75
Bute, Earl of, i. 163, 438; lived, 14; died, 80
Butler, Albian, ii. 527
Butler, Bishop, preacher, iii. 166
Butler, Charles, died, ii. 618
Butler, Joseph, rector, iii. 64
Butler, Sir Oliver (d. 1692), iii. 226
Butler, Samuel, died, iii. 170; buried, 58; monument, 476
Butterfield, William, architect, i. 11, 36, 391; ii. 6, 535; iii. 57
Butterworth, Joseph, lived, ii. 63
Button, Daniel, i. 314
Buxton, Sir Thomas Fowell, memorial fountain, ii. 93
Byer, Nicholas, buried, i. 413
Byerley, George, iii. 152
Byfield, Adoniram, preacher, ii. 179
Byng, Admiral, lived, ii. 215
Byrom, John, Merchant Taylors' School, ii. 526
Byron, William, fifth Lord, killed Mr. Chaworth, iii. 14, 305; trial, 486
Byron, George, Lord, i. 29, 220, 412, 440; ii. 26, 403; born, 226; baptized, 497; lived, i. 12, 15, 160; ii. 304; iii. 91, 253; in the Thames, 366; body lay in state, ii. 92
Byron, Henry James, buried, i. 282

CABANEL, Rudolph, architect, i. 431; iii. 435
Cabanel, Rudolph, jun., architect, iii. 337
Cade, Jack, ii. 465; iii. 285, 300, 497; head on London Bridge, ii. 419
Cadell, Thomas, lived, iii. 323; died, i. 206
Cademan, Will., lived, ii. 583
Cadogan, Lords, of Oakley, ii. 607
Cadogan, Charles, second Lord, i. 316, 375
Cæsar, Sir Julius, ii. 320, 322; monument, 304
Caius, Dr., lived, i. 110
Calamy, Benjamin, minister, ii. 490
Calamy, Edmund, i. 336; Merchant Taylors' School, ii. 526; lived, 246; at Trig Stairs, iii. 407; died, 6; buried, ii. 490
Calamy, Edmund, jun., minister, i. 484; ii. 490
Calcott, Dr., lived, ii. 457
Calcott, Sir Augustus Wall, R.A., lived, ii. 457; buried, 328

Caldwell, Richard, M.D., buried, i. 159
Call, Sir John, lived, i. 309
Calmazel, Angelus Franciscus de Talaru de, Bishop of Coutance, buried, iii. 18
Calton, Sir Francis, ii. 323
Cambridge, George Augustus, Duke of, lived, iii. 90
Cambridge, Adolphus, Duke of, died, i. 318
Cambridge, George, Duke of, ii. 118; iii. , 33; opened Charing Cross Road, i. 318, 359; iii. 237
Camden, Charles Pratt, first Earl, i. 319; baptism, ii. 327; grocer, 161; died, 215; portrait, iii. 232
Camden, Marquis, i. 449; ii. 93; lived, i. 64
Camden, William, i. 319, 455; ii. 200; born, 612; at Christ's Hospital, i. 396; school, iii. 63; headmaster, Westminster School, 488; lived, i. 494; buried, iii. 463; monument, 477; portrait, 5
Camelford, Lord, lived, i. 90, 220; duel with Captain Best, 450; ii. 398; buried, i. 50
Cameron, Dr., executed, iii. 416; monument, ii. 500
Campbell, Lady Augusta, eloped with Mr. Clavering, i. 479
Campbell, Colin, architect, i. 306; iii. 119, 166
Campbell, Duncan, lived, i. 290
Campbell, John, banker, ii. 484
Campbell, John, LL.D., lived, iii. 133; buried, ii. 102
Campbell, John, Lord, i. 250, 287, 347; club, ii. 456; lived, 259, 352, 586, 614; iii. 28, 302, 349, 452; portrait, 232
Campbell, Thomas, iii. 206; founder, 422; married, ii. 468; lived, i. 29, 169, 142, 357, 534, 535; ii. 4, 50, 67, 188, 304, 306, 470; iii. 225, 336, 328, 435; buried, 463; statue, 477
Campden, Sir Baptist Hicks, Viscount, lived, i. 320; ii. 213; iii. 274
Campden, Baptist Noel, third Viscount, lived, i. 320
Campion, Jesuit, executed, iii. 415
Campion, Dr. Thomas, buried, i. 538
Canaletto, lived, iii. 248
Canne, John, minister, iii. 340
Canning, Earl, born, ii. 119
Canning, Elizabeth, trial, ii. 611
Canning, George, father of statesman, ii. 497
Canning, Right Hon. George, i. 221, 425; ii. 422; student, 391; church, 326; grocer, 161; lived, i. 12, 289, 361, 450; ii. 118; iii. 28, 296, 302, 463, 472; statue, 8, 478; his son's monument, ii. 386
Cantlow, Sir John, i. 416

INDEX

Capel, Lord, beheaded, iii. 7.
Capel, Sir William, i. 327; lived, iii. 315
Capell, Edward, died, i. 237
Carden, Sir R. W., i. 246
Cardigan, Lord, lived (1669), iii. 112
Cardwell, Lord, portrait, ii. 575
Careless, Betty, buried, iii. 59
Carew, Lord, quoted, iii. 304
Carew, Sir Alexander, buried, ii. 179
Carew, Sir George, lived, iii. 388
Carew, Sir Nicholas, monument, i. 226
Carew, Thomas, lived, ii. 338
Carey, Henry, lived, i. 512; died, iii. 449
Carey, John, ii. 509
Carey, Nicholas, i. 327
Carey, Sir George, i. 327
Carey, Sir Henry, ii. 509
Carey, Sir Phil, ii. 509
Carey, Thomas, i. 327
Carleton, Henry Boyle, Lord, lived, i. 331
Carleton, Sir Dudley, lived, iii. 129; buried, 464; monument, 468
Carlington, Abbot, tomb, iii. 465
Carlini, Agostino, died, i. 330
Carlisle, Bishops of, residence, i. 329; iii. 321, 533
Carlisle, Countess of, ii. 28; lived, i. 327; ii. 206
Carlisle, Howards, Earls of, i. 329, 330
Carlisle, Charles Howard, first Earl of, lived, ii. 597
Carlisle, Charles Howard, third Earl of, lived, iii. 265, 267
Carlisle, seventh Earl of, born, ii. 215
Carlisle, Sir Anthony, lived, iii. 267
Carlyle, Dr. Alexander, i. 439
Carlyle, Thomas, i. 333; club, iii. 313; lecturer, ii. 7; lived, ii. 43, 380, 589; ii. 570; iii. 283; statue, i. 383
Carmarthen, Marquis of, lived, ii. 382
Carnarvon, Earl of, lived, i. 289
Caroline, Queen of George II., ii. 285, 287, 294, 338; iii. 141, 233, 298; buried, 463, 467
Caroline, Queen of George IV., i. 80; lived, 451; ii. 301; Italian witnesses at her trial, i. 460
Caron, Abbé, buried, iii. 268
Caron, Sir Noel de, i. 334; ii. 323; lived, 357
Carpenter, John, town clerk, i. 403
Carpenter, Lord, lived, ii. 186
Carr, Henry, architect, iii. 206
Carr, James, architect, ii. 277; lived, i. 14
Carr, Mrs., ii. 459
Carr, Rev. W. Holwell, ii. 573
Carr, Sir John, lived, ii. 85
Carrington, Lord, charge of assault, ii. 474
Carte, Samuel, lived, i. 336
Carte, Thomas, historian, lived, i. 494; ii. 597
Carter, sculptor, ii. 605

Carter, Mrs. Elizabeth, lived, iii. 54; died, i. 411
Carteret, Lord, lived, i. 63; ii. 307
Cartwright, architect, i. 51
Cartwright, Major, statue, i. 309
Cartwright, William, school, iii. 488; lived, 99
Cary, Lord, i. 414
Cary, Rev. Henry, ii. 310; lived, i. 40, 344, 361, 519; iii. 35; buried, 477
Cary, Thomas, ii. 28
Caryll, Joseph, minister, ii. 471
Casaubon, Isaac, buried, iii. 463; monument, 477
Casimir, Duke, ii. 250
Caslon, William, lived (1766), ii. 206; iii. 452; died, i. 179; buried, ii. 450
Castellani, Alessandro, i. 255
Castile, King of, lived, i. 112
Castlehaven, Elizabeth, Countess of, memorial, iii. 19
Castlemaine, Countess of. See Cleveland, Duchess of
Castlemaine, Earl of, lived, i. 166
Castlereagh, Lord, lived, i. 423; ii. 301; buried, iii. 463, 472
Catalani, Madame, lived, i. 281, 361
Catherine of Valois, Queen, buried, iii. 465
Catherine, Queen of Charles II., i. 339, 390; ii. 79; iii. 88; lived, 271; portrait, 5
Catton, Charles, iii. 5
Cavallo, Tiberius, buried, iii. 21
Cavanagh, fives player, i. 454
Cave, Edward, lived, ii. 314
Cave, William, rector, i. 34
Cavendish, Henry, lived, i. 204; ii. 474
Cavendish, Sir William, buried, i. 226
Cawarden, Sir Thomas, i. 194, 199; ii. 505
Cawood, Robert, buried, i. 226
Cawthorne, Mrs., i. 489
Caxton, William, i. 39; buried, ii. 468; tablet, 467
Cecil, Rev. Richard, i. 146; born, 391
Cecil, William, baptized, i. 413
Centlivre, Susan, died, i. 290; buried, iii. 59
Chadwicke, John, died, ii. 13
Chalmers, Alexander, lived, iii. 380
Chalmers, Dr., preacher, iii. 339
Chalmers, George, died, ii. 274
Chaloner, Sir Thomas, died, i. 419
Chamberlain, Dr. Hugh, lived, ii. 18
Chamberlain, John, lived, ii. 610
Chamberlayne, Dr. Edward, lived, i. 380; monument, ii. 449
Chamberlin, Mason, died, i. 121
Chambers, Ephraim, died, i. 326
Chambers, Sir Robert, lived, ii. 67
Chambers, Sir William, lived, i. 169; ii. 605; iii. 101; died, ii. 606; buried, iii. 463; portrait, 180; architect, i. 12; iii. 177, 272; state coach, i. 295

Chandler, Dr. S., portrait, iii. 188
Chandos, Duchess of, iii. 446
Chandos, James Brydges, Duke of, i. 341, 348
Chandos, George Brydges, sixth Lord, i. 289
Chandos, William Brydges, seventh Lord, i. 348
Chantrey, Sir Francis, lived, i. 350, 487; ii. 5; died, i. 152; bequest, iii. 180; statues, i. 274
Chapman, George, buried, ii. 112
Chapman, J., bequest, ii. 499
Chapone, Mrs., lived, i. 328, 330, 493
Chardin, Sir John, lived, ii. 224
Charlemont, Lord, lived, ii. 212
Charles I., i. 360, 370; ii. 289; at Guildhall, 172; at Paul's Cross, iii. 62; in the tilt-yard, 381; during his trial, i. 459; iii. 485; prisoner, ii. 286; death-warrant signed, iii. 4; execution, 511; portrait, ii. 523; iii. 358; statue, i. 355, 428; ii. 503; iii. 135, 183, 317
Charles II., i. 361, 371, 383, 451; ii. 99, 292, 293, 295; iii. 377; born, ii. 286; in Privy Garden, iii. 125; in the Thames, 365; speech to House of Commons, 506; Pall Mall, ii. 458; benefactor, iii. 250; buried, 463, 467; founder of Mathematical School, i. 396; Master of Grocers' Company, ii. 161; bust, iii. 188; portrait, i. 366, 395; ii. 523; iii. 5, 358, 438; statue, i. 384; iii. 267, 317
Charles V., lived, i. 194, 240; iii. 300, 528
Charles X., of France, lived, i. 80
Charles Edward, Prince, the Young Pretender, i. 218; ii. 19; iii. 12
Charlotte, Princess of Wales, i. 451; iii. 449, 452; born, i. 332; married, 332; lived, 320; iii. 33
Charlotte, Queen of George III., i. 293, 362; ii. 201, 597; iii. 272; portrait, ii. 523; iii. 179; statue, 133
Charnock, conspirator, i. 212
Charteris, Francis, lived, ii. 93
Chartres, William, otherwise Sautre, i. 160
Chastillon, Mons de, lived, i. 541
Chateaubriand, ii. 404; lived, iii. 390
Chatelain, J. B., lived, iii. 246; died, 491
Chatham, William Pitt, Earl of, i. 367, 520; ii. 137; baptism, 281; lived, 301; grocer, 161; lay in state, iii. 4; buried, 463; monument, ii. 170; iii. 472; statue, ii. 242; wax effigy, iii. 479
Chatham, second Earl of, i. 164; lived, iii. 212
Chatris, Sir William, burned, iii. 255
Chatterton, Thomas, lived, iii. 245; died, i. 285; buried, 44; iii. 243

Chaucer, Geoffrey, ii. 80; fined, 64; lived, i. 27; buried, iii. 463; portrait, ii. 525; monument, iii. 475
Chaucer, John, lived, iii. 368
Chauncey, Dr., minister, ii. 471
Chaworth, duel with Lord Byron, iii. 14, 305; died, i. 165
Chaworth, William (d. 1582), brass, ii. 499
Chedsey, William, rector, i. 32
Cheere, John, i. 341
Cheke, Sir John, ii. 372; died, iii. 530; buried, i. 11
Chelmsford, Frederick, first Lord, buried, i. 282
Cheney, Prof., buried, i. 282
Cheselden, William, buried, i. 384
Chester, Bishops of, residence, iii. 321
Chester, Colonel, lived, i. 210
Chesterfield, Countess of, ii. 619; lived, 586
Chesterfield, Philip, second Earl of, ii. 111
Chesterfield, Philip, fourth Earl of, baptism, ii. 281; at White's, iii. 494; club, 14; lived, i. 148; ii. 164, 300; iii. 296; died, i. 207, 388
Cheyne, Charles, Viscount, i. 375, 389
Cheyne, Lady Jane, monument, ii. 449
Cheyne, Sir William, buried, i. 159
Chicheley, Abp., ii. 361; portrait, 362, 364
Chicheley, Sir Robert, iii. 311
Chichester, Bishops of, i. 346; iii. 343
Chichester, Earls of, i. 255
Chichester, Sir Arthur, lived, i. 523
Chichley, John, lived, ii. 193
Chiffinch, Thomas, buried, iii. 478
Child, Aylwin, i. 167
Child, Francis, lived, ii. 63; banker, i. 390; portrait, 395
Child, Messrs., i. 501; iii. 359
Chilmead, Rev. Edward, buried, i. 226
Chippendale, workshops, ii. 485; lived, iii. 137
Chiswell, Richard, tablet, i. 226
Cholmondeley, Marquis of, lived, i. 318
Cholmondeley, Sir Richard, tomb, iii. 77
Christian VII., King of Denmark, i. 490
Christian, Ewan, architect, i. 393
Christie, James, auctioneer, iii. 14; buried, ii. 275, 281, sale-rooms, 337
Christie, duel with John Scott, i. 345; iii. 120
Christmas, Gerard, architect, i. 21; ii. 603
Christy, Henry, i. 255, 266
Chudleigh, Miss, marriage, i. 487
Churchill, Admiral, lived, ii. 296
Churchill, Arabella, lived, ii. 298
Churchill, Awnsham and John, lived, iii. 39

INDEX

Churchill, Charles, ii. 312; school, iii.
488; teacher, 132; married, ii. 60;
lived, 165; iii. 35, 425
Churchill, General, i. 528
Churchman, John, i. 488
Churchman, Mrs., lived, iii. 246
Churchyard, Thomas, buried, ii. 468
Cibber, Caius Gabriel, i. 172; ii. 379;
iii. 46, 184; buried, i. 490; bas relief,
ii. 557
Cibber, Colley, i. 214; lived, 360; ii.
296; died, i. 164; ii. 270; buried, i.
490
Cibber, Mrs., lived, ii. 121, 336; iii. 225,
buried, 464
Cibber, Theophilus, lived, iii. 514
Cioli, Germayne, i. 477
Cipriani, J. B., R.A., i. 295; iii. 509;
teacher, 162; lived, ii. 203; city coach,
464; buried, 450
Claggett, Mr., i. 55
Clare, John Holles, first Earl of, i. 406;
iii. 301; death of his wife, 301
Clare, John Holles, second Earl of, i. 405;
ii. 22
Clare, Gilbert Holles, third Earl of, i.
496; lived, iii. 450; died, ii. 108
Clare, Viscount, lived, ii. 92
Clarence, George, Duke of, murdered, iii.
395
Clarendon, Edward Hyde, Earl of, i. 334,
449; iii. 338; Middle Temple, 357;
married, ii. 468; lived, i. 166, 408; ii.
298; iii. 533; buried, 463; statue, ii.
242
Clarges, Anne. See Albemarle, Ann, Duchess of
Clarges, farrier, ii. 518
Clarges, Sir Thomas, lived, iii. 88
Clarges, Sir Walter, i. 411; iii. 89
Clark, menagerie keeper, ii. 26
Clarke, Dr. Adam, iii. 336; monument,
i. 405
Clarke, Dr. Samuel, i. 159; rector, ii. 279;
lived, iii. 89
Clarke, Francis, bequest, ii. 573
Clarke, Joseph, architect, ii. 149
Clarke, Mary Anne, i. 348; lived, iii.
348
Clarke, S., architect, i. 79; iii. 383
Clarke, Sir Edward, ii. 344
Clarke, Sir Simon, lived, ii. 119
Clarke, T. Chatfeild, architect, i. 45, 503;
iii. 380
Clarke, Thomas, lived, iii. 99
Claydon, John, burned, ii. 233
Claypole, Elizabeth, daughter of Oliver
Cromwell, buried, iii. 468
Clayton, Dr., pastor, iii. 117
Clayton, Sir Robert, i. 394; ii. 431; lived,
614
Clayton and Bell, glass, ii. 360, 491;
mosaic, iii. 471

Cleland, John, died, iii. 79
Cleland, William, lived, ii. 296
Clemence, architect, i. 362
Clement, Gregory, executed, i. 354
Clere, Thomas, brass, ii. 495
Cleveland, Duchess of, i. 421, 422;
baptized, ii. 468; letter, 448; lived, i.
62, 166; iii. 506
Cleveland, Duke of, died, ii. 300
Cleveland, John, buried, ii. 535
Clifford, family, i. 324
Clifford, Lady Jane, tomb, iii. 465
Clifford, Hugh, Lord, iii. 297
Clifford, Lord-Treasurer, lived, i. 361;
iii. 443
Clifford, Martin, lived, i. 365
Clifford, Robert de, i. 423
Clifton, Edward, ii. 38; architect, 3, 23,
377, 378
Cline, Henry, lived, i. 277; ii. 493; died,
396
Clint, George, A.R.A., lived, ii. 134
Clinton General, Sir Henry, lived, iii.
109
Clinton, Lord, lived, i. 289
Clive, Kitty, lived, ii. 208
Clive, Robert Lord, Merchant Taylors'
School, ii. 526; died, i. 163; portrait,
ii. 616
Closterman, John, lived, iii. 85
Cloudesley, family, i. 429
Clun, actor, murdered, ii. 333; iii. 347
Clutton, Henry, architect, ii. 31
Clyde, Lord, lived, i. 165; buried, iii.
463; statue, 454; monument, 474
Caut, King, ii. 419
Coade's artificial stone, iii. 482
Coan, Norfolk dwarf, ii. 50
Cobb, cabinetmaker, ii. 485
Cobbett, William, lived, i. 217
Cobden, Richard, lived, iii. 333; statue,
i. 319
Cobham, Sir John Oldcastle, Lord, lived,
i. 419, 454; executed, ii. 113
Cobham, Lord, i. 197; ii. 79, 548
Cobham, Lord, Pope's, lived, ii. 187
Cochrane, Lord. See Dundonald
Cock, Mr., surgeon, ii. 305
Cockaine, Sir Thomas, ii. 33
Cockaine, Sir William, i. 435; lived, 278
Cocker, Edward, lived, iii. 52; died, ii.
341; buried, 103
Cockerell, C. R., R.A., architect, i. 96,
117; ii. 2, 51, 186, 430, 443; iii. 159,
333, 360, 422
Cockerell, F. Pepys, architect, ii. 77
Cockerell, S. P., architect, i. 8, 49; ii.
481; iii. 209
Cockes, Dr., Dean of Canterbury, ii. 271
Cocks's auction rooms, iii. 84
Codrington, Admiral Sir Edward, died,
ii. 4; buried, iii. 74
Coigny, Maréchal Duc de, lived, iii. 291

Coke, Sir Edward, i. 424; ii. 11, 27, 195; reader, 453; Inner Temple, iii. 354; marriage, i. 44; lived, iii. 232; portrait, 232
Coke, Justice William, i. 108
Coke, Lady Mary, lived, ii. 565
Coke, Robert, buried, i. 44
Coke, Sir John, lived, ii. 85
Coke of Holkham, i. 164; lived, iii. 33
Colbert, lived, ii. 380
Colborne, Lord, lived, ii. 215
Colburn, Henry, died, i. 289
Colby, Sir Thomas, i. 441
Cole, J. J., architect, iii. 315
Cole, Lieutenant H. H., architect, ii. 569
Cole, Sir Henry, K.C.B., iii. 222, 223, 277; at Christ's Hospital, i. 396; buried, 282
Coleman, Robert, i. 443
Colepepper, Colonel, i. 214; at Whitehall, iii. 512
Coleridge, S. T., ii. 37, 593; "Grecian," i. 396; lectures, 471; ii. 66; iii. 336; monetary relief, 188; tavern, 207; lived, i. 204; ii. 7, 601; iii. 280
Coleridge, Sara, died, i. 387
Colet, Dean John, born, i. 52; vicar, 538; founder, iii. 63; tomb, 43; monument, 42; portrait, ii. 520
Colet, Humfrey, M.P., ii. 91
Colet, Sir Henry, lived, i. 539
Coley, Henry, ii. 144; lived, iii. 173
Collcutt, T. E., architect, ii. 256; iii. 237
College, Stephen, buried, ii. 154
Collier, Jeremy, prison, ii. 90; buried, iii. 20
Collier, J. Payne, iii. 153, 307
Collingwood, Lord, monument, iii. 48
Collingwood, Sir John, grave, iii. 49
Collins, Anthony, lived, i. 341
Collins, Arthur, lived, ii. 63; buried, i. 128
Collins, Charles A., buried, i. 282
Collins, John, died, ii. 85
Collins, William, poet, i. 380; lived, 330; ii. 270
Collins, William, R.A., born, ii. 382; lived, 110; died, i. 501; buried, iii. 3
Collins, William Wilkie, died, iii. 523
Collinson, Peter, F.R.S., lived, ii. 136
Colman, George, the elder, school, iii. 488; lived, i. 123; iii. 266; manager, ii. 200; monument, 326
Colman, George, the younger, manager, ii. 201; married, 450; lived, 519; died, i. 281; monument, ii. 326
Colman, Thomas, monument, ii. 326
Colquhoun, Patrick, died, ii. 274
Colton, Rev. C. C., lived, iii. 121
Combe, William, prisoner, ii. 342
Combermere, Field-Marshal, Lord, school, iii. 488; buried, 77
Compton, Henry, Bishop of London, i. 49; iii. 46; lived, i. 94

Compton, Sir Francis, i. 449
Comyn, Sir Robert, Merchant Taylors' School, ii. 526
Concanen, ii. 141
Condé, Prince of, lived, ii. 384
Condé, Princess of, buried, iii. 268
Condell, Henry, buried, ii. 490; will, 206
Congleton, H. B. Parnell, first Lord, buried, i. 134
Congreve, William, ii. 397, 414, 440, 446; Middle Temple, iii. 357; lived, 337; buried, 463; monument, 473
Conquest, George, ii. 148
Constable, Amy, memorial, iii. 19
Constable, John, R.A., lived, ii. 335; died, i. 362
Constance of Castile, John of Gaunt's second wife, tomb, iii. 41
Constantine, a Greek, ii. 147
Conway, Field-Marshal, lived, iii. 265, 452
Conyngham, Marchioness of, lived, ii. 183
Cook, Captain James, i. 254; club, ii. 484; lived, 542
Cook, Henry, painter, iii. 266
Cooke, George Frederick, actor, ii. 126, 200; lived, i. 311; ii. 4, 336, 489; iii. 91, 332
Cooke, Henry, lived, ii. 349
Cooke, Thomas, buried, ii. 495
Cooke, T. P., Sadler's Wells, iii. 201; buried, i. 282
Cooper, J., i. 490
Cooper, Samuel, miniature painter, lived, ii. 207; memorial, iii. 17
Cooper, Sir Astley, lived, i. 277; ii. 305, 493, 586; died, i. 450; buried, ii. 176; monument, iii. 48
Coote, Sir Eyre, portrait, ii. 616
Cope, C. W., R.A., frescoes, ii. 241, 242
Cope, Lady, lived, i. 522
Cope, Sir John, lived, i. 411; ii. 296
Cope, Sir Walter, ii. 223
Copeland, Alderman, W. T., i. 478; iii. 335
Copeland, William, lived, ii. 63, 443
Copland, William, lived, iii. 377
Copley, John Singleton, R.A., lived, ii. 93; portraits by, i. 395
Coram, Captain Thomas, i. 455; founder, ii. 71; died, 383
Corbet, Bp., school, iii. 488
Corbet, D. A., architect, i. 544
Corbet, Mrs., monument, ii. 468
Cork, Countess of, lived, i. 360; died, 308
Cornelys, Mrs. Teresa, i. 329; lived, iii. 265; prison, ii. 60
Cornwall, John of Eltham, Duke of, buried, i. 197
Cornwallis, Abp., portrait, ii. 364
Cornwallis, Charles, Marquis, grocer, ii. 161; duel, 253; lived, i. 309; ii. 137, 165, 462; monument, iii. 48

INDEX

Cornwallis, Lady, lived, ii. 596
Corticelli, iii. 331
Coryat, Tom, lived, i. 228
Cosin, William, i. 459
Costa, Sir Michael, conductor, iii. 197; buried, ii. 325
Cosway, Richard, R.A., married, ii. 96; lived, i. 165; ii. 616; iii. 13, 220, 327; monument, ii. 497
Cotes, F., R.A., died, i. 342
Cottenham, Lord, student, ii. 391
Cottington, Francis, Lord, ii. 323; lived, i. 278; monument, iii. 468
Cotton, Mr., Governor of the Bank, i. 97
Cotton, Charles, buried, ii. 280
Cotton, Sir Allen, Lord Mayor, monument, ii. 481
Cotton, Sir John, i. 253, 459
Cotton, Sir Robert, i. 253, 266; lived, 459
Courtenay, William, Abp. of Canterbury, i. 194
Courtin, Antoine, French Ambassador, lived, ii. 299
Cousins, Samuel, lived, ii. 619
Coutts, (Mrs.) See St. Alban's (Duchess of)
Coutts, Thomas, i. 5; lived, 476
Coventry, Wm., fifth Earl of, lived, ii. 186
Coventry, George, sixth Earl of, i. 466; ii. 515; died, iii. 89
Coventry, Henry, Secretary, lived, iii. 332; i. 467; tomb, ii. 478
Coventry, Lord Keeper, lived, i. 325, 542; ii. 269; died, i. 467
Coventry, Sir John, i. 231; lived, iii. 332
Coventry, Sir William, i. 467; prisoner, ii. 89; iii. 399
Coverdale, Miles, rector, ii. 455; buried, i. 117
Cowley, Abraham, ii. 298; school, iii. 486; candidate for office of Master of the Savoy, 218; lived, i. 128; ii. 62; died iii. 363; buried, 463; monument, 476
Cowley, Richard, buried, ii. 387
Cowper, Ashley, lived, iii. 283
Cowper, James, lived, iii. 112
Cowper, Lord Chancellor, lived, ii. 93, 187, 395
Cowper, William, poet, i. 488; ii. 335, 469; iii. 72; school, 488; Inner Temple, 354; lived, ii. 258
Cowper, William, Earl (d. 1793), lived, iii. 193
Cowper, Sir William, i. 469; lived, iii. 112
Cox, Richard, Bp. of Ely, ii. 10
Coxe, Archdeacon, born, i. 517
Coxe, Peter, auctioneer, lived, iii. 221
Crabbe, George, ii. 248; lived, i. 7, 189, 311, 458; on Westminster Bridge, iii. 482
Crace, F., i. 255, 267
Crace, J. G., decorator, iii. 23
Cracherode, Rev. C. M., i. 254, 267; born, iii. 134

Cradock, James, buried, ii. 501
Cradock, Thomas, jumped from monument, ii. 559
Cragg, James, i. 469
Craggs, Secretary, lived, ii. 307; buried, iii. 463, 467; monument, 473
Craig, Joseph, i. 469
Cramer, William, buried, ii. 496
Crane, Sir Francis, iii. 382
Cranmer, Abp., prisoner, iii. 398; portrait, ii. 364
Crashaw, Richard, school, i. 365
Cratwell, London hangman, i. 420
Craufurd, Dr., i. 386
Craven, Sir William, iii. 104
Craven, William, first Earl of, i. 166, 334; ii. 232; iii. 72; died, i. 472; portrait, 366
Craythorne, John, i. 155
Creede, Thomas, i. 336; lived, ii. 372
Cremorne, Lord, i. 376; lived, 473
Cresswell, Sir Cresswell, school, i. 365
Creswell, Madame, i. 243
Creswick, Mr., actor, lived, i. 209; manager, iii. 337
Cresy, Edward, lived, iii. 333
Crew, Nathaniel, Lord, Bp. of Durham, lived, iii. 84
Crewe, John, first Lord, i. 287; lived, ii. 166
Crewe, Mrs., lived, ii. 166
Crispe, Sir Nicholas, buried, ii. 539
Crispin, Dr., lived at Pimlico 1687, iii. 97
Crockford, John, i. 475; lived, iii. 324
Crodacott, chaplain, iii. 216
Croft, William, buried, iii. 464
Crofts, Lord, lived, ii. 596; iii. 296
Crofts, Sir William, duel, ii. 130
Croke, Sir George, lived, ii. 62
Croker, J. Crofton, buried, i. 282
Croly, Rev. George, LL.D., lived, i. 169, 282; iii. 133; rector, 311; bust, 312
Cromarty, Earl of, died, iii. 101
Cromwell, Mrs. Elizabeth, died, i. 146
Cromwell, Henry, Pope's correspondent, lived, iii. 121, 515; buried, i. 414
Cromwell, Henry, son of Oliver, Gray's Inn, ii. 140; married, i. 475; ii. 326
Cromwell, Mary, lived, ii. 30
Cromwell, Oliver, i. 210, 259, 443, 535; ii. 160, 252, 373, 290; student, ii. 390; married, 110; lived, i. 437, 523; ii. 338, 437; iii. 340; at Temple Bar, 358; keys of City delivered to him, ii. 269; inaugurated as Lord Protector, iii. 485; offered the Crown, 511; lay in state, 270; corpse, 155; buried, 468; body at Tyburn, 419; letter, 183; proclamation, ii. 283; his mother buried, 468; his tall porter, i. 175
Cromwell, Richard, temp. Henry VIII., ii. 203

Cromwell, Richard, son of Henry, baptism, ii. 178
Cromwell, Richard, student, ii. 390
Cromwell, Thomas, Lord, i. 325
Cromwell, Thomas (d. 1748), iii. 260
Crook, Japhet, pillory, i. 355
Crooke, Dr. Hilkiah, i. 172
Croom, Dr., trial, iii. 214
Crosby, Brass, died, i. 367; obelisk in honour of, ii. 607
Crosby, Sir John, i. 476; monument, ii. 304
Cross, highwayman, ii. 591
Cross, menagerie keeper, ii. 26; iii. 338
Crosse and Blackwell, iii. 267
Croton, William, iii. 326
Cruden, Alex., lived, iii. 219; died, ii. 270; buried, i. 491
Cruikshank, George, lived, ii. 184, 563
Cruikshank, William Cumberland, died, ii. 384
Crundale, Richard de, i. 353
Crundale, Roger de, i. 353
Crunden, John, i. 222
Cubitt, J., architect, i. 198
Cubitt, Lewis, architect, i. 131; ii. 146, 147
Cubitt, Thomas, i. 16, 153; ii. 323
Cubitt, Sir William, iii. 275
Cubitt, Mr., ii. 425
Cubitt, Messrs., ii. 4; iii. 83
Cullum, Sir John, lived, i. 482
Culver, William, ii. 415
Cumberland, William, Duke of, i. 482, 483; ii. 71, 166, 235; iii. 220; born, ii. 381; lived, iii. 12; buried, 463, 467; statue, i. 343
Cumberland, Duke of, brother of George III., lived, iii. 347
Cumberland, Cliffords, Earls of, lived, i. 324; iii. 381
Cumberland, George, third Earl of, buried, ii. 500
Cumberland, Richard, school, iii. 488; lived, i. 2; iii. 139; died, i. 145
Cumberland, Richard, Bishop of Peterborough, lived, i. 324
Cundy, Thomas, architect, i. 108, 152, 387; ii. 160, 533; iii. 3
Cundy, Messrs., architects, ii. 318
Cunningham, Allan, i. 295; lived, 152; buried, ii. 325
Cunningham, Thomas, buried, ii. 312
Cunningham, William, lived, i. 443
Cuper, Boydell, i. 483
Cure, Thomas, i. 484; lord of manor, iii. 30; monument, 215
Curll, Edmund, i. 349, 494; lived, ii. 63; iii. 170; pillory, i. 355; treatment by the Westminster scholars, iii. 489
Curll, William, lived, i. 229; club, 480
Curran, John Philpot, i. 352; lived, 42; ii. 14; died, i. 281; buried, iii. 2

Currey, Henry, architect, ii. 494; iii. 374
Curtis, William, lived, ii. 136; buried, i. 128
Curzon, Lady Diana, lived, iii. 112
Cutler, Sir John, grocer, ii. 161; buried, 468
Cuvier, Baron, lived, ii. 385
Cuzzoni, Francesca, singer, ii. 200

DABORNE, prisoner, i. 126
Dacre family, i. 141
Dacre, Anne, Lady, benefactor, ii. 14; monument, 449
Dacres, Lords, of the South, residence, iii. 329, 388
Dacre, Thomas, eighth Lord, executed, iii. 414
Dacre, Gregory, ninth Lord, i. 324, 377; ii. 14; buried, iii. 330; monument, ii. 449
Daffy, Mrs. Catherine, ii. 457; died, iii. 203
Dahl, Michael, buried, ii. 280
Dale, Rev. Thomas, "deputy Grecian," i. 306
Dalhousie, Countess of, monument, ii. 499
Dallington, Sir Robert, lived, i. 365
Dalton's print warehouse, iii. 74
Damer, Hon. John, i. 142; lived, ii. 164
Damer, Hon. Mrs., died, i. 283
Danby, Henry Danvers, Earl of, ii. 283
Dance, George, sen., architect, i. 178, 226; ii. 386, 450, 463
Dance, George, jun., R.A., architect, i. 29, 35, 116, 120; ii. 114, 134, 170, 306, 451, 463, 591, 611; iii. 287, 335
Dance, Giles, architect, i. 227
Dancett, Mr., lived, ii. 596
Dandulo, baptized, ii. 28
Dangerfield, ii. 194, 221
Daniel, George, lived, i. 326
Daniel, Samuel, lived, ii. 615
Daniel, Thomas, i. 236
Daniell, Thomas, R.A., lived, ii. 245; buried, 325
Danvers, Sir John, lived, i. 376, 377, 490
Danvers, Lord, lived, ii. 196
Darbishire, H. A., architect, i. 446; iii. 434
D'Arblay, Madame, married, i. 533; lived, 218, 387; ii. 181, 489, 565
Darbyshire, Richard, rector, ii. 178
Darcy, Thomas, Lord, monument, i. 226
Darnley, James, natural son of James II., buried, iii. 466
Darrell, Dr., bequest, ii. 579
Darson, John, i. 213
Dartequenave, Charles, ii. 345; lived, i. 309
Dartmouth, William, first Earl of, i. 410; lived, i. 490; buried, iii. 407
Dartmouth, William, second Earl of, buried, iii. 407

Darwin, Charles, statue, i. 274
Daubeny, Sir Giles, altar-tomb, iii. 468
Daukes, Samuel W., architect, i. 530
Daukes and Hamilton, architects, iii. 458
Davenant, Lady, lived, iii. 202; died, i. 337; buried, 239
Davenant, Sir William, i. 24, 85, 436; ii. 397, 607; prisoner, iii. 399; died, i. 112; buried, 463, 476; revival of the stage, 191
Davenport, Mrs., lived, i. 280
Davidge, —, manager, iii. 337
Davids, Miss, lived, i. 337
Davidson, Alexander, lived, ii. 301
Davies, James, i. 139
Davies, John, architect, i. 478
Davies, Sir John, expelled the Middle Temple, iii. 356; readmitted, 356
Davies, Mary, marriage to Sir Thomas Grosvenor, i. 414
Davies, Mary, married to Lord George Bentinck, ii. 517
Davies, Tom, lived, i. 531; iii. 194; buried, 59
Davies, Sir Thomas, i. 79
Davies of Hereford (d. 1617), buried, i. 538
Davis, Sir John, ii. 387
Davis, Lockyer, monument, i. 116
Davis, Moll, lived, ii. 298; iii. 331
Davison, Thomas, lived, iii. 504
Davy, Sir Humphry, iii. 186; founder, 542; married to Mrs. Apreece, 109; lived, ii. 165; iii. 34; portrait, 188; bust, 471
Dawe, George, R.A., lived, i. 236
Dawes, John, ii. 214
Dawes, Sir William, Abp. of York, Merchant Taylors' School, ii. 526; lived, i. 343
Dawncey, William, founder, iii. 212
Dawson, Bully, died, ii. 413
Dawson, Jemmy, executed, ii. 324
Dawson, Nancy, buried, ii. 102
Day, Bp., rector, i. 34
Day, Thomas, market keeper, i. 463
Day, Thomas, born, iii. 458; school, i. 365; lived, iii. 318
Daye, John, lived, i. 21
Dayes, Edward, lived, ii. 76
Dean, George, builder, ii. 56
Deane, Mr., Pope's schoolfellow, i. 519
De Beauvoir, Richard, i. 93
De Cort, H. F. J., buried, iii. 21
De Critz, John, lived, iii. 242
Defoe, Daniel, i. 114; ii. 68; prisoner, 501; lived, i. 494; ii. 76, 185; iii. 318; died, ii. 109; iii. 168; buried, i. 303
Defoe, Mrs., buried, i. 303
Defoe, Sophia, baptism, ii. 178
De Grey, Lord Chief Justice, lived, ii. 396
Dekker, prisoner, iii. 117

De la Bêche, Sir H. T., ii. 567
Delany, Mrs., i. 422; lived, 218, 283, 340, 412; iii. 170; died, ii. 297; buried, 281
Delaval, Lord, i. 330
De Moivre, Abraham, iii. 253
Denbigh, William, Earl of, lived, i. 325
Denham, Lieut.-Col. Dixon, Merchant Taylors' School, ii. 526
Denham, Sir John, i. 305, 495; student, ii. 390; married, i. 239; died, iii. 224; buried, 463
Denham, Lady, buried, ii. 468
Denison, J., lived, ii. 493
Denman, Lord Chief Justice, lived, iii. 109; portrait, 232
Denman, Maria, ii. 51
Denney, Lord, ii. 27
Denny, Sir Anthony, school, iii. 63
Denny, Hugh, ii. 139
Dent, Mr., died, ii. 213
Denys, Peter, lived, iii. 65
De Quincey, Thomas, lived, i. 380; iii. 540
Derby, Thomas Stanley, first Earl of, lived, i. 496; ii. 208; iii. 191
Derby, Edward, third Earl of, i. 324, 496
Derby, William, sixth Earl of, lived, i. 496
Derby, Edward, twelfth Earl of, married to Miss Farren, ii. 165
Derby, Edward, fourteenth Earl of, i. 254; bust, ii. 513; statue, iii. 8
Derby, Edward, fifteenth Earl of, ii. 302; Peabody Buildings, iii. 66
Dering, Sir Cholmley, duel, iii. 386
Dermody, Thomas, lived, ii. 620
Derrick, —, ii. 18
Derrick, hangman, iii. 417
Derwentwater, Earl of, ii. 74; prisoner, iii. 399; executed, 401
Desaguliers, Dr. J. T., died, i. 143
De Tabley, Lord, lived, ii. 215
Dethike, Gilbert, ii. 209
De Valangin, Dr., lived, ii. 211
Devone, Mons., i. 358
Devonshire, Countess of, ii. 48; died, i. 502
Devonshire, Duchess of, ii. 438
Devonshire, William, first Duke of, i. 61; 163, 214; at Whitehall, ii. 556; iii. 512; died, i. 502; iii. 89
Devonshire, William, third Duke of, i. 163; lived, 501
Devonshire, fourth Duke of, i. 306
Devonshire, Hugh Courtenay, Earl of, i. 475; benefactor, iii. 503
Devonshire, Mountjoy, Earl of, buried, iii. 464
Devonshire, William, first Earl of, died, ii. 596
Devonshire, William, second Earl of, died, i. 502; buried, 227

D'Ewes, Sir Symonds, iii. 302; lived, i. 494; ii. 61, 269
De Wint, Peter, lived, ii. 134; iii. 152; memorial, ii. 500
Dibdin, Charles, ii. 336, 452; manager, iii. 337; died, i. 61; buried, 319
Dibdin, Thomas, iii. 209; born, ii. 569; lessee, iii. 337; lived, i. 362; ii. 126, 562, 570
Dibdin, Rev. Thomas Frognal, D.D., i. 289; rector, ii. 493
Dickens, Charles, i. 181; ii. 249; lived, i. 131, 161, 503, 516; ii. 600; iii. 349; died, ii. 84; buried, iii. 461, 477
Dickenson, Dr. Edmund, lived, ii. 483
Dicker, Walter, ii. 523
Dickson, Dr., Bp. of Down, buried, ii. 275
Digby, Sir Everard, executed, ii. 431, 448
Digby, Sir Kenelm, lived, ii. 155, 221, 483; iii. 84; arrested, 501; prisoner, i. 478; iii. 525; buried, i. 392
Digby, Lady Venetia, buried, i. 392
Dighton, William de, lived, i. 206
Dillon, A. R., Abp. of Narbonne, buried, iii. 18
Dillon, Dr., i. 291, 362
Dillon's print warehouse, iii. 177
Dilly, Edward, bookseller, lived, iii. 117; buried, ii. 102
Dingley, Mr., i. 404; ii. 454
Disraeli, Benjamin. See Beaconsfield
Disraeli, Isaac, lived, i. 6, 7, 209; ii. 273
Ditton, Humphry, i. 479; buried, 398
Dives, Sir Lewis, lived, ii. 207
Dixon, John, i. 417
Dobson, William, buried, ii. 478
Docminique, Paul, lived, ii. 489
Dockwra, William, iii. 69; Penny Post, 114; lived, ii. 388
Docwra, Thomas, Prior of the Hospital of St. John of Jerusalem, Clerkenwell, ii. 211, 313
Dodd, actor, died, iii. 283
Dodd, Rev. Dr., i. 290, 362; ii. 97, 126; chaplain, iii. 458; lived, 283; trial, ii. 611; executed, iii. 416
Dodd, Ralph, iii. 453
Dodington, Bubb, Lord Melcombe, lived, iii. 12
Dodington, Eliza, ii. 121
Dodington, William, iii. 230
Dodsley, James, buried, ii. 281
Dodsley, Robert, lived, iii. 12
Dodson, Sir John, Merchant Taylors' School, ii. 526
Doggett, Thomas, ii. 49; prize, iii. 364
Dolben, David, Bp. of Bangor, i. 94; monument, ii. 178
Dolben, John, Bp. of Rochester, i. 393
Dollond, John, born, iii. 292
Dollond, Peter, died, ii. 357; tomb, 495
Dolman, Master, i. 344

Donaldson, Thomas L., buried, i. 282; architect, 280, 471, 489; ii. 130; iii. 91, 226, 422
Donegal, Barbara, Marchioness of, lived, i. 491
Donne, John, mercer, ii. 498
Donne, Dr., lived, i. 522; student, ii. 300; preacher, 391, 449; vicar, i. 538; prison, ii. 59; tomb, iii. 41, 48; his wife buried, i. 414; his son lived, iii. 540
Donyngtone, Thomas de, thief, iii. 241
Doolittle, Thomas, minister, ii. 554
Dorchester, Countess of, i. 50; lived, ii. 300
Dorchester, Damers, Earls of, i. 512
Dorchester, Marquis of, lived, i. 22, 24
Dorchester, Viscount, monument, iii. 468
D'Orsay, Count, lived, ii. 130
Dorset, Anne Clifford, Countess of, lived, i. 324
Dorset, Cicely, Dowager Countess of, lived, i. 515; prison (1610), ii. 59
Dorset, Lionel, first Duke of, lived, ii. 73, 198
Dorset, Richard, Earl of, lived, i. 515; iii. 202
Dorset, Thomas Sackville, Earl of (d. 1608), i. 515; buried, 229
Dorset and Middlesex, Charles, Earl of, Master of Grocers' Company, ii. 161; lived, i. 229, 296, 357; ii. 299; verses on Whitehall, iii. 507
Doubleday, John, i. 254
Douce, Francis, lived, ii. 134; iii. 348
Doughty, William, lived, iii. 382
Douglas, Gawin, Bp. of Dunkeld, brass, ii. 500
Douglas, James, lived, iii. 328
Douglas, John, Bp. of Salisbury, i. 433
Douglas, Miss, i. 250
Douglas, Sir Robert and Lady, monument, ii. 499
Dove, Bp., Merchant Taylors' School, ii. 526
Dover, Henry Carey, Earl of, lived, i. 278
Dover, Henry Jermyn, Earl of, lived, i. 516; iii. 88
Dover, George Agar Ellis, Lord, lived, ii. 519
Dow, Robert, monument, i. 226; portrait, ii. 523
Dowbiggin, Launcelot, architect, ii. 494
Dowe, Robert, gift to St. Sepulchre's, iii. 229; buried, 229
Downing, Dr. Calybute, rector, ii. 178
Downing, Sir George, i. 519
Doyley's warehouse, iii. 324
D'Oyley, Mrs., lived, i. 487
Drake, Sir Francis, lived, i. 518; ii. 15; portrait, iii. 408
Drayton, Michael, lived, ii. 61; buried, iii. 463; monument, 476

INDEX

Drogheda, Countess of, lived, ii. 194
Drope, Sir Robert, i. 457
Drummond, Mr., lived, i. 330
Drummond, Messrs., i. 5
Drury, Elizabeth, i. 522
Drury, Sir Robert, i. 522
Drury, Sir William, i. 522
Dryden, Erasmus, grocers, ii. 160; lived, 339
Dryden, John, ii. 37; school, iii. 488; attack on, 170, 519; married to Lady Elizabeth Howard, 343; lived, ii. 105, 437; buried, iii. 463; bust, 476
Dryden, Thomas, school, i. 365
Dubourg, Matthew, buried, iii. 2
Ducarel, Dr., died, ii. 320
Duck, Stephen, ii. 294
Ducrow, buried, ii. 324
Dudley, Alice, Duchess of, lived, i. 530; died, ii. 407; monument, 112
Dudley, Earl (d. 1833), lived, i. 64, 530
Dudley, Earl of, ii. 8; iii. 33
Dudley, Lord Guilford, prisoner, iii. 395; executed, 401; buried, 76
Dudley, Edmund, lived, iii. 206
Dudley, John, iii. 319 (d. 1580), monument, 318
Dudley, Lady Mary, monument, ii. 467
Duesbury, W., i. 380
Duffet, Thomas, lived, ii. 582
Dugdale, Sir William, lived, ii. 208
Duggan, William, ii. 235
Duke, John, lived, ii. 228; prisoner, i. 426
Duke, Mr., ii. 202
Dumergue, Charles, lived, iii. 90
Dun, hangman, iii. 417
Duncan, Lord, monument, iii. 48; bust, 408
Dunch, Mrs., died, iii. 225
Duncombe, Mrs. Lydia, murdered, iii. 346
Duncombe, William, lived, ii. 81
Dundonald, Thomas, tenth Earl of, lived, ii. 152, 296, 619; prisoner, 341; died, iii. 141; buried, 463
Dunmore, Earl of, lived, i. 379; li. 186
Dunster, Roger, i. 428
Dunton, John, lived, ii. 309; buried, i. 303
Dupont, Gainsborough, picture, iii. 408
Durel, Dr., preacher, iii. 218
D'Urfey, Tom, ii. 593; buried, 280
Durham, Bps. of, residence, iii. 321
Durrant, John Rowland, ii. 87
Dusillon, architect, iii. 91
Dutch ambassador, iii. 35
Duval, Claude, i. 348
Dyce, Rev. Alexander, library, iii. 272
Dyce, W., R.A., frescoes, ii. 240, 241; director, ii. 222
Dyer, Charles, architect, i. 544
Dyer, Sir Edward, prisoner, iii. 525; buried, 215

Dyer, George, i. 424, 442; buried, ii. 325
Dyer, J., author of *Grongar Hill*, school, iii. 488
Dyer, Samuel, died, i. 337
Dyot, Richard, lived, i. 544
Dyson, Jeremiah, iii. 232
Dyves, Sir Lewis, iii. 285

EARDLEY-WILMOT, Sir J., lived, ii. 618
Earle, Nathaniel and Jane, lived, i. 313
Earlom, Richard, born, i. 458; lived, 441; iii. 174; died, ii. 29; buried, 494
Eastfield, Sir William, i. 20; ii. 55
Eastlake, Sir Charles L., P.R.A., school, i. 365; club, iii. 313; lived, ii. 50; buried, 225
Eaton, H. W., M.P., iii. 493
Ebury, Lord, ii. 545
Edgeworth, Maria, lived, i. 80
Edinburgh, Duke of, i. 408; ii. 151; iii. 468
Edis, Robert William, architect, i. 452
Edmeston, J. S., architect, ii. 36
Edmeston, James, lived, iii. 298
Edridge, Henry, A.R.A., lived, ii. 470
Edward the Black Prince, li. 47, 323
Edward the Confessor, founder, iii. 461; died, 4; buried, 463; shrine, 468
Edward I., i. 193; benefactor, iii. 503; buried, 463; altar-tomb, 468
Edward III., ii. 3, 113; buried, iii. 463; altar-tomb, 469
Edward V., born, iii. 208; and his brother buried, 393, 394
Edward VI., i. 194, 241, 394; portrait, 395, 397, 496; at Whitehall, iii. 510; buried, 463; statue, ii. 502
Edwards, meeting with Dr. Johnson, i. 313
Edwards, Major Arthur, i. 253
Edwards, Bryan, lived, ii. 92
Edwards, Daniel, ii. 532
Edwards, Edward (d. 1806), buried, iii. 21
Edwards, Talbot, ii. 404; memorial, iii. 77
Edwin, first Abbot of Westminster, buried, i. 351
Edwin, John, lived, i. 148
Elliot, George, died, i. 389
Egerton (d. 1836), actor, ii. 450
Egerton, John, duel, ii. 269
Egerton, Lord Chancellor, student, ii. 390; lived, 269; iii. 537
Eggylston, Richard, murdered, ii. 436
Egremont, Earl of, lived, i. 318
Eldon, Lady, died, ii. 184
Eldon, Lord Chancellor, i. 470; ii. 96; Middle Temple, iii. 358; lived, i. 146, 328, 485; ii. 134, 183, 618; iii. 90, 233; portrait, ii. 523; iii. 232; bust, 356
Eleanor, Queen, widow of Henry III., ii. 359

INDEX

Eleanor, Queen, wife of Edward I., i. 197, 353; ii. 319; buried, iii. 463; altar-tomb, 469
Elgin, Earl of, i. 260; lived, iii. 90; duel (1638), ii. 130
Eliot, George, lived, i. 204
Eliot, Sir John, prison, ii. 89, 477; died, iii. 398; buried, 76
Elizabeth, widow of Edward IV., died, i. 167
Elizabeth of York, lay in state, iii. 394
Elizabeth, Queen, i. 36, 363, 373, 378, 541; iii. 218; buried, 463; tomb, 466; statue, i. 538; ii. 444, 502; iii. 181
Elizabeth, Queen of Bohemia, prisoner when Princess, ii. 380; marriage to the Prince Palatine, iii. 126; lived, i. 472; died, ii. 380; buried, iii. 463, 466
Ellenborough, Lord Chief Justice, school, i. 365; lived, 208; ii. 301; iii. 28; died (1818), ii. 213; buried, i. 365
Ellesmere, Francis, Earl of, i. 325; ii. 151; lived, i. 246
Ellice, Edward, M.P., lived, i. 63
Elliot, Adam, ii. 278
Elliot, Sir Henry, K.C.B., born, i. 236
Elliot, Lady, lived, ii. 352
Elliotson, Dr., lived, i. 450
Elliott, Dame, ii. 281
Ellis, Sir Henry, i. 272; Merchant Taylors' School, ii. 526
Ellis, J., architect, iii. 338
Ellis, John, i. 117
Ellis, Wynn, bequest, ii. 573
Ellison, Mrs., collection of water-colour paintings, iii. 276
Elliston, R. W., actor, ii. 201; manager, 615; lived, iii. 328, 540; buried, ii. 312
Ellwood, Thomas, i. 242, 300, 503; ii. 308; prisoner, 593
Elmes, James, architect, i. 91
Elmsley, bookseller, i. 452; ii. 304
Elphinstone, J., translator of *Martial*, lived, ii. 327; monument, 326
Elphinstone, Hon. Mountstuart, lived, i. 13; portrait, ii. 16
Elsing, William, i. 40; founder, ii. 10
Elstob, Rev. William, rector, iii. 343
Elsynge, Henry, born, i. 127; buried, ii. 468
Elways, Sir Gervase, hanged, iii. 401
Emanuel and Davis, architects, i. 403
Emden, Walter, architect, ii. 88; iii. 361
Emery, J., actor, tablet, i. 44
Emmet, Maurice, i. 512
Emmett, J. T., architect, ii. 318
Empson, Sir Richard, lived, i. 241; iii. 206
Ent, Sir George, buried, ii. 371
Entick, Rev. John, buried, i. 539
Eon, Chevalier d', iii. 412; lived, i. 235; died, ii. 546; buried, iii. 21

Epine, Francesca Margherita de l', singer, ii. 200
Erasmus, lived, i. 83
Erkenwald, Bp. of London, i. 188; iii. 39
Erskine, Sir Harry, ii. 18
Erskine, Lord, student, ii. 391; club, i. 480; lived, 58, 166, 289; ii. 48, 166, 396; iii. 13, 155; statue, ii. 399
Esher, Lord, ii. 344
Essex, Countess of (Miss Stephens, singer), iii. 25; died, i. 153
Essex, Robert Devereux, Earl of, Queen Elizabeth's favourite, iii. 144, 510; lived, ii. 16; prisoner, 362; iii. 398, 517; buried, 76, 470
Essex, Robert, Earl of, Parliamentary general, born, ii. 17; baptized, 609; iii. 227; died, ii. 17; effigy in Westminster Abbey destroyed, iii. 477
Essex, Thomas Cromwell, Earl of, ii. 140; iii. 396; lived, i. 520; executed, iii. 401; buried, 76
Essex, William, ii. 129; lived, 619
Estcourt, Dick, died, iii. 284; buried, 58
Ethelbert, King of Kent, i. 20; iii. 39
Ethelgoda, buried, i. 351
Etty, William, R.A., lived, i. 296; paintings, ii. 7
Eugene, Prince, lived, ii. 381
Eurett, Lady, lived, ii. 596
Evans, Rev. —, ii. 174
Evans, General, lived, ii. 186
Evans, Henry, i. 199
Evans, Maurice, i. 213
Evans, Mrs., i. 483
Evans, William, giant, ii. 592
Evelyn, John, Middle Temple, iii. 357; lived, i. 72; ii. 16, 448; iii. 194, 336, 436; marriage of his father and mother, 373
Everington and Graham, ii. 447
Evyngar, Andrew, brass, i. 31
Ewens, Ralph, died, i. 223
Ewin, John, lay brother, ii. 157
Exeter, Bps. of, residence, iii. 321
Exeter, John Holland, Duke of, tomb, ii. 322
Exeter, Thomas Cecil, Earl of, lived, ii. 27; altar-tomb, iii. 470
Exeter, Countess Dowager of, lived, i. 473
Exmouth, Lord, portrait, ii. 264
Eyre, Charles, lived, iii. 122
Eyre, Simon, mayor, ii. 375, 417; buried, 508

Fabyan, Robert, buried, ii. 534
Fairborne, Sir Palmes, monument, iii. 473
Fairchild, Thomas, ii. 386
Fairfax, Bryan, lived, iii. 211
Fairfax, General, lived, i. 160; iii. 539; Constable of the Tower, 400; married, ii. 179; lived, 224; iii. 136
Fairbolt, F. W., buried, i. 282

INDEX

Faithorne, William, lived, i. 21; iii. 16, 124, 323; buried, i. 49
Falconberg, Lady, died, ii. 30
Falconer, Thomas, ii. 563
Falkland, Lucius Carey, Viscount, i. 509; prison, ii. 59; statue, 242
Falmouth, Charles, Earl of, i. 359
Falstolfe, Sir John, i. 215, 528; ii. 33; lived, 233
Fane, Colonel, lived, ii. 186
Fanhope, Lord, lived, ii. 48
Fanshawe, Lady, i. 327; born, ii. 193; lived, i. 223
Fanshawe, Sir Richard, lived, i. 223; ii. 395
Fantom, Captain Carlo, i. 524
Faraday, Michael, i. 78, 513; iii. 186; born, ii. 593; Trinity House, iii. 409; lived, i. 204, 361; ii. 108, 272; iii. 291, 490
Farindone, William le, ii. 31
Farinelli, singer, ii. 200
Farnaby, Thomas, lived, ii. 123
Farnborough, Lord, ii. 573
Farquhar, G., dramatist, buried, ii. 479
Farquhar, Sir Walter, lived, i. 450
Farr, James, iii. 146
Farrar, Archdeacon, ii. 344
Farren, William, died, i. 281
Farren, Miss, lived, ii. 152; married to Earl of Derby, 165
Farrington, Joseph, R.A., lived, i. 362
Farryner, king's baker, iii. 127
Fascet, Abbot, tomb, iii. 470
Faunleroy, H., lived, i. 134, 170; ii. 611
Fawcett, Colonel, duel, i. 235
Fawcett, Right Hon. H., lived, iii. 430
Fawcett, John, born, iii. 258
Fawkes, Guy, prisoner, iii. 394; executed, 5
Fawkes, Richard, lived, i. 543
Featherstone, Cuthbert, ii. 33
Featherstonhaugh, Sir Matthew, lived, ii. 519
Fell, Rev. John, ii. 229
Fellows, Sir Charles, i. 255, 260
Felton, Eleanor, lived, ii. 64
Felton, John, bought the knife with which he stabbed the first Duke of Buckingham, iii. 401; executed, 415, 430
Fenning, Eliza, i. 347
Fenton, Lavinia, actress, ii. 398; lived, i. 218
Fenwick, Sir John, ii. 377; executed, iii. 401
Fergusson, James, F.R.S., lived, ii. 366; died, i. 217; monument, ii. 496
Ferrabosco, Alphonso, buried, ii. 468
Ferrar, Mr., i. 160
Ferrars, Bp., trial, iii. 214
Ferrers, Earl, trial, iii. 486; executed, 415
Ferrers, Sir John, i. 226
Ferrey, E. B., architect, iii. 40

Ferrey, Benjamin, architect, i. 276, 391; 538; iii. 166, 312
Fetherstone, hanged, iii. 256
Feversham, Lewis de Duras, Earl of, ii. 233; lived, ii. 298; iii. 271; buried, ii. 500
Ffolkes, Richard, lived, ii. 596
Field, Nathan, christened, ii. 110; buried, i. 49
Field, Theophilus, rector, iii. 73
Fielding, Basil, killed in a duel with his brother, iii. 228
Fielding, Henry, lived, i. 140, 230; iii. 131
Fielding, Lord, duel, ii. 352
Fielding, Sir John, ii. 454, 470; lived, i. 230; buried, ii. 450
Fielding, Timothy, i. 115, 212; iii. 288, 345
Fife, James Duff, second Earl of, ii. 40; lived, iii. 126
Figg, James, ii. 40, 510; lived, i. 3; buried, ii. 496
Filby, John, Goldsmith's tailor, iii. 452
Finch, Sir Heneage. See Nottingham
Finch, Lady Isabella, lived, i. 163
Finden, William, lived, i. 389
Finden, —, architect, i. 30
Finett, Sir John, lived, ii. 483
Finke, Robert, ii. 41
Fish, Simon (d. 1531), buried, i. 528
Fisher, Edward, lived, ii. 383
Fisher, John, Bp. of Rochester, lived, i. 328; preacher, iii. 61; prisoner, 394; executed, 401; buried, i. 31; head on London Bridge, ii. 419
Fisher, Jasper, ii. 42; lived, i. 503
Fisher, John, ground plan of Whitehall, iii. 507
Fisher, Kitty, lived, i. 336
Fisher, Payne, buried, iii. 231
Fitz Aylwin, Henry, lived, ii. 434
Fitzgerald, Lady Margaret, died, i. 359
Fitzgerard, Robert, i. 131
Fitzharding, Lady, lived, iii. 112
Fitzherbert, Mrs., lived, ii. 137; iii. 33
Fitz-Mary, Simon, i. 171
Fitzpatrick, General, lived, i. 63
Fitzroy, Admiral, lived, ii. 615
Fitzwalter, Archbishop Hubert, ii. 360
Fitzwalter, Robert, i. 131; iii. 528
Fitzwilliam, Earl, ii. 165
Flamsteed, lived, i. 479; portrait, iii. 188
Flatman, Thomas, born, i. 24; died, ii. 378; buried, i. 239
Flaxman, John, R.A., i. 238; ii. 51, 297; lived, i. 295; ii. 586; iii. 442; buried, ii. 113; modelled for Coade, i. 430; sculpture, 393
Fleetwood, Bridget, buried, iii. 319
Fleetwood, General Charles, lived, iii. 442; buried, i. 303
Fleetwood, William, Recorder of London, lived, i. 86; ii. 69

INDEX

Fleming, Abraham, rector, iii. 23
Fleming, Major-General, monument, iii. 474
Fleming, Mrs. Elizabeth, i. 326
Fletcher, head at Temple Bar, iii. 359
Fletcher, Rev. Alexander, i. 205
Fletcher, Bp., lived, L 328
Fletcher, Elizabeth, buried, ii. 449
Fletcher, Giles, school, iii. 488
Fletcher, John, lived, i. 101, 107; buried, iii. 214
Fletcher, Lawrence, lived, i. 102; buried, iii. 215
Flint, Bet, lived, ii. 518
Flint, Ernest, architect, iii. 73
Flitcroft, Henry, architect, ii. 111, 296, 610
Flood, Henry, lived, L 423
Florio, John, lived, iii. 242
Flower, Henry, architect, ii. 154
Fludd, Dr. William, died, i. 443
Fludyer, Sir Samuel, ii. 66
Foe, James, lived, ii. 68
Foley, Lord, ii. 66
Foliot, Gilbert, iii. 70
Folkes Martin, married, ii. 265; portrait, iii. 182
Follett, Sir William, died, L 483; statue, iii. 472
Fontana, Count Filippo N., buried, iii. 21
Foote, Miss. See Harrington, Countess of
Foote, Samuel, manager, ii. 200; lived, iii. 332; buried, 464, 480
Ford, John, Middle Temple, iii. 357
Ford, Parson, ii. 248; prison, 60
Ford, Richard, lived, iii. 34
Fordyce, Dr. George, club, ii. 484
Fordyce, Sir William, M.D., lived, i. 283
Forest, Miles, murderer, ii. 487
Forester, Sir William, duel, ii. 399
Forman, Simon, lived, ii. 357; buried, 495
Forrest, Prior, burned, iii. 255
Forset, Edward, ii. 509
Forshall, Rev. J., buried, ii. 73
Forster, Dame Agnes, ii. 445
Forster, John, his library, iii. 277
Fort, Edward, i. 523
Fortescue, Sir John, student, ii. 390; lived, iii. 448
Fortescue, William, Pope's friend, lived, i. 156; ii. 190; iii. 383
Fortune, John, i. 488
Foscolo, Ugo, lived, i. 40; ii. 207; iii. 274
Foster, Elizabeth, granddaughter of Milton, i. 431; lived, iii. 69
Foster, Dr. James, i. 107; preacher, ii. 614; minister, iii. 98
Fothergill, Dr. Anthony, buried, ii. 505
Fothergill, Dr. John, lived, iii. 497; died, ii. 193
Foubert, Major, ii. 70; lived, i. 235
Foulis, Sir Henry, i. 452

Fourmantel, Catherine, lived, ii. 519
Fowke, Captain Francis, architect, i. 17, 273; ii. 235; buried, i. 282
Fowler, Bp., rector, i. 32
Fowler, Charles, architect, i. 464; ii. 248
Fowler, J., architect, ii. 504
Fowler, J., engineer, ii. 531
Fowlers, Lords, of Manor of Barnsbury, ii. 270
Fox, founder of Corpus Christi College, Oxford, vicar, i. 538
Fox, Charles James, i. 287; born, 450; gambling, 38; trial, iii. 339; duel, ii. 253; lived, i. 15, 63, 165, 422; ii. 120, 137, 285, 296, 304; iii. 279; buried, 463, 472; monument, 474; statues, i. 209; ii. 242; iii. 191
Fox, Bp. Edward, iii. 214; buried, ii. 504
Fox, George, ii. 417; lived, 596; died, 136; buried, i. 304
Fox, Mrs., wife of Charles James, lived, ii. 181
Fox, Nevison, lived, iii. 336
Fox, Sir Stephen, i. 383; ii. 249
Fox, W. J., minister, iii. 278
Foxe, John, the martyrologist, lived, i. 21, 28; died, ii. 168; buried, 109
Franchotti, Horatio, iii. 173
Francis, F. J., architect, i. 452
Francis, Messrs., architects, ii. 365, 418
Francis, Rev. Dr. Philip, i. 384; ii. 28; lived, 572
Francis, Sir Philip, school, iii. 63; lived, ii. 301
Francklin, Dr., translator of Lucian, lived, iii. 137
Francklin, R., bookseller, lived, iii. 384
Franklin, executed, iii. 375
Franklin, B., i. 186, 511; ii. 152; club, 426; skater, iii. 234; lived, i. 110, 473, 533; ii. 406
Franklin, Sir John, monument, iii. 471; statue, 454
Fraxinet, Gilbert de, ii. 389
Frederick, Prince of Wales, i. 111, 331; iii. 211; saddler, 198; married, ii. 277; lived, 285, 381, 595, 600; buried, iii. 467; portrait, 198
Frederick, Sir Christopher, lived, ii. 76
Frederick, Sir John, lived, ii. 76; i. 394
Freeman, Mr., i. 526
Freind, Dr., prisoner, iii. 399; portrait, 82
Freind, Sir John, executed, iii. 415; quarters on Temple Bar, 359
Freke, John, i. 118
Frith, Mary, buried, i. 239
Frith, Richard, ii. 81
Frobisher, Sir Martin, buried, ii. 109
Fromont, M., i. 329
Frost, famous runner, i. 454
Fry, Mrs., i. 478

Fuller, Isaac, ii. 35; paintings, iii. 5
Fuller, Thomas, i. 415; lecturer, iii. 218; lived, 250
Fuller, Dr., William, rector, ii. 110
Fullerton, duel with Lord Melbourne, ii. 253
Fulwood, Christopher, ii. 82
Furnival, Sir William, ii. 83
Fuseli, Henry, R.A., lived, i. 169, 277, 470; ii. 484; iii. 137, 139; grave, 49
Fussell, Joseph, i. 249

GABRIEL, E., architect, ii. 36
Gadbury, John, died, i. 236; buried, ii. 468
Gage, Lord, lived, iii. 126
Gahagan, ii. 8
Gainsborough, Thomas, lived, iii. 13, 221; died, 221; portrait, 280; pictures, 178
Gale, Theophilus, ii. 177
Gale, Dr. Thomas, inscription, ii. 557
Gallini, Sir John, ii. 188
Galt, John, student, ii. 391; lived, 181; iii. 348
Gamble, Ellis, i. 470
Gandy-Deering, J. P., architect, i. 80; ii. 5, 26; iii. 331, 421
Gape, Mrs., i. 224
Gardelle, Theodore, lived, ii. 383
Gardiner, Stephen, Bp. of Winchester, lived, iii. 524; died, 510
Gardner, Sir Alan, lived, iii. 109
Garnault, Samuel, ii. 85
Garnerin, balloon ascents, iii. 429
Garnet, Jesuit, trial, ii. 172
Garrard, George, lived, i. 365
Garret, burned, iii. 256
Garret, Thomas, i. 34
Garrett, Daniel, architect, ii. 605
Garrett, John, Lord Mayor, ii. 424
Garrick, David, i. 254, 287; ii. 127, 315, 526; student, 391; club, i. 287 note; iii. 141; coffee-house, ii. 281; life governor, 452; married, i. 80; iii. 194; lived, i. 229, 360, 543; ii. 462, 874, 336; iii. 284; died, i. 6; buried, iii. 464; monument, 478
Garrick, Mrs., died, i. 6
Garrow, Sir W., lived, i. 146
Garrow, William, jun., lived, ii. 92
Garth, Sir Samuel, lived, ii. 198; portrait, iii. 82
Garvagh, Lady, lived, iii. 111
Garway, Thomas, iii. 384; lived, ii. 86
Garway, contractor (1610), ii. 509
Gascoigne, Sir Crisp, Lord Mayor, ii. 463
Gascoigne, George, ii. 140
Gascoigne, Sir William, ii. 140
Gastigny, M. de, ii. 78
Gateacre, William, i. 437
Gaunt, Elizabeth, executed, iii. 417

Gay, John, i. 306, 349; lived, 305; iii. 424; lay in state, ii. 25; buried, iii. 463; monument, 476
Gayer, Sir John, ii. 322
Gayton, Edmund, Merchant Taylors' School, ii. 596
Geddes, A., A.R.A., altar-piece, ii. 278
Geddes, Dr. Alexander, buried, iii. 2
Geldorp, George, lived, i. 59
Gell, Dr. Robert, minister, ii. 492
Gell, Sir William, lived, i. 13
Gellibrand, Rev. Henry, buried, iii. 75
Gentilis, Albericus, buried, ii. 205
George I., ii. 293, 469; statues, 97, 385; iii. 194
George II., i. 253; when Prince of Wales, lived, 14; ii. 381; died, 330; buried, iii. 463, 467; statues, ii. 122; iii. 184
George III., i. 245, 253, 269, 293; ii. 201; born, 299, 600; portrait, 523; iii. 179; bust, 188; statues, i. 165, 439; iii. 15, 184, 273
George IV., iii. 188; i. 254, 269, 293; ii. 197; in the Watch House when Prince of Wales, 565; laying first stone, i. 463; married, ii. 277; coronation dinner, iii. 486; lived, i. 332; bust, iii. 82; statues, 184, 405
George, Prince, of Denmark, i. 8; died, ii. 330; portrait, iii. 438
Georgeirenes, Joseph, ii. 506
Gerarde, John, ii. 99; lived, 221
Gerbier, Sir Balthazar, i. 179; iii. 135, 542; lived, 504
Gericault, J. L. T. A., exhibited, ii. 8
Germany, Emperor William of, i. 333
Germany, Empress Frederick of, married, ii. 277
Gerrard, Charles Lord, ii. 543; lived, 596
Gerrard, Mr., iii. 74
Gibbon, Benj. Phelps, died, i. 13
Gibbon, Dr., ii. 177
Gibbon, Edward, i. 39, 222, 287, 440; lived, 445; ii. 172, 195; school, 488; member of Brooks's, i. 287 note; lived, i. 160, 219, 451; ii. 304; iii. 13, 401
Gibbon, Edmund, monument, iii. 351
Gibbon, John, ii. 320
Gibbon, Matthew, lived, ii. 377
Gibbons, Alderman, portrait, iii. 207
Gibbons, Charles, ii. 107
Gibbons, Dr. Christopher, lived, ii. 587
Gibbons, Grinling, i. 355, 384, 434, 506, 515; ii. 279, 465; born, i. 473; lived, 156, 229; iii. 297; buried, 58; carvings, i. 536; ii. 109, 490, 535, 536, 539; iii. 47, 229
Gibbs, James, lived, ii. 207; architect, i. 190, 413; ii. 177, 501; iii. 405, 431; monument, ii. 496
Gibbs, Sir Vicary, lived, i. 206; died, iii. 192

Gibson, Bp. Edmund, ii. 98; librarian, 363
Gibson, J., landscape gardener, ii. 385
Gibson, Jesse, architect, i. 190; iii. 75, 198
Gibson, John, R.A., models, iii. 179
Gibson, Mrs., buried, ii. 102
Gibson, William, executed, ii. 324
Giffard, Henry, manager, ii. 127, 398
Giffard, William, Bp. of Winchester, iii. 212; lived, 524
Gifford, William, died, ii. 274; buried, iii. 478
Gilbart, James William, died, i. 281
Gilbert, A. T., Bp. of Chichester, lived, iii. 139
Giles, John, architect, iii. 202
Giles and Murray, architects, ii. 366
Gill, Alexander, D.D., Master of St. Paul's School, iii. 63; buried, i. 226
Gilliver, Lawton, lived, ii. 63
Gillray, James, lived, ii. 304; buried, 281
Girtin, Thomas, buried, iii. 59
Gladstone, Right Hon. W. E., lived, i. 333; ii. 192
Glanville, Gilbert de, Bp. of Rochester, i. 328
Glassington, John, ii. 351
Gleig, Rev. W. R., i. 384
Glenelg, Lord, lived, i. 13
Glenham, Anne, Lady, i. 343
Glenvarloch, Lord, iii. 65
Gloucester, Eleanor Cobham, Duchess of, penance, ii. 533; iii. 340
Gloucester, Eleanora de Bohun, Duchess of, brass, iii. 465
Gloucester, Maria, Duchess of, lived, ii. 118; iii. 99
Gloucester, Humphry, Duke of, i. 531; lived, 131; iii. 536
Gloucester, Thomas of Woodstock, Duke of, monument, iii. 469
Gloucester, Duke of, son of Charles I., prisoner, ii. 380
Gloucester, Duke of, son of Queen Anne, i. 320
Gloucester, Duke of, brother of George III., ii. 162, 166, 382; iii. 265
Gloucester, Duke of, son of George III., i. 492; ii. 118
Glover, Alex. and Vincent, ii. 359
Glover, Richard, born, ii. 482; lived, i. 160; ii. 274, 373; died, i. 15
Glover, Robert, buried, ii. 109
Goda, Countess, ii. 156
Goddard, Dr., Jonathan, lived, iii. 186, 530; buried, ii. 205
Godden, John, i. 141
Goderich, Lord (1782), buried, ii. 212
Godfrey, —, Keeper of the Bears, i. 138
Godfrey, Colonel Charles, lived, iii. 527
Godfrey, Sir Edmund Berry, i. 344, 414; ii. 193; lived, 151; murder, iii. 22, 120, 271; monument, 480

Godfrey, Mary, lived, i. 491
Godfrey, Michael, i. 95; monument, iii. 343
Godfrey and Cooke, chemists, ii. 457; iii. 284
Godolphin, Sidney, Earl of, monument, iii. 423
Godwin, Earl, iii. 286 *
Godwin, Mary Jane, tomb, iii. 19
Godwin, Mary Wollstonecraft, lived, iii. 319; died, 101; tomb, 19
Godwin, William, ii. 246; married to Mary Wollstonecraft, iii. 19; lived, i. 345; ii. 135, 189; iii. 101, 251, 268, 349; died, 8; tomb, 19
Gold, James, architect, i. 227
Golde, Henry, hanged, ii. 491
Goldie, G., architect, ii. 594
Golding, Dr. buried, i. 281
Goldney, Henry, lived, ii. 136
Goldsmith, Oliver, i. 71; ii. 18, 294; iii. 243, 359; the Cock Lane ghost, i. 433; coffee-house, ii. 148, 281; at Temple Bar, iii. 359; usher, 67; lived, i. 84, 102, 234, 326; ii. 6, 85, 141, 150, 270, 343, 559; iii. 38, 203, 528; died, i. 236; buried, iii. 352; grave-stone; 352; memorial tablet, 477
Gondomar, Count, lived, i. 105; ii. 11
Gooch, J. M., i. 285
Gooch, Dr. Robert, lived, i. 170
Good, J. H., jun., architect, i. 64
Goodall, Frederick, R.A., iii. 267
Goodchild, Ralph, remarriage, ii. 502
Goodge, Mr., i. 125
Goodman, Bp., lived, ii. 338
Goodman, Dean, tomb, iii. 465
Goodrich, Thomas, rector, iii. 72
Goodwin, John, i. 443; books burned by hangman, ii. 612
Goodwin, Dr. Thomas, pastor, iii. 65; buried, i. 303
Gooscal, Sir John, ii. 51
Gordon, Alexander, Duke of, lived, i. 291
Gordon, General, tomb, iii. 48; statue, 406
Gordon, Lord George, i. 430; ii. 100; iii. 176; born, i. 283; lived, iii. 457, prisoner. 399; died, ii. 591; buried, 275
Gorges, Sir Arthur, i. 141, 378; monument, ii. 449
Goring, Lord, ii. 566
Goring, Mr., duel, ii. 352
Gosling, Sir Francis, ii. 444
Gosling, Humphrey, vintner, iii. 498
Gosson, Stephen, i. 194; buried, 227
Gough, Sir John, i. 376
Gough, Richard, born, i. 84; iii. 526
Gough and Roumieu, architects, iii. 17
Gould, John, died, i. 361
Gower, John, benefactor, ii. 10; lived, 555; monument, iii. 214

Grabe, John Ernest, buried, iii. 20
Grafton, Isabella, Duchess of, i. 61
Grafton, Dukes of, ii. 20, 137; iii. 389;
  lived, i. 412; ii. 50, 137; iii. 410
Grafton, Henry, first Duke of, lived at
  Pimlico, iii. 97
Grafton, Augustus, third Duke of, Prime
  Minister, i. 438
Graham, Alexander, architect, i. 322
Graham, Dr., lived, iii. 220
Graham, Lord George, prisoner, ii. 485
Graham, Thomas, Master of the Mint, ii.
  549
Granby, Marquis of, ii. 211; at Hercules
  Pillars, iii. 91
Grandison, Oliver St. John, Viscount,
  monument, i. 128
Grant, —, executed, ii. 431
Grant, Albert, ii. 326, 385
Grant, Charles, lived, iii. 192
Grant, Donald, D.D., buried, ii. 312
Grant, Sir Francis, portraits by, i. 395
Grant, Sir R., lived, iii. 192
Grant, William, lived, ii. 215
Grant, Sir William, i. 429; lived, ii. 396;
  iii. 167; portrait, ii. 398
Grantham, Earl of, ii. 137; lived, i. 14
Grantley, Sir Fletcher Norton, Lord, died,
  ii. 396
Granville, Earl, i. 402; lived, 289
Granville, Sir Richard, fined, ii. 209
Grasse, Count de, lived, iii. 13
Grattan, Right Hon. Henry, lived, i. 90;
  iii. 35; buried, 472; statue, ii. 242
Graunt, John, lived, i. 186; buried, 538
Graves, Alexander, builder, iii. 156
Gravet, William, vicar, iii. 230
Gray, Edmund, Lord, ii. 139; lived, i.
  343
Gray, John, iii. 75
Gray, John, executed, i. 209
Gray, Sir Richard, founder, iii. 503
Gray, Robert, portrait, ii. 523
Gray, Sarah, ii. 329
Gray, Thomas, born, i. 458; in Cran-
  bourne Alley, 470; lived, ii. 307, 327;
  iii. 283; monument, 477; his father
  buried, ii. 534
Gray de Wilton, Lord, lived, iii. 388
Gray and Davison, organ, iii. 290; ii.
  535
Grayson, —, architect, i. 402
Greaves, John, buried, i. 160
Greaves, Samuel, ii. 18
Green, balloon ascents, iii. 429
Green, Joseph Henry, lived, ii. 396
Green, Matthew, died, ii. 136, 570
Green, "Paddy," ii. 21
Green, Richard, statue, iii. 106
Green, T. K., architect, ii. 481
Green, Valentine, i. 251
Green, William, jumped from monument,
  ii. 559

Greene, Fortunatus, buried, ii. 387
Greene, Robert, i. 24; died, 518; buried,
  171
Greenwell, Rev. William, i. 255, 265
Grenville, Lord, lived, i. 320
Grenville, Right Hon. George, i. 283;
  lived, 218
Grenville, Right Hon. Thomas, i. 254,
  268; lived, ii. 184
Grenwich, John de, ii. 153
Gresham, Sir John, i. 171
Gresham, Sir Thomas, founder, ii. 154;
  iii. 182; mercer, ii. 521; lived, i. 190;
  ii. 416; monument, 204; portrait, 520;
  statue, iii. 181
Gresse, John Alexander, iii. 156
Gresse, Stephen Jaspar, iii. 312
Greville, Colonel, iii. 158
Greville, Fulke, lived, i. 83; iii. 510
Grey, Earl, lived, i. 164; ii. 213
Grey, Lord, lived, iii. 134
Grey, Lady Jane, prisoner, iii. 395, 398;
  trial, ii. 172; buried, iii. 76
Gribelin, Simon, i. 93; lived, ii. 437
Griffin, Edward, lived, iii. 11
Griffith, Philip, lived, iii. 99
Griffith, William, ii. 30
Griffith, W. P., architect, ii. 277, 315;
  iii. 228
Griffith and Dawson, architects, iii. 39
Griffiths, bookseller, iii. 38
Grignion, Charles, lived, ii. 274; died,
  334
Grimaldi, J., born, iii. 302; Sadler's Wells,
  201; lived, ii. 85; died, iii. 283; buried,
  70
Grimaldi, L. A., Bp. of Noyon, buried,
  iii. 18
Grimston, Sir Harbottle, arms, iii. 166
Grimthorpe, Lord, ii. 242
Grisi, Madame, singer, ii. 200
Groot, Isaac de, lived, i. 366; iii. 131
Grose, Francis, ii. 210
Grosvenor, Mary Davies, Lady, i. 490
Grosvenor, Sir Richard (d. 1732), ii. 164
Grosvenor, Sir Robert, lived, ii. 545
Grosvenor, Sir Thomas, marriage, i. 414
Grote, George, school, i. 365; lived, 152;
  buried, iii. 463, 477
Grove, Captain, i. 69
Gruner, L., decorator, i. 294
Gruning, Edward A., architect, i. 79
Gryffyth, Richard ap, ii. 268
Guiccioli, Countess, lived, ii. 385
Guildford, Lord Keeper, Middle Temple,
  iii. 357; lived, i. 346; ii. 9, 297; iii.
  232
Guiscard, i. 438; buried, 392
Guizot, F., lived, i. 281; ii. 461; iii. 68
Guizot, Madame, died, iii. 69
Gull, Sir William, lived, i. 283
Gundulph, Bp. of Rochester, architect, iii.
  392

Gunnell, Richard, iii. 203
Gunner, hairdresser, iii. 127
Gunning, Mrs., lived, i. 219; died, iii. 271
Gunning, Rev. Peter, ii. 28
Gunning, Elizabeth, marriage to Duke of Hamilton, i. 487; ii. 516; died, i. 59
Gunning, John, died, iii. 271
Gunstor, Thomas, iii. 319
Gunter, Rev. Edmund, buried, iii. 75
Gurney, Sir John, tomb, iii. 19
Gurwood, Colonel, buried, iii. 77
Guthrie, G. J., founder, iii. 487
Guthrie, William, died, iii. 110; buried, ii. 496
Guy, John, lived, i. 121
Guy, Thomas, ii. 417; born, 29, 233; apprentice, 521; founder, 175; lived, i. 458
Gwilt, Joseph, architect, ii. 159, 234, 498; iii. 214; his map of Southwark, 984
Gwydyr, Lord, ii. 176
Gwynn, John, lived, ii. 383, 484
Gwynne, Nell, i. 87, 385; born, 431; lived, 523; ii. 288; iii. 11; buried, ii. 478

HAAK, Theodore, F.R.S., iii. 186; buried, i. 44
Habershon, E., architect, i. 223
Hacker, Colonel Francis, ii. 598; lived, 528; executed, iii. 415
Hacket, Bp., rector, i. 44
Hacket, William, lived, ii. 350; hanged, i. 280
Hackman, Rev. James, i. 142; lived, 473; murderer, iii. 348; executed, 417
Hadeleye, John, ii. 542
Hadfield, Mrs., lived, ii. 93
Haggerty, murderer, i. 545
Haines, Joe, actor, ii. 607; died, 193
Hakewell, Henry, architect, iii. 74
Hakluyt, Richard, school, iii. 488; buried, 464
Hale, Sir Matthew, i. 424; student, ii. 390; bequest, 398; portrait, iii. 232; ii. 398
Halford, Sir Henry, College of Physicians, iii. 82; lived, i. 487
Halifax, C. Montague, Earl of, school, iii. 488; President of the Royal Society, 187; lived, ii. 298; monument, iii. 467
Halifax, Savile, Marquis of, lived, ii. 332; buried, iii. 463; monument, 467
Hall, Chambers, i. 267
Hall, Vice-Chancellor Sir Charles, died, i. 135
Hall, Edward, ii. 140; buried, i. 160
Hall, John, lived, i. 170
Hall, John, engraver, buried, iii. 2
Hall, Bp., i. 522
Hall, Rev. Newman, minister, iii. 177
Hall, Mrs. (1768), i. 512
Hall, Mrs. S. C., school, ii. 189

Hall, Timothy, ii. 514; rector, i. 36; buried, ii. 179
Hallam, Henry, lived, iii. 523; monument, 48
Hallenge, Jasper, ii. 566
Halley, Dr. Edmund, i. 390; born, ii. 180; school, iii. 63; coffee-house, ii. 148; lived, iii. 121, 526; portraits, 188
Halsal, Bp., brass, ii. 500
Halsey, E., i. 107
Hamilton, Colonel, ii. 252
Hamilton, James, first Duke of, i. 375; iii. 285; beheaded, 7
Hamilton, James, fourth Duke of, duel with Lord Mohun, ii. 252; iii. 165, 172
Hamilton, James, sixth Duke of, married to Elizabeth Gunning, i. 487; ii. 516
Hamilton, Alexander, tenth Duke of, lived, i. 64; iii. 111
Hamilton, Elizabeth, ii. 183
Hamilton, Gavin, ii. 366; lived, iii. 101
Hamilton, James, ii. 183; iii. 89
Hamilton, Lady, ii. 165; lived, i. 220, 367, 412
Hamilton, Lady Anne, ii. 448
Hamilton, Marquis of, died (1625), ii. 47
Hamilton, William, R.A., lived, i. 492; monument, 50
Hamilton, Sir William, i. 254; ii. 165; married, 96; lived, 337; died, iii. 89
Hamilton, William Gerard (Single-speech), lived, ii. 187; died, i. 283
Hammersley, Sir Hugh, monument, i. 46
Hampden, John, lived, ii. 144; statue, 242
Hand, Richard, i. 381
Handel, G. F., ii. 200; benefactor, 73; lived, i. 283, 306; buried, iii. 464; monument, 478; portrait, ii. 574
Hanmer, Sir Thomas, lived, iii. 12
Hannes, Sir Edward, ii. 86
Hanson, Sheriff, lived, i. 190
Hanway, Jonas, ii. 454, 470; died, iii. 156
Harborne, John, ii. 38
Harcourt, Charles, died, i. 359
Harcourt, Simon, Lord Chancellor (d. 1727), lived, i. 74; ii. 12, 190, 395
Harcourt, John, M.P., ii. 402
Hardcastle, Dean, i. 413
Hardinge, Agnes, ii. 190
Hardinge, Field-Marshal, first Viscount, lived, iii. 302
Hardman, Mr., stained glass, ii. 241; iron gates, iii. 8
Hardwick, Philip, R.A., architect, i. 57, 153, 175, 391, 402; ii. 123, 147, 318, 323, 353, 398, 432; iii. 319
Hardwick, P. C., architect, i. 364, 402; ii. 359, 418, 443, 495
Hardwick, Thomas, architect, i. 116; ii. 275, 318, 497; iii. 57; died, i. 170

INDEX

Hardwicke, Philip Yorke, Earl of, i. 285;
  lived, ii. 396, 617; iii. 119, 131, 155;
  died, ii. 164
Hardwidge, James, tablet, i. 167
Hardy, Thomas, trial, ii. 611; buried, i. 394
Hardy, Sir T. Duffus, at Christ's Hospital, i. 396
Hardyman, John, parson, ii. 481
Hare, John, manager, ii. 305
Hare, Archdeacon, Julius Charles, school, i. 365; club, iii. 313
Hare, Nicholas, ii. 190
Harewood, Earl of, ii. 188
Hargrave, Lieut.-General, monument, iii. 474
Hargreave, Francis, lived, i. 224
Harley, J. P., lived, ii. 134
Harlow, Mrs. Elizabeth, lived, iii. 138
Harlow, George Henry, lived, iii. 138;
  died, i. 492; buried, ii. 281
Harness, Rev. William, ii. 351
Harold, Earl, i. 166
Harpefield, Archdeacon, John, ii. 8
Harper, Justice Richard, i. 108
Harpur, Sir William, i. 145; ii. 193
Harrington, Miss Foote, Countess of, i. 145; lived, ii. 335; died, iii. 163
Harrington, Earl of, lived, ii. 303; iii. 126
Harrington, James, club, ii. 542; iii. 7, 410; lived, i. 40; buried, ii. 468
Harris, —, actor, lived, iii. 202
Harris, Lady, lived, ii. 596
Harris, Renatus, organ, i. 31, 43; ii. 515; iii. 229
Harris, Richard, clock, iii. 57
Harris, Thomas, i. 537
Harrison, Elizabeth, murdered, iii. 346
Harrison, Henry, architect, ii. 169, 452
Harrison, John, i. 156; lived, iii. 53
Harrison, Major-General, executed, i. 354
Harrison, Ralph, iii. 389
Harrowby, Earl of, i. 340; lived, ii. 164
Hart, Sir John, lived, ii. 620
Harte, executed, iii. 415
Hartington, Marquis of, lived, i. 14
Hartlib, Nan, marriage, ii. 131
Hartlib, Samuel, lived, i. 85, 533
Hartopp, Sir John, lived, iii. 319; monument, 318
Harvard, John, iii. 216
Harvey, Daniel and Eliab, lived, ii. 372
Harvey, Daniel Whittle, ii. 614
Harvey, Sir Eliab, i. 435, 440
Harvey, Henry, i. 507
Harvey, Dr. William, i. 118, 435; lecturer, iii. 82; preparations, 82; lived, ii. 372; portrait, iii. 82; bust, 82; statue, 83
Haselrigge, Sir Arthur, i. 284; married, 32
Haslang, Count, lived, ii. 122
Hastings, Lord, arrested, iii. 394
Hastings, Marquis of, ii. 296

Hastings, Warren, school, iii. 288; lived, i. 283; ii. 297; trial, iii. 486; monument, 472
Hatfield, Thomas, Bp. of Durham, lived, i. 540
Hatfield, lunatic, i. 526
Hatherley, Lord Chancellor, died, ii. 92
Hatherly, John, i. 372
Hatten, John, iii. 194
Hatton, Sir Christopher, i. 399; ii. 194; iii. 510; lived, ii. 10; monument, iii. 41, 49
Hatton, Lord, died, ii. 13
Hatton, Lady, ii. 195, 582; lived, ii. 27
Haughton, Prior of the Charter-house, executed, iii. 414
Haughton, John, i. 363
Haughton, Sir John Hotles, Lord, ii. 196
Haughton, William, prisoner, i. 426
Havelock, Sir Henry, school, i. 365; Middle Temple, iii. 158; monument, 474; statue, 405
Haward, Francis, lived, ii. 474
Hawes, —, jumped from monument, ii. 559
Hawes, Dr. William, born, ii. 270; founder, 247
Hawke, Admiral Sir Edward, i. 8; lived, ii. 93
Hawker, Colonel Peter, died, i. 515
Hawkesworth, Dr., lived, ii. 158, 618; died, 388
Hawkins, Cæsar, at Christ's Hospital, i. 396
Hawkins, Edward, i. 255, 267
Hawkins, Dr. Edward, Merchant Taylors' School, ii. 526
Hawkins, Dr. Francis, Merchant Taylors' School, ii. 526
Hawkins, John, editor of Cocker's *Works*, buried, ii. 103
Hawkins, Sir John, author of the *History of Music*, died, iii. 209
Hawkins, Sir John, Naval Commander, monument, i. 536
Hawkins, R. M., architect, ii. 176
Hawkshaw, Sir John, engineer, i. 358, 324
Hawksmoor, Nicholas, architect, i. 49, 393; ii. 97, 98, 310, 389, 508; iii. 462
Hay, Charles, baptized, ii. 17
Hay, Thomas Atte, ii. 230
Haydn, Joseph, at St. Paul's, iii. 52; lived, 130
Haydon, B. R., exhibited, ii. 8; lived, 402, 474; iii. 156; prisoner, ii. 342; died, i. 310; buried, iii. 3
Hayley, William, lived, i. 108; iii. 137, i. 138
Hayman, Francis, lived, i. 492; ii. 483
Haynau, General, i. 107
Haynes, Joseph, lived, iii. 99
Hayter, Sir George, lived, i. 187, 204

Hayward, John, iii. 81
Hayward, Sir John, buried, i. 116
Hayward, Sir Rowland, lived, i. 284; monument, 40
Haywood, W., engineer, ii. 222, 223
Hazlitt, William, lecturer, iii. 336; marriage, i. 44; lived, 228, 519; ii. 181; iii. 79, 281, 543; died, ii. 82; buried, i. 50
Head, Richard, lived, iii. 141
Heath, engraver, lived, ii. 402
Heath, Nicholas, Abp. of York, i. 52, 328; lived, iii. 536
Heath, James, lived, ii. 595; buried, i. 117
Heathcote, Sir Gilbert, Lord Mayor, ii. 464
Heathfield, Lord, lived, i. 487; monument, iii. 48
Heber, Bp., married, ii. 468; preacher, 392; monument, iii. 48
Heber, Richard, ii. 274; lived, i. 236; died, iii. 97
Heberden, Dr., portrait, iii. 82
Heidegger, J. J., lived, iii. 133
Heinch, Mademoiselle, dancer, ii. 453
Heine, Heinrich, lived, i. 473
Hemens, Giles, i. 495
Hemings, John, lived ii. 206
Hemynge, John, grocer, ii. 160; buried, 490
Henchman, Bp. Humphry, died, i. 24; ii. 430
Henderson, Alexander, i. 52
Henderson, John, i. 255, 265, 266, 267; ii. 270; actor, 221; died, i. 296; buried, iii. 464
Heneage, Thomas, i. 180; ii. 207
Heneage, Sir Thomas, i. 310; died, iii. 219
Henley, John, "orator," i. 407; ii. 595
Henley, Robert, lived, iii. 112
Henning, jun., ii. 254
Henrietta Maria, Queen, ii. 207; iii. 418; lived, 270; statue, 135
Henry III., i. 351; Westminster Abbey, iii. 462; buried, 463; altar-tomb, 468
Henry IV., died, iii. 479
Henry V., i. 352; ii. 220; prisoner when Prince of Wales, 341; Smithfield, when Prince of Wales, iii. 255; buried, 463; altar-tomb, 469
Henry VII., lived, i. 132; buried, iii. 463; altar-tomb, 466
Henry VIII., i. 194, 249, 363, 375; ii. 113, 285, 320; portrait, 523
Henry, Prince of Wales, ii. 104, 589; iii. 121; benefactor, ii. 477; died, 286; buried, iii. 466
Henry, John, hanged, iii. 375
Henry, Matthew, preacher, ii. 179
Heneyko, builder, iii. 182
Henslowe, Francis, ii. 166

Henslowe, Philip, ii. 68, 116, 239; iii. 31, 95, 172, 174; manager, ii. 594; lived, i. 101, 426; buried, iii. 215
Herbert, George, school, iii. 488
Herbert, Sir Henry, ii. 389, 477; lived, i. 337; iii. 388; died, ii. 274; buried, iii. 58
Herbert, Magdalen, buried, ii. 449
Herbert, Mr., ii. 444
Herbert, J. R., R.A., frescoes, ii. 241, 242
Herbert, William, lived, ii. 138
Herbert of Cherbury, Edward Lord, lived, ii. 613; iii. 136; died, 136; buried, ii. 112
Herbert, of Lea, Lord, statue, iii. 447
Hereford, Bps. of, ii. 45, 504
Hereicke, Elizabeth, tablet, ii. 468
Heriot, Alison, wife of George, buried, ii. 154
Heriot, George, buried, ii. 428
Herrick, Nicholas, lived, iii. 431
Herrick, Robert, baptised, iii. 430; lived, i. 51
Herring, Abp., portrait, ii. 363
Herringman, Henry, i. 210; lived, ii. 583
Herschel, Sir John, Master of the Mint, ii. 549; buried, iii. 464; monument, 473
Hertford, Countess of, lived, ii. 165; tomb, iii. 465
Hertford, William Seymour, Earl of, lived, i. 324; ii. 17
Hertford, Marquis of, i. 537; iii. 90; lived, ii. 461; iii. 161; died, 33
Hervey, Bp. of Cloyne, in Cranbourne Alley, i. 470
Hervey, John, lived, ii. 299
Hervey, John, Lord, ii. 293; duel, ii. 151; lived, i. 309; ii. 299
Hervilly, L. C., Comte d', buried, iii. 18
Hesketh, Lady, lived, ii. 609
Heton, Dr. Martin, Bp. of Ely, ii. 11
Hewer, William, i. 428; lived, 296
Hewett, Dr. John, executed, ii. 153
Hewson, Hugh, buried, i. 319
Heydon, Alderman, ii. 197
Heyward, Edward, iii. 27
Hickes, Dr. George, vicar, i. 31; lived, ii. 617; buried, 468
Hicks, Sir Baptist, ii. 223; lived, i. 320
Higgins, J. M., architect, ii. 78
Higgins, M. J., lived, ii. 4
Higgons, Bevil, buried, iii. 22
Highland, Mr., M.P., iii. 286
Hill, Aaron, i. 540; born, 140; lived, iii. 79
Hill, Sir John, i. 316; lived, 134, 279
Hill, Joseph, lived, iii. 212
Hill, General Lord, lived, i. 153; iii. 460
Hill, Captain Richard, ii. 244
Hill, Sir Richard, M.P., lived, ii. 191
Hill, Matthew Davenport, lived, i. 380
Hill, Rowland, minister, iii. 176; dislikes William Huntington, 54; died, i. 199

INDEX 573

Hill, Sir Rowland, Post Office, iii. 114;
 lived, ii. 616; buried, iii. 463; bust,
 468
Hill, Bp. Rowley, "Grecian," i. 396
Hill, Thomas, Mayor, ii. 135
Hill, Thomas, lived, i. 7; ii. 273; iii.
 144
Hill, T. J., architect, i. 37, 125
Hilliard, Nicholas, buried, ii. 478
Hillier, Charles Parker, died, i. 359
Hills, Richard, benefactor, ii. 524
Hillsborough, Lord, lived, ii. 186
Hilton, William, R.A., lived, ii. 134; altar-
 pieces, 535; iii. 74; memorial, ii. 500
Hinchman, Dr., Bp. of London, iii. 46
Hind, Andrew, iii. 27
Hinde, Jacob, ii. 215, 510
Hinde, Peter, ii. 215
Hingham, Ralph de, Chief Justice, iii. 6
Hoadly, Benj., Bp. of Winchester, lecturer,
 ii. 540; rector, iii. 74
Hoadly, Benjamin, M.D., born, i. 278;
 lived, 380; died, 376
Hoare, Prince, lived, iii. 349
Hoare, Richard, lived, ii. 63
Hobbes, of Malmesbury, lived, ii. 37;
 portraits, iii. 188
Hobhey, Sir Edward, lived, i. 324
Hobhouse, Sir John, arrested, ii. 581
Hobhouse, Lord, lived, i. 289
Hobson, Cambridge carrier, i. 298
Hobson, Thomas, ii. 509
Hodges, Dr. Nathaniel, lived, iii. 456;
 memorial, 311
Hodgkins, hanged, iii. 340
Hogarth, Mary and Ann, ii. 440
Hogarth, William, i. 129, 143, 490, 492,
 501 ii. 36, 73, 114, 149, 403, 406;
 iii. 297, 350, 452; baptism, i. 116;
 club, ii. 106; Vauxhall Gardens, iii.
 428 married to Jane Thornhill, 3;
 lived, ii. 364, 383, 612; iii. 196;
 pictures, ii. 399, 496, 570; iii. 57, 84,
 95, 102, 172, 190, 201, 261, 346, 376,
 389, 419, 492; shopbill, 27; bust, ii.
 385
Hogg, James, lived, iii. 454; dinner, ii.
 77
Holbein, Hans, i. 395; ii. 275, 321;
 lived, i. 377; died, 46; pictures, 102,
 243; ii. 555; iii. 308
Holcroft, Thomas, born, ii. 616; club, iii.
 107; lived, i. 80; iii. 280; died, i.
 427; buried, ii. 496
Holden, Thomas, architect, ii. 264
Holderness, Lord, iii. 220
Holford, R. S., i. 512; iii. 33
Holgate, Abp., i. 127
Holl, William, engraver, lived, i. 131
Holland, Henry, lived, iii. 65; architect,
 i. 201, 286, 332, 527; ii. 189, 519
Holland, Sir Henry, M.D., lived, i. 283;
 ii. 565

Holland, Henry Rich, Earl of, lived, ii.
 223
Holland, Robert Rich, second Earl of, i.
 361; ii. 596
Holland, Lady (1845), died, iii. 279
Holland, Henry Fox, first Lord, died, ii.
 224
Holland, Stephen, second Lord, lived, i. 12
Holland, Henry Vassall, third Lord, i. 3;
 died, ii. 225; monument, iii. 474
Hollar, Wenceslaus, lived, i. 73; died, ii.
 85; buried, 468, 579; drawings, iii. 44;
 views, 57, 183
Holles, Denail, Lord, i. 496; lived, iii. 84
Holles, Sir John, i. 416; ii. 589
Hollis, Charles, architect, iii. 106
Hollis, —, lived, ii. 596
Holloway, murderer, i. 545
Holmes, J. L., architect, ii. 378
Holscombe, Ellis, ii. 359
Holt, Lord Chief Justice, Gray's Inn, ii.
 140; died, i. 126
Home, John, author of *Douglas*, lived, i. 80
Home, architect, ii. 321
Home, Earl of, ii. 165
Home, Sir Everard, lived, iii. 197
Hone, Horace, buried, i. 134
Hone, Nathaniel, R.A., died, iii. 151;
 exhibited, ii. 484
Hone, William, lived, ii. 63, 136, 271,
 365, 612; prisoner, 342; buried, i. 3
Hood, Admiral Lord, lived, iii. 523; por-
 trait, ii. 264
Hood, Thomas, ii. 26; born, iii. 117;
 lived, 165; died, ii. 9, 42; buried, 325
Hook, James, ii. 533
Hook, Theodore, ii. 319; born, i. 361;
 spunging-house, iii. 241; hoax, i. 170;
 lived, 423
Hooke, Dr. Robert, buried, ii. 205; archi-
 tect, i. 76, 173; ii. 555; professor, i.
 155
Hooker, Richard, Master of the Temple,
 iii. 353; lived, 246
Hoole, Charles, lived, i. 72
Hoole, John, translator of *Tasso*, ii. 3;
 lived, iii. 137
Hooper, Bp., i. 48; trial, iii. 214; prisoner,
 i. 426; ii. 59; iii. 535
Hope, Henry Thomas, i. 78; lived, iii. 91
Hope, Philip Henry, i. 528; ii. 462
Hope, Tho., lived, i. 528; died, ii. 462
Hopetoun, Earl of, i. 342
Hopkins, Bp., Merchant Taylors' School,
 ii. 526
Hopper, Tho., architect, i. 65; ii. 494
Hoppner, J., lived, i. 361; buried, ii. 275
Hore, James, lived, ii. 63
Hornby, John, ii. 38
Horne, J., surveyor, ii. 72
Horne, Bp. Robert, rector, i. 32
Horne, Rev. Thomas Hartwell, "deputy
 Grecian," i. 396; died, 209

Horneck, Mrs., iii. 25
Horner, Francis, club, ii. 335; lived, 85; statue, iii. 472
Horner, Messrs., i. 297
Hornor, —, founder of Colosseum, i. 446
Horsley, Bp., rector, ii. 505
Horsley, J. C., R.A., fresco, ii. 241, 242
Hosiar, Ralph, i. 481
Hoskin, John, lived, i. 148
Hotham, John de, Bp. of Ely, ii. 10
Houblon, Sir John, lived, i. 95
Houghton, Lord, club, iii. 313
Houlker, Thomas, i. 424
House, Sam, lived, iii. 447
Howard, Hon. Charles, lived, iii. 336
Howard, Hon. Esme, buried, iii. 20
Howard, Sir George, lived, iii. 267
Howard, Hon. James, quoted, ii. 251
Howard, John, i. 217; born, ii. 179; lived, 618; iii. 318; statue, 48; his father, ii. 440
Howard, Queen Katherine, prisoner, iii. 398; buried, 76
Howard, Lady Mary, lived, iii. 11
Howard, Mrs., lived, i. 165
Howard, Sir Philip, ii. 233; lived (1665-1672), iii. 332
Howard, Sir Robert, prison, ii. 89
Howard, Sir William, lived, ii. 596
Howard of Effingham, Katherine, Lady, i. 375; brass, ii. 495
Howard of Effingham (William, first Lord), Lord Admiral, lived, ii. 337
Howard of Effingham, Francis, fifth Lord, i. 476
Howard of Effingham, Thomas, sixth Lord, born, i. 476
Howe, John, minister, iii. 98; lived, i. 80, 366; buried, 32
Howe, Admiral Lord, i. 8; lived, ii. 137; bust, iii. 408; monument, 48
Howe, Earl, lived, i. 80
Howe, George, third Viscount, i. 486
Howell, James, lived, i. 278; prison, ii. 59; monument, iii. 351
Howell, Thomas, i. 522
Howland, John, Lord, i. 447; ii. 245
Howland, Mrs., iii. 74
Howley, Abp., ii. 362, 363; portrait, 364
Howson, J., Bp. of Durham, i. 542
Hoyle, Edmund, died, iii. 457; buried, ii. 496
Hubbard, J. G., M.P., i. 11
Hubert, hanged for setting fire to London, iii. 128
Hucks, William, ii. 97
Hudson, Geo., Railway King, lived, i. 16
Hudson, Sir Jeffrey, prison, ii. 90
Hudson, Philip, i. 66
Hudson, Thomas, lived, iii. 137
Hugan, —, iii. 529

Huggins, —, ii. 57
Hughes, —, manager, iii. 337; exhibits feats of horsemanship, i. 476
Hughes, John, buried, i. 44
Hughes, Thomas, i. 540
Hugo, Rev. T., quoted, ii. 180
Hugolin, buried, i. 351
Hull, J. F., i. 254
Hullah, John, ii. 438
Humble, Alderman, monument, iii. 215
Hume, Sir Abraham, lived, ii. 216
Hume, David, i. 287; member of Brooks's, 287 note, lived, 235, 296; ii. 402
Hume, Joseph, M.P., died, i. 289; buried, ii. 325
Humphrey, Duke, tomb at St. Paul's, iii. 41. See Gloucester, Humphrey, Duke of
Humphrey, Ozias, R.A., lived, i. 219; ii. 597; iii. 151
Humphreys, Samuel, lived, ii. 269; died, i. 326
Humphries, Mrs., lived, ii. 571
Hungerford, Sir Edward, lived, iii. 296; died, ii. 248
Hungerford, Thomas, monument, ii. 449
Hunlock, Sir Hugh, i. 466; iii. 80
Hunne, Richard, prisoner, ii. 414; hanged, iii. 245
Hunsdon, Henry Carey, Lord, K.G., ii. 447; iii. 269; lived, i. 196, 284; monument, iii. 470
Hunt, F. W., architect, iii. 413
Hunt, Holman, studio, i. 423
Hunt, Leigh, i. 424; "deputy Grecian," 396; prisoner, ii. 234; lived, i. 389; ii. 334, 403; iii. 119; buried, ii. 325
Hunt, Roger, iii. 173
Hunt, William, bequest, ii. 176; born, i. 157
Hunt, Orator, iii. 290
Hunter, John, i. 119, 342; iii. 527; club, ii. 484; founder, iii. 334; lived, ii. 1, 307, 383; died, 101; buried, 479; iii. 464; grave, 473; portrait, 336; bust, ii. 385; his widow died, 226
Hunter, Rev. Joseph, lived, iii. 385
Hunter, Dr. William, lived, ii. 307; i. 12, 527; buried, ii. 280; portrait, iii. 82
Huntingdon, Catherine, Countess of, tomb, ii. 449
Huntingdon, Selina, Countess of, died, i. 419; iii. 290
Huntingdon, Theophilus, Earl of, lived, i. 473
Huntington, William, S.S., i. 117; ii. 144; minister, iii. 382; died, ii. 211
Hurd, Bp., preacher, iii. 392; lived, i. 424
Hurst and Blackett, ii. 474
Huskisson, William, lived, ii. 165; statue, 410
Hutchinson, Colonel, i. 127; iii. 536; student, ii. 300; marriage, i. 44

INDEX

Hutchinson, Mrs., born, iii. 399
Hutton, Matthew, Abp. of Canterbury, died, i. 534
Huysman, James, buried, ii. 289
Hyde, Lord Chief Justice (d. 1631), lived, i. 346; iii. 232; Treasurer of Middle Temple, 357

I'Anson, Edward, architect, i. 120, 181, 456; ii. 523, 525; iii. 184
Iddesleigh, Earl of, lived, ii. 192; portrait, 575
Ilchester, Stephen, Earl of, i. 309
Ilive, Jacob, lived, i. 94
Illidge, S., lived, iii. 232
Impey, Sir Elijah, lived, iii. 523
Inchbald, Mrs., lived, ii. 81, 384; iii. 324; died, ii. 327; monument, 326
Inchiquin, Earl of, lived, ii. 384
Incledon, Charles, lived, i. 281
Ingelric, Earl of Essex, founder, ii. 486
Ingram, Sir Arthur, lived, ii. 257
Innes, C., architect, ii. 491
Inwood, Henry William, architect, iii. 23, 158, 486
Inwood, W., architect, i. 319; ii. 312; iii. 23, 158, 209, 486
Ireland, J., quoted, ii. 72
Ireland, Samuel, lived, ii. 601
Ireland, William, ii. 262; iii. 129
Ireton, Colonel, Middle Temple, iii. 357; corpse, 155; body at Tyburn, 419
Ironside, Bp. Gilbert, buried, ii. 505
Irving, Rev. Edward, i. 479; preacher, iii. 158; lived, ii. 20, 119, 570
Irving, Washington, quoted, ii. 534
Isaacs, L. H., architect, ii. 425
Isabel, Queen of Edward II., buried, ii. 157
Islip, Abbot, tomb, iii. 470

Jackson, Bp., tomb, iii. 48
Jackson, John, R.A., buried, ii. 318; tomb, i. 282
Jackson, John, pugilist, lived, i. 220; ii. 166
Jacob, Sir Hildebrand, buried, i. 50
Jacob, Lady, lived, i. 523
Jacobsen, Theodore, architect, ii. 71; buried, i. 34
Jaggard, John, lived, ii. 62
James I., ii. 229; Pall Mall, iii. 8; at Paul's Cross, 61; buried, 463, 466, 467; portrait, 358, 408; statue, i. 428; bust, iii. 509
James II., i. 373, 451; ii. 231; as Duke of York, 271, 286; grocer, 161; revenues of Post Office, iii. 113; in Priory Garden, 325; in Spring Gardens, 295; escape, ii. 401; flight from Whitehall, iii. 363, 512; portraits, i. 395; ii. 523; iii. 408, 438; statue, 513
James I. of Scotland, marriage to Johanna Beaufort, iii. 213, 524

James IV. of Scotland, head buried, ii. 536
James, the old Pretender, born ii. 286
James, Sir Henry, ii. 316
James, John, i. 301
James, John, architect, ii. 95
James, John, executed, ii. 546
James, Mrs. benefactor, iii. 250
James, Dr. Robert, died, i. 289
James, Sir Walter, lived, i. 502
James, William, Bp. of Durham, i. 542
Jameson, Mrs., lived, i. 289, 387
Jamford, William de, ii. 608
Jamieson, Dr., monetary relief, iii. 188
Jamrach, Charles, iii. 151
Jansen, Mr., i. 363
Jansen, Bernard, ii. 603
Jansen, Cornelius, iii. 4; lived, i. 196
Jansen, Sir Theodore, iii. 134; lived, ii. 186
Jarvis, Messrs., iii. 444
Jebb, Major R., architect, iii. 71
Jeffrey, Francis, duel with Moore, i. 344; iii. 120
Jeffreys, Judge, married, i. 31; Inner Temple, iii. 354; at Wapping, 444; lived, i. 20, 534; ii. 288, 439; prisoner, iii. 399; buried, ii. 491
Jekyll, Sir Joseph, accident, ii. 395; iii. 166
Jekyll, J., lived, ii. 343, 586
Jenkins, gardener, i. 295
Jenkins, bank clerk, buried, i. 399
Jenner, Rev. Charles, quoted, ii. 268; iii. 497
Jenner, Dr., lived, ii. 213; iii. 193
Jenner, Sir William, lived, i. 283
Jennings, Henry Constantine, lived, ii. 400; died, i. 157
Jennings, Joseph, architect, i. 68, 405
Jenyns, Soame, ii. 41; born, 617
Jerdan, William, lived, i. 281
Jerman, Edw., architect, i. 521; ii. 8, 259, 520; iii. 183
Jermyn, Henry, duel, ii. 283
Jerome, William, vicar, i. 538; burned, iii. 256
Jerrold, Douglas, born, ii. 149; lived, i. 277, 400
Jersey, Earl of, i. 164; iii. 302
Jervas, Charles, lived, iii. 221; died, i. 421
Jessop, William, engineer, iii. 459
Jevon, T., actor and dramatist, ii. 414
Jewel, John, Bp. of Salisbury, i. 515
Jocelyn, Lord Chancellor of Ireland, i. 285
John, King, i. 481
John, King of France, prisoner, iii. 217
John of Eltham, monument, iii. 465
John of Gaunt, iii. 217; tomb, 41
John of Northampton, i. 351
Johnson, tavern proprietor, i. 406
Johnson, Gerard, lived, iii. 373
Johnson, Hector, ii. 254

Johnson, Sir Henry, i. 202
Johnson, J., lived. iii. 54
Johnson, Joel, architect, ii. 311
Johnson, John, architect, ii. 548
Johnson, Marmaduke, ii. 445
Johnson, Rev. Samuel, ii. 221; mock ceremony of degradation, iii. 55
Johnson, Dr. Samuel, i. 71, 350, 413; ii. 90, 302, 314, 336, 353; the Cock Lane ghost, i. 432; meeting with Edwards, 313; at Temple Bar, iii. 359; dined, ii. 586; at the Mitre, 551; clubs, i. 480, 500; ii. 18, 106, 271, 403; iii. 141; lived, i. 224, 230, 337, 491, 544; ii. 28, 131, 221, 257, 318, 406; iii. 393, 531; died, i. 216; buried, iii. 463, 478; his will, 516; statue, 48
Johnstone, "Irish," lived, iii. 349
Jones, clockmaker, ii. 259
Jones, Mrs. Ann, licence to eat flesh in Lent, ii. 505
Jones, Gale, ii. 100
Jones, Sir Horace, lived, i. 502; architect, 183; ii. 32, 170, 171, 173, 424, 530; iii. 338, 359
Jones, Inigo, ii. 112, 225, 360, 560; iii. 4; baptism, i. 116; lived, iii. 224; died, 276; buried, i. 159; architect, ii. 23, 74, 102, 143, 461; ii. 84, 104, 321, 391, 393, 401, 604; iii. 40, 56, 83, 269, 505, 508, 509, 523; his will, 516
Jones, John, bequest, iii. 276
Jones, John, engraver, lived, iii. 110
Jones, John, executed, i. 354
Jones, Owen, school, i. 365; architect, ii. 283; iii. 159
Jones, Thomas, chaplain, iii. 216
Jones, William, architect, iii. 147
Jones, Rev. William, of Nayland, school, i. 365
Jones, Sir William, lived, i. 80; ii. 354; monument, iii. 48
Jones, J. Winter, i. 268, 272
Jonson, Ben, i. 509; ii. 110, 390; school, iii. 488; duel, ii. 245, 387; club, i. 497; lived, 195; ii. 193; buried, iii. 461, 473; monumental tablet, 476; burial of his infant son, i. 227
Jordaens, iii. 509
Jordan, Master Westminster School, iii. 488
Jordan, Mrs., lived, i. 316
Jortin, John, monument, ii. 326
Jortin, Roger (d. 1795), i. 536
Joseph, N. S., architect, iii. 110
Judd, Sir Andrew, ii. 319; monument, 204; portrait, iii. 252
Jullien, C. manager, iii. 338; concerts, i. 466
Junius, ii. 456
Jupp, Richard, architect, ii. 2; iii. 252
Jupp, William, lived, ii. 434
Juxon, Abp., ii. 362; school, 526; Gray's Inn, 140; portrait, 364

KATHARINE, Queen of Charles II., i. 187
Katherine of Aragon, ii. 99, 320
Katterfelto, lived, iii. 91
Kay, John, i. 19
Kayes, Robert, iii. 425
Kean, Charles, manager, iii. 122
Kean, Edmund, i. 350; ii. 616; iii. 209; born, i. 336; club, ii. 75; lived, i. 344, 412; ii. 81, 402
Keats, John, born, ii. 562; baptism, i. 227; student, ii. 176; lived, i. 493; iii. 116, 140
Keble, Henry, buried, ii. 491
Keble, John, bust, iii. 473
Keck, Robert, lived, iii. 346
Keeley, Robert, born, ii. 138; died, iii. 69; buried, i. 282
Keeling, F. B., architect, ii. 84
Keir, Dr., i. 386; ii. 484
Keith, Rev. Alexander, ii. 516; chapel, i. 487; prison, ii. 69; died, 517
Keith, Admiral Lord, lived, ii. 192
Kelly, Hugh, lived, ii. 132
Kelly, Miss, manager, iii. 189
Kem, Rev. —, preached in buff coat, iii. 77
Kemble, Charles, lived, ii. 107, 595; buried, 325
Kemble, Mrs. Fanny, born, ii. 595; school, 189; lived, 107
Kemble, John Philip, i. 465; lived, ii. 334; iii. 193; farewell dinner, ii. 77; statue, iii. 471
Kemp, W., actor, i. 101
Kemp, Thomas, Bp. of London, iii. 60; mortuary chapel, 41
Kemp, T. R., i. 153
Kempenfelt, Admiral, monument, iii. 471
Ken, Thomas (d. 1631), lived, ii. 84
Kendal, Duchess of, lived, ii. 164, 287
Kendal, Mr. and Mrs., ii. 305
Kendall, H. E., architect, ii. 153
Kene, Antony, ii. 201
Kenmuir, Lord, prisoner, iii. 399; executed, 401
Kennet, Dr. White, Bp. of Peterborough, rector, i. 227; ii. 490; satire on, 503; lived, i. 481; died, ii. 396
Kenney, J., dramatist, died, i. 281
Kenrick, James, ii. 454
Kenrick, William, LL.D., i. 501; buried, ii. 450
Kensington, William Edwards, Lord, ii. 2, 224; married, 517
Kent, Duchess of, lived, i. 408
Kent, Duke of, lived, ii. 331; statue, iii. 33, 109
Kent, Henry Grey, ninth Earl of, i. 214; lived, iii. 504
Kent, William, i. 306, 332; architect, 63, 163, 501; ii. 238, 532; iii. 141, 407; landscape gardener, ii. 329

INDEX 577

Kenyon, Lord, lived, ii. 396
Keppel, Lord, i. 8; school, iii. 488
Kerbye, Charles, bookseller, ii. 192
Kerr, Prof. Robert, architect, ii. 4
Kerwyn, And., ii. 531
Kerwyn, William and Magdalen, monument, ii. 205
Ketch, John, hangman, iii. 418
Kettlewell, John, i. 120; buried, 31
Key, Sir John, Lord Mayor, ii. 451
Keys, —, prison, ii. 59
Keyes, —, executed, iii. 5
Keyse, Thomas, i. 168
Kidd, Captain William, hanged, ii. 25
Kiffen, William, i. 502
Kildare, Gerald, ninth Earl of, buried, iii. 76
Killigrew, Anne, buried, iii. 218; monument, ii. 499
Killigrew, Dr., Master of the Savoy, iii. 218; buried, 464
Killigrew, Sir Robert, prison, ii. 59
Killigrew, Thomas, ii. 335, 607; iii. 153, 431; manager, i. 436; ii. 397; born, 442; lived, iii. 84; buried, ii. 397; iii. 473
Kilmarnock, Lord, prisoner, iii. 399; trial, 486; executed, 401; buried, 76
Kilwardby, Robert, Abp. of Canterbury, i. 193
King, Charles, executed, i. 209
King, Sir Edmund, portrait, iii. 82
King, Gregory, buried, i. 159; builder, ii. 149
King, John, Bp. of London, ii. 311
King, Peter, first Lord, ii. 469; portrait, iii. 233
King, Peter, seventh Lord, died, i. 517
King, William, LL.D., iii. 116, 313
King, Tom, lived, ii. 343
Kingston, Duchess of, lived, ii. 327, 352; marriage, 96; trial, iii. 486
Kingston, Duke of, marriage, i. 487
Kinnaird, Hon. Douglas, lived, i. 412
Kinski, Count, lived, ii. 186
Kip, John, died, ii. 439
Kippis, Andrew, F.R.S., ii. 246; lived, i. 481; ii. 179; buried, i. 303
Kirby, John, lived, i. 179
Kirk, Captain, ii. 293
Kirkall, Edward, lived, i. 507
Kirkeby, John de, Bp. of Ely, ii. 10
Kirkley, Ralph, ii. 198
Kitchener, Dr. Wm., lived, iii. 449; died, 449; buried, i. 415
Knapton, George, painter, i. 505
Knatchbull, Sir Edward, lived, ii. 92
Kneller, Sir Godfrey, ii. 348; lived, i. 543; iii. 85, 137; monument, 475
Knevet, Sir Edmund, i. 213
Knight, surgeon to Charles II, lived, iii. 194
Knight, Charles, lived, iii. 349

Knight, Gowin, M.D., i. 272
Knight, Henry Gally, lived, ii. 165
Knight, John, lived, i. 140
Knight, Mary, lived, iii. 11
Knight, Richard Payne, i. 254, 266, 267; died, iii. 266
Knight, Robert, cashier of the South Sea Company, i. 445
Knight, Samuel, school, iii. 63
Knollys, Sir Francis, marriage, i. 35
Knowles, James, died, i. 29
Knowles, J., architect, ii. 385
Knowles, Sheridan, lived, i. 29
Knowles, Thomas, ii. 171
Knox, John, i. 32
Knox, Vicesimus, i. 536; Merchant Taylors' School, ii. 526
Koningsmarck, Count, ii. 71, 198; trial, 214
Koops, Matthias, ii. 578
Kosciusko, lived, ii. 385; iii. 196
Kossuth, Louis, lived, i. 40
Kyllingham, John, i. 336
Kynaston, Edward, lived, i. 148, 149; buried, iii. 58
Kynaston, Sir Francis, lived, i. 148
Kyngescote, William, warden, ii. 444

LABELYE, Charles, architect, iii. 481
Lackington, George, i. 391; ii. 7; lived, 43
Lacy, Bp. of Exeter, lived, ii. 21
Lacy, John, lived, i. 523; buried, ii. 478
Ladbroke, Sir Robert, monument, i. 393
Laguerre, Louis, painter, i. 524; died, 526; buried, ii. 479
Laing, David, architect, i. 487, 535
Lake, General Lord, lived, i. 283
La Marche, J. F., Comte de, Bp. of St. Pol de Leon, buried, iii. 18
Lamb, auctioneer, iii. 14, 177
Lamb, Lady Caroline, school, ii. 189
Lamb, Charles, i. 204; ii. 3, 20, 34, 82, 141, 593; born, i. 489; school, 121; "deputy Grecian," 396; tavern, iii. 207; lived, i. 350, 442; ii. 258, 270, 551; iii. 138, 280, 195
Lamb, Dr., the conjurer, iii. 528; prisoner, 117
Lamb, E. B., architect, i. 222, 452
Lamb, John, iii. 279
Lamb, Mary, school, i. 121; stabbed her mother, iii. 138; lived, i. 350, 442
Lambe, William, i. 428; ii. 212, 354
Lambert, George, i. 150
Lambert, General, lived, ii. 224
Lancaster, Henry Plantagenet, first Duke of, iii. 212
Lancaster, John of Gaunt, Duke of, i. 528; died, ii. 10
Lancaster, Edmund Crouchback, Earl of, iii. 217; tomb, 471

VOL. III 2 P

578   INDEX

Lancaster, Joseph, i. 250; ii. 365; schools, i. 223; lived, ii. 273.
Lander, Richard, monument, ii. 500
Landon, Miss L. E., born, ii. 189; married, i. 289; ii. 493
Landor, Walter Savage, lived, i. 142, 224
Landseer, Charles, R.A., died, ii. 318
Landseer, Sir Edwin, R.A., lions in Trafalgar Square, iii. 405; lived, ii. 67, 166; died, 318
Landseer, John, lived, ii. 67
Landseer, Thomas, A.R.A., lived, ii. 318
Lane, William, highwayman, ii. 352
Lanesborough, Earl of, iii. 48, 302
Laney, Benjamin, Bp. of Ely, ii. 13
Lange, Robert, Lord Mayor, iii. 528
Langford's auction rooms, iii. 84
Langham, S., Abp. of Canterbury, tomb, iii. 465
Langham, Sir James, ii. 66, 365
Langham, Sir John, lived, i. 478
Langborne, John, ii. 144, 312; assistant preacher, 392
Langley, Batty, lived, ii. 519
Langton, Bennet, lived, i. 219
Langton, Thomas, monument, ii. 204
Langton, Abp., rector, i. 32; Constable of the Tower, iii. 399
Lankrink, Prosper Henry, lived, iii. 85
La Noye, Cornelius de, lived, iii. 269
Lansdowne, George Granville, Viscount, lived, ii. 187; prisoner, iii. 399; buried, i. 415
Lansdowne, first Marquis of, i. 163; ii. 366
Lant, family of, ii. 367
Large, Robert, buried, ii. 609
Larke, John, rector, ii. 450
Laroone, Capt. Marcellus, club, ii. 208; lived, i. 229
Latham, Mrs., lived, ii. 502
Latimer, Dr. Hugh, ii. 357, 364, 372; preacher, 357, 364, 468, 490; iii. 246
Latimer, Lady Lucy, monument, ii. 178
Laud, Abp., ii. 360, 386, 579; Gray's Inn, 140; consecration, 117; prisoner, iii. 27, 398; trials, ii. 361, 364; executed, iii. 401; buried, i. 31; portrait, ii. 363
Lauder, Wm., lived, i. 11
Lauderdale, John, Duke of, lived, i. 23; ii. 362
Lawes, Henry, buried, iii. 480
Lawes, Robert, Clerk of the Works, iii. 269
Lawrence family, i. 375
Lawrences of Shurdington, i. 476
Lawrence, Dr. French, i. 184; died, ii. 19
Lawrence, Sir Henry, monument, iii. 48
Lawrence, Lord, ii. 448; lived, i. 376; ii. 205; buried, iii. 463; statue, 454
Lawrence, General Stringer, lived, i. 289; monument, iii. 474; portrait, ii. 616

Lawrence, Sir Thomas, iii. 150; lived, ii. 149; i. 219; died, iii. 192; grave, 49; monument ii. 449
Lawrence, William, epitaph, iii. 480
Lawson, Sir John, buried, i. 536
Layard, Sir A. H., i. 255, 258, 259
Leach, John, Master of the Rolls, drawings, iii. 319
Leadbetter, S., architect, ii. 66; iii. 62
Leake, Dr. John, ii. 452
Leake, Admiral Sir John, born, iii. 175
Leathercoat, porter, iii. 172
Le Bas, Dr., rector, iii. 447
Lechmere, Sir Edmund, ii. 315
Lechmere, Lord, lived, i. 320; ii. 224
Ledru Rollin, lived, i. 281; iii. 69
Loe, E. C., architect, i. 128; ii. 299, 503
Lee, Sir George, died, ii. 300
Lee, Sir Henry, of Ditchley, iii. 381, 510
Lee, John, LL.D., ii. 141
Lee, Nat, i. 175; school, iii. 488; died, i. 313; buried, 414
Lee, W. W., architect, i. 110
Lee Boo, Prince, monument, iii. 174
Leech, John, school, i. 365; lived, i. 288; iii. 119; buried, ii. 325; his father, 426
Leeds, Duke of, lived, ii. 302
Leeke, Henry, founder, iii. 140
Le Fevre, Ralph, ii. 31
Lefevre, Roland, died, i. 139
Le Galeys, Henry, i. 21, 23
Legat, Francis, lived, iii. 253
Legate, Bartholomew, burned, iii. 256
Legge, William, ii. 606
Legh, Alex., rector, i. 238
Legh, Sir Thomas, benefactor, ii. 520
Le Grice, Rev. C. V., i. 285
Leicester, Robert Dudley, Earl of, ii. 452; lived, 16, 379
Leicester, Robert Sidney, first Earl of, lived, ii. 380
Leicester, Robert Sidney, second Earl of, lived, ii. 543, 596
Leicester, John Sidney, sixth Earl of, lived, iii. 267
Leigh, Mrs., i. 114
Leighton, Dr. Alexander, pillory, iii. 7
Leighton, Abp., died, iii. 431
Leighton, Sir Frederick, frescoes, iii. 275
Leland, John, school, iii. 63; buried, ii. 536
Le Long, John, the Easterling, i. 189
Lely, Sir Peter, lived, iii. 84; buried, 58
Le Marchant, Sir Denis, died, i. 152
Le Mintier, Bp., buried, iii. 18
Lemon, Mark, lived, iii. 535
Lempriere, Dr., died, iii. 284
Le Neve, John, born, iii. 193; lived, 371
Le Neve, Peter, Merchant Taylors' School, ii. 526
Le Neve, Sir William, buried, i. 159
Lennard, Sampson, buried, i. 159

INDEX

Lennox, Mrs. Charlotte, lived, iii. 271; died, i. 494
Lennox, Duchess of, i. 378
Lennox, Duke of, ii. 12
Lennox, Lady Margaret, lived, ii. 179
Lennox, Lady Sarah, lived, i. 316
Le Notre, André, ii. 290
Lens, Bernard, lived, ii. 55
Lenthall, Speaker, lived, ii. 336, 566
Leoni, G., architect, iii. 424
Leoni, James, buried, iii. 21
Leopold, king of the Belgians, i. 431; lived, 320; ii. 473; iii. 33
Lepel, Molly, lived, ii. 296
Leslie, C. R., R.A., lived, i. 295; ii. 403, 426; iii. 98, 449; died, i. 2
Le Sœur, Hubert, i. 355; lived, 110; buried, 116
L'Estrange, Sir Roger, lived, ii. 108, 271; buried, 112
Le Tellier, Abp., i. 543
Lettsom, John Coakley, M.D., lived, i. 123; died, iii. 208
Leventhorpe, John, monument, ii. 204
Lever, Sir Ashton, lived, ii. 381
Leveridge, Richard, lived, iii. 349
Leverton, Thomas, architect, ii. 158
Leverton, W., architect, ii. 112
Levett, Robert, buried, i. 244
Levi, Lyon, jumped from monument, ii. 559
Lewes, Priors of, residence, iii. 385, 443
Lewes, G. H., lived, i. 204
Lewis, Mr., actor, lived, i. 277
Lewis, Mr. bookseller, iii. 195, 384
Lewis, Erasmus, lived, i. 455
Lewis, Sir Frankland, lived, ii. 137
Lewis, Sir George Cornewall, lived, ii. 137, 207, 213, 331, 396
Lewis, James, architect, i. 175; iii. 335
Lewis, M. G., lived, i. 12, 502
Lewis, T. D., bequest, ii. 573
Lewis, T. Hayter, architect, i. 30, 115; iii. 422
Lewknor, Sir Lewis, ii. 387
Leyre, William de, ii. 15
Lichfield, Anson, Earl of, lived, ii. 301
Lichfield, Lee, Lord, i. 519
Liddell, Hon. and Rev. R., iii. 63
Lieven, Prince, lived, i. 517
Ligonier, Colonel, lived, i. 309
Ligonier, Viscount, duel, ii. 151
Lightfoot, Hannah, ii. 25, 285, 471, 517
Lilburne, John, i. 25; lived, ii. 434; iii. 525; prison, ii. 59; buried, i. 171; ii. 565; iii. 79
Lillie, Charles, lived, i. 140; ii. 75; iii. 324
Lillo, George, buried, ii. 387
Lilly, grammar master of St. Paul's School, iii. 63; lived, 53; buried, 42
Lilly the astrologer, i. 51; ii. 174; married, 103; lived, 394; iii. 323

Limerick, Thomas, Earl of, buried, iii. 20
Linacre, founder, iii. 82; lived, ii. 350; buried, iii. 42; statue, 82
Lincoln, Henry Fiennes, Earl of, i. 141, 377; lived, 324; ii. 460
Lincoln, De Lacies, Earls of, ii. 390
Lincoln, Henry Lacy, Earl of, lived, i. 346
Lindsay, Sir Coutts, i. 220; ii. 161
Lindsay, John, i. 25
Lindsey, Robert Bertie, first Earl of, lived, ii. 401
Lindsey, Montague Bertie, second Earl of, died, i. 320
Lindsey, Robert Bertie, third Earl of, lived, ii. 400
Lindsey, Earls of, i. 376
Lindsey, Rev. Theophilus, buried, i. 304
Linley, Thomas, died, iii. 284
Linley, William, died, ii. 84; buried, iii. 59
Lintot, Bernard, lived, ii. 63, 483, 571
Linwood, Miss, needlework, iii. 211
Lisle, Robert, Lord, friar, ii. 157
Lister, Lady Theresa, lived, ii. 331
Liston, John, i. 337; ii. 201; lived, i. 281; died, ii. 101; buried, 325
Litlington, Abbot, iii. 489
Littledale, Sir John, died, i. 147
Littleton, Adam, i. 393
Littleton, Sir Richard, lived, i. 473
Liverpool, Charles, first Earl of, died, ii. 40, 213
Liverpool, second Earl of, school, i. 365; lived, iii. 126
Livingstone, David, buried, iii. 463; grave 472
Llandaff, Bishops of, residence, iii. 321
Llanover, Sir Benjamin Hall, Lord, lived, iii. 523
Lloyd, Captain, ii. 402
Lloyd, Dr., Bp. of St. Asaph, lived, ii. 382
Lloyd, Edward, ii. 407
Lloyd, Miss, i. 222
Lloyd, Robert, prison, ii. 60; buried, i. 239
Locke, Charles, lived, ii. 596
Locke, John, ii. 15; school, iii. 488; lived, i. 23, 512; ii. 28, 395
Lockett, Adam, ii. 413
Lockhart, Anne Scott, buried, ii. 325
Lockhart, John Gibson, lived, i. 1; iii. 14, 338
Lockhart, John Hugh, buried, ii. 325
Lockhart, Sophia, buried, ii. 325
Lockwood and Mawson, architects, i. 405
Lockyer, Lionel, monument, iii. 215
Lodge, Edmund, ii. 210; lived, 274; died, i. 209; buried, ii. 97
Lodge, Dr. Thomas, lived, ii. 502
Loftus, W. K., i. 258, 259

Logan, Rev. John, died, i. 474
Loggan, David, lived, ii. 382
Londesborough, Lord, ii. 165; died, i. 333
London, Bishops of, ii. 301
London, George, gardener, i. 331; lived, iii. 451
London and Wise, i. 282
London, John, ii. 434
Londonderry, Marquis of, iii. 33
Long, tavernkeeper, iii. 170
Long, Benjamin, ii. 441
Long, John St. John, lived, ii. 192; buried, 324
Long, William, iii. 517
Long Meg, buried, iii. 480
Longford, Earl of, lived, i. 289
Longland, Will, lived, i. 13
Longman and Co., iii. 39
Longueville, William, lived, i. 229
Lonsdale, J., lived, i. 169
Lonsdale, Bp., preacher, ii. 392
Lopes, Dr., executed, iii. 415
Lord, Thomas, ii. 441
Lort, Michael, monument, ii. 514
Lostange, Marquis de, buried, iii. 18
Loten, John, lived, ii. 284
Loudon, J. C., buried, iii. 325
Loughborough, Lord, lived, i. 146; ii. 396
Louis XVIII., lived, i. 15, 80; when Monsieur, 90
Louis Phillippe, lived, ii. 93
Loutherbourg, P. J., R.A., lived, iii. 382
Loval, Simon, Lord, prisoner, iii. 399; trial, 486; execution, i. 108; iii. 401; buried, 76
Loveing, Mr., i. 414
Lovell, Sir Thomas, K.G., i. 346; ii. 228, 390
Lovell, Mathild, ii. 443
Lovelace, Ada, Countess of, died, i. 483
Lovelace, Richard, i. 24; prison, ii. 89; died, 174; buried, ii. 239
Lovelace, Thomas, pillory, iii. 7
Low, David, first London hotel-keeper, i. 463
Lowe, Mr., ii. 513
Lowe, Sir H., lived, ii. 7; buried, i. 80
Lowe, Mauritius, lived, ii. 203
Lowe, Rev. Richard T., i. 254
Lowen, J., marriage, i. 227; buried, 414
Lowndes, H., lived, ii. 63
Lowndes, William, ii. 443
Lowth, William, Merchant Taylors' School, ii. 526
Lowther, Sir James, ii. 94
Lucas, John, his token, i. 2
Lucas, R. C., i. 261
Lucchese, Count Ferdinand, buried, iii. 21
Lucius, King, iii. 73
Lucy, Sir Fulke, lived, ii. 298
Lucy, Margaret, monument, ii. 109
Luda, William de, Bp. of Ely, ii. 19

Ludlow, Edmund, lived, iii. 280
Luke, Sir Samuel, lived, i. 49
Lullius, Raimondus, lived, ii. 320
Lumley, Lady, lived, ii. 437
Lumley, Lord, lived, ii. 451
Lumsden, Archibald, iii. 9
Lunardi, the aeronaut, i. 3, 69; balloon ascent, iii. 390
Lush, Lord Justice Sir Robert, died, i. 84
Luttrell, Henry, lived, i. 281
Lydekker, John, ii. 410
Lyell, Sir Charles, buried, iii. 464
Lyly, John, lived, i. 117
Lyndhurst, Lord, student, ii. 391; lived, i. 480; ii. 16, 40, 93; portrait, iii. 232
Lyndwood, Bp., rector, i. 32
Lynedoch, Lord, died, iii. 328
Lyons, Lord, monument, iii. 48
Lyons, Sir Daniel, Constable of the Tower, iii. 400
Lysons, Samuel, lived, ii. 343
Lyttelton, Charles, Bp. of Carlisle, died, i. 424
Lyttelton, Sir Charles, ii. 232; lived, i. 361
Lyttelton, Sir Edward, lived, i. 223
Lyttelton, Lord, "the good," lived, i. 60; ii. 215; club, iii. 313
Lyttelton, Lord, "the wicked," lived, ii. 215
Lyttelton, Sir Thomas, ii. 476; Inner Temple, iii. 354; lived, 431
Lytton, Edward, first Lord, born, i. 91; lived, ii. 359; ii. 213; buried, iii. 463, 465

M'Ardell, James, lived, ii. 208
Macartney, General, iii. 172; ii. 252
Macartney, Lord, lived, i. 487
Macaulay, Dr., lived, iii. 100
Macaulay, Lord, i. 288; church, ii. 326; lived, i. 12, 187, 321, 412, 521; ii. 41, 92, 327, 618; buried, iii. 463, 477
Macaulay, Mrs., lived, i. 170; statue, iii. 311
Macaulay, Zachary, lived, i. 187; buried, ii. 102
Macbean, Alexander, lived, i. 366
Macclesfield, Countess of, lived, i. 219
Macclesfield, Charles Gerard, first Earl of, ii. 104, 453; lived, 396; iii. 163; died, 265
Macclesfield, Charles, second Earl of, P.R.S., lived, iii. 265
M'Culloch, J. R., lived, iii. 307; buried, i. 281
Macdonald, Sir John, died, i. 289
Mackenzie, John, ii. 40
Mackintosh, Sir James, married to his first wife, Catherine Stuart, ii. 497; first wife buried, i. 415; lectures, ii. 399; lived, i. 15, 316, 362, 427, 483; ii. 169, 600; iii. 232; died, ii. 366
Mackonochie, Rev. A. ii., i. 11

Mackreth, Robert, proprietor of White's club, i. 65; iii. 492
Mackworth, Dr. John, i. 108
Mackworth, Sir Thomas, buried, iii. 20
Maclean, James, highwayman, lived, ii. 305; iii. 457
Macklin, Charles, i. 531; lecturer, iii. 80; manager, ii. 200; lived, i. 229; iii. 348; buried, 59
Maclise, Daniel, frescoes, ii. 240, 241; died, i. 389
M'Naghten, ——, i. 176
Macpherson, James, lived, ii. 56, 460; will, 40; buried, iii. 463, 478
Macpherson, Sir John, monument, i. 50
M'Pherson, Mr., i. 98
Macready, W. C., born, i. 361; lived, ii. 82
Madan, Rev. Martin, buried, ii. 327
Madan, Mrs., died, iii. 299
Madden, Thomas, sculptor, i. 46
Maddox, Sir Benjamin, ii. 454
Magheramorne, Lord, Chairman, ii. 528
Maginn, Dr., spunging-house, iii. 241
Magniac, Charles, i. 288
Maiano, John de, iii. 513
Maiden, Thomas, ii. 433
Maine, Sir H. Sumner, K.C.S.I., "Grecian," i. 396
Mainwaring, Boulton, surveyor, ii. 429
Maitland, Dr. Samuel Roffy, ii. 361; librarian, 363
Major, John, lived, i. 366
Major, Thomas, lived, ii. 484; died, iii. 349; buried, i. 318
Malcolm, James Peller, buried, iii. 21
Malcolm, Sir John, ii. 616; lived, i. 2; died, iii. 121; buried, ii. 281; statue, iii. 472
Malcolm, Sarah, buried, iii. 230; executed, ii. 553; iii. 346
Mallet, David, lived, i. 63; ii. 93; buried, i. 80
Malme, George H., ii. 338
Malmesbury, first Earl of, lived, iii. 126, 296; died, ii. 215
Malone, Edmund, lived, ii. 67, 514; iii. 138; died, 139
Maltby, Bp., preacher, ii. 392
Maltby, W., librarian, ii. 431
Malthus, Thomas, lived, iii. 21
Maltravers, Henry Howard, Lord, iii. 382
Man, Alexander, ii. 460
Man, Mr., lived, ii. 596
Manchester, Duke of, iii. 302; lived, i. 324
Manchester, Montagues, Earls of, ii. 460
Manchester, Earl of, lived, ii. 105, 269
Mandeville, Bernard, lived, ii. 179
Mandeville, Geoffrey de, ii. 5; iii. 70; Constable of the Tower, 399
Manley, Mrs., buried, i. 159
Manning, William, M.P., lived, i. 185

Manning, Cardinal, ii. 14, 594; club, iii. 313
Manningham, Thomas, Bp. of Gloucester, died, ii. 156
Manny, Sir Walter de, i. 363
Mansel, Sir Thomas, lived, iii. 267
Mansfield, Earl of, school, iii. 488; student, ii. 391; Inner Temple, iii. 354; lived, i. 208; ii. 343, 400, 614; iii. 193; portrait, 232; statue, ii. 242; iii. 472
Mantell, Dr. Gideon, died, i. 387
Manton, minister, iii. 98
Manton, Joe, lived, i. 491
Mapp, Mrs., bone setter, ii. 148
Marat, Jean Paul, lived, i. 400
Marchmont, Lord, lived, i. 486
Margaret of Anjou, ii. 113
Margaret, Queen of Edward I., buried, ii. 152
Margaret of York, infant daughter of Edward IV., tomb, iii. 469
Marillac, French Ambassador, lived, iii. 400
Mario, G., singer, ii. 200
Markeby, William, brass, i. 116
Markham, Abp., lived, i. 80
Markham, Sir George, fined ii. 209
Markham, Lady, penance, iii. 62
Markland, Jeremiah, "Grecian," i. 396
Marks, H. S., R.A., picture, iii. 175
Marlborough, Henrietta, Duchess of, iii. 473
Marlborough, Sarah, Duchess of, lived, ii. 395; died, 473
Marlborough, John Churchill, Duke of, school, iii. 63; lived, ii. 306, 472; iii. 12; prisoner, 399
Marmion, Robert, iii. 30
Marnock, Robert, i. 225
Marochetti, Baron, lived, ii. 615
Marquand, John, ii. 176
Marr, murdered, iii. 150
Marrable, Frederick, architect, ii. 87, 529; iii. 297
Marriot, Richard, publisher, lived, i. 538; ii. 152
Marryat, Captain, born, ii. 92
Marshall, ——, ii. 203
Marshall, John, i. 393
Marshall, Joshua, i. 355
Marshall, Robert, Bp. of Hereford, benefactor, iii. 503
Martin, Baron, buried, i. 282
Martin, John, lived, i. 42; ii. 400; iii. 369
Martin, Jonathan, i. 176
Martin, Richard, iii. 356; monument, 351
Martin, Samuel, M.P., duel with Wilkes, ii. 253; iii. 165
Martin and Co., bankers, ii. 416
Martindale, John, proprietor of White's club, iii. 493

Martineau, Harriet, lived, ii. 66
Marvell, Andrew, ii. 308; lived, 456; buried, 112
Mary I., Queen, i. 27, 241; conspiracy to kill her, ii. 289; buried, iii. 463, 466
Mary II., Queen, died, ii. 330; buried, iii. 467, 463
Mary, Queen of Scots, buried, iii. 463; tomb, 466
Mary of Modena, Queen of James II., ii. 358; portrait, iii. 438
Maryatt, Richard, ii. 33
Masham, Mrs. Abigail, died, i. 455
Maskell, Rev. J., ii. 15
Maskell, W., i. 255
Maskelyne and Cooke, ii. 8
Maseres, Baron, lived, iii. 152
Mason, Cartwright, i. 521
Mason, H. A., architect, ii. 534
Mason, Rev. H. H. Cox, i. 168, 492
Mason, Matt., iii. 116
Mason, Rev. William, lived, i. 422, 487; monument, iii. 477
Massinger, Philip, prisoner, i. 426; died, 102; buried, iii. 214
Master, Sir Streynsham, ii. 101
Mathew, Rev. Henry, i. 362; minister, iii. 71, 151
Mathew, Tobias, Bp. of Durham, i. 542
Mathews, Sir Tobie, prison, ii. 59
Mathews, —, duel with Sheridan, ii. 208
Mathews, Charles, i. 7; ii. 87; iii. 246; born, 323; Merchant Taylors' School, ii. 526; lived, 334, 402; died, iii. 193; buried, ii. 325
Mathews, Charles James, Merchant Taylors' School, ii. 526
Mathews, J., bookseller, lived, iii. 323
Mathews, J. Douglass, architect, ii. 8, 259
Mathison, Mr., ii. 471
Matilda, wife of King Stephen, ii. 319
Matilda, Queen of Henry I., i. 532; ii. 113; iii. 407
Matry, Mathew, M.D., i. 272
Maud, C. T., collection of water-colour paintings, iii. 276
Maudslay, Henry, lived, ii. 470
Maule, Justice, lived, iii. 27
Maunsell, Sir John, ii. 22; lived, iii. 385
Maurice, Bp., iii. 39
Maurice, Rev. Frederick Denison, club, iii. 313; chaplain, ii. 176; incumbent, iii. 431
Mawman, bookseller, lived, iii. 117
Maxey, Thomas, ii. 345
May, builder, ii. 515
May, Baptist, i. 86; ii. 298
May, Hugh, architect, i. 162
May, Sir Humphrey, lived, ii. 269
May, Thomas, buried and exhumed, iii. 468, 477
Mayer, Henry, lived, iii. 156

Mayerne, Elizabeth, monument, ii. 449
Mayerne, Sir Theodore, ii. 400; lived, i. 378, 379; ii. 483; tomb, 478; portrait, iii. 82
Maynard, Sir John, lived, iii. 112
Mayne, Jasper, school, iii. 488
Maynwaring, Arthur, lived, ii. 18
Mayo, Charles, Merchant Taylors' School, ii. 526
Mazarin, Duchess of, i. 378; lived, ii. 400
Mazzinghi, Thomas, buried, iii. 21
Mead, Matthew, buried, i. 539; iii. 313
Mead, Dr. Richard, i. 126, 390; born, iii. 313; lived, i. 14, 84, 207, 481; ii. 617; duel with Dr. Woodward, 156; buried, iii. 464; monument, 474; portrait, 82; bust, 82
Mee, A., architect, ii. 101
Meg, Long, of Westminster, buried, iii. 480
Melbourne, first Viscount, lived, i. 12
Melbourne, Viscount, Prime Minister, born, ii. 519; lived, i. 218; iii. 279; monument, 48
Melker, William, ii. 386
Mellish, Lord Justice, buried, i. 282
Mellitus, Bp., iii. 19
Mellon, Miss. See St. Albans, Duchess of
Melville, Dundas, first Viscount, lived, i. 63; trial, iii. 486; portrait, ii. 575
Mendelssohn, i. 60
Mendip, Welbore Ellis, Lord, died, i. 283
Mennis, Sir John, memorial, ii. 609
Merivale, Herman, buried, i. 282
Metcalf, Charles, Lord, lived, ii. 462; iii. 109
Methven, Paul, lived, ii. 165
Metzler, Messrs., ii. 474
Mews, Bp., Merchant Taylors' School, ii. 526
Mexborough, Earl of, i. 518
Meyrick, Sir S., iii. 398
Michael de Cantuaria, i. 372
Middlemore, Samuel, i. 415
Middlesex, Lionel Cranfield, Earl of, i. 141, 378; tomb, iii. 465
Middleton, goldsmith, ii. 484
Middleton, Thomas, surgeon, ii. 372
Middleton, Thomas Fanshaw, Bp. of Calcutta, i. 396
Milbanke, Sir Ralph, lived, ii. 191; iii. 109
Milbourne, Luke, rector, ii. 19
Mildmay, Carew, i. 449
Mildmay, Sir Walter, lived, iii. 65; monument, i. 116
Milford, Lord, lived, iii. 307
Mill, James, ii. 3; monument, 326
Mill, John Stuart, ii. 3; club, iii. 313
Millais, Sir J. E., R.A., lived, ii. 134 studio, i. 423

INDEX

Millar, Andrew, ii. 346; lived, iii. 323;
 buried, ii. 450
Miller Joe, iii. 111; buried, i. 414; iii. 112
Miller, Philip, lived, i. 225; monument,
 ii. 449
Milles, Jeremiah, Dean of Exeter, i. 254;
 died, ii. 101; monument, 6
Millington, lived, ii. 406
Mills, Mrs. Isabella, buried, iii. 21
Milman, Dr. Henry Hart, born, i. 283;
 lived, 75; died, 494; tomb, iii. 48
Milner, Rev. John, schoolmaster, iii. 67
Milton, Katherine, Milton's second wife
 (d. 1658) buried, ii. 468
Milton, John, gardener, ii. 615
Milton, John, sen., died, i. 106
Milton, John; i. 535; born, 233; baptized,
 32; school, iii. 63; married to Katherine
 Woodcocke, second wife, ii. 468, 491;
 married to Elizabeth Minshull, 308, 492;
 lived, i. 25, 70, 106, 110, 226, 240,
 300, 301; ii. 221, 288, 308, 486; iii.
 29, 225, 490, 541; buried, ii. 109; bust,
 iii. 476; books burned by hangman, ii.
 612
Mingay, James, lived, i. 146
Minshull, Elizabeth, ii. 308, 492
Minto, Gilbert, first Earl of, lived, iii.
 296
Mirfeld, John, i. 118
Mirabeau, lived, ii. 194
Misaubin, Dr., lived, ii. 484
Mitchell, Thomas, "Grecian," i. 396
Mitford, Dr., i. 180
Mitford, Mary Russell, school, ii. 189
Mohun, Lord, i. 89, 524; lived, ii. 105,
 474; trial, 245; duel with Duke of
 Hamilton, 252; iii. 165, 172; buried, ii.
 479
Mohun, Major Michael, lived, i. 229, 288;
 iii. 99, 194; buried, ii. 112
Molesworth, Sir William, buried, ii. 325
Molins, James, tablet, i. 239
Molony, Mrs. Jane, tablet, i. 135
Monce, David de, ii. 206
Money, Major, lived, ii. 106
Monk, General. See Albemarle, Duke of
Monk, Bp., school, i. 365
Monkhouse, Thomas, M.P., lived, ii. 119
Monmouth, Duchess of, lived, i. 380
Monmouth, James, Duke of, i. 2, 23; ii.
 233, 554; installed Chancellor of the
 University of Oxford, iii. 534; at
 Whitehall, 512; lived, i. 123; ii. 202;
 iii. 263, 264; executed, 401; buried, 76;
 portrait, i. 366
Monmouth, Carey, Earl of, ii. 554
Monmouth, Humphrey, i. 536
Monroe, James, American Minister, lived,
 iii. 109
Montagu, Captain, monument, iii. 474
Montagu, Duchess of (d. 1734), lived, ii.
 587

Montagu, Ralph, Duke of, ii. 201, 555;
 Master of the Wardrobe, iii. 449; lived,
 193
Montagu, Lady Mary Wortley, baptism,
 iii. 58; lived, i. 62, 342, 462; ii. 93;
 iii. 85; buried, i. 80
Montagu, Anthony Brown, Viscount, ii.
 555
Montagu, W., architect, ii. 32
Montagu, Edward Wortley, married, ii. 517
Montagu, Mrs., ii. 557; lived, 215; iii. 110
Montague, Basil, lived, i. 147
Montalembert, Baronesse de, buried, iii.
 19
Montboissier, Comte de, buried, iii. 18
Monteagle, Lord, lived, iii. 35
Montes, Lola, lived, ii. 181; married, 97
Montfort, Simon de, iii. 286; lived, 524
Montgomery, Rev. Robert, i. 362;
 minister, iii. 71
Montpensier, Duc de, brother of Louis
 Philippe, monument, iii. 467
Montrose, Duke of, lived, ii. 186
Moone, Nicholas, lived, iii. 99
Moore, Abp., tomb, ii. 495
Moore, Edward, died, ii. 357; buried,
 495
Moore, Francis, lived, ii. 357
Moore, George, i. 228
Moore, G. B., architect, iii. 252
Moore, John, lived, i. 1
Moore, Sir John, Lord Mayor (d. 1702),
 i. 397; monument, 536
Moore, General Sir John, monument, iii.
 48
Moore, Sir Jonas, buried, iii. 76
Moore, Peter, M.P., lived, ii. 92
Moore, Thomas, i. 221, 470; Middle
 Temple, iii. 358; lived, i. 311, 491; ii.
 93, 397; iii. 541; duel with Jeffrey, i.
 344; iii. 120
More, Dean, iii. 29
More, Sheriff, i. 443
More, Sir Thomas, i. 52; ii. 84; born, 544;
 student, 390; agent, iii. 310; lectures,
 ii. 370; lived, i. 140, 298, 376, 477;
 ii. 583; prisoner, iii. 398; trial, 485;
 executed, 401; buried, 76; head on
 London Bridge, ii. 489; memorial
 tablet, 448
More, Sir William, i. 199
Moreton, chaplain, iii. 216
Morgan, James, architect, i. 506; engineer,
 iii. 160
Morgan, John, ii. 41
Morgan, Lady, lived, iii. 522; buried, i.
 282
Morgan, Octavius, i. 265
Morgan, Sylvanus, i. 117
Morgan, Sir T. C., M.D., tablet, i. 282
Morgan, Sir William, iii. 30
Morison, Dr., ii. 290
Morison, Fynes, i. 25

Morison, Robert, died, ii. 152
Morland, George, i. 387; born, ii. 198; lived, iii. 312; died, ii. 29; buried, 275
Morland, Mrs. George, buried, ii. 275
Morland, Henry Robert, lived, iii. 312
Morland, Sir Samuel, i. 455; lived, iii. 425
Morley, Atkinson, benefactor, ii. 101
Morley, George, Bp. of Winchester, i. 393; born, 374; portrait, 366
Morley, Prof. Henry, ii. 344
Mornington, Anne, Countess of, died, ii. 207
Mornington, Earl of, lived, ii. 327
Morrice, High Bailiff of Westminster, ii. 224
Morrice, William, lived, i. 495
Morris, Peter, i. 458; iii. 301
Morris, Sir William, lived, iii. 296
Morrison, Sir Richard, lived, ii. 547
Mortellari, A. M. D., buried, iii. 18
Mortimer, Roger, prisoner, iii. 398; executed, ii. 9; iii. 255; buried, ii. 157
Mortimer, J. H., painter, lived, ii. 601
Mortimer, Rev. Thomas, i. 117
Morton, Abp., ii. 363; consecrated, 360, 362
Morton, Charles, M.D., i. 272
Morton, Mr., i. 327
Moseley, Messrs., architects, i. 421
Moser, Michael, keeper, iii. 74
Mosse, Capt., monument, iii. 48
Mossop, Henry, buried, ii. 450
Motteux, Peter Anthony, lived, ii. 377, 564; died, i. 313; buried, 46
Mounsey, Messenger, died, i. 384
Mountague, W., architect, ii. 463
Mountfiquet, Baron of, ii. 565
Mountfort, William, lived, ii. 244, 601; buried, i. 474
Mountjoy, Lord, lived, i. 508
Mowbray, John de, i. 425
Mowbrays, Dukes of Norfolk, i. 282
Moxhay, Edward, ii. 183
Moyes, Margaret, jumped from monument, ii. 559
Moyle, Walter, ii. 372
Moyses, —, ii. 465
Mudge, Thomas, buried, i. 538
Muggleton, Lodowick, born, i. 191; lived, ii. 237; prisoner, 591; buried, i. 171
Mulgrave, Lord, club, ii. 484
Mulready, W., R.A., buried, ii. 325
Munday, Anthony, monument, iii. 310
Munden, Joseph, i. 344; born, 286; died, 169; buried, ii. 97
Munden, Vice-Admiral, i. 511
Munro, —, of Novar, lived, ii. 184
Munro, Lieut., duel, i. 235
Munro, Dr. Thomas, lived, i. 7
Murchison, Sir Roderick, died, i. 153; buried, 281; legacy, ii. 568

Murphy, Arthur, lived, ii. 82, 399, 585; died, 353; portrait, 574
Murray, Sir George, died, i. 153
Murray, Hen., lived, ii. 596
Murray, John (d. 1843), i. 15; ii. 30, 63; buried, 325
Murray, Sir John, lived, i. 495
Murray, Robert, Post Office, iii. 69, 114
Murray, Sir Robert, President of the Royal Society, iii. 187
Musgrave, Thomas, Abp. of York, buried, ii. 325
Musgrave, Sir Wm., i. 254; lived, iii. 33
Muskerry, Viscountess, lived, iii. 85
Muss, Mr., i. 238
Myddelton, Sir Hugh, i. 344; ii. 570, 584; buried, 514; statue, 270; iii. 181
Mylling, Abbot, tomb, iii. 470
Mylne, Robert, grave, iii. 49; architect, i. 37, 197, 405; ii. 570, 604; iii. 48, 306, 522
Mynn, Mrs., i. 114
Mytens, Daniel, lived, ii. 483

NAPIER, Adm., Sir Charles, lived, i. 13, 166
Napier, General Sir Charles, monument, iii. 48; statue, 405
Napier, James Murdoch, i. 97
Napier, Lady Sarah, lived, i. 326
Napier of Magdala, Lord, Constable of the Tower, iii. 400
Napier, Sir William, monument, iii. 48
Napoleon I., his will, iii. 516; portrait, 261; miniature, 261
Napoleon III., lived, i. 400; ii. 337
Nares, Archdeacon, ii. 193; rector, i. 35
Nash, John, architect, i. 9, 36, 60, 293, 388; ii. 66, 199, 201, 295, 365; iii. 132, 158, 159, 331, 420; lived, i. 517; died, iii. 93
Nash, Thomas, prison, ii. 59
Nasmith, James, rector, ii. 490
Nasmyth, James, tomb, ii. 495
Nasmyth, Patrick, picture, i. 374; died, ii. 357
Nathan and Pearson, architects, i. 134
Naunton, Sir Robert, lived, iii. 404
Naylor, James, flogged, iii. 325
Neal, Daniel, Merchant Taylors' School, ii. 526
Needham, Marchmont, prison, ii. 90; died, i. 496; buried, 414
Needham, Mother, lived, iii. 33
Neilson, Adelaide, buried, i. 282
Nelson, John, lived, iii. 331; buried, ii. 372
Nelson, Frances, Dowager Viscountess, died, ii. 192
Nelson, Horatio, Viscount, i. 236; ii. 165, 301; lived, i. 63, 220, 342; ii. 337, meeting with Wellington, i. 415; at Somerset House, iii. 373; body

INDEX

brought in state from Greenwich to Whitehall, 363; lay in state, i. 8; sarcophagus, iii. 49; monument, ii. 170; iii. 48; bust, 408; wax effigy, 479
Nelson, Maurice, ii. 577
Nelson, Robert, i. 91; born, iii. 331; baptized, ii. 372; school, iii. 63; lived, ii. 119, 382, 559, 617; iii. 380; died, ii. 327; buried, 109
Nelson, T. M., architect, iii. 122
Nelson and Innes, architects, iii. 159, 421
Nesfield, Mr., ii. 235
Nevill, Sir Hugh, ii. 373
Nevill, Ralph, Bp. of Chichester, i. 390; ii. 579; lived, 390; died, i. 346
Newbery, John, lived, i. 326; iii. 54
Newburgh, Lady, lived, ii. 298
Newcastle, Margaret Cavendish, Duchess of, lived, i. 419; ii. 587; buried, iii. 464; monument, 472
Newcastle, William Cavendish, Duke of, lived, i. 418, 419, 515; ii. 587; buried, iii. 464; monument, 472
Newcastle, John Holles, Duke of, ii. 509; lived, 588, 589; iii. 128
Newcastle, Thomas Pelham Holles, Duke of, ground landlord of Clare Market, i. 407; Prime Minister, 255; lived, 379; ii. 396
Newcome, Richard, buried, ii. 179
Newland, Abraham, born, i. 339; lived, ii. 214; portrait, i. 97; monument, iii. 215
Newman, Cardinal, i. 359
Newman, Mr., builder, ii. 595
Newman, A. S., architect, ii. 102
Newman, John, architect, i. 205; iii. 167
Newport, Montjoy, Earl of, ii. 596; lived, 543
Newton, Sir C. T., i. 255, 260, 261
Newton, Gilbert Stuart, lived, ii. 474
Newton, Sir Isaac, i. 299; Master of the Mint, ii. 549; President of the Royal Society, iii. 187; lived, i. 380; ii. 307, 384, 489; iii. 245; died, ii. 327; lay in state, iii. 480; buried, 464; his will, 516; monument, 474; bust, ii. 385; iii. 188, 272; portraits, 188
Newton, Rev. John, lived, i. 359, 444; ii. 246; memorial, 508
Newton, Thomas, Bp. of Bristol, died, i. 494; monument, ii. 498
Newton, Sir William J., lived, i. 60
Nicholas, Sir Ambrose, lived, ii. 620
Nicholas, Secretary, lived, iii. 323
Nicholl, W. G., bas reliefs, ii. 622
Nicholls, Sutton, lived, i. 95
Nicholls, S. T., architect, ii. 325
Nichols, Gregory, iii. 370
Nichols, John, lived, ii. 270; iii. 154; buried, ii. 494
Nichols, John Gough, Merchant Taylors' School, ii. 526

Nicholson, Francis, buried, i. 282
Nicholson, Bp., lived, ii. 460
Nicholson, Peg, i. 176
Nicholson, Renton, i. 231
Nicolas, Ambrose, iii. 172
Nicolas, Sir Nicholas Harris, lived, iii. 348, 385
Nithsdale, Earl of, prisoner, iii. 399
Nivernois, Duc de, lived, i. 14
Nixon, Bp., Merchant Taylors' School, ii. 526
Nixon, Samuel, ii. 340
Noble, Matthew, buried, i. 282
Nollekens, Joseph, ii. 138; iii. 324; baptized, i. 533; lived, iii. 437; died, ii. 563; buried, iii. 2; monument, 3; sculpture by, i. 421
Nollekens, Joseph Francis (d. 1747), buried, iii. 2
Norfolk, Dukes of, ii. 356, 600
Norfolk, Thomas Howard, Duke of, i. 363, 532; lived, 28
Norfolk, Henry Howard, Duke of, ii. 601; Royal Society, iii. 187; lived, i. 73
Norgate, Edward, buried, i. 159
Norman, John, Lord Mayor, ii. 464; burial, i. 34
Norman, Dr., i. 34
Norris, Lord, monument, iii. 471
North, Dr. Brownlow, Bp. of Winchester, lived, i. 376; died, iii. 524
North, Sir Dudley, in the Thames, iii. 365; married, ii. 179; tavern, iii. 529; lived, i. 122; iii. 85, 376; buried, 58
North, Frederick, lived, i. 450
North, John, ii. 602
North, Edward, first Lord (d. 1564), i. 363
North, Roger, second Lord, i. 363
North, Dudley, fourth Lord (d. 1677), lived, ii. 339
North, William, sixth Lord, iii. 134
North, Frederick, Lord, Prime Minister, i. 418; lived, ii. 164; died, 165, 207
North, Roger, lived, iii. 85
Northampton, Henry Howard, Earl of, lived, ii. 603
Northampton, Spencer Compton, Earl of, i. 418; lived, 478; in the Thames, iii. 365
Northampton, Marquis of, lived, i. 325
Northcote, James, R.A., lived, i. 60, 219; iii. 323; died, i. 59; buried, ii. 497
Northington, Lord Chancellor, married, i. 80; lived, ii. 273, 395
Northumberland, Countess of, lived, ii. 303, 306
Northumberland, Jane Dudley, Duchess of, monument, ii. 449
Northumberland, Dukes of, lived, ii. 603
Northumberland, John Dudley, Duke of, i. 325, 363, 375; lived, 541; ii. 10, 113; executed, iii. 401; buried, 76

Northumberland, George Fitzroy, Duke of, lived, ii. 300
Northumberland, Hugh Smithson, Duke of, ii. 604
Northumberland, Earls of, lived, ii. 602, 603
Northumberland, Henry Percy, sixth Earl of, died, i. 284; ii. 178
Northumberland, Henry Percy, ninth Earl of, K.G., ii. 262; lived, 547, 602
Northumberland, Algernon, tenth Earl of, ii. 603, 604
Northumberland, Joseeline, eleventh Earl of, died, ii. 604
Norton, Hon. Mrs. Caroline, lived, i. 187
Norwich, George Goring, Earl of, lived, ii. 130
Notary, Julian, lived, ii. 337; iii. 53
Nott, Sir W., portrait, ii. 616
Nottingham, Countess Dowager of, monument, ii. 499
Nottingham, Charles Howard, first Earl of, lived, i. 73. 422
Nottingham, Heneage Finch, first Earl of, ii. 328, 330; "grocer," 161; Inner Temple, iii. 354, 355; lived, 136
Nottingham, Daniel Finch, second Earl of, lived, iii. 267
Nourse, Edward, i. 119
Novosielski, Michael, lived, i. 280; architect, ii. 199
Nowell, Alexander, Headmaster of Westminster School, iii. 488; buried, 42
Noy, William, Attorney-General, student, ii. 390; benefactor, 391
Nurse, Wm., builder, i. 483
Nutford, William, lived, i. 412
Nycolson, James, printer, iii. 286
Nye, Philip, preacher, ii. 179; buried, 534

OAKEY, Mrs., buried, i. 539
Oates, Titus, i. 518; ii. 221, 332, 345; Merchant Taylors' School, 526; pillory, iii. 7; lived, i. 439
O'Brian, Charles, the Irish giant, ii. 1; died, i. 439
O'Brien, Lady Susan, married, iii. 58
O'Brien, Nelly, lived, iii. 12; died, 34
Ochterlony, Sir David, portrait, ii. 616
O'Connell, Daniel, i. 287; lived, 311, 412; ii. 92
O'Connor, Feargus, ii. 324
Odell, Thomas, ii. 126
Oddie, Henry Hoyle, i. 328
Odo, Bp. of Bayeux, iii. 285
Offa, King of Mercia, iii. 461
Offor, George, buried, i. 3
Ogilby, F., author of *Britannia*, ii. 86; lottery, iii. 431; lived, ii. 345; iii. 504; buried, i. 239
Ogle, Henry Cavendish, Earl of, ii. 604
O'Keefe, J., lived, i. 362; ll. 489; iii. 299
Okey, Colonel, regicide, lived, ii. 401; executed, iii. 415; buried, 76

Oldcastle, Sir John, executed, ii. 110
Oldenburg, Grand-Duchess of, lived, iii. 90
Oldenburgh, Henry, lived, iii. 11
Oldfield, Mrs. Anne, lived, ii. 165, 198, 285, 553; iii. 284; buried, 464, 473
Oldham, Bp. Hugh, rector, ii. 539
Oldmixon, John, died, iii. 130
Oldys, William, ii. 612; died, 210; buried, i. 159
O'Leary, Father, buried, iii. 18
Oliver, Isaac, lived, i. 196; buried, 49
Oliver, Peter, buried, i. 49
O'Meara, Barry, died, ii. 6
O'Neill, Miss, actress, lived, i. 412
Oniate, Conde de, Spanish Ambassador, iii. 135
Onslow, Speaker, ii. 309; "grocer," 161; died, iii. 193
Onslow, Thomas, Lord, ii. 148
Opie, John, lived, i. 169; ii. 616; iii. 137; grave, 49
Orange, Prince of, suitor to the Princess Charlotte of Wales, lived, i. 425
Ordish, F. W., architect, i. 221
Ordish, R. M., architect, i. 16, 17
Orford, Margaret, Countess of, married to the Hon. Sewallis Shirley, ii. 517
Orford, Edward Russell, Earl of, lived, i. 463; ii. 21; iii. 85
Orleans, Charles Duc d', prisoner, iii. 398
Orleans, Philippe Egalité, Duc d', lived, iii. 279
Orme, Robert, lived, ii. 191
Ormond, Duchess of (1655), lived, iii. 514
Ormond, James Butler, Duke of, ii. 304; lived, i. 410; ii. 299, 619; installed Chancellor of the University of Oxford, iii. 534
Ormond, James, second Duke of, lived, ii. 299; buried, iii. 464
Orrery, Countess of, lived, iii. 33
Orrery, Roger Boyle, first Earl of, married to Lady Margaret Howard, iii. 329
Orrery, Charles Boyle, Earl of, lived, i. 534; ii. 115
Osborne, Peter, lived, iii. 530
Osborne, Ralph Bernal, school, i. 365
Osborne, Admiral Sherard, died, i. 360
Osborne, T., bookseller, lived, ii. 143; buried, 494
Osborne, Sir Thomas, i. 438
Ossory, Earl of, ii. 619
Osswich, Martin, Nicholas, William and John de, founders, ii. 481
Otho, Papal Legate, lived, i. 540
Otway, Thomas, i. 513; died, 299; iii. 401; buried, i. 414
Oude, Queen of, lived, ii. 191
Ouseley, Sir Gore, i. 254
Outram, Sir James, buried, iii. 463; monument, 474

Overbury, Sir Thomas, Middle Temple, iii. 357; prisoner, 398; buried, 76
Overstone, Lord, lived, ii. 600
Owen, Alice, benefactor, ii. 619
Owen, Dr. John, minister, iii. 98; buried, i. 303
Owen, Robert, lived, i. 310
Owen, T. E., architect, ii. 78
Owen, William, R.A., lived, i. 289
Oxford, Henrietta, Countess of, ii. 207, 226
Oxford, Earls of, lived, ii. 620
Oxford, John de Vere, twelfth Earl of, buried, i. 82
Oxford, John de Vere, sixteenth Earl of, i. 214
Oxford, Edward de Vere, seventeenth Earl of, lived, ii. 47
Oxford, Henry de Vere, eighteenth Earl of, lived, ii. 62
Oxford, Aubrey de Vere, twentieth Earl of, i. 361; ii. 232; lived, i. 519; ii. 298; iii. 84; buried, 464
Oxford, Robert Harley, first Earl of, i. 252, 438; born, 229; lived, 296, 517; iii. 536; prisoner, 399
Oxford, Edward Harley, second Earl of, i. 341; ii. 7, 191, 346, 563; lived, i. 517
Oxford, Edward, fired at the Queen, i. 176, 452
Oxman, hanged, iii. 340

PACE, Richard, vicar, i. 538
Pack, Major, i. 136
Packer, J. Hayman, buried, iii. 21
Packington, Dame Anne, tomb, i. 225
Page, Robert, right hand cut off, iii. 7
Page, S., architect, iii. 211
Page, Thomas, engineer, i. 129, 381; iii. 482
Paget, Wm., first Lord, lived, i. 324; ii. 16; iii. 3
Paget, Henry, second Lord, iii. 3
Paine, James, architect, ii. 451, 484, 519, 537; iii. 205
Paine, Tom, author of *Rights of Man*, lived, ii. 37
Palastron, Comtesse de, buried, iii. 18
Paleotti, Ferdinando, Marquis, executed, iii. 415
Paley, Archdeacon, prebend, iii. 23; lived, i. 209
Palliser, Sir Hugh, lived, iii. 13
Palliser, Sir William, buried, i. 282
Palmer, Henry R., engineer, ii. 427
Palmer, James, B.D., iii. 15
Palmer, John, actor, iii. 289, 338
Palmer, John, Post Office, iii. 114
Palmerston, Viscount, i. 287; ii. 461; lived, i. 318, 323; iii. 90, 302; buried, 463, 472; statue, 8, 472
Paltock, Robert, i. 416
Panizzi, Sir Anthony, i. 271, 272; died, 209

Panton, Colonel Thomas, i. 11; ii. 202; iii. 25, 87, 527
Paoli, General Pasquale, lived, i. 80; iii. 236; died, ii. 6; buried, iii. 21; remains exhumed, 21; bust, 475
Papworth, John B., director, iii. 222; lived, i. 334; architect, 140, 222, 238; ii. 7
Papworth, Wyatt, ii. 605 note; architect, 337
Park, Sir James Allan, lived, i. 147; ii. 396
Parker, mutineer, buried, ii. 504
Parker, Charles, architect, iii. 290
Parker, Admiral Sir Hyde, died, i. 483
Parker, Matthew, Abp. of Canterbury, i. 53; ii. 80; iii. 35; buried, ii. 360; portrait, 364; his wife, 600
Parker, Peter, ii. 322
Parker, Philip, lived, iii. 35
Parker, Lord Chief Baron Thomas, i. 285
Parkes, Dr. Edmund, at Christ's Hospital, i. 396
Parkins, Sir William, head and quarters on Temple Bar, iii. 359
Parkyns, Sir William, executed, iii. 415
Parnell, C., architect, ii. 418
Parnell and Smith, architects, i. 65
Parnell, Sir John, buried, i. 134
Parnell, Thomas, lived, ii. 296
Parr, Queen Katherine, i. 375, 378
Parr, Rev. Richard, buried, i. 317
Parr, Dr. Samuel, lived, i. 227; portrait, ii. 574
Parr, Th., "Old," buried, iii. 464, 478
Parris, E. T., i. 446
Parry, Sefton, ii. 118
Parry, Sir Thomas, lived, i. 454
Parry, William, hanged, iii. 7
Parsons, Dr., died, iii. 156
Parsons, the comedian, i. 228; died, ii. 357; Cock Lane ghost, i. 432
Parsons, J. M., bequest, iii. 276
Parsons, Nancy, lived, i. 296
Partridge, almanac maker, lived, iii. 205
Partridge, Sir Miles, ii. 29
Pasqualino, Peter, buried, iii. 21
Pate, Robert, i. 318
Paten, William, iii. 319
Paterson, Samuel, lived, ii. 17, 336
Paterson, William, i. 95; ii. 81
Patrick, Mr., buried, ii. 387
Patrick, Simon, Bp. of Ely, rector, iii. 59; vicar, i. 128; lived, ii. 13
Pattison, Sir James, lived, i. 147
Paulet, Lady, ii. 403
Paulet, Sir Amias, prisoner, iii. 356
Paulett, Earl, i. 410
Paulson, Thomas, lived, ii. 612
Paxton, Sir Joseph, ii. 253
Paxton, Robert, buried, iii. 21
Payne, Roger, buried, i. 320
Payne, Thomas, bookseller, ii. 532

Payne, William, iii. 376
Peabody, George, benefactor, iii. 65; died, ii. 4; statue, iii. 67, 184
Peake, Sir Robert, buried, iii. 230
Pearson, Bp., rector, i. 415
Pearson, J. L., R.A., architect, iii. 156, 430, 463, 486
Peck, Frederick, architect, i. 10
Pedley, Mr., M.P., i. 406
Peel, first Sir Robert, lived, ii. 166
Peel, second Sir Robert, married, iii. 236; lived, 302; died, i. 452; ii. 126; statue, i. 374; iii. 8, 472; pictures, ii. 573
Peel, William, born, iii. 302
Peele, George, ii. 80; at an alehouse, iii. 227
Pegge, Samuel, died, iii. 225
Peke, Elizabeth, buried, iii. 377
Pelham family, i. 255
Pelham, Henry, lived, i. 63
Pell, Walter, portrait, ii. 503
Pellatt, Apsley, M.P., ii. 226
Pemberton, Hugh, tomb, ii. 481
Pembroke, Countess-Dowager of, lived, i. 478; died, 24
Pembroke, Dorset, and Montgomery, Anne, Countess of, i. 132; iii. 369; married, i. 83
Pembroke, William Marshall, Earl of, tomb, iii. 351
Pembroke, Aymer de Valence, Earl of, iii. 350; buried, 463; tomb, 471
Pembroke, William de Valence, Earl of, monument, iii. 465
Pembroke and Montgomery, Philip Herbert, Earl of, i. 132; ii. 442, 531; lived, i. 549; died, 437
Pembroke, Thomas, Earl of, i. 8; lived, ii. 300
Pembroke, William Herbert, Earl of, i. 132; prison, ii. 59; lived, i. 284; benefactor, ii. 391
Pembroke, Henry, Earl of, in the Thames, iii. 365
Pender, Sir John, M.P., lived, i. 63
Penderell, Richard, buried, ii. 112
Penn, Granville, lived, i. 474
Penn, W., ii. 417; born, iii. 400; baptized, i. 31; lived, ii. 224, 353, 601; prisoner, 60, 591
Pennant, Sir Charles, Lord Mayor, ii. 463
Pennant, Thomas, lived, ii. 93
Pennell, Mr., i. 483
Pennethorne, Sir James, i. 209; architect, 294, 308, 391; ii. 337, 473, 568; iii. 153, 272, 307, 423
Pennington, Isaac, i. 373; ii. 49; lii, 62
Penny, Stephen Jarvis, ii. 97
Penrose, F. C., architect, iii. 51, 59
Penry, John, lived, ii. 439; prisoner, 341
Penton, Henry, iii. 70

Pepusch, J. C., died, i. 366
Pepys, Sir Lucas, lived, i. 283
Pepys, Samuel, i. 428; school, iii. 63; married, ii. 468; buys a coach, i. 468; President of the Royal Society, iii. 187; prison, ii. 89; lived, i. 85, 296; ii. 576; iii. 227, 536; portrait, 188; buried, ii. 609; memorial, 609; monument to his wife, 609
Pepys, Tom, buried, ii. 609
Perceval, Spencer, born, i. 79; lived, ii. 396; monument, iii. 474
Percival, H., proprietor of White's club, iii. 493
Percy, James, claimant, lived, iii. 528
Percy, Earl, ii. 165
Percy, "Harry Hotspur," lived, ii. 486, 603
Percy, Sir Thomas, head on London Bridge, ii. 419
Perkins, John, i. 213
Perkins, Richard, buried, ii. 277
Perreau, Daniel, executed, iii. 416
Perreau, Robert, lived, ii. 122; executed, iii. 416
Perry, James, lived, ii. 365; iii. 349
Persiani, Madame, singer, ii. 200
Peter of Colechurch, ii. 418; chaplain, 493
Peter de Rupibus, Bp. of Winchester, iii. 213
Peter the Great, i. 397; iii. 483; lived, i. 135, 296; ii. 601; iii. 536
Peter of Savoy, lived, iii. 321
Peterborough, Bps. of, residence, iii. 77
Peterborough, Henry, second Earl of, lived, ii. 437
Peterborough, Charles, third Earl of (d. 1735), lived, i. 218; ii. 105, 327, 545, 587
Peters, Hugh, ii. 202; preacher, 469
Petiver, James, lived, i. 25
Peto, Henry, statue, ii. 84
Peto, William, builder, ii. 84
Petre, Lord, lived, i. 22, 24
Pettigrew, T. J., buried, ii. 282
Petty, Sir William, iii. 383; club, 7, 410; lived, 89, 197
Phelps, Richard, bell, iii. 49
Phelps, Samuel, Sadler's Wells, iii. 201
Philip, John, R.A., buried, ii. 325
Philpot, John, buried, i. 159; ii. 430
Philippa, Queen of Edward III., ii. 319; buried, iii. 463; altar-tomb, 469
Philips, Ambrose, lived. ii. 483; died, 187; iii. 425; buried, i. 80
Philips, Sir Edward, lived, i. 223
Philips, John, monument, iii. 475
Philips, Katherine, i. 108; lived, ii. 62; buried, i. 160
Philips, Theresa Constantia, lived, i. 469; iii. 134
Phillimore, Sir R. J., lived, i. 63
Phillips, Augustine, lived, ii. 234

Phillips, John, lived. i. 297
Phillips, R., ii. 568
Phillips, Sir Richard, lived, i. 281
Phillips, Thomas, R.A., lived, i. 11; ii. 93
Philpot family, ii. 542
Philpot, martyr, ii. 415
Philpot, Sir John, lived, iii. 81
Phipps, Sir Constantine, Lord Chancellor of Ireland, lived, ii. 617
Phipps, C. J., architect, i. 501; ii. 84, 201; iii. 122, 201, 237
Pickering, Danby, ii. 453
Pickering, William, i. 347
Pickering, Sir William, monument, ii. 204
Pickersgill, F. R., R.A., fresco, ii. 242; lived, 563
Pickersgill, W. H., R.A., lived, iii. 267
Picket, Alderman, iii. 92
Picton, Sir Thomas, lived, i. 220; ii. 7; buried, i. 134; monument, iii. 48
Pidgeon, Bat, iii. 324
Pierce, Edward, i. 413; ii. 557
Pigott, Adam, i. 463
Pilcher, Mr., lived, iii. 264
Pilkington, Mrs., lived, iii. 499
Pilkington, Wm., architect, i. 213, 325; iii. 513
Pinchbeck, buried, i. 538
Pinckney, Major, lived, ii. 64
Pinkerton, John, lived, ii. 4; iii. 348, 390
Pinkethman, actor, ii. 516
Pindar, Sir Paul, lived, i. 191; monument, 227
Pine, John, engraver, lived, i. 25
Piozzi, Mrs., i. 357; ii. 336; lived, i. 60, 491, 493; ii. 564; iii. 457
Piper, Francis, buried, ii. 502
Pisani, Father Nicholas, buried, iii. 18
Pitcairn, Dr. David, i. 119
Pitcairn, Dr. William, i. 119
Pite, A. R., architect, ii. 26
Pitt, William, i. 164, 287; student, ii. 391; member of Brooks's, i. 287 note; club, 480; "grocer," ii. 161; lived, i. 90, 91, 450, 520; ii. 191, 396; iii. 33, 212, 319, 540; lay in state, 4; buried, 463, 472; monument, ii. 170; iii. 474; statue, ii. 188, 242; portrait, 523; iii. 408
Planché, J. R., iii. 398; lived, i. 281
Planta, Joseph, i. 272
Platt, William, memorial, iii. 17
Plaw, John, architect, iii. 2
Playfair, Professor John, i. 386; lived, 74; ii. 269
Plot, Dr. Robert, quoted, ii. 406
Plowden, Edmund, iii. 102; Treasurer of Middle Temple, 356, 357; tomb, 351
Plumpton, Sir Richard, lived, i. 48
Plunket, Oliver, Abp. of Armagh, executed, iii. 415; buried, ii. 112
Pocock, Sir George, died, i. 360
Pocock, W. F., architect, i. 236; ii. 379; iii. 439

Pocock, W. W., architect, i. 335; ii. 593
Poe, Edgar Allan, school, iii. 318
Poelemberg, lived, i. 58
Pole, Long Tylney Wellesley, died, iii. 371
Polito, menagerie keeper, ii. 25
Pollock, Sir Frederick, Lord Chief Baron, school, iii. 69; bust, ii. 523
Pollock, Sir George, buried, iii. 463; portrait, ii. 616
Pomfret, Thomas, Earl of, i. 528; ii. 294
Ponsonby, General, monument, iii. 48
Pont de l'Arche, William, founder, iii. 212
Pontcarré, Seigneur de, buried, iii. 19
Poole, Edmund and Arthur, prisoners, iii. 395
Poole, Henry, master mason of Westminster Abbey, iii. 100
Pope, Alex., sen., lived, i. 278
Pope, Alexander, i. 165, 218; born, ii. 417; iii. 99; school, i. 503; Sun Fire Office, iii. 333; lived, i. 248, 422, 517; ii. 303
Pope, Mrs. Magdalen, buried, i. 158
Pope, Miss, actress (d. 1818), i. 280
Pope, Mrs., actress (d. 1797), ii. 181
Pope, Morgan, i. 137
Pope, Sir Thomas, i. 168
Popham, Sir Francis, iii. 319
Popham, Lord Chief Justice, lived, iii. 318
Popham, General, funeral, ii. 27; monument, iii. 470
Porden, C., architect, i. 276
Porson, Professor, i. 337; ii. 456; librarian, 431; lived, iii. 280, 605, 614
Porten, Mrs. Catherine, lived, i. 445, 494
Porter, F. W., architect, i. 348; iii. 198
Porter, Joseph, lived, ii. 263
Porter, Mrs., lived, i. 74
Porter, Phil, Piccadilly Hall, iii. 87
Porter, Sir R. Ker, ii. 452
Porter, Rev. William, pastor, iii. 65
Porteus, Dr. B., Bp. of London, ii. 481
Portington, William, portrait, i. 335
Portland family, i. 160
Portland, Countess of, lived, iii. 11
Portland, Margaret Harley, Duchess of, i. 264, 528; ii. 470
Portland, Dukes of, residences, ii. 190; iii. 126
Portland, William Bentinck, second Duke of, i. 533; ii. 509; married to Lady Margaret Cavendish Harley, iii. 431
Portland, William, third Duke of, i. 307
Portland, William Bentinck, Earl of, iii. 263; lived, ii. 390
Portman, Lord, i. 289; ii. 616
Portman, William Henry, iii. 116
Portsmouth, Duchess of, lived, ii. 327; iii. 162
Pott, Perceval, i. 119; lived, ii. 187; buried, 491
Potter, Abp., portrait, ii. 363

INDEX

Potter, John, builder, ii. 200
Pottinger, Sir H., portrait, ii. 616
Poultney, Sir John, i. 441 ; ii. 371, 525
Poultney, Sir William, club, iii. 7
Poussin, M., French Ambassador, i. 212
Povey, John, iii. 333 ; Post Office, 114
Powell, hanged, iii. 256
Powell, George, actor, buried, i. 414
Powell, Martin, actor, lived, iii. 99
Powell, Mrs., lived, i. 367
Powell, Richard, died, i. 106
Power, Tyrone, lived, i. 19
Power, music publisher, lived, i. 297
Powerscourt, Lord, lived, i. 473
Powis, William, first Marquis of, lived, ii. 588 ; iii. 118
Powis, William, second Marquis of, lived, iii. 118
Pownall, F. H., architect, i. 421
Poynter, Ambrose, architect, ii. 78, 322, 580
Poynter, E. J., R.A., ii. 240
Pozzo di Borgo, Prince, lived, i. 517
Praed, W. Mackworth, died, i. 237 ; buried, ii. 325
Pratt, Sir Roger, architect, i. 408
Pratt, Rev. Josiah, vicar, iii. 311
Pratt, Rev. J. W., vicar, iii. 311
Prescott, Mrs., iii. 220
Preston, Keeper of the Bears, ii. 216
Preston, Elizabeth, ii. 216
Prior, player on salt-box, ii. 33
Price, Ann, murdered, iii. 346
Price, D., and Co., feather merchants, iii. 96
Price, F. G. Hilton, ii. 418
Price, John, architect, ii. 102
Price, Peter, i. 213
Price, Dr. Richard, club, ii. 426 ; minister, 179, 594 ; iii. 318 ; preacher, ii. 614 ; buried, i. 303 ; portrait, iii. 188
Pride, Col., ii. 202
Prideaux, Edmund, M.P., iii. 113
Priestley, Dr. Joseph, club, ii. 426 ; minister, 179 ; lived, 366
Primrose, Lady, ii. 19
Pringle, Sir John, lived, iii. 11 ; died, ii. 337 ; portrait, iii. 188
Prior, Matthew, ii. 294 ; school, iii. 488 ; lived, i. 357, 534 ; buried, iii. 463 ; monument, 476 ; portrait, 306
Prior, Samuel, iii. 190 ; lived, i. 357
Pritchard, hanged, iii. 340
Pritchard, Mrs., i. 114 ; lived, iii. 540 ; monument, 478
Procter, Adelaide, born, i. 147
Procter, Bryan Waller, lived, i. 147, 288 ; ii. 166, 192 ; iii. 490
Proctor, Thomas, sculptor, died, ii. 457
Proctor, William, vintner, lived, ii. 553
Proger, Art., ii. 531
Prosser, Richard, iii. 36
Prujean, Sir Francis, lived, iii. 127

Prynne, William, student, ii. 190 ; in the Star Chamber, iii. 303 ; prison, ii. 59 ; buried, 392
Psalmanazar, George, lived, ii. 263 ; iii. 12 ; died, ii. 615
Puckering, Lord Keeper, lived, iii. 191 ; died, 537
Puget, Pierre, architect, ii. 556
Pugin, Augustus, lived, iii. 193
Pugin, Augustus Welby, born, iii. 193 ; architect, i. 506 ; ii. 95
Pullison, Sir Thomas, i. 518 ; ii. 15
Pulteney, Sir William, lived, iii. 130
Pulteney, William, afterwards Earl of Bath, duel, ii. 151
Purbeck, Viscount, lived, ii. 298
Purbeck, Frances Viscountess, prison, ii. 89
Purcell, Henry, organist, i. 415 ; lived, 51, 92 ; buried, iii. 464 ; memorial tablet, 472
Purcell, Mrs., lived, i. 494
Purchas, Samuel, rector, ii. 480
Purfoote, lived, iii. 54
Puttick and Simpson, ii. 384
Pye, Henry James, lived, ii. 274
Pye, Sir Robert, ii. 579 ; lived, iii. 131
Pym, Sir John, ii. 469 ; Middle Temple, iii. 357 ; lived, i. 379 ; ii. 144 ; died, i. 496
Pynson, Richard, lived, ii. 62 ; iii. 359

Quare, Daniel, buried, i. 304
Quarles, Francis, buried, ii. 386
Queensberry, Duchess of, lived, i. 305 ; iii. 424
Queensberry, Charles, third Duke of, lived, iii. 424
Queensberry, William, fourth Duke of, club, iii. 15 ; lived, 90 ; died, 90 ; buried, ii. 281
Quick, John, lived, i. 277 ; buried, ii. 227
Quin, James, actor, ii. 308 ; born, 116 ; killed Bowen, iii. 105 ; lived, i. 148
Quyney, Richard, i. 336 ; lived, 298

Racket, Henry, buried, iii. 20
Racket, Robert, buried, iii. 20
Radcliffe, Alexander, iii. 263
Radcliffe, Dr. John, i. 120, 301, 390, 407 ; gold-headed cane, iii. 82 ; quarrel with Kneller, 85 ; lived, i. 207, 229 ; portrait, iii. 82
Radcliffe, Mrs., died, iii. 299 ; buried, i. 114
Radford, Thomas, and his wife Ann Clarges, ii. 582
Radnor, first Earl of, lived, i. 378
Radnor, second Earl of, ii. 340 ; lived, 300
Radstock, Admiral Lord, lived, iii. 109
Raffles, Lady, i. 255
Raffles, Sir Stamford, founder, iii. 512 ; statue, 472

INDEX

Ragget, proprietor of White's club, iii. 493, 496
Raglan, Lord, school, iii. 488; lived, 302
Rahere, founder, i. 115, 117; iii. 145
Railton, William, architect, iii. 405
Raimbach, Abraham, born, ii. 484; lived, iii. 449
Raine, Matthew, D.D., monument, i. 365; club, ii. 456
Rainham, James, i. 81
Raleigh, Carew, born, iii. 398, 399; lived, ii. 483; buried, 468
Raleigh, Lady, lived, i. 223; iii. 400
Raleigh, Sir Walter, iii. 510; Gray's Inn, ii. 145; Middle Temple, iii. 357; lived, i. 542; ii. 269, 542; iii. 149; prison, ii. 89; iii. 393, 398; buried, ii. 468; iii. 26; portrait, ii. 574; brass tablet, 467
Ramsay, Allan, portrait painter, lived, ii. 191, 615; buried, 496, 497
Ramsay, Andrew, killed, ii. 35
Ramsay, Col. John, lived, ii. 192
Ramsden, Jesse, club, ii. 484
Ramsey, Dame Mary, buried, ii. 508
Randall, prize-fighter, lived, iii. 390
Ranelagh, Richard, Earl, lived, iii. 147; design, 149
Ranelagh, Lady, lived, iii. 12
Rann, John, executed, iii. 230, 416
Rassam, Hormuzd, i. 258, 259
Rastell, John, lived, ii. 62
Rastell, Thomas, lived, ii. 528
Rastrick, Mr., ii. 424
Ravenet, S. F., buried, iii. 20
Ravenscroft, George, i. 213
Rawdon, Sir Marmaduke, lived, iii. 452
Rawlins, T., medallist, lived, i. 348
Rawlinson, Dan, lived, ii. 35
Rawlinson, Dr. Rich., library sold, iii. 56
Rawlinson, Sir Henry C., i. 259
Rawlinson, Mrs., died, ii. 35
Rawlinson, Thomas, lived, i. 24; ii. 430; buried, i. 226
Rawthmell, John, iii. 152
Raymond, Lord Chief Justice, died, iii. 156
Reach, —, nurseryman, i. 187
Read, Robert, landlord of a Mug-house, iii. 203
Reay, Martha, lived, iii. 348; murdered, 348
Recorde, Richard, rector, ii. 492
Reed, Rev. Andrew, D.D., born, i. 313
Reed, Sir Charles, M.P., buried, i. 3
Reed, Isaac, lived, iii. 303
Rees, Dr. Abraham, ii. 246; lived, 249; died, i. 69; buried, 304
Rees, Rev. Thomas, minister, ii. 594
Reeve, Justice Edmund, i. 109
Reeve, John, died, i. 281; buried, 171
Reid, Captain Mayne, died, i. 205
Reinagle, Philip, ii. 191
Rendel, J. M., engineer, ii. 295

Rennell, James, lived, iii. 333; buried, 463
Rennie, John, engineer, i. 18; ii. 424, 427; iii. 324, 453; died, 300; buried, 453; grave, 49
Rennie, Sir John, engineer, ii. 262, 424; iii. 287
Rennie, J. and G., engineers, ii. 254, 329; iii. 233
Repton, G. S., architect, ii. 199; iii. 80, 159
Repton, Humphry, landscape-gardener, ii. 329; iii. 191
Revett, Nicholas, lived, ii. 488
Reynolds, Frances, died, iii. 134
Reynolds, Frederic, born, ii. 388; lived, iii. 449
Reynolds, Sir Joshua, i. 39, 287; club, 480; ii. 106, 403; iii. 15; i. 287 note; President R.A., iii. 14; Discourse, 177; member of Painter Stainers' Company, 5; lived, ii. 384, 483, 597; iii. 137; grave, 49; statue, 48; bust, ii. 385; picture, iii. 178
Reynolds, Miss, lived, i. 517
Rhodes, —, manager, i. 436; lived, 357
Rhodoway, John, i. 215
Ricardo, J. L., buried, i. 281
Riccard, Sir Andrew, ii. 609
Ricci, Sebastian, i. 306, 384
Ricci, Marco, i. 306
Rich, Christopher, manager, ii. 397
Rich, John, i. 150, 465; manager, ii. 398
Rich, Richard, ii. 333
Richard, Prior of Bermondsey, founder, iii. 373
Richard II., buried, iii. 463; altar-tomb, 469; portrait, 471; ii. 575
Richard III., i. 132, 477; ii. 15
Richards, Brinsley, buried, i. 282
Richardson, Mr., pastor, iii. 65
Richardson, Charles, jun., i. 316
Richardson, C. J., lived, i. 281
Richardson, Jonathan, died, iii. 134; buried, ii. 102
Richardson, Lady, monument, i. 226
Richardson, Mrs., portrait, iii. 306
Richardson, Lord Chief Justice, lived, i. 148; bust, iii. 475
Richardson, Samuel, ii. 132; at Christ's Hospital, i. 306; lived, iii. 202; buried, i. 239; portrait, iii. 306
Richmond, Margaret, Countess of, altar-tomb, iii. 466
Richmond, Duchess of, ii. 27
Richmond, "La Belle Stuart," Duchess of, i. 500; lived, ii. 306; buried, iii. 464; monument, 467; wax effigy, 478
Richmond, Lodowick Stuart, Duke of, lived, ii. 306; died, 12; monument, iii. 467
Richmond, Charles, second Duke of (d. 1750), iii. 162
Richmond, Charles, third Duke of, iii. 162

Rickman, J., friend of Southey, lived, ii. 551
Rider, Mark, iii. 341
Rider, Sir William, lived, i. 178
Ridley, Bp., i. 241, 394
Ridley, Dr. Gloucester, buried, iii. 106
Ridley, Sir Thomas, buried, i. 159
Ridgway. —, bookseller, iii. 91, 541
Rigaud, J. F., R.A., altar-piece, ii. 487
Rigby, Francis Hale, lived, ii. 166
Rigby, Right Hon. Richard, lived, ii. 296; duel, 253
Riley, John, buried, i. 227
Rimmel, Eugene, i. 140
Riou, —, monument, iii. 48
Ripley, Thomas, architect, i. 8, 488; ii. 345; lived, iii. 530
Ripperda, Duke de, lived, iii. 265
Ritson, Joseph, lived, ii. 141; buried, i. 303
Rivers, James, bust, i. 116
Rivers, Richard, Earl, lived, iii. 136
Rivett, John, i. 356
Roberts, David, R.A., lived, i. 2; ii. 50; died, i. 170
Roberts, Edward, i. 266
Roberts, Emma, school, ii. 189
Roberts, Henry, architect, i. 507, 545; ii. 48, 424
Roberts, John, singer, i. 493
Roberts, John, bookseller, iii. 451
Robertson, Joseph Clinton, iii. 152
Robertson, Rev. F. W., born, iii. 449
Robertson, Dr. Wm., i. 250
Robins, E. C., architect, i. 128
Robins, George, auctioneer, iii. 84; buried, ii. 324
Robinson, Anastasia, "Perdita," lived, ii. 121, 297; iii. 137
Robinson, Bp., lived, i. 94
Robinson, Sir Christopher, buried, i. 159
Robinson, Dick, buried, i. 49
Robinson, Frederick, lived, i. 309
Robinson, H. Crabb, ii. 93; lived, iii. 212
Robinson, Jacob, lived, ii. 63
Robinson, John, monument, ii. 205
Robinson, Sir John, lived, ii. 547
Robinson, P. F., architect, ii. 7
Robinson, Wm., architect, ii. 83
Robson, E. R., architect, ii. 262; iii. 121, 223
Rocheford, Lady, prisoner, iii. 398
Rochester, Laurence Hyde, Earl of, i. 410; lived, ii. 298
Rochester, Wilmot, Earl of, lived, iii. 112; in Tower Street, 403
Rock, Rich., quack doctor, lived, i. 156
Rock, Dr., buried, ii. 325
Rockingham, Charles, second Marquis of, school, iii. 488; married, ii. 122; lived, 164
Rodney, Admiral Lord, lived, ii. 187; monument, iii. 48

Roe, Sir John, buried, i. 414
Roe, Sir Thomas, i. 171
Roger de Lincoln, prisoner, ii. 487
Rogers, John, rector, ii. 465; vicar, iii. 230; trial, 214; burnt, ii. 10
Rogers, Mrs., benefactor, ii. 491
Rogers, Samuel, i. 165, 417; ii. 77; born, 594; lived, i. 362; ii. 151, 297, 594; iii. 28
Rogers, Thomas, architect, i. 421
Rogers, Thomas, carvings, ii. 533, 492
Rogers, Prof. Thorold, ii. 344
Roget, Dr., lived, i. 169
Rokeby, Sir Richard and Lady, tomb, ii. 500
Rokesley, Gregory, i. 193; ii. 174
Rolfe, Sir R. M., lived, ii. 586
Romaine, Rev. William, lecturer, i. 536; preacher, ii. 586; monument, i. 47
Romilly, John Lord, buried, i. 282
Romilly, Sir Samuel, born, ii. 81; manager, iii. 191; lived, ii. 399, 513; iii. 192
Romney, Charles Marsham, Earl of, ii. i. 477
Romney, Henry Sidney, Earl of, died, ii. 300; buried, 280
Romney, George, lived, i. 469, 342; ii. 597; iii. 98
Ronquillo, Spanish Ambassador, ii. 394; lived, iii. 514
Rooker, Michael Angelo, buried, i. 320
Rookwood, executed, iii. 5
Roos, Lord, lived, i. 367
Roos, Sir Thomas, i. 203
Roper, Margaret, born, i. 298
Roper, D. R., architect, ii. 324
Roper, Wm., i. 477
Roscommon, Earl, buried, iii. 463
Rose, John, gardener, i. 331; buried, ii. 479
Rose, Henry, architect, i. 223; iii. 214
Rose, Sir George, quoted, i. 473
Rose, Richard, i. 328; ii. 356
Rose, Samuel, lived, i. 347; iii. 72
Rosebery, Earl of, ii. 426
Rosee, Pasqua, coffee-house, ii. 532
Rosoman, —, iii. 174
Ross, Sir John, died, ii. 114
Ross, Sir William C., lived, ii. 50
Rossetti, Dante Gabriel, born, i. 362; studio, 423; lived, 389; statue, 383
Rossi, J. C. F., R.A., ii. 403
Rossi, C. and H., terra-cotta, iii. 23
Rosslyn, first Earl of, lived, iii. 192
Roth, Richard, burned, ii. 269
Rothes, Countess of, lived, i. 283
Rothschild, Baron Ferdinand de, ii. 21
Rothschild, N. M., lived, i. 501
Rotier, John, buried, iii. 76
Roubiliac, L. F., i. 226, 493; iii. 253, 478; studio, 73; lived, ii. 484; buried, 479; monuments in Westminster Abbey, iii. 471, 472; statue of Handel, 428

Rouelle, innkeeper, ii. 307
Rough, John, burned, ii. 269
Roumieu, Robert Louis, architect, ii. 78
Rousseau, J. J., ii. 402; lived, i. 296; ii. 151
Row, Sir Thomas, portrait, ii. 503
Rowe family, ii. 177
Rowe, John, ii. 177
Rowe, Nicholas, school, iii. 488; lived, ii. 437; died, 336; buried, iii. 463; monument, 476
Rowe, Owen, buried, ii. 179
Rowe, Thomas, ii. 177
Rowlandson, Thomas, died, i. 7
Roxburgh, Duke of, lived, ii. 186
Roxburgh, John, Duke of, lived, ii. 188, 301
Royston, Richard, lived, ii. 271
Rudd, Mrs. Margaret Caroline, iii. 416; died, ii. 122
Rudyerd, Sir Benjamin, lived, ii. 483
Rumford, Count, founder, iii. 185; lived, i. 281
Rumsey, Colonel, lived, iii. 264
Rupert, Prince, ii. 246; iii. 190; lived, i. 149; iii. 296; buried, 463
Rushworth, John, student, ii. 390; buried, 103; died, 341
Russell, draper, iii. 191
Russell family, i. 447
Russell, Earls of Bedford, lived, iii. 191
Russell, Colonel, ii. 232
Russell, Earl, school, iii. 488
Russell, Elizabeth, statue, iii. 465
Russell, Lady Rachel, i. 143; died, iii. 281
Russell, Lord William, i. 1; ii. 221; iii. 138; lived, i. 206; trial, ii. 213, 611; prisoner, 591; iii. 399; executed, ii. 393
Russell, Richard (1374), iii. 37
Russell, Richard (1784), ii. 50
Russell, Sir William (d. 1705), monument, i. 516
Russia, Nicholas, Emperor of, in 1814, lived, iii. 90
Russian Ambassador (1663), lived, iii. 539
Rustat, Tobias, i. 384; iii. 513
Ruthven, Patrick, died, ii. 341; buried, 103
Rutland, Countess of, buried, ii. 387
Rutland, John, third Duke of, died, iii. 196
Rutland, John, fifth Duke of, lived, i. 64
Rutland, Edw., third Earl of, lived, iii. 129
Rutland, Fran., sixth Earl of, lived, ii. 451
Ryder, Captain, iii. 196; lived, ii. 596
Ryder, Richard, lived, i. 471
Ryland, William Wynne, lived, iii. 299; executed, 417
Rymer, Thomas, lived, i. 74; buried, 414
Ryplingham, William, i. 47
Rysbrack, J. M., lived, iii. 431; buried, ii. 496; statues, i. 224

VOL. III

Sabernes, William, i. 481
Sabine, Sir Edward, K.C.B., lived, i. 75
Sacheverell, Dr., chaplain, iii. 216; rector, i. 44; trial, iii. 486
Sackville, Lord George, born, ii. 198
Sackville, Isabel, Lady Prioress, ii. 277
Sackville, Sir Richard, lived, i. 496
Sadleir, Sir Ralph, lived, ii. 179
Sadler, surveyor, iii. 199
Sadler, John, lived, i. 298
Sadler, Thomas, thief, ii. 393; executed, iii. 415
Saffin, Thomas, buried, i. 539
St. Albans, Duchess of (Miss Mellon), iii. 90; lived, ii. 489; iii. 328
St. Albans, Charles, first Duke of, lived, i. 218
St. Albans, George, third Duke of, i. 5
St. Albans, Henry Jermyn, Earl of, ii. 278; iii. 88, 263; lived, ii. 298, 299
St. André, Nathaniel, lived, ii. 605
St. Antoine, M., ii. 532
St. Augustin, Abbots of, residence, iii. 385
St. Croix, L. C. Bigot de, buried, iii. 18
St. Evremond, Chevalier de, i. 187, 378, 528; ii. 294; lived, i. 11; ii. 400; buried, iii. 464; monument, 478
St. Helens, Lord, iii. 193
St. John family, i. 127
St. John, Oliver, third Lord, of Bletsoe, lived, ii. 245
St. Leger family, i. 84; residence, iii. 385
St. Leger, Sir Warham, iii. 30
St. Leonards, Lord, student, ii. 391
St. Vincent, Earl, i. 8; lived, ii. 165, 564; monument, iii. 48; bust, 408
Sala, G. A., ii. 130
Sale, George, died, iii. 337
Salis, Count de, i. 266
Salisbury, Bishops of, residence, iii. 202
Salisbury, Margaret, Countess of, buried, iii. 76
Salisbury, Richard Nevill, Earl of, ii. 15
Salisbury, Robert Cecil, Earl of, i. 141, 377; iii. 204; baptized, i. 413; lived, 343; arms, iii. 166
Salisbury, William, second Earl of, prisoner, iii. 399
Salisbury, Marquis of, i. 467
Salisbury, Marquis of, i. 63; ii. 151
Salisbury, Mr., i. 316
Salkeld, Mr., i. 385
Salmon, Mrs., ii. 61; lived, iii. 206
Salter, "Don Saltero," barber, i. 390, 511
Salter, Stephen, architect, ii. 391
Salvage, Elizabeth, ii. 547
Salvin, Anthony, architect, iii. 75
Sambrook, Sir Jeremy, i. 123; lived, iii. 208
Sampson, George, architect, i. 96
Sampson, Richard, rector, ii. 178
Sams, W. T., architect, ii. 161

2 Q

INDEX

Sancho, Ignatius, died, i. 360
Sancroft, William, Abp. of Canterbury, i. 183; ii. 178; Dean of St. Paul's, iii. 15; lived, i. 494; ii. 456; iii. 16; portrait, ii. 364
Sandby, Paul, R.A., buried, i. 134
Sandby, Thomas, R.A., iii. 513; architect, ii. 77
Sanders, John, architect, iii. 186
Sandford, Francis, ii. 210; lived, iii. 193; prison, ii. 59; buried, i. 239
Sandford, actor, lived, ii. 202
Sandwich, Edward, first Earl of, i. 518; lived, ii. 395; buried, iii. 463; portrait, 408
Sandwich, J. fourth Earl of, died, ii. 212
Sandwich Islands, King and Queen of, died, i. 6
Sandys, Sir Edwin, Merchant Taylors' School, ii. 526; quarrel, i. 169
Sandys, William, Lord, i. 375
Sanquhar, Lord. iii. 504; hanged, 7
Saul, Edwin and Susan, ii. 221
Saumerez, Richard, F.R.S., buried, ii. 505
Saunders, Mr., trial, iii. 214
Saunders, Adm. Sir Charles, died, iii. 296
Saunders, Lawrence, rector, i. 32
Saunders, Lord Chief Justice, lived, i. 313
Saunders, Richard, ii. 171
Savage, James, architect, i. 304; ii. 450, 492; iii. 253
Savage, John, i. 301
Savage, Richard, ii. 75, 302, 317; baptism, i. 44; trial, ii. 611; prison, 60, 90
Savery, T., i. 320; his fire engine tried, iii. 535
Savile, Sir George, lived, ii. 385; iii. 211
Savile, Sir Henry, prison, ii. 89
Saville, Henry, lived, ii. 306
Savoy and Richmond, Peter, Earl, of, iii. 217
Say, Frederick Richard, lived, ii. 192
Sayers, Tom, lived, i. 9
Scarborough, Earl of, lived, ii. 300
Scarlett, Sir James, lived, i. 480
Scawen, Capt., iii. 25
Scheemakers, Thomas, lived, iii. 437; buried, 21
Schiavonetti, Louis, lived, i. 280; buried, iii. 2
Schlesinger, Dr. Max, died, ii. 145
Schmydt, Bernard, organ, iii. 48
Schnebbelie, Jacob, lived, iii. 101; buried, ii. 275
Scholefield, James, "Grecian," i. 396
Schomberg, Frederick, first Duke of, iii. 18, 220
Schomberg, Charles, second Duke of, iii. 220
Schomberg, Mindhardt, third Duke of, lived, iii. 220
Scoles, J. J., architect, i. 280; ii. 31, 166

Scot, Colonel, ii. 362
Scot, Thomas, executed, i. 354
Scott, Sir G. Gilbert, R.A., architect, i. 131, 357, 351, 357, 495, 494; ii. 20, 132, 326, 399, 466, 533, 534, 538; iii. 318, 462, 471; Memorial to Old Westminsters, 209; lived, 208, 297; buried, 463
Scott, General H.Y.D., architect, i. 17, 180
Scott, John, alias Rotherham, Abp. of York, buried, iii. 430
Scott, J., of Amwell, born, i. 168; ii. 118
Scott, John, i. 7
Scott, J., duel with Christie, i. 344; iii. 120
Scott, J. O., architect, ii. 324
Scott, Robert, monument, ii. 495
Scott, Samuel, lived, ii. 208
Scott, Rev. Thomas, founder, ii. 412; lived, 183
Scott, Sir Walter, i. 221; lived, ii. 308, 447; iii. 14, 99
Scroggs, Sir William, died, ii. 18
Scroope, Sir Carr, lived, i. 534
Scrope, Robert, executed, i. 354
Scudamore, Lord, lived, iii. 541
Seamer, Joan, monument, ii. 204
Sebert, King of the East Saxons, iii. 461; buried, i. 351; tomb, iii. 471
Seeker, Archbishop, ii. 362; rector, 279; tomb, 495; portrait, 363
Sedding, J. D., architect, iii. 253
Seddon, Mr., upholsterer, i. 24
Sedley, Catherine, lived, ii. 300
Sedley, Sir Charles, i. 231; ii. 182; baptized, i. 413; died, 207
Sedley, Sir John, lived, iii. 240
Sefton, Lord, lived, i. 64
Selby, Mrs., iii. 73
Selden, J., i. 424; ii. 453; Inner Temple, iii. 354; lived, 27, 504; prison, ii. 89; iii. 398; monument, 351; statue, ii. 242
Selous, Henry, lived, i. 131
Selwyn, George, i. 287; club, iii. 15, 305; lived, i. 389; died, 422
Selywn, Mrs., lived, i. 422
Serle, Henry, ii. 399; iii. 232
Sermon, Dr. William, lived, ii. 190
Serres, John Dominick, buried, ii. 496
Settle, Elkanah, i. 371; died, 365
Seward, William, school, i. 365; lived, iii. 110
Seymour, Lady Arabella, ii. 357
Seymour, Conway, ii. 293
Seymour, Sir Edward, i. 357
Seymour, Lord George, lived, ii. 331
Seymour of Sudeley, Thomas Lord, lived, i. 72, 124; beheaded, iii. 401; buried, 76
Shaa, Sir John, ii. 170
Shackelton, portrait painter, lived, i. 165
Shadwell, Sir John, lived, i. 379, 399, 533; iii. 527
Shadwell, Thomas, Middle Temple, iii. 357; lived, i. 379; iii. 202; died, i. 399; buried, ii. 440; monument, iii. 476

Shaftesbury, Anthony, first Earl of, student, ii. 390; lived, L 23; ii. 27, 483; trial, 611; prisoner, iii. 399; portrait, L 366
Shaftesbury, Anthony, third Earl of, author of *Characteristics*, born, ii. 27; baptized, L 413; lived, 379
Shakespeare, Edmund, lived, i. 102; buried, iii. 214
Shakespeare, William, house in Blackfriars, i. 26, 195; ii. 262; iii. 129; lived, L 101, 426, 478; his will, iii. 516; Chandos portrait, ii. 574; memorial window, 205; monument, iii. 475; statue, ii. 385
Sharp, John, Abp. of York, rector, ii. 111; lived, iii. 541
Sharp, William, born, ii. 548; lived, i. 121, 361
Sharpe, Richard, i. 425; club, 480
Shatrell, Robert, lived, iii. 99
Shaw, Dr., preacher, iii. 61
Shaw, Sir James, Lord Mayor, ii. 464
Shaw, John, architect, i. 395, 536
Shaw, John, jun., architect, L 395
Shaw, Mr., lived, ii. 299
Shaw, R. Norman, R.A., architect, ii. 378; lived, i. 190
Shee, Sir Martin Archer, P.R.A., married, iii. 3; lived, i. 343
Sheepshanks, John, lived, iii. 196; collection of pictures, 276
Sheffield, John Holroyd, Lord, died, iii. 169
Sheffield, Sir Charles, i. 293
Shelburne, Earl of, duel, ii. 253
Sheldon, Daniel, iii. 2
Sheldon, Gilbert, Abp. of Canterbury, iii. 2; Gray's Inn, ii. 140; rector, 178; portrait, i. 366; ii. 354
Sheldon, Sir Joseph, i. 336; iii. 2
Sheldon, Mr., lived, ii. 186
Shelley, Mrs. Harriet, lived, ii. 565; suicide, 152
Shelley, Mrs. Mary, died, i. 387
Shelley, Percy B., married Mary Godwin, ii. 540; in St. Pancras Churchyard, iii. 19 lived, L 349; ii. 181, 189; iii. 101
Shelley, Sir Thomas, i. 86; lived, ii. 600
Shelton, William, iii. 35
Shenstone, William, lived, ii. 62
Shepherd, Edward, i. 465, 487; ii. 127, 515
Shepherd, Sir Samuel, lived, ii. 586
Shepherd, Thomas, lived, i. 2
Sheppard, Jack, i. 407; ii. 388; iii. 111, 190; trial, ii. 611; executed, iii. 415; buried, ii. 478
Sheppy, John de, Bp. of Rochester, L 328
Sherard, William, Merchant Taylors' School, ii. 526
Sheridan, R. B., L 287; ii. 92, 265; Middle Temple, iii. 352; member of Brooks's, i. 287 note; Spunging-house, iii. 384; duel, ii. 208; married, 497; lived, 93, 213, 616; iii. 212, 137; buried, 463, 477

Sheridan, Thomas, lived, L 148; ii. 93
Sherlock, Thomas, Bp. of London, i. 24
Sherlock, William, Dean of St. Asaph, rector, ii. 95
Sherrington, Walter, iii. 29
Sherwin, John Keyes, lived, i. 161; ii. 277, 304; died, iii. 339
Sherwood, Mr., lived, 235
Shield, William, composer, club, iii. 107; died, L 170; buried, iii. 464
Shipley, Bp. Jonathan, died, L 218
Shipley, William, i. 70; lived, 337
Shippen, William "Downright," M.P., lived, ii. 224, 601; prisoner, iii. 399
Shirley, Sir Anthony, prison, ii. 59
Shirley, James, Merchant Taylors' School, ii. 526; lived, 62; buried, 112; his child baptized, 110; his son, 84
Shirley, John, traveller, brass, i. 116
Shirley, Hon. Sewallis, married to Margaret, Countess of Orford, ii. 517
Shoppee, C. J., architect, i. 102
Shore, Jane, penance, iii. 62; her husband, ii. 416
Short, Dudley, lived, iii. 246
Shorter, Catherine, married, ii. 351
Shorter, Sir Robert, died, L 111
Shovel, Sir Cloudesley, lived, iii. 120, 265; buried, 463; monument, 475
Shrewsbury, Margaret, Countess of, executed, iii. 401
Shrewsbury, profligate Countess of, buried, ii. 112
Shrewsbury, Charles Talbot, Duke of, portrait, i. 366
Shrewsbury, John Talbot, first Earl of, portrait, ii. 209
Shrewsbury, George, fourth Earl of, L 441
Shrewsbury, Francis, fifth Earl of, i. 441; ii. 83
Shrewsbury, George, sixth Earl of, i. 441; ii. 83
Shrewsbury, Gilbert, seventh Earl of, lived, L 278
Shuckburgh, Sir G., club, ii. 484
Shudi, harpsichord maker, iii. 130
Shuter, Ned, lived, i. 496; ii. 489
Shuttleworth, Sir James P. Kay, buried, ii. 282
Sibbes, Dr. Richard, Gray's Inn, ii. 140
Sibthorp, Colonel, died, L 4
Sicard, —, buried, i. 351
Sicigniano, Duke of, buried, iii. 21
Siddons, Mrs., i. 217; lived, 90; ii. 134, 474; iii. 460; buried, 2; monument, 3; statue, 471
Sidmouth, Viscount, born, i. 246; baptism, 44; student, ii. 391; lived, i. 424; ii. 119, 586; iii. 328
Sidney, Algernon, L 2; lived, ii. 612; prisoner, iii. 399; executed, 401
Sidney, Sir Henry, lived, L 543; iii. 376

INDEX

Sidney, Sir Philip, iii. 510; "grocer," ii. 160; lived, i. 133; monumental tablet, iii. 41
Simmons, Samuel, i. 25
Simon, Sir John, ii. 344
Simon, Thomas, medallist, died, i. 414
Simond, Thomas, buried, iii. 343
Sims, Valentine, lived, i. 4
Simson, Cuthbert, prisoner, ii. 269
Simson, Dr. John, benefactor, iii. 248
Sinclair, Mary, ii. 5
Sinclair, Matilda, ii. 50
Singleton, Hugh, lived, i. 473
Sisson, John, iii. 172
Skelton, John, lived, iii. 208; buried, ii. 468
Skepworth, William, ii. 139
Skinner, Cyriack, club, ii. 542; iii. 410; lived, ii. 471
Skip, Bp., buried, ii. 504
Slade, Felix, i. 255, 266, 267
Slater, William, architect, i. 115
Slater and Carpenter, architects, ii. 507
Slaughter's coffee-house, ii. 484; iii. 253
Sleep, Thomas, ii. 316
Slingsby, Sir William, ii. 437
Sloane, Sir Hans, i. 56, 141, 251, 266, 267, 275, 325, 390, 511; ii. 189; iii. 253; coffee-house, ii. 148; President of the Royal Society, iii. 187; lived, i. 207; died, 389; monument, ii. 449; statue, i. 224; portrait, iii. 82, 188
Slye, William, lived, ii. 234; buried, 387
Smallwood, William, portrait, iii. 80
Smart, Christopher, lived, i. 326; died, ii. 341
Smart, Sir George, lived, iii. 110; died, i. 147
Smeaton, John, ii. 563; club, 484
Smellie, Dr., lived, iii. 12
Smethwick, J., lived, i. 537
Smirke, Sir Robert, R.A., architect, i. 252, 330, 465, 488; ii. 343, 344, 493, 548, 622; iii. 4, 82, 115, 259, 272, 405, 420; lived, i. 169; died, ii. 619
Smirke, Sydney, R.A. architect, i. 175, 271, 307, 330, 451, 480; ii. 85, 235, 303, 500, 622; iii. 25, 28, 180, 354; lived, i. 165; ii. 344
Smith, Albert, ii. 8; buried, i. 282
Smith, Anker, lived, iii. 535
Smith, Charlotte, born, ii. 337
Smith, Elizabeth, monument, i. 226
Smith, George, print-seller, lived, ii. 402
Smith, George, architect, i. 456; ii. 154, 521; iii. 63
Smith, Rev. Henry, lecturer at St. Clement's Church, i. 413
Smith, Henry, buried, ii. 69
Smith, Horace, born, i. 123
Smith, Hugh, architect, i. 362
Smith, James, born, i. 123; lived, 84; died, 473; buried, ii. 479

Smith, Sir James, iii. 968
Smith, John (1705), executed, iii. 415
Smith, Capt. John, buried, iii. 230
Smith, John Edward, Vestry Clerk, iii. 461
Smith, Dr. J. Pye, ii. 229
Smith, John Thomas, i. 161, 492; lived, ii. 106; died, iii. 424; buried, i. 134
Smith, Nathaniel, iii. 324
Smith, Nicholas, token, i. 92
Smith, Raphael, lived, i. 123
Smith, Richard, ii. 75
Smith, General Richard, lived, ii. 191
Smith, Robert, solicitor, lived, i. 123
Smith, Robert, "Bobus," club, i. 480; ii. 335; lived, iii. 212
Smith, Sir Sidney, lived, i. 423; iii. 193
Smith, Rev. Sydney, ii. 310; lived, i. 42, 283, 359, 516; ii. 169, 307, 616; iii. 328, 409; died, ii. 152; buried, 305
Smith, William, "father of geology," i. 275; lived, 297
Smith, William, M.P., lived, iii. 34
Smith, William, lived, ii. 402; collection of water-colour paintings, iii. 276
Smithson, Sir Hugh. See Northumberland (Duke of)
Smollett, Tobias, i. 439; lived, 380, 520; prisoner, ii. 341
Snell, Hannah, i. 176
Snelling, T., lived, ii. 62
Snooke, W., architect, i. 76
Soames, Sir William, lived, ii. 306
Soane, Sir John, R.A., i. 384; architect, 96, 152, 178, 291; ii. 77, 164, 240; iii. 77, 260, 306, 407, 444, 483, 486, 509; tomb, 19; portrait, 261; bust, 262
Solander, Dr. club, ii. 484; buried, iii. 151, 342
Somere, Richard, beheaded, ii. 541
Somers, Lord Chancellor, Middle Temple, iii. 357; President of the Royal Society, 187; lived, ii. 382, 396, 588; iii. 118; statue, ii. 242; portrait, i. 366; iii. 188
Somers, Will, buried, ii. 387
Somerset, negro prisoner, iii. 118
Somerset, Anne, Duchess of, i. 375; lived, 324; monument, iii. 265
Somerset, Elizabeth, Duchess of, lived, ii. 604
Somerset, Seymours, Dukes of, iii. 236
Somerset, Edward Seymour, first Duke of, i. 460; Protector, ii. 314; iii. 29; lived, 268, 321; trial, 485; prisoner, 398; executed, 401; buried, 76
Somerset, William Seymour, second Duke of, escaped out of the Tower (1611), iii. 398
Somerset, Charles Seymour, sixth Duke of, lived, ii. 396, 401, 604
Somerset, Robert Carr, Earl of, i. 197; lived, iii. 194; married to Countess of Essex, ii. 522; trial, iii. 458; buried, 58

INDEX

Somerville, Mrs., bust, iii. 188
Sophia, Princess, daughter of James I., buried, iii. 466
Sophia, Princess, daughter of George III., buried, ii. 324
Sotheby, James, monument, ii. 178
Sotheby, William, lived, ii. 165
Sothern, E. A., died, iii. 431
South, Sir James, lived, i. 321
South, Dr. Robert, ii. 223; baptism, 178; school, iii. 488; school oration, 489; chaplain, ii. 524; lay in state, iii. 480; buried, 464; monument, 475
Southampton, Wriothesley, Earls of, iii. 279, 281
Southampton, Thomas, first Earl of, Lord Treasurer, i. 143; born, 105; lived, 206; ii. 17; buried, i. 45
Southampton, Henry, third Earl of, ii. 16; benefactor, 391; prisoner, 362
Southampton, Charles Fitzroy, Lord, iii. 389
Southcott, Joanna, i. 24; died, ii. 462; buried, 318
Southerne, Thomas, lived, iii. 389; Middle Temple, 357; died, 258
Southesk, Countess of, lived, iii. 11
Southey, Robert, school, iii. 488; lived, i. 276; ii. 141, 593; bust, iii. 477
Southwell, Robert, executed, iii. 415
Southwell, Sir Robert, i. 168; portrait, iii. 188
Sowerby, James, died, ii. 357; tomb, 495
Sowerby, Leonard, publisher, iii. 412
Soyer, Alexis, ii. 130; iii. 158
Spang, M. H., statues, iii. 291
Sparke, Michael, lived, ii. 150
Spedding, James, club, iii. 313
Speed, John, baptism, i. 158; Merchant Taylor, ii. 524; buried, 109
Spelman, Sir Henry, ii. 61, 140; student, 390; died, i. 106; buried, iii. 463, 477; portrait, 188
Spencer, Earls, residence, i. 127; ii. 296; iii. 291
Spencer, Gabriel, lived, ii. 218
Spencer, Jack, prisoner, ii. 485
Spencer, Sir John, lived, i. 325, 477; monument, ii. 205
Spencer, Hon. W., lived, i. 311
Spenser, Edmund, i. 236; ii. 16; born, 3; iii. 258; Merchant Taylors' School, ii. 526; died, 338; buried, iii. 463, monument, 475
Spenser, Florence, baptized, i. 413
Spenser, Gabriel, killed, ii. 245; buried, 387
Spert, Sir Thomas, founder, iii. 408; buried, i. 539
Spiggot, highwayman, ii. 591
Spiller, James, buried, i. 415
Spiller, John, architect, ii. 429
Spohr, Ludwig, composer, i. 69

Spottiswoode, Abp., tomb, iii. 465
Spragg, Sir Edward, lived, iii. 332; buried, 463
Sprat, Thomas, Bp. of Rochester, lived, i. 494; monument, iii. 473
Spurgeon, Rev. C. H., preacher, iii. 338; pastor, ii. 593
Squibb, auctioneer, i. 308
Squire, Mr., iii. 297
Squire, executed, iii. 415
Stacey, Wm., ii. 509
Stacy, Robert, ii. 317
Stahl, Madame de, lived, i. 60; ii. 93
Stafford, John, Abp. of Canterbury, ii. 465
Stafford, Lady, lived at Pimlico (1687), iii. 97
Stafford, William Howard, Viscount, iii. 299; lived, 346; executed, 401
Stafford, Richard, i. 175
Stafford, Simon, lived, i. 4
Staines, Sir William, builder, i. 40
Stallworth, William, i. 490
Stamford, Earl of, lived, iii. 264
Standish, Sir Frank, i. 222
Stanfield, Clarkson, R.A., iii. 189; lived, i. 296; ii. 563; buried, 325
Stanhope, Countess, lived, i. 412
Stanhope, Earl, monument, iii. 474
Stanhope, John, first Lord, i. 375
Stanley, Sir Robert, monument, ii. 449
Stanley, Thomas, died, iii. 332; buried, ii. 478
Staple, Alderman (1594), monument, ii. 481
Stapylton, Walter, Bp. of Exeter, lived, ii. 26; beheaded, iii. 350
Staunton, Sir George, buried, iii. 463
Steele, Mr., murdered, i. 545
Steele, Sir Richard, i. 310, 407; school, 365; coffee-house, ii. 281; spunginghouse, iii. 431; his wife Prue buried, 428; lived, i. 208, 380; iii. 258, 436; portrait, 306
Steevens, George, iii. 303; baptized, 106; buried, 106
Stephen, Cardinal Abp., ii. 271
Stephen, Sir James Fitzjames, ii. 344
Stephens, Edward B., died, i. 295
Stephens, Joel, lived, ii. 62
Stephenson, George, statue, ii. 20
Stephenson, Robert, buried, iii. 463; grave, 473; statue, ii. 20
Stepney, George, school, iii. 488
Sterling, the elder, lived, iii. 278
Sterling, John, club, iii. 313; lived, ii. 617
Stern, Lieut., hanged, iii. 14
Sterne, Laurence, ii. 107; died, i. 219; buried, 134; ii. 97
Stevens, A., Wellington monument, iii. 48
Stevens, George Alexander, lecture, iii. 199
Stevenson, Mrs., i. 321
Steward, Alicia, monument, ii. 500
Stewart, James, buried, ii. 494

INDEX

Stewart, Sir James, duel, ii. 269
Stewart, John, lived, i. 296
Stewart, Mr., duel with Duke of Bolton, ii. 511
Stewart, Mr., prisoner, ii. 485
Stewart, Lieut.-General, ii. 96; lived, 186
Stiddolph, Sir Richard, i. 449
Stillingfleet, Benj., buried, ii. 280
Stillingfleet, Edward, Bp. of Worcester, at Christ's Hospital, i. 396; rector, 44; lived, iii. 34
Stirling, Sir William Alexander, Earl of, lived, i. 523; ii. 483, 543; iii. 84
Stirling Maxwell, Sir William, M.P., lived, iii. 34
Stody, John de, benefactor, iii. 438
Stone, Frank, A.R.A., lived, i. 169; iii. 349
Stone, Henry, lived, ii. 437
Stone, John, in hiding, ii. 437
Stone, Nicholas, i. 363; sculptor, ii. 205, 225; iii. 346, 475; pay, 509, 542; lived, ii. 437; buried, 478
Stonehewer, Richard, lived, i. 486
Storace, Madame, monument, ii. 496
Storace, Stephen, monument, ii. 496
Store, Dr. John, prisoner, iii. 395
Storer, Anthony Morris, lived, ii. 122
Storer, Henry Sargant (d. 1837), buried, iii. 71
Storer, James (d. 1853), buried, iii. 71
Storey, Edward, iii. 319
Storketh, Mr., ii. 539
Stothard, Thomas, R.A., i. 294; born, ii. 438; baptized, 479; lived, 595; buried, i. 304
Stow, Henry, i. 441
Stow, John, Merchant Taylor, ii. 504; monument, i. 46
Stowell, Lord, Middle Temple, iii. 358; lived, ii. 137; bust, iii. 356
Strachan, Sir Richard, died, i. 289
Stradling, Sir Edward, lived, iii. 514
Strafford, Thomas Wentworth, Earl of, born, i. 346; baptized, 538; lived, 83; ii. 37, 207; trial, iii. 485; prisoner, 398; executed, 401
Strafford, second Earl of, lived, ii. 382
Strahan, William, lived, iii. 122
Strange, Sir John, i. 285
Strange, Sir Robert, lived, ii. 208; i. 337; iii. 137; died, 137; buried, 59
Strangeways, Major, ii. 591
Strangford, Lord, died, ii. 192
Strangways, hanged, i. 245
Stratford, Ralph, Bp. of London, iii. 29
Streater, Robert, paintings, ii. 614
Streatfield, Sophy, lived, i. 425
Street, A. E., architect, ii. 368
Street, G. E., R.A., architect, i. 187, 341, 596; ii. 295, 368
Street, Peter, builder, ii. 68, 116
Stretes, Guillim, i. 244
Stringer, Anthony, ii. 38

Stringfellow, Rev. —, i. 449
Strode, General, iii. 133, 327
Strode, Ralph, i. 21
Strode, Sir William, buried, iii. 470
Strong, Bp. Edward, rector, i. 34
Strong, Edward, master mason, ii. 535; iii. 46
Strong, Thomas, master mason, iii. 46
Strong, William, ii. 177
Strudwick, Mr., grocer, lived, i. 303; ii. 190; iii. 262
Strutt, Joseph, lived, i. 534; died, 360; buried, 44
Stryp, John van, buried, i. 529
Strype, Gherardt van, iii. 78
Strype, Mrs. Hester, lived, ii. 257
Strype, John, born, iii. 329; school, 63; died, ii. 178
Stuart, Lady Arabella, i. 454; lived, iii. 129; prisoner, 398, 425; buried, 464, 466
Stuart, James, "Athenian," architect, ii. 296, 301; iii. 119, 291; born, i. 473; lived, ii. 192, 383; buried, 479
Stuart, Lady Louisa, lived, ii. 119
Stubbs, George, A.R.A., lived, iii. 273; buried, ii. 496
Stubbs, John, right hand cut off, iii. 7
Stukeley, Dr. William, i. 130, 248; iii. 267, 301; rector, ii. 101; lived, 334, 617; iii. 133
Styllington, M. R., ii. 540
Suckling, Sir John, i. 136; lived, 513; ii. 483; Piccadilly Hall, iii. 87
Suckling, Capt. Maurice, lived, ii. 577
Suckling, William, ii. 577
Sudbury, John, lived, iii. 104
Suffolk, Henrietta, Countess of, lived, i. 80; ii. 287; iii. 211
Suffolk, Catherine, Duchess of, ii. 401; escape, i. 104
Suffolk, Frances Grey, Duchess of, effigy, iii. 465
Suffolk, Dukes of, i. 530
Suffolk, Charles Brandon, Duke of, ii. 550; lived, i. 104; ii. 372; iii. 286, 330
Suffolk, Henry Grey, Duke of, head, iii. 407
Suffolk, Thomas Howard, Earl of, i. 363, 532; iii. 168; lived, ii. 603
Suffolk, James, third Earl of, lived, iii. 332
Sullivan, engraver, died, iii. 491
Sully, Duc de, lived, i. 74, 313; 477
Summer, John, buried, ii. 277
Sunderland, Lady, ii. 199
Surrey, Henry, Earl of, ii. 373; trial, 172; prison, 59; executed, 401; buried, i. 31
Surridge, Obadiah, token, i. 47
Sussex, Augustus Frederick, Duke of, i. 358; marriage, ii. 96, 504; died, 330; buried, 324

INDEX 599

Sussex, Robert Ratcliffe, first Earl of, buried, ii. 372
Sussex, Henry Ratcliffe, second Earl of, lived, ii. 10; buried, 372
Sussex, Thomas Ratcliffe, third Earl of, lived, i. 168, 324
Sutcliffe, Dr. Matthew, Dean of Exeter, i. 382
Sutherland, Colonel, lived, ii. 134
Sutherland, George, first Duke of, iii. 215; lived, 298
Sutton, Sir Richard, lived, i. 318
Sutton, Roger, i. 364
Sutton, Thomas, i. 362; portrait, 366; iii. 319; lived, i. 280; ii. 179
Sutton, chaplain, iii. 216
Sutton, C. Manners, Abp. of Canterbury, school, i. 365; portrait, ii. 364
Swallow, Thomas, iii. 338
Swedenborg, Emanuel, iii. 151; buried, 342; died, i. 125, 419
Swieten, Henry, iii. 342
Swift, Dr. Jonathan, i. 26, 415; lived, ii. 219, 310, 379, 381, 400; ii. 327, 382; iii. 196, 332
Swinnerton, John, i. 83
Sydenham, Dr. William, lived, iii. 10; buried, ii. 280; statue, iii. 83; bust, 82; portrait, 82
Sydney, Anne, baptized, ii. 17
Sydney, Viscount, i. 423
Sylvester, Joshua, lived, i. 117
Sylvester, Matthew, i. 336
Symington, William, buried, i. 227
Symondes, Thomasin, iii. 172
Symons, —, Lord Camelford's mistress, i. 450

Tait, Abp., ii. 360, 499
Talbot, Edward, buried, ii. 280
Talbot, Lord Chancellor, Inner Temple, iii. 355
Talbot, Sir Gilbert, iii. 396
Talfourd, Sir Th., Middle Temple, iii. 358; lived, 192
Talleyrand, Travellers' Club, iii. 406; lived, ii. 188, 461; iii. 109
Talma, school, i. 533; lived, 342; ii. 384
Tamburini, singer, ii. 200
Tanfield, Sir Laurence, iii. 346
Tanner, J. Sigismund, died, ii. 7
Tappen, George, architect, i. 317
Tarlton, Richard, i. 299; lived, 510; ii. 136; iii. 38; buried, iii. 387
Tarring, J., and Son, architects, i. 451
Tassie, James, i. 251
Taswell, Dr., ii. 30
Tatam, Boniface, ii. 528
Tate, Nahum, died, ii. 550; buried, 103
Tattersall, Richard, iii. 347
Taylor, Brook, LL.D., buried, i. 50
Taylor, Jeremy, preacher, ii. 154

Taylor, John, architect, i. 231; ii. 573; iii. 75
Taylor, John, the Water Poet, i. 23, 26
Taylor, Joseph, lived, iii. 194
Taylor, Michael Angelo, died, iii. 296
Taylor, Rev. Robert, "Devil's Chaplain," iii. 336
Taylor, Sir Robert, died, iii. 296; architect, i. 96, 232, 517; ii. 418; iii. 319; alto-relievo, ii. 463
Taylor, Thomas, the Platonist, died, iii. 444
Taylor, Tom, buried, i. 282
Taylor, Watson, i. 342; lived, ii. 137
Taylor, Messrs., of Loughborough, iii. 49, 50
Telford, Thomas, ii. 262; engineer, 323; lived, i. 357; iii. 206; died, i. 2; buried, iii. 463; grave, 473
Tempest, Pierce, lived, iii. 323; buried, 58
Temple, Right Hon. Sir William, i. 254, 266; lived, iii. 11; buried, 463; monument, 473
Templeman, Peter, M.D., school, i. 365
Tenison, Abp., ii. 362; rector, 279; lived, 483; tomb, 495
Tennyson, Lord, i. 434; club, iii. 313
Tenterden, Lord Chief Justice, died, iii. 192; buried, ii. 73
Terry, Daniel, i. 7; buried, ii. 318
Teulon, S. S., architect, i. 169
Thackeray, W. M., school, i. 365; church, ii. 326; lecturer, iii. 338; lived, i. 237, 455; ii. 615; iii. 540; buried, ii. 325; bust, iii. 477
Thanet, Tuftons, Earls of, lived, i. 22, 23; iii. 193
Thavie, John, iii. 370
Thayer, Miss, ii. 215
Thellusson, Peter, lived, iii. 81
Thelwall, John, lived, i. 745; trial, ii. 611
Theobald, Lewis, lived, iii. 193, 534; buried, 20
Theodore, King of Corsica, i. 350; lived, 493; prisoner, ii. 341; tablet, i. 50
Thesiger, Lord Justice, buried, i. 282
Thirlby, Thomas, Bp. of Westminster, iii. 461; buried, ii. 495
Thirlwall, Bp., school, i. 365; student, ii. 391; club, iii. 313; buried, 463, 477
Thistlewood, Arthur, i. 340; ii. 164; trial, 611; prisoner, iii. 399; hanged, i. 341
Thomas, Elizabeth, lived, i. 545; iii. 534; buried, i. 239
Thomas, John, architect, i. 506; sculptor, ii. 240; bas reliefs, 432
Thomas, Dr. John, died, i. 376
Thomas, Mrs., prison, ii. 60
Thomas, Moy, i. 285
Thomas, William, architect, iii. 176
Thompson, Abp., preacher, ii. 392

Thompson, Colonel (1666), ii. 100; iii. 286
Thompson, Horatia Nelson, baptized, ii. 497; lived, iii. 389
Thoms, W. J., buried, i. 282
Thomson, James, lived, ii. 365; iii. 134, 403; monument, 477
Thomson, James, architect, i. 483; iii. 101, 158
Thomson, J. J., architect, i. 348
Thoresby, Ralph, ii. 569; lived, 350
Thornhill, Sir James, i. 206; club, ii. 106; lived, i. 492; ii. 274, 383, 483; iii. 85; painting, ii. 490; iii. 47
Thornton, Bonnell, i. 231; ii. 456; iii. 148; monument, 480
Thornton, Henry, M.P., i. 492; lived, 129; ii. 340
Thorpe, John, architect, ii. 223; designs, iii. 261, 269
Thrale, Henry, i. 107; lived, 491; ii. 164
Thrale, Miss, "Queeny," lived, iii. 457
Thrale, Mrs. See Piozzi
Throgmorton, Francis, lived, iii. 65
Throgmorton, Sir Nicholas, iii. 379; trial, ii. 179; died, 16; monument, 321
Thurloe, John, i. 419; lived, ii. 400; died, 400; buried, 392; his wife died, i. 337
Thurlow, Lord Chancellor, iii. 283; ii. 335, 571; iii. 350; lived, ii. 40, 92, 301, 617; buried, iii. 352
Thurtell, murderer, i. 450; lived, ii. 460
Thwaites, Sir John, chairman, ii. 528
Thynne, Thomas, of Longleat, murdered, ii. 198, 604; iii. 14; monument, 475
Thynne, William, brass, i. 31; monument, iii. 474
Tichborn, Sir Robert, Lord Mayor, lived, ii. 49
Tierney, Right Hon. G., lived, ii. 92, 137, 212; died, iii. 212
Tillier, Comte de, i. 196
Tillotson, Abp., ii. 490; lecturer, 370; preacher, 391; married, 371; lived, i. 347, 494; portrait, ii. 363
Timbs, John, i. 215
Tindal, Sir Nicholas, lived, i. 147
Tite, Sir William, architect, ii. 23, 121, 443; iii. 158, 181
Tobin, Sir James, memorial, iii. 19
Todd, Henry John, librarian, ii. 363
Todd, Silas, ii. 73
Tofts, Katherine, singer, ii. 200; lived, 382
Tomkins, Charles, ii. 254
Tomkins, Nathaniel, buried, i. 44
Tompion, Thomas, died, iii. 452
Toms, William Henry, lived, iii. 420
Tomson, Bp., Merchant Taylors' School, ii. 526
Tonson, Jacob, i. 231; ii. 347; warehouse, iii. 219; patent, 307; lived, i. 347; ii. 142, 63; iii. 323
Tooke, Rev. Andrew, lived, i. 365

Tooke, J. Horne, baptism, i. 50; school, iii. 488; lived, i. 493; ii. 595; trial, 611; iii. 339; prisoner, ii. 591
Tooke, William, i. 92
Tooley, Alexander, ii. 101
Topham, Thomas, lived, i. 125
Toplady, Augustus, buried, iii. 391; monument, 502
Torell, W., goldsmith, iii. 469
Torré, pyrotechnist, ii. 512
Torrigiano, Peter, sculptor, iii. 166, 466
Torvor or Turver, Richard, i. 503
Tottel, Richard, privilege, iii. 307; lived, ii. 62
Tottingham, Mrs., lived, i. 170
Tournour, John, iii. 241
Towers, Dr., minister, iii. 318
Townley, Charles, lived, iii. 35; died, 35; head on Temple Bar, 359
Townley, Rev. James, tablet, i. 158
Townley, Peregrine, i. 254, 266
Townsend, Rev. John, i. 168, 492
Townsend, Bow St. Officer, born, ii. 538
Townshend, Right Hon. Charles, lived, iii. 302; bequest, 276
Townshend, Lord Charles, i. 425
Townshend, George, duel, ii. 511
Townshend, Charles, second Viscount, scuffle with Walpole, i. 422; duel, ii. 511
Tracy, "Handsome," married, ii. 516
Tradescant, J., lived, ii. 356; tomb, 495
Traherne, John, monument, iii. 215
Trapp, vicar, i. 392
Travers, lecturer, iii. 353
Tredgold, Thomas, buried, ii. 318
Trench, Abp., club, iii. 313
Tresham, Sir Thomas, ii. 314
Tresilian, Sir Robert, i. 20
Tress, William, architect, i. 317
Tress and Chambers, architects, iii. 135
Trevor, Sir John, died, i. 347, 457
Treyssac de Vergy, Peter Henry, buried, iii. 21
Trimen, R., architect, i. 317
Trimnell, Charles, Bp. of Norwich, lived, iii. 79
Trollope, Anthony, buried, ii. 325
Trotman, Samuel, highwayman, ii. 353
Trotter, Mr., iii. 267
Troughton, Edward, died, ii. 62
Trowbridge, Sir Thomas, lived, i. 283
Truefitt, G., architect, iii. 400
Trundle, John, his sign, i. 106
Truro, Lord Chancellor, i. 518; born, 337; school, iii. 63; died, ii. 4; portrait, iii. 232
Trusler, Rev. John, LL.D., Marylebone Gardens, ii. 512; lived, iii. 157
Tufnell, William, iii. 409
Tufton, Sir Richard, iii. 400
Tuke, Sir Samuel, died, iii. 271
Tullum, Daniel, memorial, iii. 19

INDEX

Tunstal, Cuthbert, Bp. of Durham, i. 344,
441, 541; buried, ii. 495
Turke, Robert, ii. 415
Turle, Mr., organist, lived, i. 75
Turner, fencing-master, lived, iii. 504
Turner, Mrs. Anne, lived, iii. 38
Turner, Charles, lived, iii. 449
Turner, J. M. W., R.A., born, ii. 457;
baptized, iii. 58; lived, ii. 186, 192,
606; iii. 139; died, i. 389; grave, iii.
49; bequest, ii. 573; picture, iii. 175;
monument, 48
Turner, Mrs., executed, iii. 415; buried,
ii. 478
Turner, Sharon, lived, iii. 156
Turner, T., architect, ii. 424
Turner, Dr. William, lived, i. 481;
memorial, ii. 609
Turner, William, father of the artist,
married, iii. 58; buried, 58
Turpin, Dick, iii. 157; lived, i. 279
Turton, Th., Bp. of Ely, buried, ii. 325
Tussaud, Madame, died, i. 91; iii. 413
Tusser, Thomas, buried, ii. 540
Tutchin, John, died, ii. 550
Twiss, Horace, lived, i. 347; died, 245
Twiss, Richard, monument, iii. 3
Twyford, Henry, lived, iii. 437
Twyford, Nicholas, founder, ii. 313;
arrested, 544
Twysden, Heneage, monument, iii. 473
Tyers, Jonathan, iii. 428
Tyler, H. E., architect, ii. 188
Tyler, Rev. James Endell, ii. 15
Tyler, Wat, ii. 313; iii. 217, 300, 314
Tyler, William, R.A., architect, ii. 77
Tyndal, William, i. 536; died, ii. 13
Tyrrell, Rear Admiral, monument, iii.
474
Tyrconnell, Frances, Duchess of, ii. 583
Tyrwhitt, Thomas, i. 254; lived, iii. 457
Tyson, Dr. Edward, monument, i. 35
Tyssen, family, ii. 178

UDALL, Nicholas, master, Westminster
School, iii. 488; buried, ii. 468
Ude, cook, lived, i. 64
Underhill, Cave, iii. 202
Unwin, Rev. W. C., school, i. 365
Upcott, William, lived, ii. 270
Uphome, Robert, ii. 113
Urswick, Christopher, altar-tomb, ii. 178
Urwin, William, iii. 517
Usher, Abp., i. 354; iii. 442; preacher,
59, 153; buried, 463, 468
Uwins, Thomas, R.A., born, ii. 211

VALANGIN, Dr. de, lived, iii. 70
Valentia, Lord, lived, i. 13
Vanbrugh, Sir John, ii. 210; architect,
199; lived, iii. 235, 506; buried, 311

Vancouver, Capt., insulted by Lord Camel-
ford, i. 450
Vanderbank, John, buried, ii. 496
Vanderborcht, lived, i. 73
Vanderdoort, Abraham, lived, ii. 483
Vandergucht, Benjamin, born, i. 283
Vandergucht, Gerard, lived, i. 283
Vanderput, Mr., i. 310
Vandervelde, Wm., the elder, buried, ii. 280
Vandervelde, William, the younger, died,
iii. 349; buried, ii. 280
Van de Weyer, Sylvain, lived, i. 64
Van Dun, Cornelius, founder, iii. 424;
monument, ii. 467; iii. 424
Vandyck, Sir A., iii. 4; lived, i. 196;
died, 49; buried, iii. 42; his will, 516
Vane, Sir Harry, the elder, lived, iii. 327
Vane, Sir Harry, the younger, school, iii.
488; lived, i. 357; iii. 84; prisoner,
399; executed, 401
Vane, Lady, died, ii. 215
Vane, Miss, lived, ii. 165, 287
Vane, Sir Walter, ii. 232
Vanhomrigh, Mrs., i. 310; iii. 332
Van Limput, Remigius, lived, i. 148
Van Mildert, Bp., Merchant Taylors
School, ii. 526
Van Nost, lived, ii. 483
Vansittart, Right Hon. P., lived, ii. 92
Vansomer, Paul, buried, ii. 478
Van Stryp, John, buried, i. 539
Vardy, John, ii. 232; architect, 396, 473
iii. 291, 424
Varley, John, lived, i. 277
Vaughan, B., i. 386
Vaulx, Viscomte de, buried, iii. 18
Vaux, W. S. W., buried, i. 282
Vavasour, Sir Thomas, iii. 432
Venalinie, Jacob, ii. 115
Venge, E., lived, iii. 377
Venner, Millennarian, hanged, i. 443; iii.
340; head on London Bridge, ii. 419
Vere, Elizabeth, iii. 431
Vere, Sir Francis, buried, iii. 463; monu-
ment, 470
Verelst, Simon, lived, ii. 284, 306
Vergil, Polydore, lived, iii. 53
Verity, Thomas, architect, i. 475
Verney, Sir Edmund, lived, iii. 83
Vernon, Admiral, born, iii. 134; lived,
209; monument, 472
Vernon, John, portrait, ii. 523
Vernon, Robert, ii. 573
Verrio, Antonio, lived, ii. 286; iii. 89;
paintings, i. 395; ii. 555
Verselyn, James, ii. 115
Verstegan, Richard, born, ii. 320
Vertue, George, lived, i. 288; ii. 569;
monument, iii. 480
Vesey, Mrs., lived, i. 218, 411
Vestris, Madame, ii. 451; born, i. 493;
lived, 487; manager, ii. 615
Vicars, John, buried, i. 392

INDEX

Vicary, Thomas, i. 118
Victoria (Queen), born, ii. 330; married, 27; at Temple Bar, iii. 358; portrait, i. 375; statue, iii. 181, 359
Villiers, Sir John, married, ii. 195
Vincent, Augustine, buried, i. 159
Vincent, William, Dean of Westminster, rector, i. 34; iii. 436
Violante, descended from St. Martin's steeple, ii. 479
Vivares, Francis, lived, ii. 597; buried, iii. 2
Voltaire, i. 185; lived, ii. 456
Voss, Mrs., ii. 285
Voysey, Rev. C., minister, iii. 339
Vratz, Col., hanged, iii. 14
Vulliamy, George, architect, i. 486
Vulliamy, Lewis, architect, i. 512; ii. 369; iii. 33, 185, 529
Vyner, Sir Robert, iii. 317; lived, ii. 417
Vyse, Edward, i. 309

Wacr, Dr., ii. 344
Wade, Field-Marshal, lived, i. 456; buried, iii. 463; monument, 474
Wadloe, J., innkeeper, i. 497; iii. 334
Wadloe, Simon, i. 497; buried, 538
Waghorn, Lieut. Thomas, died, i. 109
Wagstaffe, Thomas, rector, ii. 466
Waithman, Alderman Robert, tablet, i. 239; obelisk, ii. 32, 55
Wake, William, Abp. of Canterbury, lived, i. 494; rector, ii. 379; portrait, 363
Wakefield, Gilbert, died, ii. 179
Walcott, Rev. Mackenzie, buried, i. 282
Waldeby, Robert de, Abp. of York, brass, iii. 465
Waldegrave, Sir Charles, lived, iii. 112
Waldegrave, Countess of, lived, i. 163; iii. 21
Waldegrave, Earl, K.G., lived, i. 14
Waldegrave, General, lived, iii. 211
Waldo, Daniel, i. 429
Waldo, Sir Timothy, ii. 588
Wale, Samuel, R.A., lived, ii. 484
Waleis, Henry le, Lord Mayor, i. 455, 457; iii. 316, 409
Wales, Frederick, Prince of, i. 331
Wales, Albert Edward, Prince of, i. 119; ii. 473; iii. 15, 498; married, ii. 277; Bencher of the Middle Temple, iii. 357; Thanksgiving Service at St. Paul's, 51; statue, 359
Wales, Princess Dowager of, i. 332
Walker, Fowler, ii. 470
Walker, Hubert, Abp. of Canterbury, i. 328
Walker, John, memorial, iii. 19
Walker, J. L., bequest, ii. 573
Walker, Obadiah, buried, iii. 20

Walker, Thomas, iii. 525
Walker, William, iii. 294
Walkley, Thomas, lived, ii. 582
Wall, Governor, trial, ii. 611
Wallace, Sir Richard, lived, ii. 461
Wallace, Robert, iii. 214
Wallace, Sir William, i. 36; prisoner, ii. 35; iii. 398; trial, 485; executed, ii. 9; iii. 255; head on London Bridge, ii. 419
Wallen, J., architect, i. 405; ii. 262, 471; engineer, iii. 425; died, ii. 92
Waller, Edmund, married, ii. 468; lived, i. 229; ii. 303; speech, iii. 4
Waller, Sir William, buried, ii. 579
Wallington, John, common crier, i. 474
Wallis, Albany, lived, ii. 601
Wallis, John, D.D., ii. 84; iii. 186; portrait, 188
Walmesley, Sir Thomas, i. 109
Walpole, Sir Edward, lived, iii. 12
Walpole, Edward, of Dunston (d. 1740), buried, iii. 20
Walpole, Horatio Lord, married, ii. 278
Walpole, Horatio, i. 287; student, ii. 390; member of Brooks's, i. 287 note; robbed, ii. 253; lived, iii. 109; died, i. 163
Walpole, Lady, first wife of Sir Robert Walpole, statue, iii. 466
Walpole, Sir Robert, ii. 600; club, 208; married, 351; scuffle with Lord Townshend, i. 422; lived, 62, 379, 519; ii. 300; iii. 12 prisoner, 399; statue, ii. 242
Walsingham, Sir Francis, lived, iii. 28; died, 227; monumental tablet, 41
Walsingham, George de Grey, third Lord, died, ii. 192
Walsingham, Mrs., lived, iii. 328
Walter, John (d. 1812), iii. 124
Walter, John (d. 1847), iii. 124
Walters, John, architect, i. 78; iii. 64
Waltham, John de, Bp. of Salisbury, brass, iii. 469
Walton, Bp. Bryan, i. 415; ii. 110; rector, 503; died, i. 24
Walton, Isaac, lived, i. 346, 419; his will, iii. 516; portrait, ii. 262
Walton, Isaak, jun., buried, ii. 278
Walworth, John, ii. 56
Walworth, Sir William, ii. 49; leaseholder of the Stews, iii. 314; slays Wat Tyler, 255; lived, ii. 534
Wanley, Humphrey, lived, i. 517; ii. 533; monument, 496
Waple, Rev. E., benefactor, iii. 250
Wapshott, Thomas, builder, iii. 2
Warbeck, Perkin, executed, iii. 414
Warburton, Bp., preacher, ii. 391; lived, i. 146; ii. 141, 164
Warburton, John, buried, i. 159
Ward, Artemus, ii. 8

INDEX 603

Ward, E. M., R.A., fresco, ii. 242
Ward, James, R.A., lived, i. 492; picture, iii. 161
Ward, John, lived, ii. 179
Ward, John, LL.D., buried, i. 303
Ward, Ned, died, ii. 83; buried, iii. 20
Ward, Sir Patience, Lord Mayor, lived, ii. 373; monument, 490
Ward, Seth, Bp. of Salisbury, rector, ii. 370; died, 353
Ward, W. B., lived, iii. 458
Wardle, Colonel, lived, ii. 274
Ware, Isaac, architect, i. 209, 388
Ware, Samuel, lived, i. 14; architect, 304
Warham, Abp., portrait, ii. 363
Warren, Dr., portrait, iii. 82
Warren, Mrs., monument, iii. 472
Warren, Sir Peter, monument, iii. 472
Warton, Dr. Joseph, lived, iii. 197
Warwick, Countess of, wife of Addison (d. 1731), lived, i. 309; ii. 224
Warwick, Countess of (1676), lived, ii. 298
Warwick, Earl of, ii. 592
Warwick, Thomas de Beauchamp, Earl of, prisoner, iii. 395
Warwick, Richard Nevill, Earl of, lived, ii. 15
Warwick, John Dudley, Earl of, prisoner, iii. 395
Warwick, Robert Rich, second Earl of, i. 169; lived, iii. 450
Warwick, Charles, fourth Earl of, i. 37
Warwick, Edward, seventh Earl of, ii. 224; monument, 326
Warwick, Sir Philip, born, iii. 449; lived, 296, 449, 451
Waterhouse, Alfred, R.A., architect, i. 273, 286, 328, 402; ii. 221; iii. 431
Watier, cook, i. 218
Watson, Sir Brook, portrait, i. 395
Watson, Caroline, monument, ii. 496
Watson, Daniel, i. 197
Watson, General, i. 340
Watson, James, lived, iii. 138
Watson, J. B., architect, ii. 295
Watson, John Webbe, ii. 518
Watson, L. M., sculptor, ii. 183
Watson, Richard, Bp. of Llandaff, lived, i. 517; ii. 92
Watson, Thomas, buried, i. 117
Watt, James, i. 18; articled, ii. 41; meeting, 27; lived, 434; statue, iii. 468
Watts, G. F., R.A., fresco, ii. 398
Watts, Dr. Isaac, i. 310; ii. 177; minister, 471; iii. 98; lived, i. 3; iii. 319; buried, i. 303; monument, ii. 475
Watts, Joseph, iii. 68
Watts, Mr., i. 225
Watts, Thomas, iii. 68
Waynflete, William, Bp. of Winchester, ii. 465; lived, iii. 524
Weare, William, lived, ii. 453

Webb, Aston, architect, i. 115
Webb, John, architect, i. 143, 305, 542; iii. 135; scenes painted by him, 196
Weber, C. M. von, i. 60; died, iii. 110; buried, ii. 42, 407; iii. 167
Webster, Benjamin, i. 7; buried, 282
Webster, John, i. 45; Merchant Taylor, ii. 524; lived, 228
Wedgwood, Josiah, iii. 266; lived, ii. 302, 597; showrooms, 149
Weedon, Cavendish, ii. 400; Whitehall, iii. 506
Weekes, Henry, R.A., lived, i. 152
Weever, John, died, i. 419; buried, ii. 277
Welby, Henry, died, ii. 169
Welch, Joseph, iii. 158
Welch, Saunders, ii. 454
Weld, Humphrey, lived, iii. 514
Wellesley, Marquis, lived, i. 57; died, ii. 327
Wellington, Duke of, ii. 277; meeting with Nelson, i. 445; duel, 129; Constable of the Tower, iii. 400; gift, 312; lived, i. 56, 425; ii. 184, 192; buried, iii. 51; lay in state, i. 384; monument, ii. 170; iii. 48; sarcophagus, 49; statue, ii. 216; iii. 182; portrait, ii. 523, 616; iii. 207
Wells, Mother, lived, i. 2
Wells, William Charles, tablet, i. 239
Weltzie Club, i. 516; ii. 303
Welwood, Dr., died, i. 296
Wentworth, Lady Elizabeth, lived, i. 219
Wentworth, Thomas, Lord, i. 325
Wenzel, Baron de, buried, iii. 21
Wesket, John, executed, iii. 416
Wesley, Charles, i. 404; preacher, ii. 324; monument, i. 405; ii. 496
Wesley, Rev. John, i. 25; ii. 73; Gray's Inn, 146; school, i. 365; preacher, ii. 324, 562; iii. 459; died, i. 404; buried, 404; his wife buried, 318
Wesley, Samuel, lived, i. 494
Wesley, Susannah, buried, i. 303; monument, 405
West, Benjamin, P.R.A., ii. 138; skater, iii. 234; lived, ii. 148, 337; ii. 594; grave, iii. 49; modelled for Coade, i. 430; altarpiece, ii. 497; iii. 311; bust, 179
West, Sir Henry, monument, ii. 178
West, James, lived, i. 463; ii. 21
West, Richard, lived, i. 219
West, Captain Thomas, iii. 383
Westall, Richard, R.A., lived, i. 362
Westbrook, Harriet, suicide, ii. 152
Westbury, Lord, lived, i. 145
Westmacott, Sir Richard, R.A., i. 209; died, 80
Westmacott, Richard, R.A., architect, ii. 438; sculpture, iii. 181
Westminster, Duke of, ii. 162

Westminster, second Marquis of, born, ii. 545
Westmoreland, Nevilles, Earls of, lived, i. 23
Weston, executed, iii. 415
Weston, Lord Treasurer, i. 356; lived, 278
Weston, Prior, ii. 314; monument, 277
Whalley, Rev. Peter, rector, ii. 466
Wharncliffe, Lord, lived, i. 487
Wharton, Sir George, duel, ii. 269; buried, 494
Wharton, Henry, librarian, ii. 363
Wharton, Maria Theresa, Duchess of, buried, iii. 21
Wharton, Duke of, lived, ii. 407
Wharton, Marquis of, lived, i. 517
Whashe, —, ii. 5
Wheatley, Francis, i. 278; buried, ii. 496
Wheatly, Charles, lecturer, ii. 540; Merchant Taylors' School, 526
Wheeler, John, banker, i. 390
Wheeler, R. C., bequest, ii. 573
Wheeler, William, iii. 490
Whetstone, William, iii. 490
Whichcote, Benjamin, rector, ii. 371
Whichcott, Sir Jeremy, i. 335
Whiston, William, i. 44, 390; lived, 479
Whitaker, William, school, iii. 63
Whitbread, Sam., M.P., i. 391; died, 517
Whitbread, Samuel, jun., lived, ii. 165
Whitbread, Thomas, ii. 18
Whitbrook, Sir John, ii. 58
White, Francis, i. 160
White, John Francis, died, ii. 13
White, Miss Lydia, lived, iii. 34
White, Robert, died, i. 206
White, Dr. Thomas, vicar, i. 538; founder, iii. 248
White, T., bookseller, lived, ii. 63
White, Dr. Thomas, deprived Bishop of Peterborough, rector, i. 34; buried, ii. 154
White, Sir Thomas, founder, ii. 524; statue, 525; portrait, 523
White, William, i. 255
Whitefield, Rev. George, iii. 502; minister, 345; preacher, ii. 324, 562
Whitefield, Mrs., monument, iii. 391, 502
Whitefoord, Caleb, buried, iii. 2
Whitehead, George, buried, i. 303
Whitehead, Paul, i. 313; born, 337; lived, ii. 208
Whitehead, William, buried, i. 80
Whitehurst, Mr., i. 386
Whitelocke, Bulstrode, i. 136, 141, 378, 499; born, ii. 62; baptized, i. 538; Merchant Taylors' School, ii. 526; Middle Temple, iii. 357; lived, 202, 274
Whitelocke, General, trial, i. 384
Whitelocke, Sir James, Merchant Taylors' School, ii. 526
Whitelocke, Sir William, Reader, Inner Temple, iii. 355

Whitfield, Sir Ralph, lived, i. 106
Whitgift, Abp., i. 52; Gray's Inn, ii. 140
Whitley, Roger and Thomas, ii. 544
Whitmore, Sir George, i. 93; lived, ii. 245
Whitney, Constance, monument, ii. 109
Whittington, Sir Richard, i. 301, 302, 444; ii. 157, 445, 589; iii. 463; mercer, ii. 521; lived, 193, 535; statue, iii. 181; executors, ii. 535
Whitwell, T., architect, i. 288
Whitworth, Charles, Lord, died, ii. 106
Whyte, Mr., ii. 216
Wicliffe, John, ii. 361
Wigan, Alfred, lived, i. 321; ii. 189
Wigan, Edward, i. 255, 266
Wigg, F., surveyor, ii. 139
Wigg and Pownall, architects, iii. 303
Wigram, Sir Robert, i. 202
Wilberforce, W., i. 287; member of Brooks's, 287 note; governor, ii. 452; church, 326; Percy Chapel, iii. 71; lived, i. 129, 281, 450; ii. 130; iii. 100; died, i. 317; buried, iii. 463; statue, 472
Wilberforce, Bp. Samuel, ii. 610; club, iii. 313
Wilbraham, Sir Roger, lived, ii. 314
Wilcocks, Dean, monument, iii. 473
Wild, Jonathan, married to his third wife, iii. 20; lived, ii. 388, 611, 612; executed, iii. 415; buried, 20
Wild, J. W., architect, i. 276
Wildman, i. 143
Wildman, Major, club, iii. 410
Wilkes, Israel, ii. 246
Wilkes, John, iii. 515; duel, ii. 253; iii. 165; King's Bench Prison, 379; prisoner, ii. 341; iii. 399; alderman, ii. 32; obelisk, 32, 55; lived, 91, 126, 296; iii. 120, 155; died, ii. 164; tablet, i. 80
Wilkie, Sir David, iii. 253; lived, ii. 184, 327, 606; iii. 110; exhibition of pictures, 13; statue, ii. 574
Wilkins, Bp. John, rector, ii. 370; died, i. 347
Wilkins, Serjeant, lived, ii. 327
Wilkins, Thomas, lived at Pimlico (1687), iii. 97
Wilkins, William, R.A., architect, ii. 2, 100, 522; iii. 331, 421, 422
Wilkinson, Jane, ii. 306
Wilkinson, alias Tooley, Nicholas, benefactor, ii. 387
Wilks, Mark, lived, iii. 109
Wilks, Robert, lived, i. 229; buried, iii. 59
Willes, Chief Justice, died 1761, i. 208
Willes, Justice, buried (1872), i. 282
William, son of William the goldsmith, founder, ii. 203
William de Colchester, Abbot, tomb, iii. 470
William of Windsor, tomb, iii. 465
William of Wykeham, dean, ii. 487

INDEX

William III., ii. 99, 286, 328; offered the crown at Whitehall, iii. 513; Master of Grocers' Company, ii. 161; died, 330; buried, iii. 463, 467; statue, ii. 302; portrait, 523; iii. 5
William IV., i. 8, 293, 408; ii. 564; statue, i. 215; ii. 340
William, Major, shot, iii. 55
Williams, landlord of White Horse Cellar, iii. 89
Williams, murderer, iii. 150
Williams, Dr. Daniel, minister, ii. 185; buried, i. 303; library, iii. 522
Williams, David, ii. 404, 470; died, 107; buried, i. 50
Williams, Gilly, club, iii. 305; died, i. 422
Williams, G. Barnes, architect, i. 453; iii. 63
Williams, Herbert, architect, i. 521
Williams, H. W., builder, iii. 413
Williams, J., architect, iii. 115
Williams, John, bookseller, pillory, iii. 7
Williams, Miss, ii. 336; lived, i. 216; benefactor, ii. 354
Williams, Sir W. F., of Kars, buried, i. 282
Williamson, murdered, iii. 150
Williamson, Sir Joseph, lived, ii. 299; President of the Royal Society, iii. 187
Willis, proprietor, iii. 522
Willis, Browne, lived, ii. 483
Willis, Rev. Francis, rector, iii. 447
Willis, Dr. Richard, died, i. 376
Willis, Dr. Th. (d. 1675), lived, ii. 483
Willmore, J. T., lived, iii. 101
Wilmot, John, iii. 189
Wilmot, Lord, iii. 377
Wilson, proprietor, iii. 527
Wilson, Benjamin, died, iii. 193
Wilson, D., Bp. of Calcutta, born, iii. 293
Wilson, C. H., director, iii. 222
Wilson, Dr., rector, iii. 311
Wilson, Edward, architect, ii. 190; engineer, 146
Wilson, Sir Erasmus, i. 417; iii. 367; benefactor, 335; surgeon, ii. 538
Wilson, G. A., architect, ii. 379
Wilson, James, architect, ii. 232
Wilson, Mrs., lived, i. 80
Wilson, General Sir Robert T., died, i. 343
Wilson, Richard, R.A., iii. 253; club, ii. 107; lived, i. 362; ii. 606; iii. 84, 110, 137, 382, 391; pictures, ii. 438
Wilson, Sir Robert, born, iii. 193; buried, 473
Wilson, Thomas, i. 543
Wilton, Joseph, R.A., lived, ii. 67, 203; iii. 110; teacher, 162
Wiltshire, Earl of, lived, i. 541
Wimbledon, Sir Edward Cecil, Viscount, lived, iii. 523

Winchester, Bps. of, i. 376, 426; ii. 301; residence, iii. 286, 524
Winchester, William, first Marquis of, ii. 547; lived, i. 82, 141, 377; iii. 523
Winchester, John, second Marquis of, died, i. 377
Winchilsea, Daniel Finch, sixth Earl of, lived, iii. 265
Winchilsea, George, eighth Earl of, lived, iii. 333
Winde, Capt. William, architect, i. 291; ii. 588; iii. 118
Windham, Rt. Hon. William, i. 437, 450; born, ii. 122; lived, 215, 301; iii. 13, 34; 139
Windsor, William, second Lord, lived, ii. 554
Wing, Tycho, portrait, iii. 307
Winsor, introducer of gas-lighting, iii. 15
Winston, Charles, ii. 467
Winter, Mrs., died, ii. 181
Winter, Robert, executed, ii. 431, 448
Winter, Thomas, executed, ii. 5
Winter, Sir William, ii. 576
Winwood, Sir Ralph, lived, ii. 405; buried, i. 117
Wise, gardener, ii. 398
Wiseman, Cardinal, lived, ii. 122; enthroned, 95; died, iii. 540; buried, ii. 325
Wither, George, student, ii. 390; prisoner, 477; buried, 500
Withers, Lieut.-General, monument, iii. 480
Woffington, Peg, i. 150; lived, 229; died, iii. 134
Wolcott, Dr. John, ii. 248; iii. 91; lived, i. 350; ii. 245, 597; iii. 119, 137, 349; died, ii. 20; iii. 268; buried, 59
Wolfe, John, prisoner, i. 426
Wolfe, an Esterling, hanged, ii. 579
Wolfe, General, lived, i. 309; ii. 303; monument, iii. 470
Wollaston, Dr., F.R.S., lived, i. 295, 344, 515; died, 366; portrait, iii. 188
Wollstonecraft, Mary, lived, i. 483; ii. 91, 246, 319, 594; died, i. 345
Wolsey, Cardinal, i. 352; ii. 46, 320; lived, i. 245; iii. 505
Wood, Sir Henry, iii. 389
Wood, J. T., architect, i. 255, 260
Wood, Sir Matthew, ii. 183; lived, i. 80
Wood, Michael, quoted, iii. 419
Wood, Thomas, sheriff, i. 369; lived, iii. 529
Wood, Thomas, monument, ii. 178
Wood, William, coined his halfpence in Seven Dials, iii. 81
Woodcroft, Bennet, iii. 36
Woodfall, Henry Sampson, i. 469; lived, 380; iii. 38; buried, ii. 450
Woodhead, Abraham, buried, iii. 19
Woodhouse, Mr., i. 266
Woodman, James, iii. 517

Woodmason, James and Mary, family burnt, iii. 73
Woods, J., architect, i. 456
Woods, Sir William, buried, i. 159
Woodthorpe, Edmund, architect, ii. 109
Woodward, Dr., duel with Dr. Mead, ii. 156; buried, iii. 464
Woodward, George M., lived, i. 230
Woolaston, Mary, i. 192
Woollett, William, lived, i. 362; died, ii. 152; monument, iii. 480; memorial, 19
Woolley, Mr., i. 321
Woolston, Thomas, buried, ii. 103
Wootton, John, died, i. 342
Worcester, Bps. of, residence, iii. 321
Worcester, Margaret, Countess of, lived, iii. 533
Worcester, John Tiptoft, Earl of, lived, iii. 534; buried, i. 197
Worcester, Henry, first Marquis of, i. 330; lived, iii. 313
Worcester, Edward, second Marquis of, lived, iii. 533
Worde, Wynkin de, lived, ii. 30, 62; buried, i. 239
Wordsworth, William, married, i. 281; lived, iii. 34; statue, 473
Worlidge, Thomas, lived, iii. 137
Woronzow, Count, lived, ii. 191
Worsdale, James, buried, iii. 59
Wotton, Sir Henry, iii. 242; lived, 338, 483
Wotton, Dr. Nicholas, lived, ii. 8; brass, 481
Wotton, W., lived, i. 422
Woulfe, Peter, lived, i. 108; buried, iii. 21
Wraxall, Sir Nicholas, lived, i. 411
Wray, C. J., architect, iii. 290
Wray, Daniel, tablet, i. 226
Wren, Sir C., i. 355, 438; ii. 249; school, iii. 468; tavern, 207; married, ii. 277; professor, 155; President of the Royal Society, iii. 187; lived, i. 318, 374; ii. 30; iii. 192, 225, 243, 443; architect, i. 11, 32, 33, 35, 43, 47, 48, 51, 81, 117, 157, 158, 238, 352, 383, 392, 399, 413, 415, 488, 505, 515, 525, 535; ii. 6, 8, 95, 176, 259, 278, 330, 370, 455, 465, 466, 472, 480, 490, 491, 492, 497, 502, 505, 508, 514, 520, 533, 534, 535, 536, 539, 540, 557, 558, 598, 609; iii. 5, 44, 45, 73, 99, 228, 310, 311, 343, 346, 356, 358, 393, 430, 438, 451, 462; grave, 49; inscription to, in St. Paul's, 48; portrait, 188
Wren, Matthew, Bp. of Ely, died, ii. 13
Wright, bookseller, iii. 91
Wright, Gilbert, lived, iii. 323
Wright, Sir Nathan, lived, ii. 588
Wright, Sir Robert, died, ii. 502
Wright, Dr. Samuel, monument, iii. 318
Wright, Thomas, i. 215; iii. 388

Wroth, Richard, burned, ii. 269
Wroughton, Richard, lived, i. 170, 277
Wyat, Sir Thomas, i. 155; ii. 446, 451; iii. 286 (1554): lived, i. 481; prisoner (1554), iii. 398; executed, 401; head set up, ii. 196
Wyatt, Benj., architect, i. 527; iii. 298, 536
Wyatt, Benj. and Philip, architects, i. 57, 475
Wyatt, James, R.A., architect, ii. 297, 391; iii. 24, 509; lived, ii. 67; buried, iii. 463
Wyatt, Sir M. Digby, architect, ii. 2, 295; lived, iii. 348
Wyatt, Samuel, architect, i. 18; iii. 407
Wyatt, S. and B., architects, iii. 33
Wyatt, Thomas Henry, architect, i. 7; ii. 353, 494, 538; iii. 33
Wyatville, Sir Jeffrey, lived, i. 283
Wych, Sir Cyril, lived, ii. 298
Wycherley, William, ii. 194; Middle Temple, iii. 357; lived, i. 229; prisoner, ii. 59; buried, iii. 58
Wylgeforte, St., iii. 419
Wylson and Long, architects, ii. 248
Wyndham, Sir William, lived, i. 14, 517
Wyndesore, Henry, i. 215
Wynford, Lord, ii. 165; lived, i. 147
Wynn, Charles, lived, ii. 137
Wynne, Sir William, buried, i. 159
Wynter, Sir Edward, monument, i. 128
Wyrley, William, buried, i. 159
Wyseman, Sir Robert, buried, i. 159

YARBOROUGH, Earl of, i. 63
Yarmouth, Countess of, lived, iii. 118
Yarrell, William, lived, i. 534
Yates, Anna Maria, lived, iii. 299; died, 299
Yates, Frederick Henry, i. 7; school, 365; lived, 281
Yelverton, Sir Henry, lived, ii. 269
Yeowell, James, died, i. 366
Yevele, Henry, ii. 454
York, Abps. of, i. 127; residences, iii. 79, 321, 536, 537
York, Anne Hyde, Duchess of, married, iii. 534; buried, 463, 466
York, Frederica, Duchess of, iii. 234
York, Philippa, Duchess of (d. 1433), buried, iii. 465
York, Richard, Duke of, lived, iii. 536
York, Frederick, Duke of, son of George III., i. 395; ii. 519, 619; iii. 89, 298, 536; lived, i. 12, 79; died, 64; statue, iii. 454, 536; portrait, ii. 523
York, Thomas, iii. 540
Yorke, Hon. Charles, lived, ii. 300; died, i. 208
Young, Arthur, lived, iii. 197

Young, Dr. John, Master of the Rolls, monument, iii. 166
Young, Robert, executed, iii. 455
Young, Dr. Thomas, club, iii. 14; lived, 457; marriage, ii. 492; medallion, iii. 471
Young, Rev. William, buried, i. 384
Young, Witherden, architect, ii. 444
Yule, Major William, i. 254
Yuseph, Emin, iii. 106

ZACHARY, Thomas, ii. 313
Zetland, Earl of, i. 63
Zincke, Christian Frederick (d. 1767), lived, iii. 349
Zinzendorf, Count, Gray's Inn, ii. 146; lived, 400
Zoffany, John, R.A., lived, i. 15, 160, 495; iii. 85
Zouch, Edward, twelfth Lord, lived, iii. 80
Zucchi, Antonio, A.R.A., i. 6

THE END

Printed by R. & R. CLARK, *Edinburgh*.

www.ingramcontent.com/pod-product-compliance
Lightning Source LLC
Chambersburg PA
CBHW021228300426
44111CB00007B/463